Collins
English
School
Dictionary
& Thesaurus
T0321763

Published by Collins
An imprint of HarperCollins Publishers
Westerhill Road
Bishopbriggs
Glasgow
G64 2QT

HarperCollins *Publishers*
Macken House, 39 40 Mayor Street Upper,
Dublin 1, D01 C9W8, Ireland

Third edition 2018

10 9 8 7 6

ISBN 978-0-00-825795-8

www.collins.co.uk

Typeset by Davidson Publishing Solutions

Printed in India by Replika Press Pvt. Ltd.

A catalogue record for this book is available from the British Library.

If you would like to comment on any aspect of this book, please contact us at the given address or online.
E-mail: dictionaries@harpercollins.co.uk

Acknowledgements
We would like to thank those authors and publishers who kindly gave permission for copyright material to be used in the Collins Corpus. We would also like to thank Times Newspapers Ltd for providing valuable data.

Contents

EDITORIAL STAFF

EDITORS
Sandra Anderson
Ian Brookes
Alice Grandison
Lucy Hollingworth
Helen Hucker
Michael Munro
Mary O'Neill

SUPPLEMENT
Penny Hands

FOR THE PUBLISHER
Vaila Donnachie
Laura Waddell

COMPUTING SUPPORT
Ross Taggart
Agnieszka Urbanowicz
Thomas Widmann

Australian Editor
W. A. Krebs

New Zealand Editor
Elizabeth Gordon

South African Editor
Geoffrey Hughes

Teacher Consultants
Tracey Baxter
Emma Espley
Karen Gordon
Beth Kemp
Victoria Marston
Rob Orme
Robert Peal
Colin Stobart

Introduction

The ability to read, understand and write good English is vital for both success in exams and, ultimately, success in the world beyond school. ***Collins School Dictionary & Thesaurus*** is an essential tool in achieving that knowledge.

Collins School Dictionary & Thesaurus has been researched with teachers and students to ensure that it includes the information on language that students need to allow them to improve their performance and achieve exam success, not just in English but in all other school subjects.

The up-to-date dictionary allows students to find out what a word means and how to spell it correctly. The thesaurus entries are a perfect complement, offering students thousands of synonyms to use in order to make their writing more vibrant.

In addition, a section called **Get It Right** recognises the importance of spelling, punctuation and grammar. It explains the use and relevance of word classes, sentence types and punctuation marks, and it lists words that students have been found to misspell, helping them to master the trickiest spelling problems.

Collins School Dictionary & Thesaurus is accessible and student-friendly, and it provides two essential resources in a handy format.

How to Use the Dictionary & Thesaurus

In the Dictionary Entries

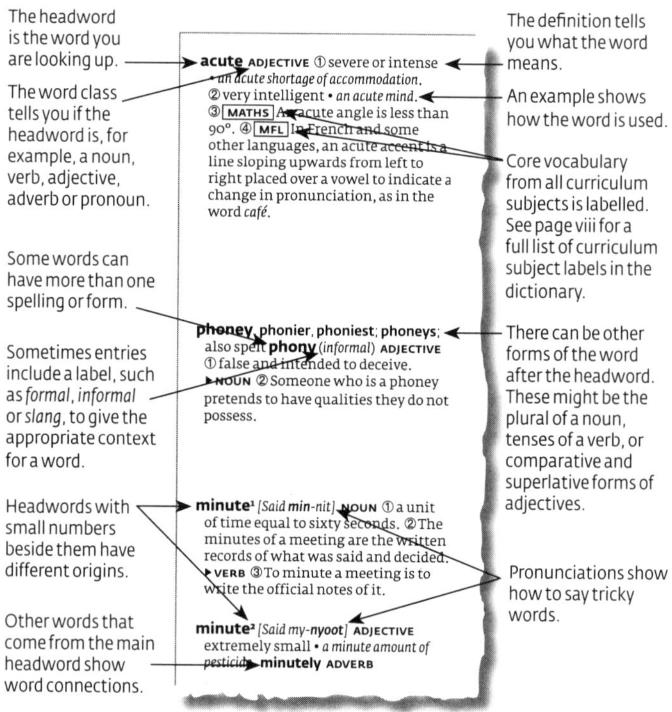

The headword is the word you are looking up.
The word class tells you if the headword is, for example, a noun, verb, adjective, adverb or pronoun.
The definition tells you what the word means.
An example shows how the word is used.
Core vocabulary from all curriculum subjects is labelled. See page viii for a full list of curriculum subject labels in the dictionary.
acute ADJECTIVE ① severe or intense • an acute shortage of accommodation. ② very intelligent • an acute mind. ③ MATHS An acute angle is less than 90°. ④ MFL In French and some other languages, an acute accent is a line sloping upwards from left to right placed over a vowel to indicate a change in pronunciation, as in the word café.
Some words can have more than one spelling or form.
Sometimes entries include a label, such as formal, informal or slang, to give the appropriate context for a word.
There can be other forms of the word after the headword. These might be the plural of a noun, tenses of a verb, or comparative and superlative forms of adjectives.
phoney, phonier, phoniest; phoneys; also spelt phony (informal) ADJECTIVE ① false and intended to deceive. ▸ NOUN ② Someone who is a phoney pretends to have qualities they do not possess.
Headwords with small numbers beside them have different origins.
Other words that come from the main headword show word connections.
Pronunciations show how to say tricky words.
minute¹ [Said min-nit] NOUN ① a unit of time equal to sixty seconds. ② The minutes of a meeting are the written records of what was said and decided. ▸ VERB ③ To minute a meeting is to write the official notes of it.
minute² [Said my-nyoot] ADJECTIVE extremely small • a minute amount of pesticide ▸ minutely ADVERB

In the Thesaurus Entries

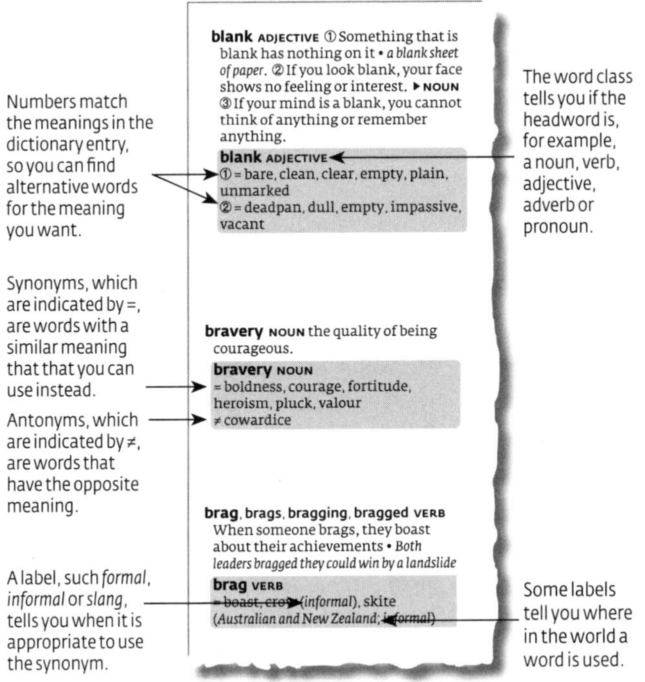

Numbers match the meanings in the dictionary entry, so you can find alternative words for the meaning you want.
Synonyms, which are indicated by =, are words with a similar meaning that that you can use instead.
Antonyms, which are indicated by ≠, are words that have the opposite meaning.
A label, such *formal*, *informal* or *slang*, tells you when it is appropriate to use the synonym.
blank ADJECTIVE ① Something that is blank has nothing on it • *a blank sheet of paper*. ② If you look blank, your face shows no feeling or interest. ▶ NOUN ③ If your mind is a blank, you cannot think of anything or remember anything.
blank ADJECTIVE
① = bare, clean, clear, empty, plain, unmarked
② = deadpan, dull, empty, impassive, vacant
bravery NOUN the quality of being courageous.
bravery NOUN
= boldness, courage, fortitude, heroism, pluck, valour
≠ cowardice
brag, brags, bragging, bragged VERB When someone brags, they boast about their achievements • *Both leaders bragged they could win by a landslide*
brag VERB
= boast, crow (*informal*), skite (*Australian and New Zealand; informal*)
The word class tells you if the headword is, for example, a noun, verb, adjective, adverb or pronoun.
Some labels tell you where in the world a word is used.

Curriculum Subject Labels

Collins School Dictionary & Thesaurus gives you clear explanations of many words you need to know, not just for English but for many other school curriculum subjects.

If a word is important in a particular subject, you will find an eye-catching label with the name of the subject in the entry for that word.

An entry may also have a label if the word is particularly relevant to exams or using the library.

Here is a list of the subject labels used.

ART	Art
CITIZENSHIP	Citizenship
D&T	Design and technology
DRAMA	Drama
ENGLISH	English
EXAM TERM	Word used in exam questions
GEOGRAPHY	Geography
HISTORY	History
ICT	Information and communication technology
LIBRARY	Library skills
MATHS	Maths
MFL	Modern foreign languages
MUSIC	Music
PE	Physical education
PSHE	Personal, social and health education
RE	Religious education
SCIENCE	Science

Dictionary & Thesaurus A–Z

Aa

a or **an** ADJECTIVE The indefinite article 'a', or 'an' if the next sound is a vowel, is used when you are talking about one of something • *an apple* • *There was a car parked behind the hedge.*

aback ADVERB If you are taken aback, you are very surprised.

abalone *[Said ab-a-**lone**-ee]* NOUN a shellfish which can be eaten.

abandon VERB ① If you abandon someone or something, you leave them or give them up for good. ▶ NOUN ② If you do something with abandon, you do it in an uncontrolled way • *He began to laugh with abandon.* **abandoned** ADJECTIVE **abandonment** NOUN

> **abandon** VERB
> ① = desert, jilt, leave, leave behind
> ▶ NOUN ② = recklessness, wildness
> ≠ control

abate VERB If something abates, it becomes less • *His anger abated.*

> **abate** VERB
> = decrease, diminish, ebb, lessen, subside, wane

abattoir *[Said **ab**-a-twahr]* NOUN a place where animals are killed for meat.

abbey NOUN a church with buildings attached to it in which monks or nuns live.

abbot NOUN the monk or priest in charge of all the monks in a monastery.

abbreviate VERB To abbreviate something is to make it shorter.

abbreviation NOUN a short form of a word or phrase. An example is 'W', which is short for 'West'.

abdicate VERB If a king or queen abdicates, he or she gives up being a king or queen. **abdication** NOUN

abdomen NOUN the front part of your body below your chest, containing your stomach and intestines. **abdominal** ADJECTIVE

abduct VERB To abduct someone is to take them away by force. **abduction** NOUN

aberration NOUN something that is not normal or usual.

abet, **abets**, **abetting**, **abetted** VERB If you abet someone, you help them to do something • *You've aided and abetted criminals to evade justice.*

abhor, **abhors**, **abhorring**, **abhorred** VERB (*formal*) If you abhor something, you hate it. **abhorrence** NOUN **abhorrent** ADJECTIVE

abide, **abides**, **abiding**, **abided** VERB ① If you can't abide something, you dislike it very much. ② If you abide by a decision or law, you act in agreement with it.

abiding ADJECTIVE lasting for ever • *an abiding interest in history.*

ability, **abilities** NOUN the intelligence or skill needed to do something • *the ability to get on with others.*

> **ability** NOUN
> = capability, competence, expertise, skill, talent
> ≠ inability

abject ADJECTIVE very bad • *abject failure.* **abjectly** ADVERB

ablaze ADJECTIVE on fire.

able, **abler**, **ablest** ADJECTIVE ① If you are able to do something, you can do it. ② PSHE Someone who is able is very clever or talented.

> **able** ADJECTIVE
> ② = accomplished, capable, efficient, expert, first-rate, skilled, talented

-able SUFFIX ① forming adjectives which have the meaning 'capable of' an action • *enjoyable* • *breakable*. ② forming adjectives with the meaning 'able to' or 'causing' • *comfortable* • *miserable*.

ably [*Said* ***ay****-blee*] ADVERB skilfully and successfully • *He is ably supported by the cast*.

abnormal ADJECTIVE not normal or usual. **abnormally** ADVERB

abnormality, **abnormalities** NOUN something that is not normal or usual.

aboard PREPOSITION, ADVERB on a ship or plane.

abode NOUN (*old-fashioned*) Your abode is your home.

abolish VERB To abolish something is to do away with it • *the campaign to abolish hunting*. **abolition** NOUN

> **abolish** VERB
> = annul, do away with, overturn, put an end to

abominable ADJECTIVE very unpleasant or shocking. **abominably** ADVERB

Aboriginal [*Said ab-or-****rij****-in-al*] ADJECTIVE descended from the people who lived in Australia before Europeans arrived.

abort VERB If a plan or activity is aborted, it is stopped before it is finished.

abortion NOUN If a woman has an abortion, the pregnancy is ended deliberately before the foetus can live independently.

abortive ADJECTIVE unsuccessful • *an abortive bank raid*.

abound VERB If things abound, there are very large numbers of them.

about PREPOSITION, ADVERB ① of or concerning. ② approximately and not exactly. ▸ ADVERB ③ in different directions • *There were some bottles scattered about*. ▸ ADJECTIVE ④ present or in a place • *Is Jane about?* ▸ PHRASE ⑤ If you are **about to** do something, you are just going to do it.

> **about** PREPOSITION, ADVERB
> ① = concerning, on, regarding, relating to
> ② = almost, approximately, around, nearly, roughly

above PREPOSITION, ADVERB ① directly over or higher than something • *above the clouds*. ② greater than a level or amount • *The temperature didn't rise above freezing point*.

> **above** PREPOSITION, ADVERB
> ① = higher than, over
> ≠ below
> ② = beyond, exceeding

above board ADJECTIVE completely open and legal • *They assured me it was above board and properly licensed*.

abrasion NOUN ① an area where your skin has been broken. ② GEOGRAPHY erosion caused by the small stones, etc. carried by a river or glacier scraping against a surface.

abrasive ADJECTIVE ① An abrasive substance is rough and can be used to clean hard surfaces. ② Someone who is abrasive is unpleasant and rude.

abreast ADJECTIVE ① side by side • *youths riding their motorbikes four abreast*. ② If you keep abreast of a subject, you know all the most recent facts about it.

abroad ADVERB in a foreign country.

abrupt ADJECTIVE ① sudden and quick • *His career came to an abrupt end.* ② not friendly or polite. **abruptly** ADVERB **abruptness** NOUN

abrupt ADJECTIVE
① = sudden, unexpected, unforeseen
② = curt, rude, short, terse
≠ polite

abscess *[Said **ab**-sess]* NOUN a painful swelling filled with pus.

abseiling NOUN Abseiling is the sport of going down a cliff or a tall building by sliding down ropes.

absent ADJECTIVE *[Said **ab**-sent]* Something that is absent is not present in a place or situation. **absence** NOUN

absent ADJECTIVE
= away, elsewhere, gone, missing
≠ present

absentee NOUN someone who is not present when they should be.

absolute ADJECTIVE ① total and complete • *absolute honesty*. ② having total power • *the absolute ruler*. **absolutely** ADVERB

absolute ADJECTIVE
① = complete, downright, pure, sheer, thorough, total, utter
② = dictatorial, supreme, tyrannical

absolve VERB To absolve someone of something is to state they are not to blame for it.

absorb VERB [SCIENCE] If something absorbs liquid or gas, it soaks it up or takes it in.

absorb VERB
= digest, soak up, take in

absorbent ADJECTIVE Absorbent materials soak up liquid easily.

absorption NOUN ① the soaking up of a liquid or taking in of a gas. ② great interest in something • *the artists' total absorption in their work*.

abstain VERB ① If you abstain from something, you do not do it or have it • *The patients had to abstain from fatty foods*. ② If you abstain in a vote, you do not vote. **abstainer** NOUN **abstention** NOUN

abstain VERB
① = avoid, deny yourself, forgo, give up, refrain

abstinence NOUN Abstinence is deliberately not doing something you enjoy.

abstract ADJECTIVE *[Said **ab**-strakt]* ① An abstract idea is based on thoughts and ideas rather than physical objects or events, for example 'bravery'. ② [ART] Abstract art is a style of art which uses shapes rather than images of people or objects. ③ Abstract nouns refer to qualities or ideas rather than to physical objects, for example 'happiness' or 'a question'. **abstraction** NOUN

absurd ADJECTIVE ridiculous and stupid. **absurdly** ADVERB **absurdity** NOUN

absurd ADJECTIVE
= crazy (*informal*), illogical, ludicrous, nonsensical, ridiculous

abundance NOUN Something that exists in abundance exists in large numbers • *an abundance of wildlife*.

abundance NOUN
= bounty, plenty, wealth
≠ shortage

abundant ADJECTIVE present in large quantities. **abundantly** ADVERB

abundant ADJECTIVE
= ample, copious, plentiful
≠ scarce

abuse VERB *[Said ab-**yooze**]* ① If you abuse someone, you speak insultingly to them. ② [PSHE] To abuse someone also means to treat them cruelly. ③ If you abuse something, you use it wrongly or for a bad purpose. ▶ **NOUN** *[Said ab-**yoose**]* ④ PSHE prolonged cruel treatment of someone. ⑤ rude and unkind remarks directed towards someone. ⑥ the wrong use of something • *an abuse of power* • *alcohol abuse*. **abuser** **NOUN**

> **abuse** **NOUN**
> ④ = exploitation, harm, hurt, ill-treatment, oppression
> ⑤ = curses, derision, insults, invective

abusive **ADJECTIVE** rude and unkind. **abusively** **ADVERB** **abusiveness** **NOUN**

> **abusive** **ADJECTIVE**
> = disparaging, insulting, offensive, rude, scathing

abysmal *[Said ab-**biz**-ml]* **ADJECTIVE** very bad indeed • *an abysmal performance*. **abysmally** **ADVERB**

abyss **NOUN** a very deep hole.

> **abyss** **NOUN**
> = chasm, fissure, gorge, pit, void

acacia *[Said a-**kay**-sha]* **NOUN** a type of thorny shrub with small yellow or white flowers.

academic **ADJECTIVE** ① Academic work is work done in a school, college or university. ▶ **NOUN** ② someone who teaches or does research in a college or university. **academically** **ADVERB**

academy, **academies** **NOUN** ① a school or college, especially one that specialises in one particular subject • *the Royal Academy of Dramatic Art*. ② in England, a school that is funded by the central government rather than by a local authority. ③ an organisation of scientists, artists, writers or musicians.

accelerate **VERB** SCIENCE To accelerate is to go faster.

> **accelerate** **VERB**
> = hurry, quicken, speed up
> ≠ decelerate

acceleration **NOUN** the rate at which the speed of something is increasing.

accelerator **NOUN** the pedal in a vehicle which you press to make it go faster.

accent **NOUN** ① a way of pronouncing a language • *She had an Australian accent*. ② MFL a mark placed above or below a letter in some languages, which affects the way the letter is pronounced. ③ ENGLISH stress placed on a particular word, syllable or note • *In Icelandic the accent usually falls on the first syllable of a word*. ④ an emphasis on something • *The accent is on action and special effects*.

accentuate **VERB** To accentuate a feature of something is to make it more noticeable.

accept **VERB** ① If you accept something, you say yes to it or take it from someone. ② If you accept a situation, you realise that it cannot be changed • *He accepts criticism as part of his job*. ③ If you accept a statement or story, you believe it is true • *The teacher accepted his explanation*. ④ If a group accepts you, they treat you as one of the group. **acceptance** **NOUN**

> **accept** **VERB**
> ① = acknowledge, agree to, concur with (*formal*), consent to, take
> ≠ refuse

acceptable **ADJECTIVE** good enough to be accepted. **acceptably** **ADVERB**

> **acceptable** **ADJECTIVE**
> = adequate, all right, fair, good enough, passable, satisfactory, tolerable

access **NOUN** ① the right or opportunity to enter a place or to use something. ▶ **VERB** ② If you access information from a computer, you get it.

accessible ADJECTIVE ① easily reached or seen • *The village was accessible by foot only.* ② easily understood or used • *guidebooks which present information in a clear and accessible style.* **accessibility** NOUN

accession NOUN A ruler's accession is the time when he or she becomes the ruler of a country.

accessory, accessories NOUN ① an extra part. ② someone who helps another person commit a crime.

accident NOUN ① an unexpected event in which people are injured or killed. ② Something that happens by accident happens by chance.

accidental ADJECTIVE happening by chance. **accidentally** ADVERB

> **accidental** ADJECTIVE
> = casual, chance, inadvertent, random
> ≠ deliberate

accolade NOUN (*formal*) great praise or an award given to someone.

accommodate VERB ① If you accommodate someone, you provide them with a place to sleep, live or work. ② If a place can accommodate a number of things or people, it has enough room for them.

> **accommodate** VERB
> ① = house, put up, shelter

accommodating ADJECTIVE willing to help and to adjust to new situations.

> **accommodating** ADJECTIVE
> = considerate, helpful, hospitable, kind, obliging

accommodation NOUN a place provided for someone to sleep, live or work in.

> **accommodation** NOUN
> = house, housing, lodgings, quarters

accompaniment NOUN ① The accompaniment to a song is the music played to go with it. ② An accompaniment to something is another thing that comes with it • *Melon is a good accompaniment to cold meats.*

accompany, accompanies, accompanying, accompanied VERB ① If you accompany someone, you go with them. ② If one thing accompanies another, the two things exist at the same time • *severe pain accompanied by fever.* ③ If you accompany a singer or musician, you play an instrument while they sing or play the main tune.

> **accompany** VERB
> ① = conduct (*formal*), escort, go with, usher
> ② = come with, go together with

accomplice NOUN a person who helps someone else to commit a crime.

accomplish VERB If you accomplish something, you succeed in doing it.

> **accomplish** VERB
> = achieve, bring about, complete, do, fulfil, manage

accomplished ADJECTIVE very talented at something • *an accomplished cook.*

accomplishment NOUN Someone's accomplishments are the skills they have gained.

accord VERB ① If you accord someone or something a particular treatment, you treat them in that way • *She was accorded a proper respect for her status.* ▶ NOUN ② agreement. ▶ PHRASE ③ If you do something **of your own accord**, you do it willingly and not because you have been forced to do it.

accordance PHRASE If you act **in accordance with** a rule or belief, you act in the way the rule or belief says you should.

accordingly ADVERB in a way that is appropriate for the circumstances • *The street had changed its character, and the shops had changed accordingly.*

according to PREPOSITION ① If something is true according to a particular person, that person says that it is true. ② If something is done according to a principle or plan, that principle or plan is used as the basis for it.

accordion NOUN a musical instrument like an expanding box. It is played by squeezing the two sides together while pressing the keys on it.

accost VERB If someone accosts you, especially someone you do not know, they come up and speak to you • *She says she is accosted when she goes shopping.*

account NOUN ① a written or spoken report of something. ② If you have a bank account, you can leave money in the bank and take it out when you need it. ③ (*in plural*) Accounts are records of money spent and received by a person or business. ▸ PHRASE ④ If you **take something into account**, you include it in your planning. ⑤ **On account of** means because of. ▸ VERB ⑥ To account for something is to explain it • *This might account for her strange behaviour.* ⑦ If something accounts for a particular amount of something, it is that amount • *The brain accounts for three per cent of body weight.*

accountable ADJECTIVE If you are accountable for something, you are responsible for it and have to explain your actions • *The committee is accountable to Parliament.* **accountability** NOUN

accountancy NOUN the job of keeping or inspecting financial accounts.

accountant NOUN a person whose job is to keep or inspect financial accounts.

accounting NOUN the keeping and checking of financial accounts.

accrue, **accrues**, **accruing**, **accrued** VERB If money or interest accrues, it increases gradually.

accumulate VERB If you accumulate things or they accumulate, they collect over a period of time.

accurate ADJECTIVE completely correct or precise. **accurately** ADVERB **accuracy** NOUN

> **accurate** ADJECTIVE
> = correct, exact, faithful, precise, right, strict, true
> ≠ inaccurate

accuse VERB If you accuse someone of doing something wrong, you say they have done it. **accusation** NOUN **accuser** NOUN

> **accuse** VERB
> = blame, censure (*formal*), charge, cite, denounce

accustom VERB If you accustom yourself to something new or different, you get used to it.

accustomed ADJECTIVE used to something.

> **accustomed** ADJECTIVE
> = adapted, familiar, used
> ≠ unaccustomed

ace NOUN ① In a pack of cards, an ace is a card with a single symbol on it. ▸ ADJECTIVE ② (*informal*) good or skilful • *an ace squash player.*

acerbic [*Said as-**ser**-bik*] ADJECTIVE (*formal*) Acerbic remarks are harsh and bitter.

ache VERB ① If you ache, you feel a continuous dull pain in a part of your body. ② If you are aching for something, you want it very much. ▸ NOUN ③ a continuous dull pain.

achieve VERB [PSHE] If you achieve something, you successfully do it or cause it to happen.

achieve VERB
= accomplish, carry out, complete, do, fulfil, perform

achievement NOUN [PSHE] something which you succeed in doing, especially after a lot of effort.

achievement NOUN
= accomplishment, deed, exploit, feat

acid NOUN ① [SCIENCE] An acid is a substance with a pH value of less than 7. There are many different acids; some are used in chemical processes and others in household substances. ▶ ADJECTIVE ② Acid tastes are sharp or sour. ③ Acid comments are unkind and critical. ▶ PHRASE ④ Something that is an **acid test** is used as a way of testing whether something is true or not, or whether it is of good quality or not. **acidly** ADVERB **acidic** ADJECTIVE **acidity** NOUN

acid rain NOUN [GEOGRAPHY] rain polluted by acid in the atmosphere which has come from factories.

acknowledge VERB ① If you acknowledge a fact or situation, you agree or admit it is true. ② If you acknowledge someone, you show that you have seen and recognised them. ③ If you acknowledge a message, you tell the person who sent it that you have received it. **acknowledgment**; also spelt **acknowledgement** NOUN

acne *[Said* ***ak****-nee]* NOUN lumpy spots that cover someone's face.

acoustic *[Said a-****koo****-stik]* ADJECTIVE ① relating to sound or hearing. ② An acoustic guitar is not made louder with an electric amplifier.

acoustics PLURAL NOUN The acoustics of a room are its structural features which are responsible for how clearly you can hear sounds made in it.

acquaintance NOUN someone you know slightly but not well.

acquire VERB If you acquire something, you obtain it.

acquire VERB
= attain, gain, get, obtain, pick up, procure, secure

acquisition NOUN something you have obtained.

acquit, **acquits**, **acquitting**, **acquitted** VERB ① If someone is acquitted of a crime, they have been tried in a court and found not guilty. ② If you acquit yourself well on a particular occasion, you behave or perform well. **acquittal** NOUN

acre NOUN a unit for measuring areas of land. One acre is equal to 4840 square yards or about 4047 square metres.

acrid ADJECTIVE sharp and bitter • *the acrid smell of burning plastic.*

acrimony *[Said* ***ak****-rim-on-ee]* NOUN *(formal)* bitterness and anger. **acrimonious** ADJECTIVE

acrobat NOUN an entertainer who performs gymnastic tricks. **acrobatic** ADJECTIVE **acrobatics** PLURAL NOUN

acronym NOUN a word made up of the initial letters of a phrase. An example of an acronym is 'BAFTA', which stands for 'British Academy of Film and Television Arts'.

across PREPOSITION, ADVERB ① going from one side of something to the other. ② on the other side of a road or river.

acrylic *[Said a-****kril****-lik]* NOUN ① Acrylic is a type of synthetic cloth. ② [ART] Acrylics, or acrylic paints, are thick artists' paints which can be used like oil paints or thinned down with water.

act VERB ① If you act, you do something • *It would be irresponsible not to act swiftly.* ② If you act in a particular way, you behave in that way. ③ If a person or thing acts as something else, it has the function or does the job of that thing • *She was able to act as an interpreter.* ④ If you act in a play or film, you play a part. ▶ NOUN ⑤ a single thing someone does • *It was an act of disloyalty to the King.* ⑥ An Act of Parliament is a law passed by the government. ⑦ In a play, ballet or opera, an act is one of the main parts it is divided into.

> **act** VERB
> ① = function, operate, perform, work
> ④ = act out, perform, play, play the part of, portray
> ▶ NOUN ⑤ = accomplishment, achievement, deed, feat, undertaking

acting NOUN the profession of performing in plays or films.

action NOUN ① the process of doing something. ② something that is done. ③ a physical movement. ④ In law, an action is a legal proceeding • *a libel action.*

> **action** NOUN
> ① = activity, operation, process
> ② = accomplishment, achievement, deed, exploit, feat

activate VERB To activate something is to make it start working.

active ADJECTIVE ① PE full of energy. ② busy and hardworking. ③ ENGLISH In grammar, a verb in the active voice is one where the subject does the action, rather than having it done to them. **actively** ADVERB

> **active** ADJECTIVE
> ① = energetic, lively, restless, sprightly, vivacious
> ② = busy, engaged, enthusiastic, hardworking, industrious, involved, occupied

activist NOUN a person who tries to bring about political and social change.

activity, **activities** NOUN ① Activity is a situation in which a lot of things are happening at the same time. ② PE something you do for pleasure • *sport and leisure activities.*

> **activity** NOUN
> ① = action, bustle, energy, liveliness
> ② = hobby, interest, pastime, pursuit

actor NOUN a man or woman whose profession is acting.

actress NOUN a woman whose profession is acting.

actual ADJECTIVE real, rather than imaginary or guessed at • *That is the official figure: the actual figure is much higher.* **actually** ADVERB

> **actual** ADJECTIVE
> = authentic, genuine, realistic, true, verified

acumen NOUN the ability to make good decisions quickly • *business acumen.*

acupuncture NOUN the treatment of illness or pain by sticking small needles into specific places on a person's body.

acute ADJECTIVE ① severe or intense • *an acute shortage of accommodation.* ② very intelligent • *an acute mind.* ③ MATHS An acute angle is less than 90°. ④ MFL In French and some other languages, an acute accent is a line sloping upwards from left to right placed over a vowel to indicate a change in pronunciation, as in the word *café.*

> **acute** ADJECTIVE
> ① = critical, extreme, grave (*formal*), great, intense, serious, severe
> ② = alert, astute, bright, keen, perceptive, quick, sharp, shrewd

ad NOUN (*informal*) an advertisement.

AD You use 'AD' in dates to indicate the number of years after the birth of Jesus Christ.

adage [*Said* ***ad****-dij*] **NOUN** a saying that expresses some general truth about life.

adamant **ADJECTIVE** If you are adamant, you are determined not to change your mind. **adamantly** **ADVERB**

adapt **VERB** ① If you adapt to a new situation, you change so you can deal with it successfully. ② If you adapt something, you change it so it is suitable for a new purpose or situation. **adaptable** **ADJECTIVE** **adaptation** **NOUN**

> **adapt** **VERB**
> ② = adjust, alter, change, convert, modify

adaptor; also spelt **adapter** **NOUN** a type of electric plug which can be used to connect two or more plugs to one socket.

add **VERB** ① If you add something to a number of things, you put it with the things. ② If you add numbers together or add them up, you work out the total.

> **add** **VERB**
> ① = attach, include, supplement
> ② = add up, count up, total
> ≠ subtract

addict **NOUN** PSHE someone who cannot stop doing something, especially something harmful. **addicted** **ADJECTIVE** **addiction** **NOUN**

addictive **ADJECTIVE** If something is addictive, people cannot stop once they have started to do it.

addition **NOUN** ① something that has been added to something else. ② MATHS the process of adding numbers together.

> **addition** **NOUN**
> ① = increase, supplement

additional **ADJECTIVE** extra or more • *They made the decision to take on additional staff*. **additionally** **ADVERB**

additive **NOUN** something added to something else, usually in order to improve it.

address, **addresses**, **addressing**, **addressed** **NOUN** ① the number of the house where you live, together with the name of the street and the town or village. ② a group of words or letters that identifies a location on the internet • *my email address*. ③ a speech given to a group of people. ▸ **VERB** ④ If a letter is addressed to you, it has your name and address written on it. ⑤ If you address a problem or task, you start to deal with it.

adept **ADJECTIVE** very skilful at doing something • *She is adept at motivating others*.

adequate **ADJECTIVE** enough in amount or good enough for a purpose • *an adequate diet*. **adequately** **ADVERB** **adequacy** **NOUN**

> **adequate** **ADJECTIVE**
> = acceptable, ample, enough, satisfactory, sufficient
> ≠ insufficient

adhere **VERB** ① If one thing adheres to another, it sticks firmly to it. ② If you adhere to a rule or agreement, you do what it says. ③ If you adhere to an opinion or belief, you firmly hold that opinion or belief. **adherence** **NOUN**

adherent **NOUN** An adherent of a belief is someone who holds that belief.

adhesive **NOUN** ① any substance used to stick two things together, for example glue. ▸ **ADJECTIVE** ② Adhesive substances are sticky and able to stick to things.

adjacent *[Said ad-jay-sent]* ADJECTIVE (*formal*) ① If two things are adjacent, they are next to each other • *a hotel adjacent to the beach.* ② MATHS Adjacent angles share one side and have the same point opposite to their bases.

adjective NOUN ENGLISH MFL a word that adds to the description given by a noun. For example, in 'They live in a large white Georgian house', 'large', 'white' and 'Georgian' are all adjectives. **adjectival** ADJECTIVE

adjoining ADJECTIVE If two rooms are next to each other and are connected, they are adjoining.

adjourn VERB ① If a meeting or trial is adjourned, it stops for a time • *The case was adjourned until September.* ② If people adjourn to another place, they go there together after a meeting • *We adjourned to the lounge.*
adjournment NOUN

adjust VERB ① If you adjust something, you change its position or alter it in some other way. ② If you adjust to a new situation, you get used to it. **adjustment** NOUN **adjustable** ADJECTIVE

administer VERB ① To administer an organisation is to be responsible for managing it. ② To administer the law or administer justice is to put it into practice and apply it. ③ If medicine is administered to someone, it is given to them.

> **administer** VERB
> ① = be in charge of, command, control, direct, manage, run, supervise
> ② = carry out, deal, dispense, execute, impose, inflict, perform

administration NOUN ① Administration is the work of organising and supervising an organisation. ② Administration is also the process of administering something • *the administration of criminal justice.* ③ The administration is the group of people that manages an organisation or a country.
administrative ADJECTIVE
administrator NOUN

admirable ADJECTIVE very good and deserving to be admired. **admirably** ADVERB

admiral NOUN the commander of a navy.

admiration NOUN a feeling of great liking and respect.

> **admiration** NOUN
> = appreciation, approval, esteem, regard, respect

admire VERB If you admire someone or something, you respect and approve of them. **admirer** NOUN **admiring** ADJECTIVE **admiringly** ADVERB

> **admire** VERB
> = appreciate, look up to, respect, value
> ≠ scorn

admission NOUN ① If you are allowed admission to a place, you are allowed to go in. ② If you make an admission of something, you agree, often reluctantly, it is true • *It was an admission of guilt.*

admit, **admits**, **admitting**, **admitted** VERB ① If you admit something, you agree, often reluctantly, it is true. ② To admit someone or something to a place or organisation is to allow them to enter it. ③ If you are admitted to hospital, you are taken there to stay until you are better.

> **admit** VERB
> ① = accept, acknowledge, grant
> ≠ deny
> ② = accept, let in, receive, take in
> ≠ exclude

A B C D E F G H I J K L M N O P Q R S T U V W X Y Z

admittedly ADVERB People use 'admittedly' to show that what they are saying contrasts with something they have already said or are about to say, and weakens their argument • *My studies, admittedly only from books, taught me much.*

adolescent NOUN SCIENCE a young person who is no longer a child but who is not yet an adult. **adolescence** NOUN

adopt VERB ① If you adopt a child that is not your own, you take him or her into your family as your son or daughter. ② (*formal*) If you adopt a particular attitude, you start to have it. **adoption** NOUN

adorable ADJECTIVE sweet and attractive.

adore VERB If you adore someone, you feel deep love and admiration for them. **adoration** NOUN

adorn VERB To adorn something is to decorate it • *The cathedral is adorned with statues.* **adornment** NOUN

adrenalin [*Said a-**dren**-al-in*]; also spelt **adrenaline** NOUN Adrenalin is a hormone which is produced by your body when you are angry, nervous or excited. Adrenalin makes your heart beat faster, and gives you more energy.

adrift ADJECTIVE, ADVERB If a boat is adrift or goes adrift, it floats on the water without being controlled.

adulation [*Said ad-yoo-**lay**-shn*] NOUN great admiration and praise for someone. **adulatory** ADJECTIVE

adult NOUN a mature and fully developed person or animal.

> **adult** NOUN
> = grown-up, man, woman
> ≠ child

adulthood NOUN the time during someone's life when they are an adult.

advance VERB ① To advance is to move forward. ② To advance a cause or interest is to help it to be successful. ③ If you advance someone a sum of money, you lend it to them. ▶ NOUN ④ Advance in something is progress in it • *scientific advance.* ⑤ a sum of money lent to someone. ▶ ADJECTIVE ⑥ happening before an event • *The event received little advance publicity.* ▶ PHRASE ⑦ If you do something **in advance**, you do it before something else happens • *We booked the room well in advance.*

> **advance** VERB
> ① = make inroads, press on, proceed (*formal*), progress
> ▶ NOUN ④ = breakthrough, development, gain, progress, step

advantage NOUN ① a benefit or something that puts you in a better position. ▶ PHRASE ② If you **take advantage of** someone, you treat them unfairly for your own benefit. ③ If you **take advantage of** something, you make use of it.

> **advantage** NOUN
> ① = ascendancy (*formal*), benefit, dominance, superiority
> ≠ disadvantage

advantageous ADJECTIVE likely to benefit you in some way • *an advantageous marriage.*

advent NOUN ① The advent of something is its start or its coming into existence • *The advent of the submarine changed naval warfare.* ② Advent is the season just before Christmas in the Christian calendar.

adventure NOUN a series of events that are unusual and exciting.

adventurer NOUN someone who enjoys doing dangerous and exciting things.

adventurous ADJECTIVE willing to take risks and do new and exciting things. **adventurously** ADVERB

adverb NOUN [ENGLISH] [MFL] a word that adds information about a verb or a following adjective or other adverb, for example, 'slowly', 'now' and 'here', which say how, when or where something is done. **adverbial** ADJECTIVE

adversary, **adversaries** *[Said **ad**-ver-sar-ee]* NOUN someone who is your enemy or who opposes what you are doing.

adverse ADJECTIVE not helpful to you, or opposite to what you want or need • *adverse weather conditions*. **adversely** ADVERB

adversity, **adversities** NOUN a time of danger or difficulty.

advert NOUN (*informal*) an advertisement.

advertise VERB ① If you advertise something, you tell people about it in a newspaper or poster, or on TV or the internet. ② To advertise is to make an announcement in a newspaper or poster, or on TV or the internet. **advertiser** NOUN **advertising** NOUN

> **advertise** VERB
> ① = plug (*informal*), promote, publicise, push

advertisement *[Said ad-**ver**-tiss-ment]* NOUN an announcement about something in a newspaper or poster, or on TV or the internet.

> **advertisement** NOUN
> = ad (*informal*), advert (*informal*), banner ad, commercial, notice, plug (*informal*)

advice NOUN a suggestion from someone about what you should do.

> **advice** NOUN
> = counsel (*formal*), drum (*Australian; informal*), guidance, opinion, suggestion

advisable ADJECTIVE sensible and likely to achieve the result you want • *It is advisable to buy the visa before travelling*. **advisably** ADVERB **advisability** NOUN

advise VERB ① If you advise someone to do something, you tell them you think they should do it. ② (*formal*) If you advise someone of something, you inform them of it. **advisory** ADJECTIVE

> **advise** VERB
> ① = caution, counsel, recommend, suggest, urge
> ② = inform, make known, notify

adviser NOUN a person whose job is to give advice.

> **adviser** NOUN
> = aide, consultant, guru, mentor, tutor

advocate VERB ① If you advocate a course of action or plan, you support it publicly. ▶ NOUN ② An advocate of something is someone who supports it publicly. ③ (*formal*) a lawyer who represents clients in court. **advocacy** NOUN

> **advocate** VERB
> ① = back, champion, endorse, favour, promote, recommend, support, uphold

aerial *[Said **air**-ee-al]* ADJECTIVE ① Aerial means happening in the air • *aerial combat*. ▶ NOUN ② a piece of wire for receiving television or radio signals.

aerobics NOUN a type of fast physical exercise, which increases the oxygen in your blood and strengthens your heart and lungs.

aerodynamic ADJECTIVE having a streamlined shape that moves easily through the air.

aeroplane NOUN a vehicle with wings and engines that enable it to fly.

aerosol NOUN [SCIENCE] a small metal container in which liquid is kept under pressure so that it can be forced out as a spray.

aerospace ADJECTIVE involved in making and designing aeroplanes and spacecraft.

aesthetic [*Said eess-**thet**-ik*]; also spelt **esthetic** ADJECTIVE DGT (*formal*) relating to the appreciation of beauty or art. **aesthetically** or **esthetically** ADVERB **aesthetics** or **esthetics** NOUN

afar NOUN (*literary*) From afar means from a long way away.

affable ADJECTIVE pleasant and easy to talk to. **affably** ADVERB **affability** NOUN

affair NOUN ① an event or series of events • *The funeral was a sad affair.* ② To have an affair is to have a secret romantic relationship, especially when one of the people involved is married. ③ (*in plural*) Your affairs are your private and personal life • *Why had he meddled in her affairs?*

> **affair** NOUN
> ① = business, event, issue, matter, question, situation, subject

affect VERB ① If something affects you, it influences you in some way. ② (*formal*) If you affect a particular way of behaving, you behave in that way • *He affected an Italian accent.*

> **affect** VERB
> ① = act on, alter, change, impinge on

affectation NOUN An affectation is behaviour that is not genuine but is put on to impress people.

affection NOUN ① a feeling of love and fondness for someone. ② (*in plural*) Your affections are feelings of love you have for someone.

> **affection** NOUN
> ① = attachment, fondness, liking, love, warmth
> ≠ dislike

affectionate ADJECTIVE full of fondness for someone • *an affectionate embrace.* **affectionately** ADVERB

> **affectionate** ADJECTIVE
> = caring, fond, loving, tender
> ≠ cold

affiliate VERB If a group affiliates itself to another, larger group, it forms a close association with it • *organisations affiliated to the ANC.* **affiliation** NOUN

affinity, **affinities** NOUN a close similarity or understanding between two things or people • *There are affinities between the two poets.*

affirm VERB If you affirm an idea or belief, you clearly indicate your support for it • *We affirm our commitment to broadcast quality programmes.* **affirmation** NOUN

affirmative ADJECTIVE An affirmative word or gesture is one that means yes.

afflict VERB If illness or pain afflicts someone, they suffer from it • *She was afflicted by depression.* **affliction** NOUN

affluent ADJECTIVE having a lot of money and possessions. **affluence** NOUN

afford VERB ① If you can afford to do something, you have enough money or time to do it. ② If you cannot afford something to happen, it would be harmful or embarrassing for you if it happened • *We cannot afford to be complacent.*

affordable ADJECTIVE If something is affordable, most people have enough money to buy it • *the availability of affordable housing.*

affray NOUN (*formal*) a noisy and violent fight.

affront VERB ① If you are affronted by something, you are insulted and angered by it. ▶ NOUN ② something that is an insult • *He took my question as a personal affront.*

afield ADVERB Far afield means a long way away • *competitors from as far afield as Russia and China.*

afloat ADVERB, ADJECTIVE ① floating on water. ② successful and making enough money • *Companies are struggling hard to stay afloat.*

afoot ADJECTIVE, ADVERB happening or being planned, especially secretly • *Plans are afoot to build a new museum.*

afraid ADJECTIVE ① If you are afraid, you think that something bad is going to happen. ② If you are afraid something might happen, you are worried it might happen.

> **afraid** ADJECTIVE
> ① = apprehensive, fearful, frightened, nervous, scared
> ≠ unafraid

afresh ADVERB again and in a new way • *The couple moved abroad to start life afresh.*

Africa NOUN Africa is the second largest continent. It is almost surrounded by sea, with the Atlantic on its west side, the Mediterranean to the north, and the Indian Ocean and the Red Sea to the east.

African ADJECTIVE ① belonging or relating to Africa. ▶ NOUN ② someone, especially a Black person, who comes from Africa.

African-American NOUN an American whose ancestors came from Africa.

Afrikaans [*Said af-rik-**ahns***] NOUN a language spoken in South Africa, similar to Dutch.

Afrikaner NOUN a white South African with Dutch ancestors.

aft ADVERB, ADJECTIVE towards the back of a ship or boat.

after PREPOSITION, ADVERB ① later than a particular time, date or event. ② behind and following someone or something • *They ran after her.*

> **after** PREPOSITION, ADVERB
> ① = afterwards, following, later, subsequently
> ≠ before

afterlife NOUN The afterlife is a life some people believe begins when you die.

aftermath NOUN The aftermath of a disaster is the situation that comes after it.

afternoon NOUN the part of the day between noon and about six o'clock.

aftershave NOUN a pleasant-smelling liquid men put on their faces after shaving.

afterthought NOUN something you do or say as an addition to something else you have already done or said.

afterwards ADVERB after an event or time.

again ADVERB ① happening one more time • *He looked forward to becoming a father again.* ② returning to the same state or place as before • *there and back again.*

> **again** ADVERB
> ① = afresh, anew, once more

against PREPOSITION ① touching and leaning on • *He leaned against the wall.* ② in opposition to • *the Test match against England.* ③ in preparation for or in case of something • *precautions against fire.* ④ in comparison with • *The pound is now at its lowest rate against the dollar.*

> **against** PREPOSITION
> ② = averse to, hostile to, in opposition to, versus
> ③ = in anticipation of, in expectation of, in preparation for

age, **ages**, **ageing** or **aging**, **aged** NOUN ① The age of something or someone is the number of years they have lived or existed. ② Age is the quality of being old • *The fabric was showing signs* *of age.* ③ a particular period in history • *the Iron Age.* ④ (*in plural, informal*) Ages means a very long time • *He's been talking for ages.* ▸ VERB ⑤ To age is to grow old or to appear older.

aged ADJECTIVE ① [*Rhymes with* ***raged***] having a particular age • *people aged 16 to 24.* ② [*Said* ***ay****-jid*] very old • *an aged horse.*

agency, **agencies** NOUN an organisation or business which provides certain services • *a detective agency.*

agenda NOUN a list of items to be discussed at a meeting.

agent NOUN ① someone who arranges work or business for other people, especially actors or singers. ② someone who works for their country's secret service.

aggravate VERB ① To aggravate a bad situation is to make it worse. ② (*informal*) If someone or something aggravates you, they make you annoyed. **aggravating** ADJECTIVE **aggravation** NOUN

aggregate NOUN a total that is made up of several smaller amounts.

aggression NOUN violent and hostile behaviour.

aggressive ADJECTIVE full of hostility and violence. **aggressively** ADVERB **aggressiveness** NOUN

> **aggressive** ADJECTIVE
> = assertive, hostile
> ≠ peaceful

aggressor NOUN a person or country that starts a fight or a war.

aggrieved ADJECTIVE upset and angry about the way you have been treated.

aghast [*Said a-****gast***] ADJECTIVE shocked and horrified.

agile ADJECTIVE [PE] able to move quickly and easily • *He is as agile as a cat.* **agilely** ADVERB **agility** NOUN

> **agile** ADJECTIVE
> = lithe, nimble, sprightly, supple
> ≠ clumsy

agitate VERB ① If you agitate for something, you campaign energetically to get it. ② If something agitates you, it worries you. **agitation** NOUN **agitator** NOUN

> **agitate** VERB
> ① = campaign, demonstrate, protest, push
> ② = bother, distress, disturb, trouble, upset, worry

agnostic NOUN [RE] someone who believes we cannot know definitely whether God exists or not. **agnosticism** NOUN

ago ADVERB in the past • *He came to Britain six years ago.*

agog ADJECTIVE excited and eager to know more about an event or situation • *She was agog to hear his news.*

agonising; also spelt **agonizing** ADJECTIVE extremely painful, either physically or mentally • *an agonising decision.*

agony NOUN very great physical or mental pain.

agrarian [*Said ag-****rare****-ee-an*] ADJECTIVE (*formal*) relating to farming and agriculture • *agrarian economies.*

agree, **agrees**, **agreeing**, **agreed** VERB ① If you agree with someone, you have the same opinion as them. ② If you agree to do something, you say you will do it. ③ If two stories or totals agree, they are the same. ④ Food that doesn't agree with you makes you ill.

> **agree** VERB
> ① = assent (*formal*), be of the same opinion, concur (*formal*), see eye to eye
> ≠ disagree
> ③ = accord (*formal*), conform, match, square, tally

agreeable ADJECTIVE ① pleasant or enjoyable. ② If you are agreeable to something, you are willing to allow it or to do it • *She was agreeable to the project.* **agreeably** ADVERB

agreeable ADJECTIVE
① = delightful, enjoyable, lovely, nice, pleasant, pleasurable
≠ disagreeable
② = game, happy, prepared, ready, willing

agreement NOUN ① a decision that has been reached by two or more people. ② Two people who are in agreement have the same opinion about something.

agreement NOUN
① = arrangement, contract, deal (*informal*), pact, settlement, treaty

agriculture NOUN Agriculture is farming. **agricultural** ADJECTIVE

aground ADVERB If a boat runs aground, it becomes stuck in a shallow stretch of water.

ahead ADVERB ① in front • *He looked ahead.* ② more advanced than someone or something else • *We are five years ahead of the competition.* ③ in the future • *I haven't had time to think far ahead.*

aid NOUN ① Aid is money, equipment or services provided for people in need • *food and medical aid.* ② something that makes a task easier • *teaching aids.* ▶ VERB ③ (*formal*) If you aid a person or an organisation, you help or support them.

aide NOUN an assistant to an important person, especially in the government or the army • *the Prime Minister's closest aides.*

AIDS NOUN a disease which destroys the body's natural system of immunity to diseases. AIDS is an abbreviation for 'acquired immune deficiency syndrome'.

ailing ADJECTIVE ① sick or ill, and not getting better. ② getting into difficulties, especially with money • *an ailing company.*

ailment NOUN a minor illness.

aim VERB ① If you aim an object or weapon at someone or something, you point it at them. ② If you aim to do something, you are planning or hoping to do it. ▶ NOUN ③ Your aim is what you intend to achieve. ④ If you take aim, you point an object or weapon at someone or something.

aim VERB
② = aspire, attempt, intend, plan, propose, strive
▶ NOUN ③ = ambition, goal, intention, objective, plan, target

aimless ADJECTIVE having no clear purpose or plan. **aimlessly** ADVERB **aimlessness** NOUN

air NOUN ① Air is the mixture of oxygen and other gases which we breathe and which forms the earth's atmosphere. ② 'Air' is used to refer to travel in aircraft • *I have to travel by air a great deal.* ③ An air someone or something has is the impression they give • *an air of defiance.* ④ (*in plural*) If you give yourself airs, you behave as if you were more important than you really are. ⑤ An air is a simple tune. ▶ VERB ⑥ If you air your opinions, you talk about them to other people.

airborne ADJECTIVE in the air and flying.

air-conditioning NOUN a system of providing cool, clean air in buildings. **air-conditioned** ADJECTIVE

aircraft NOUN any vehicle which can fly.

airfield NOUN an open area of ground with runways where small aircraft take off and land.

air force NOUN the part of a country's

armed services that fights using aircraft.

airlift NOUN an operation to move people or goods by air, especially in an emergency.

airline NOUN a company which provides air travel.

airliner NOUN a large passenger plane.

airman, **airmen** NOUN a man who serves in his country's air force.

airport NOUN a place where people go to catch planes.

air raid NOUN an attack by enemy aircraft, in which bombs are dropped.

airship NOUN a large, light aircraft, consisting of a rigid balloon filled with gas and powered by an engine, with a passenger compartment underneath.

airstrip NOUN a stretch of land that has been cleared for aircraft to take off and land.

airtight ADJECTIVE not letting air in or out.

airy, **airier**, **airiest** ADJECTIVE full of fresh air and light. **airily** ADVERB

aisle *[Rhymes with **mile**]* NOUN a long narrow gap that people can walk along between rows of seats or shelves.

ajar ADJECTIVE A door or window that is ajar is slightly open.

akin ADJECTIVE (*formal*) similar • *The taste is akin to peach.*

alacrity NOUN (*formal*) eager willingness • *He seized this offer with alacrity.*

alarm NOUN ① a feeling of fear and worry • *The cat sprang back in alarm.* ② an automatic device used to warn people of something • *a car alarm.* ▶ VERB ③ If something alarms you, it makes you worried and anxious.
alarming ADJECTIVE

alarm NOUN
① = anxiety, apprehension, fright, nervousness, panic, scare
≠ calm
② = distress signal, siren, warning
▶ VERB ③ = distress, frighten, panic, scare, startle, unnerve
≠ calm

alas ADVERB unfortunately or regrettably • *But, alas, it would not be true.*

albatross NOUN a large white sea bird.

albeit *[Said awl-**bee**-it]* CONJUNCTION (*formal*) although • *He was making progress, albeit slowly.*

albino, **albinos** NOUN a person or animal with very white skin, white hair, and pink eyes.

album NOUN ① a recording with a number of songs on it. ② a book in which you keep a collection of things such as photographs or stamps.

alchemy *[Said **al**-kem-ee]* NOUN a medieval science that attempted to change ordinary metals into gold.
alchemist NOUN

alcohol NOUN Alcohol is any drink that can make people drunk; also the colourless flammable liquid found in these drinks, produced by fermenting sugar.

alcoholic ADJECTIVE ① An alcoholic drink contains alcohol. ▶ NOUN ② someone who is addicted to alcohol. **alcoholism** NOUN

alcove NOUN an area of a room which is set back slightly from the main part.

ale NOUN a type of beer.

alert ADJECTIVE ① paying full attention to what is happening • *The criminal was spotted by an alert member of the public.* ▶ NOUN ② a situation in which people prepare themselves for danger • *The troops were on a war alert.*

▸ **VERB** ③ If you alert someone to a problem or danger, you warn them of it. **alertness** **NOUN**

alert **ADJECTIVE**
① = attentive, observant, on guard, vigilant, wary
≠ unaware
▸ **VERB** ③ = forewarn, inform, notify, warn

A level **NOUN** an advanced exam taken by students in many British schools and colleges, usually following GCSEs.

algae *[Said* ***al****-jee]* **PLURAL NOUN** plants that grow in water or on damp surfaces.

algebra **NOUN** [MATHS] a branch of mathematics in which symbols and letters are used instead of numbers to express relationships between quantities. **algebraic** **ADJECTIVE**

Algerian **ADJECTIVE** ① belonging or relating to Algeria. ▸ **NOUN** ② someone who comes from Algeria.

alias, **aliases** *[Said* ***ay****-lee-ass]* **NOUN** a false name • *Zachary Quinto, alias Mr Spock.*

alibi, **alibis** *[Said* ***al****-li-bye]* **NOUN** An alibi is evidence proving you were somewhere else when a crime was committed.

alien *[Said* ***ay****-lee-an]* **ADJECTIVE** ① not normal to you • *a totally alien culture.* ▸ **NOUN** ② someone who is not a citizen of the country in which he or she lives. ③ In science fiction, an alien is a creature from outer space.

alienate **VERB** If you alienate someone, you do something that makes them stop being sympathetic to you • *The Council's approach alienated many local residents.* **alienation** **NOUN**

alight **ADJECTIVE** ① Something that is alight is burning. ▸ **VERB** ② If a bird or insect alights somewhere, it lands there. ③ *(formal)* When passengers alight from a vehicle, they get out of it at the end of a journey.

align *[Said a-****line****]* **VERB** ① If you align yourself with a particular group, you support them. ② If you align things, you place them in a straight line. **alignment** **NOUN**

alike **ADJECTIVE** ① Things that are alike are similar in some way. ▸ **ADVERB** ② If people or things are treated alike, they are treated in a similar way.

alike **ADJECTIVE**
① = analogous, close, identical, similar, the same
≠ different
▸ **ADVERB** ② = equally, in the same way, similarly, uniformly

alimony *[Said* ***al****-li-mon-ee]* **NOUN** money someone has to pay regularly to their wife or husband after they are divorced.

alive **ADJECTIVE** ① living. ② lively and active.

alive **ADJECTIVE**
① = animate, breathing, living
≠ dead
② = active, alert, animated, energetic, full of life, lively, vivacious
≠ dull

alkali *[Said* ***al****-kal-eye]* **NOUN** [SCIENCE] a chemical substance that turns litmus paper blue. **alkaline** **ADJECTIVE**

all **ADJECTIVE, PRONOUN, ADVERB** ① used when referring to the whole of something • *Why did he have to say all that?* • *She managed to finish it all.* ▸ **ADVERB** ② 'All' is also used when saying the two sides in a game or contest have the same score • *The final score was six points all.*

all **ADJECTIVE, PRONOUN, ADVERB**
① = each, every one, everything, the whole amount, the (whole) lot

Allah **PROPER NOUN** [RE] the Arabic word for God.

allay VERB To allay someone's fears or doubts is to stop them feeling afraid or doubtful.

allege [*Said a-**lej***] VERB If you allege that something is true, you say it is true but do not provide any proof • *It is alleged that she died as a result of neglect.* **allegation** NOUN **alleged** ADJECTIVE

allegiance [*Said al-**lee**-jenss*] NOUN loyal support for a person or organisation.

allegory, allegories [*Said **al**-li-gor-ee*] NOUN a piece of writing or art in which the characters and events are symbols for something else. Allegories usually make some moral, religious or political point. For example, George Orwell's novel *Animal Farm* is an allegory in that the animals who revolt in the farmyard are symbols of the political leaders in the Russian Revolution. **allegorical** ADJECTIVE

allergy, allergies [*Said **al**-er-jee*] NOUN a sensitivity someone has to something, so that they become ill when they eat it or touch it • *an allergy to cows' milk.* **allergic** ADJECTIVE

alleviate VERB To alleviate pain or a problem is to make it less severe • *measures to alleviate poverty.* **alleviation** NOUN

alley NOUN a narrow passage between buildings.

alliance NOUN a group of people, organisations or countries working together for similar aims.

alligator NOUN a large animal, similar to a crocodile.

allocate VERB If you allocate something, you decide it should be given to a person or place, or used for a particular purpose • *funds allocated for nursery education.* **allocation** NOUN

allot, allots, allotting, allotted VERB If something is allotted to you, it is given to you as your share • *Space was allotted for visitors' cars.*

allotment NOUN ① a piece of land which people can rent to grow vegetables on. ② a share of something.

allow VERB ① If you allow something, you say it is all right or let it happen. ② If you allow a period of time or an amount of something, you set it aside for a particular purpose • *Allow four hours for the paint to dry.* **allowable** ADJECTIVE

> **allow** VERB
> ① = approve, authorise, let, permit, stand for, tolerate
> ≠ forbid
> ② = allocate, allot, assign, grant, set aside

allowance NOUN ① money given regularly to someone for a particular purpose • *a petrol allowance.* ▶ PHRASE ② If you **make allowances** for something, you take it into account • *The school made allowances for different cultural customs.*

alloy NOUN SCIENCE a mixture of two or more metals.

all right; also spelt **alright** ADJECTIVE ① If something is all right, it is acceptable. ② If someone is all right, they are safe and not harmed. ③ You say 'all right' to agree to something.

> **all right** ADJECTIVE
> ① = acceptable, adequate, average, fair, okay, OK

allude VERB If you allude to something, you refer to it in an indirect way.

allure NOUN The allure of something is an exciting quality that makes it attractive • *the allure of foreign travel.* **alluring** ADJECTIVE

allusion NOUN ENGLISH an indirect reference to or comment about something • *English literature is full of classical allusions.*

ally, **allies, allying, allied** NOUN ① a person or country that helps and supports another. ▶ VERB ② If you ally yourself with someone, you agree to help and support each other.

almighty ADJECTIVE ① very great or serious • *I've just had an almighty row with my dad.* ▶ PROPER NOUN ② The Almighty is another name for God.

almond NOUN a pale brown oval nut.

almost ADVERB very nearly • *Prices have almost doubled.*

> **almost** ADVERB
> = about, approximately, close to, nearly, not quite, practically

aloft ADVERB up in the air or in a high position • *He held aloft the trophy.*

alone ADJECTIVE, ADVERB not with other people or things • *He just wanted to be alone.*

> **alone** ADJECTIVE, ADVERB
> = detached, isolated, separate, single

along PREPOSITION ① moving, happening or existing continuously from one end to the other of something, or at various points beside it • *Put rivets along the top edge.* ▶ ADVERB ② moving forward • *We marched along, singing as we went.* ③ with someone • *Why could she not take her along?* ▶ PHRASE ④ **All along** means from the beginning of a period of time right up to now • *You've known that all along.*

alongside PREPOSITION, ADVERB ① next to something • *They had a house in the park alongside the river.* ▶ PREPOSITION ② If you work alongside other people, you are working in the same place and cooperating with them • *He was thrilled to work alongside Robert De Niro.*

aloof ADJECTIVE emotionally distant from someone or something.

aloud ADVERB When you read or speak aloud, you speak loudly enough for other people to hear you.

> **aloud** ADVERB
> = audibly, out loud

alphabet NOUN [LIBRARY] a set of letters in a fixed order that is used in writing a language. **alphabetical** ADJECTIVE **alphabetically** ADVERB

alpine ADJECTIVE existing in or relating to high mountains • *alpine flowers.*

already ADVERB having happened before the present time or earlier than expected • *She has already gone to bed.*

alright another spelling of **all right**.

also ADVERB in addition to something that has just been mentioned.

> **also** ADVERB
> = as well, besides, furthermore, into the bargain, moreover, too

altar NOUN a holy table in a church or temple.

alter VERB If something alters or if you alter it, it changes. **alteration** NOUN

altercation NOUN (*formal*) a noisy disagreement.

alternate VERB [*Said* ***ol****-tern-ate*] ① If one thing alternates with another, the two things regularly occur one after the other. ▶ ADJECTIVE [*Said ol-****tern****-at*] ② If something happens on alternate days, it happens on the first day but not the second, and happens again on the third day but not the fourth, and so on. ③ [MATHS] Alternate angles are two angles on opposite sides of a line that crosses two other lines. **alternately** ADVERB **alternation** NOUN

alternative NOUN ① something you can do or have instead of something else • *alternatives to prison such as community service.* ▶ ADJECTIVE

A B C D E F G H I J K L M N O P Q R S T U V W X Y Z

② Alternative plans or actions can happen or be done instead of what is already happening or being done. **alternatively** ADVERB

although CONJUNCTION in spite of the fact that • *He wasn't well-known in America, although he did make a film there.*

altitude NOUN [GEOGRAPHY] The altitude of something is its height above sea level • *The mountain range reaches an altitude of 1330 metres.*

altogether ADVERB ① entirely • *She wasn't altogether sorry to be leaving.* ② in total; used of amounts • *I get paid £1000 a month altogether.*

aluminium NOUN [SCIENCE] Aluminium is a light silvery-white metallic element. It is used to make aircraft and other equipment, usually in the form of aluminium alloys.

always ADVERB all the time or for ever • *She's always moaning.*

> **always** ADVERB
> = continually, every time, forever, invariably, perpetually

am the first person singular, present tense of **be**.

a.m. used to specify times between 12 midnight and 12 noon, eg *I get up at 6 a.m.* It is an abbreviation for the Latin phrase 'ante meridiem', which means 'before noon'.

amalgamate VERB If two organisations amalgamate, they join together to form one new organisation. **amalgamation** NOUN

amass VERB If you amass something such as money or information, you collect large quantities of it • *He amassed a huge fortune.*

amateur NOUN someone who does something as a hobby rather than as a job.

amateurish ADJECTIVE not skilfully made or done. **amateurishly** ADVERB

amaze VERB If something amazes you, it surprises you very much.

> **amaze** VERB
> = astonish, astound, shock, stagger, stun, surprise

amazement NOUN complete surprise.

> **amazement** NOUN
> = astonishment, shock, surprise, wonder

amazing ADJECTIVE very surprising or remarkable. **amazingly** ADVERB

> **amazing** ADJECTIVE
> = astonishing, astounding, staggering, startling, stunning, surprising

ambassador NOUN a person sent to a foreign country as the representative of his or her own government.

amber NOUN ① a hard, yellowish-brown substance used for making jewellery. ▶ NOUN, ADJECTIVE ② orange-brown.

ambience NOUN (*formal*) The ambience of a place is its atmosphere.

ambient ADJECTIVE ① surrounding • *low ambient temperatures.* ② creating a relaxing atmosphere • *ambient music.*

ambiguous ADJECTIVE A word or phrase that is ambiguous has more than one meaning. **ambiguously** ADVERB **ambiguity** NOUN

ambition NOUN ① If you have an ambition to achieve something, you want very much to achieve it • *His ambition is to be an actor.* ② a great desire for success, power and wealth • *He's talented and full of ambition.*

ambitious ADJECTIVE ① Someone who is ambitious has a strong desire for success, power and wealth. ② An ambitious plan is a large one and requires a lot of work • *an ambitious rebuilding schedule.*

ambivalent ADJECTIVE having or showing two conflicting attitudes or emotions. **ambivalence** NOUN

amble VERB If you amble, you walk slowly and in a relaxed manner.

ambulance NOUN a vehicle for taking sick and injured people to hospital.

ambush VERB ① To ambush someone is to attack them after hiding and lying in wait for them. ▸ NOUN ② an attack on someone after hiding and lying in wait for them.

amenable *[Said am-**mee**-na-bl]* ADJECTIVE willing to listen to suggestions, or to cooperate with someone • *Both brothers were amenable to the arrangement.* **amenably** ADVERB **amenability** NOUN

amend VERB To amend something that has been written or said is to alter it slightly • *Our constitution had to be amended.* **amendment** NOUN

amenity, **amenities** *[Said am-**mee**-nit-ee]* NOUN GEOGRAPHY Amenities are things that are available for the public to use, such as sports facilities or shopping centres.

America NOUN America refers to the United States, or to the whole of North, South and Central America.

American ADJECTIVE ① belonging or relating to the United States, or to the whole of North, South and Central America. ▸ NOUN ② someone who comes from the United States.

amiable ADJECTIVE pleasant and friendly • *The hotel staff were very amiable.* **amiably** ADVERB **amiability** NOUN

amicable ADJECTIVE fairly friendly • *an amicable agreement.* **amicably** ADVERB

amid or **amidst** PREPOSITION *(formal)* ① If something happens amid events of some kind, it happens at the same time as those events • *The trial began amid scenes of chaos.* ② surrounded by • *The house is set amid trees and bushes.*

amiss ADJECTIVE If something is amiss, there is something wrong.

ammonia NOUN Ammonia is a colourless, strong-smelling gas or alkaline liquid. It is used in household cleaning materials, explosives and fertilisers. It has the chemical formula NH_3.

ammunition NOUN anything that can be fired from a gun or other weapon, for example bullets and shells.

amnesia NOUN loss of memory.

amnesty, **amnesties** NOUN an official pardon for political or other prisoners.

amok *[Said am-**muk**]* PHRASE If a person or animal **runs amok**, they behave in a violent and uncontrolled way.

among or **amongst** PREPOSITION ① surrounded by • *The bike lay among piles of chains and pedals.* ② in the company of • *He was among friends.* ③ between more than two • *The money will be divided among seven charities.*

> **among** PREPOSITION
> ① = amid, amidst, in the middle of, in the thick of, surrounded by
> ③ = between, to each of

amoral ADJECTIVE Someone who is amoral has no moral standards by which to live.

amorous ADJECTIVE passionately affectionate • *an amorous relationship.* **amorously** ADVERB **amorousness** NOUN

amount NOUN ① An amount of something is how much there is of it. ▸ VERB ② If something amounts to a particular total, all the parts of it add up to that total • *Her vocabulary amounted to only 50 words.*

> **amount** NOUN
> ① = expanse, quantity, volume

amp NOUN An amp is the same as an amplifier.

amphetamine NOUN a drug that increases people's energy and makes them excited. It can have dangerous and unpleasant side effects.

amphibian NOUN [SCIENCE] a creature that lives partly on land and partly in water, for example a frog or a newt.

amphibious ADJECTIVE An amphibious animal, such as a frog, lives partly on land and partly in water.

amphitheatre NOUN [HISTORY] An amphitheatre is a large, circular open area with sloping sides covered with rows of seats. Amphitheatres were built originally by the Greeks and Romans as venues for sport and entertainment.

ample ADJECTIVE If there is an ample amount of something, there is more than enough of it. **amply** ADVERB

> **ample** ADJECTIVE
> = abundant, enough, plenty of, sufficient

amplifier NOUN a piece of equipment which causes sounds or electrical signals to become louder.

amplify, **amplifies**, **amplifying**, **amplified** VERB If you amplify a sound, you make it louder. **amplification** NOUN

amputate VERB To amputate an arm or a leg is to cut it off as a surgical operation. **amputation** NOUN

amuse VERB ① If something amuses you, you think it is funny. ② If you amuse yourself, you find things to do which stop you from being bored. **amused** ADJECTIVE **amusing** ADJECTIVE

amusement NOUN ① Amusement is the state of thinking something is funny. ② Amusement is also the pleasure you get from being entertained or from doing something interesting. ③ Amusements are ways of passing the time pleasantly.

an ADJECTIVE 'An' is used instead of 'a' in front of words that begin with a vowel sound.

-an SUFFIX '-an' comes at the end of nouns and adjectives which show where or what someone or something comes from or belongs to • *American* • *Victorian* • *Christian*.

anachronism *[Said an-**ak**-kron-izm]* NOUN something that belongs or seems to belong to another time. **anachronistic** ADJECTIVE

anaemia *[Said a-**nee**-mee-a]* NOUN a medical condition resulting from too few red cells in a person's blood. People with anaemia look pale and feel very tired. **anaemic** ADJECTIVE

anaesthetic *[Said an-niss-**thet**-ik]* NOUN a substance that stops you feeling pain. A general anaesthetic stops you from feeling pain in the whole of your body by putting you to sleep, and a local anaesthetic makes just one part of your body go numb.

anaesthetist; also spelt **anesthetist** NOUN a doctor who is specially trained to give anaesthetics.

anagram NOUN a word or phrase formed by changing the order of the letters of another word or phrase. For example, 'triangle' is an anagram of 'integral'.

anal *[Said **ay**-nl]* ADJECTIVE relating to the anus.

analogy, **analogies** *[Said an-**al**-o-jee]* NOUN a comparison showing that two things are similar in some ways. **analogous** ADJECTIVE

analyse VERB [EXAM TERM] To analyse something is to break it down into parts, or investigate it carefully, so that you can describe its main aspects, or find out what it consists of.

analysis, **analyses** NOUN the process of investigating something in order to understand it or find out what it consists of • *a full analysis of the problem.*

analyst NOUN a person whose job is to analyse things to find out about them.

analytic or **analytical** ADJECTIVE using logical reasoning • *Planning in detail requires an acute analytical mind.* **analytically** ADVERB

anarchy *[Said **an**-nar-kee]* NOUN a situation where nobody obeys laws or rules.

anatomy, **anatomies** NOUN ① the study of the structure of the human body or of the bodies of animals. ② An animal's anatomy is the structure of its body. **anatomical** ADJECTIVE **anatomically** ADVERB

ANC NOUN one of the main political parties in South Africa. ANC is an abbreviation for 'African National Congress'.

ancestor NOUN Your ancestors are the members of your family who lived many years ago and from whom you are descended. **ancestral** ADJECTIVE

> **ancestor** NOUN
> = forebear, forefather

ancestry, **ancestries** NOUN Your ancestry consists of the people from whom you are descended • *a French citizen of Greek ancestry.*

anchor NOUN ① a heavy, hooked object at the end of a chain, dropped from a boat into the water to keep the boat in one place. ▸ VERB ② To anchor a boat or another object is to stop it from moving by dropping an anchor or attaching it to something solid.

anchorage NOUN a place where a boat can safely be anchored.

anchovy, **anchovies** NOUN a type of small edible fish with a very strong salty taste.

ancient *[Said **ayn**-shent]* ADJECTIVE ① existing or happening in the distant past • *ancient Greece.* ② very old or having a very long history • *an ancient monastery.*

ancillary *[Said an-**sil**-lar-ee]* ADJECTIVE The ancillary workers in an institution are the people such as cooks and cleaners, whose work supports the main work of the institution.

and CONJUNCTION You use 'and' to link two or more words or phrases together.

androgynous *[Said an-**droj**-in-uss]* ADJECTIVE (*formal*) having both male and female characteristics.

android NOUN In science fiction, an android is a robot that looks like a human being.

anecdote NOUN a short, entertaining story about a person or event. **anecdotal** ADJECTIVE

anew ADVERB If you do something anew, you do it again • *They left their life in Britain to start anew in France.*

angel NOUN Angels are spiritual beings some people believe live in heaven and act as messengers for God. **angelic** ADJECTIVE

anger NOUN ① the strong feeling you get when you feel someone has behaved in an unfair or cruel way. ▸ VERB ② If something angers you, it makes you feel angry.

> **anger** NOUN
> ① = fury, outrage, rage, wrath
> ▸ VERB ② = enrage, infuriate, outrage
> ≠ calm

angina *[Said an-**jy**-na]* NOUN a brief but very severe heart pain, caused by lack of blood supply to the heart. It is also known as 'angina pectoris'.

angle **NOUN** ① [MATHS] the difference in direction between two lines or surfaces. Angles are measured in degrees. ② the direction from which you look at something • *He had painted the vase from all angles.* ③ An angle on something is a particular way of considering it • *the same story from a German angle.*

angler **NOUN** someone who fishes with a fishing rod as a hobby. **angling** **NOUN**

Anglican **NOUN, ADJECTIVE** [RE] (a member of one of the churches) belonging to the Anglican Communion, a group of Protestant churches which includes the Church of England.

Anglo-Saxon **NOUN** ① [HISTORY] The Anglo-Saxons were a race of people who settled in England from the fifth century AD and were the dominant people until the Norman invasion in 1066. They were composed of three West Germanic tribes, the Angles, Saxons and Jutes. ② Anglo-Saxon is another name for **Old English**.

Angolan *[Said ang-**goh**-ln]* **ADJECTIVE** ① belonging or relating to Angola. ▶ **NOUN** ② someone who comes from Angola.

angry, **angrier**, **angriest** **ADJECTIVE** very cross or annoyed. **angrily** **ADVERB**

> **angry** **ADJECTIVE**
> = cross, enraged, furious, mad (*informal*)

anguish **NOUN** extreme suffering. **anguished** **ADJECTIVE**

angular **ADJECTIVE** Angular things have straight lines and sharp points • *He has an angular face and pointed chin.*

animal **NOUN** any living being except a plant, or any mammal except a human being.

> **animal** **NOUN**
> = beast, creature

animate **VERB** To animate something is to make it lively and interesting.

animated **ADJECTIVE** lively and interesting • *an animated conversation.* **animatedly** **ADVERB**

animation **NOUN** ① a method of film-making in which a series of drawings are photographed. When the film is projected, the characters in the drawings appear to move. ② Someone who has animation shows liveliness in the way they speak and act • *The crowd showed no sign of animation.* **animator** **NOUN**

animosity, **animosities** **NOUN** a feeling of strong dislike and anger towards someone.

> **animosity** **NOUN**
> = antagonism, antipathy (*formal*), dislike, hatred, hostility, ill will, malice, resentment

ankle **NOUN** the joint which connects your foot to your leg.

annex; also spelt **annexe** **NOUN** ① an extra building which is joined to a larger main building. ② an extra part added to a document. ▶ **VERB** ③ If one country annexes another, it seizes the other country and takes control of it. **annexation** **NOUN**

annihilate *[Said an-**nye**-ill-ate]* **VERB** If something is annihilated, it is completely destroyed. **annihilation** **NOUN**

anniversary, **anniversaries** **NOUN** a date which is remembered because something special happened on that date in a previous year.

announce **VERB** If you announce something, you tell people about it publicly or officially • *The team was announced on Friday morning.*

announce VERB
= advertise, make known, proclaim, reveal, tell

announcement NOUN a statement giving information about something.

announcement NOUN
= advertisement, broadcast, bulletin, declaration, report, statement

announcer NOUN someone who introduces programmes on radio and television.

annoy VERB If someone or something annoys you, they irritate you and make you fairly angry. **annoyed** ADJECTIVE

annoy VERB
= bother, displease, get on someone's nerves (*informal*), hack off (*British and New Zealand; slang*), irritate, plague, vex

annoyance NOUN ① a feeling of irritation. ② something that causes irritation.

annoyance NOUN
① = displeasure, irritation
② = bore, drag (*informal*), nuisance, pain (*informal*), pain in the neck (*informal*), pest

annual ADJECTIVE ① happening or done once a year • *their annual conference.* ② happening or calculated over a period of one year • *the United States' annual budget for national defence.* ▸ NOUN ③ a book or magazine published once a year. ④ a plant that grows, flowers and dies within one year. **annually** ADVERB

annuity, annuities NOUN a fixed sum of money paid to someone every year from an investment or insurance policy.

annul, annuls, annulling, annulled VERB If a marriage or contract is annulled, it is declared invalid, so that legally it is considered never to have existed. **annulment** NOUN

anoint VERB To anoint someone is to put oil on them as part of a ceremony. **anointment** NOUN

anomaly, anomalies [*Said an-**nom**-al-ee*] NOUN Something is an anomaly if it is unusual or different from normal. **anomalous** ADJECTIVE

anon. an abbreviation for **anonymous**.

anonymous ADJECTIVE If something is anonymous, nobody knows who is responsible for it • *The police received an anonymous phone call.* **anonymously** ADVERB **anonymity** NOUN

anorak NOUN a warm waterproof jacket, usually with a hood.

anorexia NOUN a psychological condition in which a person may eat too little in order to keep their weight as low as possible. **anorexic** ADJECTIVE

another ADJECTIVE, PRONOUN Another thing or person is an additional thing or person.

answer VERB ① If you answer someone, you reply to them using words or actions or in writing. ▸ NOUN ② the reply you give when you answer someone. ③ a solution to a problem.

answer VERB
① = reply, respond, retort
≠ ask
▸ NOUN ② = reply, response, retort
≠ question

answerable ADJECTIVE If you are answerable to someone for something, you are responsible for it • *He must be made answerable for these terrible crimes.*

ant NOUN Ants are small insects that live in large groups.

-ant SUFFIX '-ant' is used to form adjectives • *important.*

antagonise; also spelt **antagonize** VERB If someone is antagonised, they are made to feel anger and hostility.

antagonism NOUN hatred or hostility.

antagonist NOUN an enemy or opponent.

antagonistic ADJECTIVE Someone who is antagonistic towards you shows hate or hostility. **antagonistically** ADVERB

Antarctic NOUN The Antarctic is the region south of the Antarctic Circle.

Antarctic Circle NOUN The Antarctic Circle is an imaginary circle around the southern part of the world.

ante- PREFIX 'Ante-' means 'before'. For example, *antenatal* means 'before birth'.

antelope NOUN an animal which looks like a deer.

antenatal ADJECTIVE concerned with the care of pregnant women and their unborn children • *an antenatal clinic*.

antenna, **antennae** or **antennas** NOUN ① The antennae of insects and certain other animals are the two long, thin parts attached to their heads which they use to feel with. ② In Australian, New Zealand and American English, an antenna is a radio or television aerial.

anthem NOUN a hymn written for a special occasion.

anthology, **anthologies** NOUN LIBRARY a collection of writings by various authors published in one book.

anthropology NOUN the study of human beings and their society and culture. **anthropological** ADJECTIVE **anthropologist** NOUN

anti- PREFIX 'Anti-' means opposed to or opposite to something • *antiwar marches*.

antibiotic NOUN a drug or chemical used in medicine to kill bacteria and cure infections.

antibody, **antibodies** NOUN a substance produced in the blood which can kill the harmful bacteria that cause disease.

anticipate VERB If you anticipate an event, you are expecting it and are prepared for it • *She had anticipated his visit*. **anticipation** NOUN

anticlimax NOUN something that disappoints you because it is not as exciting as expected, or because it occurs after something that was very exciting.

anticlockwise ADJECTIVE, ADVERB moving in the opposite direction to the hands of a clock.

antics PLURAL NOUN funny or silly ways of behaving.

antidote NOUN a chemical substance that acts against the effect of a poison.

antipathy NOUN a strong feeling of dislike or hostility towards something or someone.

antiquarian ADJECTIVE relating to or involving old and rare objects • *antiquarian books*.

antiquated ADJECTIVE very old-fashioned • *an antiquated method of teaching*.

antique *[Said an-**teek**]* NOUN ① an object from the past that is collected because of its value or beauty. ▶ ADJECTIVE ② from or concerning the past • *antique furniture*.

antiquity, **antiquities** NOUN ① Antiquity is the distant past, especially the time of the ancient Egyptians, Greeks and Romans. ② Antiquities are interesting works of art and buildings from the distant past.

anti-Semitism NOUN hatred of Jewish people. **anti-Semitic** ADJECTIVE **anti-Semite** NOUN

antiseptic ADJECTIVE Something that is antiseptic kills germs.

antisocial ADJECTIVE ① An antisocial person is unwilling to meet and be friendly with other people. ② Antisocial behaviour is annoying or upsetting to other people • *Smoking in public is antisocial.*

antithesis, **antitheses** *[Said an-**tith**-iss-iss]* NOUN *(formal)* The antithesis of something is its exact opposite • *Work is the antithesis of leisure.*

anus NOUN the hole between the buttocks.

anvil NOUN a heavy iron block on which hot metal is beaten into shape.

anxiety, **anxieties** NOUN nervousness or worry.

> **anxiety** NOUN
> = apprehension, concern, fear, misgiving, nervousness, unease, worry

anxious ADJECTIVE ① If you are anxious, you are nervous or worried. ② If you are anxious to do something or anxious that something should happen, you very much want to do it or want it to happen • *He was anxious to get back to playing football.* **anxiously** ADVERB

> **anxious** ADJECTIVE
> ① = apprehensive, bothered, concerned, fearful, nervous, troubled, uneasy, worried

any ADJECTIVE, PRONOUN ① one, some or several • *Do you have any paperclips I could borrow?* ② even the smallest amount or even one • *He was unable to tolerate any dairy products.* ③ whatever or whichever, no matter what or which • *Any type of cooking oil will do.*

anybody PRONOUN any person.

anyhow ADVERB ① in any case. ② in a careless way • *They were all shoved in anyhow.*

anyone PRONOUN any person.

anything PRONOUN any object, event, situation or action.

anyway ADVERB in any case.

anywhere ADVERB in, at or to any place.

Anzac NOUN ① HISTORY In World War I, an Anzac was a soldier with the Australia and New Zealand Army Corps. ② an Australian or New Zealand soldier.

aorta *[Said ay-**or**-ta]* NOUN SCIENCE the main artery in the body, which carries blood away from the heart.

apart ADVERB, ADJECTIVE ① When something is apart from something else, there is a space or a distance between them • *The couple separated and lived apart for four years* • *The gliders landed about seventy metres apart.* ▶ ADVERB ② If you take something apart, you separate it into pieces.

apartheid *[Said ap-**par**-tide]* NOUN HISTORY In South Africa, apartheid was the government policy and laws which kept people of different races apart. It was abolished in 1994.

apartment NOUN a set of rooms for living in, usually on one floor of a building.

apathetic ADJECTIVE not interested in anything.

> **apathetic** ADJECTIVE
> = cool, indifferent, passive, uninterested
> ≠ enthusiastic

apathy *[Said **ap**-path-ee]* NOUN a state of mind in which you do not care about anything.

ape NOUN ① Apes are animals with a very short tail or no tail. They are closely related to humans. Apes include chimpanzees, gorillas and gibbons. ▶ VERB ② If you ape someone's speech or behaviour, you imitate it.

aphid NOUN a small insect that feeds by sucking the juices from plants.

apiece ADVERB If people have a particular number of things apiece, they have that number each.

aplomb [*Said uh-**plom***] NOUN If you do something with aplomb, you do it with great confidence.

apocalypse [*Said uh-**pok**-ka-lips*] NOUN The Apocalypse is the end of the world. **apocalyptic** ADJECTIVE

apocryphal ADJECTIVE A story that is apocryphal is generally believed not to have really happened.

apolitical [*Said ay-poll-**it**-i-kl*] ADJECTIVE not interested in politics.

apologetic ADJECTIVE showing or saying you are sorry. **apologetically** ADVERB

apologise; also spelt **apologize** VERB When you apologise to someone, you say you are sorry for something you have said or done.

> **apologise** VERB
> = ask forgiveness, beg someone's pardon, express regret, say sorry

apology, **apologies** NOUN something you say or write to tell someone you are sorry.

apostle NOUN [RE] The apostles are the twelve followers who were chosen by Christ.

apostrophe [*Said ap-**poss**-troff-ee*] NOUN [ENGLISH] a punctuation mark that is used to show that one or more letters have been missed out of a word. Apostrophes are also used with -s at the end of a noun to show that what follows belongs to or relates to the noun.

app NOUN [ICT] a computer program designed to do a particular task, especially one that you can download to a mobile electronic device.

appal, **appals**, **appalling**, **appalled** VERB If something appals you, it shocks you because it is very bad.

appalling ADJECTIVE so bad as to be shocking • *She escaped with appalling injuries.*

apparatus NOUN The apparatus for a particular task is the equipment used for it.

apparent ADJECTIVE ① seeming real rather than actually being real • *an apparent hit and run accident.* ② obvious • *It was apparent that he had lost interest.* **apparently** ADVERB

apparition NOUN something you think you see but that is not really there • *a ghostly apparition on the windscreen.*

appeal VERB ① If you appeal for something, you make an urgent request for it • *The police appealed for witnesses to come forward.* ② If you appeal to someone in authority against a decision, you formally ask them to change it. ③ If something appeals to you, you find it attractive or interesting. ▶ NOUN ④ a formal or serious request • *an appeal for peace.* ⑤ The appeal of something is the quality it has which people find attractive or interesting • *the rugged appeal of the Rockies.* **appealing** ADJECTIVE

> **appeal** VERB
> ① = beg, call upon, plead, request
> ③ = attract, fascinate, interest, please
> ▶ NOUN ④ = petition, plea, request

appear VERB ① When something which you could not see appears, it moves (or you move) so that you can see it. ② When something new appears, it begins to exist. ③ When an actor or actress appears in a film or show, they take part in it. ④ If something appears to be a certain way, it seems or looks that way • *He appeared to be searching for something.*

appear VERB
① = come into view, crop up (*informal*), emerge, show up (*informal*), surface, turn up
≠ disappear
② = become available, be invented, come into being, come into existence, come out

appearance NOUN ① The appearance of someone in a place is their arrival there, especially when it is unexpected. ② The appearance of something new is the time when it begins to exist • *the appearance of computer technology.* ③ Someone's or something's appearance is the way they look to other people • *We were taken aback by his tired appearance.*

appearance NOUN
② = advent, arrival, coming, debut, emergence, introduction
③ = bearing, image, look, looks

appease VERB If you try to appease someone, you try to calm them down when they are angry, for example by giving them what they want.
appeasement NOUN

appendage NOUN a less important part attached to a main part.

appendicitis [*Said app-end-i-**site**-uss*] NOUN a painful illness in which a person's appendix becomes infected.

appendix, **appendices** or **appendixes** NOUN ① a small closed tube forming part of your digestive system. ② An appendix to a book is extra information placed after the end of the main text.

appetising; also spelt **appetizing** ADJECTIVE Food that is appetising looks and smells good, and makes you want to eat it.

appetite NOUN ① Your appetite is your desire to eat. ② If you have an appetite for something, you have a strong desire for it and enjoyment of it • *She had lost her appetite for air travel.*

applaud VERB ① When a group of people applaud, they clap their hands in approval or praise. ② When an action or attitude is applauded, people praise it.

applause NOUN Applause is clapping by a group of people.

apple NOUN a round fruit with smooth skin and firm white flesh.

appliance NOUN any machine in your home you use to do a job like cleaning or cooking • *kitchen appliances.*

applicable ADJECTIVE Something that is applicable to a situation is relevant to it • *The rules are applicable to everyone.*

applicant NOUN someone who is applying for something • *We had problems recruiting applicants for the post.*

application NOUN ① a formal request for something, usually in writing. ② The application of a rule, system or skill is the use of it in a particular situation.

apply, **applies**, **applying**, **applied** VERB ① If you apply for something, you formally ask for it, usually by sending an email or writing a letter. ② If you apply a rule or skill, you use it in a situation • *He applied his mind to the problem.* ③ If something applies to a person or a situation, it is relevant to that person or situation • *The legislation applies only to people living in England and Wales.* ④ If you apply something to a surface, you put it on • *She applied lipstick to her mouth.*

appoint VERB ① If you appoint someone to a job or position, you formally choose them for it. ② If you appoint a time or place for something to happen, you decide

when or where it will happen.
appointed ADJECTIVE

appointment NOUN ① an arrangement you have with someone to meet them. ② The appointment of a person to do a particular job is the choosing of that person to do it. ③ a job or a position of responsibility • *He applied for an appointment in Russia.*

appointment NOUN
① = date, interview, meeting, rendezvous
② = election, naming, nomination, selection
③ = assignment, job, place, position, post

apposite [*Said* ***app**-o-zit*] ADJECTIVE well suited for a particular purpose • *He went before Cameron could think of anything apposite to say.*

appraise VERB If you appraise something, you think about it carefully and form an opinion about it. **appraisal** NOUN

appreciable [*Said a-**pree**-shuh-bl*] ADJECTIVE large enough to be noticed • *an appreciable difference.* **appreciably** ADVERB

appreciate VERB ① If you appreciate something, you like it because you recognise its good qualities • *He appreciates fine art.* ② If you appreciate a situation or problem, you understand it and know what it involves. ③ If you appreciate something someone has done for you, you are grateful to them for it • *I really appreciate you coming to visit me.* ④ If something appreciates over a period of time, its value increases • *The property appreciated by 50% in two years.*

appreciate VERB
① = admire, prize, rate highly, respect, treasure, value
≠ scorn
② = be aware of, perceive, realise, recognise, understand

appreciative ADJECTIVE
① understanding and enthusiastic • *They were a very appreciative audience.* ② thankful and grateful • *I am particularly appreciative of the help my family and friends have given me.*
appreciatively ADVERB

apprehend VERB (*formal*) ① When the police apprehend someone, they arrest them and take them into custody. ② If you apprehend something, you understand it fully • *They were unable to apprehend his hidden meaning.*

apprehensive ADJECTIVE afraid something bad may happen • *I was a little apprehensive about meeting him.*
apprehensively ADVERB
apprehension NOUN

apprentice NOUN a person who works with someone for a period of time in order to learn their skill or trade. **apprenticeship** NOUN

approach VERB ① To approach something is to come near or nearer to it. ② When a future event approaches, it gradually gets nearer • *As winter approached, tents were set up to accommodate refugees.* ③ If you approach someone about something, you ask them about it. ④ If you approach a situation or problem in a particular way, you think about it or deal with it in that way. ▸ NOUN ⑤ The approach of something is the process of it coming closer • *the approach of spring.* ⑥ An approach to a situation or problem is a way of thinking about it or dealing with it. ⑦ a road or path that leads to a place.
approaching ADJECTIVE

appropriate ADJECTIVE [*Said a-**proh**-pri-it*] ① suitable or acceptable for a particular situation • *He didn't think jeans were appropriate for a vice-president.* ▸ VERB [*Said a-**proh**-pri-ate*] ② (*formal*) If you appropriate something which does not belong to you, you take it without permission. **appropriately** ADVERB **appropriation** NOUN

> **appropriate** ADJECTIVE
> ① = apt, correct, fitting, proper, suitable
> ≠ inappropriate

approval NOUN ① Approval is agreement given to a plan or request • *The plan will require approval from the local authority.* ② PSHE Approval is also admiration • *She looked at James with approval.*

> **approval** NOUN
> ① = agreement, authorisation, blessing, endorsement, permission, sanction
> ② = admiration, esteem, favour, praise, respect
> ≠ disapproval

approve VERB ① PSHE If you approve of something or someone, you think that thing or person is acceptable or good. ② If someone in a position of authority approves a plan or idea, they formally agree to it. **approved** ADJECTIVE **approving** ADJECTIVE

> **approve** VERB
> ① = admire, favour, praise, respect, think highly of
> ≠ disapprove
> ② = authorise, consent to, endorse, permit, sanction
> ≠ veto

approximate ADJECTIVE MATHS almost exact • *What was the approximate distance between the cars?* **approximately** ADVERB

> **approximate** ADJECTIVE
> = estimated, inexact, loose, rough
> ≠ exact

apricot NOUN a small, soft, yellowish-orange fruit.

April NOUN the fourth month of the year. April has 30 days.

apron NOUN a piece of clothing worn over the front of normal clothing to protect it.

apt ADJECTIVE ① suitable or relevant • *a very apt description.* ② having a particular tendency • *They are apt to jump to the wrong conclusions.*

aptitude NOUN Someone's aptitude for something is their ability to learn it quickly and to do it well • *I have a natural aptitude for painting.*

aquarium, **aquaria** or **aquariums** NOUN a glass tank filled with water in which fish are kept.

Aquarius NOUN Aquarius is the eleventh sign of the zodiac, represented by a person carrying water. People born between January 20th and February 18th are born under this sign.

aquatic ADJECTIVE ① An aquatic animal or plant lives or grows in water. ② involving water • *aquatic sports.*

Arab NOUN a member of a group of people who used to live in Arabia but who now live throughout the Middle East and North Africa.

Arabic NOUN a language spoken by many people in the Middle East and North Africa.

arable ADJECTIVE Arable land is used for growing crops.

arbiter NOUN the person who decides about something.

arbitrary ADJECTIVE An arbitrary decision or action is one that is not based on a plan or system. **arbitrarily** ADVERB

arc NOUN ① a smoothly curving line. ② MATHS in geometry, a section of the circumference of a circle.

arcade NOUN a covered passage with shops or market stalls along one or both sides.

arcane ADJECTIVE mysterious and difficult to understand.

arch NOUN ① a structure that has a curved top supported on either side by a pillar or wall. ② the curved part of bone at the top of the foot. ▶ VERB ③ When something arches, it forms a curved line or shape. ▶ ADJECTIVE ④ most important • *my arch enemy*.

archaeology [*Said ar-kee-**ol**-loj-ee*]; also spelt **archeology** NOUN the study of the past by digging up and examining the remains of buildings, tools and other things. **archaeological**; also spelt **archeological** ADJECTIVE **archaeologist**; also spelt **archeologist** NOUN

archaic [*Said ar-**kay**-ik*] ADJECTIVE very old or old-fashioned.

archbishop NOUN [RE] a bishop of the highest rank in a Christian Church.

archeology another spelling of **archaeology**.

archer NOUN someone who shoots with a bow and arrow.

archery NOUN a sport in which people shoot at a target with a bow and arrow.

archipelago, **archipelagos** [*Said ar-kip-**pel**-lag-oh*] NOUN a group of small islands.

architect [*Said **ar**-kit-tekt*] NOUN [ART] a person who designs buildings.

architecture NOUN [ART] the art or practice of designing buildings. **architectural** ADJECTIVE

archive [*Said **ar**-kive*] NOUN Archives are collections of documents and records about the history of a family or some other group of people.

arctic NOUN ① The Arctic is the region north of the Arctic Circle. ▶ ADJECTIVE ② Arctic means very cold indeed • *arctic conditions*.

Arctic Circle NOUN The Arctic Circle is an imaginary circle around the northern part of the world.

ardent ADJECTIVE full of enthusiasm and passion. **ardently** ADVERB

> **ardent** ADJECTIVE
> = avid, devoted, enthusiastic, fervent, intense, keen, passionate
> ≠ apathetic

ardour NOUN a strong and passionate feeling of love or enthusiasm.

arduous [*Said **ard**-yoo-uss*] ADJECTIVE tiring and needing a lot of effort • *the arduous task of rebuilding the country*.

are the plural form of the present tense of **be**.

area NOUN ① a particular part of a place, country or the world • *a built-up area of the city*. ② The area of a piece of ground or a surface is the amount of space it covers, measured in square metres or square feet. ③ [MATHS] The area of a geometric object is the amount of space enclosed within its lines.

> **area** NOUN
> ① = district, locality, neighbourhood, region, zone
> ② = expanse, extent, range, size

arena NOUN ① a place where sports and other public events take place. ② A particular arena is the centre of attention or activity in a particular situation • *the political arena*.

Argentinian [*Said ar-jen-**tin**-ee-an*] ADJECTIVE ① belonging or relating to Argentina. ▶ NOUN ② someone who comes from Argentina.

arguable ADJECTIVE An arguable idea or point is not necessarily true or correct and should be questioned. **arguably** ADVERB

argue, **argues**, **arguing**, **argued** VERB ① If you argue with someone about something, you disagree with them about it, sometimes in an angry way. ② If you argue that something is the case, you give reasons why you think it is so • *She argued that her client had been wrongly accused.*

argue VERB
① = bicker, disagree, fall out (*informal*), feud, fight, quarrel, row, squabble, wrangle
② = assert, claim, debate, maintain, reason

argument NOUN ① a disagreement between two people which causes a quarrel. ② a point or a set of reasons you use to try to convince people about something.

argument NOUN
① = barney (*British, Australian and New Zealand; informal*), blue (*Australian; slang*), clash, dispute, feud, fight, row, squabble
② = case, grounds, logic, reasoning

argumentative ADJECTIVE An argumentative person is always disagreeing with other people.

aria *[Said* ***ah****-ree-a]* NOUN a song sung by one of the leading singers in an opera.

arid ADJECTIVE Arid land is very dry because it has very little rain.

Aries *[Said* ***air****-reez]* NOUN Aries is the first sign of the zodiac, represented by a ram. People born between March 21st and April 19th are born under this sign.

arise, arises, arising, arose, arisen VERB ① When something such as an opportunity or problem arises, it begins to exist. ② (*formal*) To arise also means to stand up from a sitting, kneeling or lying position.

aristocracy, aristocracies NOUN a class of people who have a high social rank and special titles.

aristocrat NOUN someone whose family has a high social rank, and who has a title. **aristocratic** ADJECTIVE

arithmetic NOUN the part of mathematics which is to do with the addition, subtraction, multiplication and division of numbers.
arithmetical ADJECTIVE
arithmetically ADVERB

ark NOUN [RE] In the Bible, the ark was the boat built by Noah for his family and the animals during the Flood.

arm NOUN ① Your arms are the part of your body between your shoulder and your wrist. ② The arms of a chair are the parts on which you rest your arms. ③ An arm of an organisation is a section of it • *the political arm of the armed forces.* ④ (*in plural*) Arms are weapons used in a war. ▶ VERB ⑤ To arm someone is to provide them with weapons.

armada *[Said ar-****mah****-da]* NOUN An armada is a large fleet of warships. In 1588, the Spanish Armada was sent against England by Philip II of Spain, but was defeated in the Channel by the English and destroyed.

Armageddon NOUN In Christianity, Armageddon is the final battle between good and evil at the end of the world.

armament NOUN Armaments are the weapons and military equipment that belong to a country.

armchair NOUN a comfortable chair with a support on each side for your arms.

armed ADJECTIVE A person who is armed is carrying a weapon or weapons.

armistice *[Said* ***ar****-miss-tiss]* NOUN [HISTORY] an agreement in a war to stop fighting in order to discuss peace.

armour NOUN [HISTORY] In the past, armour was metal clothing worn for protection in battle.

armoured ADJECTIVE covered with

thick steel for protection from gunfire and other missiles • *an armoured car*.

armoury, **armouries** **NOUN** a place where weapons are stored.

armpit **NOUN** the area under your arm where your arm joins your shoulder.

army, **armies** **NOUN** a large group of soldiers organised into divisions for fighting on land.

aroma **NOUN** a strong, pleasant smell. **aromatic** **ADJECTIVE**

aromatherapy **NOUN** a type of therapy that involves massaging the body with special fragrant oils.

arose the past tense of **arise**.

around **PREPOSITION** ① placed at various points in a place or area • *There are many seats around the building.* ② from place to place inside an area • *We walked around the showroom.* ③ at approximately the time or place mentioned • *The attacks began around noon.* ▸ **ADVERB** ④ here and there • *His papers were scattered around.*

arouse **VERB** If something arouses a feeling in you, it causes you to begin to have this feeling • *The song arouses sad memories.* **arousal** **NOUN**

arrange **VERB** ① If you arrange to do something, you make plans for it. ② If you arrange something for someone, you make it possible for them to have it or do it • *The bank has arranged a loan for her.* ③ If you arrange objects, you set them out in a particular position • *He started to arrange the books in piles.* **arrangement** **NOUN**

arrange **VERB**
① = fix up, organise, plan, schedule
③ = classify, group, order, organise, sort

array **NOUN** An array of different things is a large number of them displayed together.

arrears **PLURAL NOUN** ① Arrears are amounts of money you owe • *mortgage arrears.* ▸ **PHRASE** ② If you are paid **in arrears**, you are paid at the end of the period for which the payment is due.

arrest **VERB** ① If the police arrest someone, they take them into custody to decide whether to charge them with an offence. ▸ **NOUN** ② An arrest is the act of taking a person into custody. **arresting** **ADJECTIVE**

arrest **VERB**
① = apprehend, capture, nick (*British; slang*), seize, take prisoner
▸ **NOUN** ② = apprehension, capture, seizure

arrival **NOUN** ① the act or time of arriving • *The arrival of the train was delayed.* ② something or someone that has arrived • *The tourist authority reported record arrivals over Christmas.*

arrive **VERB** ① When you arrive at a place, you reach it at the end of your journey. ② When a letter or a piece of news arrives, it is brought to you • *A letter arrived at her lawyer's office.* ③ When you arrive at an idea or decision you reach it. ④ When a moment, event or new thing arrives, it begins to happen • *The Easter holidays arrived.*

arrogant **ADJECTIVE** Someone who is arrogant behaves as if they are better than other people. **arrogantly** **ADVERB** **arrogance** **NOUN**

arrow **NOUN** a long, thin weapon with a sharp point at one end, shot from a bow.

arsenal **NOUN** a place where weapons and ammunition are stored or produced.

arsenic **NOUN** SCIENCE Arsenic is a strongly poisonous element used in insecticides and weedkillers. Arsenic's atomic number is 33 and its symbol is As.

arson NOUN the crime of deliberately setting fire to something, especially a building.

art NOUN ① Art is the creation of objects such as paintings and sculptures, which are thought to be beautiful or which express a particular idea; also used to refer to the objects themselves. ② An activity is called an art when it requires special skill or ability • *the art of diplomacy*. ③ (*in plural*) The arts are literature, music, painting and sculpture, considered together.

artefact [*Said* ***ar****-tif-fact*] NOUN any object made by people.

artery, **arteries** NOUN ① Your arteries are the tubes that carry blood from your heart to the rest of your body. ② a main road or major section of any system of communication or transport.

artful ADJECTIVE clever and skilful, often in a cunning way. **artfully** ADVERB

arthritis NOUN [SCIENCE] a condition in which the joints in someone's body become swollen and painful. **arthritic** ADJECTIVE

artichoke NOUN ① the round, green, partly edible flower head of a thistle-like plant; the flower head is made up of clusters of leaves that have a soft fleshy part that is eaten as a vegetable. ② A Jerusalem artichoke is a small yellowish-white vegetable that grows underground and looks like a potato.

article NOUN ① [LIBRARY] a piece of writing in a newspaper or magazine. ② a particular item • *an article of clothing*. ③ In English grammar, 'a' and 'the' are sometimes called articles: 'a' (or 'an') is the indefinite article; 'the' is the definite article.

> **article** NOUN
> ① = feature, item, piece, story
> ② = item, object, thing

articulate ADJECTIVE ① If you are articulate, you are able to express yourself well in words. ▶ VERB ② When you articulate your ideas or feelings, you express in words what you think or feel • *She could not articulate her grief*. ③ When you articulate a sound or word, you speak it clearly. **articulation** NOUN

artificial ADJECTIVE ① created by people rather than occurring naturally • *artificial colouring*. ② pretending to have attitudes and feelings which other people realise are not real • *an artificial smile*. **artificially** ADVERB

artillery NOUN ① Artillery consists of large, powerful guns such as cannons. ② The artillery is the branch of an army which uses large, powerful guns.

artist NOUN ① a person who draws or paints or produces other works of art. ② a person who is very skilled at a particular activity.

artistic ADJECTIVE ① able to create good paintings, sculpture or other works of art. ② concerning or involving art or artists. **artistically** ADVERB

artistry NOUN Artistry is the creative skill of an artist, writer, actor or musician • *a supreme demonstration of his artistry as a cellist*.

arty, **artier**, **artiest** ADJECTIVE (*informal*) interested in painting, sculpture and other works of art.

as CONJUNCTION ① at the same time that • *She waved at fans as she arrived for the concert*. ② in the way that • *They had talked as only the best of friends can*. ③ because • *As I won't be back tonight, don't bother to cook a meal*. ④ You use the structure **as ... as** when you are comparing things that are similar • *It was as big as four football pitches*. ▶ PREPOSITION ⑤ You use 'as' when you are saying what role someone or something has • *She worked as a waitress.* ▶ **PHRASE** ⑥ You use **as if** or **as though** when you are giving a possible explanation for something • *He looked at me as if I were mad.*

asbestos **NOUN** a grey heat-resistant material used in the past to make fireproof articles.

ascend [*Said ass-**end***] **VERB** (*formal*) To ascend is to move or lead upwards • *We finally ascended to the brow of a steep hill.*

ascendancy **NOUN** (*formal*) If one group has ascendancy over another, it has more power or influence than the other.

ascendant **ADJECTIVE** ① rising or moving upwards. ▶ **PHRASE** ② Someone or something **in the ascendant** is increasing in power or popularity.

ascent **NOUN** an upward journey, for example up a mountain.

ascertain [*Said ass-er-**tain***] **VERB** (*formal*) If you ascertain that something is the case, you find out it is the case • *The police were still trying to ascertain the facts about the incident.*

ascribe **VERB** ① If you ascribe an event or state of affairs to a particular cause, you think that it is the cause of it • *Global warming is often ascribed to human activity.* ② If you ascribe a quality to someone, you think they have it.

ash **NOUN** ① the grey or black powdery remains of anything that has been burnt. ② a tree with grey bark and hard tough wood used for timber.

ashamed **ADJECTIVE** ① feeling embarrassed or guilty. ② If you are ashamed of someone, you feel embarrassed to be connected with them.

> **ashamed** **ADJECTIVE**
> ① = embarrassed, guilty, humiliated, sheepish, sorry
> ≠ proud

ashore **ADVERB** on land or onto the land.

ashtray **NOUN** a small dish for ash from cigarettes and cigars.

Asia **NOUN** Asia is the largest continent. It has Europe on its western side, with the Arctic to the north, the Pacific to the east, and the Indian Ocean to the south. Asia includes several island groups, including Japan, Indonesia and the Philippines.

Asian **ADJECTIVE** ① belonging or relating to Asia. ▶ **NOUN** ② someone who comes from Asia.

aside **ADVERB** ① If you move something aside, you move it to one side. ▶ **NOUN** ② a comment made away from the main conversation or dialogue that all those talking are not meant to hear.

ask **VERB** ① If you ask someone a question, you put a question to them for them to answer. ② If you ask someone to do something or give you something, you tell them you want them to do it or to give it to you. ③ If you ask someone's permission or forgiveness, you try to obtain it. ④ If you ask someone somewhere, you invite them there • *Not everybody had been asked to the wedding.*

> **ask** **VERB**
> ① = inquire, interrogate, query, question, quiz
> ≠ answer
> ② = appeal, beg, demand, implore, plead, seek
> ④ = bid (*literary*), invite

askew **ADJECTIVE** not straight.

asleep **ADJECTIVE** sleeping.

asparagus **NOUN** a vegetable that has long shoots which are cooked and eaten.

A B C D E F G H I J K L M N O P Q R S T U V W X Y Z

aspect NOUN ① An aspect of something is one of its features • *Exam results illustrate only one aspect of a school's success.* ② The aspect of a building is the direction it faces • *The southern aspect of the cottage faces over fields.*

> **aspect** NOUN
> ① = consideration, element, factor, feature, part, point, side

asphalt NOUN a black substance used to make road surfaces and playgrounds.

aspiration NOUN Someone's aspirations are their desires and ambitions.

aspire VERB If you aspire to something, you have an ambition to achieve it • *He aspired to work in music journalism.* **aspiring** ADJECTIVE

aspirin NOUN ① a white drug used to relieve pain, fever and colds. ② a tablet of this drug.

ass NOUN a donkey.

assailant NOUN someone who attacks another person.

assassin NOUN someone who has murdered a political or religious leader.

assassinate VERB To assassinate a political or religious leader is to murder him or her. **assassination** NOUN

assault NOUN ① a violent attack on someone. ▶ VERB ② To assault someone is to attack them violently.

assemble VERB ① To assemble is to gather together. ② If you assemble something, you fit the parts of it together.

> **assemble** VERB
> ① = collect, come together, congregate, convene, gather, mass
> ② = build, construct, erect, make, put together

assembly, **assemblies** NOUN ① a group of people who have gathered together for a meeting. ② The assembly of an object is the fitting together of its parts • *DIY assembly of units.*

assent [*Said as-sent*] NOUN ① If you give your assent to something, you agree to it. ▶ VERB ② If you assent to something, you agree to it.

assert VERB ① If you assert a fact or belief, you state it firmly and forcefully. ② If you assert yourself, you speak and behave in a confident and direct way, so that people pay attention to you.

assertion NOUN a statement or claim.

assertive ADJECTIVE If you are assertive, you speak and behave in a confident and direct way, so that people pay attention to you. **assertively** ADVERB **assertiveness** NOUN

assess VERB EXAM TERM If you assess something, you consider it carefully and make a judgment about it. **assessment** NOUN

assessor NOUN someone whose job is to assess the value of something.

asset NOUN ① a person or thing considered useful • *He will be a great asset to the club.* ② (*in plural*) The assets of a person or company are all the things they own that could be sold to raise money.

assign VERB ① To assign something to someone is to give it to them officially or to make them responsible for it. ② If someone is assigned to do something, they are officially told to do it.

assignment NOUN a job someone is given to do.

assimilate VERB ① If you assimilate ideas or experiences, you learn and understand them. ② When people are assimilated into a group, they become part of it. **assimilation** NOUN

assist VERB To assist someone is to help them do something. **assistance** NOUN

assistant NOUN someone whose job is to help another person in their work.

> **assistant** NOUN
> = aide, ally, colleague, helper, right-hand man

associate VERB ① If you associate one thing with another, you connect the two things in your mind. ② If you associate with a group of people, you spend a lot of time with them. ▸ NOUN ③ Your associates are the people you work with or spend a lot of time with.

> **associate** VERB
> ① = connect, couple, identify, link
> ② = hang out (*informal*), mingle, mix, run around (*informal*), socialise
> ▸ NOUN ③ = colleague, co-worker, workmate

association NOUN ① an organisation for people who have similar interests, jobs or aims. ② Your association with a person or group is the connection or involvement you have with them. ③ An association between two things is a link you make in your mind between them • *The place contained associations for her.*

> **association** NOUN
> ① = body, club, company, confederation, group, institution, league, society, syndicate
> ② = affiliation, attachment, bond, connection, relationship, tie

assorted ADJECTIVE Assorted things are different in size and colour • *assorted swimsuits.*

assortment NOUN a group of similar things that are different sizes and colours • *an amazing assortment of old toys.*

assume VERB ① If you assume that something is true, you accept it is true even though you have not thought about it • *I assumed that he would turn up.* ② To assume responsibility for something is to put yourself in charge of it.

> **assume** VERB
> ① = believe, guess (*informal*), imagine, suppose, think
> ② = accept, shoulder, take on, undertake

assumption NOUN ① a belief that something is true, without thinking about it. ② Assumption of power or responsibility is the taking of it.

assurance NOUN ① something said which is intended to make people less worried • *She was emphatic in her assurances that she wanted to stay.* ② Assurance is a feeling of confidence • *He handled the car with ease and assurance.* ③ Life assurance is a type of insurance that pays money to your dependants when you die.

assure VERB If you assure someone that something is true, you tell them it is true.

asterisk NOUN the symbol (*) used in printing and writing.

astern ADVERB, ADJECTIVE (*Nautical*) backwards or at the back.

asteroid NOUN one of the large number of very small planets that move around the sun between the orbits of Jupiter and Mars.

asthma [*Said ass-ma*] NOUN SCIENCE a disease of the chest which causes wheezing and difficulty in breathing. **asthmatic** ADJECTIVE

astonish VERB If something astonishes you, it surprises you very much. **astonished** ADJECTIVE **astonishing** ADJECTIVE **astonishingly** ADVERB **astonishment** NOUN

astound VERB If something astounds you, it shocks and amazes you. **astounded** ADJECTIVE **astounding** ADJECTIVE

astray PHRASE ① To **lead someone astray** is to influence them to do something wrong. ② If something **goes astray**, it gets lost • *The money had gone astray.*

astride PREPOSITION with one leg on either side of something • *He is pictured astride his new motorbike.*

astringent *[Said ass-**trin**-jent]* NOUN a liquid that makes skin less greasy and stops bleeding.

astrology NOUN the study of the sun, moon and stars in order to predict the future. **astrological** ADJECTIVE **astrologer** NOUN

astronaut NOUN a person who operates a spacecraft.

astronomical ADJECTIVE ① involved with or relating to astronomy. ② extremely large in amount • *astronomical legal costs.* **astronomically** ADVERB

astronomy NOUN the scientific study of stars and planets. **astronomer** NOUN

astute ADJECTIVE clever and quick at understanding situations and behaviour • *an astute diplomat.*

> **astute** ADJECTIVE
> = alert, clever, keen, perceptive, quick, sharp, shrewd, smart

asunder ADVERB (*literary*) If something is torn asunder, it is violently torn apart.

asylum *[Said ass-**eye**-lum]* NOUN ① (*old-fashioned*) a hospital for psychiatric patients. ② Political asylum is protection given by a government to someone who has fled from their own country for political reasons.

asymmetrical *[Said ay-sim-**met**-ri-kl]* or **asymmetric** ADJECTIVE unbalanced or with one half not exactly the same as the other half. **asymmetry** NOUN

at PREPOSITION ① used to say where someone or something is • *Bert met us at the airport.* ② used to mention the direction something is going in • *He threw his plate at the wall.* ③ used to say when something happens • *The game starts at 3 o'clock.* ④ used to mention the rate or price of something • *The shares were priced at fifty pence.*

ate the past tense of **eat**.

atheist *[Said **ayth**-ee-ist]* NOUN [RE] someone who believes there is no God. **atheistic** ADJECTIVE **atheism** NOUN

athlete NOUN [PE] someone who is good at sport and takes part in sporting events.

athletic ADJECTIVE ① [PE] strong, healthy and good at sports. ② involving athletes or athletics • *I lost two years of my athletic career because of injury.*

athletics PLURAL NOUN Sporting events such as running, jumping and throwing are called athletics.

Atlantic NOUN The Atlantic is the ocean separating North and South America from Europe and Africa.

atlas, atlases NOUN [GEOGRAPHY] a book of maps.

atmosphere NOUN ① [SCIENCE] [GEOGRAPHY] the air and other gases that surround a planet; also the air in a particular place • *a musty atmosphere.* ② the general mood of a place • *a relaxed atmosphere.* ③ [ENGLISH] the mood created by the writer of a novel or play. **atmospheric** ADJECTIVE

atom NOUN [SCIENCE] the smallest part of an element that can take part in a chemical reaction.

atomic ADJECTIVE relating to atoms or to the power released by splitting atoms • *atomic energy*.

atomic bomb NOUN an extremely powerful bomb which explodes because of the energy that comes from splitting atoms.

atone VERB (*formal*) If you atone for something wrong you have done, you say you are sorry and try to make up for it. **atonement** NOUN

atrocious ADJECTIVE extremely bad. **atrociously** ADVERB

atrocity, **atrocities** NOUN an extremely cruel and shocking act.

attach VERB If you attach something to something else, you join or fasten the two things together.

> **attach** VERB
> = affix, connect, couple, fasten, join, link, tie
> ≠ separate

attached ADJECTIVE If you are attached to someone, you are very fond of them.

attachment NOUN ① Attachment to someone is a feeling of love and affection for them. ② Attachment to a cause or ideal is a strong belief in it and support for it. ③ a piece of equipment attached to a tool or machine to do a particular job. ④ an extra document attached to or included with another document. ⑤ a file that is attached to an electronic message.

attack VERB ① To attack someone is to use violence against them so as to hurt or kill them. ② If you attack someone or their ideas, you criticise them strongly • *He attacked the government's economic policies*. ③ If a disease or chemical attacks something, it damages or destroys it • *fungal diseases that attack crops*. ④ In a game such as football or hockey, to attack is to get the ball into a position from which a goal can be scored. ▸ NOUN ⑤ An attack is violent physical action against someone. ⑥ An attack on someone or on their ideas is strong criticism of them. ⑦ An attack of an illness is a short time in which you suffer badly with it. **attacker** NOUN

> **attack** VERB
> ① = assault, charge, invade, raid, set upon, storm
> ② = blast, censure (*formal*), criticise, have a go at (*British*; *informal*), put down (*informal*), vilify (*formal*)
> ▸ NOUN ⑤ = assault, charge, invasion, offensive, onslaught, raid

attain VERB (*formal*) If you attain something, you manage to achieve it • *He eventually attained the rank of major*. **attainable** ADJECTIVE **attainment** NOUN

attempt VERB ① If you attempt to do something, you try to do it or achieve it, but may not succeed • *They attempted to escape*. ▸ NOUN ② an act of trying to do something • *He made no attempt to go for the ball*.

> **attempt** VERB
> ① = endeavour, seek, strive, try, try your hand at
> ▸ NOUN ② = bid, crack (*informal*), go (*informal*), shot (*informal*), stab (*informal*), try

attend VERB ① If you attend an event, you are present at it. ② To attend school, church or hospital is to go there regularly. ③ If you attend to something, you deal with it • *We have business to attend to first*. **attendance** NOUN

attendant NOUN someone whose job is to look after people in a place such as a cloakroom or swimming pool.

attention NOUN Attention is the thought or care you give to something

A B C D E F G H I J K L M N O P Q R S T U V W X Y Z

• *The woman needed medical attention.*

attentive ADJECTIVE paying close attention to something • *an attentive audience.* **attentively** ADVERB **attentiveness** NOUN

attest VERB (*formal*) To attest something is to show or declare it is true. **attestation** NOUN

attic NOUN a room at the top of a house immediately below the roof.

attire NOUN (*formal*) Attire is clothing • *We will be wearing traditional wedding attire.*

attitude NOUN Your attitude to someone or something is the way you think about them and behave towards them.

> **attitude** NOUN
> = outlook, perspective, point of view, position, stance

attorney [*Said at-**turn**-ee*] NOUN In America, an attorney is the same as a lawyer.

attract VERB ① If something attracts people, it interests them and makes them want to go to it • *The trials have attracted many leading riders.* ② If someone attracts you, you like and admire them • *He was attracted to her outgoing personality.* ③ If something attracts support or publicity, it gets it. ④ SCIENCE If something attracts objects to it, it has a force that pulls them towards it.

> **attract** VERB
> ① = appeal to, draw, entice, lure, pull (*informal*), tempt
> ≠ repel

attraction NOUN ① Attraction is a feeling of liking someone or something very much. ② something people visit for interest or pleasure • *The temple is a major tourist attraction.* ③ a quality that attracts someone or something • *the attraction of moving to seaside resorts.*

attractive ADJECTIVE ① interesting and possibly advantageous • *an attractive proposition.* ② pleasant to look at or be with • *an attractive woman* • *an attractive personality.* **attractively** ADVERB **attractiveness** NOUN

> **attractive** ADJECTIVE
> ② = appealing, charming, fetching, handsome, lovely, pretty
> ≠ unattractive

attribute VERB [*Said a-**trib**-yoot*] ① If you attribute something to a person or thing, you believe it was caused or created by that person or thing • *a painting attributed to Raphael* • *Water pollution was attributed to the use of fertilisers.* ▶ NOUN [*Said **at**-rib-yoot*] ② a quality or feature someone or something has. **attribution** NOUN **attributable** ADJECTIVE

> **attribute** NOUN
> ② = characteristic, feature, property, quality, trait

attrition NOUN ① Attrition is the constant wearing down of an enemy. ② GEOGRAPHY the process by which rocks gradually become smaller and smoother as they rub against one another in moving water.

attuned ADJECTIVE accustomed or well adjusted to something • *His eyes quickly became attuned to the dark.*

aubergine [*Said **oh**-ber-jeen*] NOUN a dark purple, pear-shaped fruit that is eaten as a vegetable. It is also called an **eggplant**.

auburn ADJECTIVE Auburn hair is reddish brown.

auction NOUN ① a public sale in which goods are sold to the person who offers the highest price. ▶ VERB ② To auction something is to sell it in an auction.

auctioneer NOUN the person in charge of an auction.

audacious ADJECTIVE very daring • *an audacious escape from jail.* **audaciously** ADVERB **audacity** NOUN

audible ADJECTIVE loud enough to be heard • *She spoke in a barely audible whisper.* **audibly** ADVERB **audibility** NOUN

audience NOUN ① the group of people who are watching or listening to a performance. ② a private or formal meeting with an important person • *an audience with the Queen.*

audio ADJECTIVE used in recording and reproducing sound • *audio equipment.*

audit VERB ① To audit a set of financial accounts is to examine them officially to check they are correct. ▶ NOUN ② an official examination of an organisation's accounts. **auditor** NOUN

audition NOUN a short performance given by an actor or musician, so that a director can decide whether they are suitable for a part in a play or film or for a place in an orchestra.

auditorium, **auditoriums** or **auditoria** NOUN the part of a theatre where the audience sits.

augment VERB (*formal*) To augment something is to add something to it.

> **augment** VERB
> = add to, boost, complement, increase, reinforce, supplement, top up

August NOUN the eighth month of the year. August has 31 days.

aunt NOUN Your aunt is the sister of your mother or father, or the wife of one of your parents' siblings.

au pair [*Said oh* ***pair***] NOUN a young foreign person who lives with a family to help with the children and housework and sometimes to learn the language.

aura NOUN an atmosphere that surrounds a person or thing • *She has a great aura of calmness.*

aural [*Rhymes with* ***floral***] ADJECTIVE relating to or done through the sense of hearing • *an aural comprehension test.*

auspices [*Said* ***aw****-spiss-eez*] PLURAL NOUN (*formal*) If you do something under the auspices of a person or organisation, you do it with their support • *military intervention under the auspices of the United Nations.*

auspicious ADJECTIVE (*formal*) favourable and seeming to promise success • *It was an auspicious start to the month.*

austere ADJECTIVE plain and simple, and without luxury • *an austere grey office block.* **austerity** NOUN

Australasia [*Said ost-ral-****lay****-sha*] NOUN Australasia consists of Australia, New Zealand and neighbouring islands in the Pacific. **Australasian** ADJECTIVE

Australia NOUN Australia is the smallest continent and the largest island in the world, situated between the Indian Ocean and the Pacific.

Austrian ADJECTIVE ① belonging or relating to Austria. ▶ NOUN ② someone who comes from Austria.

authentic ADJECTIVE real and genuine. **authentically** ADVERB **authenticity** NOUN

> **authentic** ADJECTIVE
> = bona fide, dinkum (*Australian and New Zealand; informal*), genuine, real, true
> ≠ fake

author NOUN ENGLISH The author of a book is the person who wrote it.

authorise; also spelt **authorize** VERB To authorise something is to give official permission for it to happen. **authorisation** NOUN

authoritarian ADJECTIVE believing in strict obedience • *thirty years of authoritarian government.* **authoritarianism** NOUN

A B C D E F G H I J K L M N O P Q R S T U V W X Y Z

authoritative ADJECTIVE ① having authority • *a deep, authoritative voice*. ② accepted as being reliable and accurate • *an authoritative biography of the President*. **authoritatively** ADVERB

authority, **authorities** NOUN ① Authority is the power to control people • *the authority of the state*. ② In Britain, an authority is a local government department • *local health authorities*. ③ Someone who is an authority on something knows a lot about it • *the world's leading authority on fashion*. ④ (*in plural*) The authorities are the people who have the power to make decisions.

autobiography, **autobiographies** NOUN Someone's autobiography is an account of their life which they have written themselves. **autobiographical** ADJECTIVE

autograph NOUN the signature of a famous person.

automatic ADJECTIVE ① An automatic machine is programmed to perform tasks without needing a person to operate it • *The plane was flying on automatic pilot*. ② Automatic actions or reactions take place without involving conscious thought. ③ A process or punishment that is automatic always happens as a direct result of something • *Certain crimes carry an automatic prison sentence*. **automatically** ADVERB

> **automatic** ADJECTIVE
> ① = automated, mechanical, robot, self-propelled
> ② = instinctive, involuntary, natural, reflex

automobile NOUN In American English, an automobile is a car.

> **automobile** NOUN
> = car, motor (*old-fashioned*), vehicle

autonomous [*Said aw-**ton**-nom-uss*] ADJECTIVE An autonomous country governs itself rather than being controlled by anyone else. **autonomy** NOUN

autopsy, **autopsies** NOUN a medical examination of a dead body to discover the cause of death.

autumn NOUN the season between summer and winter. **autumnal** ADJECTIVE

auxiliary, **auxiliaries** NOUN ① a person employed to help other members of staff • *nursing auxiliaries*. ▶ ADJECTIVE ② Auxiliary equipment is used when necessary in addition to the main equipment • *Auxiliary fuel tanks were stored in the bomb bay*.

avail PHRASE If something you do is **of no avail** or **to no avail**, it is not successful or helpful.

available ADJECTIVE ① Something that is available can be obtained • *Artichokes are available in supermarkets*. ② Someone who is available is ready for work or free for people to talk to • *She will no longer be available at weekends*. **availability** NOUN

> **available** ADJECTIVE
> ① = accessible, at hand, at someone's disposal, free, handy, to hand
> ≠ unavailable

avalanche [*Said **av**-a-lahnsh*] NOUN a huge mass of snow and ice that falls down a mountain side.

avant-garde [*Said av-vong-**gard***] ADJECTIVE extremely modern or experimental, especially in art, literature or music.

avarice NOUN (*formal*) greed for money and possessions. **avaricious** ADJECTIVE

avenge VERB If you avenge something harmful someone has done to you or your family, you punish or harm the other person in return • *He was prepared to avenge the death of his friend*. **avenger** NOUN

avenue NOUN a street, especially one with trees along it.

average NOUN ① MATHS a measure which represents the typical central or normal value in a set of data • *Six pupils were examined in a total of 39 subjects, an average of 6.5 subjects per pupil.* ▸ ADJECTIVE ② Average means standard or normal • *the average American teenager.* ▸ VERB ③ To average a number is to produce that number as an average over a period of time • *Monthly sales averaged more than 110,000.* ▸ PHRASE ④ You say **on average** when mentioning what usually happens in a situation • *Men are, on average, taller than women.*

> **average** ADJECTIVE
> ② = normal, regular, standard, typical, usual
> ▸ PHRASE ④ = as a rule, generally, normally, typically, usually

averse ADJECTIVE unwilling to do something • *He was averse to eating vegetables.*

aversion NOUN If you have an aversion to someone or something, you dislike them very much.

avert VERB ① If you avert an unpleasant event, you prevent it from happening. ② If you avert your eyes from something, you turn your eyes away from it.

aviary, **aviaries** NOUN a large cage or group of cages in which birds are kept.

aviation NOUN the science of flying aircraft.

aviator NOUN (*old-fashioned*) a pilot of an aircraft.

avid ADJECTIVE eager and enthusiastic for something. **avidly** ADVERB

avocado, **avocados** NOUN a pear-shaped fruit, with dark green skin, soft greenish yellow flesh, and a large stone.

avoid VERB ① If you avoid doing something, you make a deliberate effort not to do it. ② If you avoid someone, you keep away from them. **avoidable** ADJECTIVE **avoidance** NOUN

> **avoid** VERB
> ① = dodge, duck out of (*informal*), fight shy of, refrain from, shirk
> ② = dodge, elude, eschew (*formal*), evade, shun, sidestep, steer clear of

avowed ADJECTIVE (*formal*) ① If you are an avowed supporter or opponent of something, you have declared that you support it or oppose it. ② An avowed belief or aim is one you hold very strongly.

avuncular ADJECTIVE friendly and helpful in manner towards younger people, rather like an uncle.

await VERB ① If you await something, you expect it. ② If something awaits you, it will happen to you in the future.

awake, **awakes**, **awaking**, **awoke**, **awoken** ADJECTIVE ① Someone who is awake is not sleeping. ▸ VERB ② When you awake, you wake up. ③ If you are awoken by something, it wakes you up.

awaken VERB If something awakens an emotion or interest in you, you start to feel this emotion or interest.

award NOUN ① a prize or certificate for doing something well. ② a sum of money an organisation gives to students for training or study. ▸ VERB ③ If you award someone something, you give it to them formally or officially.

aware ADJECTIVE ① If you are aware of something, you realise it is there. ② If you are aware of something, you know about it. **awareness** NOUN

aware ADJECTIVE
① = acquainted with, conscious of, familiar with, mindful of
≠ unaware
② = informed, in the picture, knowledgeable

awash ADJECTIVE, ADVERB covered with water • *After the downpour the road was awash.*

away ADVERB ① moving from a place • *I saw them walk away.* ② at a distance from a place • *Our nearest vet is 12 kilometres away.* ③ in its proper place • *He put his wallet away.* ④ not at home, school or work • *She had been away from home for years.*

awe NOUN (*formal*) a feeling of great respect mixed with amazement and sometimes slight fear.

awesome ADJECTIVE ① Something that is awesome is very impressive and frightening. ② (*informal*) Awesome also means excellent or outstanding.

awful ADJECTIVE ① very unpleasant or very bad. ② (*informal*) very great • *It took an awful lot of courage.* **awfully** ADVERB

awful ADJECTIVE
① = appalling, dreadful, frightful (*old-fashioned*), ghastly, horrendous, terrible

awkward ADJECTIVE ① clumsy and uncomfortable • *an awkward gesture.* ② embarrassed or nervous • *He was a shy, awkward young man.* ③ difficult to deal with • *I found myself in an awkward situation.*

awning NOUN a large roof of canvas or plastic attached to a building or vehicle.

awoke the past tense of **awake**.

awoken the past participle of **awake**.

awry [*Said a-**rye***] ADJECTIVE wrong or not as planned • *Why had their plans gone so badly awry?*

axe, **axes**, **axing**, **axed** NOUN ① a tool with a handle and a sharp blade, used for chopping wood. ▶ VERB ② To axe something is to end it.

axiom NOUN a statement or saying that is generally accepted to be true. **axiomatic** ADJECTIVE

axis, **axes** [*Said **ak**-siss*] NOUN ① MATHS an imaginary line through the centre of something, around which it moves. ② MATHS one of the two sides of a graph.

axle NOUN the long bar that connects a pair of wheels on a vehicle.

azure [*Said **az**-yoor*] ADJECTIVE (*literary*) bright blue.

Bb

babble VERB When someone babbles, they talk in a confused or excited way.

> **babble** VERB
> = burble, chatter, gabble, prattle

baboon NOUN an African monkey with a pointed face, large teeth, and a long tail.

baby, babies NOUN a child in the first year or two of its life. **babyhood** NOUN **babyish** ADJECTIVE

> **baby** NOUN
> = ankle-biter (*Australian and New Zealand; slang*), bairn (*Scottish*), child, infant

bach [*Said* **batch**] NOUN ① In New Zealand, a bach is a small holiday cottage. ▶ VERB ② (*informal*) In Australian and New Zealand English, to bach is to live and keep a house on your own, especially when you are not used to it.

bachelor NOUN a man who has never been married.

back ADVERB ① When people or things move back, they move in the opposite direction from the one they are facing. ② When people or things go back to a place or situation, they return to it • *She went back to sleep.* ③ If you get something back, it is returned to you. ④ If you do something back to someone, you do to them what they have done to you • *I smiled back at them.* ⑤ Back also means in the past • *It happened back in the early eighties.* ▶ NOUN ⑥ the rear part of your body. ⑦ the part of something that is behind the front. ▶ ADJECTIVE ⑧ The back parts of something are the ones near the rear • *an animal's back legs.* ▶ VERB ⑨ If a building backs onto something, its back faces in that direction. ⑩ When a car backs, it moves backwards. ⑪ To back a person or organisation means to support or finance that person or organisation. **back down** VERB If you back down on a demand or claim, you withdraw and give up. **back out** VERB If you back out of a promise or commitment, you decide not to do what you had promised to do.
back up VERB ① If you back up a claim or story, you produce evidence to show that it is true. ② If you back someone up, you help and support them.

> **back** NOUN
> ⑦ = end, rear, reverse, stern
> ≠ front
> ▶ VERB ⑪ = advocate, encourage, endorse, favour, promote, support
> ≠ oppose

backbone NOUN ① the column of linked bones along the middle of a person's or animal's back. ② strength of character.

backdate VERB If an arrangement is backdated, it is valid from a date earlier than the one on which it is completed or signed.

backdrop NOUN the background to a situation or event • *The visit occurred against the backdrop of the political crisis.*

backer NOUN The backers of a project are the people who give it financial help.

A B C D E F G H I J K L M N O P Q R S T U V W X Y Z

backfire VERB ① If a plan backfires, it fails. ② When a car backfires, there is a small but noisy explosion in its exhaust pipe.

background NOUN ① the circumstances which help to explain an event or caused it to happen. ② the kind of home you come from and your education and experience • *a rich background.* ③ If sounds are in the background, they are there but no one really pays any attention to them • *She could hear voices in the background.*

> **background** NOUN
> ② = culture, environment, history, upbringing

backing NOUN support or help • *The project got government backing.*

backlash NOUN a hostile reaction to a new development or a new policy.

backlog NOUN a number of things which have not yet been done, but which need to be done.

backpack NOUN a large bag that hikers or campers carry on their backs.

backside NOUN (*informal*) the part of your body that you sit on.

backward ADJECTIVE ① Backward means directed behind you • *without a backward glance.* ② A backward country or society is one that does not have modern industries or technology. **backwardness** NOUN

backwards ADVERB ① Backwards means behind you • *Lucille looked backwards.* ② If you do something backwards, you do it the opposite of the usual way • *He instructed them to count backwards.*

bacon NOUN meat from the back or sides of a pig, which has been salted or smoked.

bacteria PLURAL NOUN [SCIENCE] Bacteria are very tiny organisms which live in air, water, soil, plants and the bodies of animals. Some bacteria provide food for plants, others cause diseases such as typhoid. **bacterial** ADJECTIVE

bad, **worse**, **worst** ADJECTIVE ① Anything harmful or upsetting can be described as bad • *Is the pain bad?* • *I have some bad news.* ② insufficient or of poor quality • *bad roads.* ③ evil or immoral in character or behaviour • *a bad person.* ④ lacking skill in something • *I was bad at sports.* ⑤ Bad language consists of swearwords. ⑥ If you have a bad temper, you become angry easily. **badness** NOUN

> **bad** ADJECTIVE
> ① = damaging, disturbing, harmful, serious, severe, terrible, unpleasant
> ≠ good
> ② = faulty, imperfect, inferior, poor, unsatisfactory
> ≠ satisfactory
> ③ = corrupt, depraved, evil, immoral, wicked
> ≠ good

bade a form of the past tense of **bid**.

badge NOUN a piece of plastic or metal with a design or message on it that you can pin to your clothes.

badger NOUN ① a wild animal that has a white head with two black stripes on it. ▸ VERB ② If you badger someone, you keep asking them questions or pestering them to do something.

badly ADVERB in an inferior or unimpressive way.

> **badly** ADVERB
> = inadequately, ineptly, poorly, shoddily, unsatisfactorily
> ≠ well

badminton NOUN [PE] Badminton is a game in which two or four players use rackets to hit a shuttlecock over a high net. It was first played at

Badminton House in Gloucestershire.

baffle VERB If something baffles you, you cannot understand or explain it • *The symptoms baffled the doctors.* **baffled** ADJECTIVE **baffling** ADJECTIVE

bag NOUN ① a container for carrying things in. ② (*in plural, informal*) Bags of something is a lot of it • *bags of fun.*

baggage NOUN the suitcases and bags that you take on a journey.

baggy, **baggier**, **baggiest** ADJECTIVE Baggy clothing hangs loosely.

bagpipes PLURAL NOUN [MUSIC] a musical instrument played by squeezing air out of a leather bag through pipes, on which a tune is played.

bail NOUN ① Bail is a sum of money paid to a court to allow an accused person to go free until the time of the trial • *He was released on bail.* ▸ VERB ② If you bail water from a boat, you scoop it out. **bail out**; also spelt **bale out** VERB ① To bail out of an aircraft means to jump out of it with a parachute. ② If you bail someone out, you help them out of a difficult situation.

bailiff NOUN ① a law officer who makes sure that the decisions of a court are obeyed. ② a person employed to look after land or property for the owner.

bait NOUN ① a small amount of food placed on a hook or in a trap, to attract a fish or wild animal so that it gets caught. ② something used to tempt a person to do something. ▸ VERB ③ If you bait a hook or trap, you put some food on it to catch a fish or wild animal.

> **bait** NOUN
> ② = bribe, decoy, inducement, lure, temptation

bake VERB ① To bake food means to cook it in an oven without using liquid or fat. ② To bake earth or clay means to heat it until it becomes hard.

baker NOUN a person who makes and sells bread and cakes.

bakery, **bakeries** NOUN a building where bread and cakes are baked and sold.

bakkie [*Said* **buck-ee**] NOUN In South African English, a bakkie is a small truck.

balance VERB ① When someone or something balances, they remain steady and do not fall over. ▸ NOUN ② Balance is the state of being upright and steady. ③ Balance is also a situation in which all the parts involved have a stable relationship with each other • *the chemical balance of the brain* • *a good work-life balance.* ④ The balance in someone's bank account is the amount of money in it.

> **balance** VERB
> ① = level, stabilise, steady
> ▸ NOUN ③ = equilibrium, equity, parity

balanced ADJECTIVE A balanced account or report presents information in a fair and objective way.

balcony, **balconies** NOUN ① a platform on the outside of a building with a wall or railing round it. ② an area of upstairs seats in a theatre or cinema.

bald ADJECTIVE ① A bald person has little or no hair on their head. ② A bald statement or question is made in the simplest way without any attempt to be polite. **baldly** ADVERB **baldness** NOUN

bale NOUN ① a large bundle of something, such as paper or hay, tied tightly. ▸ VERB ② If you bale water from a boat, you remove it using a container; also spelt **bail**. **bale out**;

also spelt **bail out** VERB To bale out of an aircraft means to jump out of it with a parachute.

balk; also spelt **baulk** VERB If you balk at something, you object to it and may refuse to do it • *He balked at the cost.*

ball NOUN ① a round object, especially one used in games such as cricket and soccer. ② The ball of your foot or thumb is the rounded part where your toes join your foot or your thumb joins your hand. ③ a large formal social event at which people dance.

> **ball** NOUN
> ① = drop, globe, pellet, sphere

ballad NOUN ① ENGLISH a long song or poem which tells a story. ② a slow, romantic pop song.

ballast NOUN any heavy material placed in a ship to make it more stable.

ballerina NOUN a female ballet dancer.

ballet [*Said* ***bal**-lay*] NOUN Ballet is a type of artistic dancing based on precise steps.

balloon NOUN ① a small bag made of thin rubber that you blow into until it becomes larger and rounder. ② a large, strong bag filled with gas or hot air, which travels through the air carrying passengers in a compartment underneath.

ballot NOUN ① a secret vote in which people select a candidate in an election, or express their opinion about something. ▸ VERB ② When a group of people are balloted, they are asked questions to find out what they think about a particular problem or question.

ballpoint NOUN a pen with a small metal ball at the end which transfers the ink onto the paper.

ballroom NOUN a very large room used for dancing or formal balls.

balmy, **balmier**, **balmiest** ADJECTIVE mild and pleasant • *balmy summer evenings.*

balustrade NOUN a railing or wall on a balcony or staircase.

bamboo NOUN Bamboo is a tall tropical plant with hard, hollow stems used for making furniture. It is a species of giant grass. The young shoots can be eaten.

ban, **bans**, **banning**, **banned** VERB ① If something is banned, or if you are banned from doing it or using it, you are not allowed to do it or use it. ▸ NOUN ② If there is a ban on something, it is not allowed.

> **ban** VERB
> ① = bar, disqualify, exclude, forbid, outlaw, prohibit
> ≠ permit
> ▸ NOUN ② = disqualification, embargo, prohibition, suppression
> ≠ permit

banal [*Said ba-**nahl***] ADJECTIVE very ordinary and not at all interesting • *He made some banal remark.* **banality** NOUN

banana NOUN a long curved fruit with a yellow skin.

band NOUN ① a group of musicians who play jazz or pop music together, or a group who play brass instruments together. ② a group of people who share a common purpose • *a band of rebels.* ③ a narrow strip of something used to hold things together or worn as a decoration • *an elastic band* • *a headband.* **band together** VERB When people band together, they join together for a particular purpose.

> **band** NOUN
> ① = group, orchestra
> ② = bunch, company, crowd, gang, party, troupe

bandage NOUN ① a strip of cloth wrapped round a wound to protect it. ▸ VERB ② If you bandage a wound, you tie a bandage round it.

bandit NOUN (*old-fashioned*) a member of an armed gang who rob travellers.

bandwagon PHRASE To **jump on the bandwagon** means to become involved in something because it is fashionable or likely to be successful.

bandwidth NOUN The bandwidth of a telecommunications signal is the range of frequencies used to transmit it.

bandy, **bandies, bandying, bandied** VERB If a name is bandied about, many people mention it.

bane NOUN (*literary*) Someone or something that is the bane of a person or organisation causes a lot of trouble for them • *the bane of my life.*

bang VERB ① If you bang something, you hit it or put it somewhere violently, so that it makes a loud noise • *He banged down the receiver.* ② If you bang a part of your body against something, you accidentally bump it. ▸ NOUN ③ a sudden, short, loud noise. ④ a hard or painful bump against something.

> **bang** VERB
> ① = beat, hammer, hit, knock, pound, slam, thump
> ▸ NOUN ③ = blast, boom, crack, detonation, explosion, thump
> ④ = blow, clout (*informal*), knock, thump, whack (*informal*)

Bangladeshi [*Said bang-glad-**desh**-ee*] ADJECTIVE ① belonging or relating to Bangladesh. ▸ NOUN ② someone who comes from Bangladesh.

bangle NOUN an ornamental band worn round someone's wrist or ankle.

banish VERB ① To banish someone means to send them into exile. ② To banish something means to get rid of it • *It will be a long time before poverty is banished.* **banishment** NOUN

> **banish** VERB
> ① = deport, eject, evict, exile, expel, transport
> ② = discard, dismiss, dispel, eliminate, eradicate, remove

banjo, **banjos** or **banjoes** NOUN a musical instrument, like a small guitar with a round body.

bank NOUN ① a business that looks after people's money. ② A bank of something is a store of it kept ready for use • *a blood bank.* ③ the raised ground along the edge of a river or lake. ④ the sloping side of an area of raised ground. ▸ VERB ⑤ When you bank money, you pay it into a bank. ⑥ If you bank on something happening, you expect it and rely on it.

> **bank** NOUN
> ② = fund, hoard, reserve, stock, store
> ③ = brink, edge, shore, side

banker, **bankers** NOUN a senior worker in a bank.

bank holiday NOUN a public holiday, when banks are officially closed.

banking NOUN the business of looking after people's money.

banknote NOUN a piece of paper money.

bankrupt ADJECTIVE ① People or organisations that go bankrupt do not have enough money to pay their debts. ▸ NOUN ② someone who has been declared bankrupt. ▸ VERB ③ To bankrupt someone means to make them bankrupt • *Restoring the house nearly bankrupted them.* **bankruptcy** NOUN

banner NOUN a long strip of cloth with a message or slogan on it.

banquet NOUN a grand formal dinner, often followed by speeches.

banter NOUN Banter is friendly joking and teasing.

baptise; also spelt **baptize** VERB When someone is baptised, water is sprinkled on them, or they are immersed in water, as a sign that they have become a Christian.

baptism NOUN [RE] a ceremony in which someone is baptised.

Baptist NOUN [RE] a member of a Protestant church who believe that people should be baptised when they are adults rather than when they are babies.

bar, **bars**, **barring**, **barred** NOUN ① a long, straight piece of metal. ② a piece of something made in a rectangular shape • *a bar of soap*. ③ a counter or room where alcoholic drinks are served. ④ The bars in a piece of music are the many short parts of equal length that the piece is divided into. ⑤ [GEOGRAPHY] In meteorology, a bar is a unit of pressure, equivalent to 100,000 newtons per square metre. ▶ VERB ⑥ If you bar a door, you place something across it to stop it being opened. ⑦ If you bar someone's way, you stop them going somewhere by standing in front of them.

> **bar** NOUN
> ① = pole, rail, rod, shaft
> ▶ VERB ⑦ = obstruct, prevent

barb NOUN a sharp curved point on the end of an arrow or fish-hook.

barbarian NOUN a member of a wild or uncivilised people.

barbaric ADJECTIVE cruel or brutal • *The judge described the crime as barbaric*.
barbarity NOUN

barbecue, **barbecues**, **barbecuing**, **barbecued** NOUN ① a grill with a charcoal fire on which you cook food, usually outdoors; also an outdoor party where you eat food cooked on a barbecue. ▶ VERB ② When food is barbecued, it is cooked over a charcoal grill.

barbed ADJECTIVE A barbed remark is one that seems straightforward but is really unkind or spiteful.

barbed wire NOUN Barbed wire is strong wire with sharp points sticking out of it, used to make fences.

barber NOUN a person who cuts men's hair.

bar code NOUN a small pattern of numbers and lines on something you buy in a shop, which can be electronically scanned at a checkout to give the price.

bard NOUN (*literary*) A bard is a poet. Some people call Shakespeare the Bard.

bare, **barer**, **barest** ADJECTIVE ① If a part of your body is bare, it is not covered by any clothing. ② If something is bare, it has nothing on top of it or inside it • *bare floorboards* • *a small bare office*. ③ When trees are bare, they have no leaves on them. ④ The bare minimum or bare essentials means the very least that is needed • *They were fed the bare minimum*. ▶ VERB ⑤ If you bare something, you uncover or show it.

> **bare** ADJECTIVE
> ① = exposed, uncovered
> ≠ covered
> ② = empty, open, spartan

barefoot ADJECTIVE, ADVERB not wearing anything on your feet.

barely ADVERB only just • *The girl was barely sixteen*.

> **barely** ADVERB
> = almost, hardly, just, scarcely

bargain NOUN ① an agreement in which two people or groups discuss and agree what each will do, pay or

A B C D E F G H I J K L M N O P Q R S T U V W X Y Z

receive in a matter which involves them both. ② something which is sold at a low price and which is good value. ▶ VERB ③ When people bargain with each other, they discuss and agree terms about what each will do, pay or receive in a matter which involves both. **bargain for** VERB If you had not bargained for or on something, you were not prepared for it.

barge NOUN ① a boat with a flat bottom used for carrying heavy loads, especially on canals. ▶ VERB ② (*informal*) If you barge into a place, you push into it in a rough or rude way.

bark VERB ① When a dog barks, it makes a short, loud noise, once or several times. ▶ NOUN ② the short, loud noise that a dog makes. ③ the tough material that covers the outside of a tree.

barley NOUN a cereal that is grown for food and is also used for making beer and whisky.

barmy, **barmier**, **barmiest** ADJECTIVE (*slang*) eccentric or very foolish.

barn NOUN a large farm building used for storing crops or animal food.

barometer NOUN GEOGRAPHY an instrument that measures air pressure and shows when the weather is changing.

baron NOUN a member of the lowest rank of the nobility. **baronial** ADJECTIVE

baroness NOUN a woman who has the rank of baron, or who is the wife of a baron.

barracks PLURAL NOUN a building where soldiers live.

barrage NOUN ① A barrage of questions or complaints is a lot of them all coming at the same time. ② A barrage is continuous artillery fire over a wide area, to prevent the enemy from moving.

barrel NOUN ① a wooden container with rounded sides and flat ends. ② The barrel of a gun is the long tube through which the bullet is fired.

barren ADJECTIVE ① Barren land has soil of such poor quality that plants cannot grow on it. ② A barren female animal is not able to have young. **barrenness** NOUN

> **barren** ADJECTIVE
> ① = arid, desert, desolate, dry, empty, waste
> ≠ fertile

barricade NOUN ① a temporary barrier put up to stop people getting past. ▶ VERB ② If you barricade yourself inside a room or building, you put something heavy against the door to stop people getting in.

barrier NOUN ① a fence or wall that prevents people or animals getting from one area to another. ② If something is a barrier, it prevents two people or groups from agreeing or communicating, or prevents something from being achieved
• *Cost is a major barrier to using the law.*

> **barrier** NOUN
> ① = barricade, fence, obstruction, wall
> ② = handicap, hindrance, hurdle, impediment, obstacle

barrister NOUN a lawyer who is qualified to represent people in the higher courts.

barrow NOUN ① the same as a **wheelbarrow**. ② a large cart from which fruit or other goods are sold in the street.

barter VERB ① If you barter goods, you exchange them for other goods, rather than selling them for money. ▶ NOUN ② Barter is the activity of exchanging goods.

base NOUN ① the lowest part of something, which often supports the rest. ② a place which part of an army, navy or air force works from. ③ SCIENCE In chemistry, a base is any compound that reacts with an acid to form a salt. ④ MATHS In mathematics, a base is a system of counting and expressing numbers. The decimal system uses base 10, and the binary system uses base 2. ⑤ MATHS The base of a shape is the side or face that is at the bottom. ▸ VERB ⑥ To base something on something else means to use the second thing as a foundation or starting point of the first • *The film is based on a traditional folk tale.* ⑦ If you are based somewhere, you live there or work from there.

> **base** NOUN
> ① = bed, bottom, foot, foundation, pedestal, stand
> ≠ top
> ② = camp, centre, headquarters, post, station
> ▸ VERB ⑥ = build, derive, found, ground, hinge

baseball NOUN Baseball is a team game played with a bat and a ball, similar to rounders.

basement NOUN a floor of a building built completely or partly below the ground.

bases PLURAL NOUN ① *[Said* ***bay****-seez]* the plural of **basis**. ② *[Said* ***bay****-siz]* the plural of **base**.

bash *(informal)* VERB ① If you bash someone or bash into them, you hit them hard. ▸ NOUN ② A bash is a hard blow. ▸ PHRASE ③ If you **have a bash** at something, you try to do it.

bashful ADJECTIVE shy and easily embarrassed.

basic ADJECTIVE ① The basic aspects of something are the most necessary ones • *the basic necessities of life.* ② Something that is basic has only the necessary features without any extras or luxuries • *The accommodation is pretty basic.* **basically** ADVERB

> **basic** ADJECTIVE
> ① = elementary, essential, fundamental, key, necessary, vital

basics PLURAL NOUN The basics of something are the things you need to know or understand • *the basics of map-reading.*

basin NOUN ① a round wide container which is open at the top. ② The basin of a river is a bowl of land from which water runs into the river.

basis NOUN ① The basis of something is the essential main principle from which it can be developed • *The same colour theme is used as the basis for several patterns.* ② The basis for a belief is the facts that support it • *There is no basis for this assumption.*

> **basis** NOUN
> ① = core, fundamental, heart, premise, principle

bask VERB If you bask in the sun, you sit or lie in it, enjoying its warmth.

basket NOUN a container made of thin strips of cane woven together.

basketball NOUN Basketball is a game in which two teams try to score goals by throwing a large ball through one of two circular nets suspended high up at each end of the court.

bass[1] *[Rhymes with* ***lace****]* NOUN ① MUSIC a man with a very deep singing voice. ② MUSIC A bass is also a musical instrument that provides the rhythm and lowest part in the harmonies. A bass may be either a large guitar or a very large member of the violin family.

bass[2] *[Rhymes with* ***gas****]* NOUN a type of edible sea fish.

bastion NOUN (*literary*) something that protects a system or way of life • *The country is the last bastion of communism.*

bat, **bats, batting, batted** NOUN ① a specially shaped piece of wood with a handle, used for hitting the ball in a game such as cricket or table tennis. ② a small flying animal, active at night, that looks like a mouse with wings. ▶ VERB ③ In certain sports, when someone is batting, it is their turn to try to hit the ball and score runs.

batch NOUN a group of things of the same kind produced or dealt with together.

bated PHRASE **With bated breath** means very anxiously.

bath NOUN a long container which you fill with water and sit in to wash yourself.

bathe VERB ① When you bathe, you swim or play in open water. ② When you bathe a wound, you wash it gently. ③ (*literary*) If a place is bathed in light, a lot of light reaches it • *The room was bathed in spring sunshine.* **bather** NOUN **bathing** NOUN

bathroom NOUN a room with a bath or shower, a washbasin, and often a toilet in it.

baton NOUN ① a light, thin stick that a conductor uses to direct an orchestra or choir. ② In athletics, the baton is a short stick passed from one runner to another in a relay race. ③ A baton is also a short stick used as a weapon by police officers in some countries.

batsman, **batsmen** NOUN In cricket, the batsman is the person who is batting.

battalion NOUN an army unit consisting of three or more companies.

batten NOUN a strip of wood that is fixed to something to strengthen it or hold it firm. **batten down** VERB If you batten something down, you make it secure by fixing battens across it.

batter VERB ① To batter someone or something means to hit them many times • *The waves kept battering the life raft.* ▶ NOUN ② Batter is a mixture of flour, eggs and milk, used to make pancakes, or to coat food before frying it. **battering** NOUN

battery, **batteries** NOUN ① a device, containing two or more cells, for storing and producing electricity, for example in a torch or a car. ② a large group of things or people. ▶ ADJECTIVE ③ A battery hen is one of a large number of hens kept in small cages for the mass production of eggs.

battle NOUN ① HISTORY a fight between armed forces or a struggle between two people or groups with conflicting aims • *the battle between town and country.* ② A battle for something difficult is a determined attempt to obtain or achieve it • *the battle for equality in the workplace.*

battlefield NOUN a place where a battle is or has been fought.

battleship NOUN a large, heavily armoured warship.

batty, **battier, battiest** ADJECTIVE (*informal*) foolish or eccentric.

bauble NOUN a pretty but cheap ornament or piece of jewellery.

baulk another spelling of **balk**.

bawl VERB ① (*informal*) To bawl at someone means to shout at them loudly and harshly. ② When a child is bawling, it is crying very loudly and angrily.

bay NOUN ① GEOGRAPHY a part of a coastline where the land curves inwards. ② a space or area used for a particular purpose • *a loading bay.*

③ Bay is a kind of tree similar to the laurel, with leaves used for flavouring in cooking. ▶ PHRASE ④ If you **keep something at bay**, you prevent it from reaching you • *Eating oranges keeps colds at bay*. ▶ VERB ⑤ When a hound or wolf bays, it makes a deep howling noise.

bay NOUN
① = cove, gulf, inlet, sound
▶ VERB ⑤ = bark, cry, howl, yelp

bayonet NOUN a sharp blade that can be fixed to the end of a rifle and used for stabbing.

bazaar NOUN ① an area with many small shops and stalls, especially in Asia or North Africa. ② a sale to raise money for charity.

BC BC means 'before Christ'. You use 'BC' in dates to indicate the number of years before the traditional date of the birth of Jesus Christ • *in 49 BC*.

be, **am**, **is**, **are**; **being**; **was**, **were**; **been** AUXILIARY VERB ① 'Be' is used with a present participle to form the continuous tense • *Crimes of violence are increasing*. ② 'Be' is also used to say that something will happen • *We are going to America next month*. ③ 'Be' is used to form the passive voice • *The walls were being repaired*. ▶ VERB ④ 'Be' is used to give more information about the subject of a sentence • *Her name is Melanie*.

beach NOUN an area of sand or pebbles beside the sea.

beach NOUN
= coast, sands, seashore, seaside, shore, strand

beacon NOUN In the past, a beacon was a light or fire on a hill, which acted as a signal or warning.

bead NOUN ① Beads are small pieces of coloured glass or wood with a hole through the middle, strung together to make necklaces. ② Beads of liquid are drops of it.

beady, **beadier**, **beadiest** ADJECTIVE Beady eyes are small and bright like beads.

beagle NOUN a short-haired dog with long ears and short legs.

beak NOUN A bird's beak is the hard part of its mouth that sticks out.

beam NOUN ① a broad smile. ② A beam of light is a band of light that shines from something such as a torch. ③ a long, thick bar of wood or metal, especially one that supports a roof. ▶ VERB ④ If you beam, you smile because you are happy.

bean NOUN Beans are the seeds or pods of a climbing plant, which are eaten as a vegetable; also used of some other seeds, for example the seeds from which coffee is made.

bear, **bears**, **bearing**, **bore**, **borne** NOUN ① a large, strong wild animal with thick fur and sharp claws. ▶ VERB ② (*formal*) To bear something means to carry it or support its weight • *The ice wasn't thick enough to bear their weight*. ③ If something bears a mark or typical feature, it has it • *The room bore all the signs of a violent struggle*. ④ If you bear something difficult, you accept it and are able to deal with it • *He bore his last illness with courage*. ⑤ If you can't bear someone or something, you dislike them very much. ⑥ (*formal*) When a plant or tree bears flowers, fruit or leaves, it produces them. **bearable** ADJECTIVE **bear out** VERB To bear someone out or to bear out their story or report means to support what they are saying • *These claims are not borne out by the evidence*.

bear VERB
② = carry, convey (*formal*), hold, support, take
③ = exhibit, harbour, have
④ = abide, endure, stand, stomach, suffer, tolerate

beard NOUN the hair that grows on the lower part of a man's face. **bearded** ADJECTIVE

bearer NOUN The bearer of something is the person who carries or presents it • *the bearer of bad news.*

bearing NOUN ① If something has a bearing on a situation, it is relevant to it. ② the way in which a person moves or stands.

beast NOUN ① (*old-fashioned*) a large wild animal. ② (*informal*) If you call someone a beast, you mean that they are cruel or spiteful.

beastly, **beastlier**, **beastliest** ADJECTIVE (*old-fashioned, informal*) cruel or spiteful.

beat, **beats**, **beating**, **beat**, **beaten** VERB ① To beat someone or something means to hit them hard and repeatedly. ② If you beat someone in a race or game, you defeat them or do better than them. ③ When a bird or insect beats its wings, it moves them up and down. ④ When your heart is beating, it is pumping blood with a regular rhythm. ⑤ If you beat eggs or butter, you mix them vigorously using a fork or a whisk. ▸ NOUN ⑥ The beat of your heart is its regular pumping action. ⑦ [MUSIC] The beat of a piece of music is its main rhythm. ⑧ A police officer's beat is the area which he or she patrols. **beater** NOUN **beating** NOUN **beat up** VERB To beat someone up means to hit or kick them repeatedly.

beat VERB
① = batter, buffet, hit, pound, strike, thrash
② = defeat, outdo, outstrip, overcome, overwhelm, vanquish (*literary*)
▸ NOUN ⑦ = cadence, metre, rhythm, stress, time

beaut (*informal*) NOUN ① In Australian and New Zealand English, a beaut is an outstanding person or thing. ▸ ADJECTIVE ② In Australian and New Zealand English, beaut means good or excellent • *a beaut house.*

beautiful ADJECTIVE very attractive or pleasing • *a beautiful girl* • *beautiful music.* **beautifully** ADVERB

beautiful ADJECTIVE
= attractive, delightful, fine, gorgeous, lovely, pleasing
≠ ugly

beauty, **beauties** NOUN ① Beauty is the quality of being beautiful. ② (*old-fashioned*) a very attractive woman. ③ The beauty of an idea or plan is what makes it attractive or worthwhile • *The beauty of the idea is its simplicity.*

beauty NOUN
① = attractiveness, charm, elegance, loveliness
≠ ugliness
③ = advantage, asset, attraction, benefit

beaver NOUN an animal with a big, flat tail and webbed hind feet. Beavers build dams.

became the past tense of **become**.

because CONJUNCTION ① 'Because' is used with a clause that gives the reason for something • *I went home because I was tired.* ▸ PHRASE ② **Because of** is used with a noun that gives the reason for something • *He quit playing because of a knee injury.*

because CONJUNCTION
① = as, since

beck PHRASE If you are at someone's **beck and call**, you are always available to do what they ask.

beckon VERB ① If you beckon to someone, you signal with your hand that you want them to come to you.

② If you say that something beckons, you mean that you find it very attractive • *A career in journalism beckons.*

become, **becomes**, **becoming**, **became**, **become** VERB To become something means to start feeling or being that thing • *I became very angry* • *He became an actor.*

bed NOUN ① a piece of furniture that you lie on when you sleep. ② A bed in a garden is an area of ground in which plants are grown. ③ The bed of a sea or river is the ground at the bottom of it.

bedding NOUN Bedding is sheets, blankets and other covers that are used on beds.

bedlam NOUN You can refer to a noisy and disorderly place or situation as bedlam • *The delay caused bedlam at the station.*

bedraggled ADJECTIVE A bedraggled person or animal is in a messy or untidy state.

bedridden ADJECTIVE Someone who is bedridden is too ill to get out of bed.

bedrock NOUN ① Bedrock is the solid rock under the soil. ② The bedrock of something is the foundation and principles on which it is based • *His life was built on the bedrock of integrity.*

bedroom NOUN a room used for sleeping in.

bedspread NOUN a cover put over a bed, on top of the sheets and blankets.

bee NOUN a winged insect that makes honey and lives in large groups.

beech NOUN a tree with a smooth grey trunk and shiny leaves.

beef NOUN Beef is the meat of a cow, bull or ox.

beefy, **beefier**, **beefiest** ADJECTIVE (*informal*) A beefy person is strong and muscular.

beehive NOUN a container in which bees live and make their honey.

beeline PHRASE (*informal*) If you **make a beeline** for a place, you go there as quickly and directly as possible.

been the past participle of **be**.

beer NOUN an alcoholic drink made from malt and flavoured with hops.

beetle NOUN a flying insect with hard wings which cover its body when it is not flying.

beetroot NOUN A beetroot is the round, dark red root of a type of beet. It is cooked and eaten, especially cold as a salad vegetable or preserved in vinegar.

befall, **befalls**, **befalling**, **befell**, **befallen** VERB (*old-fashioned*) If something befalls you, it happens to you • *A similar fate befell my cousin.*

before ADVERB, PREPOSITION, CONJUNCTION ① 'Before' is used to refer to a previous time • *Apply the ointment before going to bed.* ▶ ADVERB ② If you have done something before, you have done it on a previous occasion • *Never before had he seen such poverty.* ▶ PREPOSITION ③ (*formal*) Before also means in front of • *They stopped before a large white villa.*

> **before** ADVERB, PREPOSITION, CONJUNCTION
> ① = earlier, formerly, in advance, previously, sooner
> ≠ after

beforehand ADVERB before • *It had been agreed beforehand that they would spend the night there.*

befriend VERB If you befriend someone, you act in a kind and helpful way and so become friends with them.

beg, **begs**, **begging**, **begged** VERB ① When people beg, they ask for food or money, because they are very poor. ② If you beg someone to do something, you ask them very anxiously to do it.

> **beg** VERB
> ② = beseech (*literary*), implore, petition, plead

began the past tense of **begin**.

beggar NOUN someone who lives by asking people for money or food.

begin, **begins**, **beginning**, **began**, **begun** VERB If you begin to do something, you start doing it. When something begins, it starts.

> **begin** VERB
> = commence (*formal*), inaugurate (*formal*), initiate, originate, set about, start
> ≠ end

beginner NOUN someone who has just started learning to do something and cannot do it very well yet.

> **beginner** NOUN
> = apprentice, learner, novice, starter, trainee
> ≠ expert

beginning NOUN The beginning of something is the first part of it or the time when it starts • *They had now reached the beginning of the city.*

> **beginning** NOUN
> = birth, commencement (*formal*), opening, origin, outset, start
> ≠ end

begrudge VERB If you begrudge someone something, you are angry or envious because they have it • *No one could begrudge him the glory.*

begun the past participle of **begin**.

behalf PHRASE To do something **on behalf of** someone or something means to do it for their benefit or as their representative.

behave VERB ① If you behave in a particular way, you act in that way • *They were behaving like animals.* ② To behave yourself means to act correctly or properly.

> **behave** VERB
> ① = act, function, operate, work

behaviour NOUN Your behaviour is the way in which you behave.

behead VERB To behead someone means to cut their head off.

behind PREPOSITION ① at the back of • *He was seated behind the desk.* ② responsible for or causing • *He was the driving force behind the move.* ③ supporting someone • *The whole country was behind him.* ▶ ADVERB ④ If you stay behind, you remain after other people have gone. ⑤ If you leave something behind, you do not take it with you.

behold, **beholds**, **beholding**, **beheld** (*literary*) VERB ① To behold something means to notice it or look at it. ▶ INTERJECTION ② You say 'behold' when you want someone to look at something. **beholder** NOUN

beige [*Said* ***bayj***] NOUN, ADJECTIVE pale creamy-brown.

being ① Being is the present participle of **be**. ▶ NOUN ② Being is the state or fact of existing • *The party came into being in 1923.* ③ a living creature, either real or imaginary • *alien beings from a distant galaxy.*

belated ADJECTIVE (*formal*) A belated action happens later than it should have done • *a belated birthday present.* **belatedly** ADVERB

belch VERB ① If you belch, you make a sudden noise in your throat because air has risen up from your stomach. ② If something belches smoke or fire, it sends it out in large amounts • *Smoke belched from the steelworks.* ▶ NOUN ③ the noise you make when you belch.

beleaguered ADJECTIVE ① struggling against difficulties or criticism • *the* *beleaguered aviation industry*. ② besieged by an enemy • *the beleaguered garrison*.

Belgian ADJECTIVE ① belonging or relating to Belgium. ▶ NOUN ② someone who comes from Belgium.

belief NOUN ① a feeling of certainty that something exists or is true. ② one of the principles of a religion or moral system.

> **belief** NOUN
> ① = confidence, conviction, judgment, opinion, trust, view
> ② = creed, doctrine, dogma, faith, ideology, principle, tenet (*formal*)

believable ADJECTIVE possible or likely to be the case.

> **believable** ADJECTIVE
> = credible, imaginable, likely, plausible, possible, probable
> ≠ unbelievable

believe VERB ① If you believe that something is true, you accept that it is true. ② If you believe someone, you accept that they are telling the truth. ③ If you believe in things such as God and miracles, you accept that they exist or happen. ④ If you believe in something such as a plan or system, you are in favour of it • *They really believe in education*. **believer** NOUN

> **believe** VERB
> ① = accept, assume, presume, swallow (*informal*), trust
> ≠ doubt

belittle VERB If you belittle someone or something, you make them seem unimportant • *He belittled my opinions*.

> **belittle** VERB
> = deride (*formal*), detract from, downgrade, scorn, undervalue
> ≠ praise

bell NOUN ① a cup-shaped metal object with a piece inside that swings and hits the sides, producing a ringing sound. ② an electrical device that rings or buzzes in order to attract attention.

belligerent ADJECTIVE aggressive and keen to start a fight or an argument. **belligerently** ADVERB **belligerence** NOUN

bellow VERB ① When an animal such as a bull bellows, it makes a loud, deep roaring noise. ② If someone bellows, they shout in a loud, deep voice.

belly, **bellies** NOUN ① Your belly is your stomach or the front of your body below your chest. ② An animal's belly is the underneath part of its body.

belong VERB ① If something belongs to you, it is yours and you own it. ② To belong to a group means to be a member of it. ③ If something belongs in a particular place, that is where it should be • *It did not belong in the music room*.

belongings PLURAL NOUN Your belongings are the things that you own.

beloved [*Said bil-**luv**-id*] ADJECTIVE A beloved person or thing is one that you feel great affection for.

> **beloved** ADJECTIVE
> = adored, cherished, darling, dearest, precious, treasured
> ≠ despised

below PREPOSITION, ADVERB ① If something is below a line or the surface of something else, it is lower down • *six inches below soil level*. ② Below also means at or to a lower point, level or rate • *The temperature fell below zero degrees*.

> **below** PREPOSITION, ADVERB
> ① = beneath, down, lower, under, underneath
> ≠ above

belt NOUN ① a strip of leather or cloth

that you fasten round your waist to hold your trousers or skirt up. ② In a machine, a belt is a circular strip of rubber that drives moving parts or carries objects along. ③ a specific area of a country • *Poland's industrial belt*. ▶ VERB ④ (*informal*) To belt someone means to hit them very hard.

bemused ADJECTIVE If you are bemused, you are puzzled or confused.

bench NOUN ① a long seat that two or more people can sit on. ② a long, narrow table for working at, for example in a laboratory.

bend, **bends**, **bending**, **bent** VERB ① When you bend something, you use force to make it curved or angular. ② When you bend, you move your head and shoulders forwards and downwards. ▶ NOUN ③ a curved part of something.

> **bend** VERB
> ① = buckle, curve, turn, twist, warp
> ② = arch, bow, crouch, incline, lean, stoop
> ▶ NOUN ③ = arc, corner, curve, loop, turn

beneath PREPOSITION, ADJECTIVE, ADVERB ① an old-fashioned word for **underneath**. ▶ PREPOSITION ② If someone thinks something is beneath them, they think that it is too unimportant for them to bother with it.

benefactor NOUN a person who helps to support a person or institution by giving money.

beneficial ADJECTIVE Something that is beneficial is good for people • *the beneficial effects of exercise*. **beneficially** ADVERB

> **beneficial** ADJECTIVE
> = advantageous, good for you, healthy, helpful, useful, wholesome

beneficiary, **beneficiaries** NOUN A beneficiary of something is someone who receives money or other benefits from it.

benefit NOUN ① The benefits of something are the advantages that it brings to people • *the benefits of relaxation*. ② Benefit is money given by the government to people who are unemployed or ill. ▶ VERB ③ If you benefit from something or something benefits you, it helps you.

> **benefit** NOUN
> ① = advantage, asset, boon, gain, good, help, profit, use
> ≠ disadvantage
> ▶ VERB ③ = aid, assist, enhance, further, help, profit
> ≠ harm

benevolent ADJECTIVE kind and helpful. **benevolence** NOUN **benevolently** ADVERB

> **benevolent** ADJECTIVE
> = benign, charitable, compassionate, humane, kind

benign [*Said be-nine*] ADJECTIVE ① Someone who is benign is kind and gentle. ② A benign tumour is one that will not cause death or serious illness. **benignly** ADVERB

bent ① Bent is the past tense and past participle of **bend**. ▶ PHRASE ② If you are **bent on** doing something, you are determined to do it.

berate VERB (*formal*) If you berate someone, you scold them angrily • *He berated them for getting caught*.

bereaved ADJECTIVE (*formal*) You say that someone is bereaved when a close relative or friend of theirs has recently died. **bereavement** NOUN

bereft ADJECTIVE (*literary*) If you are bereft of something, you no longer have it • *The government seems bereft of ideas*.

beret *[Said* **ber**-*ray]* **NOUN** a circular flat hat with no brim.

berry, **berries** **NOUN** Berries are small, round fruits that grow on bushes or trees.

berserk **PHRASE** If someone **goes berserk**, they lose control of themselves and become very violent.

berth **NOUN** ① a space in a harbour where a ship stays when it is being loaded or unloaded. ② In a boat or caravan, a berth is a bed.

beset **ADJECTIVE** *(formal)* If you are beset by difficulties or doubts, you have a lot of them.

beside **PREPOSITION** If one thing is beside something else, they are next to each other.

beside **PREPOSITION**
= adjacent to, alongside, close to, near, next to

besiege **VERB** ① When soldiers besiege a place, they surround it and wait for the people inside to surrender. ② If you are besieged by people, many people want something from you and continually bother you.

best **ADJECTIVE, ADVERB** ① the superlative of **good** and **well**. ▶ **ADVERB** ② The thing that you like best is the thing that you prefer to everything else. ▶ **NOUN** ③ the thing most preferred.

best **ADJECTIVE, ADVERB**
① = finest, first-rate, foremost, greatest, leading, outstanding, pre-eminent, principal, superlative, supreme, top
≠ worst
▶ **NOUN** ③ = cream, elite, finest, pick
≠ worst

best man **NOUN** The best man at a wedding is the man who acts as the bridegroom's attendant.

bestow **VERB** *(formal)* If you bestow something on someone, you give it to them.

bet, **bets**, **betting**, **bet** **VERB** ① If you bet on the result of an event, you will win money if something happens and lose money if it does not. ▶ **NOUN** ② the act of betting on something, or the amount of money that you agree to risk. ▶ **PHRASE** ③ *(informal)* You say **I bet** to indicate that you are sure that something is or will be so • *I bet the answer is no*. **betting** **NOUN**

betray **VERB** ① If you betray someone who trusts you, you do something which harms them, such as helping their enemies. ② If you betray your feelings or thoughts, you show them without intending to. **betrayal** **NOUN** **betrayer** **NOUN**

betray **VERB**
① = break your promise, double-cross *(informal)*, inform on
② = expose, manifest *(formal)*, reveal, show

better **ADJECTIVE, ADVERB** ① the comparative of **good** and **well**. ▶ **ADVERB** ② If you like one thing better than another, you like it more than the other thing. ▶ **ADJECTIVE** ③ If you are better after an illness, you are no longer ill.

better **ADJECTIVE, ADVERB**
① = finer, grander, greater, higher-quality, nicer, preferable, superior, surpassing, worthier
≠ inferior
▶ **ADJECTIVE** ③ = cured, fitter, fully recovered, healthier, improving, on the mend *(informal)*, recovering, stronger, well
≠ worse

between **PREPOSITION, ADVERB** ① If something is between two other things, it is situated or happens in the space or time that separates them

• *flights between Europe and Asia.* ② A relationship or difference between two people or things involves only those two.

beverage NOUN (*formal*) a drink.

bevy, **bevies** NOUN a group of people • *a bevy of lawyers.*

beware VERB If you tell someone to beware of something, you are warning them that it might be dangerous or harmful.

> **beware** VERB
> = be careful, be cautious, be wary, guard against, look out, watch out

bewilder VERB If something bewilders you, it is too confusing or difficult for you to understand. **bewildered** ADJECTIVE **bewildering** ADJECTIVE **bewilderment** NOUN

bewitch VERB ① To bewitch someone means to cast a spell on them. ② If something bewitches you, you are so attracted to it that you cannot pay attention to anything else. **bewitched** ADJECTIVE **bewitching** ADJECTIVE

beyond PREPOSITION ① If something is beyond a certain place, it is on the other side of it • *Beyond the hills was the Sahara.* ② If something continues beyond a particular point, it continues further than that point • *an education beyond the age of 16.* ③ If someone or something is beyond understanding or help, they cannot be understood or helped.

bias NOUN Someone who shows bias favours one person or thing unfairly.

> **bias** NOUN
> = bigotry, favouritism, prejudice

biased; also spelt **biassed** ADJECTIVE favouring one person or thing unfairly • *biased attitudes.*

> **biased** ADJECTIVE
> = one-eyed (*Australian and New Zealand*), one-sided, partial, prejudiced, slanted, weighted
> ≠ neutral

bib NOUN a piece of cloth or plastic which is worn under the chin of very young children when they are eating, to keep their clothes clean.

Bible NOUN [RE] The Bible is the sacred book of the Christian and Jewish religions. **biblical** ADJECTIVE

bicentenary, **bicentenaries** NOUN The bicentenary of an event is its two-hundredth anniversary.

biceps NOUN [PE] the large muscle on your upper arms.

bicker VERB When people bicker, they argue or quarrel about unimportant things.

bicycle NOUN a two-wheeled vehicle which you ride by pushing two pedals with your feet.

bid, **bids**, **bidding**, **bade** or **bid**, **bidden** or **bid** NOUN ① an attempt to obtain or do something • *He made a bid for freedom.* ② an offer to buy something for a certain sum of money. ▸ VERB ③ If you bid for something, you offer to pay a certain sum of money for it. ④ (*old-fashioned*) If you bid someone a greeting or a farewell, you say it to them.

bide, **bides**, **biding**, **bided** PHRASE If you **bide your time**, you wait for a good opportunity before doing something.

big, **bigger**, **biggest** ADJECTIVE ① of a large size. ② of great importance. **biggish** ADJECTIVE **bigness** NOUN

> **big** ADJECTIVE
> ① = enormous, huge, immense, massive, vast
> ≠ small
> ② = important, major, powerful, prominent, significant
> ≠ unimportant

a b c d e f g h i j k l m n o p q r s t u v w x y z

bigot NOUN someone who has strong and unreasonable opinions which they refuse to change. **bigoted** ADJECTIVE **bigotry** NOUN

bike NOUN (*informal*) a bicycle or motorcycle.

bikini, **bikinis** NOUN a small two-piece swimming costume worn by women.

bilateral ADJECTIVE A bilateral agreement is one made between two groups or countries.

bile NOUN Bile is a bitter yellow liquid produced by the liver which helps the digestion of fat. In the Middle Ages, it was believed to cause anger.

bilge NOUN the lowest part of a ship, where dirty water collects.

bilingual ADJECTIVE involving or using two languages • *bilingual street signs*.

bill NOUN ① a written statement of how much is owed for goods or services. ② a formal statement of a proposed new law that is discussed and then voted on in Parliament. ③ a notice or a poster. ④ A bird's bill is its beak. ▸ VERB ⑤ If you bill someone, you give or send them a bill for goods or services you have supplied.

> **bill** NOUN
> ① = account, charges, invoice, statement

billboard NOUN a large board on which advertisements are displayed.

billiards NOUN Billiards is a game played on a large table, in which a long stick called a cue is used to strike one of three balls. The aim is to hit a second ball with the first so that either the third ball is also hit or one of the balls goes into one of the six pockets at the edges of the table.

billion NOUN a thousand million. Formerly, a billion was a million million. **billionth** ADJECTIVE

billow VERB ① When things made of cloth billow, they swell out and flap slowly in the wind. ② When smoke or cloud billows, it spreads upwards and outwards. ▸ NOUN ③ a large wave.

bin NOUN a container, especially one that you put rubbish in.

binary [*Said by-nar-ee*] ADJECTIVE ICT The binary system expresses numbers using only two digits, 0 and 1.

bind, **binds**, **binding**, **bound** VERB ① If you bind something, you tie rope or string round it so that it is held firmly. ② If something binds you to a course of action, it makes you act in that way • *He was bound by that decision*.

binding ADJECTIVE ① If a promise or agreement is binding, it must be obeyed. ▸ NOUN ② The binding of a book is its cover.

binge NOUN (*informal*) a wild bout of drinking or eating too much.

bingo NOUN Bingo is a game in which players aim to match the numbers that someone calls out with the numbers on the card that they have been given.

binoculars PLURAL NOUN Binoculars are an instrument with lenses for both eyes, which you look through in order to see objects far away.

biochemistry NOUN Biochemistry is the study of the chemistry of living things. **biochemical** ADJECTIVE **biochemist** NOUN

biodegradable ADJECTIVE If something is biodegradable, it can be broken down into its natural elements by the action of bacteria • *biodegradable cleaning products*.

biodiversity NOUN SCIENCE the existence of a wide variety of plant and animal species in a particular area.

biography, **biographies** NOUN A biography is an account of someone's life, written by someone else. Compare **autobiography**. **biographer** NOUN **biographical** ADJECTIVE

biology NOUN Biology is the study of living things. **biological** ADJECTIVE **biologically** ADVERB **biologist** NOUN

bionic ADJECTIVE having a part of the body that works electronically.

biopsy, **biopsies** NOUN an examination under a microscope of tissue from a living body to find out the cause of a disease.

birch NOUN a tall deciduous tree with thin branches and thin bark.

bird NOUN an animal with two legs, two wings, and feathers.

birth NOUN ①The birth of a baby is when it comes out of its mother's womb at the beginning of its life. ②The birth of something is its beginning • *the birth of modern art*.

birthday NOUN Your birthday is the anniversary of the date on which you were born.

biscuit NOUN a small flat cake made of baked dough.

bisexual ADJECTIVE attracted to both males and females.

bishop NOUN ① RE a high-ranking member of the clergy in some Christian Churches. ② In chess, a bishop is a piece that is moved diagonally across the board.

bison NOUN A bison is a large hairy animal, related to cattle, with a large head and shoulders. Bison used to be very common on the prairies in North America, but they are now almost extinct.

bistro, **bistros** [*Said* ***bee**-stroh*] NOUN a small informal restaurant.

bit ① Bit is the past tense of **bite**. ▸NOUN ② A bit of something is a small amount of it • *a bit of coal*. ▸PHRASE ③ **A bit** means slightly or to a small extent • *That's a bit tricky*.

bit NOUN
② = crumb, fragment, grain, part, piece, scrap

bitch NOUN a female dog.

bite, **bites**, **biting**, **bit**, **bitten** VERB ① To bite something or someone is to cut it or cut through it with the teeth. ▸NOUN ② a small amount that you bite off something with your teeth. ③ the injury you get when an animal or insect bites you.

bite VERB
① = chew, gnaw, nibble, nip

bitter ADJECTIVE ① If someone is bitter, they feel angry and resentful. ② A bitter disappointment or experience makes people feel angry or unhappy for a long time afterwards. ③ In a bitter argument or war, people argue or fight fiercely and angrily • *a bitter power struggle*. ④ A bitter wind is an extremely cold wind. ⑤ Something that tastes bitter has a sharp, unpleasant taste. **bitterly** ADVERB **bitterness** NOUN

bitter ADJECTIVE
① = acrimonious (*formal*), begrudging, embittered, rancorous (*formal*), resentful, sour
⑤ = acid, acrid, astringent, sharp, sour, tart
≠ sweet

bizarre [*Said biz-**zahr***] ADJECTIVE very strange or eccentric.

bizarre ADJECTIVE
= curious, eccentric, extraordinary, odd, outlandish, peculiar, queer (*old-fashioned*), strange, weird
≠ ordinary

black NOUN, ADJECTIVE ① Black is the darkest possible colour, like tar or soot. ② Someone who is Black is a member of a dark-skinned race. ③ Black coffee or tea has no milk or cream added to it. ④ Black humour involves jokes about death or suffering. **blackness** NOUN **black out** VERB If you black out, you lose consciousness.

blackberry, **blackberries** NOUN Blackberries are small black fruits that grow on prickly bushes called brambles.

blackboard NOUN a dark-coloured board on which people can write or draw using chalk.

black box NOUN A black box is an electronic device in an aircraft which collects and stores information during flights. This information can be used to provide evidence if an accident occurs.

blackcurrant NOUN Blackcurrants are very small dark purple fruits that grow in bunches on bushes.

blacken VERB To blacken something means to make it black • *The smoke from the chimney blackened the roof.*

blacklist NOUN ① a list of people or organisations who are thought to be untrustworthy or disloyal. ▸ VERB ② When someone is blacklisted, they are put on a blacklist.

blackmail VERB ① If someone blackmails another person, they threaten to reveal an unpleasant secret about them unless that person gives them money or does something for them. ▸ NOUN ② Blackmail is the action of blackmailing people. **blackmailer** NOUN

black market NOUN If something is bought or sold on the black market, it is bought or sold illegally.

blackout NOUN If you have a blackout, you lose consciousness for a short time.

blacksmith NOUN a person whose job is making things out of iron, such as horseshoes.

bladder NOUN the part of your body where urine is held until it leaves your body.

blade NOUN ① The blade of a weapon or cutting tool is the sharp part of it. ② The blades of a propeller are the thin, flat parts that turn round. ③ A blade of grass is a single piece of it.

blame VERB ① If someone blames you for something bad that has happened, they believe you caused it. ▸ NOUN ② The blame for something bad that happens is the responsibility for letting it happen.

blame VERB
① = accuse, charge, hold responsible
▸ NOUN ② = accountability, fault, guilt, liability, rap (*slang*), responsibility

blameless ADJECTIVE Someone who is blameless has not done anything wrong.

blanch VERB If you blanch, you suddenly become very pale.

bland ADJECTIVE tasteless, dull or boring • *a bland diet* • *bland pop music.* **blandly** ADVERB

blank ADJECTIVE ① Something that is blank has nothing on it • *a blank sheet of paper.* ② If you look blank, your face shows no feeling or interest. ▸ NOUN ③ If your mind is a blank, you cannot think of anything or remember anything.

blank ADJECTIVE
① = bare, clean, clear, empty, plain, unmarked
② = deadpan, dull, empty, impassive, vacant

blanket NOUN ① a large rectangle of thick cloth that is put on a bed to keep people warm. ② A blanket of something such as snow is a thick covering of it.

blare VERB To blare means to make a loud, unpleasant noise • *The radio blared pop music.*

blasphemy NOUN Blasphemy is speech or behaviour that shows disrespect for God or religion.
blasphemous ADJECTIVE

blast VERB ① When people blast a hole in something they make a hole with an explosion. ▶ NOUN ② a big explosion, especially one caused by a bomb. ③ a sudden strong rush of wind or air.

blatant ADJECTIVE If you describe something you think is bad as blatant, you mean that rather than hide it, those responsible actually seem to be making it obvious • *a blatant disregard for the law.*

blaze NOUN ① a large, hot fire. ② A blaze of light or colour is a great or strong amount of it • *a blaze of red.* ③ A blaze of publicity or attention is a lot of it. ▶ VERB ④ If something blazes, it burns or shines brightly.

blazer NOUN a kind of jacket, often in the colours of a school or sports team.

bleach VERB ① To bleach material or hair means to make it white, usually by using a chemical. ▶ NOUN ② Bleach is a chemical that is used to make material white or to clean thoroughly and kill germs.

bleak ADJECTIVE ① If a situation is bleak, it is bad and seems unlikely to improve. ② If a place is bleak, it is cold, bare and exposed to the wind.

bleat VERB ① When sheep or goats bleat, they make a high-pitched cry. ▶ NOUN ② the high-pitched cry that a sheep or goat makes.

bleed, bleeds, bleeding, bled VERB When you bleed, you lose blood as a result of an injury.

bleep NOUN a short high-pitched sound made by an electrical device such as an alarm.

blemish NOUN a mark that spoils the appearance of something.

blend VERB ① When you blend substances, you mix them together to form a single substance. ② When colours or sounds blend, they combine in a pleasing way. ▶ NOUN ③ A blend of things is a mixture of them, especially one that is pleasing. ④ a word formed by joining together the beginning and the end of two other words; for example, 'brunch' is a blend of 'breakfast' and 'lunch'.

> **blend** VERB
> ① = combine, merge, mingle, mix
> ≠ separate
> ② = go well, harmonise
> ▶ NOUN ③ = alloy, amalgamation, combination, compound, fusion, mix, mixture

blender NOUN a machine used for mixing liquids and foods at high speed.

bless, blesses, blessing, blessed or **blest** VERB When a priest blesses people or things, he or she asks for God's protection for them.

> **bless** VERB
> = anoint, consecrate, dedicate, hallow
> ≠ curse

blessed [*Said* ***blest***] ADJECTIVE If someone is blessed with a particular quality or skill, they have it • *He was blessed with a sense of humour.*

blessing NOUN ① something good that you are thankful for • *Good health is the greatest blessing.* ▶ PHRASE ② If something is done **with someone's blessing**, they approve of it and support it.

> **blessing** NOUN
> ① = benefit, boon, gift, godsend, help
> ≠ disadvantage
> ▶ PHRASE ② = approval, backing, consent, leave, permission, support
> ≠ disapproval

blew the past tense of **blow**.

blight NOUN ① something that damages or spoils other things • *the blight of the recession.* ▶ VERB ② When something is blighted, it is seriously harmed • *His life had been blighted by sickness.*

blind ADJECTIVE ① Someone who is blind cannot see. ② If someone is blind to a particular fact, they are not aware of it. ▶ VERB ③ If something blinds you, you become unable to see, either for a short time or permanently. ▶ NOUN ④ a roll of cloth or paper that you pull down over a window to keep out the light. **blindly** ADVERB **blindness** NOUN

blindfold NOUN ① a strip of cloth tied over someone's eyes so that they cannot see. ▶ VERB ② To blindfold someone means to cover their eyes with a strip of cloth.

blinding ADJECTIVE A blinding light is so bright that it hurts your eyes • *There was a blinding flash.*

blindingly ADVERB (*informal*) If something is blindingly obvious, it is very obvious indeed.

bling (*informal*) NOUN ① jewellery that looks expensive in a vulgar way. ▶ ADJECTIVE ② flashy; expensive-looking in a vulgar way.

blink VERB When you blink, you close your eyes rapidly for a moment. Blinking is an involuntary action that keeps the eyes moist.

blinkers PLURAL NOUN Blinkers are two pieces of leather placed at the side of a horse's eyes so that it can only see straight ahead.

bliss NOUN Bliss is a state of complete happiness. **blissful** ADJECTIVE **blissfully** ADVERB

blister NOUN ① a small bubble on your skin containing watery liquid, caused by a burn or rubbing. ▶ VERB ② If someone's skin blisters, blisters appear on it as result of burning or rubbing.

blistering ADJECTIVE ① Blistering heat is very hot. ② A blistering remark expresses great anger or criticism.

blitz NOUN ① HISTORY a bombing attack by enemy aircraft on a city. ② a sudden intensive attack or concerted effort.

blizzard NOUN a heavy snowstorm with strong winds.

bloated ADJECTIVE Something that is bloated is much larger than normal, often because there is a lot of liquid or gas inside it.

blob NOUN a small amount of a thick or sticky substance.

blob NOUN
= bead, dab, drop, droplet

bloc NOUN A group of countries or political parties with similar aims acting together is often called a bloc • *the world's largest trading bloc.*

block NOUN ① A block of flats or offices is a large building containing flats or offices. ② In a town, a block is an area of land with streets on all its sides • *He lives a few blocks down.* ③ A block of something is a large rectangular piece of it. ▶ VERB ④ To block a road or channel means to put something across it so that nothing can get through. ⑤ If something blocks your view, it is in the way and prevents you from seeing what you want to see. ⑥ If someone blocks something, they prevent it from happening • *The council blocked his plans.*

block NOUN
③ = bar, brick, chunk, ingot, lump, piece
▶ VERB ④ = choke, clog, obstruct, plug
≠ unblock
⑥ = bar, check, halt, obstruct, stop, thwart

blockade NOUN ① an action that prevents goods from reaching a place. ▸ VERB ② When a place is blockaded, supplies are prevented from reaching it.

blockage NOUN When there is a blockage in a pipe or tunnel, something is clogging it.

blockage NOUN
= block, obstruction, stoppage

blog, **blogs**, **blogging**, **blogged** NOUN a person's online diary that he or she puts on the internet so that other people can read it. **blogging** NOUN

blogger NOUN a person who keeps a blog.

bloke NOUN (*informal*) a man.

blonde; also spelt **blond** ADJECTIVE ① Blonde hair is pale yellow in colour. The spelling 'blond' is used when referring to men. ▸ NOUN ② A blonde, or blond, is a person with light-coloured hair.

blood NOUN ① Blood is the red liquid that is pumped by the heart round the bodies of human beings and other mammals. ▸ PHRASE ② If something cruel is done **in cold blood**, it is done deliberately and without showing any emotion.

bloodless ADJECTIVE ① If someone's face or skin is bloodless, it is very pale. ② In a bloodless coup or revolution, nobody is killed.

blood pressure NOUN Your blood pressure is a measure of the force with which your blood is being pumped round your body.

bloodshed NOUN When there is bloodshed, people are killed or wounded.

bloodshot ADJECTIVE If a person's eyes are bloodshot, the white parts have become red.

bloodstream NOUN the flow of blood through your body.

bloodthirsty ADJECTIVE Someone who is bloodthirsty enjoys using or watching violence.

blood transfusion NOUN a process in which blood is injected into the body of someone who has lost a lot of blood.

blood vessel NOUN Blood vessels are the narrow tubes in your body through which your blood flows.

bloody, **bloodier**, **bloodiest** ADJECTIVE, ADVERB ① 'Bloody' is a common swearword, used to express anger or annoyance. ▸ ADJECTIVE ② A bloody event is one in which a lot of people are killed • *a bloody revolution*. ③ Bloody also means covered with blood • *a bloody gash on his head*.

bloom NOUN ① a flower on a plant. ▸ VERB ② When a plant blooms, it produces flowers. ③ When something like a feeling blooms, it grows • *Romance can bloom where you least expect it*.

blossom NOUN ① Blossom is the growth of flowers that appears on a tree before the fruit. ▸ VERB ② When a tree blossoms, it produces blossom.

blot, **blots**, **blotting**, **blotted** NOUN ① a drop of ink that has been spilled on a surface. ② A blot on someone's reputation is a mistake or piece of bad behaviour that spoils their reputation. **blot out** VERB To blot something out means to be in front of it and prevent it from being seen • *The smoke blotted out the sky*.

blouse NOUN a light shirt, worn by a girl or a woman.

blow, **blows**, **blowing**, **blew**, **blown** VERB ① When the wind blows, the air moves. ② If something blows or is blown somewhere, the wind moves it there. ③ If you blow a whistle or horn, you make a sound by blowing into it. ▸ NOUN ④ If you receive a blow, someone or something hits you. ⑤ something that makes you very disappointed or unhappy • *Marc's death was a terrible blow.*

blow up VERB ① To blow something up means to destroy it with an explosion. ② To blow up a balloon or a tyre means to fill it with air.

> **blow** VERB
> ② = buffet, drive, flutter, sweep, waft, whirl
> ▸ NOUN ④ = bang, clout (*informal*), knock, smack, thump, whack (*informal*)
> ⑤ = bombshell, disappointment, misfortune, setback, shock, upset

blubber NOUN The blubber of animals such as whales and seals is the layer of fat that protects them from the cold.

bludgeon VERB To bludgeon someone means to hit them several times with a heavy object.

blue, **bluer**, **bluest**; **blues** ADJECTIVE, NOUN ① Blue is the colour of the sky on a clear, sunny day. ▸ PHRASE ② If something happens **out of the blue**, it happens suddenly and unexpectedly. **bluish**; also spelt **blueish** ADJECTIVE

blue-collar ADJECTIVE Blue-collar workers do physical work as opposed to office work.

blueprint NOUN a plan of how something is expected to work • *the blueprint for a successful school career.*

blues NOUN The blues is a type of music which is similar to jazz, but is always slow and sad.

bluff NOUN ① an attempt to make someone wrongly believe that you are in a strong position. ▸ VERB ② If you are bluffing, you are trying to make someone believe that you are in a position of strength.

blunder VERB ① If you blunder, you make a silly mistake. ▸ NOUN ② a silly mistake.

blunt ADJECTIVE ① A blunt object has a rounded point or edge, rather than a sharp one. ② If you are blunt, you say exactly what you think, without trying to be polite.

> **blunt** ADJECTIVE
> ① = dull, rounded, unsharpened
> ≠ sharp
> ② = bluff, brusque, forthright, frank, outspoken, straightforward
> ≠ tactful

blur, **blurs**, **blurring**, **blurred** NOUN ① a shape or area which you cannot see clearly because it has no distinct outline or because it is moving very fast. ▸ VERB ② To blur the differences between things means to make them no longer clear • *The dreams blurred confusingly with her memories.* **blurred** ADJECTIVE

blush VERB ① If you blush, your face becomes red, because you are embarrassed or ashamed. ▸ NOUN ② the red colour on someone's face when they are embarrassed or ashamed.

> **blush** VERB
> ① = colour, flush, go red, turn crimson, turn red, turn scarlet
> ▸ NOUN ② = colour, flush, glow

bluster VERB ① When someone blusters, they behave aggressively because they are angry or frightened. ▸ NOUN ② Bluster is aggressive behaviour by someone who is angry or frightened.

blustery ADJECTIVE Blustery weather is rough and windy.

boa NOUN ① A boa, or a boa constrictor, is a large snake that kills its prey by coiling round it and crushing it. ② a long thin scarf of feathers or fur.

boar NOUN a male wild pig, or a male domestic pig used for breeding.

board NOUN ① a long, flat piece of

wood. ② the group of people who control a company or organisation. ③ Board is the meals provided when you stay somewhere • *The price includes full board.* ▶ **VERB** ④ If you board a ship or aircraft, you get on it or in it. ▶ **PHRASE** ⑤ If you are **on board** a ship or aircraft, you are on it or in it.

boarder NOUN a pupil who lives at school during the term.

boarding school NOUN a school where the pupils live during the term.

boardroom NOUN a room where the board of a company meets.

boast VERB ① If you boast about your possessions or achievements, you talk about them proudly. ▶ **NOUN** ② something that you say which shows that you are proud of what you own or have done.

> **boast** VERB
> ① = brag, crow (*informal*), skite (*Australian and New Zealand; informal*)

boastful ADJECTIVE tending to brag about things.

> **boastful** ADJECTIVE
> = bragging, cocky, conceited, crowing, egotistical, swaggering
> ≠ modest

boat NOUN a small vehicle for travelling across water.

bob, **bobs**, **bobbing**, **bobbed** VERB ① When something bobs, it moves up and down. ▶ **NOUN** ② a woman's hair style in which her hair is cut level with her chin.

bode PHRASE (*literary*) If something **bodes ill**, or **bodes well**, it makes you think that something bad, or good, will happen.

bodice NOUN the upper part of a dress.

bodily ADJECTIVE ① relating to the body • *bodily contact.* ▶ **ADVERB** ② involving the whole of someone's body • *He was carried bodily up the steps.*

body, **bodies** NOUN ① Your body is either all your physical parts, or just the main part not including your head, arms and legs. ② a person's dead body. ③ the main part of a car or aircraft, not including the engine. ④ A body of people is also an organised group.

> **body** NOUN
> ① = build, figure, form, frame, physique, shape
> ② = carcass, corpse, dead body, remains
> ④ = association, band, company, confederation, organisation, society

bodyguard NOUN a person employed to protect someone.

bodywork NOUN the outer part of a motor vehicle.

bog NOUN an area of land which is always wet and spongy.

boggle VERB If your mind boggles at something, you find it difficult to imagine or understand.

bogus ADJECTIVE not genuine • *a bogus doctor.*

bohemian [*Said boh-**hee**-mee-an*] ADJECTIVE Someone who is bohemian does not behave in the same way as most other people in society, and is usually involved in the arts.

boil VERB ① When a hot liquid boils, bubbles appear in it and it starts to give off steam. ② When you boil a kettle, you heat it until the water in it boils. ③ When you boil food, you cook it in boiling water. ▶ **NOUN** ④ a red swelling on your skin.

> **boil** VERB
> ① = bubble, fizz, foam, froth
> ▶ NOUN ④ = blister, swelling, tumour

boiler NOUN a piece of equipment which burns fuel to provide hot water.

boiling ADJECTIVE (*informal*) very hot.

boisterous ADJECTIVE Someone who is boisterous is noisy and lively.

bold ADJECTIVE ① confident and not shy or embarrassed • *He was not bold enough to ask them.* ② not afraid of risk or danger. ③ clear and noticeable • *bold colours.* **boldly** ADVERB **boldness** NOUN

> **bold** ADJECTIVE
> ① = brash, brazen, cheeky, confident, forward, impudent
> ≠ shy
> ② = adventurous, brave, courageous, daring, fearless, intrepid
> ≠ cowardly
> ③ = bright, flashy, loud, striking, strong, vivid
> ≠ dull

bolster VERB To bolster something means to support it or make it stronger • *She relied on others to bolster her self-esteem.*

bolt NOUN ① a metal bar that you slide across a door or window in order to fasten it. ② a metal object which screws into a nut and is used to fasten things together. ▸ VERB ③ If you bolt a door or window, you fasten it using a bolt. If you bolt things together, you fasten them together using a bolt. ④ To bolt means to escape or run away. ⑤ To bolt food means to eat it very quickly.

> **bolt** VERB
> ④ = dash, escape, flee, fly, run away, run off, rush

bomb NOUN ① a container filled with material that explodes when it hits something or is set off by a timer. ▸ VERB ② When a place is bombed, it is attacked with bombs.

> **bomb** NOUN
> ① = device, explosive, missile, rocket, shell, torpedo
> ▸ VERB ② = attack, blow up, bombard, destroy, shell, torpedo

bombard VERB ① To bombard a place means to attack it with heavy gunfire or bombs. ② If you are bombarded with something you are made to face a great deal of it • *I was bombarded with criticism.* **bombardment** NOUN

bomber NOUN an aircraft that drops bombs.

bombshell NOUN a sudden piece of shocking or upsetting news.

bona fide [*Said boh-na fie-dee*] ADJECTIVE genuine • *We are happy to donate to bona fide charities.*

bond NOUN ① a close relationship between people. ② (*literary*) Bonds are chains or ropes used to tie a prisoner up. ③ a certificate which records that you have lent money to a business and that it will repay you the loan with interest. ④ SCIENCE In chemistry, a bond is the means by which atoms or groups of atoms are combined in molecules. ⑤ Bonds are also feelings or obligations that force you to behave in a particular way • *the social bonds of community.* ▸ VERB ⑥ When two things bond or are bonded, they become closely linked or attached.

> **bond** NOUN
> ① = attachment, connection, link, relation, tie, union
> ⑤ = agreement, contract, obligation, pledge, promise, word
> ▸ VERB ⑥ = bind, fasten, fuse, glue, paste

bondage NOUN Bondage is the condition of being someone's slave.

bone NOUN Bones are the hard parts that form the framework of a person's or animal's body. **boneless** ADJECTIVE

bonfire NOUN a large fire made outdoors, often to burn rubbish.

bonnet NOUN ① the metal cover over a car's engine. ② a baby's or woman's hat tied under the chin.

bonus NOUN ① an amount of money added to your usual pay. ② Something that is a bonus is a good thing that you get in addition to something else • *The view from the hotel was an added bonus.*

bony, bonier, boniest ADJECTIVE Bony people or animals are thin, with very little flesh covering their bones.

boo NOUN ① a shout of disapproval. ▸ VERB ② When people boo, they shout 'boo' to show their disapproval.

book NOUN ① a number of pages held together inside a cover. ▸ VERB ② When you book something such as a room, you arrange to have it or use it at a particular time.

> **book** NOUN
> ① = publication, textbook, volume, work
> ▸ VERB ② = charter, engage, organise, reserve, schedule

bookcase NOUN a piece of furniture with shelves for books.

booking NOUN an arrangement to book something such as a hotel room.

booklet NOUN a small book with a paper cover.

bookmaker NOUN a person who makes a living by taking people's bets and paying them when they win.

bookmark NOUN ① a piece of card which you put between the pages of a book to mark your place. ② In computing, a bookmark is the address of a website that you put into a list on your computer so that you can return to it easily. ▸ VERB ③ If you bookmark a website, you put its address into a list on your computer so that you can return to it easily.

boom NOUN ① a rapid increase in something • *the baby boom.* ② a loud deep echoing sound. ▸ VERB ③ When something booms, it increases rapidly • *Sales are booming.* ④ To boom means to make a loud deep echoing sound.

boomerang NOUN a curved wooden missile that can be thrown so that it returns to the thrower, originally used as a weapon by native Australians.

boon NOUN Something that is a boon makes life better or easier • *Subtitles are a boon for deaf people.*

boost VERB ① To boost something means to cause it to improve or increase • *The campaign had boosted sales.* ▸ NOUN ② an improvement or increase • *a boost to the economy.* **booster** NOUN

boot NOUN ① Boots are strong shoes that come up over your ankle and sometimes your calf. ② the covered space in a car, usually at the back, for carrying things in. ▸ VERB ③ (*informal*) If you boot something, you kick it. ▸ PHRASE ④ **To boot** means also or in addition • *The story was compelling and well written to boot.*

booth NOUN ① a small partly enclosed area • *a photo booth.* ② a stall where you can buy goods.

booty NOUN Booty is valuable things taken from a place, especially by soldiers after a battle.

booze (*informal*) NOUN ① Booze is alcoholic drink. ▸ VERB ② When people booze, they drink alcohol. **boozer** NOUN **boozy** ADJECTIVE

border NOUN ① the dividing line between two places or things. ② a strip or band round the edge of something • *plain tiles with a bright border.* ③ a long flower bed in a garden. ▸ VERB ④ To border something means to form a boundary along the side of it • *Tall poplar trees bordered the fields.*

a b c d e f g h i j k l m n o p q r s t u v w x y z

border NOUN
① = borderline, boundary, frontier, line
② = bounds, edge, limits, margin, rim
▶ VERB ④ = edge, fringe, hem, rim, trim

borderline ADJECTIVE only just acceptable as a member of a class or group • *a borderline case*.

bore VERB ① If something bores you, you find it dull and not at all interesting. ② If you bore a hole in something, you make it using a tool such as a drill. ③ Bore is also the past tense of **bear**. ▶ NOUN ④ someone or something that bores you.

bored ADJECTIVE If you are bored, you are impatient because you do not find something interesting or because you have nothing to do.

bored ADJECTIVE
= fed up, tired, uninterested, wearied
≠ interested

boredom NOUN a lack of interest.

boredom NOUN
= apathy, dullness, flatness, monotony, tedium, weariness
≠ interest

boring ADJECTIVE dull and lacking interest.

boring ADJECTIVE
= dull, flat, humdrum, monotonous, tedious, tiresome
≠ interesting

born VERB ① When a baby is born, it comes out of its mother's womb at the beginning of its life. ▶ ADJECTIVE ② You use 'born' to mean that someone has a particular quality from birth • *He was a born pessimist*.

borne the past participle of **bear**.

borough [*Said* **bur**-*uh*] NOUN a town, or a district within a large town, that has its own council.

borrow VERB If you borrow something that belongs to someone else, they let you have it for a period of time. **borrower** NOUN

Bosnian ADJECTIVE ① belonging or relating to Bosnia. ▶ NOUN ② someone who comes from Bosnia.

bosom NOUN ① A woman's bosom is her chest. ▶ ADJECTIVE ② A bosom friend is a very close friend.

boss, bosses, bossing, bossed NOUN ① Someone's boss is the person in charge of the place where they work. ▶ VERB ② If someone bosses you around, they keep telling you what to do.

boss NOUN
① = chief, director, employer, head, leader, manager

bossy, bossier, bossiest ADJECTIVE A bossy person enjoys telling other people what to do. **bossiness** NOUN

bossy ADJECTIVE
= authoritarian, dictatorial, domineering, imperious, overbearing

botany NOUN Botany is the scientific study of plants. **botanic** or **botanical** ADJECTIVE **botanist** NOUN

botch VERB (*informal*) If you botch something, you do it badly or clumsily.

botch VERB
= bungle (*informal*), mar, mess up

both ADJECTIVE, PRONOUN 'Both' is used when saying something about two things or people.

bother VERB ① If you do not bother to do something, you do not do it because it takes too much effort or it seems unnecessary. ② If something bothers you, you are worried or concerned about it. If you do not bother about it, you are not concerned about it • *She is not bothered* *about money.* ③ If you bother someone, you interrupt them when they are busy. ▶ **NOUN** ④ Bother is trouble, fuss or difficulty. **bothersome** **ADJECTIVE**

bother VERB
② = annoy, concern, disturb, get on someone's nerves (*informal*), trouble, worry
▶ **NOUN** ④ = annoyance, difficulty, inconvenience, irritation, trouble, worry

bottle NOUN ① a glass or plastic container for keeping liquids in. ▶ **VERB** ② To bottle something means to store it in bottles. **bottle up VERB** If you bottle up strong feelings, you do not let yourself think about them.

bottleneck NOUN a narrow section of road where traffic has to slow down or stop.

bottom NOUN ① The bottom of something is its lowest part. ② Your bottom is your buttocks. ▶ **ADJECTIVE** ③ The bottom thing in a series of things is the lowest one. **bottomless** **ADJECTIVE**

bottom NOUN
① = base, bed, depths, floor, foot
≠ top
▶ **ADJECTIVE** ③ = base, basement, ground, lowest
≠ highest

bought the past tense and past participle of **buy**.

boulder NOUN a large rounded rock.

boulevard *[Said* ***boo****-le-vard]* **NOUN** a wide street in a city, usually with trees along each side.

bounce VERB ① When an object bounces, it springs back from something after hitting it. ② To bounce also means to move up and down • *Her long black hair bounced as she walked.*

bounce VERB
① = rebound, ricochet
② = bob, bound, bump, jump

bouncy, bouncier, bounciest **ADJECTIVE** ① Someone who is bouncy is lively and enthusiastic. ② Something that is bouncy is capable of bouncing or being bounced on • *a bouncy ball* • *a bouncy castle.*

bound ADJECTIVE ① If you say that something is bound to happen, you mean that it is certain to happen. ② If a person or a vehicle is bound for a place, they are going there. ③ If someone is bound by an agreement or regulation, they must obey it. ▶ **NOUN** ④ a large leap. ⑤ (*in plural*) Bounds are limits which restrict or control something • *Their enthusiasm knew no bounds.* ▶ **PHRASE** ⑥ If a place is **out of bounds**, you are forbidden to go there. ▶ **VERB** ⑦ When animals or people bound, they move quickly with large leaps • *He bounded up the stairway.* ⑧ Bound is also the past tense and past participle of **bind**.

boundary, boundaries NOUN something that indicates the farthest limit of anything • *the city boundary.*

boundless ADJECTIVE without end or limit • *her boundless energy.*

bountiful ADJECTIVE (*literary*) freely available in large amounts • *a bountiful harvest.*

bounty NOUN ① (*literary*) Bounty is a generous supply • *autumn's bounty of fruits.* ② Someone's bounty is their generosity in giving a lot of something.

bouquet *[Said boo-****kay****]* **NOUN** an attractively arranged bunch of flowers.

bout NOUN ① If you have a bout of something such as an illness, you have it for a short time • *a bout of flu.* ② If you have a bout of doing something, you do it enthusiastically for a short time. ③ a boxing or wrestling match.

boutique *[Said boo-**teek**]* **NOUN** a small shop that sells fashionable clothes.

bovine **ADJECTIVE** (*technical*) relating to cattle.

bow[1] *[Rhymes with **now**]* **VERB** ① When you bow, you bend your body or lower your head as a sign of respect or greeting. ② If you bow to something, you give in to it • *He bowed to pressure from his friends.* ▸ **NOUN** ③ the movement you make when you bow. ④ the front part of a ship.

bow[2] *[Rhymes with **low**]* **NOUN** ① a knot with two loops and two loose ends. ② a long thin piece of wood with horsehair stretched along it, which you use to play a violin. ③ a long flexible piece of wood used for shooting arrows.

bowel *[Rhymes with **towel**]* **NOUN** Your bowels are the tubes leading from your stomach, through which waste passes before it leaves your body.

bowl *[Rhymes with **mole**]* **NOUN** ① A bowl is a round container with a wide uncovered top, used for holding liquid or for serving food. ② A bowl is also the hollow, rounded part of something • *a toilet bowl* • *the bowl of his pipe.* ③ PE A bowl is a large heavy ball used in the game of bowls or in bowling. ▸ **VERB** ④ PE In cricket, to bowl means to throw the ball towards the batsman; if a batsman is bowled, or bowled out, their wicket is knocked over by the ball and they are out. **bowler** **NOUN**

bowling **NOUN** Bowling is a game in which you roll a heavy ball down a narrow track towards a group of wooden objects called pins and try to knock them down.

bowls **NOUN** Bowls is a game in which the players try to roll large wooden balls as near as possible to a small ball.

box **NOUN** ① a container with a firm base and sides and usually a lid. ② On a form, a box is a rectangular space which you have to fill in. ③ In a theatre, a box is a small separate area where a few people can watch the performance together. ▸ **VERB** ④ To box means to fight someone according to the rules of boxing.

> **box** **NOUN**
> ① = carton, case, chest, container, trunk

boxer **NOUN** ① a person who boxes. ② a type of medium-sized, smooth-haired dog with a flat face.

boxing **NOUN** Boxing is a sport in which two people fight using their fists, wearing padded gloves.

box office **NOUN** the place where tickets are sold in a theatre or cinema.

boy **NOUN** a male child. **boyhood** **NOUN** **boyish** **ADJECTIVE**

> **boy** **NOUN**
> = kid (*informal*), lad (*informal*), schoolboy, youngster, youth

boycott **VERB** ① If you boycott an organisation or event, you refuse to have anything to do with it. ▸ **NOUN** ② the boycotting of an organisation or event • *a boycott of the elections.*

> **boycott** **VERB**
> ① = blacklist, embargo, exclude

boyfriend **NOUN** Someone's boyfriend is the man or boy with whom they are having a romantic relationship.

bra **NOUN** a piece of underwear worn by a woman to support her breasts.

braaivleis *[Said **bry**-flayss]* or **braai**, **braais** **NOUN** In South African English, a braaivleis is a picnic where meat is cooked on an open fire.

brace VERB ① When you brace yourself, you stiffen your body to steady yourself • *The ship lurched and he braced himself.* ② If you brace yourself for something unpleasant, you prepare yourself to deal with it • *The country braced itself for an invasion.* ▸ NOUN ③ an object fastened to something to straighten or support it • *a neck brace.* ④ (*in plural*) Braces are a pair of straps worn over the shoulders and fastened to the trousers to hold them up.

bracelet NOUN a chain or band worn around someone's wrist as an ornament.

bracing ADJECTIVE Something that is bracing makes you feel fit and full of energy • *the bracing sea air.*

bracken NOUN Bracken is a plant like a large fern that grows on hills and in woods.

bracket NOUN ① ENGLISH Brackets are a pair of written marks, ( ) or [ ], placed round a word or sentence that is not part of the main text, or to show that the items inside the brackets belong together. ② a range between two limits, for example of ages or prices • *the four-figure price bracket.* ③ a piece of metal or wood fastened to a wall to support something such as a shelf.

brag, **brags, bragging, bragged** VERB When someone brags, they boast about their achievements • *Both leaders bragged they could win by a landslide.*

> **brag** VERB
> = boast, crow (*informal*), skite (*Australian and New Zealand; informal*)

braid NOUN ① Braid is a strip of decorated cloth used to decorate clothes or curtains. ② a length of hair which has been plaited and tied. ▸ VERB ③ To braid hair or thread means to plait it.

Braille NOUN Braille is a system of printing for blind people in which letters are represented by raised dots that can be felt with the fingers. It was invented by the French inventor Louis Braille in the 19th century.

brain NOUN ① Your brain is the mass of nerve tissue inside your head that controls your body and enables you to think and feel; also used to refer to your mind and the way that you think • *I admired his legal brain.* ② (*in plural*) If you say that someone has brains, you mean that they are very intelligent.

brainchild NOUN (*informal*) Someone's brainchild is something that they have invented or created.

brainwash VERB If people are brainwashed into believing something, they accept it without question because they are told it repeatedly. **brainwashing** NOUN

brainwave NOUN (*informal*) a clever idea you think of suddenly.

brainy, **brainier, brainiest** ADJECTIVE (*informal*) clever.

braise VERB To braise food means to fry it for a short time, then cook it slowly in a little liquid.

brake NOUN ① a device for making a vehicle stop or slow down. ▸ VERB ② When a driver brakes, he or she makes a vehicle stop or slow down by using its brakes.

bran NOUN Bran is the ground husks that are left over after flour has been made from wheat grains.

branch NOUN ① The branches of a tree are the parts that grow out from its trunk. ② A branch of an organisation is one of a number of its offices or shops. ③ A branch of a subject is one of its areas of study or activity • *specialists in certain branches of medicine.* ▸ VERB ④ A road that branches off from another road splits off from it to lead in a different direction. **branch out** VERB To branch out means to take up an additional pursuit.

brand NOUN ① A brand of something is a particular kind or make of it • *a popular brand of chocolate.* ▸ VERB ② When an animal is branded, a mark is burned on its skin to show who owns it.

brandish VERB (*literary*) If you brandish something, you wave it vigorously • *He brandished his sword over his head.*

brand-new ADJECTIVE completely new.

brandy, **brandies** NOUN a strong alcoholic drink, usually made from wine.

brash ADJECTIVE If someone is brash, they are overconfident or rather rude.

brass NOUN ① Brass is a yellow-coloured metal made from copper and zinc. ② In an orchestra, the brass or brass section consists of instruments made of brass such as trumpets and trombones.

brat NOUN (*informal*) A badly behaved child may be referred to as a brat.

bravado [*Said bra-**vah**-doh*] NOUN Bravado is a display of courage intended to impress other people.

brave ADJECTIVE ① A brave person is willing to do dangerous things and does not show any fear. ▸ VERB ② If you brave an unpleasant or dangerous situation, you face up to it in order to do something • *His fans braved the rain to hear him sing.* **bravely** ADVERB

> **brave** ADJECTIVE
> ① = bold, courageous, fearless, heroic, plucky, valiant
> ≠ cowardly
> ▸ VERB ② = face, stand up to

bravery NOUN the quality of being courageous.

> **bravery** NOUN
> = boldness, courage, fortitude, heroism, pluck, valour
> ≠ cowardice

brawl NOUN ① a rough fight. ▸ VERB ② When people brawl, they take part in a rough fight.

brawn NOUN Brawn is physical strength. **brawny** ADJECTIVE

brazen ADJECTIVE When someone's behaviour is brazen, they do not care if other people think they are behaving wrongly. **brazenly** ADVERB

Brazilian ADJECTIVE ① belonging or relating to Brazil. ▸ NOUN ② someone who comes from Brazil.

breach VERB ① (*formal*) If you breach an agreement or law, you break it. ② To breach a barrier means to make a gap in it • *The river breached its banks.* ▸ NOUN ③ A breach of an agreement or law is an action that breaks it • *a breach of contract.* ④ a gap or break.

> **breach** NOUN
> ③ = infringement, offence, trespass, violation
> ④ = crack, gap, hole, opening, rift, split

bread NOUN a food made from flour and water, usually raised with yeast, and baked.

breadth NOUN The breadth of something is the distance between its two sides.

breadwinner NOUN the person who earns the money in a family.

break, **breaks**, **breaking**, **broke**, **broken** VERB ① When an object breaks, it is damaged and separates into pieces. ② If you break a rule or promise, you fail to keep it. ③ When a boy's voice breaks, it becomes permanently deeper. ④ When a wave breaks, it falls and becomes foam. ▸ **NOUN** ⑤ a short period during which you rest or do something different. **breakable** **ADJECTIVE** **break down** **VERB** ① When a machine or a vehicle breaks down, it stops working. ② When a discussion or relationship breaks down, it ends because of problems or disagreements. **break up** **VERB** If something breaks up, it ends • *The marriage broke up after a year.*

break **VERB**
① = crack, shatter, smash, snap, split, wreck
② = breach, contravene, infringe, violate
▸ **NOUN** ⑤ = interlude, interval, pause, recess, respite, rest

breakaway **ADJECTIVE** A breakaway group is one that has separated from a larger group.

breakdown **NOUN** ① The breakdown of something such as a system is its failure • *a breakdown in communications.* ② the same as a nervous breakdown. ③ If a driver has a breakdown, their car stops working. ④ A breakdown of something complex is a summary of its important points • *He demanded a breakdown of the costs.*

breaker **NOUN** Breakers are big sea waves.

breakfast **NOUN** the first meal of the day.

break-in **NOUN** the illegal entering of a building, especially by a burglar.

breakneck **ADJECTIVE** (*informal*) Someone or something that is travelling at breakneck speed is travelling dangerously fast.

breakthrough **NOUN** a sudden important development • *a medical breakthrough.*

breakwater **NOUN** a wall extending into the sea which protects a coast from the force of the waves.

bream **NOUN** an edible fish.

breast **NOUN** ① A woman's breasts are the two soft, fleshy parts on her chest, which secrete milk after she has had a baby. ② (*literary or old-fashioned*) The human breast is the upper front part of the body, sometimes regarded as the place where emotions are felt • *His breast was red with blood* • *I felt hope rise in my breast.*

breath **NOUN** ① Your breath is the air you take into your lungs and let out again when you breathe. ▸ **PHRASE** ② If you are **out of breath**, you are breathing with difficulty after doing something energetic. ③ If you say something **under your breath**, you say it in a very quiet voice.

breathe **VERB** When you breathe, you take air into your lungs and let it out again.

breathless **ADJECTIVE** If you are breathless, you are breathing fast or with difficulty. **breathlessly** **ADVERB** **breathlessness** **NOUN**

breathtaking **ADJECTIVE** If you say that something is breathtaking, you mean that it is very beautiful or exciting.

bred the past tense and past participle of **breed**.

breeches [*Said* ***brit****-chiz*] **PLURAL NOUN** Breeches are trousers reaching to just below the knee, worn especially for riding.

breed, **breeds**, **breeding**, **bred** **NOUN** ① A breed of a species of domestic animal is a particular type of it. ▸ **VERB** ② Someone who breeds animals or plants keeps them in order to produce more animals or plants with particular qualities. ③ When animals breed, they mate and produce offspring.

breed NOUN
① = kind, species, stock, strain, type, variety
▶ VERB ② = cultivate, develop, keep, nurture, raise, rear
③ = multiply, produce, propagate, reproduce

breeze NOUN a gentle wind.

brevity NOUN (*formal*) Brevity means shortness • *the brevity of his report*.

brew VERB ① If you brew tea or coffee, you make it in a pot by pouring hot water over it. ② To brew beer means to make it, by boiling and fermenting malt. ③ If an unpleasant situation is brewing, it is about to happen • *Another scandal is brewing*. **brewer** NOUN

brewery, **breweries** NOUN a place where beer is made, or a company that makes it.

bribe NOUN ① a gift or money given to an official to persuade them to make a favourable decision. ▶ VERB ② To bribe someone means to give them a bribe. **bribery** NOUN

bric-a-brac NOUN Bric-a-brac consists of small ornaments or pieces of furniture of no great value.

brick NOUN Bricks are rectangular blocks of baked clay used in building.

bricklayer NOUN a person whose job is to build with bricks.

bride NOUN a woman who is getting married or who has just got married. **bridal** ADJECTIVE

bridegroom NOUN a man who is getting married or who has just got married.

bridesmaid NOUN a woman who helps and accompanies a bride on her wedding day.

bridge NOUN ① a structure built over a river, road or railway so that vehicles and people can cross. ② the platform from which a ship is steered and controlled. ③ the hard ridge at the top of your nose. ④ Bridge is a card game for four players based on whist.

bridle NOUN a set of straps round a horse's head and mouth, which the rider uses to control the horse.

brief ADJECTIVE ① Something that is brief lasts only a short time. ▶ VERB ② DGT When you brief someone on a task, you give them all the necessary instructions and information about it. **briefly** ADVERB

brief ADJECTIVE
① = fleeting, momentary, quick, short, swift
≠ long
▶ VERB ② = advise, fill in (*informal*), inform, instruct, prepare, prime

briefcase NOUN a small flat case for carrying papers.

briefing NOUN a meeting at which information and instructions are given.

brigade NOUN an army unit consisting of three battalions.

brigadier [*Said brig-ad-**ear***] NOUN an army officer of the rank immediately above colonel.

bright ADJECTIVE ① strong and startling • *a bright light*. ② clever • *my brightest student*. ③ cheerful • *a bright smile*. **brightly** ADVERB **brightness** NOUN

bright ADJECTIVE
① = brilliant, dazzling, glowing, luminous, radiant, vivid
≠ dull
② = brainy (*informal*), brilliant, clever, ingenious, intelligent, smart
≠ dim
③ = cheerful, happy, jolly, light-hearted, lively, merry

brighten VERB ① If something brightens, it becomes brighter • *The weather had brightened*. ② If someone brightens, they suddenly look happier. **brighten up** VERB To brighten something up means to make it more attractive and cheerful.

brilliant ADJECTIVE ① A brilliant light or colour is extremely bright. ② A brilliant person is extremely clever. ③ A brilliant career is extremely successful. **brilliantly** ADVERB **brilliance** NOUN

> **brilliant** ADJECTIVE
> ① = bright, dazzling, gleaming, glowing, luminous, radiant, sparkling, vivid
> ≠ dull
> ② = acute, brainy (*informal*), bright, clever, intelligent, perceptive, sharp, smart
> ≠ stupid
> ③ = first-class, great, magnificent, marvellous, outstanding, superb, tremendous, wonderful
> ≠ terrible

brim NOUN ① the wide part of a hat that sticks outwards at the bottom. ▸ PHRASE ② If a container is filled **to the brim**, it is filled right to the top.

brine NOUN Brine is salt water.

bring, **brings**, **bringing**, **brought** VERB ① If you bring something or someone with you when you go to a place, you take them with you • *You can bring a friend to the party*. ② To bring something to a particular state means to cause it to be like that • *Bring the vegetables to the boil*. **bring about** VERB To bring something about means to cause it to happen • *We must try to bring about a better world*. **bring off** VERB If you bring off something difficult, you succeed in doing it. **bring out** VERB ① To bring out a new product means to produce it and offer it for sale. ② If something brings out a particular kind of behaviour, it causes it to occur • *Sunny days seem to bring out the best in us*. **bring up** VERB ① To bring up children means to look after them while they grow up. ② If you bring up a subject, you introduce it into the conversation • *She brought up the subject at dinner*.

> **bring** VERB
> ① = bear, carry, convey (*formal*), lead, take, transport
> ② = cause, create, inflict, produce, result in, wreak
> ▸ **bring about** = cause, create, generate, make happen, produce, provoke

brink NOUN If you are on the brink of something, you are just about to do it or experience it.

brisk ADJECTIVE ① A brisk action is done quickly and energetically • *A brisk walk restores your energy*. ② If someone's manner is brisk, it shows that they want to get things done quickly and efficiently. **briskly** ADVERB **briskness** NOUN

bristle NOUN ① Bristles are strong animal hairs used to make brushes. ▸ VERB ② If the hairs on an animal's body bristle, they rise up, because it is frightened. **bristly** ADJECTIVE

British ADJECTIVE belonging or relating to the United Kingdom of Great Britain and Northern Ireland.

Briton NOUN someone who comes from the United Kingdom of Great Britain and Northern Ireland.

brittle ADJECTIVE An object that is brittle is hard but breaks easily.

broach VERB When you broach a subject, you introduce it into a discussion.

broad ADJECTIVE ① wide • *a broad smile*. ② having many different aspects or concerning many different people • *A broad range of issues was discussed*. ③ general rather than detailed • *the broad concerns of the movement*. ④ If someone has a broad accent, the way that they speak makes it very clear where they come from • *She spoke in a broad Irish accent.*

broad ADJECTIVE
① = expansive, extensive, large, thick, vast, wide
≠ narrow
② = comprehensive, extensive, general, sweeping, universal, wide, wide-ranging
③ = approximate, general, non-specific, rough, sweeping, vague

broadband NOUN Broadband is a digital system used on the internet and in other forms of telecommunication which can process and transfer information input from various sources, such as from telephones, computers or televisions.

broadcast, **broadcasts**, **broadcasting**, **broadcast** NOUN ① a programme or announcement on radio or television. ▶ VERB ② To broadcast something means to send it out by radio waves, so that it can be seen on television or heard on radio. **broadcaster** NOUN **broadcasting** NOUN

broaden VERB ① When something broadens, it becomes wider • *His smile broadened.* ② To broaden something means to cause it to involve more things or concern more people • *We must broaden the scope of this job.*

broadly ADVERB true to a large extent or in most cases • *There are broadly two schools of thought on this.*

broadsheet NOUN ENGLISH a newspaper with large pages and detailed news stories.

brocade NOUN Brocade is a heavy, expensive material, often made of silk, with a raised pattern.

broccoli NOUN Broccoli is a green vegetable, similar to cauliflower.

brochure *[Said **broh**-sher]* NOUN a booklet which gives information about a product or service.

broke ① the past tense of **break**. ▶ ADJECTIVE ② *(informal)* If you are broke, you have no money.

broken ① the past participle of **break**. ▶ ADJECTIVE ② in pieces. ③ not kept.

broker NOUN a person whose job is to buy and sell shares for other people.

bronchitis NOUN Bronchitis is an illness in which the two tubes which connect your windpipe to your lungs become infected, making you cough.

bronze NOUN Bronze is a yellowish-brown metal which is a mixture of copper and tin; also the yellowish-brown colour of this metal.

brooch *[Rhymes with **coach**]* NOUN a piece of jewellery with a pin at the back for attaching to clothes.

brood NOUN ① a family of baby birds. ▶ VERB ② If you brood about something, you keep thinking about it in a serious or unhappy way.

brook NOUN a stream.

broom NOUN ① a long-handled brush. ② Broom is a shrub with yellow flowers.

broth NOUN Broth is soup, usually with vegetables in it.

brother NOUN Your brother is a boy or man who has the same parents as you. **brotherly** ADJECTIVE

brotherhood NOUN ① Brotherhood is the affection and loyalty that brothers or close male friends feel for each other. ② a group of men with common interests or beliefs.

brother-in-law, **brothers-in-law** NOUN Someone's brother-in-law is the brother of their husband or wife, or their sibling's husband.

A B C D E F G H I J K L M N O P Q R S T U V W X Y Z

brought the past tense and past participle of **bring**.

brow NOUN ① Your brow is your forehead. ② Your brows are your eyebrows. ③ The brow of a hill is the top of it.

brown ADJECTIVE, NOUN Brown is the colour of earth or wood.

browse VERB ① If you browse through a book or magazine, you look through it in a casual way. ② If you browse in a shop, you look at the things in it for interest rather than because you want to buy something. ③ If you browse on a computer, you search for information on the World Wide Web.

browser NOUN a piece of computer software that lets you look at websites on the World Wide Web.

bruise NOUN ① a purple mark that appears on your skin after something has hit it. ▸ VERB ② If something bruises you, it hits you so that a bruise appears on your skin.

brumby, **brumbies** NOUN In Australia and New Zealand, a brumby is a wild horse.

brunette NOUN a girl or woman with dark brown hair.

brunt PHRASE If you **bear the brunt** of something unpleasant, you are the person who suffers most • *Young people bear the brunt of unemployment.*

brush NOUN ① an object with bristles which you use for cleaning things, painting, or tidying your hair. ▸ VERB ② If you brush something, you clean it or tidy it with a brush. ③ To brush against something means to touch it while passing it • *Her lips brushed his cheek.* **brush up** VERB If you brush up on a subject, you improve your knowledge of it • *They need to brush up their French.*

brusque *[Said broosk]* ADJECTIVE Someone who is brusque deals with people quickly and without considering their feelings. **brusquely** ADVERB **brusqueness** NOUN

brussels sprout, **brussels sprouts** NOUN Brussels sprouts are vegetables that look like tiny cabbages.

brutal ADJECTIVE Brutal behaviour is cruel and violent • *a brutal murder.* **brutally** ADVERB **brutality** NOUN

brute NOUN ① a rough and insensitive man. ▸ ADJECTIVE ② Brute force is strength alone, without any skill • *You have to use brute force to open the gates.* **brutish** ADJECTIVE

bubble NOUN ① a ball of air in a liquid. ② a hollow, delicate ball of soapy liquid. ▸ VERB ③ When a liquid bubbles, bubbles form in it. ④ If you are bubbling with something like excitement, you are full of it. **bubbly** ADJECTIVE

bucket NOUN a deep round container with an open top and a handle.

buckle NOUN ① a fastening on the end of a belt or strap. ▸ VERB ② If you buckle a belt or strap, you fasten it. ③ If something buckles, it becomes bent because of severe heat or pressure.

bud, **buds**, **budding**, **budded** NOUN ① a small, tight swelling on a tree or plant, which develops into a flower or a cluster of leaves. ▸ VERB ② When a tree or plant buds, new buds appear on it.

Buddhism NOUN [RE] an Eastern religion which teaches that the way to end suffering is by overcoming your desires. It was founded in the 6th century BC by the Buddha (a title meaning 'the enlightened one'), Gautama Siddhartha, a nobleman and religious teacher of northern India. **Buddhist** NOUN, ADJECTIVE

budding ADJECTIVE just beginning to develop • *a budding artist.*

budge VERB If something will not budge, you cannot move it.

budgerigar NOUN A budgerigar is a small brightly coloured pet bird. Budgerigars originated in Australia.

budget NOUN ① CITIZENSHIP a plan showing how much money will be available and how it will be spent. ▶ VERB ② CITIZENSHIP If you budget for something, you plan your money carefully, so that you are able to afford it. **budgetary** ADJECTIVE

budgie NOUN (*informal*) a budgerigar.

buff ADJECTIVE ① a pale brown colour. ▶ NOUN ② (*informal*) someone who knows a lot about a subject • *a film buff.*

buffalo, **buffaloes** NOUN a wild animal like a large cow with long curved horns.

buffer NOUN ① Buffers on a train or at the end of a railway line are metal discs on springs that reduce shock when they are hit. ② something that prevents something else from being harmed • *Keep savings as a buffer against unexpected cash needs.*

buffet[1] [*Said* ***boof**-ay or **buf**-ay*] NOUN ① a café at a station. ② a meal at which people serve themselves.

buffet[2] [*Said* ***buff**-it*] VERB If the wind or sea buffets a place or person, it strikes them violently and repeatedly.

bug, **bugs**, **bugging**, **bugged** NOUN ① an insect, especially one that causes damage. ② a small error in a computer program which means that the program will not work properly. ③ (*informal*) a virus or minor infection • *a stomach bug.* ▶ VERB ④ If a place is bugged, tiny microphones are hidden there to pick up what people are saying.

bugle NOUN MUSIC a brass musical instrument that looks like a small trumpet. **bugler** NOUN

build, **builds**, **building**, **built** VERB ① To build something such as a house means to make it from its parts. ② To build something such as an organisation means to develop it gradually. ▶ NOUN ③ Your build is the shape and size of your body. **builder** NOUN

> **build** VERB
> ① = assemble, construct, erect, fabricate, form, make
> ≠ dismantle
> ② = develop, extend, increase, intensify, strengthen
> ▶ NOUN ③ = body, figure, form, frame, physique, shape

building NOUN a structure with walls and a roof.

> **building** NOUN
> = edifice, structure

building society NOUN a business in which some people invest their money, while others borrow from it to buy a house.

bulb NOUN ① the glass part of an electric lamp. ② an onion-shaped root that grows into a flower or plant.

Bulgarian ADJECTIVE ① belonging or relating to Bulgaria. ▶ NOUN ② someone who comes from Bulgaria. ③ the main language spoken in Bulgaria.

bulge VERB ① If something bulges, it swells out from a surface. ▶ NOUN ② a lump on a normally flat surface.

> **bulge** VERB
> ① = expand, protrude (*formal*), stick out, swell
> ▶ NOUN ② = bump, hump, lump, protrusion, swelling

bulk NOUN ① a large mass of something • *The book is more impressive* *for its bulk than its content.* ② The bulk of something is most of it • *the bulk of the world's great poetry.* ▸ PHRASE ③ To buy something **in bulk** means to buy it in large quantities.

bulky, **bulkier**, **bulkiest** ADJECTIVE large and heavy • *a bulky package.*

bull NOUN the male of some species of animals, including the cow family, elephants and whales.

bulldog NOUN a squat dog with a broad head and muscular body.

bulldozer NOUN a powerful tractor with a broad blade in front, which is used for moving earth or knocking things down.

bullet NOUN a small piece of metal fired from a gun.

bulletin NOUN ① a short news report on radio or television. ② a leaflet or small newspaper regularly produced by a group or organisation.

bullion NOUN Bullion is gold or silver in the form of bars.

bully, **bullies**, **bullying**, **bullied** NOUN ① someone who repeatedly tries to hurt or frighten other people. ▸ VERB ② If you bully someone, you frighten or hurt them deliberately. ③ If someone bullies you into doing something, they make you do it by using force or threats.

> **bully** NOUN
> ① = oppressor, persecutor
> ▸ VERB ② = intimidate, oppress, persecute, pick on, tease, torment
> ③ = force, intimidate, pressurise

bump VERB ① If you bump or bump into something, you knock it with a jolt. ▸ NOUN ② a soft or dull noise made by something knocking into something else. ③ a raised, uneven part of a surface. **bumpy** ADJECTIVE **bump off** VERB (*informal*) To bump someone off means to kill them.

> **bump** VERB
> ① = bang, collide, hit, jolt, knock, strike
> ▸ NOUN ② = bang, knock, thud, thump
> ③ = bulge, hump, knob, lump, swelling

bumper NOUN ① Bumpers are bars on the front and back of a vehicle which protect it if there is a collision. ▸ ADJECTIVE ② A bumper crop or harvest is larger than usual.

bun NOUN a small, round cake.

bunch NOUN ① a group of people. ② a number of flowers held or tied together. ③ a group of things. ④ a group of bananas or grapes growing on the same stem. ▸ VERB ⑤ When people bunch together or bunch up, they stay very close to each other.

> **bunch** NOUN
> ① = band, crowd, gaggle, gang, group, lot, multitude
> ② = bouquet, posy, spray
> ③ = batch, bundle, cluster, heap, load, pile, set

bundle NOUN ① a number of things tied together or wrapped up in a cloth. ▸ VERB ② If you bundle someone or something somewhere, you push them there quickly and roughly.

bung NOUN ① a stopper used to close a hole in something such as a barrel. ▸ VERB ② (*informal*) If you bung something somewhere, you put it there quickly and carelessly.

bungalow NOUN a one-storey house.

bungle VERB To bungle something means to fail to do it properly.

bunk NOUN a bed fixed to a wall in a ship or caravan.

bunker NOUN ① On a golf course, a bunker is a large hole filled with sand. ② an underground shelter with strong walls to protect it from bombing.

bunting NOUN Bunting is strips of small coloured flags displayed on streets and buildings on special occasions.

buoy *[Said **boy**]* NOUN a floating object anchored to the bottom of the sea, marking a channel or warning of danger.

buoyant ADJECTIVE ① able to float. ② lively and cheerful • *She was in a buoyant mood.* **buoyancy** NOUN

burden NOUN ① a heavy load. ② If something is a burden to you, it causes you a lot of worry or hard work. **burdensome** ADJECTIVE

> **burden** NOUN
> ① = load, weight
> ② = anxiety, care, strain, stress, trouble, worry

bureau, **bureaux** *[Said **byoo**-roh]* NOUN ① an office that provides a service • *an employment bureau.* ② a writing desk with shelves and drawers.

bureaucracy NOUN Bureaucracy is the complex system of rules and procedures which operates in government departments. **bureaucratic** ADJECTIVE

> **bureaucracy** NOUN
> = administration, officialdom, red tape (*informal*), regulations

bureaucrat NOUN a person who works in a government department, especially one who follows rules and procedures strictly.

burgeoning ADJECTIVE growing or developing rapidly • *a burgeoning political crisis.*

burglar NOUN a thief who breaks into a building.

burglary, **burglaries** NOUN Burglary is the act of breaking into a building in order to steal things.

burgle VERB If your house is burgled, someone breaks into it and steals things.

burial NOUN a ceremony held when a dead person is buried.

burly, **burlier**, **burliest** ADJECTIVE If you are burly, you have a broad body and strong muscles.

burn, **burns**, **burning**, **burned** or **burnt** VERB ① If something is burning, it is on fire. ② To burn something means to destroy it with fire. ③ If you burn yourself or are burned, you are injured by fire or by something hot. ▸ NOUN ④ an injury caused by fire or by something hot.

> **burn** VERB
> ① = be ablaze, be on fire, blaze, flame, flare, flicker
> ② = char, incinerate, scorch, shrivel, singe

burrow NOUN ① a tunnel or hole in the ground dug by a small animal. ▸ VERB ② When an animal burrows, it digs a burrow.

bursary, **bursaries** NOUN a sum of money given to someone to help fund their education.

burst, **bursts**, **bursting**, **burst** VERB ① When something bursts, it splits open because of pressure from inside it. ② If you burst into a room, you enter it suddenly. ③ To burst means to happen or come suddenly and with force • *The aircraft burst into flames.* ④ (*informal*) If you are bursting with something, you find it difficult to keep it to yourself • *We were bursting with joy.* ▸ NOUN ⑤ A burst of something is a short period of it • *He had a sudden burst of energy.*

> **burst** VERB
> ① = break, crack, explode, puncture, rupture, split
> ② = barge, rush
> ③ = break, erupt
> ▸ NOUN ⑤ = fit, outbreak, rush, spate, surge, torrent

bury, **buries**, **burying**, **buried** VERB ① When a dead person is buried, their body is put into a grave and covered with earth. ② To bury something means to put it in a hole in the ground and cover it up. ③ If something is buried under something, it is covered by it • *My bag was buried under a pile of old newspapers.*

bus NOUN a large motor vehicle that carries passengers.

bush NOUN ① a thick plant with many stems branching out from ground level. ② In Australia and South Africa, the bush is an area of land in its natural state outside of city areas. ③ In New Zealand, the bush is land covered with rainforest.

bushman, **bushmen** NOUN ① In Australia and New Zealand, a bushman is someone who lives or travels in the bush. ② In New Zealand, a bushman is also someone whose job it is to clear the bush for farming.

Bushman, **Bushmen** NOUN A Bushman is a member of a group of people in southern Africa who live by hunting and gathering food.

bushranger NOUN In Australia and New Zealand in the past, a bushranger was an outlaw living in the bush.

bushy, **bushier**, **bushiest** ADJECTIVE Bushy hair or fur grows very thickly • *bushy eyebrows.*

business NOUN ① Business is work relating to the buying and selling of goods and services. ② an organisation which produces or sells goods or provides a service. ③ You can refer to any event, situation or activity as a business • *This whole business has upset me.* **businessman** NOUN **businesswoman** NOUN

business NOUN
① = commerce, dealings, industry, trade, trading, transaction
② = company, corporation, enterprise, establishment, firm, organisation
③ = affair, issue, matter, problem, question, subject

businesslike ADJECTIVE dealing with things in an efficient way.

busker NOUN someone who plays music or sings for money in public places.

bust, **busts**, **busting**, **bust** or **busted** NOUN ① a statue of someone's head and shoulders • *a bust of Beethoven.* ② A woman's bust is her chest and her breasts. ▶ VERB ③ (*informal*) If you bust something, you break it. ▶ ADJECTIVE ④ (*informal*) If a business goes bust, it becomes bankrupt and closes down.

bustle VERB ① When people bustle, they move in a busy, hurried way. ▶ NOUN ② Bustle is busy, noisy activity.

bustle VERB
① = dash, fuss, hurry, rush, scurry, scuttle
▶ NOUN ② = activity, commotion, excitement, flurry, fuss, hurry
≠ peace

busy, **busier**, **busiest**; **busies**, **busying**, **busied** ADJECTIVE ① If you are busy, you are in the middle of doing something. ② A busy place is full of people doing things or moving about • *a busy seaside resort.* ▶ VERB ③ If you busy yourself with something, you occupy yourself by doing it. **busily** ADVERB

busy ADJECTIVE
① = active, employed, engaged, engrossed, occupied, working
≠ idle
② = active, full, hectic, lively, restless
▶ VERB ③ = absorb, employ, engage, immerse, occupy

A B C D E F G H I J K L M N O P Q R S T U V W X Y Z

but CONJUNCTION ① used to introduce an idea that is opposite to what has gone before • *I don't like apples, but I do like oranges.* ② used when apologising • *I'm sorry, but I can't come tonight.* ③ except • *We can't do anything but wait.*

> **but** CONJUNCTION
> ① = although, though, while, yet
> ③ = except, except for, other than, save

butcher NOUN a shopkeeper who sells meat.

butler NOUN the chief male servant in a rich household.

butt NOUN ① The butt of a weapon is the thick end of its handle. ② If you are the butt of teasing, you are the target of it. ▸ VERB ③ If you butt something, you ram it with your head. **butt in** VERB If you butt in, you join in a private conversation or activity without being asked to.

butter NOUN ① Butter is a soft fatty food made from cream, which is spread on bread and used in cooking. ▸ VERB ② To butter bread means to spread butter on it.

butterfly, **butterflies** NOUN a type of insect with large colourful wings.

buttocks PLURAL NOUN Your buttocks are the part of your body that you sit on.

button NOUN ① Buttons are small, hard objects sewn on to clothing, and used to fasten two surfaces together. ② a small object on a piece of equipment that you press to make it work. ▸ VERB ③ If you button a piece of clothing, you fasten it using its buttons.

buxom ADJECTIVE A buxom woman is large, healthy and attractive.

buy, **buys**, **buying**, **bought** VERB If you buy something, you obtain it by paying money for it. **buyer** NOUN

> **buy** VERB
> = acquire, get, invest in, pay for, procure, purchase
> ≠ sell

buzz VERB ① If something buzzes, it makes a humming sound, like a bee. ▸ NOUN ② the sound something makes when it buzzes.

buzzer NOUN a device that makes a buzzing sound, to attract attention.

by PREPOSITION ① used to indicate who or what has done something • *The class was taken by a new teacher.* ② used to indicate how something is done • *He frightened her by hiding behind the door.* ③ located next to • *I sat by her bed.* ④ before a particular time • *It should be ready by next spring.* ▸ PREPOSITION, ADVERB ⑤ going past • *We drove by his house.*

by-election NOUN an election held to choose a new member of parliament after the previous member has resigned or died.

bygone ADJECTIVE (*literary*) happening or existing a long time ago • *the ceremonies of a bygone era.*

bypass NOUN a main road which takes traffic round a town rather than through it.

bystander NOUN someone who is not included or involved in something but is there to see it happen.

byte NOUN [ICT] a unit of computer memory size.

Cc

cab NOUN ① a taxi. ② In a lorry, bus or train, the cab is where the driver sits.

cabaret *[Said **kab**-bar-ray]* NOUN a show consisting of dancing, singing or comedy acts.

cabbage NOUN a large green or reddish-purple leafy vegetable.

cabin NOUN ① a room in a ship where a passenger sleeps. ② a small house, usually in the country and often made of wood. ③ the area where the passengers or the crew sit in a plane.

cabinet NOUN ① a small cupboard. ② The cabinet in a government is a group of ministers who advise the leader and decide policies.

cable NOUN ① a strong, thick rope or chain. ② a bundle of wires with a rubber covering, which carries electricity. ③ a message sent abroad by using electrical signals sent along a wire.

cable car NOUN a vehicle pulled by a moving cable, for taking people up and down mountains.

cable television NOUN a television service people can receive from underground wires which carry the signals.

cache *[Said **kash**]* NOUN a store of things hidden away • *a cache of guns.*

cachet *[Said **kash**-shay]* NOUN (*formal*) Cachet is the status and respect something has • *the cachet of shopping at Harrods.*

cackle VERB ① If you cackle, you laugh harshly. ▸ NOUN ② a harsh laugh.

cacophony *[Said kak-**koff**-fon-nee]* NOUN (*formal*) a loud, unpleasant noise • *a cacophony of barking dogs.*

cactus, **cacti** or **cactuses** NOUN a thick, fleshy plant that grows in deserts and is usually covered in spikes.

caddie; also spelt **caddy** NOUN ① a person who carries golf clubs for a golf player. ② A tea caddy is a box for keeping tea in.

cadence *[Said **kay**-denss]* NOUN The cadence of someone's voice is the way it goes up and down as they speak.

cadet NOUN a young person being trained in the armed forces or police.

caesarean *[Said siz-**air**-ee-an]*; also spelt **caesarian** or **cesarean** NOUN A caesarean or caesarean section is an operation in which a baby is lifted out of a woman's womb through a cut in her abdomen.

café *[Said **kaf**-fay]* NOUN ① a place where you can buy light meals and drinks. ② In South African English, a café is a corner shop or grocer's shop.

cafeteria *[Said kaf-fit-**ee**-ree-ya]* NOUN a restaurant where you serve yourself.

caffeine *[Said **kaf**-feen]* NOUN Caffeine is a chemical in coffee and tea which makes you more active.

cage NOUN a box made of wire or bars in which birds or animals are kept. **caged** ADJECTIVE

cagey, **cagier**, **cagiest** *[Said **kay**-jee]* ADJECTIVE (*informal*) cautious and not open • *They're very cagey when they talk to me.*

cahoots PHRASE (*informal*) If you are **in cahoots** with someone, you are working closely with them on a secret plan.

cajole VERB If you cajole someone into doing something, you persuade them to do it by saying nice things to them.

cake NOUN ① a sweet food made by baking flour, eggs, fat and sugar. ② a block of a hard substance such as soap. ▸ VERB ③ If something cakes or is caked, it forms or becomes covered with a solid layer • *caked with mud*.

calamity, **calamities** NOUN an event that causes disaster or distress. **calamitous** ADJECTIVE

calcium [*Said* ***kal**-see-um*] NOUN SCIENCE Calcium is a soft white element found in bones and teeth. Its atomic number is 20 and its symbol is Ca.

calculate VERB MATHS If you calculate something, you work it out, usually by doing some arithmetic. **calculation** NOUN

> **calculate** VERB
> = count, determine, reckon, work out

calculating ADJECTIVE carefully planning situations to get what you want • *Toby was always a calculating type*.

calculator NOUN a small electronic machine used for doing mathematical calculations.

calculus NOUN Calculus is a branch of mathematics concerned with amounts that can change and rates of change.

calendar NOUN ① a chart showing the date of each day in a particular year. ② a system of dividing time into fixed periods of days, months and years • *the Jewish calendar*.

calf, **calves** NOUN ① a young cow, bull, elephant, whale or seal. ② the thick part at the back of your leg below your knee.

calibre [*Said* ***kal**-lib-ber*] NOUN ① the ability or intelligence someone has • *a player of her calibre*. ② The calibre of a gun is the width of the inside of the barrel of the gun.

call VERB ① If someone or something is called a particular name, that is their name • *a man called Jeffrey*. ② If you call people or situations something, you use words to describe your opinion of them • *They called me unfriendly*. ③ If you call someone, you telephone them. ④ If you call or call out something, you say it loudly • *He called out his daughter's name*. ⑤ If you call on someone, you pay them a short visit • *Don't hesitate to call on me*. ▸ NOUN ⑥ If you get a call from someone, they telephone you or pay you a visit. ⑦ a cry or shout • *a call for help*. ⑧ a demand for something • *The call for art teachers was small*. **call off** VERB If you call something off, you cancel it. **call up** VERB If someone is called up, they are ordered to join the army, navy or air force.

> **call** VERB
> ① = christen, designate, dub, name
> ③ = contact, phone, ring, telephone
> ④ = announce, cry, cry out, shout, yell
> ▸ NOUN ⑦ = cry, shout, yell

call centre NOUN an office in which most staff are employed to answer telephone calls on behalf of a particular company or organisation.

calling NOUN ① a profession or career. ② If you have a calling to a particular job, you have a strong feeling that you should do it.

callous ADJECTIVE cruel and not concerned with other people's feelings. **callously** ADVERB **callousness** NOUN

> **callous** ADJECTIVE
> = cold, heartless, indifferent, insensitive
> ≠ caring

calm, **calmest** ADJECTIVE ① Someone who is calm is quiet and does not show any worry or excitement. ② If the weather or the sea is calm, it is still because there is no strong wind. ▸ NOUN ③ Calm is a state of quietness and peacefulness • *He liked the calm of the evening.* ▸ VERB ④ To calm someone means to make them less upset or excited. **calmly** ADVERB **calmness** NOUN

calm ADJECTIVE
① = collected, composed, cool, impassive, relaxed
≠ worried
② = balmy, mild, still, tranquil
≠ rough
▸ NOUN ③ = calmness, peace, peacefulness, quiet, serenity, stillness
▸ VERB ④ = quieten, relax, soothe

calorie NOUN a unit of measurement for the energy food and drink gives you • *Chocolate cake is high in calories.* **calorific** ADJECTIVE

calves the plural of **calf**.

calypso, **calypsos** [*Said kal-**lip**-soh*] NOUN a type of song from the West Indies, accompanied by a rhythmic beat, about something happening at the time.

camaraderie [*Said kam-mer-**rah**-der-ree*] NOUN Camaraderie is a feeling of trust and friendship between a group of people.

came the past tense of **come**.

camel NOUN a large mammal with either one or two humps on its back. Camels live in hot desert areas and are sometimes used for carrying things.

cameo, **cameos** NOUN ① a small but important part in a play or film played by a well-known actor or actress. ② a brooch with a raised stone design on a flat stone of another colour.

camera NOUN a piece of equipment used for taking photographs or for filming.

camouflage [*Said **kam**-mof-flahj*] NOUN ① Camouflage is a way of avoiding being seen by having the same colour or appearance as the surroundings. ▸ VERB ② To camouflage something is to hide it by giving it the same colour or appearance as its surroundings.

camp NOUN ① a place where people live in tents or stay in tents on holiday. ② a collection of buildings for a particular group of people such as soldiers or prisoners. ③ a group of people who support a particular idea or belief • *the pro-government camp.* ▸ VERB ④ If you camp, you stay in a tent. **camper** NOUN **camping** NOUN

campaign [*Said kam-**pane***] NOUN ① a set of actions aiming to achieve a particular result • *a campaign to educate people.* ▸ VERB ② To campaign means to carry out a campaign • *He has campaigned against smoking.* **campaigner** NOUN

campaign NOUN
① = crusade, movement, operation, push

campus, **campuses** NOUN the area of land and the buildings that make up a university or college.

can[1], **could** VERB ① If you can do something, it is possible for you to do it or you are allowed to do it • *You can go to the cinema.* ② If you can do something, you have the ability to do it • *I can speak Italian.*

can[2], **cans**, **canning**, **canned** NOUN ① a metal container, often a sealed one with food or drink inside. ▸ VERB ② To can food or drink is to seal it in cans.

Canadian ADJECTIVE ① belonging or relating to Canada. ▸ NOUN ② someone who comes from Canada.

canal NOUN a long, narrow man-made stretch of water.

canary, **canaries** NOUN a small yellow bird.

cancel, **cancels**, **cancelling**, **cancelled** VERB ① If you cancel something that has been arranged, you stop it from happening. ② If you cancel a cheque or an agreement, you make sure that it is no longer valid. **cancellation** NOUN

> **cancel** VERB
> ① = abandon, call off
> ② = annul, quash, repeal, revoke

cancer NOUN ① a serious disease in which abnormal cells in a part of the body increase rapidly, causing growths. ② Cancer is also the fourth sign of the zodiac, represented by a crab. People born between June 21st and July 22nd are born under this sign. **cancerous** ADJECTIVE

candelabra or **candelabrum** NOUN an ornamental holder for a number of candles.

candid ADJECTIVE honest and frank. **candidly** ADVERB **candour** NOUN

> **candid** ADJECTIVE
> = blunt, frank, honest, open, straightforward, truthful

candidate NOUN ① a person who is being considered for a job. ② a person taking an examination. **candidacy** NOUN

> **candidate** NOUN
> ① = applicant, competitor, contender

candied ADJECTIVE covered or cooked in sugar • *candied fruit*.

candle NOUN a stick of hard wax with a wick through the middle. The lighted wick gives a flame that provides light.

candy, **candies** NOUN In America, candy is sweets.

cane NOUN ① Cane is the long, hollow stems of a plant such as bamboo. ② Cane is also strips of cane used for weaving things such as baskets. ③ a long narrow stick, often one used to beat people as a punishment. ▸ VERB ④ To cane someone means to beat them with a cane as a punishment.

canine [Said **kay**-nine] ADJECTIVE relating to dogs.

canister NOUN a container with a lid, used for storing foods such as sugar or tea.

cannabis NOUN Cannabis is an illegal drug made from the hemp plant, which some people smoke.

canned ADJECTIVE ① Canned food is kept in cans. ② Canned music or laughter on a television or radio show is recorded beforehand.

cannibal NOUN a person who eats other human beings; also used of animals that eat animals of their own type. **cannibalism** NOUN

cannon NOUN ① A cannon is a large gun, usually on wheels, used in battles to fire heavy metal balls. ▸ VERB ② To cannon into people or things means to collide into them with force.

cannot VERB Cannot is the same as can not • *She cannot come home yet*.

canny, **cannier**, **canniest** ADJECTIVE clever and cautious • *canny business people*. **cannily** ADVERB

canoe [Said ka-**noo**] NOUN a small, narrow boat that you row using a paddle. **canoeing** NOUN **canoeist** NOUN

canon NOUN ① a member of the clergy in a cathedral. ② a basic rule or principle • *the canons of political economy*. ③ In literature, a canon is all the writings by a particular author which are known to be genuine.

canopy, **canopies** NOUN a cover for something, used for shelter or decoration • *a frilly canopy over the bed*.

cantankerous ADJECTIVE Cantankerous people are quarrelsome and bad-tempered.

canteen NOUN ① In a place such as a school or office, the canteen is a place where people can go to eat. ② A canteen of cutlery is a set of cutlery in a box.

canter VERB When a horse canters, it moves at a speed between a gallop and a trot.

canvas NOUN ① Canvas is strong, heavy cloth used for making things such as sails and tents. ② a piece of canvas on which an artist does a painting.

canvass VERB ① If you canvass people or a place, you go round trying to persuade people to vote for a particular candidate or party in an election. ② If you canvass opinion, you find out what people think about a particular subject by asking them.

canyon NOUN GEOGRAPHY a narrow river valley with steep sides.

cap, **caps**, **capping**, **capped** NOUN ① a soft, flat hat, often with a peak at the front. ② the top of a bottle. ③ Caps are small explosives used in toy guns. ▶ VERB ④ To cap something is to cover it with something. ⑤ If you cap a story or a joke that someone has just told, you tell a better one.

capable ADJECTIVE ① able to do something • *a man capable of writing great books.* ② skilful or talented • *She was a very capable woman.* **capably** ADVERB **capability** NOUN

> **capable** ADJECTIVE
> ② = able, accomplished, adept, competent, efficient, proficient, skilful
> ≠ incompetent

capacity, **capacities** *[Said kap-**pas**-sit-tee]* NOUN ① the maximum amount that something can hold or produce • *a seating capacity of eleven thousand.* ② a person's power or ability to do something • *his capacity for consuming hamburgers.* ③ someone's position or role • *in his capacity as councillor.*

> **capacity** NOUN
> ① = dimensions, room, size, space, volume
> ② = ability, capability, facility, gift, potential, power

cape NOUN ① a short cloak with no sleeves. ② a large piece of land sticking out into the sea • *the Cape of Good Hope.*

caper NOUN ① Capers are the flower buds of a spiky Mediterranean shrub, which are pickled and used to flavour food. ② a light-hearted practical joke • *Jack would have nothing to do with such capers.*

capital NOUN ① The capital of a country is the city where the government meets. ② Capital is the amount of money or property owned or used by a business. ③ Capital is also a sum of money that you save or invest in order to gain interest. ④ A capital or capital letter is a larger letter used at the beginning of a sentence or a name.

capitalise; also spelt **capitalize** VERB If you capitalise on a situation, you use it to get an advantage.

capitalism NOUN Capitalism is an economic and political system where businesses and industries are not owned and run by the government, but by individuals who can make a profit from them. **capitalist** ADJECTIVE, NOUN

capital punishment NOUN Capital punishment is legally killing someone as a punishment for a crime they have committed.

capitulate VERB To capitulate is to give in and stop fighting or resisting

• *The Finns capitulated in March 1940.* **capitulation** NOUN

cappuccino, **cappuccinos** [*Said kap-poot-**sheen**-oh*] NOUN coffee made with frothy milk.

capricious [*Said kap-**prish**-uss*] ADJECTIVE often changing unexpectedly • *the capricious English weather.*

Capricorn NOUN Capricorn is the tenth sign of the zodiac, represented by a goat. People born between December 22nd and January 19th are born under this sign.

capsize VERB If a boat capsizes, it turns upside down.

capsule NOUN ① a small container with medicine inside which you swallow. ② the part of a spacecraft in which astronauts travel.

captain NOUN ① the officer in charge of a ship or aeroplane. ② an army officer of the rank immediately above lieutenant. ③ a navy officer of the rank immediately above commander. ④ the leader of a sports team • *captain of the cricket team.* ▸ VERB ⑤ If you captain a group of people, you are their leader.

caption NOUN a title printed underneath a picture or photograph.

captivate VERB To captivate someone is to fascinate or attract them so that they cannot take their attention away • *I was captivated by her.* **captivating** ADJECTIVE

captive NOUN ① a person who has been captured and kept prisoner. ▸ ADJECTIVE ② imprisoned or enclosed • *a captive bird.* **captivity** NOUN

captor NOUN someone who has captured a person or animal.

capture VERB ① To capture someone is to take them prisoner. ② To capture a quality or mood means to succeed in representing or describing it • *capturing the mood of the riots.* ▸ NOUN ③ The capture of someone or something is the action of taking them prisoner • *the fifth anniversary of his capture.*

> **capture** VERB
> ① = apprehend, arrest, catch, seize, take
> ≠ release
> ▸ NOUN ③ = arrest, seizure, taking, trapping

car NOUN ① a four-wheeled road vehicle with room for a small number of people. ② a railway carriage used for a particular purpose • *the buffet car.*

> **car** NOUN
> ① = automobile (*American*), motor (*old-fashioned*), vehicle

caramel NOUN ① a chewy sweet made from sugar, butter and milk. ② Caramel is burnt sugar used for colouring or flavouring food.

carat NOUN ① A carat is a unit for measuring the weight of diamonds and other precious stones, equal to 0.2 grams. ② A carat is also a unit for measuring the purity of gold. The purest gold is 24 carats.

caravan NOUN ① a vehicle pulled by a car in which people live or spend their holidays. ② a group of people and animals travelling together, usually across a desert.

carbohydrate NOUN [DGT] [SCIENCE] Carbohydrate is a substance that gives you energy. It is found in foods like sugar and bread.

carbon NOUN [SCIENCE] Carbon is a chemical element that is pure in diamonds and also found in coal. All living things contain carbon. Its atomic number is 6 and its symbol is C.

carbonated ADJECTIVE Carbonated drinks contain bubbles of carbon dioxide that make them fizzy.

carbon dioxide NOUN SCIENCE Carbon dioxide is a colourless, odourless gas that humans and animals breathe out. It is used in industry, for example in making fizzy drinks and in fire extinguishers.

carcass; also spelt **carcase** NOUN the body of a dead animal.

card NOUN ① a piece of stiff paper or plastic with information or a message on it • *a birthday card.* ② Cards can mean playing cards • *a poor set of cards with which to play.* ③ When you play cards, you play any game using playing cards. ④ Card is thick, stiff paper.

cardboard NOUN Cardboard is thick, stiff paper.

cardiac ADJECTIVE relating to the heart • *cardiac disease.*

cardigan NOUN a knitted jacket that fastens up the front.

cardinal NOUN ① a high-ranking member of the Roman Catholic clergy who chooses and advises the Pope. ▶ ADJECTIVE ② extremely important • *a cardinal principle of law.*

care VERB ① If you care about something, you are concerned about it and interested in it. ② If you care about someone, you feel affection towards them. ③ If you care for someone, you look after them. ▶ NOUN ④ Care is concern or worry. ⑤ Care of someone or something is treatment for them or looking after them • *the care of young children.* ⑥ If you do something with care, you do it with close attention.

> **care** VERB
> ① = be bothered, be concerned, be interested, mind
> ▶ NOUN ④ = anxiety, concern, stress, trouble, woe, worry
> ⑥ = attention, caution, pains

career NOUN ① PSHE the series of jobs that someone has in life, usually in the same occupation • *a career in insurance.* ▶ VERB ② To career somewhere is to move very quickly, often out of control • *His car careered off the road.*

carefree ADJECTIVE having no worries or responsibilities.

careful ADJECTIVE ① acting sensibly and with care • *Be careful what you say to him.* ② complete and well done • *It needs very careful planning.* **carefully** ADVERB

> **careful** ADJECTIVE
> ① = cautious, prudent
> ≠ careless
> ② = meticulous, painstaking, precise, thorough
> ≠ careless

careless ADJECTIVE ① done badly without enough attention • *careless driving.* ② relaxed and unconcerned • *careless laughter.* **carelessly** ADVERB **carelessness** NOUN

> **careless** ADJECTIVE
> ① = irresponsible, neglectful, sloppy (*informal*)
> ≠ careful
> ② = casual, nonchalant, offhand

caress VERB ① If you caress someone, you stroke them gently and affectionately. ▶ NOUN ② a gentle, affectionate stroke.

caretaker NOUN ① a person who looks after a large building such as a school. ▶ ADJECTIVE ② having an important position for a short time until a new person is appointed • *O'Leary was named caretaker manager.*

cargo, **cargoes** NOUN the goods carried on a ship or plane.

caricature NOUN ① a drawing or description of someone that exaggerates striking parts of their appearance or personality. ▶ VERB

②To caricature someone is to give a caricature of them.

A B C D E F G H I J K L M N O P Q R S T U V W X Y Z

carnage *[Said kahr-nij]* NOUN Carnage is the violent killing of large numbers of people.

carnival NOUN a public festival with music, processions and dancing.

carnivore NOUN an animal that eats meat. **carnivorous** ADJECTIVE

carol NOUN a religious song sung at Christmas time.

carousel *[Said kar-ros-sel]* NOUN a merry-go-round.

carp NOUN ① a large edible freshwater fish. ▶ VERB ② To carp means to complain about unimportant things.

carpenter NOUN a person who makes and repairs wooden structures. **carpentry** NOUN

carpet NOUN ① a thick covering for a floor, usually made of a material like wool. ▶ VERB ② To carpet a floor means to cover it with a carpet.

carriage NOUN ① one of the separate sections of a passenger train. ② an old-fashioned vehicle for carrying passengers, usually pulled by horses.

carriageway NOUN one of the sides of a road which traffic travels along in one direction only.

carrier NOUN ① a vehicle that is used for carrying things • *a troop carrier*. ② A carrier of a germ or disease is a person or animal that can pass it on to others.

carrier bag NOUN a bag made of plastic or paper, which is used for carrying shopping.

carrot NOUN a long, thin orange root vegetable.

carry, carries, carrying, carried VERB ① To carry something is to hold it and take it somewhere. ② When a vehicle carries people, they travel in it. ③ A person or animal that carries a germ can pass it on to other people or animals • *I still carry the disease*. ④ If a sound carries, it can be heard far away • *Jake's voice carried over the cheering*. ⑤ In a meeting, if a proposal is carried, it is accepted by a majority of the people there. **carry away** VERB If you are carried away, you are so excited by something that you do not behave sensibly. **carry on** VERB To carry on doing something means to continue doing it. **carry out** VERB To carry something out means to do it and complete it • *The conversion was carried out by a local builder*.

> **carry** VERB
> ① = bear, convey (*formal*), lug, take, transport
> ▶ **carry out** = accomplish, achieve, fulfil, perform

cart NOUN a vehicle with wheels, used to carry goods and often pulled by horses or cattle.

cartilage NOUN [SCIENCE] Cartilage is a strong, flexible substance found around the joints and in the nose and ears.

carton NOUN a cardboard or plastic container.

cartoon NOUN ① a drawing or a series of drawings which are funny or make a point. ② a film in which the characters and scenes are drawn. **cartoonist** NOUN

cartridge NOUN ① a tube containing a bullet and an explosive substance, used in guns. ② a plastic container full of ink that you put in a printer or pen.

carve VERB ① To carve an object means to cut it out of a substance such as stone or wood. ② To carve meat means to cut slices from it.

> **carve** VERB
> ① = chisel, cut, engrave, inscribe, sculpt

carving NOUN a carved object.

cascade NOUN ① a waterfall or group of waterfalls. ▸ VERB ② To cascade means to flow downwards quickly • *Gallons of water cascaded from the attic.*

case NOUN ① a particular situation, event or example • *a clear case of mistaken identity.* ② a container for something, or a suitcase • *a camera case.* ③ Doctors sometimes refer to a patient as a case. ④ Police detectives refer to a crime they are investigating as a case. ⑤ In an argument, the case for an idea is the reasons used to support it. ⑥ In law, a case is a trial or other inquiry. ⑦ In grammar, the case of a noun or pronoun is the form of it which shows its relationship with other words in a sentence • *the accusative case.* ▸ PHRASE ⑧ You say **in case** to explain something that you do because a particular thing might happen • *I didn't want to shout in case I startled you.* ⑨ You say **in that case** to show that you are assuming something said before is true • *In that case we won't do it.*

case NOUN
① = example, illustration, instance, occasion, occurrence
② = box, container
⑥ = action, lawsuit, proceedings, trial

cash NOUN Cash is money in notes and coins.

cashew [Said **kash**-oo] NOUN a curved, edible nut.

cash flow NOUN Cash flow is the money that a business makes and spends.

cashier NOUN the person that customers pay in a shop or get money from in a bank.

cashmere NOUN Cashmere is very soft, fine wool from goats.

cash register NOUN a machine in a shop which records sales, and where the money is kept.

casing NOUN a protective covering for something.

casino, **casinos** [Said kass-**ee**-noh] NOUN a place where people go to play gambling games.

cask NOUN a wooden barrel.

casket NOUN a small box for jewellery or other valuables.

casserole NOUN a dish made by cooking a mixture of meat and vegetables slowly in an oven; also used to refer to the pot a casserole is cooked in.

cassowary, **cassowaries** NOUN a large bird found in Australia with black feathers and a brightly coloured neck. Cassowaries cannot fly.

cast, **casts**, **casting**, **cast** NOUN ① all the people who act in a play or film. ② an object made by pouring liquid into a mould and leaving it to harden • *the casts of classical sculptures.* ③ a stiff plaster covering put on broken bones to keep them still so that they heal properly. ▸ VERB ④ To cast actors is to choose them for roles in a play or film. ⑤ When people cast their votes in an election, they vote. ⑥ To cast something is to throw it. ⑦ If you cast your eyes somewhere, you look there • *I cast my eyes down briefly.* ⑧ To cast an object is to make it by pouring liquid into a mould and leaving it to harden • *An image of him has been cast in bronze.* **cast off** VERB If you cast off, you untie the rope fastening a boat to a harbour or shore.

caste NOUN ① [RE] one of the four classes into which Hindu society is divided. ② Caste is a system of social classes decided according to family, wealth and position.

castigate VERB (*formal*) To castigate someone is to criticise them severely.

castle NOUN ① HISTORY a large building with walls or ditches round it to protect it from attack. ② In chess, a castle is the same as a rook.

castor; also spelt **caster** NOUN a small wheel fitted to furniture so that it can be moved easily.

casual ADJECTIVE ① happening by chance without planning • *a casual remark*. ② careless or without interest • *a casual glance over his shoulder*. ③ Casual clothes are suitable for informal occasions. ④ Casual work is not regular or permanent. **casually** ADVERB **casualness** NOUN

> **casual** ADJECTIVE
> ① = accidental, chance, incidental
> ≠ deliberate
> ② = careless, cursory, nonchalant, offhand, relaxed
> ≠ concerned

casualty, **casualties** NOUN a person killed or injured in an accident or war • *Many of the casualties were office workers*.

cat NOUN ① a small furry animal with whiskers, a tail, and sharp claws, often kept as a pet. ② any of the family of mammals that includes lions and tigers.

> **cat** NOUN
> ① = feline (*formal*), kitty (*informal*), moggy, moggie, pussy, puss, pussycat

catalogue, **catalogues**, **cataloguing**, **catalogued** NOUN ① a book containing pictures and descriptions of goods that you can buy in a shop or through the post. ② LIBRARY a list of things such as the objects in a museum or the books in a library. ▸ VERB ③ To catalogue a collection of things means to list them in a catalogue.

catalyst [*Said* ***kat**-a-list*] NOUN ① something that causes a change to happen • *the catalyst which provoked civil war*. ② SCIENCE a substance that speeds up a chemical reaction without changing itself.

catamaran NOUN a sailing boat with two hulls connected to each other.

catapult NOUN ① a Y-shaped object with a piece of elastic tied between the two top ends, used for shooting small stones. ▸ VERB ② To catapult something is to throw it violently through the air. ③ If someone is catapulted into a situation, they find themselves unexpectedly in that situation • *Tony has been catapulted into the limelight*.

cataract NOUN an area of the lens of someone's eye that has become white instead of clear, so that they cannot see properly.

catastrophe [*Said kat-**tass**-trif-fee*] NOUN a terrible disaster. **catastrophic** ADJECTIVE

catch, **catches**, **catching**, **caught** VERB ① If you catch a ball moving in the air, you grasp hold of it when it comes near you. ② To catch an animal means to trap it • *I caught ten fish*. ③ When the police catch criminals, they find them and arrest them. ④ If you catch someone doing something they should not be doing, you discover them doing it • *He caught me playing the church organ*. ⑤ If you catch a bus or train, you get on it and travel somewhere. ⑥ If you catch a cold or a disease, you become infected with it. ⑦ If something catches on an object, it sticks to it or gets trapped • *The white fibres caught on the mesh*. ▸ NOUN ⑧ a device that fastens something. ⑨ a problem or hidden complication in something.

catch on VERB ① If you catch on to something, you understand it. ② If something catches on, it becomes popular • *The show has never really caught*

A B C D E F G H I J K L M N O P Q R S T U V W X Y Z

on with TV viewers. **catch out** VERB To catch someone out is to trick them or trap them. **catch up** VERB ① To catch up with someone in front of you is to reach the place where they are by moving slightly faster than them. ② To catch up with someone is also to reach the same level or standard as them.

catch VERB
② = capture, snare, trap
③ = apprehend, arrest
▸ NOUN ⑧ = bolt, clasp, clip, latch
⑨ = disadvantage, drawback, snag

catching ADJECTIVE tending to spread very quickly • *Measles is catching*.

catchy, **catchier**, **catchiest** ADJECTIVE attractive and easily remembered • *a catchy little tune*.

categorical ADJECTIVE absolutely certain and direct • *a categorical denial*. **categorically** ADVERB

categorise; also spelt **categorize** VERB To categorise things is to arrange them in different categories.

category, **categories** NOUN a set of things with a particular characteristic in common • *Occupations can be divided into four categories*.

category NOUN
= class, classification, group, set, sort, type

cater VERB To cater for people is to provide them with what they need, especially food.

caterer NOUN a person or business that provides food for parties and groups.

caterpillar NOUN the larva of a butterfly or moth. It looks like a small coloured worm and feeds on plants.

catharsis, **catharses** [*Said kath-**ar**-siss*] NOUN (*formal*) Catharsis is the release of strong emotions and feelings by expressing them through drama or literature.

cathedral NOUN HISTORY an important church with a bishop in charge of it.

Catholic, **Catholics** NOUN, ADJECTIVE (a) Roman Catholic. **Catholicism**

cattle PLURAL NOUN Cattle are cows and bulls kept by farmers.

catty, **cattier**, **cattiest** ADJECTIVE unpleasant and spiteful. **cattiness** NOUN

catwalk NOUN a narrow pathway that people walk along, for example over a stage.

Caucasian [*Said kaw-**kayz**-yn*] NOUN a person belonging to a race of people with fair or light-brown skin.

caught the past tense and past participle of **catch**.

cauldron NOUN a large, round, metal cooking pot, especially one that sits over a fire.

cauliflower NOUN a large, round, white vegetable surrounded by green leaves.

cause NOUN ① The cause of something is the thing that makes it happen • *the most common cause of back pain*. ② an aim or principle which a group of people are working for • *dedication to the cause of peace*. ③ If you have cause for something, you have a reason for it • *They gave us no cause to believe that*. ▸ VERB ④ To cause something is to make it happen • *This can cause delays*. **causal** ADJECTIVE

cause NOUN
① = origin, root, source
② = aim, ideal, movement
③ = basis, grounds, justification, motivation, motive, reason
▸ VERB ④ = bring about, create, generate, produce, provoke

causeway NOUN a raised path or road across water or marshland.

A B C D E F G H I J K L M N O P Q R S T U V W X Y Z

caustic ADJECTIVE ① A caustic chemical can destroy substances • *caustic liquids such as acids.* ② bitter or sarcastic • *your caustic sense of humour.*

caution NOUN ① Caution is great care which you take to avoid danger • *You will need to proceed with caution.* ② a warning • *Sutton was let off with a caution.* ▶ VERB ③ If someone cautions you, they warn you, usually not to do something again • *A man has been cautioned by police.* **cautionary** ADJECTIVE

> **caution** NOUN
> ① = care, prudence
> ▶ VERB ③ = reprimand, tick off (*informal*), warn

cautious ADJECTIVE acting very carefully to avoid danger • *a cautious approach.* **cautiously** ADVERB

> **cautious** ADJECTIVE
> = careful, guarded, tentative, wary
> ≠ daring

cavalcade NOUN a procession of people on horses or in cars or carriages.

cavalier [*Said kav-val-**eer***] ADJECTIVE Someone who is cavalier behaves without sensitivity, or does not take something seriously enough • *a cavalier attitude to friendships.*

cavalry NOUN The cavalry is the part of an army that uses armoured vehicles or horses.

cave NOUN ① a large hole in rock, that is underground or in the side of a cliff. ▶ VERB ② If a roof caves in, it collapses inwards.

caveman, **cavemen** NOUN Cavemen were people who lived in caves in prehistoric times.

cavern NOUN a large cave.

cavernous ADJECTIVE large, deep and hollow • *a cavernous warehouse.*

caviar [*Said **kav**-vee-ar*] NOUN Caviar is the tiny salted eggs of a fish called the sturgeon.

cavity, **cavities** NOUN a small hole in something solid • *There were dark cavities in his back teeth.*

cavort VERB When people cavort, they jump around excitedly.

cc an abbreviation for 'cubic centimetres'.

CD an abbreviation for 'compact disc'.

cease VERB ① If something ceases, it stops happening. ② If you cease to do something, or cease doing it, you stop doing it.

> **cease** VERB
> ① = be over, come to an end, die away, end, finish, stop
> ≠ begin
> ② = desist from, discontinue, finish, give up, stop, suspend
> ≠ start

ceaseless ADJECTIVE going on without stopping • *ceaseless chatter.* **ceaselessly** ADVERB

cedar NOUN a large evergreen tree with wide branches and needle-shaped leaves.

cede [*Said **seed***] VERB To cede something is to give it up to someone else • *Haiti was ceded to France in 1697.*

ceiling NOUN the top inside surface of a room.

celebrate VERB ① If you celebrate or celebrate something, you do something special and enjoyable because of it • *a party to celebrate the end of the exams.* ② When a priest celebrates Mass, he performs the ceremonies of the Mass.

> **celebrate** VERB
> ① = commemorate, party, rejoice
> ≠ mourn

celebrated ADJECTIVE famous • *the celebrated Italian mountaineer.*

celebration NOUN an event in honour of a special occasion. **celebratory** ADJECTIVE

celebration NOUN
= festival, festivity, gala, party

celebrity, **celebrities** NOUN a famous person.

celebrity NOUN
= big name, name, personality, star, superstar, VIP

celery NOUN Celery is a vegetable with long, pale green stalks.

celestial [*Said sil-**lest**-yal*] ADJECTIVE (*formal*) concerning the sky or heaven • *The telescope is pointed at a celestial object.*

celibate [*Said **sel**-lib-bit*] ADJECTIVE Someone who is celibate does not marry. **celibacy** NOUN

cell NOUN ① SCIENCE In biology, a cell is the smallest part of an animal or plant that can exist by itself. Each cell contains a nucleus. ② a small room where a prisoner is kept in a prison or police station. ③ a small group of people set up to work together as part of a larger organisation. ④ DGT a device that converts chemical energy to electricity.

cellar NOUN a room underneath a building, often used to store wine.

cello, **cellos** [*Said **chel**-loh*] NOUN MUSIC a large musical stringed instrument which you play sitting down, holding the instrument upright with your knees. **cellist** NOUN

cellphone NOUN a small portable telephone.

cellular ADJECTIVE Cellular means relating to the cells of animals or plants.

Celsius [*Said **sel**-see-yuss*] NOUN SCIENCE Celsius is a scale for measuring temperature in which water freezes at 0 degrees (0°C) and boils at 100 degrees (100°C). It is named after Anders Celsius (1701–1744), who invented it. Celsius is the same as 'Centigrade'.

Celtic [*Said **kel**-tik*] ADJECTIVE A Celtic language is one of a group of languages that includes Gaelic and Welsh.

cement NOUN ① Cement is a fine powder made from limestone and clay, which is mixed with sand and water to make concrete. ▸ VERB ② To cement things is to stick them together with cement or cover them with cement. ③ Something that cements a relationship makes it stronger • *to cement relations between them.*

cemetery, **cemeteries** NOUN an area of land where dead people are buried.

cenotaph [*Said **sen**-not-ahf*] NOUN a monument built in memory of dead people, especially soldiers buried elsewhere.

censor NOUN ① a person officially appointed to examine books or films and to ban parts that are considered unsuitable. ▸ VERB ② If someone censors a book or film, they cut or ban parts of it that are considered unsuitable for the public. **censorship** NOUN

censure [*Said **sen**-sher*] NOUN ① Censure is strong disapproval of something. ▸ VERB ② To censure someone is to criticise them severely.

censure NOUN
① = blame, condemnation, criticism, disapproval, reproach
▸ VERB ② = condemn, criticise, denounce, reproach

census, **censuses** NOUN an official survey of the population of a country.

cent NOUN a unit of currency. In the USA and the Caribbean, a cent is worth one hundredth of a dollar;

in Europe, it is worth one hundredth of a euro.

centenary, **centenaries** *[Said sen-**teen**-er-ee]* **NOUN** the hundredth anniversary of something.

centimetre **NOUN** a unit of length equal to ten millimetres or one hundredth of a metre.

central **ADJECTIVE** ① in or near the centre of an object or area • *central ceiling lights*. ② main or most important • *the central idea of this work*. **centrally** **ADVERB** **centrality** **NOUN**

Central America **NOUN** Central America is the area of land joining North America to South America.

central heating **NOUN** Central heating is a system of heating a building in which water or air is heated in a tank and travels through pipes and radiators round the building.

centralise; also spelt **centralize** **VERB** To centralise a system is to bring the organisation of it under the control of one central group. **centralisation** **NOUN**

centre **NOUN** ① the middle of an object or area. ② a building where people go for activities, meetings or help • *a health centre*. ③ Someone or something that is the centre of attention attracts a lot of attention. ▶ **VERB** ④ To centre something is to move it so that it is balanced or at the centre of something else. ⑤ If something centres on or around a particular thing, that thing is the main subject of attention • *The discussion centred on his request*.

> **centre** **NOUN**
> ① = core, focus, heart, hub, middle
> ≠ edge
> ▶ **VERB** ⑤ = concentrate, focus, revolve

centurion **NOUN** HISTORY an ancient Roman officer in charge of a hundred soldiers.

century, **centuries** **NOUN** ① a period of one hundred years. ② In cricket, a century is one hundred runs scored by a batsman.

ceramic *[Said si-**ram**-mik]* **NOUN** ① SCIENCE Ceramic is a hard material made by baking clay to a very high temperature. ② Ceramics is the art of making objects out of clay.

cereal **NOUN** ① a food made from grain, often eaten with milk for breakfast. ② a plant that produces edible grain, such as wheat or oats.

cerebral *[Said **ser**-reb-ral]* **ADJECTIVE** (*formal*) relating to the brain • *a cerebral haemorrhage*.

cerebral palsy **NOUN** Cerebral palsy is an illness caused by damage to a baby's brain, which makes its muscles and limbs very weak.

ceremonial **ADJECTIVE** relating to a ceremony • *ceremonial dress*. **ceremonially** **ADVERB**

ceremony, **ceremonies** **NOUN** ① a set of formal actions performed at a special occasion or important public event • *his recent coronation ceremony*. ② Ceremony is very formal and polite behaviour • *He hung up without ceremony*.

> **ceremony** **NOUN**
> ① = observance, pomp, rite, ritual, service
> ② = decorum, etiquette, formality, niceties, protocol

certain **ADJECTIVE** ① definite or reliable • *He is certain to be in Italy*. ② having no doubt in your mind. ③ You use 'certain' to refer to a specific person or thing • *certain aspects of the job*. ④ You use 'certain' to suggest that a quality is noticeable but not obvious • *There's a certain resemblance to Joe*.

certain ADJECTIVE
① = definite, established, guaranteed, inevitable, known, sure, undeniable
≠ uncertain
② = clear, confident, convinced, definite, positive, satisfied, sure
≠ uncertain

certainly ADVERB ① without doubt • *My boss was certainly interested.* ② of course • *'Will you be there?' — 'Certainly.'*

certainly ADVERB
① = definitely, undeniably, undoubtedly, unquestionably, without doubt

certainty, **certainties** NOUN ① Certainty is the state of being certain. ② something that is known without doubt • *There are no certainties and no guarantees.*

certificate NOUN a document stating particular facts, for example of someone's birth or death • *a marriage certificate.*

certify, **certifies**, **certifying**, **certified** VERB ① To certify something means to declare formally that it is true • *certifying the cause of death.* ② To certify someone means to declare officially that they are insane.

cervical *[Said* ***ser****-vik-kl]* ADJECTIVE (*technical*) relating to the cervix.

cervix, **cervixes** or **cervices** NOUN (*technical*) The cervix is the entrance to the womb.

cessation NOUN (*formal*) The cessation of something is the stopping of it • *a swift cessation of hostilities.*

cf. cf. means 'compare'. It is written after something in a text to mention something else which the reader should compare with what has just been written.

chaff NOUN Chaff is the outer parts of grain separated from the seeds by beating.

chagrin *[Said* ***shag****-rin]* NOUN (*formal*) Chagrin is a feeling of annoyance or disappointment.

chain NOUN ① a number of metal rings connected together in a line • *a bicycle chain.* ② a number of things in a series or connected to each other • *a chain of shops.* ▶ VERB ③ If you chain one thing to another, you fasten them together with a chain • *They had chained themselves to railings.*

chair NOUN ① a seat with a back and four legs for one person. ② the person in charge of a meeting who decides when each person may speak. ▶ VERB ③ The person who chairs a meeting is in charge of it.

chairperson, **chairpersons** NOUN ① the person in charge of a meeting who decides when each person may speak. ② the head of a company or committee. **chairman** NOUN **chairwoman** NOUN

chalet *[Said* ***shall****-lay]* NOUN a wooden house with a sloping roof, especially in a mountain area or a holiday camp.

chalice *[Said* ***chal****-liss]* NOUN [RE] a gold or silver cup used in churches to hold the Communion wine.

chalk NOUN ① [ART] Chalk is a soft white rock. Small sticks of chalk are used for writing or drawing on a blackboard. ▶ VERB ② To chalk up a result is to achieve it • *He chalked up his first win.* **chalky** ADJECTIVE

challenge NOUN ① something that is new and exciting but requires a lot of effort • *It's a new challenge at the right time in my career.* ② a suggestion from someone to compete with them. ③ A challenge to something is a questioning of whether it is correct or true • *a challenge to authority.* ▶ VERB ④ If someone challenges you, they suggest that you compete with them in some way. ⑤ If you challenge something, you question whether it is correct or true. **challenger** NOUN **challenging** ADJECTIVE

> **challenge** NOUN
> ② = dare
> ▸ VERB ④ = dare, defy
> ⑤ = dispute, question

chamber NOUN ① a large room, especially one used for formal meetings • *the Council Chamber*. ② a group of people chosen to decide laws or administrative matters. ③ a hollow place or compartment inside something, especially inside an animal's body or inside a gun • *the chambers of the heart*. ④ (*in plural*) Chambers are a room where judges hear cases that are not being heard in an open court.

chameleon [*Said kam-**mee**-lee-on*] NOUN a lizard which is able to change the colour of its skin to match the colour of its surroundings.

champagne [*Said sham-**pain***] NOUN Champagne is a sparkling white wine made in France.

champion NOUN ① a person who wins a competition. ② someone who supports or defends a cause or principle • *a champion of women's causes*. ▸ VERB ③ Someone who champions a cause or principle supports or defends it.

> **champion** NOUN
> ① = hero, title holder, victor, winner
> ② = advocate, defender, guardian, protector
> ▸ VERB ③ = defend, fight for, promote, stick up for (*informal*), support, uphold

championship NOUN a competition to find the champion of a sport.

chance NOUN ① The chance of something happening is how possible or likely it is • *There's a chance of rain later*. ② an opportunity to do something • *Your chance to be a TV star!* ③ a possibility that something dangerous or unpleasant may happen • *Don't take chances, he's armed*. ④ Chance is also the way things happen unexpectedly without being planned • *I only found out by chance*. ▸ VERB ⑤ If you chance something, you try it although you are taking a risk.

> **chance** NOUN
> ① = likelihood, odds, possibility, probability, prospect
> ② = occasion, opening, opportunity, time
> ④ = accident, coincidence, fortune, luck

chancellor NOUN ① the head of government in some European countries. ② In Britain, the Chancellor is the Chancellor of the Exchequer. ③ the honorary head of a university.

Chancellor of the Exchequer NOUN In Britain, the Chancellor of the Exchequer is the minister responsible for finance and taxes.

chandelier [*Said shan-del-**leer***] NOUN an ornamental light fitting which hangs from the ceiling.

change NOUN ① a difference or alteration in something • *Steven soon noticed a change in Penny's attitude*. ② a replacement of something by something else • *a change of clothes*. ③ Change is money you get back when you have paid more than the actual price of something. ▸ VERB ④ When something changes or when you change it, it becomes different • *It changed my life*. ⑤ If you change something, you exchange it for something else. ⑥ When you change, you put on different clothes. ⑦ To change money means to exchange it for smaller coins of the same total value, or to exchange it for foreign currency.

> **change** NOUN
> ① = alteration, difference, modification, transformation
> ▶ VERB ④ = alter, convert, moderate, modify, reform, transform
> ⑤ = barter, exchange, interchange, replace, substitute, swap, trade

changeable ADJECTIVE likely to change all the time.

> **changeable** ADJECTIVE
> = erratic, fickle, irregular, unpredictable, unstable, variable, volatile
> ≠ constant

changeover NOUN a changefrom one system or activity to another • *the changeover between day and night.*

channel, **channels**, **channelling**, **channelled** NOUN ① a wavelength used to receive programmes broadcast by a television or radio station; also the station itself • *I was watching another channel.* ② a passage along which water flows or along which something is carried. ③ The Channel or the English Channel is the stretch of sea between England and France. ④ a method of achieving something • *We have tried to do things through the right channels.* ▶ VERB ⑤ To channel something such as money or energy means to direct it in a particular way • *Their efforts are being channelled into worthy causes.*

chant NOUN ① a group of words repeated over and over again • *a rousing chant.* ② a religious song sung on only a few notes. ▶ VERB ③ If people chant a group of words, they repeat them over and over again • *Crowds chanted his name.*

chaos *[Said **kay**-oss]* NOUN Chaos is a state of complete disorder and confusion. **chaotic** ADJECTIVE

chap, **chaps**, **chapping**, **chapped** NOUN ① *(informal)* a man. ▶ VERB ② If your skin chaps, it becomes dry and cracked, usually as a result of cold or wind.

chapel NOUN ① a section of a church or cathedral with its own altar. ② a type of small church.

chaperone *[Said **shap**-per-rone]*; also spelt **chaperon** NOUN an older woman who accompanies a young unmarried woman on social occasions, or any person who accompanies a group of younger people.

chaplain NOUN a member of the Christian clergy who regularly works in a hospital, school or prison. **chaplaincy** NOUN

chapter NOUN ① one of the parts into which a book is divided. ② a particular period in someone's life or in history.

char, **chars**, **charring**, **charred** VERB If something chars, it gets partly burned and goes black. **charred** ADJECTIVE

character NOUN ① all the qualities which combine to form the personality of a person or the atmosphere of a place. ② A person or place that has character has an interesting, attractive or admirable quality • *an inn of great character and simplicity.* ③ ENGLISH The characters in a film, play or book are the people in it. ④ a person • *an odd character.* ⑤ a letter, number or other written symbol.

> **character** NOUN
> ① = make-up, nature, personality, temperament
> ② = honour, integrity, strength

characterise; also spelt **characterize** VERB A quality that characterises something is typical of it • *a condition characterised by muscle stiffness.*

characteristic NOUN ① a quality that is typical of a particular person or thing • *Silence is the characteristic of the place.* ② SCIENCE a feature that is typical of a particular living thing. ▶ ADJECTIVE ③ Characteristic means typical of a particular person or thing • *Two things are very characteristic of his driving.* **characteristically** ADVERB

> **characteristic** NOUN
> ① = attribute, feature, property, quality, trait
> ▶ ADJECTIVE ③ = distinctive, distinguishing, typical
> ≠ uncharacteristic

charade [*Said shar-**rahd***] NOUN a ridiculous and unnecessary activity or pretence.

charcoal NOUN Charcoal is a black form of carbon made by burning wood without air, used as a fuel and also for drawing.

charge VERB ① If someone charges you money, they ask you to pay it for something you have bought or received • *The company charged £150 on each loan.* ② To charge someone means to accuse them formally of having committed a crime. ③ To charge the battery of an electrical device means to pass an electrical current through it to make it store electricity. ④ To charge somewhere means to rush forward, often to attack someone • *The rhino charged at her.* ▶ NOUN ⑤ the price that you have to pay for something. ⑥ a formal accusation that a person is guilty of a crime and has to go to court. ⑦ To have charge or be in charge of someone or something means to be responsible for them and be in control of them. ⑧ an explosive put in a gun or other weapon. ⑨ SCIENCE An electrical charge is the amount of electricity that something carries.

> **charge** VERB
> ① = ask (for), bill, levy
> ④ = dash, rush, stampede, storm
> ▶ NOUN ⑤ = cost, fee, payment, price

charger NOUN a device for charging or recharging batteries.

chariot NOUN a two-wheeled open vehicle pulled by horses.

charisma [*Said kar-**riz**-ma*] NOUN Charisma is a special ability to attract or influence people by your personality. **charismatic** ADJECTIVE

charity, **charities** NOUN ① an organisation that raises money to help people or animals in need. ② Charity is money or other help given to people or animals in need • *to help raise money for charity.* ③ Charity is also a kind, sympathetic attitude towards people. **charitable** ADJECTIVE

charlatan [*Said **shar**-lat-tn*] NOUN someone who pretends to have skill or knowledge that they do not really have.

charm NOUN ① Charm is an attractive and pleasing quality that some people and things have • *a man of great personal charm.* ② a small ornament worn on a bracelet. ③ a magical spell or an object that is supposed to bring good luck. ▶ VERB ④ If you charm someone, you use your charm to please them.

> **charm** NOUN
> ① = allure, appeal, attraction, fascination, magnetism
> ▶ VERB ④ = bewitch, captivate, delight, entrance

charmer NOUN someone who uses their charm to influence people.

charming ADJECTIVE very pleasant and attractive • *a rather charming man.* **charmingly** ADVERB

chart NOUN ① a diagram or table showing information • *He noted the* *score on his chart.* ② a map of the sea or stars. ▸ VERB ③ If you chart something, you observe and record it carefully.

charter NOUN ① a document stating the rights or aims of a group or organisation, often written by the government • *the new charter for commuters.* ▸ VERB ② To charter transport such as a plane or boat is to hire it for private use. **chartered** ADJECTIVE

chase VERB ① If you chase someone or something, you run after them in order to catch them. ② If you chase someone, you force them to go somewhere else. ▸ NOUN ③ the activity of chasing or hunting someone or something • *a high-speed car chase.*

chase VERB
① = hunt, pursue
② = drive, hound

chasm *[Said **kazm**]* NOUN ① a deep crack in the earth's surface. ② a very large difference between two ideas or groups of people • *the chasm between rich and poor in America.*

chassis *[Said **shas**-ee]* NOUN the frame on which a vehicle is built.

chaste *[Said **chayst**]* ADJECTIVE (*old-fashioned*) pure and well-behaved. **chastity** NOUN

chastise VERB (*formal*) If someone chastises you, they criticise you or punish you for something that you have done.

chat, **chats**, **chatting**, **chatted** NOUN ① a friendly talk with someone, usually about things that are not very important. ② the exchange of messages on a computer network. ▸ VERB ③ When people chat, they talk to each other in a friendly way. **chat up** VERB (*informal*) If you chat up someone, you talk to them in a friendly way, because you are attracted to them.

chat NOUN
① = conversation, gossip, natter (*informal*), talk
▸ VERB ③ = gossip, natter (*informal*), talk

chateau, **chateaux** *[Said **shat**-toe]* NOUN a large country house or castle in France.

chatroom NOUN an internet site where people read and post messages.

chatter VERB ① When people chatter, they talk very fast. ② If your teeth are chattering, they are knocking together and making a clicking noise because you are cold. ▸ NOUN ③ Chatter is a lot of fast unimportant talk.

chatty, **chattier**, **chattiest** ADJECTIVE talkative and friendly.

chauffeur *[Said **show**-fur]* NOUN a person whose job is to drive another person's car.

chauvinist NOUN ① a person who thinks their country is always right. ② A male chauvinist is a man who believes that men are superior to women. **chauvinistic** ADJECTIVE **chauvinism** NOUN

cheap ADJECTIVE ① costing very little money. ② inexpensive but of poor quality. ③ A cheap joke or cheap remark is unfair and unkind. **cheaply** ADVERB

cheap ADJECTIVE
① = bargain, economical, inexpensive, reasonable
≠ expensive
② = inferior, second-rate, tawdry

cheat VERB ① If someone cheats, they do wrong or unfair things to win or get something that they want. ② If you are cheated of or out of something, you do not get what you are entitled to. ▶ **NOUN** ③ a person who cheats.

> **cheat VERB**
> ① = con (*informal*), deceive, defraud, dupe, fleece, rip off (*slang*), swindle

check VERB ① To check something is to examine it in order to make sure that everything is all right. ② To check the growth or spread of something is to make it stop • *a policy to check fast population growth.* ▶ **NOUN** ③ an inspection to make sure that everything is all right. ④ (*in plural*) Checks are different coloured squares which form a pattern. ▶ **PHRASE** ⑤ If you keep something **in check**, you keep it under control • *She kept her emotions in check.* ▶ **ADJECTIVE** ⑥ Check or checked means marked with a pattern of squares • *check design.* **check in VERB** When you check in at a hotel or airport, you arrive and sign your name or show your ticket. **check out VERB** ① If you check something out, you inspect it and find out whether everything about it is right. ② When you check out of a hotel, you pay the bill and leave.

> **check VERB**
> ① = check out, examine, inspect, test
> ② = control, curb, halt, inhibit, restrain, stop
> ▶ **NOUN** ③ = examination, inspection, test

checkout NOUN a counter in a supermarket where the customers pay for their goods.

checkpoint NOUN a place where traffic has to stop in order to be checked.

checkup NOUN an examination by a doctor or dentist to see if you are healthy.

cheek NOUN ① Your cheeks are the sides of your face below your eyes. ② Cheek is speech or behaviour that is rude or disrespectful • *an expression of sheer cheek.*

> **cheek NOUN**
> ② = audacity, gall, impudence, insolence, nerve, rudeness

cheeky, **cheekier**, **cheekiest ADJECTIVE** rather rude and disrespectful.

> **cheeky ADJECTIVE**
> = impertinent, impudent, insolent, rude
> ≠ polite

cheer VERB ① When people cheer, they shout with approval or in order to show support for a person or team. ▶ **NOUN** ② a shout of approval or support. **cheer up VERB** When you cheer up, you feel more cheerful.

cheerful ADJECTIVE ① happy and in good spirits • *I had never seen her so cheerful.* ② bright and pleasant-looking • *a cheerful and charming place.* **cheerfully ADVERB cheerfulness NOUN**

> **cheerful ADJECTIVE**
> ① = bright, buoyant, cheery, happy, jaunty, jolly, light-hearted, merry
> ≠ miserable

cheery, **cheerier**, **cheeriest ADJECTIVE** happy and cheerful • *He gave me a cheery nod.*

> **cheery ADJECTIVE**
> = cheerful, chirpy, good-humoured, happy, jolly, sunny, upbeat
> ≠ gloomy

cheese NOUN a hard or creamy food made from milk.

cheesecake NOUN a dessert made of biscuit covered with smooth soft cheese.

cheetah NOUN a wild animal like a large cat with black spots.

chef NOUN a head cook in a restaurant or hotel.

chemical NOUN SCIENCE ① Chemicals are substances manufactured by chemistry. ▶ ADJECTIVE ② involved in chemistry or using chemicals • *chemical weapons*. **chemically** ADVERB

chemist NOUN ① a person who is qualified to make up drugs and medicines prescribed by a doctor. ② a shop where medicines and cosmetics are sold. ③ a scientist who does research in chemistry.

chemistry NOUN Chemistry is the scientific study of substances and the ways in which they change when they are combined with other substances.

chemotherapy *[Said keem-oh-**ther**-a-pee]* NOUN Chemotherapy is a way of treating diseases such as cancer by using chemicals.

cheque NOUN a printed form on which you write an amount of money that you have to pay. You sign the cheque and your bank pays the money from your account.

chequered *[Said **chek**-kerd]* ADJECTIVE ① covered with a pattern of squares. ② A chequered career is a varied career that has both good and bad parts.

cherish VERB ① If you cherish something, you care deeply about it and want to keep it or look after it lovingly. ② If you cherish a memory or hope, you have it in your mind and care deeply about it • *I cherish the good memories I have of him*.

cherry, **cherries** NOUN ① a small, juicy fruit with a red or black skin and a hard stone in the centre. ② a tree that produces cherries.

chess NOUN Chess is a board game for two people in which each player has 16 pieces and tries to move his or her pieces so that the other player's king cannot escape.

chest NOUN ① the front part of your body between your shoulders and your waist. ② a large wooden box with a hinged lid.

chestnut NOUN ① Chestnuts are reddish-brown nuts that grow inside a prickly green outer covering. ② a tree that produces these nuts. ▶ ADJECTIVE ③ Something that is chestnut is reddish-brown.

chest of drawers NOUN a piece of furniture with drawers in it, used for storing clothes.

chew VERB When you chew something, you use your teeth to break it up in your mouth before swallowing it. **chewy** ADJECTIVE

> **chew** VERB
> = crunch, gnaw, munch

chewing gum NOUN Chewing gum is a kind of sweet that you chew for a long time, but which you do not swallow.

chic *[Said **sheek**]* ADJECTIVE elegant and fashionable • *a chic restaurant*.

chick NOUN a young bird.

chicken NOUN a bird kept on a farm for its eggs and meat; also the meat of this bird • *roast chicken*. **chicken out** VERB (*informal*) If you chicken out of something, you do not do it because you are afraid.

chickenpox NOUN Chickenpox is an illness which produces a fever and blister-like spots on the skin.

chicory NOUN Chicory is a plant with bitter leaves that are used in salads.

chide, **chides**, **chiding**, **chided** VERB (*old-fashioned*) To chide someone is to tell them off.

chief NOUN ① the leader of a group or organisation. ▶ ADJECTIVE ② most important • *the chief source of oil*. **chiefly** ADVERB

chief NOUN
① = boss, chieftain, director, governor, head, leader, manager
▶ ADJECTIVE ② = foremost, key, main, prevailing, primary, prime, principal

chieftain NOUN the leader of a tribe or clan.

chiffon *[Said* ***shif****-fon]* NOUN Chiffon is a very thin lightweight cloth made of silk or nylon.

chihuahua *[Said chi-****wah****-wah]* NOUN a breed of very small dog with short hair and pointed ears.

child, **children** NOUN ① a young person who is not yet an adult. ② Someone's child is their son or daughter.

child NOUN
① = ankle-biter (*Australian and New Zealand; slang*), baby, bairn (*Scottish*), infant, juvenile (*formal*), kid (*informal*), minor (*formal*), offspring, toddler, tot (*informal*), youngster
≠ adult

childbirth NOUN Childbirth is the act of giving birth to a child.

childhood NOUN Someone's childhood is the time when they are a child.

childish ADJECTIVE immature and foolish • *I don't have time for childish arguments.* **childishly** ADVERB **childishness** NOUN

childish ADJECTIVE
= immature, infantile, juvenile, puerile
≠ mature

childless ADJECTIVE having no children.

childlike ADJECTIVE like a child in appearance or behaviour • *childlike enthusiasm.*

Chilean ADJECTIVE ① belonging or relating to Chile. ▶ NOUN ② someone who comes from Chile.

chill VERB ① To chill something is to make it cold • *Chill the cheesecake.* ② If something chills you, it makes you feel worried or frightened • *The thought chilled her.* ▶ NOUN ③ a feverish cold. ④ a feeling of cold • *the chill of the night air.*

chilli, **chillies** NOUN the red or green seed pod of a type of pepper which has a very hot, spicy taste.

chilly, **chillier**, **chilliest** ADJECTIVE ① rather cold • *the chilly November breeze.* ② unfriendly and without enthusiasm • *a chilly reception.*

chime VERB When a bell chimes, it makes a clear ringing sound.

chimney NOUN a vertical pipe or other hollow structure above a fireplace or furnace through which smoke from a fire escapes.

chimpanzee NOUN a small ape with dark fur that lives in forests in Africa.

chin NOUN the part of your face below your mouth.

china NOUN ① China is items like cups, saucers and plates made from very fine clay. ② (*informal*) In British and South African English, a china is a friend.

china NOUN
② = buddy (*informal*), chum (*informal*), crony (*old-fashioned*), friend, mate (*informal*), pal (*informal*)

Chinese ADJECTIVE ① belonging or relating to China. ▶ NOUN ② someone who comes from China. ③ Chinese refers to any of a group of related languages and dialects spoken by Chinese people.

chink NOUN ① a small, narrow opening • *a chink in the roof.* ② a short, light, ringing sound, like one made by glasses touching each other.

chip, **chips**, **chipping**, **chipped** NOUN ① Chips are thin strips of fried potato. ② In electronics, a chip is a tiny piece of silicon inside a computer which is used to form electronic circuits. ③ a small piece broken off an object, or the mark made when a piece breaks off. ▶ VERB ④ If you chip an object, you break a small piece off it.

chirp VERB When a bird chirps, it makes a short, high-pitched sound.

chisel, **chisels**, **chiselling**, **chiselled** NOUN ① a tool with a long metal blade and a sharp edge at the end which is used for cutting and shaping wood, stone or metal. ▶ VERB ② To chisel wood, stone or metal is to cut or shape it using a chisel.

chivalry *[Said **shiv**-val-ree]* NOUN Chivalry is polite and helpful behaviour, especially by men towards women. **chivalrous** ADJECTIVE

chive NOUN Chives are grasslike hollow leaves that have a mild onion flavour.

chlorine *[Said **klaw**-reen]* NOUN SCIENCE Chlorine is a chemical element which is a poisonous greenish-yellow gas with a strong, unpleasant smell. It is used to disinfect water and to make bleach. Its atomic number is 17 and its symbol is Cl.

chlorophyll *[Said **klor**-rof-fil]* NOUN SCIENCE Chlorophyll is a green substance in plants which enables them to use the energy from sunlight in order to grow.

chocolate NOUN ① Chocolate is a sweet food made from cacao seeds. ② a sweet made of chocolate. ▶ ADJECTIVE ③ dark brown.

choice NOUN ① a range of different things that are available to choose from • *a wider choice of treatments*. ② something that you choose • *You've made a good choice*. ③ Choice is the power or right to choose • *I had no choice*.

choice NOUN
① = range, selection, variety
③ = alternative, option, say

choir *[Said **kwire**]* NOUN MUSIC a group of singers, for example in a church.

choke VERB ① If you choke, you stop being able to breathe properly, usually because something is blocking your windpipe • *the diner who choked on a fish bone*. ② If things choke a place, they fill it so much that it is blocked or clogged up • *The canal was choked with old tyres*.

cholera *[Said **kol**-ler-ra]* NOUN Cholera is a serious disease causing severe diarrhoea and vomiting. It is caused by infected food or water.

cholesterol *[Said kol-**less**-ter-rol]* NOUN Cholesterol is a substance found in all animal fats, tissues and blood.

chook NOUN (*informal*) In Australian and New Zealand English, a chook is a chicken.

choose, **chooses**, **choosing**, **chose**, **chosen** VERB To choose something is to decide to have it or do it • *He chose to live in Kenya*.

choose VERB
= opt for, pick, select, take

choosy, **choosier**, **choosiest** ADJECTIVE fussy and difficult to satisfy • *You can't be too choosy about jobs*.

chop, **chops**, **chopping**, **chopped** VERB ① To chop something is to cut it with quick, heavy strokes using an axe or a knife. ▶ NOUN ② a small piece of lamb or pork containing a bone, usually cut from the ribs.

chop VERB
① = cut, fell, hack, lop

chopper NOUN (*informal*) a helicopter.

choppy, **choppier**, **choppiest** ADJECTIVE Choppy water has a lot of waves because it is windy.

choral ADJECTIVE relating to singing by a choir • *choral music*.

chord, **chords** NOUN MUSIC a group of three or more musical notes played together.

chore NOUN an uninteresting job that has to be done • *the chore of cleaning*.

choreography [*Said kor-ree-**og**-raf-fee*] NOUN Choreography is the art of composing dance steps and movements. **choreographer** NOUN

chorus, **choruses**, **chorusing**, **chorused** MUSIC NOUN ① a large group of singers; also a piece of music for a large group of singers. ② a part of a song which is repeated after each verse. ▸ VERB ③ If people chorus something, they all say or sing it at the same time.

chose the past tense of **choose**.

chosen the past participle of **choose**.

Christ PROPER NOUN RE Christ is the name for Jesus. Christians believe that Jesus is the son of God.

christen VERB RE When a baby is christened, it is named by a member of the clergy in a religious ceremony.

Christian NOUN RE ① a person who believes in Jesus Christ and his teachings. ▸ ADJECTIVE ② relating to Christ and his teachings • *the Christian faith*. ③ good, kind and considerate. **Christianity** NOUN

Christmas NOUN RE the Christian festival celebrating the birth of Christ, falling on December 25th.

chrome [*Said **krome***] NOUN Chrome is metal plated with chromium, a hard grey metal.

chromosome NOUN SCIENCE In biology, a chromosome is one of a number of rod-shaped parts in the nucleus of a cell which contains genes that determine the characteristics of an animal or plant.

chronic [*Said **kron**-nik*] ADJECTIVE lasting a very long time or never stopping • *a chronic illness*. **chronically** ADVERB

chronicle NOUN ① a record of a series of events described in the order in which they happened. ▸ VERB ② To chronicle a series of events is to record or describe them in the order in which they happened.

chronological [*Said kron-nol-**loj**-i-kl*] ADJECTIVE HISTORY arranged in the order in which things happened • *Tell me the whole story in chronological order*. **chronologically** ADVERB

chronology [*Said kron-**nol**-loj-jee*] NOUN HISTORY The chronology of events is the order in which they happened.

chubby, **chubbier**, **chubbiest** ADJECTIVE plump and round • *his chubby cheeks*.

chuck VERB (*informal*) To chuck something is to throw it casually.

chuckle VERB When you chuckle, you laugh quietly.

chug, **chugs**, **chugging**, **chugged** VERB When a machine or engine chugs, it makes a continuous dull thudding sound.

chum NOUN (*informal*) a friend.

chunk NOUN a thick piece of something.

chunky, **chunkier**, **chunkiest** ADJECTIVE Someone who is chunky is broad and heavy but usually short.

church NOUN ① a building where Christians go for religious services and worship. ② In the Christian religion, a church is one of the groups with their own particular beliefs, customs and clergy • *the Catholic Church*.

Church of England NOUN RE The Church of England is the Anglican church in England, where it is the state church, with the King or Queen as its head.

churchyard NOUN an area of land around a church, often used as a graveyard.

churn NOUN a container used for making milk or cream into butter.

chute *[Said **shoot**]* NOUN a steep slope or channel used to slide things down • *a rubbish chute.*

chutney NOUN Chutney is a strong-tasting thick sauce made from fruit, vinegar and spices.

cider NOUN Cider is an alcoholic drink made from apples.

cigar NOUN a roll of dried tobacco leaves which people smoke.

cigarette NOUN a thin roll of tobacco covered in thin paper which people smoke.

cinema NOUN ① a place where people go to watch films. ② Cinema is the business of making films.

cinnamon NOUN Cinnamon is a sweet spice which comes from the bark of an Asian tree.

circa *[Said **sur**-ka]* PREPOSITION *(formal)* about or approximately; used especially before dates • *portrait of a lady, circa 1840.*

circle NOUN ① MATHS a completely regular round shape. Every point on its edge is the same distance from the centre. ② a group of people with the same interest or profession • *a character well known in yachting circles.* ③ an area of seats on an upper floor of a theatre. ▸ VERB ④ To circle is to move round and round as though going round the edge of a circle • *A police helicopter circled above.*

circuit *[Said **sur**-kit]* NOUN ① any closed line or path, often circular, for example a racing track; also the distance round this path • *three circuits of the 26-lap race remaining.* ② SCIENCE An electrical circuit is a complete route around which an electric current can flow. A **closed circuit** is a complete electrical circuit around which current can flow; a **parallel circuit** is a closed circuit in which the current divides into two or more paths before coming back together to complete the circuit; a **series circuit** is an electrical circuit in which the elements are connected one after the other so that the same current flows through them all.

circular ADJECTIVE ① in the shape of a circle. ② A circular argument or theory is not valid because it uses a statement to prove a conclusion and the conclusion to prove the statement. ▸ NOUN ③ a letter or advert sent to a lot of people at the same time. **circularity** NOUN

circulate VERB ① When something circulates or when you circulate it, it moves easily around an area • *an open position where the air can circulate freely.* ② When you circulate something among people, you pass it round or tell it to all the people • *We circulate a regular newsletter.*

> **circulate** VERB
> ② = distribute, propagate, spread

circulation NOUN ① The circulation of something is the act of circulating it or the action of it circulating • *traffic circulation.* ② The circulation of a newspaper or magazine is the number of copies that are sold of each issue. ③ SCIENCE Your circulation is the movement of blood through your body.

circumference NOUN MATHS The circumference of a circle is its outer line or edge; also the length of this line.

circumstance NOUN ① The circumstances of a situation or event are the conditions that affect what happens • *He did well in the circumstances.* ② Someone's circumstances are their position and conditions in life • *Her circumstances had changed.*

circus, **circuses** NOUN a show given by a travelling group of entertainers such as clowns, acrobats and specially trained animals.

cistern NOUN a tank in which water is stored, for example one in the roof of a house or above a toilet.

citadel NOUN a fortress in or near a city.

cite VERB ① (*formal*) If you cite something, you quote it or refer to it • *He cited a letter written by Newall.* ② If someone is cited in a legal action, they are officially called to appear in court.

citizen NOUN CITIZENSHIP The citizens of a country or city are the people who live in it or belong to it • *American citizens.*

citizenship NOUN CITIZENSHIP the status of being a citizen, with all the rights and duties that go with it • *I'm applying for Australian citizenship.*

citrus fruit NOUN Citrus fruits are juicy, sharp-tasting fruits such as oranges, lemons and grapefruit.

city, **cities** NOUN a large town where many people live and work.

> **city** NOUN
> = metropolis, town

civic ADJECTIVE relating to a city or citizens • *the Civic Centre.*

civil ADJECTIVE ① relating to the citizens of a country • *civil rights.* ② relating to people or things that are not connected with the armed forces • *the history of civil aviation.* ③ polite.
civilly ADVERB **civility** NOUN

civil engineering NOUN Civil engineering is the design and construction of roads, bridges and public buildings.

civilian NOUN a person who is not in the armed forces.

civilisation; also spelt **civilization** NOUN ① HISTORY a society which has a highly developed organisation and culture • *the tale of a lost civilisation.* ② Civilisation is an advanced state of social organisation and culture.

civilised; also spelt **civilized** ADJECTIVE ① A civilised society is one with a developed social organisation and way of life. ② A civilised person is polite and reasonable.

> **civilised** ADJECTIVE
> ① = cultured, enlightened

civil servant NOUN a person who works in the civil service.

civil service NOUN The civil service is the government departments responsible for the administration of a country.

civil war NOUN a war between groups of people who live in the same country.

clad ADJECTIVE (*literary*) Someone who is clad in particular clothes is wearing them.

claim VERB ① If you claim that something is the case, you say that it is the case • *He claims to have lived in the same house all his life.* ② If you claim something, you ask for it because it belongs to you or you have a right to it • *Cartier claimed the land for the King of France.* ▶ NOUN ③ a statement that something is the case, or that you have a right to something • *She will make a claim for damages.*

> **claim** VERB
> ① = allege, assert, hold, insist, maintain, profess
> ▶ NOUN ③ = allegation, assertion

claimant NOUN someone who is making a claim, especially for money.

clairvoyant ADJECTIVE ① able to know about things that will happen in the future. ▶ NOUN ② a person who is, or claims to be, clairvoyant.

clam NOUN a kind of shellfish.

clamber VERB If you clamber somewhere, you climb there with difficulty.

clammy, clammier, clammiest ADJECTIVE unpleasantly damp and sticky • *clammy hands.*

clamour VERB ① If people clamour for something, they demand it noisily or angrily • *We clamoured for an explanation.* ▶ NOUN ② Clamour is noisy or angry shouts or demands by a lot of people.

clamp NOUN ① an object with movable parts that are used to hold two things firmly together. ▶ VERB ② To clamp things together is to fasten them or hold them firmly with a clamp. **clamp down on** VERB To clamp down on something is to become stricter in controlling it • *The Queen has clamped down on all expenditure.*

clan NOUN a group of families related to each other by being descended from the same ancestor.

clandestine ADJECTIVE secret and hidden • *a clandestine meeting with friends.*

clap, claps, clapping, clapped VERB ① When you clap, you hit your hands together loudly to show your appreciation. ② If you clap someone on the back or shoulder, you hit them in a friendly way. ③ If you clap something somewhere, you put it there quickly and firmly • *I clapped a hand over her mouth.* ▶ NOUN ④ a sound made by clapping your hands. ⑤ A clap of thunder is a sudden loud noise of thunder.

claret NOUN a type of red wine, especially one from the Bordeaux region of France.

clarify, clarifies, clarifying, clarified VERB [EXAM TERM] To clarify something is to make it clear and easier to understand • *Discussion will clarify your thoughts.* **clarification** NOUN

clarinet NOUN [MUSIC] a woodwind instrument with a straight tube and a single reed in its mouthpiece.

clarity NOUN The clarity of something is its clearness.

clash VERB ① If people clash with each other, they fight or argue. ② Ideas or styles that clash are so different that they do not go together. ③ If two events clash, they happen at the same time so you cannot go to both. ④ When metal objects clash, they hit each other with a loud noise. ▶ NOUN ⑤ a fight or argument. ⑥ A clash of ideas, styles or events is a situation in which they do not go together. ⑦ a loud noise made by metal objects when they hit each other.

> **clash** VERB
> ① = battle, fight, quarrel, wrangle
> ② = conflict, contradict, differ, disagree, go against, jar
> ▶ NOUN ⑤ = battle, conflict, confrontation, fight, skirmish, squabble, struggle

clasp VERB ① To clasp something means to hold it tightly or fasten it • *He clasped his hands.* ▶ NOUN ② a fastening such as a hook or catch.

> **clasp** VERB
> ① = clutch, embrace, grip, hold, hug, press, squeeze
> ▶ NOUN ② = buckle, catch, clip, fastener, fastening

class NOUN ① A class of people or things is a group of them of a particular type or quality • *the old class of politicians.* ② a group of pupils or students taught together, or a lesson that they have together. ③ Someone who has class is elegant in appearance or behaviour. ▶ VERB ④ To class something means to arrange it in a particular group or to consider it as belonging to a particular group

• *They are officially classed as visitors.*

> **class** NOUN
> ① = category, genre, grade, group, kind, set, sort, type
> ▶ VERB ④ = categorise, classify, designate, grade, rank, rate

classic ADJECTIVE ① typical and therefore a good model or example of something • *a classic case of misuse.* ② of very high quality • *one of the classic films of all time.* ③ simple in style and form • *the classic dinner suit.* ▶ NOUN ④ something of the highest quality • *one of the great classics of rock music.* ⑤ Classics is the study of Latin and Greek, and the literature of ancient Greece and Rome.

classical ADJECTIVE ① traditional in style, form and content • *classical ballet.* ② Classical music is serious music considered to be of lasting value. ③ characteristic of the style of ancient Greece and Rome • *Classical friezes decorate the walls.* **classically** ADVERB

classified ADJECTIVE officially declared secret by the government • *access to classified information.*

classify, **classifies**, **classifying**, **classified** VERB [LIBRARY] To classify things is to arrange them into groups with similar characteristics • *We can classify the differences into three groups.* **classification** NOUN

> **classify** VERB
> = arrange, categorise, grade, rank, sort

classroom NOUN a room in a school where pupils have lessons.

classy, **classier**, **classiest** ADJECTIVE (*informal*) stylish and elegant.

clatter VERB ① When things clatter, they hit each other with a loud rattling noise. ▶ NOUN ② a loud rattling noise made by hard things hitting each other.

clause NOUN ① a section of a legal document. ② [ENGLISH] In grammar, a clause is a group of words with a subject and a verb, which may be a complete sentence or one of the parts of a sentence.

claustrophobia [*Said klos-trof-**foe**-bee-ya*] NOUN Claustrophobia is a fear of being in enclosed spaces. **claustrophobic** ADJECTIVE

claw NOUN ① An animal's claws are hard, curved nails at the end of its feet. ② The claws of a crab or lobster are the two jointed parts, used for grasping things. ▶ VERB ③ If an animal claws something, it digs its claws into it.

clay NOUN Clay is a type of earth that is soft and sticky when wet and hard when baked dry. It is used to make pottery and bricks.

clean ADJECTIVE ① free from dirt or marks. ② free from germs or infection. ③ If humour is clean, it is not rude and does not involve bad language. ④ A clean movement is skilful and accurate. ⑤ Clean also means free from fault or error • *a clean driving licence.* ▶ VERB ⑥ To clean something is to remove dirt from it. **cleanly** ADVERB **cleaner** NOUN

> **clean** ADJECTIVE
> ① = immaculate, impeccable, laundered, spotless, washed
> ≠ dirty
> ② = antiseptic, hygienic, purified, sterilised, uncontaminated, unpolluted
> ≠ contaminated
> ▶ VERB ⑥ = cleanse, dust, scour, scrub, sponge, swab, wash, wipe
> ≠ soil

cleanliness [*Said **klen**-lin-ness*] NOUN Cleanliness is the practice of keeping yourself and your surroundings clean.

cleanse [*Said **klenz***] VERB To cleanse

something is to make it completely free from dirt.

clear ADJECTIVE ① easy to understand, see or hear • *He made it clear he did not want to talk.* ② easy to see through • *a clear liquid.* ③ free from obstructions or unwanted things • *clear of snow.* ▶ VERB ④ To clear an area is to remove unwanted things from it. ⑤ If you clear a fence or other obstacle, you jump over it without touching it. ⑥ When fog or mist clears, it disappears. ⑦ If someone is cleared of a crime, they are proved to be not guilty. **clearly** ADVERB **clear out** VERB ① If you clear out a room or cupboard, you tidy it and throw away unwanted things. ② (*informal*) To clear out means to leave • *You can clear out right now!* **clear up** VERB ① If you clear up, you tidy a place and put things away. ② When a problem or misunderstanding is cleared up, it is solved or settled.

> **clear** ADJECTIVE
> ① = apparent, blatant, conspicuous, definite, evident, explicit, obvious, plain
> ② = crystalline, glassy, translucent, transparent
> ≠ cloudy
> ▶ VERB ⑦ = absolve, acquit
> ≠ convict

clearance NOUN ① Clearance is the removal of old buildings in an area. ② If someone is given clearance to do something, they get official permission to do it.

clearing NOUN an area of bare ground in a forest.

cleaver NOUN a knife with a large square blade, used especially by butchers.

cleft NOUN a narrow opening in a rock.

clench VERB ① When you clench your fist, you curl your fingers up tightly. ② When you clench your teeth, you squeeze them together tightly.

clergy PLURAL NOUN [RE] The clergy are the ministers of the Christian Church.

clergyman, **clergymen** NOUN a male member of the clergy.

clerical ADJECTIVE ① relating to work done in an office • *clerical jobs with the City Council.* ② relating to the clergy.

clerk [*Said* ***klahrk***] NOUN a person who keeps records or accounts in an office, bank or law court.

clever ADJECTIVE ① intelligent and quick to understand things. ② very effective or skilful • *a clever plan.* **cleverly** ADVERB **cleverness** NOUN

> **clever** ADJECTIVE
> ① = brainy (*informal*), bright, intelligent, shrewd, smart
> ≠ stupid

cliché [*Said* ***klee****-shay*] NOUN [ENGLISH] an idea or phrase which is no longer effective because it has been used so much.

click VERB ① When something clicks or when you click it, it makes a short snapping sound. ② When you click on an area of a computer screen, you point the cursor at it and press one of the buttons on the mouse in order to make something happen. ▶ NOUN ③ a sound of something clicking • *I heard the click of a bolt.*

client NOUN someone who pays a professional person or company for a service.

clientele [*Said klee-on-****tell***] PLURAL NOUN The clientele of a place are its customers.

cliff NOUN a steep, high rock face by the sea.

climactic ADJECTIVE (*formal*) bringing a climax • *Her death is the climactic point of the film.*

climate NOUN ① GEOGRAPHY The climate of a place is the average weather conditions there • *The climate was dry in the summer.* ② the general attitude and opinion of people at a particular time • *the American political climate.* **climatic** ADJECTIVE

climax NOUN ENGLISH The climax of a process, story or piece of music is the most exciting moment in it, usually near the end.

climb VERB ① To climb is to move upwards. ② If you climb somewhere, you move there with difficulty • *She climbed out of the driving seat.* ▶ NOUN ③ a movement upwards • *this long climb up the slope* • *the rapid climb in murders.* **climber** NOUN

climb VERB
① = ascend, clamber, mount, scale

clinch VERB If you clinch an agreement or an argument, you settle it in a definite way • *Peter clinched a deal.*

cling, clings, clinging, clung VERB To cling to something is to hold onto it or stay closely attached to it • *still clinging to old-fashioned values.*

clinic NOUN a building where people go for medical treatment.

clinical ADJECTIVE ① relating to the medical treatment of patients • *clinical tests.* ② Clinical behaviour or thought is logical and unemotional • *the cold, clinical attitudes of his colleagues.* **clinically** ADVERB

clip, clips, clipping, clipped NOUN ① a small metal or plastic object used for holding things together. ② a short piece of a film shown by itself. ▶ VERB ③ If you clip things together, you fasten them with clips. ④ If you clip something, you cut bits from it to shape it • *clipped hedges.*

clipping NOUN an article cut from a newspaper or magazine.

clique [*Rhymes with* ***seek***] NOUN a small group of people who stick together and do not mix with other people.

cloak NOUN ① a wide, loose coat without sleeves. ▶ VERB ② To cloak something is to cover or hide it • *a land permanently cloaked in mist.*

cloakroom NOUN a room for coats or a room with toilets and washbasins in a public building.

clock NOUN ① a device that measures and shows the time. ▶ PHRASE ② If you work **round the clock**, you work all day and night.

clockwise ADJECTIVE, ADVERB in the same direction as the hands on a clock.

clockwork NOUN ① Toys that work by clockwork move when they are wound up with a key. ▶ PHRASE ② If something happens **like clockwork**, it happens with no problems or delays.

clog, clogs, clogging, clogged VERB ① To clog something is to block it • *pavements clogged up with people.* ▶ NOUN ② Clogs are heavy wooden shoes.

clone SCIENCE NOUN ① In biology, a clone is an animal or plant that has been produced artificially from the cells of another animal or plant and is therefore identical to it. ▶ VERB ② To clone an animal or plant is to produce it as a clone.

close VERB [*Said* ***kloze***] ① To close something is to shut it. ② To close a road or entrance is to block it so that no-one can go in or out. ③ If a shop closes at a certain time, then it does not do business after that time. ▶ ADJECTIVE, ADVERB [*Said* ***kloass***] ④ near to something • *a restaurant close to their home.* ▶ ADJECTIVE [*Said* ***kloass***] ⑤ People who are close to each other are very friendly and know each other well. ⑥ You say the weather is close when it is uncomfortably warm and there is not enough air. **closely** ADVERB **closeness** NOUN **closed** ADJECTIVE **close down** VERB If a business closes down, all work stops there permanently.

close VERB
① = secure, shut
≠ open
② = bar, block, obstruct, seal
▶ ADJECTIVE, ADVERB ④ = adjacent, adjoining, at hand, handy, near, nearby, neighbouring
≠ distant
▶ ADJECTIVE ⑤ = attached, dear, devoted, friendly, intimate, loving
≠ distant

closet NOUN ① a cupboard. ▶ VERB ② If you are closeted somewhere, you shut yourself away alone or in private with another person. ▶ ADJECTIVE ③ Closet beliefs or habits are kept private and secret • *a closet romantic*.

close-up NOUN a detailed close view of something, especially a photograph taken close to the subject.

closure *[Said **klohz**-yur]* NOUN ① The closure of a business is the permanent shutting of it. ② The closure of a road is the blocking of it so it cannot be used.

clot, **clots**, **clotting**, **clotted** NOUN ① a lump, especially one that forms when blood thickens. ▶ VERB ② When a substance such as blood clots, it thickens and forms a lump.

cloth NOUN ① Cloth is fabric made by a process such as weaving. ② a piece of material used for wiping or protecting things.

cloth NOUN
① = fabric, material, textile

clothe, **clothes**, **clothing**, **clothed** VERB To clothe someone is to give them clothes to wear.

clothes PLURAL NOUN the things people wear on their bodies.

clothes PLURAL NOUN
= attire (*formal*), clothing, costume, dress, garments, gear (*informal*), outfit, wardrobe, wear

clothing NOUN the clothes people wear.

cloud NOUN ① a mass of water vapour, smoke or dust that forms in the air and is seen floating in the sky. ▶ VERB ② If something clouds or is clouded, it becomes cloudy or difficult to see through • *The sky clouded over*. ③ Something that clouds an issue makes it more confusing.

cloud NOUN
① = billow, fog, haze, mist, vapour
▶ VERB ③ = confuse, distort, muddle

cloud computing NOUN [ICT] Cloud computing is a system where a person's files and programs are stored on the internet so that the person can use them at any time from any place.

cloudy, **cloudier**, **cloudiest** ADJECTIVE ① full of clouds • *the cloudy sky*. ② difficult to see through • *a glass of cloudy liquid*.

cloudy ADJECTIVE
① = dull, gloomy, leaden, overcast
≠ clear
② = muddy, murky, opaque
≠ clear

clout (*informal*) NOUN ① Someone who has clout has influence. ② A clout is a hit • *a clout on the head*. ▶ VERB ③ If you clout someone, you hit them.

clove NOUN ① Cloves are small, strong-smelling dried flower buds from a tropical tree, used as a spice in cooking. ② A clove of garlic is one of the separate sections of the bulb.

clover NOUN Clover is a small plant with leaves made up of three similar parts.

clown NOUN ① a circus performer who wears funny clothes and make-up and does silly things to make people laugh. ▶ VERB ② If you clown around, you do silly things to make people laugh.

cloying ADJECTIVE unpleasantly sickly, sweet or sentimental • *something less cloying than whipped cream.*

club, **clubs**, **clubbing**, **clubbed** NOUN ① an organisation of people with a particular interest, who meet regularly; also the place where they meet. ② a thick, heavy stick used as a weapon. ③ a stick with a shaped head that a golf player uses to hit the ball. ④ Clubs is one of the four suits in a pack of playing cards. It is marked by a black symbol in the shape of a clover leaf. ▶ VERB ⑤ To club someone is to hit them hard with a heavy object. **club together** VERB If people club together, they all join together to give money to buy something.

club NOUN
① = association, circle, group, guild, society, union
② = bat, stick, truncheon

clue NOUN something that helps to solve a problem or mystery.

clump NOUN ① a small group of things close together. ▶ VERB ② If you clump about, you walk with heavy footsteps.

clumsiness NOUN awkwardness in the way someone or something moves.

clumsiness NOUN
= awkwardness, ungainliness

clumsy, **clumsier**, **clumsiest** ADJECTIVE ① moving awkwardly and carelessly. ② said or done without thought or tact • *his clumsy attempts to catch her out.* **clumsily** ADVERB

clumsy ADJECTIVE
① = awkward, gauche, lumbering, uncoordinated, ungainly
≠ graceful

clung the past tense and past participle of **cling**.

cluster NOUN ① A cluster of things is a group of them together • *a cluster of huts at the foot of the mountains.* ▶ VERB ② If people cluster together, they stay together in a close group.

clutch VERB If you clutch something, you hold it tightly or seize it.

clutter NOUN ① Clutter is an untidy mess. ▶ VERB ② Things that clutter a place fill it and make it untidy.

cm an abbreviation for 'centimetres'.

co- PREFIX 'Co-' means 'together' • *Paula is now co-writing a book with Pierre.*

coach NOUN ① a long motor vehicle used for taking passengers on long journeys. ② a section of a train that carries passengers. ③ a four-wheeled vehicle with a roof pulled by horses, which people used to travel in. ④ a person who coaches a sport or a subject. ▶ VERB ⑤ If someone coaches you, they teach you and help you to get better at a sport or a subject.

coal NOUN ① Coal is a hard black rock obtained from under the earth and burned as a fuel. ② Coals are burning pieces of coal.

coalition NOUN a temporary alliance, especially between different political parties forming a government.

coarse ADJECTIVE ① Something that is coarse is rough in texture, often consisting of large particles • *a coarse blanket.* ② Someone who is coarse talks or behaves in a rude or rather offensive way. **coarsely** ADVERB **coarseness** NOUN

coast NOUN ① the edge of the land where it meets the sea. ▶ VERB ② A vehicle that is coasting is moving without engine power. **coastal** ADJECTIVE

> **coast** NOUN
> ① = beach, border, coastline, seaside, shore, strand

coastguard NOUN an official who watches the sea near a coast to get help for sailors when they need it, and to prevent smuggling.

coastline NOUN the outline of a coast, especially its appearance as seen from the sea or air.

coat NOUN ① a piece of clothing with sleeves which you wear over your other clothes. ② An animal's coat is the fur or hair on its body. ③ A coat of paint or varnish is a layer of it. ▶ VERB ④ To coat something means to cover it with a thin layer of something • *walnuts coated with chocolate.*

> **coat** NOUN
> ② = fleece, fur, hair, hide, pelt, skin, wool

coating NOUN a layer of something.

> **coating** NOUN
> = coat, covering, layer

coax VERB If you coax someone to do something, you gently persuade them to do it.

> **coax** VERB
> = cajole, persuade, talk into

cobalt NOUN [SCIENCE] Cobalt is a hard silvery-white metallic element which is used in alloys and for producing a blue dye. Its atomic number is 27 and its symbol is Co.

cobble NOUN Cobbles or cobblestones are stones with a rounded surface that were used in the past for making roads.

cobbler NOUN a person who makes or mends shoes.

cobra *[Said **koh**-bra]* NOUN a type of large poisonous snake from Africa and Asia.

cobweb NOUN the very thin net that a spider spins for catching insects.

cocaine NOUN Cocaine is an illegal addictive drug.

cock NOUN an adult male chicken; also used of any male bird.

cockatoo, **cockatoos** NOUN a type of parrot with a crest, found in Australia and New Guinea.

Cockney NOUN a person born in the East End of London.

cockpit NOUN The place in a small plane where the pilot sits.

cockroach NOUN a large dark-coloured insect often found in dirty rooms.

cocktail NOUN an alcoholic drink made from several ingredients.

cocky, **cockier**, **cockiest**; **cockies** (*informal*) ADJECTIVE ① cheeky or too self-confident. ▶ NOUN ② in Australian English, a cockatoo. ③ in Australian and New Zealand English, a farmer, especially one whose farm is small. **cockiness** NOUN

> **cocky** ADJECTIVE
> ① = arrogant, brash, conceited, overconfident
> ▶ NOUN ③ = crofter (*Scottish*), farmer

cocoa NOUN Cocoa is a brown powder made from the seeds of a tropical tree and used for making chocolate; also a hot drink made from this powder.

coconut NOUN a very large nut with white flesh, milky juice, and a hard hairy shell.

cocoon NOUN a silky covering over the larvae of moths and some other insects.

cod NOUN a large edible fish.

code NOUN ① a system of replacing the letters or words in a message with other letters or words, so that nobody can understand the message unless they know the system.

② a group of numbers and letters which is used to identify something • *the telephone code for Melbourne.* ▶ VERB **coded** ADJECTIVE

coffee NOUN Coffee is a substance made by roasting and grinding the beans of a tropical shrub; also a hot drink made from this substance.

coffin NOUN a box in which a dead body is buried or cremated.

cog NOUN a wheel with teeth which turns another wheel or part of a machine.

cognac *[Said* ***kon****-yak]* NOUN Cognac is a kind of brandy.

coherent ADJECTIVE ① If something such as a theory is coherent, its parts fit together well and do not contradict each other. ② If someone is coherent, what they are saying makes sense and is not jumbled or confused. **coherence** NOUN

cohesive ADJECTIVE If something is cohesive, its parts fit together well • *The team must work as a cohesive unit.* **cohesion** NOUN

coil NOUN ① a length of rope or wire wound into a series of loops; also one of the loops. ▶ VERB ② If something coils, it turns into a series of loops.

> **coil** VERB
> ② = curl, loop, spiral, twine, twist, wind

coin NOUN ① a small metal disc which is used as money. ▶ VERB ② If you coin a word or a phrase, you invent it.

coinage NOUN The coinage of a country is the coins that are used there.

coincide VERB ① If two events coincide, they happen at about the same time. ② When two people's ideas or opinions coincide, they agree • *What she said coincided exactly with his own thinking.*

coincidence NOUN ① what happens when two similar things occur at the same time by chance • *I had moved to London, and by coincidence, Helen had too.* ② the fact that two things are surprisingly the same. **coincidental** ADJECTIVE **coincidentally** ADVERB

coke NOUN Coke is a grey solid fuel produced from coal.

colander *[Said* ***kol****-an-der]* NOUN a bowl-shaped container with holes in it, used for washing or draining food.

cold ADJECTIVE ① having a low temperature. ② Someone who is cold does not show much affection. ▶ NOUN ③ You can refer to cold weather as the cold • *She was complaining about the cold.* ④ a minor illness in which you sneeze and may have a sore throat. **coldly** ADVERB **coldness** NOUN

> **cold** ADJECTIVE
> ① = arctic, biting, bitter, bleak, chilly, freezing, icy, raw, wintry
> ≠ hot
> ② = aloof, distant, frigid, lukewarm, reserved, stony
> ≠ warm

cold-blooded ADJECTIVE ① Someone who is cold-blooded does not show any pity • *two cold-blooded killers.* ② A cold-blooded animal has a body temperature that changes according to the surrounding temperature.

cold war NOUN Cold war is a state of extreme unfriendliness between countries not actually at war.

coleslaw NOUN Coleslaw is a salad of chopped cabbage and other vegetables in mayonnaise.

colic NOUN Colic is pain in a baby's stomach.

collaborate VERB When people collaborate, they work together to produce something • *The two bands have collaborated in the past.*

A B C D E F G H I J K L M N O P Q R S T U V W X Y Z

collaboration NOUN **collaborator** NOUN

collage *[Said* ***kol****-lahj]* NOUN ART a picture made by sticking pieces of paper or cloth onto a surface.

collapse VERB ① If something such as a building collapses, it falls down suddenly. If a person collapses, they fall down suddenly because they are ill. ② If something such as a system or a business collapses, it suddenly stops working • *50,000 small firms collapsed last year.* ▶ NOUN ③ The collapse of something is what happens when it stops working • *the collapse of the country's economy.*

collapse VERB
① = fall down, give way
② = fail, fold, founder
▶ NOUN ③ = downfall, failure

collapsible ADJECTIVE A collapsible object can be folded flat when it is not in use • *a collapsible ironing board.*

collar NOUN ① The collar of a shirt or coat is the part round the neck which is usually folded over. ② a leather band round the neck of a dog or cat.

collateral NOUN Collateral is money or property which is used as a guarantee that someone will repay a loan, and which the lender can take if the loan is not repaid.

colleague NOUN A person's colleagues are the people he or she works with.

colleague NOUN
= associate, co-worker, partner, workmate

collect VERB ① To collect things is to gather them together for a special purpose or as a hobby • *collecting money for charity.* ② If you collect someone or something from a place, you call there and take them away • *We had to collect her from school.* ③ When things collect in a place, they gather there over a period of time • *Food collects in holes in the teeth.* **collector** NOUN

collect VERB
① = accumulate, assemble, gather, raise
≠ scatter

collected ADJECTIVE calm and self-controlled.

collection NOUN ① ART a group of things acquired over a period of time • *a collection of paintings.* ② Collection is the collecting of something • *tax collection.* ③ the organised collecting of money, for example for charity, or the sum of money collected.

collection NOUN
① = assortment, group, store

collective ADJECTIVE ① involving every member of a group of people • *The school's teachers took a collective decision.* ▶ NOUN ② a group of people who share the responsibility both for running something and for doing the work. **collectively** ADVERB

college NOUN ① a place where students study after they have left school. ② a name given to some secondary schools. ③ one of the institutions into which some universities are divided. ④ In New Zealand English, a college can also refer to a teacher training college.

collide VERB If a moving object collides with something, it hits it.

collie NOUN a dog that is used for rounding up sheep.

colliery, **collieries** NOUN a coal mine.

collision NOUN A collision occurs when a moving object hits something.

colloquial *[Said kol-****loh****-kwee-al]* ADJECTIVE ENGLISH Colloquial words and phrases are informal and used especially in conversation.
colloquially ADVERB
colloquialism NOUN

colloquial ADJECTIVE
= conversational, everyday, informal

A **cologne** *[Said kol-**lone**]* NOUN Cologne is a kind of weak perfume.

B **colon** NOUN ① ENGLISH the punctuation mark (:). ② part of your intestine.

C

D **colonel** *[Said **kur**-nl]* NOUN an army officer with a fairly high rank.

E **colonial** ADJECTIVE ① relating to a colony. ② In Australia, 'colonial' is used to relate to the period of Australian history before the Federation in 1901.

F

G

H

I **colonise**; also spelt **colonize** VERB ① HISTORY When people colonise a place, they go to live there and take control of it • *the Europeans who colonised North America*. ② When a lot of animals colonise a place, they go there and make it their home • *Toads are colonising the whole place.* **colonisation** NOUN **colonist** NOUN

J

K

L

M

N **colony**, **colonies** NOUN ① HISTORY a country controlled by a more powerful country. ② a group of people who settle in a country controlled by their homeland.

O

P

Q

colony NOUN
① = dependency, dominion, territory
② = community, outpost, settlement

R

S **colossal** ADJECTIVE very large indeed.

T

colossal ADJECTIVE
= enormous, gigantic, huge, immense, mammoth, massive, vast
≠ tiny

U

V

W **colour** NOUN ① ART the appearance something has as a result of reflecting light. ② a substance used to give colour. ③ Someone's colour is the normal colour of their skin. ④ Colour is also a quality that makes something interesting or exciting • *bringing more culture and colour to the city*. ▸ VERB ⑤ If you colour something, you give it a colour. ⑥ If something colours your opinion, it affects the way you think about something. **coloured** ADJECTIVE **colourless** ADJECTIVE **colouring** NOUN

X

Y

Z

colour NOUN
① = hue, pigmentation, shade, tint
② = dye, paint, pigment
▸ VERB ⑤ = dye, paint, stain, tint
⑥ = bias, distort, prejudice, slant

colourful ADJECTIVE ① full of colour. ② interesting or exciting. **colourfully** ADVERB

colourful ADJECTIVE
① = bright, brilliant, intense, jazzy (*informal*), rich, vibrant, vivid
≠ dull
② = graphic, interesting, lively, rich, vivid
≠ dull

colt NOUN a young male horse.

column NOUN ① a tall solid upright cylinder, especially one supporting a part of a building. ② a group of people moving in a long line. ③ a vertical section of writing. ④ a regular article in a newspaper or magazine.

columnist NOUN a journalist who writes a regular article in a newspaper or magazine.

coma NOUN Someone who is in a coma is in a state of deep unconsciousness.

comb NOUN ① a flat object with pointed teeth used for tidying your hair. ▸ VERB ② When you comb your hair, you tidy it with a comb. ③ If you comb a place, you search it thoroughly to try to find someone or something.

combat NOUN ① Combat is fighting • *his first experience of combat*. ▸ VERB ② To combat something means to try to stop it happening or developing • *a way to combat crime*.

combination NOUN ① a mixture of things • *a combination of charm and skill*. ② a series of letters or numbers used to open a special lock.

combination NOUN
① = amalgamation, blend, mix, mixture

combine VERB ① To combine things is to cause them to exist together • *to combine a career with being a mother*. ② To combine things also means to join them together to make a single thing • *Combine all the ingredients*. ③ If something combines two qualities or features, it has them both • *a film that combines great charm and scintillating performances*.

combine VERB
② = amalgamate, blend, fuse, integrate, merge, mix, unite
≠ separate

combustion NOUN SCIENCE Combustion is the act of burning something or the process of burning.

come, comes, coming, came, come VERB ① To come to a place is to move there or arrive there. ② To come to a place also means to reach as far as that place • *The sea water came up to his waist*. ③ 'Come' is used to say that someone or something reaches a particular state • *They came to power in 2016* • *We had come to a decision*. ④ When a particular time or event comes, it happens • *The peak of his career came early in 2000*. ⑤ If you come from a place, you were born there or it is your home. ▶ PHRASE ⑥ A time or event **to come** is a future time or event • *The public will thank them in years to come*. **come about** VERB The way something comes about is the way it happens • *The discussion came about because of the proposed changes*. **come across** VERB If you come across something, you find it by chance. **come off** VERB If something comes off, it succeeds • *His rescue plan had come off*. **come on** VERB If something is coming on, it is making progress • *How is your essay coming on?* **come round** VERB ① To come round means to recover consciousness. ② To come round to an idea or situation means to eventually accept it. ③ When a regular event comes round, it happens • *Beginning of term came round too quickly*. **come to** VERB To come to means to recover consciousness. **come up** VERB If something comes up in a conversation or meeting, it is mentioned or discussed. **come up with** VERB If you come up with a plan or idea, you suggest it.

come VERB
① = appear, arrive, enter, materialise, show up (*informal*), turn up (*informal*)
④ = happen, occur, take place

comeback NOUN To make a comeback means to be popular or successful again.

comedian NOUN an entertainer whose job is to make people laugh.

comedienne [*Said kom-mee-dee-**en***] NOUN a female comedian.

comedy, comedies NOUN a light-hearted play or film with a happy ending.

comet NOUN an object that travels around the sun leaving a bright trail behind it.

comfort NOUN ① Comfort is the state of being physically relaxed • *He settled back in comfort*. ② Comfort is also a feeling of relief from worries or unhappiness • *The thought is a great comfort to me*. ③ (in plural) Comforts are things which make your life easier and more pleasant • *all the comforts of home*. ▶ VERB ④ To comfort someone is to make them less worried or unhappy.

comfort NOUN
① = ease, luxury, wellbeing
② = consolation, help, relief, satisfaction, support
▸ VERB ④ = cheer, console, reassure, soothe

comfortable ADJECTIVE ① If you are comfortable, you are physically relaxed. ② Something that is comfortable makes you feel relaxed • *a comfortable bed*. ③ If you feel comfortable in a particular situation, you are not afraid or embarrassed. **comfortably** ADVERB

comfortable ADJECTIVE
② = cosy, homely, relaxing, restful
≠ uncomfortable
③ = at ease, at home, contented, happy, relaxed
≠ uneasy

comic ADJECTIVE ① funny • *a comic monologue*. ▸ NOUN ② someone who tells jokes. ③ a magazine that contains stories told in pictures.

comical ADJECTIVE funny • *a comical sight*.

comma NOUN [ENGLISH] the punctuation mark (,).

command VERB ① To command someone to do something is to order them to do it. ② If you command something such as respect, you receive it because of your personal qualities. ③ An officer who commands part of an army or navy is in charge of it. ▸ NOUN ④ an order to do something. ⑤ Your command of something is your knowledge of it and your ability to use this knowledge • *a good command of English*.

command VERB
① = bid, demand, direct, order
③ = control, head, lead, manage, supervise
▸ NOUN ④ = bidding, decree, directive, injunction (*formal*), instruction, order
⑤ = grasp, knowledge, mastery

commandant [*Said* ***kom**-man-dant*] NOUN an army officer in charge of a place or group of people.

commander NOUN an officer in charge of a military operation or organisation.

commandment NOUN [RE] The ten commandments are ten important rules of behaviour that, according to the Old Testament, people should obey.

commando, **commandos** NOUN Commandos are soldiers who have been specially trained to carry out raids.

commemorate VERB ① An object that commemorates a person or an event is intended to remind people of that person or event. ② If you commemorate an event, you do something special to show that you remember it. **commemorative** ADJECTIVE **commemoration** NOUN

commemorate VERB
② = celebrate, honour

commence VERB (*formal*) To commence is to begin. **commencement** NOUN

commend VERB To commend someone or something is to praise them • *He has been commended for his work*. **commendation** NOUN **commendable** ADJECTIVE

comment VERB ① If you comment on something, you make a remark about it. ▸ NOUN ② a remark about something • *She received many comments about her performance*.

comment VERB
① = mention, note, observe, point out, remark, say
▸ NOUN ② = observation, remark, statement

commentary, **commentaries** NOUN a description of an event which is

A B C D E F G H I J K L M N O P Q R S T U V W X Y Z

broadcast on radio or television while the event is happening.

commentator NOUN someone who gives a radio or television commentary.

commerce NOUN Commerce is the buying and selling of goods.

commercial ADJECTIVE ① relating to commerce. ② Commercial activities involve producing goods on a large scale in order to make money • *the commercial fishing world*. ▶ NOUN ③ an advertisement on television or radio. **commercially** ADVERB

commission VERB ① If someone commissions a piece of work, they formally ask someone to do it • *a study commissioned by the government*. ▶ NOUN ② a piece of work that has been commissioned. ③ Commission is money paid to a salesperson each time a sale is made. ④ an official body appointed to investigate or control something.

commit, **commits**, **committing**, **committed** VERB ① To commit a crime or sin is to do it. ② If you commit yourself, you state an opinion or state that you will do something. ③ If someone is committed to hospital or prison, they are officially sent there. **committal** NOUN

> **commit** VERB
> ① = carry out, do, perform, perpetrate

commitment NOUN ① Commitment is a strong belief in an idea or system. ② something that regularly takes up some of your time • *business commitments*.

committed ADJECTIVE A committed person has strong beliefs • *a committed feminist*.

committee NOUN a group of people who make decisions on behalf of a larger group.

commodity, **commodities** NOUN (*formal*) Commodities are things that are sold.

common ADJECTIVE ① Something that is common exists in large numbers or happens often • *a common complaint*. ② If something is common to two or more people, they all have it or use it • *I realised we had a common interest*. ③ 'Common' is used to indicate that something is of the ordinary kind and not special. ④ If you describe someone as common, you mean they do not have good taste or good manners. ▶ NOUN ⑤ an area of grassy land where everyone can go. ▶ PHRASE ⑥ If two things or people have something **in common**, they both have it. **commonly** ADVERB

> **common** ADJECTIVE
> ① = general, popular, prevailing, prevalent, universal, widespread
> ≠ rare
> ③ = average, commonplace, everyday, ordinary, plain, standard, usual
> ≠ special
> ④ = coarse, rude, vulgar
> ≠ refined

commoner NOUN someone who is not a member of the nobility.

commonplace ADJECTIVE Something that is commonplace happens often • *Foreign holidays have become commonplace*.

common sense NOUN Your common sense is your natural ability to behave sensibly and make good judgments.

> **common sense** NOUN
> = good sense, judgment, level-headedness, prudence, wit

commotion NOUN A commotion is a lot of noise and excitement.

communal ADJECTIVE shared by a group of people • *a communal canteen*.

a b c d e f g h i j k l m n o p q r s t u v w x y z

commune *[Said* ***kom****-yoon]* NOUN a group of people who live together and share everything.

communicate VERB ① If you communicate with someone, you keep in touch with them. ② If you communicate information or a feeling to someone, you make them aware of it.

> **communicate** VERB
> ① = be in contact, be in touch, correspond
> ② = convey (*formal*), impart (*formal*), inform, pass on, spread, transmit, tweet

communication NOUN ① [PSHE] Communication is the process by which people or animals exchange information. ② (*in plural*) Communications are the systems by which people communicate or broadcast information, especially using electricity or radio waves. ③ (*formal*) a letter or telephone call.

communicative ADJECTIVE Someone who is communicative is willing to talk to people.

communion NOUN ① Communion is the sharing of thoughts and feelings. ② [RE] In Christianity, Communion is a religious service in which people share bread and wine in remembrance of the death and resurrection of Jesus Christ.

communism NOUN Communism is the doctrine that the state should own the means of production and that there should be no private property. **communist** ADJECTIVE, NOUN

community, **communities** NOUN [CITIZENSHIP] all the people living in a particular area; also used to refer to particular groups within a society • *the heart of the local community* • *the Asian community*.

commute VERB People who commute travel a long distance to work every day. **commuter** NOUN

compact ADJECTIVE taking up very little space • *a compact microwave*.

compact disc NOUN a music or video recording in the form of a plastic disc which is played using a laser on a special machine, and gives good quality sound or pictures.

companion NOUN someone you travel or spend time with. **companionship** NOUN

> **companion** NOUN
> = comrade, crony (*old-fashioned*), friend, mate (*informal*), pal (*informal*), partner

company, **companies** NOUN ① a business that sells goods or provides a service • *the record company*. ② a group of actors, opera singers or dancers • *the Royal Shakespeare Company*. ③ If you have company, you have a friend or visitor with you • *I enjoyed her company*.

> **company** NOUN
> ① = business, corporation, establishment, firm, house
> ② = assembly, band, circle, community, crowd, ensemble, group, party, troupe
> ③ = companionship, presence

comparable *[Said* ***kom****-pra-bl]* ADJECTIVE If two things are comparable, they are similar in size or quality • *The skill is comparable to playing the violin*. **comparably** ADVERB

comparative ADJECTIVE ① You add comparative to indicate that something is true only when compared with what is normal • *eight years of comparative calm*. ▶ NOUN ② [ENGLISH] In grammar, the comparative is the form of an adjective which indicates that the person or thing described has more of a particular quality than someone or something else. For example, 'quicker', 'better' and 'easier' are all comparatives. **comparatively** ADVERB

compare VERB ① EXAM TERM When you compare things, you look at them together and see in what ways they are different or similar. ② If you compare one thing to another, you say it is like the other thing • *Her voice is often compared to Adele's.*

> **compare** VERB
> ① = contrast, juxtapose, weigh up

comparison NOUN ENGLISH When you make a comparison, you consider two things together and see in what ways they are different or similar.

compartment NOUN ① a section of a railway carriage. ② one of the separate parts of an object • *a special compartment inside your vehicle.*

> **compartment** NOUN
> ② = bay, chamber, division, section

compass NOUN ① SCIENCE an instrument with a magnetic needle for finding directions. ② (*in plural*) Compasses are a hinged instrument for drawing circles.

compassion NOUN pity and sympathy for someone who is suffering.

compassionate ADJECTIVE feeling or showing sympathy and pity for others. **compassionately** ADVERB

> **compassionate** ADJECTIVE
> = caring, humane, kind, kind-hearted, merciful, sympathetic, tender

compatible ADJECTIVE If people or things are compatible, they can live or work together successfully. **compatibility** NOUN

> **compatible** ADJECTIVE
> = congenial, harmonious
> ≠ incompatible

compatriot NOUN Your compatriots are people from your own country.

compel, compels, compelling, compelled VERB To compel someone to do something is to force them to do it.

compelling ADJECTIVE ① If a story or event is compelling, it is extremely interesting • *a compelling novel.* ② A compelling argument or reason makes you believe that something is true or should be done • *compelling new evidence.*

compensate VERB ① To compensate someone is to give them money to replace something lost or damaged. ② If one thing compensates for another, it cancels out its bad effects • *The trip more than compensated for the hardship.* **compensatory** ADJECTIVE

> **compensate** VERB
> ① = atone, refund, repay, reward
> ② = balance, cancel out, counteract, make up for, offset

compensation NOUN something that makes up for loss or damage.

> **compensation** NOUN
> = amends, atonement, damages, payment

compere [*Said* ***kom****-pare*] NOUN ① the person who introduces the guests or performers in a show. ▶ VERB ② To compere a show is to introduce the guests or performers.

compete VERB ① When people or firms compete, each tries to prove that they or their products are the best. ② If you compete in a contest or game, you take part in it.

> **compete** VERB
> ① = contend, contest, fight, vie

competent ADJECTIVE Someone who is competent at something can do it satisfactorily • *a very competent engineer.* **competently** ADVERB **competence** NOUN

competition NOUN ① When there is competition between people or groups, they are all trying to get something that not everyone can have • *There's a lot of competition for places.* ② an event in which people take part to find who is best at something. ③ When there is competition between firms, each firm is trying to get people to buy its own goods.

competition NOUN
① = contention, contest, opposition, rivalry, struggle
② = championship, contest, event, tournament

competitive ADJECTIVE ① A competitive situation is one in which people or firms are competing with each other • *a crowded and competitive market.* ② A competitive person is eager to be more successful than others. ③ Goods sold at competitive prices are cheaper than other goods of the same kind. **competitively** ADVERB

competitor NOUN a person or firm that is competing to become the most successful.

competitor NOUN
= adversary, challenger, competition, contestant, opponent, opposition, rival

compilation NOUN A compilation is a book, recording or programme consisting of several items that were originally produced separately • *this compilation of his solo work.*

compile VERB When someone compiles a book or report, they make it by putting together several items.

complacent ADJECTIVE If someone is complacent, they are unconcerned about a serious situation and do nothing about it. **complacently** ADVERB **complacency** NOUN

complain VERB ① If you complain, you say that you are not satisfied with something. ② If you complain of pain or illness, you say that you have it.

complain VERB
① = carp, find fault, grouse, grumble, kick up a fuss (*informal*), moan, whine, whinge (*informal*)

complaint NOUN If you make a complaint, you complain about something.

complaint NOUN
= criticism, grievance, grumble, objection, protest

complement VERB ① If one thing complements another, the two things go well together • *The tiled floor complements the pine furniture.* ▶ NOUN ② If one thing is a complement to another, it goes well with it. ③ In grammar, a complement is a word or phrase that gives information about the subject or object of a sentence. For example, in the sentence 'Rover is a dog', 'a dog' is a complement. **complementary** ADJECTIVE

complete ADJECTIVE ① to the greatest degree possible • *a complete mess.* ② If something is complete, none of it is missing • *a complete set of tools.* ③ When a task is complete, it is finished • *The planning stage is now complete.* ▶ VERB ④ If you complete something, you finish it. ⑤ If you complete a form, you fill it in. **completely** ADVERB **completion** NOUN

complete ADJECTIVE
① = absolute, consummate, outright, perfect, thorough, total, utter
② = entire, full, intact, undivided, whole
≠ incomplete
▶ VERB ④ = conclude, end, finish

complex ADJECTIVE ① Something that is complex has many different parts

• *a very complex problem*. ▶ **NOUN** ② A complex is a group of buildings, roads or other things connected with each other in some way • *a hotel and restaurant complex*. ③ If someone has a complex, they have an emotional problem because of a past experience • *an inferiority complex*. **complexity** **NOUN**

> **complex** **ADJECTIVE**
> ① = complicated, difficult, intricate, involved, tangled
> ≠ simple
> ▶ **NOUN** ③ = fixation, obsession, phobia, preoccupation, problem, thing

complexion **NOUN** the quality of the skin on your face • *a healthy glowing complexion*.

complicate **VERB** To complicate something is to make it more difficult to understand or deal with.

complicated **ADJECTIVE** Something that is complicated has so many parts or aspects that it is difficult to understand or deal with.

> **complicated** **ADJECTIVE**
> = complex, convoluted, elaborate, intricate, involved
> ≠ simple

complication **NOUN** something that makes a situation more difficult to deal with • *One possible complication was that it was late in the year*.

compliment **NOUN** ① If you pay someone a compliment, you tell them you admire something about them. ② (*in plural, formal*) When someone sends their compliments, they formally express their good wishes • *Inspector Paget sends his compliments*. ▶ **VERB** ③ If you compliment someone, you pay them a compliment.

complimentary **ADJECTIVE** ① If you are complimentary about something, you express admiration for it. ② A complimentary seat, ticket or magazine is given to you free.

comply, **complies**, **complying**, **complied** **VERB** If you comply with an order or rule, you obey it. **compliance** **NOUN**

component **NOUN** [DGT] [SCIENCE] The components of something are the parts it is made of.

compose **VERB** ① If something is composed of particular things or people, it is made up of them. ② To compose a piece of music, letter or speech means to write it. ③ If you compose yourself, you become calm after being excited or upset.

> **compose** **VERB**
> ② = create, devise, invent, produce, write

composed **ADJECTIVE** calm and in control of your feelings.

composer **NOUN** someone who writes music.

composition **NOUN** ① The composition of something is the things it consists of • *the composition of the ozone layer*. ② [MUSIC] The composition of a poem or piece of music is the writing of it. ③ [MUSIC] a piece of music or writing.

compost **NOUN** Compost is a mixture of decaying plants and manure added to soil to help plants grow.

composure **NOUN** Someone's composure is their ability to stay calm • *Jarvis was able to recover his composure*.

compound **NOUN** ① an enclosed area of land with buildings used for a particular purpose • *the prison compound*. ② [SCIENCE] In chemistry, a compound is a substance consisting of two or more different substances or chemical elements. ▶ **VERB** ③ To compound something is to put

a b c d e f g h i j k l m n o p q r s t u v w x y z

together different parts to make a whole. ④ To compound a problem is to make it worse by adding to it • *Water shortages were compounded by taps left running.*

comprehend VERB (*formal*) To comprehend something is to understand or appreciate it • *He did not fully comprehend what was puzzling me.* **comprehension** NOUN

> **comprehend** VERB
> = appreciate, fathom, grasp, see, take in, understand, work out

comprehensible ADJECTIVE able to be understood.

comprehensive ADJECTIVE ① Something that is comprehensive includes everything necessary or relevant • *a comprehensive guide.* ▸ NOUN ② a school where children of all abilities are taught together. **comprehensively** ADVERB

compress VERB To compress something is to squeeze it or shorten it so that it takes up less space • *compressed air.* **compression** NOUN

comprise VERB (*formal*) What something comprises is what it consists of • *The district then comprised 66 villages.*

compromise NOUN ① an agreement in which people accept less than they originally wanted • *In the end they reached a compromise.* ▸ VERB ② When people compromise, they agree to accept less than they originally wanted.

compulsion NOUN a very strong desire to do something.

compulsive ADJECTIVE ① You use 'compulsive' to describe someone who cannot stop doing something • *a compulsive letter writer.* ② If you find something such as a book or television programme compulsive, you cannot stop reading or watching it.

compulsory ADJECTIVE If something is compulsory, you have to do it • *School attendance is compulsory.*

> **compulsory** ADJECTIVE
> = mandatory, obligatory, required, requisite
> ≠ voluntary

computer NOUN an electronic machine that can quickly make calculations or store and find information.

computerise; also spelt **computerize** VERB When a system or process is computerised, the work is done by computers.

computing NOUN Computing is the use of computers and the writing of programs for them.

comrade NOUN A soldier's comrades are his or her fellow soldiers, especially in battle. **comradeship** NOUN

con, **cons**, **conning**, **conned** (*informal*) VERB ① If someone cons you, they trick you into doing or believing something. ▸ NOUN ② a trick in which someone deceives you into doing or believing something.

> **con** VERB
> ① = cheat, deceive, mislead, swindle, trick
> ▸ NOUN ② = bluff, deception, fraud, swindle, trick

concave ADJECTIVE [MATHS] A concave surface curves inwards, rather than being level or bulging outwards.

conceal VERB To conceal something is to hide it • *He had concealed his gun.* **concealment** NOUN

concede [*Said kon-**seed***] VERB ① If you concede something, you admit that it is true • *I conceded that he was entitled to his views.* ② When someone concedes defeat, they accept that they have lost something such as a contest or an election.

conceit NOUN Conceit is someone's excessive pride in their appearance or abilities.

conceit NOUN
= egotism, pride, self-importance, vanity

conceited ADJECTIVE Someone who is conceited is too proud of their appearance or abilities.

conceited ADJECTIVE
= bigheaded (*informal*), cocky, egotistical, self-important, vain
≠ modest

conceivable ADJECTIVE If something is conceivable, you can believe that it could exist or be true • *It's conceivable that you also met her.* **conceivably** ADVERB

conceive VERB ① If you can conceive of something, you can imagine it or believe it • *Could you conceive of doing such a thing yourself?* ② If you conceive something such as a plan, you think of it and work out how it could be done. ③ When a woman conceives, she becomes pregnant.

concentrate VERB ① If you concentrate on something, you give it all your attention. ② When something is concentrated in one place, it is all there rather than in several places • *They are mostly concentrated in the urban areas.*
concentration NOUN

concentrate VERB
① = be engrossed in, focus your attention on, give your attention to, put your mind to
② = accumulate, collect, gather

concentrated ADJECTIVE A concentrated liquid has been made stronger by having water removed from it • *concentrated apple juice.*

concentration camp NOUN HISTORY a prison camp, especially one set up by the Nazis during World War Two.

concept NOUN an abstract or general idea • *the concept of tolerance.*
conceptual ADJECTIVE **conceptually** ADVERB

conception NOUN ① Your conception of something is the idea you have of it. ② Conception is the process by which a woman becomes pregnant.

concern NOUN ① Concern is a feeling of worry about something or someone • *public concern about violence.* ② If something is your concern, it is your responsibility. ③ a business • *a large manufacturing concern.* ▶ VERB ④ If something concerns you or if you are concerned about it, it worries you. ⑤ You say that something concerns you if it affects or involves you • *My business does not concern you.* ▶ PHRASE ⑥ If something is **of concern** to you, it is important to you. **concerned** ADJECTIVE

concern NOUN
① = anxiety, apprehension, disquiet, worry
② = affair, business, responsibility
▶ VERB ④ = bother, distress, disturb, trouble, worry
⑤ = affect, apply to, be relevant to, involve

concerning PREPOSITION You use 'concerning' to show what something is about • *studies concerning the environment.*

concert NOUN a public performance by musicians.

concerted ADJECTIVE A concerted action is done by several people together • *concerted action to cut interest rates.*

concerto, **concertos** or **concerti** *[Said kon-*cher*-toe]* NOUN MUSIC a piece of music for a solo instrument and an orchestra.

concession NOUN If you make a concession, you agree to let someone have or do something • *Her one concession was to let me come into the building.*

concise ADJECTIVE giving all the necessary information using as few words as necessary • *a concise guide.* **concisely** ADVERB

> **concise** ADJECTIVE
> = brief, short, succinct, terse
> ≠ long

conclude VERB ① If you conclude something, you decide that it is so because of the other things that you know • *An inquiry concluded that this was untrue.* ② When you conclude something, you finish it • *At that point I intend to conclude the interview.* **concluding** ADJECTIVE

> **conclude** VERB
> ① = decide, deduce, infer, judge, reckon (*informal*), suppose, surmise (*formal*)
> ② = close, end, finish, round off, wind up
> ≠ begin

conclusion NOUN ① a decision made after thinking carefully about something. ② the finish or ending of something.

> **conclusion** NOUN
> ① = deduction, inference, judgment, verdict
> ② = close, end, ending, finish, termination (*formal*)
> ≠ beginning

conclusive ADJECTIVE Facts that are conclusive show that something is certainly true. **conclusively** ADVERB

concoct VERB ① If you concoct an excuse or explanation, you invent one. ② If you concoct something, you make it by mixing several things together. **concoction** NOUN

concourse NOUN a wide hall in a building where people walk about or gather together.

concrete NOUN ① Concrete is a solid building material made by mixing cement, sand and water. ▸ ADJECTIVE ② definite, rather than general or vague • *I don't really have any concrete plans.* ③ real and physical, rather than abstract • *concrete evidence.*

concur, concurs, concurring, concurred VERB (*formal*) To concur is to agree • *She concurred with me.*

concurrent ADJECTIVE If things are concurrent, they happen at the same time. **concurrently** ADVERB

concussed ADJECTIVE confused or unconscious because of a blow to the head. **concussion** NOUN

condemn VERB ① If you condemn something, you say it is bad and unacceptable • *Teachers condemned the new plans.* ② If someone is condemned to a punishment, they are given it • *She was condemned to death.* ③ If you are condemned to something unpleasant, you must suffer it • *Many people are condemned to poverty.* ④ When a building is condemned, it is going to be pulled down because it is unsafe. **condemnation** NOUN

> **condemn** VERB
> ① = blame, censure (*formal*), criticise, damn, denounce
> ② = damn, doom, sentence

condensation NOUN SCIENCE Condensation is a coating of tiny drops formed on a surface by steam or vapour.

condense VERB ① If you condense a piece of writing or a speech, you shorten it. ② SCIENCE When a gas or vapour condenses, it changes into a liquid.

condescending ADJECTIVE If you are condescending, you behave in a way that shows you think you are superior to other people.

condition NOUN ① the state someone

or something is in. ② (*in plural*) The conditions in which something is done are the location and other factors likely to affect it • *The very difficult conditions continued to affect our performance.* ③ a requirement that must be met for something else to be possible • *He had to report to the police each week as a condition of bail.* ④ You can refer to an illness or other medical problem as a condition • *a heart condition.* ▶ PHRASE ⑤ If you are **out of condition**, you are unfit. ▶ VERB ⑥ If someone is conditioned to behave or think in a certain way, they do it as a result of their upbringing or training.

condition NOUN
① = form, shape, state
③ = prerequisite, provision, proviso, qualification, requirement, requisite, stipulation, terms

conditional ADJECTIVE If one thing is conditional on another, it can only happen if the other thing happens • *Admission to the course is conditional on you getting good grades.*

condolence NOUN Condolence is sympathy expressed for a bereaved person.

condominium NOUN In Canadian, Australian and New Zealand English, a condominium is an apartment block in which each apartment is owned by the person who lives in it.

condone VERB If you condone someone's bad behaviour, you accept it and do not try to stop it • *We cannot condone violence.*

conducive [*Said kon-**joo**-siv*] ADJECTIVE If something is conducive to something else, it makes it likely to happen • *a situation that is conducive to relaxation.*

conduct VERB ① To conduct an activity or task is to carry it out • *He seemed to be conducting a conversation.* ② (*formal*) The way you conduct yourself is the way you behave. ③ MUSIC When someone conducts an orchestra or choir, they stand in front of it and direct it. ④ SCIENCE If something conducts heat or electricity, heat or electricity can pass through it. ▶ NOUN ⑤ If you take part in the conduct of an activity or task, you help to carry it out. ⑥ Your conduct is your behaviour.

conduct VERB
① = carry out, direct, do, manage, organise, perform, run
② = act, behave
▶ NOUN ⑥ = attitude, behaviour, manners, ways

conductor NOUN ① MUSIC someone who conducts an orchestra or choir. ② someone who moves round a train, bus or tram selling tickets. ③ SCIENCE a substance that conducts heat or electricity.

cone NOUN ① a regular three-dimensional shape with a circular base and a point at the top. ② A fir cone or pine cone is the fruit of a fir or pine tree.

confectionery NOUN Confectionery is sweets.

confederation NOUN an organisation formed for business or political purposes.

confer, **confers, conferring, conferred** VERB When people confer, they discuss something in order to make a decision.

conference NOUN a meeting at which formal discussions take place.

conference NOUN
= congress, convention, discussion, forum, meeting

confess VERB If you confess to something, you admit it • *Your son has confessed to his crimes.*

confess VERB
= acknowledge, admit, own up
≠ deny

confession NOUN ① If you make a confession, you admit you have done something wrong. ② Confession is the act of confessing something, especially a religious act in which people confess their sins to a priest.

> **confession** NOUN
> ② = acknowledgment, admission

confessional NOUN [RE] a small room in some churches where people confess their sins to a priest.

confetti NOUN Confetti is small pieces of coloured paper thrown over the newly married couple after a wedding.

confidant [*Said* ***kon**-fid-dant*] NOUN (*formal*) a person you discuss your private problems with.

confide VERB If you confide in or to someone, you tell them a secret • *She confided in me that she was worried.*

confidence NOUN ① If you have confidence in someone, you feel you can trust them. ② Someone who has confidence is sure of their own abilities or qualities. ③ a secret you tell someone.

> **confidence** NOUN
> ① = belief, faith, reliance, trust
> ≠ distrust
> ② = aplomb, assurance, self-assurance, self-possession
> ≠ shyness

confident ADJECTIVE ① If you are confident about something, you are sure it will happen the way you want it to. ② People who are confident are sure of their own abilities or qualities. **confidently** ADVERB

> **confident** ADJECTIVE
> ① = certain, convinced, positive, satisfied, secure, sure
> ≠ uncertain
> ② = assured, self-assured, self-possessed
> ≠ shy

confidential ADJECTIVE Confidential information is meant to be kept secret. **confidentially** ADVERB **confidentiality** NOUN

confine VERB ① If something is confined to one place, person or thing, it exists only in that place or affects only that person or thing. ② If you confine yourself to doing or saying something, it is the only thing you do or say • *They confined themselves to discussing the weather.* ③ If you are confined to a place, you cannot leave it • *She was confined to bed for two days.* ▶ PLURAL NOUN ④ The confines of a place are its boundaries • *outside the confines of the prison.* **confinement** NOUN

> **confine** VERB
> ② = limit, restrict
> ③ = hem in, imprison, restrict, shut up

confined ADJECTIVE A confined space is small and enclosed by walls.

confirm VERB ① To confirm something is to say or show that it is true • *Police confirmed that they had received a call.* ② If you confirm an arrangement or appointment, you say it is definite. ③ [RE] When someone is confirmed, they are formally accepted as a member of a Christian Church. **confirmation** NOUN

> **confirm** VERB
> ① = bear out, endorse, prove, substantiate, validate, verify
> ② = fix, settle

confirmed ADJECTIVE You use 'confirmed' to describe someone who has a belief or way of life that is unlikely to change • *a confirmed bachelor.*

confiscate VERB To confiscate something is to take it away from someone as a punishment.

conflict NOUN *[Said* ***kon****-flikt]* ① Conflict is disagreement and argument • *conflict between teenagers and their parents*. ② HISTORY a war or battle. ③ When there is a conflict of ideas or interests, people have different ideas or interests which cannot all be satisfied. ▶ VERB *[Said kon-****flikt****]* ④ When ideas or interests conflict, they are different and cannot all be satisfied.

conflict NOUN
① = antagonism, disagreement, discord, friction, hostility, opposition, strife
② = battle, combat, fighting, strife, war
▶ VERB ④ = be at variance, be incompatible, clash, differ, disagree

conform VERB ① If you conform, you behave the way people expect you to. ② If something conforms to a law or to someone's wishes, it is what is required or wanted. **conformist** NOUN, ADJECTIVE

confront VERB ① If you are confronted with a problem or task, you have to deal with it. ② If you confront someone, you meet them face to face like an enemy. ③ If you confront someone with evidence or a fact, you present it to them in order to accuse them of something.

confrontation NOUN a serious dispute or fight • *a confrontation between police and protesters*.

confuse VERB ① If you confuse two things, you mix them up and think one of them is the other • *You are confusing facts with opinion*. ② To confuse someone means to make them uncertain about what is happening or what to do. ③ To confuse a situation means to make it more complicated.

confuse VERB
① = mistake, mix up, muddle up
② = baffle, bewilder, mystify, puzzle

confused ADJECTIVE ① uncertain about what is happening or what to do. ② in an untidy mess.

confused ADJECTIVE
① = baffled, bewildered, muddled, perplexed, puzzled
② = chaotic, disordered, disorganised, untidy
≠ tidy

confusing ADJECTIVE puzzling or bewildering.

confusing ADJECTIVE
= baffling, bewildering, complicated, puzzling

confusion NOUN ① a bewildering state. ② an untidy mess.

confusion NOUN
② = chaos, disarray, disorder, disorganisation, mess
≠ order

congenial *[Said kon-****jeen****-yal]* ADJECTIVE If something is congenial, it is pleasant and suits you • *We wanted to talk in congenial surroundings*.

congenital ADJECTIVE If someone has a congenital disease or disability, they have had it from birth but did not inherit it.

congested ADJECTIVE ① When a road is congested, it is so full of traffic that normal movement is impossible. ② If your nose is congested, it is blocked and you cannot breathe properly. **congestion** NOUN

conglomerate NOUN a large business organisation consisting of several companies.

congratulate VERB If you congratulate someone, you express pleasure at something good that has happened to them, or praise them for something they have achieved. **congratulation** NOUN **congratulatory** ADJECTIVE

congregate VERB When people

congregate, they gather together somewhere.

congregation NOUN the congregation are the people attending a service in a church.

congress NOUN a large meeting held to discuss ideas or policies • *a medical congress.*

conical ADJECTIVE shaped like a cone.

conifer NOUN any type of evergreen tree that produces cones. **coniferous** ADJECTIVE

conjecture NOUN Conjecture is guesswork about something • *There was no evidence, only conjecture.*

conjunction NOUN ① ENGLISH MFL In grammar, a conjunction is a word that links two other words or two clauses, for example 'and', 'but', 'while' and 'that'. ▶ PHRASE ② If two or more things are done **in conjunction**, they are done together.

connect VERB ① To connect two things is to join them together. ② If you connect something with something else, you think of them as being linked • *High blood pressure is closely connected to heart disease.*

connect VERB
① = affix, attach, couple, fasten, join, link
≠ separate
② = ally, associate, link, relate

connection; also spelt **connexion** NOUN ① a link or relationship between things. ② the point where two wires or pipes are joined together • *a loose connection.* ③ (*in plural*) Someone's connections are the people they know • *He had powerful connections in the army.*

connection NOUN
① = affiliation, association, bond, correlation, correspondence, link, relation, relationship
② = coupling, fastening, junction, link

connective NOUN ENGLISH MFL a word or short phrase that connects clauses, phrases or words.

connoisseur [*Said kon-nis-**sur***] NOUN someone who knows a lot about the arts, or about food or drink • *a great connoisseur of coffee.*

connotation NOUN ENGLISH The connotations of a word or name are what it makes you think of • *the word grey has connotations of dullness.*

conquer VERB ① To conquer people is to take control of their country by force. ② If you conquer something difficult or dangerous, you succeed in controlling it • *Conquer your fear!* **conqueror** NOUN

conquest NOUN ① Conquest is the conquering of a country or group of people. ② Conquests are lands captured by conquest.

conscience NOUN the part of your mind that tells you what is right and wrong.

conscience NOUN
= principles, scruples, sense of right and wrong

conscientious [*Said kon-shee-**en**-shus*] ADJECTIVE Someone who is conscientious is very careful to do their work properly. **conscientiously** ADVERB

conscious ADJECTIVE ① If you are conscious of something, you are aware of it • *She was not conscious of the time.* ② A conscious action or effort is done deliberately • *I made a conscious decision not to hide.* ③ Someone who is conscious is awake, rather than asleep or unconscious • *Still conscious, she was taken to hospital.* **consciously** ADVERB **consciousness** NOUN

consecrated ADJECTIVE A consecrated building or place is one that has been officially declared to be holy.

consecutive ADJECTIVE Consecutive

events or periods of time happen one after the other • *eight consecutive games.*

consensus NOUN Consensus is general agreement among a group of people • *The consensus was that it could be done.*

consent NOUN ① PSHE Consent is permission to do something • *Thomas reluctantly gave his consent to my writing this book.* ② Consent is also agreement between two or more people • *By common consent it was the best game of these championships.* ▸ VERB ③ PSHE If you consent to something, you agree to it or allow it.

consequence NOUN ① The consequences of something are its results or effects • *the dire consequences of major war.* ② (*formal*) If something is of consequence, it is important.

consequent ADJECTIVE Consequent describes something as being the result of something else • *an earthquake in 1980 and its consequent damage.* **consequently** ADVERB

conservation NOUN Conservation is the preservation of the environment. **conservationist** NOUN, ADJECTIVE

conservative NOUN ① In Britain, a Conservative is a member or supporter of the Conservative Party, a political party that believes that the government should interfere as little as possible in the running of the economy. ▸ ADJECTIVE ② In Britain, Conservative views and policies are those of the Conservative Party. ③ Someone who is conservative is opposed to radical change and values tradition and stability. ④ A conservative estimate or guess is a cautious or moderate one. **conservatively** ADVERB **conservatism** NOUN

> **conservative** ADJECTIVE
> ③ = conventional, traditional
> ≠ radical

conservatory, **conservatories** NOUN a room with glass walls and a glass roof attached to a house.

conserve VERB If you conserve a supply of something, you make it last • *the only way to conserve energy.*

consider VERB ① If you consider something to be the case, you think or judge it to be so • *The manager does not consider him an ideal team member.* ② EXAM TERM To consider something is to think about it carefully • *If an offer were made, we would consider it.* ③ If you consider someone's needs or feelings, you take account of them.

> **consider** VERB
> ① = believe, judge, rate, regard as, think
> ② = contemplate, deliberate, meditate, muse, ponder, reflect, think about
> ③ = bear in mind, make allowances for, respect, take into account, think about

considerable ADJECTIVE A considerable amount of something is a lot of it • *a considerable sum of money.* **considerably** ADVERB

considerate ADJECTIVE Someone who is considerate pays attention to other people's needs and feelings.

consideration NOUN ① Consideration is careful thought about something • *a decision demanding careful consideration.* ② If you show consideration for someone, you take account of their needs and feelings. ③ something that has to be taken into account • *Money was also a consideration.*

> **consideration** NOUN
> ① = attention, contemplation, deliberation, study, thought
> ② = concern, kindness, respect, tact
> ③ = factor, issue, point

considered ADJECTIVE A considered opinion or judgment is arrived at by careful thought.

considering CONJUNCTION, PREPOSITION You say 'considering' to indicate that you are taking something into account • *It's a great game considering that it's free.*

consign VERB (*formal*) To consign something to a particular place is to send or put it there.

consignment NOUN A consignment of goods is a load of them being delivered somewhere.

consist VERB What something consists of is its different parts or members • *The brain consists of millions of nerve cells.*

> **consist** VERB
> = be composed of, be made up of, comprise

consistency, **consistencies** NOUN ① Consistency is the quality of being consistent. ② The consistency of a substance is how thick or smooth it is • *the consistency of single cream.*

consistent ADJECTIVE ① If you are consistent, you keep doing something the same way • *one of our most consistent performers.* ② If something such as a statement or argument is consistent, there are no contradictions in it. **consistently** ADVERB

console VERB [*Said con-**sole***] ① To console someone who is unhappy is to make them more cheerful. ▸ NOUN [*Said **con**-sole*] ② a panel with switches or knobs for operating a machine. **consolation** NOUN

consolidate VERB To consolidate something you have gained or achieved is to make it more secure. **consolidation** NOUN

consonant NOUN ENGLISH a sound such as 'p' or 'm' which you make by stopping the air flowing freely through your mouth.

consort VERB [*Said con-**sort***] ① (*formal*) If you consort with someone, you spend a lot of time with them. ▸ NOUN [*Said **con**-sort*] ② the wife or husband of the king or queen.

consortium, **consortia** or **consortiums** NOUN a group of businesses working together.

conspicuous ADJECTIVE If something is conspicuous, people can see or notice it very easily. **conspicuously** ADVERB

> **conspicuous** ADJECTIVE
> = apparent, blatant, evident, noticeable, obvious, perceptible

conspiracy, **conspiracies** NOUN When there is a conspiracy, a group of people plan something illegal, often for a political purpose.

conspirator NOUN someone involved in a conspiracy.

conspire VERB ① When people conspire, they plan together to do something illegal, often for a political purpose. ② (*literary*) When events conspire towards a particular result, they seem to work together to cause it • *Circumstances conspired to doom the business.*

constable NOUN a police officer of the lowest rank.

constabulary, **constabularies** NOUN a police force.

constant ADJECTIVE ① Something that is constant happens all the time or is always there • *a city under constant attack.* ② If an amount or level is constant, it stays the same. ③ People who are constant stay loyal to a person or idea. **constantly** ADVERB **constancy** NOUN

> **constant** ADJECTIVE
> ① = continual, continuous, eternal, nonstop, perpetual, relentless
> ≠ periodic
> ② = even, fixed, regular, stable, steady, uniform
> ≠ changeable

constellation NOUN a group of stars.

consternation NOUN Consternation is anxiety or dismay • *There was some consternation when it began raining.*

constituency, **constituencies** NOUN a town or area represented by an MP.

constituent NOUN ① An MP's constituents are the voters who live in his or her constituency. ② The constituents of something are its parts • *the major constituents of bone.*

constitute VERB If a group of things constitute something, they are what it consists of • *Jewellery constitutes 80 per cent of the stock.*

constitution NOUN ① HISTORY The constitution of a country is a system of laws and principles by which the country should be governed. ② Your constitution is your health • *a very strong constitution.* **constitutional** ADJECTIVE **constitutionally** ADVERB

constrained ADJECTIVE If a person feels constrained to do something, they feel that they should do that.

constraint NOUN something that limits someone's freedom of action • *the financial constraints on schools.*

construct VERB To construct something is to build or make it.

> **construct** VERB
> = assemble, build, create, erect, make, put together, put up

construction NOUN ① The construction of something is the building or making of it • *the construction of the harbour.* ② something built or made • *a shoddy modern construction built of concrete.*

constructive ADJECTIVE Constructive criticisms and comments are helpful. **constructively** ADVERB

consul NOUN an official who lives in a foreign city and who looks after people there who are citizens of his or her own country. **consular** ADJECTIVE

consulate NOUN the place where a consul works.

consult VERB ① If you consult someone, you ask for their opinion or advice. ② When people consult each other, they exchange ideas and opinions. ③ If you consult a book or map, you look at it for information.

> **consult** VERB
> ① = ask for advice, confer with, refer to

consultancy NOUN an organisation whose members give expert advice on a subject.

consultant NOUN ① an experienced doctor who specialises in one type of medicine. ② someone who gives expert advice • *a management consultant.*

consultation NOUN ① a meeting held to discuss something. ② Consultation is discussion or the seeking of advice • *There has to be much better consultation with the public.* **consultative** ADJECTIVE

consume VERB ① (*formal*) If you consume something, you eat or drink it. ② To consume fuel or energy is to use it up.

consumer NOUN someone who buys things or uses services • *two new magazines for teenage consumers.*

consumerism NOUN Consumerism is the belief that a country will have a strong economy if its people buy a lot of goods and spend a lot of money.

consuming ADJECTIVE A consuming passion or interest is more important to you than anything else.

consummate VERB [*Said* ***kons**-yum-mate*] ① To consummate something is to make it complete. ▸ ADJECTIVE [*Said* ***kon**-sum-mit*] ② You use 'consummate' to describe someone who is very good at something • *a consummate politician*. **consummation** NOUN

consumption NOUN The consumption of fuel or food is the using of it, or the amount used.

contact NOUN ① If you are in contact with someone, you regularly talk to them or write to them. ② When things are in contact, they are touching each other. ③ someone you know in a place or organisation from whom you can get help or information. ▸ VERB ④ If you contact someone, you telephone them or write to them.

> **contact** NOUN
> ① = communication, touch
> ③ = acquaintance, connection
> ▸ VERB ④ = approach, communicate with, get hold of, get in touch with, reach

contagious ADJECTIVE A contagious disease can be caught by touching people or things infected with it.

contain VERB ① If a substance contains something, that thing is a part of it • *Alcohol contains sugar*. ② The things a box or room contains are the things inside it. ③ (*formal*) To contain something also means to stop it increasing or spreading • *efforts to contain the disease*.
containment NOUN

> **contain** VERB
> ① = comprise, include
> ③ = control, curb, repress, restrain, stifle

container NOUN ① something such as a box or a bottle that you keep things in. ② a large sealed metal box for transporting things.

> **container** NOUN
> ① = holder, vessel

contaminate VERB If something is contaminated by dirt, chemicals or radiation, it is made impure and harmful • *foods contaminated with lead*.
contamination NOUN

contemplate VERB ① To contemplate is to think carefully about something for a long time. ② If you contemplate doing something, you consider doing it • *I never contemplated going to university*. ③ If you contemplate something, you look at it for a long time • *He contemplated his drawings*.
contemplation NOUN
contemplative ADJECTIVE

> **contemplate** VERB
> ① = consider, examine, muse on, ponder, reflect on, think about
> ② = consider, envisage, plan, think of

contemporary, **contemporaries** ADJECTIVE ① produced or happening now • *contemporary literature*. ② produced or happening at the time you are talking about • *contemporary descriptions of Lizzie Borden*. ▸ NOUN ③ Someone's contemporaries are other people living or active at the same time as them • *Shakespeare and his contemporaries*.

contempt NOUN If you treat someone or something with contempt, you show no respect for them at all.

> **contempt** NOUN
> = derision, disdain, disregard, disrespect, scorn
> ≠ respect

contemptible ADJECTIVE not worthy of any respect • *this contemptible piece of nonsense*.

contemptuous ADJECTIVE showing contempt. **contemptuously** ADVERB

contend VERB ① To contend with a difficulty is to deal with it • *They had to contend with injuries*. ② (*formal*) If you contend that something is true, you say firmly that it is true. ③ When people contend for something, they compete for it. **contender** NOUN

content NOUN *[Said* ***con****-tent]* ① *(in plural)* The contents of something are the things inside it. ▶ ADJECTIVE *[Said con-****tent****]* ② happy and satisfied with your life. ③ willing to do or have something • *He would be content to phone her.* ▶ VERB *[Said con-****tent****]* ④ If you content yourself with doing something, you do it and do not try to do anything else • *He contented himself with an early morning lecture.*

contented ADJECTIVE happy and satisfied with your life. **contentedly** ADVERB **contentment** NOUN

contention NOUN *(formal)* ① Someone's contention is the idea or opinion they are expressing • *Is your contention that government employees should not be jailed for breaking the law?* ② Contention is disagreement and argument about something • *What had brought about all this contention?*

contest NOUN *[Said* ***con****-test]* ① a competition or game • *a boxing contest.* ② a struggle for power • *a presidential contest.* ▶ VERB *[Said con-****test****]* ③ If you contest a statement or decision, you object to it formally.

> **contest** NOUN
> ① = competition, game, match, tournament
> ② = battle, fight, struggle
> ▶ VERB ③ = challenge, dispute, oppose, question
> ≠ accept

contestant NOUN someone taking part in a competition.

context NOUN ① The context of something consists of matters related to it which help to explain it • *English history is treated in a European context.* ② ENGLISH The context of a word or sentence consists of the words or sentences before and after it.

continent NOUN ① a very large area of land, such as Africa or Asia. ② The Continent is the mainland of Europe. **continental** ADJECTIVE

contingency, contingencies *[Said kon-****tin****-jen-see]* NOUN something that might happen in the future • *I need to examine all possible contingencies.*

contingent NOUN ① a group of people representing a country or organisation • *a strong South African contingent.* ② a group of police or soldiers.

continual ADJECTIVE ① happening all the time without stopping • *continual headaches.* ② happening again and again • *the continual snide remarks.* **continually** ADVERB

> **continual** ADJECTIVE
> ① = constant, endless, eternal, nagging, perpetual, uninterrupted
> ② = frequent, recurrent, regular, repeated
> ≠ occasional

continuation NOUN ① The continuation of something is the continuing of it • *the continuation of the human race.* ② Something that is a continuation of an event follows it and seems like a part of it • *a meeting which was a continuation of a conference.*

continue, continues, continuing, continued VERB ① If you continue to do something, you keep doing it. ② If something continues, it does not stop. ③ You also say something continues when it starts again after stopping • *She continued after a pause.*

> **continue** VERB
> ① = carry on, go on, keep on, persist
> ② = carry on, endure, last, persist, remain, survive
> ③ = carry on, recommence, resume

continuous ADJECTIVE ① Continuous means happening or existing without stopping. ② MATHS A continuous line or surface has no gaps or holes in it. A continuous set

a b c d e f g h i j k l m n o p q r s t u v w x y z

of data has an unlimited amount of numbers or items in it. **continuously** ADVERB **continuity** NOUN

continuous ADJECTIVE
① = constant, continued, extended, prolonged, uninterrupted
≠ periodic

contorted ADJECTIVE twisted into an unnatural, unattractive shape.

contour NOUN ① The contours of something are its general shape. ② GEOGRAPHY On a map, a contour is a line joining points of equal height.

contraception NOUN Contraception is methods of preventing pregnancy.

contraceptive NOUN a device or pill for preventing pregnancy.

contract NOUN *[Said* ***con****-trakt]* ① a written legal agreement about the sale of something or work done for money. ▶ VERB *[Said con-****trakt****]* ② When something contracts, it gets smaller or shorter. ③ *(formal)* If you contract an illness, you get it • *Her husband contracted a virus*. **contractual** ADJECTIVE

contractor NOUN a person or company who does work for other people or companies • *a building contractor*.

contradict VERB If you contradict someone, you say that what they have just said is not true, and that something else is. **contradiction** NOUN **contradictory** ADJECTIVE

contraption NOUN a strange-looking machine or piece of equipment.

contrary ADJECTIVE ① Contrary ideas or opinions are opposed to each other and cannot be held by the same person. ▶ PHRASE ② You say **on the contrary** when you are contradicting what someone has just said.

contrast NOUN *[Said* ***con****-trast]*
① a great difference between things • *the real contrast between the two poems*. ② If one thing is a contrast to another, it is very different from it • *I couldn't imagine a greater contrast to Maxwell*. ▶ VERB *[Said con-****trast****]*
③ EXAM TERM If you contrast things, you describe or emphasise the differences between them • *The painter contrasted her image of rural America with striking representations of New York*. ④ If one thing contrasts with another, it is very different from it • *The interview completely contrasted with the one she gave after Tokyo*.

contravene VERB *(formal)* If you contravene a law or rule, you do something that it forbids.

contribute VERB ① If you contribute to something, you do things to help it succeed • *Young people have much to contribute to the community*. ② If you contribute money, you give it to help to pay for something. ③ If something contributes to an event or situation, it is one of its causes • *The dry summer has contributed to perfect conditions*. **contribution** NOUN **contributor** NOUN **contributory** ADJECTIVE

contrive VERB *(formal)* If you contrive to do something difficult, you succeed in doing it • *Anthony contrived to escape with a few companions*.

contrived ADJECTIVE Something that is contrived is unnatural • *a contrived compliment*.

control, **controls**, **controlling**, **controlled** NOUN ① Control of a country or organisation is the power to make the important decisions about how it is run. ② Your control over something is your ability to make it work the way you want it to. ③ The controls on a machine are knobs or other devices used to work it. ▶ VERB ④ To control a country or organisation means to have the power to make decisions about how it is run. ⑤ To control something such as a machine or system means to make it work the way you want it to. ⑥ If you control yourself, you make yourself behave calmly when you are angry or upset. ▸ PHRASE ⑦ If something is **out of control**, nobody has any power over it. **controller** NOUN

control NOUN
① = authority, command, direction, government, management, power, rule, supremacy
▸ VERB ④ = administer, be in charge of, command, direct, govern, have power over, manage, rule

controversial ADJECTIVE Something that is controversial causes a lot of discussion and argument, because many people disapprove of it.

controversy, **controversies** NOUN discussion and argument because many people disapprove of something.

conundrum NOUN (*formal*) a puzzling problem.

convection NOUN SCIENCE Convection is the process by which heat travels through gases and liquids.

convene VERB ① (*formal*) To convene a meeting is to arrange for it to take place. ② When people convene, they come together for a meeting.

convenience NOUN ① The convenience of something is the fact that it is easy to use or that it makes something easy to do. ② something useful.

convenient ADJECTIVE If something is convenient, it is easy to use or it makes something easy to do. **conveniently** ADVERB

convenient ADJECTIVE
= handy, helpful, useful, user-friendly
≠ inconvenient

convent NOUN a building where nuns live, or a school run by nuns.

convention NOUN ① an accepted way of behaving or doing something. ② a large meeting of an organisation or political group • *the Democratic Convention.*

convention NOUN
① = code, custom, etiquette, practice, tradition
② = assembly, conference, congress, meeting

conventional ADJECTIVE ① You say that people are conventional when there is nothing unusual about their way of life. ② Conventional methods are the ones that are usually used. **conventionally** ADVERB

conventional ADJECTIVE
① = conformist, conservative, unadventurous
② = customary, ordinary, orthodox, regular, standard, traditional

converge VERB To converge is to meet or join at a particular place.

conversation NOUN If you have a conversation with someone, you spend time talking to them. **conversational** ADJECTIVE **conversationalist** NOUN

converse VERB [*Said con-**verse***] ① (*formal*) When people converse, they talk to each other. ▸ NOUN [*Said **con**-verse*] ② The converse of something is its opposite • *Don't you think that the converse might also be possible?* **conversely** ADVERB

convert VERB [*Said con-**vert***] ① To convert one thing into another is to change it so that it becomes the other thing. ② MATHS If you convert a unit or measurement, you express it in terms of another unit or scale of measurement. For example, you can convert inches to centimetres by multiplying by 2.54. ③ If someone

a b c d e f g h i j k l m n o p q r s t u v w x y z

converts you, they persuade you to change your religious or political beliefs. ▶ **NOUN** *[Said **con**-vert]* ④ someone who has changed their religious or political beliefs. **conversion NOUN convertible ADJECTIVE**

convey VERB ① To convey information or ideas is to cause them to be known or understood. ② *(formal)* To convey someone or something to a place is to transport them there.

> **convey VERB**
> ① = communicate, express, get across, impart *(formal)*

conveyor belt NOUN a moving strip used in factories for moving objects along.

convict VERB *[Said kon-**vikt**]* ① To convict someone of a crime is to find them guilty. ▶ **NOUN** *[Said **kon**-vikt]* ② someone serving a prison sentence.

conviction NOUN ① a strong belief or opinion. ② The conviction of someone is what happens when they are found guilty in a court of law.

convince VERB To convince someone of something is to persuade them that it is true.

> **convince VERB**
> = assure, persuade, satisfy

convincing ADJECTIVE 'Convincing' is used to describe things or people that can make you believe something is true • *a convincing argument*. **convincingly ADVERB**

> **convincing ADJECTIVE**
> = conclusive, effective, persuasive, plausible, powerful, telling
> ≠ unconvincing

convoluted *[Said kon-vol-**oo**-tid]* **ADJECTIVE** Something that is convoluted has many twists and bends • *the convoluted patterns of these designs*.

convoy NOUN a group of vehicles or ships travelling together.

convulsion NOUN If someone has convulsions, their muscles move violently and uncontrollably.

coo VERB When pigeons and doves coo, they make a soft flutelike sound.

cook VERB ① To cook food is to prepare it for eating by heating it. ▶ **NOUN** ② someone who prepares and cooks food, often as their job.

> **cook VERB**
> ① = bake, barbecue, boil, fry, grill, microwave, poach, roast, steam, stew, toast

cooker NOUN a device for cooking food.

cookery NOUN Cookery is the activity of preparing and cooking food.

cookie NOUN ① a sweet biscuit. ② a small file placed on a user's computer by a website, containing information about the user's preferences that will be used on any future visits he or she may make to the site.

cool ADJECTIVE ① Something cool has a low temperature but is not cold. ② If you are cool in a difficult situation, you stay calm and unemotional. ▶ **VERB** ③ When something cools or when you cool it, it becomes less warm. **coolly ADVERB coolness NOUN**

> **cool ADJECTIVE**
> ① = chilled, chilly, cold, refreshing
> ≠ warm
> ② = calm, collected, composed, level-headed, relaxed, serene
> ≠ nervous
> ▶ **VERB** ③ = chill, cool off, freeze, refrigerate
> ≠ heat

coop NOUN a cage for chickens or rabbits.

A B C D E F G H I J K L M N O P Q R S T U V W X Y Z

cooperate *[Said koh-**op**-er-rate]* VERB ① When people cooperate, they work or act together. ② To cooperate also means to do what someone asks. **cooperation** NOUN

> **cooperate** VERB
> ① = collaborate, join forces, pull together, work together

cooperative *[Said koh-**op**-er-ut-tiv]* NOUN ① a business or organisation run by the people who work for it, and who share its benefits or profits. ▸ ADJECTIVE ② A cooperative activity is done by people working together. ③ Someone who is cooperative does what you ask them to.

coordinate, **coordinates**, **coordinating**, **coordinated** *[Said koh-**or**-din-ate]* VERB ① To coordinate an activity is to organise the people or things involved in it • *to coordinate the campaign*. ▸ NOUN ② [MATHS] *(in plural)* Coordinates are a pair of numbers or letters which tell you how far along and up or down a point is on a grid. **coordination** NOUN **coordinator** NOUN

cop NOUN *(slang)* a police officer.

cope VERB If you cope with a problem or task, you deal with it successfully.

copious ADJECTIVE *(formal)* existing or produced in large quantities • *He wrote copious notes in every class*.

copper NOUN ① [SCIENCE] Copper is a reddish-brown metallic element. Its atomic number is 29 and its symbol is Cu. ② Coppers are brown metal coins of low value. ③ *(informal)* A copper is also a police officer.

copy, **copies**, **copying**, **copied** NOUN ① something made to look like something else. ② A copy of something such as a book, magazine or DVD is one of many identical ones produced at the same time. ▸ VERB ③ If you copy what someone does, you do the same thing. ④ If you copy something, you make a copy of it. **copier** NOUN

> **copy** NOUN
> ① = counterfeit, duplicate, fake, forgery, imitation, replica, reproduction
> ▸ VERB ③ = ape, emulate, follow, imitate, mimic
> ④ = counterfeit, duplicate, reproduce

copyright NOUN [LIBRARY] If someone has the copyright on a piece of writing or music, it cannot be copied or performed without their permission.

coral NOUN Coral is a hard substance that forms in the sea from the skeletons of tiny animals called corals.

cord NOUN ① Cord is strong, thick string. ② Electrical wire covered in rubber or plastic is also called cord.

cordial ADJECTIVE ① warm and friendly • *a cordial greeting*. ▸ NOUN ② a sweet drink made from fruit juice.

cordon NOUN ① a line or ring of police or soldiers preventing people entering or leaving a place. ▸ VERB ② If police or soldiers cordon off an area, they stop people entering or leaving by forming themselves into a line or ring.

corduroy NOUN Corduroy is a thick cloth with parallel raised lines on the outside.

core NOUN ① the hard central part of a fruit such as an apple. ② the most important part of something • *the core of Asia's problems*. ③ [GEOGRAPHY] the central part of the earth that lies beneath the mantle.

cork NOUN ① Cork is the very light, spongelike bark of a Mediterranean tree. ② a piece of cork pushed into the end of a bottle to close it.

corkscrew NOUN a device for pulling corks out of bottles.

corn NOUN ① Corn refers to crops such as wheat and barley and to their seeds. ② a small painful area of hard skin on your foot.

cornea *[Said* ***kor****-nee-a]* NOUN the transparent skin that covers the outside of your eyeball.

corner NOUN ① a place where two sides or edges of something meet. ▶ VERB ② To corner a person or animal is to get them into a place they cannot escape from.

cornflour NOUN Cornflour is a fine white flour made from maize and used in cooking to thicken sauces.

corny, **cornier**, **corniest** ADJECTIVE very obvious or sentimental and not at all original • *corny old love songs*.

> **corny** ADJECTIVE
> = banal, hackneyed, maudlin, sentimental, stale, stereotyped, trite

coronary, **coronaries** NOUN If someone has a coronary, blood cannot reach their heart because of a blood clot.

coronation NOUN the ceremony at which a king or queen is crowned.

coronavirus NOUN a type of virus that causes colds and diseases such as COVID-19.

coroner NOUN an official who investigates the deaths of people who have died in a violent or unusual way.

corporal NOUN an officer of low rank in the army or air force.

corporal punishment NOUN Corporal punishment is the punishing of people by beating them.

corporate ADJECTIVE (*formal*) belonging to or done by all members of a group together.

corporation NOUN ① a large business. ② a group of people responsible for running a city.

corps *[Rhymes with* ***more****]* NOUN ① a part of an army with special duties • *the Engineering Corps*. ② a small group of people who do a special job • *the world press corps*.

corpse NOUN a dead body.

correct ADJECTIVE ① If something is correct, there are no mistakes in it. ② The correct thing in a particular situation is the right one • *Each has the correct number of coins*. ③ Correct behaviour is considered to be socially acceptable. ▶ VERB ④ If you correct something which is wrong, you make it right. **correctly** ADVERB **corrective** ADJECTIVE, NOUN

> **correct** ADJECTIVE
> ① = accurate, exact, faultless, flawless, precise, right, true
> ③ = acceptable, appropriate, fitting, okay, OK, proper, seemly (*old-fashioned*)
> ≠ wrong
> ▶ VERB ④ = amend, cure, improve, rectify, reform, remedy, right

correction NOUN the act of making something right.

> **correction** NOUN
> = adjustment, amendment, righting

correlate VERB If two things correlate or are correlated, they are closely connected or strongly influence each other • *Obesity correlates with health problems*. **correlation** NOUN

correspond VERB ① If one thing corresponds to another, it has a similar purpose, function or status. ② MATHS If numbers or amounts correspond, they are the same. ③ When people correspond, they write to each other.

> **correspond** VERB
> ① = agree, be related, coincide, correlate, fit, match, tally

correspondence NOUN ① Correspondence is the writing of letters; also the letters written. ② If there is a correspondence between two things, they are closely related or very similar.

correspondent NOUN a newspaper, television or radio reporter.

corresponding ADJECTIVE ① You use 'corresponding' to describe a change that results from a change in something else • *the rise in inflation and corresponding rise in prices*. ② You also use 'corresponding' to describe something which has a similar purpose or status to something else • *Alfard is the corresponding Western name for the star*. **correspondingly** ADVERB

corridor NOUN a passage that connects different parts of a building.

corrode VERB [SCIENCE] When metal corrodes, it is gradually destroyed by a chemical or rust. **corrosion** NOUN **corrosive** ADJECTIVE

corrugated ADJECTIVE Corrugated metal or cardboard is made in parallel folds to make it stronger.

corrupt ADJECTIVE ① Corrupt people act dishonestly or illegally in return for money or power • *corrupt ministers*. ▸ VERB ② To corrupt someone means to make them dishonest. ③ To corrupt someone also means to make them immoral. **corruptible** ADJECTIVE

> **corrupt** ADJECTIVE
> ① = crooked, dishonest, fraudulent, shady (*informal*), unscrupulous
> ≠ honest
> ▸ VERB ② = bribe, buy off, fix (*informal*)

corruption NOUN Corruption is dishonesty and illegal behaviour by people in positions of power.

> **corruption** NOUN
> = bribery, dishonesty, fraud

corset NOUN Corsets are stiff underwear worn round the hips and waist to make them look slimmer.

cosmetic NOUN ① Cosmetics are substances such as lipstick and face powder which are intended to make someone more attractive. ▸ ADJECTIVE ② Cosmetic changes improve the appearance of something without changing its basic nature.

cosmic ADJECTIVE belonging or relating to the universe.

cosmopolitan ADJECTIVE A cosmopolitan place is full of people from many countries.

cosmos NOUN The cosmos is the universe.

cost, **costs**, **costing**, **cost** NOUN ① The cost of something is the amount of money needed to buy it, do it, or make it. ② The cost of achieving something is the loss or injury in achieving it • *the total cost in human misery*. ▸ VERB ③ You use 'cost' to talk about the amount of money you have to pay for things • *The air fares were going to cost a lot*. ④ If a mistake costs you something, you lose that thing because of the mistake • *a reckless gamble that could cost him his job*.

> **cost** NOUN
> ① = charge, expense, outlay, payment, price, rate
> ② = detriment, expense, penalty
> ▸ VERB ③ = come to, sell at, set someone back (*informal*)

costly, **costlier**, **costliest** ADJECTIVE expensive • *a costly piece of furniture*.

costume NOUN ① [DRAMA] a set of clothes worn by an actor. ② Costume is the clothing worn in a particular place or during a particular period • *eighteenth-century costume*.

cosy, **cosier**, **cosiest** ADJECTIVE ① warm and comfortable • *her cosy new flat*. ② Cosy activities are pleasant and friendly • *a cosy chat*. **cosily** ADVERB **cosiness** NOUN

cosy ADJECTIVE
① = comfortable, snug, warm
② = friendly, informal, intimate, relaxed

cot NOUN a small bed for a baby, with bars or panels round it to stop the baby falling out.

cottage NOUN a small house in the country.

cottage cheese NOUN Cottage cheese is a type of soft white lumpy cheese.

cotton NOUN ① Cotton is cloth made from the soft fibres of the cotton plant. ② Cotton is also thread used for sewing.

cotton wool NOUN Cotton wool is soft fluffy cotton, often used for dressing wounds.

couch NOUN ① a long, soft piece of furniture which more than one person can sit on. ▸ VERB ② If a statement is couched in a particular type of language, it is expressed in that language • *a comment couched in impertinent terms.*

cough [*Said* ***koff***] VERB ① When you cough, you force air out of your throat with a sudden harsh noise. ▸ NOUN ② an illness that makes you cough a lot; also the noise you make when you cough.

could VERB ① You use 'could' to say that you were able or allowed to do something • *He could hear voices* • *She could come and go as she wanted.* ② You also use 'could' to say that something might happen or might be the case • *It could rain.* ③ You use 'could' when you are asking for something politely • *Could you tell me the name of that film?*

council NOUN ① CITIZENSHIP a group of people elected to look after the affairs of a town, district or county. ② Some other groups have Council as part of their name • *the World Gold Council.*

council NOUN
① = assembly, board, committee, panel

councillor NOUN CITIZENSHIP an elected member of a local council.

counsel, counsels, counselling, counselled NOUN ① (*formal*) To give someone counsel is to give them advice. ▸ VERB ② To counsel people is to give them advice about their problems. **counselling** NOUN **counsellor** NOUN

count VERB ① To count is to say all the numbers in order up to a particular number. ② If you count all the things in a group, you add them up to see how many there are. ③ What counts in a situation is whatever is most important. ④ To count as something means to be regarded as that thing • *I'm not sure whether this counts as harassment.* ⑤ If you can count on someone or something, you can rely on them. ▸ NOUN ⑥ a number reached by counting. ⑦ (*formal*) If something is wrong on a particular count, it is wrong in that respect. ⑧ a European nobleman.

count VERB
② = add up, calculate, tally
③ = carry weight, matter, rate, signify, weigh
▸ NOUN ⑥ = calculation, reckoning, sum, tally

countdown NOUN the counting aloud of numbers in reverse order before something happens, especially before a spacecraft is launched.

countenance (*formal*) NOUN ① Someone's countenance is their face. ▸ VERB ② To countenance something means to allow or accept it • *I will not countenance behaviour of this sort.*

counter NOUN ① a long, flat surface

over which goods are sold in a shop. ② a small, flat, round object used in board games. ▶ **VERB** ③ If you counter something that is being done, you take action to make it less effective • *I countered that argument with a reference to our sales report.*

counteract **VERB** To counteract something is to reduce its effect by producing an opposite effect.

counteract **VERB**
= act against, offset

counterfeit *[Said **kown**-ter-fit]* **ADJECTIVE** ① Something counterfeit is not genuine but has been made to look genuine to deceive people • *counterfeit money.* ▶ **VERB** ② To counterfeit something is to make a counterfeit version of it.

counterpart **NOUN** The counterpart of a person or thing is another person or thing with a similar function in a different place • *The Irish prime minister called his French counterpart to discuss the issue.*

counterterrorism **NOUN** Counterterrorism is action to prevent terrorist attacks or destroy terrorist groups.

countess **NOUN** the wife of a count or earl, or a woman with the same rank as a count or earl.

counting **PREPOSITION** You say 'counting' when including something in a calculation • *six students, not counting me.*

countless **ADJECTIVE** too many to count • *There had been countless demonstrations.*

countless **ADJECTIVE**
= infinite, innumerable, myriad, untold

country, **countries** **NOUN** ① GEOGRAPHY one of the political areas the world is divided into. ② The country is land away from towns and cities. ③ 'Country' is used to refer to an area with particular features or associations • *the heart of coal country.*

country **NOUN**
① = kingdom, land, state
② = bush (*New Zealand and South African*), countryside, outback (*Australian and New Zealand*), outdoors

countryman, **countrymen** **NOUN** Your countrymen are people from your own country.

countryside **NOUN** The countryside is land away from towns and cities.

county, **counties** **NOUN** GEOGRAPHY a region with its own local government.

coup *[Said **koo**]* or **coup d'état** *[Said koo day-**tah**]* **NOUN** HISTORY When there is a coup, a group of people seize power in a country.

couple **NOUN** ① two people who are married or are involved in a romantic relationship. ② A couple of things or people means two of them • *a couple of weeks ago.* ▶ **VERB** ③ If one thing is coupled with another, the two things are done or dealt with together • *Its stores offer high quality coupled with low prices.*

coupon **NOUN** ① a piece of printed paper which, when you hand it in, entitles you to pay less than usual for something. ② a form you fill in to ask for information or to enter a competition.

courage **NOUN** Courage is the quality shown by people who do things knowing they are dangerous or difficult. **courageous** **ADJECTIVE** **courageously** **ADVERB**

courage **NOUN**
= bravery, daring, guts (*informal*), heroism, nerve, pluck, valour
≠ fear

courgette *[Said koor-**jet**]* **NOUN** a type of small marrow with dark green skin. Courgettes are also called **zucchini**.

courier *[Said* ***koo****-ree-er]* **NOUN** someone employed to collect and deliver letters and packages.

course **NOUN** ① a series of lessons or lectures. ② a series of medical treatments • *a course of injections*. ③ one of the parts of a meal. ④ A course or a course of action is one of the things you can do in a situation. ⑤ a piece of land where a sport such as golf is played. ⑥ the route a ship or aircraft takes. ⑦ If something happens in the course of a period of time, it happens during that period • *One hundred people joined in the course of the day*. ▸ **PHRASE** ⑧ If you say **of course**, you are showing that something is totally expected or that you are sure about something • *Of course she wouldn't do that*.

> **course** **NOUN**
> ① = classes, curriculum
> ④ = plan, policy, procedure
> ⑥ = direction, line, path, route, trajectory, way

court **NOUN** ① CITIZENSHIP a place where legal matters are decided by a judge and jury or a magistrate. The judge and jury or magistrate can also be referred to as the court. ② a place where a game such as tennis or badminton is played. ③ the place where a king or queen lives and carries out ceremonial duties. ▸ **VERB** ④ (*old-fashioned*) If two people are courting, they are spending a lot of time together because they intend to get married.

> **court** **NOUN**
> ① = bench, law court, tribunal
> ▸ **VERB** ④ = go steady, woo

courteous *[Said* ***kur****-tee-yuss]* **ADJECTIVE** Courteous behaviour is polite and considerate.

courtesy **NOUN** Courtesy is polite, considerate behaviour.

> **courtesy** **NOUN**
> = civility, courteousness, gallantry, good manners, grace, graciousness, politeness

courtier **NOUN** Courtiers were noblemen and noblewomen at the court of a king or queen.

courtship **NOUN** (*formal*) Courtship is the activity of courting or the period of time during which two people are courting.

courtyard **NOUN** a flat area of ground surrounded by buildings or walls.

cousin **NOUN** Your cousin is the child of your uncle or aunt.

cove **NOUN** a small bay.

covenant *[Said* ***kuv****-vi-nant]* **NOUN** a formal written agreement or promise.

cover **VERB** ① If you cover something, you put something else over it to protect it or hide it. ② If something covers something else, it forms a layer over it • *Tears covered his face*. ③ If you cover a particular distance, you travel that distance • *He covered 52 kilometres in 210 laps*. ▸ **NOUN** ④ something put over an object to protect it or keep it warm. ⑤ The cover of a book or magazine is its outside. ⑥ Insurance cover is a guarantee that money will be paid if something is lost or harmed. ⑦ In the open, cover consists of trees, rocks or other places where you can shelter or hide. **cover up** **VERB** If you cover up something you do not want people to know about, you hide it from them • *He lied to cover up his crime*. **cover-up** **NOUN**

> **cover** **VERB**
> ① = cloak, conceal, cover up, hide, mask, obscure, screen, shade
> ≠ reveal

A B C D E F G H I J K L M N O P Q R S T U V W X Y Z

② = coat, overlay
▸ **NOUN** ④ = case, coating, covering, jacket, mask, screen, wrapper

coverage **NOUN** The coverage of something in the news is the reporting of it.

covering **NOUN** a layer of something which protects or conceals something else • *A morning blizzard left a covering of snow.*

covert [*Said* **koh**-*vert*] **ADJECTIVE** (*formal*) Covert activities are secret, rather than open. **covertly** **ADVERB**

COVID-19; also spelt **Covid-19** **NOUN** a serious infectious disease that affects the lungs.

cow **NOUN** a large animal kept on farms for its milk.

cow **NOUN**
= bovine (*formal*), cattle

coward **NOUN** someone who is easily frightened and who avoids dangerous or difficult situations. **cowardice** **NOUN**

coward **NOUN**
= chicken (*slang*), wimp (*informal*)

cowardly **ADJECTIVE** easily scared.

cowardly **ADJECTIVE**
= chicken (*slang*), faint-hearted, gutless (*informal*), sookie (*New Zealand*)
≠ brave

cowboy **NOUN** a man employed to look after cattle in America.

cower **VERB** When someone cowers, they crouch or move backwards because they are afraid.

cower **VERB**
= cringe, quail, shrink

coy **ADJECTIVE** If someone is coy, they pretend to be shy and modest. **coyly** **ADVERB**

coyote [*Said* koy-**ote**-*ee*] **NOUN** a North American animal like a small wolf.

crab **NOUN** a sea creature with four pairs of legs, two pincers, and a flat, round body covered by a shell.

crack **VERB** ① If something cracks, it becomes damaged, with lines appearing on its surface. ② If you crack a joke, you tell it. ③ If you crack a problem or code, you solve it. ▸ **NOUN** ④ one of the lines appearing on something when it cracks. ⑤ a narrow gap. ▸ **ADJECTIVE** ⑥ A crack soldier, sportsman or sportswoman is highly trained and skilful.

crack **VERB**
① = break, fracture, snap
③ = decipher, solve, work out
▸ **NOUN** ④ = break, cleft, crevice, fracture

cracker **NOUN** ① a thin, crisp biscuit that is often eaten with cheese. ② a paper-covered tube that pulls apart with a bang and usually has a toy and paper hat inside.

crackle **VERB** ① If something crackles, it makes a rapid series of short, harsh noises. ▸ **NOUN** ② a short, harsh noise.

cradle **NOUN** ① a box-shaped bed for a baby. ▸ **VERB** ② If you cradle something in your arms or hands, you hold it there carefully.

craft **NOUN** ① an activity such as weaving, carving or pottery. ② a skilful occupation • *the writer's craft*. ③ a boat, plane or spacecraft.

craftsman, **craftsmen** **NOUN** a man who makes things skilfully with his hands. **craftsmanship** **NOUN**

craftswoman, **craftswomen** **NOUN** a woman who makes things skilfully with her hands.

crafty, **craftier**, **craftiest** **ADJECTIVE** Someone who is crafty gets what they want by tricking people in a clever way.

crafty ADJECTIVE
= artful, cunning, devious, scheming, slippery, sly, wily

craggy, **craggier**, **craggiest** ADJECTIVE A craggy mountain or cliff is steep and rocky.

cram, **crams**, **cramming**, **crammed** VERB If you cram people or things into a place, you put more in than there is room for.

cram VERB
= jam, pack, squeeze, stuff

cramp NOUN Cramp or cramps is a pain caused by a muscle contracting.

cramped ADJECTIVE If a room or building is cramped, it is not big enough for the people or things in it.

cranberry, **cranberries** NOUN Cranberries are sour-tasting red berries, often made into a sauce.

crane NOUN ① a machine that moves heavy things by lifting them in the air. ② a large bird with a long neck and long legs. ▸ VERB ③ If you crane your neck, you extend your head in a particular direction to see or hear something better.

crank NOUN ① (*informal*) someone with strange ideas who behaves in an odd way. ② a device you turn to make something move • *The adjustment is made by turning the crank.* ▸ VERB ③ If you crank something, you make it move by turning a handle.

cranny, **crannies** NOUN a very narrow opening in a wall or rock • *nooks and crannies.*

crash NOUN ① an accident in which a moving vehicle hits something violently. ② a sudden loud noise • *the crash of the waves on the rocks.* ③ the sudden failure of a business or financial institution. ▸ VERB ④ When a vehicle crashes, it hits something and is badly damaged. ⑤ If a computer or a computer program crashes, it fails suddenly.

crash NOUN
① = accident, bump (*informal*), collision, pile-up (*informal*), smash (*informal*)
② = bang, clash, din, smash
③ = bankruptcy, collapse, depression, failure, ruin
▸ VERB ④ = bump (*informal*), collide, drive into, have an accident, plough into (*informal*), wreck

crate NOUN a large box used for transporting or storing things.

crater NOUN GEOGRAPHY a wide hole in the ground caused by something hitting it or by an explosion.

crave VERB If you crave something, you want it very much • *He craves attention.* **craving** NOUN

crawl VERB ① When you crawl, you move forward on your hands and knees. ② When a vehicle crawls, it moves very slowly. ③ (*informal*) If a place is crawling with people or things, it is full of them • *The place is crawling with tourists.* **crawler** NOUN

crawl VERB
③ = be alive with, be full of, be overrun, swarm, teem

crayfish, **crayfishes** or **crayfish** NOUN a small shellfish like a lobster.

crayon NOUN a coloured pencil or a stick of coloured wax.

craze NOUN something that is very popular for a short time.

craze NOUN
= fad, fashion, trend, vogue

crazy, **crazier**, **craziest** ADJECTIVE (*informal*) ① very strange or foolish • *The guy is crazy* • *a crazy idea.* ② If you are crazy about something, you are very keen on it • *I was crazy about dancing.* **crazily** ADVERB **craziness** NOUN

crazy ADJECTIVE
① = foolish, insane, mad, ridiculous, wild, zany
≠ sensible
② = fanatical, mad, obsessed, passionate, smitten, wild

creak VERB ① If something creaks, it makes a harsh sound when it moves or when you stand on it. ▶ NOUN ② a harsh squeaking noise. **creaky** ADJECTIVE

cream NOUN ① Cream is a thick, yellowish-white liquid taken from the top of milk. ② Cream is also a substance people can rub on their skin. ▶ ADJECTIVE ③ yellowish-white. **creamy** ADJECTIVE

crease NOUN ① an irregular line that appears on cloth or paper when it is crumpled. ② a straight line on something that has been pressed or folded neatly. ▶ VERB ③ To crease something is to make lines appear on it. **creased** ADJECTIVE

create VERB ① To create something is to cause it to happen or exist • *This is absolutely vital but creates a problem.* ② When someone creates a new product or process, they invent it. **creator** NOUN **creation** NOUN

create VERB
① = bring about, cause, lead to, occasion (*formal*)
② = coin, compose, devise, formulate, invent, originate

creative ADJECTIVE ① Creative people are able to invent and develop original ideas. ② Creative activities involve the inventing and developing of original ideas • *creative writing.* **creatively** ADVERB **creativity** NOUN

creative ADJECTIVE
① = fertile, imaginative, inspired, inventive

creature NOUN any living thing that moves about.

credence NOUN (*formal*) If something gives credence to a theory or story, it makes it easier to believe.

credentials PLURAL NOUN Your credentials are your past achievements or other things in your background that make you qualified for something.

credible ADJECTIVE If someone or something is credible, you can believe or trust them. **credibility** NOUN

credit NOUN ① If you are allowed credit, you can take something and pay for it later • *to buy goods on credit.* ② If you get the credit for something, people praise you for it. ③ If you say someone is a credit to their family or school, you mean that their family or school should be proud of them. ④ (*in plural*) The list of people who helped make a film, recording or television programme is called the credits. ▶ PHRASE ⑤ If someone or their bank account is **in credit**, their account has money in it. ▶ VERB ⑥ If you are credited with an achievement, people believe that you were responsible for it.

credit NOUN
② = commendation, glory, praise, recognition, thanks
≠ disgrace

creditable ADJECTIVE satisfactory or fairly good • *a creditable performance.*

credit card NOUN a plastic card that allows someone to buy goods on credit.

creditor NOUN Your creditors are the people you owe money to.

creed NOUN ① a religion. ② any set of beliefs • *her political creed.*

creek NOUN a narrow inlet where the sea comes a long way into the land.

creep, **creeps**, **creeping**, **crept** VERB To creep is to move quietly and slowly.

creepy, **creepier**, **creepiest** ADJECTIVE (*informal*) strange and frightening • *a creepy feeling.*

> **creepy** ADJECTIVE
> = disturbing, eerie, macabre, scary (*informal*), sinister, spooky, unnatural

cremate VERB When someone is cremated, their dead body is burned during a funeral service. **cremation** NOUN

crematorium, **crematoriums** or **crematoria** NOUN a building in which the bodies of dead people are burned.

crepe [*Said* ***krayp***] NOUN ① Crepe is a thin ridged material made from cotton, silk or wool. ② Crepe is also a type of rubber with a rough surface.

crept the past tense and past participle of **creep**.

crescendo, **crescendos** [*Said krish-**en**-doe*] NOUN MUSIC When there is a crescendo in a piece of music, the music gets louder.

crescent NOUN a curved shape that is wider in its middle than at the ends, which are pointed.

crest NOUN ① The crest of a hill or wave is its highest part. ② a tuft of feathers on top of a bird's head. ③ a small picture or design that is the emblem of a noble family, a town, or an organisation. **crested** ADJECTIVE

crevice NOUN a narrow crack or gap in rock.

crew NOUN ① The crew of a ship, aeroplane or spacecraft are the people who operate it. ② people with special technical skills who work together • *the camera crew.*

crib, **cribs**, **cribbing**, **cribbed** VERB ① (*informal*) If you crib, you copy what someone else has written and pretend it is your own work. ▸ NOUN ② (*old-fashioned*) a baby's cot.

cricket NOUN ① Cricket is an outdoor game played by two teams who take turns at scoring runs by hitting a ball with a bat. ② a small jumping insect that produces sounds by rubbing its wings together. **cricketer** NOUN

crime NOUN an action for which you can be punished by law • *a serious crime.*

> **crime** NOUN
> = misdemeanour, offence, violation, wrong

criminal NOUN ① someone who has committed a crime. ▸ ADJECTIVE ② involving or related to crime • *criminal activities.* **criminally** ADVERB

> **criminal** NOUN
> ① = crook (*informal*), culprit, delinquent, offender, skelm (*South African*), villain
> ▸ ADJECTIVE ② = corrupt, crooked, illegal, illicit, unlawful
> ≠ legal

criminology NOUN the scientific study of crime and criminals. **criminologist** NOUN

crimson NOUN, ADJECTIVE dark purplish-red.

cringe VERB If you cringe, you back away from someone or something because you are afraid or embarrassed.

cripple VERB ① To cripple someone is to injure them severely. ② To cripple a company or country is to prevent it from working. **crippled** ADJECTIVE **crippling** ADJECTIVE

> **cripple** VERB
> ② = bring to a standstill, impair, put out of action

crisis, **crises** [*Said **kry**-seez in the plural*] NOUN a serious or dangerous situation.

crisp ADJECTIVE ① Something that is crisp is pleasantly fresh and firm

• *crisp lettuce leaves*. ② If the air or the weather is crisp, it is pleasantly fresh, cold and dry • *crisp wintry days*. ▶ NOUN ③ Crisps are thin slices of potato fried until they are hard and crunchy.

crispy, **crispier**, **crispiest** ADJECTIVE Crispy food is pleasantly hard and crunchy • *a crispy salad*.

criterion, **criteria** *[Said kry-**teer**-ee-on]* NOUN a standard by which you judge or decide something.

critic NOUN ① someone who writes reviews of books, films, plays or musical performances. ② A critic of a person or system is someone who criticises them publicly • *the government's critics*.

critical ADJECTIVE ① A critical time is one which is very important in determining what happens in the future • *critical months in the history of the world*. ② A critical situation is a very serious one • *Rock music is in a critical state*. ③ If an ill or injured person is critical, they are in danger of dying. ④ If you are critical of something or someone, you express severe judgments or opinions about them. ⑤ If you are critical, you examine and judge something carefully • *Learning facts is not so important as critical thinking*.
critically ADVERB

> **critical** ADJECTIVE
> ① = crucial, deciding, decisive, momentous, pivotal, vital
> ≠ unimportant
> ② = grave (*formal*), precarious, serious
> ④ = carping, derogatory, disapproving, disparaging, scathing
> ≠ complimentary

criticise; also spelt **criticize** VERB If you criticise someone or something, you say what you think is wrong with them.

> **criticise** VERB
> = censure (*formal*), condemn, find fault with, knock (*informal*), pan (*informal*), put down (*informal*)
> ≠ praise

criticism NOUN ① When there is criticism of someone or something, people express disapproval of them. ② If you make a criticism, you point out a fault you think someone or something has.

> **criticism** NOUN
> ① = censure (*formal*), disapproval, disparagement, fault-finding, flak (*informal*), panning (*informal*)
> ≠ praise

croak VERB ① When animals and birds croak, they make harsh, low sounds. ▶ NOUN ② a harsh, low sound.

Croatian ADJECTIVE ① belonging or relating to Croatia. ▶ NOUN ② someone who comes from Croatia. ③ Croatian is the form of Serbo-Croat spoken in Croatia.

crochet, **crochets**, **crocheting**, **crocheted** *[Said **kroh**-shay]* NOUN ① Crochet is a way of making clothes and other things out of thread using a needle with a small hook at the end. ▶ VERB ② If someone crochets clothes, they make them out of thread using a needle with a small hook at the end.

crockery NOUN Crockery is plates, cups and saucers.

crocodile NOUN a large, scaly, meat-eating reptile which lives in tropical rivers.

croissant *[Said **krwah**-son]* NOUN a light, crescent-shaped roll eaten at breakfast.

crony, **cronies** NOUN (*old-fashioned*) Your cronies are the friends you spend a lot of time with.

crook NOUN ① (*informal*) a criminal.

② The crook of your arm or leg is the soft inside part where you bend your elbow or knee. ▶ ADJECTIVE ③ In Australian English, crook means ill.

crook NOUN
① = cheat, rogue, scoundrel (*old-fashioned*), shark (*informal*), swindler, thief, villain
▶ ADJECTIVE ③ = ill, nauseous, poorly (*British; informal*), queasy, sick, under the weather (*informal*), unwell

crooked [*Said **kroo**-kid*] ADJECTIVE ① bent or twisted. ② (*informal*) Someone who is crooked is dishonest.

crooked ADJECTIVE
① = bent, deformed, distorted, irregular, out of shape, twisted, warped
≠ straight
② = corrupt, criminal, dishonest, fraudulent, illegal, shady (*informal*)
≠ honest

croon VERB To croon is to sing or hum quietly and gently • *He crooned a love song*.

crop, **crops**, **cropping**, **cropped** NOUN ① Crops are plants such as wheat and potatoes that are grown for food. ② the plants collected at harvest time • *You should have two crops in the year*. ▶ VERB ③ To crop someone's hair is to cut it very short. **crop up** VERB (*informal*) If something crops up, it happens unexpectedly.

croquet [*Said **kroh**-kay*] NOUN Croquet is a game in which the players use long-handled mallets to hit balls through metal arches pushed into a lawn.

cross VERB ① If you cross something such as a room or a road, you go to the other side of it. ② Lines or roads that cross meet and go across each other. ③ If a thought crosses your mind, you think of it. ④ If you cross your arms, legs or fingers, you put one on top of the other. ▶ NOUN ⑤ a vertical bar or line crossed by a shorter horizontal bar or line; also used to describe any object shaped like this. ⑥ RE The Cross is the cross-shaped structure on which Jesus Christ was crucified. A cross is also any symbol representing Christ's Cross. ⑦ a written mark shaped like an X • *Mark the wrong answers with a cross*. ⑧ Something that is a cross between two things is neither one thing nor the other, but a mixture of both. ▶ ADJECTIVE ⑨ Someone who is cross is rather angry. **crossly** ADVERB **cross out** VERB If you cross out words on a page, you draw a line through them because they are wrong or because you do not want people to read them.

cross VERB
① = ford, go across, span, traverse
② = crisscross, intersect
▶ NOUN ⑧ = blend, combination, mixture
▶ ADJECTIVE ⑨ = angry, annoyed, fractious, fretful, grumpy, in a bad mood, irritable

crossbow NOUN HISTORY a weapon consisting of a small bow fixed at the end of a piece of wood.

cross-country NOUN ① Cross-country is the sport of running across open countryside, rather than on roads or on a track. ▶ ADVERB, ADJECTIVE ② across open countryside.

crossfire NOUN Crossfire is gunfire crossing the same place from opposite directions.

crossing NOUN ① a place where you can cross a road safely. ② a journey by ship to a place on the other side of the sea.

cross-legged ADJECTIVE If you are sitting cross-legged, you are sitting on the floor with your knees pointing outwards and your feet tucked under them.

cross section NOUN A cross section of a group of people is a representative sample of them.

crossword NOUN a puzzle in which you work out the answers to clues and write them in the white squares of a pattern of black and white squares.

crotch NOUN the part of your body between the tops of your legs.

crouch VERB If you are crouching, you are leaning forward with your legs bent under you.

> **crouch** VERB
> = bend down, squat

crow NOUN ① a large black bird which makes a loud, harsh noise. ▸ VERB ② When a cock crows, it utters a loud squawking sound.

crowbar NOUN a heavy iron bar used as a lever or for forcing things open.

crowd NOUN ① a large group of people gathered together. ▸ VERB ② When people crowd somewhere, they gather there close together or in large numbers.

> **crowd** NOUN
> ① = horde, host, mass, mob, multitude, swarm, throng
> ▸ VERB ② = congregate, gather, swarm, throng

crowded ADJECTIVE A crowded place is full of people.

> **crowded** ADJECTIVE
> = congested, full, overflowing, packed

crown NOUN ① a circular ornament worn on a royal person's head. ② The crown of something such as your head is the top part of it. ▸ VERB ③ When a king or queen is crowned, a crown is put on their head during their coronation ceremony. ④ When something crowns an event, it is the final part of it • *The news crowned a dreadful week.*

crucial *[Said **kroo**-shl]* ADJECTIVE If something is crucial, it is very important in determining how something else will be in the future.

> **crucial** ADJECTIVE
> = central, critical, decisive, momentous, pivotal, vital

crucifix NOUN [RE] a cross with a figure representing Jesus Christ being crucified on it.

crucify, **crucifies**, **crucifying**, **crucified** VERB [RE] To crucify someone is to tie or nail them to a large wooden cross and leave them there to die. **crucifixion** NOUN

crude ADJECTIVE ① rough and simple • *a crude weapon* • *a crude method of entry.* ② A crude person speaks or behaves in a rude and offensive way • *You can be quite crude at times.* **crudely** ADVERB **crudity** NOUN

> **crude** ADJECTIVE
> ① = primitive, rough, rudimentary, simple
> ② = coarse, tasteless, vulgar
> ≠ refined

cruel ADJECTIVE Cruel people deliberately cause pain or distress to other people or to animals. **cruelly** ADVERB

> **cruel** ADJECTIVE
> = barbarous, brutal, callous, cold-blooded, heartless, inhumane, sadistic, savage, vicious
> ≠ compassionate, kind

cruelty NOUN cruel behaviour.

> **cruelty** NOUN
> = barbarity, brutality, callousness, inhumanity, savagery, viciousness
> ≠ compassion, kindness

cruise NOUN ① a holiday in which you travel on a ship and visit places.

▸ **VERB** ② When a vehicle cruises, it moves at a constant moderate speed.

cruiser **NOUN** ① a motor boat with a cabin you can sleep in. ② a large, fast warship.

crumb **NOUN** Crumbs are very small pieces of bread or cake.

crumble **VERB** When something crumbles, it breaks into small pieces.

crumbly, **crumblier**, **crumbliest** **ADJECTIVE** Something crumbly easily breaks into small pieces.

crumple **VERB** To crumple paper or cloth is to squash it so that it is full of creases and folds.

> **crumple** **VERB**
> = crease, crush, screw up, wrinkle

crunch **VERB** If you crunch something, you crush it noisily, for example between your teeth or under your feet.

crunchy, **crunchier**, **crunchiest** **ADJECTIVE** Crunchy food is hard or crisp and makes a noise when you eat it.

crusade **NOUN** a long and determined attempt to achieve something • *the crusade for human rights*. **crusader** **NOUN**

crush **VERB** ① To crush something is to destroy its shape by squeezing it. ② To crush a substance is to turn it into liquid or powder by squeezing or grinding it. ③ To crush an army or political organisation is to defeat it completely. ▸ **NOUN** ④ a dense crowd of people.

> **crush** **VERB**
> ① = crumble, crumple, mash, squash
> ③ = overcome, put down, quell, stamp out, vanquish (*literary*)

crust **NOUN** ① the hard outside part of a loaf. ② a hard layer on top of something • *The snow had a fine crust on it*. ③ GEOGRAPHY the outer layer of the earth.

crusty, **crustier**, **crustiest** **ADJECTIVE** ① Something that is crusty has a hard outside layer. ② Crusty people are impatient and irritable.

crutch **NOUN** a support like a long stick which you lean on to help you walk when you have an injured foot or leg.

crux, **cruxes** **NOUN** the most important or difficult part of a problem or argument.

cry, **cries**, **crying**, **cried** **VERB** ① When you cry, tears appear in your eyes. ② To cry something is to shout it or say it loudly • *'See you soon!' they cried*. ▸ **NOUN** ③ If you have a cry, you cry for a period of time. ④ a shout or other loud sound made with your voice. ⑤ a loud sound made by some birds • *the cry of a seagull*. **cry off** **VERB** (*informal*) If you cry off, you change your mind and decide not to do something. **cry out for** **VERB** (*informal*) If something is crying out for something else, it needs it very much.

> **cry** **VERB**
> ① = blubber, howl, sob, wail, weep
> ② = call, exclaim, shout, yell
> ▸ **NOUN** ④ = call, exclamation, shout, yell

crypt **NOUN** an underground room beneath a church, usually used as a burial place.

cryptic **ADJECTIVE** A cryptic remark or message has a hidden meaning.

crystal **NOUN** ① a piece of a mineral that has formed naturally into a regular shape. ② Crystal is a type of transparent rock, used in jewellery. ③ Crystal is also a kind of very high quality glass. **crystalline** **ADJECTIVE**

crystallise; also spelt **crystallize** **VERB** ① If a substance crystallises, it turns into crystals. ② If an idea crystallises, it becomes clear in your mind.

cub NOUN ① Some young wild animals are called cubs • *a lion cub.* ② The Cubs is an organisation for young boys before they join the Scouts.

Cuban [*Said* ***kyoo****-ban*] ADJECTIVE ① belonging or relating to Cuba. ▶ NOUN ② someone who comes from Cuba.

cube MATHS NOUN ① a three-dimensional shape with six equally-sized square surfaces. ② The cube of a number is the number multiplied by itself twice. For example, the cube of 4, written 4^3, is 4 x 4 x 4. ▶ VERB ③ To cube a number is to multiply it by itself twice.

cubic ADJECTIVE MATHS used in measurements of volume • *cubic centimetres.*

cubicle NOUN a small enclosed area in a place such as a sports centre, where you can dress and undress.

cuckoo, cuckoos NOUN a grey bird with a two-note call that lays its eggs in other birds' nests.

cucumber NOUN a long, thin, green-skinned fruit eaten raw in salads.

cuddle VERB ① If you cuddle someone, you hold them affectionately in your arms. ▶ NOUN ② If you give someone a cuddle, you hold them affectionately in your arms.

cuddly, cuddlier, cuddliest ADJECTIVE Cuddly people, animals or toys are soft or pleasing in some way so that you want to cuddle them.

cue NOUN ① something said or done by a performer that is a signal for another performer to begin • *Chris never misses a cue.* ② a long stick used to hit the balls in snooker and billiards.

cuff NOUN the end part of a sleeve.

cuisine [*Said kwiz-****een***] NOUN The cuisine of a region is the style of cooking that is typical of it.

cul-de-sac [*Said* ***kul****-des-sak*] NOUN a road that does not lead to any other roads because one end is blocked off.

culinary ADJECTIVE (*formal*) connected with the kitchen or cooking.

cull VERB ① If you cull things, you gather them from different places or sources • *information culled from movies.* ② If you cull animals, you kill them in order to reduce their numbers • *culling infected chickens.* ▶ NOUN ③ When there is a cull, weaker animals are killed to reduce the numbers in a group.

culminate VERB To culminate in something is to finally develop into it • *a campaign that culminated in a stunning success.* **culmination** NOUN

culprit NOUN someone who has done something harmful or wrong.

cult NOUN ① A cult is a religious group with special rituals, usually connected with the worship of a particular person. ② 'Cult' is used to refer to any situation in which someone or something is very popular with a large group of people • *the American sports car cult.*

cultivate VERB ① To cultivate land is to grow crops on it. ② If you cultivate a feeling or attitude, you try to develop it in yourself or other people. **cultivation** NOUN

cultural ADJECTIVE ① of or relating to artistic activities • *a cultural festival.* ② of or relating to a culture or civilisation • *cultural diversity.*

culture NOUN ① Culture refers to the arts and to people's appreciation of them • *He was a man of culture.* ② The culture of a particular society is its ideas, customs and art • *Japanese culture.* ③ In science, a culture is a group of bacteria or cells grown in a laboratory. **cultured** ADJECTIVE

cumulative ADJECTIVE Something that is cumulative keeps being added to.

cunning ADJECTIVE ① Someone who is cunning uses clever and deceitful methods to get what they want. ▶ NOUN ② Cunning is the ability to get what you want using clever and deceitful methods. **cunningly** ADVERB

> **cunning** ADJECTIVE
> ① = artful, crafty, devious, sly, wily
> ≠ open
> ▶ NOUN ② = deviousness, guile

cup, **cups**, **cupping**, **cupped** NOUN ① a small, round container with a handle, which you drink out of. ② a large metal container with two handles, given as a prize. ▶ VERB ③ If you cup your hands, you put them together to make a shape like a cup.

cupboard NOUN a piece of furniture with doors and shelves.

curable ADJECTIVE If a disease or illness is curable, it can be cured.

curate NOUN a member of the clergy who helps a vicar or a priest.

curator NOUN the person in a museum or art gallery in charge of its contents.

curb VERB ① To curb something is to keep it within limits • *policies designed to curb inflation*. ▶ NOUN ② If a curb is placed on something, it is kept within limits • *the curb on spending*.

> **curb** VERB
> ① = check, contain, control, limit, restrain, suppress
> ▶ NOUN ② = brake, control, limit, limitation, restraint

cure VERB ① To cure an illness is to end it. ② To cure a sick or injured person is to make them well. ③ If something cures you of a habit or attitude, it stops you having it. ④ To cure food, tobacco or animal skin is to treat it in order to preserve it. ▶ NOUN ⑤ A cure for an illness is something that cures it.

> **cure** VERB
> ② = heal, remedy
> ▶ NOUN ⑤ = medicine, remedy, treatment

curfew NOUN If there is a curfew, people must stay indoors between particular times at night.

curiosity, **curiosities** NOUN ① Curiosity is the desire to know about something or about many things. ② something unusual and interesting.

> **curiosity** NOUN
> ① = inquisitiveness, interest
> ② = freak, marvel, novelty, oddity, rarity

curious ADJECTIVE ① Someone who is curious wants to know more about something. ② Something that is curious is unusual and hard to explain. **curiously** ADVERB

> **curious** ADJECTIVE
> ① = inquiring, inquisitive, interested, nosy (*informal*)
> ≠ incurious
> ② = bizarre, extraordinary, odd, peculiar, singular, strange, unusual
> ≠ ordinary

curl NOUN ① Curls are lengths of hair shaped in tight curves and circles. ② a curved or spiral shape • *the curls of morning fog*. ▶ VERB ③ If something curls, it moves in a curve or spiral. **curly** ADJECTIVE

curler NOUN Curlers are plastic or metal tubes that you can roll your hair round to make it curly.

currency, **currencies** NOUN ① A country's currency is its coins and banknotes or its monetary system generally • *foreign currency • a strong economy and a weak currency.* ② If something such as an idea has currency, it is used a lot at a particular time.

current NOUN ① GEOGRAPHY a strong continuous movement of the water in a river or in the sea. ② GEOGRAPHY An air current is a flowing movement in the air. ③ SCIENCE An electric current is a flow of electricity through a wire or circuit. ▸ ADJECTIVE ④ Something that is current is happening, being done, or being used now. **currently** ADVERB

current NOUN
① = flow, tide, undertow
▸ ADJECTIVE ④ = contemporary, fashionable, ongoing, present, present-day, today's, up-to-the-minute
≠ past

current affairs PLURAL NOUN Current affairs are political and social events discussed in newspapers and on television and radio.

curriculum, **curriculums** or **curricula** [*Said kur-**rik**-yoo-lum*] NOUN the different courses taught at a school or university.

curriculum vitae, **curricula vitae** [*Said **vee**-tie*] NOUN Someone's curriculum vitae is a written account of their personal details, education and work experience which they send when they apply for a job.

curry, **curries**, **currying**, **curried** NOUN ① Curry is an Indian dish made with hot spices. ▸ PHRASE ② To **curry favour** with someone means to try to please them by flattering them or doing things to help them.

curse VERB ① To curse is to swear because you are angry. ② If you curse someone or something, you say angry things about them using rude words. ▸ NOUN ③ what you say when you curse. ④ something supernatural that is supposed to cause unpleasant things to happen to someone. ⑤ a thing or person that causes a lot of trouble or distress • *the curse of summer colds.* **cursed** ADJECTIVE

cursor NOUN ICT an arrow or box on a computer screen which indicates where the next letter or symbol will be inserted.

cursory ADJECTIVE When you give something a cursory glance or examination, you look at it briefly without paying attention to detail.

curt ADJECTIVE If someone is curt, they speak in a brief and rather rude way. **curtly** ADVERB

curtail VERB (*formal*) To curtail something is to reduce or restrict it • *Injury curtailed his career.*

curtain NOUN ① a hanging piece of material which can be pulled across a window for privacy or to keep out the light. ② DRAMA a large piece of material which hangs in front of the stage in a theatre until a performance begins.

curve NOUN ① a smooth, gradually bending line. ▸ VERB ② When something curves, it moves in a curve or has the shape of a curve • *The track curved away below him • His mouth curved slightly.* **curved** ADJECTIVE **curvy** ADJECTIVE

curve NOUN
① = arc, bend, trajectory, turn
▸ VERB ② = arc, arch, bend, swerve

cushion NOUN ① a soft object put on a seat to make it more comfortable. ▸ VERB ② To cushion something is to reduce its effect • *We might have helped to cushion the shock for her.*

custard NOUN Custard is a sweet yellow sauce made from milk and eggs or milk and a powder.

A B C D E F G H I J K L M N O P Q R S T U V W X Y Z

custodian NOUN the person in charge of a collection in an art gallery or a museum.

custody NOUN ① To have custody of a child means to have the legal right to keep it and look after it • *She won custody of her younger son.* ▶ PHRASE ② Someone who is **in custody** is being kept in prison until they can be tried in a court. **custodial** ADJECTIVE

custom NOUN ① a traditional activity • *an ancient Chinese custom.* ② something usually done at a particular time or in particular circumstances by a person or by the people in a society • *It was also my custom to do Christmas shows.* ③ Customs is the place at a border, airport or harbour where you have to declare any goods you are bringing into a country. ④ (*formal*) If a shop or business has your custom, you buy things or go there regularly • *Banks are desperate to get your custom.*

> **custom** NOUN
> ① = convention, practice, ritual, tradition
> ② = habit, practice, routine, wont (*formal*)

customary ADJECTIVE usual • *his customary modesty* • *her customary greeting.* **customarily** ADVERB

custom-built or **custom-made** ADJECTIVE Something that is custom-built or custom-made is made to someone's special requirements.

customer NOUN ① A shop's or firm's customers are the people who buy its goods. ② (*informal*) You can use 'customer' to refer to someone when describing what they are like to deal with • *a tough customer.*

> **customer** NOUN
> ① = buyer, client, consumer, patron, purchaser, shopper

cut, cuts, cutting, cut VERB ① If you cut something, you use a knife, scissors or some other sharp tool to mark it or remove parts of it. ② If you cut yourself, you injure yourself on a sharp object. ③ If you cut the amount of something, you reduce it • *Some costs could be cut.* ④ When writing is cut, parts of it are not printed or broadcast. ⑤ To cut from one scene or shot to another in a film is to go instantly to the other scene or shot. ▶ NOUN ⑥ a mark or injury made with a knife or other sharp tool. ⑦ a reduction • *another cut in interest rates.* ⑧ a part in something written that is not printed or broadcast. ⑨ a large piece of meat ready for cooking. ▶ ADJECTIVE ⑩ Well cut clothes have been well designed and made • *this beautifully cut coat.* **cut back** VERB To cut back or cut back on spending means to reduce it. **cutback** NOUN **cut down** VERB If you cut down on an activity, you do it less often • *cutting down on smoking.* **cut off** VERB ① To cut someone or something off means to separate them from things they are normally connected with • *The President had cut himself off from the people.* ② If a supply of something is cut off, you no longer get it • *The water had been cut off.* ③ If your telephone or telephone call is cut off, it is disconnected. **cut out** VERB ① If you cut out something you are doing, you stop doing it • *Cut out eating fatty foods.* ② If an engine cuts out, it suddenly stops working.

> **cut** VERB
> ① = chop, clip, nick, slice, trim
> ③ = cut back, decrease, lower, reduce, slash
> ≠ increase
> ▶ NOUN ⑥ = gash, incision, slash, slit
> ⑦ = cutback, decrease, lowering, reduction, saving
> ≠ increase

cute ADJECTIVE pretty or attractive.

> **cute** ADJECTIVE
> = appealing, attractive, charming, dear, good-looking, gorgeous, pretty
> ≠ ugly

cutlery NOUN Cutlery is knives, forks and spoons.

cutlet NOUN a small piece of meat which you fry or grill.

cutting NOUN ① something cut from a newspaper or magazine. ② a part cut from a plant and used to grow a new plant. ▶ ADJECTIVE ③ A cutting remark is unkind and likely to hurt someone.

CV an abbreviation for **curriculum vitae**.

cyanide *[Said **sigh**-an-nide]* NOUN Cyanide is an extremely poisonous chemical.

cyberspace NOUN all of the data stored in a large computer or network, seen as a place.

cycle VERB ① When you cycle, you ride a bicycle. ▶ NOUN ② a bicycle or a motorcycle. ③ a series of events which is repeated again and again in the same order • *the cycle of births and deaths*. ④ a series of songs or poems intended to be performed or read together.

cyclical or **cyclic** ADJECTIVE happening over and over again in cycles • *a clear cyclical pattern*.

cyclist NOUN someone who rides a bicycle.

cyclone NOUN a violent tropical storm.

cylinder NOUN ① MATHS a three-dimensional shape with two equally-sized flat circular ends joined by a curved surface. ② the part in a motor engine in which the piston moves backwards and forwards. **cylindrical** ADJECTIVE

cynic *[Said **sin**-nik]* NOUN a cynical person.

cynical ADJECTIVE believing that people always behave selfishly or dishonestly. **cynically** ADVERB **cynicism** NOUN

> **cynical** ADJECTIVE
> = distrustful, sceptical

cypress NOUN a type of evergreen tree with small dark green leaves and round cones.

cyst *[Said **sist**]* NOUN a growth containing liquid that can form under your skin or inside your body.

czar another spelling of **tsar**.

Czech *[Said **chek**]* ADJECTIVE ① belonging or relating to the Czech Republic. ▶ NOUN ② someone who comes from the Czech Republic. ③ Czech is the language spoken in the Czech Republic.

Dd

dab, **dabs**, **dabbing**, **dabbed** VERB ① If you dab something, you touch it with quick light strokes • *He dabbed some disinfectant onto the gash.* ▶ NOUN ② a small amount of something that is put on a surface • *a dab of perfume.*

dabble VERB If you dabble in something, you work or play at it without being seriously involved in it • *All his life he dabbled in poetry.*

dad or **daddy**, **daddies** NOUN (*informal*) Your dad or your daddy is your father.

daffodil NOUN A daffodil is an early spring flowering plant, with a yellow trumpet-shaped flower grown from a bulb.

daft ADJECTIVE (*informal*) stupid and not sensible.

> **daft** ADJECTIVE
> = crazy (*informal*), foolish, ludicrous, preposterous, ridiculous, silly, stupid
> ≠ sensible

dagger NOUN a weapon like a short knife.

daily ADJECTIVE ① happening or appearing every day • *our daily visit to the gym.* ▶ ADVERB ② every day • *New messages arrived daily.*

dainty, **daintier**, **daintiest** ADJECTIVE very delicate and pretty. **daintily** ADVERB

dairy, **dairies** NOUN ① a shop or company that supplies milk and milk products. ② in New Zealand, a small shop selling groceries, often outside usual opening hours. ▶ ADJECTIVE ③ Dairy products are foods made from milk, such as butter, cheese, cream and yogurt. ④ A dairy farm is one which keeps cattle to produce milk.

dais [*Said **day**-is*] NOUN a raised platform, normally at one end of a hall and used by a speaker.

daisy, **daisies** NOUN a small wild flower with a yellow centre and small white petals.

dale NOUN a valley.

dam NOUN a barrier built across a river to hold back water.

damage VERB ① To damage something means to harm or spoil it. ▶ NOUN ② Damage to something is injury or harm done to it. ③ Damages is the money awarded by a court to compensate someone for loss or harm. **damaging** ADJECTIVE

> **damage** VERB
> ① = harm, hurt, injure
> ▶ NOUN ② = harm, injury

dame NOUN the title given to a woman who has been awarded the OBE or one of the other British orders of chivalry.

damn [*Said **dam***] VERB ① To damn something or someone means to curse or condemn them. ▶ INTERJECTION ② 'Damn' is a swearword. **damned** ADJECTIVE

damnation [*Said dam-**nay**-shun*] NOUN Damnation is eternal punishment in Hell after death.

damp ADJECTIVE ① slightly wet. ▶ NOUN ② Damp is slight wetness, especially in the air or in the walls of a building. **dampness** NOUN

damp ADJECTIVE
① = clammy, dank, humid, moist, sodden, soggy, wet
▶ NOUN ② = dampness, humidity, moisture

dampen VERB ① If you dampen something, you make it slightly wet. ② To dampen something also means to reduce its liveliness or strength • *The whole episode has rather dampened my enthusiasm.*

damper PHRASE (*informal*) To **put a damper on** something means to stop it being enjoyable.

dance VERB ① To dance means to move your feet and body rhythmically in time to music. ▶ NOUN ② a series of rhythmic movements or steps in time to music. ③ a social event where people dance with each other. **dancer** NOUN **dancing** NOUN

dandelion NOUN a wild plant with yellow flowers which form a ball of fluffy seeds.

dandruff NOUN Dandruff is small, loose scales of dead skin in someone's hair.

Dane NOUN someone who comes from Denmark.

danger NOUN ① Danger is the possibility that someone may be harmed or killed. ② something or someone that can hurt or harm you.

danger NOUN
① = hazard, jeopardy, menace, peril, risk, threat
≠ safety

dangerous ADJECTIVE able to or likely to cause hurt or harm. **dangerously** ADVERB

dangerous ADJECTIVE
= hazardous, perilous, risky, treacherous
≠ safe

dangle VERB When something dangles or when you dangle it, it swings or hangs loosely.

Danish ADJECTIVE ① belonging or relating to Denmark. ▶ NOUN ② Danish is the main language spoken in Denmark.

dank ADJECTIVE A dank place is unpleasantly damp and chilly.

dapper ADJECTIVE slim and neatly dressed.

dappled ADJECTIVE marked with patches of a different or darker shade.

dare VERB ① To dare someone means to challenge them to do something in order to prove their courage. ② To dare to do something means to have the courage to do it. ▶ NOUN ③ a challenge to do something dangerous.

dare VERB
① = challenge, defy, throw down the gauntlet
② = risk, venture

daredevil NOUN a person who enjoys doing dangerous things.

daring ADJECTIVE ① bold and willing to take risks. ▶ NOUN ② the courage required to do things which are dangerous.

daring ADJECTIVE
① = adventurous, audacious, bold, brave, fearless
≠ cautious
▶ NOUN ② = audacity, boldness, bravery, courage, guts (*informal*), nerve (*informal*)
≠ caution

dark ADJECTIVE ① If it is dark, there is not enough light to see properly. ② Dark colours or surfaces reflect little light and so look deep-coloured or dull. ③ 'Dark' is also used to describe thoughts or ideas which are sinister or unpleasant. ▶ **NOUN** ④ The dark is the lack of light in a place. **darkly ADVERB darkness NOUN**

dark ADJECTIVE
① = cloudy, dim, dingy, murky, overcast, shadowy
≠ light
② = black, swarthy
▶ **NOUN** ④ = darkness, dimness, dusk, gloom
≠ light

darken VERB If something darkens, or if you darken it, it becomes darker than it was.

darling NOUN ① Someone who is lovable or a favourite may be called a darling. ▶ **ADJECTIVE** ② much admired or loved • *his darling daughter*.

darn VERB ① To darn a hole in a garment means to mend it with crossing stitches. ▶ **NOUN** ② a part of a garment that has been darned.

dart NOUN ① a small pointed arrow. ② Darts is a game in which the players throw darts at a round board divided into numbered sections. ▶ **VERB** ③ To dart about means to move quickly and suddenly from one place to another.

dash VERB ① To dash somewhere means to rush there. ② If something is dashed against something else, it strikes it or is thrown violently against it. ③ If hopes or ambitions are dashed, they are ruined or frustrated. ▶ **NOUN** ④ a sudden movement or rush. ⑤ a small quantity of something. ⑥ ENGLISH the punctuation mark (—) which shows a change of subject, or which may be used instead of brackets.

dash VERB
① = bolt, fly, race, run, rush, sprint, tear
② = break, crash, hurl, slam, smash
③ = crush, destroy, disappoint, foil, frustrate, shatter, thwart
▶ **NOUN** ④ = bolt, race, run, rush, sprint, stampede
⑤ = drop, pinch, splash, sprinkling

dashboard NOUN the instrument panel in a motor vehicle.

dashing ADJECTIVE A dashing man is stylish and confident • *He was a dashing figure in forties cinema*.

data NOUN ① information, usually in the form of facts or statistics. ② ICT any information put into a computer and which the computer works on or processes.

database NOUN ICT a collection of information stored in a computer.

date NOUN ① a particular day or year that can be named. ② If you have a date, you have an appointment to meet someone; also used to refer to the person you are meeting. ③ a small dark-brown sticky fruit with a stone inside, which grows on palm trees. ▶ **VERB** ④ If you are dating someone, you have a romantic relationship with them. ⑤ If you date something, you find out the time when it began or was made. ⑥ If something dates from a particular time, that is when it happened or was made. ▶ **PHRASE** ⑦ If something is **out of date**, it is old-fashioned or no longer valid.

dated ADJECTIVE no longer fashionable.

datum the singular form of **data**.

daub VERB If you daub something such as mud or paint on a surface, you smear it there.

daughter NOUN Someone's daughter is their female child.

daughter-in-law, daughters-in-law NOUN Someone's daughter-in-law is the wife of their grown-up child.

daunt VERB If something daunts you,

you feel worried about whether you can succeed in doing it • *He was not the type of man to be daunted by adversity.* **daunting** ADJECTIVE

dawn NOUN ① the time in the morning when light first appears in the sky. ② the beginning of something • *the dawn of the radio age.* ▸ VERB ③ If day is dawning, morning light is beginning to appear. ④ If an idea or fact dawns on you, you realise it.

day NOUN ① one of the seven 24-hour periods of time in a week, measured from one midnight to the next. ② Day is the period of light between sunrise and sunset. ③ You can refer to a particular day or days meaning a particular period in history • *in Gladstone's day.*

daybreak NOUN Daybreak is the time in the morning when light first appears in the sky.

daydream NOUN ① a series of pleasant thoughts about things that you would like to happen. ▸ VERB ② When you daydream, you drift off into a daydream.

daydream NOUN
① = dream, fantasy
▸ VERB ② = dream, fantasise

daylight NOUN ① Daylight is the period during the day when it is light. ② Daylight is also the light from the sun.

day-to-day ADJECTIVE happening every day as part of ordinary routine life.

day trip NOUN a journey for pleasure to a place and back again on the same day.

daze PHRASE If you are **in a daze**, you are confused and bewildered.

dazed ADJECTIVE If you are dazed, you are stunned and unable to think clearly.

dazed ADJECTIVE
= bewildered, confused, dizzy, light-headed, numbed, stunned

dazzle VERB ① If someone or something dazzles you, you are very impressed by their brilliance. ② If a bright light dazzles you, it blinds you for a moment. **dazzling** ADJECTIVE

deacon NOUN ① In the Church of England or Roman Catholic Church, a deacon is a member of the clergy below the rank of priest. ② In some other churches, a deacon is a church official appointed to help the minister. **deaconess** NOUN

dead ADJECTIVE ① no longer living or supporting life. ② no longer used or no longer functioning • *a dead language.* ③ If part of your body goes dead, it loses sensation and feels numb. ▸ PHRASE ④ **The dead of night** is the middle part of the night, when it is most quiet and dark.

dead ADJECTIVE
① = deceased (*formal*), departed, extinct, late
≠ alive
② = defunct, not working

dead end NOUN a street that is closed off at one end.

deadline NOUN a time or date before which something must be completed.

deadlock NOUN a situation in which neither side in a dispute is willing to give in.

deadly, **deadlier**, **deadliest** ADJECTIVE ① likely or able to cause death. ▸ ADVERB, ADJECTIVE ② 'Deadly' is used to emphasise how serious or unpleasant a situation is • *He is deadly serious about his comeback.*

deadly ADJECTIVE
① = destructive, fatal, lethal, mortal

deadpan ADJECTIVE, ADVERB showing no emotion or expression.

deaf ADJECTIVE ① partially or totally unable to hear. ② refusing to listen or pay attention to something • *He was deaf to all pleas for financial help.* **deafness** NOUN

deafening ADJECTIVE If a noise is deafening, it is so loud that you cannot hear anything else.

deal, **deals**, **dealing**, **dealt** NOUN ① an agreement or arrangement, especially in business. ▶ VERB ② If you deal with something, you do what is necessary to sort it out • *He must learn to deal with stress.* ③ If you deal in a particular type of goods, you buy and sell those goods. ④ If you deal someone or something a blow, you hurt or harm them • *Competition from abroad dealt a heavy blow to the industry.*

> **deal** VERB
> ② = attend to, cope with, handle, manage, see to, take care of

dealer NOUN a person or firm whose business involves buying or selling things.

dealings PLURAL NOUN Your dealings with people are the relations you have with them or the business you do with them.

dean NOUN ① In a university or college, a dean is a person responsible for administration or for the welfare of students. ② In the Church of England, a dean is a member of the clergy who is responsible for administration.

dear NOUN ① 'Dear' is used as a sign of affection • *What's the matter, dear?* ▶ ADJECTIVE ② much loved • *my dear son.* ③ Something that is dear is expensive. ④ You use 'dear' at the beginning of a letter before the name of the person you are writing to. **dearly** ADVERB

> **dear** NOUN
> ① = angel, beloved (*old-fashioned*), darling, treasure (*informal*)
> ▶ ADJECTIVE ② = beloved, cherished, darling, esteemed, precious, prized, treasured
> ③ = costly, expensive, pricey (*informal*)

dearth [*Said* ***derth***] NOUN a shortage of something.

death NOUN Death is the end of the life of a person or animal.

debacle [*Said day-****bah****-kl*] NOUN (*formal*) a sudden disastrous failure.

debatable ADJECTIVE not absolutely certain • *The justness of these wars is debatable.*

debate NOUN ① Debate is argument or discussion • *There is some debate as to what causes global warming.* ② CITIZENSHIP a formal discussion in which opposing views are expressed. ▶ VERB ③ When people debate something, they discuss it in a fairly formal manner. ④ If you are debating whether or not to do something, you are considering it • *He was debating whether or not he should tell her.*

debilitating ADJECTIVE (*formal*) If something is debilitating, it makes you very weak • *a debilitating illness.*

debit VERB ① to take money from a person's bank account. ▶ NOUN ② a record of the money that has been taken out of a person's bank account.

debrief VERB When someone is debriefed, they are asked to give a report on a task they have just completed. **debriefing** NOUN

debris [*Said* ***day****-bree*] NOUN Debris is fragments or rubble left after something has been destroyed.

debt [*Said* ***det***] NOUN ① a sum of money that is owed to one person by another. ② Debt is the state of owing money.

debtor NOUN a person who owes money.

A B C D E F G H I J K L M N O P Q R S T U V W X Y Z

debut *[Said **day**-byoo]* NOUN a performer's first public appearance.

debutante *[Said **deb**-yoo-tant]* NOUN (*old-fashioned*) a girl from the upper classes who has started going to social events.

decade NOUN a period of ten years.

decadence NOUN Decadence is a decline in standards of morality and behaviour. **decadent** ADJECTIVE

decapitate VERB To decapitate someone means to cut off their head.

decathlon *[Said de-**cath**-lon]* NOUN a sports contest in which athletes compete in ten different events.

decay VERB ① When things decay, they rot or go bad. ▶ NOUN ② Decay is the process of decaying.

deceased (*formal*) ADJECTIVE ① A deceased person is someone who has recently died. ▶ NOUN ② The deceased is someone who has recently died.

deceit NOUN Deceit is behaviour that is intended to make people believe something that is not true. **deceitful** ADJECTIVE

deceive VERB If you deceive someone, you make them believe something that is not true.

> **deceive** VERB
> = con (*informal*), double-cross, dupe, fool, mislead, take in, trick

December NOUN December is the twelfth and last month of the year. It has 31 days.

decency NOUN ① Decency is behaviour that is respectable and follows accepted moral standards. ② Decency is also behaviour which shows kindness and respect towards people • *No one had the decency to tell me to my face.*

decent ADJECTIVE ① of an acceptable standard or quality • *She went to a decent school.* ② Decent people are honest and respectable • *a decent man.* **decently** ADVERB

> **decent** ADJECTIVE
> ① = adequate, passable, reasonable, respectable, satisfactory, tolerable
> ② = proper, respectable
> ≠ improper

deception NOUN ① something that is intended to trick or deceive someone. ② Deception is the act of deceiving someone.

deceptive ADJECTIVE likely to make people believe something that is not true. **deceptively** ADVERB

> **deceptive** ADJECTIVE
> = false, fraudulent, illusory, misleading, unreliable

decibel NOUN [SCIENCE] a unit of the intensity of sound.

decide VERB If you decide to do something, you choose to do it.

> **decide** VERB
> = choose, come to a decision, determine (*formal*), elect (*formal*), make up your mind, reach a decision, resolve (*formal*)

deciduous ADJECTIVE Deciduous trees lose their leaves in the autumn every year.

decimal [MATHS] ADJECTIVE ① The decimal system expresses numbers using all the digits from 0 to 9. ▶ NOUN ② a fraction in which a dot called a decimal point is followed by numbers representing tenths, hundredths and thousandths. For example, 0.5 represents $^5/_{10}$ (or $^1/_2$); 0.05 represents $^5/_{100}$ (or $^1/_{20}$).

decimate VERB To decimate a group of people or animals means to kill or destroy a large number of them.

decipher VERB If you decipher a piece of writing or a message, you work out its meaning.

A B C D E F G H I J K L M N O P Q R S T U V W X Y Z

decision NOUN a choice or judgment that is made about something • *The editor's decision is final.*

decision NOUN
= conclusion, finding, judgment, resolution, ruling, verdict

decisive [*Said dis-**sigh**-siv*] ADJECTIVE ① having great influence on the result of something • *It was the decisive moment of the race.* ② A decisive person is able to make decisions firmly and quickly. **decisively** ADVERB **decisiveness** NOUN

deck NOUN ① a floor or platform built into a ship, or one of the two floors on a bus. ② a pack of cards.

declaration NOUN a firm, forceful statement, often an official announcement • *a declaration of war.*

declaration NOUN
= affirmation, protestation (*formal*), statement, testimony

declare VERB ① If you declare something, you state it forcefully or officially. ② If you declare goods or earnings, you state what you have bought or earned, in order to pay tax or duty.

declare VERB
① = affirm, announce, assert, certify, proclaim, profess (*formal*), pronounce, state

decline VERB ① If something declines, it becomes smaller or weaker. ② If you decline something, you politely refuse to accept it or do it. ▶ NOUN ③ a gradual weakening or decrease • *a decline in the birth rate.*

decline VERB
① = decrease, diminish, drop, fall, go down, plummet, reduce
≠ increase
② = abstain (*formal*), excuse yourself, refuse, turn down
≠ accept
▶ NOUN ③ = decrease, downturn, drop, fall, recession, shrinkage, slump
≠ increase

decode VERB If you decode a coded message, you convert it into ordinary language. **decoder** NOUN

decommission VERB When something such as a nuclear reactor or large machine is decommissioned, it is taken to pieces or removed from service because it is no longer going to be used.

decompose VERB SCIENCE If something decomposes, it decays through chemical or bacterial action. **decomposition** NOUN

decor [*Said **day**-kor*] NOUN The decor of a room or house is the style in which it is decorated and furnished.

decorate VERB ① If you decorate something, you make it more attractive by adding some ornament or colour to it. ② If you decorate a room or building, you paint or wallpaper it.

decorate VERB
① = adorn, deck, ornament
② = do up (*informal*), renovate

decoration NOUN ① Decorations are features added to something to make it more attractive. ② The decoration in a building or room is the style of the furniture and wallpaper.

decorative ADJECTIVE intended to look attractive.

decorator NOUN a person whose job is painting and putting up wallpaper in rooms and buildings.

decorum [*Said dik-**ore**-um*] NOUN (*formal*) Decorum is polite and correct behaviour.

decoy NOUN a person or object that is used to lead someone or something into danger.

decrease VERB ① If something decreases or if you decrease it, it becomes less in quantity or size. ▶ NOUN ② a lessening in the amount of something; also the amount by which something becomes less. **decreasing** ADJECTIVE

> **decrease** VERB
> ① = cut down, decline, diminish, drop, dwindle, lessen, lower, reduce, shrink
> ≠ increase
> ▶ NOUN ② = cutback, decline, drop, lessening, reduction
> ≠ increase

decree, decrees, decreeing, decreed VERB ① If someone decrees something, they state formally that it will happen. ▶ NOUN ② an official decision or order, usually by governments or rulers.

dedicate VERB If you dedicate yourself to something, you devote your time and energy to it. **dedication** NOUN

deduce VERB If you deduce something, you work it out from other facts that you know are true.

deduct VERB To deduct an amount from a total amount means to subtract it from the total.

deduction NOUN ① an amount which is taken away from a total. ② a conclusion that you have reached because of other things that you know are true.

deed NOUN ① something that is done. ② a legal document, especially concerning the ownership of land or buildings.

deem VERB (*formal*) If you deem something to be true, you judge or consider it to be true • *His ideas were deemed unacceptable.*

deep ADJECTIVE ① situated or extending a long way down from the top surface of something, or a long way inwards • *a deep hole.* ② great or intense • *deep suspicion.* ③ low in pitch • *a deep voice.* ④ strong and fairly dark in colour • *The juice was deep orange in colour.* **deeply** ADVERB

> **deep** ADJECTIVE
> ① = bottomless, yawning
> ≠ shallow
> ② = extreme, grave (*formal*), great, intense, profound, serious
> ③ = bass, low
> ≠ high

deepen VERB If something deepens or is deepened, it becomes deeper or more intense.

deer, deer NOUN a large, hoofed mammal that lives wild in parts of Britain.

deface VERB If you deface a wall or notice, you spoil it by writing or drawing on it • *She spitefully defaced her sister's poster.*

default VERB ① If someone defaults on something they have legally agreed to do, they fail to do it • *He defaulted on repayment of the loan.* ▶ PHRASE ② If something happens **by default**, it happens because something else which might have prevented it has failed to happen.

defeat VERB ① If you defeat someone or something, you win a victory over them, or cause them to fail. ▶ NOUN ② the state of being beaten or of failing or an occasion on which someone is beaten or fails to achieve something • *He was gracious in defeat.*

> **defeat** VERB
> ① = beat, conquer, crush, rout, trounce, vanquish (*literary*)
> ▶ NOUN ② = conquest, debacle (*formal*), rout, trouncing
> ≠ victory

defect NOUN ① a fault or flaw in something. ▶ VERB ② If someone

A B C D E F G H I J K L M N O P Q R S T U V W X Y Z

defects, they leave their own country or organisation and join an opposing one. **defection** NOUN

defect NOUN
① = deficiency, failing, fault, flaw, imperfection, shortcoming, weakness

defective ADJECTIVE imperfect or faulty • *defective eyesight*.

defence NOUN ① Defence is action that is taken to protect someone or something from attack. ② any arguments used in support of something that has been criticised or questioned. ③ the case presented, in a court of law, by a lawyer for the person on trial; also the person on trial and his or her lawyers. ④ HISTORY A country's defences are its military resources, such as its armed forces and weapons.

defence NOUN
① = cover, protection, resistance, safeguard, security
② = argument, excuse, explanation, justification, plea

defend VERB ① To defend someone or something means to protect them from harm or danger. ② If you defend a person or their ideas and beliefs, you argue in support of them. ③ To defend someone in court means to represent them and argue their case for them. ④ In a game such as football or hockey, to defend means to try to prevent goals being scored by your opponents.

defend VERB
① = cover, guard, protect, safeguard, shelter, shield
② = endorse, justify, stick up for (*informal*), support, uphold

defendant NOUN a person who has been accused of a crime in a court of law.

defender NOUN ① a person who protects someone or something from harm or danger. ② a person who argues in support of something. ③ a person who tries to stop goals being scored in certain sports.

defender NOUN
② = advocate, champion, supporter

defensible ADJECTIVE able to be defended against criticism or attack.

defensive ADJECTIVE ① intended or designed for protection • *defensive weapons*. ② Someone who is defensive feels unsure and threatened by other people's opinions and attitudes • *Don't get defensive, I was only joking about your cooking*. **defensively** ADVERB **defensiveness** NOUN

defer, defers, deferring, deferred VERB ① If you defer something, you delay or postpone it until a future time. ② If you defer to someone, you agree with them or do what they want because you respect them.

deference [*Said* ***def**-er-enss*] NOUN Deference is polite and respectful behaviour. **deferential** ADJECTIVE **deferentially** ADVERB

defiance NOUN Defiance is behaviour which shows that you are not willing to obey or behave in the expected way • *a gesture of defiance*. **defiant** ADJECTIVE **defiantly** ADVERB

deficiency, deficiencies NOUN a lack of something • *vitamin deficiency*.

deficiency NOUN
= deficit, deprivation, inadequacy, lack, want (*formal*)
≠ abundance

deficient ADJECTIVE lacking in something.

deficient ADJECTIVE
= inadequate, lacking, poor, short, wanting

deficit [*Said* ***def**-iss-it*] NOUN the amount by which money received by an organisation is less than money spent.

define VERB [EXAM TERM] If you define something, you say clearly what it is or what it means • *Culture can be defined in hundreds of ways.*

definite ADJECTIVE ① firm and unlikely to be changed • *The answer is a definite 'yes'.* ② certain or true rather than guessed or imagined • *definite proof.* **definitely** ADVERB

> **definite** ADJECTIVE
> ① = assured, certain, decided, fixed, guaranteed, settled
> ② = clear, positive

definition NOUN a statement explaining the meaning of a word or idea.

definitive ADJECTIVE ① final and unable to be questioned or altered • *a definitive answer.* ② most complete, or the best of its kind • *a definitive history of science fiction.* **definitively** ADVERB

deflate VERB ① If you deflate something such as a tyre or balloon, you let out all the air or gas in it. ② If you deflate someone, you make them seem less important.

deflect VERB To deflect something means to turn it aside or make it change direction. **deflection** NOUN

deforestation NOUN [GEOGRAPHY] Deforestation is the cutting down of all the trees in an area.

deformed ADJECTIVE disfigured or abnormally shaped.

> **deformed** ADJECTIVE
> = disfigured, distorted

defraud VERB If someone defrauds you, they cheat you out of something that should be yours.

defrost VERB ① If you defrost a freezer or refrigerator, you remove the ice from it. ② If you defrost frozen food, you let it thaw out.

deft ADJECTIVE Someone who is deft is quick and skilful in their movements. **deftly** ADVERB

defunct ADJECTIVE no longer existing or functioning.

defuse VERB ① To defuse a dangerous or tense situation means to make it less dangerous or tense. ② To defuse a bomb means to remove its fuse or detonator so that it cannot explode.

defy, **defies**, **defying**, **defied** VERB ① If you defy a person or a law, you openly refuse to obey. ② (*formal*) If you defy someone to do something that you think is impossible, you challenge them to do it.

degenerate VERB [*Said de-**jen**-er-ate*] ① If something degenerates, it becomes worse • *The election campaign degenerated into farce.* ▶ ADJECTIVE [*Said de-**jen**-e-rit*] ② having low standards of morality. ▶ NOUN [*Said de-**jen**-e-rit*] ③ someone whose standards of morality are so low that people find their behaviour shocking or disgusting. **degeneration** NOUN

degradation NOUN Degradation is a state of poverty and misery.

degrade VERB If something degrades people, it humiliates them and makes them feel that they are not respected. **degrading** ADJECTIVE

> **degrade** VERB
> = demean, humiliate

degree NOUN ① an amount of a feeling or quality • *a degree of pain.* ② [SCIENCE] a unit of measurement of temperature; often written as ° after a number • *20°C.* ③ [MATHS] a unit of measurement of angles in mathematics, and of latitude and longitude • *The yacht was 20° off course.* ④ a course of study at a university or college; also the qualification awarded after passing the course.

dehydrate VERB ① If something is

dehydrated, water is removed or lost from it. ② If someone is dehydrated, they are weak or ill because they have lost too much water from their body. **dehydrated** ADJECTIVE **dehydration** NOUN

deity, **deities** NOUN a god or goddess.

deja vu *[Said* ***day****-ja* ***voo****]* NOUN Deja vu is the feeling that you have already experienced in the past exactly the same sequence of events as is happening now.

dejected ADJECTIVE miserable and unhappy. **dejectedly** ADVERB **dejection** NOUN

delay VERB ① If you delay doing something, you put it off until a later time. ② If something delays you, it hinders you or slows you down. ▶ NOUN ③ Delay is time during which something is delayed.

> **delay** VERB
> ① = defer, postpone, put off, shelve, suspend
> ② = check, hinder, impede, obstruct, set back
> ≠ hurry
> ▶ NOUN ③ = interruption, obstruction, setback

delectable ADJECTIVE very pleasing or delightful.

delegate NOUN ① a person appointed to vote or to make decisions on behalf of a group of people. ▶ VERB ② If you delegate duties, you give them to someone who can then act on your behalf.

delegation NOUN ① a group of people chosen to represent a larger group of people. ② Delegation is the giving of duties, responsibilities or power to someone who can then act on your behalf.

delete VERB ICT To delete something means to cross it out or remove it • *He had deleted the computer file by mistake.* **deletion** NOUN

> **delete** VERB
> = cross out, erase, rub out

deliberate ADJECTIVE *[Said di-****lib****-er-it]* ① done on purpose or planned in advance • *It was a deliberate insult.* ② careful and not hurried in speech and action • *She was very deliberate in her movements.* ▶ VERB *[Said di-****lib****-er-ayt]* ③ If you deliberate about something, you think about it seriously and carefully. **deliberately** ADVERB

> **deliberate** ADJECTIVE
> ① = calculated, conscious, intentional, premeditated, studied
> ≠ accidental
> ② = careful, cautious, measured, methodical
> ≠ casual
> ▶ VERB ③ = debate, meditate, mull over, ponder, reflect

deliberation NOUN Deliberation is careful consideration of a subject.

delicacy, **delicacies** NOUN ① Delicacy is grace and attractiveness. ② Something said or done with delicacy is said or done tactfully so that nobody is offended. ③ Delicacies are rare or expensive foods that are considered especially nice to eat.

delicate ADJECTIVE ① fine, graceful or subtle in character • *a delicate fragrance.* ② fragile and needing to be handled carefully • *delicate antique lace.* ③ precise or sensitive, and able to notice very small changes • *a delicate instrument.* **delicately** ADVERB

delicatessen NOUN a shop selling unusual or imported foods.

delicious ADJECTIVE very pleasing, especially to taste. **deliciously** ADVERB

> **delicious** ADJECTIVE
> = appetising, delectable, luscious, tasty

delight NOUN ① Delight is great pleasure or joy. ▶ VERB ② If something delights you or if you are delighted by it, it gives you a lot of pleasure. **delighted** ADJECTIVE

> **delight** NOUN
> ① = glee, happiness, joy, pleasure, rapture, satisfaction
> ▶ VERB ② = amuse, captivate, charm, enchant, please, thrill

delightful ADJECTIVE very pleasant and attractive. **delightfully** ADVERB

delinquent NOUN a young person who commits minor crimes. **delinquency** NOUN

delirious ADJECTIVE ① unable to speak or act in a rational way because of illness or fever. ② wildly excited and happy. **deliriously** ADVERB

deliver VERB ① If you deliver something to someone, you take it to them and give them it. ② To deliver a lecture or speech means to give it.

delivery, **deliveries** NOUN ① Delivery or a delivery is the bringing of letters or goods to a person or firm. ② Someone's delivery is the way in which they give a speech.

delta NOUN GEOGRAPHY a low, flat area at the mouth of a river where the river has split into several branches to enter the sea.

delude VERB To delude people means to deceive them into believing something that is not true.

deluge NOUN ① a sudden, heavy downpour of rain. ▶ VERB ② To be deluged with things means to be overwhelmed by a great number of them.

delusion NOUN a mistaken or misleading belief or idea.

delve VERB If you delve into something, you seek out more information about it.

demand VERB ① If you demand something, you ask for it forcefully and urgently. ② If a job or situation demands a particular quality, it needs it • *This situation demands hard work.* ▶ NOUN ③ a forceful request for something. ④ If there is a demand for something, a lot of people want to buy it or have it.

> **demand** VERB
> ② = involve, need, require, take, want

demean VERB If you demean yourself, you do something which makes people have less respect for you. **demeaning** ADJECTIVE

demeanour NOUN Your demeanour is the way you behave and the impression that this creates.

demented ADJECTIVE Someone who is demented behaves in a wild or violent way.

dementia [*Said dee-**men**-sha*] NOUN Dementia is a serious illness of the brain that affects people's ability to think clearly and remember things.

demise [*Said dee-**myz***] NOUN (*formal*) Someone's demise is their death.

demo, **demos** NOUN (*informal*) a demonstration.

democracy, **democracies** NOUN CITIZENSHIP Democracy is a system of government in which the people choose their leaders by voting for them in elections.

democrat NOUN a person who believes in democracy, personal freedom and equality.

democratic ADJECTIVE having representatives elected by the people. **democratically** ADVERB

demolish VERB To demolish a building means to pull it down or break it up. **demolition** NOUN

demon NOUN ① an evil spirit or devil. ▶ ADJECTIVE ② skilful, keen and energetic • *a demon squash player*. **demonic** ADJECTIVE

A B C D E F G H I J K L M N O P Q R S T U V W X Y Z

demonstrate VERB ① EXAM TERM To demonstrate a fact or theory means to prove or show it to be true. ② If you demonstrate something to somebody, you show and explain it by using or doing the thing itself • *She demonstrated how to apply the make-up*. ③ If people demonstrate, they take part in a march or rally to show their opposition or support for something.

demonstration NOUN ① a talk or explanation to show how to do or use something. ② Demonstration is proof that something exists or is true. ③ a public march or rally in support of or opposition to something. **demonstrator** NOUN

demote VERB A person who is demoted is put in a lower rank or position, often as a punishment. **demotion** NOUN

demure ADJECTIVE Someone who is demure is quiet and shy and behaves very modestly. **demurely** ADVERB

den NOUN ① the home of some wild animals such as lions or foxes. ② a secret place where people meet.

denial NOUN ① A denial of something is a statement that it is untrue • *He published a firm denial of the report*. ② The denial of a request or something to which you have a right is the refusal of it • *the denial of human rights*.

denigrate VERB (*formal*) To denigrate someone or something means to criticise them in order to damage their reputation.

denim NOUN ① Denim is strong cotton cloth, used for making clothes. ② (*in plural*) Denims are jeans made from denim.

denomination NOUN ① a particular group which has slightly different religious beliefs from other groups within the same faith. ② a unit in a system of weights, values or measures • *bank notes of different denominations*.

denominator NOUN MATHS In maths, the denominator is the bottom part of a fraction.

denote VERB If one thing denotes another, it is a sign of it or it represents it • *Red eyes denote tiredness*.

denounce VERB ① If you denounce someone or something, you express very strong disapproval of them • *He publicly denounced government nuclear policy*. ② If you denounce someone, you give information against them • *He was denounced as a dangerous agitator*.

dense ADJECTIVE ① thickly crowded or packed together • *the dense crowd*. ② difficult to see through • *dense black smoke*. **densely** ADVERB

density, **densities** NOUN the degree to which something is filled or occupied • *a very high population density*.

dent VERB ① To dent something means to damage it by hitting it and making a hollow in its surface. ▶ NOUN ② a hollow in the surface of something.

dental ADJECTIVE relating to the teeth.

dentist NOUN a person who is qualified to treat people's teeth.

dentistry NOUN Dentistry is the branch of medicine concerned with disorders of the teeth.

dentures PLURAL NOUN Dentures are false teeth.

denunciation NOUN A denunciation of someone or something is severe public criticism of them.

deny, **denies**, **denying**, **denied** VERB ① If you deny something that has been said, you state that it is untrue. ② If you deny that something is the case, you refuse to believe it • *He denied the existence of God*. ③ If you deny someone something, you refuse to give it to them • *They were denied permission to attend.*

deny VERB
① = contradict, refute
≠ admit
② = reject, renounce
③ = refuse, withhold

deodorant NOUN a substance or spray used to hide the smell of sweat.

depart VERB When you depart, you leave. **departure** NOUN

department NOUN one of the sections into which an organisation is divided • *the art department.* **departmental** ADJECTIVE

department NOUN
= division, office, section, unit

depend VERB ① If you depend on someone or something, you trust them and rely on them. ② If one thing depends on another, it is influenced by it • *Success depends on how hard you work.*

depend VERB
① = bank on, count on, rely on, trust
② = be determined by, hinge on

dependable ADJECTIVE reliable and trustworthy.

dependant NOUN PSHE someone who relies on another person for financial support.

dependence NOUN Dependence is a constant need that someone has for something or someone in order to survive or operate properly • *She was frustrated by her dependence on her sister.*

dependency, **dependencies** NOUN ① PSHE Dependency is relying on someone or something to give you what you need • *drug dependency.* ② a country or area controlled by another country.

dependent ADJECTIVE reliant on someone or something.

depict VERB To depict someone or something means to represent them in painting or sculpture.

deplete VERB To deplete something means to reduce greatly the amount of it available. **depletion** NOUN

deplorable ADJECTIVE shocking or regrettable • *deplorable conditions.*

deplore VERB If you deplore something, you condemn it because you feel it is wrong.

deploy VERB To deploy troops or resources means to organise or position them so that they can be used effectively. **deployment** NOUN

deport VERB If a government deports someone, it sends them out of the country because they have committed a crime or because they do not have the right to be there. **deportation** NOUN

depose VERB If someone is deposed, they are removed from a position of power.

deposit VERB ① If you deposit something, you put it down or leave it somewhere. ② If you deposit money or valuables, you put them somewhere for safekeeping. ③ GEOGRAPHY If something is deposited on a surface, a layer of it is left there as a result of chemical or geological action. ▶ NOUN ④ a sum of money given in part payment for goods or services.

deposit VERB
① = drop, lay, leave, place, put down

depot [*Said* ***dep****-oh*] NOUN a place where large supplies of materials or equipment may be stored.

depraved ADJECTIVE morally bad.

depress VERB ① If something depresses you, it makes you feel sad and gloomy. ② If wages or prices are depressed, their value falls. **depressive** ADJECTIVE

a b c d e f g h i j k l m n o p q r s t u v w x y z

A B C D E F G H I J K L M N O P Q R S T U V W X Y Z

depressed ADJECTIVE ① unhappy and gloomy. ② A place that is depressed has little economic activity and therefore low incomes and high unemployment • *depressed industrial areas.*

depression NOUN ① a state of mind in which someone feels unhappy and has no energy or enthusiasm. ② a time of industrial and economic decline. ③ GEOGRAPHY In meteorology, a depression is a mass of air that has low pressure and brings cloud, wind and rain. ④ GEOGRAPHY A depression in the surface of something is a part which is lower than the rest.

deprive VERB If you deprive someone of something, you take it away or prevent them from having it. **deprived** ADJECTIVE **deprivation** NOUN

depth NOUN ① The depth of something is the measurement or distance between its top and bottom, or between its front and back. ② The depth of something such as emotion is its intensity • *the depth of her hostility.*

deputy, **deputies** NOUN Someone's deputy is a person appointed to act in their place.

deranged ADJECTIVE behaving in a wild and uncontrolled way • *a deranged and motiveless rampage.*

derby, **derbies** [*Said* ***dar**-bee*] NOUN A local derby is a sporting event between two teams from the same area.

derelict ADJECTIVE abandoned and falling into ruins.

> **derelict** ADJECTIVE
> = abandoned, dilapidated, neglected, ruined

deride VERB To deride someone or something means to mock or jeer at them with contempt.

derision NOUN Derision is an attitude of contempt or scorn towards something or someone.

derivative NOUN ① something which has developed from an earlier source. ▸ ADJECTIVE ② not original, but based on or copied from something else • *The record was not deliberately derivative.*

derive VERB ① (*formal*) If you derive something from someone or something, you get it from them • *He derived so much joy from music.* ② If something derives from something else, it develops from it.

derogatory ADJECTIVE critical and scornful • *He made derogatory remarks about them.*

descend VERB ① To descend means to move downwards. ② If you descend on people or on a place, you arrive unexpectedly.

> **descend** VERB
> ① = dip, dive, fall, go down, plummet, sink
> ≠ ascend

descendant NOUN A person's descendants are the people in later generations who are related to them.

descent NOUN ① a movement or slope from a higher to a lower position or level. ② Your descent is your family's origins.

describe VERB To describe someone or something means to give an account or a picture of them in words.

> **describe** VERB
> = define, depict, portray

description NOUN an account or picture of something in words. **descriptive** ADJECTIVE

desert[1] [*Said* ***dez**-ert*] NOUN GEOGRAPHY a region of land with very little plant life, usually because of low rainfall.

desert[2] [*Said dez-**zert***] VERB To desert a

person means to leave or abandon them • *His friends had deserted him.* **desertion** NOUN

deserter NOUN someone who leaves the armed forces without permission.

deserve VERB If you deserve something, you are entitled to it or earn it because of your qualities, achievements or actions • *He deserved a rest.*

> **deserve** VERB
> = be entitled to, be worthy of, earn, justify, merit, warrant

deserving ADJECTIVE worthy of being helped, rewarded or praised • *a deserving charity.*

design DGT VERB ① To design something means to plan it, especially by preparing a detailed sketch or drawings from which it can be built or made. ▸ NOUN ② a drawing or plan from which something can be built or made. ③ The design of something is its shape and style. **designer** NOUN

> **design** VERB
> ① = draft, draw up, plan
> ▸ NOUN ② = model, plan
> ③ = form, pattern, shape, style

designate [Said *dez-ig-nate*] VERB ① To designate someone or something means to formally label or name them • *The cathedral was designated a World Heritage site.* ② If you designate someone to do something, you appoint them to do it • *He designated his son as his successor.*

designation NOUN a name or title.

designing ADJECTIVE crafty and cunning.

desirable ADJECTIVE worth having or doing • *a desirable job.* **desirability** NOUN

desire VERB ① If you desire something, you want it very much. ▸ NOUN ② a strong feeling of wanting something.

> **desire** VERB
> ① = crave, fancy, long for, want, wish, yearn
> ▸ NOUN ② = appetite, craving, hankering, longing, wish, yearning, yen (*informal*)

desist VERB (*formal*) To desist from doing something means to stop doing it.

desk NOUN ① a piece of furniture designed for working at or writing on. ② a counter or table in a public building behind which a receptionist sits.

desktop ADJECTIVE of a convenient size to be used on a desk or table • *a desktop computer.*

desolate ADJECTIVE ① deserted and bleak • *a desolate mountainous region.* ② lonely, very sad, and without hope • *He was desolate without her.* **desolation** NOUN

despair NOUN ① Despair is a total loss of hope. ▸ VERB ② If you despair, you lose hope • *He despaired of finishing it.* **despairing** ADJECTIVE

> **despair** NOUN
> ① = dejection, despondency, gloom, hopelessness
> ▸ VERB ② = feel dejected, feel despondent, lose heart, lose hope

despatch another spelling of **dispatch**.

desperate ADJECTIVE ① If you are desperate, you are so worried or frightened that you will try anything to improve your situation • *a desperate attempt to win.* ② A desperate person is violent and dangerous. ③ A desperate situation is extremely dangerous or serious. **desperately** ADVERB **desperation** NOUN

despicable ADJECTIVE deserving contempt.

despise VERB If you despise someone or something, you dislike them very much.

despite PREPOSITION in spite of • *He fell asleep despite all the coffee he'd drunk.*

> **despite** PREPOSITION
> = in spite of, notwithstanding (*formal*), regardless of

despondent ADJECTIVE dejected and unhappy. **despondency** NOUN

dessert *[Said diz-**ert**]* NOUN a sweet food served after the main course of a meal.

destination NOUN a place to which someone or something is going or is being sent.

destined ADJECTIVE meant or intended to happen • *I was destined for fame and fortune.*

destiny, **destinies** NOUN ① Your destiny is all the things that happen to you in your life, especially when they are considered to be outside human control. ② Destiny is the force which some people believe controls everyone's life.

destitute ADJECTIVE without money or possessions, and therefore in great need. **destitution** NOUN

destroy VERB ① To destroy something means to damage it so much that it is completely ruined. ② To destroy something means to put an end to it • *The holiday destroyed their friendship.*

> **destroy** VERB
> ① = annihilate, demolish, devastate, obliterate, raze, ruin, wreck

destruction NOUN Destruction is the act of destroying something or the state of being destroyed.

> **destruction** NOUN
> = annihilation, demolition, devastation, obliteration

destructive ADJECTIVE causing or able to cause great harm, damage or injury. **destructiveness** NOUN

desultory *[Said **dez**-ul-tree]* ADJECTIVE passing from one thing to another in a fitful or random way • *A desultory, embarrassed chatter began again.* **desultorily** ADVERB

detach VERB To detach something means to remove it • *The hood can be detached.* **detachable** ADJECTIVE

detached ADJECTIVE ① separate or standing apart • *a detached house.* ② having no real interest or emotional involvement in something • *He observed me with a detached curiosity.*

detachment NOUN ① Detachment is the feeling of not being personally involved with something • *A stranger can view your problems with detachment.* ② a small group of soldiers sent to do a special job.

detail NOUN ① an individual fact or feature of something • *We discussed every detail of the performance.* ② Detail is all the small features that make up the whole of something • *Look at the detail.* **detailed** ADJECTIVE

> **detail** NOUN
> ① = aspect, element, particular, point, respect

detain VERB ① To detain someone means to force them to stay • *She was being detained for interrogation.* ② If you detain someone, you delay them • *I mustn't detain you.*

detect VERB ① If you detect something, you notice it • *I detected a glimmer of interest in his eyes.* ② To detect something means to find it • *Bone injuries can be detected by X-rays.* **detectable** ADJECTIVE

detection NOUN ① Detection is the act of noticing, discovering or sensing something. ② Detection is also the work of investigating crime.

detective NOUN a person, usually a police officer, whose job is to investigate crimes.

detector NOUN an instrument which is used to detect the presence of something • *a metal detector.*

detention NOUN The detention of someone is their arrest or imprisonment.

deter, **deters**, **deterring**, **deterred** VERB To deter someone means to discourage or prevent them from doing something by creating a feeling of fear or doubt • *Many burglars are deterred by the sight of an alarm box.*

detergent NOUN a chemical substance used for washing or cleaning things.

deteriorate VERB If something deteriorates, it gets worse • *My father's health has deteriorated lately.*
deterioration NOUN

determination NOUN Determination is great firmness, after you have made up your mind to do something • *They shared a determination to win the war.*

> **determination** NOUN
> = perseverance, persistence, resolution, resolve (*formal*), tenacity

determine VERB ① If something determines a situation or result, it causes it or controls it • *The track surface determines his tactics in a race.* ② To determine something means to decide or settle it firmly • *The date has still to be determined.* ③ To determine something means to find out or calculate the facts about it • *He bit the coin to determine whether it was genuine.*

> **determine** VERB
> ① = control, decide, dictate, govern, shape
> ② = arrange, choose, decide, fix, resolve, settle
> ③ = ascertain (*formal*), confirm, discover, establish, find out, verify

determined ADJECTIVE firmly decided • *She was determined not to repeat her error.*
determinedly ADVERB

> **determined** ADJECTIVE
> = bent on, dogged, intent on, persistent, purposeful, resolute (*formal*), single-minded, tenacious

deterrent NOUN something that prevents you from doing something by making you afraid of what will happen if you do it • *The cameras act as a deterrent to would-be thieves.*
deterrence NOUN

detest VERB If you detest someone or something, you strongly dislike them.

detonate VERB To detonate a bomb or mine means to cause it to explode.
detonator NOUN

detour NOUN an alternative, less direct route.

detract VERB To detract from something means to make it seem less good or valuable.

detriment NOUN Detriment is disadvantage or harm • *a detriment to their health.* **detrimental** ADJECTIVE

deuce [*Said* **joos**] NOUN In tennis, deuce is the score of forty all.

devalue VERB To devalue something means to lower its status, importance or worth. **devaluation** NOUN

devastate VERB To devastate an area or place means to damage it severely or destroy it. **devastation** NOUN

devastated ADJECTIVE very shocked or upset • *The family are devastated by the news.*

develop VERB ① When something develops or is developed, it grows or becomes more advanced • *The sneezing developed into a full-blown cold.* ② To develop an area of land means to build on it. ③ To develop an illness or a fault means to become affected by it.

develop VERB
① = advance, evolve, grow, mature, progress, result, spring
③ = catch, contract (*formal*), fall ill with, get, go down with, pick up, succumb to (*formal*)

developer NOUN a person or company that builds on land.

development NOUN ① Development is gradual growth or progress. ② The development of land or water is the process of making it more useful or profitable by the expansion of industry or housing • *the development of the old docks*. ③ a new stage in a series of events • *developments in technology*. **developmental** ADJECTIVE

deviant ADJECTIVE ① Deviant behaviour is unacceptable or different from what people consider as normal. ▸ NOUN ② someone whose behaviour or beliefs are different from what people consider to be acceptable. **deviance** NOUN

deviate VERB To deviate means to differ or depart from what is usual or acceptable. **deviation** NOUN

device NOUN ① a machine or tool that is used for a particular purpose • *a device to warn you when the batteries need changing*. ② a plan or scheme • *a device to pressurise him into selling*.

devil NOUN ① RE In Christianity and Judaism, the Devil is the spirit of evil and enemy of God. ② an evil spirit.

devious ADJECTIVE insincere and dishonest. **deviousness** NOUN

devious ADJECTIVE
= calculating, scheming, underhand, wily

devise VERB To devise something means to work it out • *Besides diets, he devised punishing exercise routines*.

devoid ADJECTIVE lacking in a particular thing or quality • *His glance was devoid of expression*.

devolution NOUN Devolution is the transfer of power from a central government or organisation to local government departments or smaller organisations.

devote VERB If you devote yourself to something, you give all your time, energy or money to it • *She has devoted herself to women's causes*.

devoted ADJECTIVE very loving and loyal.

devoted ADJECTIVE
= constant, dedicated, doting, faithful, loving, loyal, true

devotee NOUN a fanatical or enthusiastic follower of something.

devotion NOUN Devotion to someone or something is great love or affection for them. **devotional** ADJECTIVE

devour VERB If you devour something, you eat it hungrily or greedily.

devout ADJECTIVE deeply and sincerely religious • *a devout Buddhist*. **devoutly** ADVERB

dew NOUN Dew is drops of moisture that form on the ground and other cool surfaces at night.

dexterity NOUN Dexterity is skill or agility in using your hands or mind • *He had learned to use the crutches with dexterity*. **dexterous** ADJECTIVE

diabetes [*Said dy-a-***bee***-tiss*] NOUN Diabetes is a disease in which someone has too much sugar in their blood, because they do not produce enough insulin to absorb it. **diabetic** ADJECTIVE

diabolical ADJECTIVE ① (*informal*) dreadful and very annoying • *The pain was diabolical*. ② extremely wicked and cruel.

diagnose VERB To diagnose an illness or problem means to identify exactly what is wrong.

diagnosis NOUN the identification of what is wrong with someone who is ill. **diagnostic** ADJECTIVE

diagonal ADJECTIVE in a slanting direction. **diagonally** ADVERB

diagram NOUN a drawing that shows or explains something.

dial, **dials, dialling, dialled** NOUN ① the face of a clock or meter, with divisions marked on it so that a time or measurement can be recorded and read. ② a part of a device, such as a radio, used to control or tune it. ▸ VERB ③ To dial a telephone number means to press the number keys to select the required number.

dialect NOUN a form of a language spoken in a particular geographical area.

dialogue NOUN ① ENGLISH In a novel, play or film, dialogue is conversation. ② Dialogue is communication or discussion between people or groups of people • *The union sought dialogue with the council.*

dialysis NOUN Dialysis is a treatment used for some kidney diseases, in which blood is filtered by a special machine to remove waste products.

diameter NOUN MATHS The diameter of a circle is the length of a straight line drawn across it through its centre.

diamond NOUN ① A diamond is a precious stone made of pure carbon. Diamonds are the hardest known substance in the world and are used for cutting substances and for making jewellery. ② A diamond is also a shape with four straight sides of equal length forming two opposite angles less than 90° and two opposite angles greater than 90°. ③ Diamonds is one of the four suits in a pack of playing cards. It is marked by a red diamond-shaped symbol. ▸ ADJECTIVE ④ A diamond anniversary is the 60th anniversary of an event • *a diamond wedding.*

diaphragm *[Said dy-a-fram]* NOUN SCIENCE In mammals, the diaphragm is the muscular wall that separates the lungs from the stomach.

diarrhoea *[Said dy-a-ree-a]* NOUN Diarrhoea is a condition in which the faeces are more liquid and frequent than usual.

diary, **diaries** NOUN a book which has a separate space or page for each day of the year on which to keep a record of appointments. **diarist** NOUN

dice NOUN ① a small cube which has each side marked with dots representing the numbers one to six. ▸ VERB ② To dice food means to cut it into small cubes. **diced** ADJECTIVE

dictate VERB ① If you dictate something, you say or read it aloud for someone else to write down. ② To dictate something means to command or state what must happen • *What we wear is largely dictated by our daily routine.* **dictation** NOUN

dictator NOUN HISTORY A dictator is a ruler who has complete power in a country, especially one who has taken power by force. **dictatorial** ADJECTIVE

diction NOUN Someone's diction is the clarity with which they speak or sing.

dictionary, **dictionaries** NOUN LIBRARY a book in which words are listed alphabetically and explained, or equivalent words are given in another language.

did the past tense of **do**.

didgeridoo NOUN an Australian musical wind instrument made in the shape of a long wooden tube.

die, **dies, dying, died** VERB ① When people, animals or plants die, they stop living. ② When something dies, dies away or dies down, it gradually fades away • *The footsteps died away.* ▸ NOUN ③ a dice. **die out** VERB When something dies out, it ceases to exist.

die VERB
① = cark it (*Australian and New Zealand; informal*), expire (*formal*), pass away, pass on, perish (*formal*)
② = fade away, fade out, peter out
▸ **die out** = disappear, fade, vanish

diesel [*Said* ***dee**-zel*] NOUN ① a heavy fuel used in trains, buses, lorries and some cars. ② a vehicle with a diesel engine.

diet NOUN ① Someone's diet is the usual food that they eat • *a vegetarian diet.* ② PSHE a special restricted selection of foods that someone eats to improve their health or regulate their weight. **dietary** ADJECTIVE **dieter** NOUN

dietician; also spelt **dietitian** NOUN a person trained to advise people about healthy eating.

differ VERB ① If two or more things differ, they are unlike each other. ② If people differ, they have opposing views or disagree about something.

difference NOUN ① The difference between things is the way in which they are unlike each other. ② The difference between two numbers is the amount by which one is less than another. ③ A difference in someone or something is a significant change in them • *You wouldn't believe the difference in her.*

difference NOUN
① = contrast, discrepancy, disparity, distinction, divergence, variation
≠ similarity
② = balance, remainder

different ADJECTIVE ① unlike something else. ② unusual and out of the ordinary. ③ distinct and separate, although of the same kind • *The school supports a different charity each year.* **differently** ADVERB

different ADJECTIVE
① = contrasting, disparate (*formal*), dissimilar, divergent (*formal*), opposed, unlike
≠ similar
② = special, unique
③ = another, discrete (*formal*), distinct, individual, separate

differentiate VERB ① To differentiate between things means to recognise or show how one is unlike the other. ② Something that differentiates one thing from another makes it distinct and unlike the other. **differentiation** NOUN

difficult ADJECTIVE ① not easy to do, understand or solve • *a very difficult decision to make.* ② hard to deal with, especially because of being unreasonable or unpredictable • *a difficult child.*

difficult ADJECTIVE
① = arduous, demanding, hard, intractable (*formal*), laborious, uphill
≠ easy
② = demanding, troublesome, trying

difficulty, **difficulties** NOUN ① a problem • *The main difficulty is memorising the shortcut keys.* ② Difficulty is the fact or quality of being difficult.

difficulty NOUN
① = complication, hassle (*informal*), hurdle, obstacle, pitfall, problem, snag, trouble
② = hardship, strain, tribulation (*formal*)

diffident ADJECTIVE timid and lacking in self-confidence. **diffidently** ADVERB **diffidence** NOUN

diffuse VERB [*Said dif-**yooz***] ① If something diffuses, it spreads out or scatters in all directions. ② SCIENCE

If particles of a gas, liquid or solid diffuse, they mix together, especially by moving from an area where they are very concentrated to one where there are fewer of them. ▸ **ADJECTIVE** *[Said dif-**yoos**]* ③ spread out over a wide area. **diffusion NOUN**

dig VERB ① If you dig, you break up soil or sand, especially with a spade or garden fork. ② To dig something into an object means to push, thrust or poke it in. ▸ **NOUN** ③ a prod or jab, especially in the ribs. ④ *(informal)* A dig at someone is a spiteful or unpleasant remark intended to hurt or embarrass them.

> **dig VERB**
> ① = burrow, excavate, gouge, hollow out, quarry, till, tunnel
> ② = jab, poke, thrust
> ▸ **NOUN** ③ = jab, poke, prod, thrust

digest VERB ① To digest food means to break it down in the gut so that it can be easily absorbed and used by the body. ② If you digest information or a fact, you understand it and take it in. **digestible ADJECTIVE**

digestion NOUN ① [SCIENCE] Digestion is the process of digesting food. ② Your digestion is your ability to digest food • *Camomile tea aids poor digestion*. **digestive ADJECTIVE**

digger NOUN In Australian English, digger is a friendly name to call a man.

digit *[Said **dij**-it]* **NOUN** ① *(formal)* Your digits are your fingers or toes. ② [MATHS] a written symbol for any of the numbers from 0 to 9.

digital ADJECTIVE ① Digital technology involves recording or transmitting information in the form of thousands of very small electronic signals • *a digital camera* • *digital shopping*. ② Digital displays show information, especially time, by numbers, rather than by a pointer moving round a dial • *a digital watch*. **digitally ADVERB**

dignified ADJECTIVE full of dignity.

dignitary, dignitaries NOUN a person who holds a high official position.

dignity NOUN Dignity is behaviour which is serious, calm and controlled • *She conducted herself with dignity*.

dilapidated ADJECTIVE falling to pieces and generally in a bad condition • *a dilapidated castle*.

dilemma NOUN [PSHE] a situation in which a choice has to be made between alternatives that are equally difficult or unpleasant.

diligent ADJECTIVE hard-working, and showing care and perseverance. **diligently ADVERB diligence NOUN**

dill NOUN Dill is a herb with yellow flowers and a strong sweet smell.

dilute VERB To dilute a liquid means to add water or another liquid to it to make it less concentrated. **dilution NOUN**

dim, dimmer, dimmest; dims, dimming, dimmed ADJECTIVE ① badly lit and lacking in brightness. ② very vague and unclear in your mind • *dim recollections*. ③ *(informal)* stupid or mentally dull • *He is rather dim*. ▸ **VERB** ④ If lights dim or are dimmed, they become less bright. **dimly ADVERB dimness NOUN**

> **dim ADJECTIVE**
> ① = dark, dull, grey, murky, poorly lit, shadowy
> ② = faint, hazy, indistinct, obscure, shadowy, vague
> ≠ clear
> ③ = dumb *(informal)*, obtuse *(formal)*, slow, stupid, thick *(informal)*
> ≠ bright

dimension NOUN ① A dimension of a situation is an aspect or factor that influences the way you understand it

• *This process had a domestic and a foreign dimension.* ② You can talk about the size or extent of something as its dimensions • *It was an explosion of major dimensions.* ③ ART The dimensions of something are also its measurements, for example its length, breadth, height or diameter.

diminish VERB If something diminishes or if you diminish it, it becomes reduced in size or importance.

> **diminish** VERB
> = contract, decrease, lessen, lower, reduce, shrink, weaken

diminutive ADJECTIVE very small.

din NOUN a loud and unpleasant noise.

dinar [*Said* **dee**-*nar*] NOUN a unit of currency in several countries in southern Europe, North Africa and the Middle East.

dine VERB (*formal*) To dine means to eat dinner in the evening • *We dined together in the hotel.*

diner NOUN ① a person who is having dinner in a restaurant. ② a small restaurant.

dinghy, **dinghies** [*Said* **ding**-*ee*] NOUN a small boat which is rowed, sailed or powered by outboard motor.

dingo, **dingoes** NOUN an Australian wild dog.

dingy, **dingier**, **dingiest** [*Said* **din**-*jee*] ADJECTIVE dusty, dark and rather depressing • *a dingy room.*

dinkum ADJECTIVE (*informal*) In Australian and New Zealand English, dinkum means genuine or right • *a fair dinkum offer.*

> **dinkum** ADJECTIVE
> = genuine, guileless, honest, sincere

dinner NOUN ① the main meal of the day, eaten either in the evening or at lunchtime. ② a formal social occasion in the evening, at which a meal is served.

dinosaur [*Said* **dy**-*no-sor*] NOUN a large reptile which lived in prehistoric times.

dint PHRASE **By dint of** means by means of • *He succeeds by dint of hard work.*

diocese NOUN a district controlled by a bishop. **diocesan** ADJECTIVE

dip, **dips**, **dipping**, **dipped** VERB ① If you dip something into a liquid, you lower it or plunge it quickly into the liquid. ② If something dips, it slopes downwards or goes below a certain level • *The sun dipped below the horizon.* ③ To dip also means to make a quick, slight downward movement • *She dipped her fingers into the cool water.* ▶ NOUN ④ a rich creamy mixture which you scoop up with biscuits or raw vegetables and eat • *an avocado dip.* ⑤ (*informal*) a swim.

diploma NOUN a certificate awarded to a student who has successfully completed a course of study.

diplomacy NOUN ① Diplomacy is the managing of relationships between countries. ② Diplomacy is also skill in dealing with people without offending or upsetting them. **diplomatic** ADJECTIVE **diplomatically** ADVERB

diplomat NOUN an official who negotiates and deals with another country on behalf of his or her own country.

dire ADJECTIVE disastrous, urgent or terrible • *people in dire need.*

direct ADJECTIVE ① moving or aimed in a straight line or by the shortest route • *the direct route.* ② straightforward, and without delay or evasion • *his direct manner.* ③ without anyone or anything intervening • *Schools can take direct* *control of their own funding*. ④ exact • *the direct opposite*. ▶ VERB ⑤ To direct something means to guide and control it. ⑥ To direct people or things means to send them, tell them, or show them the way. ⑦ To direct a film, a play, or a television programme means to organise the way it is made and performed.

direct ADJECTIVE
① = straight, uninterrupted
≠ indirect
② = blunt, candid, forthright, frank, straight, straightforward
≠ devious
③ = first-hand, immediate, personal
≠ indirect
▶ VERB ⑤ = control, guide, lead, manage, oversee, run, supervise

direction NOUN ① the general line that someone or something is moving or pointing in. ② Direction is the controlling and guiding of something • *He was chopping vegetables under the chef's direction*. ③ (*in plural*) Directions are instructions that tell you how to do something or how to get somewhere.

direction NOUN
① = course, path, route, way
② = charge, command, control, guidance, leadership, management

directive NOUN an instruction that must be obeyed • *a directive banning cigarette advertising*.

directly ADVERB in a straight line or immediately • *He looked directly at Rose*.

director NOUN ① a member of the board of a company or institution. ② DRAMA the person responsible for the making and performance of a programme, play or film. **directorial** ADJECTIVE

directorate NOUN a board of directors of a company or organisation.

directory, **directories** NOUN ① a book which gives lists of facts, such as names and addresses, and is usually arranged in alphabetical order. ② ICT another name for **folder**.

dirt NOUN ① Dirt is any unclean substance, such as dust, mud or stains. ② Dirt is also earth or soil.

dirt NOUN
① = dust, filth, grime, muck, mud
② = earth, soil

dirty, **dirtier**, **dirtiest** ADJECTIVE ① marked or covered with dirt. ② unfair, unscrupulous or dishonest • *She accused her opponents of running a dirty campaign*.

dirty ADJECTIVE
① = filthy, grimy, grubby, mucky, muddy, soiled, unclean
≠ clean
② = corrupt, crooked
≠ honest

disability, **disabilities** NOUN a physical or mental condition or illness that restricts someone's ability to move or use his or her senses.

disable VERB ① If something disables someone, it restricts his or her ability to move or use his or her senses. ② If someone or something disables a system or mechanism, they stop it working, usually temporarily. **disablement** NOUN

disabled ADJECTIVE having a physical or mental condition that restricts your ability to move or use your senses.

disadvantage NOUN an unfavourable or harmful circumstance. **disadvantaged** ADJECTIVE

disadvantage NOUN
= drawback, handicap, minus, weakness
≠ advantage

A B C D E F G H I J K L M N O P Q R S T U V W X Y Z

disaffected ADJECTIVE If someone is disaffected with an idea or organisation, they no longer believe in it or support it • *disaffected voters.*

disagree, **disagrees**, **disagreeing**, **disagreed** VERB ① If you disagree with someone, you have a different view or opinion from theirs. ② If you disagree with an action or proposal, you disapprove of it and believe it is wrong • *He detested her and disagreed with her policies.* ③ If food or drink disagrees with you, it makes you feel unwell.

> **disagree** VERB
> ① = differ, dispute, dissent
> ≠ agree
> ② = object, oppose, take issue with

disagreeable ADJECTIVE unpleasant or unhelpful and unfriendly • *a disagreeable odour.*

> **disagreeable** ADJECTIVE
> = horrible, horrid (*old-fashioned*), nasty, objectionable, obnoxious, unfriendly, unpleasant
> ≠ agreeable

disagreement NOUN ① a dispute about something. ② an objection to something.

> **disagreement** NOUN
> ① = altercation (*formal*), argument, difference, dispute, quarrel, row, squabble, tiff
> ≠ agreement
> ② = dissent, objection, opposition

disappear VERB ① If something or someone disappears, they go out of sight or become lost. ② To disappear also means to stop existing or happening • *The pain has disappeared.* **disappearance** NOUN

> **disappear** VERB
> ① = be lost to view, drop out of sight, fade, recede, vanish
> ≠ appear
> ② = cease (*formal*), die out, go away, melt away, pass, vanish

disappoint VERB If someone or something disappoints you, it fails to live up to what you expected of it.

disappointed ADJECTIVE sad because something has not happened.

> **disappointed** ADJECTIVE
> = dejected, despondent, disenchanted, disillusioned, downcast, saddened
> ≠ satisfied

disappointment NOUN ① a feeling of being disappointed. ② something that disappoints you.

> **disappointment** NOUN
> ① = dejection, despondency, regret
> ② = blow, setback

disapproval NOUN the belief that something is wrong or inappropriate.

> **disapproval** NOUN
> = censure (*formal*), condemnation, criticism
> ≠ approval

disapprove VERB To disapprove of something or someone means to believe they are wrong or bad • *Everyone disapproved of their marrying so young.* **disapproving** ADJECTIVE

> **disapprove** VERB
> = condemn, deplore (*formal*), dislike, find unacceptable, take a dim view of
> ≠ approve

disarm VERB ① To disarm means to get rid of weapons. ② If someone disarms you, they overcome your anger or doubt by charming or soothing you • *Mahoney was almost disarmed by his frankness.* **disarming** ADJECTIVE

disarmament NOUN Disarmament is the reducing or getting rid of military forces and weapons.

disarray NOUN Disarray is a state of disorder and confusion • *Our army was* *in disarray and practically weaponless.*

disaster NOUN ① an event or accident that causes great distress or destruction. ② a complete failure. **disastrous** ADJECTIVE **disastrously** ADVERB

disaster NOUN
① = calamity (*formal*), catastrophe, misfortune, tragedy

disband VERB When a group of people disbands, it officially ceases to exist.

disc; also spelt **disk** NOUN ① a flat round object • *a metal disc.* ② one of the thin circular pieces of cartilage that separate the bones in your spine. ③ ICT in computing, another spelling of **disk**.

discard VERB To discard something means to get rid of it, because you no longer want it or find it useful.

discard VERB
= cast aside, dispose of, dump (*informal*), jettison, shed, throw away, throw out

discern [*Said dis-**ern***] VERB (*formal*) To discern something means to notice or understand it clearly • *The film had no plot that I could discern.*

discern VERB
= detect, make out, notice, observe, perceive, see, spot

discernible ADJECTIVE able to be seen or recognised • *no discernible talent.*

discerning ADJECTIVE having good taste and judgment. **discernment** NOUN

discharge VERB ① If something discharges or is discharged, it is given or sent out • *Oil discharged into the world's oceans.* ② To discharge someone from hospital means to allow them to leave. ③ If someone is discharged from a job, they are dismissed from it. ▸ NOUN ④ a substance that is released from the inside of something • *a thick nasal discharge.* ⑤ a dismissal or release from a job or an institution.

discharge VERB
① = emit, empty, expel, flush, give off, release
② = free, let go, liberate, release, set free
③ = dismiss, eject, fire (*informal*), sack (*informal*)
▸ NOUN ⑤ = dismissal, ejection, expulsion, the sack (*informal*)

disciple [*Said dis-**sigh**-pl*] NOUN RE a follower of someone or something, especially one of the twelve men who were followers and helpers of Christ.

discipline NOUN ① Discipline is making people obey rules and punishing them when they break them. ② Discipline is the ability to behave and work in a controlled way. ▸ VERB ③ If you discipline yourself, you train yourself to behave and work in an ordered way. ④ To discipline someone means to punish them. **disciplinary** ADJECTIVE **disciplined** ADJECTIVE

disc jockey NOUN someone who introduces and plays music on the radio or at a night club.

disclose VERB To disclose something means to make it known or allow it to be seen. **disclosure** NOUN

disco, **discos** NOUN a party or a club where people dance to recorded music.

discomfort NOUN ① Discomfort is distress or slight pain. ② Discomfort is also a feeling of worry or embarrassment. ③ Discomforts are things that make you uncomfortable.

disconcert VERB If something disconcerts you, it makes you feel uneasy or embarrassed. **disconcerting** ADJECTIVE

disconnect VERB ① To disconnect something means to detach it from something else. ② If someone disconnects your fuel supply or telephone, they cut you off.

discontent NOUN Discontent is a feeling of dissatisfaction with conditions or with life in general • *He was aware of the discontent this policy had caused.* **discontented** ADJECTIVE

discontinue, **discontinues**, **discontinuing**, **discontinued** VERB To discontinue something means to stop doing it.

discord NOUN Discord is unpleasantness or quarrelling between people.

discount NOUN ① a reduction in the price of something. ▸ VERB ② If you discount something, you reject it or ignore it • *We shouldn't discount the possibility that things could get a lot worse.*

discourage VERB To discourage someone means to take away their enthusiasm to do something. **discouraging** ADJECTIVE **discouragement** NOUN

> **discourage** VERB
> = daunt, deter, dissuade, put off
> ≠ encourage

discourse (*formal*) NOUN ① a formal talk or piece of writing intended to teach or explain something. ② Discourse is serious conversation between people on a particular subject.

discover VERB When you discover something, you find it or find out about it. **discovery** NOUN **discoverer** NOUN

> **discover** VERB
> = come across, find, find out, learn, realise, stumble on, stumble across, unearth

discredit VERB ① To discredit someone means to damage their reputation. ② To discredit an idea means to cause it to be doubted or not believed.

discreet ADJECTIVE If you are discreet, you avoid causing embarrassment when dealing with secret or private matters. **discreetly** ADVERB

discrepancy, **discrepancies** NOUN a difference between two things which ought to be the same • *discrepancies in his police interviews.*

discrete ADJECTIVE ① (*formal*) separate and distinct • *two discrete sets of nerves.* ② [MATHS] A discrete line or set of data is made up of a limited number of separate points or items.

discretion NOUN ① Discretion is the quality of behaving with care and tact so as to avoid embarrassment or distress to other people • *You can count on my discretion.* ② Discretion is also freedom and authority to make decisions and take action according to your own judgment • *Class teachers have some discretion in decision-making.* **discretionary** ADJECTIVE

discriminate VERB ① To discriminate between things means to recognise and understand the differences between them. ② [PSHE] To discriminate against a person or group means to treat them unfairly, for example because of their gender, race or colour. ③ To discriminate in favour of a person or group means to treat them more favourably than others. **discrimination** NOUN **discriminatory** ADJECTIVE

discus, **discuses** NOUN a disc-shaped object with a heavy middle, thrown by athletes.

discuss VERB ① When people discuss something, they talk about it in detail. ② [EXAM TERM] To discuss a question is to look at the points or arguments of both sides and try to reach your own opinion.

discuss VERB
① = debate, exchange views on, go into, talk about

discussion NOUN PSHE a conversation or piece of writing in which a subject is considered in detail.

discussion NOUN
= consultation, conversation, debate, dialogue, discourse, talk

disdain NOUN Disdain is a feeling of superiority over or contempt for someone or something • *The candidates showed disdain for the press.* **disdainful** ADJECTIVE

disease NOUN SCIENCE an unhealthy condition in people, animals or plants. **diseased** ADJECTIVE

disembark VERB To disembark means to land or unload from a ship, aircraft or bus.

disembodied ADJECTIVE ① separate from or existing without a body • *a disembodied skull.* ② seeming not to be attached or to come from anyone • *disembodied voices.*

disenchanted ADJECTIVE disappointed with something, and no longer believing that it is good or worthwhile • *Students can become disenchanted with learning.* **disenchantment** NOUN

disfigure VERB To disfigure something means to spoil its appearance • *Graffiti or posters disfigured every wall.*

disgrace NOUN ① Disgrace is a state in which people disapprove of someone. ② If something is a disgrace, it is unacceptable • *The overcrowded prisons were a disgrace.* ③ If someone is a disgrace to a group of people, their behaviour makes the group feel ashamed • *You're a disgrace to the school.* ▸ VERB ④ If you disgrace yourself or disgrace someone else, you cause yourself or them to be strongly disapproved of by other people.

disgrace NOUN
① = scandal, shame
≠ credit
▸ VERB ④ = discredit, shame

disgraceful ADJECTIVE If something is disgraceful, people disapprove of it strongly and think that those who are responsible for it should be ashamed. **disgracefully** ADVERB

disgraceful ADJECTIVE
= scandalous, shameful, shocking

disgruntled ADJECTIVE discontented or in a bad mood.

disguise VERB ① To disguise something means to change its appearance so that people do not recognise it. ② To disguise a feeling means to hide it • *I tried to disguise my relief.* ▸ NOUN ③ something you wear or something you do to alter your appearance so that you cannot be recognised by other people.

disgust NOUN ① Disgust is a strong feeling of dislike or disapproval. ▸ VERB ② To disgust someone means to make them feel a strong sense of dislike or disapproval. **disgusted** ADJECTIVE

disgust NOUN
① = loathing, repulsion, revulsion
▸ VERB ② = repel, revolt, sicken

disgusting ADJECTIVE very unpleasant and offensive.

disgusting ADJECTIVE
= foul, gross, obnoxious, repellent, revolting, sickening, vile

dish NOUN ① a shallow container for cooking or serving food. ② food of a particular kind or food cooked in a particular way • *two fish dishes to choose from.*

dishearten VERB If you dishearten

someone, you take away their hope and confidence in something.

dishevelled *[Said dish-**ev**-ld]* ADJECTIVE If someone looks dishevelled, their clothes or hair look untidy.

dishonest ADJECTIVE not truthful or able to be trusted. **dishonestly** ADVERB

> **dishonest** ADJECTIVE
> = corrupt, crooked, deceitful, fraudulent, lying
> ≠ honest

dishonesty NOUN Dishonesty is behaviour which is meant to deceive people, either by not telling the truth or by cheating.

> **dishonesty** NOUN
> = cheating, corruption, deceit, trickery
> ≠ honesty

disillusion VERB If something or someone disillusions you, you discover that you were mistaken about something you valued, and so you feel disappointed with it. **disillusionment** NOUN

disillusioned ADJECTIVE If you are disillusioned with something, you are disappointed because it is not as good as you had expected.

disinfectant NOUN a chemical substance that kills germs.

disintegrate VERB ① If something disintegrates, it becomes weakened and is not effective • *My confidence disintegrated.* ② If an object disintegrates, it breaks into many pieces and so is destroyed. **disintegration** NOUN

> **disintegrate** VERB
> ② = break up, crumble, fall apart, fall to pieces, fragment

disinterest NOUN ① Disinterest is a lack of interest. ② Disinterest is also a lack of personal involvement in a situation.

disinterested ADJECTIVE If someone is disinterested, they are not going to gain or lose from the situation they are involved in, and so can act in a way that is fair to both sides • *a disinterested judge.*

disjointed ADJECTIVE If thought or speech is disjointed, it jumps from subject to subject and so is difficult to follow.

disk NOUN ① [ICT] In a computer, the disk is the part where information is stored • *The program takes up 2.5 megabytes of disk space.* ② another spelling of **disc**.

dislike VERB ① If you dislike something or someone, you think they are unpleasant and do not like them. ▸ NOUN ② Dislike is a feeling that you have when you do not like someone or something.

> **dislike** VERB
> ① = abhor (*formal*), be averse to, detest, hate, loathe, not be able to abide, not be able to bear, not be able to stand
> ≠ like
> ▸ NOUN ② = animosity, antipathy (*formal*), aversion, distaste, hatred, hostility, loathing
> ≠ liking

dislocate VERB To dislocate your bone or joint means to put it out of place.

dislodge VERB To dislodge something means to move it or force it out of place.

dismal *[Said **diz**-mal]* ADJECTIVE rather gloomy and depressing • *dismal weather.* **dismally** ADVERB

dismantle VERB To dismantle something means to take it apart.

dismay NOUN ① Dismay is a feeling of fear and worry. ▸ VERB ② If someone or something dismays you, it fills you with alarm and worry.

dismember VERB (*formal*) To dismember

a person or animal means to cut or tear their body into pieces.

dismiss VERB ① If you dismiss something, you decide to ignore it because it is not important enough for you to think about. ② To dismiss an employee means to ask that person to leave their job. ③ If someone in authority dismisses you, they tell you to leave. **dismissal** NOUN

dismissive ADJECTIVE If you are dismissive of something or someone, you show that you think they are of little importance or value • *a dismissive gesture*.

disobey VERB To disobey a person or an order means to deliberately refuse to do what you are told.

> **disobey** VERB
> = break, defy, flout, infringe, violate
> ≠ obey

disorder NOUN ① Disorder is a state of untidiness. ② Disorder is also a lack of organisation • *The men fled in disorder*. ③ a disease • *a stomach disorder*.

> **disorder** NOUN
> ① = clutter, disarray, muddle
> ≠ order
> ② = chaos, confusion, disarray, turmoil
> ③ = affliction, complaint, condition, disease, illness

disorganised; also spelt **disorganized** ADJECTIVE If something is disorganised, it is confused and badly prepared or badly arranged. **disorganisation** NOUN

disown VERB To disown someone or something means to refuse to admit any connection with them.

disparaging ADJECTIVE critical and scornful • *disparaging remarks*.

disparate ADJECTIVE (*formal*) Things that are disparate are utterly different from one another. **disparity** NOUN

dispatch; also spelt **despatch** VERB ① To dispatch someone or something to a particular place means to send them there for a special reason • *The president dispatched him on a fact-finding visit*. ▸ NOUN ② an official written message, often sent to an army or government headquarters.

dispel, **dispels, dispelling, dispelled** VERB To dispel fears or beliefs means to drive them away or to destroy them • *The myths are being dispelled*.

dispensary, **dispensaries** NOUN a place where medicines are prepared and given out.

dispense VERB ① (*formal*) To dispense something means to give it out • *They dispense advice*. ② To dispense medicines means to prepare them and give them out. ③ To dispense with something means to do without it or do away with it • *When she stood up to speak she dispensed with her notes*.

dispenser NOUN a machine or container from which you can get things • *a cash dispenser*.

disperse VERB ① When something disperses, it scatters over a wide area. ② When people disperse or when someone disperses them, they move apart and go in different directions. **dispersal** NOUN **dispersion** NOUN

dispirited ADJECTIVE depressed and having no enthusiasm for anything.

dispiriting ADJECTIVE Something dispiriting makes you depressed • *a dispiriting defeat*.

displace VERB ① If one thing displaces another, it forces the thing out of its usual place and occupies that place itself. ② If people are displaced, they are forced to leave their home or country.

displacement NOUN ① Displacement is the removal of something from its usual or correct place or position.

② SCIENCE In physics, displacement is the weight or volume of liquid displaced by an object submerged or floating in it.

display VERB ① If you display something, you show it or make it visible to people. ② If you display something such as an emotion, you behave in a way that shows you feel it. ▶ NOUN ③ ART an arrangement of things designed to attract people's attention.

displease VERB If someone or something displeases you, they make you annoyed, dissatisfied or offended. **displeasure** NOUN

disposable ADJECTIVE designed to be thrown away after use • *disposable nappies*.

disposal NOUN Disposal is the act of getting rid of something that is no longer wanted or needed.

dispose VERB ① To dispose of something means to get rid of it. ② If you are not disposed to do something, you are not willing to do it.

dispose VERB
① = discard, dispense with, dump, get rid of, jettison, throw away

disprove VERB If someone disproves an idea, belief or theory, they show that it is not true.

disprove VERB
= discredit, give the lie to, invalidate, prove false, refute
≠ prove

dispute NOUN ① an argument. ▶ VERB ② To dispute a fact or theory means to question the truth of it.

dispute NOUN
① = argument, clash, conflict, disagreement, feud, row, wrangle
▶ VERB ② = challenge, contest, contradict, deny, query, question
≠ accept

disqualify, disqualifies, disqualifying, disqualified VERB If someone is disqualified from a competition or activity, they are officially stopped from taking part in it • *He was disqualified from driving for 18 months*. **disqualification** NOUN

disquiet NOUN Disquiet is worry or anxiety. **disquieting** ADJECTIVE

disregard VERB ① To disregard something means to pay little or no attention to it. ▶ NOUN ② Disregard is a lack of attention or respect for something • *He exhibited a flagrant disregard of the law*.

disrepair PHRASE If something is **in disrepair** or **in a state of disrepair**, it is broken or in poor condition.

disrespect NOUN Disrespect is contempt or lack of respect • *his disrespect for authority*. **disrespectful** ADJECTIVE

disrupt VERB To disrupt something such as an event or system means to break it up or throw it into confusion • *Ash from the volcano disrupted air traffic*. **disruption** NOUN **disruptive** ADJECTIVE

dissatisfied ADJECTIVE not pleased or not contented. **dissatisfaction** NOUN

dissect VERB To dissect a plant or a dead body means to cut it up so that it can be scientifically examined. **dissection** NOUN

dissent NOUN ① Dissent is strong difference of opinion • *political dissent*. ▶ VERB ② When people dissent, they express a difference of opinion about something. **dissenting** ADJECTIVE

dissertation NOUN a long essay, especially for a university degree.

disservice NOUN To do someone a disservice means to do something that harms them.

dissident NOUN someone who disagrees with and criticises the government of their country.

dissimilar ADJECTIVE If things are dissimilar, they are unlike each other.

dissipate VERB ① (*formal*) When something dissipates or is dissipated, it completely disappears • *The cloud seemed to dissipate there.* ② If someone dissipates time, money or effort, they waste it.

dissipated ADJECTIVE Someone who is dissipated shows signs of indulging too much in things such as food and drink.

dissolve VERB ① SCIENCE If you dissolve something or if it dissolves in a liquid, it becomes mixed with and absorbed in the liquid. ② To dissolve an organisation or institution means to officially end it.

dissuade [*Said dis-**wade***] VERB To dissuade someone from doing something or from believing something means to persuade them not to do it or not to believe it.

distance NOUN ① The distance between two points is how far it is between them. ② Distance is the fact of being far away in space or time. ▸ VERB ③ If you distance yourself from someone or something or are distanced from them, you become less involved with them.

distant ADJECTIVE ① far away in space or time. ② A distant relative is one who is not closely related to you. ③ Someone who is distant is cold and unfriendly. **distantly** ADVERB

distant ADJECTIVE
① = far, outlying, out-of-the-way, remote
≠ close
③ = aloof, detached, reserved, withdrawn
≠ friendly

distaste NOUN Distaste is a dislike of something which you find offensive.

distasteful ADJECTIVE If you find something distasteful, you think it is unpleasant or offensive.

distil, distils, distilling, distilled VERB SCIENCE When a liquid is distilled, it is heated until it evaporates and then cooled to enable purified liquid to be collected. **distillation** NOUN

distillery, distilleries NOUN a place where whisky or other strong alcoholic drink is made, using a process of distillation.

distinct ADJECTIVE ① If one thing is distinct from another, it is recognisably different from it • *A word may have two quite distinct meanings.* ② If something is distinct, you can hear, smell or see it clearly and plainly • *There was a distinct buzzing noise.* ③ If something such as a fact, idea or intention is distinct, it is clear and definite • *She had a distinct feeling that someone was watching them.* **distinctly** ADVERB

distinction NOUN ① a difference between two things • *a distinction between the body and the soul.* ② Distinction is a quality of excellence and superiority • *a man of distinction.* ③ a special honour or claim • *It had the distinction of being the largest square in Europe.* ④ A distinction is the highest level of achievement in an examination.

distinctive ADJECTIVE Something that is distinctive has a special quality which makes it recognisable • *a distinctive voice.* **distinctively** ADVERB

distinguish VERB ① To distinguish between things means to recognise the difference between them • *I've learned to distinguish business and friendship.* ② To distinguish something means to make it out by seeing, hearing or tasting it • *I heard shouting but was unable to distinguish the words.* ③ If you distinguish yourself, you do something that makes people think highly of you. **distinguishable** ADJECTIVE **distinguishing** ADJECTIVE

distinguish VERB
① = differentiate, discriminate, tell, tell apart, tell the difference
② = discern, make out, pick out, recognise

distinguished ADJECTIVE ① dignified in appearance or behaviour. ② having a very high reputation • *He was a distinguished professor.*

distort VERB ① If you distort a statement or an argument, you represent it in an untrue or misleading way. ② If something is distorted, it is changed so that it seems strange or unclear • *His voice was distorted.* ③ If an object is distorted, it is twisted or pulled out of shape. **distorted** ADJECTIVE **distortion** NOUN

distract VERB If something distracts you, your attention is taken away from what you are doing. **distracted** ADJECTIVE **distractedly** ADVERB **distracting** ADJECTIVE

distract VERB
= divert, draw away

distraction NOUN ① something that takes people's attention away from something. ② an activity that is intended to amuse or relax someone.

distraught ADJECTIVE so upset and worried that you cannot think clearly • *He was distraught over the accident.*

distress NOUN ① Distress is great suffering caused by pain or sorrow. ② Distress is also the state of needing help because of difficulties or danger. ▸ VERB ③ To distress someone means to make them feel alarmed or unhappy • *Her letter had profoundly distressed me.*

distress NOUN
① = heartache, pain, sorrow, suffering
② = difficulty, need, straits, trouble
▸ VERB ③ = bother, disturb, grieve, pain, sadden, trouble, upset, worry

distressing ADJECTIVE very worrying or upsetting.

distribute VERB ① To distribute something such as leaflets means to hand them out or deliver them • *They publish and distribute brochures.* ② If things are distributed, they are spread throughout an area or space • *Distribute the cheese evenly on top of the pizza.* ③ To distribute something means to divide it and share it out among a number of people.

distribute VERB
① = circulate, hand out, pass around, pass round
② = diffuse, disperse, scatter, spread
③ = allocate, allot, dispense (*formal*), divide, dole out, share out

distribution NOUN ① Distribution is the delivering of something to various people or organisations • *the distribution of political leaflets.* ② Distribution is the sharing out of something to various people • *distribution of power.*

distributor NOUN a company that supplies goods to other businesses who then sell them to the public.

district NOUN an area of a town or country • *a residential district.*

distrust VERB ① If you distrust someone, you are suspicious of them because you are not sure whether they are honest. ▸ NOUN ② Distrust is suspicion. **distrustful** ADJECTIVE

disturb VERB ① If you disturb someone, you break their peace or privacy. ② If something disturbs you, it makes you feel upset or worried. ③ If something is disturbed, it is moved out of position or meddled with. **disturbing** ADJECTIVE

disturb VERB
① = bother, disrupt, intrude on
② = agitate, distress, shake, trouble, unsettle, upset, worry

disturbance NOUN ① Disturbance is the state of being disturbed. ② a violent or unruly incident in public.

disuse NOUN Something that has fallen into disuse is neglected or no longer used. **disused** ADJECTIVE

ditch NOUN a channel at the side of a road or field, to drain away excess water.

dither VERB To dither means to be unsure and hesitant.

ditto 'Ditto' means 'the same'. In written lists, 'ditto' is represented by a mark (") to avoid repetition.

ditty, ditties NOUN (*old-fashioned*) a short simple song or poem.

diva NOUN a great or leading female singer, especially in opera.

dive, dives, diving, dived VERB ① To dive means to jump into water with your arms held straight above your head, usually head first. ② If you go diving, you go down under the surface of the sea or a lake using special breathing equipment. ③ If an aircraft or bird dives, it flies in a steep downward path, or drops sharply. **diver** NOUN **diving** NOUN

dive VERB
① = jump, leap, submerge

diverge VERB ① If opinions or facts diverge, they differ • *Theory and practice sometimes diverged.* ② If two things such as roads or paths which have been going in the same direction diverge, they separate and go off in different directions. **divergence** NOUN **divergent** ADJECTIVE

diverse ADJECTIVE ① CITIZENSHIP If a group of people or things is diverse, it is made up of several different kinds • *a racially diverse community.* ② People, ideas or objects that are diverse are very different from each other. **diversity** NOUN

diversify, diversifies, diversifying, diversified VERB To diversify means to increase the variety of something • *Has the company diversified into new areas?* **diversification** NOUN

diversion NOUN ① a special route arranged for traffic when the usual route is closed. ② something that takes your attention away from what you should be concentrating on • *A break for tea created a welcome diversion.* ③ a pleasant or amusing activity.

divert VERB To divert something means to change the course or direction it is following.

divide VERB ① When something divides or is divided, it is split up and separated into two or more parts. ② If something divides two areas, it forms a barrier between them. ③ If people divide over something or if something divides them, it causes strong disagreement between them. ④ MATHS When you divide one number by another, you calculate how many times the first number contains the other. ▸ NOUN ⑤ a separation • *the class divide.*

divide VERB
① = cut up, partition, segregate, separate, split, split up
≠ join
② = bisect, separate
③ = come between, set against one another, split

dividend NOUN a portion of a company's profits that is paid to shareholders.

divine ADJECTIVE ① having the qualities of a god or goddess. ▶ VERB ② To divine something means to discover it by guessing. **divinely** ADVERB

divinity, **divinities** NOUN ① Divinity is the study of religion. ② Divinity is the state of being a god. ③ a god or goddess.

division NOUN ① Division is the separation of something into two or more distinct parts. ② MATHS Division is also the process of dividing one number by another. ③ a difference of opinion that causes separation between ideas or groups of people • *There were divisions in the Party on economic policy.* ④ any one of the parts or groups into which something is split • *the Research Division.* **divisional** ADJECTIVE

> **division** NOUN
> ① = partition, separation
> ③ = breach, difference of opinion, rupture, split
> ④ = department, section, sector

divisive ADJECTIVE causing hostility between people so that they split into different groups • *He was seen as a divisive and meddling figure.*

divorce NOUN ① Divorce is the formal and legal ending of a marriage. ▶ VERB ② When a married couple divorce, their marriage is legally ended. **divorced** ADJECTIVE **divorcee** NOUN

divulge VERB To divulge information means to reveal it.

DIY NOUN DIY is the activity of making or repairing things yourself. DIY is an abbreviation for 'do-it-yourself'.

dizzy, **dizzier**, **dizziest** ADJECTIVE having or causing a whirling sensation. **dizziness** NOUN

> **dizzy** ADJECTIVE
> = giddy, light-headed

DNA NOUN SCIENCE DNA is deoxyribonucleic acid, a substance found in the cells of all living things. It determines the structure of every cell and is responsible for characteristics being passed on from parents to their children.

do, **does**, **doing**, **did**, **done**; **dos** VERB ① 'Do' is an auxiliary verb, which is used to form questions and negatives and to give emphasis to the main verb of a sentence. ② If someone does a task or activity, they perform it and finish it • *He just didn't want to do any work.* ③ If you ask what people do, you want to know what their job is • *What will you do when you leave school?* ④ If you do well at something, you are successful. If you do badly, you are unsuccessful. ⑤ If something will do, it is adequate but not the most suitable option • *If you don't have a tennis ball, a rolled-up sock will do.* ▶ NOUN ⑥ (*informal*) a party or other social event. **do away with** VERB To do away with something means to get rid of it. **do up** VERB ① To do something up means to fasten it. ② To do up something old means to repair and decorate it.

> **do** VERB
> ② = carry out, execute (*formal*), perform, undertake
> ④ = fare, get on, manage
> ⑤ = be adequate, be sufficient, suffice (*formal*)

docile ADJECTIVE quiet, calm and easily controlled.

dock NOUN ① an enclosed area in a harbour where ships go to be loaded, unloaded or repaired. ② In a court of law, the dock is the place where the accused person stands or sits. ③ a stand in which a portable electronic device can be placed to charge its battery or to connect it to other devices. ▸ **VERB** ④ When a ship docks, it is brought into dock at the end of its voyage. ⑤ To dock someone's wages means to deduct an amount from the sum they would normally receive. ⑥ To dock an animal's tail means to cut part of it off. **docker** **NOUN**

doctor **NOUN** ① a person who is qualified in medicine and treats people who are ill. ② A doctor of an academic subject is someone who has been awarded the highest academic degree • *She is a doctor of philosophy.* ▸ **VERB** ③ To doctor something means to alter it in order to deceive people • *Stamps can be doctored.*

doctorate **NOUN** the highest university degree. **doctoral** **ADJECTIVE**

doctrine **NOUN** a set of beliefs or principles held by a group. **doctrinal** **ADJECTIVE**

document **NOUN** ① HISTORY a piece of paper which provides an official record of something. ② ICT a piece of text or graphics stored in a computer as a file that can be amended or altered by document processing software. ▸ **VERB** ③ HISTORY If you document something, you make a detailed record of it. **documentation** **NOUN**

documentary, **documentaries** **NOUN** ① a radio or television programme, or a film, which gives information on real events. ▸ **ADJECTIVE** ② Documentary evidence is made up of written or official records.

dodge **VERB** ① If you dodge or dodge something, you move suddenly to avoid being seen, hit or caught. ② If you dodge something such as an issue or accusation, you avoid dealing with it.

dodge **VERB**
① = duck, swerve
② = avoid, elude, evade, get out of, shirk, sidestep

dodgy, **dodgier**, **dodgiest** **ADJECTIVE** (*informal*) dangerous, risky or unreliable • *He has a dodgy knee.*

dodo, **dodos** **NOUN** A dodo was a large, flightless bird that lived in Mauritius and became extinct in the late 17th century.

doe **NOUN** a female deer, rabbit or hare.

does the third person singular of the present tense of **do**.

dog, **dogs**, **dogging**, **dogged** **NOUN** ① a four-legged, meat-eating animal, kept as a pet, or to guard property or go hunting. ▸ **VERB** ② If you dog someone, you follow them very closely and never leave them.

dog **NOUN**
① = brak (*South African*), canine (*formal*), mongrel, mutt (*slang*), pooch (*slang*)

dogged [*Said* ***dog****-ged*] **ADJECTIVE** showing determination to continue with something, even if it is very difficult • *dogged persistence.* **doggedly** **ADVERB**

dogma **NOUN** a belief or system of beliefs held by a religious or political group.

dogmatic **ADJECTIVE** Someone who is dogmatic about something is convinced that they are right about it. **dogmatism** **NOUN**

doldrums **PHRASE** (*informal*) If you are **in the doldrums**, you are depressed or bored.

dole **VERB** If you dole something out, you give a certain amount of it to each individual in a group.

doll **NOUN** a child's toy which looks like a baby or person.

dollar NOUN the main unit of currency in Australia, New Zealand, the USA, Canada and some other countries. A dollar is worth 100 cents.

dollop NOUN an amount of food, served casually in a lump.

dolphin NOUN a mammal which lives in the sea and looks like a large fish with a long snout.

domain NOUN ① a particular area of activity or interest • *the domain of science.* ② an area over which someone has control or influence • *This reservation was the largest of the Apache domains.*

dome NOUN a round roof. **domed** ADJECTIVE

domestic ADJECTIVE ① happening or existing within one particular country • *domestic and foreign politics.* ② involving or concerned with the home and family • *routine domestic tasks.*

domesticated ADJECTIVE If a wild animal or plant has been domesticated, it has been controlled or cultivated.

domesticity NOUN (*formal*) Domesticity is life at home with your family.

dominance NOUN ① Dominance is power or control. ② If something has dominance over other similar things, it is more powerful or important than they are • *the dominance of the United States in the film business.* **dominant** ADJECTIVE

dominate VERB ① If something or someone dominates a situation or event, they are the most powerful or important thing in it and have control over it • *The artist dominated the music charts this year.* ② If a person or country dominates other people or places, they have power or control over them. ③ If something dominates an area, it towers over it • *The valley was dominated by high surrounding cliffs.* **dominating** ADJECTIVE **domination** NOUN

domineering ADJECTIVE Someone who is domineering tries to control other people.

dominion NOUN Dominion is control or authority that a person or a country has over other people.

domino, dominoes NOUN Dominoes are small rectangular blocks marked with two groups of spots on one side, used for playing the game called dominoes.

don, dons, donning, donned VERB (*literary*) If you don clothing, you put it on.

donate VERB To donate something to a charity or organisation means to give it as a gift. **donation** NOUN

done the past participle of **do**.

donkey NOUN an animal like a horse, but smaller and with longer ears.

donor NOUN ① someone who gives some of their blood or an organ to be used to help someone who is ill • *a kidney donor.* ② someone who gives something such as money to a charity or other organisation.

doom NOUN Doom is a terrible fate or event in the future which you can do nothing to prevent.

doomed ADJECTIVE If someone or something is doomed to an unpleasant or unhappy experience, they are certain to suffer it • *doomed to failure.*

> **doomed** ADJECTIVE
> = condemned, hopeless, ill-fated

doomsday NOUN Doomsday is the end of the world.

door NOUN a swinging or sliding panel for opening or closing the entrance to something; also the entrance itself.

doorway NOUN an opening in a wall for a door.

dope NOUN ① (*informal*) Dope is an illegal drug. ▶ VERB ② If someone dopes you, they put a drug into your food or drink.

dormant ADJECTIVE Something that is dormant is not active, growing or being used • *The buds will remain dormant until spring.*

dormitory, **dormitories** NOUN a large bedroom where several people sleep.

dosage NOUN the amount of a medicine or a drug that should be taken.

dose NOUN a measured amount of a medicine or drug.

dossier [*Said* ***doss-ee-ay***] NOUN a collection of papers with information on a particular subject or person.

dot, **dots**, **dotting**, **dotted** NOUN ① a very small, round mark. ▶ VERB ② If things dot an area, they are scattered all over it • *Fishing villages dot the coastline.* ▶ PHRASE ③ If you arrive somewhere **on the dot**, you arrive there at exactly the right time.

dotcom NOUN a company that does most of its business on the internet.

dote VERB If you dote on someone, you love them very much. **doting** ADJECTIVE

double ADJECTIVE ① twice the usual size • *a double portion of cheesecake.* ② consisting of two parts • *a double album.* ▶ VERB ③ If something doubles, it becomes twice as large. ④ To double as something means to have a second job or use as well as the main one • *Their home doubles as an office.* ▶ NOUN ⑤ Your double is someone who looks exactly like you. ⑥ Doubles is a game of tennis or badminton which two people play against two other people. **doubly** ADVERB

> **double** ADJECTIVE
> ① = twice, twofold
> ② = dual, twin, twofold

double bass NOUN a musical instrument like a large violin, which you play standing up.

double-decker ADJECTIVE ① having two tiers or layers. ▶ NOUN ② a bus with two floors.

double glazing NOUN Double glazing is a second layer of glass fitted to windows to keep the building quieter or warmer.

doubt NOUN ① Doubt is a feeling of uncertainty about whether something is true or possible. ▶ VERB ② If you doubt something, you think that it is probably not true or possible.

> **doubt** NOUN
> ① = misgiving, qualm, scepticism, uncertainty
> ≠ certainty
> ▶ VERB ② = be dubious, be sceptical, query, question
> ≠ believe

doubtful ADJECTIVE unlikely or uncertain.

> **doubtful** ADJECTIVE
> = debatable, dubious, questionable, uncertain
> ≠ certain

dough [*Rhymes with* ***go***] NOUN ① Dough is a mixture of flour and water and sometimes other ingredients, used to make bread, pastry or biscuits. ② (*slang*) Dough is money.

doughnut NOUN a ring or ball of sweet dough cooked in hot fat.

dour [*Rhymes with* ***poor***] ADJECTIVE severe and unfriendly • *a dour portrait of his personality.*

douse; also spelt **dowse** VERB If you douse a fire, you stop it burning by throwing water over it.

dove NOUN a bird like a small pigeon.

dovetail VERB If two things dovetail together, they fit together closely or neatly.

dowdy, **dowdier**, **dowdiest** ADJECTIVE wearing dull and unfashionable clothes.

down PREPOSITION, ADVERB ① Down means towards the ground, towards a lower level, or in a lower place. ② If you go down a road or river, you go along it. ▸ ADVERB ③ If you put something down, you place it on a surface. ④ If an amount of something goes down, it decreases. ▸ ADJECTIVE ⑤ If you feel down, you feel unhappy. ▸ VERB ⑥ If you down a drink, you drink it quickly. ▸ NOUN ⑦ Down is the small, soft feathers on young birds.

> **down** PREPOSITION, ADVERB
> ① = downwards, downstairs
> ≠ up
> ▸ ADJECTIVE ⑤ = dejected, depressed, dispirited, fed up (*informal*), glum, melancholy (*literary*), miserable

downcast ADJECTIVE ① feeling sad and dejected. ② If your eyes are downcast, they are looking towards the ground.

downfall NOUN ① The downfall of a successful or powerful person or institution is their failure. ② Something that is someone's downfall is the thing that causes their failure • *His pride may be his downfall.*

> **downfall** NOUN
> ① = collapse, fall, ruin

downgrade VERB If you downgrade something, you give it less importance or make it less valuable.

downhill ADVERB ① moving down a slope. ② becoming worse • *The press has gone downhill in the last 10 years.*

download ICT VERB ① If you download data, you transfer it from the memory of a large computer system to a smaller computer. ▸ NOUN ② a piece of data transferred in this way.

downpour NOUN a heavy fall of rain.

downright ADJECTIVE, ADVERB You use 'downright' to emphasise that something is extremely unpleasant or bad • *Staff are often discourteous and sometimes downright rude.*

downstairs ADVERB ① If you go downstairs in a building, you go down to a lower floor. ▸ ADJECTIVE, ADVERB ② on a lower floor or on the ground floor. ▸ NOUN ③ The downstairs of a building is its lower floor or floors.

downstream ADVERB towards the mouth of a river • *The raft drifted downstream.*

down-to-earth ADJECTIVE sensible and practical • *a down-to-earth approach.*

downtrodden ADJECTIVE People who are downtrodden are treated badly by those with power and do not have the ability to fight back.

downturn NOUN a decline in the economy or in the success of a company or industry.

down under (*informal*) NOUN ① Australia or New Zealand. ▸ ADVERB ② in or to Australia or New Zealand.

downwards ADVERB ① If you move or look downwards, you move or look towards the ground or towards a lower level • *His eyes travelled downwards.* ② If an amount or rate moves downwards, it decreases. **downward** ADJECTIVE

downwind ADVERB If something

moves downwind, it moves in the same direction as the wind • *Sparks drifted downwind.*

dowry, dowries NOUN In some societies, a woman's dowry is money or property which her father gives to the man she marries.

doze VERB ① When you doze, you sleep lightly for a short period. ▶ NOUN ② a short, light sleep.

dozen NOUN A dozen things are twelve of them.

Dr ① *[Said* ***dock**-ter]* 'Dr' is short for 'Doctor' and is used before the name of someone with the highest form of academic degree or who practises medicine. ② 'Dr' is short for 'drive' in addresses.

drab, drabber, drabbest ADJECTIVE dull and unattractive. **drabness** NOUN

> **drab** ADJECTIVE
> = dingy, dismal, dreary, gloomy, grey, sombre
> ≠ bright

draft NOUN ① an early rough version of a document or speech. ▶ VERB ② When you draft a document or speech, you write the first rough version of it. ③ To draft people somewhere means to move them there so that they can do a specific job • *Various different presenters were drafted in.* ④ In Australian and New Zealand English, to draft cattle or sheep is to select some from a herd or flock.

drag, drags, dragging, dragged VERB ① If you drag a heavy object somewhere, you pull it slowly and with difficulty. ② If you drag someone somewhere, you make them go although they may be unwilling. ③ If things drag behind you, they trail along the ground as you move along. ④ If an event or a period of time drags, it is boring and seems to last a long time. ▶ NOUN ⑤ SCIENCE Drag is the resistance to the motion of a body passing through air or a fluid.

> **drag** VERB
> ① = draw, haul, lug, tow, trail

dragon NOUN In stories and legends, a dragon is a fierce animal like a large lizard with wings and claws that breathes fire.

drain VERB ① If you drain something, you cause liquid to flow out of it. ② If you drain a glass, you drink all its contents. ③ If liquid drains somewhere, it flows there. ④ If something drains strength or resources, it gradually uses them up • *The job seems to have drained him of energy.* ▶ NOUN ⑤ a pipe or channel that carries water or sewage away from a place. ⑥ a metal grid in a road, through which rainwater flows.

> **drain** VERB
> ① = draw off, pump
> ③ = discharge, empty, flow, seep
> ④ = consume, exhaust, sap, tax, use up

drainage NOUN ① Drainage is the system of pipes, drains or ditches used to drain water or other liquid away from a place. ② Drainage is also the process of draining water away, or the way in which a place drains • *To grow these plants well, all you need is good drainage.*

drama NOUN ① a serious play for the theatre, television or radio. ② Drama is plays and the theatre in general • *Japanese drama.* ③ You can refer to the exciting events or aspects of a situation as drama • *the drama of real life.*

dramatic ADJECTIVE A dramatic change or event happens suddenly and is very noticeable • *a dramatic departure from tradition.* **dramatically** ADVERB

dramatist NOUN DRAMA a person who writes plays.

drank the past tense of **drink**.

drape VERB If you drape a piece of cloth, you arrange it so that it hangs down or covers something in loose folds.

drastic ADJECTIVE A drastic course of action is very severe and is usually taken urgently • *It's time for drastic measures to stop people littering.* **drastically** ADVERB

drastic ADJECTIVE
= extreme, harsh, radical, severe

draught *[Said draft]* NOUN ① a current of cold air. ② an amount of liquid that you swallow. ③ Draughts is a game for two people played on a chessboard with round pieces. ▸ ADJECTIVE ④ Draught beer is served straight from barrels rather than in bottles.

draughtsman, **draughtsmen** NOUN a person who prepares detailed drawings or plans.

draughty, **draughtier**, **draughtiest** ADJECTIVE A place that is draughty has currents of cold air blowing through it.

draw, **draws**, **drawing**, **drew**, **drawn** VERB ① When you draw, you use a pen or crayon to make a picture or diagram. ② To draw near means to move closer. To draw away or draw back means to move away. ③ If you draw something in a particular direction, you pull it there smoothly and gently • *He drew his feet under the chair.* ④ If you draw a deep breath, you breathe in deeply. ⑤ If you draw the curtains, you pull them so that they cover or uncover the window. ⑥ If something such as water or energy is drawn from a source, it is taken from it. ⑦ If you draw a conclusion, you arrive at it from the facts you know. ⑧ If you draw a distinction or a comparison between two things, you point out that it exists. ▸ NOUN ⑨ the result of a game or competition in which nobody wins. **draw up** VERB To draw up a plan, document or list means to prepare it and write it out.

draw VERB
① = paint, sketch, trace
② = move, pull
③ = drag, haul, pull

drawback NOUN a problem that makes something less acceptable or desirable • *Shortcuts usually have a drawback.*

drawback NOUN
= difficulty, hitch, problem, snag, trouble

drawer NOUN a sliding box-shaped part of a piece of furniture used for storing things.

drawing NOUN ① a picture made with a pencil, pen or crayon. ② Drawing is the skill or work of making drawings.

drawing room NOUN (*old-fashioned*) a room in a house where people relax or entertain guests.

drawl VERB If someone drawls, they speak slowly with long vowel sounds.

drawn Drawn is the past participle of **draw**.

dread VERB ① If you dread something, you feel very worried and frightened about it • *He was dreading the journey.* ▸ NOUN ② Dread is a feeling of great fear or anxiety. **dreaded** ADJECTIVE

dreadful ADJECTIVE very bad or unpleasant. **dreadfully** ADVERB

dreadful ADJECTIVE
= appalling, atrocious, awful, frightful (*old-fashioned*), ghastly, horrendous, terrible
≠ wonderful

dream, **dreams**, **dreaming**, **dreamed** or **dreamt** NOUN ① a series of events that you experience in your mind while asleep. ② a situation or event which you often think about because you would very much like it to happen • *his dream of winning the lottery.* ▶ VERB ③ When you dream, you see events in your mind while you are asleep. ④ When you dream about something happening, you often think about it because you would very much like it to happen. ⑤ If someone dreams up a plan or idea, they invent it. ⑥ If you say you would not dream of doing something, you are emphasising that you would not do it • *I wouldn't dream of giving the plot away.* ▶ ADJECTIVE ⑦ too good to be true • *a dream holiday.*
dreamer NOUN

> **dream** NOUN
> ① = hallucination, trance, vision
> ② = ambition, aspiration, daydream, fantasy

Dreamtime NOUN In Australian Aboriginal culture, Dreamtime is the time when the world was being made and the first people were created.

dreamy, **dreamier**, **dreamiest** ADJECTIVE Someone with a dreamy expression looks as if they are thinking about something very pleasant.

dreary, **drearier**, **dreariest** ADJECTIVE dull or boring.

> **dreary** ADJECTIVE
> = boring, drab, dull, humdrum, monotonous, tedious, uneventful
> ≠ exciting

dregs PLURAL NOUN The dregs of a liquid are the last drops left at the bottom of a container, and any sediment left with it.

drenched ADJECTIVE soaking wet.

dress NOUN ① a piece of clothing made up of a skirt and top attached. ② Dress is any clothing. ▶ VERB ③ When you dress, you put clothes on. ④ If you dress for a special occasion, you put on formal clothes. ⑤ To dress a wound means to clean it up and treat it.

> **dress** NOUN
> ① = frock, gown, robe
> ② = attire (*formal*), clothes, clothing, costume, garb (*formal*)
> ▶ VERB ③ = attire (*formal*), clothe, garb (*formal*)
> ≠ undress

dresser NOUN a piece of kitchen or dining room furniture with cupboards or drawers in the lower part and open shelves in the top part.

dressing gown NOUN an item of clothing shaped like a coat and put on over nightwear.

dressing room NOUN a room used for getting changed and putting on make-up, especially a backstage room at a theatre.

dress rehearsal NOUN the last rehearsal of a show or play, using costumes, scenery and lighting.

drew the past tense of **draw**.

dribble VERB ① When liquid dribbles down a surface, it trickles down it in drops or a thin stream. ② If a person or animal dribbles, saliva trickles from their mouth. ③ In sport, to dribble a ball means to move it along by repeatedly tapping it with your foot or a stick. ▶ NOUN ④ a small quantity of liquid flowing in a thin stream or drops.

drift VERB ① When something drifts, it is carried along by the wind or by water. ② When people drift somewhere, they wander or move there gradually. ③ When people drift in life, they move without any aims from place to place or from one activity to another. ④ If you drift off to sleep, you gradually fall asleep. ▸ **NOUN** ⑤ A snow drift is a pile of snow heaped up by the wind. ⑥ The drift of an argument or speech is its main point. **drifter** **NOUN**

drill **NOUN** ① DGT a tool for making holes • *an electric drill.* ② Drill is a routine exercise or routine training • *lifeboat drill.* ▸ **VERB** ③ DGT To drill into something means to make a hole in it using a drill. ④ If you drill people, you teach them to do something by repetition.

drink, **drinks**, **drinking**, **drank**, **drunk** **VERB** ① When you drink, you take liquid into your mouth and swallow it. ② To drink also means to drink alcohol • *He drinks little and eats carefully.* ▸ **NOUN** ③ an amount of liquid suitable for drinking. ④ an alcoholic drink. **drinker** **NOUN**

drink **VERB**
① = gulp, guzzle, sip, swig (*informal*)

drip, **drips**, **dripping**, **dripped** **VERB** ① When liquid drips, it falls in small drops. ② When an object drips, drops of liquid fall from it. ▸ **NOUN** ③ a drop of liquid falling from something. ④ a device for allowing liquid food or medicine to enter the bloodstream of a person who is ill.

drip **VERB**
① = dribble, splash, trickle
▸ **NOUN** ③ = bead, drop, droplet

drive, **drives**, **driving**, **drove**, **driven** **VERB** ① To drive a vehicle means to operate it and control its movements. ② If something or someone drives you to do something, they force you to do it • *His lack of progress drove him to start again.* ③ If you drive a post or nail into something, you force it in by hitting it with a hammer. ④ If something drives a machine, it supplies the power that makes it work. ▸ **NOUN** ⑤ a journey in a vehicle. ⑥ a private road that leads from a public road to a person's house. ⑦ Drive is energy and determination. **driver** **NOUN** **driving** **NOUN**

drive **VERB**
① = operate, pilot, power, propel, run, steer, work
② = compel, force, lead, motivate, prompt, push, spur
③ = hammer, knock, ram, sink, thrust
▸ **NOUN** ⑤ = excursion, jaunt, journey, ride, run, spin (*informal*), trip
⑦ = ambition, determination, energy, enterprise, initiative, motivation, vigour

drive-in **NOUN** a restaurant, cinema or other commercial place that is specially designed for customers to use while staying in their cars.

drivel **NOUN** Drivel is nonsense • *He is still writing mindless drivel.*

drizzle **NOUN** Drizzle is light rain.

drone **VERB** ① If something drones, it makes a low, continuous humming noise. ② If someone drones on, they keep talking or reading aloud in a boring way. ▸ **NOUN** ③ a low, continuous humming sound.

drool **VERB** If someone drools, saliva dribbles from their mouth without them being able to stop it.

droop **VERB** If something droops, it hangs or sags downwards with no strength or firmness.

drop, **drops**, **dropping**, **dropped** **VERB** ① If you drop something, you let it fall. ② If something drops, it falls straight down. ③ If a level or amount drops, it becomes less. ④ If your voice drops, or if you drop your voice, you speak more quietly. ⑤ If you drop something that you are doing or dealing with, you stop doing it or dealing with it • *She dropped the subject and never mentioned it again.* ⑥ If you drop a hint, you give someone a hint in a casual way. ⑦ If you drop something or someone somewhere, you deposit or leave them there. ▶ **NOUN** ⑧ A drop of liquid is a very small quantity of it that forms or falls in a round shape. ⑨ a decrease • *a huge drop in income.* ⑩ the distance between the top and bottom of something tall, such as a cliff or building • *It is a sheer drop to the foot of the cliff.*

> **drop** VERB
> ② = descend, fall, plummet, sink, tumble
> ③ = decline, decrease, diminish, fall, plummet, sink, slump, tumble
> ≠ rise
> ▶ NOUN ⑧ = bead, drip, droplet

droplet NOUN a small drop.

droppings PLURAL NOUN Droppings are the faeces of birds and small animals.

drought *[Rhymes with **shout**]* NOUN GEOGRAPHY a long period during which there is no rain.

drove ① Drove is the past tense of **drive**. ▶ VERB ② To drove cattle or sheep is to drive them over a long distance.

drown VERB ① When someone drowns or is drowned, they die because they have gone under water and cannot breathe. ② If a noise drowns a sound, it is louder than the sound and makes it impossible to hear it.

drowsy, **drowsier**, **drowsiest** ADJECTIVE sleepy.

drudgery NOUN Drudgery is hard boring work.

drug, **drugs**, **drugging**, **drugged** NOUN ① a chemical given to people to treat disease. ② PSHE Drugs are chemical substances that some people smoke, swallow, inhale or inject because of their stimulating effects. ▶ VERB ③ To drug a person or animal means to give them a drug to make them unconscious. ④ To drug food or drink means to add a drug to it in order to make someone unconscious. **drugged** ADJECTIVE

> **drug** NOUN
> ① = medication, medicine
> ② = narcotic, stimulant

drum, **drums**, **drumming**, **drummed** NOUN ① a musical instrument consisting of a skin stretched tightly over a round frame. ② an object or container shaped like a drum • *an oil drum.* ③ *(informal)* In Australian English, the drum is information or advice • *The manager gave me the drum.* ▶ VERB ④ If something is drumming on a surface, it is hitting it regularly, making a continuous beating sound. ⑤ If you drum something into someone, you keep saying it to them until they understand it or remember it. **drummer** NOUN

drunk ① Drunk is the past participle of **drink**. ▶ ADJECTIVE ② If someone is drunk, they have drunk so much alcohol that they cannot speak clearly or behave sensibly. ▶ NOUN ③ a person who is drunk, or who often gets drunk. **drunken** ADJECTIVE **drunkenly** ADVERB **drunkenness** NOUN

> **drunk** ADJECTIVE
> ② = babalas *(South African)*, intoxicated *(formal)*, tipsy
> ≠ sober

dry, **drier** or **dryer**, **driest** or **dryest**; **dries**, **drying**, **dried** ADJECTIVE ① Something that is dry contains or uses no water or liquid. ② Dry bread or toast is eaten without a topping.

③ Dry sherry or wine does not taste sweet. ④ Dry also means plain and sometimes boring • *the dry facts*. ⑤ Dry humour is subtle and sarcastic. ▶ VERB ⑥ When you dry something, or when it dries, liquid is removed from it. **dryness** NOUN **drily** ADVERB

dry up VERB ① If something dries up, it becomes completely dry. ② (*informal*) If you dry up, you forget what you were going to say, or find that you have nothing left to say.

> **dry** ADJECTIVE
> ① = arid, dried-up, parched
> ≠ wet
> ▶ VERB ⑥ = dehydrate, drain
> ≠ moisten

dryer; also spelt **drier** NOUN a device for removing moisture from something by heating or by hot air • *a hair dryer*.

dual ADJECTIVE having two parts, functions or aspects • *a dual-purpose trimmer*.

dub, **dubs**, **dubbing**, **dubbed** VERB ① If something is dubbed a particular name, it is given that name • *Smiling has been dubbed 'nature's secret weapon'*. ② If a film is dubbed, the voices on the soundtrack are not those of the actors, but those of other actors speaking in a different language.

dubious [*Said **dyoo**-bee-uss*] ADJECTIVE ① not entirely honest, safe or reliable • *dubious sales techniques*. ② doubtful • *I felt dubious about the entire proposition*. **dubiously** ADVERB

> **dubious** ADJECTIVE
> ① = crooked, dishonest, questionable, suspect, suspicious, unreliable
> ② = doubtful, nervous, sceptical, suspicious, unconvinced, undecided, unsure

duchess NOUN a woman who has the same rank as a duke, or who is a duke's wife or widow.

duck, **ducks**, **ducking**, **ducked** NOUN ① a bird that lives in water and has webbed feet and a large flat bill. ▶ VERB ② If you duck, you move your head quickly downwards in order to avoid being hit by something. ③ If you duck a duty or responsibility, you avoid it. ④ To duck someone means to push them briefly under water.

duckling NOUN a young duck.

duct NOUN ① a pipe or channel through which liquid or gas is sent. ② a bodily passage through which liquid such as tears can pass.

dud NOUN something which does not function properly.

due ADJECTIVE ① expected to happen or arrive • *The baby is due at Christmas*. ② If you give something due consideration, you give it the consideration it needs. ▶ PHRASE ③ **Due to** means caused by • *Headaches can be due to stress*. ▶ ADVERB ④ Due means exactly in a particular direction • *About a mile due west lay the ocean*. ▶ NOUN ⑤ (*in plural*) Dues are sums of money that you pay regularly to an organisation you belong to.

duel NOUN ① a fight arranged between two people using deadly weapons, to settle a quarrel. ② Any contest or conflict between two people can be referred to as a duel.

duet NOUN MUSIC a piece of music sung or played by two people.

dug Dug is the past tense and past participle of **dig**.

dugout NOUN ① a canoe made by hollowing out a log. ② (*Military*) a shelter dug in the ground for protection.

duke NOUN a nobleman with a rank just below that of a prince.

dull ADJECTIVE ① not at all interesting

in any way. ② not bright, sharp or clear. ③ A dull day or dull sky is very cloudy. ④ Dull feelings are weak and not intense • *He should have been angry but felt only dull resentment.* ▶ **VERB** ⑤ If something dulls or is dulled, it becomes less bright, sharp or clear. **dully ADVERB dullness NOUN**

dull ADJECTIVE
① = boring, drab, humdrum, monotonous, tedious, uninteresting
≠ interesting
② = drab, gloomy, muted, sombre, subdued
≠ bright
③ = cloudy, leaden, murky, overcast
≠ bright

duly ADVERB ① (*formal*) If something is duly done, it is done in the correct way • *I wish to record my support for the duly elected council.* ② If something duly happens, it is something that you expected to happen • *Two chicks duly emerged from their eggs.*

dumb ADJECTIVE ① unable to speak • *She was dumb with rage.* ② (*informal*) slow to understand or stupid.

dumb ADJECTIVE
① = mute, silent, speechless
② = dim, obtuse (*formal*), stupid, thick (*informal*)
≠ smart

dumbfounded ADJECTIVE speechless with amazement • *She was too dumbfounded to answer.*

dummy, dummies NOUN ① a rubber teat which a baby sucks or bites on. ② an imitation or model of something which is used for display. ▶ **ADJECTIVE** ③ imitation or substitute.

dump VERB ① When unwanted waste is dumped, it is left somewhere. ② If you dump something, you throw it down or put it down somewhere in a careless way. ▶ **NOUN** ③ a place where rubbish is left. ④ a storage place, especially used by the military for storing supplies. ⑤ (*informal*) You refer to a place as a dump when it is unattractive and unpleasant to live in.

dump VERB
① = discharge, dispose of, get rid of, jettison, throw away, throw out
② = deposit, drop

dumpling NOUN a small lump of dough that is cooked and eaten with meat and vegetables.

dunce NOUN a person who cannot learn what someone is trying to teach them.

dune NOUN A dune or sand dune is a hill of sand near the sea or in the desert.

dung NOUN Dung is the faeces from large animals, sometimes called manure.

dungeon [*Said* ***dun**-jen*] **NOUN** an underground prison.

dunk VERB To dunk something means to dip it briefly into a liquid • *He dunked a single tea bag into two cups.*

duo, duos NOUN ① a pair of musical performers; also a piece of music written for two players. ② Any two people doing something together can be referred to as a duo.

dupe VERB ① If someone dupes you, they trick you. ▶ **NOUN** ② someone who has been tricked.

dupe VERB
① = cheat, con (*informal*), deceive, delude, fool, play a trick on, trick

duplicate VERB [*Said* ***dyoop**-lik-ayt*] ① To duplicate something means to make an exact copy of it. ▶ **NOUN** [*Said* ***dyoop**-lik-it*] ② something that is identical to something else. ▶ **ADJECTIVE** [*Said* ***dyoop**-lik-it*] ③ identical to or an exact copy of • *a duplicate key.* **duplication NOUN**

durable ADJECTIVE strong and lasting for a long time. **durability** NOUN

duration NOUN The duration of something is the length of time during which it happens or exists.

duress [*Said dyoo-ress*] NOUN If you do something under duress, you are forced to do it, and you do it very unwillingly.

during PREPOSITION happening throughout a particular time or at a particular point in time • *The mussels will open naturally during cooking.*

dusk NOUN Dusk is the time just before nightfall when it is not completely dark.

dust NOUN ① Dust is dry fine powdery material such as particles of earth, dirt or pollen. ▸ VERB ② When you dust furniture or other objects, you remove dust from them using a duster. ③ If you dust a surface with powder, you cover it lightly with the powder.

dustbin NOUN a large container for rubbish.

duster NOUN a cloth used for removing dust from furniture and other objects.

dusty, **dustier**, **dustiest** ADJECTIVE covered with dust.

Dutch ADJECTIVE ① belonging or relating to Holland. ▸ NOUN ② Dutch is the main language spoken in Holland.

dutiful ADJECTIVE doing everything you are expected to do. **dutifully** ADVERB

duty, **duties** NOUN ① something you ought to do or feel you should do, because it is your responsibility • *Adults have a duty to listen to children.* ② a task which you do as part of your job. ③ Duty is tax paid to the government on some goods, especially imports.

duty NOUN
① = obligation, responsibility
② = assignment, job, responsibility, role
③ = excise, levy (*formal*), tariff, tax

duty-free ADJECTIVE Duty-free goods are sold at airports or on planes or ships at a cheaper price than usual because they are not taxed.

duvet [*Said doo-vay*] NOUN a cotton quilt filled with feathers or other material, which you put over yourself in bed.

DVD NOUN A DVD is a disc that can store large amounts of video and sound information. DVD is an abbreviation for 'digital video disc' or 'digital versatile disc'.

dwarf VERB ① If one thing dwarfs another, it is so much bigger that it makes it look very small. ▸ ADJECTIVE ② smaller than average. ▸ NOUN ③ a person who is much smaller than average size.

dwell, **dwells**, **dwelling**, **dwelled** or **dwelt** VERB ① (*literary*) To dwell somewhere means to live there. ② If you dwell on something or dwell upon it, you think or write about it a lot.

dwelling NOUN (*formal*) Someone's dwelling is the house or other place where they live.

dwindle VERB If something dwindles, it becomes smaller or weaker.

dye, **dyes**, **dyeing**, **dyed** VERB ① To dye something means to change its colour by applying coloured liquid to it. ▸ NOUN ② a colouring substance which is used to change the colour of something such as cloth or hair.

dying ADJECTIVE ① likely to die soon. ② (*informal*) If you are **dying for something**, you want it very much.

dying ADJECTIVE
② = ache for, be hungry for, long for, pine for, yearn for

dyke; also spelt **dike** NOUN a thick wall that prevents water flooding onto land from a river or from the sea.

dynamic ADJECTIVE ① A dynamic person is full of energy, ambition and new ideas. ② relating to energy or forces which produce motion.

dynamics PLURAL NOUN ① The dynamics of a society or a situation are the forces that cause it to change. ② MUSIC Dynamics is the various degrees of loudness needed in the performance of a piece of music, or the symbols used to indicate this in written music.

dynamite NOUN Dynamite is an explosive made of nitroglycerine.

dynamo, **dynamos** NOUN SCIENCE a device that converts mechanical energy into electricity.

dynasty, **dynasties** NOUN HISTORY a series of rulers of a country all belonging to the same family.

dysentery *[Said **diss**-en-tree]* NOUN an infection of the bowel which causes fever, stomach pain and severe diarrhoea.

dyslexia *[Said dis-**lek**-see-a]* NOUN Dyslexia is difficulty with reading and spelling caused by a slight disorder of the brain. **dyslexic** ADJECTIVE

Ee

A B C D E F G H I J K L M N O P Q R S T U V W X Y Z

each ADJECTIVE, PRONOUN ① every one taken separately • *Each time she went out, she would buy a plant.* ▸ PHRASE ② If people do something to **each other**, each person does it to the other or others • *She and Chris smiled at each other.*

eager ADJECTIVE wanting very much to do or have something. **eagerly** ADVERB **eagerness** NOUN

> **eager** ADJECTIVE
> = anxious, ardent, avid, enthusiastic, keen, raring to go (*informal*)

eagle NOUN a large bird of prey.

ear NOUN ① the parts of your body on either side of your head with which you hear sounds. ② An ear of corn or wheat is the top part of the stalk which contains seeds.

earl NOUN a British nobleman.

early, **earlier**, **earliest** ADJECTIVE ① before the arranged or expected time • *He wasn't late for our meeting, I was early.* ② near the beginning of a day, evening or other period of time • *the early 2000s.* ▸ ADVERB ③ before the arranged or expected time • *I arrived early.*

> **early** ADJECTIVE
> ① = advance, premature, untimely
> ≠ late
> ③ = primeval, primitive
> ▸ ADVERB ③ = ahead of time, beforehand, in advance, in good time, prematurely

earmark VERB If you earmark something for a special purpose, you keep it for that purpose.

earn VERB ① If you earn money, you get it in return for work that you do. ② If you earn something such as praise, you receive it because you deserve it. **earner** NOUN

> **earn** VERB
> ① = bring in, draw, get, make, obtain
> ② = acquire, attain (*formal*), win

earnest ADJECTIVE ① sincere in what you say or do • *I answered with an earnest smile.* ▸ PHRASE ② If something begins **in earnest**, it happens to a greater or more serious extent than before • *The battle began in earnest.* **earnestly** ADVERB

earnings PLURAL NOUN Your earnings are money that you earn.

earphones PLURAL NOUN small speakers which you wear on your ears to listen to sounds from an electronic device.

earring NOUN Earrings are pieces of jewellery that you wear on your ear lobes.

earshot PHRASE If you are **within earshot** of something, you can hear it.

earth NOUN ① The earth is the planet on which we live. ② Earth is the dry land on the surface of the earth, especially the soil in which things grow. ③ a hole in the ground where a fox lives. ④ The earth in a piece of electrical equipment is the wire through which electricity can pass into the ground and so make the equipment safe for use.

earth NOUN
① = globe, planet, world
② = clay, dirt, ground, soil

earthenware NOUN pottery made of baked clay.

earthly, **earthlier**, **earthliest** ADJECTIVE concerned with life on earth rather than heaven or life after death.

earthquake NOUN [SCIENCE] [GEOGRAPHY] a shaking of the ground caused by movement of the earth.

earthy, **earthier**, **earthiest** ADJECTIVE ① looking or smelling like earth. ② Someone who is earthy is open and direct, often in a crude way • *earthy language.*

ease NOUN ① lack of difficulty, worry or hardship • *He had sailed through life with relative ease.* ▶ VERB ② When something eases, or when you ease it, it becomes less severe or less intense • *to ease the pain.* ③ If you ease something somewhere, you move it there slowly and carefully • *He eased himself into his chair.*

ease NOUN
① = leisure, relaxation, simplicity
▶ VERB ② = abate, calm, relax, relieve, slacken
③ = creep, edge, guide, inch, lower, manoeuvre, squeeze

easel NOUN [ART] an upright frame which supports a picture that someone is painting.

easily ADVERB ① without difficulty. ② without a doubt • *The song is easily one of their finest.*

east NOUN ① East is the direction in which you look to see the sun rise. ② The east of a place is the part which is towards the east when you are in the centre • *the east of Africa.* ③ The East is the countries in the south and east of Asia. ▶ ADJECTIVE, ADVERB ④ East means in or towards the east • *The entrance faces east.* ▶ ADJECTIVE ⑤ An east wind blows from the east.

Easter NOUN [RE] a Christian religious festival celebrating Jesus Christ's coming back to life after he had been killed.

easterly ADJECTIVE ① Easterly means to or towards the east. ② An easterly wind blows from the east.

eastern ADJECTIVE in or from the east • *a remote eastern corner of the country.*

eastward or **eastwards** ADVERB ① Eastward or eastwards means towards the east • *The city expanded eastward.* ▶ ADJECTIVE ② The eastward part of something is the east part.

easy, **easier**, **easiest** ADJECTIVE ① able to be done without difficulty • *It's easy to fall.* ② comfortable and without any worries • *an easy life.*

easy ADJECTIVE
① = light, painless, simple, smooth, straightforward
≠ hard
② = carefree, comfortable, leisurely, quiet, relaxed

eat, **eats**, **eating**, **ate**, **eaten** VERB ① To eat means to chew and swallow food. ② When you eat, you have a meal • *We like to eat early.* **eat away** VERB If something is eaten away, it is slowly destroyed • *The sea had eaten away at the headland.*

eat VERB
① = chew, consume, devour, feed on, scoff, swallow
② = breakfast (*formal*), dine (*formal*), feed, have a meal, lunch (*formal*), picnic
▶ **eat away** = corrode, destroy, dissolve, erode, rot, wear away

eaves PLURAL NOUN The eaves of a roof are the lower edges which jut out over the walls.

eavesdrop, **eavesdrops**, **eavesdropping**, **eavesdropped** VERB If you eavesdrop, you listen secretly to what other people are saying.

ebb VERB ① When the sea or the tide ebbs, it flows back. ② If a person's feeling or strength ebbs, it gets weaker • *The strength ebbed from his body*.

ebony NOUN ① a hard, dark-coloured wood, used for making furniture. ▶ NOUN, ADJECTIVE ② very deep black.

ebullient ADJECTIVE (*formal*) lively and full of enthusiasm. **ebullience** NOUN

eccentric [*Said ik-**sen**-trik*] ADJECTIVE ① having habits or opinions which other people think are odd or peculiar. ▶ NOUN ② someone who is eccentric. **eccentricity** NOUN **eccentrically** ADVERB

> **eccentric** ADJECTIVE
> ① = bizarre, outlandish, quirky, strange, weird, whimsical
> ▶ NOUN ② = character (*informal*), crank

ecclesiastical [*Said ik-leez-ee-**ass**-ti-kl*] ADJECTIVE of or relating to the Christian Church.

echelon [*Said **esh**-el-on*] NOUN ① An echelon is a level of power or responsibility in an organisation; also used of the group of people at that level. ② An echelon is also a military formation in the shape of an arrowhead.

echidna, **echidnas** or **echidnae** [*Said ik-**kid**-na*] NOUN a small, spiny mammal that lays eggs and has a long snout and claws, found in Australia.

echo, **echoes**, **echoing**, **echoed** NOUN ① [SCIENCE] a sound which is caused by sound waves reflecting off a surface. ② a repetition, imitation or reminder of something • *Echoes of the past are everywhere*. ▶ VERB ③ If a sound echoes, it is reflected off a surface so that you can hear it again after the original sound has stopped.

eclipse NOUN An eclipse occurs when one planet passes in front of another and hides it from view for a short time.

eco-friendly, **eco-friendlier**, **eco-friendliest** ADJECTIVE If a product is eco-friendly, it does not cause any damage to the environment • *eco-friendly washing powder*.

ecology NOUN [SCIENCE] the relationship between living things and their environment; also used of the study of this relationship. **ecological** ADJECTIVE **ecologically** ADVERB **ecologist** NOUN

economic ADJECTIVE ① concerning the management of the money, industry and trade of a country. ② concerning making a profit • *economic ways to produce dairy foods*.

> **economic** ADJECTIVE
> ① = budgetary, commercial, financial
> ② = productive, profitable, viable

economical ADJECTIVE ① another word for **economic**. ② Something that is economical is cheap to use or operate. ③ Someone who is economical spends money carefully and sensibly. **economically** ADVERB

> **economical** ADJECTIVE
> ② = cheap, cost-effective, economic, inexpensive
> ③ = careful, frugal, prudent, thrifty

economics NOUN Economics is the study of the production and distribution of goods, services and wealth in a society and the organisation of its money, industry and trade.

economist NOUN a person who studies or writes about economics.

economy, **economies** NOUN ① [HISTORY] The economy of a country is the system it uses to organise and manage its money, industry and trade; also used of the wealth that a country gets from business and industry. ② Economy is the careful use of things to save money, time or energy • *There is a wonderful economy of effort about this recipe.*

economy NOUN
② = frugality (*formal*), prudence, restraint, thrift

ecosystem NOUN SCIENCE the relationship between plants and animals and their environment.

ecstasy, **ecstasies** NOUN Ecstasy is a feeling of extreme happiness.
ecstatic ADJECTIVE **ecstatically** ADVERB

ecstasy NOUN
= bliss, delight, elation, euphoria, exaltation, joy, rapture

eczema [*Said* ***ek**-sim-ma or ek-**see**-ma*] NOUN a skin disease that causes the surface of the skin to become rough and itchy.

edge NOUN ① The edge of something is a border or line where it ends or meets something else. ② The edge of a blade is its thin, sharp side. ③ If you have the edge over someone, you have an advantage over them. ▶ VERB ④ If you edge something, you make a border for it • *The veil was edged with matching lace.* ⑤ If you edge somewhere, you move there very gradually • *The ferry edged its way out into the river.*

edge NOUN
① = border, boundary, brim, fringe, lip, margin, rim
≠ centre
▶ VERB ⑤ = creep, inch, sidle

edgy, **edgier**, **edgiest** ADJECTIVE anxious and irritable.

edible ADJECTIVE safe and pleasant to eat.

edifice [*Said* ***ed**-if-iss*] NOUN (*formal*) a large and impressive building.

edit VERB ① If you edit a piece of writing, you correct it so that it is fit for publishing. ② To edit a film or television programme means to select different parts of it and arrange them in a particular order. ③ Someone who edits a newspaper or magazine is in charge of it.

edition NOUN ① ENGLISH An edition of a book, magazine or newspaper is a particular version of it printed at one time; also the total number of copies printed at one time. ② An edition of a television or radio programme is a single programme that is one of a series • *tonight's edition of the news.*

editor NOUN ① a person who is responsible for the content of a newspaper or magazine. ② LIBRARY a person who checks books and makes corrections to them before they are published. ③ a person who selects different parts of a television programme or a film and arranges them in a particular order.
editorship NOUN

editorial ADJECTIVE ① involved in preparing a newspaper, book or magazine for publication. ② involving the contents and the opinions of a newspaper or magazine • *an editorial comment.* ▶ NOUN ③ an article in a newspaper or magazine which gives the opinions of the editor or publisher on a particular topic. **editorially** ADVERB

educate VERB To educate someone means to teach them so that they gain knowledge about something.

educated ADJECTIVE having a high standard of learning and culture.

educated ADJECTIVE
= cultivated, cultured, intellectual, learned

education NOUN the process of gaining knowledge and understanding through learning or the system of teaching people. **educational** ADJECTIVE **educationally** ADVERB

> **education** NOUN
> = coaching, e-learning, instruction, schooling, training, tuition

eel NOUN a long, thin, snakelike fish.

eerie, **eerier**, **eeriest** ADJECTIVE strange and frightening • *an eerie silence*. **eerily** ADVERB

effect NOUN ① a direct result of someone or something on another person or thing • *the effects of bullying on children*. ② An effect that someone or something has is the overall impression or result that they have • *The effect of the decor was cosy and antique*. ▶ PHRASE ③ If something **takes effect** at a particular time, it starts to happen or starts to produce results at that time • *The law will take effect next year*.

> **effect** NOUN
> ① = consequence, end result, fruit, result, upshot

effective ADJECTIVE ① working well and producing the intended results. ② coming into operation or beginning officially • *The agreement has become effective immediately*. **effectively** ADVERB

effeminate ADJECTIVE A man who is effeminate behaves, looks or sounds like a woman.

efficient ADJECTIVE capable of doing something well without wasting time or energy. **efficiently** ADVERB **efficiency** NOUN

> **efficient** ADJECTIVE
> = businesslike, competent, economic, effective, organised, productive
> ≠ inefficient

effigy, **effigies** [*Said* ***ef**-fij-ee*] NOUN a statue or model of a person.

effluent [*Said* ***ef**-loo-ent*] NOUN Effluent is liquid waste that comes out of factories or sewage works.

effort NOUN ① PSHE Effort is the physical or mental energy needed to do something. ② an attempt or struggle to do something • *The town has banned cars in an effort to cut pollution*.

> **effort** NOUN
> ① = application, energy, exertion, trouble, work
> ② = attempt, bid, stab (*informal*), struggle

effortless ADJECTIVE done easily. **effortlessly** ADVERB

eg or **e.g.** Eg means 'for example', and is abbreviated from the Latin expression 'exempli gratia'.

egalitarian ADJECTIVE favouring equality for all people • *an egalitarian country*.

egg NOUN ① an oval or rounded object laid by female birds, reptiles, fishes and insects. A baby creature develops inside the egg until it is ready to be born. ② a hen's egg used as food. ③ In a female animal, an egg is a cell produced in its body which can develop into a baby if it is fertilised. **egg on** VERB If you egg someone on, you encourage them to do something foolish or daring.

eggplant NOUN a dark purple pear-shaped fruit eaten as a vegetable. It is also called **aubergine**.

ego, **egos** [*Said* ***ee**-goh*] NOUN Your ego is your opinion of what you are worth • *It'll do her good and boost her ego*.

egocentric ADJECTIVE only thinking of yourself.

egoism or **egotism** NOUN Egoism is behaviour and attitudes which show that you believe that you are more important than other people.

egoist or **egotist** NOUN **egoistic** or **egotistic** or **egotistical** ADJECTIVE

Egyptian *[Said ij-**jip**-shn]* ADJECTIVE ① belonging or relating to Egypt. ▶ NOUN ② An Egyptian is someone who comes from Egypt.

eight ① the number 8. ▶ NOUN ② In rowing, an eight is the crew of a narrow racing boat, consisting of eight rowers. **eighth** ADJECTIVE

eighteen the number 18. **eighteenth** ADJECTIVE

eighty, **eighties** the number 80. **eightieth** ADJECTIVE

either ADJECTIVE, PRONOUN, CONJUNCTION ① one or the other of two possible alternatives • *You can spell it either way* • *Either of these schemes would cost billions of pounds* • *Either take it or leave it.* ▶ ADJECTIVE ② both one and the other • *on either side of the head.*

eject VERB If you eject something or someone, you forcefully push or send them out • *He was ejected from the club.* **ejection** NOUN

elaborate ADJECTIVE *[Said e-**la**-bor-it]* ① having many different parts • *an elaborate system of drains.* ② carefully planned, detailed and exact • *elaborate plans.* ③ highly decorated and complicated • *elaborate designs.* ▶ VERB *[Said e-**la**-bor-ate]* ④ If you elaborate on something, you add more information or detail about it. **elaborately** ADVERB **elaboration** NOUN

> **elaborate** ADJECTIVE
> ① = complex, complicated, detailed, intricate, involved
> ≠ simple
> ③ = fancy, fussy, ornate
> ▶ VERB ④ = develop, enlarge, expand

elapse VERB When time elapses, it passes by • *Eleven years elapsed before you got this job.*

elastic ADJECTIVE ① able to stretch easily. ▶ NOUN ② Elastic is rubber material which stretches and returns to its original shape. **elasticity** NOUN

elation NOUN Elation is a feeling of great happiness. **elated** ADJECTIVE

elbow NOUN ① Your elbow is the joint between the upper part of your arm and your forearm. ▶ VERB ② If you elbow someone aside, you push them away with your elbow.

elder ADJECTIVE ① Your elder brother or sister is older than you. ▶ NOUN ② a senior member of a group who has influence or authority. ③ a bush or small tree with dark purple berries.

elderly ADJECTIVE Elderly is a polite way to describe an old person • *our elderly relatives.*

elect VERB ① CITIZENSHIP If you elect someone, you choose them to fill a position, by voting • *He's just been elected president.* ② (formal) If you elect to do something, you choose to do it • *I have elected to stay.* ▶ ADJECTIVE ③ (formal) voted into a position, but not yet carrying out the duties of the position • *the vice-president elect.*

election NOUN CITIZENSHIP the selection of one or more people for an official position by voting. **electoral** ADJECTIVE

electorate NOUN all the people who have the right to vote in an election.

electric ADJECTIVE ① powered or produced by electricity. ② very tense or exciting • *The atmosphere is electric.*

electrical ADJECTIVE using or producing electricity • *electrical goods.* **electrically** ADVERB

electrician NOUN a person whose job is to install and repair electrical equipment.

electricity NOUN Electricity is a form of energy used for heating and lighting, and to provide power for machines.

A B C D E F G H I J K L M N O P Q R S T U V W X Y Z

electrified ADJECTIVE connected to a supply of electricity.

electrifying ADJECTIVE Something that is electrifying makes you feel very excited.

electrocute VERB If someone is electrocuted, they are killed by touching something that is connected to electricity.
electrocution NOUN

electrode NOUN a small piece of metal which allows an electric current to pass between a source of power and a piece of equipment.

electron NOUN ① SCIENCE In physics, an electron is a tiny particle of matter, smaller than an atom. ② SCIENCE An **electron shell** is the orbit of an electron around the nucleus of an atom.

electronic ADJECTIVE ICT having transistors or silicon chips which control an electric current.
electronically ADVERB

electronics NOUN Electronics is the technology of electronic devices such as televisions and computers; also the study of how these devices work.

elegant ADJECTIVE attractive and graceful or stylish • *an elegant and beautiful city*. **elegantly** ADVERB
elegance NOUN

element NOUN ① a part of something which combines with others to make a whole. ② SCIENCE In chemistry, an element is a substance that is made up of only one type of atom. ③ A particular element within a large group of people is a section of it which is similar • *criminal elements*. ④ An element of a quality is a certain amount of it • *Their attack has largely lost the element of surprise*. ⑤ The elements of a subject are the basic and most important points. ⑥ The elements are the weather conditions • *Our open boat is exposed to the elements*.

elemental ADJECTIVE (*formal*) simple and basic, but powerful • *elemental emotions*.

elementary ADJECTIVE simple, basic and straightforward • *an elementary course in woodwork*.

elephant NOUN a very large four-legged mammal with a long trunk, large ears, and ivory tusks.

elevate VERB ① To elevate someone to a higher status or position means to give them greater status or importance • *He was elevated to the rank of major in the army*. ② To elevate something means to raise it up.

elevation NOUN ① The elevation of someone or something is the raising of them to a higher level or position. ② The elevation of a place is its height above sea level or above the ground.

eleven ① the number 11. ▶ NOUN ② a team of cricket or soccer players.
eleventh ADJECTIVE

elf NOUN In folklore, an elf is a small mischievous fairy.

elicit [*Said il-iss-it*] VERB ① (*formal*) If you elicit information, you find it out by asking careful questions. ② If you elicit a response or reaction, you make it happen • *He elicited sympathy from the audience*.

eligible [*Said* ***el****-lij-i-bl*] ADJECTIVE suitable or having the right qualifications for something • *You will be eligible for a grant in the future*.
eligibility NOUN

eliminate VERB ① If you eliminate something or someone, you get rid of them • *They eliminated him from their inquiries*. ② If a team or a person is eliminated from a competition, they can no longer take part. **elimination** NOUN

> **eliminate** VERB
> ① = cut out, do away with, eradicate, get rid of, remove, stamp out
> ② = knock out, put out

elite *[Said ill-**eet**]* NOUN a group of the most powerful, rich or talented people in a society.

Elizabethan HISTORY ADJECTIVE Someone or something that is Elizabethan lived or was made during the reign of Elizabeth I.

elk NOUN a large kind of deer.

elm NOUN a tall tree with broad leaves.

elongated ADJECTIVE long and thin.

eloquent ADJECTIVE able to speak or write skilfully and with ease • *an eloquent politician.* **eloquently** ADVERB **eloquence** NOUN

else ADVERB ① other than this or more than this • *Can you think of anything else?* ▸ PHRASE ② You say **or else** to introduce a possibility or an alternative • *You have to go with the flow or else be left behind in the rush.*

elsewhere ADVERB in or to another place • *He would rather be elsewhere.*

elude *[Said ill-**ood**]* VERB ① If a fact or idea eludes you, you cannot understand it or remember it. ② If you elude someone or something, you avoid them or escape from them • *He eluded the authorities.*

elusive ADJECTIVE difficult to find, achieve, describe or remember • *the elusive million dollar prize.*

elves the plural of **elf**.

emaciated *[Said im-**may**-see-ate-ed]* ADJECTIVE extremely thin and weak, because of illness or lack of food.

email; also spelt **e-mail** NOUN ① the sending of messages from one computer to another. ② a message sent in this way. ▸ VERB ③ If you email someone, you send an email to them. ④ If you email something to someone, you send it to them by email.

emancipation NOUN The emancipation of a person means the act of freeing them from harmful or unpleasant restrictions.

embargo, **embargoes** NOUN an order made by a government to stop trade with another country.

embark VERB ① If you embark, you go onto a ship at the start of a journey. ② If you embark on something, you start it • *He embarked on a huge spending spree.*

embarrass VERB If you embarrass someone, you make them feel ashamed or awkward • *I won't embarrass you by asking for details.* **embarrassing** ADJECTIVE

> **embarrass** VERB
> = disconcert, fluster, humiliate, shame

embarrassed ADJECTIVE ashamed or awkward.

> **embarrassed** ADJECTIVE
> = ashamed, awkward, humiliated, red-faced, self-conscious, sheepish

embarrassment, **embarrassments** NOUN shame and awkwardness.

> **embarrassment** NOUN
> = awkwardness, bashfulness, humiliation, self-consciousness, shame

embassy, **embassies** NOUN the building in which an ambassador and his or her staff work; also used of the ambassador and his or her staff.

embedded ADJECTIVE Something that is embedded is fixed firmly and deeply • *glass decorated with embedded threads.*

ember NOUN Embers are glowing pieces of coal or wood from a dying fire.

embittered ADJECTIVE If you are embittered, you are angry and resentful about things that have happened to you.

emblazoned *[Said im-**blaze**-nd]* ADJECTIVE If something is emblazoned with designs, it is decorated with them • *vases emblazoned with bold and colourful images.*

emblem NOUN an object or a design representing an organisation or an idea • *a flower emblem of Japan.*

embody, **embodies**, **embodying**, **embodied** VERB ① To embody a quality or idea means to contain it or express it • *A young dancer embodies the spirit of fun.* ② If a number of things are embodied in one thing, they are contained in it • *the principles embodied in his report.* **embodiment** NOUN

embossed ADJECTIVE decorated with designs that stand up slightly from the surface • *embossed wallpaper.*

embrace VERB ① If you embrace someone, you hug them to show affection or as a greeting. ② If you embrace a belief or cause, you accept it and believe in it. ▸ NOUN ③ a hug.

embroider VERB If you embroider fabric, you sew a decorative design onto it.

embroidery NOUN Embroidery is decorative designs sewn onto fabric; also the art or skill of embroidering.

embroiled ADJECTIVE If someone is embroiled in an argument or conflict, they are deeply involved in it and cannot get out of it • *The two companies are now embroiled in the courts.*

embryo *[Said **em**-bree-oh]* NOUN SCIENCE an animal or human being in the very early stages of development in the womb.
embryonic ADJECTIVE

emerald NOUN ① a bright green precious stone. ▸ NOUN, ADJECTIVE ② bright green.

emerge VERB ① If someone emerges from a place, they come out of it so that they can be seen. ② If something emerges, it becomes known or begins to be recognised as existing • *It later emerged that he had left the band.*
emergence NOUN **emergent** ADJECTIVE

emergency, **emergencies** NOUN an unexpected and serious event which needs immediate action to deal with it.

> **emergency** NOUN
> = crisis, pinch

emigrant NOUN HISTORY someone who leaves their native country and goes to live permanently in another one. **emigrate** VERB **emigration** NOUN

eminence NOUN ① Eminence is the quality of being well-known and respected for what you do • *lawyers of eminence.* ② 'Your Eminence' is a title of respect used to address a Roman Catholic cardinal.

eminent ADJECTIVE well-known and respected for what you do • *an eminent scientist.*

eminently ADVERB *(formal)* very • *eminently reasonable.*

emir *[Said em-**eer**]* NOUN a Muslim ruler or nobleman.

emission NOUN *(formal)* The emission of something such as gas or radiation is the release of it into the atmosphere.

emit, **emits**, **emitting**, **emitted** VERB To emit something means to give it out or release it • *She emitted a long, low whistle.*

> **emit** VERB
> = exude, give off, give out, release, send out, utter

emotion NOUN PSHE a strong feeling, such as love or fear.

emotional ADJECTIVE ① causing strong feelings • *an emotional appeal for help.* ② PSHE to do with feelings rather than your physical condition • *emotional support.* ③ showing your feelings openly • *The child is in a very emotional state.* **emotionally** ADVERB

emotive ADJECTIVE concerning emotions, or stirring up strong emotions • *emotive language.*

empathise; also spelt **empathize** VERB PSHE If you empathise with someone, you understand how they are feeling. **empathy** NOUN

emperor NOUN a male ruler of an empire.

emphasis, **emphases** NOUN Emphasis is special importance or extra stress given to something.

> **emphasis** NOUN
> = accent, importance, prominence, weight

emphasise; also spelt **emphasize** VERB If you emphasise something, you make it known that it is very important • *It was emphasised that the matter was of international concern.*

> **emphasise** VERB
> = accent, accentuate, highlight, play up, stress, underline

emphatic ADJECTIVE expressed strongly and with force to show how important something is • *I answered both questions with an emphatic 'Yes'.* **emphatically** ADVERB

empire NOUN ① a group of countries controlled by one country. ② a powerful group of companies controlled by one person.

employ VERB ① If you employ someone, you pay them to work for you. ② If you employ something for a particular purpose, you make use of it • *the techniques employed in turning milk into cheese.*

> **employ** VERB
> ① = appoint, commission, engage (*formal*), hire, take on
> ② = bring to bear, make use of, use, utilise

employee NOUN a person who is paid to work for another person or for an organisation.

> **employee** NOUN
> = hand, worker, workman

employer NOUN Someone's employer is the person or organisation that they work for.

> **employer** NOUN
> = boss, gaffer (*informal*)

employment NOUN GEOGRAPHY Employment is the state of having a paid job, or the activity of recruiting people for a job.

> **employment** NOUN
> = engagement, enlistment, hiring, recruitment, taking on

empower VERB If you are empowered to do something, you have the authority or power to do it.

empress NOUN a woman who rules an empire, or the wife of an emperor.

empty, **emptier**, **emptiest**; **empties**, **emptying**, **emptied** ADJECTIVE ① having nothing or nobody inside. ② without purpose, value or meaning • *empty promises.* ▸ VERB ③ If you empty something, or empty its contents, you remove the contents. **emptiness** NOUN

> **empty** ADJECTIVE
> ① = bare, blank, clear, deserted, unfurnished, uninhabited, vacant
> ≠ full
> ② = inane, meaningless, worthless
> ▸ VERB ③ = clear, drain, evacuate, unload
> ≠ fill

emu [*Said* ***ee**-myoo*] NOUN a large Australian bird which can run fast but cannot fly.

emulate VERB If you emulate someone or something, you imitate them because you admire them. **emulation** NOUN

emulsion NOUN a water-based paint.

enable VERB To enable something to happen means to make it possible.

enact VERB ① If a government enacts a law or bill, it officially passes it so that it becomes law. ② If you enact a story or play, you act it out. **enactment** NOUN

enamel, **enamels**, **enamelling**, **enamelled** NOUN ① a substance like glass, used to decorate or protect metal or china. ② The enamel on your teeth is the hard, white substance that forms the outer part. ▸ VERB ③ If you enamel something, you decorate or cover it with enamel. **enamelled** ADJECTIVE

enamoured *[Said in-**am**-erd]* ADJECTIVE If you are enamoured of someone or something, you like them very much.

encapsulate VERB If something encapsulates facts or ideas, it contains or represents them in a small space.

encased ADJECTIVE Something that is encased is surrounded or covered with a substance • *encased in plaster.*

enchanted ADJECTIVE If you are enchanted by something or someone, you are fascinated or charmed by them.

enchanting ADJECTIVE attractive, delightful or charming • *an enchanting baby.*

encircle VERB To encircle something or someone means to completely surround them.

enclave NOUN a place that is surrounded by areas that are different from it in some important way, for example because the people there are from a different culture • *an Armenian enclave in Azerbaijan.*

enclose VERB To enclose an object or area means to surround it with something solid. **enclosed** ADJECTIVE

> **enclose** VERB
> = encircle, fence off, hem in, surround, wrap

enclosure NOUN an area of land surrounded by a wall or fence and used for a particular purpose.

encompass VERB To encompass a number of things means to include all of those things • *The book encompassed all aspects of maths.*

encore *[Said **ong**-kor]* NOUN a short extra performance given by an entertainer because the audience asks for it.

encounter VERB ① If you encounter someone or something, you meet them or are faced with them • *She was the most gifted child he ever encountered.* ▸ NOUN ② a meeting, especially when it is difficult or unexpected.

encourage VERB ① [PSHE] If you encourage someone, you give them courage and confidence to do something. ② If someone or something encourages a particular activity, they support it • *The government will encourage the creation of nursery places.* **encouraging** ADJECTIVE **encouragement** NOUN

> **encourage** VERB
> ① = cheer, hearten, reassure
> ≠ discourage
> ② = aid, boost, favour, help, incite, support

encroach VERB If something encroaches on a place or on your time or rights, it gradually takes up or takes away more and more of it. **encroachment** NOUN

encrusted ADJECTIVE covered with a crust or layer of something • *a necklace encrusted with gold.*

encyclopedia *[Said en-sigh-klo-**pee**-dee-a]*; also spelt **encyclopaedia** NOUN [LIBRARY] a book or set of books giving information about many different subjects.

encyclopedic; also spelt **encyclopaedic** ADJECTIVE knowing or giving information about many different things.

end NOUN ① The end of a period of time or an event is the last part. ② The end of something is the farthest point of it • *the room at the end of the passage.* ③ the purpose for which something is done • *He made friends with me for his own ends.* ▶ VERB ④ If something ends or if you end it, it comes to a finish.

> **end** NOUN
> ① = climax, close, conclusion, culmination, ending, expiry, finale, finish
> ≠ beginning
> ② = boundary, bounds, edge, extremity, limit, margin
> ③ = aim, goal, intention, object, objective, purpose, reason
> ▶ VERB ④ = bring to an end, cease, conclude, finish, stop, terminate (*formal*)
> ≠ begin

endanger VERB To endanger something means to cause it to be in a dangerous and harmful situation • *a driver who endangers the safety of others.*

> **endanger** VERB
> = compromise, jeopardise, put at risk, risk, threaten

endear VERB If someone's behaviour endears them to you, it makes you fond of them. **endearing** ADJECTIVE **endearingly** ADVERB

endeavour [*Said in-**dev**-er*] VERB ① (*formal*) If you endeavour to do something, you try very hard to do it. ▶ NOUN ② an effort to do or achieve something.

endless ADJECTIVE having or seeming to have no end. **endlessly** ADVERB

endorse VERB ① If you endorse someone or something, you give approval and support to them. ② If you endorse a document, you write your signature or a comment on it, to show that you approve of it. **endorsement** NOUN

endowed ADJECTIVE If someone is endowed with a quality or ability, they have it or are given it • *She was endowed with great willpower.*

endurance NOUN Endurance is the ability to put up with a difficult situation for a period of time.

endure VERB ① If you endure a difficult situation, you put up with it calmly and patiently. ② If something endures, it lasts or continues to exist • *The old alliance still endures.* **enduring** ADJECTIVE

> **endure** VERB
> ① = cope with, experience, go through, stand, suffer
> ② = last, live on, remain, survive

enemy, **enemies** NOUN a person or group that is hostile or opposed to another person or group.

> **enemy** NOUN
> = adversary, antagonist, foe, opponent
> ≠ friend

energetic ADJECTIVE having or showing energy or enthusiasm. **energetically** ADVERB

> **energetic** ADJECTIVE
> = animated, dynamic, indefatigable, spirited, tireless, vigorous

energy, **energies** NOUN ① the physical strength to do active things. ② the power which drives machinery. ③ SCIENCE In physics, energy is the capacity of a body or system to do work. It is measured in joules.

> **energy** NOUN
> ① = drive, life, spirit, strength, vigour, vitality

A B C D E F G H I J K L M N O P Q R S T U V W X Y Z

enforce VERB If you enforce a law or a rule, you make sure that it is obeyed. **enforceable** ADJECTIVE **enforcement** NOUN

engage VERB ① If you engage in an activity, you take part in it • *Officials have declined to engage in a debate.* ② To engage someone or their attention means to make or keep someone interested in something • *He engaged the driver in conversation.*

engaged ADJECTIVE ① When two people are engaged, they have agreed to marry each other. ② If someone or something is engaged, they are occupied or busy • *Mr Anderson was otherwise engaged* • *The emergency number was always engaged.*

engagement NOUN ① an appointment that you have with someone. ② an agreement that two people have made with each other to get married.

engine NOUN ① a machine designed to convert heat or other kinds of energy into mechanical movement. ② a railway locomotive.

engineer NOUN ① a person trained in designing and building machinery and electrical devices, or roads and bridges. ② a person who repairs mechanical or electrical devices. ▶ VERB ③ If you engineer an event or situation, you arrange it cleverly, usually for your own advantage.

engineering NOUN Engineering is the profession of designing and constructing machinery and electrical devices, or roads and bridges.

English ADJECTIVE ① belonging or relating to England. ▶ NOUN ② English is the main language spoken in the United Kingdom, the USA, Canada, Australia, New Zealand and many other countries.

Englishman, **Englishmen** NOUN a man who comes from England.

Englishwoman, **Englishwomen** NOUN a woman who comes from England.

engrave VERB To engrave means to cut letters or designs into a hard surface with a tool.

engraving NOUN a picture or design that has been cut into a hard surface. **engraver** NOUN

engrossed ADJECTIVE If you are engrossed in something, it holds all your attention • *He was engrossed in a video game.*

engulf VERB To engulf something means to completely cover or surround it • *Black smoke engulfed him.*

enhance VERB To enhance something means to make it more valuable or attractive • *an outfit that really enhances your colouring.* **enhancement** NOUN

enigma NOUN anything which is puzzling or difficult to understand.

enigmatic ADJECTIVE mysterious, puzzling or difficult to understand • *an enigmatic stranger.* **enigmatically** ADVERB

enjoy VERB ① If you enjoy something, you find pleasure and satisfaction in it. ② If you enjoy something, you are lucky to have it or experience it • *She has enjoyed a long life.*

> **enjoy** VERB
> ① = appreciate, delight in, like, love, relish, revel in, take pleasure from, take pleasure in

enjoyable ADJECTIVE giving pleasure or satisfaction.

enjoyment NOUN Enjoyment is the feeling of pleasure or satisfaction you get from something nice.

enlarge VERB ① When you enlarge something, it gets bigger. ② If you enlarge on a subject, you give more details about it.

enlarge VERB
① = add to, expand, extend, increase, magnify
② = develop, elaborate on, expand on

enlargement NOUN ① An enlargement of something is the action of making it bigger. ② something, especially a photograph, which has been made bigger.

enlighten VERB To enlighten someone means to give them more knowledge or understanding of something. **enlightening** ADJECTIVE **enlightenment** NOUN

enlightened ADJECTIVE well-informed and willing to consider different opinions • *an enlightened government*.

enlist VERB ① If someone enlists, they join the army, navy or air force. ② If you enlist someone's help, you persuade them to help you in something you are doing.

enliven VERB To enliven something means to make it more lively or more cheerful.

en masse [*Said on* ***mass***] ADVERB If a group of people do something en masse, they do it together and at the same time.

enormity, **enormities** NOUN ① The enormity of a problem or difficulty is its great size and seriousness. ② something that is thought to be a terrible crime or offence.

enormous ADJECTIVE very large in size or amount. **enormously** ADVERB

enormous ADJECTIVE
= colossal, gigantic, huge, immense, massive, tremendous, vast
≠ tiny

enough ADJECTIVE, ADVERB ① as much or as many as required • *He did not have enough money for sweets*. ▶ NOUN ② Enough is the quantity necessary for something • *There's not enough to go round*. ▶ ADVERB ③ very or fairly • *She could manage well enough without me*.

enquire; also spelt **inquire** VERB If you enquire about something or someone, you ask about them.

enquiry; also spelt **inquiry** NOUN ① a question that you ask in order to find something out. ② an investigation into something that has happened and that needs explaining.

enrage VERB If something enrages you, it makes you very angry. **enraged** ADJECTIVE

enrich VERB To enrich something means to improve the quality or value of it • *new woods to enrich our countryside*. **enriched** ADJECTIVE **enrichment** NOUN

enrol, **enrols**, **enrolling**, **enrolled** VERB If you enrol for something such as a course or a college, you register to join or become a member of it. **enrolment** NOUN

en route [*Said on* ***root***] ADVERB If something happens en route to a place, it happens on the way there.

ensconced ADJECTIVE If you are ensconced in a particular place, you are settled there firmly and comfortably.

ensemble [*Said on-****som****-bl*] NOUN ① a group of things or people considered as a whole rather than separately. ② a small group of musicians who play or sing together.

enshrine VERB If something such as an idea or a right is enshrined in a society, constitution or a law, it is protected by it • *Freedom of speech is enshrined in the American Constitution*.

ensue, **ensues**, **ensuing**, **ensued** [*Said en-****syoo***] VERB If something ensues, it happens after another event, usually as a result of it • *He entered the house and an argument ensued*. **ensuing** ADJECTIVE

ensure VERB To ensure that something happens means to make certain that it happens • *We make every effort to ensure the information given is correct.*

ensure VERB
= guarantee, make certain, make sure

entangled ADJECTIVE If you are entangled in problems or difficulties, you are involved in them.

enter VERB ① To enter a place means to go into it. ② If you enter an organisation or institution, you join and become a member of it • *He entered Parliament in 2015.* ③ If you enter a competition or examination, you take part in it. ④ If you enter data into a form or database, you record it by writing or typing it in an empty space.

enterprise NOUN ① a business or company. ② a project or task, especially one that involves risk or difficulty.

enterprise NOUN
① = business, company, concern, establishment, firm, operation
② = effort, endeavour, operation, project, undertaking, venture

enterprising ADJECTIVE ready to start new projects and tasks and full of boldness and initiative • *an enterprising company.*

entertain VERB ① If you entertain people, you keep them amused or interested. ② If you entertain guests, you receive them into your house and give them food and hospitality.

entertain VERB
① = amuse, charm, delight, enthral, please

entertainer, **entertainers** NOUN someone whose job is to amuse and please audiences, for example a comedian or singer.

entertaining ADJECTIVE ① amusing and full of interest. ▶ NOUN ② Entertaining is the hospitality that you give to guests • *He enjoys entertaining at home.*

entertainment, **entertainments** NOUN anything people watch or do for pleasure.

entertainment NOUN
= amusement, enjoyment, fun, pleasure, recreation

enthuse [Said inth-**yooz**] VERB If you enthuse about something, you talk about it with enthusiasm and excitement.

enthusiasm NOUN Enthusiasm is interest, eagerness or delight in something.

enthusiasm NOUN
= eagerness, excitement, interest, keenness, warmth

enthusiastic ADJECTIVE showing great excitement, eagerness or approval for something • *She was enthusiastic about poetry.*
enthusiastically ADVERB

enthusiastic ADJECTIVE
= ardent, avid, devoted, eager, excited, keen, passionate
≠ apathetic

entice VERB If you entice someone to do something, you tempt them to do it • *We tried to entice the mouse out of the hole.*

enticing ADJECTIVE extremely attractive and tempting.

entire ADJECTIVE including all of something • *the entire month of July.*

entirely ADVERB wholly and completely • *He and I were entirely different.*

entirety [Said en-**tire**-it-tee] PHRASE If something happens to something **in its entirety**, it happens to all of it • *This message will now be repeated in its entirety.*

A B C D E F G H I J K L M N O P Q R S T U V W X Y Z

entitle VERB If something entitles you to have or do something, it gives you the right to have or do it.
entitlement NOUN

entity, **entities** [*Said* ***en****-tit-ee*] NOUN any complete thing that is not divided and not part of anything else.

entourage [*Said* ***on****-too-rahj*] NOUN a group of people who follow or travel with a famous or important person.

entrails PLURAL NOUN Entrails are the inner parts, especially the intestines, of people or animals.

entrance[1] [*Said* ***en****-trunss*] NOUN ① The entrance of a building or area is its doorway or gate. ② A person's entrance is their arrival in a place, or the way in which they arrive • *She likes to make a dramatic entrance.* ③ DRAMA In the theatre, an actor makes his or her entrance when he or she comes onto the stage. ④ Entrance is the right to enter a place • *He had gained entrance by pretending to be a heating engineer.*

> **entrance** NOUN
> ① = door, doorway, entry, gate, way in
> ② = appearance, arrival, entry
> ④ = access, admission, entry

entrance[2] [*Said en-****trahnss***] VERB If something entrances you, it gives you a feeling of wonder and delight.
entrancing ADJECTIVE

> **entrance** VERB
> = bewitch, captivate, charm, delight, enthral, fascinate

entrant NOUN a person who officially enters a competition or an organisation.

entrenched ADJECTIVE If a belief, custom or power is entrenched, it is firmly established.

entrepreneur [*Said on-tre-pren-****ur***] NOUN a person who sets up business deals, especially ones in which risks are involved, in order to make a profit. **entrepreneurial** ADJECTIVE

entrust VERB If you entrust something to someone, you give them the care and protection of it • *Miss Fry was entrusted with the children's education.*

entry, **entries** NOUN ① Entry is the act of entering a place. ② a place through which you enter somewhere. ③ anything which is entered or recorded • *Send your entry to the address below.*

> **entry** NOUN
> ① = appearance, arrival, entrance
> ② = door, doorway, entrance, gate, way in
> ③ = item, note, record

envelop VERB To envelop something means to cover or surround it completely • *A dense fog enveloped the area.*

envelope NOUN a flat covering of paper with a flap that can be folded over to seal it, which is used to hold a letter.

enviable ADJECTIVE If you describe something as enviable, you mean that you wish you had it yourself.

envious ADJECTIVE full of envy.
enviously ADVERB

environment NOUN ① Your environment is the circumstances and conditions in which you live or work • *a good environment to grow up in.* ② SCIENCE The environment is the natural world around us • *the waste which is dumped in the environment.*
environmental ADJECTIVE
environmentally ADVERB

environmentalist NOUN a person who is concerned with the problems of the natural environment, such as pollution.

envisage VERB If you envisage a

situation or state of affairs, you can picture it in your mind as being true or likely to happen.

envoy NOUN a messenger, sent especially from one government to another.

envy, **envies**, **envying**, **envied** NOUN ① Envy is a feeling of resentment you have when you wish you could have what someone else has. ▸ VERB ② If you envy someone, you wish that you had what they have.

> **envy** NOUN
> ① = jealousy, resentment
> ▸ VERB ② = be envious, begrudge, be jealous, covet, resent

enzyme NOUN [SCIENCE] a chemical substance, usually a protein, produced by cells in the body.

ephemeral [Said if-**em**-er-al] ADJECTIVE lasting only a short time.

epic NOUN ① a long story of heroic events and actions. ▸ ADJECTIVE ② very impressive or ambitious • *epic adventures*.

epidemic NOUN ① an occurrence of a disease in one area, spreading quickly and affecting many people. ② a rapid development or spread of something • *the country's crime epidemic*.

epilepsy NOUN Epilepsy is a condition of the brain which causes fits and periods of unconsciousness. **epileptic** ADJECTIVE

episode NOUN ① an event or period • *After this episode, she found it impossible to trust him*. ② [ENGLISH] one of several parts of a novel or drama appearing for example on television • *I never miss an episode of the show*.

epitaph [Said **ep**-it-ahf] NOUN some words on a tomb about the person who has died.

epithet NOUN a word or short phrase used to describe some characteristic of a person.

epitome [Said ip-**pit**-om-ee] NOUN (*formal*) The epitome of something is the most typical example of its sort • *She was the epitome of the successful woman*.

epoch [Said **ee**-pok] NOUN a long period of time.

eponymous [Said ip-**on**-im-uss] ADJECTIVE (*formal*) The eponymous hero or heroine of a play or book is the person whose name forms its title • *the eponymous hero of 'Eric the Viking'*.

equal, **equals**, **equalling**, **equalled** ADJECTIVE ① having the same size, amount, value or standard. ② If you are equal to a task, you have the necessary ability to deal with it. ▸ NOUN ③ Your equals are people who have the same ability, status or rights as you. ▸ VERB ④ If one thing equals another, it is as good or remarkable as the other • *He equalled the course record of 63*. **equally** ADVERB **equality** NOUN

> **equal** ADJECTIVE
> ① = equivalent, identical, the same
> ② = capable of, up to
> ▸ VERB ④ = be equal to, match

equate VERB If you equate a particular thing with something else, you believe that it is similar or equal • *You can't equate lives with money*.

equation NOUN [MATHS] a mathematical statement showing that two expressions are equal.

equator [Said ik-**way**-tor] NOUN [GEOGRAPHY] an imaginary line drawn round the middle of the earth, lying halfway between the North and South poles. **equatorial** ADJECTIVE

equestrian [Said ik-**west**-ree-an] ADJECTIVE relating to or involving horses.

equilibrium NOUN a state of balance or stability in a situation.

equine ADJECTIVE relating to horses.

equip, **equips**, **equipping**, **equipped** VERB If a person or thing is equipped with something, they have it or are provided with it • *The test boat was equipped with a folding propeller.*

> **equip** VERB
> = arm, endow, fit out, provide, supply

equipment NOUN Equipment is all the things that are needed or used for a particular job or activity.

> **equipment** NOUN
> = apparatus, gear (*informal*), paraphernalia, stuff, tackle

equitable ADJECTIVE fair and reasonable.

equity NOUN Equity is the quality of being fair and reasonable • *It is important to distribute income with some sense of equity.*

equivalent ADJECTIVE ① equal in use, size, value or effect. ▶ NOUN ② something that has the same use, value or effect as something else • *911 is the American equivalent of the British 999 service.* **equivalence** NOUN

era [*Said* **ear**-*a*] NOUN a period of time distinguished by a particular feature • *a new era of prosperity.*

eradicate VERB To eradicate something means to get rid of it or destroy it completely. **eradication** NOUN

erase VERB To erase something means to remove it.

erect VERB ① To erect something means to put it up or construct it • *The building was erected in 1900.* ▶ ADJECTIVE ② in a straight and upright position • *She held herself erect and looked directly at him.*

erection, **erections** NOUN ① the process of erecting something. ② anything which has been erected.

erode VERB If something erodes or is eroded, it is gradually worn or eaten away and destroyed.

> **erode** VERB
> = corrode, destroy, deteriorate, disintegrate

erosion NOUN GEOGRAPHY the gradual wearing away and destruction of something • *soil erosion.*

err VERB If you err, you make a mistake.

> **err** VERB
> = blunder, go wrong, make a mistake, miscalculate

errand NOUN a short trip you make in order to do a job for someone.

erratic ADJECTIVE not following a regular pattern or a fixed course • *Police officers noticed his erratic driving.* **erratically** ADVERB

erroneous [*Said ir*-**rone**-*ee-uss*] ADJECTIVE Ideas or methods that are erroneous are incorrect or only partly correct. **erroneously** ADVERB

error NOUN a mistake or something which you have done wrong.

> **error** NOUN
> = blunder, fault, lapse, mistake, slip

erudite [*Said* **eh**-*roo-dite*] ADJECTIVE having great academic knowledge.

erupt VERB ① When a volcano erupts, it violently throws out a lot of hot lava and ash. ② When a situation erupts, it starts up suddenly and violently • *A family row erupted.* **eruption** NOUN

escalate VERB If a situation escalates, it becomes greater in size, seriousness or intensity.

escalator NOUN a mechanical moving staircase.

escapade NOUN an adventurous or daring incident that causes trouble.

escape VERB ① To escape means to

get free from someone or something. ② If you escape something unpleasant or difficult, you manage to avoid it • *He escaped the death penalty.* ③ If something escapes you, you cannot remember it • *It was an actor whose name escapes me for the moment.* ▸ **NOUN** ④ an act of escaping from a particular place or situation • *his escape from North Korea.* ⑤ a situation or activity which distracts you from something unpleasant • *Television provides an escape.*

> **escape VERB**
> ① = break free, break out, get away, make your escape, run away, run off
> ② = avoid, dodge, duck, elude, evade
> ▸ **NOUN** ⑤ = distraction, diversion, relief

escapee *[Said is-kay-**pee**]* **NOUN** someone who has escaped, especially an escaped prisoner.

escapism **NOUN** avoiding the real and unpleasant things in life by thinking about pleasant or exciting things • *Most horror movies are simple escapism.* **escapist** **ADJECTIVE**

eschew *[Said is-**chew**]* **VERB** *(formal)* If you eschew something, you deliberately avoid or keep away from it.

escort **NOUN** ① a person or vehicle that travels with another in order to protect or guide them. ② a person who accompanies another person to a social event. ▸ **VERB** ③ If you escort someone, you go with them somewhere, especially in order to protect or guide them.

Eskimo, **Eskimos** **NOUN** *(offensive)* a name that was formerly used for the Inuit and their language.

especially **ADVERB** You say especially to show that something applies more to one thing, person or situation than to any other • *Regular eye tests are important, especially for older people.*

espionage *[Said **ess**-pee-on-ahj]* **NOUN** Espionage is the act of spying to get secret information, especially to find out military or political secrets.

espouse **VERB** *(formal)* If you espouse a particular policy, cause or plan, you give your support to it • *They espoused the values of freedom and human rights.*

espresso **NOUN** Espresso is strong coffee made by forcing steam through ground coffee.

essay **NOUN** a short piece of writing on a particular subject, for example one done as an exercise by a student.

essence **NOUN** ① The essence of something is its most basic and most important part, which gives it its identity • *the very essence of life.* ② a concentrated liquid used for flavouring food • *vanilla essence.*

> **essence NOUN**
> ① = core, heart, nature, soul, spirit
> ② = concentrate, extract

essential **ADJECTIVE** ① vitally important and absolutely necessary • *Good ventilation is essential in the greenhouse.* ② very basic, important and typical • *the essential aspects of international banking.* **essentially** **ADVERB**

> **essential ADJECTIVE**
> ① = crucial, indispensable, vital
> ② = basic, cardinal, fundamental, key, main, principal

establish **VERB** ① To establish something means to set it up in a permanent way. ② If you establish yourself or become established as something, you achieve a strong reputation for a particular activity • *He had just established himself as a film star.* ③ If you establish a fact or establish the truth of something, you discover it and can prove it • *Our first priority is to establish the cause of the accident.* **established** **ADJECTIVE**

establishment NOUN ① The establishment of an organisation or system is the act of setting it up. ② a shop, business or some other sort of organisation or institution. ③ The Establishment is the group of people in a country who have power and influence • *lawyers and other pillars of the Establishment*.

estate NOUN ① a large area of privately owned land in the country, together with all the property on it. ② an area of land, usually in or near a city, which has been developed for housing or industry. ③ (*Law*) A person's estate consists of all the possessions they leave behind when they die.

estate agent NOUN a person who works for a company that sells houses and land.

esteem NOUN admiration and respect that you feel for another person.
esteemed ADJECTIVE

esteem NOUN
= admiration, estimation, regard, respect, reverence

estimate VERB ① MATHS If you estimate an amount or quantity, you calculate it approximately. ② If you estimate something, you make a guess about it based on the evidence you have available • *Often it's possible to estimate a person's age just by knowing their name*. ▶ NOUN ③ a guess at an amount, quantity or outcome, based on the evidence you have available. ④ a formal statement from a company who may do some work for you, telling you how much it is likely to cost.

estimate NOUN
③ = appraisal, assessment, estimation, guess, quote, reckoning, valuation

estimation NOUN ① an approximate calculation of something that can be measured. ② the opinion or impression you form about a person or situation.

estranged ADJECTIVE ① If someone is estranged from their husband or wife, they no longer live with them. ② If someone is estranged from their family or friends, they have quarrelled with them and no longer keep in touch with them.

estrogen NOUN SCIENCE a female hormone which regulates the reproductive cycle.

estuary, **estuaries** [*Said* **est**-*yoo-ree*] NOUN GEOGRAPHY the wide part of a river near where it joins the sea and where fresh water mixes with salt water.

etc. a written abbreviation for **et cetera**.

et cetera [*Said it* **set**-*ra*] 'Et cetera' is used at the end of a list to indicate that other items of the same type you have mentioned could have been mentioned if there had been time or space.

etch VERB ① If you etch a design or pattern on a surface, you cut it into the surface by using acid or a sharp tool. ② If something is etched on your mind or memory, it has made such a strong impression on you that you feel you will never forget it.
etched ADJECTIVE

etching NOUN a picture printed from a metal plate that has had a design cut into it.

eternal ADJECTIVE lasting forever, or seeming to last forever • *eternal life*.
eternally ADVERB

eternal ADJECTIVE
= everlasting, immortal, unchanging

eternity, **eternities** NOUN ① Eternity is time without end, or a state of existing outside time, especially the state some people believe they will pass into when they die. ② a period of time which seems to go on forever • *We arrived there after an eternity.*

ether *[Said* ***eeth****-er]* **NOUN** a colourless liquid that burns easily, used in industry as a solvent and in medicine as an anaesthetic.

ethereal *[Said ith-****ee****-ree-al]* **ADJECTIVE** light and delicate • *misty ethereal landscapes.* **ethereally** **ADVERB**

ethical **ADJECTIVE** in agreement with accepted principles of behaviour that are thought to be right • *teenagers who become vegetarian for ethical reasons.* **ethically** **ADVERB**

ethics **PLURAL NOUN** Ethics are moral beliefs about right and wrong • *The medical profession has a code of ethics.*

Ethiopian *[Said eeth-ee-****oh****-pee-an]* **ADJECTIVE** ① belonging or relating to Ethiopia. ▶ **NOUN** ② someone who comes from Ethiopia.

ethnic **ADJECTIVE** ① involving different racial groups of people • *ethnic minorities.* ② relating to a particular racial or cultural group, especially when very different from modern western culture • *ethnic food.* **ethnically** **ADVERB**

ethos *[Said* ***eeth****-oss]* **NOUN** a set of ideas and attitudes that is associated with a particular group of people • *the ethos of journalism.*

etiquette *[Said* ***et****-ik-ket]* **NOUN** a set of rules for behaviour in a particular social situation.

EU an abbreviation for **European Union**.

eucalyptus, **eucalyptuses** or **eucalypt**, **eucalypts** **NOUN** an evergreen tree, grown mostly in Australia; also the wood and oil from this tree.

Eucharist *[Said* ***yoo****-kar-rist]* **NOUN** RE a religious ceremony in which Christians remember and celebrate Christ's last meal with his disciples.

euphemism **NOUN** a polite word or expression that you can use instead of one that might offend or upset people • *'Passing on' is a euphemism for death.* **euphemistic** **ADJECTIVE** **euphemistically** **ADVERB**

euphoria **NOUN** a feeling of great happiness. **euphoric** **ADJECTIVE**

euro, **euros** **NOUN** the official unit of currency in some countries of the European Union, replacing their old currencies at the beginning of January 2002.

Europe **NOUN** Europe is the second smallest continent. It has Asia on its eastern side, with the Arctic to the north, the Atlantic to the west, and the Mediterranean and Africa to the south.

European **ADJECTIVE** ① belonging or relating to Europe. ▶ **NOUN** ② someone who comes from Europe.

European Union **NOUN** The group of countries who have joined together under the Treaty of Rome for economic and trade purposes are officially known as the European Union.

euthanasia *[Said yooth-a-****nay****-zee-a]* **NOUN** Euthanasia is the act of painlessly killing a dying person in order to stop their suffering.

evacuate **VERB** If someone is evacuated, they are removed from a place of danger to a place of safety • *A crowd of shoppers had to be evacuated from a store after a bomb scare.* **evacuation** **NOUN** **evacuee** **NOUN**

evade **VERB** ① If you evade something or someone, you keep moving in order to keep out of their way • *For two months he evaded police.* ② If you evade a problem or question, you avoid dealing with it.

evaluate VERB EXAM TERM If you evaluate something, you assess its strengths and weaknesses.

evaluation, **evaluations** NOUN ① Evaluation is assessing the strengths and weaknesses of something. ② DGT To carry out an evaluation of a design, product or system is to do an assessment to find out how well it works or will work.

evangelical *[Said ee-van-**jel**-ik-kl]* ADJECTIVE Evangelical beliefs are Christian beliefs that stress the importance of the gospels and a personal belief in Christ.

evangelist, **evangelists** *[Said iv-**van**-jel-ist]* NOUN RE a person who travels from place to place preaching Christianity. **evangelise** VERB **evangelism** NOUN

evaporate VERB ① SCIENCE When a liquid evaporates, it gradually changes into a gas. ② SCIENCE If a substance has been evaporated, all the liquid has been taken out so that it is dry or concentrated. **evaporation** NOUN

evasion NOUN deliberately avoiding doing something • *evasion of arrest.*

evasive ADJECTIVE deliberately trying to avoid talking about or doing something • *He was evasive about his past.*

eve NOUN the evening or day before an event or occasion • *on the eve of the battle.*

even ADJECTIVE ① flat and level • *an even layer of chocolate.* ② regular and without variation • *an even temperature.* ③ In maths, numbers that are even can be divided exactly by two • *4 is an even number.* ④ Scores that are even are exactly the same. ▸ ADVERB ⑤ 'Even' is used to suggest that something is unexpected or surprising • *I haven't even got a bank account.* ⑥ 'Even' is also used to say that something is greater in degree than something else • *This was an opportunity to obtain even more money.* ▸ PHRASE ⑦ **Even if** or **even though** is used to introduce something that is surprising in relation to the main part of the sentence • *She was too kind to say anything, even though she was jealous.* **evenly** ADVERB

> **even** ADJECTIVE
> ① = flat, horizontal, level, smooth ≠ uneven
> ② = constant, regular, smooth, steady, uniform
> ④ = equal, identical, level, neck and neck

evening NOUN the part of the day between late afternoon and night.

event NOUN ① something that happens, especially when it is unusual or important. ② one of the competitions that are part of an organised occasion, especially in sports. ▸ PHRASE ③ If you say **in any event**, you mean whatever happens • *In any event we must get on with our own lives.*

> **event** NOUN
> ① = affair, business, circumstance, episode, experience, incident, matter
> ② = bout, competition, contest

eventful ADJECTIVE full of interesting and important events.

eventual ADJECTIVE happening or being achieved in the end • *He remained confident of eventual victory.*

eventuality, **eventualities** NOUN a possible future event or result • *equipment to cope with most eventualities.*

eventually ADVERB in the end • *Eventually I got to Berlin.*

ever ADVERB ① at any time • *Have you ever seen anything like it?* ② more all the time • *They grew ever further apart.* ③ 'Ever' is used to give emphasis to what you are saying • *I'm as happy here* *as ever I was in England.* ▶ PHRASE ④ (*informal*) **Ever so** means very • *Thank you ever so much.*

evergreen NOUN a tree or bush which has green leaves all the year round.

everlasting ADJECTIVE never coming to an end.

every ADJECTIVE ① 'Every' is used to refer to all the members of a particular group, separately and one by one • *We eat out every night.* ② 'Every' is used to mean the greatest or the best possible degree of something • *He has every reason to avoid the subject.* ③ 'Every' is also used to indicate that something happens at regular intervals • *renewable every five years.* ▶ PHRASE ④ **Every other** means each alternate • *I see Lisa at least every other week.*

everybody PRONOUN ① all the people in a group • *He obviously thinks everybody in the place knows him.* ② all the people in the world • *Everybody has a hobby.*

everyday ADJECTIVE usual or ordinary • *the everyday drudgery of work.*

> **everyday** ADJECTIVE
> = common, daily, day-to-day, mundane, ordinary, routine

everyone PRONOUN ① all the people in a group. ② all the people in the world.

everything PRONOUN ① all or the whole of something. ② the most important thing • *Friends were everything to me.*

everywhere ADVERB in or to all places.

evict VERB To evict someone means to officially force them to leave a place they are occupying. **eviction** NOUN

evidence NOUN ① Evidence is anything you see, read or are told which gives you reason to believe something. ② Evidence is the information used in court to attempt to prove or disprove something.

evident ADJECTIVE easily noticed or understood • *His love of nature is evident in his paintings.* **evidently** ADVERB

> **evident** ADJECTIVE
> = apparent, clear, noticeable, obvious, palpable, plain, visible

evil NOUN ① Evil is a force or power that is believed to cause wicked or bad things to happen. ② a very unpleasant or harmful situation or activity • *the evils of war.* ▶ ADJECTIVE ③ Someone or something that is evil is morally wrong or bad • *evil influences.*

> **evil** NOUN
> ① = badness, immorality, sin, vice, wickedness
> ≠ good
> ② = affliction, ill, misery, sorrow
> ▶ ADJECTIVE ③ = bad, depraved, malevolent, sinful, vile, wicked
> ≠ good

evoke VERB To evoke an emotion, memory or reaction means to cause it • *Enthusiasm was evoked by the appearance of the Prince.*

evolution [*Said ee-vol-**oo**-shn*] NOUN ① SCIENCE Evolution is a process of gradual change taking place over many generations during which living things slowly change as they adapt to different environments. ② Evolution is also any process of gradual change and development over a period of time • *the evolution of the European Union.* **evolutionary** ADJECTIVE

evolve VERB ① If something evolves or if you evolve it, it develops gradually over a period of time • *I was given a brief to evolve a system of training.* ② When living things evolve, they gradually change and develop into different forms over a period of time.

ewe [*Said **yoo***] NOUN a female sheep.

ex- PREFIX 'Ex-' means 'former' • *her ex-husband.*

exacerbate *[Said ig-zass-er-bate]* VERB To exacerbate something means to make it worse.

exact ADJECTIVE ① correct and complete in every detail • *an exact replica of the Santa Maria.* ② accurate and precise, as opposed to approximate • *Mystery surrounds the exact circumstances of his death.* ▶ VERB ③ *(formal)* If somebody or something exacts something from you, they demand or obtain it from you, especially through force • *The navy was on its way to exact a terrible revenge.*

exact ADJECTIVE
① = accurate, authentic, faithful, faultless, precise, true
≠ approximate
▶ VERB ③ = command, extract, impose, insist on, insist upon, wring

exactly ADVERB ① with complete accuracy and precision • *That's exactly what happened.* ② You can use 'exactly' to emphasise the truth of a statement, or a similarity or close relationship between one thing and another • *It's exactly the same colour.* ▶ INTERJECTION ③ an expression implying total agreement.

exactly ADVERB
① = accurately, faithfully, just, on the dot, precisely, quite
≠ approximately
▶ INTERJECTION ③ = absolutely, indeed, precisely, quite

exaggerate VERB ① If you exaggerate, you make the thing you are describing seem better, worse, bigger or more important than it really is. ② To exaggerate something means to make it more noticeable than usual • *He exaggerated his Irish accent for the benefit of the joke he was telling.* **exaggeration** NOUN

exaggerate VERB
① = overdo, overestimate, overstate

exalted ADJECTIVE *(formal)* Someone who is exalted is very important.

exam NOUN an official test set to find out your knowledge or skill in a subject.

exam NOUN
= examination, oral, test

examination NOUN ① an exam. ② If you make an examination of something, you inspect it very carefully • *I carried out a careful examination of the hull.* ③ A medical examination is a check by a doctor to find out the state of your health.

examination NOUN
② = analysis, inspection, study
③ = check, checkup, medical

examine VERB ① If you examine something, you inspect it very carefully. ② EXAM TERM To examine a subject is to look closely at the issues involved and form your own opinion. ③ To examine someone means to find out their knowledge or skill in a particular subject by testing them. ④ If a doctor examines you, he or she checks your body to find out the state of your health.

examine VERB
① = analyse, go over, go through, inspect, look over, study
④ = check, inspect, look at, test

examiner NOUN a person who sets or marks an exam.

example NOUN ① something which represents or is typical of a group or set • *some examples of early Spanish music.* ② If you say someone or something is an example to people, you mean that people can imitate and learn from them. ▶ PHRASE ③ You use **for example** to give an example of something you are talking about.

a b c d e f g h i j k l m n o p q r s t u v w x y z

example NOUN
① = illustration, sample, specimen
② = ideal, model, paragon, prototype

exasperate VERB If someone or something exasperates you, they irritate you and make you angry.
exasperating ADJECTIVE
exasperation NOUN

excavate VERB To excavate means to remove earth from the ground by digging. **excavation** NOUN

exceed VERB To exceed something such as a limit means to go beyond it or to become greater than it • *the first aircraft to exceed the speed of sound.*

exceedingly ADVERB extremely or very much.

excel, **excels**, **excelling**, **excelled** VERB If someone excels in something, they are very good at doing it.

Excellency, **Excellencies** NOUN a title used to address an official of very high rank, such as an ambassador or a governor.

excellent ADJECTIVE very good indeed.
excellence NOUN

excellent ADJECTIVE
= beaut (*Australian and New Zealand; informal*), brilliant, cracking (*British, Australian and New Zealand; informal*), fine, first-class, great, outstanding, superb
≠ terrible

except PREPOSITION Except or except for means other than or apart from • *All my family were musicians except my father.*

except PREPOSITION
= apart from, but, other than, save (*formal*), with the exception of

exception, **exceptions** NOUN somebody or something that is not included in a general statement or rule • *English, like every language, has exceptions to its rules.*

exceptional ADJECTIVE ① unusually talented or clever. ② unusual and likely to happen very rarely.
exceptionally ADVERB

exceptional ADJECTIVE
① = excellent, extraordinary, outstanding, phenomenal, remarkable, talented
≠ mediocre
② = isolated, out of the ordinary, rare, special, unheard-of, unusual
≠ common

excerpt NOUN a short piece of writing or music which is taken from a larger piece.

excess NOUN ① Excess is behaviour which goes beyond normally acceptable limits • *a life of excess.* ② a larger amount of something than is needed, usual or healthy • *an excess of energy.* ▶ ADJECTIVE ③ more than is needed, allowed or healthy • *excess weight.* ▶ PHRASE ④ **In excess of** a particular amount means more than that amount • *a fortune in excess of 150 million pounds.* ⑤ If you do something **to excess**, you do it too much • *She exercised to excess.*

excess NOUN
① = extravagance, indulgence
② = glut, overdose, surfeit, surplus
≠ shortage
▶ ADJECTIVE ③ = extra, superfluous, surplus

excessive ADJECTIVE too great in amount or degree • *using excessive force.*
excessively ADVERB

excessive ADJECTIVE
= exaggerated, undue, unreasonable

exchange VERB ① To exchange things means to give or receive one thing in return for another • *They exchange small presents on Christmas Eve.* ▶ NOUN ② the act of giving or receiving something in return for something else • *an exchange of letters*

• *exchanges of gunfire*. ③ a place where people trade and do business • *the stock exchange*.

exchange VERB
① = barter, change, swap, switch, trade
▸ NOUN ② = interchange, swap, switch, trade

exchequer *[Said iks-**chek**-er]* NOUN The exchequer is the department in the government in Britain and other countries which is responsible for money belonging to the state.

excise NOUN Excise is a tax put on goods produced for sale in the country that produces them.

excitable ADJECTIVE easily excited.

excite VERB ① If somebody or something excites you, they make you feel very happy and nervous or very interested and enthusiastic. ② If something excites a particular feeling, it causes somebody to have that feeling • *This excited my suspicion*.

excite VERB
① = agitate, animate, thrill, titillate
② = arouse, elicit, evoke, incite, inspire, provoke, stir up

excited ADJECTIVE happy and unable to relax. **excitedly** ADVERB

excited ADJECTIVE
= agitated, enthusiastic, feverish, high (*informal*), thrilled
≠ bored

excitement NOUN happiness and enthusiasm.

excitement NOUN
= activity, adventure, agitation, commotion, enthusiasm, thrill

exciting ADJECTIVE making you feel happy and enthusiastic.

exciting ADJECTIVE
= dramatic, electrifying, exhilarating, rousing, stimulating, thrilling
≠ boring

exclaim VERB When you exclaim, you cry out suddenly or loudly because you are excited or shocked.

exclamation NOUN ENGLISH a word or phrase spoken suddenly to express a strong feeling.

exclude VERB ① If you exclude something, you deliberately do not include it or do not consider it. ② If you exclude somebody from a place or an activity, you prevent them from entering the place or taking part in the activity. **exclusion** NOUN

exclude VERB
① = eliminate, ignore, leave out, omit, rule out
≠ include
② = ban, bar, forbid, keep out

exclusive ADJECTIVE ① available to or for the use of a small group of rich or privileged people • *an exclusive club*. ② belonging to a particular person or group only • *exclusive rights to coverage of the concerts*. ▸ NOUN ③ a story or interview which appears in only one newspaper or on only one television programme. **exclusively** ADVERB

exclusive ADJECTIVE
① = chic, classy, posh (*informal*), select, up-market

excrement *[Said **eks**-krim-ment]* NOUN Excrement is the solid waste matter that is passed out of a person's or animal's body through their bowels.

excruciating *[Said iks-**kroo**-shee-ate-ing]* ADJECTIVE unbearably painful. **excruciatingly** ADVERB

excursion NOUN a short journey or outing.

excuse NOUN *[Said iks-**kyoos**]* ① a reason which you give to explain why something has been done, has not been done, or will not be done. ▸ VERB *[Said iks-**kyooz**]* ② If you excuse yourself or something that you have done, you give reasons defending your actions. ③ If you excuse somebody for something wrong they have done, you forgive them for it. ④ If you excuse somebody from a duty or responsibility, you free them from it • *He was excused from standing trial because of ill health.* ▶ PHRASE ⑤ You say **excuse me** to try to catch somebody's attention or to apologise for an interruption or for rude behaviour.

excuse NOUN
① = explanation, justification, pretext, reason
▶ VERB ③ = forgive, overlook, pardon, turn a blind eye to

execute VERB ① To execute somebody means to kill them as a punishment for a crime. ② If you execute something such as a plan or an action, you carry it out or perform it • *The crime had been planned and executed in Montreal.* **execution** NOUN

executioner, **executioners** NOUN a person whose job is to execute criminals.

executive NOUN ① a person who is employed by a company at a senior level. ② The executive of an organisation is a committee which has the authority to make decisions and ensure that they are carried out. ▶ ADJECTIVE ③ concerned with making important decisions and ensuring that they are carried out • *the commission's executive director.*

executor *[Said ig-**zek**-yoo-tor]* NOUN a person you appoint to carry out the instructions in your will.

exemplary ADJECTIVE ① being a good example and worthy of imitation • *an exemplary performance.* ② serving as a warning • *an exemplary tale.*

exemplify, **exemplifies**, **exemplifying**, **exemplified** VERB ① To exemplify something means to be a typical example of it • *This aircraft exemplifies the advantages of European technological cooperation.* ② If you exemplify something, you give an example of it.

exempt ADJECTIVE ① excused from a rule or duty • *people exempt from prescription charges.* ▶ VERB ② To exempt someone from a rule, duty or obligation means to excuse them from it. **exemption** NOUN

exempt ADJECTIVE
① = excused, immune, not liable

exercise NOUN ① [PE] Exercise is any activity which you do to get fit or remain healthy. ② Exercises are also activities which you do to practise and train for a particular skill • *piano exercises* • *a mathematical exercise.* ▶ VERB ③ When you exercise, you do activities which help you to get fit and remain healthy. ④ If you exercise your rights or responsibilities, you use them.

exercise NOUN
① = activity, exertion, training, work

exert VERB ① To exert pressure means to apply it. ② If you exert yourself, you make a physical or mental effort to do something.

exertion, **exertions** NOUN Exertion is vigorous physical effort or exercise.

exhale VERB [SCIENCE] When you exhale, you breathe out. **exhalation** NOUN

exhaust VERB ① To exhaust somebody means to make them very tired • *Several lengths of the pool left her exhausted.* ② If you exhaust a supply of something such as money or food, you use it up completely. ③ If you exhaust a subject, you talk about it so much that there is nothing else to say about it. ▶ NOUN ④ a pipe which carries the gas or steam out of the engine of a vehicle. ⑤ Exhaust is the gas or steam produced by the engine of a vehicle. **exhaustion** NOUN

exhaust VERB
① = drain, fatigue, tire out, wear out
② = consume, deplete, run through, use up

exhaustive ADJECTIVE thorough and complete • *an exhaustive series of tests.* **exhaustively** ADVERB

exhibit VERB ① To exhibit things means to show them in a public place for people to see. ② If you exhibit your feelings or abilities, you display them so that other people can see them. ▶ NOUN ③ anything which is put on show for the public to see.

exhibition NOUN ART a public display of works of art, products or skills.

exhibitor NOUN a person whose work is being shown in an exhibition.

exhilarating ADJECTIVE Something that is exhilarating makes you feel very happy and excited.

exile NOUN ① If somebody lives in exile, they live in a foreign country because they cannot live in their own country, usually for political reasons. ② a person who lives in exile. ▶ VERB ③ If somebody is exiled, they are sent away from their own country and not allowed to return.

exist VERB If something exists, it is present in the world as a real or living thing.

existence NOUN ① Existence is the state of being or existing. ② a way of living or being • *an idyllic existence.*

exit NOUN ① a way out of a place. ② If you make an exit, you leave a place. ▶ VERB ③ To exit means to go out. ④ DRAMA An actor exits when he or she leaves the stage.

exodus NOUN An exodus is the departure of a large number of people from a place.

exotic ADJECTIVE ① attractive or interesting through being unusual • *exotic fabrics.* ② coming from a foreign country • *exotic plants.*

expand VERB ① If something expands or you expand it, it becomes larger in number or size. ② If you expand on something, you give more details about it • *Use the following paragraphs to expand on the points you made in the first.* **expansion** NOUN

expand VERB
① = develop, enlarge, extend, fill out, grow, increase, swell
≠ decrease
② = develop, elaborate on, enlarge on

expanse NOUN a very large or widespread area • *a vast expanse of pine forests.*

expansive ADJECTIVE ① Something that is expansive is very wide or extends over a very large area • *the expansive countryside.* ② Someone who is expansive is friendly, open or talkative.

expatriate [*Said eks-**pat**-ree-it*] NOUN someone who is living in a country which is not their own.

expect VERB ① If you expect something to happen, you believe that it will happen • *The group is expected to arrive today.* ② If you are expecting somebody or something, you believe that they are going to arrive or to happen • *Mr Jenkins was expecting you this morning.* ③ If you expect something, you believe that it is your right to get it or have it • *He seemed to expect a reply.*

expect VERB
① = anticipate, assume, believe, imagine, presume, reckon (*informal*), think
③ = demand, rely on, require

expectancy NOUN Expectancy is the feeling that something is about to happen, especially something exciting.

a b c d e f g h i j k l m n o p q r s t u v w x y z

expectant ADJECTIVE ① If you are expectant, you believe that something is about to happen, especially something exciting. ② An expectant mother or father is someone whose baby is going to be born soon. **expectantly** ADVERB

expectation NOUN Expectation or an expectation is a strong belief or hope that something will happen.

expedient [Said iks-**pee**-dee-ent] NOUN ① an action or plan that achieves a particular purpose but that may not be morally acceptable • *Many firms have improved their profitability by the simple expedient of cutting staff*. ▶ ADJECTIVE ② Something that is expedient is useful or convenient in a particular situation. **expediency** NOUN

expedition NOUN ① an organised journey made for a special purpose, such as to explore; also the party of people who make such a journey. ② a short journey or outing • *shopping expeditions*. **expeditionary** ADJECTIVE

expel, **expels**, **expelling**, **expelled** VERB ① If someone is expelled from a school or club, they are officially told to leave because they have behaved badly. ② If a gas or liquid is expelled from a place, it is forced out of it.

expend VERB To expend energy, time or money means to use it up or spend it.

expendable ADJECTIVE no longer useful or necessary, and therefore able to be got rid of.

expenditure NOUN Expenditure is the total amount of money spent on something.

expense NOUN ① Expense is the money that something costs • *the expense of installing a burglar alarm*. ② (*in plural*) Expenses are the money somebody spends while doing something connected with their work, which is paid back to them by their employer • *travelling expenses*.

expensive ADJECTIVE costing a lot of money. **expensively** ADVERB

> **expensive** ADJECTIVE
> = costly, dear, pricey (*informal*)
> ≠ cheap

experience NOUN ① Experience consists of all the things that you have done or that have happened to you. ② the knowledge or skill you have in a particular activity. ③ something that you do or something that happens to you, especially something new or unusual. ▶ VERB ④ If you experience a situation or feeling, it happens to you or you are affected by it.

> **experience** NOUN
> ② = expertise, know-how, knowledge, training, understanding
> ③ = adventure, affair, encounter, episode, incident, ordeal
> ▶ VERB ④ = encounter, have, meet, undergo

experienced ADJECTIVE skilled or knowledgeable through doing something for a long time.

> **experienced** ADJECTIVE
> = expert, knowledgeable, practised, seasoned, well-versed
> ≠ inexperienced

experiment NOUN ① the testing of something, either to find out its effect or to prove something. ▶ VERB ② If you experiment with something, you do a scientific test on it to prove or discover something.
experimentation NOUN
experimental ADJECTIVE
experimentally ADVERB

expert NOUN ① a person who is very skilled at doing something or very knowledgeable about a particular subject. ▶ ADJECTIVE ② having or requiring special skill or knowledge • *expert advice*. **expertly** ADVERB

expert NOUN
① = ace (*informal*), authority, buff (*informal*), geek (*informal*), guru, master, professional, specialist, wizard
≠ beginner
▸ ADJECTIVE ② = able, adept, experienced, knowledgeable, proficient, skilful, skilled

expertise [*Said eks-per-**teez***] NOUN Expertise is special skill or knowledge.

expire VERB When something expires, it reaches the end of the period of time for which it is valid • *My contract expires in the summer.* **expiry** NOUN

explain VERB If you explain something, you give details about it or reasons for it so that it can be understood.

explain VERB
= define, describe, illustrate

explanation NOUN a helpful or clear description. **explanatory** ADJECTIVE

explanation NOUN
= clarification, definition, description, exposition

explicit ADJECTIVE shown or expressed clearly and openly • *an explicit warning.* **explicitly** ADVERB

explode VERB ① If something such as a bomb explodes, it bursts loudly and with great force, often causing damage. ② If somebody explodes, they express strong feelings suddenly or violently • *I half expected him to explode in anger.* ③ When something increases suddenly and rapidly, it can be said to explode • *Sales of men's toiletries have exploded.*

explode VERB
① = blow up, burst, detonate, go off, set off
② = blow up, go berserk, go mad
③ = rocket, shoot up, soar

exploit VERB [*Said iks-**ploit***] ① If somebody exploits a person or a situation, they take advantage of them for their own ends • *Critics claim the record label exploited young musicians.* ② If you exploit something, you make the best use of it, often for profit • *The company wants to exploit the power of social media.* ▸ NOUN [*Said **eks**-ploit*] ③ something daring or interesting that somebody has done • *The diver's courage and exploits were legendary.* **exploitation** NOUN

explore VERB ① If you explore a place, you travel in it to find out what it is like. ② If you explore an idea, you think about it carefully. **exploration** NOUN **exploratory** ADJECTIVE **explorer** NOUN

explosion NOUN a sudden violent burst of energy, for example one caused by a bomb.

explosion NOUN
= bang, blast

explosive ADJECTIVE ① capable of exploding or likely to explode. ② happening suddenly and making a loud noise. ③ An explosive situation is one which is likely to have serious or dangerous effects. ▸ NOUN ④ a substance or device that can explode.

exponent NOUN ① An exponent of an idea or plan is someone who puts it forward. ② (*formal*) An exponent of a skill or activity is someone who is good at it.

export VERB [*Said ik-**sport***] ① If you export goods, you send them to another country and sell them there. ② [ICT] If you export data, you save it in a format that can be used by another software program. ▸ NOUN [*Said **ek**-sport*] ③ Exports are goods which are sent to another country and sold there. **exporter** NOUN

expose VERB ① To expose something means to uncover it and make it visible. ② To expose a person to something dangerous means to put them in a situation in which it might harm them • *exposed to tobacco smoke*. ③ To expose a person or situation means to reveal the truth about them.

> **expose** VERB
> ① = reveal, show, uncover
> ③ = bring to light, reveal, show up, uncover, unearth

exposition NOUN [ENGLISH] a detailed explanation of a particular subject.

exposure NOUN ① Exposure is the exposing of something. ② Exposure is the harmful effect on the body caused by very cold weather.

express VERB ① When you express an idea or feeling, you show what you think or feel by saying or doing something. ② If you express a quantity in a particular form, you write it down in that form • *The result of the equation is usually expressed as a percentage*. ▶ ADJECTIVE ③ very fast • *express delivery service*. ▶ NOUN ④ a fast train or coach which stops at only a few places.

> **express** VERB
> ① = communicate, couch, phrase, put, put across, voice
> ▶ ADJECTIVE ③ = direct, fast, high-speed, nonstop

expression NOUN ① Your expression is the look on your face which shows what you are thinking or feeling. ② [ENGLISH] The expression of ideas or feelings is the showing of them through words, actions or art. ③ a word or phrase used in communicating • *the expression 'nosey parker'*. ④ [MATHS] a symbol or equation that represents a quantity or problem.

> **expression** NOUN
> ① = countenance (*formal*), face
> ③ = idiom, phrase, remark, term

expressive ADJECTIVE ① showing feelings clearly. ② full of expression.

expressway NOUN a road designed for fast-moving traffic.

expulsion NOUN The expulsion of someone from a place or institution is the act of officially banning them from that place or institution • *the high number of school expulsions*.

exquisite ADJECTIVE extremely beautiful and pleasing.

extend VERB ① If something extends for a distance, it continues and stretches into the distance. ② If something extends from a surface or an object, it sticks out from it. ③ If you extend something, you make it larger or longer • *The table had been extended to seat fifty*.

> **extend** VERB
> ① = continue, hang, reach, stretch
> ② = jut out, project, protrude (*formal*), stick out
> ③ = add to, develop, enlarge, expand, widen

extension, **extensions** NOUN ① a room or building which is added to an existing building. ② an extra period of time for which something continues to exist or be valid • *an extension to his visa*. ③ an additional telephone connected to the same line as another telephone.

extensive ADJECTIVE ① covering a large area. ② very great in effect • *extensive repairs*. **extensively** ADVERB

> **extensive** ADJECTIVE
> ① = broad, expansive, large, spacious, sweeping, vast, wide
> ② = comprehensive, considerable, far-reaching, great, pervasive, untold, widespread

extent NOUN The extent of something is its length, area or size.

> **extent** NOUN
> = degree, level, measure, scale, size

exterior NOUN ① The exterior of something is its outside. ② Your exterior is your outward appearance.

exterminate VERB When animals or people are exterminated, they are deliberately killed. **extermination** NOUN

external ADJECTIVE existing or happening on the outside or outer part of something. **externally** ADVERB

extinct ADJECTIVE ① [SCIENCE] An extinct species of animal or plant is no longer in existence. ② [SCIENCE] An extinct volcano is no longer likely to erupt. **extinction** NOUN

extinguish VERB To extinguish a light or fire means to put it out.

extortionate ADJECTIVE more expensive than you consider to be fair.

extra ADJECTIVE ① more than is usual, necessary or expected. ▶ NOUN ② anything which is additional. ③ a person who is hired to play a very small and unimportant part in a film.

> **extra** ADJECTIVE
> ① = added, additional, excess, further, more, new, spare
> ▶ NOUN ② = accessory, addition, bonus

extract VERB *[Said iks-**tract**]* ① To extract something from a place means to take it out or get it out, often by force. ② If you extract information from someone, you get it from them with difficulty. ▶ NOUN *[Said **eks**-tract]* [LIBRARY] ③ a small section taken from a book or piece of music.

> **extract** VERB
> ① = draw, mine, obtain, pull out, remove, take out
> ② = draw, elicit (*formal*), get, glean, obtain
> ▶ NOUN ③ = excerpt, passage, reading, section, snatch, snippet

extraction NOUN ① Your extraction is the country or people that your family originally comes from • *a Malaysian citizen of Australian extraction*. ② Extraction is the process of taking or getting something out of a place.

extraordinary ADJECTIVE unusual or surprising. **extraordinarily** ADVERB

> **extraordinary** ADJECTIVE
> = amazing, bizarre, odd, singular, strange, surprising, unusual
> ≠ ordinary

extravagant ADJECTIVE ① spending or costing more money than is reasonable or affordable. ② going beyond reasonable limits. **extravagantly** ADVERB **extravagance** NOUN

extravaganza NOUN a spectacular and expensive public show.

extreme ADJECTIVE ① very great in degree or intensity • *extreme caution*. ② going beyond what is usual or reasonable • *extreme weather conditions*. ③ at the furthest point or edge of something • *the extreme northern corner of Spain*. ▶ NOUN ④ the highest or furthest degree of something. **extremely** ADVERB

> **extreme** ADJECTIVE
> ① = acute, deep, dire, great, intense, profound, severe
> ② = drastic, exceptional, excessive, extravagant, radical, unreasonable
> ▶ NOUN ④ = boundary, depth, end, height, limit, ultimate

extremist NOUN a person who uses unreasonable or violent methods to bring about political change. **extremism** NOUN

extremity, **extremities** NOUN The extremities of something are its furthest ends or edges.

extricate VERB To extricate someone from a place or a situation means to free them from it.

extrovert NOUN a person who is more interested in other people and the world around them than their own thoughts and feelings.

exuberant ADJECTIVE full of energy and cheerfulness. **exuberantly** ADVERB **exuberance** NOUN

exude VERB If someone exudes a quality or feeling, they seem to have it to a great degree.

eye, **eyes**, **eyeing** or **eying**, **eyed** NOUN ① the organ of sight. ② the small hole at the end of a needle through which you pass the thread. ▶ VERB ③ To eye something means to look at it carefully or suspiciously.

eyeball NOUN the whole of the ball-shaped part of the eye.

eyebrow NOUN Your eyebrows are the lines of hair which grow on the ridges of bone above your eyes.

eyelash NOUN Your eyelashes are hairs that grow on the edges of your eyelids.

eyelid NOUN Your eyelids are the folds of skin which cover your eyes when they are closed.

eyesight NOUN Your eyesight is your ability to see.

eyesore NOUN Something that is an eyesore is extremely ugly.

eyewitness NOUN a person who has seen an event and can describe what happened.

Ff

fable NOUN a story intended to teach a moral lesson.

fabled ADJECTIVE well-known because many stories have been told about it • *the fabled city of Troy*.

fabric NOUN ① DGT cloth • *tough fabric for tents*. ② The fabric of a building is its walls, roof and other parts. ③ The fabric of a society or system is its structure, laws and customs • *the democratic fabric of American society*.

fabricate VERB ① If you fabricate a story or an explanation, you invent it in order to deceive people. ② To fabricate something is to make or manufacture it. **fabrication** NOUN

fabulous ADJECTIVE ① wonderful or very impressive • *a fabulous picnic*. ② not real, but happening in stories and legends • *fabulous creatures*.

facade [*Said fas-**sahd***] NOUN ① the front outside wall of a building. ② a false outward appearance • *the facade of honesty*.

face NOUN ① the front part of your head from your chin to your forehead. ② the expression someone has or is making • *a grim face*. ③ a surface or side of something, especially the most important side • *the north face of Everest*. ④ the main aspect or general appearance of something • *We have changed the face of language study*. ▶ VERB ⑤ To face something or someone is to be opposite them or to look at them or towards them • *a room that faces onto the street*. ⑥ If you face something difficult or unpleasant, you have to deal with it • *She faced a terrible dilemma*. ▶ PHRASE ⑦ **On the face of it** means judging by the appearance of something or your initial reaction to it • *On the face of it the palace looks gigantic*.

> **face** NOUN
> ① = countenance (*formal*), features, mug (*slang*)
> ③ = aspect, exterior, front, side, surface
> ▶ VERB ⑤ = be opposite, look at, overlook

faceless ADJECTIVE without character or individuality • *anonymous shops and faceless coffee-bars*.

facet [*Said **fas**-it*] NOUN ① a single part or aspect of something • *the many facets of his talent*. ② one of the flat, cut surfaces of a precious stone.

facial [*Said **fay**-shal*] ADJECTIVE appearing on or being part of the face • *facial expressions*.

facilitate VERB To facilitate something is to make it easier for it to happen • *a process that will facilitate individual development*.

facility, **facilities** NOUN ① a service or piece of equipment which makes it possible to do something • *excellent shopping facilities*. ② A facility for something is an ability to do it easily or well • *a facility for novel-writing*.

fact NOUN ① a piece of knowledge or information that is true or something that has actually happened. ▶ PHRASE ② **In fact**, **as a matter of fact** and **in point of fact**

mean 'actually' or 'really' and are used for emphasis or when making an additional comment • *Very few people, in fact, have this type of skin.*
factual ADJECTIVE **factually** ADVERB

fact NOUN
① = certainty, reality, truth
≠ lie

faction NOUN a small group of people belonging to a larger group, but differing from the larger group in some aims or ideas • *a conservative faction in the Church.*

fact of life NOUN ① The facts of life are details about how babies are conceived and born. ② If you say that something is a fact of life, you mean that it is something that people expect to happen, even though they might find it shocking or unpleasant • *War is a fact of life.*

factor NOUN ① something that helps to cause a result • *House dust mites are a major factor in asthma.* ② The factors of a number are the whole numbers that will divide exactly into it. For example, 2 and 5 are factors of 10. ③ If something increases by a particular factor, it is multiplied that number of times • *The amount of energy used has increased by a factor of eight.*

factor NOUN
① = aspect, cause, consideration, element, influence, part

factory, **factories** NOUN a building or group of buildings where goods are made in large quantities.

factory NOUN
= mill, plant, works

faculty, **faculties** NOUN ① Your faculties are your physical and mental abilities • *My mental faculties are as sharp as ever.* ② In some universities, a Faculty is a group of related departments • *the Science Faculty.*

fad NOUN a temporary fashion or craze • *the latest exercise fad.*

fade VERB If something fades, the intensity of its colour, brightness or sound is gradually reduced.

fade VERB
= die away, dim, discolour, dull, wash out

faeces [*Said* ***fee**-seez*]; also spelt **feces** PLURAL NOUN the solid waste substances discharged from a person's or animal's body.

fag NOUN (*informal*) a cigarette.

Fahrenheit [*Said* ***far**-ren-hite*] NOUN a scale of temperature in which the freezing point of water is 32° and the boiling point is 212°.

fail VERB ① If someone fails to achieve something, they are not successful. ② If you fail an exam, your marks are too low and you do not pass. ③ If you fail to do something that you should have done, you do not do it • *They failed to phone her.* ④ If something fails, it becomes less effective or stops working properly • *The power failed* • *His grandmother's eyesight began to fail.* ▸ NOUN ⑤ In an exam, a fail is a piece of work that is not good enough to pass. ▸ PHRASE ⑥ **Without fail** means definitely or regularly • *Every Sunday her mum would ring without fail.*

fail VERB
① = be defeated, be in vain, be unsuccessful, come to grief, fall through, flunk (*informal*)
≠ succeed
③ = neglect, omit
④ = crash, give out, stop working

failing NOUN ① a fault in something or someone. ▸ PREPOSITION ② used to introduce an alternative • *Failing that, get a market stall.*

failure NOUN ① lack of success • *Not all conservation programmes ended in failure.* ② an unsuccessful person, thing or action • *The venture was a complete failure.* ③ Your failure to do something is not doing something that you were expected to do • *a statement explaining his failure to turn up as a speaker.* ④ a weakness in something.

failure NOUN
① = breakdown, collapse, defeat, downfall
≠ success
② = disappointment, fiasco, flop (*informal*), loser (*informal*), no-hoper (*informal*)
④ = deficiency, shortcoming

faint ADJECTIVE ① A sound, colour or feeling that is faint is not very strong or intense. ② If you feel faint, you feel weak, dizzy and unsteady. ▸ VERB ③ If you faint, you lose consciousness for a short time. **faintly** ADVERB

faint ADJECTIVE
① = dim, faded, indistinct, low, muted, vague
≠ strong
② = dizzy, giddy, light-headed
▸ VERB ③ = black out, collapse, pass out, swoon (*literary*)

fair ADJECTIVE ① reasonable and just • *fair and prompt trials for political prisoners.* ② quite large • *a fair size.* ③ moderately good or likely to be correct • *He had a fair idea of what to expect.* ④ having light-coloured hair or pale skin. ⑤ with pleasant and dry weather • *Ireland's fair weather months.* ▸ NOUN ⑥ a form of entertainment that takes place outside, with stalls, sideshows and machines to ride on. ⑦ an exhibition of goods produced by a particular industry • *International Food Fair.* **fairly** ADVERB **fairness** NOUN

fair ADJECTIVE
① = equal, equitable, impartial, legitimate, proper, upright
≠ unfair
④ = blonde, blond, light
≠ dark
▸ NOUN ⑥ = bazaar, carnival, exhibition, festival, fete, show

fairground NOUN an outdoor area where a fair is set up.

fairway NOUN the area of trimmed grass between a tee and a green on a golf course.

fairy, **fairies** NOUN In stories, fairies are small, supernatural creatures with magical powers.

fairy tale NOUN a story of magical events.

faith NOUN ① Faith is a feeling of confidence, trust or optimism about something. ② [RE] Someone's faith is their religion.

faith NOUN
① = confidence, trust
② = belief, creed, persuasion, religion

faithful ADJECTIVE ① loyal to someone or something and remaining firm in support of them. ② accurate and truthful • *a faithful copy of an original.* **faithfully** ADVERB **faithfulness** NOUN

faithful ADJECTIVE
① = devoted, loyal, staunch, true
≠ unfaithful
② = accurate, exact, strict, true

fake NOUN ① an imitation of something made to trick people into thinking that it is genuine. ▸ ADJECTIVE ② imitation and not genuine • *fake fur.* ▸ VERB ③ If you fake a feeling, you pretend that you are experiencing it.

fake NOUN
① = copy, forgery, fraud, imitation, reproduction, sham
▸ ADJECTIVE ② = artificial, counterfeit, false, imitation, phoney, phony
≠ real
▸ VERB ③ = feign, pretend, simulate

falcon NOUN a bird of prey that can be trained to hunt other birds or small animals.

fall, falls VERB ① If someone or something falls or falls over, they drop towards the ground. ② If something falls somewhere, it lands there • *The spotlight fell on her.* ③ If something falls in amount or strength, it becomes less • *Steel production fell about 25 per cent.* ④ If a person or group in a position of power falls, they lose their position and someone else takes control. ⑤ Someone who falls in battle is killed. ⑥ If, for example, you fall asleep, fall ill, or fall in love, you change quite quickly to that new state. ⑦ If you fall for someone, you become strongly attracted to them and fall in love. ⑧ If you fall for a trick or lie, you are deceived by it. ⑨ Something that falls on a particular date occurs on that date. ▸ NOUN ⑩ If you have a fall, you accidentally fall over. ⑪ A fall of snow, soot or other substance is a quantity of it that has fallen to the ground. ⑫ A fall in something is a reduction in its amount or strength. ⑬ In America, autumn is called fall. **fall down** VERB An argument or idea that falls down on a particular point is weak on that point and as a result will be unsuccessful. **fall out** VERB If people fall out, they disagree and quarrel. **fall through** VERB If an arrangement or plan falls through, it fails or is abandoned.

> **fall** VERB
> ① = collapse, drop, plunge, topple, trip
> ≠ rise
> ③ = decline, decrease, diminish, dwindle, plummet, subside
> ≠ increase
> ▸ NOUN ⑫ = decline, decrease, drop, reduction, slump
> ≠ rise

fallacy, fallacies [*Said* ***fal**-lass-ee*] NOUN something false that is generally believed to be true.

fallout NOUN radioactive particles that fall to the earth after a nuclear explosion.

fallow ADJECTIVE Land that is fallow is not being used for crop growing so that it has the chance to rest and improve.

false ADJECTIVE ① untrue or incorrect • *I think that's a false argument.* ② not real or genuine but intended to seem real • *false teeth.* ③ unfaithful or deceitful. **falsely** ADVERB **falseness** NOUN **falsity** NOUN

> **false** ADJECTIVE
> ① = erroneous (*formal*), fictitious, incorrect, mistaken, untrue
> ≠ true
> ② = artificial, bogus, fake, forged, simulated
> ≠ genuine
> ③ = deceitful, disloyal, insincere, unfaithful

falsehood NOUN ① the quality or fact of being untrue • *the difference between truth and falsehood.* ② a lie.

falsify, falsifies, falsifying, falsified VERB If you falsify something, you change it in order to deceive people. **falsification** NOUN

falter VERB If someone or something falters, they hesitate or become unsure or unsteady • *Her voice faltered.*

fame NOUN the state of being very well-known.

> **fame** NOUN
> = eminence, glory, prominence, renown, reputation

famed ADJECTIVE very well-known • *an area famed for its beauty.*

familiar ADJECTIVE ① well-known or easy to recognise • *familiar faces.* ② knowing or understanding something well • *Most children are familiar with stories.* **familiarity** NOUN **familiarise** VERB

familiar ADJECTIVE
② = acquainted with, aware of, knowledgeable about, versed in
≠ unfamiliar

family, **families** NOUN ① a group consisting of parents and their children; also all the people who are related to each other, including aunts and uncles, cousins and grandparents. ② a group of related species of animals or plants. It is smaller than an order and larger than a genus. **familial** ADJECTIVE

family NOUN
① = descendants, relations, relatives
② = class, classification, kind

famine NOUN a serious shortage of food which may cause many deaths.

famous ADJECTIVE very well-known.

famous ADJECTIVE
= celebrated, distinguished, illustrious, legendary, noted, renowned
≠ unknown

famously ADVERB (*old-fashioned*) If people get on famously, they enjoy each other's company very much.

fan, **fans**, **fanning**, **fanned** NOUN ① If you are a fan of someone or something, you like them very much and are very enthusiastic about them. ② a hand-held or mechanical object which creates a draught of cool air when it moves. ▸ VERB ③ To fan someone or something is to create a draught in their direction • *The gentle wind fanned her from all sides*. **fan out** VERB If things or people fan out, they move outwards in different directions.

fan NOUN
① = adherent (*formal*), admirer, devotee, geek (*informal*), lover, supporter, zealot

fanatic NOUN a person who is very extreme in their support for a cause or in their enthusiasm for a particular activity. **fanaticism** NOUN

fanatic NOUN
= activist, devotee, extremist, militant, zealot

fanatical ADJECTIVE If you are fanatical about something, you are very extreme in your enthusiasm or support for it. **fanatically** ADVERB

fanatical ADJECTIVE
= fervent, obsessive, passionate, rabid, wild

fancy, **fancies**, **fancying**, **fancied**; **fancier**, **fanciest** VERB ① If you fancy something, you want to have it or do it • *She fancied living in Canada*. ▸ ADJECTIVE ② special and elaborate • *dressed up in some fancy clothes*. **fanciful** ADJECTIVE

fancy VERB
① = be attracted to, hanker after, have a yen for, would like
▸ ADJECTIVE ② = decorated, elaborate, extravagant, intricate, ornate
≠ plain

fancy dress NOUN clothing worn for a party at which people dress up to look like a particular character or animal.

fanfare NOUN a short, loud musical introduction to a special event, usually played on trumpets.

fantasise; also spelt **fantasize** VERB If you fantasise, you imagine pleasant but unlikely events or situations.

fantastic ADJECTIVE ① wonderful and very pleasing • *a fantastic view of the sea*. ② extremely large in degree or amount • *fantastic debts*. ③ strange and difficult to believe • *fantastic animals found nowhere else on earth*. **fantastically** ADVERB

fantasy, **fantasies** NOUN ① an imagined story or situation.

② Fantasy is the activity of imagining things or the things that you imagine • *She can't distinguish between fantasy and reality.* ③ In books and films, fantasy is the people or situations which are created in the writer's imagination and do not reflect reality.

far, farther, farthest; further, furthest ADVERB ① If something is far away from other things, it is a long distance away. ② Far also means very much or to a great extent or degree • *far more important.* ▶ ADJECTIVE ③ Far means very distant • *in the far south of Africa.* ④ Far also describes the more distant of two things rather than the nearer one • *the far corner of the goal.* ▶ PHRASE ⑤ **By far** and **far and away** are used to say that something is so to a great degree • *Walking is by far the best way to get around.* ⑥ **So far** means up to the present moment • *So far, it's been good news.* ⑦ **As far as, so far as** and **in so far as** mean to the degree or extent that something is true • *As far as I know he is progressing well.*

far ADVERB
① = afar, a great distance, a long way, deep, miles
② = considerably, incomparably, much, very much
▶ ADJECTIVE ③ = distant, long, outlying, remote
≠ near

farce NOUN ① a humorous play in which ridiculous and unlikely situations occur. ② a disorganised and ridiculous situation. **farcical** ADJECTIVE

fare NOUN ① the amount charged for a journey on a bus, train or plane. ▶ VERB ② How someone fares in a particular situation is how they get on • *The team have not fared well in this tournament.*

Far East NOUN The Far East consists of the countries of East Asia, including China, Japan and Malaysia. **Far Eastern** ADJECTIVE

farewell INTERJECTION ① Farewell means goodbye. ▶ ADJECTIVE ② A farewell act is performed by or for someone who is leaving a particular job or career • *a farewell speech.*

far-fetched ADJECTIVE unlikely to be true.

farm NOUN ① an area of land together with buildings, used for growing crops and raising animals. ▶ VERB ② Someone who farms uses land to grow crops and raise animals. **farmer** NOUN **farming** NOUN

farmhouse NOUN the main house on a farm.

farmyard NOUN an area surrounded by farm buildings.

fascinate VERB If something fascinates you, it interests you very much. **fascinating** ADJECTIVE

fascinate VERB
= absorb, bewitch, captivate, enthral, intrigue

fascism [Said *fash*-izm] NOUN HISTORY an extreme political ideology or system of government with a powerful dictator and state control of most activities. Nationalism is encouraged and political opposition is not allowed. **fascist** NOUN, ADJECTIVE

fashion NOUN ① a style of dress or way of behaving that is popular at a particular time. ② The fashion in which someone does something is the way in which they do it. ▶ VERB ③ If you fashion something, you make or shape it.

fashion NOUN
① = craze, fad, style, trend, vogue
② = manner, method, mode, way
▶ VERB ③ = construct, create, make, mould, shape, work

fashionable ADJECTIVE Something that is fashionable is very popular with a lot of people at the same time. **fashionably** ADVERB

> **fashionable** ADJECTIVE
> = current, in (*informal*), latest, popular, prevailing
> ≠ old-fashioned

fast ADJECTIVE ① moving or done at great speed. ② If a clock is fast, it shows a time that is later than the real time. ▶ ADVERB ③ quickly and without delay. ④ Something that is held fast is firmly fixed. ▶ PHRASE ⑤ If you are **fast asleep**, you are in a deep sleep. ▶ VERB ⑥ If you fast, you eat no food at all for a period of time, usually for religious reasons. ▶ NOUN ⑦ a period of time during which someone does not eat food.

> **fast** ADJECTIVE
> ① = accelerated, hurried, quick, rapid, speedy, swift
> ≠ slow
> ▶ ADVERB ③ = hastily, hurriedly, quickly, rapidly, swiftly
> ≠ slowly
> ④ = firmly, securely, tightly

fasten VERB ① To fasten something is to close it or attach it firmly to something else. ② If you fasten your hands or teeth around or onto something, you hold it tightly with them. **fastener** NOUN **fastening** NOUN

> **fasten** VERB
> ① = attach, fix, join, lock, secure, tie

fast food NOUN hot food that is prepared and served quickly after you have ordered it.

fastidious ADJECTIVE extremely choosy and concerned about neatness and cleanliness.

fast-track VERB To fast-track something is to make it happen or put it into effect as quickly as possible, usually giving it priority over other things.

fat, **fatter**, **fattest**; **fats** ADJECTIVE ① Someone who is fat has too much weight on their body. ② large or great • *a fat pile of letters.* ▶ NOUN ③ Fat is the greasy, cream-coloured substance that animals and humans have under their skin, which is used to store energy and to help keep them warm. ④ Fat is also the greasy solid or liquid substance obtained from animals and plants and used in cooking. **fatness** NOUN **fatty** ADJECTIVE

> **fat** ADJECTIVE
> ① = obese, overweight, plump, portly
> ≠ thin

fatal ADJECTIVE ① causing death • *fatal injuries.* ② very important or significant and likely to have an undesirable effect • *The mistake was fatal to my plans.* **fatally** ADVERB

> **fatal** ADJECTIVE
> ① = deadly, incurable, lethal, mortal, terminal
> ② = calamitous, catastrophic, disastrous, lethal

fatality, **fatalities** NOUN a death caused by accident or violence.

fate NOUN ① Fate is a power that is believed to control events. ② Someone's fate is what happens to them • *She was resigned to her fate.*

> **fate** NOUN
> ① = chance, destiny, fortune, providence

fateful ADJECTIVE having an important, often disastrous, effect • *fateful political decisions.*

father NOUN ① A person's father is their male parent. ② The father of something is the man who invented or started it • *the father of Italian painting.* ③ 'Father' is used to address a priest in some Christian churches. ④ Father is another name for God. **fatherly** ADJECTIVE **fatherhood** NOUN

father-in-law, **fathers-in-law** NOUN A person's father-in-law is the father of their husband or wife.

fathom NOUN ① a unit for measuring the depth of water. It is equal to 6 feet or about 1.83 metres. ▶ VERB ② If you fathom something, you understand it after careful thought • *Daisy tries to fathom what it means.*

fatigue, **fatigues**, **fatiguing**, **fatigued** [*Said fat-**eeg***] NOUN ① Fatigue is extreme tiredness. ▶ VERB ② If you are fatigued by something, it makes you extremely tired.

fault NOUN ① If something bad is your fault, you are to blame for it. ② a weakness or imperfection in someone or something. ③ GEOGRAPHY a large crack in rock caused by movement of the earth's crust. ▶ PHRASE ④ If you are **at fault**, you are mistaken or are to blame for something • *If you were at fault, you accept it.* ▶ VERB ⑤ If you fault someone, you criticise them for what they are doing because they are not doing it well. **faultless** ADJECTIVE

> **fault** NOUN
> ① = blame, liability, responsibility
> ② = blemish, defect, deficiency, drawback, failing, flaw, imperfection, weakness
> ≠ strength
> ▶ VERB ⑤ = blame, censure (*formal*), criticise

faulty, **faultier**, **faultiest** ADJECTIVE containing flaws or errors.

> **faulty** ADJECTIVE
> = defective, flawed, imperfect, invalid, unsound

favour NOUN ① If you regard someone or something with favour, you like or support them. ② If you do someone a favour, you do something helpful for them. ▶ PHRASE ③ Something that is **in someone's favour** is a help or advantage to them • *The arguments seemed to be in our favour.* ④ If you are **in favour of** something, you agree with it and think it should happen. ▶ VERB ⑤ If you favour something or someone, you prefer that person or thing.

> **favour** NOUN
> ① = approval, esteem, grace, support
> ≠ disapproval
> ② = courtesy, good turn, kindness, service
> ≠ wrong
> ▶ VERB ⑤ = prefer, single out

favourable ADJECTIVE ① of advantage or benefit to someone. ② positive and expressing approval. **favourably** ADVERB

> **favourable** ADJECTIVE
> ① = advantageous, beneficial, good, opportune, suitable
> ≠ unfavourable
> ② = affirmative, amicable, approving, friendly, positive, sympathetic, welcoming
> ≠ unfavourable

favourite ADJECTIVE ① Your favourite person or thing is the one you like best. ▶ NOUN ② Someone's favourite is the person or thing they like best. ③ the animal or person expected to win in a race or contest.

> **favourite** ADJECTIVE
> ① = best-loved, dearest, favoured, preferred
> ▶ NOUN ② = darling, idol, pet, pick

favouritism NOUN Favouritism is behaviour in which you are unfairly more helpful or more generous to one person than to other people.

> **favouritism** NOUN
> = bias, one-sidedness
> ≠ impartiality

fawn NOUN, ADJECTIVE ① pale yellowish-brown. ▸ NOUN ② a very young deer. ▸ VERB ③ To fawn on someone is to seek their approval by flattering them.

fear NOUN ① Fear is an unpleasant feeling of danger. ② a thought that something undesirable or unpleasant might happen • *You have a fear of failure.* ▸ VERB ③ If you fear someone or something, you are frightened of them. ④ If you fear something unpleasant, you are worried that it is likely to happen • *Artists feared that their pictures would be forgotten.* **fearless** ADJECTIVE **fearlessly** ADVERB

> **fear** NOUN
> ① = alarm, awe, dread, fright, panic, terror
> ▸ VERB ③ = be afraid, be frightened, be scared, dread, take fright

fearful ADJECTIVE ① afraid and full of fear. ② extremely unpleasant or worrying • *The world's in such a fearful mess.* **fearfully** ADVERB

fearsome ADJECTIVE terrible or frightening • *a powerful, fearsome weapon.*

feasible ADJECTIVE possible and likely to happen • *The proposal is just not feasible.* **feasibility** NOUN

feast NOUN a large and special meal for many people.

feat NOUN an impressive and difficult achievement • *It was an astonishing feat for Leeds to score six away from home.*

feather NOUN one of the light fluffy things covering a bird's body. **feathery** ADJECTIVE

feature NOUN ① an interesting or important part or characteristic of something. ② Someone's features are the various parts of their face. ③ a special article or programme dealing with a particular subject. ④ the main film in a cinema programme. ▸ VERB ⑤ To feature something is to include it or emphasise it as an important part or subject. **featureless** ADJECTIVE

> **feature** NOUN
> ① = aspect, attribute, characteristic, mark, property, quality
> ③ = article, column, item, piece, report, story
> ▸ VERB ⑤ = emphasise, give prominence to, spotlight, star

February NOUN February is the second month of the year. It has 28 days, except in a leap year, when it has 29 days.

fed the past tense and past participle of **feed**.

federal ADJECTIVE relating to a system of government in which a group of states is controlled by a central government, but each state has its own local powers • *The United States of America is a federal country.*

federation NOUN a group of organisations or states that have joined together for a common purpose.

fed up ADJECTIVE (*informal*) unhappy or bored.

fee NOUN a charge or payment for a job, service or activity.

feeble ADJECTIVE weak or lacking in power or influence • *feeble and stupid arguments.*

feed, feeds, feeding, fed VERB ① To feed a person or animal is to give them food. ② When an animal or baby feeds, it eats. ③ To feed something is to supply what is needed for it to operate or exist • *The information was fed into a computer database.* ▸ NOUN ④ Feed is food for animals.

feedback NOUN ① Feedback is comments and information about the quality or success of something.

② Feedback is also a condition in which some of the power, sound or information produced by electronic equipment goes back into it.

feel, **feels**, **feeling**, **felt** VERB ① If you feel an emotion or sensation, you experience it • *I felt a bit ashamed.* ② If you feel that something is the case, you believe it to be so • *She feels that she is in control of her life.* ③ If you feel something, you touch it. ④ If something feels warm or cold, for example, you experience its warmth or coldness through the sense of touch • *Real marble feels cold to the touch.* ⑤ To feel the effect of something is to be affected by it • *The shock waves of this fire will be felt by people from all over the world.* ▶ NOUN ⑥ The feel of something is how it feels to you when you touch it • *skin with a velvety smooth feel.* ▶ PHRASE ⑦ If you **feel like** doing something, you want to do it.

> **feel** VERB
> ① = experience, suffer, undergo
> ② = believe, consider, deem, judge, think
> ③ = finger, fondle, stroke, touch

feeling NOUN ① an emotion or reaction • *feelings of envy.* ② a physical sensation • *a feeling of pain.* ③ Feeling is the ability to experience the sense of touch in your body • *He had no feeling in his hands.* ④ (*in plural*) Your feelings about something are your general attitudes or thoughts about it • *He has strong feelings about our national sport.*

> **feeling** NOUN
> ① = emotion, fervour, heat, passion
> ② = sensation, sense
> ④ = inclination, opinion, point of view, sentiment, view

feet the plural of **foot**.

feign [*Rhymes with* ***rain***] VERB If you feign an emotion or state, you pretend to experience it • *I feigned a headache.*

feline [*Said* ***fee****-line*] ADJECTIVE belonging or relating to the cat family.

fell ① the past tense of **fall**. ▶ VERB ② To fell a tree is to cut it down.

fellow NOUN ① (*old-fashioned, informal*) a man • *I knew a fellow by that name.* ② a senior member of a learned society or a university college. ③ Your fellows are the people who share work or an activity with you. ▶ ADJECTIVE ④ You use 'fellow' to describe people who have something in common with you • *his fellow editors.*

fellowship NOUN ① a feeling of friendliness that a group of people have when they are doing things together. ② a group of people that join together because they have interests in common • *the Dickens Fellowship.* ③ an academic post at a university which involves research work.

> **fellowship** NOUN
> ① = brotherhood, camaraderie, companionship
> ② = association, brotherhood, club, league, society

felt ① the past tense and past participle of **feel**. ▶ NOUN ② DGT Felt is a thick cloth made by pressing short threads together.

female NOUN ① a person or animal belonging to the sex that can have babies or lay eggs. ▶ ADJECTIVE ② concerning or relating to females.

> **female** NOUN
> ① = girl, lady, sheila (*Australian and New Zealand; informal*), woman
> ≠ male
> ▶ ADJECTIVE ② = feminine, girlish, womanly
> ≠ male

feminine ADJECTIVE ① relating to women or considered to be typical of women. ② belonging to a particular class of nouns in some languages, such as French, German and Latin. **femininity** NOUN

feminism NOUN Feminism is the belief that women should have the same rights and opportunities as men. **feminist** NOUN, ADJECTIVE

fence NOUN ① a wooden or wire barrier between two areas of land. ② a barrier or hedge for the horses to jump over in horse racing or show jumping. ▶ VERB ③ To fence an area of land is to surround it with a fence. ④ When two people fence, they use special swords to fight each other as a sport.

fend PHRASE If you have to **fend for yourself**, you have to look after yourself. **fend off** VERB If you fend off an attack or unwelcome questions or attention, you defend and protect yourself.

ferment VERB When wine, beer or fruit ferments, a chemical change takes place in it, often producing alcohol. **fermentation** NOUN

fern NOUN a plant with long feathery leaves and no flowers.

ferocious ADJECTIVE violent and fierce • *ferocious dogs* • *ferocious storms*. **ferociously** ADVERB **ferocity** NOUN

ferret NOUN a small, fierce animal related to the weasel and kept for hunting rats and rabbits.

ferry, **ferries**, **ferrying**, **ferried** NOUN ① a boat that carries people and vehicles across short stretches of water. ▶ VERB ② To ferry people or goods somewhere is to transport them there, usually on a short, regular journey.

fertile ADJECTIVE ① capable of producing offspring or plants. ② creative • *fertile minds*. **fertility** NOUN

> **fertile** ADJECTIVE
> ① = fruitful, productive, prolific, rich
> ≠ barren

fertilise; also spelt **fertilize** VERB ① [SCIENCE] When an egg, plant or female is fertilised, the process of reproduction begins by sperm joining with the egg, or by pollen coming into contact with the reproductive part of a plant. ② To fertilise land is to put manure or chemicals onto it to feed the plants.

fertiliser; also spelt **fertilizer** NOUN [GEOGRAPHY] a substance put onto soil to improve plant growth.

fervent ADJECTIVE showing strong, sincere and enthusiastic feeling • *a fervent nationalist*. **fervently** ADVERB

> **fervent** ADJECTIVE
> = ardent, committed, devout, enthusiastic, impassioned, passionate, zealous

fervour NOUN a very strong feeling for or belief in something • *a wave of revolutionary fervour*.

fester VERB If a wound festers, it becomes infected and produces pus.

festival NOUN ① an organised series of events and performances • *the Cannes Film Festival*. ② [RE] a day or period of religious celebration.

> **festival** NOUN
> ① = carnival, entertainment, fair, fete, gala
> ② = anniversary, holiday

festive ADJECTIVE full of happiness and celebration • *a festive time of singing and dancing*.

festivity, **festivities** NOUN celebration and happiness • *the wedding festivities*.

festooned ADJECTIVE If something is festooned with objects, the objects are hanging across it in large numbers.

fetch VERB ① If you fetch something, you go to where it is and bring it back. ② If something fetches a particular sum of money, it is sold for that amount • *Portraits fetch the highest prices.*

fetching ADJECTIVE attractive in appearance • *a fetching purple frock.*

fete *[Rhymes with* ***date****]* NOUN ① an outdoor event with competitions, displays and goods for sale. ▶ VERB ② Someone who is feted receives a public welcome or entertainment as an honour.

feud *[Said* ***fyood****]* NOUN ① a long-term and very bitter quarrel, especially between families. ▶ VERB ② When people feud, they take part in a feud.

fever NOUN ① Fever is a condition occurring during illness, in which the patient has a very high body temperature. ② A fever is extreme excitement or agitation • *a fever of impatience.*

feverish ADJECTIVE ① in a state of extreme excitement or agitation • *increasingly feverish activity.* ② suffering from a high body temperature. **feverishly** ADVERB

few ADJECTIVE, NOUN ① used to refer to a small number of things • *I saw him a few moments ago* • *one of only a few.* ▶ PHRASE ② **Quite a few** or **a good few** means quite a large number of things.

> **few** ADJECTIVE, NOUN
> ① = infrequent, meagre, not many, scanty, scarce, sparse
> ≠ many

fiancé *[Said fee-****on****-say]* NOUN A person's fiancé is the man to whom they are engaged.

fiancée *[Said fee-****on****-say]* NOUN A person's fiancée is the woman to whom they are engaged.

fiasco, fiascos *[Said fee-****ass****-koh]* NOUN an event or attempt that fails completely, especially in a ridiculous or disorganised way • *The game ended in a complete fiasco.*

fib, fibs, fibbing, fibbed NOUN ① a small, unimportant lie. ▶ VERB ② If you fib, you tell a small lie.

fibre NOUN ① [DGT] a thin thread of a substance used to make cloth. ② [SCIENCE] Fibre is also a part of plants that can be eaten but not digested; it helps food pass quickly through the body. **fibrous** ADJECTIVE

fickle ADJECTIVE A fickle person keeps changing their mind about who or what they like or want.

fiction NOUN ① Fiction is stories about people and events that have been invented by the author. ② something that is not true. **fictional** ADJECTIVE **fictitious** ADJECTIVE

fiddle VERB ① If you fiddle with something, you keep moving it or touching it restlessly. ② *(informal)* If someone fiddles something such as an account, they alter it dishonestly to get money for themselves. ▶ NOUN *(informal)* ③ a dishonest action or scheme to get money. ④ a violin. **fiddler** NOUN

fiddly, fiddlier, fiddliest ADJECTIVE small and difficult to do or use • *fiddly nuts and bolts.*

fidelity NOUN Fidelity is remaining firm in your beliefs, friendships or loyalty to another person.

field NOUN ① an area of land where crops are grown or animals are kept. ② [PE] an area of land where sports are played • *a hockey field.* ③ A coal field, oil field or gold field is an area where coal, oil or gold is found. ④ a particular subject or area of interest • *He was doing well in the field of chemistry.* ▶ ADJECTIVE ⑤ A field trip or a field study involves research or activity in the natural environment rather than theoretical or laboratory work. ⑥ In an athletics competition, the field events are the events such as the high jump and the javelin which do not take place on a running track. ▸ VERB ⑦ In cricket, when you field the ball, you stop it after the batsman has hit it. ⑧ To field questions is to answer or deal with them skilfully.

field NOUN
① = green, meadow, pasture
④ = area, department, domain, province, speciality, territory

fielder NOUN In cricket, the fielders are the team members who stand at various parts of the pitch and try to get the batsmen out or to prevent runs from being scored.

fieldwork NOUN Fieldwork is the study of something in the environment where it naturally lives or occurs, rather than in a class or laboratory.

fiend *[Said **feend**]* NOUN ① a devil or evil spirit. ② a very wicked or cruel person. ③ *(informal)* someone who is very keen on a particular thing • *a fitness fiend*.

fierce ADJECTIVE ① very aggressive or angry. ② extremely strong or intense • *a sudden fierce pain* • *a fierce storm*.
fiercely ADVERB

fierce ADJECTIVE
① = aggressive, dangerous, ferocious, murderous
≠ gentle
② = intense, keen, relentless, strong

fiery, **fierier**, **fieriest** ADJECTIVE ① involving fire or seeming like fire • *a huge fiery sun*. ② showing great anger, energy or passion • *a fiery debate*.

fifteen the number 15. **fifteenth** ADJECTIVE

fifth ADJECTIVE ① The fifth item in a series is the one counted as number five. ▸ NOUN ② one of five equal parts.

fifty, **fifties** the number 50. **fiftieth** ADJECTIVE

fig NOUN a soft, sweet fruit full of tiny seeds. It grows in hot countries and is often eaten dried.

fight, **fights**, **fighting**, **fought** VERB ① When people fight, they take part in a battle, a war, a boxing match, or in some other attempt to hurt or kill someone. ② To fight for something is to try in a very determined way to achieve it • *I must fight for respect*. ▸ NOUN ③ a situation in which people hit or try to hurt each other. ④ a determined attempt to prevent or achieve something • *the fight for independence*. ⑤ an angry disagreement.

fight VERB
① = battle, brawl, grapple, struggle
▸ NOUN ③ = action, battle, bout, combat, duel, skirmish
⑤ = argument, blue (*Australian; slang*), dispute, row, squabble

fighter NOUN someone who physically fights another person.

fighter NOUN
= soldier, warrior

figurative ADJECTIVE ENGLISH If you use a word or expression in a figurative sense, you use it with a more abstract or imaginative meaning than its ordinary one.
figuratively ADVERB

figure NOUN ① a written number or the amount a number stands for. ② a geometrical shape. ③ a diagram or table in a written text. ④ the shape of a human body, sometimes one that you cannot see properly • *his slim and supple figure* • *A human figure leaped at him*. ⑤ a person • *He was a major figure in the trial*. ▸ VERB ⑥ To figure in something is to appear or be included in it • *the many people who have figured in his life*. ⑦ *(informal)* If you figure that something is the case, you guess or conclude this • *We figure the fire broke out around four in the morning*.

figure NOUN
① = amount, digit, number, numeral, statistic, total
④ = body, build, form, physique, shape, silhouette
⑤ = character, dignitary, person, personality, player
▶ VERB ⑦ = expect, guess, reckon (*informal*), suppose

figurehead NOUN the leader of a movement or organisation who has no real power.

file NOUN ① a box or folder in which a group of papers or records is kept; also used of the information kept in the file. ② In computing, a file is a stored set of related data with its own name. ③ a line of people one behind the other. ④ DGT a long steel tool with a rough surface, used for smoothing and shaping hard materials. ▶ VERB ⑤ When someone files a document, they put it in its correct place with similar documents. ⑥ When a group of people file somewhere, they walk one behind the other in a line. ⑦ If you file something, you smooth or shape it with a file.

fill VERB ① If you fill something or if it fills up, it becomes full. ② If something fills a need, it satisfies the need • *Ella had in some small way filled the gap left by Molly's absence.* ③ To fill a job vacancy is to appoint someone to do that job. ▶ NOUN ④ If you have had your fill of something, you do not want any more. **fill in** VERB ① If you fill in a form, you write information in the appropriate spaces. ② If you fill someone in, you give them information to bring them up to date.

fill VERB
① = cram, gorge, pack, stock, stuff
≠ empty

fillet NOUN ① a strip of tender, boneless beef, veal or pork. ② a piece of fish with the bones removed. ▶ VERB ③ To fillet meat or fish is to prepare it by cutting out the bones.

filling NOUN ① the soft food mixture inside a sandwich, cake or pie. ② a small amount of metal or plastic put into a hole in a tooth by a dentist.

filly, fillies NOUN a female horse or pony under the age of four.

film NOUN ① a series of moving pictures projected onto a screen and shown at the cinema or on television. ② a thin flexible strip of plastic used in some cameras to record images when exposed to light. ③ a very thin layer of powder or liquid on a surface. ④ Plastic film is a very thin sheet of plastic used for wrapping things. ▶ VERB ⑤ If you film someone, you use a video camera to record their movements.

filter NOUN ① a device that allows some things to pass through it, but not others • *a filter against the harmful rays of the sun* • *a filter to block unwanted email.* ▶ VERB ② To filter something is to pass it through a filter. ③ If something filters somewhere, it gets there slowly or faintly • *Traffic filtered into the city.* **filtration** NOUN

filth NOUN ① Filth is disgusting dirt and muck. ② People often use the word filth to refer to very bad language or to things that are thought to be crude and offensive. **filthy** ADJECTIVE **filthiness** NOUN

fin NOUN a thin, flat structure on the body of a fish, used to help guide it through the water.

final ADJECTIVE ① last in a series or happening at the end of something. ② A decision that is final cannot be changed or questioned. ▶ NOUN ③ the last game or contest in a series which decides the overall winner.

④ (*in plural*) Finals are the last and most important examinations of a university or college course.

final ADJECTIVE
① = closing, concluding, eventual, last, ultimate
≠ first
② = absolute, conclusive, definite, definitive

finale [*Said fin-**nah**-lee*] NOUN the last section of a piece of music or show.

finalise; also spelt **finalize** VERB If you finalise something, you complete all the arrangements for it.

finalist NOUN a person taking part in the final of a competition.

finally ADVERB ① If something finally happens, it happens after a long delay. ② You use 'finally' to introduce a final point, question or topic that you are talking or writing about.

finally ADVERB
① = at last, at the last moment, eventually, in the end, in the long run
② = in conclusion, in summary, lastly

finance VERB ① To finance a project or a large purchase is to provide the money for it. ▶ NOUN ② Finance for something is the money or loans used to pay for it. ③ Finance is also the management of money, loans and investments.

finance VERB
① = back, fund, pay for, support
▶ NOUN ③ = banking, budgeting, commerce, economics, investment

financial ADJECTIVE relating to or involving money. **financially** ADVERB

financial ADJECTIVE
= economic, fiscal, money

financier NOUN a person who deals with the finance for large businesses.

find, **finds**, **finding**, **found** VERB ① If you find someone or something, you discover them, either as a result of searching or by coming across them unexpectedly. ② If you find that something is the case, you become aware of it or realise it • *I found my fists were clenched.* ③ Something that is found in a particular place typically lives or exists there. ④ When a court or jury finds a person guilty or not guilty, they decide that the person is guilty or innocent • *He was found guilty and sentenced to life imprisonment.* ▶ NOUN ⑤ If you describe something or someone as a find, you mean that you have recently discovered them and they are valuable or useful. **finder** NOUN **find out** VERB ① If you find out something, you learn or discover something that you did not know. ② If you find someone out, you discover that they have been doing something they should not have been doing.

find VERB
① = come across, discover, locate, track down, turn up, unearth
≠ lose
② = become aware, detect, discover, learn, realise

findings PLURAL NOUN Someone's findings are the conclusions they reach as a result of investigation.

fine ADJECTIVE ① very good or very beautiful • *a fine school* • *fine clothes.* ② satisfactory or suitable • *If you're on a diet, pasta dishes are fine if not served with a rich sauce.* ③ very narrow or thin. ④ A fine detail, adjustment or distinction is very delicate, exact or subtle. ⑤ When the weather is fine, it is not raining and is bright or sunny. ▶ NOUN ⑥ a sum of money paid as a punishment. ▶ VERB ⑦ Someone who is fined has to pay a sum of money as a punishment.

fine ADJECTIVE
① = admirable, beautiful, excellent, magnificent, outstanding, splendid
③ = delicate, lightweight, powdery, sheer, small
④ = fastidious, keen, precise, refined, sensitive, subtle

finery NOUN Finery is very beautiful clothing and jewellery.

finesse *[Said fin-**ness**]* NOUN If you do something with finesse, you do it with skill and subtlety.

finger NOUN ① Your fingers are the four long jointed parts of your hands, sometimes including the thumbs. ▶ VERB ② If you finger something, you feel it with your fingers.

fingernail NOUN Your fingernails are the hard coverings at the ends of your fingers.

fingerprint NOUN a mark made showing the pattern on the skin at the tip of a person's finger.

finish VERB ① When you finish something, you reach the end of it and complete it. ② When something finishes, it ends or stops. ▶ NOUN ③ The finish of something is the end or last part of it. ④ DGT The finish that something has is the texture or appearance of its surface • *a healthy, glossy finish.*

finish VERB
① = close, complete, conclude, end, finalise
≠ start
▶ NOUN ③ = close, completion, conclusion, end, ending, finale
≠ start
④ = grain, lustre, polish, shine, surface, texture

finite *[Said **fie**-nite]* ADJECTIVE having a particular size or limit which cannot be increased • *There's only finite money to spend.*

Finn NOUN someone who comes from Finland.

Finnish ADJECTIVE ① belonging or relating to Finland. ▶ NOUN ② Finnish is the main language spoken in Finland.

fir NOUN a tall, pointed evergreen tree that has thin, needle-like leaves and produces cones.

fire NOUN ① Fire is the flames produced when something burns. ② a pile or mass of burning material. ③ a piece of equipment that is used as a heater • *a gas fire.* ▶ VERB ④ If you fire a weapon or fire a bullet, you operate the weapon so that the bullet or missile is released. ⑤ If you fire questions at someone, you ask them a lot of questions very quickly. ⑥ (*informal*) If an employer fires someone, he or she dismisses that person from their job. ▶ PHRASE ⑦ If someone **opens fire**, they start shooting.

fire NOUN
① = blaze, combustion, flames, inferno
▶ VERB ④ = detonate, explode, launch, set off, shoot
⑥ = discharge, dismiss, make redundant, sack (*informal*)

firearm NOUN a gun.

fire brigade NOUN the organisation which has the job of putting out fires.

fire engine NOUN a large vehicle that carries equipment for putting out fires.

fire extinguisher NOUN a metal cylinder containing water or foam for spraying onto a fire.

firefighter NOUN a person whose job is to put out fires and rescue trapped people.

fireplace NOUN the opening beneath a chimney where a fire can be lit.

fire station NOUN a building where fire engines are kept and where firefighters wait to be called out.

firework NOUN a small container of gunpowder and other chemicals which explodes and produces coloured sparks or smoke when lit.

firm ADJECTIVE ① Something that is firm does not move easily when pressed or pushed, or when weight is put on it. ② A firm grasp or push is one with controlled force or pressure. ③ A firm decision is definite. ④ Someone who is firm behaves with authority that shows they will not change their mind. ▸ NOUN ⑤ a business selling or producing something. **firmly** ADVERB **firmness** NOUN

> **firm** ADJECTIVE
> ① = compressed, congealed, hard, rigid, set, solid, stiff
> ≠ soft
> ④ = adamant, determined, inflexible, resolute, staunch, unshakable
> ▸ NOUN ⑤ = business, company, corporation, enterprise, organisation

first ADJECTIVE ① done or in existence before anything else. ② more important than anything else • *Her story won first prize.* ▸ ADVERB ③ done or occurring before anything else. ▸ NOUN ④ something that has never happened or been done before. **firstly** ADVERB

> **first** ADJECTIVE
> ① = earliest, initial, opening, original, primeval
> ≠ last
> ② = chief, foremost, leading, main, prime, principal
> ▸ ADVERB ③ = beforehand, earlier, firstly, initially, to begin with

first aid NOUN First aid is medical treatment given to an injured person.

first-class ADJECTIVE ① Something that is first-class is of the highest quality or standard • *This machine produces first-class results.* ② First-class services are more expensive and therefore faster or more comfortable than second-class ones.

first-hand ADJECTIVE First-hand knowledge or experience is gained directly rather than from books or other people.

First Lady NOUN The First Lady of a country is the wife of its president.

first-rate ADJECTIVE excellent.

> **first-rate** ADJECTIVE
> = excellent, exceptional, first-class, marvellous, outstanding, splendid, superb

fiscal ADJECTIVE involving government or public money, especially taxes.

fish, **fish** or **fishes** NOUN ① a cold-blooded creature living in water that has a spine, gills, fins and a scaly skin. ② Fish is the flesh of fish eaten as food. ▸ VERB ③ To fish is to try to catch fish for food or sport. ④ If you fish for information, you try to get it in an indirect way. **fishing** NOUN **fisherman** NOUN

fishery, **fisheries** NOUN an area of the sea where fish are caught commercially.

fishmonger NOUN a shopkeeper who sells fish; also the shop itself.

fishy, **fishier**, **fishiest** ADJECTIVE ① smelling of fish. ② (*informal*) suspicious or doubtful • *He spotted something fishy going on.*

fist NOUN a hand with the fingers curled tightly towards the palm.

fit, **fits**, **fitting**, **fitted**; **fitter**, **fittest** VERB ① Something that fits is the right shape or size for a particular person or position. ② If you fit something somewhere, you put it there carefully or securely • *Very carefully he fitted the files inside the compartment.* ③ If something fits a particular situation, person or thing, it is suitable or appropriate • *a sentence that fitted the crime*. ▸ NOUN ④ The fit of something is how it fits • *This bolt must be a good fit*. ⑤ If someone has a fit, their muscles suddenly start contracting violently and they may lose consciousness. ⑥ A fit of laughter, coughing, anger or panic is a sudden uncontrolled outburst. ▸ ADJECTIVE ⑦ good enough or suitable • *Housing fit for young families*. ⑧ Someone who is fit is healthy and has strong muscles as a result of regular exercise. **fitness** NOUN

fit out VERB To fit someone or something out means to provide them with the necessary equipment.

> **fit** VERB
> ① = belong, correspond, dovetail, go, match
> ② = adapt, arrange, place, position
> ▸ ADJECTIVE ⑧ = healthy, in good condition, robust, trim, well
> ≠ unfit

fitful ADJECTIVE happening at irregular intervals and not continuous • *a fitful breeze*. **fitfully** ADVERB

fitter NOUN a person who assembles or installs machinery.

fitting ADJECTIVE ① right or suitable • *a fitting reward for his efforts*. ▸ NOUN ② a small part that is fixed to a piece of equipment or furniture. ③ If you have a fitting, you try on a garment that is being made to see if it fits properly.

> **fitting** ADJECTIVE
> ① = appropriate, correct, proper, right, suitable
> ▸ NOUN ② = accessory, attachment, component, part, unit

five ① the number 5. ▸ NOUN ② Fives is a ball game similar to squash, in which you hit the ball with your hand.

fix VERB ① If you fix something somewhere, you attach it or put it there securely. ② If you fix something broken, you mend it. ③ If you fix your attention on something, you concentrate on it. ④ If you fix something, you make arrangements for it • *The opening party is fixed for the 24th September*. ⑤ (*informal*) To fix something is to arrange the outcome unfairly or dishonestly. ▸ NOUN ⑥ (*informal*) something that has been unfairly or dishonestly arranged. ⑦ (*informal*) If you are in a fix, you are in a difficult situation. **fixed** ADJECTIVE **fixedly** ADVERB

> **fix** VERB
> ① = attach, bind, fasten, secure, stick
> ② = correct, mend, patch up, repair
> ▸ NOUN ⑦ = difficulty, mess, predicament, quandary

fixation NOUN an extreme and obsessive interest in something.

fixture NOUN ① a piece of furniture or equipment that is fixed into position in a house. ② a sports event due to take place on a particular date • *a series of difficult away fixtures*.

fizz VERB Something that fizzes makes a hissing sound.

fizzle VERB Something that fizzles makes a weak hissing or spitting sound.

fizzy, **fizzier**, **fizziest** ADJECTIVE Fizzy drinks have carbon dioxide in them to make them bubbly.

fjord [*Said fee-ord*]; also spelt **fiord** NOUN a long, narrow inlet of the sea between very high cliffs, especially in Norway.

flab NOUN Flab is large amounts of surplus fat on someone's body.

flabbergasted ADJECTIVE extremely surprised.

flabby, **flabbier**, **flabbiest** ADJECTIVE Someone who is flabby is rather fat and unfit, with loose flesh on their body.

flabby ADJECTIVE
= sagging, slack
≠ taut

flag, flags, flagging, flagged NOUN ① a rectangular or square cloth which has a particular colour and design, and is used as the symbol of a nation or as a signal. ▸ VERB ② If you or your spirits flag, you start to lose energy or enthusiasm. **flag down** VERB If you flag down a vehicle, you signal to the driver to stop.

flagrant *[Said flay-grant]* ADJECTIVE very shocking and bad in an obvious way • *a flagrant defiance of the rules.* **flagrantly** ADVERB

flagship NOUN ① a ship carrying the commander of the fleet. ② the most modern or impressive product or asset of an organisation.

flail VERB If someone's arms or legs flail about, they move in a wild, uncontrolled way.

flair NOUN Flair is a natural ability to do something well or stylishly.

flak NOUN ① Flak is anti-aircraft fire. ② If you get flak for doing something, you get a lot of severe criticism.

flake NOUN ① a small, thin piece of something. ▸ VERB ② When something such as paint flakes, small thin pieces of it come off. **flaky** ADJECTIVE **flaked** ADJECTIVE **flake out** VERB (*informal*) If you flake out, you collapse, go to sleep, or lose consciousness.

flamboyant ADJECTIVE behaving in a very showy and confident way. **flamboyance** NOUN

flame NOUN ① a hot bright stream of burning gas. ② A flame of passion, desire or anger is a sudden strong feeling.

flamenco NOUN Flamenco is a type of very lively, fast Spanish dancing, accompanied by guitar music.

flammable ADJECTIVE likely to catch fire and burn easily.

flan NOUN an open sweet or savoury tart with a pastry or cake base.

flank NOUN ① the side of an animal between the ribs and the hip. ▸ VERB ② Someone or something that is flanked by a particular thing or person has them at their side • *He was flanked by four bodyguards.*

flannel NOUN ① Flannel is a lightweight woollen fabric. ② a small square of towelling, used for washing yourself. In Australian English it is called a **washer**.

flap, flaps, flapping, flapped VERB ① Something that flaps moves up and down or from side to side with a snapping sound. ▸ NOUN ② a loose piece of something such as paper or skin that is attached at one edge.

flare NOUN ① a device that produces a brightly coloured flame, used especially as an emergency signal. ▸ VERB ② If a fire flares, it suddenly burns much more vigorously. ③ If violence or a conflict flares or flares up, it suddenly starts or becomes more serious.

flash NOUN ① a sudden, short burst of light. ▸ VERB ② If a light flashes, it shines for a very short period, often repeatedly. ③ Something that flashes past moves or happens so fast that you almost miss it. ④ If you flash something, you show it briefly • *Rihanna flashed her face at the crowd.* ▸ PHRASE ⑤ Something that happens **in a flash** happens suddenly and lasts a very short time.

flash NOUN
① = burst, flare, sparkle
▸ VERB ② = flare, glint, glitter, sparkle, twinkle

flashback NOUN a scene in a film, play or book that returns to events in the past.

flashlight NOUN a large, powerful torch.

flashy, **flashier**, **flashiest** ADJECTIVE expensive and fashionable in appearance, in a vulgar way • *flashy clothes*.

> **flashy** ADJECTIVE
> = flamboyant, garish, showy, tacky (*informal*), tasteless
> ≠ modest

flask NOUN a bottle used for carrying alcoholic or hot drinks around with you.

flat NOUN ① a self-contained set of rooms, usually on one level, for living in. ② In music, a flat is a note or key a semitone lower than that described by the same letter. It is represented by the symbol (♭). ▶ VERB ③ In Australian and New Zealand English, to flat is to live in a flat • *flatting in London*. ▶ ADJECTIVE ④ Something that is flat is level and smooth. ⑤ A flat object is not very tall or deep • *a low, flat building*. ⑥ A flat tyre or ball has not got enough air in it. ⑦ A flat battery has lost its electrical charge. ⑧ A flat refusal or denial is complete and firm. ⑨ Something that is flat is without emotion or interest. ⑩ A flat rate or price is fixed and the same for everyone • *The company charges a flat fee for its advice*. ⑪ A musical instrument or note that is flat is slightly too low in pitch. ▶ ADVERB ⑫ Something that is done in a particular time flat, takes exactly that time • *They would find them in two minutes flat*. **flatly** ADVERB **flatness** NOUN

> **flat** NOUN
> ① = apartment, rooms
> ▶ ADJECTIVE ④ = horizontal, level, levelled, smooth, unbroken
> ≠ uneven
> ⑨ = boring, dull, insipid, monotonous, weak

flathead NOUN a common Australian edible fish.

flatten VERB If you flatten something or if it flattens, it becomes flat or flatter.

flatter VERB ① If you flatter someone, you praise them in an exaggerated way, either to please them or to persuade them to do something. ② If you are flattered by something, it makes you feel pleased and important • *He was very flattered because she liked him*. ③ If you flatter yourself that something is the case, you believe, perhaps mistakenly, something good about yourself or your abilities. ④ Something that flatters you makes you appear more attractive. **flattering** ADJECTIVE

> **flatter** VERB
> ① = compliment, fawn
> ④ = enhance, set off, suit

flattery NOUN Flattery is flattering words or behaviour.

> **flattery** NOUN
> = adulation, fawning

flatulence NOUN Flatulence is the uncomfortable state of having too much gas in your stomach or intestine.

flaunt VERB If you flaunt your possessions or talents, you display them too obviously or proudly.

flautist NOUN someone who plays the flute.

flavour NOUN ① DGT The flavour of food is its taste. ② The flavour of something is its distinctive characteristic or quality. ▶ VERB ③ DGT If you flavour food with a spice or herb, you add it to the food to give it a particular taste. **flavouring** NOUN

flaw NOUN ① a fault or mark in a piece of fabric or glass, or in a decorative pattern. ② a weak point or undesirable quality in a theory, plan or person's character. **flawed** ADJECTIVE **flawless** ADJECTIVE

> **flaw** NOUN
> ① = blemish, defect, fault, imperfection

flax NOUN Flax is a plant used for making rope and cloth.

flea NOUN a small wingless jumping insect which feeds on blood.

fled the past tense and past participle of **flee**.

fledgling NOUN ① a young bird that is learning to fly. ▶ ADJECTIVE ② Fledgling means new, or young and inexperienced • *the fledgling American President*.

flee, **flees**, **fleeing**, **fled** VERB To flee from someone or something is to run away from them.

> **flee** VERB
> = bolt, escape, fly, leave, run away, take flight

fleece NOUN ① A sheep's fleece is its coat of wool. ▶ VERB ② (*informal*) To fleece someone is to swindle them or charge them too much money.

fleet NOUN a group of ships or vehicles owned by the same organisation or travelling together.

fleeting ADJECTIVE lasting for a very short time.

Flemish NOUN Flemish is a language spoken in many parts of Belgium.

flesh NOUN ① Flesh is the soft part of the body. ② The flesh of a fruit or vegetable is the soft inner part that you eat. **fleshy** ADJECTIVE

flew the past tense of **fly**.

flex NOUN ① a length of wire covered in plastic, which carries electricity to an appliance. ▶ VERB ② If you flex your muscles, you bend and stretch them.

flexible ADJECTIVE ① able to be bent easily without breaking. ② able to adapt to changing circumstances. **flexibility** NOUN

> **flexible** ADJECTIVE
> ① = elastic, lithe, pliable, supple
> ② = adaptable, discretionary, open

flick VERB ① If you flick something, you move it sharply with your finger. ② If something flicks somewhere, it moves with a short sudden movement • *His foot flicked forward*. ▶ NOUN ③ a short sudden movement or sharp touch with the finger • *a sideways flick of the head*.

flicker VERB ① If a light or a flame flickers, it shines and moves unsteadily. ▶ NOUN ② a short unsteady light or movement of light • *the flicker of candlelight*. ③ A flicker of a feeling is a very brief experience of it • *a flicker of interest*.

flight NOUN ① a journey made by aeroplane. ② Flight is the action of flying or the ability to fly. ③ Flight is also the act of running away. ④ A flight of stairs or steps is a set running in a single direction.

flight attendant NOUN a person who looks after passengers on an aircraft.

flimsy, **flimsier**, **flimsiest** ADJECTIVE ① made of something very thin or weak and not providing much protection. ② not very convincing • *flimsy evidence*.

flinch VERB If you flinch, you make a sudden small movement in fear or pain.

> **flinch** VERB
> = cringe, shrink, start, wince

fling, **flings**, **flinging**, **flung** VERB ① If you fling something, you throw it with a lot of force. ▶ NOUN ② a short period devoted to pleasure and free from any restrictions or rules.

A B C D E F G H I J K L M N O P Q R S T U V W X Y Z

flint NOUN Flint is a hard greyish-black form of quartz. It produces a spark when struck with steel.

flip, flips, flipping, flipped VERB If you flip something, you turn or move it quickly and sharply • *He flipped over the first page.*

flippant ADJECTIVE showing an inappropriate lack of seriousness • *a flippant attitude to money.* **flippantly** ADVERB **flippancy** NOUN

flipper NOUN ① one of the broad, flat limbs of sea animals, for example seals or penguins, used for swimming. ② Flippers are broad, flat pieces of rubber that you can attach to your feet to help you swim.

flirt VERB ① If you flirt with someone, you behave as if you are attracted to them but without serious intentions. ② If you flirt with an idea, you consider it without seriously intending to do anything about it. ▸ NOUN ③ someone who often flirts with people. **flirtation** NOUN **flirtatious** ADJECTIVE

flit, flits, flitting, flitted VERB To flit somewhere is to fly or move there with quick, light movements.

float VERB ① Something that floats is supported by water. ② Something that floats through the air moves along gently, supported by the air. ③ If a company is floated, shares are sold to the public for the first time and the company gains a listing on the stock exchange. ▸ NOUN ④ a light object that floats and either supports something or someone or regulates the level of liquid in a tank or cistern. ⑤ In Australian English, a float is also a vehicle for transporting horses.

> **float** VERB
> ① = be on the surface, bob, drift, lie on the surface, stay afloat
> ≠ sink
> ② = drift, glide, hang, hover

flock NOUN ① a group of birds, sheep or goats. ▸ VERB ② If people flock somewhere, they go there in large numbers.

flog, flogs, flogging, flogged VERB ① (*informal*) If you flog something, you sell it. ② To flog someone is to beat them with a whip or stick. **flogging** NOUN

flood NOUN ① a large amount of water covering an area that is usually dry. ② A flood of something is a large amount of it suddenly occurring • *a flood of angry language.* ▸ VERB ③ If liquid floods an area, or if a river floods, the water or liquid overflows, covering the surrounding area. ④ If people or things flood into a place, they come there in large numbers • *Tourists have flooded into the city in recent years.*

> **flood** NOUN
> ① = deluge, downpour, spate, torrent
> ② = rush, stream, torrent
> ▸ VERB ③ = deluge, drown, overflow, submerge, swamp

floodgates PHRASE To **open the floodgates** is suddenly to give a lot of people the opportunity to do something they could not do before.

floodlight NOUN a very powerful outdoor lamp used to light up public buildings and sports grounds. **floodlit** ADJECTIVE

floor NOUN ① the part of a room you walk on. ② one of the levels in a building • *the top floor of a factory.* ③ the ground at the bottom of a valley, forest or the sea. ▸ VERB ④ If a remark or question floors you, you are completely unable to deal with it or answer it.

floorboard NOUN one of the long planks of wood from which a floor is made.

flop, flops, flopping, flopped VERB ① If someone or something flops, they fall loosely and rather heavily. ② (*informal*) Something that flops fails. ▶ NOUN ③ (*informal*) something that is completely unsuccessful.

floppy, **floppier**, **floppiest** ADJECTIVE tending to hang downwards in a rather loose way • *a floppy, outsize jacket*.

floral ADJECTIVE patterned with flowers or made from flowers • *floral cotton dresses*.

florid [*Rhymes with* **horrid**] ADJECTIVE ① highly elaborate and extravagant • *florid language*. ② having a red face.

florist NOUN a person or shop selling flowers.

floss NOUN Dental floss is soft silky threads or fibre which you use to clean between your teeth.

flotation NOUN ① The flotation of a business is the issuing of shares in order to launch it or to raise money. ② Flotation is the act of floating.

flotilla [*Said* flot-**til**-la] NOUN a small fleet or group of small ships.

flotsam NOUN Flotsam is rubbish or wreckage floating at sea or washed up on the shore.

flounder VERB ① To flounder is to struggle to move or stay upright, for example in water or mud. ② If you flounder in a conversation or situation, you find it difficult to decide what to say or do. ▶ NOUN ③ a type of edible flatfish.

flour NOUN [DGT] Flour is a powder made from finely ground grain, usually wheat, and used for baking and cooking. **floured** ADJECTIVE **floury** ADJECTIVE

flourish VERB ① Something that flourishes develops or functions successfully or healthily. ② If you flourish something, you wave or display it so that people notice it. ▶ NOUN ③ a bold sweeping or waving movement.

flourish VERB
① = bloom, boom, come on, do well, prosper, succeed, thrive
≠ fail
② = brandish (*literary*), display, hold aloft, wave
▶ NOUN ③ = flick, sweep, wave

flout VERB If you flout a convention or law, you deliberately disobey it.

flow VERB ① If something flows, it moves or happens in a steady continuous stream. ▶ NOUN ② A flow of something is a steady continuous movement of it; also the rate at which it flows • *a steady flow of complaints*.

flow VERB
① = circulate, glide, roll, run, slide
▶ NOUN ② = current, drift, flood, stream, tide

flower NOUN ① [SCIENCE] the part of a plant containing the reproductive organs from which the fruit or seeds develop. A **complete flower** is a flower that has all the flower parts, particularly the stamens and pistils; an **incomplete flower** is a flower without one or more of the main flower parts; a **perfect flower** is a flower that has both stamens and pistils. ▶ VERB ② When a plant flowers, it produces flowers.

flowery ADJECTIVE Flowery language is full of elaborate expressions.

flown the past participle of **fly**.

flu NOUN Flu is an illness similar to a very bad cold, which causes headaches, sore throat, weakness and aching muscles. Flu is short for 'influenza'.

fluctuate VERB Something that fluctuates is irregular and changeable • *fluctuating between feeling well and not so well*. **fluctuation** NOUN

flue NOUN a pipe which takes fumes and smoke away from a stove or boiler.

fluent ADJECTIVE ① able to speak a foreign language correctly and without hesitation. ② able to express yourself clearly and without hesitation. **fluently** ADVERB

> **fluent** ADJECTIVE
> ② = articulate, easy, effortless, flowing, ready
> ≠ hesitant

fluff NOUN ① Fluff is soft, light, woolly threads or fibres bunched together. ▸ VERB ② If you fluff something up or out, you brush or shake it to make it seem larger and lighter • *Fluff the rice up with a fork before serving*. **fluffy** ADJECTIVE

fluid NOUN ① a liquid. ▸ ADJECTIVE ② Fluid movement is smooth and flowing. ③ A fluid arrangement or plan is flexible and without a fixed structure. **fluidity** NOUN

fluke NOUN an accidental success or piece of good luck.

flung the past tense and past participle of **fling**.

fluorescent *[Said floo-er-**ess**-nt]* ADJECTIVE ① having a very bright appearance when light is shone on it, as if it is shining itself • *fluorescent yellow dye*. ② A fluorescent light is in the form of a tube and shines with a hard bright light.

fluoride NOUN Fluoride is a mixture of chemicals that is meant to prevent tooth decay.

flurry, **flurries** NOUN a short rush of activity or movement.

flush NOUN ① A flush is a rosy red colour • *The flowers are cream with a pink flush*. ② In cards, a flush is a hand all of one suit. ▸ VERB ③ If you flush, your face goes red. ④ If you flush a toilet or something such as a pipe, you force water through it to clean it. ▸ ADJECTIVE ⑤ (*informal*) Someone who is flush has plenty of money. ⑥ Something that is flush with a surface is level with it or flat against it.

flustered ADJECTIVE If you are flustered, you feel confused, nervous and rushed.

flute NOUN a musical wind instrument consisting of a long metal tube with holes and keys. It is held sideways to the mouth and played by blowing across a hole in its side.

flutter VERB ① If something flutters, it flaps or waves with small, quick movements. ▸ NOUN ② If you are in a flutter, you are excited and nervous. ③ (*informal*) If you have a flutter, you have a small bet.

flux NOUN Flux is a state of constant change • *stability in a world of flux*.

fly, **flies**, **flying**, **flew**, **flown** NOUN ① an insect with two pairs of wings. ② The front opening on a pair of trousers is the fly or the flies. ③ The fly or fly sheet of a tent is either a flap at the entrance or an outer layer providing protection from rain. ▸ VERB ④ When a bird, insect or aircraft flies, it moves through the air. ⑤ If someone or something flies, they move or go very quickly. ⑥ If you fly at someone or let fly at them, you attack or criticise them suddenly and aggressively. **flying** ADJECTIVE, NOUN **flyer** NOUN

> **fly** VERB
> ④ = flit, flutter, sail, soar
> ⑤ = dart, dash, hurry, race, rush, speed, tear

fly-fishing NOUN Fly-fishing is a method of fishing using imitation flies as bait.

flying fox NOUN ① a large bat that eats fruit, found in Australia and Africa. ② In Australia and New Zealand, a flying fox is a cable car used to carry people over rivers and gorges.

A B C D E F G H I J K L M N O P Q R S T U V W X Y Z

flyover NOUN a structure carrying one road over another at a junction or intersection.

foal NOUN ① a young horse. ▶ VERB ② When a female horse foals, she gives birth.

foam NOUN ① Foam is a mass of tiny bubbles. ② DGT Foam is light spongy material used, for example, in furniture or packaging. ▶ VERB ③ When something foams, it forms a mass of small bubbles.

> **foam** NOUN
> ① = bubbles, froth, lather
> ▶ VERB ③ = bubble, fizz, froth

focus, **focuses** or **focusses**, **focusing** or **focussing**, **focused** or **focussed**; **focuses** or **foci** VERB ① If you focus your eyes or an instrument on an object, you adjust them so that the image is clear. ▶ NOUN ② The focus of something is its centre of attention • *The focus of the conversation had moved around during the meal*. **focal** ADJECTIVE

> **focus** VERB
> ① = aim, concentrate, direct, fix
> ▶ NOUN ② = centre, focal point, hub, target

fodder NOUN Fodder is food for farm animals or horses.

foe NOUN an enemy.

foetus *[Said **fee**-tus]*; also spelt **fetus** NOUN SCIENCE an unborn child or animal in the womb. **foetal** ADJECTIVE

fog, **fogs**, **fogging**, **fogged** NOUN ① Fog is a thick mist of water droplets suspended in the air. ▶ VERB ② If glass fogs up, it becomes clouded with steam or condensation. **foggy** ADJECTIVE

foil VERB ① If you foil someone's attempt at something, you prevent them from succeeding. ▶ NOUN ② Foil is thin, paper-like sheets of metal used to wrap food. ③ Something that is a good foil for something else contrasts with it and makes its good qualities more noticeable. ④ a thin, light sword with a button on the tip, used in fencing.

> **foil** VERB
> ① = check, counter, defeat, frustrate, thwart
> ▶ NOUN ③ = antithesis, background, complement, contrast

foist VERB If you foist something on someone, you force or impose it on them.

fold VERB ① If you fold something, you bend it so that one part lies over another. ② *(informal)* If a business folds, it fails and closes down. ③ In cooking, if you fold one ingredient into another, you mix it in gently. ▶ NOUN ④ a crease or bend in paper or cloth. ⑤ a small enclosed area for sheep.

> **fold** VERB
> ① = bend, crease, crumple, tuck, turn under
> ▶ NOUN ④ = bend, crease, pleat, wrinkle

folder NOUN ① a thin piece of folded cardboard for keeping loose papers together. ② In computing, a folder is a named area of a computer disk where you can group together files and subdirectories.

foliage NOUN Foliage is leaves and plants.

folk PLURAL NOUN ① Folk or folks are people. ▶ ADJECTIVE ② Folk music, dance or art is traditional or representative of the ordinary people of an area.

folklore NOUN Folklore is the traditional stories and beliefs of a community.

follicle NOUN a small sac or cavity in the body • *hair follicles*.

follow VERB ① If you follow someone, you move along behind them. If you follow a path or a sign, you move along in that direction. ② Something that follows a particular thing happens after it. ③ Something that follows is true or logical as a result of something else being the case • *Just because she is pretty, it doesn't follow that she can sing.* ④ If you follow instructions or advice, you do what you are told. ⑤ If you follow an explanation or the plot of a story, you understand each stage of it. ⑥ If you follow a person on a social networking site, you regularly read the messages he or she writes.
follow up VERB If you follow up a suggestion or discovery, you find out more about it or act upon it.

follow VERB
① = hound, pursue, stalk, track
② = come after, succeed, supersede
≠ precede
④ = comply, conform, obey, observe

follower NOUN ① The followers of a person or belief are the people who support them. ② On a social networking site, the followers of a person are the people who regularly read their messages.

follower NOUN
① = believer, disciple, fan, henchman, supporter
≠ leader

folly, **follies** NOUN Folly is a foolish act or foolish behaviour.

fond ADJECTIVE ① If you are fond of someone or something, you like them. ② A fond hope or belief is thought of with happiness but is unlikely to happen. **fondly** ADVERB **fondness** NOUN

fond ADJECTIVE
① = adoring, affectionate, devoted, doting, having a liking for, loving
② = deluded, empty, foolish, naive, vain

fondle VERB To fondle something is to stroke it affectionately.

font NOUN ① In printing, a font is a set of characters of the same style and size. ② a large stone bowl in a church that holds the water for baptisms.

food NOUN Food is any substance consumed by an animal or plant to provide energy.

food NOUN
= diet, fare, foodstuffs, grub (*informal*), kai (*New Zealand; informal*), nourishment, provisions, refreshment, tucker (*Australian and New Zealand; informal*)

food chain NOUN SCIENCE a series of living things which are linked because each one feeds on the next one in the series. For example, a plant may be eaten by a rabbit which may be eaten by a fox.

foodstuff NOUN anything used for food.

fool NOUN ① someone who behaves in a silly or stupid way. ② a dessert made from fruit, cream and sugar whipped together. ▶ VERB ③ If you fool someone, you deceive or trick them.

fool NOUN
① = dope (*informal*), dunce, idiot, ignoramus
▶ VERB ③ = con (*informal*), deceive, dupe, mislead, trick

foolhardy ADJECTIVE foolish and involving too great a risk.

foolish ADJECTIVE very silly or unwise. **foolishly** ADVERB **foolishness** NOUN

foolish ADJECTIVE
= inane, nonsensical, senseless, silly, unintelligent, unwise
≠ wise

foolproof ADJECTIVE Something that is foolproof is so well designed or simple to use that it cannot fail.

foot, **feet** NOUN ① the part of your body at the end of your leg. ② the bottom, base or lower end of something • *the foot of the mountain.* ③ a unit of length equal to 12 inches or about 30.5 centimetres. ④ ENGLISH In poetry, a foot is the basic unit of rhythm containing two or three syllables. ▸ ADJECTIVE ⑤ A foot brake, pedal or pump is operated by your foot.

footage NOUN Footage is a length of film • *exclusive footage of the summer festivals.*

football NOUN ① Football is any game in which the ball can be kicked, such as soccer, Australian Rules, rugby union and American football. ② a ball used in any of these games. **footballer** NOUN

foothills PLURAL NOUN GEOGRAPHY Foothills are hills at the base of mountains.

foothold NOUN ① a place where you can put your foot when climbing. ② a position from which further progress can be made.

footing NOUN ① Footing is a secure grip by or for your feet • *He missed his footing and fell flat.* ② a footing is the basis or nature of a relationship or situation • *Steps to put the nation on a war footing.*

footman, **footmen** NOUN a male servant in a large house who wears uniform.

footnote NOUN a note at the bottom of a page or an additional comment giving extra information.

footpath NOUN a path for people to walk on.

footprint NOUN a mark left by a foot or shoe.

footstep NOUN the sound or mark made by someone walking.

for PREPOSITION ① meant to be given to or used by a particular person, or done in order to help or benefit them • *private beaches for their exclusive use.* ② 'For' is used when explaining the reason, cause or purpose of something • *This is my excuse for going to Italy.* ③ You use 'for' to express a quantity, time or distance • *I'll play for ages* • *the only house for miles around.* ④ If you are for something, you support it or approve of it • *votes for or against independence.*

forage VERB When a person or animal forages, they search for food.

foray NOUN ① a brief attempt to do or get something • *her first foray into acting.* ② an attack or raid by soldiers.

forbid, **forbids**, **forbidding**, **forbade**, **forbidden** VERB If you forbid someone to do something, you order them not to do it. **forbidden** ADJECTIVE

forbid VERB
= ban, exclude, outlaw, prohibit, veto
≠ allow

force VERB ① To force someone to do something is to make them do it. ② To force something is to use violence or great strength to move or open it. ▸ NOUN ③ a pressure to do something, sometimes with the use of violence or great strength. ④ The force of something is its strength or power • *The force of the explosion shook buildings.* ⑤ a person or thing that has a lot of influence or effect • *She became the dominant force in tennis.* ⑥ an organised group of soldiers or police. ⑦ SCIENCE In physics, force is a pushing or pulling influence that changes a body from a state of rest to one of motion, or changes its rate of motion. ▸ PHRASE ⑧ A law or rule that is **in force** is currently valid and must be obeyed.

> **force** VERB
> ① = compel, drive, make, oblige, pressurise
> ▸ NOUN ③ = compulsion, duress, pressure
> ④ = impact, might, power, pressure, strength

forceful ADJECTIVE powerful and convincing • *a forceful, highly respected lawyer*. **forcefully** ADVERB

forceps PLURAL NOUN Forceps are a pair of long tongs or pincers used by a doctor or surgeon.

forcible ADJECTIVE ① involving physical force or violence. ② convincing and making a strong impression • *a forcible reminder*. **forcibly** ADVERB

ford NOUN ① a shallow place in a river where it is possible to cross on foot or in a vehicle. ▸ VERB ② To ford a river is to cross it on foot or in a vehicle.

fore PHRASE Someone or something that comes **to the fore** becomes important or popular.

forearm NOUN the part of your arm between your elbow and your wrist.

forebear NOUN Your forebears are your ancestors.

foreboding NOUN a strong feeling of approaching disaster.

forecast, **forecasts**, **forecasting**, **forecast** or **forecasted** NOUN ① a prediction of what will happen, especially a statement about what the weather will be like. ▸ VERB ② To forecast an event is to predict what will happen.

forecourt NOUN an open area at the front of a petrol station or large building.

forefinger NOUN the finger next to your thumb.

forefront NOUN The forefront of something is the most important and progressive part of it.

forego, **foregoes**, **foregoing**, **forewent**, **foregone**; also spelt **forgo** VERB If you forego something pleasant, you give it up or do not insist on having it.

foregoing PHRASE (*formal*) You can say **the foregoing** when talking about something that has just been said • *The foregoing discussion has highlighted the difficulties*.

foregone conclusion NOUN A foregone conclusion is a result or conclusion that is bound to happen.

foreground NOUN [ART] In a picture, the foreground is the part that seems nearest to you.

forehand NOUN, ADJECTIVE [PE] (a stroke in tennis, squash or badminton) made with the palm of your hand facing in the direction that you hit the ball.

forehead NOUN the area at the front of your head, above your eyebrows and below your hairline.

foreign ADJECTIVE ① belonging to or involving countries other than your own • *foreign coins* • *foreign travel*. ② unfamiliar or uncharacteristic • *Such daft enthusiasm was foreign to him*. ③ A foreign object has got into something, usually by accident, and should not be there • *a foreign object in my eye*. **foreigner** NOUN

> **foreign** ADJECTIVE
> ① = distant, exotic, overseas

foreman, **foremen** NOUN ① a person in charge of a group of workers, for example on a building site. ② The foreman of a jury is its spokesperson.

foremost ADJECTIVE The foremost of a group of things is the most important or the best.

> **foremost** ADJECTIVE
> = best, chief, first, greatest, leading, most important, prime, principal, top

forensic ADJECTIVE ① relating to or involving the scientific examination of objects involved in a crime. ② relating to or involving the legal profession.

forerunner NOUN The forerunner of something is the person who first introduced or achieved it, or the first example of it.

foresee, **foresees**, **foreseeing**, **foresaw**, **foreseen** VERB If you foresee something, you predict or expect that it will happen. **foreseeable** ADJECTIVE

foresight NOUN Foresight is the ability to know what is going to happen in the future.

forest NOUN a large area of trees growing close together.

forestry NOUN Forestry is the study and work of growing and maintaining forests.

foretaste NOUN a slight taste or experience of something in advance.

forever ADVERB permanently or continually.

forewent the past tense of **forego**.

foreword NOUN an introduction in a book.

forfeit VERB ① If you forfeit something, you have to give it up as a penalty. ▸ NOUN ② something that you have to give up or do as a penalty.

forgave the past tense of **forgive**.

forge NOUN ① a place where a blacksmith works making metal goods by hand. ▸ VERB ② To forge metal is to hammer and bend it into shape while hot. ③ To forge a relationship is to create a strong and lasting relationship. ④ To forge money, documents or paintings is to make illegal copies of them. ⑤ To forge ahead is to progress quickly.

forgery, **forgeries** NOUN Forgery is the crime of forging money, documents or paintings; also something that has been forged. **forger** NOUN

forget, **forgets**, **forgetting**, **forgot**, **forgotten** VERB ① If you forget something, you fail to remember or think about it. ② If you forget yourself, you behave in an unacceptable, uncontrolled way. **forgetful** ADJECTIVE

forget VERB
① = fail to remember, omit, overlook
≠ remember

forgive, **forgives**, **forgiving**, **forgave**, **forgiven** VERB If you forgive someone for doing something bad, you stop feeling angry and resentful towards them. **forgiving** ADJECTIVE

forgive VERB
= absolve, condone, excuse, pardon
≠ blame

forgiveness NOUN the act of forgiving.

forgiveness NOUN
= mercy, pardon

forgo another spelling of **forego**.

forgot the past tense of **forget**.

forgotten the past participle of **forget**.

fork NOUN ① a pronged instrument used for eating food. ② a large garden tool with three or four prongs. ③ a Y-shaped junction or division in a road, river or branch. ▸ VERB ④ To fork something is to move or turn it with a fork. **fork out** VERB (*informal*) If you fork out for something, you pay for it, often unwillingly.

forlorn ADJECTIVE ① lonely, unhappy and pitiful. ② desperate and without any expectation of success • *a forlorn fight for a draw*. **forlornly** ADVERB

form NOUN ① A particular form of something is a type or kind of it • *a new form of weapon*. ② The form of something is the shape or pattern of something • *a brooch in the form of a bright green lizard*. ③ a sheet of paper with questions and spaces for you to fill in the answers. ④ a class in a school. ▸ **VERB** ⑤ The things that form something are the things it consists of • *events that were to form the basis of her novel*. ⑥ When someone forms something or when it forms, it is created, organised or started.

form NOUN
① = class, kind, sort, type, variant, variety
② = contours, layout, outline, shape, structure
▸ **VERB** ⑤ = compose, constitute, make up, serve as
⑥ = assemble, create, develop, draw up, establish, fashion, make

formal ADJECTIVE ① correct, serious and conforming to accepted conventions • *a very formal letter of apology*. ② official and publicly recognised • *the first formal agreement of its kind*. **formally** ADVERB

formal ADJECTIVE
① = conventional, correct, precise, stiff
≠ informal
② = approved, legal, official, prescribed, regular

formaldehyde *[Said for-**mal**-di-hide]* NOUN Formaldehyde is a poisonous, strong-smelling gas, used in the manufacture of plastics and for preserving biological specimens. Its formula is HCHO.

formality, **formalities** NOUN an action or process that is carried out as part of an official procedure.

format NOUN ① the way in which something is arranged or presented. ② [ICT] The format of a computer file is the way in which the data is stored in it.

formation NOUN ① The formation of something is the process of developing and creating it. ② the pattern or shape of something.

formative ADJECTIVE having an important and lasting influence on character and development • *the formative days of his young manhood*.

former ADJECTIVE ① happening or existing before now or in the past • *a former tennis champion*. ▸ NOUN ② You use 'the former' to refer to the first of two things just mentioned • *If I had to choose between happiness and money, I would have the former*. **formerly** ADVERB

former ADJECTIVE
① = ancient, bygone, old, past

formidable ADJECTIVE very difficult to deal with or overcome, and therefore rather frightening or impressive • *formidable enemies*.

formidable ADJECTIVE
= challenging, daunting, difficult, intimidating, mammoth, onerous

formula, **formulae** or **formulas** NOUN ① [MATHS] a group of letters, numbers and symbols which stand for a mathematical or scientific rule. ② [SCIENCE] a list of quantities of substances that when mixed make another substance, for example in chemistry. ③ a plan or set of rules for dealing with a particular problem • *my secret formula for keeping myself fit*.

formulate VERB If you formulate a plan or thought, you create it and express it in a clear and precise way.

forsake, **forsakes**, **forsaking**, **forsook**, **forsaken** VERB To forsake someone or something is to give them up or abandon them.

fort NOUN ① a strong building built for defence. ▸ PHRASE ② If you **hold the fort** for someone, you manage their affairs while they are away.

fort NOUN
① = castle, citadel, fortification, fortress

forte *[Said **for**-tay]* ADVERB ① MUSIC In music, forte is an instruction to play or sing something loudly. ▶ NOUN ② If something is your forte, you are particularly good at doing it.

forth ADVERB ① out and forward from a starting place • *Christopher Columbus set forth on his epic voyage of discovery.* ② into view • *He brought forth a slim volume of his newly published verse.*

forthcoming ADJECTIVE ① planned to happen soon • *their forthcoming holiday.* ② given or made available • *Medical aid might be forthcoming.* ③ willing to give information • *He was not too forthcoming about this.*

forthright ADJECTIVE Someone who is forthright is direct and honest about their opinions and feelings.

fortification NOUN Fortifications are buildings, walls and ditches used to protect a place.

fortitude NOUN Fortitude is calm and patient courage.

fortnight NOUN a period of two weeks. **fortnightly** ADVERB, ADJECTIVE

fortress NOUN a castle or well-protected town built for defence.

fortuitous *[Said for-**tyoo**-it-uss]* ADJECTIVE happening by chance or good luck • *a fortuitous winning goal.*

fortunate ADJECTIVE ① Someone who is fortunate is lucky. ② Something that is fortunate brings success or advantage. **fortunately** ADVERB

fortune NOUN ① Fortune or good fortune is good luck. ② A fortune is a large amount of money. ▶ PHRASE ③ If someone **tells your fortune**, they predict your future.

forty, **forties** the number 40. **fortieth** ADJECTIVE

forum NOUN ① a place or meeting in which people can exchange ideas and discuss public issues. ② a website where people discuss a particular topic. ③ a square in Roman towns where people met to discuss business and politics.

forward ADVERB, ADJECTIVE ① Forward or forwards means in the front or towards the front • *A photographer moved forward to capture the moment.* ② Forward means in or towards a future time • *a positive atmosphere of looking forward and making fresh starts.* ③ Forward or forwards also means developing or progressing • *The new committee would push forward government plans.* ▶ ADVERB ④ If someone or something is put forward, they are suggested as being suitable for something. ▶ VERB ⑤ If you forward a message or document that you have received, you send it on to another person. ▶ NOUN ⑥ In a game such as football or hockey, a forward is a player in an attacking position.

fossil NOUN SCIENCE the remains or impression of an animal or plant from a previous age, preserved in rock. **fossilise** VERB

fossil fuel NOUN GEOGRAPHY SCIENCE Fossil fuels are fuels such as coal, oil and natural gas, which have been formed by rotting animals and plants from millions of years ago.

foster VERB ① If someone fosters a child, they are paid to look after the child for a period, but do not become its legal parent. ② If you foster something such as an activity or an idea, you help its development and growth by encouraging people to do or think it • *to foster and maintain this goodwill.* **foster child** NOUN **foster home** NOUN **foster parent** NOUN

fought the past tense and past participle of **fight**.

foul ADJECTIVE ① Something that is foul is very unpleasant, especially because it is dirty, wicked or obscene.

▸ VERB ② To foul something is to make it dirty, especially with faeces • *Dogs must not be allowed to foul the pavement.* ▸ NOUN ③ In sport, a foul is an act of breaking the rules.

found ① Found is the past tense and past participle of **find**. ▸ VERB ② If someone founds an organisation or institution, they start it and set it up.

foundation NOUN ① The foundation of a belief or way of life is the basic ideas or attitudes on which it is built. ② a solid layer of concrete or bricks in the ground, on which a building is built to give it a firm base. ③ an organisation set up by money donated to or left in someone's will for research or charity.

founder NOUN ① The founder of an institution or organisation is the person who sets it up. ▸ VERB ② If something founders, it fails.

foundry, **foundries** NOUN a factory where metal is melted and cast.

fountain NOUN an ornamental structure consisting of a jet of water forced into the air by a pump.

fountain pen NOUN a pen which is supplied with ink from a container inside the pen.

four ① the number 4. ▸ PHRASE ② If you are **on all fours**, you are on your hands and knees.

four-poster NOUN a bed with a tall post at each corner supporting a canopy and curtains.

fourteen the number 14. **fourteenth** ADJECTIVE

fourth ADJECTIVE The fourth item in a series is the one counted as number four.

fowl NOUN a bird such as chicken or duck that is kept or hunted for its meat or eggs.

fox NOUN ① a dog-like wild animal with reddish-brown fur, a pointed face and ears, and a thick tail. ▸ VERB ② If something foxes you, it is too confusing or puzzling for you to understand.

foyer [*Said* ***foy-ay***] NOUN a large area just inside the main doors of a cinema, hotel or public building.

fracas [*Said* ***frak-ah***] NOUN a rough noisy quarrel or fight.

fracking NOUN Fracking is the extraction of oil or gas by forcing liquid into rock at high pressure.

fraction NOUN ① MATHS In arithmetic, a fraction is a part of a whole number. A **proper fraction** is a fraction in which the number above the line is lower than the number below it; an **improper fraction** has the greater number above the line • *$^3/_4$ is a proper fraction.* ② a tiny proportion or amount of something • *an area a fraction of the size of London.* **fractional** ADJECTIVE **fractionally** ADVERB

fractious ADJECTIVE When small children are fractious, they become upset or angry very easily, often because they are tired.

fracture NOUN ① a crack or break in something, especially a bone. ▸ VERB ② If something fractures, it breaks.

fragile ADJECTIVE easily broken or damaged • *fragile glass* • *a fragile relationship.* **fragility** NOUN

fragile ADJECTIVE
= breakable, dainty, delicate, flimsy, frail
≠ tough

fragment NOUN ① a small piece or part of something. ▸ VERB ② If something fragments, it breaks into small pieces or different parts. **fragmentation** NOUN **fragmented** ADJECTIVE

fragmentary ADJECTIVE made up of small pieces, or parts that are not connected • *fragmentary notes in a journal.*

fragrance NOUN a sweet or pleasant smell.

> **fragrance** NOUN
> = aroma, perfume, scent, smell

fragrant ADJECTIVE Something that is fragrant smells sweet or pleasant.

> **fragrant** ADJECTIVE
> = aromatic, perfumed, sweet-smelling
> ≠ smelly

frail ADJECTIVE ① Someone who is frail is not strong or healthy. ② Something that is frail is easily broken or damaged. **frailty** NOUN

frame NOUN ① the structure surrounding a door, window or picture. ② an arrangement of connected bars over which something is built. ③ The frames of a pair of glasses are the wire or plastic parts that hold the lenses. ④ Your frame is your body • *his large frame*. ⑤ one of the many separate photographs of which a cinema film is made up. ▶ VERB ⑥ To frame a picture is to put it into a frame • *I've framed pictures I've pulled out of magazines*. ⑦ The language something is framed in is the language used to express it.

framework NOUN ① DGT a structure acting as a support or frame. ② a set of rules, beliefs or ideas which you use to decide what to do.

franc NOUN the main unit of currency in Switzerland, and formerly in France and Belgium. A franc is worth 100 centimes.

franchise NOUN ① The franchise is the right to vote in an election • *a franchise that gave the vote to less than 2% of the population*. ② the right given by a company to someone to allow them to sell its goods or services.

frank ADJECTIVE If you are frank, you say things in an open and honest way. **frankly** ADVERB **frankness** NOUN

> **frank** ADJECTIVE
> = blunt, candid, honest, open, plain, straightforward

frantic ADJECTIVE If you are frantic, you behave in a wild, desperate way because you are anxious or frightened. **frantically** ADVERB

fraternal ADJECTIVE 'Fraternal' is used to describe friendly actions and feelings between groups of people • *an affectionate fraternal greeting*.

fraternity, **fraternities** NOUN ① Fraternity is friendship between groups of people. ② a group of people with something in common • *the golfing fraternity*.

fraud NOUN ① Fraud is the crime of getting money by deceit or trickery. ② something that deceives people in an illegal or immoral way. ③ Someone who is not what they pretend to be.

> **fraud** NOUN
> ① = deceit, deception, guile, trickery
> ② = fake, forgery, hoax
> ③ = charlatan, cheat, imposter, quack

fraudulent ADJECTIVE dishonest or deceitful • *fraudulent use of credit cards*.

fraught ADJECTIVE If something is fraught with problems or difficulties, it is full of them • *Modern life was fraught with hazards*.

fray VERB ① If cloth or rope frays, its threads or strands become worn and it is likely to tear or break. ▶ NOUN ② a fight or argument.

freak NOUN ① someone whose appearance or behaviour is very unusual. ▶ ADJECTIVE ② A freak event is very unusual and unlikely to happen • *a freak snowstorm in summer*.

free, **freer**, **freest**; **frees**, **freeing**, **freed** ADJECTIVE ① not controlled or limited • *the free flow of aid* • *free trade*. ② Someone who is free is no longer a prisoner. ③ To be free of something unpleasant is not to have it • *She wanted her aunt's life to be free of worry.* ④ If someone is free, they are not busy or occupied. If a place, seat or machine is free, it is not occupied or not being used • *Are you free for dinner?* ⑤ If something is free, you can have it without paying for it. ▸ VERB ⑥ If you free someone or something that is imprisoned, fastened or trapped, you release them.

> **free** ADJECTIVE
> ② = at large, at liberty, liberated, loose
> ≠ captive
> ⑤ = complimentary, gratis, unpaid, without charge
> ▸ VERB ⑥ = discharge, liberate, release, set at liberty, set loose
> ≠ imprison

freedom NOUN ① If you have the freedom to do something, you have the scope or are allowed to do it • *We have the freedom to decide our own futures.* ② When prisoners gain their freedom, they escape or are released. ③ When there is freedom from something unpleasant, people are not affected by it • *freedom from guilt.*

> **freedom** NOUN
> ① = discretion, latitude, leeway, licence, scope
> ② = emancipation, liberty, release
> ≠ captivity
> ③ = exemption, immunity

freehold NOUN the right to own a house or piece of land for life without conditions.

freelance ADJECTIVE, ADVERB A freelance journalist or photographer is not employed by one organisation, but is paid for each job he or she does.

freely ADVERB Freely means without restriction • *the pleasure of being able to walk about freely.*

free-range ADJECTIVE Free-range eggs are laid by hens that can move and feed freely on an area of open ground.

freestyle NOUN Freestyle refers to sports competitions, especially swimming, in which competitors can use any style or method.

freeway NOUN In Australia, South Africa and the United States, a freeway is a road designed for fast-moving traffic.

free will PHRASE If you do something **of your own free will**, you do it by choice and not because you are forced to.

freeze, **freezes**, **freezing**, **froze**, **frozen** VERB ① [SCIENCE] When a liquid freezes, it becomes solid because it is very cold. ② If you freeze, you suddenly become very still and quiet. ③ [DRAMA] To freeze the action in a film is to stop the film at a particular frame. ④ If you freeze food, you put it in a freezer to preserve it. ⑤ When wages or prices are frozen, they are officially prevented from rising. ▸ NOUN ⑥ an official action taken to prevent wages or prices from rising. ⑦ a period of freezing weather.

freezer NOUN a large refrigerator which freezes and stores food for a long time.

freezing ADJECTIVE extremely cold.

freight NOUN Freight is goods moved by lorries, ships or other transport; also the moving of these goods.

French ADJECTIVE ① belonging or relating to France. ▸ NOUN ② French is the main language spoken in France, and is also spoken by many people in Belgium, Switzerland and Canada.

Frenchman, **Frenchmen** NOUN a man who comes from France.

Frenchwoman, **Frenchwomen** NOUN a woman who comes from France.

frenetic ADJECTIVE Frenetic behaviour

is wild and excited. **frenetically** ADVERB

frenzy, **frenzies** NOUN If someone is in a frenzy, their behaviour is wild and uncontrolled. **frenzied** ADJECTIVE

> **frenzy** NOUN
> = agitation, fury, hysteria, madness, rage

frequency, **frequencies** NOUN ① The frequency of an event is how often it happens • *He did not call anyone with great frequency*. ② SCIENCE The frequency of a sound or radio wave is the rate at which it vibrates. ③ MATHS In statistics, the frequency of a particular class is the number of individuals in it.

frequent ADJECTIVE *[Said* ***free****-kwuhnt]* ① often happening • *His visits were frequent* • *They move at frequent intervals*. ▸ VERB *[Said free-****kwent****]* ② If you frequent a place, you go there often. **frequently** ADVERB

> **frequent** ADJECTIVE
> ① = common, continual, everyday, habitual, recurrent, repeated
> ≠ rare
> ▸ VERB ② = attend, haunt, patronise, visit
> ≠ avoid

fresco, **frescoes** NOUN a picture painted on a plastered wall while the plaster is still wet.

fresh ADJECTIVE ① A fresh thing replaces a previous one, or is added to it • *footprints filled in by fresh snow* • *fresh evidence*. ② Fresh food is newly made or obtained, and not tinned or frozen. ③ Fresh water is not salty, for example the water in a stream. ④ If the weather is fresh, it is fairly cold and windy. ⑤ If you are fresh from something, you have experienced it recently • *a teacher fresh from college*. **freshly** ADVERB **freshness** NOUN

freshwater ADJECTIVE ① A freshwater lake or pool contains water that is not salty. ② A freshwater creature lives in a river, lake or pool that is not salty.

fret, **frets**, **fretting**, **fretted** VERB ① If you fret about something, you worry about it. ▸ NOUN ② The frets on a stringed instrument, such as a guitar, are the metal ridges across its neck. **fretful** ADJECTIVE

friction NOUN ① SCIENCE the force that stops things from moving freely when they rub against each other. ② Friction between people is disagreement and quarrels.

Friday NOUN the day between Thursday and Saturday.

fridge NOUN the same as a **refrigerator**.

friend NOUN ① Your friends are people you know well and like to spend time with. ② someone with whom you can exchange posts and messages on a social networking site.

> **friend** NOUN
> ① = buddy (*informal*), china (*British and South African*; *informal*), chum (*informal*), companion, confidant, confidante, crony (*old-fashioned*), mate (*British*; *informal*), pal (*informal*)
> ≠ enemy

friendly, **friendlier**, **friendliest** ADJECTIVE ① If you are friendly to someone, you behave in a kind and pleasant way to them. ② People who are friendly with each other like each other and enjoy spending time together. **friendliness** NOUN

> **friendly** ADJECTIVE
> ① = affectionate, amiable, close, cordial, genial, welcoming
> ≠ unfriendly

friendship NOUN ① Your friendships are the special relationships that you have with your friends. ② Friendship is the state of being friends with someone.

friendship NOUN
② = affection, attachment, closeness, goodwill
≠ hostility

frieze NOUN ① a strip of decoration or carving along the top of a wall or column. ② ART a picture on a long strip of paper which is hung along a wall.

frigate [*Said* ***frig****-it*] NOUN a small, fast warship.

fright NOUN Fright is a sudden feeling of fear.

frighten VERB If something frightens you, it makes you afraid.

frighten VERB
= alarm, intimidate, scare, startle, terrify, terrorise, unnerve

frightened ADJECTIVE having feelings of fear about something.

frightened ADJECTIVE
= afraid, alarmed, petrified, scared, startled, terrified

frightening ADJECTIVE causing someone to feel fear.

frightening ADJECTIVE
= alarming, hair-raising, intimidating, menacing, terrifying

frightful ADJECTIVE very bad or unpleasant • *a frightful bully*.
frightfully ADVERB

frigid ADJECTIVE Frigid behaviour is cold and unfriendly • *frigid stares*.

frill NOUN a strip of cloth with many folds, attached to something as a decoration. **frilly** ADJECTIVE

fringe NOUN ① the hair that hangs over a person's forehead. ② a decoration on clothes and other objects, consisting of a row of hanging strips or threads. ③ The fringes of a place are the parts farthest from its centre • *the western fringe of the Amazon basin*. **fringed** ADJECTIVE

frisky, **friskier**, **friskiest** ADJECTIVE A frisky animal or child is energetic and wants to have fun.

fritter NOUN ① Fritters consist of food dipped in batter and fried • *apple fritters*. ▶ VERB ② If you fritter away your time or money, you waste it on unimportant things.

frivolous ADJECTIVE Someone who is frivolous behaves in a silly or light-hearted way, especially when they should be serious or sensible.
frivolity NOUN

frivolous ADJECTIVE
= flippant, foolish, juvenile, puerile, silly
≠ serious

frock NOUN (*old-fashioned*) a dress.

frog NOUN a small amphibious creature with smooth skin, prominent eyes, and long back legs which it uses for jumping.

frolic, **frolics**, **frolicking**, **frolicked** VERB When animals or children frolic, they run around and play in a lively way.

from PREPOSITION ① You use 'from' to say what the source, origin or starting point of something is • *a call from a mobile phone* • *people from a city 100 miles away*. ② If you take something from an amount, you reduce the amount by that much • *A sum of money was wrongly taken from his account*. ③ You also use 'from' when stating the range of something • *a score from one to five*.

front NOUN ① The front of something is the part that faces forward. ② In a war, the front is the place where two armies are fighting. ③ In meteorology, a front is the line where a mass of cold air meets a mass of warm air. ④ A front is an outward appearance, often one that is false • *I put up a brave front* • *He's no more than a* *respectable front for some very dubious happenings.* ▸ **PHRASE** ⑤ **In front** means ahead or further forward. ⑥ If you do something **in front of** someone, you do it when they are present. **frontal** **ADJECTIVE**

front **NOUN**
① = facade, face, frontage
≠ back
④ = appearance, exterior, facade, face, show
▸ **PHRASE** ⑤ = ahead of, before

frontage **NOUN** The frontage of a building is the wall that faces a street.

frontier **NOUN** a border between two countries.

frost **NOUN** When there is a frost, the temperature outside falls below freezing.

frostbite **NOUN** Frostbite is damage to your fingers, toes or ears caused by extreme cold.

frosty, **frostier**, **frostiest** **ADJECTIVE** ① If it is frosty, the temperature outside is below freezing point. ② If someone is frosty, they are unfriendly or disapproving. **frostily** **ADVERB**

froth **NOUN** ① Froth is a mass of small bubbles on the surface of a liquid. ▸ **VERB** ② If a liquid froths, small bubbles appear on its surface. **frothy** **ADJECTIVE**

frown **VERB** ① If you frown, you move your eyebrows closer together, because you are annoyed, worried or concentrating. ▸ **NOUN** ② a cross expression on someone's face.

frown **VERB**
① = glare, glower, knit your brows, scowl

froze the past tense of **freeze**.

frozen ① Frozen is the past participle of **freeze**. ▸ **ADJECTIVE** ② If you say you are frozen, you mean you are extremely cold.

frozen **ADJECTIVE**
② = arctic, chilled, frigid, icy, numb

frugal **ADJECTIVE** ① Someone who is frugal spends very little money. ② A frugal meal is small and cheap. **frugally** **ADVERB** **frugality** **NOUN**

fruit **NOUN** ① the part of a plant that develops after the flower and contains the seeds. Many fruits are edible. ② (*in plural*) The fruits of something are its good results • *the fruits of his labours.*

fruitful **ADJECTIVE** Something that is fruitful has good and useful results • *a fruitful experience.*

fruitless **ADJECTIVE** Something that is fruitless does not achieve anything • *a fruitless effort.*

fruit salad **NOUN** a mixture of pieces of different fruits served in a juice as a dessert.

fruity, **fruitier**, **fruitiest** **ADJECTIVE** Something that is fruity smells or tastes of fruit.

frustrate **VERB** ① If something frustrates you, it prevents you doing what you want and makes you upset and angry • *Everyone gets frustrated with their work.* ② To frustrate something such as a plan is to prevent it • *She hopes to frustrate the building of the new road.* **frustrated** **ADJECTIVE** **frustrating** **ADJECTIVE** **frustration** **NOUN**

frustrate **VERB**
② = block, check, foil, thwart

fry, **fries**, **frying**, **fried** **VERB** When you fry food, you cook it in a pan containing hot fat or oil.

fuchsia *[Said fyoo-sha]* **NOUN** a plant or small bush with pink, purple or white flowers that hang downwards.

a b c d e f g h i j k l m n o p q r s t u v w x y z

fudge NOUN ① Fudge is a soft brown sweet made from butter, milk and sugar. ▶ VERB ② If you fudge something, you avoid making clear or definite decisions or statements about it • *He was carefully fudging his message.*

fuel, **fuels**, **fuelling**, **fuelled** NOUN ① Fuel is a substance such as coal or petrol that is burned to provide heat or power. ▶ VERB ② A machine or vehicle that is fuelled by a substance works by burning the substance as a fuel • *power stations fuelled by wood.*

fugitive *[Said **fyoo**-jit-tiv]* NOUN someone who is running away or hiding, especially from the police.

-ful SUFFIX ① '-ful' is used to form adjectives with the meaning 'full of' • *careful.* ② '-ful' is used to form nouns which mean 'the amount needed to fill' • *spoonful.*

fulcrum, **fulcrums** or **fulcra** NOUN DGT the point at which something is balancing or pivoting.

fulfil, **fulfils**, **fulfilling**, **fulfilled** VERB ① If you fulfil a promise, hope or duty, you carry it out or achieve it. ② If something fulfils you, it gives you satisfaction. **fulfilling** ADJECTIVE **fulfilment** NOUN

fulfil VERB
① = accomplish, achieve, carry out, perform, realise, satisfy

full ADJECTIVE ① containing or having as much as it is possible to hold • *His room is full of posters.* ② complete or whole • *They had taken a full meal* • *a full 20 years later.* ③ loose and made from a lot of fabric • *full sleeves.* ④ rich and strong • *a full, pungent cheese.* ▶ ADVERB ⑤ completely and directly • *Turn the taps full on.* ▶ PHRASE ⑥ Something that has been done or described **in full** has been dealt with completely. **fullness** NOUN **fully** ADVERB

full ADJECTIVE
① = filled, loaded, packed, saturated ≠ empty
② = comprehensive, detailed, exhaustive, extensive, maximum, thorough
③ = baggy, loose, voluminous

full-blooded ADJECTIVE having great commitment and enthusiasm • *a full-blooded sprint for third place.*

full-blown ADJECTIVE complete and fully developed • *a full-blown crisis.*

full moon NOUN the moon when it appears as a complete circle.

full stop NOUN ENGLISH the punctuation mark (.) used at the end of a sentence and after an abbreviation or initial.

full-time ADJECTIVE ① involving work for the whole of each normal working week. ▶ NOUN ② In games such as football, full time is the end of the match.

fully-fledged ADJECTIVE completely developed • *I was a fully-fledged and mature human being.*

fulsome ADJECTIVE exaggerated and elaborate, and often sounding insincere • *His most fulsome praise was reserved for his mother.*

fumble VERB If you fumble, you feel or handle something clumsily.

fume NOUN ① Fumes are unpleasant-smelling gases and smoke, often toxic, that are produced by burning and by some chemicals. ▶ VERB ② If you are fuming, you are very angry.

fun NOUN ① Fun is pleasant, enjoyable and light-hearted activity. ▶ PHRASE ② If you **make fun** of someone, you tease them or make jokes about them.

fun NOUN
① = amusement, enjoyment, entertainment, pleasure, recreation
▶ PHRASE ② = deride (*formal*), laugh at, mock, ridicule, taunt, tease

function NOUN ① The function of something or someone is their purpose or the job they have to do. ② a large formal dinner, reception or party. ③ MATHS A function is a variable whose value depends on the value of other independent variables. 'y is a function of x' is written y = f(x). ▸ VERB ④ When something functions, it operates or works.

> **function** NOUN
> ① = duty, job, purpose, remit, responsibility, role
> ② = dinner, gathering, party, reception
> ▸ VERB ④ = go, operate, perform, run, work

functional ADJECTIVE ① relating to the way something works. ② designed for practical use rather than for decoration or attractiveness • *The buildings are functional but not nice to look at.* ③ working properly • *fully functional smoke alarms.*

fund NOUN ① an amount of available money, usually for a particular purpose • *a pension fund.* ② A fund of something is a lot of it • *He had a fund of hilarious tales on the subject.* ▸ VERB ③ Someone who funds something provides money for it • *research funded by pharmaceutical companies.*

> **fund** NOUN
> ① = capital, foundation, pool, reserve, supply
> ② = hoard, mine, reserve, reservoir, store
> ▸ VERB ③ = finance, pay for, subsidise, support

fundamental ADJECTIVE ① basic and central • *the fundamental right of freedom of choice* • *fundamental changes.* ▸ NOUN ② The fundamentals of something are its most basic and important parts • *teaching small children the fundamentals of road safety.*

funeral *[Said fyoo-ner-al]* NOUN a ceremony or religious service for the burial or cremation of a dead person.

funereal *[Said few-nee-ree-al]* ADJECTIVE depressing and gloomy.

funfair NOUN a place of entertainment with things like amusement arcades and rides.

fungicide NOUN a chemical used to kill or prevent fungus.

fungus, fungi or **funguses** NOUN SCIENCE a plant such as a mushroom or mould that does not have leaves and grows on other living things. **fungal** ADJECTIVE

funnel, funnels, funnelling, funnelled NOUN ① an open cone narrowing to a tube, used to pour substances into containers. ② a metal chimney on a ship or steam engine. ▸ VERB ③ If something is funnelled somewhere, it is directed through a narrow space into that place.

funny, funnier, funniest ADJECTIVE ① strange or puzzling • *Young children get some very funny ideas sometimes!* ② causing amusement or laughter • *a funny old film.* **funnily** ADVERB

> **funny** ADJECTIVE
> ① = mysterious, odd, peculiar, puzzling, strange, unusual, weird
> ② = amusing, comic, comical, hilarious, humorous, witty
> ≠ serious

fur NOUN ① Fur is the soft thick body hair of many animals. ② a coat made from an animal's fur. **furry** ADJECTIVE

furious ADJECTIVE ① extremely angry. ② involving great energy, effort or speed • *the furious speed of technological development.* **furiously** ADVERB

> **furious** ADJECTIVE
> ① = enraged, fuming, infuriated, livid, mad, raging
> ② = breakneck, fierce, frantic, frenzied, intense, manic

furlong NOUN a unit of length equal to 220 yards or about 201.2 metres. Furlong originally referred to the length of the average furrow.

furnace NOUN a container for a very large, hot fire used, for example, in the steel industry for melting ore.

furnish VERB ① If you furnish a room, you put furniture into it. ② (*formal*) If you furnish someone with something, you supply or provide it for them.

furnishings PLURAL NOUN The furnishings of a room or house are the furniture and fittings in it.

furniture NOUN Furniture is movable objects such as tables, chairs and wardrobes.

furore [*Said fyoo-**roh**-ree*] NOUN an angry and excited reaction or protest.

furrow NOUN ① a long, shallow trench made by a plough. ▸ VERB ② When someone furrows their brow, they frown.

further ① a comparative form of **far**. ▸ ADJECTIVE ② additional or more • *There was no further rain.* ▸ VERB ③ If you further something, you help it to progress • *He wants to further his acting career.*

further education NOUN Further education is education at a college after leaving school, but not at a university.

furthermore ADVERB (*formal*) used to introduce additional information • *There is no record of such a letter. Furthermore, it is company policy never to send such letters.*

furthest a superlative form of **far**.

furtive ADJECTIVE secretive, sly and cautious • *a furtive smile.* **furtively** ADVERB

fury NOUN Fury is violent or extreme anger.

fuse NOUN ① a safety device in a plug or electrical appliance consisting of a piece of wire which melts to stop the electric current if a fault occurs. ② a long cord attached to some types of simple bomb which is lit to detonate. ▸ VERB ③ When an electrical appliance fuses, it stops working because the fuse has melted to protect it. ④ If two things fuse, they join or become combined • *Christianity slowly fused with existing beliefs.*

fuselage [*Said **fyoo**-zil-ahj*] NOUN the main part of an aeroplane or rocket.

fusion NOUN ① Fusion is what happens when two substances join by melting together. ② Fusion is also nuclear fusion. ▸ ADJECTIVE ③ Fusion is used to refer to food or a style of cooking that brings together ingredients or cooking techniques from several different countries.

fuss NOUN ① Fuss is unnecessarily anxious or excited behaviour. ▸ VERB ② If someone fusses, they behave with unnecessary anxiety and concern for unimportant things.

> **fuss** NOUN
> ① = agitation, bother, commotion, confusion, stir, to-do (*informal*)
> ▸ VERB ② = bustle, fidget, fret

fussy, **fussier**, **fussiest** ADJECTIVE ① likely to fuss a lot • *He was unusually fussy about keeping things perfect.* ② with too much elaborate detail or decoration • *fussy chiffon evening wear.*

> **fussy** ADJECTIVE
> ① = choosy (*informal*), discriminating, exacting, fastidious, particular

futile ADJECTIVE having no chance of success • *a futile attempt to calm the storm.* **futility** NOUN

> **futile** ADJECTIVE
> = abortive, forlorn, unsuccessful, useless, vain
> ≠ successful

future NOUN ① The future is the period of time after the present. ② Something that has a future is likely to succeed • *She sees no future in a modelling career*. ▶ ADJECTIVE ③ relating to or occurring at a time after the present • *to predict future events*. ④ ENGLISH | MFL The future tense of a verb is the form used to express something that will happen in the future.

future ADJECTIVE
③ = approaching, coming, forthcoming, impending, later, prospective
≠ past

futuristic ADJECTIVE very modern and strange, as if belonging to a time in the future • *futuristic cars*.

fuzz NOUN short fluffy hair. **fuzzy** ADJECTIVE

Gg

A B C D E F **G** H I J K L M N O P Q R S T U V W X Y Z

g an abbreviation for 'gram' or 'grams'.

gable NOUN Gables are the triangular parts at the top of the outside walls at each end of a house.

gadget NOUN a small machine or tool. **gadgetry** NOUN

> **gadget** NOUN
> = appliance, device, machine, tool

Gaelic *[Said **gay**-lik]* NOUN a language spoken in some parts of Scotland and Ireland.

gaffe *[Said **gaf**]* NOUN a social blunder or mistake.

gaffer NOUN (*informal*) a boss.

gag, gags, gagging, gagged NOUN ① a strip of cloth that is tied round someone's mouth to stop them speaking. ② (*informal*) a joke told by a comedian. ▸ VERB ③ To gag someone means to put a gag round their mouth. ④ If you gag, you choke and nearly vomit.

gaggle NOUN ① a group of geese. ② (*informal*) a noisy group • *a gaggle of schoolboys.*

gaiety *[Said **gay**-yet-tee]* NOUN liveliness and fun.

gaily ADVERB in a happy and cheerful way.

gain VERB ① If you gain something, you get it gradually • *I spent years at night school trying to gain qualifications.* ② If you gain from a situation, you get some advantage from it. ③ If you gain on someone, you gradually catch them up. ▸ NOUN ④ an increase • *a gain in speed.* ⑤ an advantage that you get for yourself • *People use whatever influence they have for personal gain.*

> **gain** VERB
> ① = achieve, acquire, earn, obtain, secure (*formal*), win
> ② = benefit, profit
> ▸ NOUN ④ = advance, growth, improvement, increase, rise

gait NOUN Someone's gait is their way of walking • *an awkward gait.*

gala NOUN a special public celebration or performance • *the opening gala of the London Film Festival.*

galaxy, galaxies NOUN [SCIENCE] A galaxy is an enormous group of stars that extends over many millions of miles. The galaxy to which the earth's solar system belongs is called the Milky Way. **galactic** ADJECTIVE

gale NOUN an extremely strong wind.

gall *[Rhymes with **ball**]* NOUN ① If someone has the gall to do something, they have enough courage or impudence to do it • *He even has the gall to visit her.* ▸ VERB ② If something galls you, it makes you extremely annoyed.

gallant ADJECTIVE ① brave and honourable • *They have put up a gallant fight for pensioners' rights.* ② polite and considerate towards women. **gallantly** ADVERB **gallantry** NOUN

gall bladder NOUN an organ in your body which stores bile and which is next to your liver.

gallery, galleries NOUN ① [ART] a building or room where works of art are shown. ② In a theatre or large hall, the gallery is a raised area at the back or sides • *the public gallery in Parliament.*

galley NOUN ① a kitchen in a ship or aircraft. ② a ship, driven by oars, used in ancient and medieval times.

Gallic [*Said* ***gal**-lik*] ADJECTIVE (*formal or literary*) French.

gallon NOUN a unit of liquid volume equal to eight pints or about 4.55 litres.

gallop VERB ① When a horse gallops, it runs very fast, so that during each stride all four feet are off the ground at the same time. ▸ NOUN ② a very fast run.

gallows NOUN A gallows is a framework on which criminals used to be hanged.

galore ADJECTIVE in very large numbers • *chocolates galore.*

galvanised; also spelt **galvanized** ADJECTIVE Galvanised metal has been coated with zinc by an electrical process to protect it from rust.

gambit NOUN something which someone does to gain an advantage in a situation • *Commentators are calling the plan a clever political gambit.*

gamble VERB ① When people gamble, they bet money on the result of a game or race. ② If you gamble something, you risk losing it in the hope of gaining an advantage • *The company gambled everything on the new factory.* ▸ NOUN ③ If you take a gamble, you take a risk in the hope of gaining an advantage. **gambler** NOUN **gambling** NOUN

> **gamble** VERB
> ① = back, bet
> ② = chance, risk, stake
> ▸ NOUN ③ = chance, lottery, risk

game NOUN ① an enjoyable activity with a set of rules which is played by individuals or teams against each other. ② an enjoyable imaginative activity played by small children • *childhood games of cowboys and Indians.* ③ You might describe something as a game when it is designed to gain advantage • *the political game.* ④ Game is wild animals or birds that are hunted for sport or for food. ⑤ (*in plural*) Games are sports played at school or in a competition. ▸ ADJECTIVE ⑥ (*informal*) Someone who is game is willing to try something unusual or difficult. **gamely** ADVERB

> **game** NOUN
> ① = clash, contest, match

gamekeeper NOUN a person employed to look after game animals and birds on a country estate.

gamut [*Said* ***gam**-mut*] NOUN (*formal*) The gamut of something is the whole range of things that can be included in it • *the whole gamut of human emotions.*

gang NOUN a group of people who join together for some purpose, for example to commit a crime. **gang up** VERB (*informal*) If people gang up on you, they join together to oppose you.

gangrene [*Said* ***gang**-green*] NOUN Gangrene is decay in the tissues of part of the body, caused by inadequate blood supply. **gangrenous** ADJECTIVE

gangster NOUN a violent criminal who is a member of a gang.

gap NOUN ① a space between two things or a hole in something solid. ② a period of time. ③ A gap between things, people or ideas is a great difference between them • *the gap between fantasy and reality.*

> **gap** NOUN
> ① = break, chink, crack, hole, opening, space
> ② = hiatus (*formal*), interlude, interval, lull, pause
> ③ = difference, disparity (*formal*), inconsistency

a b c d e f g h i j k l m n o p q r s t u v w x y z

gape VERB ① If you gape at someone or something, you stare at them with your mouth open in surprise. ② Something that gapes is wide open • *gaping holes in the wall*.

garage NOUN ① a building where a car can be kept. ② a place where cars are repaired and where petrol is sold.

garb NOUN (*formal*) Someone's garb is their clothes • *his usual garb of a dark suit*.

garbage NOUN ① Garbage is rubbish, especially household rubbish. ② (*informal*) If you say something is garbage, you mean it is nonsense.

> **garbage** NOUN
> ① = debris, junk (*informal*), litter, refuse (*formal*), rubbish, trash, waste
> ② = drivel, gibberish, nonsense, rubbish

garbled ADJECTIVE Garbled messages are jumbled and the details may be wrong.

> **garbled** ADJECTIVE
> = confused, distorted, incomprehensible, jumbled, unintelligible

garden NOUN ① an area of land next to a house, where flowers, fruit or vegetables are grown. ② (*in plural*) Gardens are a type of park in a town or around a large house. ▶ VERB ③ If you garden, you do work in your garden such as weeding or planting.
gardening NOUN

gardener NOUN a person who looks after a garden as a job or as a hobby.

garish [*Said* ***gair****-rish*] ADJECTIVE bright and harsh to look at • *garish bright red boots*.

garland NOUN a circle of flowers and leaves which is worn around the neck or head.

garlic NOUN Garlic is the small white bulb of an onion-like plant which has a strong taste and smell and is used in cooking.

garment NOUN a piece of clothing.

garnish NOUN ① something such as a sprig of parsley, that is used in cooking for decoration. ▶ VERB ② To garnish food means to decorate it with a garnish.

garrison NOUN a group of soldiers stationed in a town in order to guard it; also used of the buildings in which these soldiers live.

gas, **gases**; **gasses**, **gassing**, **gassed** NOUN ① SCIENCE any airlike substance that is not liquid or solid, such as oxygen or the gas used as a fuel in heating. ② In American English, gas is petrol. ▶ VERB ③ To gas people or animals means to kill them with poisonous gas.

gash NOUN ① a long, deep cut. ▶ VERB ② If you gash something, you make a long, deep cut in it.

gasoline NOUN In American English, gasoline is petrol.

gasp VERB ① If you gasp, you quickly draw in your breath through your mouth because you are surprised or in pain. ▶ NOUN ② a sharp intake of breath through the mouth.

> **gasp** VERB
> ① = choke, gulp, pant, puff
> ▶ NOUN ② = gulp, pant, puff

gastric ADJECTIVE occurring in the stomach or involving the stomach • *gastric pain*.

gate NOUN ① a barrier which can open and shut and is used to close the entrance to a garden or field. ② The gate at a sports event is the number of people who have attended it.

gatecrash VERB If you gatecrash a party, you go to it when you have not been invited.

gateway NOUN ① an entrance through a wall or fence where there is a gate. ② Something that is considered to be the entrance to a larger or more important thing can be described as the gateway to the larger thing • *New York is the great gateway to America.*

gather VERB ① When people gather, they come together in a group. ② If you gather a number of things, you bring them together in one place. ③ If something gathers speed or strength, it gets faster or stronger. ④ If you gather something, you learn it, often from what someone says.

> **gather** VERB
> ① = assemble, congregate, flock, mass, round up
> ≠ scatter
> ② = accumulate, amass, collect, hoard, stockpile
> ④ = assume, conclude, hear, learn, understand

gathering NOUN a meeting of people who have come together for a particular purpose.

> **gathering** NOUN
> = assembly, congregation, get-together (*informal*), meeting, rally

gauche [*Said* ***gohsh***] ADJECTIVE (*formal*) socially awkward.

gaudy, **gaudier**, **gaudiest** [*Said* ***gaw****-dee*] ADJECTIVE very colourful in a vulgar way.

> **gaudy** ADJECTIVE
> = bright, flashy, garish, loud, showy, tacky (*informal*), vulgar

gauge [*Said* ***gayj***] VERB ① If you gauge something, you estimate it or calculate it • *He gauged the wind at over 30 knots.* ▶ NOUN ② a piece of equipment that measures the amount of something • *a rain gauge.* ③ something that is used as a standard by which you judge a situation • *They see profit as a gauge of efficiency.* ④ On railways, the gauge is the distance between the two rails on a railway line.

gaunt ADJECTIVE A person who looks gaunt is thin and bony.

gauntlet NOUN ① Gauntlets are long thick gloves worn for protection, for example by motorcyclists. ▶ PHRASE ② If you **throw down the gauntlet**, you challenge someone. ③ If you **run the gauntlet**, you have an unpleasant experience in which you are attacked or criticised by people.

gave the past tense of **give**.

gay ADJECTIVE ① Someone who is gay is homosexual. ② (*old-fashioned*) Gay people or places are lively and full of fun. ▶ NOUN ③ a homosexual person.

gaze VERB If you gaze at something, you look steadily at it for a long time.

gazette NOUN a newspaper or journal.

GB an abbreviation for **Great Britain**.

GCSE NOUN In Britain, the GCSE is an examination taken by school students aged 15 and 16. GCSE is an abbreviation for 'General Certificate of Secondary Education'.

gear NOUN ① [DGT] a piece of machinery which controls the rate at which energy is converted into movement. Gears in vehicles control the speed and power of the vehicle. ② [PE] The gear for an activity is the clothes and equipment that you need for it. ▶ VERB ③ If someone or something is geared to a particular event or purpose, they are prepared for it.

geek NOUN (*informal*) a person who is obsessive about an interest or hobby, especially computers.

geese the plural of **goose**.

gel, **gels**, **gelling**, **gelled** [*Said* ***jel***] NOUN ① a smooth, soft, jelly-like substance • *shower gel.* ▶ VERB ② If a liquid gels, it turns into a gel. ③ If a vague thought or plan gels, it becomes more definite.

gelatine or **gelatin** *[Said* ***jel****-lat-tin]* NOUN a clear tasteless substance, obtained from meat and bones, used to make liquids firm and jelly-like.

gem NOUN ① a jewel or precious stone. ② You can describe something or someone that is extremely good or beautiful as a gem • *a gem of a novel*.

Gemini *[Said* ***jem****-in-nye]* NOUN Gemini is the third sign of the zodiac, represented by a pair of twins. People born between May 21st and June 20th are born under this sign.

gen NOUN *(informal)* The gen on something is information about it.

gender NOUN ① PSHE The gender of a person or animal is whether they are male or female • *the female gender*. ② MFL the classification of nouns as masculine, feminine and neuter in certain languages.

gene *[Said* ***jeen****]* NOUN SCIENCE one of the parts of a living cell which controls the physical characteristics of an organism and which are passed on from one generation to the next.

genera the plural of **genus**.

general ADJECTIVE ① relating to the whole of something or to most things in a group • *your general health*. ② true, suitable or relevant in most situations • *the general truth of science*. ③ including or involving a wide range of different things • *a general hospital*. ④ having complete responsibility over a wide area of work or a large number of people • *the general secretary*. ▸ NOUN ⑤ an army officer of very high rank. ▸ PHRASE ⑥ **In general** means usually. **generally** ADVERB

> **general** ADJECTIVE
> ① = broad, comprehensive, overall
> ≠ specific
> ② = accepted, broad, common, universal, widespread
> ≠ special

general election NOUN an election for a new government, which all the people of a country may vote in.

generalise; also spelt **generalize** VERB To generalise means to say that something is true in most cases, ignoring minor details. **generalisation** NOUN

general practitioner NOUN a doctor who works in the community rather than in a hospital.

generate VERB To generate something means to create or produce it • *using wind power to generate electricity*.

generation NOUN all the people of about the same age; also the period of time between one generation and the next, usually considered to be about 25–30 years.

generator NOUN a machine which produces electricity from another form of energy such as wind or water power.

generic ADJECTIVE A generic term is a name that applies to all the members of a group of similar things.

generosity NOUN PSHE the willingness to give money, time or help.

> **generosity** NOUN
> = benevolence, charity, kindness
> ≠ meanness

generous ADJECTIVE ① PSHE A generous person is very willing to give money or time. ② Something that is generous is very large • *a generous waist*. **generously** ADVERB

> **generous** ADJECTIVE
> ① = charitable, hospitable, kind, lavish, liberal
> ≠ mean
> ② = abundant, ample, plentiful
> ≠ meagre

genesis NOUN *(formal)* The genesis of

something is its beginning.

genetics NOUN SCIENCE Genetics is the science of the way that characteristics are passed on from generation to generation by means of genes. **genetic** ADJECTIVE **genetically** ADVERB

genial ADJECTIVE cheerful, friendly and kind. **genially** ADVERB

genie [*Said* ***jee**-nee*] NOUN a magical being that obeys the wishes of the person who controls it.

genitals PLURAL NOUN The genitals are the reproductive organs. The technical name is **genitalia**. **genital** ADJECTIVE

genius NOUN ① a highly intelligent, creative or talented person. ② Genius is great intelligence, creativity or talent • *a poet of genius*.

genius NOUN
① = brain, master, mastermind, virtuoso
② = brains, brilliance, intellect

genocide [*Said* ***jen**-nos-side*] NOUN (*formal*) Genocide is the systematic murder of all members of a particular race or group.

genome [*Said* ***jee**-nome*] NOUN SCIENCE all of the genes contained in a single cell of an organism.

genre [*Said* ***jahn**-ra*] NOUN ENGLISH LIBRARY (*formal*) a particular style in literature or art.

genteel ADJECTIVE very polite and refined.

Gentile [*Said* ***jen**-tile*] NOUN RE a person who is not Jewish.

gentle ADJECTIVE mild and calm; not violent or rough • *a gentle man*. **gently** ADVERB **gentleness** NOUN

gentle ADJECTIVE
= benign, kind, kindly, meek, mild, placid, soft, tender
≠ cruel

gentleman, **gentlemen** NOUN a man who is polite and well-educated; also a polite way of referring to any man. **gentlemanly** ADJECTIVE

gentry PLURAL NOUN The gentry are wealthy landowners who are not members of the nobility.

genuine [*Said* ***jen**-yoo-in*] ADJECTIVE ① real and not false or pretend • *a genuine smile* • *genuine silver*. ② A genuine person is sincere and honest. **genuinely** ADVERB **genuineness** NOUN

genuine ADJECTIVE
① = authentic, bona fide, dinkum (*Australian and New Zealand; informal*), real
≠ fake

genus, **genera** [*Said* ***jee**-nuss*] NOUN SCIENCE In biology, a genus is a class of animals or closely related plants. It is smaller than a family and larger than a species.

geography NOUN the study of the physical features of the earth, together with the climate, natural resources and population in different parts of the world. **geographic** or **geographical** ADJECTIVE **geographically** ADVERB

geology NOUN the study of the earth's structure, especially the layers of rock and soil that make up the surface of the earth. **geological** ADJECTIVE **geologist** NOUN

geometric or **geometrical** ADJECTIVE ① consisting of regular lines and shapes, such as squares, triangles and circles • *bold geometric designs*. ② involving geometry.

geometry NOUN Geometry is the branch of mathematics that deals with lines, angles, curves and spaces.

Georgian ADJECTIVE HISTORY belonging to or typical of the time from 1714 to 1830, when George I to

George IV reigned in Britain.

geranium NOUN a garden plant with red, pink or white flowers.

geriatrics [*Said jer-ree-**at**-riks*] NOUN Geriatrics is the medical care of elderly people. **geriatric** ADJECTIVE

germ NOUN ① a very small organism that causes disease. ② (*formal*) The germ of an idea or plan is the beginning of it.

German ADJECTIVE ① belonging or relating to Germany. ▶ NOUN ② someone who comes from Germany. ③ German is the main language spoken in Germany and Austria and is also spoken by many people in Switzerland.

Germanic ADJECTIVE ① typical of Germany or the German people. ② The Germanic group of languages includes English, Dutch, German, Danish, Swedish and Norwegian.

germinate VERB ① SCIENCE When a seed germinates, it starts to grow. ② When an idea or plan germinates, it starts to develop. **germination** NOUN

gestation [*Said jes-**tay**-shn*] NOUN SCIENCE Gestation is the time during which a foetus is growing inside its mother's womb.

gesture NOUN ① a movement of your hands or head that conveys a message or feeling. ② an action symbolising something • *a gesture of support.* ▶ VERB ③ If you gesture, you move your hands or head in order to communicate a message or feeling.

get, gets, getting, got VERB ① Get often means the same as become • *People draw the curtains once it gets dark.* ② If you get into a particular situation, you put yourself in that situation • *We are going to get into a hopeless muddle.* ③ If you get something done, you do it or someone does it for you • *You can get your homework done in time.* ④ If you get somewhere, you go there • *I must get home.* ⑤ If you get something, you fetch it or are given it • *I'll get us all a cup of coffee* • *I got your message.* ⑥ If you get a joke or get the point of something, you understand it. ⑦ If you get a train, bus or plane, you travel on it • *You can get a bus.*

get across VERB If you get an idea across, you make people understand it. **get at** VERB ① If someone is getting at you, they are criticising you in an unkind way. ② If you ask someone what they are getting at, you are asking them to explain what they mean. **get away with** VERB If you get away with something dishonest, you are not found out or punished for doing it. **get by** VERB If you get by, you have just enough money to live on. **get on** VERB ① If two people get on well together, they like each other's company. ② If you get on with a task, you do it.

get over with VERB If you want to get something unpleasant over with, you want it to be finished quickly.

get through VERB ① If you get through to someone, you make them understand what you are saying. ② If you get through to someone on the telephone, you succeed in talking to them.

> **get** VERB
> ① = become, grow, turn
> ⑤ = acquire, fetch, obtain, procure (*formal*), receive, secure (*formal*)
> ▶ **get on** ① = be compatible, hit it off (*informal*)

getaway NOUN an escape made by criminals.

get-together NOUN (*informal*) an informal meeting or party.

Ghanaian [*Said gah-**nay**-an*] ADJECTIVE ① belonging or relating to Ghana.

▸ **NOUN** ② someone who comes from Ghana.

ghastly, **ghastlier**, **ghastliest** **ADJECTIVE** extremely horrible and unpleasant • *a ghastly crime* • *ghastly food.*

ghetto, **ghettoes** or **ghettos** **NOUN** a part of a city where many poor people of a particular ethnic group live.

ghost **NOUN** the spirit of a dead person, believed to haunt people or places.

> **ghost** **NOUN**
> = apparition, phantom, spectre, spirit

ghoulish *[Said* ***gool****-ish]* **ADJECTIVE** very interested in unpleasant things such as death and murder.

giant **NOUN** ① a huge person in a myth or legend. ▸ **ADJECTIVE** ② much larger than other similar things • *giant prawns* • *a giant wave.*

gibberish *[Said* ***jib****-ir-ish]* **NOUN** Gibberish is speech that makes no sense at all.

gibe; also spelt **jibe** **NOUN** an insulting remark.

giddy, **giddier**, **giddiest** **ADJECTIVE** If you feel giddy, you feel unsteady on your feet usually because you are ill. **giddily** **ADVERB**

gift **NOUN** ① a present. ② a natural skill or ability • *a gift for comedy.*

> **gift** **NOUN**
> ① = bequest (*formal*), bonsela (*South African*), contribution, donation, legacy, present
> ② = ability, aptitude, flair, talent

gifted **ADJECTIVE** having a special ability • *gifted tennis players.*

gig **NOUN** a rock or jazz concert.

gigabyte **NOUN** [ICT] a unit of computer memory size, equal to 1024 megabytes.

gigantic **ADJECTIVE** extremely large.

giggle **VERB** ① To giggle means to laugh in a silly or nervous way. ▸ **NOUN** ② a silly or nervous laugh. **giggly** **ADJECTIVE**

gilded **ADJECTIVE** Something which is gilded is covered with a thin layer of gold.

gill **NOUN** ① *[Said* ***gil****]* The gills of a fish are the organs on its sides which it uses for breathing. ② *[Said* ***jil****]* a unit of liquid volume equal to one quarter of a pint or about 0.142 litres.

gilt **NOUN** ① a thin layer of gold. ▸ **ADJECTIVE** ② covered with a thin layer of gold • *a gilt writing-table.*

gimmick **NOUN** a device that is not really necessary but is used to attract interest • *All pop stars need a good gimmick.* **gimmicky** **ADJECTIVE**

gin **NOUN** Gin is a strong, colourless alcoholic drink made from grain and juniper berries.

ginger **NOUN** ① Ginger is a plant root with a hot, spicy flavour, used in cooking. ▸ **ADJECTIVE** ② bright orange or red • *ginger hair.*

gingerbread **NOUN** Gingerbread is a sweet, ginger-flavoured cake.

gingerly **ADVERB** If you move gingerly, you move cautiously • *They walked gingerly down the stairs.*

giraffe **NOUN** a tall, four-legged African mammal with a very long neck.

girl **NOUN** a female child. **girlhood** **NOUN** **girlish** **ADJECTIVE**

girlfriend **NOUN** Someone's girlfriend is the woman or girl with whom they are having a romantic relationship.

girth **NOUN** The girth of something is the measurement round it.

gist *[Said* ***jist****]* **NOUN** the general meaning or most important points in a piece of writing or speech.

give, **gives**, **giving**, **gave**, **given** **VERB** ① If you give someone something, you hand it to them or provide it for them • *I gave her a card* • *George gave me my job.* ② 'Give' is also used to express physical actions and speech • *He gave a fierce smile* • *Rosa gave a lovely performance.* ③ If you give a party or a meal, you are the host at it. ④ If something gives, it collapses under pressure. ▶ NOUN ⑤ If material has give, it will bend or stretch when pulled or put under pressure. ▶ PHRASE ⑥ You use **give or take** to indicate that an amount you are mentioning is not exact • *About two years, give or take a month or so.* ⑦ If something **gives way** to something else, it is replaced by it. ⑧ If something **gives way**, it collapses. **give in** VERB If you give in, you admit that you are defeated. **give out** VERB If something gives out, it stops working • *the electricity gave out.* **give up** VERB ① If you give something up, you stop doing it • *I can't give up my job.* ② If you give up, you admit that you cannot do something. ③ If you give someone up, you let the police know where they are hiding.

give VERB
① = award, deliver, donate, grant, hand, present, provide, supply
≠ take
④ = buckle, cave in, collapse, give way, yield
▶ **give in** = capitulate, concede, submit, succumb (*formal*), surrender, yield (*formal*)

given ① the past participle of **give**. ▶ ADJECTIVE ② fixed or specified • *My style can change at any given moment.*

glacier [*Said glass-yer*] NOUN GEOGRAPHY a huge frozen river of slow-moving ice.

glad, **gladder**, **gladdest** ADJECTIVE happy and pleased • *They'll be glad to get away from it all.* **gladly** ADVERB **gladness** NOUN

glad ADJECTIVE
= delighted, happy, joyful, overjoyed, pleased
≠ sorry

gladiator NOUN HISTORY In ancient Rome, gladiators were slaves trained to fight in arenas to provide entertainment.

glamour NOUN The glamour of a fashionable or attractive person or place is the charm and excitement that they have • *the glamour of Paris.* **glamorous** ADJECTIVE

glance VERB ① If you glance at something, you look at it quickly. ② If one object glances off another, it hits it at an angle and bounces away in another direction. ▶ NOUN ③ a quick look.

glance VERB
① = glimpse, look, peek, peep, scan
② = bounce, brush, skim
▶ NOUN ③ = glimpse, look, peek, peep

gland NOUN an organ in your body, such as the thyroid gland and the sweat glands, which either produce chemical substances for your body to use, or which help to get rid of waste products from your body. **glandular** ADJECTIVE

glare VERB ① If you glare at someone, you look at them angrily. ▶ NOUN ② a hard, angry look. ③ Glare is extremely bright light.

glare VERB
① = frown, glower, scowl
▶ NOUN ② = frown, scowl
③ = blaze, glow

glass NOUN ① Glass is a hard, transparent substance that is easily broken, used to make windows and bottles. ② a container for drinking out of, made from glass.

glasses PLURAL NOUN Glasses are two lenses in a frame, which some people wear over their eyes to improve their eyesight.

glassy, **glassier**, **glassiest** ADJECTIVE ① smooth and shiny like glass • *glassy water*. ② A glassy look shows no feeling or expression.

glaze NOUN ① A glaze on pottery or on food is a smooth shiny surface. ▶ VERB ② To glaze pottery or food means to cover it with a glaze. ③ To glaze a window means to fit a sheet of glass into a window frame. **glaze over** VERB If your eyes glaze over, they lose all expression, usually because you are bored.

glazed ADJECTIVE Someone who has a glazed expression looks bored.

gleam VERB ① If something gleams, it shines and reflects light. ▶ NOUN ② a pale shining light.

glean VERB To glean information means to collect it from various sources.

glee NOUN (*old-fashioned*) Glee is joy and delight. **gleeful** ADJECTIVE **gleefully** ADVERB

glen NOUN a deep, narrow valley, especially in Scotland or Ireland.

glide VERB ① To glide means to move smoothly • *cygnets gliding up the stream*. ② When birds or aeroplanes glide, they float on air currents.

glider NOUN an aeroplane without an engine, which flies by floating on air currents.

glimmer NOUN ① a faint, unsteady light. ② A glimmer of a feeling or quality is a faint sign of it • *a glimmer of intelligence*.

glimpse NOUN ① a brief sight of something • *They caught a glimpse of their hero*. ▶ VERB ② If you glimpse something, you see it very briefly.

glint VERB ① If something glints, it reflects quick flashes of light. ▶ NOUN ② a quick flash of light. ③ A glint in someone's eye is a brightness expressing some emotion • *A glint of mischief in her blue-grey eyes*.

glisten [*Said* ***gliss-sn***] VERB If something glistens, it shines or sparkles.

glitter VERB ① If something glitters, it shines in a sparkling way • *a glittering crown*. ▶ NOUN ② Glitter is sparkling light.

gloat VERB If you gloat, you cruelly show your pleasure about your own success or someone else's failure • *Their rivals were gloating over their triumph*.

global ADJECTIVE concerning the whole world • *a global tour*.

globalisation; also spelt **globalization** NOUN ① the process by which a company expands so that it can do business internationally. ② the process by which cultures throughout the world become more and more similar for a variety of reasons including increased global business and better international communications.

global warming NOUN [GEOGRAPHY] [SCIENCE] an increase in the world's overall temperature believed to be caused by the greenhouse effect.

globe NOUN ① a ball-shaped object, especially one with a map of the earth on it. ② [GEOGRAPHY] You can refer to the world as the globe. ③ In South African, Australian and New Zealand English, a globe is an electric light bulb.

gloom NOUN ① Gloom is darkness or dimness. ② Gloom is also a feeling of unhappiness or despair.

gloomy, **gloomier**, **gloomiest** ADJECTIVE ① dark and depressing. ② feeling very sad. **gloomily** ADVERB

gloomy ADJECTIVE
① = dark, dismal, dreary, dull
≠ sunny
② = dejected, down, glum, miserable, sad
≠ cheerful

glorify, glorifies, glorifying, glorified VERB If you glorify someone or something, you make them seem better than they really are • *songs glorifying war.* **glorification** NOUN

glorious ADJECTIVE ① beautiful and impressive to look at • *glorious beaches.* ② very pleasant and giving a feeling of happiness • *glorious sunshine.* ③ involving great fame and success • *a glorious career.* **gloriously** ADVERB

glory, glories, glorying, gloried NOUN ① Glory is fame and admiration for an achievement. ② something considered splendid or admirable • *the true glories of the Alps.* ▸ VERB ③ If you glory in something, you take great delight in it.

glory NOUN
① = fame, honour, immortality, praise, prestige
≠ disgrace
② = grandeur, magnificence, majesty, splendour
▸ VERB ③ = gloat, relish, revel

gloss NOUN ① Gloss is a bright shine on a surface. ② Gloss is also an attractive appearance which may hide less attractive qualities • *to put a positive gloss on the events.*

gloss NOUN
① = brilliance, gleam, polish, sheen, shine

glossary, glossaries NOUN [LIBRARY] a list of explanations of specialist words, usually found at the back of a book.

glossy, glossier, glossiest ADJECTIVE smooth and shiny • *glossy lipstick* • *glossy paper.*

glossy ADJECTIVE
= bright, brilliant, polished, shiny, sleek

glove NOUN Gloves are coverings which you wear over your hands for warmth or protection.

glow NOUN ① a dull, steady light. ② a strong feeling of pleasure or happiness. ▸ VERB ③ If something glows, it shines with a dull, steady light • *A light glowed behind the curtains.* ④ If you are glowing, you look very happy or healthy.

glow NOUN
① = gleam, glimmer, light
▸ VERB ③ = gleam, glimmer, shine, smoulder

glowing ADJECTIVE A glowing description praises someone or something very highly • *a glowing character reference.*

glucose NOUN [SCIENCE] Glucose is a type of sugar found in plants and that animals and people make in their bodies from food to provide energy.

glue, glues, gluing or **glueing, glued** NOUN ① a substance used for sticking things together. ▸ VERB ② If you glue one object to another, you stick them together using glue.

glue VERB
② = fix, paste, seal, stick

glum, glummer, glummest ADJECTIVE miserable and depressed. **glumly** ADVERB

glut NOUN a greater quantity of things than is needed.

gluten [*Said* ***gloo****-ten*] NOUN a sticky protein found in cereal grains, such as wheat.

gnarled [*Said* ***narld***] ADJECTIVE old, twisted and rough • *gnarled fingers.*

gnome [*Said* ***nome***] NOUN a tiny old man in fairy stories.

go, **goes**, **going**, **went**, **gone** VERB ① If you go somewhere, you move or travel there. ② You can use 'go' to mean become • *She felt she was going mad*. ③ You can use 'go' to describe the state that someone or something is in • *Our arrival went unnoticed*. ④ If something goes well, it is successful. If it goes badly, it is unsuccessful. ⑤ If you are going to do something, you will do it. ⑥ If a machine or clock goes, it works and is not broken. ⑦ You use 'go' before giving the sound something makes or before quoting a song or saying • *The bell goes ding-dong*. ⑧ If something goes on something or to someone, it is allotted to them. ⑨ If one thing goes with another, they are appropriate together. ⑩ If one number goes into another, it can be divided into it. ▸ NOUN ⑪ an attempt at doing something. ▸ PHRASE ⑫ If someone is always **on the go**, they are always busy and active. ⑬ **To go** means remaining • *I've got one more year of my course to go*. **go back on** VERB If you go back on a promise or agreement, you do not do what you promised or agreed. **go down** VERB ① If something goes down well, people like it. If it goes down badly, they do not like it. ② If you go down with an illness, you catch it. **go for** VERB If someone goes for you, they attack you. **go in** VERB If you go in for something, you decide to do it as your job. **go off** VERB ① If you go off someone or something, you stop liking them. ② If a bomb goes off, it explodes. **go on** VERB ① If you go on doing something, you continue to do it. ② If you go on about something, you keep talking about it in a rather boring way. ③ Something that is going on is happening. **go out** VERB If you go out with someone, you have a romantic relationship with them. **go over** VERB If you go over something, you think about it or discuss it carefully. **go through** VERB ① If you go through an unpleasant event, you experience it. ② If a law or agreement goes through, it is approved and becomes official. ③ If you go through with something, you do it even though it is unpleasant.

> **go** VERB
> ① = advance, drive, fly, journey (*formal*), leave, proceed (*formal*), set off, travel
> ⑥ = function, work
> ▸ NOUN ⑪ = attempt, shot (*informal*), stab (*informal*), try
> ▸ **go through** ① = endure, experience, undergo

goad VERB If you goad someone, you encourage them to do something by making them angry or excited • *He had goaded the man into losing his temper*.

go-ahead NOUN If someone gives you the go-ahead for something, they give you permission to do it.

goal NOUN ① the space, in games like football or hockey, into which the players try to get the ball in order to score a point. ② an instance of this. ③ Your goal is something that you hope to achieve.

> **goal** NOUN
> ③ = aim, end, intention, object, objective, purpose, target

goalkeeper NOUN the player, in games like soccer or hockey, who stands in the goal and tries to stop the other team from scoring.

goat NOUN an animal, like a sheep, with coarse hair, a beard and horns.

gob NOUN (*informal*) Your gob is your mouth.

gobble VERB ① If you gobble food, you eat it very quickly. ② When a turkey gobbles, it makes a loud gurgling sound.

gobble VERB
① = bolt, devour, wolf

god PROPER NOUN ① RE The name God is given to the being who is worshipped by Christians, Jews and Muslims as the creator and ruler of the world. ▸ NOUN ② any of the beings that are believed in many religions to have power over an aspect of life or a part of the world • *Mars, the Roman god of war.* ③ If someone is your god, you admire them very much. ④ (*in plural*) In a theatre, the gods are the highest seats farthest from the stage.

goddess NOUN a female god.

godsend NOUN something that comes unexpectedly and helps you very much.

goggles PLURAL NOUN Goggles are special glasses that fit closely round your eyes to protect them.

going NOUN The going is the conditions that affect your ability to do something • *He found the going very slow indeed.*

gold NOUN ① SCIENCE Gold is a valuable, yellow-coloured metallic element. It is used for making jewellery and as an international currency. Its atomic number is 79 and its symbol is Au. ② 'Gold' is also used to mean things that are made of gold. ▸ ADJECTIVE ③ bright yellow.

golden ADJECTIVE ① gold in colour • *golden syrup.* ② made of gold • *a golden chain.* ③ excellent or ideal • *a golden hero.*

golden rule NOUN a very important rule to remember in order to be able to do something successfully.

goldfish NOUN a small orange-coloured fish, often kept in ponds or bowls.

golf NOUN Golf is a game in which players use special clubs to hit a small ball into holes that are spread out over a large area of grassy land.
golfer NOUN

golf course NOUN an area of grassy land where people play golf.

gondola [*Said* ***gon**-dol-la*] NOUN a long narrow boat used in Venice, which is propelled with a long pole.

gone the past participle of **go**.

gong NOUN a flat, circular piece of metal that is hit with a hammer to make a loud sound, often as a signal for something.

good, **better**, **best** ADJECTIVE ① pleasant, acceptable or satisfactory • *good news* • *a good film.* ② skilful or successful • *good at art.* ③ kind, thoughtful and loving • *She was grateful to her parents for being so good to her.* ④ well-behaved • *Have the children been good?* ⑤ used to emphasise something • *a good few million pounds.* ▸ NOUN ⑥ Good is moral and spiritual justice and virtue • *the forces of good and evil.* ⑦ Good also refers to anything that is desirable or beneficial as opposed to harmful • *The break has done me good.* ⑧ (*in plural*) Goods are objects that people own or that are sold in shops • *leather goods.* ▸ PHRASE ⑨ **For good** means for ever. ⑩ **As good as** means almost • *The election is as good as decided.*

good ADJECTIVE
① = excellent, fine, first-class, first-rate, splendid, superb
≠ bad
② = able, capable, competent, skilful, talented
≠ incompetent
③ = decent, generous, kind, kind-hearted, thoughtful
≠ unkind

goodbye INTERJECTION You say goodbye when you are leaving someone or ending a telephone conversation.

Good Friday NOUN [RE] Good Friday is the Friday before Easter, when Christians remember the crucifixion of Christ.

good-natured ADJECTIVE friendly, pleasant and even-tempered.

goodness NOUN ① Goodness is the quality of being kind. ▶ INTERJECTION ② People say 'Goodness!' or 'My goodness!' when they are surprised.

goodwill NOUN Goodwill is kindness and helpfulness • *Messages of goodwill were exchanged.*

goodwill NOUN
= benevolence, favour, friendliness, friendship

goody, **goodies** NOUN (*informal*) ① Goodies are enjoyable things, often food. ② You can call a hero in a film or book a goody.

goose, **geese** NOUN a fairly large bird with webbed feet and a long neck.

gooseberry, **gooseberries** NOUN a round, green berry that grows on a bush and has a sharp taste.

gore VERB ① If an animal gores someone, it wounds them badly with its horns or tusks. ▶ NOUN ② Gore is clotted blood from a wound.

gorge NOUN ① [GEOGRAPHY] a deep, narrow valley. ▶ VERB ② If you gorge yourself, you eat a lot of food greedily.

gorgeous ADJECTIVE extremely pleasant or attractive • *a gorgeous view.*

gorilla NOUN a very large, strong ape with very dark fur.

gorse NOUN Gorse is a dark green wild shrub that has sharp prickles and small yellow flowers.

gory, **gorier**, **goriest** ADJECTIVE Gory situations involve people being injured in horrible ways.

gospel NOUN ① [RE] The Gospels are the four books in the New Testament which describe the life and teachings of Jesus Christ. ② a set of ideas that someone strongly believes in • *The chef wants to spread the gospel of good food.* ▶ ADJECTIVE ③ Gospel music is a style of religious music popular among Black Christians in the United States.

gossip, **gossips**, **gossiping**, **gossiped** NOUN ① Gossip is informal conversation, often concerning people's private affairs. ② Someone who is a gossip enjoys talking about other people's private affairs. ▶ VERB ③ If you gossip, you talk informally with someone, especially about other people.

gossip NOUN
① = dirt, hearsay

got ① Got is the past tense and past participle of **get**. ② You can use 'have got' instead of the more formal 'have' when talking about possessing things • *The director has got a map.* ③ You can use 'have got to' instead of the more formal 'have to' when talking about something that must be done • *He has got to win.*

gouge [*Said gowj*] VERB ① If you gouge a hole in something, you make a hole in it with a pointed object. ② If you gouge something out, you force it out of position with your fingers or a sharp tool.

gourmet [*Said goor-may*] NOUN a person who enjoys good food and drink and knows a lot about it.

gout NOUN Gout is a disease which causes someone's joints to swell painfully, especially in their toes.

govern VERB ① To govern a country means to control it. ② Something that governs a situation influences it • *Our thinking is as much governed by habit as by behaviour.*

governess NOUN a woman who is employed to teach the children in a family and who lives with the family.

A B C D E F G H I J K L M N O P Q R S T U V W X Y Z

government NOUN ① CITIZENSHIP The government is the group of people who govern a country. ② CITIZENSHIP Government is the control and organisation of a country. **governmental** ADJECTIVE

governor NOUN ① a person who controls and organises a state or an institution. ② In Australia, the Governor is the representative of the King or Queen in a State.

gown NOUN ① a long, formal dress. ② a long, dark cloak worn by people such as judges and lawyers.

GP an abbreviation for **general practitioner**.

grab, grabs, grabbing, grabbed VERB ① If you grab something, you take it or pick it up roughly. ② If you grab an opportunity, you take advantage of it eagerly. ③ (*informal*) If an idea grabs you, it excites you. ▸ NOUN ④ A grab at an object is an attempt to grab it.

> **grab** VERB
> ① = clutch, grasp, seize, snatch

grace NOUN ① Grace is an elegant way of moving. ② Grace is also a pleasant, kind way of behaving. ③ Grace is also a short prayer of thanks said before a meal. ④ Dukes and archbishops are addressed as 'Your Grace' and referred to as 'His Grace'. ▸ VERB ⑤ Something that graces a place makes it more attractive. ⑥ If someone important graces an event, they kindly agree to be present at it. **graceful** ADJECTIVE **gracefully** ADVERB

> **grace** NOUN
> ① = elegance, poise
> ≠ clumsiness

gracious ADJECTIVE ① kind, polite and pleasant. ▸ INTERJECTION ② 'Good gracious' is an exclamation of surprise. **graciously** ADVERB

grade VERB ① To grade things means to arrange them according to quality. ▸ NOUN ② The grade of something is its quality. ③ the mark that you get for an exam or piece of written work. ④ Your grade in a company or organisation is your level of importance or your rank.

> **grade** VERB
> ① = class, classify, group, rate, sort

gradient NOUN a slope or the steepness of a slope.

gradual ADJECTIVE happening or changing slowly over a long period of time. **gradually** ADVERB

> **gradual** ADJECTIVE
> = continuous, progressive, slow, steady
> ≠ sudden

graduate NOUN [*Said* ***grad**-yoo-it*] ① a person who has completed a first degree at a university or college. ▸ VERB [*Said* ***grad**-yoo-ate*] ② When students graduate, they complete a first degree at a university or college. ③ To graduate from one thing to another means to progress gradually towards the second thing. **graduation** NOUN

graffiti [*Said graf-**fee**-tee*] NOUN Graffiti is slogans or drawings scribbled on walls.

graft NOUN ① a piece of living tissue which is used to replace by surgery a damaged or unhealthy part of a person's body. ② (*informal*) Graft is hard work. ▸ VERB ③ To graft one thing to another means to attach it.

grain NOUN ① a cereal plant, such as wheat, that is grown as a crop and used for food. ② Grains are seeds of a cereal plant. ③ A grain of sand or salt is a tiny particle of it. ④ The grain of a piece of wood is the pattern of lines made by the fibres in it. ▸ PHRASE ⑤ If something **goes against the grain**, you find it difficult to accept because it is against your principles.

gram; also spelt **gramme** NOUN a unit of weight equal to one thousandth of a kilogram.

grammar NOUN [ENGLISH] [MFL] Grammar is the rules of a language relating to the ways you can combine words to form sentences.

grammar school NOUN ① a secondary school for pupils of high academic ability. ② In Australia, a grammar school is a private school, usually one controlled by a church.

grammatical ADJECTIVE ① relating to grammar • *grammatical knowledge*. ② following the rules of grammar correctly • *grammatical sentences*. **grammatically** ADVERB

gran NOUN (*informal*) Your gran is your grandmother.

grand ADJECTIVE ① magnificent in appearance and size • *a grand house*. ② very important • *the grand scheme of your life*. ③ (*informal*) very pleasant or enjoyable • *It was a grand day*. ④ A grand total is the final complete amount. ▶ NOUN ⑤ (*informal*) a thousand pounds or dollars. **grandly** ADVERB

> **grand** ADJECTIVE
> ① = imposing, impressive, magnificent, majestic, monumental, splendid
> ③ = brilliant, fantastic (*informal*), great (*informal*), marvellous, terrific, tremendous, wonderful

grandad NOUN (*informal*) Your grandad is your grandfather.

grandchild, **grandchildren** NOUN Someone's grandchildren are the children of their son or daughter.

granddaughter NOUN Someone's granddaughter is the daughter of their son or daughter.

grandeur [*Said **grand**-yer*] NOUN Grandeur is great beauty and magnificence.

grandfather NOUN Your grandfather is your father's father or your mother's father.

grandiose [*Said **gran**-dee-ose*] ADJECTIVE intended to be very impressive, but seeming ridiculous • *a grandiose gesture of love*.

grandma NOUN (*informal*) Your grandma is your grandmother.

grandmother NOUN Your grandmother is your father's mother or your mother's mother.

grandparent NOUN Your grandparents are your parents' parents.

grand piano NOUN a large flat piano with horizontal strings.

grandson NOUN Someone's grandson is the son of their son or daughter.

grandstand NOUN a structure with a roof and seats for spectators at a sports ground.

granite [*Said **gran**-nit*] NOUN Granite is a very hard rock used in building.

granny, **grannies** NOUN (*informal*) Your granny is your grandmother.

grant NOUN ① an amount of money that an official body gives to someone for a particular purpose • *a grant to carry out repairs*. ▶ VERB ② If you grant something to someone, you allow them to have it. ③ If you grant that something is true, you admit that it is true. ▶ PHRASE ④ If you **take something for granted**, you believe it without thinking about it. If you **take someone for granted**, you benefit from them without showing that you are grateful.

> **grant** NOUN
> ① = allocation, allowance, award, handout, subsidy
> ▶ VERB ② = allocate, allow, award, give, permit
> ≠ deny
> ③ = accept, acknowledge, admit, allow, concede
> ≠ deny

a b c d e f g h i j k l m n o p q r s t u v w x y z

grape NOUN a small green or purple fruit, eaten raw or used to make wine.

grapefruit NOUN a large, round, yellow citrus fruit.

grapevine NOUN ① a climbing plant which grapes grow on. ▸ PHRASE ② If you hear some news **on the grapevine**, it has been passed on from person to person, usually unofficially or secretly.

graph NOUN [MATHS] a diagram which shows how sets of numbers or measurements are related.

-graph SUFFIX '-graph' means a writer or recorder of some sort or something made by writing, drawing or recording • *telegraph* • *autograph*.

graphic ADJECTIVE ① A graphic description is very detailed and lifelike. ② relating to drawing or painting. **graphically** ADVERB

graphics PLURAL NOUN [ICT] Graphics are drawings and pictures composed of simple lines and strong colours • *computerised graphics*.

graphite NOUN a black form of carbon that is used in pencil leads.

grapple VERB ① If you grapple with someone, you struggle with them while fighting. ② If you grapple with a problem, you try hard to solve it.

grasp VERB ① If you grasp something, you hold it firmly. ② If you grasp an idea, you understand it. ▸ NOUN ③ a firm hold. ④ Your grasp of something is your understanding of it.

> **grasp** VERB
> ① = clutch, grab, grip, hold, seize, snatch
> ② = absorb, appreciate, assimilate, realise, take in, understand
> ▸ NOUN ③ = clasp, embrace, grip, hold
> ④ = awareness, comprehension (*formal*), grip, knowledge, understanding

grass NOUN Grass is the common green plant that grows on lawns and in parks. **grassy** ADJECTIVE

grasshopper NOUN an insect with long back legs which it uses for jumping and making a high-pitched sound.

grate NOUN ① a framework of metal bars in a fireplace. ▸ VERB ② To grate food means to shred it into small pieces by rubbing it against a metal tool. ③ When something grates on something else, it rubs against it making a harsh sound. ④ If something grates on you, it irritates you.

grateful ADJECTIVE If you are grateful for something, you are glad you have it and want to thank the person who gave it to you. **gratefully** ADVERB

> **grateful** ADJECTIVE
> = appreciative, indebted, thankful
> ≠ ungrateful

gratify, **gratifies**, **gratifying**, **gratified** VERB ① If you are gratified by something, you are pleased by it. ② If you gratify a wish or feeling, you satisfy it.

grating NOUN ① a metal frame with bars across it fastened over a hole in a wall or in the ground. ▸ ADJECTIVE ② A grating sound is harsh and unpleasant • *grating melodies*.

gratitude NOUN Gratitude is the feeling of being grateful.

> **gratitude** NOUN
> = appreciation, recognition, thanks
> ≠ ingratitude

gratuitous [*Said grat-**yoo**-it-tuss*] ADJECTIVE unnecessary • *a gratuitous attack*. **gratuitously** ADVERB

grave[1] [*Rhymes with **save***] NOUN ① a place where a corpse is buried. ▸ ADJECTIVE ② (*formal*) very serious • *grave danger*.

grave NOUN
① = mausoleum, pit, sepulchre (*literary*), tomb
▸ ADJECTIVE ② = acute, critical, heavy (*informal*), serious

grave² [*Said grahv*] ADJECTIVE MFL In French and some other languages, a grave accent is a line sloping downwards from left to right placed over a vowel to indicate a change in pronunciation, as in the word *lièvre* (a hare).

gravel NOUN Gravel is small stones used for making roads and paths.

gravestone NOUN a large stone placed over someone's grave, with their name on it.

graveyard NOUN an area of land where corpses are buried.

gravitate VERB When people gravitate towards something, they go towards it because they are attracted by it.

gravity NOUN ① SCIENCE Gravity is the force that makes things fall when you drop them. ② (*formal*) The gravity of a situation is its seriousness.

gravy NOUN Gravy is a brown sauce made from meat juices.

graze VERB ① When animals graze, they eat grass. ② If something grazes a part of your body, it scrapes against it, injuring you slightly. ▸ NOUN ③ a slight injury caused by something scraping against your skin.

graze VERB
② = scrape, scratch, skin
▸ NOUN ③ = abrasion (*formal*), scratch

grease NOUN ① Grease is an oily substance used for lubricating machines. ② Grease is also melted animal fat, used in cooking. ③ Grease is also an oily substance produced by your skin and found in your hair. ▸ VERB ④ If you grease something, you lubricate it with grease. **greasy** ADJECTIVE

great ADJECTIVE ① very large • *a great sea* • *great efforts*. ② very important • *a great artist*. ③ (*informal*) very good • *Paul had a great time*. **greatly** ADVERB **greatness** NOUN

great ADJECTIVE
① = big, colossal, huge, large, enormous, extensive, gigantic, immense, massive, stupendous, tremendous, vast
≠ small
② = celebrated, chief, distinguished, eminent, famed, famous, illustrious, important, main, major, momentous, notable, principal, prominent, renowned, serious, significant
③ = beaut (*Australian and New Zealand; informal*), excellent, fantastic (*informal*), fine, first-rate, marvellous, outstanding, superb, terrific, tremendous, wonderful
≠ terrible

Great Britain NOUN Great Britain is the largest of the British Isles, consisting of England, Scotland and Wales.

great-grandfather NOUN Your great-grandfather is your father's or mother's grandfather.

great-grandmother NOUN Your great-grandmother is your father's or mother's grandmother.

greed NOUN Greed is a desire for more of something than you really need.

greedy, **greedier**, **greediest** ADJECTIVE wanting more of something than you really need. **greedily** ADVERB **greediness** NOUN

greedy ADJECTIVE
= materialistic, snoep (*South African; informal*)

Greek ADJECTIVE ① belonging or relating to Greece. ▸ NOUN ② someone who comes from Greece. ③ Greek is the main language spoken in Greece.

green ADJECTIVE, NOUN ① Green is a colour between yellow and blue on the spectrum. ▶ NOUN ② an area of grass in the middle of a village. ③ A putting green or bowling green is a grassy area on which putting or bowls is played. ④ an area of smooth short grass around each hole on a golf course. ⑤ (*in plural*) Greens are green vegetables. ▶ ADJECTIVE ⑥ 'Green' is used to describe political movements which are concerned with environmental issues. ⑦ (*informal*) Someone who is green is young and inexperienced.

> **green** ADJECTIVE
> ⑥ = conservationist, ecological

greenery NOUN Greenery is a lot of trees, bushes or other green plants together in one place.

greengrocer NOUN a shopkeeper who sells vegetables and fruit.

greenhouse NOUN a glass building in which people grow plants that need to be kept warm.

greenhouse effect NOUN GEOGRAPHY | SCIENCE the gradual rise in temperature in the earth's atmosphere due to heat being absorbed from the sun and being trapped by gases such as carbon dioxide in the air around the earth.

green paper NOUN In Britain, Australia and New Zealand, a green paper is a report published by the government containing proposals to be discussed before decisions are made about them.

greet VERB ① If you greet someone, you say something friendly like 'hello' to them when you meet them. ② If you greet something in a particular way, you react to it in that way • *He was greeted with deep suspicion.*

> **greet** VERB
> ① = meet, receive (*formal*), welcome

greeting NOUN something friendly that you say to someone when you meet them • *Her greeting was warm.*

gregarious [*Said grig-**air**-ee-uss*] ADJECTIVE (*formal*) Someone who is gregarious enjoys being with other people.

grenade NOUN a small bomb, containing explosive or tear gas, which can be thrown.

grew the past tense of **grow**.

grey ADJECTIVE, NOUN ① Grey is a colour between black and white. ▶ ADJECTIVE ② dull and boring • *He's a bit of a grey man.* ▶ VERB ③ If someone is greying, their hair is going grey.
greyness NOUN

greyhound NOUN a thin dog with long legs that can run very fast.

grid NOUN ① a pattern of lines crossing each other to form squares. ② The grid is the network of wires and cables by which electricity is distributed throughout a country.

grief NOUN ① Grief is extreme sadness. ▶ PHRASE ② If someone or something **comes to grief**, they fail or are injured.

> **grief** NOUN
> ① = distress, heartache, misery, sadness, sorrow, unhappiness
> ≠ happiness

grievance NOUN a reason for complaining.

grieve VERB ① If you grieve, you are extremely sad, especially because someone has died. ② If something grieves you, it makes you feel very sad.

> **grieve** VERB
> ① = lament, mourn
> ② = distress, pain, sadden, upset
> ≠ cheer

grievous ADJECTIVE (*formal*) extremely serious • *grievous damage*. **grievously** ADVERB

grill NOUN ① a part on a cooker where food is cooked by strong heat from above. ② a metal frame on which you cook food over a fire. ▶ VERB ③ If you grill food, you cook it on or under a grill. ④ (*informal*) If you grill someone, you ask them a lot of questions in a very intense way.

grille [*Rhymes with* ***pill***]; also spelt **grill** NOUN a metal framework over a window or piece of machinery, used for protection.

grim, **grimmer**, **grimmest** ADJECTIVE ① If a situation or piece of news is grim, it is very unpleasant and worrying • *There are grim times ahead*. ② Grim places are unattractive and depressing. ③ If someone is grim, they are very serious or stern. **grimly** ADVERB

> **grim** ADJECTIVE
> ③ = grave (*formal*), severe, solemn, stern

grimace [*Said* ***grim****-iss or* ***grim****-****mace***] NOUN ① a twisted facial expression indicating disgust or pain. ▶ VERB ② When someone grimaces, they make a grimace.

grime NOUN Grime is thick dirt which gathers on the surface of something. **grimy** ADJECTIVE

grin, **grins**, **grinning**, **grinned** VERB ① If you grin, you smile broadly. ▶ NOUN ② a broad smile. ▶ PHRASE ③ If you **grin and bear it**, you accept a difficult situation without complaining.

grind, **grinds**, **grinding**, **ground** VERB ① If you grind something such as pepper, you crush it into a fine powder. ② If you grind your teeth, you rub your upper and lower teeth together. ▶ PHRASE ③ If something **grinds to a halt**, it stops • *Progress ground to a halt*.

grip, **grips**, **gripping**, **gripped** NOUN ① a firm hold. ② a handle on a bat or a racket. ③ Your grip on a situation is your control over it. ▶ VERB ④ If you grip something, you hold it firmly. ▶ PHRASE ⑤ If you **get to grips with** a situation or problem, you start to deal with it effectively.

> **grip** NOUN
> ① = clasp, grasp, hold
> ③ = clutches, control, influence, power
> ▶ VERB ④ = clutch, grasp, hold

grisly, **grislier**, **grisliest** ADJECTIVE very nasty and horrible • *a grisly murder scene*.

grit, **grits**, **gritting**, **gritted** NOUN ① Grit consists of very small stones. It is put on icy roads to make them less slippery. ▶ VERB ② When workmen grit an icy road, they put grit on it. ▶ PHRASE ③ To **grit your teeth** means to decide to carry on in a difficult situation. **gritty** ADJECTIVE

grizzled ADJECTIVE Grizzled hair is grey. A grizzled person has grey hair.

groan VERB ① If you groan, you make a long, low sound of pain, unhappiness or disapproval. ▶ NOUN ② the sound you make when you groan.

grocer NOUN a shopkeeper who sells many kinds of food and other household goods.

grocery, **groceries** NOUN ① a grocer's shop. ② (*in plural*) Groceries are the goods that you buy in a grocer's shop.

grog NOUN (*informal*) In Australian and New Zealand English, grog is any alcoholic drink.

groin NOUN the area where your legs join the main part of your body at the front.

groom NOUN ① someone who looks after horses in a stable. ② At a wedding, the groom is the bridegroom. ▶ VERB

③ To groom an animal means to clean its fur. ④ If you groom someone for a job, you prepare them for it by teaching them the skills they will need.

groove NOUN a deep line cut into a surface. **grooved** ADJECTIVE

grope VERB ① If you grope for something you cannot see, you search for it with your hands. ② If you grope for something such as the solution to a problem, you try to think of it.

gross ADJECTIVE ① extremely bad • *a gross betrayal*. ② Gross speech or behaviour is very rude. ③ Gross things are ugly • *gross holiday outfits*. ④ Someone's gross income is their total income before any deductions are made. ⑤ The gross weight of something is its total weight including the weight of its container. ▸ VERB ⑥ If you gross an amount of money, you earn that amount in total. **grossly** ADVERB

grotesque [*Said groh-**tesk***] ADJECTIVE ① exaggerated and absurd • *It was the most grotesque thing she had ever heard*. ② very strange and ugly • *grotesque animal puppets*. **grotesquely** ADVERB

grotto, **grottoes** or **grottos** NOUN a small cave that people visit because it is attractive.

ground NOUN ① The ground is the surface of the earth. ② a piece of land that is used for a particular purpose • *the training ground*. ③ The ground covered by a book or course is the range of subjects it deals with. ④ (*in plural*) The grounds of a large building are the land belonging to it and surrounding it. ⑤ (*in plural, formal*) The grounds for something are the reasons for it • *genuine grounds for caution*. ▸ VERB ⑥ (*formal*) If something is grounded in something else, it is based on it. ⑦ If an aircraft is grounded, it has to remain on the ground. ⑧ Ground is the past tense and past participle of **grind**.

> **ground** NOUN
> ① = dirt, earth, land, soil, terrain
> ④ = estate, gardens, land
> ⑤ = basis, cause, excuse, justification, reason

ground floor NOUN The ground floor of a building is the floor that is approximately level with the ground.

grounding NOUN If you have a grounding in a skill or subject, you have had basic instruction in it.

groundless ADJECTIVE not based on reason or evidence • *groundless accusations*.

group NOUN ① A group of things or people is a number of them that are linked together in some way. ② a number of musicians who perform pop music together. ▸ VERB ③ When things or people are grouped together, they are linked together in some way.

> **group** NOUN
> ① = band, bunch, collection, crowd, gang, pack, party, set
> ▸ VERB ③ = arrange, class, classify, organise, sort

grouping NOUN a number of things or people that are linked together in some way.

grouse, **grouse** NOUN a fat brown or grey bird, often shot for sport.

grove NOUN (*literary*) a group of trees growing close together.

grovel, **grovels**, **grovelling**, **grovelled** VERB If you grovel, you behave in an unpleasantly humble way towards someone you regard as important.

grow, **grows**, **growing**, **grew**, **grown** VERB ① To grow means to increase in size or amount. ② If a tree or plant grows somewhere, it is alive there.

③ When people grow plants, they plant them and look after them. ④ If a man grows a beard or moustache, he lets it develop by not shaving. ⑤ To grow also means to pass gradually into a particular state. ⑥ If one thing grows from another, it develops from it. ⑦ (*informal*) If something grows on you, you gradually get to like it. **grow up** VERB When a child grows up, he or she becomes an adult.

grow VERB
① = develop, expand, increase, multiply
≠ shrink
② = flourish, germinate, sprout
⑤ = become, get, turn

growl VERB ① When an animal growls, it makes a low rumbling sound, usually because it is angry. ② If you growl something, you say it in a low, rough, rather angry voice. ▸ NOUN ③ the sound an animal makes when it growls.

grown-up NOUN ① (*informal*) an adult. ▸ ADJECTIVE ② Someone who is grown-up is adult, or behaves like an adult.

growth NOUN ① When there is a growth in something, it gets bigger • *the growth of the fishing industry*. ② Growth is the process by which something develops to its full size. ③ an abnormal lump that grows inside or on a person, animal or plant.

growth NOUN
① = development, enlargement, expansion, increase

grub NOUN ① a wormlike insect that has just hatched from its egg. ② (*informal*) Grub is food.

grubby, **grubbier**, **grubbiest** ADJECTIVE rather dirty.

grudge NOUN ① If you have a grudge against someone, you resent them because they have harmed you in the past. ▸ VERB ② If you grudge someone something, you give it to them unwillingly, or are displeased that they have it.

grudging ADJECTIVE done or felt unwillingly • *grudging admiration*.
grudgingly ADVERB

gruelling ADJECTIVE difficult and tiring • *a gruelling race*.

gruesome ADJECTIVE shocking and horrible • *gruesome pictures*.

gruff ADJECTIVE If someone's voice is gruff, it sounds rough and unfriendly.

grumble VERB ① If you grumble, you complain in a bad-tempered way. ▸ NOUN ② a bad-tempered complaint.

grumble VERB
① = carp, complain, groan, moan, mutter, whine, whinge
▸ NOUN ② = complaint, moan, murmur, objection, protest, whinge

grumpy, **grumpier**, **grumpiest** ADJECTIVE bad-tempered and fed-up.

grumpy ADJECTIVE
= irritable, sulky, sullen, surly

grunt VERB ① If a person or a pig grunts, they make a short, low, gruff sound. ▸ NOUN ② the sound a person or a pig makes when they grunt.

guarantee, **guarantees**, **guaranteeing**, **guaranteed** NOUN ① If something is a guarantee of something else, it makes it certain that it will happen. ② a written promise that if a product develops a fault it will be replaced or repaired free. ▸ VERB ③ If something or someone guarantees something, they make certain that it will happen • *Money may not guarantee success*.
guarantor NOUN

guarantee NOUN
① = assurance, pledge, promise, undertaking, word
▶ VERB ③ = ensure, pledge, promise

guard VERB ① If you guard a person or object, you stay near to them to protect them. ② If you guard a person, you stop them making trouble or escaping. ③ If you guard against something, you are careful to avoid it happening. ▶ NOUN ④ a person or group of people who guard a person, object or place. ⑤ a railway official in charge of a train. ⑥ Any object which covers something to prevent it causing harm can be called a guard • *a fire guard*.

guard VERB
① = defend, protect, safeguard, shelter, shield, watch over
② = patrol, police, supervise
▶ NOUN ④ = sentry, warden

guardian NOUN ① someone who has been legally appointed to look after a child. ② A guardian of something is someone who protects it • *a guardian of the law*. **guardianship** NOUN

guernsey NOUN ① In Australian and New Zealand English, a jersey. ② a sleeveless top worn by an Australian Rules football player.

guerrilla [*Said ger-**ril**-la*]; also spelt **guerilla** NOUN a member of a small unofficial army fighting an official army.

guess VERB ① If you guess something, you form or express an opinion that it is the case, without having much information. ▶ NOUN ② an attempt to give the correct answer to something without having much information, or without working it out properly.

guess VERB
① = estimate, imagine, reckon (*informal*), speculate, suppose, suspect, think
▶ NOUN ② = feeling, reckoning, speculation

guest NOUN ① someone who stays at your home or who attends an occasion because they have been invited. ② The guests in a hotel are the people staying there.

guidance NOUN Guidance is help and advice.

guide NOUN ① someone who shows you round places, or leads the way through difficult country. ② a book which gives you information or instructions • *a Sydney street guide*. ③ A Guide is a girl who is a member of an organisation that encourages discipline and practical skills. ▶ VERB ④ If you guide someone in a particular direction, you lead them in that direction. ⑤ If you are guided by something, it influences your actions or decisions.

guide VERB
④ = accompany, direct, escort, lead
⑤ = counsel (*formal*), govern, influence

guidebook NOUN a book which gives information about a place.

guide dog NOUN a dog that has been trained to lead a blind person.

guideline NOUN a piece of advice about how something should be done.

guild NOUN a society of people • *the Screen Writers' Guild*.

guile [*Rhymes with **mile***] NOUN Guile is cunning and deceit. **guileless** ADJECTIVE

guillotine [*Said **gil**-lot-teen*] NOUN ① HISTORY In the past, the guillotine was a machine used for beheading people, especially in France. It was named after Joseph-Ignace Guillotin, who first recommended its use. ② A guillotine is also a piece of equipment with a long sharp blade, used for cutting paper.

guilt NOUN ① Guilt is an unhappy feeling of having done something wrong. ② Someone's guilt is the fact that they have done something wrong • *The law will decide their guilt.*

guilty, guiltier, guiltiest ADJECTIVE ① If you are guilty of doing something wrong, you did it • *He was guilty of theft.* ② If you feel guilty, you are unhappy because you have done something wrong. **guiltily** ADVERB

> **guilty** ADJECTIVE
> ① = convicted, criminal
> ≠ innocent
> ② = ashamed, regretful, remorseful (*formal*), sorry

guinea [*Said **gin**-ee*] NOUN an old British unit of money, worth 21 shillings.

guinea pig NOUN ① a small furry animal without a tail, often kept as a pet. ② a person used to try something out on • *a guinea pig for a new drug.*

guise [*Rhymes with **prize***] NOUN a misleading appearance • *political statements in the guise of religious talk.*

guitar NOUN a musical instrument with six strings which are strummed or plucked. **guitarist** NOUN

gulf NOUN ① GEOGRAPHY a very large bay. ② a wide gap or difference between two things or people.

gull NOUN a sea bird with long wings, white and grey or black feathers, and webbed feet.

gullible ADJECTIVE easily tricked. **gullibility** NOUN

> **gullible** ADJECTIVE
> = naive, trusting
> ≠ suspicious

gully, gullies NOUN a long, narrow valley.

gulp VERB ① If you gulp food or drink, you swallow large quantities of it. ② If you gulp, you swallow air, because you are nervous. ▶ NOUN ③ A gulp of food or drink is a large quantity of it swallowed at one time.

gum NOUN ① Gum is a soft flavoured substance that people chew but do not swallow. ② Gum is also glue for sticking paper. ③ Your gums are the firm flesh in which your teeth are set.

gun NOUN a weapon which fires bullets or shells.

gunfire NOUN Gunfire is the repeated firing of guns.

gunpowder NOUN Gunpowder is an explosive powder made from a mixture of potassium nitrate and other substances.

gunshot NOUN the sound of a gun being fired.

gurgle VERB ① To gurgle means to make a bubbling sound. ▶ NOUN ② a bubbling sound.

guru [*Said **goo**-rooh*] NOUN RE a spiritual leader and teacher, especially in India.

gush VERB ① When liquid gushes from something, it flows out of it in large quantities. ② When people gush, they express admiration or pleasure in an exaggerated way. **gushing** ADJECTIVE

> **gush** VERB
> ① = flow, pour, spurt, stream

gust NOUN a sudden rush of wind. **gusty** ADJECTIVE

gusto NOUN Gusto is energy and enthusiasm • *Her gusto for life was amazing.*

gut, guts, gutting, gutted NOUN (*in plural*) ① Your guts are your internal organs, especially your intestines. ② (*informal*) Guts is courage. ▶ VERB ③ To gut a dead fish means to remove its internal organs. ④ If a building is gutted, the inside of it is destroyed, especially by fire.

gutter NOUN ① the edge of a road next to the pavement, where rain collects and flows away. ② a channel fixed to the edge of a roof, where rain collects and flows away. **guttering** NOUN

guy NOUN ① (*informal*) a man or boy. ② a crude model of Guy Fawkes, that is burnt on top of a bonfire on Guy Fawkes Day (November 5).

guzzle VERB To guzzle something means to drink or eat it quickly and greedily.

gym NOUN ① a gymnasium. ② [PE] Gym is gymnastics.

gymnasium NOUN a room with special equipment for physical exercises.

gymnast NOUN someone who is trained in gymnastics. **gymnastic** ADJECTIVE

gymnastics NOUN [PE] Gymnastics is physical exercises, especially ones using equipment such as bars and ropes.

gynaecology [*Said gie-nak-**kol**-loj-ee*]; also spelt **gynecology** NOUN Gynaecology is the branch of medical science concerned with the female reproductive system. **gynaecologist** NOUN **gynaecological** ADJECTIVE

Hh

habit NOUN ① something that you do often • *He got into the habit of eating out.* ② something that you keep doing and find it difficult to stop doing • *a habit of picking at her spots.* ③ A monk's or nun's habit is a garment like a loose dress. **habitual** ADJECTIVE **habitually** ADVERB

> **habit** NOUN
> ① = convention, custom, practice, routine, tradition

habitat NOUN GEOGRAPHY the natural home of a plant or animal.

> **habitat** NOUN
> = environment, territory

hack VERB ① If you hack at something, you cut it using rough strokes. ② If you hack into a computer system, you gain access to it without permission. ▸ NOUN ③ a writer or journalist who produces work fast without worrying about quality.

hacker NOUN someone who uses a computer to break into the computer system of a company or government.

hackles PLURAL NOUN ① A dog's hackles are the hairs on the back of its neck which rise when it is angry. ▸ PHRASE ② Something that **makes your hackles rise** makes you angry.

hackneyed ADJECTIVE A hackneyed phrase is meaningless because it has been used too often.

> **hackneyed** ADJECTIVE
> = banal, clichéd, stale, tired, trite
> ≠ original

had the past tense and past participle of **have**.

haddock, **haddocks** NOUN an edible sea fish.

haemoglobin *[Said hee-moh-**gloh**-bin]* NOUN SCIENCE Haemoglobin is a substance in red blood cells which carries oxygen round the body.

haemorrhage *[Said **hem**-er-rij]* NOUN A haemorrhage is serious bleeding especially inside a person's body.

haggard ADJECTIVE A person who is haggard looks very tired and ill.

haggis NOUN Haggis is a Scottish dish made of the internal organs of a sheep, boiled together with oatmeal and spices in a skin.

haggle VERB If you haggle with someone, you argue with them, usually about the cost of something.

hail NOUN ① Hail is frozen rain. ② A hail of things is a lot of them falling together • *a hail of bullets* • *a hail of protest.* ▸ VERB ③ When it is hailing, frozen rain is falling. ④ If someone hails you, they call you to attract your attention or greet you • *He hailed a taxi.*

> **hail** NOUN
> ② = barrage, bombardment, shower, storm, volley
> ▸ VERB ④ = call, signal to, wave down

hair NOUN Hair consists of the long, threadlike strands that grow from the skin of animals and humans.

haircut NOUN the cutting of someone's hair; also the style in which it is cut.

hairdo, **hairdos** NOUN a hairstyle.

hairdresser NOUN someone who is trained to cut and style people's hair; also a shop where this is done. **hairdressing** NOUN, ADJECTIVE

hairline NOUN ① the edge of the area on your forehead where your hair grows. ▸ ADJECTIVE ② A hairline crack is so fine that you can hardly see it.

hairpin NOUN ① a U-shaped wire used to hold hair in position. ▸ ADJECTIVE ② A hairpin bend is a U-shaped bend in the road.

hair-raising ADJECTIVE very frightening or exciting.

hairstyle NOUN Someone's hairstyle is the way in which their hair is arranged or cut.

hairy, **hairier**, **hairiest** ADJECTIVE ① covered in a lot of hair. ② (*informal*) difficult, exciting and rather frightening • *He had lived through many hairy adventures.*

hajj [*Rhymes with* ***badge***] NOUN RE The hajj is the pilgrimage to Mecca that every Muslim must make at least once in their life if they are healthy and wealthy enough to do so.

haka NOUN ① In New Zealand, a haka is a ceremonial Māori dance made up of various postures and accompanied by a chant. ② an imitation of this dance performed by New Zealand sports teams before matches as a challenge.

halcyon [*Said* ***hal****-see-on*] ADJECTIVE ① (*literary*) peaceful, gentle and calm • *halcyon colours of yellow and turquoise.* ▸ PHRASE ② **Halcyon days** are a happy and carefree time in the past • *halcyon days in the sun.*

half NOUN, ADJECTIVE, ADVERB ① Half refers to one of two equal parts that make up a whole • *the two halves of the brain* • *They chatted for another half hour* • *The bottle was only half full.* ▸ ADVERB ② You can use 'half' to say that something is only partly true • *I half expected him to explode in anger.*

half-baked ADJECTIVE (*informal*) Half-baked ideas or plans have not been properly thought out.

half-brother NOUN Your half-brother is the son of either your mother or your father but not of your other parent.

half-hearted ADJECTIVE showing no real effort or enthusiasm.

half-sister NOUN Your half-sister is the daughter of either your mother or your father but not of your other parent.

half-time NOUN Half-time is a short break between two parts of a game when the players have a rest.

halfway ADVERB at the middle of the distance between two points in place or time • *He stopped halfway down the ladder* • *halfway through the term.*

halibut NOUN a large edible flat fish.

hall NOUN ① the room just inside the front entrance of a house which leads into other rooms. ② a large room or building used for public events • *a concert hall.*

hallmark NOUN ① The hallmark of a person or group is their most typical quality • *A warm, hospitable welcome is the hallmark of island people.* ② an official mark on gold or silver indicating the quality of the metal.

hallowed [*Said* ***hal****-lode*] ADJECTIVE respected as being holy • *hallowed ground.*

Halloween NOUN Halloween is October 31st, and is celebrated by children dressing up, often as ghosts and witches.

hallucinate [*Said hal-****loo****-sin-ate*] VERB If you hallucinate, you see strange things in your mind because of illness or drugs. **hallucination** NOUN **hallucinatory** ADJECTIVE

halo, haloes or **halos** NOUN a circle of light around the head of a holy figure.

halt VERB ① To halt when moving means to stop. ② To halt development or action means to stop it. ▶ NOUN ③ a short standstill.

halt VERB
① = draw up, pull up, stop
② = cease, check, curb, cut short, end, terminate (*formal*)
≠ begin
▶ NOUN ③ = close, end, pause, standstill, stop, stoppage

halter NOUN a strap fastened round a horse's head so that it can be led easily.

halve [*Said* ***hahv***] VERB ① If you halve something, you divide it into two equal parts. ② To halve something also means to reduce its size or amount by half.

ham NOUN ① Ham is meat from the hind leg of a pig, salted and cured. ② (*informal*) a bad actor who exaggerates emotions and gestures. ③ someone who is interested in amateur radio.

hamburger NOUN a flat disc of minced meat, seasoned and fried; often eaten in a bread roll.

hammer NOUN ① a tool consisting of a heavy piece of metal at the end of a handle, used for hitting nails into things. ▶ VERB ② If you hammer something, you hit it repeatedly, with a hammer or with your fist. ③ If you hammer an idea into someone, you keep repeating it and telling them about it. ④ (*informal*) If you hammer someone, you criticise or attack them severely.

hammock NOUN a piece of net or canvas hung between two supports and used as a bed.

hamper NOUN ① a rectangular wicker basket with a lid, used for carrying food. ▶ VERB ② If you hamper someone, you make it difficult for them to move or progress.

hamper VERB
② = frustrate, hinder, impede, obstruct, restrict

hamster NOUN a small furry rodent which is often kept as a pet.

hamstring NOUN [PE] Your hamstring is a tendon behind your knee joining your thigh muscles to the bones of your lower leg.

hand NOUN ① Your hand is the part of your body beyond the wrist, with four fingers and a thumb. ② Your hand is also your writing style. ③ The hand of someone in a situation is their influence or the part they play in it • *He had a hand in its design.* ④ If you give someone a hand, you help them to do something. ⑤ When an audience gives someone a big hand, they applaud. ⑥ The hands of a clock or watch are the pointers that point to the numbers. ⑦ In cards, your hand is the cards you are holding. ▶ VERB ⑧ If you hand something to someone, you give it to them. ▶ PHRASE ⑨ Something that is **at hand, to hand** or **on hand** is available, close by, and ready for use. ⑩ You use **on the one hand** to introduce the first part of an argument or discussion with two different points of view. ⑪ You use **on the other hand** to introduce the second part of an argument or discussion with two different points of view. ⑫ If you do something **by hand**, you do it using your hands rather than a machine.
hand down VERB Something that is handed down is passed from one generation to another.

▶ **hand down** = bequeath, give, pass down, pass on

A B C D E F G H I J K L M N O P Q R S T U V W X Y Z

handbag NOUN a small bag used mainly by women to carry money and personal items.

handbook NOUN a book giving information and instructions about something.

handcuff NOUN Handcuffs are two metal rings linked by a chain which are locked around a prisoner's wrists.

handful NOUN ① A handful of something is the amount of it you can hold in your hand • *He picked up a handful of seeds.* ② a small quantity • *Only a handful of people knew.* ③ Someone who is a handful is difficult to control • *He is a bit of a handful.*

handicap, handicaps, handicapping, handicapped NOUN ① (*old-fashioned, offensive*) a physical or mental disability. ② something that makes it difficult for you to achieve something. ③ In sport, a handicap is a disadvantage or advantage given to competitors according to their skill, in order to give them an equal chance of winning. ▸ VERB ④ If something handicaps someone, it makes it difficult for them to achieve something.

> **handicap** NOUN
> ② = barrier, disadvantage, drawback, hindrance, impediment, obstacle
> ▸ VERB ④ = burden, hamper, hinder, impede, restrict

handiwork NOUN Your handiwork is something that you have done or made yourself.

handkerchief NOUN a small square of fabric used for blowing your nose.

handle NOUN ① The handle of an object is the part by which it is held or controlled. ② a small lever used to open and close a door or window. ▸ VERB ③ If you handle an object, you hold it in your hands to examine it. ④ If you handle something, you deal with it or control it • *I have learned how to handle pressure.*

> **handle** NOUN
> ① = grip, hilt
> ▸ VERB ③ = feel, finger, grasp, hold, touch
> ④ = administer, conduct, deal with, manage, supervise, take care of

handlebar NOUN Handlebars are the bar and handles at the front of a bicycle, used for steering.

handout NOUN ① a gift of food, clothing or money given to a person in need. ② a piece of paper giving information about something.

hand-picked ADJECTIVE carefully chosen • *a hand-picked team of bodyguards.*

handset NOUN The handset of a telephone is the part that you speak into and listen with.

handshake NOUN the grasping and shaking of a person's hand by another person.

handsome ADJECTIVE ① very attractive in appearance. ② large and generous • *a handsome profit.*
handsomely ADVERB

> **handsome** ADJECTIVE
> ① = attractive, good-looking
> ≠ ugly
> ② = ample, considerable, generous, liberal, plentiful, sizable, sizeable
> ≠ small

handwriting NOUN Someone's handwriting is their style of writing as it looks on the page.

handy, handier, handiest ADJECTIVE ① conveniently near. ② easy to handle or use. ③ skilful.

> **handy** ADJECTIVE
> ① = at hand, at your fingertips, close, convenient, nearby, on hand
> ② = convenient, easy to use, helpful, neat, practical, useful, user-friendly

hang, **hangs**, **hanging**, **hung** VERB ① If you hang something somewhere, you attach it to a high point • *She hung heavy red velvet curtains in the sitting room.* ② If something is hanging on something, it is attached by its top to it • *His jacket hung from a hook behind the door.* ③ If a future event or possibility is hanging over you, it worries or frightens you • *She has an eviction notice hanging over her.* ④ When you hang wallpaper, you stick it onto a wall. ⑤ To hang someone means to kill them by suspending them by a rope around the neck. ▶ PHRASE ⑥ When you **get the hang of something**, you understand it and are able to do it. **hang about** or **hang around** VERB ① (*informal*) To hang about or hang around means to wait somewhere. ② To hang about or hang around with someone means to spend a lot of time with them. **hang back** VERB To hang back means to wait or hesitate. **hang on** VERB ① If you hang on to something, you hold it tightly or keep it. ② (*informal*) To hang on means to wait. **hang out** VERB (*informal*) If you hang out somewhere or with someone, you spend a lot of time there or with them. **hang up** VERB When you hang up, you end a telephone call.

> **hang** VERB
> ① = attach, drape, fasten, fix, suspend
> ② = dangle, droop

hangar NOUN a large building where aircraft are kept.

hangover NOUN a feeling of sickness and headache after drinking too much alcohol.

hanker VERB If you hanker after something, you continually want it. **hankering** NOUN

hanky, **hankies** NOUN a handkerchief.

Hanukkah [*Said* ***hah**-na-ka*]; also spelt **Chanukah** NOUN RE Hanukkah is an eight-day Jewish festival of lights.

haphazard [*Said hap-**haz**-ard*] ADJECTIVE not organised or planned. **haphazardly** ADVERB

hapless ADJECTIVE (*literary*) unlucky.

happen VERB ① When something happens, it occurs or takes place. ② If you happen to do something, you do it by chance. **happening** NOUN

> **happen** VERB
> ① = come about, follow, occur, result, take place

happiness NOUN a feeling of great contentment or pleasure.

> **happiness** NOUN
> = delight, ecstasy, elation, joy, pleasure, satisfaction
> ≠ sadness

happy, **happier**, **happiest** ADJECTIVE ① feeling, showing or producing contentment or pleasure • *a happy smile* • *a happy atmosphere.* ② satisfied that something is right • *I wasn't very happy about the layout.* ③ willing • *I would be happy to help.* ④ fortunate or lucky • *a happy coincidence.* **happily** ADVERB

> **happy** ADJECTIVE
> ① = cheerful, delighted, jolly, joyful, jubilant, merry
> ≠ sad
> ④ = auspicious, convenient, favourable, fortunate, lucky, opportune, timely
> ≠ unlucky

happy-go-lucky ADJECTIVE carefree and unconcerned.

harass [*Said **har**-rass*] VERB If someone harasses you, they trouble or annoy you continually. **harassed** ADJECTIVE **harassment** NOUN

harbinger [*Said **har**-bin-jer*] NOUN a person or thing that announces or indicates the approach of a future event • *The cold wind was a harbinger of winter.*

harbour NOUN ① a protected area of deep water where boats can be moored. ▸ VERB ② To harbour someone means to hide them secretly in your house. ③ If you harbour a feeling, you have it for a long time • *She's still harbouring great bitterness.*

hard ADJECTIVE ① Something that is hard is firm, solid or stiff • *a hard piece of cheese.* ② requiring a lot of effort • *hard work.* ③ difficult • *That is a hard question.* ④ Someone who is hard has no kindness or pity • *Don't be hard on him.* ⑤ A hard colour or voice is harsh and unpleasant. ⑥ Hard evidence or facts can be proved to be true. ⑦ Hard water contains a lot of lime and does not easily produce a lather. ▸ ADVERB ⑧ earnestly or intently • *They tried hard to attract tourists.* ⑨ An event that follows hard upon something takes place immediately afterwards.
hardness NOUN

> **hard** ADJECTIVE
> ① = firm, rigid, solid, stiff, strong, tough
> ≠ soft
> ② = arduous, exhausting, laborious, rigorous, strenuous, tough
> ≠ easy
> ③ = baffling, complex, complicated, difficult, puzzling
> ≠ simple

hard and fast ADJECTIVE fixed and not able to be changed • *hard and fast rules.*

hardback NOUN a book with a stiff cover.

hard core NOUN The hard core in an organisation is the group of people who most resist change.

harden VERB To harden means to become hard or get harder.
hardening NOUN **hardened** ADJECTIVE

> **harden** VERB
> = bake, cake, freeze, set, stiffen
> ≠ soften

hard labour NOUN physical work which is difficult and tiring, used in some countries as a punishment for a crime.

hardly ADVERB ① almost not or not quite • *I could hardly believe it.* ② certainly not • *It's hardly a secret.*

> **hardly** ADVERB
> ① = barely, just, only just, scarcely

hard-nosed ADJECTIVE tough, practical and realistic.

hardship NOUN Hardship is a time or situation of suffering and difficulty.

> **hardship** NOUN
> = adversity, destitution, difficulty, misfortune, want

hard shoulder NOUN the area at the edge of a motorway where a driver can stop in the event of a breakdown.

hard up ADJECTIVE (*informal*) having hardly any money.

hardware NOUN ① Hardware is tools and equipment for use in the home and garden. ② [ICT] Hardware is also computer machinery rather than computer programs.

hard-wearing ADJECTIVE strong, well-made and long-lasting.

hardwood NOUN strong, hard wood from a tree such as an oak; also the tree itself.

hardy, **hardier**, **hardiest** ADJECTIVE tough and able to endure very difficult or cold conditions • *The environment produced hardy and independent people.* **hardiness** NOUN

hare NOUN ① an animal like a large rabbit, but with longer ears and legs. ▸ VERB ② To hare means to run very fast • *He hared off down the corridor.*

harem *[Said har-**reem**]* NOUN in the past, the place in a Muslim house or palace where the women lived.

hark VERB ① *(old-fashioned)* To hark means to listen. ② To hark back to something in the past means to refer back to it or recall it.

harlequin *[Said **har**-lik-win]* ADJECTIVE having many different colours.

harm VERB ① To harm someone or something means to injure or damage them. ▶ NOUN ② Harm is injury or damage.

> **harm** VERB
> ① = abuse, damage, hurt, ill-treat, ruin, wound
> ▶ NOUN ② = abuse, damage, hurt, injury

harmful ADJECTIVE having a bad effect on something • *Whilst most stress is harmful, some is beneficial.*

> **harmful** ADJECTIVE
> = damaging, destructive, detrimental, hurtful, pernicious
> ≠ harmless

harmless ADJECTIVE ① safe to use or be near. ② unlikely to cause problems or annoyance • *He's harmless really.*
harmlessly ADVERB

> **harmless** ADJECTIVE
> ① = innocuous, nontoxic, not dangerous, safe
> ≠ harmful

harmonic ADJECTIVE using musical harmony.

harmonica NOUN a small musical instrument which you play by blowing and sucking while moving it across your lips.

harmonious *[Said har-**moh**-nee-uss]* ADJECTIVE ① showing agreement, peacefulness and friendship • *a harmonious relationship.* ② consisting of parts which blend well together making an attractive whole • *harmonious interior decor.*
harmoniously ADVERB

harmony, **harmonies** NOUN ① Harmony is a state of peaceful agreement and cooperation • *the promotion of racial harmony.* ② MUSIC Harmony is the structure and relationship of chords in a piece of music. ③ Harmony is the pleasant combination of two or more notes played at the same time.

harness NOUN ① a set of straps and fittings fastened round a horse so that it can pull a vehicle, or fastened round someone's body to attach something • *a safety harness.* ▶ VERB ② If you harness something, you bring it under control to use it • *harnessing your natural energy.*

harp NOUN ① a musical instrument consisting of a triangular frame with vertical strings which you pluck with your fingers. ▶ VERB ② *(informal)* If someone harps on about something, they keep talking about it, especially in a boring way. **harpist** NOUN

harpoon NOUN a barbed spear attached to a rope, thrown or fired from a gun and used for catching whales or large fish.

harpsichord NOUN a musical instrument like a small piano, with strings which are plucked when the keys are pressed.

harrowing ADJECTIVE very upsetting or disturbing • *a harrowing experience.*

harsh ADJECTIVE severe, difficult and unpleasant • *harsh weather conditions* • *harsh criticism.* **harshly** ADVERB
harshness NOUN

> **harsh** ADJECTIVE
> = austere, cruel, hard, ruthless, severe, stern
> ≠ mild

harvest NOUN ① the cutting and gathering of a crop; also the ripe crop when it is gathered and the time of gathering. ▶ **VERB** ② To harvest food means to gather it when it is ripe. **harvester** **NOUN**

has-been **NOUN** (*informal*) a person who is no longer important or successful.

hash **PHRASE** ① If you **make a hash of** a job, you do it badly. ▶ **NOUN** ② the name for the symbol #. ③ Hash is a dish made of small pieces of meat and vegetables cooked together.

hashtag **NOUN** ICT a word or phrase that is used to indicate the topic of a post on a social networking website.

hassle (*informal*) **NOUN** ① Something that is a hassle is difficult or causes trouble. ▶ **VERB** ② If you hassle someone, you annoy them by repeatedly asking them to do something.

> **hassle** **NOUN**
> ① = bother, effort, inconvenience, trouble, upheaval
> ▶ **VERB** ② = badger, bother, go on at, harass, nag, pester

haste **NOUN** Haste is doing something quickly, especially too quickly.

hasten [*Said* ***hay**-sn*] **VERB** To hasten means to move quickly or do something quickly.

hasty, **hastier**, **hastiest** **ADJECTIVE** done or happening suddenly and quickly, often without enough care or thought. **hastily** **ADVERB**

> **hasty** **ADJECTIVE**
> = brisk, hurried, prompt, rapid, swift

hat **NOUN** a covering for the head.

hatch **VERB** ① When an egg hatches, or when a bird or reptile hatches, the egg breaks open and the young bird or reptile emerges. ② To hatch a plot means to plan it. ▶ **NOUN** ③ a covered opening in a floor or wall.

hatchback **NOUN** a car with a door at the back which opens upwards.

hatchet **NOUN** ① a small axe. ▶ **PHRASE** ② To **bury the hatchet** means to resolve a disagreement and become friends again.

hate **VERB** ① If you hate someone or something, you have a strong dislike for them. ▶ **NOUN** ② Hate is a strong dislike.

> **hate** **VERB**
> ① = abhor (*formal*), be sick of, despise, detest, dislike, loathe
> ≠ love
> ▶ **NOUN** ② = animosity, aversion, dislike, hatred, hostility, loathing
> ≠ love

hateful **ADJECTIVE** extremely unpleasant.

> **hateful** **ADJECTIVE**
> = abhorrent (*formal*), despicable, horrible, loathsome, obnoxious, offensive

hatred [*Said* ***hay**-trid*] **NOUN** Hatred is an extremely strong feeling of dislike.

> **hatred** **NOUN**
> = animosity, antipathy (*formal*), aversion, dislike, hate, revulsion
> ≠ love

hat trick **NOUN** In sport, a hat trick is three achievements, for example when a footballer scores three goals in a match • *Crawford completed his hat trick in the 60th minute.*

haughty, **haughtier**, **haughtiest** [*Rhymes with* ***naughty***] **ADJECTIVE** showing excessive pride • *He behaved in a haughty manner.* **haughtily** **ADVERB**

> **haughty** **ADJECTIVE**
> = arrogant, conceited, disdainful, proud, snobbish, stuck-up (*informal*)
> ≠ humble

haul **VERB** ① To haul something somewhere means to pull it with great effort. ▸ NOUN ② a quantity of something obtained • *a good haul of fish.* ▸ PHRASE ③ Something that you describe as **a long haul** takes a lot of time and effort to achieve • *So women began the long haul to equality.*

haulage [*Said* ***hawl**-lij*] NOUN Haulage is the business or cost of transporting goods by road.

haunches PLURAL NOUN Your haunches are your buttocks and the tops of your legs • *He squatted on his haunches.*

haunt VERB ① If a ghost haunts a place, it is seen or heard there regularly. ② If a memory or a fear haunts you, it continually worries you. ▸ NOUN ③ A person's favourite haunt is a place they like to visit often.

haunted ADJECTIVE ① regularly visited by a ghost • *a haunted house.* ② very worried or troubled • *a haunted expression.*

haunting ADJECTIVE extremely beautiful or sad so that it makes a lasting impression on you • *haunting landscapes.*

have, has, having, had VERB ① Have is an auxiliary verb, used to form the past tense or to express completed actions • *They have never met* • *I have lost it.* ② If you have something, you own or possess it • *We have two tickets for the concert.* ③ If you have something, you experience it, it happens to you, or you are affected by it • *I have an idea!* • *He had a marvellous time.* ④ To have a child or baby animal means to give birth to it • *When is she having the baby?* ▸ PHRASE ⑤ If you **have to** do something, you must do it. If you **had better** do something, you ought to do it.

> **have** VERB
> ② = hold, keep, own, possess
> ③ = endure, enjoy, experience, feel, sustain, undergo

haven [*Said* ***hay**-ven*] NOUN a safe place.

havoc NOUN ① Havoc is disorder and confusion. ▸ PHRASE ② To **play havoc** with something means to cause great disorder and confusion • *Food allergies often play havoc with the immune system.*

hawk NOUN ① a bird of prey with short rounded wings and a long tail. ▸ VERB ② To hawk goods means to sell them by taking them around from place to place.

hawthorn NOUN a small, thorny tree producing white blossom and red berries.

hay NOUN Hay is grass which has been cut and dried and is used as animal feed.

hay fever NOUN Hay fever is an allergy to pollen, causing sneezing and watering eyes.

haystack NOUN a large, firmly built pile of hay, usually covered and left out in the open.

hazard NOUN ① [SCIENCE] a substance, object or action which could be dangerous to you. ▸ VERB ② If you hazard something, you put it at risk • *hazarding the health of his crew.* ▸ PHRASE ③ If you **hazard a guess**, you make a guess. **hazardous** ADJECTIVE

haze NOUN If there is a haze, you cannot see clearly because there is moisture or smoke in the air.

hazel NOUN ① a small tree producing edible nuts. ▸ ADJECTIVE ② greenish brown in colour.

hazy, hazier, haziest ADJECTIVE dim or vague • *hazy sunshine* • *a hazy memory.*

he PRONOUN 'He' is used to refer to a man, boy or male animal.

head NOUN ① Your head is the part of your body which has your eyes, brain and mouth in it. ② Your head is also your mind and mental abilities • *He has a head for figures.* ③ The head of something is the top, start or most important end • *at the head of the table.* ④The head of a group or organisation is the person in charge. ⑤The head on beer is the layer of froth on the top. ⑥The head on a computer or tape recorder is the part that can read or write information. ⑦When you toss a coin, the side called heads is the one with the head on it. ▸VERB ⑧To head a group or organisation means to be in charge • *Bryce heads the aid organisation.* ⑨To head in a particular direction means to move in that direction • *She is heading for the city centre.* ⑩To head a ball means to hit it with your head. ▸PHRASE ⑪If you **lose your head**, you panic. ⑫If you say that someone is **off their head**, you mean that they are mad. ⑬If something is **over someone's head**, it is too difficult for them to understand. ⑭If you **can't make head nor tail of something**, you cannot understand it. **head off** VERB If you head off someone or something, you make them change direction or prevent something from happening • *He hopes to head off a public squabble.*

head NOUN
②= aptitude, brain, common sense, intelligence, mind, wits
③= beginning, front, source, start, top
≠ tail
④= boss, chief, director, leader, manager, president, principal
▸VERB ⑧= be in charge of, control, direct, lead, manage, run

headache NOUN ①a pain in your head. ②Something that is a headache is causing a lot of difficulty or worry • *Homework can be a headache for school students.*

header NOUN A header in soccer is hitting the ball with your head.

heading NOUN a piece of writing that is written or printed at the top of a page or section.

headland NOUN GEOGRAPHY a narrow piece of land jutting out into the sea.

headlight NOUN The headlights on a motor vehicle are the large powerful lights at the front.

headline NOUN ①A newspaper headline is the title of a newspaper article printed in large, bold type. ②The headlines are the main points of the radio or television news.

headmaster NOUN a man who is the head teacher of a school.

headmistress NOUN a woman who is the head teacher of a school.

headphones PLURAL NOUN Headphones are a pair of small speakers which you wear in or over your ears to listen to music without other people hearing.

headquarters NOUN The headquarters of an organisation is the main place or the place from which it is run.

headroom NOUN Headroom is the amount of space below a roof or surface under which an object must pass or fit.

headstone NOUN a large stone standing at one end of a grave and showing the name of the person buried there.

headstrong ADJECTIVE determined to do something in your own way and ignoring other people's advice.

head teacher NOUN the teacher who is in charge of a school.

headway PHRASE If you are **making headway**, you are making progress.

headwind NOUN a wind blowing in the opposite direction to the way you are travelling.

heady, **headier**, **headiest** ADJECTIVE extremely exciting • *the heady days of the civil rights era.*

heal VERB If something heals or if you heal it, it becomes healthy or normal again • *He had a nasty wound which had not healed properly.*

healer, **healers** NOUN a person who heals people.

health NOUN ① PSHE Your health is the condition of your body • *His health is not good.* ② Health is also the state of being free from disease and feeling well.

health NOUN
① = condition, constitution, shape
② = fitness, good condition, wellbeing
≠ illness

health food NOUN food which is free from added chemicals and is considered to be good for your health.

healthy, **healthier**, **healthiest** ADJECTIVE ① PSHE Someone who is healthy is fit and strong and does not have any diseases. ② Something that is healthy is good for you • *a healthy diet.* ③ An organisation or system that is healthy is successful • *a healthy economy.* **healthily** ADVERB

healthy ADJECTIVE
① = fit, in good shape (*informal*), robust, strong, well
≠ ill
② = beneficial, bracing, good for you, nourishing, nutritious, wholesome
≠ unhealthy

heap NOUN ① a pile of things. ② (*in plural, informal*) Heaps of something means plenty of it • *His performance earned him heaps of praise.* ▸ VERB ③ If you heap things, you pile them up. ④ To heap something such as praise on someone means to give them a lot of it.

heap NOUN
① = hoard, mass, mound, pile, stack
② = loads (*informal*), lots (*informal*), plenty, stacks (*informal*), tons (*informal*)
▸ VERB ③ = pile, stack

hear, **hears**, **hearing**, **heard** VERB ① When you hear sounds, you are aware of them because they reach your ears. ② When you hear from someone, they write to you or phone you. ③ When you hear about something, you are informed about it. ④ When a judge hears a case, he or she listens to it in court in order to make a decision on it. ▸ PHRASE ⑤ If you say that you **won't hear of** something, you mean you refuse to allow it. **hear out** VERB If you hear someone out, you listen to all they have to say without interrupting.

hear VERB
① = catch, eavesdrop, heed, listen in, listen to, overhear
③ = ascertain, discover, find out, gather, learn, understand

hearing NOUN ① Hearing is the sense which makes it possible for you to be aware of sounds • *My hearing is poor.* ② a court trial or official meeting to hear facts about an incident. ③ If someone gives you a hearing, they let you give your point of view and listen to you.

hearsay NOUN Hearsay is information that you have heard from other people rather than something that you know personally to be true.

hearse [*Rhymes with **verse***] NOUN a large car that carries the coffin at a funeral.

heart NOUN ① the organ in your chest that pumps the blood around your body. ② Your heart is also thought of as the centre of your emotions. ③ Heart is courage, determination or enthusiasm • *They were losing heart.* ④ The heart of something is the most central and important part of it. ⑤ a shape similar to a heart, used especially as a symbol of love. ⑥ Hearts is one of the four suits in a pack of playing cards. It is marked by a red heart-shaped symbol.

heartache NOUN Heartache is very great sadness and emotional suffering.

heart attack NOUN a serious medical condition in which the heart suddenly beats irregularly or stops completely.

heartbreak NOUN Heartbreak is great sadness and emotional suffering. **heartbreaking** ADJECTIVE

heartbroken ADJECTIVE very sad and emotionally upset • *She was heartbroken when her cat was lost.*

heartburn NOUN Heartburn is a painful burning sensation in your chest, caused by indigestion.

heartening ADJECTIVE encouraging or uplifting • *heartening news.*

heart failure NOUN Heart failure is a serious condition in which someone's heart does not work as well as it should, sometimes stopping completely.

heartfelt ADJECTIVE sincerely and deeply felt • *Our heartfelt sympathy goes out to you.*

hearth [*Said* **harth**] NOUN the floor of a fireplace.

heartless ADJECTIVE cruel and unkind.

heart-rending ADJECTIVE causing great sadness and pity • *a heart-rending story.*

heart-throb NOUN someone who is attractive to a lot of people.

heart-to-heart NOUN a discussion in which two people talk about their deepest feelings.

hearty, **heartier**, **heartiest** ADJECTIVE ① cheerful and enthusiastic • *hearty congratulations.* ② strongly felt • *a hearty dislike for her teacher.* ③ A hearty meal is large and satisfying. **heartily** ADVERB

heat NOUN ① Heat is warmth or the quality of being hot; also the temperature of something that is warm or hot. ② Heat is strength of feeling, especially of anger or excitement. ③ a contest or race in a competition held to decide who will play in the final. ▸ VERB ④ To heat something means to raise its temperature. ▸ PHRASE ⑤ When a female animal is **on heat**, she is ready for mating.

heat NOUN
① = high temperature, warmth
≠ cold
② = excitement, fervour, intensity, passion, vehemence
▸ VERB ④ = reheat, warm up
≠ cool

heater, **heaters** NOUN a piece of equipment or a machine which is used to raise the temperature of something.

heath NOUN an area of open land covered with rough grass or heather.

heather NOUN a plant with small purple or white flowers that grows wild on hills and moorland.

heating NOUN Heating is the equipment used to heat a building; also the process and cost of running the equipment to provide heat.

heatwave NOUN a period of time during which the weather is much hotter than usual.

heave VERB ① To heave something means to move or throw it with a lot of effort. ② If your stomach heaves, you vomit or suddenly feel sick. ③ If you heave a sigh, you sigh loudly. ▸ NOUN ④ If you give something a heave, you move or throw it with a lot of effort.

heaven NOUN ① RE a place of happiness where God is believed to live and where good people are believed to go when they die. ② (*informal*) If you describe something as heaven, you mean that it is wonderful • *The cake was pure heaven.* ▶ PHRASE ③ You say **Good heavens** to express surprise.

> **heaven** NOUN
> ① = next world, paradise
> ≠ hell
> ② = bliss, ecstasy, paradise, rapture

heavenly ADJECTIVE ① relating to heaven • *a heavenly choir.* ② (*informal*) wonderful • *heavenly chocolate ice cream.*

heavy, **heavier**, **heaviest**; **heavies** ADJECTIVE ① great in weight or force • *How heavy are you?* • *a heavy blow.* ② great in degree or amount • *heavy casualties.* ③ solid and thick in appearance • *heavy shoes.* ④ using a lot of something quickly • *The van is heavy on petrol.* ⑤ serious and difficult to deal with or understand • *It all got a bit heavy when the police arrived* • *a heavy speech.* ⑥ Food that is heavy is solid and difficult to digest • *a heavy meal.* ⑦ When it is heavy, the weather is hot, humid and still. ⑧ Someone with a heavy heart is very sad. ▶ NOUN ⑨ (*informal*) a large, strong man employed to protect someone or something. **heavily** ADVERB **heaviness** NOUN

> **heavy** ADJECTIVE
> ① = bulky, massive
> ≠ light
> ⑤ = deep, grave (*formal*), profound, serious, solemn, weighty
> ≠ trivial

heavy-duty ADJECTIVE Heavy-duty equipment is strong and hard-wearing.

heavy-handed ADJECTIVE showing a lack of care or thought and using too much authority • *The demonstration was broken up in a heavy-handed way.*

heavyweight NOUN ① a boxer in the heaviest weight group. ② an important person with a lot of influence.

Hebrew [*Said* ***hee****-broo*] NOUN ① Hebrew is an ancient language now spoken in Israel, where it is the official language. ② In the past, the Hebrews were Hebrew-speaking Jews who lived in Israel. ▶ ADJECTIVE ③ relating to the Hebrews and their customs.

heckle VERB If members of an audience heckle a speaker, they interrupt and shout rude remarks. **heckler** NOUN

hectare NOUN a unit for measuring areas of land, equal to 10,000 square metres or about 2.471 acres.

hectic ADJECTIVE involving a lot of rushed activity • *a hectic schedule.*

hedge NOUN ① a row of bushes forming a barrier or boundary. ▶ VERB ② If you hedge against something unpleasant happening, you protect yourself. ③ If you hedge, you avoid answering a question or dealing with a problem. ▶ PHRASE ④ If you **hedge your bets**, you support two or more people or courses of action to avoid the risk of losing a lot.

hedgehog NOUN a small, brown animal with sharp spikes covering its back.

hedonism [*Said* ***hee****-dn-izm*] NOUN Hedonism is the belief that gaining pleasure is the most important thing in life. **hedonistic** ADJECTIVE

heed VERB ① If you heed someone's advice, you pay attention to it. ▶ NOUN ② If you take or pay heed to something, you give it careful attention.

heed VERB
① = follow, listen to, pay attention to, take notice of
▶ NOUN ② = attention, notice

heel NOUN ① the back part of your foot. ② The heel of a shoe or sock is the part that fits over your heel. ▶ VERB ③ To heel a pair of shoes means to put a new piece on the heel. ▶ PHRASE ④ A person or place that looks **down at heel** looks untidy and in poor condition.

hefty, **heftier**, **heftiest** ADJECTIVE of great size, force or weight • *a hefty fine* • *hefty volumes*.

height NOUN ① The height of an object is its measurement from the bottom to the top. ② a high position or place • *Their nesting rarely takes place at any great height*. ③ The height of something is its peak, or the time when it is most successful or intense • *the height of the tourist season* • *at the height of his career*. ④ MATHS In maths, the height of a triangle is the point where two sides meet at a peak opposite the base.

heighten VERB If something heightens a feeling or experience, it increases its intensity.

heinous [*Said* ***hay**-nuss or **hee**-nuss*] ADJECTIVE evil and terrible • *heinous crimes*.

heir [*Said* ***air***] NOUN A person's heir is the person who is entitled to inherit their property or title.

heiress [*Said* ***air**-iss*] NOUN a female with the right to inherit property or a title.

heirloom [*Said* ***air**-loom*] NOUN something belonging to a family that has been passed from one generation to another.

held the past tense and past participle of **hold**.

helicopter NOUN an aircraft with rotating blades above it which enable it to take off vertically, hover and fly.

helium [*Said* ***hee**-lee-um*] NOUN SCIENCE Helium is an element which is a colourless inert gas. It occurs in some natural gases, and is used in air balloons. Its atomic number is 2 and its symbol is He.

hell NOUN ① RE Hell is the place where souls of evil people are believed to go to be punished after death. ② (*informal*) If you say that something is hell, you mean it is very unpleasant. ▶ INTERJECTION ③ 'Hell' is also a swearword.

hell NOUN
① = abyss, inferno
≠ heaven
② = agony, anguish, misery, nightmare, ordeal

hell-bent ADJECTIVE determined to do something whatever the consequences.

hellish ADJECTIVE (*informal*) very unpleasant.

hello INTERJECTION You say 'Hello' as a greeting or when you answer the phone.

hello INTERJECTION
= gidday (*Australian and New Zealand*), good afternoon (*formal*), good evening (*formal*), good morning (*formal*), hi (*informal*), how do you do? (*formal*)
≠ goodbye

helm NOUN ① The helm on a boat is the position from which it is steered and the wheel or tiller. ▶ PHRASE ② **At the helm** means in a position of leadership or control.

helmet NOUN a hard hat worn to protect the head.

help VERB ① To help someone means to make something easier or better for them. ▶ NOUN ② If you need or give help, you need or give assistance. ③ someone or something that helps you • *He really is a good help.* ▶ PHRASE ④ If you **help yourself** to something, you take it. ⑤ If you **can't help** something, you cannot control it or change it • *I can't help feeling sorry for him.*

help VERB
① = aid, assist, lend a hand, support
▶ NOUN ② = advice, aid, assistance, guidance, helping hand, support

helper NOUN a person who gives assistance.

helper NOUN
= aide, assistant, deputy, henchman, right-hand man, supporter

helpful ADJECTIVE ① If someone is helpful, they help you by doing something for you. ② Something that is helpful makes a situation more pleasant or easier to tolerate. **helpfully** ADVERB

helpful ADJECTIVE
① = accommodating, cooperative, kind, supportive
≠ unhelpful
② = advantageous, beneficial, constructive, profitable, useful

helping NOUN an amount of food that you get in a single serving.

helpless ADJECTIVE ① unable to cope on your own • *a helpless child.* ② weak or powerless • *helpless despair.* **helplessly** ADVERB **helplessness** NOUN

helpless ADJECTIVE
① = defenceless, powerless, unprotected, vulnerable, weak

hem, **hems**, **hemming**, **hemmed** NOUN ① The hem of a garment is an edge which has been turned over and sewn in place. ▶ VERB ② To hem something means to make a hem on it. **hem in** VERB If someone is hemmed in, they are surrounded and prevented from moving.

hemisphere *[Said* ***hem****-iss-feer]* NOUN one half of the earth, the brain or a sphere. **hemispherical** ADJECTIVE

hemp NOUN Hemp is a tall plant, some varieties of which are used to make rope, and others to produce the drug cannabis.

hen NOUN a female chicken; also any female bird.

hence ADVERB ① *(formal)* for this reason • *I was tired when I sat the test, hence I made mistakes.* ② from now or from the time mentioned • *The convention is due to start two weeks hence.*

henceforth ADVERB *(formal)* from this time onwards • *His life henceforth was to revolve around her.*

henchman, **henchmen** NOUN The henchmen of a powerful person are the people employed to do violent or dishonest work for that person.

hepatitis NOUN Hepatitis is a serious infectious disease causing inflammation of the liver.

her PRONOUN, ADJECTIVE 'Her' is used to refer to a woman, girl or female animal that has already been mentioned, or to show that something belongs to a particular female.

herald NOUN ① In the past, a herald was a messenger. ▶ VERB ② Something that heralds a future event is a sign of that event.

herb NOUN a plant whose leaves are used in medicine or to flavour food. **herbal** ADJECTIVE **herbalist** NOUN

herd NOUN ① a large group of animals. ▶ VERB ② To herd animals or people means to make them move together as a group.

here ADVERB ① at, to or in the place where you are, or the place mentioned or indicated. ▶ PHRASE ② **Here and there** means in various unspecified places • *dense forests broken here and there by small towns.*

hereafter ADVERB (*formal*) after this time or point • *the South China Morning Post (referred to hereafter as SCMP).*

hereby ADVERB (*formal*) used in documents and statements to indicate that a declaration is official • *All leave is hereby cancelled.*

hereditary ADJECTIVE passed on to a child from a parent • *a hereditary disease.*

herein ADVERB (*formal*) in this place or document.

heresy, **heresies** [*Said **herr**-ess-ee*] NOUN Heresy is belief or behaviour considered to be wrong because it disagrees with what is generally accepted, especially with regard to religion. **heretic** NOUN **heretical** ADJECTIVE

heritage NOUN the possessions or traditions that have been passed from one generation to another.

hermit NOUN a person who lives alone with a simple way of life, especially for religious reasons.

hernia [*Said **her**-nee-a*] NOUN a medical condition in which part of the intestine sticks through a weak point in the surrounding tissue.

hero, **heroes** NOUN ① the main male character in a book, film or play. ② a person who has done something brave or good.

heroic ADJECTIVE brave, courageous and determined. **heroically** ADVERB

heroin [*Said **herr**-oh-in*] NOUN Heroin is a powerful drug formerly used as an anaesthetic and now taken illegally by some people for pleasure.

heroine [*Said **herr**-oh-in*] NOUN ① the main female character in a book, film or play. ② a woman who has done something brave or good.

heroism [*Said **herr**-oh-izm*] NOUN Heroism is great courage and bravery.

heron NOUN a wading bird with very long legs and a long beak and neck.

herring NOUN a silvery fish that lives in large shoals in northern seas.

hers PRONOUN 'Hers' refers to something that belongs or relates to a woman, girl or female animal.

herself PRONOUN ① 'Herself' is used when the same woman, girl or female animal does an action and is affected by it • *She pulled herself out of the water.* ② 'Herself' is used to emphasise 'she' • *She herself was not a keen gardener.*

hesitant ADJECTIVE If you are hesitant, you do not do something immediately because you are uncertain or worried. **hesitantly** ADVERB

> **hesitant** ADJECTIVE
> = diffident, doubtful, reluctant, unsure, wavering

hesitate VERB To hesitate means to pause or show uncertainty. **hesitation** NOUN

> **hesitate** VERB
> = dither, pause, waver

hessian NOUN Hessian is a thick, rough fabric used for making sacks.

heterosexual [*Said het-roh-**seks**-yool*] NOUN ① a person who is attracted to people of the opposite sex. ▸ ADJECTIVE ② attracted to people of the opposite sex.

hewn ADJECTIVE carved from a substance • *a cave, hewn out of the hillside.*

heyday [*Said **hay**-day*] NOUN The heyday of a person or thing is the period when they are most successful or popular • *Hollywood in its heyday.*

hi INTERJECTION 'Hi!' is an informal greeting.

hiatus, **hiatuses** [*Said high-**ay**-tuss*] NOUN (*formal*) a pause or gap.

hibernate VERB Animals that hibernate spend the winter in a state like deep sleep. **hibernation** NOUN

hibiscus, **hibiscuses** *[Said hie-**bis**-kuss]* NOUN a type of tropical shrub with brightly coloured flowers.

hiccup, **hiccups**, **hiccupping**, **hiccupped** *[Said **hik**-kup]* NOUN ① Hiccups are short, uncontrolled choking sounds in your throat that you sometimes get if you have been eating or drinking too quickly. ② *(informal)* a minor problem. ▶ VERB ③ When you hiccup, you make little choking sounds.

hide, **hides**, **hiding**, **hid**, **hidden** VERB ① To hide something means to put it where it cannot be seen, or to prevent it from being discovered • *He was unable to hide his disappointment.* ▶ NOUN ② the skin of a large animal.

> **hide** VERB
> ① = cache, conceal, secrete, stash *(informal)*
> ▶ NOUN ② = pelt, skin

hideous *[Said **hid**-ee-uss]* ADJECTIVE extremely ugly or unpleasant.
hideously ADVERB

hideout NOUN a hiding place.

hiding NOUN *(informal)* To give someone a hiding means to beat them severely.

hierarchy, **hierarchies** *[Said **high**-er-ar-kee]* NOUN a system in which people or things are ranked according to how important they are.
hierarchical ADJECTIVE

high ADJECTIVE ① tall or a long way above the ground. ② great in degree, quantity or intensity • *high interest rates* • *There is a high risk of failure.* ③ towards the top of a scale of importance or quality • *high fashion.* ④ close to the top of a range of sound or notes • *the human voice reaches a very high pitch.* ▶ ADVERB ⑤ at or to a height. ▶ NOUN ⑥ a high point or level • *Morale reached a new high.* ▶ PHRASE ⑦ *(informal)* Someone who is **on a high** is in a very excited and optimistic mood.

> **high** ADJECTIVE
> ① = elevated, lofty, soaring, steep, tall, towering
> ≠ low
> ② = acute, excessive, extraordinary, extreme, great, severe
> ≠ low

highbrow ADJECTIVE concerned with serious, intellectual subjects.

higher education NOUN Higher education is education at universities and colleges.

high jump NOUN The high jump is an athletics event involving jumping over a high bar.

highlands PLURAL NOUN Highlands are mountainous or hilly areas of land.

highlight VERB ① If you highlight a point or problem, you emphasise and draw attention to it. ▶ NOUN ② The highlight of something is the most interesting part of it • *His show was the highlight of the Festival.* ③ ART a lighter area of a painting, showing where light shines on things. ④ Highlights are also light-coloured streaks in someone's hair.

highly ADVERB ① extremely • *It is highly unlikely I'll be able to replace it.* ② towards the top of a scale of importance, admiration or respect • *She thought highly of him* • *highly qualified personnel.*

high-minded ADJECTIVE Someone who is high-minded has strong moral principles.

Highness NOUN 'Highness' is used in titles and forms of address for members of the royal family other than a king or queen • *Her Royal Highness, Princess Alexandra.*

high-pitched ADJECTIVE A high-pitched sound is high and often rather shrill.

a b c d e f g h i j k l m n o p q r s t u v w x y z

high-rise ADJECTIVE High-rise buildings are very tall.

high school NOUN a secondary school.

high tide NOUN On a coast, high tide is the time, usually twice a day, when the sea is at its highest level.

highway NOUN a road along which vehicles have the right to pass.

hijab NOUN a head-covering worn by some Muslim women.

hijack VERB If someone hijacks a plane or vehicle, they illegally take control of it during a journey. **hijacker** NOUN **hijacking** NOUN

hike NOUN ① a long country walk. ▸ VERB ② To hike means to walk long distances in the country. **hiker** NOUN

hilarious ADJECTIVE very funny. **hilariously** ADVERB

hilarity NOUN Hilarity is great amusement and laughter.

hill NOUN a rounded area of land higher than the land surrounding it. **hilly** ADJECTIVE

hillbilly, **hillbillies** NOUN someone who lives in the country away from other people, especially in remote areas in the southern United States.

hilt NOUN The hilt of a sword or knife is its handle.

him PRONOUN You use 'him' to refer to a man, boy or male animal that has already been mentioned.

himself PRONOUN ① 'Himself' is used when the same man, boy or male animal does an action and is affected by it • *He discharged himself from hospital.* ② 'Himself' is used to emphasise 'he' • *He himself was not keen to join the others.*

hind *[Rhymes with* ***blind****]* ADJECTIVE ① used to refer to the back part of an animal • *the hind legs.* ▸ NOUN ② a female deer.

hinder VERB ① *[Said* ***hin****-der]* If you hinder someone or something, you get in their way and make something difficult for them. ▸ ADJECTIVE ② *[Said* ***hine****-der]* The hinder parts of an animal are the parts at the back.

Hindi *[Said* ***hin****-dee]* NOUN Hindi is a language spoken in northern India.

hindrance NOUN ① Someone or something that is a hindrance causes difficulties or is an obstruction. ② Hindrance is the act of hindering someone or something.

hindsight NOUN Hindsight is the ability to understand an event after it has actually taken place • *With hindsight, I realised how odd he is.*

Hindu *[Said* ***hin****-doo]* NOUN [RE] a person who believes in Hinduism, an Indian religion which has many gods and believes that people have another life on earth after death. **Hinduism** NOUN

hinge NOUN ① the movable joint which attaches a door or window to its frame. ▸ VERB ② Something that hinges on a situation or event depends entirely on that situation or event • *Victory or defeat hinged on her final putt.*

hint NOUN ① an indirect suggestion. ② a helpful piece of advice. ▸ VERB ③ If you hint at something, you suggest it indirectly.

> **hint** NOUN
> ① = clue, indication, intimation, suggestion
> ② = advice, pointer, suggestion, tip
> ▸ VERB ③ = imply, indicate, insinuate, intimate, suggest

hinterland NOUN The hinterland of a coastline or a port is the area of land behind it or around it.

hip NOUN Your hips are the two parts at the sides of your body between your waist and your upper legs.

hippopotamus, **hippopotamuses** or **hippopotami** NOUN a large African animal with thick wrinkled skin and short legs, that lives near rivers.

hippy, **hippies**; also spelt **hippie** NOUN In the 1960s and 1970s hippies were people who rejected conventional society and tried to live a life based on peace and love.

hire VERB ① If you hire something, you pay money to be able to use it for a period of time. ② If you hire someone, you pay them to do a job for you. ▶ PHRASE ③ Something that is **for hire** is available for people to hire.

> **hire** VERB
> ① = charter, lease, rent
> ② = appoint, commission, employ, engage, sign up

hirsute [*Said* **hir**-*syoot*] ADJECTIVE (*formal*) hairy.

his ADJECTIVE, PRONOUN 'His' refers to something that belongs or relates to a man, boy or male animal that has already been mentioned, and sometimes also to any person whose gender is not known.

hiss VERB ① To hiss means to make a long 's' sound, especially to show disapproval or aggression. ▶ NOUN ② a long 's' sound.

historian NOUN a person who studies and writes about history.

historic ADJECTIVE important in the past or likely to be seen as important in the future.

historical ADJECTIVE ① occurring in the past, or relating to the study of the past • *historical events*. ② describing or representing the past • *historical novels*. **historically** ADVERB

history, **histories** NOUN History is the study of the past. A history is a record of the past • *The village is steeped in history* • *my family history*.

histrionic [*Said hiss-tree*-**on**-*ik*] ADJECTIVE ① Histrionic behaviour is very dramatic and full of exaggerated emotion. ② (*formal*) relating to drama and acting • *a young man of marked histrionic ability*.

histrionics PLURAL NOUN Histrionics are dramatic behaviour full of exaggerated emotion.

hit, **hits**, **hitting**, **hit** VERB ① If you hit someone, you strike them forcefully, usually causing hurt or damage. ② If you hit an object, you collide with it. ③ To hit a ball or other object means to make it move by hitting it with something. ④ If something hits you, it affects you badly and suddenly • *The recession has hit the tourist industry hard*. ⑤ If something hits a particular point or place, it reaches it • *The book hit Britain just at the right time*. ⑥ If you hit on an idea or solution, you suddenly think of it. ▶ NOUN ⑦ a person or thing that is popular and successful. ⑧ the action of hitting something • *Give it a good hard hit with the hammer*. ▶ PHRASE ⑨ (*informal*) If you **hit it off** with someone, you become friendly with them the first time you meet them.

> **hit** VERB
> ① = beat, knock, slap, smack, strike, thump, wallop
> ② = bang into, bump, collide with, meet head-on, run into, smash into
> ▶ NOUN ⑧ = blow, knock, rap, slap, smack, stroke

hit and miss ADJECTIVE happening in an unpredictable way or without being properly organised.

hit-and-run ADJECTIVE A hit-and-run car accident is one in which the person who has caused the damage drives away without stopping.

hitch NOUN ① A hitch is a slight problem or difficulty • *The whole process was completed without a hitch* • *an administrative hitch*. ▶ VERB ② (*informal*) If you hitch, you hitchhike • *Which country is the safest to hitch round?* ③ To hitch something somewhere means to hook it or fasten it there • *Each wagon was hitched onto the one in front.* ▸ PHRASE ④ (*informal*) If you **get hitched**, you get married.

hitchhiking NOUN Hitchhiking is travelling by getting free lifts from passing vehicles.

hither (*old-fashioned*) ADVERB ① used to refer to movement towards the place where you are. ▸ PHRASE ② Something that moves **hither and thither** moves in all directions.

hitherto ADVERB (*formal*) until now • *What he was aiming at had not hitherto been attempted.*

HIV NOUN HIV is a virus that reduces people's resistance to illness and can cause AIDS. HIV is an abbreviation for 'human immunodeficiency virus'.

hive NOUN ① a beehive. ② A place that is a hive of activity is very busy with a lot of people working hard. ▸ VERB ③ If part of something such as a business is hived off, it is transferred to new ownership • *The company is poised to hive off its music interests.*

hoard VERB ① To hoard things means to save them even though they may no longer be useful. ▸ NOUN ② a store of things that has been saved or hidden.

> **hoard** VERB
> ① = save, stockpile, store
> ▸ NOUN ② = cache, fund, reserve, stockpile, store, supply

hoarding NOUN a large advertising board by the side of the road.

hoarse ADJECTIVE A hoarse voice sounds rough and unclear. **hoarsely** ADVERB

> **hoarse** ADJECTIVE
> = croaky, gruff, husky, rasping
> ≠ clear

hoax NOUN ① a trick or an attempt to deceive someone. ▸ VERB ② To hoax someone means to trick or deceive them. **hoaxer** NOUN

hob NOUN a surface on top of a cooker which can be heated in order to cook things.

hobble VERB ① If you hobble, you walk awkwardly because of pain or injury. ② If you hobble an animal, you tie its legs together to restrict its movement.

hobby, **hobbies** NOUN something that you do for enjoyment in your spare time.

> **hobby** NOUN
> = diversion, leisure activity, leisure pursuit, pastime

hock NOUN The hock of a horse or other animal is the angled joint in its back leg.

hockey NOUN Hockey is a game in which two teams use long sticks with curved ends to try to hit a small ball into the other team's goal.

hoe, **hoes**, **hoeing**, **hoed** NOUN ① a long-handled gardening tool with a small square blade, used to remove weeds and break up the soil. ▸ VERB ② To hoe the ground means to use a hoe on it.

hog, **hogs**, **hogging**, **hogged** NOUN ① a castrated male pig. ▸ VERB ② (*informal*) If you hog something, you take more than your share of it, or keep it for too long. ▸ PHRASE ③ (*informal*) If you **go the whole hog**, you do something completely or thoroughly in a bold or extravagant way.

hoist VERB ① To hoist something means to lift it, especially using a crane or other machinery. ▸ NOUN ② a machine for lifting heavy things.

hold, **holds**, **holding**, **held** VERB ① To hold something means to carry or keep it in place, usually with your hand or arms. ② Someone who holds power, office or an opinion has it or possesses it. ③ If you hold something such as a meeting or an election, you arrange it and cause it to happen. ④ If something holds, it is still available or valid • *The offer still holds.* ⑤ If you hold someone responsible for something, you consider them responsible for it. ⑥ If something holds a certain number or amount, it can contain that number or amount • *The theatre holds 150 people.* ⑦ If you hold something such as theatre tickets, a telephone call, or the price of something, you keep or reserve it for a period of time • *The line is engaged – will you hold?* ⑧ To hold something down means to keep it or to keep it under control • *I managed to hold down a job for years.* ⑨ If you hold on to something, you continue it or keep it even though it might be difficult • *They are keen to hold on to their culture.* ⑩ To hold something back means to prevent it, keep it under control, or not reveal it • *She failed to hold back the tears.* ▸ NOUN ⑪ If someone or something has a hold over you, they have power, control or influence over you • *The party has a considerable hold over its own leader.* ⑫ a way of holding something or the act of holding it • *He grabbed the rope and got a hold on it.* ⑬ the place where cargo or luggage is stored in a ship or a plane. **holder** NOUN **hold out** VERB If you hold out, you stand firm and manage to resist opposition in difficult circumstances • *The rebels could hold out for ten years.* **hold up** VERB If something holds you up, it delays you.

hold VERB
① = carry, clasp, clutch, embrace, grasp, grip
▸ NOUN ⑪ = control, dominance, sway
⑫ = grasp, grip

holdall NOUN a large, soft bag for carrying clothing.

hole NOUN ① an opening or hollow in something. ② (*informal*) If you are in a hole, you are in a difficult situation. ③ (*informal*) A hole in a theory or argument is a weakness or error in it. ④ In golf, a hole is one of the small holes into which you have to hit the ball. ▸ VERB ⑤ When you hole the ball in golf, you hit the ball into one of the holes.

hole NOUN
① = gap, hollow, opening, pit, split, tear
② = fix (*informal*), hot water (*informal*), mess, predicament, tight spot (*informal*)
③ = defect, error, fault, flaw, loophole

holiday NOUN ① a period of time spent away from home for enjoyment. ② a time when you are not working or not at school. ▸ VERB ③ When you holiday somewhere, you take a holiday there • *She is currently holidaying in Italy.*

holiday NOUN
① = break, leave, recess, staycation (*informal*), time off, vacation

holidaymaker NOUN a person who is away from home on holiday.

holiness NOUN ① Holiness is the state or quality of being holy. ② 'Your Holiness' and 'His Holiness' are titles used to address or refer to the Pope or to leaders of some other religions.

hollow ADJECTIVE ① Something that is hollow has space inside it rather than being solid. ② An opinion or situation that is hollow has no real value or worth • *a hollow gesture.* ③ A hollow sound is dull and has a slight echo • *the hollow sound of his footsteps on the stairs.* ▸ NOUN ④ a hole in something or a part of a surface that is lower than the rest • *It is a pleasant* *village in a lush hollow.* ▶ **VERB** ⑤ To hollow means to make a hollow • *They hollowed out crude dwellings from the soft rock.*

holly **NOUN** Holly is an evergreen tree or shrub with spiky leaves. It often has red berries in winter.

holocaust *[Said* ***hol****-o-kawst]* **NOUN** ① a large-scale destruction or loss of life, especially the result of war or fire. ② HISTORY The Holocaust was the mass murder of the Jews in Europe by the Nazis during World War II.

holster **NOUN** a holder for a hand gun, worn at the side of the body or under the arm.

holy, **holier**, **holiest** **ADJECTIVE** ① RE relating to God or to a particular religion • *the holy city.* ② Someone who is holy is religious and leads a pure and good life.

> **holy** **ADJECTIVE**
> ① = blessed, consecrated, hallowed, sacred, sacrosanct, venerated (*formal*)
> ② = devout, pious, religious, saintly, virtuous
> ≠ wicked

homage *[Said* ***hom****-ij]* **NOUN** Homage is an act of respect and admiration • *The thronging crowds paid homage to their assassinated president.*

home **NOUN** ① Your home is the building or place in which you live or feel you belong. ② a building in which elderly or ill people live and are looked after • *He has been living in a nursing home since his stroke.* ▶ **ADJECTIVE** ③ connected with or involving your home or country • *He gave them his home phone number* • *coverage of both home and overseas news.* **home in** **VERB** If something homes in on a target, it moves directly and quickly towards it.

> **home** **NOUN**
> ① = abode (*old-fashioned*), dwelling (*formal*), house, residence (*formal*)
> ▶ **ADJECTIVE** ③ = domestic, internal, national, native
> ≠ foreign

homeland **NOUN** Your homeland is your native country.

homeless **ADJECTIVE** ① having no home. ▶ **PLURAL NOUN** ② The homeless are people who have no home. **homelessness** **NOUN**

homely, **homelier**, **homeliest** **ADJECTIVE** simple, ordinary and comfortable • *The room was small and homely.*

> **homely** **ADJECTIVE**
> = comfortable, cosy, modest, simple, welcoming
> ≠ grand

homeopathy *[Said home-ee-****op****-path-ee]* **NOUN** Homeopathy is a way of treating illness by giving the patient tiny amounts of a substance that would normally cause illness in a healthy person. **homeopathic** **ADJECTIVE** **homeopath** **NOUN**

homeowner **NOUN** a person who owns the home in which he or she lives.

homesick **ADJECTIVE** unhappy because of being away from home and missing family and friends. **homesickness** **NOUN**

homespun **ADJECTIVE** not sophisticated or complicated • *The book contains simple homespun philosophy.*

homestead **NOUN** a house and its land and other buildings, especially a farm.

homeward or **homewards** **ADJECTIVE, ADVERB** towards home • *the homeward journey.*

homework **NOUN** ① Homework is school work given to pupils to be done in the evening at home. ② Homework is also research and preparation • *You certainly need to do your homework before buying a horse.*

A B C D E F G H I J K L M N O P Q R S T U V W X Y Z

homicide NOUN Homicide is the crime of murder. **homicidal** ADJECTIVE

homing ADJECTIVE A homing device is able to guide itself to a target. An animal with a homing instinct is able to guide itself home.

homosexual NOUN ① a person who is attracted to people of the same sex. ▸ ADJECTIVE ② attracted to people of the same sex. **homosexuality** NOUN

hone VERB ① If you hone a tool, you sharpen it. ② If you hone a quality or ability, you develop and improve it • *He had a sharply honed sense of justice.*

honest ADJECTIVE truthful and trustworthy. **honestly** ADVERB

> **honest** ADJECTIVE
> = law-abiding, reputable, trustworthy, truthful, virtuous
> ≠ dishonest

honesty NOUN Honesty is the quality of being truthful and trustworthy.

honey NOUN ① Honey is a sweet, edible, sticky substance produced by bees. ② 'Honey' means 'sweetheart' or 'darling' • *What is it, honey?*

honeycomb NOUN a wax structure consisting of rows of six-sided cells made by bees for storage of honey and eggs.

honeymoon NOUN a holiday taken by a couple who have just got married.

honeysuckle NOUN Honeysuckle is a climbing plant with fragrant pink or cream flowers.

honk NOUN ① a short, loud sound like that made by a car horn or a goose. ▸ VERB ② When something honks, it makes a short, loud sound.

honorary ADJECTIVE An honorary title or job is given as a mark of respect, and does not involve the usual qualifications or work • *She was awarded an honorary degree.*

honour NOUN ① Your honour is your good reputation and the respect that other people have for you • *This is a war fought by men totally without honour.* ② an award or privilege given as a mark of respect. ③ Honours is a class of university degree which is higher than a pass or ordinary degree. ▸ PHRASE ④ If something is done **in honour of** someone, it is done out of respect for them • *Egypt celebrated frequent minor festivals in honour of the dead.* ▸ VERB ⑤ If you honour someone, you give them special praise or attention, or an award. ⑥ If you honour an agreement or promise, you do what was agreed or promised • *There is enough cash to honour the existing pledges.*

> **honour** NOUN
> ① = decency, goodness, honesty, integrity
> ≠ dishonour
> ② = accolade, commendation, homage, praise, recognition, tribute
> ▸ VERB ⑤ = commemorate, commend, decorate, glorify, praise

honourable ADJECTIVE worthy of respect or admiration • *He should do the honourable thing and resign.*

hood NOUN ① a loose covering for the head, usually part of a coat or jacket. ② a cover on a piece of equipment or vehicle, usually curved and movable • *The mechanic had the hood up to work on the engine.* **hooded** ADJECTIVE

-hood SUFFIX '-hood' is added at the end of words to form nouns that indicate a state or condition • *childhood* • *priesthood.*

hoof, **hooves** or **hoofs** NOUN the hard bony part of certain animals' feet.

hook NOUN ① a curved piece of metal or plastic that is used for catching, holding or hanging things • *picture hooks.* ② a curving movement, for example of the fist in boxing, or of a golf ball. ▸ VERB ③ If you hook one thing onto another, you attach it there using a hook. ▸ PHRASE ④ If you are **let off the hook**, something happens so that you avoid punishment or a difficult situation.

hooked ADJECTIVE addicted to something; also obsessed by something • *hooked on soap operas* • *I'm hooked on exercise*.

hooligan NOUN a destructive and violent young person. **hooliganism** NOUN

> **hooligan** NOUN
> = delinquent, hoon (*Australian and New Zealand; informal*), lout, vandal, yob (*British and Australian; slang*)

hoop NOUN a large ring, often used as a toy.

hooray INTERJECTION another spelling of **hurray**.

hoot VERB ① To hoot means to make a long 'oo' sound like an owl • *hooting with laughter*. ② If a car horn hoots, it makes a loud honking noise. ▸ NOUN ③ a sound like that made by an owl or a car horn.

hooves a plural of **hoof**.

hop, hops, hopping, hopped VERB ① If you hop, you jump on one foot. ② When animals or birds hop, they jump with two feet together. ③ (*informal*) If you hop into or out of something, you move there quickly and easily • *You only have to hop on the ferry to get there*. ▸ NOUN ④ a jump on one leg. ⑤ Hops are flowers of the hop plant, which are dried and used for making beer.

hope VERB ① If you hope that something will happen or hope that it is true, you want it to happen or be true. ▸ NOUN ② Hope is a wish or feeling of desire and expectation • *There was little hope of recovery*. **hopeful** ADJECTIVE **hopefully** ADVERB

> **hope** NOUN
> ② = ambition, dream, expectation

hopeless ADJECTIVE ① having no hope • *She shook her head in hopeless bewilderment*. ② certain to fail or be unsuccessful. ③ bad or inadequate • *I'm hopeless at remembering birthdays* • *hopeless athletes*. **hopelessly** ADVERB **hopelessness** NOUN

> **hopeless** ADJECTIVE
> ② = forlorn, futile, impossible, pointless, useless, vain
> ③ = inadequate, pathetic, poor, useless (*informal*)

hopper NOUN a large, funnel-shaped container for storing things such as grain or sand.

horde [*Rhymes with **bored***] NOUN a large group or number of people or animals • *hordes of tourists*.

horizon [*Said hor-**eye**-zn*] NOUN ① the distant line where the sky seems to touch the land or sea. ② Your horizons are the limits of what you want to do or are interested in • *Travel broadens your horizons*. ▸ PHRASE ③ If something is **on the horizon**, it is almost certainly going to happen or be done in the future • *Political change was on the horizon*.

horizontal [*Said hor-riz-**zon**-tl*] ADJECTIVE [MATHS] flat and parallel with the horizon or with a line considered as a base • *a patchwork of vertical and horizontal black lines*. **horizontally** ADVERB

hormone NOUN a chemical made by one part of your body that stimulates or has a specific effect on another part of your body. **hormonal** ADJECTIVE

horn NOUN ① one of the hard, pointed growths on the heads of animals such as goats. ② a musical instrument made of brass, consisting of a tube that is narrow at one end and wide at the other. ③ On vehicles, a horn is a warning device which makes a loud noise.

hornet NOUN a type of very large wasp.

horoscope *[Said* ***hor****-ros-kope]* NOUN a prediction about what is going to happen to someone, based on the position of the stars when they were born.

horrendous ADJECTIVE very unpleasant and shocking • *horrendous injuries*.

horrible ADJECTIVE ① disagreeable and unpleasant • *A horrible nausea rose within him*. ② causing shock, fear or disgust • *horrible crimes*. **horribly** ADVERB

> **horrible** ADJECTIVE
> ① = awful, disagreeable, horrid (*old-fashioned*), mean, nasty, unpleasant
> ② = appalling, dreadful, grim, gruesome, terrifying

horrid ADJECTIVE (*old-fashioned*) very unpleasant indeed • *We were all so horrid to him*.

horrific ADJECTIVE so bad or unpleasant that people are horrified • *a horrific attack*.

horrify, **horrifies**, **horrifying**, **horrified** VERB If something horrifies you, it makes you feel dismay or disgust • *a crime trend that will horrify parents*. **horrifying** ADJECTIVE

> **horrify** VERB
> = appal, disgust, dismay, outrage, shock, sicken

horror NOUN ① a strong feeling of alarm, dismay and disgust • *He gazed in horror at the knife*. ② If you have a horror of something, you fear it very much • *He had a horror of fire*.

> **horror** NOUN
> ① = alarm, dread, fear, fright, panic, terror
> ② = abhorrence (*formal*), aversion, disgust, hatred, loathing, revulsion

horse NOUN ① a large animal with a mane and long tail, on which people can ride. ② a piece of gymnastics equipment with four legs, used for jumping over.

> **horse** NOUN
> ① = brumby (*Australian and New Zealand*), equine (*formal*), moke (*Australian and New Zealand; slang*), nag (*informal*), pony

horseback NOUN, ADJECTIVE You refer to someone who is riding a horse as someone 'on horseback', or a horseback rider.

horsepower NOUN Horsepower is a unit used for measuring how powerful an engine is, equal to about 746 watts.

horseradish NOUN Horseradish is the white root of a plant made into a hot-tasting sauce, often served cold with beef.

horseshoe NOUN a U-shaped piece of metal, nailed to the hard surface of a horse's hoof to protect it; also anything of this shape, often regarded as a good luck symbol.

horticulture NOUN Horticulture is the study and practice of growing flowers, fruit and vegetables. **horticultural** ADJECTIVE

hose NOUN ① a long flexible tube through which liquid or gas can be passed • *He left the garden hose on*. ▶ VERB ② If you hose something, you wash or water it using a hose • *The street cleaners need to hose the square down*.

hosiery *[Said* ***hoze****-ee-yer-ee]* NOUN Hosiery consists of tights, socks and similar items, especially in shops.

hospice *[Said* ***hoss****-piss]* NOUN a hospital which provides care for people who are dying.

hospitable ADJECTIVE friendly, generous and welcoming to guests or strangers. **hospitality** NOUN

A B C D E F G H I J K L M N O P Q R S T U V W X Y Z

hospital NOUN a place where sick and injured people are treated and cared for.

host NOUN ① The host of an event is the person that welcomes guests and provides food or accommodation for them • *He is a most generous host who takes his guests to the best restaurants in town.* ② The host of a radio or television show is the person who introduces it and talks to other people who take part in it • *the host of a comedy quiz show.* ③ a plant or animal with smaller plants or animals living on or in it. ④ A host of things is a large number of them • *a host of close friends.* ⑤ In the Christian Church, the Host is the consecrated bread used in Mass or Holy Communion. ▸ VERB ⑥ To host an event or programme means to act as its host.

hostage NOUN a person who is illegally held prisoner and threatened with injury or death unless certain demands are met by other people.

hostel NOUN a large building in which people can stay or live • *a hostel for homeless people.*

hostess NOUN a woman who welcomes guests or visitors and provides food or accommodation for them.

hostile ADJECTIVE ① unfriendly, aggressive and unpleasant • *a hostile audience.* ② relating to or involving the enemies of a country • *hostile territory.*

> **hostile** ADJECTIVE
> ① = antagonistic, belligerent, malevolent, unkind
> ≠ friendly

hostility, **hostilities** NOUN aggression or unfriendly behaviour towards a person or thing.

> **hostility** NOUN
> = animosity, antagonism, hatred, ill will, malice, resentment
> ≠ friendship

hot, **hotter**, **hottest** ADJECTIVE ① having a high temperature • *a hot climate.* ② very spicy and causing a burning sensation in your mouth • *a hot curry.* ③ new, recent and exciting • *hot news from Tinseltown.* ④ dangerous or difficult to deal with • *Animal testing is a hot issue.* **hotly** ADVERB

> **hot** ADJECTIVE
> ① = boiling, heated, scalding, scorching, warm
> ≠ cold
> ② = peppery, spicy
> ≠ bland

hotbed NOUN A hotbed of some type of activity is a place that seems to encourage it • *The city was a hotbed of rumour.*

hot dog NOUN a sausage served in a roll split lengthways.

hotel NOUN a building where people stay, paying for their room and sometimes also meals.

hothouse NOUN ① a large heated greenhouse. ② a place or situation of intense intellectual or emotional activity • *a hothouse of radical ideas.*

hot seat NOUN (*informal*) Someone who is in the hot seat has to make difficult decisions for which they will be held responsible.

hound NOUN ① a dog, especially one used for hunting or racing. ▸ VERB ② If someone hounds you, they constantly pursue or trouble you.

hour NOUN ① a unit of time equal to 60 minutes, of which there are 24 in a day. ② The hour for something is the time when it happens • *The hour for launching approached.* ③ The hour is also the time of day • *What are you doing up at this hour?* ④ an important or

difficult time • *The hour has come* • *He is the hero of the hour.* ⑤ *(in plural)* The hours that you keep are the times that you usually go to bed and get up.
hourly ADJECTIVE, ADVERB

house NOUN *[Said* ***hows****]* ① a building where a person or family lives. ② a building used for a particular purpose • *an auction house* • *the opera house.* ③ In a theatre or cinema, the house is the part where the audience sits; also the audience itself • *The show had a packed house calling for more.* ▶ VERB *[Said* ***howz****]* ④ To house something means to keep it or contain it • *The west wing housed a store of valuable antiques.*

house NOUN
① = abode *(old-fashioned)*, building, dwelling *(formal)*, home, residence *(formal)*

houseboat NOUN a small boat which people live on that is tied up at a particular place on a river or canal.

household NOUN ① all the people who live as a group in a house or flat. ▶ PHRASE ② Someone who is **a household name** is very well-known.
householder NOUN

housekeeper NOUN a person who is employed to do the cooking and cleaning in a house.

House of Commons NOUN The House of Commons is the more powerful of the two parts of the British Parliament. Its members are elected by the public.

House of Lords NOUN The House of Lords is the less powerful of the two parts of the British Parliament. Its members are unelected and come from noble families or are appointed by the monarch as an honour for a life of public service.

House of Representatives NOUN ① In Australia, the House of Representatives is the larger of the two parts of the Federal Parliament. ② In New Zealand, the House of Representatives is the Parliament.

housewife, housewives NOUN a married woman who does the chores in her home, and does not have a paid job.

housing NOUN Housing is the buildings in which people live • *the serious housing shortage.*

hover VERB ① When a bird, insect or aircraft hovers, it stays in the same position in the air. ② If someone is hovering, they are hesitating because they cannot decide what to do • *He was hovering nervously around the sick animal.*

hovercraft NOUN a vehicle which can travel over water or land supported by a cushion of air.

how ADVERB ① 'How' is used to ask about, explain or refer to the way in which something is done, known or experienced • *How did this happen?* • *He knew how quickly rumours could spread.* ② 'How' is used to ask about or refer to a measurement or quantity • *How much is it for the weekend?* • *I wonder how old he is.* ③ 'How' is used to emphasise the following word or statement • *How odd!*

however ADVERB ① You use 'however' when you are adding a comment that seems to contradict or contrast with what has just been said • *For all his compassion, he is, however, surprisingly restrained.* ② You use 'however' to say that something makes no difference to a situation • *However hard she tried, nothing seemed to work.*

howl VERB ① To howl means to make a long, loud wailing noise such as that made by a dog when it is upset • *A distant coyote howled at the moon* • *The wind howled through the trees.* ▶ NOUN ② a long, loud wailing noise.

a b c d e f g h i j k l m n o p q r s t u v w x y z

HQ an abbreviation for **headquarters**.

hub NOUN ① the centre part of a wheel. ② the most important or active part of a place or organisation • *The kitchen is the hub of most households.*

hubbub NOUN Hubbub is great noise or confusion • *the general hubbub of conversation.*

huddle VERB ① If you huddle up or are huddled, you are curled up with your arms and legs close to your body. ② When people or animals huddle together, they sit or stand close to each other, often for warmth. ▸ NOUN ③ A huddle of people or things is a small group of them.

hue NOUN ① (*literary*) a colour or a particular shade of a colour. ▸ PHRASE ② If people raise a **hue and cry**, they are very angry about something and protest.

huff PHRASE (*informal*) If you are **in a huff**, you are sulking or offended about something. **huffy** ADJECTIVE **huffily** ADVERB

hug, hugs, hugging, hugged VERB ① If you hug someone, you put your arms round them and hold them close to you. ② To hug the ground or a stretch of water or land means to keep very close to it • *The road hugs the coast for hundreds of miles.* ▸ NOUN ③ If you give someone a hug, you hold them close to you.

> **hug** VERB
> ① = clasp, cuddle, embrace, squeeze
> ▸ NOUN ③ = cuddle, embrace

huge ADJECTIVE extremely large in amount, size or degree • *a huge success* • *a huge crowd.* **hugely** ADVERB

> **huge** ADJECTIVE
> = colossal, enormous, giant, immense, massive, vast
> ≠ tiny

hulk NOUN ① a large, heavy person or thing. ② the body of a ship that has been wrecked or abandoned. **hulking** ADJECTIVE

hull NOUN The hull of a ship is the main part of its body that sits in the water.

hum, hums, humming, hummed VERB ① To hum means to make a continuous low noise • *The generator hummed faintly.* ② If you hum, you sing with your lips closed. ▸ NOUN ③ a continuous low noise • *the hum of the fridge.*

human ADJECTIVE ① relating to, concerning or typical of people • *Intolerance appears deeply ingrained in human nature.* ▸ NOUN ② a person. **humanly** ADVERB

human being NOUN a person.

humane ADJECTIVE showing kindness and sympathy towards others • *Medicine is regarded as the most humane of professions.* **humanely** ADVERB

> **humane** ADJECTIVE
> = benevolent, caring, charitable, compassionate, kind, merciful, thoughtful

humanism NOUN [RE] Humanism is the belief in mankind's ability to achieve happiness and fulfilment without depending on religion or superstition.

humanitarian NOUN ① a person who works for the welfare of mankind. ▸ ADJECTIVE ② concerned with the welfare of mankind • *humanitarian aid.* **humanitarianism** NOUN

humanity NOUN ① Humanity is people in general • *I have faith in humanity.* ② Humanity is also the condition of being human • *He is so full of hatred he has lost his humanity.* ③ Someone who has humanity is kind and sympathetic.

human rights PLURAL NOUN [CITIZENSHIP] Human rights are the rights of individuals to freedom and justice.

humble ADJECTIVE ① A humble person is modest and thinks that he or she has very little value. ② Something that is humble is small, or not very important or special • *Just a splash of this sauce will transform a humble casserole.* ▶ VERB ③ To humble someone means to make them feel humiliated. **humbly** ADVERB **humbled** ADJECTIVE

> **humble** ADJECTIVE
> ① = meek, modest, unassuming
> ≠ haughty
> ② = lowly, modest, ordinary, simple
> ▶ VERB ③ = disgrace, humiliate

humbug NOUN ① a hard black and white striped sweet that tastes of peppermint. ② Humbug is speech or writing that is obviously dishonest or untrue • *hypocritical humbug.*

humdrum ADJECTIVE ordinary, dull and boring • *humdrum domestic tasks.*

humid ADJECTIVE If it is humid, the air feels damp, heavy and warm.

> **humid** ADJECTIVE
> = clammy, muggy, steamy, sticky

humidity NOUN Humidity is the amount of moisture in the air, or the state of being humid.

humiliate VERB To humiliate someone means to make them feel ashamed or appear stupid to other people. **humiliation** NOUN

> **humiliate** VERB
> = disgrace, embarrass, humble, put down, shame

humility NOUN Humility is the quality of being modest and humble.

humour NOUN ① Humour is the quality of being funny • *They discussed it with tact and humour.* ② Humour is also the ability to be amused by certain things • *Helen's got a peculiar sense of humour.* ③ Someone's humour is the mood they are in • *He hasn't been in a good humour lately.* ▶ VERB ④ If you humour someone, you are especially kind to them and do whatever they want. **humorous** ADJECTIVE

> **humour** NOUN
> ① = comedy, wit
> ③ = frame of mind, mood, spirits, temper
> ▶ VERB ④ = flatter, indulge, mollify, pander to

hump NOUN ① a small, rounded lump or mound • *a camel's hump.* ▶ VERB ② (*informal*) If you hump something heavy, you carry or move it with difficulty.

hunch NOUN ① a feeling or suspicion about something, not based on facts or evidence. ▶ VERB ② If you hunch your shoulders, you raise your shoulders and lean forwards.

hundred the number 100. **hundredth** ADJECTIVE

hung a past tense and past participle of **hang**.

Hungarian [*Said hung-**gair**-ee-an*] ADJECTIVE ① belonging or relating to Hungary. ▶ NOUN ② someone who comes from Hungary. ③ Hungarian is the main language spoken in Hungary.

hunger NOUN ① Hunger is the need to eat or the desire to eat. ② A hunger for something is a strong need or desire for it • *a hunger for winning.* ▶ VERB ③ If you hunger for something, you want it very much.

hunger strike NOUN a refusal to eat anything at all, especially by prisoners, as a form of protest.

hungry, **hungrier**, **hungriest** ADJECTIVE needing or wanting to eat • *People are going hungry.* **hungrily** ADVERB

> **hungry** ADJECTIVE
> = famished, ravenous, starving

hunk NOUN A hunk of something is a large piece of it.

hunt VERB ① To hunt means to chase wild animals to kill them for food or for sport. ② If you hunt for something, you search for it. ▶ NOUN ③ the act of hunting • *Police launched a hunt for an abandoned car.* **hunter** NOUN **hunting** ADJECTIVE, NOUN

hurdle NOUN ① one of the frames or barriers that you jump over in an athletics race called hurdles • *She won the 400-metre hurdles.* ② a problem or difficulty • *Several hurdles exist for anyone seeking to do postgraduate study.*

hurl VERB ① To hurl something means to throw it with great force. ② If you hurl insults at someone, you insult them aggressively and repeatedly.

hurray or **hurrah** or **hooray** INTERJECTION an exclamation of excitement or approval.

hurricane NOUN GEOGRAPHY A hurricane is a violent wind or storm, usually force 12 or above on the Beaufort scale.

hurry, hurries, hurrying, hurried VERB ① To hurry means to move or do something as quickly as possible • *She hurried through the empty streets.* ② To hurry something means to make it happen more quickly • *You can't hurry nature.* ▶ NOUN ③ Hurry is the speed with which you do something quickly • *He was in a hurry to leave.* **hurried** ADJECTIVE **hurriedly** ADVERB

> **hurry** VERB
> ① = dash, fly, get a move on (*informal*), rush, scurry
> ② = accelerate, hasten, quicken, speed up
> ≠ slow down

hurt, hurts, hurting, hurt VERB ① To hurt someone means to cause them physical pain. ② If a part of your body hurts, you feel pain there. ③ If you hurt yourself, you injure yourself. ④ To hurt someone also means to make them unhappy by being unkind or thoughtless towards them • *I didn't want to hurt his feelings.* ▶ ADJECTIVE ⑤ If someone feels hurt, they feel unhappy because of someone's unkindness towards them • *He felt hurt by all the lies.* **hurtful** ADJECTIVE

> **hurt** VERB
> ① = harm, injure, wound
> ④ = distress, sadden, upset, wound
> ▶ ADJECTIVE ⑤ = aggrieved, offended, upset, wounded

hurtle VERB To hurtle means to move or travel very fast indeed, especially in an uncontrolled way.

husband NOUN A person's husband is the man they are married to.

husbandry NOUN ① Husbandry is the art or skill of farming. ② Husbandry is also the art or skill of managing something carefully and economically.

hush VERB ① If you tell someone to hush, you are telling them to be quiet. ② To hush something up means to keep it secret, especially something dishonest involving important people • *The government has hushed up a series of scandals.* ▶ NOUN ③ If there is a hush, it is quiet and still • *A graveyard hush fell over the group.* **hushed** ADJECTIVE

husk NOUN Husks are the dry outer coverings of grain or seed.

husky, huskier, huskiest; huskies ADJECTIVE ① A husky voice is rough or hoarse. ▶ NOUN ② a large, strong dog with a thick coat, often used to pull sledges across snow. **huskily** ADVERB

hustle VERB To hustle someone means to make them move by pushing and jostling them • *The guards hustled him out of the car.*

hut NOUN a small, simple building, with one or two rooms.

hybrid NOUN ① a plant or animal that has been bred from two different types of plant or animal. ② anything that is a mixture of two other things.

hydraulic *[Said high-**drol**-lik]* ADJECTIVE operated by water or other fluid which is under pressure.

hydraulics NOUN Hydraulics is the study and use of systems that work using hydraulic pressure.

hydrogen NOUN SCIENCE Hydrogen is the lightest gas and the simplest chemical element. It is colourless and odourless. Its atomic number is 1 and its symbol is H.

hyena *[Said high-**ee**-na]*; also spelt **hyaena** NOUN a wild doglike animal of Africa and Asia that hunts in packs.

hygiene *[Said **high**-jeen]* NOUN D&T Hygiene is the practice of keeping yourself and your surroundings clean, especially to stop the spread of disease. **hygienic** ADJECTIVE **hygienically** ADVERB

> **hygiene** NOUN
> = cleanliness, sanitation

hymn NOUN RE a Christian song in praise of God.

hyperactive ADJECTIVE A hyperactive person is unable to relax and is always in a state of restless activity.

hyperbole *[Said high-**per**-bol-lee]* NOUN Hyperbole is a style of speech or writing which uses exaggeration.

hypertension NOUN Hypertension is a medical condition in which a person has high blood pressure.

hyphen NOUN ENGLISH a punctuation mark used to join together words or parts of words, as for example in the word 'left-handed'. **hyphenate** VERB **hyphenation** NOUN

hypnosis *[Said hip-**noh**-siss]* NOUN Hypnosis is an artificially produced state of relaxation in which the mind is very receptive to suggestion.

hypocrisy, **hypocrisies** NOUN Hypocrisy is pretending to have beliefs or qualities that you do not really have, so that you seem a better person than you are. **hypocritical** ADJECTIVE **hypocritically** ADVERB **hypocrite** NOUN

hypothermia NOUN SCIENCE Hypothermia is a condition in which a person is very ill because their body temperature has been unusually low for a long time.

hypothesis, **hypotheses** NOUN SCIENCE an explanation or theory which has not yet been proved to be correct.

hypothetical ADJECTIVE based on assumption rather than on fact or reality. **hypothetically** ADVERB

hysterectomy, **hysterectomies** *[Said his-ter-**rek**-tom-ee]* NOUN an operation to remove a woman's womb.

hysteria *[Said hiss-**teer**-ee-a]* NOUN Hysteria is a state of uncontrolled excitement or panic.

hysterical ADJECTIVE ① Someone who is hysterical is in a state of uncontrolled excitement or panic. ② *(informal)* Something that is hysterical is extremely funny. **hysterically** ADVERB **hysterics** NOUN

> **hysterical** ADJECTIVE
> ① = frantic, frenzied, overwrought, raving
> ② = comical, hilarious

Ii

A B C D E F G H I J K L M N O P Q R S T U V W X Y Z

I PRONOUN A speaker or writer uses 'I' to refer to himself or herself • *I like the colour*.

ibis, ibises [*Said* **eye**-*biss*] NOUN a large wading bird with a long, thin, curved bill that lives in warm countries.

-ible SUFFIX another form of the suffix **-able**.

-ic or **-ical** SUFFIX '-ic' and '-ical' form adjectives from nouns. For example, *ironic* or *ironical* can be formed from *irony*.

ice NOUN ① water that has frozen solid. ② an ice cream. ▸ VERB ③ If you ice cakes, you cover them with icing. ④ If something ices over or ices up, it becomes covered with a layer of ice. ▸ PHRASE ⑤ If you do something to **break the ice**, you make people feel relaxed and comfortable.

Ice Age NOUN a period of time lasting thousands of years when a lot of the earth's surface was covered with ice.

iceberg NOUN a large mass of ice floating in the sea.

ice cream NOUN a very cold sweet food made from frozen cream.

ice hockey NOUN a type of hockey played on ice, with two teams of six players.

Icelandic ADJECTIVE ① belonging or relating to Iceland. ▸ NOUN ② the main language spoken in Iceland.

icing NOUN a mixture of powdered sugar and water or egg whites, used to decorate cakes.

icon [*Said* **eye**-*kon*] NOUN ① ICT a picture on a computer screen representing a program that can be activated by moving the cursor over it. ② in the Orthodox Churches, a holy picture of Christ, the Virgin Mary or a saint.

ICT an abbreviation for 'Information and Communication Technology'.

icy, icier, iciest ADJECTIVE ① Something which is icy is very cold • *an icy wind*. ② An icy road has ice on it. **icily** ADVERB

id NOUN In psychology, your id is your basic instincts and unconscious thoughts.

idea NOUN ① a plan, suggestion or thought that you have after thinking about a problem. ② an opinion or belief • *old-fashioned ideas about women*. ③ An idea of something is what you know about it • *They had no idea of their position*.

> **idea** NOUN
> ① = plan, recommendation, scheme, solution, suggestion
> ② = belief, conviction, impression, notion, opinion, view
> ③ = clue, guess, hint, inkling, notion, suspicion

ideal NOUN ① a principle or idea that you try to achieve because it seems perfect to you. ② Your ideal of something is the person or thing that seems the best example of it. ▸ ADJECTIVE ③ The ideal person or thing is the best possible person or thing for the situation.

ideal NOUN
① = principle, standard, value
② = epitome, example, model, paragon, prototype, standard
▸ ADJECTIVE ③ = classic, complete, consummate, model, perfect, supreme

idealism *[Said eye-**dee**-il-izm]* NOUN behaviour that is based on a person's ideals. **idealist** NOUN **idealistic** ADJECTIVE

ideally ADVERB ① If you say that ideally something should happen, you mean that you would like it to happen but you know that it is not likely. ② Ideally means perfectly • *The hotel is ideally placed for business travellers.*

identical ADJECTIVE exactly the same • *identical twins.* **identically** ADVERB

identification NOUN ① The identification of someone or something is the act of identifying them. ② Identification is a document, such as a driving licence or passport, which proves who you are.

identify, **identifies**, **identifying**, **identified** VERB ① To identify someone or something is to recognise them or name them. ② If you identify with someone, you understand their feelings and ideas. **identifiable** ADJECTIVE

identify VERB
① = diagnose, label, name, pinpoint, place, recognise
② = associate with, empathise with, feel for, relate to, respond to

identity, **identities** NOUN ① the characteristics that make you who you are. ② MATHS an equation that is valid for all values of its variables.

ideology, **ideologies** NOUN a set of political beliefs. **ideological** ADJECTIVE **ideologically** ADVERB

idiom NOUN ENGLISH a group of words whose meaning together is different from all the words taken individually. For example, 'It's raining cats and dogs' is an idiom.

idiot NOUN someone who is stupid or foolish.

idiot NOUN
= fool, galah (*Australian; informal*), imbecile, oaf, twit (*informal*)

idiotic ADJECTIVE extremely foolish or silly. **idiotically** ADVERB

idiotic ADJECTIVE
= crazy (*informal*), daft (*British; informal*), dumb (*informal*), foolish, senseless, stupid

idle ADJECTIVE If you are idle, you are doing nothing. **idleness** NOUN **idly** ADVERB

idle ADJECTIVE
= jobless, redundant, unemployed
≠ busy

idol *[Said **eye**-doll]* NOUN ① a famous person who is loved and admired by fans. ② RE a picture or statue which is worshipped as if it were a god.

idyll *[Said **id**-ill]* NOUN a situation which is peaceful and beautiful. **idyllic** ADJECTIVE

i.e. i.e. means 'that is', and is used before giving more information. It is an abbreviation for the Latin expression 'id est'.

if CONJUNCTION ① on the condition that • *I shall stay if I can.* ② whether • *I asked her if she wanted to go.*

igloo, **igloos** NOUN a dome-shaped house built out of blocks of snow by Inuit.

ignite VERB If you ignite something or if it ignites, it starts burning.

ignition NOUN In a car, the ignition is the part of the engine where the fuel is ignited.

ignominious ADJECTIVE shameful or considered wrong • *It was an ignominious end to a brilliant career*. **ignominiously** ADVERB **ignominy** NOUN

ignorant ADJECTIVE ① If you are ignorant of something, you do not know about it • *He was completely ignorant of the rules*. ② Someone who is ignorant does not know about things in general • *I thought of asking, but didn't want to seem ignorant*. **ignorantly** ADVERB **ignorance** NOUN

> **ignorant** ADJECTIVE
> ① = inexperienced, innocent, oblivious, unaware, unconscious
> ② = green (*informal*), naive, unaware

ignore VERB If you ignore someone or something, you deliberately do not take any notice of them.

> **ignore** VERB
> = blank (*slang*), discount, disregard, neglect, overlook

iguana [*Said ig-**wah**-na*] NOUN a large, tropical lizard.

ill ADJECTIVE ① unhealthy or sick. ② harmful or unpleasant • *ill effects*. ▶ PLURAL NOUN ③ Ills are difficulties or problems. ▶ PHRASE ④ If you feel **ill at ease**, you feel unable to relax.

> **ill** ADJECTIVE
> ① = ailing, poorly (*British; informal*), queasy, sick, unhealthy, unwell
> ≠ healthy

illegal ADJECTIVE forbidden by the law. **illegally** ADVERB **illegality** NOUN

> **illegal** ADJECTIVE
> = banned, criminal, illicit, outlawed, prohibited, unlawful
> ≠ legal

illegible [*Said il-**lej**-i-bl*] ADJECTIVE Writing which is illegible is unclear and very difficult to read.

ill-fated ADJECTIVE doomed to end unhappily • *his ill-fated attempt on the world record*.

illicit [*Said il-**liss**-it*] ADJECTIVE not allowed by law or not approved of by society • *illicit drugs*.

illiterate ADJECTIVE unable to read or write. **illiteracy** NOUN

illness NOUN ① Illness is the experience of being ill. ② a particular disease • *the treatment of common illnesses*.

> **illness** NOUN
> ② = affliction, ailment, complaint, disease, disorder, lurgy (*British, Australian and New Zealand; informal*), sickness

illogical ADJECTIVE An illogical feeling or action is not reasonable or sensible. **illogically** ADVERB

illuminate VERB To illuminate something is to shine light on it to make it easier to see.

illumination NOUN ① Illumination is lighting. ② Illuminations are the coloured lights put up to decorate a town, especially at Christmas.

illusion NOUN ① a false belief which you think is true • *Their hopes proved to be an illusion*. ② ART a false appearance of reality which deceives the eye • *Painters create the illusion of space*.

> **illusion** NOUN
> ① = delusion, fallacy, fancy, misconception
> ② = hallucination, mirage, semblance

illusory [*Said ill-**yoo**-ser-ee*] ADJECTIVE seeming to be true, but actually false • *an illusory truce*.

illustrate VERB ① EXAM TERM If you illustrate a point, you explain it or make it clearer, often by using examples. ② If you illustrate a book, you put pictures in it. **illustrator** NOUN **illustrative** ADJECTIVE

illustration NOUN ① an example or a

story which is used to make a point clear. ② a picture in a book.

illustrious ADJECTIVE An illustrious person is famous and respected.

ill will NOUN Ill will is a feeling of hostility.

image NOUN ① a mental picture of someone or something. ② the appearance which a person, group or organisation presents to the public.

imagery NOUN [ENGLISH] The imagery of a poem or book is the descriptive language used in it.

imaginary ADJECTIVE Something that is imaginary exists only in your mind, not in real life.

> **imaginary** ADJECTIVE
> = fictional, fictitious, hypothetical, ideal, illusory, invented, mythological
> ≠ real

imagination NOUN the ability to form new and exciting ideas.

> **imagination** NOUN
> = creativity, ingenuity, inventiveness, originality, vision

imaginative ADJECTIVE Someone who is imaginative can easily form new or exciting ideas in their mind. **imaginatively** ADVERB

imagine VERB ① If you imagine something, you form an idea of it in your mind, or you think you have seen or heard it but you have not really. ② If you imagine that something is the case, you believe it is the case • *I imagine that's what you aim to do*. **imaginable** ADJECTIVE

> **imagine** VERB
> ① = conceive, envisage, fantasise, picture, visualise
> ② = assume, believe, gather, guess (*informal*), suppose, suspect

imam [*Said ih-**mam***] NOUN [RE] a person who leads a group in prayer in a mosque.

imbalance NOUN If there is an imbalance between things, they are unequal • *the imbalance between rich and poor*.

imitate VERB To imitate someone or something is to copy them. **imitator** NOUN **imitative** ADJECTIVE

> **imitate** VERB
> = ape, copy, emulate, impersonate, mimic, simulate

imitation NOUN a copy of something else.

immaculate [*Said im-**mak**-yoo-lit*] ADJECTIVE ① completely clean and tidy • *The flat was immaculate*. ② without any mistakes at all • *his usual immaculate guitar accompaniment*. **immaculately** ADVERB

immaterial ADJECTIVE Something that is immaterial is not important.

immature ADJECTIVE ① Something that is immature has not finished growing or developing. ② A person who is immature does not behave in a sensible adult way. **immaturity** NOUN

immediate ADJECTIVE ① Something that is immediate happens or is done without delay. ② Your immediate relatives and friends are the ones most closely connected or related to you. **immediacy** NOUN

> **immediate** ADJECTIVE
> ① = instant, instantaneous
> ② = close, direct, near

immediately ADVERB ① If something happens immediately, it happens right away. ② Immediately means very near in time or position • *immediately behind the house*.

> **immediately** ADVERB
> ① = at once, directly, instantly, now, promptly, right away, straight away
> ② = closely, directly, right

immemorial ADJECTIVE If something

has been happening from time immemorial, it has been happening longer than anyone can remember.

immense ADJECTIVE very large or huge. **immensely** ADVERB **immensity** NOUN

> **immense** ADJECTIVE
> = colossal, enormous, giant, gigantic, huge, massive, vast
> ≠ tiny

immerse VERB ① If you are immersed in an activity, you are completely involved in it. ② If you immerse something in a liquid, you put it into the liquid so that it is completely covered. **immersion** NOUN

immigrant NOUN [HISTORY] someone who has come to live permanently in a new country. **immigrate** VERB **immigration** NOUN

imminent ADJECTIVE If something is imminent, it is going to happen very soon. **imminently** ADVERB **imminence** NOUN

> **imminent** ADJECTIVE
> = close, coming, forthcoming, impending, looming, near, upcoming

immobile ADJECTIVE not moving. **immobility** NOUN

immoral ADJECTIVE [RE] If you describe someone or their behaviour as immoral, you mean that they do not fit in with most people's idea of what is right and proper. **immorality** NOUN

immortal ADJECTIVE ① Something that is immortal is famous and will be remembered for a long time • *Emily Brontë's immortal love story*. ② In stories, someone who is immortal will never die.

immortality NOUN [RE] Immortality is never dying. In many religions, people believe that the soul or some other essential part of a person lives forever or continues to exist in some form.

immovable; also spelt **immoveable** ADJECTIVE Something that is immovable is fixed and cannot be moved. **immovably** ADVERB

immune [*Said im-**yoon***] ADJECTIVE ① If you are immune to a particular disease, you cannot catch it. ② If someone or something is immune to something, they are able to avoid it or are not affected by it • *The captain was immune to prosecution*. **immunity** NOUN

> **immune** ADJECTIVE
> ② = exempt, free, protected, resistant, safe, unaffected

immune system NOUN [SCIENCE] Your body's immune system consists of your white blood cells, which fight disease by producing antibodies or germs to kill germs which come into your body.

impact NOUN ① The impact that someone or something has is the impression that they make or the effect that they have. ② Impact is the action of one object hitting another, usually with a lot of force • *The aircraft crashed into a ditch, exploding on impact*.

impair VERB To impair something is to damage it so that it stops working properly • *Travel had made him weary and impaired his judgement*.

impart VERB (*formal*) To impart information to someone is to pass it on to them.

impartial ADJECTIVE Someone who is impartial has a view of something which is fair or not biased. **impartially** ADVERB **impartiality** NOUN

impasse [*Said **am**-pass*] NOUN a difficult situation in which it is impossible to find a solution.

impassioned ADJECTIVE full of emotion • *an impassioned plea*.

impassive ADJECTIVE showing no emotion. **impassively** ADVERB

impatient ADJECTIVE ① Someone who is impatient becomes annoyed easily or is quick to lose their temper when things go wrong. ② If you are impatient to do something, you are eager and do not want to wait • *He was impatient to get back.* **impatiently** ADVERB **impatience** NOUN

> **impatient** ADJECTIVE
> ① = brusque, curt, irritable
> ≠ patient
> ② = eager, restless

impeccable [*Said im-**pek**-i-bl*] ADJECTIVE excellent, without any faults. **impeccably** ADVERB

impede VERB If you impede someone, you make their progress difficult.

> **impede** VERB
> = block, delay, disrupt, get in the way, hamper, hinder, obstruct

impediment NOUN something that makes it difficult to move, develop or do something properly • *a speech impediment.*

impending ADJECTIVE (*formal*) You use 'impending' to describe something that is going to happen very soon • *a sense of impending doom.*

impenetrable ADJECTIVE impossible to get through.

imperative ADJECTIVE ① Something that is imperative is extremely urgent or important. ▶ NOUN ② ENGLISH In grammar, an imperative is the form of a verb that is used for giving orders.

imperfect ADJECTIVE ① Something that is imperfect has faults or problems. ▶ NOUN ② ENGLISH MFL In grammar, the imperfect is a tense used to describe continuous or repeated actions which happened in the past. **imperfectly** ADVERB **imperfection** NOUN

> **imperfect** ADJECTIVE
> ① = broken, damaged, defective, faulty, flawed
> ≠ perfect

imperial ADJECTIVE ① HISTORY Imperial means relating to an empire or an emperor or empress • *the Imperial Palace.* ② The imperial system of measurement is the measuring system which uses inches, feet and yards, ounces and pounds, and pints and gallons.

imperialism NOUN HISTORY a system of rule in which a rich and powerful nation controls other nations. **imperialist** ADJECTIVE, NOUN

imperious ADJECTIVE proud and domineering • *an imperious manner.* **imperiously** ADVERB

impersonal ADJECTIVE Something that is impersonal makes you feel that individuals and their feelings do not matter • *impersonal cold rooms.* **impersonally** ADVERB

> **impersonal** ADJECTIVE
> = aloof, cold, detached, formal, neutral, remote

impersonate VERB If you impersonate someone, you pretend to be that person. **impersonation** NOUN **impersonator** NOUN

impertinent ADJECTIVE disrespectful and rude • *impertinent questions.* **impertinently** ADVERB **impertinence** NOUN

impetuous ADJECTIVE If you are impetuous, you act quickly without thinking • *an impetuous gamble.* **impetuously** ADVERB **impetuosity** NOUN

impetus NOUN ① An impetus is the stimulating effect that something has on a situation, which causes it to develop more quickly. ② In physics, impetus is the force that starts an object moving and resists changes in speed or direction.

impinge VERB If something impinges on your life, it has an effect on you and influences you • *My private life doesn't impinge on my professional life.*

implacable *[Said im-**plak**-a-bl]* ADJECTIVE Someone who is implacable is being harsh and refuses to change their mind. **implacably** ADVERB **implacability** NOUN

implant VERB *[Said im-**plant**]* ① To implant something into a person's body is to put it there, usually by means of an operation. ▶ NOUN *[Said **im**-plant]* ② something that has been implanted into someone's body.

implausible ADJECTIVE very unlikely • *implausible stories.* **implausibly** ADVERB

implement VERB ① If you implement something such as a plan, you carry it out • *The government has failed to implement promised reforms.* ▶ NOUN ② An implement is a tool. **implementation** NOUN

implicate VERB If you are implicated in a crime, you are shown to be involved in it.

implication NOUN something that is suggested or implied but not stated directly.

implicit *[Said im-**pliss**-it]* ADJECTIVE ① expressed in an indirect way • *implicit criticism.* ② If you have an implicit belief in something, you have no doubts about it • *He had implicit faith in the noble intentions of the Emperor.* **implicitly** ADVERB

implore VERB If you implore someone to do something, you beg them to do it.

> **implore** VERB
> = beg, beseech (*literary*), plead with

imply, **implies**, **implying**, **implied** VERB If you imply that something is the case, you suggest it in an indirect way.

import VERB *[Said im-**port**]* ① If you import something from another country, you bring it into your country or have it sent there. ② ICT If you import data, you open it using a different software program. ▶ NOUN *[Said **im**-port]* ③ Imports are goods that are made in another country and sent to your own country to be sold there. **importation** NOUN **importer** NOUN

important ADJECTIVE ① Something that is important is very valuable, necessary or significant. ② An important person has great influence or power. **importantly** ADVERB **importance** NOUN

> **important** ADJECTIVE
> ① = momentous, serious, significant, weighty
> ≠ unimportant
> ② = eminent, foremost, influential, leading, notable, powerful

impose VERB ① If you impose something on people, you force it on them • *Many companies imposed a pay freeze on their employees.* ② If someone imposes on you, they unreasonably expect you to do something for them. **imposition** NOUN

> **impose** VERB
> ① = dictate, enforce, inflict, levy, ordain
> ② = abuse, take advantage of, use

imposing ADJECTIVE having an impressive appearance or manner • *an imposing building.*

impossible ADJECTIVE Something that is impossible cannot happen, be done, or be believed. **impossibly** ADVERB **impossibility** NOUN

A B C D E F G H I J K L M N O P Q R S T U V W X Y Z

impossible ADJECTIVE
= absurd, hopeless, inconceivable, ludicrous, out of the question, unthinkable
≠ possible

imposter; also spelt **impostor** NOUN a person who pretends to be someone else in order to get things they want.

impotent ADJECTIVE Someone who is impotent has no power to influence people or events. **impotently** ADVERB **impotence** NOUN

impound VERB If something you own is impounded, the police or other officials take it.

impoverished ADJECTIVE Someone who is impoverished is very poor.

impractical ADJECTIVE not practical, sensible or realistic.

impregnable ADJECTIVE A building or other structure that is impregnable is so strong that it cannot be broken into or captured.

impresario, impresarios *[Said im-pris-**sar**-ee-oh]* NOUN a person who manages theatrical or musical events or companies.

impress VERB ① If you impress someone, you make them admire or respect you. ② If you impress something on someone, you make them understand the importance of it.

impression NOUN An impression of someone or something is the way they look or seem to you.

impression NOUN
= feeling, hunch, idea, notion, sense
▶ PHRASE = cause a stir, influence, make an impact

impressionable ADJECTIVE easy to influence • *impressionable young children*.

impressionable ADJECTIVE
= gullible, open, receptive, sensitive, susceptible, vulnerable

impressive ADJECTIVE If something is impressive, it impresses you • *an impressive display of old-fashioned American cars*.

impressive ADJECTIVE
= awesome, exciting, grand, powerful, stirring, striking

imprint NOUN *[Said **im**-print]* ① If something leaves an imprint on your mind, it has a strong and lasting effect. ② the mark left by the pressure of one object on another. ▶ VERB *[Said im-**print**]* ③ If something is imprinted on your memory, it is firmly fixed there.

imprison VERB If you are imprisoned, you are locked up, usually in a prison. **imprisonment** NOUN

imprison VERB
= confine, detain, incarcerate, jail, lock up, send to prison
≠ free

improbable ADJECTIVE not probable or likely to happen. **improbably** ADVERB **improbability** NOUN

improbable ADJECTIVE
= doubtful, dubious, far-fetched, implausible, unbelievable, unlikely
≠ probable

impromptu *[Said im-**prompt**-yoo]* ADJECTIVE An impromptu action is one done without planning or organisation.

improper ADJECTIVE ① rude or shocking • *improper behaviour*. ② illegal or dishonest • *improper dealings*. ③ not suitable or correct • *an improper diet*. **improperly** ADVERB

impropriety NOUN *(formal)* Impropriety is improper behaviour.

improve VERB If something improves or if you improve it, it gets better or becomes more valuable.

improve VERB
= advance, better, enhance, look up *(informal)*, progress, upgrade
≠ worsen

improvement NOUN ① the fact or process of getting better. ② An improvement in something is a change in something that makes it better.

> **improvement** NOUN
> ① = advance, development, enhancement, progress, upturn

improvise VERB ① If you improvise something, you make or do something without planning in advance, and with whatever materials are available. ② DRAMA MUSIC When musicians or actors improvise, they make up the music or words as they go along. **improvised** ADJECTIVE **improvisation** NOUN

impulse NOUN a strong urge to do something • *She felt a sudden impulse to confide in her*.

impulsive ADJECTIVE If you are impulsive, you do things suddenly, without thinking about them carefully. **impulsively** ADVERB

impure ADJECTIVE Something which is impure contains small amounts of other things, such as dirt.

impurity, **impurities** NOUN ① Impurity is the quality of being impure • *the impurity of the water*. ② If something contains impurities, it contains small amounts of dirt or other substances that should not be there.

in PREPOSITION, ADVERB 'In' is used to indicate position, direction, time and manner • *boarding schools in England* • *in the past few years*.

inability NOUN a lack of ability to do something.

> **inability** NOUN
> = impotence, inadequacy, incompetence, ineptitude
> ≠ ability

inaccessible ADJECTIVE impossible or very difficult to reach.

inaccurate ADJECTIVE not accurate or correct.

inadequate ADJECTIVE ① If something is inadequate, there is not enough of it. ② not good enough in quality for a particular purpose. ③ If someone feels inadequate, they feel they do not possess the skills necessary to do a particular job or to cope with life in general. **inadequately** ADVERB **inadequacy** NOUN

> **inadequate** ADJECTIVE
> ① = insufficient, lacking, poor, scarce, short
> ≠ adequate
> ② = deficient, incapable, incompetent, inept, pathetic, useless (*informal*)

inadvertent ADJECTIVE not intentional • *The insult had been inadvertent*. **inadvertently** ADVERB

inane ADJECTIVE silly or stupid. **inanely** ADVERB **inanity** NOUN

inanimate ADJECTIVE An inanimate object is not alive.

inappropriate ADJECTIVE not suitable for a particular purpose or occasion • *It was quite inappropriate to ask such questions*. **inappropriately** ADVERB

> **inappropriate** ADJECTIVE
> = improper, incongruous, unfit, unseemly, unsuitable, untimely
> ≠ appropriate

inarticulate ADJECTIVE If you are inarticulate, you are unable to express yourself well or easily in speech.

inaudible ADJECTIVE not loud enough to be heard. **inaudibly** ADVERB

inaugurate [*Said in-**awg**-yoo-rate*] VERB ① To inaugurate a new scheme is to start it. ② To inaugurate a new leader is to officially establish them in their new position in a special ceremony • *Albania's Orthodox Church inaugurated its first archbishop in 25 years.* **inauguration** NOUN **inaugural** ADJECTIVE

incandescent ADJECTIVE Something which is incandescent gives out light when it is heated. **incandescence** NOUN

incapable ADJECTIVE ① Someone who is incapable of doing something is not able to do it • *He is incapable of changing a fuse.* ② An incapable person is weak and helpless.

incarcerate *[Said in-**kar**-ser-rate]* VERB To incarcerate someone is to lock them up. **incarceration** NOUN

incendiary *[Said in-**send**-yer-ee]* ADJECTIVE An incendiary weapon is one which sets fire to things • *incendiary bombs.*

incense NOUN Incense is a spicy substance which is burned to create a sweet smell, especially during religious services.

incensed ADJECTIVE If you are incensed by something, it makes you extremely angry.

incentive NOUN something that encourages you to do something.

> **incentive** NOUN
> = bait, encouragement, inducement, motivation, stimulus

inception NOUN *(formal)* The inception of a project is the start of it.

incessant ADJECTIVE continuing without stopping • *her incessant talking.* **incessantly** ADVERB

inch NOUN ① a unit of length equal to about 2.54 centimetres. ▶ VERB ② To inch forward is to move forward slowly.

incident NOUN an event • *a shooting incident.*

> **incident** NOUN
> = circumstance, episode, event, happening, occasion, occurrence

incidental ADJECTIVE occurring as a minor part of something • *full of vivid incidental detail.* **incidentally** ADVERB

incinerator NOUN a furnace for burning rubbish.

incipient ADJECTIVE beginning to happen or appear • *incipient panic.*

incision NOUN a sharp cut, usually made by a surgeon operating on a patient.

incisive ADJECTIVE Incisive language is clear and forceful.

incite VERB If you incite someone to do something, you encourage them to do it by making them angry or excited. **incitement** NOUN

> **incite** VERB
> = agitate for, goad, instigate, provoke, whip up

inclination NOUN If you have an inclination to do something, you want to do it.

incline VERB ① If you are inclined to behave in a certain way, you often behave that way or you want to behave that way. ▶ NOUN ② a slope.

include VERB If one thing includes another, it has the second thing as one of its parts. **including** PREPOSITION

> **include** VERB
> = contain, cover, embrace, encompass, incorporate, involve
> ≠ exclude

inclusion NOUN The inclusion of one thing in another is the act of making it part of the other thing.

inclusive ADJECTIVE A price that is inclusive includes all the goods and services that are being offered, with no extra charge for any of them.

incognito *[Said in-kog-**nee**-toe]* ADVERB If you are travelling incognito, you are travelling in disguise.

incoherent ADJECTIVE If someone is incoherent, they are talking in an unclear or rambling way. **incoherently** ADVERB **incoherence** NOUN

income NOUN the money a person earns.

> **income** NOUN
> = earnings, pay, profits, salary, takings, wages

income tax NOUN Income tax is a part of someone's salary which they have to pay regularly to the government.

incoming ADJECTIVE coming in • *incoming trains* • *an incoming phone call.*

incomparable ADJECTIVE Something that is incomparable is so good that it cannot be compared with anything else. **incomparably** ADVERB

> **incomparable** ADJECTIVE
> = inimitable, peerless (*literary*), superlative, supreme, unparalleled, unrivalled

incompatible ADJECTIVE Two things or people are incompatible if they are unable to live or exist together because they are completely different. **incompatibility** NOUN

incompetent ADJECTIVE Someone who is incompetent does not have the ability to do something properly. **incompetently** ADVERB **incompetence** NOUN

> **incompetent** ADJECTIVE
> = bungling, cowboy (*British; informal*), incapable, inept, unable, useless (*informal*)
> ≠ competent

incomplete ADJECTIVE not complete or finished. **incompletely** ADVERB

> **incomplete** ADJECTIVE
> = deficient, half-pie (*New Zealand; informal*), insufficient, partial
> ≠ complete

incomprehensible ADJECTIVE not able to be understood.

inconceivable ADJECTIVE impossible to believe.

inconclusive ADJECTIVE not leading to a decision or to a definite result.

incongruous ADJECTIVE Something that is incongruous seems strange because it does not fit in to a place or situation. **incongruously** ADVERB

inconsequential ADJECTIVE Something that is inconsequential is not very important.

inconsistent ADJECTIVE Someone or something that is inconsistent is unpredictable and behaves differently in similar situations. **inconsistently** ADVERB **inconsistency** NOUN

inconspicuous ADJECTIVE not easily seen or obvious. **inconspicuously** ADVERB

inconvenience NOUN ① If something causes inconvenience, it causes difficulty or problems. ▸ VERB ② To inconvenience someone is to cause them trouble, difficulty or problems. **inconvenient** ADJECTIVE **inconveniently** ADVERB

incorporate VERB If something is incorporated into another thing, it becomes part of that thing. **incorporation** NOUN

incorrect ADJECTIVE wrong or untrue. **incorrectly** ADVERB

increase VERB ① If something increases, it becomes larger in amount. ▸ NOUN ② a rise in the number, level or amount of something. **increasingly** ADVERB

A B C D E F G H I J K L M N O P Q R S T U V W X Y Z

increase VERB
① = enlarge, expand, extend, grow, multiply, swell
≠ decrease
▸ NOUN ② = gain, growth, increment, rise, upsurge
≠ decrease

incredible ADJECTIVE ① totally amazing. ② impossible to believe. **incredibly** ADVERB

incredible ADJECTIVE
① = amazing, astonishing, astounding, extraordinary, marvellous, sensational (*informal*)
② = absurd, far-fetched, improbable, unbelievable, unimaginable, unthinkable

incredulous ADJECTIVE If you are incredulous, you are unable to believe something because it is very surprising or shocking. **incredulously** ADVERB **incredulity** NOUN

increment NOUN the amount by which something increases, or a regular increase in someone's salary. **incremental** ADJECTIVE

incriminate VERB If something incriminates you, it suggests that you are involved in a crime.

incubator NOUN a piece of hospital equipment in which sick or weak newborn babies are kept warm.

incumbent (*formal*) ADJECTIVE ① If it is incumbent on you to do something, it is your duty to do it. ▸ NOUN ② the person in a particular official position.

incur, incurs, incurring, incurred VERB If you incur something unpleasant, you cause it to happen.

incurable ADJECTIVE ① An incurable disease is one which cannot be cured. ② An incurable habit is one which cannot be changed • *an incurable romantic*. **incurably** ADVERB

indebted ADJECTIVE If you are indebted to someone, you are grateful to them. **indebtedness** NOUN

indecent ADJECTIVE Something that is indecent is shocking or rude • *indecent images*. **indecently** ADVERB **indecency** NOUN

indecent ADJECTIVE
= crude, improper, rude, vulgar

indeed ADVERB You use 'indeed' to strengthen a point that you are making • *The desserts are very good indeed*.

indefatigable [Said in-dif-**fat**-ig-a-bl] ADJECTIVE People who never get tired of doing something are indefatigable.

indefinite ADJECTIVE ① If something is indefinite, no time to finish has been decided • *an indefinite strike*. ② Indefinite also means vague or not exact • *indefinite words and pictures*. **indefinitely** ADVERB

indelible ADJECTIVE unable to be removed • *indelible ink*. **indelibly** ADVERB

indemnity NOUN (*formal*) Indemnity is protection against damage or loss.

independence NOUN
① Independence is not relying on anyone else. ② HISTORY A nation or state gains its independence when it stops being ruled or governed by another country and has its own government and laws.

independent ADJECTIVE
① Something that is independent happens or exists separately from other people or things • *Results are assessed by an independent panel*.
② Someone who is independent does not need other people's help • *a fiercely independent teenager*. ③ An independent nation is one that is not ruled or governed by another country. **independently** ADVERB

a b c d e f g h i j k l m n o p q r s t u v w x y z

independent ADJECTIVE
① = autonomous, free, separate, unrelated
② = individualistic, liberated, self-sufficient, unaided

indeterminate ADJECTIVE not certain or definite • *some indeterminate point in the future.*

index, **indexes** or **indices** NOUN ① ENGLISH An index is an alphabetical list at the back of a book, referring to items in the book. ② LIBRARY An index is also an alphabetical list of all the books in a library, arranged by title, author or subject. ③ MATHS a number or symbol placed above and to the right of a number, indicating the number of times the number is to be multiplied by itself. ▶ VERB ④ To index a book or collection of information means to provide an index for it.

index finger NOUN your first finger, next to your thumb.

Indian ADJECTIVE ① belonging or relating to India. ▶ NOUN ② someone who comes from India. ③ someone descended from the people who lived in North, South or Central America before Europeans arrived.

indicate VERB ① If something indicates something, it shows that it is true • *a gesture which clearly indicates his relief.* ② If you indicate something to someone, you point to it. ③ If you indicate a fact, you mention it. ④ If the driver of a vehicle indicates, they give a signal to show which way they are going to turn.

indicate VERB
① = denote, reveal, show, signal, signify

indication NOUN a sign of what someone feels or what is likely to happen.

indication NOUN
= clue, hint, sign, signal, suggestion, warning

indicative ADJECTIVE ① If something is indicative of something else, it is a sign of that thing • *Clean, pink tongues are indicative of a good, healthy digestion.* ▶ NOUN ② ENGLISH If a verb is used in the indicative, it is in the form used for making statements.

indicator NOUN ① something which tells you what something is like or what is happening. ② A car's indicators are the lights at the front and back which are used to show when it is turning left or right. ③ SCIENCE a substance used in chemistry that shows if another substance is an acid or alkali by changing colour when it comes into contact with it.

indict [*Said in-**dite***] VERB (*formal*) To indict someone is to charge them officially with a crime. **indictment** NOUN **indictable** ADJECTIVE

indifferent ADJECTIVE ① If you are indifferent to something, you have no interest in it. ② If something is indifferent, it is of a poor quality or low standard • *a pair of rather indifferent paintings.* **indifferently** ADVERB **indifference** NOUN

indigenous [*Said in-**dij**-in-uss*] ADJECTIVE If something is indigenous to a country, it comes from that country • *a plant indigenous to Asia.*

indigestion NOUN Indigestion is a pain you get when you find it difficult to digest food.

indignant ADJECTIVE If you are indignant, you feel angry about something that you think is unfair. **indignantly** ADVERB

indignation NOUN Indignation is anger about something that you think is unfair.

indignity, **indignities** NOUN something that makes you feel embarrassed or humiliated • *the indignity of having to flee angry protesters.*

indigo, **indigos** or **indigoes** NOUN, ADJECTIVE dark violet-blue.

indirect ADJECTIVE ① not moving in a straight line or by the shortest route . ② not done or caused directly by a particular person or thing, but by someone or something else. **indirectly** ADVERB

> **indirect** ADJECTIVE
> ① = meandering, oblique, rambling, roundabout, tortuous, wandering
> ≠ direct

indiscriminate ADJECTIVE not involving careful thought or choice • *an indiscriminate bombing campaign.* **indiscriminately** ADVERB

indispensable ADJECTIVE If something is indispensable, you cannot do without it • *A good pair of walking shoes is indispensable.*

indistinct ADJECTIVE not clear • *indistinct voices.* **indistinctly** ADVERB

individual ADJECTIVE ① relating to one particular person or thing • *Each family needs individual attention.* ② Someone who is individual behaves quite differently from the way other people behave. ▶ NOUN ③ a person, different from any other person • *wealthy individuals.* **individually** ADVERB

> **individual** ADJECTIVE
> ① = discrete (*formal*), independent, separate, single
> ② = characteristic, distinctive, idiosyncratic, original, personal, special, unique
> ▶ NOUN ③ = character, party, person, soul

individuality NOUN If something has individuality, it is different from all other things, and therefore is very interesting and noticeable.

indomitable ADJECTIVE (*formal*) impossible to overcome • *an indomitable spirit.*

Indonesian [*Said in-don-**nee**-zee-an*] ADJECTIVE ① belonging or relating to Indonesia. ▶ NOUN ② someone who comes from Indonesia. ③ Indonesian is the official language of Indonesia.

indoor ADJECTIVE situated or happening inside a building.

indoors ADVERB If something happens indoors, it takes place inside a building.

induce VERB ① To induce a state is to cause it • *His manner was rough and suspicious but he did not induce fear.* ② If you induce someone to do something, you persuade them to do it.

inducement NOUN something offered to encourage someone to do something.

indulge VERB ① If you indulge in something, you allow yourself to do something that you enjoy. ② If you indulge someone, you let them have or do what they want, often in a way that is not good for them.

indulgence NOUN ① something you allow yourself to have because it gives you pleasure. ② Indulgence is the act of indulging yourself or another person.

indulgent ADJECTIVE If you are indulgent, you treat someone with special kindness • *a rich, indulgent father.* **indulgently** ADVERB

industrial ADJECTIVE relating to industry.

industrial action NOUN Industrial action is action such as striking taken by workers in protest over pay or working conditions.

industrialist NOUN a person who owns or controls a lot of factories.

Industrial Revolution NOUN HISTORY The Industrial Revolution was a period when machines began to be used more in factories and more goods were produced as a result. It started in Britain in the late eighteenth and early nineteenth century.

industrious ADJECTIVE An industrious person works very hard.

> **industrious** ADJECTIVE
> = busy, conscientious, diligent, hard-working, tireless
> ≠ lazy

industry, **industries** NOUN ① Industry is the work and processes involved in manufacturing things in factories. ② all the people and processes involved in manufacturing a particular thing.

inedible ADJECTIVE too nasty or poisonous to eat.

inefficient ADJECTIVE badly organised, wasteful and slow • *a corrupt and inefficient administration*. **inefficiently** ADVERB **inefficiency** NOUN

> **inefficient** ADJECTIVE
> = disorganised, incapable, incompetent, inept, sloppy
> ≠ efficient

inept ADJECTIVE without skill • *an inept lawyer*. **ineptitude** NOUN

inequality, **inequalities** NOUN a difference in size, status, wealth or position, between different things, groups or people.

inert ADJECTIVE ① Something that is inert does not move and appears lifeless • *an inert body lying on the floor*. ② In chemistry, an inert gas does not react with other substances. The inert gases are also called **noble gases**.

inertia *[Said in-**ner**-sha]* NOUN If you have a feeling of inertia, you feel very lazy and unwilling to do anything.

inevitable ADJECTIVE certain to happen. **inevitably** ADVERB **inevitability** NOUN

inexhaustible ADJECTIVE Something that is inexhaustible will never be used up • *an inexhaustible supply of ideas*.

inexorable ADJECTIVE (*formal*) Something that is inexorable cannot be prevented from continuing • *the inexorable increase in the number of cars*. **inexorably** ADVERB

inexpensive ADJECTIVE not costing much.

inexperienced ADJECTIVE lacking experience of a situation or activity • *inexperienced drivers*. **inexperience** NOUN

> **inexperienced** ADJECTIVE
> = green (*informal*), new, raw, unaccustomed
> ≠ experienced

inexplicable ADJECTIVE If something is inexplicable, you cannot explain it • *For some inexplicable reason I still felt uneasy*. **inexplicably** ADVERB

inextricably ADVERB If two or more things are inextricably linked, they cannot be separated.

infallible ADJECTIVE never wrong • *No machine is infallible*. **infallibility** NOUN

infamous *[Said **in**-fe-muss]* ADJECTIVE well-known because of something bad or evil • *a book about the country's most infamous murder cases*.

infant NOUN ① a baby or very young child. ▸ ADJECTIVE ② designed for young children • *an infant school*. **infancy** NOUN **infantile** ADJECTIVE

infantry NOUN In an army, the infantry are soldiers who fight on foot rather than in tanks or on horses.

infatuated ADJECTIVE If you are infatuated with someone, you have such strong feelings of love or passion that you cannot think sensibly about them. **infatuation** NOUN

infect VERB To infect someone or something is to cause disease in them.

> **infect** VERB
> = affect, blight, contaminate, taint

infection NOUN ① a disease caused by germs • *a chest infection.* ② Infection is the state of being infected • *a very small risk of infection.*

infectious ADJECTIVE spreading from one person to another • *an infectious disease.*

> **infectious** ADJECTIVE
> = catching, contagious, spreading

infer, **infers**, **inferring**, **inferred** VERB If you infer something, you work out that it is true on the basis of information that you already have. **inference** NOUN

inferior ADJECTIVE ① having a lower position than something or someone else. ② of low quality • *inferior quality DVDs.* ▶ NOUN ③ Your inferiors are people in a lower position than you. **inferiority** NOUN

> **inferior** ADJECTIVE
> ① = lesser, lower, minor, secondary, second-class, subordinate
> ≠ superior
> ② = mediocre, poor, second-class, second-rate, shoddy
> ≠ superior
> ▶ NOUN ③ = junior, menial, subordinate, underling
> ≠ superior

infernal ADJECTIVE (*old-fashioned*) very unpleasant • *an infernal bore.*

inferno, **infernos** NOUN a very large dangerous fire.

infertile ADJECTIVE ① Infertile soil is of poor quality and plants cannot grow well in it. ② Someone who is infertile cannot have children. **infertility** NOUN

infested ADJECTIVE Something that is infested has a large number of animals or insects living on or in it and causing damage • *The flats are damp and infested with rats.* **infestation** NOUN

infighting NOUN Infighting is quarrelling or rivalry between members of the same organisation.

infiltrate VERB If people infiltrate an organisation, they gradually enter it in secret to spy on its activities. **infiltration** NOUN **infiltrator** NOUN

infinite ADJECTIVE without any limit or end • *an infinite number of possibilities.* **infinitely** ADVERB

> **infinite** ADJECTIVE
> = boundless, endless, eternal, everlasting, inexhaustible, perpetual

infinity NOUN ① Infinity is a number that is larger than any other number and can never be given an exact value. ② Infinity is also a point that can never be reached, further away than any other point • *skies stretching on into infinity.*

infirmary, **infirmaries** NOUN a hospital.

inflamed ADJECTIVE If part of your body is inflamed, it is red and swollen, usually because of infection.

inflammation NOUN Inflammation is painful redness or swelling of part of the body.

inflammatory ADJECTIVE Inflammatory actions are likely to make people very angry.

inflate VERB When you inflate something, you fill it with air or gas to make it swell. **inflatable** ADJECTIVE

inflation NOUN Inflation is an increase in the price of goods and services in a country. **inflationary** ADJECTIVE

inflection; also spelt **inflexion** NOUN [MFL] a change in the form of a word that shows its grammatical function, for example a change that makes a noun plural.

inflexible ADJECTIVE fixed and unable to be altered • *an inflexible routine*.

inflict VERB If you inflict something unpleasant on someone, you make them suffer it.

influence NOUN ① Influence is power that a person has over other people. ② An influence is also the effect that someone or something has • *under the influence of alcohol*. ▸ VERB ③ To influence someone or something means to have an effect on them.

> **influence** NOUN
> ① = authority, control, importance, power, sway
> ② = effect, hold, magnetism, spell, weight
> ▸ VERB ③ = affect, control, direct, guide, manipulate, sway

influential ADJECTIVE Someone who is influential has a lot of influence over people.

influenza NOUN (*formal*) Influenza is flu.

influx NOUN a steady arrival of people or things • *a large influx of tourists*.

inform VERB ① If you inform someone of something, you tell them about it. ② If you inform on a person, you tell the police about a crime they have committed. **informant** NOUN

> **inform** VERB
> ① = advise (*formal*), enlighten, notify, tell
> ② = betray, denounce, grass on (*British*; *slang*), tell on (*informal*)

informal ADJECTIVE relaxed and casual • *an informal meeting*. **informally** ADVERB **informality** NOUN

> **informal** ADJECTIVE
> = casual, colloquial, easy, familiar, natural, relaxed
> ≠ formal

information NOUN If you have information on or about something, you know something about it.

> **information** NOUN
> = data, drum (*Australian*; *informal*), facts, material, news, notice, word

informative ADJECTIVE Something that is informative gives you useful information.

informer NOUN someone who tells the police that another person has committed a crime.

infrastructure NOUN [GEOGRAPHY] The infrastructure of a country consists of things like factories, schools and roads, which show how much money the country has and how strong its economy is.

infringe VERB ① If you infringe a law, you break it. ② To infringe people's rights is to not allow them the rights to which they are entitled. **infringement** NOUN

infuriate VERB If someone infuriates you, they make you very angry. **infuriating** ADJECTIVE

infuse VERB ① If you infuse someone with a feeling such as enthusiasm or joy, you fill them with it. ② If you infuse a substance such as a herb or medicine, you pour hot water onto it and leave it for the water to absorb the flavour. **infusion** NOUN

ingenious [*Said in-**jeen**-yuss*] ADJECTIVE very clever and using new ideas • *his ingenious invention*. **ingeniously** ADVERB

ingenuity [*Said in-jen-**yoo**-it-ee*] NOUN Ingenuity is cleverness and skill at inventing things or working out plans.

ingrained ADJECTIVE If habits and

beliefs are ingrained, they are difficult to change or destroy.

ingredient NOUN [DGT] Ingredients are the things that something is made from, especially in cookery.

> **ingredient** NOUN
> = component, constituent, element

inhabit VERB If you inhabit a place, you live there.

> **inhabit** VERB
> = dwell (*formal*), live, lodge, occupy, populate, reside (*formal*)

inhabitant NOUN The inhabitants of a place are the people who live there.

> **inhabitant** NOUN
> = citizen, inmate, native, occupant, resident

inhale VERB [SCIENCE] When you inhale, you breathe in. **inhalation** NOUN

inherent ADJECTIVE Inherent qualities or characteristics in something are a natural part of it • *her inherent common sense*. **inherently** ADVERB

inherit VERB ① If you inherit money or property, you receive it from someone who has died. ② [SCIENCE] If you inherit a quality or characteristic from a parent or ancestor, it is passed on to you at birth. **inheritor** NOUN

inheritance NOUN something that is passed on from another person.

> **inheritance** NOUN
> = bequest, heritage, legacy

inhibit VERB If you inhibit someone from doing something, you prevent them from doing it.

inhibited ADJECTIVE People who are inhibited find it difficult to relax and to show their emotions.

inhibition NOUN Inhibitions are feelings of fear or embarrassment that make it difficult for someone to relax and to show their emotions.

inhospitable ADJECTIVE ① An inhospitable place is unpleasant or difficult to live in. ② If someone is inhospitable, they do not make people who visit them feel welcome.

inhuman ADJECTIVE not human or not behaving like a human • *the inhuman killing of their enemies*.

inhumane ADJECTIVE extremely cruel. **inhumanity** NOUN

inimitable ADJECTIVE If you have an inimitable characteristic, no one else can imitate it • *her inimitable sense of style*.

initial *[Said in-**nish**-l]* ADJECTIVE ① first, or at the beginning • *Shock and dismay were my initial reactions*. ▶ NOUN ② the first letter of a name. **initially** ADVERB

initiate *[Said in-**nish**-ee-ate]* VERB ① If you initiate something, you make it start or happen. ② If you initiate someone into a group or club, you allow them to become a member of it, usually by means of a special ceremony. **initiation** NOUN

initiative *[Said in-**nish**-at-ive]* NOUN ① an attempt to get something done. ② If you have initiative, you decide what to do and then do it, without needing the advice of other people.

inject VERB ① If a doctor or nurse injects you with a substance, they use a needle and syringe to put the substance into your body. ② If you inject something new into a situation, you add it. **injection** NOUN

injunction NOUN an order issued by a court of law to stop someone doing something.

injure VERB To injure someone is to damage part of their body.

> **injure** VERB
> = harm, hurt, maim, wound

injury, **injuries** NOUN [PE] hurt or damage, especially to part of a person's body or to their feelings • *The knee injury forced him to retire from the professional game* • *He suffered acute injury to his pride.*

> **injury** NOUN
> = damage, harm, wound

injustice NOUN ① Injustice is lack of justice and fairness. ② If you do someone an injustice, you judge them too harshly.

> **injustice** NOUN
> ① = bias, discrimination, inequality, prejudice, unfairness, wrong
> ≠ justice

ink NOUN Ink is the coloured liquid used for writing or printing.

inkling NOUN a vague idea about something.

inlaid ADJECTIVE decorated with small pieces of wood, metal or stone • *decorative plates inlaid with brass.* **inlay** NOUN

inland ADJECTIVE ① near the middle of a country, away from the sea. ▸ ADVERB ② towards the middle of a country, away from the sea.

in-law NOUN Your in-laws are members of your husband's or wife's family.

inlet NOUN a narrow bay.

inmate NOUN someone who lives in a prison or psychiatric hospital.

inn NOUN a small old country pub or hotel.

innards PLURAL NOUN The innards of something are its inside parts.

innate ADJECTIVE An innate quality is one that you were born with • *an innate sense of fairness.* **innately** ADVERB

inner ADJECTIVE contained inside a place or object • *an inner room.*

innermost ADJECTIVE deepest and most secret • *our innermost feelings.*

innings NOUN In cricket, an innings is a period when a particular team is batting.

innocence NOUN inexperience of evil or unpleasant things.

> **innocence** NOUN
> = gullibility, inexperience, naivety, simplicity

innocent ADJECTIVE ① not guilty of a crime. ② without experience of evil or unpleasant things • *an innocent child.* **innocently** ADVERB

> **innocent** ADJECTIVE
> ① = blameless, clear, not guilty
> ≠ guilty
> ② = childlike, guileless, naive, pure, spotless

innocuous *[Said in-**nok**-yoo-uss]* ADJECTIVE not harmful.

innovation NOUN [DGT] a completely new idea, product or system of doing things.

innuendo, **innuendos** or **innuendoes** *[Said in-yoo-**en**-doe]* NOUN an indirect reference to something rude or unpleasant.

innumerable ADJECTIVE too many to be counted • *innumerable cups of tea.*

input NOUN ① Input consists of all the money, information and other resources that are put into a job, project or company to make it work. ② [ICT] In computing, input is information which is fed into a computer.

inquest NOUN an official inquiry to find out what caused a person's death.

inquire; also spelt **enquire** VERB If you inquire about something, you ask for information about it. **inquiring** ADJECTIVE **inquiry** NOUN

inquisition NOUN an official investigation, especially one which is very thorough and uses harsh methods of questioning.

inquisitive ADJECTIVE Someone who is inquisitive is keen to find out about things. **inquisitively** ADVERB

inroads PLURAL NOUN If something makes inroads on or into something, it starts affecting it.

insane ADJECTIVE Someone who is insane has a serious mental illness that causes their mind not to work normally. **insanely** ADVERB **insanity** NOUN

insatiable *[Said in-**saysh**-a-bl]* ADJECTIVE A desire or urge that is insatiable is very great • *an insatiable curiosity about the world*. **insatiably** ADVERB

inscribe VERB If you inscribe words on an object, you write or carve them on it.

inscription NOUN the words that are written or carved on something.

inscrutable *[Said in-**skroot**-a-bl]* ADJECTIVE Someone who is inscrutable does not show what they are really thinking.

insect NOUN SCIENCE a small creature with six legs, and usually wings.

insecticide NOUN SCIENCE a poisonous chemical used to kill insects.

insecure ADJECTIVE ① If you are insecure, you feel unsure of yourself and doubt whether other people like you. ② Something that is insecure is not safe or well protected • *People still feel their jobs are insecure*. **insecurity** NOUN

insensitive ADJECTIVE If you are insensitive, you do not notice when you are upsetting people. **insensitivity** NOUN

insert VERB If you insert an object into something, you put it inside. **insertion** NOUN

> **insert** VERB
> = enter, implant, introduce, place, put, set

inshore ADJECTIVE at sea but close to the shore • *inshore boats*.

inside NOUN ① the part of something that is surrounded by the main part and often hidden • *The inside of the house was painted white*. ② (*in plural*) Your insides are the parts inside your body. ▶ ADJECTIVE ③ surrounded by the main part and often hidden • *an inside pocket*. ▶ PREPOSITION ④ in or to the interior of • *inside the house*. ▶ PHRASE ⑤ **Inside out** means with the inside part facing outwards.

> **inside** NOUN
> ② = entrails, guts, innards, internal organs
> ▶ ADJECTIVE ③ = inner, innermost, interior, internal
> ≠ outside

insider NOUN a person who is involved in a situation and so knows more about it than other people.

insidious ADJECTIVE Something that is insidious is unpleasant and develops slowly without being noticed • *the insidious progress of the disease*. **insidiously** ADVERB

insight NOUN If you gain insight into a problem, you gradually get a deep and accurate understanding of it.

insignia *[Said in-**sig**-nee-a]* NOUN the badge or a sign of a particular organisation.

insignificant ADJECTIVE small and unimportant. **insignificance** NOUN

> **insignificant** ADJECTIVE
> = irrelevant, little, minor, petty, trifling, trivial, unimportant
> ≠ significant

insincere ADJECTIVE Someone who is insincere pretends to have feelings which they do not really have.

insincerely ADVERB **insincerity** NOUN

insincere ADJECTIVE
= deceitful, dishonest, false, two-faced
≠ sincere

insinuate VERB If you insinuate something unpleasant, you hint about it. **insinuation** NOUN

insipid ADJECTIVE ① An insipid person or activity is dull and boring. ② Food that is insipid has very little taste.

insist VERB If you insist on something, you demand it forcefully. **insistent** ADJECTIVE **insistence** NOUN

insist VERB
= demand, press, urge

insoluble [*Said in-**soll**-yoo-bl*] ADJECTIVE ① impossible to solve • *an insoluble problem.* ② SCIENCE unable to dissolve • *substances which are insoluble in water.*

insolvent ADJECTIVE unable to pay your debts. **insolvency** NOUN

insomnia NOUN Insomnia is difficulty in sleeping. **insomniac** NOUN

inspect VERB To inspect something is to examine it carefully to check that everything is all right. **inspection** NOUN

inspect VERB
= check, examine, eye, investigate, scan, survey

inspector NOUN ① someone who inspects things. ② a police officer just above a sergeant in rank.

inspire VERB ① If something inspires you, it gives you new ideas and enthusiasm to do something. ② To inspire an emotion in someone is to make them feel this emotion. **inspired** ADJECTIVE **inspiring** ADJECTIVE **inspiration** NOUN

instability NOUN Instability is a lack of stability in a place • *political instability.*

install VERB ① If you install a piece of equipment in a place, you put it there so it is ready to be used. ② If you install software on a computer, you transfer it there and make it ready to be used. ③ To install someone in an important job is to officially give them that position. ④ If you install yourself in a place, you settle there and make yourself comfortable. **installation** NOUN

instalment NOUN ① If you pay for something in instalments, you pay small amounts of money regularly over a period of time. ② one of the parts of a story or television series.

instance NOUN ① a particular example or occurrence of an event, situation or person • *a serious instance of corruption.* ▶ PHRASE ② You use **for instance** to give an example of something you are talking about.

instant NOUN ① a moment or short period of time • *In an instant they were gone.* ▶ ADJECTIVE ② immediate and without delay • *The record was an instant success.* **instantly** ADVERB

instant NOUN
① = flash, minute, moment, second, split second, trice
▶ ADJECTIVE ② = immediate, instantaneous, prompt

instantaneous ADJECTIVE happening immediately and without delay • *The applause was instantaneous.* **instantaneously** ADVERB

instead ADVERB in place of something • *Take the stairs instead of the lift.*

instigate VERB Someone who instigates a situation makes it happen. **instigation** NOUN **instigator** NOUN

instil, **instils**, **instilling**, **instilled** VERB If you instil an idea or feeling into someone, you make them feel or think it.

instinct NOUN a natural tendency to do something • *My first instinct was to protect myself.* **instinctive** ADJECTIVE **instinctively** ADVERB

instinct NOUN
= feeling, impulse, intuition, sixth sense, urge

institute NOUN ① an organisation for teaching or research. ▶ VERB ② (*formal*) If you institute a rule or system, you introduce it.

institution NOUN ① a custom or system regarded as an important tradition within a society • *the institution of marriage.* ② a large, important organisation, for example a university or bank. **institutional** ADJECTIVE

instruct VERB ① If you instruct someone to do something, you tell them to do it. ② If someone instructs you in a subject or skill, they teach you about it. **instructor** NOUN **instructive** ADJECTIVE **instruction** NOUN

instruct VERB
① = command, direct, order, tell
≠ forbid
② = coach, educate, school, teach, train, tutor

instrument NOUN ① a tool or device used for a particular job • *a special instrument which cut through the metal.* ② MUSIC A musical instrument is an object, such as a piano or flute, played to make music.

instrumental ADJECTIVE ① If you are instrumental in doing something, you help to make it happen. ② MUSIC Instrumental music is performed using only musical instruments, and not voices.

insufficient ADJECTIVE not enough for a particular purpose. **insufficiently** ADVERB

insufficient ADJECTIVE
= deficient, inadequate, lacking, scant, short
≠ sufficient

insular [*Said inss-yoo-lar*] ADJECTIVE Someone who is insular is unwilling to meet new people or to consider new ideas. **insularity** NOUN

insulate VERB ① If you insulate a person from harmful things, you protect them from those things. ② If materials such as feathers, fur or foam insulate something, they keep it warm by covering it in a thick layer. ③ SCIENCE You insulate an electrical or metal object by covering it with rubber or plastic. This is to stop electricity passing through it and giving you an electric shock. **insulation** NOUN **insulator** NOUN

insulin [*Said inss-yoo-lin*] NOUN Insulin is a substance which controls the level of sugar in the blood. People who have diabetes do not produce insulin naturally and have to take regular doses of it.

insult VERB ① If you insult someone, you offend them by being rude to them. ▶ NOUN ② a rude remark which offends you. **insulting** ADJECTIVE

insult VERB
① = abuse, affront, offend, put down, slag off (*British; informal*), slight, snub
≠ compliment
▶ NOUN ② = abuse, affront, offence, slight, snub
≠ compliment

insure VERB ① If you insure something or yourself, you pay money regularly to a company so that if there is an accident or damage, the company will pay for medical treatment or repairs. ② If you do something to insure against something unpleasant happening, you do it to prevent the unpleasant thing from happening or to protect yourself if it does happen. **insurance** NOUN

insurrection NOUN a violent action taken against the rulers of a country.

intact ADJECTIVE complete, and not changed or damaged in any way • *The rear of the aircraft remained intact when it crashed.*

intake NOUN A person's intake of food, drink or air is the amount they take in.

integral ADJECTIVE If something is an integral part of a whole thing, it is an essential part.

integrate VERB ① If a person integrates into a group, they become part of it. ② To integrate things is to combine them so that they become closely linked or form one thing • *his plan to integrate the coal and steel industries.* **integration** NOUN

integrity NOUN ① Integrity is the quality of being honest and following your principles. ② The integrity of a group of people is their being united as one whole.

intellect NOUN Intellect is the ability to understand ideas and information.

intellectual ADJECTIVE ① involving thought, ideas and understanding • *an intellectual exercise.* ▶ NOUN ② someone who enjoys thinking about complicated ideas. **intellectually** ADVERB

intelligence NOUN A person's intelligence is their ability to understand and learn things quickly and well.

> **intelligence** NOUN
> = cleverness, comprehension, intellect, perception, sense, understanding, wit

intelligent ADJECTIVE able to understand and learn things quickly and well. **intelligently** ADVERB

> **intelligent** ADJECTIVE
> = acute, brainy (*informal*), bright, clever, quick, sharp, smart
> ≠ stupid

intelligentsia [*Said in-tell-lee-**jent**-sya*] NOUN The intelligentsia are intellectual people, considered as a group.

intelligible ADJECTIVE able to be understood • *very few intelligible remarks.*

intend VERB ① If you intend to do something, you have decided or planned to do it • *She intended to move back to Cape Town.* ② If something is intended for a particular use, you have planned that it should have this use • *The booklet is intended to be kept handy.*

> **intend** VERB
> ① = aim, be determined, mean, plan, propose, resolve
> ② = aim, design, earmark, mean

intense ADJECTIVE ① very great in strength or amount • *intense heat.* ② If a person is intense, they take things very seriously and have very strong feelings. **intensely** ADVERB **intensity** NOUN

> **intense** ADJECTIVE
> ① = acute, deep, extreme, fierce, great, powerful, profound, severe
> ② = ardent, earnest, fervent, fierce, impassioned, passionate, vehement

intensify, **intensifies**, **intensifying**, **intensified** VERB To intensify something is to make it greater or stronger.

intensive ADJECTIVE involving a lot of energy or effort over a very short time • *an intensive training course.*

intent NOUN ① (*formal*) A person's intent is their purpose or intention.

▸ ADJECTIVE ② If you are intent on doing something, you are determined to do it. **intently** ADVERB

intention NOUN If you have an intention to do something, you have a plan of what you are going to do.

> **intention** NOUN
> = aim, goal, idea, object, objective, purpose

intentional ADJECTIVE If something is intentional, it is done on purpose. **intentionally** ADVERB

interact VERB The way two people or things interact is the way they work together, communicate or react with each other. **interaction** NOUN

interactive ADJECTIVE ICT Interactive television, computers and games react to decisions taken by the viewer, user or player.

intercept *[Said in-ter-**sept**]* VERB If you intercept someone or something that is going from one place to another, you stop them.

interchange NOUN An interchange is the act or process of exchanging things or ideas. **interchangeable** ADJECTIVE

intercom NOUN a device consisting of a microphone and a loudspeaker, which you use to speak to people in another room.

interest NOUN ① If you have an interest in something or if something is of interest, you want to learn or hear more about it. ② Your interests are your hobbies. ③ If you have an interest in something being done, you want it to be done because it will benefit you. ④ Interest is an extra payment made to the lender by someone who has borrowed a sum of money, or by a bank or company to someone who has invested money in them. Interest is worked out as a percentage of the sum of money borrowed or invested. ▸ VERB ⑤ Something that interests you attracts your attention so that you want to learn or hear more about it. **interested** ADJECTIVE

> **interest** NOUN
> ① = attention, concern, curiosity, fascination
> ② = activity, hobby, pastime, pursuit
> ▸ VERB ⑤ = appeal, captivate, fascinate, intrigue, stimulate
> ≠ bore

interesting ADJECTIVE making you want to know, learn or hear more. **interestingly** ADVERB

> **interesting** ADJECTIVE
> = absorbing, compelling, entertaining, gripping, intriguing, stimulating
> ≠ boring

interface NOUN ① The interface between two subjects or systems is the area in which they affect each other or are linked. ② ICT The user interface of a computer program is how it is presented on the computer screen and how easy it is to operate.

interfere VERB ① If you interfere in a situation, you try to influence it, although it does not really concern you. ② Something that interferes with a situation has a damaging effect on it. **interference** NOUN **interfering** ADJECTIVE

> **interfere** VERB
> ① = butt in, intervene, intrude, meddle, tamper
> ② = conflict, disrupt

interim ADJECTIVE intended for use only until something permanent is arranged • *an interim government.*

interior NOUN ① the inside part of something. ▸ ADJECTIVE ② Interior means inside • *They painted the interior walls white.*

interlude *[Rhymes with **rude**]* NOUN a short break from an activity.

intermediary, intermediaries *[Said in-ter-**meed**-yer-ee]* NOUN someone who tries to get two groups of people to come to an agreement.

intermediate ADJECTIVE An intermediate level occurs in the middle, between two other stages • *intermediate students*.

interminable ADJECTIVE If something is interminable, it goes on for a very long time • *an interminable wait for the bus*. **interminably** ADVERB

intermission NOUN an interval between two parts of a film or play.

intermittent ADJECTIVE happening only occasionally. **intermittently** ADVERB

internal ADJECTIVE happening inside a person, place or object. **internally** ADVERB

international ADJECTIVE [GEOGRAPHY] ① involving different countries. ▶ NOUN ② a sports match between two countries. **internationally** ADVERB

internet or **Internet** NOUN [ICT] The internet is a global communication system of interconnected computer networks which supports the world wide web, email and instant messaging.

interplay NOUN The interplay between two things is the way they react with one another.

interpret VERB ① If you interpret what someone writes, says or does, you decide what it means. ② If you interpret a foreign language that someone is speaking, you translate it. **interpretation** NOUN **interpreter** NOUN

interrogate VERB If you interrogate someone, you question them thoroughly to get information from them. **interrogation** NOUN **interrogator** NOUN

> **interrogate** VERB
> = examine, grill (*informal*), question, quiz

interrupt VERB ① If you interrupt someone, you start talking while they are talking. ② If you interrupt a process or activity, you stop it continuing for a time. **interruption** NOUN

> **interrupt** VERB
> ① = butt in, heckle
> ② = break, discontinue, suspend

intersect VERB When two roads or lines intersect, they cross each other.

intersection, **intersections** NOUN ① An intersection is where two roads meet. ② [MATHS] In maths, an intersection is the point where two straight lines meet.

interspersed ADJECTIVE If something is interspersed with things, these things occur at various points in it.

interval NOUN ① the period of time between two moments or dates. ② a short break during a play or concert. ③ [MUSIC] In music, an interval is the difference in pitch between two musical notes.

> **interval** NOUN
> ① = break, gap, hiatus (*formal*), interlude, intermission, pause

intervene VERB If you intervene in a situation, you step in to prevent conflict between people. **intervention** NOUN

> **intervene** VERB
> = arbitrate, mediate

intervening ADJECTIVE An intervening period of time is one which separates two events.

interview NOUN ① a meeting at which someone asks you questions about yourself to see if you are suitable for a particular job. ② a conversation in which a journalist asks a famous person questions. ▶ VERB ③ If you interview someone, you ask them questions about themselves. **interviewer** NOUN **interviewee** NOUN

intestine NOUN Your intestines are a long tube which carries food from your stomach through to your bowels, and in which the food is digested. **intestinal** ADJECTIVE

intimate ADJECTIVE *[Said **in**-ti-mit]* ① If two people are intimate, there is a close relationship between them. ② An intimate matter is very private and personal. ③ An intimate knowledge of something is very deep and detailed. ▶ VERB *[Said **in**-ti-mate]* ④ If you intimate something, you hint at it • *He did intimate that he might give up.* **intimately** ADVERB **intimacy** NOUN **intimation** NOUN

intimidate VERB If you intimidate someone, you frighten them in a threatening way. **intimidated** ADJECTIVE **intimidating** ADJECTIVE **intimidation** NOUN

into PREPOSITION ① If something goes into something else, it goes inside it. ② If you bump or crash into something, you hit it. ③ *(informal)* If you are into something, you like it very much • *Nowadays I'm really into healthy food.*

intolerable ADJECTIVE If something is intolerable, it is so bad that it is difficult to put up with it. **intolerably** ADVERB

intonation NOUN Your intonation is the way that your voice rises and falls as you speak.

intoxicated ADJECTIVE If someone is intoxicated, they are drunk. **intoxicating** ADJECTIVE **intoxication** NOUN

intractable ADJECTIVE *(formal)* stubborn and difficult to deal with or control.

intravenous *[Said in-trav-**vee**-nuss]* ADJECTIVE Intravenous foods or drugs are given to sick people through their veins. **intravenously** ADVERB

intrepid ADJECTIVE not worried by danger • *an intrepid explorer.* **intrepidly** ADVERB

intricate ADJECTIVE Something that is intricate has many fine details • *walls and ceilings covered with intricate patterns.* **intricately** ADVERB **intricacy** NOUN

intrigue NOUN ① Intrigue is the making of secret plans, often with the intention of harming other people • *political intrigue.* ▶ VERB ② If something intrigues you, you are fascinated by it and curious about it. **intriguing** ADJECTIVE

intrinsic ADJECTIVE *(formal)* The intrinsic qualities of something are its basic qualities. **intrinsically** ADVERB

introduce VERB ① If you introduce one person to another, you tell them each other's name so that they can get to know each other. ② When someone introduces a radio or television show, they say a few words at the beginning to tell you about it. ③ If you introduce someone to something, they learn about it for the first time. **introductory** ADJECTIVE

introduction NOUN ① The introduction of someone or something is the act of presenting them for the first time. ② [ENGLISH] a piece of writing at the beginning of a book, which usually tells you what the book is about.

> **introduction** NOUN
> ① = establishment, inauguration *(formal)*, initiation, institution, launch
> ② = foreword, preface, prologue

introvert NOUN someone who spends more time thinking about their private feelings than about the world around them, and who often finds it difficult to talk to others.
introverted ADJECTIVE

intrude VERB To intrude on someone or something is to disturb them • *I don't want to intrude on your parents.*
intruder NOUN **intrusion** NOUN
intrusive ADJECTIVE

intrude VERB
= butt in, encroach, infringe, interrupt, trespass, violate

intuition *[Said int-yoo-**ish**-n]* NOUN Your intuition is a feeling you have about something that you cannot explain • *My intuition is right about him.* **intuitive** ADJECTIVE **intuitively** ADVERB

Inuit; also spelt **Innuit** NOUN one of a group of peoples who live in Northern Canada, Greenland, Alaska and Eastern Siberia.

inundated ADJECTIVE If you are inundated by messages or requests, you receive so many that you cannot deal with them all.

invade VERB ① If an army invades a country, it enters it by force. ② If someone invades your privacy, they disturb you when you want to be alone. **invader** NOUN

invade VERB
① = attack, enter, occupy, violate

invalid[1] *[Said **in**-va-lid]* NOUN someone who is so ill that they need to be looked after by someone else.

invalid[2] *[Said in-**val**-id]* ADJECTIVE ① If an argument or result is invalid, it is not acceptable because it is based on a mistake. ② If a law, marriage or election is invalid, it is illegal because it has not been carried out properly. **invalidate** VERB

invaluable ADJECTIVE extremely useful • *This book contains invaluable tips.*

invariably ADVERB If something invariably happens, it almost always happens.

invasion NOUN ① HISTORY The invasion of a country or territory is the act of entering it by force. ② an unwanted disturbance or intrusion • *an invasion of her privacy.*

invective NOUN *(formal)* Invective is abusive language used by someone who is angry.

invent VERB ① If you invent a device or process, you are the first person to think of it or to use it. ② If you invent a story or an excuse, you make it up.
inventor NOUN **invention** NOUN
inventive ADJECTIVE **inventiveness** NOUN

invent VERB
① = coin, come up with *(informal)*, conceive, create, formulate, originate
② = concoct, fabricate, make up, manufacture

inventory, **inventories** *[Said **in**-vin-to-ri]* NOUN a written list of all the objects in a place.

inverse ADJECTIVE *(formal)* If there is an inverse relationship between two things, one decreases as the other increases.

invertebrate NOUN SCIENCE An invertebrate is a creature which does not have a spine. Some invertebrates, for example crabs, have an external skeleton.

inverted ADJECTIVE upside down or back to front.

invest VERB ① If you invest money, you pay it into a bank or buy shares so that you will receive a profit. ② If you invest in something useful, you buy it because it will help you do something better. ③ If you invest money, time or energy in something, you try to make it a success. **investor**

NOUN **investment** NOUN

investigate VERB To investigate something is to try to find out all the facts about it. **investigator** NOUN **investigation** NOUN

investigate VERB
= examine, explore, probe, research, sift, study

inveterate ADJECTIVE having lasted for a long time and not likely to stop • *an inveterate gambler.*

invincible ADJECTIVE unable to be defeated. **invincibility** NOUN

invincible ADJECTIVE
= impregnable, indomitable, unbeatable

invisible ADJECTIVE If something is invisible, you cannot see it, because it is hidden, very small or imaginary. **invisibly** ADVERB **invisibility** NOUN

invisible ADJECTIVE
= concealed, disguised, hidden, inconspicuous, unseen
≠ visible

invite VERB ① If you invite someone to an event, you ask them to come to it. ② If you invite someone to do something, you ask them to do it • *Andrew has been invited to speak at the conference.* **inviting** ADJECTIVE **invitation** NOUN

invoice NOUN a bill for services or goods.

invoke VERB ① (*formal*) If you invoke a law, you use it to justify what you are doing. ② If you invoke certain feelings, you cause someone to have these feelings.

involuntary ADJECTIVE sudden and uncontrollable. **involuntarily** ADVERB

involve VERB PSHE If a situation involves someone or something, it includes them as a necessary part. **involvement** NOUN

involve VERB
= incorporate, require, take in

inward ADJECTIVE, ADVERB ① Inward means towards the inside or centre of something • *inward motion.* ▸ ADJECTIVE ② Your inward thoughts and feelings are private • *She gave an inward sigh of relief.* **inwardly** ADVERB

inwards ADVERB towards the centre or inside • *Let your fingers curl inwards.*

iodine [*Said* ***eye***-*oh-deen*] NOUN SCIENCE Iodine is a bluish-black element whose compounds are used in medicine and photography. Its atomic number is 53 and its symbol is I.

ion [*Said* ***eye***-*on*] NOUN Ions are electrically charged atoms.

iota NOUN an extremely small amount • *He did not have an iota of proof.*

IQ NOUN Your IQ is your level of intelligence shown by the results of a special test. IQ is an abbreviation for 'intelligence quotient'.

Iranian [*Said ir-****rain****-ee-an*] ADJECTIVE ① belonging or relating to Iran. ▸ NOUN ② someone who comes from Iran. ③ Iranian is the main language spoken in Iran. It is also known as Farsi.

Iraqi [*Said ir-****ah****-kee*] ADJECTIVE ① belonging or relating to Iraq. ▸ NOUN ② someone who comes from Iraq.

irate [*Said eye-****rate***] ADJECTIVE very angry.

iris, irises [*Said* ***eye***-*riss*] NOUN ① the round, coloured part of your eye. ② a tall plant with long leaves and large blue, yellow or white flowers.

Irish ADJECTIVE ① belonging or relating to the Irish Republic, or to the whole of Ireland. ▸ NOUN ② Irish or Irish Gaelic is a language spoken in some parts of Ireland.

Irishman, Irishmen NOUN a man who comes from Ireland.

Irishwoman, Irishwomen NOUN a woman who comes from Ireland.

irk VERB If something irks you, it annoys you. **irksome** ADJECTIVE

iron NOUN ① SCIENCE Iron is a strong hard metallic element found in rocks. It is used in making tools and machines, and is also an important component of blood. Its atomic number is 26 and its symbol is Fe. ② An iron is a device which heats up and which you rub over clothes to remove creases. ▸VERB ③ If you iron clothes, you use a hot iron to remove creases from them. **ironing** NOUN **iron out** VERB If you iron out difficulties, you solve them.

Iron Age NOUN HISTORY The Iron Age was a time about 3000 years ago when people first started to make tools out of iron.

irony, ironies *[Said* ***eye****-ron-ee]* NOUN ① ENGLISH Irony is a form of humour in which you say the opposite of what you really mean • *This group could be described, without irony, as the fortunate ones.* ② There is irony in a situation when there is an unexpected or unusual connection between things or events • *It's a sad irony of life: once you are lost, a map is useless.* **ironic** or **ironical** ADJECTIVE **ironically** ADVERB

irrational ADJECTIVE ① Irrational feelings are not based on logical reasons • *irrational fears.* ② MATHS An irrational number is a number that cannot be expressed as the ratio of two whole numbers. **irrationally** ADVERB **irrationality** NOUN

> **irrational** ADJECTIVE
> ① = absurd, crazy (*informal*), illogical, nonsensical, unsound

irregular ADJECTIVE ① not smooth or even • *irregular walls.* ② not forming a regular pattern. ③ MATHS Irregular things are uneven or unequal, or are not symmetrical. **irregularly** ADVERB **irregularity** NOUN

> **irregular** ADJECTIVE
> ① = asymmetrical, bumpy, jagged, lopsided, ragged, uneven
> ≠ regular
> ② = erratic, haphazard, occasional, patchy, random, variable
> ≠ regular

irrelevant ADJECTIVE not directly connected with a subject • *He either ignored questions or gave irrelevant answers.* **irrelevance** NOUN

irrepressible ADJECTIVE Someone who is irrepressible is lively and cheerful.

irresistible ADJECTIVE ① unable to be controlled • *an irresistible urge to yawn.* ② extremely attractive • *irresistible freshly baked bread.* **irresistibly** ADVERB

irrespective ADJECTIVE If you say something will be done irrespective of certain things, you mean it will be done without taking those things into account.

irresponsible ADJECTIVE An irresponsible person does things without considering the consequences • *an irresponsible driver.* **irresponsibly** ADVERB **irresponsibility** NOUN

> **irresponsible** ADJECTIVE
> = careless, reckless, thoughtless, wild
> ≠ responsible

irrigate VERB To irrigate land is to supply it with water brought through pipes or ditches. **irrigated** ADJECTIVE **irrigation** NOUN

irritable ADJECTIVE easily annoyed.

> **irritable** ADJECTIVE
> = bad-tempered, cantankerous, petulant, ratty (*British and New Zealand; informal*)

irritate VERB ① If something irritates

you, it annoys you. ② If something irritates part of your body, it makes it tender, sore or itchy. **irritant** NOUN **irritation** NOUN

> **irritate** VERB
> ① = anger, annoy, bother, exasperate, needle (*informal*), ruffle

is the third person singular, present tense of **be**.

-ise or **-ize** SUFFIX '-ise' and '-ize' form verbs. Most verbs can be spelt with either ending, though there are some that can only be spelt with '-ise', for example *advertise*, *improvise* and *revise*.

-ish SUFFIX '-ish' forms adjectives that mean 'fairly' or 'rather' • *smallish* • *greenish*.

Islam [*Said* **iz**-*lahm*] NOUN RE Islam is the Muslim religion, which teaches that there is only one God, Allah, and Mohammed is his prophet. The holy book of Islam is the Qur'an. **Islamic** ADJECTIVE

island [*Said* **eye**-*land*] NOUN a piece of land surrounded on all sides by water. **islander** NOUN

isle [*Rhymes with* **mile**] NOUN (*literary*) an island.

-ism SUFFIX ① '-ism' forms nouns that refer to an action or condition • *criticism* • *heroism*. ② '-ism' forms nouns that refer to a political or economic system or a system of beliefs • *Marxism* • *Sikhism*. ③ '-ism' forms nouns that refer to a type of prejudice • *racism* • *sexism*.

isolate VERB ① If something isolates you or if you isolate yourself, you are set apart from other people. ② If you isolate something, you separate it from everything else. **isolated** ADJECTIVE **isolation** NOUN

ISP an abbreviation for 'internet service provider'.

Israeli, **Israelis** [*Said iz*-**rail**-*ee*] ADJECTIVE ① belonging or relating to Israel. ▶ NOUN ② someone who comes from Israel.

issue, **issues**, **issuing**, **issued** [*Said* **ish**-*yoo*] NOUN ① an important subject that people are talking about. ② a particular edition of a newspaper or magazine. ▶ VERB ③ If you issue a statement or a warning, you say it formally and publicly. ④ If someone issues something, they officially give it • *Staff were issued with plastic cards*.

> **issue** NOUN
> ① = concern, matter, problem, question, subject, topic
> ② = copy, edition, instalment
> ▶ VERB ③ = deliver, give, make, pronounce, read out, release
> ≠ withdraw
> ④ = equip, furnish (*formal*), give out, provide, supply

-ist SUFFIX ① '-ist' forms nouns and adjectives which refer to someone who is involved in a certain activity, or who believes in a certain system or religion • *chemist* • *motorist* • *Buddhist*. ② '-ist' forms nouns and adjectives which refer to someone who has a certain prejudice • *racist*.

it PRONOUN ① 'It' is used to refer to something that has already been mentioned, or to a situation or fact • *It was a difficult decision*. ② 'It' is used to refer to people or animals whose gender is not known • *If a baby is thirsty, it feeds more often*. ③ You use 'it' to make statements about the weather, time or date • *It's noon*.

Italian ADJECTIVE ① belonging or relating to Italy. ▶ NOUN ② someone who comes from Italy. ③ Italian is the main language spoken in Italy.

italics PLURAL NOUN Italics are letters printed in a special sloping way, and are often used to emphasise something. All the example sentences in this dictionary are in italics. **italic** ADJECTIVE

itch VERB ① When your skin itches, it has an unpleasant feeling and you want to scratch it. ② If you are itching to do something, you are impatient to do it. ▶ NOUN ③ an unpleasant feeling on your skin that you want to scratch. **itchy** ADJECTIVE

item NOUN ① one of a collection or list of objects. ② a newspaper or magazine article.

item NOUN
① = article, matter, point, thing
② = article, feature, notice, piece, report

itinerary, **itineraries** NOUN a plan of a journey, showing a route to follow and places to visit.

-itis SUFFIX '-itis' is added to the name of a part of the body to refer to disease or inflammation in that part • *appendicitis* • *tonsillitis*.

its ADJECTIVE, PRONOUN 'Its' refers to something belonging to or relating to things, children or animals that have already been mentioned • *The lion lifted its head*.

itself PRONOUN ① 'Itself' is used when the same thing, child or animal does an action and is affected by it • *The cat was washing itself*. ② 'Itself' is used to emphasise 'it'.

-ity SUFFIX '-ity' forms nouns that refer to a state or condition • *continuity* • *technicality*.

-ive SUFFIX '-ive' forms adjectives and some nouns • *massive* • *detective*.

ivory NOUN ① the valuable creamy-white bone which forms the tusk of an elephant. It is used to make ornaments. ▶ NOUN, ADJECTIVE ② creamy-white.

ivy NOUN an evergreen plant which creeps along the ground and up walls.

iwi, **iwi** or **iwis** NOUN In New Zealand, an iwi is a Māori tribe.

jab, **jabs**, **jabbing**, **jabbed** VERB ① To jab something means to poke at it roughly. ▸ NOUN ② a sharp or sudden poke. ③ (*informal*) an injection.

jack NOUN ① a piece of equipment for lifting heavy objects, especially for lifting a car when changing a wheel. ② In a pack of cards, a jack is a card with a picture of a young prince on it. ▸ VERB ③ To jack up an object means to raise it, especially by using a jack. ④ (*informal*) In New Zealand English, to jack something up is to organise or prepare something.

jacket NOUN ① a short coat reaching to the waist or hips. ② an outer covering for something • *a book jacket*. ③ The jacket of a baked potato is its skin.

jackpot NOUN In a gambling game, the jackpot is the top prize.

jade NOUN Jade is a hard green stone used for making jewellery and ornaments.

jagged ADJECTIVE sharp and spiky.

> **jagged** ADJECTIVE
> = barbed, craggy, rough, serrated
> ≠ smooth

jaguar NOUN A jaguar is a large member of the cat family with spots on its back. Jaguars live in South and Central America.

jail; also spelt **gaol** NOUN ① a building where people convicted of a crime are locked up. ▸ VERB ② To jail someone means to lock them up in a jail.

> **jail** NOUN
> ① = nick (*British, Australian and New Zealand; slang*), prison
> ▸ VERB ② = detain, imprison, incarcerate

jam, **jams**, **jamming**, **jammed** NOUN ① a food, made by boiling fruit and sugar together until it sets. ② a situation in which it is impossible to move • *a traffic jam*. ③ (*informal*) If someone is in a jam, they are in a difficult situation. ▸ VERB ④ If people or things are jammed into a place, they are squeezed together so closely that they can hardly move. ⑤ To jam something somewhere means to push it there roughly • *He jammed his foot on the brake*. ⑥ If something is jammed, it is stuck or unable to work properly. ⑦ To jam a radio signal means to interfere with it and prevent it from being received clearly.

> **jam** NOUN
> ② = crowd, crush, mass, mob, multitude, throng
> ③ = dilemma, fix (*informal*), hole (*slang*), plight, predicament, quandary, trouble
> ▸ VERB ⑤ = cram, force, ram, stuff
> ⑥ = stall, stick

Jamaican [*Said jam-**may**-kn*] ADJECTIVE ① belonging or relating to Jamaica. ▸ NOUN ② someone who comes from Jamaica.

jamboree NOUN a gathering of large numbers of people enjoying themselves.

janitor NOUN the caretaker of a building.

January NOUN January is the first month of the year. It has 31 days.

Japanese ADJECTIVE ① belonging or relating to Japan. ▶ NOUN ② someone who comes from Japan. ③ Japanese is the main language spoken in Japan.

jar, jars, jarring, jarred NOUN ① a glass container with a wide top used for storing food. ▶ VERB ② If something jars on you, you find it unpleasant or annoying.

jargon NOUN Jargon consists of words that are used in special or technical ways by particular groups of people, often making the language difficult to understand.

jarrah NOUN an Australian eucalypt tree that produces wood used for timber.

jasmine NOUN Jasmine is a climbing plant with small sweet-scented white flowers.

jaundice NOUN Jaundice is an illness affecting the liver, in which the skin and the whites of the eyes become yellow.

jaundiced ADJECTIVE pessimistic and lacking enthusiasm • *He takes a rather jaundiced view of politicians.*

jaunt NOUN a journey or trip you go on for pleasure.

jaunty, jauntier, jauntiest ADJECTIVE expressing cheerfulness and self-confidence • *a jaunty tune.* **jauntily** ADVERB

javelin NOUN a long spear that is thrown in sports competitions.

jaw NOUN ① A person's or animal's jaw is the bone in which the teeth are set. ② A person's or animal's jaws are their mouth and teeth.

jay NOUN a kind of noisy chattering bird.

jazz NOUN ① Jazz is a style of popular music with a forceful rhythm. ▶ VERB ② (*informal*) To jazz something up means to make it more colourful or exciting.

jazzy, jazzier, jazziest ADJECTIVE (*informal*) bright and showy.

jealous ADJECTIVE ① If you are jealous, you feel bitterness towards someone who has something that you would like to have. ② If you are jealous of something you have, you feel you must try to keep it from other people. **jealously** ADVERB **jealousy** NOUN

> **jealous** ADJECTIVE
> ① = envious, resentful

jeans PLURAL NOUN Jeans are casual denim trousers.

Jeep NOUN (*trademark*) a small road vehicle with four-wheel drive.

jeer VERB ① If you jeer at someone, you insult them in a loud, unpleasant way. ▶ NOUN ② Jeers are rude and insulting remarks. **jeering** ADJECTIVE

Jehovah [*Said ji-**hove**-ah*] PROPER NOUN RE Jehovah is a name of God in the Old Testament.

jelly, jellies NOUN ① a clear, sweet food eaten as a dessert. ② a type of clear, set jam.

jellyfish NOUN a sea animal with a clear soft body and tentacles which may sting.

jeopardise [*Said **jep**-par-dyz*]; also spelt **jeopardize** VERB To jeopardise something means to do something which puts it at risk • *Elaine jeopardised her health.*

jeopardy NOUN If someone or something is in jeopardy, they are at risk of failing or of being destroyed.

jerk VERB ① To jerk something means to give it a sudden, sharp pull. ② If something jerks, it moves suddenly and sharply. ▶ NOUN ③ a sudden sharp movement. ④ (*informal*) If you call someone a jerk, you mean they are stupid. **jerky** ADJECTIVE **jerkily** ADVERB

jersey NOUN ① a knitted garment for the upper half of the body. ② Jersey is a type of knitted woollen or cotton fabric used to make clothing.

jest NOUN ① a joke. ▶ VERB ② To jest means to speak jokingly.

jester NOUN In the past, a jester was a man who was kept to amuse the king or queen.

jet, jets, jetting, jetted NOUN ① a plane which is able to fly very fast. ② a stream of liquid, gas or flame forced out under pressure. ③ Jet is a hard black stone, usually highly polished and used in jewellery and ornaments. ▶ VERB ④ To jet somewhere means to fly there in a plane, especially a jet.

jet lag NOUN Jet lag is a feeling of tiredness or confusion that people have after a long flight across different time zones.

jettison VERB If you jettison something, you throw it away because you no longer want it.

jetty, jetties NOUN a wide stone wall or wooden platform at the edge of the sea or a river, where boats can be moored.

Jew *[Said joo]* NOUN [RE] a person who practises the religion of Judaism, or who is of Hebrew descent. **Jewish** ADJECTIVE

jewel NOUN a precious stone used to decorate valuable ornaments or jewellery. **jewelled** ADJECTIVE

jeweller NOUN a person who makes jewellery or who sells and repairs jewellery and watches.

jewellery NOUN Jewellery consists of ornaments that people wear, such as rings or necklaces, made of valuable metals and sometimes decorated with precious stones.

jib NOUN a small sail towards the front of a sailing boat.

jibe another spelling of **gibe**.

jig, jigs, jigging, jigged NOUN ① A jig is a type of lively folk dance; also the music that accompanies it. ▶ VERB ② If you jig, you dance or jump around in a lively bouncy manner.

jigsaw NOUN a puzzle consisting of a picture on cardboard that has been cut up into small pieces which have to be put together again.

jihad *[Said jee-had]* NOUN ① [RE] a holy war waged to defend or further the ideals of Islam. ② [RE] Jihad also means the personal struggle of a Muslim against sin.

jingle NOUN ① a short, catchy phrase or rhyme set to music and used to advertise something on radio or television. ② the sound of something jingling. ▶ VERB ③ When something jingles, it makes a tinkling sound like small bells.

jinks PLURAL NOUN High jinks is boisterous and mischievous behaviour.

jinx NOUN someone or something that is thought to bring bad luck • *He was beginning to think he was a jinx.*

jinxed ADJECTIVE If something is jinxed it is considered to be unlucky • *I think this house is jinxed.*

jitters PLURAL NOUN (*informal*) If you have got the jitters, you are feeling very nervous. **jittery** ADJECTIVE

job NOUN ① the work that someone does to earn money. ② a duty or responsibility • *It is a captain's job to lead from the front.* ▶ PHRASE ③ If something is **just the job**, it is exactly right or exactly what you wanted.

> **job** NOUN
> ① = employment, occupation, position, post, profession, trade
> ② = concern, duty, function, responsibility, role, task

jobless ADJECTIVE without any work.

jockey NOUN ① someone who rides a horse in a race. ▶ VERB ② To jockey for position means to manoeuvre in order to gain an advantage over other people.

jocular ADJECTIVE A jocular comment is intended to make people laugh. **jocularly** ADVERB

jog, jogs, jogging, jogged VERB ① To jog means to run slowly and rhythmically, often as a form of exercise. ② If you jog something, you knock it slightly so that it shakes or moves. ③ If someone or something jogs your memory, they remind you of something. ▶ NOUN ④ a slow run. **jogger** NOUN **jogging** NOUN

join VERB ① When two things join, or when one thing joins another, they come together. ② If you join a club or organisation, you become a member of it or start taking part in it. ③ To join two things means to fasten them. ▶ NOUN ④ a place where two things are fastened together. **join up** VERB If someone joins up, they become a member of the armed forces.

> **join** VERB
> ② = enlist, enrol, sign up
> ≠ resign
> ③ = attach, connect, couple, fasten, link, tie
> ≠ separate

joiner NOUN a person who makes wooden window frames, doors and furniture.

joinery NOUN Joinery is the work done by a joiner.

joint ADJECTIVE ① shared by or belonging to two or more people • *a joint building society account.* ▶ NOUN ② SCIENCE a part of the body where two bones meet and are joined together so that they can move, for example a knee or hip. ③ DGT a place where two things are fixed together. ④ a large piece of meat suitable for roasting. ⑤ (*informal*) any place of entertainment, such as a nightclub or pub. ▶ VERB ⑥ To joint meat means to cut it into large pieces according to where the bones are. **jointly** ADVERB **jointed** ADJECTIVE

joke NOUN ① something that you say or do to make people laugh, such as a funny story. ② anything that you think is ridiculous and not worthy of respect • *The decision was a joke.* ▶ VERB ③ If you are joking, you are teasing someone. **jokingly** ADVERB

> **joke** NOUN
> ① = gag (*informal*), jest, lark, prank, quip, wisecrack (*informal*), witticism
> ▶ VERB ④ = banter, jest, kid (*informal*), quip, tease

joker NOUN In a pack of cards, a joker is an extra card that does not belong to any of the four suits, but is used in some games.

jolly, jollier, jolliest; jollies, jollying, jollied ADJECTIVE ① happy, cheerful and pleasant. ▶ ADVERB ② (*informal*) Jolly also means very • *It all sounds like jolly good fun.* ▶ VERB ③ If you jolly someone along, you encourage them in a cheerful and friendly way. **jolliness** NOUN

jolt VERB ① To jolt means to move or shake roughly and violently. ② If you are jolted by something, it gives you an unpleasant surprise. ▶ NOUN ③ a sudden jerky movement. ④ an unpleasant shock or surprise.

jostle VERB To jostle means to push roughly against people in a crowd.

jot, jots, jotting, jotted VERB ① If you jot something down, you write it quickly in the form of a short informal note. ▶ NOUN ② a very small amount. **jotting** NOUN

journal NOUN ① a magazine that

deals with a particular subject, trade or profession. ② a diary which someone keeps regularly.

journalism NOUN Journalism is the work of collecting, writing and publishing news in newspapers and magazines, and on television and radio. **journalist** NOUN **journalistic** ADJECTIVE

journey NOUN ① the act of travelling from one place to another. ▶ VERB ② (*formal*) To journey somewhere means to travel there • *He intended to journey up the Amazon.*

> **journey** NOUN
> ① = excursion, expedition, passage, tour, trek, trip, voyage
> ▶ VERB ② = go, proceed (*formal*), tour, travel, trek, voyage

joust HISTORY NOUN In medieval times, a joust was a competition between knights fighting on horseback, using lances.

jovial ADJECTIVE cheerful and friendly. **jovially** ADVERB **joviality** NOUN

joy NOUN ① Joy is a feeling of great happiness. ② (*informal*) Joy also means success or luck • *Any joy with getting cup final tickets?* ③ something that makes you happy or gives you pleasure.

> **joy** NOUN
> ① = bliss, delight, ecstasy, elation, rapture
> ≠ misery

joyful ADJECTIVE ① causing pleasure and happiness. ② Someone who is joyful is extremely happy. **joyfully** ADVERB

> **joyful** ADJECTIVE
> ② = delighted, elated, jubilant, over the moon (*informal*)

joyous ADJECTIVE (*formal*) joyful. **joyously** ADVERB

joyride NOUN a drive in a stolen car for pleasure. **joyriding** NOUN **joyrider** NOUN

joystick NOUN ① a lever in an aircraft which the pilot uses to control height and direction. ② In some computer games, the joystick is the lever used to control the movement of objects on the screen.

jubilant ADJECTIVE feeling or expressing great happiness or triumph. **jubilantly** ADVERB

jubilation NOUN Jubilation is a feeling of great happiness and triumph.

jubilee NOUN a special anniversary of an event such as a coronation • *Queen Elizabeth's Diamond Jubilee in 2012.*

Judaism [*Said **joo**-day-i-zm*] NOUN RE Judaism is the religion of the Jewish people. It is based on a belief in one God, and draws its laws and authority from the Old Testament. **Judaic** ADJECTIVE

judge NOUN ① the person in a law court who decides how the law should be applied to people who appear in the court. ② someone who decides the winner in a contest or competition. ▶ VERB ③ If you judge someone or something, you form an opinion about them based on the evidence that you have. ④ To judge a contest or competition means to decide on the winner.

> **judge** NOUN
> ① = justice, magistrate
> ② = referee, umpire
> ▶ VERB ③ = appraise, assess, consider, estimate, evaluate, rate
> ④ = referee, umpire

judgment; also spelt **judgement** NOUN an opinion or decision based on evidence.

> **judgment** NOUN
> = appraisal, assessment, conclusion, opinion, ruling, verdict, view

judicial ADJECTIVE relating to judgment or to justice • *a judicial review.*

judiciary NOUN The judiciary is the branch of government concerned with justice and the legal system.

judicious ADJECTIVE sensible and showing good judgment. **judiciously** ADVERB

judo NOUN Judo is a sport in which two people try to force each other to the ground using special throwing techniques. It originated in Japan as a form of self-defence.

jug NOUN a container with a lip or spout used for holding or serving liquids.

juggernaut NOUN a large heavy lorry.

juggle VERB ① To juggle means to throw objects into the air, catching them in sequence, and tossing them up again so there are several in the air at one time. ② If you juggle several different activities, you spend some time doing each of them rather than concentrating on just one • *He has to juggle work and family life.* **juggler** NOUN

jugular NOUN The jugular or jugular vein is one of the veins in the neck which carry blood from the head back to the heart.

juice NOUN ① Juice is the liquid that can be squeezed or extracted from fruit or other food. ② Juices in the body are fluids • *gastric juices.*

juicy, juicier, juiciest ADJECTIVE ① Juicy food has a lot of juice in it. ② Something that is juicy is interesting, exciting or scandalous • *a juicy bit of gossip.* **juiciness** NOUN

jukebox NOUN a machine which automatically plays a selected piece of music when coins are inserted.

July NOUN July is the seventh month of the year. It has 31 days.

jumble NOUN ① an untidy muddle of things. ② Jumble consists of cheap articles that are given away to a charity so that they can be sold to raise money. ▶ VERB ③ To jumble things means to mix them up untidily.

jumbo NOUN ① A jumbo or jumbo jet is a large jet aeroplane that can carry several hundred passengers. ▶ ADJECTIVE ② very large • *jumbo packs of elastic bands.*

jump VERB ① To jump means to spring off the ground using your leg muscles. ② To jump something means to spring off the ground and move over or across it. ③ If you jump at something, such as an opportunity, you accept it eagerly. ④ If you jump on someone, you criticise them suddenly and forcefully. ⑤ If someone jumps, they make a sudden sharp movement of surprise. ⑥ If an amount or level jumps, it suddenly increases. ▶ NOUN ⑦ a spring into the air, sometimes over an object.

> **jump** VERB
> ② = bound, clear, hurdle, leap, spring, vault
> ⑥ = escalate, increase, rise, surge
> ▶ NOUN ⑦ = bound, leap, vault

jumper NOUN a knitted garment for the top half of the body.

jumpy, jumpier, jumpiest ADJECTIVE nervous and worried.

junction NOUN a place where roads or railway lines meet or cross.

June NOUN June is the sixth month of the year. It has 30 days.

jungle NOUN ① a dense tropical forest. ② a tangled mass of plants or other objects.

junior ADJECTIVE ① Someone who is junior to other people has a lower position in an organisation. ② Junior also means younger. ③ relating to childhood • *a junior school.* ▶ NOUN ④ someone who holds an unimportant position in an organisation.

junior ADJECTIVE
① = inferior, lesser, lower, subordinate
≠ senior

juniper NOUN an evergreen shrub with purple berries used in cooking and medicine.

junk NOUN ① Junk is old or second-hand articles which are sold cheaply or thrown away. ② If you think something is junk, you think it is worthless rubbish. ③ a Chinese sailing boat with a flat bottom and square sails.

junk NOUN
① = clutter, odds and ends, refuse (*formal*), rubbish, scrap, trash

junk food NOUN Junk food is food low in nutritional value which is eaten as well as or instead of proper meals.

junkie NOUN (*slang*) a drug addict.

Jupiter NOUN Jupiter is the largest planet in the solar system and the fifth from the sun.

jurisdiction NOUN ① (*formal*) Jurisdiction is the power or right of the courts to apply laws and make legal judgments • *The Court held that it did not have the jurisdiction to examine the merits of the case.* ② Jurisdiction is power or authority • *The airport was under French jurisdiction.*

juror NOUN a member of a jury.

jury, **juries** NOUN a group of people in a court of law who have been selected to listen to the facts of a case on trial, and to decide whether the accused person is guilty or not.

just ADJECTIVE ① fair and impartial • *She arrived at a just decision.* ② morally right or proper • *a just reward.* ▶ ADVERB ③ If something has just happened, it happened a very short time ago. ④ If you just do something, you do it by a very small amount • *They only just won.* ⑤ simply or only • *It was just an excuse not to do any work.* ⑥ exactly • *It's just what she wanted.* ▶ PHRASE ⑦ In South African English, **just now** means in a little while. **justly** ADVERB

justice NOUN ① Justice is fairness and reasonableness. ② CITIZENSHIP The system of justice in a country is the way in which laws are maintained by the courts. ③ a judge or magistrate.

justice NOUN
① = equity, fairness, impartiality
≠ injustice
③ = judge, magistrate

justify, **justifies**, **justifying**, **justified** VERB ① If you justify an action or idea, you prove or explain why it is reasonable or necessary. ② ICT To justify text that you have typed or keyed into a computer is to adjust the spaces between the words so each full line in a paragraph fills the space between the left and right hand margins of the page. **justification** NOUN **justifiable** ADJECTIVE

justify VERB
① = defend, excuse, explain, vindicate, warrant

jut, **juts**, **jutting**, **jutted** VERB If something juts out, it sticks out beyond or above a surface or edge.

juvenile ADJECTIVE ① suitable for young people. ② childish and rather silly • *a juvenile game.* ▶ NOUN ③ a young person not old enough to be considered an adult.

juxtapose VERB If you juxtapose things or ideas, you put them close together, often to emphasise the difference between them. **juxtaposition** NOUN

Kk

A B C D E F G H I J K L M N O P Q R S T U V W X Y Z

kaleidoscope *[Said kal-**eye**-dos-skope]* **NOUN** a toy consisting of a tube with a hole at one end. When you look through the hole and twist the other end of the tube, you can see a changing pattern of colours.

kamikaze **NOUN** HISTORY In the Second World War, a kamikaze was a Japanese pilot who flew an aircraft loaded with explosives directly into an enemy target knowing he would be killed doing so.

kangaroo, **kangaroos** **NOUN** a large Australian animal with very strong back legs which it uses for jumping.

karate *[Said kar-**rat**-ee]* **NOUN** Karate is a sport in which people fight each other using only their hands, elbows, feet and legs.

karma **NOUN** RE In Buddhism, Hinduism and Sikhism, karma refers to the forces that influence people's fortune and rebirth.

Karoo, **Karoos**; also spelt **Karroo** **NOUN** In South Africa, the Karoos are areas of very dry land.

kayak *[Said **ky**-ak]* **NOUN** a covered canoe with a small opening for the person sitting in it, originally used by the Inuit.

kebab **NOUN** pieces of meat or vegetable stuck on a stick and grilled.

keel **NOUN** ① the specially shaped bottom of a ship which supports the sides and sits in the water. ▸ **VERB** ② If someone or something keels over, they fall down sideways.

keen **ADJECTIVE** ① Someone who is keen shows great eagerness and enthusiasm. ② If you are keen on someone or something, you are attracted to or fond of them. ③ quick to notice or understand things. ④ Keen senses let you see, hear, smell and taste things very clearly or strongly. **keenly** **ADVERB** **keenness** **NOUN**

> **keen** **ADJECTIVE**
> ① = ardent, avid, eager, enthusiastic, fond of, into *(informal)*
> ③ = astute, brilliant, perceptive, quick, shrewd

keep, **keeps**, **keeping**, **kept** **VERB** ① To keep someone or something in a particular condition means to make them stay in that condition • *We'll walk to keep warm.* ② If you keep something, you have it and look after it. ③ To keep something also means to store it in the usual place. ④ If you keep doing something, you do it repeatedly or continuously • *I kept phoning the hospital.* ⑤ If you keep a promise, you do what you promised to do. ⑥ If you keep a secret, you do not tell anyone else. ⑦ If you keep a diary, you write something in it every day. ⑧ If you keep someone from going somewhere, you delay them so that they are late. ⑨ To keep someone means to provide them with money, food and clothing. ▸ **NOUN** ⑩ Your keep is the cost of the food you eat, your housing and your clothing • *He does not contribute towards his keep.* ⑪ HISTORY the main tower inside the walls of a castle. **keep up** **VERB** If you keep up with other people, you move or work at the same speed as they do.

keep VERB
② = care for, maintain, preserve
③ = deposit, hold, store
⑤ = carry out, fulfil, honour

keeper NOUN ① a person whose job is to look after the animals in a zoo. ② a goalkeeper in soccer or hockey.

keeping NOUN ① If something is in your keeping, it has been given to you to look after for a while. ▶ PHRASE ② If one thing is **in keeping with** another, the two things are suitable or appropriate together.

keepsake NOUN something that someone gives you to remind you of a particular person or event.

keg NOUN a small barrel.

kennel NOUN ① a shelter for a dog. ② A kennels is a place where dogs can be kept for a time, or where they are bred.

Kenyan *[Said **ken**-yan or **keen**-yan]* ADJECTIVE ① belonging or relating to Kenya. ▶ NOUN ② someone who comes from Kenya.

kept the past tense and past participle of **keep**.

kerb NOUN the raised edge at the point where a pavement joins onto a road.

kernel NOUN the part of a nut that is inside the shell.

kerosene NOUN Kerosene is the same as paraffin.

ketchup NOUN Ketchup is a cold sauce, usually made from tomatoes.

kettle NOUN a metal container with a spout, in which you boil water.

key NOUN ① a shaped piece of metal that fits into a hole so that you can unlock a door, wind something that is clockwork, or start a car. ② The keys on a computer keyboard, piano or cash register are the buttons that you press to use it. ③ an explanation of the symbols used in a map or diagram. ④ MUSIC In music, a key is a scale of notes. ⑤ The key to a situation or result is the way in which it can be achieved • *The key to success is to be ready from the start.* ▶ VERB ⑥ ICT If you key in information on a computer keyboard, you type it. ▶ ADJECTIVE ⑦ The key person or thing in a group is the most important one.

keyboard NOUN ICT a row of buttons or levers on a computer, piano or cash register.

kg an abbreviation for 'kilogram' or 'kilograms'.

khaki *[Said **kah**-kee]* NOUN ① Khaki is a strong yellowish-brown material, used especially for military uniforms. ▶ NOUN, ADJECTIVE ② yellowish-brown.

kibbutz, **kibbutzim** *[Said kib-**boots**]* NOUN a place of work in Israel, for example a farm or factory, where the workers live together and share all the duties and income.

kick VERB ① If you kick something, you hit it with your foot. ▶ NOUN ② If you give something a kick, you hit it with your foot. ③ (*informal*) If you get a kick out of doing something, you enjoy doing it very much. **kick off** VERB When players kick off, they start a soccer or rugby match. **kick-off** NOUN

kid, **kids**, **kidding**, **kidded** NOUN ① (*informal*) a child. ② a young goat. ▶ VERB ③ If you kid people, you tease them by deceiving them in fun.

kidnap, **kidnaps**, **kidnapping**, **kidnapped** VERB To kidnap someone is to take them away by force and demand a ransom in exchange for returning them. **kidnapper** NOUN **kidnapping** NOUN

kidnap VERB
= abduct, capture, seize

kidney NOUN ① Your kidneys are two organs in your body that remove waste products from your blood. ② Kidney is also the kidneys of some animals, which may be cooked and eaten.

kill VERB ① To kill a person, animal or plant is to make them die. ② (*informal*) If something is killing you, it is causing you severe pain or discomfort • *My arms are killing me*. ▶ NOUN ③ The kill is the moment when a hunter kills an animal. **killer** NOUN

kill VERB
① = assassinate, butcher (*informal*), destroy, execute, exterminate, massacre, murder, slaughter, slay (*literary*)

kiln NOUN ART an oven for baking china or pottery until it becomes hard and dry.

kilo, **kilos** NOUN a kilogram.

kilobyte NOUN ICT a unit of computer memory size, equal to 1024 bytes.

kilogram NOUN a unit of weight equal to 1000 grams.

kilometre NOUN MATHS a unit of distance equal to 1000 metres.

kilowatt NOUN SCIENCE a unit of power equal to 1000 watts.

kilt NOUN a tartan skirt worn by men as part of Scottish Highland dress.

kimono, **kimonos** NOUN a long, loose garment with wide sleeves and a sash, worn in Japan.

kin PLURAL NOUN Your kin are your relatives.

kin PLURAL NOUN
= family, kindred, people, relations, relatives

kind NOUN ① A particular kind of thing is something of the same type or sort as other things • *that kind of film*. ▶ ADJECTIVE ② Someone who is kind is considerate and generous towards other people. **kindly** ADVERB

kind NOUN
① = brand, breed, category, class, classification, genre, grade, sort, species, type, variety
▶ ADJECTIVE ② = benevolent, benign, charitable, compassionate, considerate, good, humane, kind-hearted, kindly, thoughtful, unselfish
≠ cruel

kindergarten NOUN a school for children who are too young to go to primary school.

kindness NOUN the quality of being considerate towards other people.

kindness NOUN
= benevolence, charity, compassion, gentleness, humanity
≠ cruelty

kindred ADJECTIVE If you say that someone is a kindred spirit, you mean that they have the same interests or opinions as you.

king NOUN ① HISTORY The king of a country is a man who is the head of state in the country, and who inherited his position from his parents. ② In chess, the king is a piece which can only move one square at a time. When a king cannot move away from a position where it can be taken, the game is lost. ③ In a pack of cards, a king is a card with a picture of a king on it.

kingdom NOUN ① HISTORY a country that is governed by a king or queen. ② The largest divisions of the living organisms in the natural world are called kingdoms • *the animal kingdom*.

king-size or **king-sized** ADJECTIVE

larger than the normal size • *a king-size bed.*

kinship NOUN Kinship is a family relationship to other people.

kiosk *[Said* ***kee****-osk]* NOUN a covered stall on a street where you can buy newspapers, sweets or cigarettes.

kip, kips, kipping, kipped *(informal)* NOUN ① a period of sleep. ▸VERB ② When you kip, you sleep.

kiss VERB ① When you kiss someone, you touch them with your lips as a sign of love or affection. ▸NOUN ② When you give someone a kiss, you kiss them.

kiss of life NOUN The kiss of life is a method of reviving someone by blowing air into their lungs.

kit NOUN ① a collection of things that you use for a sport or other activity. ② a set of parts that you put together to make something.

kitchen NOUN a room used for cooking and preparing food.

kite NOUN ① a frame covered with paper or cloth which is attached to a piece of string, and which you fly in the air. ② a shape with four sides, with two pairs of the same length, and none of the sides parallel to each other. ③ a large bird of prey with a long tail and long wings.

kitten NOUN a young cat.

kitty, kitties NOUN a fund of money that has been given by a group of people who will use it to pay for or do things together.

kiwi, kiwi or **kiwis** *[Said* ***kee****-wee]* NOUN ① a type of bird found in New Zealand. Kiwis cannot fly. ② *(informal)* someone who comes from New Zealand. The plural of this sense is 'kiwis'.

km an abbreviation for 'kilometres'.

knack NOUN a skilful or clever way of doing something difficult • *the knack of making friends.*

knead VERB If you knead dough, you press it and squeeze it with your hands before baking it.

knee NOUN the joint in your leg between your ankle and your hip.

kneecap NOUN Your kneecaps are the bones at the front of your knees.

kneel, kneels, kneeling, knelt VERB When you kneel, you bend your legs and lower your body until your knees are touching the ground.

knell NOUN *(literary)* the sound of a bell rung to announce a death or at a funeral.

knelt the past tense and past participle of **kneel**.

knew the past tense of **know**.

knickers PLURAL NOUN Knickers are underpants worn by women and girls.

knife, knives; knifes, knifing, knifed NOUN ① [DGT] a sharp metal tool that you use to cut things. ▸VERB ② To knife someone is to stab them with a knife.

knight NOUN ① a man who has been given the title 'Sir' by the King or Queen. ② [HISTORY] In medieval Europe, a knight was a man who served a monarch or lord as a mounted soldier. ③ a chess piece that is usually in the shape of a horse's head. ▸VERB ④ To knight a man is to give him the title 'Sir'. **knighthood** NOUN

knit, knits, knitting, knitted VERB ① If you knit a piece of clothing, you make it by working lengths of wool together, either using needles held in the hand, or with a machine. ② If you knit your brows, you frown. **knitting** NOUN

knob NOUN ① a round handle. ② a round switch on a machine • *the knobs of a radio.*

knock VERB ① If you knock on something, you strike it with your hand or fist. ② If you knock a part of your body against something, you bump into it quite forcefully. ③ (*informal*) To knock someone is to criticise them. ▶ NOUN ④ a firm blow on something solid • *There was a knock at the door*. **knock out** VERB To knock someone out is to hit them so hard that they become unconscious.

knockout NOUN ① a punch in boxing which knocks a boxer unconscious. ② a competition in which competitors are eliminated in each round until only the winner is left.

knot, **knots**, **knotting**, **knotted** NOUN ① a fastening made by looping a piece of string around itself and pulling the ends tight. ② a small lump visible on the surface of a piece of wood. ③ A knot of people is a small group of them. ④ (*technical*) a unit of speed used for ships and aircraft. ▶ VERB ⑤ If you knot a piece of string, you tie a knot in it.

know, **knows**, **knowing**, **knew**, **known** VERB ① If you know a fact, you have it in your mind and you do not need to learn it. ② People you know are not strangers because you have met them and spoken to them. ▶ PHRASE ③ (*informal*) If you are **in the know**, you are one of a small number of people who share a secret.

> **know** VERB
> ① = apprehend, be aware of, comprehend, perceive, see, understand
> ② = be acquainted with, be familiar with, recognise

know-how NOUN Know-how is the ability to do something that is quite difficult or technical.

knowing ADJECTIVE A knowing look is one that shows that you know or understand something that other people do not. **knowingly** ADVERB

knowledge NOUN Knowledge is all the information and facts that you know.

> **knowledge** NOUN
> = education, learning, scholarship, wisdom

knowledgeable ADJECTIVE Someone who is knowledgeable knows a lot about a subject • *She was very knowledgeable about Irish mythology*.

knuckle NOUN Your knuckles are the joints at the end of your fingers where they join your hand.

koala NOUN an Australian animal with grey fur and small tufted ears. Koalas live in trees and eat eucalyptus leaves.

Koran [*Said kaw-**rahn***]; also spelt **Qur'an** NOUN RE The Koran is the holy book of Islam.

Korean [*Said kor-**ree**-an*] ADJECTIVE ① relating or belonging to Korea. ▶ NOUN ② someone who comes from Korea. ③ Korean is the main language spoken in Korea.

kosher [*Said **koh**-sher*] ADJECTIVE RE Kosher food is acceptable for Jewish people to eat.

kung fu [*Said kung **foo***] NOUN Kung fu is a Chinese style of fighting which involves using your hands and feet.

Kurd NOUN The Kurds are a group of people who live mainly in eastern Turkey, northern Iraq and western Iran.

Kurdish ADJECTIVE ① belonging or relating to the Kurds • *Kurdish culture*. ▶ NOUN ② Kurdish is the language spoken by the Kurds.

Ll

l an abbreviation for 'litres'.

lab NOUN (*informal*) a laboratory.

label, **labels**, **labelling**, **labelled** NOUN ① a piece of paper or plastic attached to something as an identification. ▸ VERB ② If you label something, you put a label on it.

> **label** NOUN
> ① = sticker, tag, ticket
> ▸ VERB ② = flag, sticker, tag

laboratory, **laboratories** NOUN a place where scientific experiments are carried out.

laborious ADJECTIVE needing a lot of effort or time. **laboriously** ADVERB

Labor Party NOUN In Australia, the Labor Party is one of the major political parties.

labour NOUN ① Labour is hard work. ② The workforce of a country or industry is sometimes called its labour • *unskilled labour*. ③ In Britain, the Labour Party is a political party that believes that wealth and power should be shared more equally among the population. ④ In New Zealand, the Labour Party is one of the main political parties. ⑤ Labour is also the last stage of pregnancy when a woman gives birth to a baby. ▸ VERB ⑥ (*old-fashioned*) To labour means to work hard. **labourer** NOUN

> **labour** NOUN
> ① = effort, exertion, industry, toil, work
> ② = employees, workers, workforce
> ▸ VERB ⑥ = slave, toil, work
> ≠ relax

labrador NOUN a large dog with short black, golden or brown hair.

labyrinth [*Said* ***lab**-er-inth*] NOUN a complicated series of paths or passages.

lace NOUN ① Lace is a very fine decorated cloth made with a lot of holes in it. ② Laces are cords with which you fasten your shoes. ▸ VERB ③ When you lace up your shoes, you tie a bow in the laces. ④ To lace someone's food or drink means to put a small amount of alcohol, a drug, or poison in it. **lacy** ADJECTIVE

lack NOUN ① If there is a lack of something, it is not present when or where it is needed. ▸ VERB ② If something is lacking, it is not present when or where it is needed. ③ If someone or something is lacking in something, they do not have it or do not have enough of it • *Francis was lacking in stamina*.

> **lack** NOUN
> ① = absence, deficiency, scarcity, shortage, want
> ≠ abundance
> ▸ VERB ④ = be deficient in, be short of, miss

lacklustre [*Said* ***lak**-luss-ter*] ADJECTIVE not interesting or exciting.

laconic [*Said lak-**kon**-ik*] ADJECTIVE using very few words.

lacquer [*Said* ***lak**-er*] NOUN Lacquer is thin, clear paint that you put on wood to protect it and make it shiny.

lacrosse NOUN Lacrosse is an outdoor ball game in which two teams try to score goals using long sticks with nets on the end of them.

lad NOUN a boy or young man.

ladder NOUN ① a wooden or metal frame used for climbing which consists of horizontal steps fixed to two vertical poles. ② If your stockings or tights have a ladder in them, they have a vertical, ladder-like tear in them. ▶ VERB ③ If you ladder your stockings or tights, you get a ladder in them.

laden [*Said* ***lay**-den*] ADJECTIVE To be laden with something means to be carrying or holding a lot of it • *baskets laden with fruit.*

ladle NOUN ① a long-handled spoon with a deep, round bowl, which you use to serve soup. ▶ VERB ② If you ladle out food, you serve it with a ladle.

lady, **ladies** NOUN ① a woman, especially one who is considered to be well-mannered. ② Lady is a title used in front of the name of a woman from the nobility, such as a lord's wife.

ladylike ADJECTIVE behaving in a polite and socially correct way.

lag, **lags**, **lagging**, **lagged** VERB ① To lag behind is to make slower progress than other people. ② To lag pipes is to wrap cloth round them to stop the water inside freezing in cold weather.

> **lag** VERB
> ① = fall behind, trail

lager NOUN Lager is light-coloured beer.

lagoon NOUN an area of water separated from the sea by reefs or sand.

laid the past tense and past participle of **lay**.

lain the past participle of some meanings of **lie**[1].

lair NOUN a place where a wild animal lives.

lake NOUN an area of fresh water surrounded by land.

lamb NOUN ① a young sheep. ② Lamb is the meat from a lamb.

lame ADJECTIVE ① unable to walk easily because of an injured leg. ② A lame excuse is not very convincing.
lamely ADVERB **lameness** NOUN

> **lame** ADJECTIVE
> ② = feeble, flimsy, pathetic, poor, unconvincing, weak

lament VERB ① To lament something means to express sorrow or regret about it. ▶ NOUN ② an expression of sorrow or regret. ③ a song or poem expressing grief at someone's death.

> **lament** VERB
> ① = grieve, mourn, wail, weep
> ▶ NOUN ② = moan, wail

lamentable ADJECTIVE disappointing and regrettable.

laminated ADJECTIVE consisting of several thin sheets or layers stuck together • *laminated glass.*

lamp NOUN a device that produces light.

lamppost NOUN a tall column in a street, with a lamp at the top.

lance VERB ① To lance a boil or abscess means to stick a sharp instrument into it in order to release the fluid. ▶ NOUN ② a long spear that used to be used by soldiers on horseback.

land NOUN ① Land is an area of ground. ② Land is also the part of the earth that is not covered by water. ③ a country • *our native land.* ▶ VERB ④ When a plane lands, it arrives back on the ground after a flight. ⑤ If you land something you have been trying to get, you succeed in getting it • *She eventually landed a job with a local radio* *station*. ⑥ To land a fish means to catch it while fishing. ⑦ If you land someone with something unpleasant, you cause them to have to deal with it.

land NOUN
① = estate, grounds, property
③ = country, nation, province, region, territory
▸ VERB ④ = alight, dock, touch down

landing NOUN ① a flat area in a building at the top of a flight of stairs. ② The landing of an aeroplane is its arrival back on the ground after a flight • *a smooth landing*.

landlady, **landladies** NOUN a woman who owns a house or small hotel and who lets rooms to people.

landlord NOUN a man who owns a house or small hotel and who lets rooms to people.

landmark NOUN ① a noticeable feature in a landscape, which you can use to check your position. ② an important stage in the development of something • *The play is a landmark in Japanese theatre*.

landowner NOUN someone who owns land, especially a large area of the countryside.

landscape NOUN ① GEOGRAPHY The landscape is the view over an area of open land. ② ART a painting of the countryside.

landslide NOUN ① a large amount of loose earth and rocks falling down a mountain side. ② a victory in an election won by a large number of votes.

lane NOUN ① a narrow road, especially in the country. ② one of the strips on a road marked with lines to guide drivers.

language NOUN ① the system of words that the people of a country use to communicate with each other. ② Your language is the style in which you express yourself • *His language is often obscure*. ③ Language is the study of the words and grammar of a particular language.

language NOUN
① = dialect, idiom, jargon, lingo (*informal*), tongue, vernacular, vocabulary
② = phrasing, style, wording

languid [*Said* ***lang****-gwid*] ADJECTIVE slow and lacking energy. **languidly** ADVERB

languish VERB If you languish, you endure an unpleasant situation for a long time • *Many languished in poverty*.

lanky, **lankier**, **lankiest** ADJECTIVE Someone who is lanky is tall and thin and moves rather awkwardly.

lantern NOUN a lamp in a metal frame with glass sides.

lap, **laps**, **lapping**, **lapped** NOUN ① Your lap is the flat area formed by your thighs when you are sitting down. ② one circuit of a running track or racecourse. ▸ VERB ③ When an animal laps up liquid, it drinks using its tongue to get the liquid into its mouth. ④ If you lap someone in a race, you overtake them when they are still on the previous lap. ⑤ When water laps against something, it gently moves against it in little waves.

lapel [*Said lap-****el***] NOUN a flap which is joined on to the collar of a jacket or coat.

lapse NOUN ① a moment of bad behaviour by someone who usually behaves well. ② a slight mistake. ③ a period of time between two events. ▸ VERB ④ If you lapse into a different way of behaving, you start behaving that way • *The offenders lapsed into a sullen silence*. ⑤ If a legal document or contract lapses, it is not renewed on the date when it expires.

laptop NOUN [ICT] a type of small portable computer.

lard NOUN Lard is fat from a pig, used in cooking.

larder NOUN a room in which you store food, often next to a kitchen.

large ADJECTIVE ① Someone or something that is large is much bigger than average. ▶ PHRASE ② If a prisoner is **at large**, he or she has escaped from prison.

> **large** ADJECTIVE
> ① = big, colossal, enormous, giant, gigantic, great, huge, immense, massive, vast
> ≠ small

largely ADVERB to a great extent • *The public are largely unaware of this.*

lark NOUN ① a small brown bird with a distinctive song. ② If you do something for a lark, you do it in a high-spirited or mischievous way for fun.

larrikin NOUN (*informal*) In Australian and New Zealand English, a larrikin is a young person who behaves in a wild or irresponsible way.

larva, **larvae** NOUN an insect, which looks like a short, fat worm, at the stage before it becomes an adult.

larynx, **larynxes** or **larynges** NOUN the part of your throat containing the vocal cords, through which air passes between your nose and lungs.

lasagne [*Said laz-**zan**-ya*] NOUN Lasagne is an Italian dish made with wide flat sheets of pasta, meat and cheese sauce.

laser NOUN a machine that produces a powerful concentrated beam of light which is used to cut very hard materials and in some kinds of surgery.

lash NOUN ① Your lashes are the hairs growing on the edge of your eyelids. ② a strip of leather at the end of a whip. ③ Lashes are blows struck with a whip. **lash out** VERB To lash out at someone means to criticise them severely.

lass NOUN a girl or young woman.

last ADJECTIVE ① The last thing or event is the most recent one • *last year.* ② The last thing that remains is the only one left after all the others have gone • *The last family left in 1990.* ▶ ADVERB ③ If you last did something on a particular occasion, you have not done it since then • *They last met in Rome.* ④ The thing that happens last in a sequence of events is the final one • *He added the milk last.* ▶ VERB ⑤ If something lasts, it continues to exist or happen • *Her speech lasted fifty minutes.* ⑥ To last also means to remain in good condition • *The mixture will last for up to 2 weeks in the fridge.* ▶ PHRASE ⑦ **At last** means after a long time. **lastly** ADVERB

> **last** ADJECTIVE
> ① = latest, most recent, preceding, previous
> ≠ first
> ② = closing, concluding, final, ultimate
> ≠ first
> ▶ VERB ⑤ = carry on, continue, endure, persist, remain, survive

last-ditch ADJECTIVE A last-ditch attempt to do something is a final attempt to succeed when everything else has failed.

latch NOUN ① a simple door fastening consisting of a metal bar which falls into a hook. ② a type of door lock which locks automatically when you close the door and which has to be opened with a key. ▶ VERB ③ (*informal*) If you latch onto someone or something, you become attached to them.

late ADJECTIVE, ADVERB ① Something

that happens late happens towards the end of a period of time • *the late evening* • *late in the morning*. ② If you arrive late, or do something late, you arrive or do it after the time you were expected to. ▶ **ADJECTIVE** ③ A late event happens after the time when it usually takes place • *a late breakfast*. ④ (*formal*) Late means dead • *my late grandmother*.

late ADJECTIVE
③ = behind, behind time, belated, delayed, last-minute, overdue
≠ early
④ = dead, deceased (*formal*), departed

lately ADVERB Events that happened lately happened recently.

latent ADJECTIVE A latent quality is hidden at the moment, but may emerge in the future • *a latent talent for art*.

lateral ADJECTIVE relating to the sides of something, or moving in a sideways direction.

lathe NOUN a machine which holds and turns a piece of wood or metal against a tool to cut and shape it.

lather NOUN Lather is the foam that you get when you rub soap in water.

Latin NOUN ① Latin is the language of ancient Rome. ② Latins are people who speak languages closely related to Latin, such as French, Italian, Spanish and Portuguese.

Latin America NOUN Latin America consists of the countries in North, South and Central America where Spanish or Portuguese is the main language. **Latin American ADJECTIVE**

latitude NOUN GEOGRAPHY The latitude of a place is its distance north or south of the equator measured in degrees.

latter ADJECTIVE, NOUN ① You use 'latter' to refer to the second of two things that are mentioned • *They were eating sandwiches and cakes (the latter bought from Mrs Paul's bakery)*. ▶ **ADJECTIVE** ② 'Latter' also describes the second or end part of something • *the latter part of his career*.

latterly ADVERB (*formal*) Latterly means recently • *It's only latterly that this has become an issue*.

lattice NOUN a structure made of strips which cross over each other diagonally leaving holes in between.

laudable ADJECTIVE (*formal*) deserving praise • *It is a laudable aim*. **laudably ADVERB**

laugh VERB ① When you laugh, you make a noise which shows that you are amused or happy. ▶ **NOUN** ② the noise you make when you laugh.

laugh VERB
① = chortle, chuckle, giggle, guffaw, snigger, titter
▶ **NOUN** ② = chortle, chuckle, giggle, guffaw, snigger, titter

laughable ADJECTIVE quite absurd.

laughing stock NOUN someone who has been made to seem ridiculous.

laughter NOUN Laughter is a noise which shows that you are amused or happy.

launch VERB ① To launch a ship means to send it into the water for the first time. ② To launch a rocket means to send it into space. ③ When a company launches a new product, they have an advertising campaign to promote it as they start to sell it. ▶ **NOUN** ④ a motorboat.

launch pad NOUN A launch pad, or a launching pad, is the place from which space rockets take off.

launder VERB (*old-fashioned*) To launder clothes, sheets or towels means to wash and iron them.

laundry, **laundries NOUN** ① a business that washes and irons clothes and sheets. ② Laundry is also the dirty clothes and sheets that are being washed, or are about to be washed.

laurel NOUN an evergreen tree with shiny leaves.

lava NOUN [GEOGRAPHY] Lava is the very hot liquid rock that comes shooting out of an erupting volcano, and becomes solid as it cools.

lavatory, **lavatories** NOUN a toilet.

lavender NOUN ① Lavender is a small bush with bluish-pink flowers that have a strong, pleasant scent. ▸ ADJECTIVE ② bluish-pink.

lavish ADJECTIVE ① If you are lavish, you are very generous with your time, money or gifts. ② A lavish amount is a large amount. ▸ VERB ③ If you lavish money or affection on someone, you give them a lot of it. **lavishly** ADVERB

law NOUN ① [CITIZENSHIP] The law is the system of rules developed by the government of a country, which regulate what people may and may not do and deals with people who break these rules. ② The law is also the profession of people such as lawyers, whose job involves the application of the laws of a country. ③ [CITIZENSHIP] one of the rules established by a government or a religion, which tells people what they may or may not do. ④ a scientific fact which allows you to explain how things work in the physical world. **lawful** ADJECTIVE **lawfully** ADVERB

> **law** NOUN
> ① = charter, code, constitution
> ③ = act, code, decree, regulation, rule, statute

law-abiding ADJECTIVE obeying the law and not causing any trouble.

lawless ADJECTIVE having no regard for the law.

lawn NOUN an area of grass that is kept cut short.

lawnmower NOUN a machine for cutting grass.

lawsuit NOUN a civil court case between two people, as opposed to the police prosecuting someone for a criminal offence.

lawyer NOUN a person who is qualified in law, and whose job is to advise people about the law and represent them in court.

> **lawyer** NOUN
> = advocate, attorney, barrister, counsel, solicitor

lax ADJECTIVE careless and not keeping up the usual standards • *a lax accounting system*.

lay, **lays**, **laying**, **laid** VERB ① When you lay something somewhere, you put it down so that it lies there. ② If you lay something, you arrange it or set it out. ③ If you lay the table, you put cutlery on the table ready for a meal. ④ When a bird lays an egg, it produces the egg out of its body. ⑤ If you lay a trap for someone, you create a situation in which you will be able to catch them out. ⑥ If you lay emphasis on something, you refer to it in a way that shows you think it is very important. ⑦ If you lay odds on something, you bet that it will happen. ⑧ Lay is the past tense of **lie**[1]. ▸ ADJECTIVE ⑨ You use 'lay' to describe people who are involved with a Christian church but are not members of the clergy • *a lay preacher*. **lay off** VERB ① When workers are laid off, their employers tell them not to come to work for a while because there is a shortage of work. ② (*informal*) If you tell someone to lay off, you want them to stop doing something annoying. **lay on** VERB If you lay on a meal or entertainment, you provide it.

lay VERB
① = place, put, set, set down, settle, spread
② = arrange, set out

lay-by NOUN ① an area by the side of a main road where motorists can stop for a short while. ② In Australia and New Zealand, lay-by is a system where you pay a deposit on an item in a shop so that it will be kept for you until you pay the rest of the price.

layer NOUN a single thickness of something • *layers of clothing*.

layer NOUN
= blanket, coat, coating, covering, film, sheet, stratum

layman, **laymen** NOUN ① someone who does not have specialised knowledge of a subject • *a layman's guide to computers*. ② someone who belongs to the church but is not a member of the clergy.

layout NOUN The layout of something is the pattern in which it is arranged.

layout NOUN
= arrangement, design, format, plan

laze VERB If you laze, you relax and do no work • *We spent a few days lazing around by the pool*.

laze VERB
= idle, loaf, lounge
≠ work

lazy, **lazier**, **laziest** ADJECTIVE idle and unwilling to work. **lazily** ADVERB **laziness** NOUN

lazy ADJECTIVE
= idle, slack
≠ industrious

lb an abbreviation for 'pounds' • *3lb of sugar*.

lbw In cricket, lbw is a way of dismissing a batsman when his or her legs prevent the ball from hitting the wicket. lbw is an abbreviation for 'leg before wicket'.

leach VERB When minerals are leached from rocks, they are dissolved by water which filters through the rock.

lead[1], **leads**, **leading**, **led** *[Rhymes with* ***feed****]* VERB ① If you lead someone somewhere, you go in front of them in order to show them the way. ② If one thing leads to another, it causes the second thing to happen. ③ a person who leads a group of people is in charge of them. ▶ NOUN ④ a length of leather or chain attached to a dog's collar, so that the dog can be kept under control. ⑤ If the police have a lead, they have a clue which might help them to solve a crime.

lead VERB
① = conduct (*formal*), escort, guide, steer, usher
② = cause, contribute to, produce
③ = command, direct, govern, head, manage, supervise
▶ NOUN ⑤ = clue, indication, trace

lead[2] *[Rhymes with* ***fed****]* NOUN SCIENCE Lead is a soft metallic element. Its atomic number is 82 and its symbol is Pb.

leader NOUN ① someone who is in charge of a country, an organisation, or a group of people. ② the person who is winning in a competition or race. ③ a newspaper article that expresses the newspaper's opinions.

leader NOUN
① = boss, captain, chief, commander, director, head, principal, ringleader
≠ follower

leadership NOUN ① the group of people in charge of an organisation. ② Leadership is the ability to be a good leader.

leading ADJECTIVE particularly important, respected or advanced.

leading ADJECTIVE
= chief, eminent, key, main, major, principal, prominent, top

leaf, **leaves** NOUN ① the flat green growth on the end of a twig or branch of a tree or other plant. ▸ VERB ② If you leaf through a book, magazine or newspaper, you turn the pages over quickly. **leafy** ADJECTIVE

leaflet NOUN a piece of paper with information or advertising printed on it.

> **leaflet** NOUN
> = booklet, brochure, circular, pamphlet

league *[Said* ***leeg****]* NOUN ① PE a group of countries, clubs or people who have joined together for a particular purpose or because they share a common interest • *the League of Red Cross Societies* • *the Australian Football League*. ② a unit of distance used in former times, equal to about 3 miles.

leak VERB ① If a pipe or container leaks, it has a hole which lets gas or liquid escape. ② If liquid or gas leaks, it escapes from a pipe or container. ③ If someone in an organisation leaks information, they give the information to someone who is not supposed to have it • *The letter was leaked to the press*. ▸ NOUN ④ If a pipe or container has a leak, it has a hole which lets gas or liquid escape. ⑤ If there is a leak in an organisation, someone inside the organisation is giving information to people who are not supposed to have it. **leaky** ADJECTIVE

> **leak** VERB
> ② = escape, ooze, seep, spill
> ▸ NOUN ④ = chink, crack, fissure, hole, puncture

leakage NOUN an escape of gas or liquid from a pipe or container.

lean, **leans**, **leaning**, **leant** or **leaned** VERB ① When you lean in a particular direction, you bend your body in that direction. ② When you lean on something, you rest your body against it for support. ③ If you lean on someone, you depend on them. ④ If you lean towards particular ideas, you approve of them and follow them • *parents who lean towards strictness*. ▸ ADJECTIVE ⑤ having little or no fat • *lean cuts of meat*. ⑥ A lean period is a time when food or money is in short supply.

leap, **leaps**, **leaping**, **leapt** or **leaped** VERB ① If you leap somewhere, you jump over a long distance or high in the air. ▸ NOUN ② a jump over a long distance or high in the air.

> **leap** VERB
> ① = bounce, bound, jump, spring, vault
> ▸ NOUN ② = bound, jump, spring

leap year NOUN a year, occurring every four years, in which there are 366 days.

learn, **learns**, **learning**, **learnt** or **learned** VERB ① When you learn something, you gain knowledge or a skill through studying or training. ② If you learn of something, you find out about it • *She had first learnt of the accident that morning*. **learner** NOUN

> **learn** VERB
> ① = grasp, master, pick up
> ② = ascertain, determine, discover, find out, gather, hear, understand

learned *[Said* ***ler****-nid]* ADJECTIVE A learned person has a lot of knowledge gained from years of study.

> **learned** ADJECTIVE
> = academic, erudite, intellectual, literate, scholarly

learning NOUN Learning is knowledge that has been acquired through serious study.

lease NOUN ① an agreement which allows someone to use a house or flat in return for rent. ▸ VERB ② To lease property to someone means to allow them to use it in return for rent.

leash NOUN a length of leather or chain attached to a dog's collar so that the dog can be controlled.

least NOUN ① The least is the smallest possible amount of something. ▶ ADJECTIVE ② as small or as few as possible. ▶ ADVERB ③ Least is a superlative form of **little**. ▶ PHRASE ④ You use **at least** to show that you are referring to the minimum amount of something, and that you think the true amount is greater • *At least 200 hundred people turned up at the rally.*

least ADJECTIVE
② = fewest, lowest, minimum, slightest, smallest
≠ most

leather NOUN Leather is the tanned skin of some animals, used to make shoes and clothes. **leathery** ADJECTIVE

leave, **leaves**, **leaving**, **left** VERB ① When you leave a place, you go away from it. ② If you leave someone somewhere, they stay behind after you go away. ③ If you leave a job or organisation, you stop being part of it • *He left his job shortly after Christmas.* ④ If someone leaves money or possessions to someone, they arrange for them to be given to them after their death. ⑤ In subtraction, when you take one number from another, it leaves a third number. ▶ NOUN ⑥ a period of holiday or absence from a job.

leave VERB
① = abandon, depart, desert, forsake, go, quit, withdraw
▶ NOUN ⑥ = holiday, time off, vacation

Lebanese ADJECTIVE ① belonging or relating to Lebanon. ▶ NOUN ② someone who comes from Lebanon.

lectern NOUN a sloping desk which people use to rest books or notes on.

lecture NOUN ① a formal talk intended to teach people about a particular subject. ② a talk intended to tell someone off. ▶ VERB ③ Someone who lectures teaches in a college or university.

lecture NOUN
① = address, discourse, presentation, sermon, speech, talk
② = reprimand, scolding, telling-off (*informal*), warning
▶ VERB ③ = give a talk, speak, talk, teach

lecturer NOUN a teacher in a college or university.

led the past tense and past participle of **lead**[1].

ledge NOUN a narrow shelf on the side of a cliff or rock face, or on the outside of a building, directly under a window.

ledger NOUN a book in which accounts are kept.

lee NOUN ① the sheltered side of a place • *the lee of the mountain.* ▶ ADJECTIVE ② on the side of a ship away from the wind.

leech NOUN a small worm that lives in water and feeds by sucking the blood from other animals.

leek NOUN a long vegetable of the onion family, which is white at one end and has green leaves at the other.

leeway NOUN If something gives you some leeway, it allows you more flexibility in your plans, for example by giving you time to finish an activity.

left NOUN ① The left is one of two sides of something. For example, on a page, English writing begins on the left. ② People and political groups who hold socialist or communist views are referred to as the Left. ③ Left is the past tense and past participle of **leave**. ▶ ADJECTIVE, ADVERB ④ Left means on or towards the left side of something • *He had a mark above his left eye* • *Turn left down Govan Road*.

left-handed ADJECTIVE, ADVERB Someone who is left-handed does things such as writing with their left hand.

leftist, **leftists** NOUN, ADJECTIVE (a person) holding left-wing political views.

leftovers PLURAL NOUN the bits of food which have not been eaten at the end of a meal.

left-wing ADJECTIVE believing more strongly in socialism, or less strongly in capitalism or conservatism, than other members of the same party or group. **left-winger** NOUN

> **left-wing** ADJECTIVE
> = leftist, liberal, socialist

leg NOUN ① Your legs are the two limbs which stretch from your hips to your feet. ② The legs of a pair of trousers are the parts that cover your legs. ③ The legs of an object such as a table are the parts which rest on the floor and support the object's weight. ④ A leg of a journey is one part of it. ⑤ one of two matches played between two sports teams • *He will miss the second leg of their qualifying tie*.

legacy, **legacies** NOUN ① property or money that someone gets in the will of a person who has died. ② something that exists as a result of a previous event or time • *the legacy of a strict upbringing*.

> **legacy** NOUN
> ① = bequest, estate, heirloom, inheritance

legal ADJECTIVE ① relating to the law • *the Dutch legal system*. ② allowed by the law • *The strike was perfectly legal*. **legally** ADVERB

> **legal** ADJECTIVE
> ① = forensic, judicial, judiciary
> ② = authorised, lawful, legitimate, permissible, rightful, valid
> ≠ illegal

legal aid NOUN Legal aid is a system which provides the services of a lawyer free, or very cheaply, to people who cannot afford the full fees.

legalise; also spelt **legalize** VERB To legalise something that is illegal means to change the law so that it becomes legal. **legalisation** NOUN

legality NOUN The legality of an action means whether or not it is allowed by the law • *They challenged the legality of the scheme*.

legend NOUN ① an old story which was once believed to be true, but which is probably untrue. ② If you refer to someone or something as a legend, you mean they are very famous • *His career has become a legend*. **legendary** ADJECTIVE

leggings PLURAL NOUN ① Leggings are very close-fitting trousers made of stretch material. ② Leggings are also a waterproof covering worn over ordinary trousers to protect them.

legible ADJECTIVE Writing that is legible is clear enough to be read.

legion NOUN ① HISTORY In ancient Rome, a legion was a military unit of between 3000 and 6000 soldiers. ② a large military force • *the French Foreign Legion*. ③ Legions of people are large numbers of them.

legislate VERB (*formal*) When a government legislates, it creates new laws.

legislation NOUN Legislation is a law or set of laws created by a government.

legislative ADJECTIVE relating to the

making of new laws • *a legislative council*.

legislator NOUN (*formal*) a person involved in making or passing laws.

legislature NOUN (*formal*) the parliament in a country, which is responsible for making new laws.

legitimate [*Said lij-**it**-tim-it*] ADJECTIVE Something that is legitimate is reasonable or acceptable according to existing laws or standards • *a legitimate charge for parking the car*. **legitimacy** NOUN **legitimately** ADVERB

leisure [*Rhymes with **measure***] NOUN ① Leisure is time during which you do not have to work, and can do what you enjoy doing. ▶ PHRASE ② If you do something **at leisure**, or **at your leisure**, you do it at a convenient time.

> **leisure** NOUN
> ① = free time, recreation, relaxation, time off
> ≠ work

leisurely ADJECTIVE, ADVERB A leisurely action is done in an unhurried and calm way.

> **leisurely** ADJECTIVE, ADVERB
> = comfortable, easy, gentle, relaxed, unhurried
> ≠ hasty

lemon NOUN ① a yellow citrus fruit with a sour taste. ▶ ADJECTIVE ② pale yellow.

lemonade NOUN a sweet, fizzy drink made from lemons, water and sugar.

lend, **lends**, **lending**, **lent** VERB ① If you lend someone something, you give it to them for a period of time and then they give it back to you. ② If a bank lends money, it gives the money to someone and the money has to be repaid in the future, usually with interest. ▶ PHRASE ③ If you **lend someone a hand**, you help them. **lender** NOUN

length NOUN ① The length of something is the horizontal distance from one end to the other. ② The length of an event or activity is the amount of time it lasts for. ③ The length of something is also the fact that it is long rather than short • *Despite its length, the novel is a rewarding read*. ④ a long piece of something.

> **length** NOUN
> ① = distance, extent, span
> ② = duration, period, space, span, term

lengthen VERB To lengthen something means to make it longer.

> **lengthen** VERB
> = extend, make longer, prolong, stretch
> ≠ shorten

lengthways or **lengthwise** ADVERB If you measure something lengthways, you measure the horizontal distance from one end to the other.

lengthy, **lengthier**, **lengthiest** ADJECTIVE Something that is lengthy lasts for a long time.

lenient ADJECTIVE If someone in authority is lenient, they are less severe than expected. **leniently** ADVERB **leniency** NOUN

lens NOUN ① a curved piece of glass designed to focus light in a certain way, for example in a camera, telescope or pair of glasses. ② The lens in your eye is the part behind the iris, which focuses light.

lent ① the past tense and past participle of **lend**. ▶ NOUN ② RE Lent is the period of forty days leading up to Easter, during which Christians give up something they enjoy.

lentil NOUN Lentils are small dried red, green or brown seeds which are cooked and eaten in soups and curries.

Leo NOUN Leo is the fifth sign of the zodiac, represented by a lion. People born between July 23rd and August 22nd are born under this sign.

leopard NOUN a wild Asian or African big cat, with yellow fur and black or brown spots.

leotard [Said **lee**-eh-tard] NOUN A leotard is a tight-fitting costume covering the body, which is worn for dancing or exercise. It is named after a French acrobat called Jules Léotard.

leper NOUN (*offensive*) someone who has leprosy.

leprosy NOUN Leprosy is an infectious disease which attacks the skin and nerves, and which can lead to fingers or toes dropping off.

lesbian NOUN a homosexual woman. **lesbianism** NOUN

lesion [Said **lee**-zhen] NOUN a wound or injury.

less ADJECTIVE, ADVERB ① Less means a smaller amount, or not as much in quality • *They left less than three weeks ago* • *She had become less frightened of the dark now.* ② Less is a comparative form of **little**. ▸ PREPOSITION ③ You use 'less' to show that you are subtracting one number from another • *Eight less two leaves six.*

-less SUFFIX '-less' means without • *hopeless* • *fearless.*

lessen VERB If something lessens, it is reduced in amount, size or quality.

> **lessen** VERB
> = abate, decrease, diminish, dwindle, lower, minimise, reduce, shrink
> ≠ increase

lesser ADJECTIVE smaller in importance or amount than something else.

lesson NOUN ① a fixed period of time during which a class of pupils is taught by a teacher. ② an experience that makes you understand something important which you had not realised before.

> **lesson** NOUN
> ① = class, coaching, lecture, period, tutoring

lest CONJUNCTION (*old-fashioned*) as a precaution in case something unpleasant or unwanted happens • *I was afraid to open the door lest he should follow me.*

let, lets, letting, let VERB ① If you let someone do something, you allow them to do it. ② If someone lets a house or flat that they own, they rent it out. ③ You can say 'let's' or 'let us' when you want to suggest doing something with someone else • *Let's go.* ④ If you let yourself in for something, you agree to do it although you do not really want to. **let down** VERB If you let someone down, you fail to do something you had agreed to do for them. **let off** VERB ① If someone in authority lets you off, they do not punish you for something you have done wrong. ② If you let off a firework or explosive, you light it or detonate it.

> **let** VERB
> ① = allow, give permission, permit, sanction
> ≠ forbid
> ② = hire out, lease, rent

lethal [Said **lee**-thal] ADJECTIVE able to kill someone • *a lethal weapon.*

lethargic [Said lith-**ar**-jik] ADJECTIVE If you feel lethargic, you have no energy or enthusiasm.

lethargy [Said **leth**-ar-jee] NOUN Lethargy is a lack of energy and enthusiasm.

letter NOUN ① Letters are written symbols which go together to make words. ② a piece of writing addressed to someone, and usually sent through the post.

lettering NOUN Lettering is writing, especially when you are describing the type of letters used • *bold lettering.*

lettuce NOUN a vegetable with large green leaves eaten raw in salad.

leukaemia [*Said loo-**kee**-mee-a*]; also spelt **leukemia** NOUN Leukaemia is a serious illness which affects the blood.

level, levels, levelling, levelled ADJECTIVE ① A surface that is level is smooth, flat and parallel to the ground. ▸ VERB ② To level a piece of land means to make it flat. ③ If you level a criticism at someone, you say or write something critical about them. ▸ ADVERB ④ If you draw level with someone, you get closer to them so that you are moving next to them. ▸ NOUN ⑤ a point on a scale which measures the amount, importance or difficulty of something. ⑥ The level of a liquid is the height it comes up to in a container. **level off** or **level out** VERB If something levels off or levels out, it stops increasing or decreasing • *Profits are beginning to level off.*

> **level** ADJECTIVE
> ① = flat, horizontal
> ≠ uneven
> ▸ VERB ② = flatten, plane, smooth
> ▸ NOUN ⑤ = grade, rank, stage, standard, status

level crossing NOUN a place where road traffic is allowed to drive across a railway track.

level-headed ADJECTIVE Someone who is level-headed is sensible and calm in emergencies.

lever NOUN ① a handle on a machine that you pull in order to make the machine work. ② a long bar that you wedge underneath a heavy object and press down on to make the object move.

leverage NOUN Leverage is knowledge or influence that you can use to make someone do something.

levy, levies, levying, levied [*Said **lev**-ee*] (*formal*) NOUN ① an amount of money that you pay in tax. ▸ VERB ② When a government levies a tax, it makes people pay the tax and organises the collection of the money.

liability, liabilities NOUN ① Someone's liability is their responsibility for something they have done wrong. ② In business, a company's liabilities are its debts. ③ (*informal*) If you describe someone as a liability, you mean that they cause a lot of problems or embarrassment.

liable ADJECTIVE ① If you say that something is liable to happen, you mean that you think it will probably happen. ② If you are liable for something you have done, you are legally responsible for it.

liaise [*Said lee-**aze***] VERB To liaise with someone or an organisation means to cooperate with them and keep them informed.

liaison [*Said lee-**aze**-on*] NOUN Liaison is communication between two organisations or two sections of an organisation.

liar NOUN a person who tells lies.

libel, libels, libelling, libelled [*Said **lie**-bel*] NOUN ① Libel is something written about someone which is not true, and for which the writer can be made to pay damages in court. ▸ VERB ② To libel someone means to write or say something untrue about them. **libellous** ADJECTIVE

liberal NOUN ① someone who believes in political progress, social welfare and individual freedom. ▸ ADJECTIVE ② Someone who is liberal is tolerant of a wide range of behaviour, standards or opinions. ③ To be liberal with something means to be generous with it. ④ A liberal quantity of something is a large amount of it. **liberally** ADVERB **liberalism** NOUN

Liberal Democrat NOUN In Britain, the Liberal Democrats are a political party that believes that individuals should have more rights and freedom.

liberate VERB To liberate people means to free them from prison or from an unpleasant situation. **liberation** NOUN **liberator** NOUN

liberty NOUN CITIZENSHIP Liberty is the freedom to choose how you want to live, without government restrictions.

Libra NOUN Libra is the seventh sign of the zodiac, represented by a pair of scales. People born between September 23rd and October 22nd are born under this sign.

librarian NOUN LIBRARY a person who works in, or is in charge of, a library.

library, **libraries** NOUN ① a building in which books are kept for people to come and read or borrow. ② a collection of things such as books or music.

Libyan ADJECTIVE ① belonging or relating to Libya. ▸ NOUN ② someone who comes from Libya.

lice the plural of **louse**.

licence NOUN ① an official document which entitles you to carry out a particular activity, for example to drive a car. ② Licence is the freedom to do what you want, especially when other people consider that it is being used irresponsibly.

license VERB To license an activity means to give official permission for it to be carried out.

lichen *[Said **lie**-ken]* NOUN Lichen is a green, moss-like growth on rocks or tree trunks.

lick VERB ① If you lick something, you move your tongue over it. ▸ NOUN ② the action of licking.

lid NOUN the top of a container, which you open in order to reach what is inside.

lie[1], **lies**, **lying**, **lay**, **lain** VERB ① To lie somewhere means to rest there horizontally. ② If you say where something lies, you are describing where it is • *The farm lies between two valleys.*

> **lie** VERB
> ① = loll, lounge, recline, sprawl

lie[2], **lies**, **lying**, **lied** VERB ① To lie means to say something that is not true. ▸ NOUN ② something you say that is not true.

> **lie** VERB
> ① = fib (*informal*), perjure yourself, tell a lie
> ▸ NOUN ② = deceit, fabrication, falsehood, fib (*informal*), fiction

lieu *[Said **lyoo**]* PHRASE If one thing happens **in lieu** of another, it happens instead of it.

lieutenant *[Said loo-**ten**-ant or lef-**ten**-ent]* NOUN a junior officer in the army or navy.

life, **lives** NOUN ① Life is the quality of being able to grow and develop, which is present in people, plants and animals. ② Your life is your existence from the time you are born until the time you die. ③ The life of a machine is the period of time for which it is likely to work. ④ If you refer to the life in a place, you are talking about the amount of activity there • *The town was full of life.* ⑤ If criminals are sentenced to life, they are sent to prison for the rest of their lives, or until they are granted parole.

> **life** NOUN
> ② = existence, life span, lifetime, time

A B C D E F G H I J K L M N O P Q R S T U V W X Y Z

life assurance NOUN Life assurance is an insurance which provides a sum of money in the event of the policy holder's death.

lifeblood NOUN The lifeblood of something is the most essential part of it.

lifeboat NOUN ① a boat kept on shore, which is sent out to rescue people who are in danger at sea. ② a small boat kept on a ship, which is used if the ship starts to sink.

life expectancy NOUN GEOGRAPHY Your life expectancy is the number of years you can expect to live.

lifeguard NOUN a person whose job is to rescue people who are in difficulty in the sea or in a swimming pool.

life jacket NOUN a sleeveless inflatable jacket that keeps you afloat in water.

lifeless ADJECTIVE ① Someone who is lifeless is dead. ② If you describe a place or person as lifeless, you mean that they are dull.

lifelike ADJECTIVE A picture or sculpture that is lifelike looks very real or alive.

lifeline NOUN ① something which helps you to survive or helps an activity to continue. ② a rope thrown to someone who is in danger of drowning.

lifelong ADJECTIVE existing throughout someone's life • *He had a lifelong interest in music.*

lifesaver NOUN In Australia and New Zealand, a lifesaver is a person whose job is to rescue people who are in difficulty in the sea.

life span NOUN ① Someone's life span is the length of time during which they are alive. ② The life span of a product or organisation is the length of time it exists or is useful.

lifestyle NOUN PSHE the living conditions, behaviour and habits that a person chooses to have.

lifetime NOUN Your lifetime is the period of time during which you are alive.

lift VERB ① To lift something means to move it to a higher position. ② When fog or mist lifts, it clears away. ③ To lift a ban on something means to remove it. ④ (*informal*) To lift things means to steal them. ▶ NOUN ⑤ a machine like a large box which carries passengers from one floor to another in a building. ⑥ If you give someone a lift, you drive them somewhere in a car or on a motorcycle.

lift VERB
① = elevate, hoist, pick up, raise
≠ lower
③ = cancel, end, relax, remove

ligament NOUN SCIENCE a piece of tough tissue in your body which connects your bones.

light, lights, lighting, lighted or **lit** NOUN ① Light is brightness from the sun, fire or lamps, that enables you to see things. ② a lamp or other device that gives out brightness. ③ If you give someone a light, you give them a match or lighter to light their cigarette. ▶ ADJECTIVE ④ A place that is light is bright because of the sun or the use of lamps. ⑤ A light colour is pale. ⑥ A light object does not weigh much. ⑦ A light task is fairly easy. ⑧ Light books or music are entertaining and are not intended to be serious. ▶ VERB ⑨ To light a place means to cause it to be filled with light. ⑩ To light a fire means to make it start burning. ⑪ To light upon something means to find it by accident. **lightly** ADVERB **lightness** NOUN

light NOUN
① = brightness, brilliance, glare, glow, illumination, radiance
≠ dark
▶ ADJECTIVE ⑤ = bleached, blonde, blond, fair, pale, pastel
≠ dark
⑥ = flimsy, lightweight, portable, slight
≠ heavy
▶ VERB ⑨ = brighten, illuminate, light up
≠ darken
⑩ = ignite, kindle
≠ extinguish

lighten VERB ① When something lightens, it becomes less dark. ② To lighten a load means to make it less heavy.

lighter NOUN a device for lighting a cigarette or cigar.

light-hearted ADJECTIVE Someone who is light-hearted is cheerful and has no worries.

lighthouse NOUN a tower by the sea, which sends out a powerful light to guide ships and warn them of danger.

lighting NOUN ① The lighting in a room or building is the way that it is lit. ② DRAMA Lighting in the theatre or for a film is the special lights that are directed on the performers or scene.

lightning NOUN Lightning is the bright flashes of light in the sky which are produced by natural electricity during a thunderstorm.

lightweight NOUN ① a boxer in one of the lighter weight groups. ▶ ADJECTIVE ② Something that is lightweight does not weigh very much • *a lightweight jacket*.

likable; also spelt **likeable** ADJECTIVE Someone who is likable is very pleasant and friendly.

like PREPOSITION ① If one thing is like another, it is similar to it. ▶ NOUN ② 'The like' means other similar things of the sort just mentioned • *nappies, prams, cots and the like*. ▶ PHRASE ③ If you **feel like** something, you want to do it or have it • *I feel like a walk*. ▶ VERB ④ If you like something or someone, you find them pleasant.

like PREPOSITION
① = akin, analogous, parallel, similar
≠ unlike
▶ VERB ④ = adore (*informal*), appreciate, be fond of, be keen on, be partial to, enjoy, go for, have a soft spot for, have a weakness for, love, relish, revel in
≠ dislike

-like SUFFIX '-like' means resembling or similar to • *a balloonlike object*.

likelihood NOUN If you say that there is a likelihood that something will happen, you mean that you think it will probably happen.

likely ADJECTIVE Something that is likely will probably happen or is probably true.

likely ADJECTIVE
= anticipated, expected, liable, possible, probable
≠ unlikely

liken VERB If you liken one thing to another, you say that they are similar.

likeness NOUN If two things have a likeness to each other, they are similar in appearance.

likewise ADVERB Likewise means similarly • *She sat down and he did likewise*.

liking NOUN If you have a liking for someone or something, you like them.

lilac NOUN ① a shrub with large clusters of pink, white or mauve flowers. ▶ ADJECTIVE ② pale mauve.

lilt NOUN A lilt in someone's voice is a pleasant rising and falling sound in it. **lilting** ADJECTIVE

lily, lilies NOUN a plant with trumpet-shaped flowers of various colours.

limb NOUN ① Your limbs are your arms and legs. ② The limbs of a tree are its branches. ▶ PHRASE ③ If you have gone **out on a limb**, you have said or done something risky.

limbo NOUN ① If you are in limbo, you are in an uncertain situation over which you feel you have no control. ② The limbo is a West Indian dance in which the dancer has to pass under a low bar while leaning backwards.

lime NOUN ① a small, green citrus fruit, rather like a lemon. ② A lime tree is a large tree with pale green leaves. ③ Lime is a chemical substance that is used in cement and as a fertiliser.

limelight NOUN If someone is in the limelight, they are getting a lot of attention.

limestone NOUN Limestone is a white rock which is used for building and making cement.

limit NOUN ① a boundary or an extreme beyond which something cannot go • *the speed limit*. ▶ VERB ② To limit something means to prevent it from becoming bigger, spreading or making progress • *He did all he could to limit the damage*.

> **limit** NOUN
> ① = bounds, deadline, maximum, ultimate, utmost
> ▶ VERB ② = confine, curb, fix, ration, restrict

limitation NOUN ① The limitation of something is the reducing or controlling of it. ② If you talk about the limitations of a person or thing, you are talking about the limits of their abilities.

limited ADJECTIVE Something that is limited is rather small in amount or extent • *a limited number of bedrooms*.

limousine [*Said* **lim**-o-zeen] NOUN a large, luxurious car, usually driven by a chauffeur.

limp VERB ① If you limp, you walk unevenly because you have hurt your leg or foot. ▶ NOUN ② an uneven way of walking. ▶ ADJECTIVE ③ Something that is limp is soft and floppy, and not stiff or firm • *a limp lettuce*.

> **limp** ADJECTIVE
> ③ = drooping, flabby, floppy, slack, soft
> ≠ stiff

line NOUN ① a long, thin mark. ② a number of people or things positioned one behind the other. ③ a route along which someone or something moves • *a railway line*. ④ In a piece of writing, a line is a number of words together • *I often used to change my lines as an actor*. ⑤ MATHS In maths, a line is the straight, one-dimensional space between two points. ⑥ Someone's line of work is the kind of work they do. ⑦ The line someone takes is the attitude they have towards something • *He took a hard line with truancy*. ⑧ In a shop or business, a line is a type of product • *That line has been discontinued*. ▶ VERB ⑨ To line something means to cover its inside surface or edge with something • *Cottages lined the edge of the harbour*. **line up** VERB ① When people line up, they stand in a line. ② When you line something up, you arrange it for a special occasion • *A tour is being lined up for July*.

> **line** NOUN
> ① = rule, score, streak, stripe
> ② = column, file, queue, rank, row
> ③ = course, path, route, track, trajectory

lineage *[Said* **lin**-*ee-ij]* **NOUN** Someone's lineage is all the people from whom they are directly descended.

linear *[Said* **lin**-*ee-ar]* **ADJECTIVE** arranged in a line or in a strict sequence, or happening at a constant rate.

linen **NOUN** ① DGT Linen is a type of cloth made from a plant called flax. ② Linen is also household goods made of cloth, such as sheets and tablecloths.

liner **NOUN** a large passenger ship that makes long journeys.

linesman, linesmen **NOUN** an official at a sports match who watches the lines of the field or court and indicates when the ball goes outside them.

-ling **SUFFIX** '-ling' means 'small' • *duckling*.

linger **VERB** To linger means to remain for a long time • *The smell of the flowers lingered in the air*.

lingerie *[Said* **lan**-*jer-ee]* **NOUN** Lingerie is women's nightclothes and underclothes.

lingo, lingoes **NOUN** (*informal*) a foreign language.

linguist **NOUN** MFL someone who studies foreign languages or the way in which language works.

lining **NOUN** any material used to line the inside of something.

link **NOUN** ① a relationship or connection between two things • *the link between good diet and health*. ② a physical connection between two things or places • *a high-speed rail link between the cities*. ③ one of the rings in a chain. ④ In computing, a link is a connection between different documents, or between different parts of the same document. ▶ **VERB** ⑤ To link people, places or things means to join them together.
linkage **NOUN**

link **NOUN**
① = affiliation, association, attachment, bond, connection, relationship, tie
▶ **VERB** ⑤ = attach, connect, couple, fasten, join, tie
≠ separate

lino **NOUN** Lino is the same as linoleum.

linoleum **NOUN** a floor covering with a shiny surface.

lint **NOUN** soft cloth made from linen, used to dress wounds.

lion **NOUN** a large member of the cat family which comes from Africa. Lions have light brown fur, and the male has a long mane. A female lion is called a lioness.

lip **NOUN** ① Your lips are the edges of your mouth. ② The lip of a jug is the slightly pointed part through which liquids are poured out.

lipstick **NOUN** a coloured substance which is worn on the lips.

liqueur *[Said lik-***yoor***]* **NOUN** a strong sweet alcoholic drink, usually drunk after a meal.

liquid **NOUN** ① SCIENCE any substance which is not a solid or a gas, and which can be poured. ▶ **ADJECTIVE** ② Something that is liquid is in the form of a liquid • *liquid nitrogen*. ③ In commerce and finance, a person's or company's liquid assets are the things that can be sold quickly to raise cash.

liquid **NOUN**
① = fluid, liquor, solution
▶ **ADJECTIVE** ② = fluid, molten, runny

liquidate **VERB** To liquidate a company means to close it down and use its assets to pay off its debts.
liquidation **NOUN** **liquidator** **NOUN**

liquor **NOUN** Liquor is any strong alcoholic drink.

liquorice [*Said* **lik**-*ker-iss*] **NOUN** Liquorice is a root used to flavour sweets; also the sweets themselves.

list NOUN ① a set of words or items written one below the other. ▶ **VERB** ② If you list a number of things, you make a list of them.

> **list NOUN**
> ① = catalogue, directory, index, inventory, listing, record, register
> ▶ **VERB** ② = catalogue, index, record, register

listen VERB If you listen to something, you hear it and pay attention to it. **listener NOUN**

> **listen VERB**
> = attend (*formal*), hark (*literary*), hear, pay attention

listless ADJECTIVE lacking energy and enthusiasm. **listlessly ADVERB**

lit a past tense and past participle of **light**.

litany, **litanies NOUN** ① a part of a church service in which the priest says or chants prayers and the people give responses. ② something, especially a list of things, that is repeated often or in a boring or insincere way • *a tedious litany of complaints*.

literacy NOUN Literacy is the ability to read and write. **literate ADJECTIVE**

literal ADJECTIVE ① [ENGLISH] The literal meaning of a word is its most basic meaning. ② A literal translation from a foreign language is one that has been translated exactly word for word. **literally ADVERB**

literary ADJECTIVE [ENGLISH] connected with literature • *literary critics*.

literature NOUN ① [ENGLISH] Literature consists of novels, plays and poetry. ② The literature on a subject is everything that has been written about it.

lithe ADJECTIVE supple and graceful.

litmus NOUN [SCIENCE] In chemistry, litmus is a substance that turns red under acid and blue under alkali conditions.

litmus test NOUN something which is regarded as a simple and accurate test of a particular thing, such as a person's attitude to an issue • *The match will be a litmus test of the team's confidence*.

litre NOUN [MATHS] a unit of liquid volume equal to about 1.76 pints.

litter NOUN ① Litter is rubbish in the street and other public places. ② Cat litter is a gravelly substance you put in a container where you want your cat to urinate and defecate. ③ a number of baby animals born at the same time to the same mother. ▶ **VERB** ④ If things litter a place, they are scattered all over it.

little, **less**, **lesser**, **least ADJECTIVE** ① small in size or amount. ▶ **NOUN** ② A little is a small amount or degree • *Would you like a little of this?* ③ Little also means not much • *He has little to say*. ▶ **ADVERB** ④ to a small amount or degree • *a little afraid* • *She ate little*.

> **little ADJECTIVE**
> ① = dainty, dwarf, meagre, measly, mini, miniature, minute, paltry, pygmy, scant, small, tiny, wee (*Scottish*)
> ≠ large
> ▶ **NOUN** ② = hardly any, not much

live [*Said* **liv**] **VERB** ① If you live in a place, that is where your home is. ② To live means to be alive. ③ If something lives up to your expectations, it is as good as you thought it would be. ▶ **ADJECTIVE**, **ADVERB** [*Rhymes with* **hive**] ④ Live television or radio is broadcast while

the event is taking place • *a live football match* • *The concert will go out live*.
▸ **ADJECTIVE** ⑤ Live animals or plants are alive, rather than dead or artificial • *a live spider*. ⑥ Something is live if it is directly connected to an electricity supply • *Careful – those wires are live*. ⑦ Live bullets or ammunition have not yet been exploded.

live down **VERB** If you cannot live down a mistake or failure, you cannot make people forget it.

live **VERB**
① = dwell (*formal*), inhabit, reside (*formal*), stay (*Scottish and South African*)
② = be alive, exist
▸ **ADJECTIVE** ⑤ = alive, animate, living

livelihood **NOUN** Someone's livelihood is their job or the source of their income.

lively, **livelier**, **liveliest** **ADJECTIVE** full of life and enthusiasm • *lively conversation*. **liveliness** **NOUN**

lively **ADJECTIVE**
= active, animated, energetic, perky, sparkling, sprightly, vivacious
≠ dull

liver **NOUN** ① Your liver is a large organ in your body which cleans your blood and helps digestion. ② Liver is also the liver of some animals, which may be cooked and eaten.

livestock **NOUN** Livestock is farm animals.

livid **ADJECTIVE** ① extremely angry. ② dark purple or bluish • *livid bruises*.

living **ADJECTIVE** ① If someone is living, they are alive • *her only living relative*. ▸ **NOUN** ② The work you do for a living is the work you do in order to earn money to live.

living room **NOUN** the room where people relax and entertain in their homes.

lizard **NOUN** a long, thin, dry-skinned reptile found in hot, dry countries.

llama **NOUN** a South American animal related to the camel.

load **NOUN** ① something being carried. ② (*informal*) Loads means a lot • *loads of work*. ▸ **VERB** ③ To load a vehicle or animal means to put a large number of things into it or onto it.

load **NOUN**
① = cargo, consignment, freight, shipment
▸ **VERB** ③ = fill, pack, pile, stack

loaf, **loaves**; **loafs**, **loafing**, **loafed** **NOUN** ① a large piece of bread baked in a shape that can be cut into slices. ▸ **VERB** ② To loaf around means to be lazy and not do any work.

loan **NOUN** ① a sum of money that you borrow. ② the act of borrowing or lending something • *I am grateful to Jane for the loan of her book*. ▸ **VERB** ③ If you loan something to someone, you lend it to them.

loan **NOUN**
① = advance, credit, mortgage
▸ **VERB** ③ = advance, lend

loath [*Rhymes with* ***both***] **ADJECTIVE** If you are loath to do something, you are very unwilling to do it.

loathe **VERB** To loathe someone or something means to feel strong dislike for them. **loathing** **NOUN** **loathsome** **ADJECTIVE**

lob, **lobs**, **lobbing**, **lobbed** **VERB** ① If you lob something, you throw it high in the air. ▸ **NOUN** ② In tennis, a lob is a stroke in which the player hits the ball high in the air.

lobby, **lobbies**, **lobbying**, **lobbied** **NOUN** ① The lobby in a building is the main entrance area with corridors and doors leading off it. ② a group of people trying to persuade an organisation that something should be done • *the environmental lobby*. ▸ **VERB** ③ To lobby an MP or an organisation means to try to persuade them to do

A B C D E F G H I J K L M N O P Q R S T U V W X Y Z

something, for example by writing them lots of letters.

lobe NOUN ① The lobe of your ear is the rounded soft part at the bottom. ② any rounded part of something • *the frontal lobe of the brain*.

lobster NOUN an edible shellfish with two front claws and eight legs.

local ADJECTIVE ① Local means in, near or belonging to the area in which you live • *the local newspaper*. ② A local anaesthetic numbs only one part of your body and does not send you to sleep. ▶ NOUN ③ The locals are the people who live in a particular area. ④ (*informal*) Someone's local is the pub nearest their home. **locally** ADVERB

> **local** ADJECTIVE
> ① = community, district, neighbourhood, parish, regional
> ▶ NOUN ③ = inhabitant, native, resident

localised; also spelt **localized** ADJECTIVE existing or happening in only one place • *localised pain*.

locality, **localities** NOUN an area of a country or city • *a large map of the locality*.

locate VERB ① To locate someone or something means to find out where they are. ② If something is located in a place, it is in that place.

> **locate** VERB
> ① = find, pinpoint, track down
> ② = placed, sited, situated

location NOUN ① GEOGRAPHY a place, or the position of something. ② In South Africa, a location was a small town where only Black people or Coloured people were allowed to live.

> **location** NOUN
> ① = place, point, position, site, situation, spot, whereabouts

loch NOUN In Scottish English, a loch is a lake.

lock VERB ① If you lock something, you close it and fasten it with a key. ② If something locks into place, it moves into place and becomes firmly fixed there. ▶ NOUN ③ a device on something which fastens it and prevents it from being opened except with a key. ④ A lock on a canal is a place where the water level can be raised or lowered to allow boats to go between two parts of the canal which have different water levels. ⑤ A lock of hair is a small bunch of hair.

> **lock** VERB
> ① = latch, padlock
> ≠ unlock
> ▶ NOUN ③ = latch, padlock

lockdown NOUN If there is a lockdown, or a place is in lockdown, people must stay indoors in order to keep themselves and other people safe.

locker NOUN a small cupboard for your personal belongings, for example in a changing room.

locomotive NOUN a railway engine.

locust NOUN an insect like a large grasshopper, which travels in huge swarms and eats crops.

lodge NOUN ① a small house in the grounds of a large country house, or a small house used for holidays. ▶ VERB ② If you lodge in someone else's house, you live there and pay them rent. ③ If something lodges somewhere, it gets stuck there.

lodger NOUN a person who lives in someone's house and pays rent.

loft NOUN the space immediately under the roof of a house, often used for storing things.

lofty, **loftier**, **loftiest** ADJECTIVE ① very high • *a lofty hall*. ② very noble and important • *lofty ideals*. ③ proud and superior • *her lofty manner*.

log, **logs**, **logging**, **logged** NOUN ① a thick branch or piece of tree trunk which has fallen or been cut down. ② the captain's official record of everything that happens on board a ship. ▶ **VERB** ③ If you log something, you officially make a record of it, for example in a ship's log. ④ To log into a computer system means to gain access to it, usually by giving your name and password. To log out means to finish using the system.

logic **NOUN** Logic is a way of reasoning involving a series of statements, each of which must be true if the statement before it is true.

logical **ADJECTIVE** ① A logical argument uses logic. ② A logical course of action or decision is sensible or reasonable in the circumstances. **logically** **ADVERB**

> **logical** **ADJECTIVE**
> ① = consistent, rational, reasoned, sound, valid
> ≠ illogical
> ② = judicious (*formal*), obvious, plausible, reasonable, sensible, wise
> ≠ illogical

logistics **NOUN** (*formal*) The logistics of a complicated undertaking is the skilful organisation of it.

logo, **logos** [*Said* ***loh**-goh*] **NOUN** The logo of an organisation is a special design that is put on all its products.

-logy **SUFFIX** '-logy' is used to form words that refer to the study of something • *biology* • *geology* • *anthropology*.

loin **NOUN** ① (*old-fashioned*) Your loins are the front part of your body between your waist and your thighs. ② Loin is a piece of meat from the back or sides of an animal • *loin of pork*.

loiter **VERB** To loiter means to stand about idly with no real purpose.

lollipop **NOUN** a hard sweet on the end of a stick.

lolly, **lollies** **NOUN** ① a lollipop. ② a piece of flavoured ice or ice cream on a stick. ③ In Australian and New Zealand English, a lolly is a sweet.

lone **ADJECTIVE** A lone person or thing is the only one in a particular place • *a lone climber*.

lonely, **lonelier**, **loneliest** **ADJECTIVE** ① If you are lonely, you are unhappy because you are alone. ② A lonely place is an isolated one which very few people visit • *a lonely hillside*.
loneliness **NOUN**

> **lonely** **ADJECTIVE**
> ① = alone, forlorn, forsaken, lonesome
> ② = deserted, desolate, isolated, remote, secluded, uninhabited

loner **NOUN** a person who likes to be alone.

lonesome **ADJECTIVE** lonely and sad.

long **ADJECTIVE** ① continuing for a great amount of time • *There had been no rain for a long time*. ▶ **ADJECTIVE** ② great in length or distance • *a long dress* • *a long road*. ▶ **ADVERB** ③ for a certain period of time • *How long will it last?* ④ for an extensive period of time • *long into the following year*. ▶ **PHRASE** ⑤ If something **no longer** happens, it does not happen any more. ⑥ **Before long** means soon. ⑦ If one thing is true **as long as** another thing is true, it is true only if the other thing is true. ▶ **VERB** ⑧ If you long for something, you want it very much.

> **long** **ADJECTIVE**
> ① = extended, interminable, lengthy, lingering, long-drawn-out, prolonged, protracted, slow, sustained
> ≠ short
> ▶ **ADJECTIVE** ② = elongated, extensive, lengthy
> ≠ short
> ▶ **VERB** ⑧ = ache, covet, crave, hunger, lust, pine, yearn

longevity [*Said lon-**jev**-it-ee*] NOUN (*formal*) Longevity is long life.

longing NOUN a strong wish for something.

> **longing** NOUN
> = craving, desire, hankering, hunger, thirst, yearning

longitude NOUN GEOGRAPHY The longitude of a place is its distance east or west of a meridian line passing through Greenwich, measured in degrees.

long jump NOUN The long jump is an athletics event in which you jump as far as possible after taking a long run.

long-range ADJECTIVE ① able to be used over a great distance • *long-range artillery*. ② extending a long way into the future • *a long-range weather forecast*.

long-standing ADJECTIVE having existed for a long time • *a long-standing tradition*.

long-suffering ADJECTIVE very patient • *her long-suffering father*.

long-term ADJECTIVE extending a long way into the future • *a long-term investment*.

long-winded ADJECTIVE long and boring • *a long-winded letter*.

loo NOUN (*informal*) a toilet.

look VERB ① If you look at something, you turn your eyes towards it so that you can see it. ② If you look at a subject or situation, you study it or judge it. ③ If you look down on someone, you think that they are inferior to you. ④ If you are looking forward to something, you want it to happen because you think you will enjoy it. ⑤ If you look up to someone, you admire and respect them. ⑥ If you describe the way that something or someone looks, you are describing the appearance of it or them. ▶ NOUN ⑦ If you have a look at something, you look at it. ⑧ the way someone or something appears, especially the expression on a person's face. ⑨ If you talk about someone's looks, you are talking about how attractive they are. ▶ INTERJECTION ⑩ You say 'look out' to warn someone of danger. **look after** VERB If you look after someone or something, you take care of them. **look for** VERB If you look for someone or something, you try to find them. **look up** VERB ① To look up information means to find it out in a book. ② If you look someone up, you go to see them after not having seen them for a long time. ③ If a situation is looking up, it is improving.

> **look** VERB
> ① = gaze, glance, glimpse, peek, peep, scan, stare, view
> ⑥ = appear, look like, seem, seem to be
> ▶ NOUN ⑦ = gaze, glance, glimpse, peek
> ⑧ = air, appearance, bearing, expression, face, semblance
> ▶ **look after** = care for, mind, nurse, take care of, tend, watch ▶ **look for** = forage, hunt, search, seek

lookalike NOUN a person who looks very like someone else • *an Elvis lookalike*.

> **lookalike** NOUN
> = dead ringer (*informal*), double, spitting image (*informal*)

lookout NOUN ① someone who is watching for danger, or a place where they watch for danger. ▶ PHRASE ② If you are **on the lookout** for something, you are watching for it or waiting expectantly for it.

loom NOUN ① a machine for weaving cloth. ▶ VERB ② If something looms in front of you, it suddenly appears as a tall, unclear and sometimes frightening shape. ③ If a situation or event is looming, it is likely to happen soon and is rather worrying.

loony, loonier, looniest; loonies (*slang*) ADJECTIVE ① Behaviour can be described as loony if it is very foolish or eccentric. ▶ NOUN ② a very foolish or eccentric person.

loop NOUN ① a curved or circular shape in something long such as a piece of string. ▶ VERB ② If you loop rope or string around an object, you place it in a loop around the object.

loophole NOUN a small mistake or omission in the law which allows you to do something that the law really intends that you should not do.

loose ADJECTIVE ① If something is loose, it is not firmly held, fixed or attached. ② Loose clothes are rather large and do not fit closely. ▶ ADVERB ③ To set animals loose means to set them free after they have been tied up or kept in a cage. **loosely** ADVERB

loose ADJECTIVE
① = free, unsecured, wobbly
≠ secure
② = baggy, slack, sloppy
≠ tight

loosen VERB To loosen something means to make it looser.

loosen VERB
= slacken, undo, untie
≠ tighten

loot VERB ① To loot shops and houses means to steal goods from them during a battle or riot. ▶ NOUN ② Loot is stolen money or goods.

loot VERB
① = pillage, plunder, raid, ransack
▶ NOUN ② = booty, haul, plunder, spoils, swag (*slang*)

lop, lops, lopping, lopped VERB If you lop something off, you cut it off with one quick stroke.

lopsided ADJECTIVE Something that is lopsided is uneven because its two sides are different sizes or shapes.

lord NOUN ① a nobleman. ② Lord is a title used in front of the names of some noblemen, and of bishops, archbishops, judges and some high-ranking officials • *the Lord Mayor of London*. ③ In Christianity, Lord is a name given to God and Jesus Christ.

Lordship NOUN You address a lord, judge or bishop as Your Lordship.

lore NOUN The lore of a place, people or subject is all the traditional knowledge and stories about it.

lorry, lorries NOUN a large vehicle for transporting goods by road.

lose, loses, losing, lost VERB ① If you lose something, you cannot find it, or you no longer have it because it has been taken away from you • *I lost my jacket*. ② If you lose a relative or friend, they die • *She lost her brother in the war*. ③ If you lose a fight or an argument, you are beaten. ④ If a business loses money, it is spending more money than it is earning.

lose VERB
① = drop, mislay, misplace
≠ find
③ = be beaten, be defeated
≠ win

loser NOUN ① a person who is defeated in a game, contest or struggle. ② (*informal*) If you refer to someone as a loser, you have a low opinion of them because you think they are always unsuccessful.

loss NOUN ① The loss of something is the losing of it. ▶ PHRASE ② If you are **at a loss**, you do not know what to do.

lost ADJECTIVE ① If you are lost, you do not know where you are. ② If something is lost, you cannot find it. ③ Lost is the past tense and past participle of **lose**.

lost ADJECTIVE
① = adrift, astray, off course
② = mislaid, misplaced, missing, vanished

lot PHRASE ① **A lot** of something, or lots of something, is a large amount of it. ② **A lot** means very much or very often • *I love him a lot.* ▸ NOUN ③ an amount of something or a number of things • *I've answered the first lot of questions.* ④ In an auction, a lot is one of the things being sold.

lot PHRASE
① = abundance, a great deal, masses (*informal*), piles (*informal*), plenty, quantities, scores
▸ NOUN ③ = batch, bunch (*informal*), crowd, group, quantity, set

lotion NOUN a liquid that you put on your skin to protect or soften it • *suntan lotion.*

lottery, **lotteries** NOUN a method of raising money by selling tickets by which a winner is selected at random.

lotus NOUN a large water lily, found in Africa and Asia.

loud ADJECTIVE ① A loud noise has a high volume of sound • *a loud explosion.* ② If you describe clothing as loud, you mean that it is too bright • *a loud tie.* **loudly** ADVERB **loudness** NOUN

loud ADJECTIVE, ADVERB
① = blaring, deafening, noisy, resounding, strident, thunderous
≠ quiet
② = flamboyant, flashy, garish, gaudy, lurid
≠ dull

loudspeaker NOUN a piece of equipment that makes your voice louder when you speak into a microphone connected to it.

lounge NOUN ① a room in a house or hotel with comfortable chairs where people can relax. ② The lounge or lounge bar in a pub or hotel is a more expensive and comfortably furnished bar. ▸ VERB ③ If you lounge around, you lean against something or sit or lie around in a lazy and comfortable way.

louse, **lice** NOUN Lice are small insects that live on people's bodies • *head lice.*

lousy, **lousier**, **lousiest** ADJECTIVE (*informal*) ① of bad quality or very unpleasant • *The weather is lousy.* ② ill or unhappy.

lout NOUN a young man who behaves in an aggressive and rude way.

lovable; also spelt **loveable** ADJECTIVE having very attractive qualities and therefore easy to love • *a lovable black mongrel.*

lovable ADJECTIVE
= adorable, charming, enchanting, endearing, sweet
≠ hateful

love VERB ① If you love someone, you have strong emotional feelings of affection for them. ② If you love something, you like it very much • *We both love fishing.* ③ If you would love to do something, you want very much to do it • *I would love to live there.* ▸ NOUN ④ Love is a strong emotional feeling of affection for someone or something. ⑤ a strong liking for something. ⑥ In tennis, love is a score of zero. ▸ PHRASE ⑦ If you are **in love** with someone, you feel strongly attracted to them romantically.

love VERB
① = adore, cherish, worship
≠ hate
② = appreciate, enjoy, like, relish
≠ hate
▸ NOUN ④ = adoration, affection, ardour, devotion, infatuation, passion
≠ hatred

⑤ = devotion, fondness, liking, weakness
≠ hatred

A B C D E F G H I J K L M N O P Q R S T U V W X Y Z

love affair NOUN a romantic relationship between two people.

love life NOUN a person's romantic relationships.

lovely, **lovelier**, **loveliest** ADJECTIVE very beautiful, attractive and pleasant. **loveliness** NOUN

lovely ADJECTIVE
= attractive, beautiful, delightful, enjoyable, pleasant, pretty
≠ horrible

lover NOUN Someone who is a lover of something, for example art or music, is very fond of it.

loving ADJECTIVE feeling or showing love. **lovingly** ADVERB

loving ADJECTIVE
= affectionate, devoted, doting, fond, tender, warm
≠ cold

low ADJECTIVE ① Something that is low is close to the ground, or measures a short distance from the ground to the top • *a low stool.* ② Low means small in value or amount. ③ 'Low' is used to describe people who are considered not respectable • *mixing with low company.* ▸ ADVERB ④ in a low position, level or degree. ▸ NOUN ⑤ a level or amount that is less than before • *Sales hit a new low.*

low ADJECTIVE
① = little, short, small, squat, stunted, sunken
≠ high
② = minimal, modest, poor, reduced, scant, small
≠ high
③ = common, contemptible, despicable, disreputable, lowly, vulgar

lower VERB ① To lower something means to move it downwards. ② To lower something also means to make it less in value or amount.

lower VERB
① = drop, let down, take down
≠ raise
② = cut, decrease, diminish, lessen, minimise, reduce, slash
≠ increase

lowlands PLURAL NOUN Lowlands are an area of flat, low land. **lowland** ADJECTIVE

lowly, **lowlier**, **lowliest** ADJECTIVE low in importance, rank or status.

low tide NOUN On a coast, low tide is the time, usually twice a day, when the sea is at its lowest level.

loyal ADJECTIVE firm in your friendship or support for someone or something. **loyally** ADVERB **loyalty** NOUN

loyal ADJECTIVE
= constant, dependable, faithful, staunch, true, trusty
≠ treacherous

loyalist NOUN a person who remains firm in their support for a government or ruler.

Ltd an abbreviation for 'limited'; used after the names of some companies.

lucid ADJECTIVE ① Lucid writing or speech is clear and easy to understand. ② Someone who is lucid after having been ill or delirious is able to think clearly again.

luck NOUN Luck is anything that seems to happen by chance and not through your own efforts.

luck NOUN
= accident, chance, destiny, fate, fortune

luckless ADJECTIVE unsuccessful or unfortunate • *We reduced our luckless opponents to shattered wrecks.*

lucky, **luckier**, **luckiest** ADJECTIVE ① Someone who is lucky has a lot of good luck. ② Something that is lucky happens by chance and has good effects or consequences. **luckily** ADVERB

lucky ADJECTIVE
① = blessed, charmed, fortunate
≠ unlucky
② = fortuitous, fortunate, opportune, timely
≠ unlucky

lucrative ADJECTIVE Something that is lucrative earns you a lot of money • *a lucrative sponsorship deal.*

ludicrous ADJECTIVE completely foolish, unsuitable or ridiculous.

lug, lugs, lugging, lugged VERB If you lug a heavy object around, you carry it with difficulty.

luggage NOUN Your luggage is the bags and suitcases that you take with you when you travel.

lukewarm ADJECTIVE ① slightly warm • *a mug of lukewarm tea.* ② not very enthusiastic or interested • *The report was given a polite but lukewarm response.*

lull NOUN ① a pause in something, or a short time when it is quiet and nothing much happens • *There was a temporary lull in the fighting.* ▶ VERB ② If you are lulled into feeling safe, someone or something causes you to feel safe at a time when you are not safe • *We had been lulled into a false sense of security.*

lullaby, lullabies NOUN a song used for sending a baby or child to sleep.

lumber NOUN ① Lumber is wood that has been roughly cut up. ② Lumber is also old unwanted furniture and other items. ▶ VERB ③ If you lumber around, you move heavily and clumsily. ④ (*informal*) If you are lumbered with something, you are given it to deal with even though you do not want it • *I was lumbered with looking after my little brother.*

luminary, luminaries NOUN (*literary*) a person who is famous or an expert in a particular subject.

luminous ADJECTIVE Something that is luminous glows in the dark, usually because it has been treated with a special substance • *The luminous dial on her clock.* **luminosity** NOUN

lump NOUN ① A lump of something is a solid piece of it, of any shape or size • *a big lump of dough.* ② a bump on the surface of something. ▶ VERB ③ If you lump people or things together, you combine them into one group or consider them as being similar in some way. **lumpy** ADJECTIVE

lump NOUN
① = ball, cake, chunk, hunk, piece, wedge
② = bulge, bump, hump, swelling

lump sum NOUN a large sum of money given or received all at once.

lunacy NOUN ① Lunacy is extremely foolish or eccentric behaviour. ② (*old-fashioned*) Lunacy is also insanity.

lunar ADJECTIVE relating to the moon.

lunatic NOUN ① If you call someone a lunatic, you mean that they are very foolish • *He drives like a lunatic!* ▶ ADJECTIVE ② Lunatic behaviour is very stupid, foolish or dangerous.

lunch NOUN ① a meal eaten in the middle of the day. ▶ VERB ② When you lunch, you eat lunch.

luncheon [*Said* **lun**-*shen*] NOUN (*formal*) Luncheon is lunch.

lung NOUN Your lungs are the two organs inside your ribcage with which you breathe.

lunge NOUN ① a sudden forward movement • *He made a lunge for the door.* ▶ VERB ② To lunge means to make a sudden movement in a particular direction.

lurch VERB ① To lurch means to make a sudden, jerky movement. ▸ NOUN ② a sudden, jerky movement.

lure VERB ① To lure someone means to attract them into going somewhere or doing something. ▸ NOUN ② something that you find very attractive.

> **lure** VERB
> ① = attract, beckon, draw, entice, tempt
> ▸ NOUN ② = attraction, bait, magnet, pull, temptation

lurid [*Said* ***loo**-rid*] ADJECTIVE ① involving a lot of sensational detail • *lurid stories in the press*. ② very brightly coloured or patterned.

lurk VERB To lurk somewhere means to remain there hidden from the person you are waiting for.

> **lurk** VERB
> = lie in wait, loiter, skulk

luscious ADJECTIVE very tasty • *luscious fruit*.

lush ADJECTIVE In a lush field or garden, the grass or plants are healthy and growing thickly.

lust NOUN ① A lust for something is a strong desire to have it • *a lust for money*. ▸ VERB ② If you lust for or after something, you have a very strong desire to possess it • *She lusted after fame*.

lustre [*Said* ***lus**-ter*] NOUN Lustre is soft shining light reflected from the surface of something • *the lustre of silk*.

luxuriant ADJECTIVE Luxuriant plants, trees and gardens are large, healthy and growing strongly.

luxurious ADJECTIVE very expensive and full of luxury. **luxuriously** ADVERB

> **luxurious** ADJECTIVE
> = de luxe, lavish, opulent, plush (*informal*), sumptuous
> ≠ plain

luxury, **luxuries** NOUN ① Luxury is great comfort in expensive and beautiful surroundings • *a life of luxury*. ② something that you enjoy very much but do not have very often, usually because it is expensive.

> **luxury** NOUN
> ① = affluence, opulence, sumptuousness
> ② = extra, extravagance, indulgence, treat

-ly SUFFIX ① '-ly' forms adjectives that describe a quality • *friendly*. ② '-ly' forms adjectives that refer to how often something happens or is done • *yearly*. ③ '-ly' forms adverbs that refer to how or in what way something is done • *quickly* • *nicely*.

lying NOUN ① Lying is telling lies. ▸ ADJECTIVE ② A lying person is telling lies. ③ Lying is also the present participle of **lie**².

> **lying** NOUN
> ① = deceit, dishonesty, fabrication, fibbing, perjury
> ▸ ADJECTIVE ② = deceitful, dishonest, false, untruthful
> ≠ honest

lynch VERB If a crowd lynches someone, it kills them in a violent way without first holding a legal trial.

lynx, **lynxes** NOUN a wildcat with a short tail and tufted ears.

lyric NOUN ① MUSIC The lyrics of a song are the words. ▸ ADJECTIVE ② Lyric poetry is written in a simple and direct style, and is usually about love.

lyrical ADJECTIVE poetic and romantic.

Mm

m an abbreviation for 'metres' or 'miles'.

macabre *[Said mak-**kahb**-ra]* ADJECTIVE A macabre event or story is strange and horrible • *a macabre horror story*.

macadamia *[Said ma-ka-**dame**-ee-a]* NOUN an Australian tree, also grown in New Zealand, that produces edible nuts.

macaroni NOUN Macaroni is short hollow tubes of pasta.

mace NOUN an ornamental pole carried by an official during ceremonies as a symbol of authority.

machete *[Said mash-**ett**-ee]* NOUN a large, heavy knife with a big blade.

machine NOUN ① DGT a piece of equipment which uses electricity or power from an engine to make it work. ▸ VERB ② If you machine something, you make it or work on it using a machine.

> **machine** NOUN
> ① = apparatus, appliance, contraption, device, instrument, mechanism

machine-gun NOUN a gun that works automatically, firing bullets one after the other.

machinery NOUN Machinery is machines in general.

machismo *[Said mak-**kiz**-moe]* NOUN Machismo is exaggerated aggressive male behaviour.

macho *[Said **mat**-shoh]* ADJECTIVE A man who is described as macho behaves in an aggressively masculine way.

mackerel NOUN a sea fish with blue and silver stripes.

mad, **madder**, **maddest** ADJECTIVE ① Someone who is mad does not think in a normal way and may behave in strange ways. ② (*informal*) If you describe someone as mad, you mean that they are very foolish • *He said we were mad to share a flat*. ③ (*informal*) Someone who is mad is angry. ④ (*informal*) If you are mad about someone or something, you like them very much • *Alan was mad about golf*. **madness** NOUN **madman** NOUN

> **mad** ADJECTIVE
> ① = crazy (*informal*), deranged, insane, nuts (*slang*)
> ≠ sane
> ② = barmy (*slang*), crazy (*informal*), daft (*British; informal*), foolhardy, foolish, stupid
> ③ = angry, enraged, fuming, furious, incensed, infuriated, irate, livid

madam NOUN 'Madam' is a very formal way of addressing a woman.

maddening ADJECTIVE irritating or frustrating • *She had many maddening habits*.

made the past tense and past participle of **make**.

madly ADVERB If you do something madly, you do it in a fast, excited way.

Mafia NOUN The Mafia is a large crime organisation operating in Italy and the USA.

magazine NOUN ① LIBRARY a weekly or monthly publication with articles and photographs. ② a compartment in a gun for cartridges.

magenta *[Said maj-**jen**-ta]* NOUN, ADJECTIVE dark reddish-purple.

maggot NOUN a creature that looks like a small worm and lives on decaying things. Maggots turn into flies.

magic NOUN ① In fairy stories, magic is a special power that can make impossible things happen. ② Magic is the art of performing tricks to entertain people.

> **magic** NOUN
> ① = sorcery, witchcraft

magical ADJECTIVE wonderful and exciting. **magically** ADVERB

> **magical** ADJECTIVE
> = bewitching, enchanting

magician NOUN ① a person who performs tricks as entertainment. ② In fairy stories, a magician is a man with magical powers.

magistrate NOUN an official who acts as a judge in a law court that deals with less serious crimes.

magnanimous ADJECTIVE generous and forgiving.

magnate NOUN someone who is very rich and powerful in business.

magnet NOUN SCIENCE a piece of iron which attracts iron or steel towards it, and which points towards north if allowed to swing freely. A **permanent magnet** is a magnet that is still magnetic when the magnetic field that produced it is taken away; a **temporary magnet** is a magnet that loses its magnetism when the magnetic field that produced it is taken away. **magnetic** ADJECTIVE **magnetism** NOUN

magnificent ADJECTIVE extremely beautiful or impressive. **magnificently** ADVERB **magnificence** NOUN

magnify, **magnifies**, **magnifying**, **magnified** VERB SCIENCE When a microscope or lens magnifies something, it makes it appear bigger than it actually is. **magnification** NOUN

magnifying glass NOUN a lens which makes things appear bigger than they really are.

magnitude NOUN The magnitude of something is its great size or importance.

magnolia NOUN a tree which has large white or pink flowers in spring.

magpie NOUN a large black and white bird with a long tail.

mahogany NOUN Mahogany is a hard, reddish-brown wood used for making furniture.

maid NOUN a female servant.

maiden NOUN ① *(literary)* a young woman. ▸ ADJECTIVE ② first • *a maiden voyage*.

maiden name NOUN the surname a woman had before she married.

mail NOUN ① Your mail is the letters and parcels delivered to you by the post office. ▸ VERB ② If you mail a letter, you send it by post.

mail order NOUN Mail order is a system of buying goods by post.

maim VERB To maim someone is to injure them very badly for life.

main ADJECTIVE ① most important • *the main event*. ▸ NOUN ② The mains are large pipes or wires that carry gas, water or electricity.

> **main** ADJECTIVE
> ① = cardinal, chief, foremost, leading, major, predominant, primary, prime, principal

mainframe NOUN a large computer which can be used by many people at the same time.

mainland NOUN The mainland is the

main part of a country in contrast to islands around its coast.

mainly ADVERB true in most cases.

> **mainly** ADVERB
> = chiefly, generally, largely, mostly, predominantly, primarily, principally

mainstay NOUN The mainstay of something is the most important part of it.

mainstream NOUN The mainstream is the most ordinary and conventional group of people or ideas in a society.

maintain VERB ① If you maintain something, you keep it going or keep it at a particular rate or level • *I wanted to maintain our friendship.* ② If you maintain someone, you provide them regularly with money for what they need. ③ To maintain a machine or a building is to keep it in good condition. ④ If you maintain that something is true, you believe it is true and say so.

maintenance NOUN ① Maintenance is the process of keeping something in good condition. ② Maintenance is also money that a person sends regularly to someone to provide for the things they need.

maize NOUN Maize is a tall plant which produces sweet corn.

majesty NOUN ① Majesty is great dignity and impressiveness. ② 'Majesty' is used in the title and form of address for kings and queens • *Her Majesty, Queen Victoria.* **majestic** ADJECTIVE **majestically** ADVERB

major ADJECTIVE ① more important or more significant than other things • *the major political parties.* ② MUSIC A major key is one of the keys in which most European music is written. In a major key the third note is four semitones higher than the first. ▸ NOUN ③ an army officer of the rank immediately above captain.

> **major** ADJECTIVE
> ① = critical, crucial, leading, outstanding, significant
> ≠ minor

majority, **majorities** NOUN ① The majority of people or things in a group is more than half of the group. ② In an election, the majority is the difference between the number of votes gained by the winner and the number gained by the runner-up.

> **majority** NOUN
> ① = best part, better part, bulk, mass, most

make, **makes**, **making**, **made** VERB ① To make something is to produce or construct it, or to cause it to happen. ② To make something is to do it • *He was about to make a speech.* ③ To make something is to prepare it • *I'll make some salad dressing.* ④ If someone makes you do something, they force you to do it • *Mum made me clean the bathroom.* ▸ NOUN ⑤ The make of a product is the name of the company that manufactured it • *'What make of car do you drive?'—'A Toyota.'* **make up** VERB ① If a number of things make up something, they form that thing. ② If you make up a story, you invent it. ③ If you make yourself up, you put make-up on. ④ If two people make it up, they become friends again after a quarrel.

> **make** VERB
> ① = assemble, build, construct, create, fabricate, fashion, form, manufacture, produce
> ④ = compel, drive, force, oblige
> ▸ NOUN ⑤ = brand, model
> ▸ **make up** ① = compose, comprise, constitute, form ② = concoct, fabricate, invent

make-up NOUN ① Make-up is coloured creams and powders which people put on their faces to make themselves look more attractive. ② Someone's make-up is their character or personality.

making NOUN ① The making of something is the act or process of creating or producing it. ▶ PHRASE ② When you describe someone as something **in the making**, you mean that they are gradually becoming that thing • *a captain in the making*.

> **making** NOUN
> ① = assembly, building, construction, creation, fabrication, manufacture, production
> ▶ PHRASE ② = budding, emergent, potential, up-and-coming

malaise [*Said mal-**laze***] NOUN (*formal*) Malaise is a feeling of dissatisfaction or unhappiness.

malaria [*Said mal-**lay**-ree-a*] NOUN Malaria is a tropical disease caught from mosquitoes which causes fever and shivering.

Malaysian ADJECTIVE ① belonging or relating to Malaysia. ▶ NOUN ② someone who comes from Malaysia.

male NOUN ① a person or animal belonging to the sex that cannot give birth or lay eggs. ▶ ADJECTIVE ② concerning or relating to males.

> **male** ADJECTIVE
> ② = manly, masculine
> ≠ female

malevolent [*Said mal-**lev**-oh-lent*] ADJECTIVE (*formal*) wanting or intending to cause harm.
malevolence NOUN

malfunction VERB ① If a machine or part of the body malfunctions, it fails to work properly. ▶ NOUN ② the failure of a machine or part of the body to work properly.

malice NOUN Malice is a desire to cause harm to people.

malicious ADJECTIVE Malicious talk or behaviour is intended to harm someone.

> **malicious** ADJECTIVE
> = cruel, malevolent (*formal*), mean, spiteful, vicious

malign (*formal*) VERB ① To malign someone means to say unpleasant and untrue things about them. ▶ ADJECTIVE ② intended to harm someone.

malignant ADJECTIVE ① harmful and cruel. ② A malignant disease or tumour could cause death if it is allowed to continue.

mall NOUN a very large enclosed shopping area.

mallet NOUN a wooden hammer with a square head.

malnutrition NOUN SCIENCE Malnutrition is not eating enough food, or enough healthy food.

malpractice NOUN If someone such as a doctor or lawyer breaks the rules of their profession, their behaviour is called malpractice.

malt NOUN Malt is roasted grain, usually barley, that is used in making beer and whisky.

malware NOUN Computer programs that are designed to damage or disrupt a system are known as malware.

mammal NOUN SCIENCE Animals that give birth to live babies and feed their young with milk from the mother's body are called mammals. Human beings, dogs and whales are all mammals.

mammoth ADJECTIVE ① very large indeed • *a mammoth outdoor concert*. ▶ NOUN ② a huge animal that looked like a hairy elephant with long tusks.

Mammoths became extinct a long time ago.

man, **men**; **mans**, **manning**, **manned** NOUN ① an adult male human being. ▸ PLURAL NOUN ② 'Man' is sometimes used to refer to human beings in general, including men and women • *Man's responsibility to look after the planet.* ▸ VERB ③ To man something is to be in charge of it or operate it • *Two officers were manning the radar screens.*

> **man** NOUN
> ① = bloke (*British, Australian and New Zealand; informal*), chap (*informal*), gentleman, guy (*informal*), male
> ≠ woman
> ▸ PLURAL NOUN ② = humanity, human race, mankind

manage VERB ① If you manage to do something, you succeed in doing it • *We managed to find somewhere to sit.* ② If you manage an organisation or business, you are responsible for controlling it.

> **manage** VERB
> ① = cope with, succeed in
> ② = be in charge of, command, control, direct, run

manageable ADJECTIVE able to be dealt with.

management NOUN ① The management of a business is the controlling and organising of it. ② The people who control an organisation are called the management.

> **management** NOUN
> ① = control, direction, running
> ② = administration, board, bosses, directors, employers

manager NOUN a person responsible for running a business or organisation • *a bank manager.*

> **manager** NOUN
> = boss, director, executive

manageress NOUN a woman responsible for running a business or organisation.

managing director NOUN a company director who is responsible for the way the company is managed.

mandarin NOUN a type of small orange which is easy to peel.

mandate NOUN (*formal*) A government's mandate is the authority it has to carry out particular policies as a result of winning an election.

mandatory ADJECTIVE If something is mandatory, there is a law or rule stating that it must be done • *Attendance at the meeting is mandatory.*

mandolin NOUN a musical instrument like a small guitar with a deep, rounded body.

mane NOUN the long hair growing from the neck of a lion or horse.

manger [*Said* ***main****-jir*] NOUN a feeding box in a barn or stable.

mangle VERB ① If something is mangled, it is crushed and twisted. ▸ NOUN ② an old-fashioned piece of equipment consisting of two large rollers which squeeze water out of wet clothes.

mango, **mangoes** or **mangos** NOUN a sweet yellowish fruit which grows in tropical countries.

manhole NOUN a covered hole in the ground leading to a drain or sewer.

manhood NOUN Manhood is the state of being a man rather than a boy.

mania NOUN ① a strong liking for something • *a mania for plant collecting.* ② a mental condition characterised by periods of great excitement.

maniac NOUN a person who is violent and dangerous.

manic ADJECTIVE energetic and excited • *a manic rush to the airport.*

manicure VERB ① If you manicure your hands, you care for them by softening the skin and shaping and polishing the nails. ▶ NOUN ② A manicure is a special treatment for the hands and nails. **manicurist** NOUN

manifest (*formal*) ADJECTIVE ① obvious or easily seen • *his manifest enthusiasm.* ▶ VERB ② To manifest something is to make people aware of it • *Fear can manifest itself in many ways.*

manifest ADJECTIVE
① = blatant, clear, conspicuous, glaring, obvious, patent, plain

manifestation NOUN (*formal*) A manifestation of something is a sign that it is happening or exists • *The illness may be a manifestation of stress.*

manifesto, **manifestoes** or **manifestos** NOUN a published statement of the aims and policies of a political party.

manipulate VERB ① To manipulate people or events is to control or influence them to produce a particular result. ② If you manipulate a piece of equipment, you control it in a skilful way. **manipulation** NOUN **manipulator** NOUN **manipulative** ADJECTIVE

mankind NOUN 'Mankind' is used to refer to all human beings • *a threat to mankind.*

manly, **manlier**, **manliest** ADJECTIVE having qualities that are typically masculine • *He laughed a deep, manly laugh.*

manner NOUN ① The manner in which you do something is the way you do it. ② Your manner is the way in which you behave and talk • *his kind manner.* ③ (*in plural*) If you have good manners, you behave very politely.

manner NOUN
① = fashion, mode, style, way
② = bearing, behaviour, conduct, demeanour

mannerism NOUN a gesture or a way of speaking which is characteristic of a person.

manoeuvre [*Said man-**noo**-ver*] VERB ① If you manoeuvre something into a place, you skilfully move it there • *It took expertise to manoeuvre the boat so close to the shore.* ▶ NOUN ② a clever move you make in order to change a situation to your advantage.

manoeuvre VERB
① = guide, navigate, negotiate, steer
▶ NOUN ② = dodge, ploy, ruse, tactic

manor NOUN a large country house with land.

manpower NOUN Workers can be referred to as manpower.

mansion NOUN a very large house.

manslaughter NOUN (*Law*) Manslaughter is the accidental killing of a person.

mantelpiece NOUN a shelf over a fireplace.

mantle NOUN ① (*literary*) To take on the mantle of something is to accept the status or duties associated with it • *He has taken over the mantle of England's greatest living poet.* ② GEOGRAPHY the part of the earth between the crust and the core.

mantra NOUN RE a word or short piece of sacred text or prayer continually repeated to help concentration.

manual ADJECTIVE ① Manual work involves physical strength rather than mental skill. ② operated by hand rather than by electricity or by motor • *a manual typewriter.* ▶ NOUN ③ an instruction book which tells you how to use a machine. **manually** ADVERB

manufacture DGT VERB ① To manufacture goods is to make them in a factory. ▶ NOUN ② The manufacture of goods is the making of them in a factory • *the manufacture of computers*. **manufacturer** NOUN

manufacture VERB
① = assemble, fabricate, make, mass-produce, process, produce
▸ NOUN ② = assembly, fabrication, making, mass production, production

manure NOUN Manure is animal faeces used to fertilise the soil.

manuscript NOUN a handwritten or typed document, especially a version of a book before it is printed.

Manx ADJECTIVE belonging or relating to the Isle of Man.

many ADJECTIVE ① If there are many people or things, there is a large number of them. ② You also use 'many' to ask how great a quantity is or to give information about it • *How many tickets do you require?* ▸ PRONOUN ③ a large number of people or things • *Many are too weak to walk*.

many ADJECTIVE
① = countless, innumerable, myriad, numerous, umpteen (*informal*)
≠ few
▸ PRONOUN ③ = a lot, a mass, a multitude, large numbers, lots (*informal*), plenty, scores
≠ few

Māori, **Māoris** NOUN ① someone descended from the people who lived in New Zealand before Europeans arrived. ② Māori is a language spoken by Māoris. ▸ ADJECTIVE ③ belonging or relating to Māoris.

map, **maps**, **mapping**, **mapped** NOUN ① a detailed drawing of an area as it would appear if you saw it from above. ② MATHS the relationship between elements of a set and elements in the same or another set. **map out** VERB If you map out a plan, you work out in detail what you will do.

maple NOUN a tree that has large leaves with five points.

mar, **mars**, **marring**, **marred** VERB To mar something is to spoil it • *The presentation was marred by technical problems*.

marathon NOUN ① a race in which people run 26 miles along roads. ▸ ADJECTIVE ② A marathon task is a large one that takes a long time.

marble NOUN ① Marble is a very hard, cold stone which is often polished to show the coloured patterns in it. ② Marbles is a children's game played with small coloured glass balls. These balls are also called marbles.

march NOUN ① March is the third month of the year. It has 31 days. ② an organised protest in which a large group of people walk somewhere together. ▸ VERB ③ When soldiers march, they walk with quick regular steps in time with each other. ④ To march somewhere is to walk quickly in a determined way • *He marched out of the room*.

mare NOUN an adult female horse.

margarine [*Said* ***mar****-jar-reen*] NOUN Margarine is a substance that is similar to butter but is made from vegetable oil and animal fats.

margin NOUN ① If you win a contest by a large or small margin, you win it by a large or small amount. ② an extra amount that allows you more freedom in doing something • *a small margin of error*. ③ the blank space at each side on a written or printed page.

marginal ADJECTIVE ① small and not very important • *a marginal increase*. ② A marginal seat or constituency is a political constituency where the previous election was won by a very small majority. **marginally** ADVERB

marijuana [*Said mar-rih-****wan****-a*] NOUN Marijuana is an illegal drug which people smoke.

marina NOUN a harbour for pleasure boats and yachts.

marinate VERB To marinate food is to soak it in a mixture of oil, vinegar, spices and herbs to flavour it before cooking.

marine NOUN ① a soldier who serves with the navy. ▶ ADJECTIVE ② relating to or involving the sea • *marine life*.

marital ADJECTIVE relating to or involving marriage.

maritime ADJECTIVE relating to the sea and ships • *maritime trade*.

mark NOUN ① a small stain or damaged area on a surface • *I can't get this mark off the curtain*. ② a written or printed symbol • *He made a few marks with his pen*. ③ a letter or number showing how well you have done in homework or in an exam. ▶ VERB ④ If something marks a surface, it damages it in some way. ⑤ If you mark something, you write a symbol on it or identify it in some other way. ⑥ When a teacher marks your work, he or she decides how good it is and gives it a mark. ⑦ To mark something is to be a sign of it • *The accident marked a tragic end to the day*. ⑧ In soccer or hockey, if you mark your opposing player, you stay close to them, trying to prevent them from getting the ball.

> **mark** NOUN
> ① = blot, line, smudge, spot, stain, streak
> ▶ VERB ④ = smudge, stain, streak

marked ADJECTIVE very obvious • *a marked improvement*. **markedly** ADVERB

market NOUN ① a place where goods or animals are bought and sold. ② The market for a product is the number of people who want to buy it • *the market for cars*. ▶ VERB ③ To market a product is to organise its sale, by deciding its price, where it should be sold, and how it should be advertised.

> **market** NOUN
> ① = bazaar, fair

marketing NOUN DGT Marketing is the part of a business concerned with the way a product is sold.

market research NOUN DGT Market research is research into what people want and buy.

marksman, **marksmen** NOUN someone who can shoot very accurately.

marlin NOUN a large fish found in tropical seas which has a very long upper jaw.

marmalade NOUN Marmalade is a jam made from citrus fruit, usually eaten at breakfast.

maroon NOUN, ADJECTIVE dark reddish-purple.

marooned ADJECTIVE If you are marooned in a place, you are stranded there and cannot leave it.

marquee [*Said mar-**kee***] NOUN a very large tent used at a fair or other outdoor entertainment.

marriage NOUN ① the legal relationship between a couple. ② Marriage is the act of marrying someone.

> **marriage** NOUN
> ① = matrimony (*formal*), wedlock (*formal*)

marrow NOUN a long, thick, green-skinned fruit with cream-coloured flesh eaten as a vegetable.

marry, **marries**, **marrying**, **married** VERB ① When two people marry, they become each other's partner during a special ceremony. ② When a member of the clergy or a registrar marries a couple, he or she is in charge of their marriage ceremony. **married** ADJECTIVE

Mars NOUN Mars is the planet in the solar system which is fourth from the sun.

marsh NOUN an area of land which is permanently wet.

marshal, **marshals, marshalling, marshalled** VERB ① If you marshal things or people, you gather them together and organise them • *The students were marshalled into the assembly room.* ▶ NOUN ② an official who helps to organise a public event.

marshmallow NOUN a soft, spongy, pink or white sweet made using gelatine.

marsupial *[Said mar-**syoo**-pee-al]* NOUN an animal that carries its young in a pouch. Koalas and kangaroos are marsupials.

martial arts PLURAL NOUN The martial arts are the techniques of self-defence that come from East Asia, for example karate or judo.

Martian *[Said **mar**-shan]* NOUN an imaginary creature from the planet Mars.

martyr RE NOUN ① someone who suffers or is killed rather than change their beliefs. ▶ VERB ② If someone is martyred, they are killed because of their beliefs. **martyrdom** NOUN

marvel, **marvels, marvelling, marvelled** VERB ① If you marvel at something, it fills you with surprise or admiration • *Modern designers can only marvel at his genius.* ▶ NOUN ② something that makes you feel great surprise or admiration • *a marvel of high technology.*

marvellous ADJECTIVE wonderful or excellent. **marvellously** ADVERB

> **marvellous** ADJECTIVE
> = brilliant, excellent, first-rate, magnificent, remarkable, splendid, superb, wonderful
> ≠ terrible

Marxism NOUN Marxism is a political philosophy based on the writings of Karl Marx. It states that society will develop towards communism through the struggle between different social classes. **Marxist** ADJECTIVE, NOUN

marzipan NOUN Marzipan is a paste made of almonds, sugar and egg. It is put on top of cakes or used to make small sweets.

mascara NOUN Mascara is a substance that can be used to colour eyelashes and make them look longer.

mascot NOUN a person, animal or toy which is thought to bring good luck.

masculine ADJECTIVE ① typical of men, rather than women • *masculine characteristics like facial hair.* ② belonging to a particular class of nouns in some languages, such as French, German and Latin. **masculinity** NOUN

mash VERB If you mash vegetables, you crush them after they have been cooked.

mask NOUN ① something you wear over your face for protection or disguise • *a surgical mask.* ▶ VERB ② If you mask something, you cover it so that it is protected or cannot be seen.

mason NOUN a person who is skilled at making things with stone.

masonry NOUN Masonry is pieces of stone which form part of a wall or building.

masquerade *[Said mass-ker-**raid**]* VERB If you masquerade as something, you pretend to be it • *He masqueraded as a doctor.*

mass NOUN ① a large amount of something. ② The masses are the ordinary people in society considered as a group • *opera for the masses.*

③ SCIENCE In physics, the mass of an object is the amount of physical matter that it has. ④ RE In the Roman Catholic Church, Mass is a religious service in which people share bread and wine in remembrance of the death and resurrection of Jesus Christ. ▶ ADJECTIVE ⑤ involving a large number of people • *mass unemployment*. ▶ VERB ⑥ When people mass, they gather together in a large group.

mass NOUN
① = crowd, heap, load, lump, mob, pile, throng
▶ ADJECTIVE ⑤ = general, popular, universal, widespread
▶ VERB ⑥ = assemble, congregate, gather, group

massacre *[Said* ***mass****-ik-ker]* NOUN ① the killing of a very large number of people in a violent and cruel way. ▶ VERB ② To massacre people is to kill large numbers of them in a violent and cruel way.

massage VERB ① To massage someone is to rub their body in order to help them relax or to relieve pain. ▶ NOUN ② A massage is treatment which involves rubbing the body.

massive ADJECTIVE extremely large • *a massive iceberg*. **massively** ADVERB

mast NOUN the tall upright pole that supports the sails of a boat.

master NOUN ① a man who has authority over others, such as the employer of servants especially servants or slaves. ② the owner of an animal. ③ If you are master of a situation, you have control over it • *He was master of his own destiny*. ④ a male teacher at some schools. ▶ VERB ⑤ If you master a difficult situation, you succeed in controlling it. ⑥ If you master something, you learn how to do it properly • *She found it easy to master the game*.

master NOUN
③ = instructor, teacher, tutor
▶ VERB ⑤ = become proficient in, get the hang of (*informal*), grasp, learn

masterful ADJECTIVE showing control and authority.

masterly ADJECTIVE extremely clever or well done • *a masterly exhibition of batting*.

mastermind VERB ① If you mastermind a complicated activity, you plan and organise it. ▶ NOUN ② The mastermind behind something is the person responsible for planning it.

masterpiece NOUN an extremely good painting or other work of art.

mat NOUN ① a small round or square piece of cloth, card or plastic that is placed on a table to protect it from plates or glasses. ② a small piece of carpet or other thick material that is placed on the floor.

matador NOUN a man who fights and tries to kill bulls as part of a public entertainment, especially in Spain.

match NOUN ① an organised game of football, cricket or some other sport. ② a small, thin stick of wood that produces a flame when you strike it against a rough surface. ▶ VERB ③ If one thing matches another, the two things look the same or have similar qualities.

match NOUN
① = competition, contest, game
▶ VERB ③ = agree, correspond, fit, go with, suit, tally

mate NOUN ① (*informal*) Your mates are your friends. ② The first mate on a ship is the officer who is next in importance to the captain. ③ An animal's mate is its partner for reproduction. ▶ VERB ④ When a male and female animal mate, they come together in order to breed.

material NOUN ① [DGT] Material is cloth. ② [DGT] a substance from which something is made • *the materials to make red dye.* ③ [DGT] The equipment for a particular activity can be referred to as materials • *building materials.* ④ Material for a book, play or film is the information or ideas on which it is based. ▸ ADJECTIVE ⑤ involving possessions and money • *concerned with material comforts.* **materially** ADVERB

material NOUN
① = cloth, fabric
② = matter, stuff, substance

materialise; also spelt **materialize** VERB If something materialises, it actually happens or appears • *Fortunately, the attack did not materialise.*

materialism NOUN Materialism is thinking that money and possessions are the most important things in life. **materialistic** ADJECTIVE

maternal ADJECTIVE relating to or involving a mother • *her maternal instincts.*

maternity ADJECTIVE relating to or involving pregnant women and birth • *a maternity hospital.*

mathematics NOUN Mathematics is the study of numbers, quantities and shapes. **mathematical** ADJECTIVE **mathematically** ADVERB **mathematician** NOUN

maths NOUN Maths is mathematics.

Matilda NOUN (*old-fashioned, informal*) In Australia, Matilda is the pack of belongings carried by a swagman in the bush. The word is now used only in the phrase 'waltzing Matilda', meaning travelling in the bush with few possessions.

matrimony NOUN (*formal*) Matrimony is marriage. **matrimonial** ADJECTIVE

matrix, **matrices** [*Said **may**-trix*] NOUN ① (*formal*) the framework in which something grows and develops. ② In maths, a matrix is a set of numbers or elements set out in rows and columns.

matron NOUN In a hospital, a senior nurse in charge of all the nursing staff used to be known as matron.

matt ADJECTIVE A matt surface is dull rather than shiny • *matt black plastic.*

matted ADJECTIVE Hair that is matted is tangled with the strands sticking together.

matter NOUN ① something that you have to deal with. ② Matter is any substance • *The atom is the smallest divisible particle of matter.* ③ Books and magazines are reading matter. ▸ VERB ④ If something matters to you, it is important. ▸ PHRASE ⑤ If you ask **What's the matter?**, you are asking what is wrong.

matter NOUN
① = affair, business, issue, question, situation, subject
② = material, stuff, substance
▸ VERB ④ = be of consequence, count, make a difference

matter-of-fact ADJECTIVE showing no emotion.

matting NOUN Matting is thick woven material such as rope or straw, used as a floor covering.

mattress NOUN a large thick pad filled with springs, foam or other material that is put on a bed to make it comfortable.

mature VERB ① When a child or young animal matures, it becomes an adult. ② When something matures, it reaches complete development. ▸ ADJECTIVE ③ Mature means fully developed and emotionally balanced. **maturely** ADVERB **maturity** NOUN

mature VERB
① = come of age, grow up, reach adulthood
▸ ADJECTIVE ③ = adult, full-grown, fully-fledged, grown, grown-up

maudlin ADJECTIVE Someone who is maudlin is sad and sentimental, especially when they are drunk.

maul VERB If someone is mauled by an animal, they are savagely attacked and badly injured by it.

mausoleum [*Said maw-sal-**lee**-um*] NOUN a building which contains the grave of a famous person.

mauve [*Rhymes with **grove***] NOUN, ADJECTIVE pale purple.

maxim NOUN a short saying which gives a rule for good or sensible behaviour • *Instant action: that's my maxim.*

maximise; also spelt **maximize** VERB To maximise something is to make it as great or effective as possible • *Their objective is to maximise profits.*

maximum ADJECTIVE ① The maximum amount is the most that is possible • *the maximum recommended intake.* ▸ NOUN ② The maximum is the most that is possible • *a maximum of 50 people.*

maximum ADJECTIVE
① = top, utmost
≠ minimum
▸ NOUN ② = ceiling, height, most, upper limit, utmost
≠ minimum

may VERB ① If something may happen, it is possible that it will happen • *It may rain today.* ② If someone may do something, they are allowed to do it • *Please may I be excused?* ③ You can use 'may' when saying that although something is true, something else is also true • *This may be true, but it is only part of the story.* ④ (*formal*) You also use 'may' to express a wish that something will happen • *May you live to be a hundred.* ▸ NOUN ⑤ May is the fifth month of the year. It has 31 days.

maybe ADVERB You use 'maybe' when you are stating a possibility that you are not certain about • *Maybe I should lie about my age.*

maybe ADVERB
= conceivably, it could be, perhaps, possibly

mayhem NOUN You can refer to a confused and chaotic situation as mayhem • *There was complete mayhem in the classroom.*

mayonnaise [*Said may-on-**nayz***] NOUN Mayonnaise is a thick salad dressing made with egg yolks and oil.

mayor NOUN a person who has been elected to lead and represent the people of a town.

maze NOUN a system of complicated passages which it is difficult to find your way through • *a maze of dark tunnels.*

MBE NOUN a British honour granted by the King or Queen. MBE is an abbreviation for 'Member of the Order of the British Empire' • *Rory McIlroy, MBE.*

MD an abbreviation for 'Doctor of Medicine' or 'Managing Director'.

me PRONOUN A speaker or writer uses 'me' to refer to himself or herself.

meadow NOUN a field of grass.

meagre [*Said **mee**-ger*] ADJECTIVE very small and poor • *his meagre pension.*

meagre ADJECTIVE
= inadequate, measly (*informal*), paltry, scant, sparse

meal NOUN an occasion when people eat, or the food they eat at that time.

meal NOUN
= banquet, dinner, feast, kai (*New Zealand; informal*)

mean, **means**, **meaning**, **meant** VERB ① If you ask what something means, you want to know what it refers to or what its message is. ② If you mean what you say, you are serious • *The head teacher means what she says.* ③ If something means a lot to you, it is important to you. ④ If one thing means another, it shows that the second thing is true or will happen • *Major roadworks will mean long delays.* ⑤ If you mean to do something, you intend to do it • *I meant to phone you, but didn't have time.* ⑥ If something is meant to be true, it is supposed to be true • *I found a road that wasn't meant to be there.* ▶ ADJECTIVE ⑦ Someone who is mean is unwilling to spend much money. ⑧ Someone who is mean is unkind or cruel • *He apologised for being so mean to her.* ▶ NOUN ⑨ (*in plural*) A means of doing something is a method or object which makes it possible • *The tests were marked by means of a computer.* ⑩ (*in plural*) Someone's means are their money and income • *He's obviously a man of means.* ⑪ MATHS The mean of a set of numbers is the result obtained by adding all the numbers in the set and dividing the total by the number of members of the set. **meanness** NOUN **meanly** ADVERB

> **mean** VERB
> ① = denote, indicate, signify
> ⑤ = aim, intend, plan
> ▶ ADJECTIVE ⑦ = miserly, snoep (*South African; informal*), tight (*informal*) ≠ generous

meander [*Said mee-an-der*] VERB If a road or river meanders, it has a lot of bends in it.

meaning NOUN ① The meaning of a word is what it refers to or expresses. ② The meaning of what someone says, or of a book or a film, is the thoughts or ideas that it is intended to express. ③ If something has meaning, it seems to be worthwhile and to have real purpose. **meaningful** ADJECTIVE **meaningfully** ADVERB **meaningless** ADJECTIVE

> **meaning** NOUN
> ② = drift, gist, message, significance

means test NOUN a check of a person's money and income to see whether they need money or benefits from the government or other organisation.

meantime PHRASE **In the meantime** means in the period of time between two events • *I'll call the nurse; in the meantime, you must rest.*

meanwhile ADVERB Meanwhile means while something else is happening.

measles NOUN Measles is an infectious illness in which you have red spots on your skin.

measly ADJECTIVE (*informal*) very small or inadequate • *a measly 4.3 per cent.*

measure VERB ① MATHS When you measure something, you find out how big it is. ② MATHS If something measures a particular distance, its length or depth is that distance • *slivers of glass measuring a few millimetres across.* ▶ NOUN ③ A measure of something is a certain amount of it • *There has been a measure of agreement.* ④ MATHS a unit in which size, speed or depth is expressed. ⑤ Measures are actions carried out to achieve a particular result • *Tough measures are needed to maintain order.*

> **measure** VERB
> ① = gauge, survey
> ▶ NOUN ③ = amount, degree, portion, proportion
> ⑤ = expedient, manoeuvre, means, procedure, step

measured ADJECTIVE careful and deliberate • *walking at the same measured pace.*

measurement NOUN ① the result that you obtain when you measure something. ② Measurement is the activity of measuring something. ③ Your measurements are the sizes of your chest, waist and hips that you use to buy the correct size of clothes.

meat NOUN Meat is the flesh of animals that is cooked and eaten. **meaty** ADJECTIVE

Mecca NOUN ① [RE] Mecca is the holiest city of Islam, to which many Muslims make pilgrimages. ② If a place is a mecca for people of a particular kind, many of them go there because it is of special interest to them • *The island is a mecca for bird lovers.*

mechanic NOUN ① a person who repairs and maintains engines and machines. ② (*in plural*) The mechanics of something are the way in which it works or is done • *the mechanics of accounting.* ③ (*in plural*) Mechanics is also the scientific study of movement and the forces that affect objects.

mechanical ADJECTIVE ① A mechanical device has moving parts and is used to do a physical task. ② A mechanical action is done automatically without thinking about it • *He gave a mechanical smile.* **mechanically** ADVERB

mechanism NOUN ① [DGT] a part of a machine that does a particular task • *a locking mechanism.* ② part of your behaviour that is automatic • *the body's defence mechanisms.*

medal NOUN a small disc of metal given as an award for bravery or as a prize for sport.

medallion NOUN a round piece of metal worn as an ornament on a chain round the neck.

medallist NOUN a person who has won a medal in sport • *a gold medallist at the Olympics.*

meddle VERB To meddle is to interfere and try to change things without being asked.

media PLURAL NOUN You can refer to the television, radio and newspapers as the media.

median [*Said* ***mee****-dee-an*] ADJECTIVE [MATHS] The median value of a set is the middle value when the set is arranged in order.

mediate VERB If you mediate between two groups, you try to settle a dispute between them. **mediation** NOUN **mediator** NOUN

medical ADJECTIVE ① relating to the prevention and treatment of illness and injuries. ▶ NOUN ② a thorough examination of your body by a doctor. **medically** ADVERB

medication NOUN Medication is a substance that is used to treat illness.

medicinal ADJECTIVE relating to the treatment of illness • *a valuable medicinal herb.*

medicine NOUN ① Medicine is the treatment of illness and injuries by doctors and nurses. ② a substance that you drink or swallow to help cure an illness.

> **medicine** NOUN
> ② = drug, medication, muti (*South African; informal*), remedy

medieval [*Said med-dee-****ee****-vul*]; also spelt **mediaeval** ADJECTIVE [HISTORY] relating to the period between about 1100 AD and 1500 AD, especially in Europe.

mediocre [*Said meed-dee-****oh****-ker*] ADJECTIVE of rather poor quality • *a mediocre string of performances.* **mediocrity** NOUN

meditate VERB ① If you meditate on something, you think about it very deeply. ② If you meditate, you remain in a calm, silent state for a period of time, often as part of a religious training. **meditation** NOUN

Mediterranean NOUN ① The Mediterranean is the large sea between southern Europe and northern Africa. ▸ ADJECTIVE ② relating to or typical of the Mediterranean or the European countries adjoining it.

medium, **mediums** or **media** ADJECTIVE ① If something is of medium size or degree, it is neither large nor small • *a medium-sized hotel.* ▸ NOUN ② a means that you use to communicate something • *the medium of television.* ③ a person who claims to be able to speak to the dead and to receive messages from them.

> **medium** ADJECTIVE
> ① = average, medium-sized, middling
> ▸ NOUN ② = channel, vehicle

medley NOUN ① a mixture of different things creating an interesting effect. ② a number of different songs or tunes sung or played one after the other.

meek ADJECTIVE A meek person is timid and does what other people say. **meekly** ADVERB **meekness** NOUN

> **meek** ADJECTIVE
> = deferential, docile, mild, submissive, timid, unassuming
> ≠ bold

meet, **meets**, **meeting**, **met** VERB ① If you meet someone, you happen to be in the same place as them and start talking to them. ② If you meet a visitor you go to be with them when they arrive. ③ When a group of people meet, they gather together for a purpose. ④ If something meets a need, it can fulfil it • *services intended to meet the needs of people with disabilities.* ⑤ If something meets with a particular reaction, it gets that reaction from people • *I was met with silence.*

> **meet** VERB
> ① = bump into (*informal*), come across, come upon, encounter, run across, run into
> ③ = assemble, congregate, convene, gather, get together
> ④ = answer, fulfil, satisfy

meeting NOUN ① an event in which people discuss proposals and make decisions together. ② what happens when you meet someone.

> **meeting** NOUN
> ① = audience, conference, congress, convention, gathering, get-together (*informal*), reunion
> ② = assignation (*formal*), encounter, rendezvous, tryst (*literary*)

megabyte NOUN [ICT] a unit of computer memory size, equal to 1024 kilobytes.

melancholy ADJECTIVE If you feel melancholy, you feel sad.

mellow ADJECTIVE ① Mellow light is soft and golden. ② A mellow sound is smooth and pleasant to listen to • *his mellow clarinet.* ▸ VERB ③ If someone mellows, they become more pleasant or relaxed • *He certainly hasn't mellowed with age.*

melodic ADJECTIVE relating to melody.

melodious ADJECTIVE pleasant to listen to • *soft melodious music.*

melodrama NOUN a story or play in which people's emotions are exaggerated.

melodramatic ADJECTIVE behaving in an exaggerated, emotional way.

> **melodramatic** ADJECTIVE
> = histrionic, sensational, theatrical

melody, **melodies** NOUN [MUSIC] a tune.

melon NOUN a large, juicy fruit with a green or yellow skin and many seeds inside.

melt VERB ① When something melts or when you melt it, it changes from a solid to a liquid because it has been heated. ② If something melts, it disappears • *The crowd melted away* • *Her inhibitions melted*.

melt VERB
① = dissolve, thaw
② = disappear, disperse, dissolve, evaporate, vanish

member NOUN ① A member of a group is one of the people or things belonging to the group • *members of the family*. ② A member of an organisation is a person who has joined the organisation. ▸ ADJECTIVE ③ A country belonging to an international organisation is called a member country or a member state.

membership NOUN ① Membership of an organisation is the state of being a member of it. ② The people who belong to an organisation are its membership.

membrane NOUN [SCIENCE] a very thin piece of skin or tissue which connects or covers plant or animal organs or cells • *the nasal membrane*.

memento, **mementos** NOUN an object which you keep because it reminds you of a person or a special occasion • *a lasting memento of the holiday*.

memo, **memos** NOUN a note from one person to another within the same organisation. Memo is short for 'memorandum'.

memoirs *[Said* ***mem****-wahrz]* PLURAL NOUN [ENGLISH] If someone writes their memoirs, they write a book about their life and experiences.

memorable ADJECTIVE If something is memorable, it is likely to be remembered because it is special or unusual • *a memorable victory*.
memorably ADVERB

memorable ADJECTIVE
= catchy, historic, notable, striking, unforgettable

memorandum, **memorandums** or **memoranda** NOUN a memo.

memorial NOUN ① a structure built to remind people of a famous person or event • *a war memorial*. ▸ ADJECTIVE ② A memorial event or prize is in honour of someone who has died, so that they will be remembered.

memory, **memories** NOUN ① Your memory is your ability to remember things. ② something you remember about the past • *memories of their school days*. ③ [ICT] the part in which information is stored in a computer.

memory NOUN
① = recall, remembrance (*formal*)

memory card NOUN [ICT] a small device for storing information in a mobile phone or digital camera.

men the plural of **man**.

menace NOUN ① someone or something that is likely to cause serious harm • *the menace of drugs in sport*. ② Menace is the quality of being threatening • *an atmosphere of menace*. ▸ VERB ③ If someone or something menaces you, they threaten to harm you. **menacingly** ADVERB

menagerie *[Said men-****naj****-er-ree]* NOUN a collection of different wild animals.

mend VERB If you mend something that is broken, you repair it.

mend VERB
= darn, fix, patch, renovate, repair, restore

menial ADJECTIVE Menial work is boring and tiring and the people who do it have low status.

meningitis NOUN Meningitis is a serious infectious illness which affects your brain and spinal cord.

menopause NOUN The menopause is the time during which a woman gradually stops menstruating.

This usually happens when she is about fifty.

-ment SUFFIX '-ment' forms nouns which refer to a state or a feeling • *contentment* • *resentment*.

mental ADJECTIVE ① relating to the process of thinking or intelligence • *mental arithmetic*. ② relating to the health of the mind • *mental wellbeing*. **mentally** ADVERB

mentality, **mentalities** NOUN an attitude or way of thinking • *the traditional military mentality*.

mention VERB ① If you mention something, you talk about it briefly. ▶ NOUN ② a brief comment about someone or something • *He made no mention of his criminal past*.

> **mention** VERB
> ① = allude to, bring up, broach, hint, intimate, refer to, touch on, touch upon
> ▶ NOUN ② = allusion, reference

mentor NOUN Someone's mentor is a person who teaches them and gives them advice. **mentorship** NOUN

menu NOUN ① a list of the foods you can eat in a restaurant. ② [ICT] a list of different options shown on a computer screen which the user must choose from.

MEP NOUN a person who has been elected to represent people in the European Parliament. MEP is an abbreviation for 'Member of the European Parliament'.

mercenary, **mercenaries** NOUN ① a soldier who is paid to fight for a foreign country. ▶ ADJECTIVE ② Someone who is mercenary is mainly interested in getting money.

merchandise NOUN (*formal*) Merchandise is goods that are sold • *He had left me with more merchandise than I could sell*.

merchant NOUN a trader who imports and exports goods • *a coal merchant*.

merciful ADJECTIVE ① showing kindness. ② showing forgiveness. **mercifully** ADVERB

> **merciful** ADJECTIVE
> ① = compassionate, humane, kind
> ≠ merciless
> ② = forgiving, lenient
> ≠ merciless

merciless ADJECTIVE showing no kindness or forgiveness. **mercilessly** ADVERB

> **merciless** ADJECTIVE
> = callous, cruel, heartless, implacable, ruthless
> ≠ merciful

mercury NOUN ① [SCIENCE] Mercury is a silver-coloured metallic element that is liquid at room temperature. It is used in thermometers. Its atomic number is 80 and its symbol is Hg. ② Mercury is also the planet in the solar system which is nearest to the sun.

mercy, **mercies** NOUN If you show mercy, you show forgiveness and do not punish someone as severely as you could.

> **mercy** NOUN
> = compassion, kindness, pity= forgiveness, leniency

mere, **merest** ADJECTIVE used to emphasise how unimportant or small something is • *It's a mere seven-minute journey by boat*. **merely** ADVERB

merge VERB When two things merge, they combine together to make one thing • *The firms merged in 2003*.

meringue [*Said mer-**rang***] NOUN a type of crisp, sweet cake made with egg whites and sugar.

merino, **merinos** [*Said mer-**ree**-no*] NOUN a breed of sheep, common in Australia and New Zealand, with long, fine wool.

merit NOUN ① If something has merit, it is good or worthwhile. ② The merits of something are its advantages or good qualities. ▶ VERB ③ If something merits a particular treatment, it deserves that treatment • *He merits a place in the team.*

> **merit** NOUN
> ① = excellence, value, virtue, worth
> ② = advantage, asset, strength, strong point, virtue
> ▶ VERB ③ = be entitled to, be worthy of, deserve, earn, warrant

mermaid NOUN In stories, a mermaid is a woman with a fish's tail instead of legs, who lives in the sea.

merry, **merrier**, **merriest** ADJECTIVE happy and cheerful • *He was, for all his shyness, a merry man.* **merrily** ADVERB

merry-go-round NOUN a large rotating platform with models of animals or vehicles on it, on which children ride at a fair.

mesh NOUN Mesh is threads of wire or plastic twisted together like a net • *a fence made of wire mesh.*

mess NOUN ① something untidy. ② a situation which is full of problems and trouble. ③ a room or building in which members of the armed forces eat • *the officers' mess.* **messy** ADJECTIVE **mess about** or **mess around** VERB If you mess about or mess around, you do things without any particular purpose. **mess up** VERB If you mess something up, you spoil it or do it wrong.

> **mess** NOUN
> ① = chaos, disarray, disorder
> ② = fix (*informal*), jam (*informal*), muddle, turmoil

message NOUN ① a piece of information or a request that you send someone or leave for them. ② an idea that someone tries to communicate to people, for example in a play or a speech • *the story's anti-drugs message.* ▶ VERB ③ If you message someone, you send them a text message.

> **message** NOUN
> ① = bulletin, communication, despatch, dispatch, memo, memorandum, note, word
> ▶ VERB ③ = email, e-mail, IM, instant message, text

messaging NOUN Messaging or text messaging is the sending and receiving of short pieces of information between mobile phones, often using both letters and numbers to produce shortened forms of words.

messenger NOUN someone who takes a message to someone for someone else.

> **messenger** NOUN
> = courier, envoy, runner

Messiah [*Said miss-**eye**-ah*] PROPER NOUN ① RE For Jews, the Messiah is the king of the Jews, who will be sent by God. ② RE For Christians, the Messiah is Jesus Christ.

Messrs [*Said **mes**-serz*] Messrs is the plural of **Mr**. It is often used in the names of businesses • *Messrs Brown and Humberley, Solicitors.*

met the past tense and past participle of **meet**.

metabolism NOUN Your metabolism is the chemical processes in your body that use food for growth and energy. **metabolic** ADJECTIVE

metal NOUN SCIENCE a chemical element such as iron, steel, copper or lead. Metals are good conductors of heat and electricity and form positive ions. **metallic** ADJECTIVE

metamorphosis, **metamorphoses** [*Said met-am-**mor**-fiss-iss*] NOUN (*formal*) When a metamorphosis occurs, a person or thing changes into something completely different

• *the metamorphosis of a larva into an insect.*

metaphor NOUN ENGLISH an imaginative way of describing something as another thing, and so suggesting that it has the typical qualities of that other thing. For example, if you wanted to say that someone is shy, you might say they are a mouse. **metaphorical** ADJECTIVE **metaphorically** ADVERB

meteor NOUN a piece of rock or metal that burns very brightly when it enters the earth's atmosphere from space.

meteoric ADJECTIVE A meteoric rise to power or success happens very quickly.

meteorite NOUN a piece of rock from space that has landed on earth.

meteorological ADJECTIVE GEOGRAPHY relating to or involving the weather or weather forecasting. **meteorology** NOUN

meter NOUN a device that measures and records something • *a gas meter.*

methane *[Said **mee**-thane]* NOUN Methane is a colourless gas with no smell that is found in coal gas and produced by decaying vegetable matter. It burns easily and can be used as a fuel.

method NOUN a particular way of doing something • *the traditional method of making pasta.*

method NOUN
= approach, mode, procedure, technique, way

methodical ADJECTIVE Someone who is methodical does things carefully and in an organised way. **methodically** ADVERB

Methodist NOUN RE someone who belongs to the Methodist Church, a Protestant church whose members worship God in a way begun by John Wesley and his followers.

meticulous ADJECTIVE A meticulous person does things very carefully and with great attention to detail. **meticulously** ADVERB

metre NOUN ① a unit of length equal to 100 centimetres. ② ENGLISH In poetry, metre is the regular and rhythmic arrangement of words and syllables. **metrical** ADJECTIVE

metric ADJECTIVE relating to the system of measurement that uses metres, grams and litres.

metropolis NOUN a very large city.

metropolitan ADJECTIVE relating or belonging to a large, busy city • *metropolitan districts.*

mettle NOUN If you are on your mettle, you are ready to do something as well as you can because you know you are being tested or challenged.

Mexican ADJECTIVE ① belonging or relating to Mexico. ▸ NOUN ② someone who comes from Mexico.

mg an abbreviation for 'milligram' or 'milligrams'.

mice the plural of **mouse**.

microchip NOUN a very small piece of silicon inside a computer with electronic circuits on it, which can hold large quantities of information or perform mathematical or logical operations.

microphone NOUN a device that is used to make sounds louder or to record them.

microprocessor NOUN a microchip which can be programmed to do a large number of tasks or calculations.

microscope NOUN SCIENCE a piece of equipment which magnifies very small objects so that you can study them.

microscopic ADJECTIVE very small indeed • *microscopic parasites.*

microwave NOUN A microwave or microwave oven is a type of oven which cooks food very quickly by radiation.

mid- PREFIX 'Mid-' is used to form words that refer to the middle part of a place or period of time • *mid-Atlantic* • *the mid-70s.*

midday NOUN Midday is twelve o'clock in the middle of the day.

middle NOUN ① The middle of something is the part furthest from the edges, ends or outside surface. ▶ ADJECTIVE ② The middle one in a series or a row is the one that has an equal number of people or things on each side of it • *the middle house.*

> **middle** NOUN
> ① = centre, halfway point, midst
> ▶ ADJECTIVE ② = central, halfway

middle age NOUN Middle age is the period of your life when you are between about 40 and 60 years old. **middle-aged** ADJECTIVE

Middle Ages PLURAL NOUN HISTORY In European history, the Middle Ages were the period between about 1100 AD and 1500 AD.

middle class NOUN The middle classes are the people in a society who are not working-class or upper-class, for example managers and lawyers.

Middle East NOUN The Middle East consists of Iran and the countries in Asia to the west and south-west of Iran.

middle-of-the-road ADJECTIVE Middle-of-the-road opinions are moderate.

middle school NOUN In England and Wales, a middle school is for children aged between about 8 and 12.

middling ADJECTIVE of average quality or ability.

midge NOUN a small flying insect which can bite people.

midget NOUN ① a very small thing. ② (*offensive*) a very small person.

midnight NOUN Midnight is twelve o'clock at night.

midriff NOUN the middle of your body between your waist and your chest.

midst NOUN If you are in the midst of a crowd or an event, you are in the middle of it.

midsummer ADJECTIVE relating to the period in the middle of summer • *a lovely midsummer morning in July.*

midway ADVERB in the middle of a distance or period of time • *They scored midway through the second half.*

midwife, **midwives** NOUN a nurse who is trained to help women at the birth of a baby. **midwifery** NOUN

might VERB ① If you say something might happen, you mean that it is possible that it will happen • *I might stay a while.* ② If you say that someone might do something, you are suggesting that they do it • *You might like to go and see it.* ③ Might is also the past tense of **may**. ▶ NOUN ④ (*literary*) Might is strength or power • *the full might of the Navy.*

mightily ADVERB (*literary*) to a great degree or extent • *I was mightily relieved by the decision.*

mighty, **mightier**, **mightiest** ADJECTIVE (*literary*) ① very powerful or strong • *a mighty army on the march.* ② very large and impressive • *the world's mightiest mountain range.*

migraine [*Said **mee**-grane or **my**-grane*] NOUN a severe headache that makes you feel very ill.

migrant, **migrants** NOUN a person who moves from one place to another, especially to find work.

migrate VERB ① GEOGRAPHY If people migrate, they move from one place to another, especially to find work. ② SCIENCE When birds or animals migrate, they move at a particular season to a different place, usually to breed or to find new feeding grounds • *the birds migrate each year to Mexico*. **migration** NOUN **migratory** ADJECTIVE

mike NOUN (*informal*) a microphone.

mild ADJECTIVE ① Something that is mild is not strong and does not have any powerful or damaging effects • *a mild shampoo*. ② Someone who is mild is gentle and kind. ③ Mild weather is warmer than usual • *The region has mild winters and hot summers*. ④ Mild emotions or attitudes are not very great or extreme • *mild surprise*. **mildly** ADVERB

mild ADJECTIVE
① = insipid, weak
≠ strong
② = gentle, meek, placid
③ = balmy, temperate

mildew NOUN Mildew is a soft white fungus that grows on things when they are warm and damp.

mile NOUN a unit of distance equal to 1760 yards or about 1.6 kilometres.

mileage NOUN ① Your mileage is the distance that you have travelled, measured in miles. ② The amount of mileage that you get out of something is how useful it is to you.

militant ADJECTIVE ① A militant person is very active in trying to bring about extreme political or social change • *a militant party member*. ▸ NOUN ② a person who tries to bring about extreme political or social change. **militancy** NOUN

military ADJECTIVE ① related to or involving the armed forces of a country • *military bases*. ▸ NOUN ② The military are the armed forces of a country. **militarily** ADVERB

militia [*Said mil-**lish**-a*] NOUN an organisation that operates like an army but whose members are not professional soldiers.

milk NOUN ① Milk is the white liquid produced by female cows, goats and some other animals to feed their young. People drink milk and use it to make butter, cheese and yogurt. ② Milk is also the white liquid that a baby drinks from its mother's breasts. ▸ VERB ③ When someone milks a cow or a goat, they get milk from it by pulling its udders. ④ If you milk a situation, you get as much personal gain from it as possible • *They milked money from a hospital charity*.

milky, **milkier**, **milkiest** ADJECTIVE ① pale creamy white • *milky white skin*. ② containing a lot of milk • *a large mug of milky coffee*.

Milky Way NOUN The Milky Way is a strip of stars clustered closely together, appearing as a pale band in the sky.

mill NOUN ① a building where grain is crushed to make flour. ② a factory for making materials such as steel, wool or cotton. ③ a small device for grinding coffee or spices into powder • *a pepper mill*.

millennium, **millennia** or **millenniums** NOUN (*formal*) a period of 1000 years.

miller NOUN the person who operates a flour mill.

milligram NOUN a unit of weight equal to one thousandth of a gram.

millimetre NOUN a unit of length equal to one tenth of a centimetre or one thousandth of a metre.

million the number 1,000,000. **millionth** ADJECTIVE

millionaire NOUN a very rich person who has money or property worth millions of pounds or dollars.

millstone PHRASE If something is **a millstone round your neck**, it is an unpleasant problem or responsibility you cannot escape from.

A B C D E F G H I J K L M N O P Q R S T U V W X Y Z

mime NOUN ① Mime is the use of movements and gestures to express something or to tell a story without using speech. ▸ VERB ② If you mime something, you describe or express it using mime.

mimic, **mimics**, **mimicking**, **mimicked** VERB ① If you mimic someone's actions or voice, you imitate them in an amusing way. ▸ NOUN ② a person who can imitate other people.
mimicry NOUN

mince NOUN ① Mince is meat which has been chopped into very small pieces in a special machine. ▸ VERB ② If you mince meat, you chop it into very small pieces. ③ To mince about is to walk with small quick steps in an affected, effeminate way.

mind NOUN ① Your mind is your ability to think, together with all the thoughts you have and your memory. ▸ PHRASE ② If you **change your mind**, you change a decision that you have made or an opinion that you have. ▸ VERB ③ If you do not mind something, you are not annoyed by it or bothered about it. ④ If you say that you wouldn't mind something, you mean that you would quite like it • *I wouldn't mind something to eat.* ⑤ If you mind a child or mind something for someone, you look after it for a while • *My mother is minding the office.*

mind NOUN
① = brain, head, imagination, intellect, psyche
▸ VERB ③ = be bothered, care, object
⑤ = keep an eye on, look after, take care of, watch

mindful ADJECTIVE (*formal*) If you are mindful of something, you think about it carefully before taking action • *mindful of their needs.*

mindless ADJECTIVE ① Mindless actions are regarded as stupid and destructive • *mindless violence.* ② A mindless job or activity is simple and repetitive.

mine PRONOUN ① 'Mine' refers to something belonging or relating to the person who is speaking or writing • *a friend of mine.* ▸ NOUN ② a series of holes or tunnels in the ground from which diamonds, coal or other minerals are dug out • *a diamond mine.* ③ a bomb hidden in the ground or underwater, which explodes when people or things touch it. ▸ VERB ④ To mine diamonds, coal or other minerals is to obtain these substances from underneath the ground. **miner** NOUN **mining** NOUN

minefield NOUN an area of land or water where mines have been hidden.

mineral NOUN [DGT] [SCIENCE] a substance such as tin, salt or coal that is formed naturally in rocks and in the earth • *rich mineral deposits.*

mineral water NOUN Mineral water is water which comes from a natural spring.

mingle VERB If things mingle, they become mixed together • *His cries mingled with theirs.*

miniature [*Said min-nit-cher*] ADJECTIVE ① copying something on a much smaller scale. ▸ NOUN ② a very small detailed painting, often of a person.

minibus NOUN a van with seats in the back which is used as a small bus.

minimal ADJECTIVE very small in quality, quantity or degree • *He has minimal experience.* **minimally** ADVERB

minimise; also spelt **minimize** VERB If you minimise something, you reduce it to the smallest amount possible • *His route was changed to minimise jet lag.*

minimum ADJECTIVE ① The minimum amount is the smallest amount that is possible • *a minimum wage.* ▶ NOUN ② The minimum is the smallest amount that is possible • *a minimum of three weeks.*

minimum ADJECTIVE
① = least possible, minimal
≠ maximum

minister NOUN ① A minister is a person who is in charge of a particular government department • *Portugal's deputy foreign minister.* ② A minister in a Protestant church is a member of the clergy.

ministerial ADJECTIVE relating to a government minister or ministry • *ministerial duties.*

ministry, **ministries** NOUN ① a government department that deals with a particular area of work • *the Ministry of Defence.* ② Members of the clergy can be referred to as the ministry • *Her son is in the ministry.*

mink NOUN Mink is an expensive fur used to make coats or hats.

minnow NOUN a very small freshwater fish.

minor ADJECTIVE ① not as important or serious as other things • *a minor injury.* ② [MUSIC] A minor key is one of the keys in which most European music is written. In a minor key the third note is three semitones higher than the first. ▶ NOUN ③ (*formal*) a young person under the age of 18 • *laws concerning the employment of minors.*

minor ADJECTIVE
① = lesser, petty, secondary, slight, trifling, trivial
≠ major

minority, **minorities** NOUN ① The minority of people or things in a group is a number of them forming less than half of the whole • *Only a minority of people want this.* ② A minority is a group of people of a particular race or religion living in a place where most people are of a different race or religion • *ethnic minorities.*

mint NOUN ① Mint is a herb used for flavouring in cooking. ② a peppermint-flavoured sweet. ③ The mint is the place where the official coins of a country are made. ▶ VERB ④ When coins or medals are minted, they are made. ▶ ADJECTIVE ⑤ If something is in mint condition, it is in very good condition, like new.

minus ① You use 'minus' to show that one number is being subtracted from another • *Ten minus six equals four.* ▶ ADJECTIVE ② 'Minus' is used when talking about temperatures below 0°C or 0°F.

minuscule [*Said* ***min**-nus-kyool*] ADJECTIVE very small indeed.

minute[1] [*Said* ***min**-nit*] NOUN ① a unit of time equal to sixty seconds. ② The minutes of a meeting are the written records of what was said and decided. ▶ VERB ③ To minute a meeting is to write the official notes of it.

minute NOUN
① = flash, instant, moment, second, trice

minute[2] [*Said my-**nyoot***] ADJECTIVE extremely small • *a minute amount of pesticide.* **minutely** ADVERB

minute ADJECTIVE
= microscopic, negligible, slender, small, tiny
≠ vast

minutiae [*Said my-**nyoo**-shee-aye*] PLURAL NOUN (*formal*) Minutiae are small, unimportant details.

miracle NOUN ① [RE] a wonderful and surprising event, believed to have been caused by God. ② any very surprising and fortunate event • *My brother got a job. It was a miracle.* **miraculous** ADJECTIVE **miraculously** ADVERB

miracle NOUN
② = marvel, wonder

mirage *[Said mir-**ahj**]* NOUN an image which you can see in the distance in very hot weather, but which does not actually exist.

mire NOUN (*literary*) Mire is swampy ground or mud.

mirror NOUN ① a piece of glass which reflects light and in which you can see your reflection. ▶VERB ② To mirror something is to have similar features to it • *His own shock was mirrored on her face.*

mirth NOUN (*literary*) Mirth is great amusement and laughter.

misbehave VERB If a child misbehaves, he or she is naughty or behaves badly. **misbehaviour** NOUN

miscarriage NOUN ① If a woman has a miscarriage, her baby dies and she gives birth to it before it is properly formed. ② A miscarriage of justice is a wrong decision made by a court, which causes an innocent person to be punished.

miscellaneous ADJECTIVE A miscellaneous group is made up of people or things that are different from each other.

mischief NOUN Mischief is eagerness to have fun by teasing people or playing tricks. **mischievous** ADJECTIVE

misconception NOUN a wrong idea about something • *the misconception that history is boring.*

misconduct NOUN Misconduct is bad or unacceptable behaviour by a professional person • *The Football Association found him guilty of misconduct.*

misdemeanour *[Said miss-dem-**mee**-ner]* NOUN (*formal*) an act that is shocking or unacceptable.

miser NOUN a person who enjoys saving money but hates spending it. **miserly** ADJECTIVE

miserable ADJECTIVE ① If you are miserable, you are very unhappy. ② If a place or a situation is miserable, it makes you feel depressed • *a miserable little flat.* **miserably** ADVERB

miserable ADJECTIVE
① = dejected, depressed, down, downcast, low, melancholy (*literary*), mournful, sad, unhappy, wretched
≠ cheerful
② = gloomy, pathetic, sorry, wretched

misery, **miseries** NOUN Misery is great unhappiness.

misery NOUN
= despair, grief, melancholy (*literary*), sadness, sorrow, unhappiness, woe (*formal*)
≠ joy

misfire VERB If a plan misfires, it goes wrong.

misfit NOUN a person who is not accepted by other people because of being rather strange or eccentric.

misfortune NOUN an unpleasant occurrence that is regarded as bad luck • *I had the misfortune to fall off my bike.*

misfortune NOUN
= adversity, bad luck

misgiving NOUN If you have misgivings, you are worried or unhappy about something • *I had misgivings about his methods.*

misguided ADJECTIVE A misguided opinion or action is wrong because it is based on a misunderstanding or bad information.

misinterpret VERB To misinterpret something is to understand it wrongly • *You completely misinterpreted what I wrote.*

misjudge VERB If you misjudge someone or something, you form an incorrect idea or opinion about them.

mislead, **misleads**, **misleading**, **misled** **VERB** To mislead someone is to make them believe something which is not true.

misplaced **ADJECTIVE** A misplaced feeling is inappropriate or directed at the wrong thing or person • *misplaced loyalty*.

misrepresent **VERB** To misrepresent someone is to give an inaccurate or misleading account of what they have said or done.
misrepresentation **NOUN**

> **misrepresent** **VERB**
> = distort, falsify, twist

miss **VERB** ① If you miss something, you do not notice it • *You can't miss it. It's on the second floor.* ② If you miss someone or something, you feel sad that they are no longer with you • *The boys miss their father.* ③ If you miss a chance or opportunity, you fail to take advantage of it. ④ If you miss a bus, plane or train, you arrive too late to catch it. ⑤ If you miss something, you fail to hit it when you aim at it • *His shot missed the target and went wide.* ▶ **NOUN** ⑥ an act of missing something that you were aiming at. ⑦ 'Miss' is used before the name of a woman or girl who is not married as a form of address • *Did you know Miss Smith?*

> **miss** **VERB**
> ① = fail to notice, mistake, overlook
> ② = long for, pine for, yearn for

missile **NOUN** a weapon that moves long distances through the air and explodes when it reaches its target; also used of any object thrown as a weapon.

mission **NOUN** ① an important task that you have to do. ② a group of people who have been sent to a foreign country to carry out an official task. ③ a journey made by a military aeroplane or space rocket to carry out a task. ④ If you have a mission, there is something that you believe it is your duty to try to achieve. ⑤ the workplace of a group of Christians who are working for the Church.

missionary, **missionaries** **NOUN** RE a Christian who has been sent to a foreign country to work for the Church.

missive **NOUN** (*old-fashioned*) a letter or message.

mist **NOUN** ① Mist consists of a large number of tiny drops of water in the air, which make it hard to see clearly. ▶ **VERB** ② If your eyes mist, you cannot see very far because there are tears in your eyes. ③ If glass mists over or mists up, it becomes covered with condensation so that you cannot see through it.

mistake, **mistakes**, **mistaking**, **mistook**, **mistaken** **NOUN** ① an action or opinion that is wrong or is not what you intended. ▶ **VERB** ② If you mistake someone or something for another person or thing, you wrongly think that they are the other person or thing • *I mistook him for the owner of the house.*

> **mistake** **NOUN**
> ① = blunder, error, gaffe, oversight, slip
> ▶ **VERB** ② = confuse with, misinterpret as, mix up with, take for

mistaken **ADJECTIVE** ① If you are mistaken about something, you are wrong about it. ② If you have a mistaken belief or opinion, you believe something which is not true.
mistakenly **ADVERB**

mistletoe [*Said mis-sel-toe*] **NOUN** Mistletoe is a plant which grows on trees and has white berries on it. It is used as a Christmas decoration.

mistook the past tense of **mistake**.

mistreat VERB To mistreat a person or animal is to treat them badly and make them suffer.

> **mistreat** VERB
> = abuse, ill-treat

mistress NOUN ① A school mistress is a female teacher. ② A servant's mistress is the woman who is the servant's employer.

mistrust VERB ① If you mistrust someone, you do not feel that you can trust them. ▸ NOUN ② Mistrust is a feeling that you cannot trust someone.

misty, **mistier**, **mistiest** ADJECTIVE full of or covered with mist.

misunderstand, **misunderstands**, **misunderstanding**, **misunderstood** VERB If you misunderstand something, you do not properly understand what it means • *He misunderstood the problem.*

misunderstanding NOUN If two people have a misunderstanding, they have a slight quarrel or disagreement.

misuse NOUN *[Said mis-**yoos**]* ① The misuse of something is the incorrect or dishonest use of it • *the misuse of public money.* ▸ VERB *[Said mis-**yooz**]* ② To misuse something is to use it incorrectly or dishonestly.

mite NOUN a very tiny creature that lives in the fur of animals.

mitigating ADJECTIVE *(formal)* Mitigating circumstances make a crime easier to understand, and perhaps justify it.

mix VERB If you mix things, you combine them or shake or stir them together. **mix up** VERB If you mix up two things or people, you confuse them • *People often mix us up and greet us by each other's names.*

> **mix** VERB
> = amalgamate, blend, combine, merge, mingle
> ▸ **mix up** = confuse, muddle

mixed ADJECTIVE ① consisting of several things of the same general kind • *a mixed salad.* ② involving people from two or more different ethnic or religious groups • *mixed marriages.* ③ Mixed education or accommodation is for both males and females • *a mixed comprehensive.*

mixed up ADJECTIVE ① If you are mixed up, you are confused • *I was all mixed up and forgot where I was.* ② If you are mixed up in a crime or a scandal, you are involved in it.

mixer NOUN a machine used for mixing things together • *a cement mixer.*

mixture NOUN several different things mixed or shaken together.

> **mixture** NOUN
> = alloy, amalgamation, blend, combination, compound, fusion, medley

mix-up NOUN a mistake in something that was planned • *a mix-up with the bookings.*

> **mix-up** NOUN
> = mistake, misunderstanding, muddle

ml an abbreviation for 'millilitre' or 'millilitres'.

mm an abbreviation for 'millimetre' or 'millimetres'.

moan VERB ① If you moan, you make a low, miserable sound because you are in pain or suffering. ② *(informal)* If you moan about something, you complain about it. ▸ NOUN ③ a low cry of pain or misery.

> **moan** VERB
> ① = groan, grunt
> ② = complain, groan, grumble, whine, whinge *(informal)*
> ▸ NOUN ③ = groan, grunt

moat NOUN a wide, water-filled ditch around a building such as a castle.

mob, **mobs, mobbing, mobbed** NOUN ① a large, disorganised crowd of people • *A mob attacked the team bus.* ▶ VERB ② If a lot of people mob someone, they crowd around the person in a disorderly way • *The band was mobbed by over a thousand fans.*

mobile ADJECTIVE ① able to move or be moved freely and easily • *a mobile home.* ② PE If you are mobile, you are able to travel or move about from one place to another • *a mobile workforce.* ▶ NOUN ③ a decoration consisting of several small objects which hang from threads and move around when a breeze blows. ④ a mobile phone.
mobility NOUN

mobile phone NOUN a small portable telephone.

mock VERB ① If you mock someone, you say something scornful or imitate their foolish behaviour. ▶ ADJECTIVE ② not genuine • *mock surprise* • *a mock Tudor house.* ③ A mock examination is one that you do as a practice before the real examination.

mock VERB
① = deride (*formal*), laugh at, make fun of, poke fun at, ridicule, scoff at
▶ ADJECTIVE ② = artificial, bogus, counterfeit, dummy, fake, false, feigned, imitation, phoney, phony, pretended, sham

mockery NOUN Mockery is the expression of scorn or ridicule of someone.

mockery NOUN
= derision, jeering, ridicule

mode NOUN ① A mode of life or behaviour is a particular way of living or behaving. ② MATHS In mathematics, the mode is the biggest in a set of groups.

model, **models, modelling, modelled** NOUN ① a copy of something that shows what it looks like or how it works • *a model of a ship.* ② Something that is described as, for example, a model of clarity or a model of perfection, is extremely clear or absolutely perfect. ③ a type or version of a machine • *Which model of washing machine did you choose?* ④ a person who poses for a painter or a photographer. ⑤ a person who wears the clothes that are being displayed at a fashion show or in a magazine. ▶ ADJECTIVE ⑥ Someone who is described as, for example, a model student is an excellent student. ▶ VERB ⑦ If you model yourself on someone, you copy their behaviour because you admire them. ⑧ To model clothes is to display them by wearing them. ⑨ To model shapes or figures is to make them out of clay or wood.

model NOUN
① = dummy, replica, representation
② = epitome, example, ideal, paragon
▶ VERB ⑨ = carve, fashion, form, mould, sculpt, shape

modem [*Said* ***moe**-dem*] NOUN ICT a piece of equipment that links a computer to the telephone system so that data can be transferred from one machine to another via the telephone line.

moderate ADJECTIVE [*Said* ***mod**-i-rit*] ① Moderate views are not extreme, and usually favour gradual changes rather than major ones. ② A moderate amount of something is neither large nor small. ▶ NOUN [*Said* ***mod**-i-rit*] ③ a person whose political views are not extreme. ▶ VERB [*Said* ***mod**-i-rate*] ④ If you moderate something or if it moderates, it becomes less extreme or violent • *The weather moderated.* **moderately** ADVERB

moderate ADJECTIVE
② = average, fair, medium, middling, reasonable
▶ VERB ④ = abate, curb, ease, relax, soften, temper, tone down

moderation NOUN Moderation is control of your behaviour that stops you acting in an extreme way • *She showed fairness and moderation in her judgements.*

modern ADJECTIVE ① relating to the present time • *modern society.* ② new and involving the latest ideas and equipment • *modern technology.* **modernity** NOUN

modern ADJECTIVE
① = contemporary, current, present, present-day, recent
② = latest, new, up-to-date, up-to-the-minute
≠ old-fashioned

modernise; also spelt **modernize** VERB To modernise something is to introduce new methods or equipment to it.

modest ADJECTIVE ① quite small in size or amount. ② Someone who is modest does not boast about their abilities or possessions. ③ shy and easily embarrassed. **modestly** ADVERB **modesty** NOUN

modest ADJECTIVE
① = limited, middling, moderate, small
② = humble, unassuming
≠ conceited

modification NOUN a small change made to improve something • *Modifications to the undercarriage were made.*

modify, **modifies**, **modifying**, **modified** VERB If you modify something, you change it slightly in order to improve it.

module NOUN ① one of the parts which when put together form a whole unit or object • *The course is divided into three modules.* ② ICT a part of a machine, system or program that does a particular task. ③ a part of a spacecraft which can do certain things away from the main body • *the lunar module.* **modular** ADJECTIVE

mohair NOUN Mohair is very soft, fluffy wool obtained from angora goats.

moist ADJECTIVE slightly wet.

moisture NOUN Moisture is tiny drops of water in the air or on the ground.

mole NOUN ① a dark, slightly raised spot on your skin. ② a small animal with black fur. Moles live in tunnels underground. ③ (*informal*) a member of an organisation who is working as a spy for a rival organisation.

molecule NOUN SCIENCE the smallest amount of a substance that can exist. **molecular** ADJECTIVE

molest VERB If someone molests you, they annoy or pester you. **molester** NOUN

mollify, **mollifies**, **mollifying**, **mollified** VERB To mollify someone is to do something to make them less upset or angry.

molten ADJECTIVE Molten rock or metal has been heated to a very high temperature and has become a thick liquid.

moment NOUN ① a very short period of time • *He paused for a moment.* ② The moment at which something happens is the point in time at which it happens • *At that moment, the doorbell rang.* ▶ PHRASE ③ If something is happening **at the moment**, it is happening now.

moment NOUN
① = instant, minute, second, split second
② = instant, point, time

momentary ADJECTIVE Something that is momentary lasts for only a few seconds • *a momentary lapse of concentration.* **momentarily** ADVERB

momentous ADJECTIVE (*formal*) very important, often because of its future effect • *a momentous occasion.*

momentum NOUN ① Momentum is the ability that something has to keep developing • *The campaign is gaining momentum.* ② Momentum is also the ability that an object has to continue moving as a result of the speed it already has.

monarch [*Said* **mon**-*nark*] NOUN CITIZENSHIP a queen, king or other royal person who reigns over a country.

monarchy, monarchies NOUN a system in which a queen or king reigns in a country.

monastery, monasteries NOUN a building in which monks live. **monastic** ADJECTIVE

Monday NOUN Monday is the day between Sunday and Tuesday.

money NOUN Money is the coins or banknotes that you use to buy something.

> **money** NOUN
> = capital, cash, dosh (*British, Australian and New Zealand; slang*), dough (*informal*), funds

mongrel NOUN a dog with parents of different breeds.

monitor VERB ① If you monitor something, you regularly check its condition and progress • *Her health will be monitored daily.* ▶ NOUN ② a machine used to check or record things. ③ ICT the visual display unit of a computer. ④ a school pupil chosen to do special duties by the teacher.

monk NOUN a member of a male religious community.

monkey NOUN an animal which has a long tail and climbs trees. Monkeys live in hot countries.

monogamy NOUN (*formal*) Monogamy is the custom of being married to only one person at a time. **monogamous** ADJECTIVE

monologue [*Said* **mon**-*nol-og*] NOUN ENGLISH a long speech by one person during a play or a conversation.

monopoly, monopolies NOUN control of most of an industry by one or a few large firms.

monotone NOUN a tone which does not vary • *He droned on in a boring monotone.*

monotonous ADJECTIVE having a regular pattern which is very dull and boring • *monotonous work.* **monotony** NOUN

monsoon NOUN GEOGRAPHY the season of very heavy rain in South-east Asia.

monster NOUN ① a large, imaginary creature that looks very frightening. ② a cruel or frightening person. ▶ ADJECTIVE ③ extremely large • *a monster truck.*

monstrosity, monstrosities NOUN something that is large and extremely ugly • *a concrete monstrosity in the middle of the city.*

monstrous ADJECTIVE extremely shocking or unfair • *a monstrous crime.* **monstrously** ADVERB

montage [*Said mon-***tahj**] NOUN a picture or film consisting of a combination of several different items arranged to produce an unusual effect.

month NOUN one of the twelve periods that a year is divided into.

monthly ADJECTIVE ① happening or appearing once a month • *monthly spelling tests.* ▶ ADVERB ② once a month • *I get paid monthly.*

monument NOUN a large stone structure built to remind people of a famous person or event • *a monument to the dead.*

monumental ADJECTIVE ① A monumental building or sculpture is very large and important. ② very large or extreme • *We face a monumental task.*

mood NOUN the way you are feeling at a particular time • *She was in a really cheerful mood.*

> **mood** NOUN
> = frame of mind, humour, spirits, state of mind, temper

moody, moodier, moodiest ADJECTIVE ① Someone who is moody is depressed or unhappy • *Tony, despite his charm, could sulk and be moody.* ② Someone who is moody often changes their mood for no apparent reason.

> **moody** ADJECTIVE
> ① = irritable, morose, sulky, sullen
> ② = temperamental, volatile

moon NOUN The moon is an object moving round the earth which you see as a shining circle or crescent in the sky at night. Some other planets have moons.

moonlight, moonlights, moonlighting, moonlighted NOUN ① Moonlight is the light that comes from the moon at night. ▸ VERB ② (*informal*) If someone is moonlighting, they have a second job that they have not informed the tax office about. **moonlit** ADJECTIVE

moor NOUN ① a high area of open land. ▸ VERB ② If a boat is moored, it is attached to the land with a rope.

mooring NOUN a place where a boat can be tied.

moose NOUN a large North American deer with flat antlers.

moot VERB (*formal*) When something is mooted, it is suggested for discussion • *The project was first mooted in 2008.*

mop, mops, mopping, mopped NOUN ① a tool for washing floors, consisting of a sponge or string head attached to a long handle. ② a large amount of loose or untidy hair. ▸ VERB ③ To mop a floor is to clean it with a mop. ④ To mop a surface is to wipe it with a dry cloth to remove liquid.

moped [*Said* ***moe**-ped*] NOUN a type of small motorcycle.

moral NOUN ① PSHE (*in plural*) Morals are values based on beliefs about the correct and acceptable way to behave. ▸ ADJECTIVE ② concerned with whether behaviour is right or acceptable • *moral values.* **morality** NOUN **morally** ADVERB

morale [*Said mor-**rahl***] NOUN Morale is the amount of confidence and optimism that you have • *The morale of the team was high.*

morbid ADJECTIVE having a great interest in unpleasant things, especially death.

more ADJECTIVE ① More means a greater number or extent than something else • *He's got more chips than me.* ② used to refer to an additional thing or amount of something • *He found some more clues.* ▸ PRONOUN ③ a greater number or extent. ▸ ADVERB ④ to a greater degree or extent • *more amused than concerned.* ⑤ You can use 'more' in front of adjectives and adverbs to form comparatives • *You look more beautiful than ever.*

> **more** ADJECTIVE
> ① = added, additional, extra, further
> ≠ less

moreover ADVERB used to introduce a piece of information that supports or expands the previous statement • *They have accused the government of corruption. Moreover, they have named names.*

morgue *[Said **morg**]* **NOUN** a building where dead bodies are kept before being buried or cremated.

moribund **ADJECTIVE** no longer having a useful function and about to come to an end • *a moribund industry.*

morning **NOUN** the part of the day between midnight and noon • *He was born at three in the morning.*

Moroccan *[Said mor-**rok**-an]* **ADJECTIVE** ① belonging or relating to Morocco. ▶ **NOUN** ② someone who comes from Morocco.

moron **NOUN** (*informal*) a very stupid person. **moronic** **ADJECTIVE**

morose **ADJECTIVE** miserable and bad-tempered.

morphine **NOUN** Morphine is a drug which is used to relieve pain.

Morse or **Morse code** **NOUN** Morse or Morse code is a code used for sending messages in which each letter is represented by a series of dots and dashes. It is named after its American inventor, Samuel Morse.

morsel **NOUN** a small piece of food.

mortal **ADJECTIVE** ① unable to live forever • *Remember that you are mortal.* ② A mortal wound is one that causes death. ▶ **NOUN** ③ an ordinary person.

mortality **NOUN** ① Mortality is the fact that all people must die. ② Mortality also refers to the number of people who die at any particular time • *a low infant mortality rate.*

mortar **NOUN** ① a short cannon which fires missiles high into the air for a short distance. ② Mortar is a mixture of sand, water and cement used to hold bricks firmly together.

mortgage *[Said **mor**-gij]* **NOUN** ① a loan which you get from a bank or a building society in order to buy a house. ▶ **VERB** ② If you mortgage your house, you use it as a guarantee to a company in order to borrow money from them. They can take the house from you if you do not pay back the money you have borrowed.

mortuary, **mortuaries** **NOUN** a special room in a hospital where dead bodies are kept before being buried or cremated.

mosaic *[Said moe-**zay**-yik]* **NOUN** a design made of small coloured stones or pieces of coloured glass set into concrete or plaster.

Moslem an old-fashioned spelling of **Muslim**.

mosque *[Said **mosk**]* **NOUN** [RE] a building where Muslims go to worship.

mosquito, **mosquitoes** or **mosquitos** *[Said moss-**kee**-toe]* **NOUN** Mosquitoes are small insects which bite people in order to suck their blood.

moss **NOUN** Moss is a soft, low-growing, green plant which grows on damp soil or stone. **mossy** **ADJECTIVE**

most **ADJECTIVE, PRONOUN** ① Most of a group of things or people means nearly all of them • *Most people don't share your views* • *She is smarter than most.* ② The most means a larger amount than anyone or anything else • *She has the most talent.* ▶ **ADVERB** ③ You can use 'most' in front of adjectives or adverbs to form superlatives • *the most beautiful buildings in the world.*

mostly **ADVERB** 'Mostly' is used to show that a statement is generally true • *Her friends are mostly classmates.*

MOT **NOUN** In Britain, the MOT test is an annual test for road vehicles to check that they are safe to drive.

motel **NOUN** a hotel providing overnight accommodation for people in the middle of a car journey.

moth NOUN an insect like a butterfly which usually flies at night.

mother NOUN ① A person's mother is their female parent. ▸ VERB ② To mother someone is to look after them and bring them up.

motherhood NOUN Motherhood is the state of being a mother.

mother-in-law, **mothers-in-law** NOUN Someone's mother-in-law is the mother of their husband or wife.

motif [*Said moe-**teef***] NOUN a design which is used as a decoration.

motion NOUN ① Motion is the process of continually moving or changing position • *the motion of the ship.* ② an action or gesture • *Apply with a brush using circular motions.* ③ a proposal which people discuss and vote on at a meeting. ▸ VERB ④ If you motion to someone, you make a movement with your hand in order to show them what they should do • *I motioned him to proceed.*

motionless ADJECTIVE not moving at all • *He sat motionless.*

motivate VERB ① If you are motivated by something, it makes you behave in a particular way • *He is motivated by duty rather than ambition.* ② If you motivate someone, you make them feel determined to do something. **motivated** ADJECTIVE **motivation** NOUN

> **motivate** VERB
> ① = drive, inspire, lead, move, prompt, provoke

motive NOUN a reason or purpose for doing something • *There was no motive for the crime.*

motley ADJECTIVE A motley collection is made up of people or things of very different types.

motor NOUN DGT ① a part of a vehicle or a machine that uses electricity or fuel to produce movement so that the machine can work. ▸ ADJECTIVE ② concerned with or relating to vehicles with a petrol or diesel engine • *the motor industry.*

motorcycle NOUN a two-wheeled vehicle with an engine which is ridden like a bicycle. **motorcyclist** NOUN

motoring ADJECTIVE relating to cars and driving • *a motoring correspondent.*

motorist NOUN a person who drives a car.

motorway NOUN a wide road built for fast travel over long distances.

mottled ADJECTIVE covered with patches of different colours • *mottled leaves.*

motto, **mottoes** or **mottos** NOUN a short sentence or phrase that is a rule for good or sensible behaviour.

mould VERB ① To mould someone or something is to influence and change them so they develop in a particular way • *Early experiences mould our behaviour for life.* ② DGT To mould a substance is to make it into a particular shape • *Mould the mixture into flat round cakes.* ▸ NOUN ③ DGT a container used to make something into a particular shape • *a jelly mould.* ④ Mould is a soft grey or green substance that can form on old food or damp walls. **mouldy** ADJECTIVE

mound NOUN ① a small man-made hill. ② a large, untidy pile • *a mound of blankets.*

mount VERB ① To mount a campaign or event is to organise it and carry it out. ② If something is mounting, it is increasing • *Economic problems are mounting.* ③ (*formal*) To mount something is to go to the top of it • *He mounted the steps.* ④ If you mount a horse, you climb on its back. ⑤ If you mount an object in a particular place, you fix it there to display it. ▸ NOUN

⑥ 'Mount' is also used as part of the name of a mountain • *Mount Everest*.

mountain NOUN ① a very high piece of land with steep sides. ② a large amount of something • *mountains of paperwork*.

mountaineer NOUN a person who climbs mountains.

mountainous ADJECTIVE A mountainous area has a lot of mountains.

mourn VERB ① If you mourn for someone who has died, you are very sad and think about them a lot. ② If you mourn something, you are sad because you no longer have it • *He mourned the loss of his favourite pet*.

mourner NOUN a person who attends a funeral.

mournful ADJECTIVE very sad.

mourning NOUN If someone is in mourning, they wear special black clothes or behave in a quiet and restrained way because a member of their family has died.

mouse, **mice** NOUN ① a small rodent with a long tail. ② ICT a small device moved by hand to control the position of the cursor on a computer screen.

mousse [*Said* **moos**] NOUN Mousse is a light, fluffy food made from whipped eggs and cream.

moustache [*Said mus-***stahsh**] NOUN A man's moustache is hair growing on his upper lip.

mouth NOUN ① your lips, or the space behind them where your tongue and teeth are. ② The mouth of a cave or a hole is the entrance to it. ③ GEOGRAPHY The mouth of a river is the place where it flows into the sea. ▶ VERB ④ If you mouth something, you form words with your lips without making any sound • *Dad mouthed 'Thank you' to me*.

mouthful NOUN

mouthpiece NOUN ① the part you speak into on a telephone. ② the part of a musical instrument you put to your mouth. ③ The mouthpiece of an organisation is the person who publicly states its opinions and policies.

movable ADJECTIVE Something that is movable can be moved from one place to another.

move VERB ① To move means to go to a different place or position. To move something means to change its place or position. ② If you move, or move house, you go to live in a different house. ③ If something moves you, it causes you to feel a deep emotion • *Her story moved us to tears*. ▶ NOUN ④ a change from one place or position to another • *We were watching his every move*. ⑤ an act of moving house. ⑥ the act of putting a piece or counter in a game in a different position • *It's your move next*.

> **move** VERB
> ① = dart, dash, go, hurry
> ② = migrate, move house, relocate
> ③ = affect, touch

movement NOUN ① Movement involves changing position or going from one place to another. ② (*in plural, formal*) Your movements are everything you do during a period of time • *They asked him for an account of his movements during the previous morning*. ③ a group of people who share the same beliefs or aims • *the peace movement*. ④ one of the major sections of a piece of classical music.

> **movement** NOUN
> ① = flow, motion
> ③ = campaign, faction, group, organisation

movie NOUN (*informal*) a film.

moving ADJECTIVE Something that is moving makes you feel deep sadness or emotion. **movingly** ADVERB

> **moving** ADJECTIVE
> = affecting, emotional, poignant, stirring, touching

mow, **mows**, **mowing**, **mowed**, **mown** VERB To mow grass is to cut it with a lawnmower.

mower NOUN a machine for cutting grass.

MP NOUN CITIZENSHIP a person who has been elected to represent people in a country's parliament. MP is an abbreviation for 'Member of Parliament'.

mpg an abbreviation for 'miles per gallon'.

mph an abbreviation for 'miles per hour'.

Mr *[Said **miss**-ter]* NOUN 'Mr' is used before a man's name when you are speaking or referring to him.

Mrs *[Said **miss**-iz]* NOUN 'Mrs' is used before the name of a married woman when you are speaking or referring to her.

Ms *[Said **miz**]* NOUN 'Ms' is used before a woman's name when you are speaking or referring to her. Ms does not specify whether a woman is married or not.

MSP NOUN a person who has been elected to represent people in the Scottish Parliament. MSP is an abbreviation for 'Member of the Scottish Parliament'.

much ADVERB ① You use 'much' to emphasise that something is true to a great extent • *I feel much better now.* ② If something does not happen much, it does not happen very often. ▸ ADJECTIVE, PRONOUN ③ You use 'much' to ask questions or give information about the size or amount of something • *How much money do you need?* • *There isn't much left.*

muck NOUN ① *(informal)* Muck is dirt or some other unpleasant substance. ② Muck is also manure. **mucky** ADJECTIVE **muck about** VERB *(informal)* If you muck about, you behave stupidly and waste time.

mucus *[Said **myoo**-kuss]* NOUN Mucus is a liquid produced in parts of your body, for example in your nose.

mud NOUN Mud is wet, sticky earth.

muddle NOUN ① A muddle is a state of disorder or untidiness • *My room is in a muddle.* ▸ VERB ② If you muddle things, you mix them up.

> **muddle** NOUN
> ① = chaos, confusion, disarray, disorder, disorganisation, jumble, mess, tangle
> ▸ VERB ② = confuse, jumble, mix up

muddy, **muddier**, **muddiest** ADJECTIVE ① covered in mud. ② A muddy colour is dull and not clear • *a mottled, muddy brown.*

muesli *[Said **myooz**-lee]* NOUN Muesli is a mixture of chopped nuts, cereal flakes and dried fruit that you can eat for breakfast with milk.

muffin NOUN ① a small, flat, sweet bread roll, which you eat hot. ② a small, domed cake, often containing fruit pieces or chocolate chips.

muffled ADJECTIVE A muffled sound is quiet or difficult to hear • *a muffled explosion.*

mug, **mugs**, **mugging**, **mugged** NOUN ① a large, deep cup. ② *(informal)* someone who is stupid and easily deceived. ▸ VERB ③ *(informal)* If someone mugs you, they attack you in order to steal your money. **mugging** NOUN **mugger** NOUN

muggy, **muggier**, **muggiest** ADJECTIVE Muggy weather is unpleasantly warm and damp.

mule NOUN the offspring of a female horse and a male donkey.

mull VERB If you mull something over,

you think about it for a long time before making a decision.

mullet NOUN a common edible fish.

mulloway NOUN a large edible fish found in Australian waters.

multicultural ADJECTIVE consisting of or relating to people of many different nationalities and cultures • *London is an extremely multicultural city.* **multiculturalism** NOUN

multimedia NOUN ① [ICT] in computing, you use 'multimedia' to refer to products which use sound, pictures, film and ordinary text to convey information. ② In the classroom, all the things like TV, computers and books which are used as teaching aids are called multimedia.

multinational NOUN a very large company with branches in many countries.

multiple ADJECTIVE ① having or involving many different functions or things • *She displayed multiple talents at school.* ▸ NOUN ② The multiples of a number are other numbers that it will divide into exactly. For example, 6, 9 and 12 are multiples of 3.

multiple sclerosis [*Said skler-**roe**-siss*] NOUN Multiple sclerosis is a serious disease which attacks the nervous system, affecting your ability to move.

multiplication NOUN ① [MATHS] Multiplication is the process of multiplying one number by another. ② The multiplication of things is a large increase in their number • *the multiplication of universities.*

multiplicity NOUN If there is a multiplicity of things, there is a large number or variety of them.

multiply, **multiplies**, **multiplying**, **multiplied** VERB ① When something multiplies, it increases greatly in number • *The trip wore on and the hazards multiplied.* ② [MATHS] When you multiply one number by another, you calculate the total you would get if you added the first number to itself a particular number of times. For example, two multiplied by three is equal to two plus two plus two, which equals six.

> **multiply** VERB
> ① = increase, proliferate, spread

multitude NOUN (*formal*) a very large number of people or things.

mum (*informal*) NOUN ① Your mum is your mother. ▸ PHRASE ② If you **keep mum** about something, you keep it secret.

mumble VERB If you mumble, you speak very quietly and indistinctly.

> **mumble** VERB
> = murmur, mutter

mummy, **mummies** NOUN ① (*informal*) Your mummy is your mother. ② a dead body which was preserved long ago by being rubbed with special oils and wrapped in cloth.

mumps NOUN Mumps is a disease that causes painful swelling in the neck glands.

munch VERB If you munch something, you chew it steadily and thoroughly.

mundane ADJECTIVE very ordinary and not interesting or unusual • *a mundane job.*

municipal [*Said myoo-**nis**-si-pl*] ADJECTIVE belonging to a city or town which has its own local government • *a municipal golf course.*

munitions PLURAL NOUN Munitions are bombs, guns and other military supplies.

mural NOUN a picture painted on a wall.

murder NOUN ① Murder is the deliberate killing of a person. ▸ VERB

② To murder someone is to kill them deliberately. **murderer** NOUN

murder NOUN
① = assassination, homicide, killing, manslaughter, slaughter, slaying (*literary*)
▸ VERB ② = assassinate, butcher (*informal*), kill, slaughter, slay (*literary*), take the life of

murderous ADJECTIVE ① likely to murder someone • *murderous gangsters*. ② A murderous attack or other action results in the death of many people • *murderous acts of terrorism*.

murky, **murkier**, **murkiest** ADJECTIVE dark or dirty and unpleasant • *He rushed through the murky streets*.

murmur VERB ① If you murmur, you say something very softly. ▸ NOUN ② something that someone says which can hardly be heard.

muscle NOUN ① SCIENCE Your muscles are pieces of flesh which you can expand or contract in order to move parts of your body. An **agonistic muscle** is a muscle which is relaxed when another muscle is contracted; an **antagonistic muscle** is a muscle which is contracted when another muscle is relaxed, returning the limb to its original position; an **antagonistic pair of muscles** means two muscles which work together, for example one opening a joint and the other closing it. ▸ VERB ② (*informal*) If you muscle in on something, you force your way into a situation in which you are not welcome.

muscular [*Said* ***musk**-yool-lar*] ADJECTIVE ① involving or affecting your muscles • *muscular strength*. ② Someone who is muscular has strong, firm muscles.

muse VERB (*literary*) To muse is to think about something for a long time.

museum NOUN a building where many interesting or valuable objects are kept and displayed.

mush NOUN A mush is a thick, soft paste.

mushroom NOUN ① a fungus with a short stem and a round top. Some types of mushroom are edible. ▸ VERB ② If something mushrooms, it appears and grows very quickly • *The mill towns mushroomed into cities*.

mushy, **mushier**, **mushiest** ADJECTIVE ① Mushy fruits or vegetables are too soft • *mushy tomatoes*. ② (*informal*) Mushy stories are too sentimental.

music NOUN ① Music is a pattern of sounds performed by people singing or playing instruments. ② Music is also the written symbols that represent musical sounds • *I taught myself to read music*.

musical ADJECTIVE ① relating to playing or studying music • *a musical instrument*. ▸ NOUN ② a play or film that uses songs and dance to tell the story. **musically** ADVERB

musician NOUN MUSIC a person who plays a musical instrument as their job or hobby.

musk NOUN Musk is a substance with a strong, sweet smell. It is used to make perfume. **musky** ADJECTIVE

musket NOUN an old-fashioned gun with a long barrel.

Muslim NOUN RE ① a person who believes in Islam and lives according to its rules. ▸ ADJECTIVE ② relating to Islam.

muslin NOUN Muslin is a very thin cotton material.

mussel NOUN Mussels are a kind of shellfish with black shells.

must, **musts** VERB ① If something must happen, it is very important or necessary that it happens • *You must be over 18*. ② If you tell someone they must do something, you are suggesting that they do it • *You must* *try this pudding: it's delicious.* ▶ NOUN ③ something that is absolutely necessary • *The museum is a must for all visitors.*

mustard NOUN Mustard is a spicy-tasting yellow or brown paste made from seeds.

muster VERB If you muster something such as energy or support, you gather it together • *as much calm as he could muster.*

musty, **mustier**, **mustiest** ADJECTIVE smelling stale and damp • *musty old books.*

mutate VERB SCIENCE If something mutates, its structure or appearance alters in some way • *Viruses react to change and can mutate fast.* **mutation** NOUN **mutant** NOUN, ADJECTIVE

mute (*formal*) ADJECTIVE ① not giving out sound or speech • *He stared in mute amazement.* ▶ VERB ② To mute a sound means to make it quieter.

muted ADJECTIVE ① Muted colours or sounds are soft and gentle. ② A muted reaction is not very strong.

mutilate VERB ① If someone is mutilated, their body is badly injured. ② If you mutilate something, you deliberately damage or spoil it • *Almost every book had been mutilated.* **mutilation** NOUN

mutiny, **mutinies** NOUN A mutiny is a rebellion against someone in authority.

mutter VERB To mutter is to speak in a very low and perhaps cross voice • *Rory muttered something under his breath.*

mutton NOUN Mutton is the meat of an adult sheep.

mutual ADJECTIVE used to describe something that two or more people do to each other or share • *They had a mutual interest in rugby.*

mutually ADVERB Mutually describes a situation in which two or more people feel the same way about each other • *a mutually supportive relationship.*

muzzle NOUN ① the nose and mouth of an animal. ② a cover or a strap for a dog's nose and mouth to prevent it from biting. ③ the open end of a gun through which the bullets come out. ▶ VERB ④ To muzzle a dog is to put a muzzle on it.

my ADJECTIVE 'My' refers to something belonging or relating to the person speaking or writing • *I held my breath.*

myriad [*Said* **mir-ree-ad**] NOUN (*literary*) a very large number of people or things.

myself PRONOUN ① 'Myself' is used when the person speaking or writing does an action and is affected by it • *I congratulated myself.* ② 'Myself' is also used to emphasise 'I' • *I find it a bit odd myself.*

mysterious ADJECTIVE ① strange and not well understood. ② secretive about something • *Stop being so mysterious.* **mysteriously** ADVERB

> **mysterious** ADJECTIVE
> ① = arcane (*formal*), baffling, cryptic, enigmatic, mystifying
> ② = furtive, secretive

mystery, **mysteries** NOUN something that is not understood or known about.

> **mystery** NOUN
> = conundrum, enigma, puzzle, riddle

mystic NOUN ① a religious person who spends long hours meditating. ▶ ADJECTIVE ② Mystic means the same as mystical. **mysticism** NOUN

mystical ADJECTIVE involving spiritual powers and influences • *a mystical experience.*

mystify, **mystifies**, **mystifying**, **mystified** VERB If something mystifies you, you find it impossible to understand.

a b c d e f g h i j k l m n o p q r s t u v w x y z

mystique *[Said mis-**steek**]* NOUN Mystique is an atmosphere of mystery and importance associated with a particular person or thing.

myth NOUN ① an untrue belief or explanation. ② ENGLISH a story which was made up long ago to explain natural events and religious beliefs • *Viking myths*.

mythical ADJECTIVE imaginary, untrue or existing only in myths • *a mythical beast*.

mythology NOUN Mythology refers to stories that have been made up in the past to explain natural events or justify religious beliefs. **mythological** ADJECTIVE

Get It Right: Spelling, Punctuation and Grammar

Spelling

Commonly misspelt words

Here is a list of some commonly misspelt words with advice on how to avoid the difficult parts of these words.

accommodation	has double **c** and double **m**
achieve	put the **i** before **e**
across	has only one **c**
basically	ends in **ally**
believe	put the **i** before **e**
business	starts with **bus**
calendar	ends in **ar**
Caribbean	has one **r** and two **b**s
cemetery	ends in **ery**
committee	has a double **m**, a double **t**, and double **e**
completely	ends in **ely**
conscious	has **sc** in the middle
definitely	has **ite**, not **ate**, in the middle
dilemma	has one **l** and two **m**s
disappear	has one **s** and two **p**s
disappoint	has one **s** and two **p**s
embarrass	has double **r** and double **s**
environment	put an **n** before the **m**
finally	has double **l**
foreign	put the **e** before **i**
forty	has **o**, not **ou**, in the middle
friend	put the **i** before **e**
glamorous	ends in **orous**
government	put an **n** before the **m**
guard	has **ua** after **g,** not just **a**
happened	ends in **ened**
humorous	ends in **orous**

immediately	has double **m**
independent	ends in **ent**
knowledge	ends in **edge**
liaise	has an **i** in the middle
necessary	has one **c** and two **s**s
occasion	has two **c**s and one **s**
occurred, occurring	double **c**, double **r**
piece	**i** before **e**
possession	has two sets of double **s**
preferred, preferring	has one **f** and two **r**s
really	has double **l**
receive	put the **e** before **i**
referred, referring	has one **f** and two **r**s
separate	has **par**, not **per**, in the middle
successful	has double **c** and double **s**
tomorrow	has one **m** and two **r**s
tongue	ends in **gue**
until	has only one **l** at the end
weird	put the **e** before **i**
which	starts with **wh**

Remember!

The ending **-ful** always has only one **l**.
beautiful hopeful faithful painful grateful

Punctuation

☆ How does punctuation help us?

We use punctuation marks to make our writing easier to read and understand. Sometimes it is essential to add punctuation or the meaning of a sentence won't be clear:
Anika, thinks Oliver, is really annoying.
Anika thinks Oliver is really annoying.

Full stop (.)

We put a full stop:

- at the end of a sentence:
  I mustn't forget that appointment.
- at the end of a word or phrase that can stand on its own:
  Sorry. *Good morning.* *Not much.*

Question mark (?)

We put a question mark at the end of a question:
Did I leave my phone at your house?

Exclamation mark (!)

We put an exclamation mark at the end of a sentence:

- to show strong feeling like anger, surprise or excitement:
  That's ridiculous! *I can't believe it!* *We're getting a puppy!*
- when we are telling someone to do something:
  Don't touch that! *Look over here!*

Comma (,)

We use a comma:

- to separate items in a list:
  We need to pack shorts, swimming costumes, t-shirts and trainers.

- to mark a short pause between parts of a sentence:
  After a while, the sun came out.
- when we are quoting someone:
  'I've never been here before,' said Emily.
  Ricky shouted, 'It's on fire!'
- to mark off parts of a sentence:
  My cousin, who lives in New York, is coming to stay next week.

Apostrophe (')

- **Possession**: apostrophes show possession of something:
  Callum's bag   *Britain's castles*   *the car's windscreen*
  James' hat   *Mr Jones' golf clubs*
  the children's notebooks   *men's shoes*   *women's fashions*
- **Contraction**: apostrophes show that one or more letters have been removed:
  can't (= cannot)   *I'll* (= I will/I shall)
  she'd (= she would/she had)

Inverted commas (' ' or " ")

We put inverted commas (or 'speech marks') before and after words to show exactly what someone is saying:

'You can all go home early,' said the teacher.
"Help me!" cried the man.

> **Look!**
>
> A punctuation mark such as a full stop, comma or exclamation mark comes *inside* the inverted commas at the end of a piece of spoken text.

PUNCTUATION

Brackets ( )

We use brackets to separate off extra information in a sentence. The sentence still makes sense without the information in the brackets.

Bring some snacks (like chocolate or popcorn) to the sleepover.
My grandmother (my mother's mother) was born in Dundee.

Dash (–)

A dash is a short line that is longer than a hyphen. It goes above the line, and has a space either side of it. You use a dash:

- to show a break in a sentence: *Don't leave your plate there – put it in the dishwasher.*
- to mark off separate information in the same way that brackets do:
  Peter and I – the others can't make it – are going skating on Friday.

> **Look!**
>
> When you use dashes to mark off extra information, you need to use a dash before *and* after the extra information.

Semicolon (;)

We use a semicolon:

- to separate items in a list, when the items are longer than one or two words:
  The flight was late; the hotel was dirty; the food was horrible; it rained every day; and I got an ear infection.
- to mark a break in a sentence, especially when you are showing a contrast between two things:
  Jack loves football; his brother hates it.

Colon (:)

We use a colon:

- to introduce a list: *The Jamaican flag contains three colours: black, green and gold.*
- to introduce a reason for something: *You should take an umbrella: it's going to rain.*

Hyphen (-)

We use a hyphen to join two words together to make one:

- to avoid having two vowels next to each other:
  pro-independence *re-elect* *anti-ageing cream*
- to avoid confusion about how the word should be pronounced:
  no-nonsense *mis-sell* *do-able*
- to avoid confusion with another word:
  re-creation (recreation) *re-cover* (recover) *re-count* (recount)
- to avoid confusion about what a phrase means:
  fish-eating seabirds (different from *fish eating seabirds*)
  20-odd books (different from *20 odd books*)

Ellipsis (...)

The ellipsis is made up of three dots. We use it to:

- show that some words are missing, for example, in a long quotation:
  'I have a dream that one day, even the state of Mississippi ... will be transformed into an oasis of freedom and justice.'
- represent a pause in someone's speech:
  Well ... I ... I'm not sure.
- create a dramatic ending to a story:
  Two red eyes appeared in the cave ...

Grammar

Grammar is a set of rules about a language that tell you how we organise words to make sentences.

☆ How does grammar help us?

- It helps us to work out how to use language in order to create the effect we want.
- It helps us to work out why something 'doesn't sound right', and to put it right.
- It helps us to learn other languages.

Word classes

Nouns

Nouns name a person, an animal, a thing or a place.

celebrity *snake* *laptop* *park*

There are a few different types of noun.

Common nouns

Common nouns can be **concrete**, **abstract** or **collective**:

- A **concrete noun** is a person, thing or animal that you can actually touch.
  pen *dog* *house* *teacher*
- An **abstract noun** is used for talking about an idea or a feeling.
  happiness *beauty* *imagination*
- A **collective noun** is used for talking about a group or collection of things or animals.
  pack *bunch* *flock*

Proper nouns

Proper nouns refer to a particular person, place or thing. Remember that they always start with a capital letter.

Andy Murray *Italy* *Tower Bridge*

Possessive nouns

This form of the noun shows that a person or thing 'owns' something. You add **'s** to the noun to make the possessive form.

my mum's glasses *Kirsty's football boots*
the dog's water bowl *the mug's handle*

If the noun is a plural that already ends in **s**, you just add an apostrophe.

the soldiers' uniforms *those boys' bikes*

> **Don't do it!**
>
> Never use **'s** to make a plural.

Adjectives

Adjectives are words that tell people about a noun. We use adjectives to describe nouns in lots of different ways:

- how they feel or what they are like:
  a hungry caterpillar, a funny story, a strange coincidence
- what they look like:
  a huge cake, a stripy t-shirt, an idyllic beach
- what they sound, smell, taste or feel like:
  a noisy party, smelly feet, a delicious pudding, slimy seaweed
- what colour they are: *a beige purse, blond hair, black trainers*
- where they come from:
  our German cousins, my American friends, a Scottish accent
- what something is made from:
  chocolate cake, a wooden box, a velvet scarf

☆ Astounding adjectives

You can make your writing come alive by using adjectives with your nouns.

He gave us an ***angelic*** *smile.*
A ***pungent*** *smell came from the kitchen.*

Comparative and superlative forms

To compare people or things using an adjective, we use the comparative and the superlative forms of the adjective:

Holly is ***tall****. She is* ***taller*** *than Rebecca.* (comparative form)
Actually, Holly is ***the tallest*** *girl in the class.* (superlative form)

☆ Forget the rules!

A few adjectives don't follow the rules.

Adjective	Comparative form	Superlative form
good	better	best
bad	worse	worst
far	further	furthest

Verbs

Verbs are words that we use to talk about an action or a state.

Emily ***plays*** *the guitar.* *The cows* ***wandered*** *over to see us.*
We always ***listen*** *to the radio in the car.* *I* ***feel*** *exhausted.*

Tense

The tense of a verb tells us *when* the action takes place, for example, if it has already happened or if it is happening now.

1. **The present**

   The present tense has two forms:

- the **simple present**:
  *I **like** poodles.* *You always **say** that!*
  *Max never **brushes** his hair.*
- the **progressive** (the '-ing' form):
  *We'**re trying** to concentrate.*
  *Look! I'**m wearing** my new jeans!*

2. **The past**
   The past tense has two forms:
   - the **simple past**:
     *Mary **had** a baby.* *I **screamed** and **fainted**.*
     *Dad nearly **hit** the roof.*
   - the **progressive**:
     *I **was doing** my homework when Bethany messaged me.*

3. **The future**
   We can talk about the future in lots of different ways. We can use:
   - *will*: *I promise I **will** be there on time.*
   - *shall*: *We **shall** see!*
   - *going to*: *I'**m going to** get you!*
   - the progressive form of the present tense:
     *They'**re leaving** on Sunday.*
   - the simple present tense: *The train **leaves** at 4 p.m.*

Adverbs

Adverbs tell us something about a verb. Adverbs can tell us:

- how someone does something. This type of adverb often ends in **-ly**:
  *She woke up **suddenly**.* *They walked home **slowly**.*
- where something happens:
  *We live **here**.* *She went **upstairs**.*
- when something happens:
  *We're leaving **tomorrow**.* *Call the police **now**!*

- the extent to which something is true:
  *I **really** want to see that film.* *He was **absolutely** furious.*
- how often something happens: *We **never** go there any more.*
  *I **often** wonder what happened to her.*

☆ Amazing adverbs

You can create vivid images in your writing by using adverbs with your verbs.

*'I got an A in my test!' she declared **triumphantly**.*
*For a while, I just stared **vacantly** out of the window.*

GRAMMAR

Prepositions

We use prepositions before a noun or a pronoun. A preposition can tell us about:

- where a person or thing is: ***on** the table* ***under** the bed*
- movement: *The train came **into** the station.*
  *She ran **across** the road.*
- time: *It's twenty **to** six.* *I've been here **since** midday.*

Conjunctions

Conjunctions join two words or two parts of a sentence together.

- **Coordinating conjunctions** join two ideas that are equally important.
  *I love fish **and** chips.* *You can have a biscuit **or** a cake.*
  *It was dry **so** I walked home.* *I like maths **but** I don't like physics.*
- **Subordinating conjunctions** introduce a clause which is less important than the main part of the sentence.
  *Mark read his book **while** he was waiting.*
  *Some dogs go a bit crazy **when** it's windy.*

☆ Starting a sentence

Some people say that you should never start a sentence with a coordinating conjunction. Although you shouldn't do it too often, if you start a sentence with 'and' or but', it can create an interesting dramatic effect:

You have been late every day this week. And now you are complaining about me!
But you don't really mean that, do you?

Pronouns

We use pronouns in place of nouns. We use them instead of repeating the name of a person, place or thing.

- **Personal pronouns** are used instead of the subject or object of a sentence.
  ***She** is good at maths.* *I don't like **him**.*
- **Possessive pronouns** are used to show that something belongs to a person or thing.
  *Hey, that's **mine**!* *Excuse me, I think this is **yours**.*
- **Relative pronouns** are used to refer back to a noun that was mentioned earlier.
  *I have an aunt **who** lives in Australia.*
  *We took the road **that/which** leads to the sea.*

Determiners

We often use determiners in front of nouns.

- Articles: **a** and **an** are known as 'indefinite articles' and **the** is known as the 'definite article'.
- Other determiners tell you who owns something: ***my** bag*; how far something is from the speaker: ***this** book*, ***that** aeroplane*; how much of something there is: ***some** sugar*, ***a lot of** people*, ***one** melon*.

GRAMMAR

Sentences

Sentence types

- A **statement** tells you something. It ends with a full stop: *Berlin is the capital of Germany.*
- A **question** asks something. It ends with a question mark: *Have you seen my keys?*
- A **command** gives orders or instructions: *Come here, please.*
- An **exclamation** expresses strong feeling. It ends with an exclamation mark: *What a laugh!* *Hooray!* *Oh no!*

Sentence structure

- A **simple sentence** contains just one clause.
  Patrick threw the ball.
- A **compound sentence** contains two or more clauses joined by a conjunction.
  Patrick threw the ball and Sara caught it.
- A **complex sentence** has a main clause and one or more subordinate clauses.
  Patrick threw the ball to Sara, who was standing on the other side of the pitch.

☆ A change of pace

Vary your sentence structures to change the pace in your writing.

Compound and complex sentences can slow things down:
I should have gone to football training, but I just sat in front of the TV, watching anything that was on, before I decided it was time for bed.

Simple sentences can speed things up:
I got home. I wolfed down my dinner. I dashed out to football training.

Parts of a sentence

- **Subject**: the person or thing that carries out the action:
  ***Louise** fell asleep.*
- **Verb**: all sentences have a verb:
  *Angus **fainted**.*
- **Object**: the person or thing that 'receives' the action of the verb. (Not all sentences have an object.):
  *Kim loves **chocolate**.*
- **Complement**: a word or phrase that tells you about the subject:
  *The boys felt **silly**.* *Laura is an **architect**.*
- **Adverbial**: a word or phrase that tells you how the action is happening:
  ***Suddenly**, it started to rain.* *The door closed **with a loud bang**.*

☆ A change of emphasis

By moving the parts of your sentence around, you can change what you emphasise and create different effects.

Placing the adverbial at the start of your sentence gives it emphasis:

***With a deafening crash,** the plates fell from the table.*

Moving the subject of your sentence to the end can create tension:

*Down the alley, onto the street and across the road, **Karl** ran for his life.*

Active and passive voice

In an **active voice** sentence, the subject of the sentence does the action:

Nina fed the rabbit.

subject verb

In a **passive voice** sentence, the subject of the sentence has the action done to it:

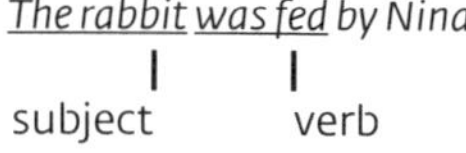

Nn

nag, **nags, nagging, nagged** VERB ① If you nag someone, you keep complaining to them about something. ② If something nags at you, it keeps worrying you.

nail NOUN ① a small piece of metal with a sharp point at one end, which you hammer into objects to hold them together. ② Your nails are the thin hard areas covering the ends of your fingers and toes. ▶ VERB ③ If you nail something somewhere, you fit it there using a nail. ④ *(informal)* If you nail someone who has done something wrong, you catch them and prove that they are guilty. ⑤ *(informal)* If you nail something, you do it extremely well or successfully.

naive *[Said ny-**eev**]*; also spelt **naïve** ADJECTIVE foolishly believing that things are easier or less complicated than they really are. **naively** ADVERB **naivety** NOUN

naked ADJECTIVE ① not wearing any clothes or not covered by anything. ② shown openly • *naked aggression.* **nakedness** NOUN

name NOUN ① a word that you use to identify a person, place or thing. ② Someone's name is also their reputation • *My only wish now is to clear my name.* ▶ VERB ③ If you name someone or something, you give them a name or you say their name. ④ If you name a price or a date, you say what you want it to be.

> **name** NOUN
> ① = designation, epithet, nickname, term, title
> ② = character, reputation
> ▶ VERB ③ = baptise, call, christen, dub, style, term

nameless ADJECTIVE You describe someone or something as nameless when you do not know their name, or when a name has not yet been given to them.

namely ADVERB that is; used to introduce more detailed information about what you have just said • *The state stripped them of their rights, namely the right to own land.*

namesake NOUN Your namesake is someone with the same name as you • *Audrey Hepburn and her namesake Katharine.*

nanny, **nannies** NOUN a person whose job is looking after young children.

nap, **naps, napping, napped** NOUN ① a short sleep. ▶ VERB ② When you nap, you have a short sleep.

napkin NOUN a small piece of cloth or paper used to wipe your hands and mouth after eating.

nappy, **nappies** NOUN a piece of towelling or paper worn round a baby's bottom.

narcotic NOUN a drug which makes you sleepy and unable to feel pain.

narrate VERB If you narrate a story, you tell it. **narration** NOUN

narrative *[Said **nar**-rat-tiv]* NOUN ENGLISH a story or an account of events.

narrator NOUN ① a person who is

reading or telling a story out loud. ② ENGLISH a character in a novel who tells the story.

narrow ADJECTIVE ① having a small distance from one side to the other • *a narrow stream.* ② concerned only with a few aspects of something and ignoring the important points • *people with a narrow point of view.* ③ A narrow escape or victory is one that you only just achieve. ▶ VERB ④ To narrow means to become less wide • *The road narrowed.* **narrowly** ADVERB **narrowness** NOUN

> **narrow** ADJECTIVE
> ① = fine, slender, slim, thin
> ≠ wide

narrow-minded ADJECTIVE unwilling to consider new ideas or opinions.

> **narrow-minded** ADJECTIVE
> = biased, bigoted, insular, opinionated, prejudiced
> ≠ tolerant

nasal [*Said nay-zal*] ADJECTIVE ① relating to the nose • *the nasal passages.* ② Nasal sounds are made by breathing out through your nose as you speak.

nasty, **nastier**, **nastiest** ADJECTIVE very unpleasant • *a nasty shock.* **nastily** ADVERB **nastiness** NOUN

> **nasty** ADJECTIVE
> = disagreeable, disgusting, foul, horrible, repellent, unpleasant, vile
> ≠ pleasant

nation NOUN GEOGRAPHY a large group of people sharing the same history and language and usually inhabiting a particular country.

national GEOGRAPHY ADJECTIVE ① relating to the whole of a country • *a national newspaper.* ② typical of a particular country • *women in Polish national dress.* ▶ NOUN ③ A national of a country is a citizen of that country • *Turkish nationals.* **nationally** ADVERB

national anthem NOUN A country's national anthem is its official song.

nationalise; also spelt **nationalize** VERB To nationalise an industry means to bring it under the control and ownership of the state. **nationalisation** NOUN

nationalism NOUN ① Nationalism is a desire for the independence of a country; also a political movement aiming to achieve such independence. ② Nationalism is also love of your own country. **nationalist** NOUN **nationalistic** ADJECTIVE

nationality, **nationalities** NOUN Nationality is the fact of belonging to a particular country.

National Party NOUN In Australia and New Zealand, the National Party is a major political party.

national service NOUN National service is a compulsory period of service in the armed forces.

nationwide ADJECTIVE, ADVERB happening all over a country • *a nationwide search.*

native ADJECTIVE ① Your native country is the country where you were born. ② Your native language is the language that you first learned to speak. ③ Animals or plants that are native to a place live or grow there naturally and have not been brought there by people. ▶ NOUN ④ A native of a place is someone who was born there.

Nativity NOUN In Christianity, the Nativity is the birth of Christ or the festival celebrating this.

natural ADJECTIVE ① normal and to be expected • *It was only natural that he was tempted.* ② not trying to pretend or hide anything • *Caitlin's natural manner reassured her.* ③ DGT existing or happening in nature • *natural disasters*

• *natural fabrics*. ④ A natural ability is one you were born with. ⑤ Your natural mother or father is your birth mother or father and not someone who has adopted you. ▶ **NOUN** ⑥ someone who is born with a particular ability • *She's a natural at tennis*. ⑦ In music, a natural is a note that is not a sharp or a flat. It is represented by the symbol (♮).
naturally ADVERB

> **natural ADJECTIVE**
> ① = common, everyday, normal, ordinary, typical, usual
> ≠ unnatural
> ② = candid, frank, genuine, real, unaffected
> ≠ false
> ④ = inborn, inherent, innate, instinctive, intuitive, native

nature NOUN ① Nature is animals, plants and all the other things in the world not made by people. ② The nature of a person or thing is their basic character • *She liked his warm, generous nature*.

> **nature NOUN**
> ② = character, make-up, personality

naughty, **naughtier**, **naughtiest ADJECTIVE** ① behaving badly. ② rude or indecent. **naughtily ADVERB naughtiness NOUN**

> **naughty ADJECTIVE**
> ① = bad, disobedient, impish, mischievous, wayward
> ≠ well-behaved

nausea *[Said* ***naw****-zee-ah]* **NOUN** Nausea is a feeling in your stomach that you are going to be sick. **nauseous ADJECTIVE**

nautical *[Said* ***naw****-tik-kl]* **ADJECTIVE** relating to ships or navigation.

naval ADJECTIVE relating to or having a navy • *naval officers* • *naval bases*.

navel NOUN the small hollow on the front of your body just below your waist.

navigate VERB ① When someone navigates, they work out the direction in which a ship, plane or car should go, using maps and sometimes instruments. ② To navigate a stretch of water means to travel safely across it • *It was the first time I had navigated the ocean*.
navigation NOUN navigator NOUN

navy, **navies NOUN** ① the part of a country's armed forces that fights at sea. ▶ **ADJECTIVE** ② dark blue.

Nazi *[Said* ***naht****-see]* **NOUN** HISTORY The Nazis were members of the National Socialist German Workers' Party, which was led by Adolf Hitler.

NB You write NB to draw attention to what you are going to write next. NB is an abbreviation for the Latin 'nota bene', which means 'note well'.

near PREPOSITION ① not far from. ▶ **ADJECTIVE** ② not far away in distance. ③ not far away in time. ④ You can also use 'near' to mean almost • *a night of near disaster*. ▶ **VERB** ⑤ When you are nearing something, you are approaching it and will soon reach it • *The dog began to bark as he neared the porch*. **nearness NOUN**

> **near PREPOSITION**
> ① = adjacent to, alongside, close to, next to, not far from
> ▶ **ADJECTIVE** ② = adjacent, adjoining, close, nearby
> ≠ far
> ③ = approaching, forthcoming, imminent, looming, near at hand, nigh, upcoming

nearby ADJECTIVE ① only a short distance away • *a nearby town*. ▶ **ADVERB** ② only a short distance away • *They built a house nearby*.

nearly ADVERB not completely but almost.

nearly ADVERB
= almost, as good as, just about, practically, virtually

neat ADJECTIVE ① tidy and smart. ② A neat alcoholic drink does not have anything added to it. **neatly** ADVERB **neatness** NOUN

neat ADJECTIVE
① = orderly, smart, spruce, tidy, trim
≠ untidy

necessarily ADVERB Something that is not necessarily the case is not always or inevitably the case.

necessary ADJECTIVE ① Something that is necessary is needed or must be done. ② (*formal*) Necessary also means certain or inevitable • *a necessary consequence of war.*

necessary ADJECTIVE
① = essential, imperative, indispensable, required, vital
≠ unnecessary
② = certain, inevitable, inexorable, unavoidable

necessity, **necessities** NOUN
① Necessity is the need to do something • *There is no necessity for any of this.* ② Necessities are things needed in order to live.

neck NOUN ① the part of your body which joins your head to the rest of your body. ② the long narrow part at the top of a bottle.

necklace NOUN a piece of jewellery worn around the neck.

nectar NOUN Nectar is a sweet liquid produced by flowers that is attractive to insects.

need VERB ① If you need something, you believe that you must have it or do it. ▶ NOUN ② Your needs are the things that you need to have. ③ a strong feeling that you must have or do something • *I just felt the need to write about it.*

need VERB
① = demand, require, want

needle NOUN ① a small thin piece of metal with a pointed end and a hole at the other, which is used for sewing. ② Needles are also long thin pieces of steel or plastic, used for knitting. ③ the part of a syringe which a doctor or nurse sticks into your body. ④ the thin piece of metal or plastic on a dial which moves to show a measurement. ⑤ The needles of a pine tree are its leaves. ▶ VERB ⑥ (*informal*) If someone needles you, they annoy or provoke you.

needless ADJECTIVE unnecessary. **needlessly** ADVERB

needy, **needier**, **neediest** ADJECTIVE very poor.

negative ADJECTIVE ① A negative answer means 'no'. ② Someone who is negative sees only problems and disadvantages • *Why are you so negative about everything?* ③ If a medical or scientific test is negative, it shows that something has not happened or is not present • *The diabetes test came back negative.* ④ MATHS A negative number is less than zero. ▶ NOUN ⑤ the image on film that is first produced when you take a photograph. **negatively** ADVERB

neglect VERB ① If you neglect something, you do not look after it properly. ② (*formal*) If you neglect to do something, you fail to do it • *He had neglected to give her his address.* ▶ NOUN ③ Neglect is failure to look after something or someone properly • *Most of her plants died from neglect.* **neglectful** ADJECTIVE

neglect VERB
① = ignore, overlook, turn your back on
② = fail, forget, omit
▶ NOUN ③ = disregard, indifference, unconcern

negligent ADJECTIVE not taking enough care • *her negligent driving.* **negligently** ADVERB **negligence** NOUN

negligible ADJECTIVE very small and unimportant • *a negligible amount of fat.*

negotiable ADJECTIVE able to be changed or agreed by discussion • *All contributions are negotiable.*

negotiate VERB ① When people negotiate, they have formal discussions in order to reach an agreement about something. ② If you negotiate an obstacle, you manage to get over it or round it. **negotiation** NOUN **negotiator** NOUN

Negro, **Negroes** NOUN (*old-fashioned, offensive*) a person with black skin who comes from Africa or whose ancestors came from Africa.

neighbour NOUN ① Your neighbour is someone who lives next door to you or near you. ② Your neighbour is also someone standing or sitting next to you • *I got chatting with my neighbour in the studio.*

neighbourhood NOUN a district where people live • *a safe neighbourhood.*

neighbouring ADJECTIVE situated nearby • *schools in neighbouring areas.*

neither ADJECTIVE, PRONOUN used to indicate that a negative statement refers to two or more things or people • *It's neither a play nor a musical* • *Neither of them spoke.*

nephew NOUN Someone's nephew is the son of their sister or brother.

Neptune NOUN Neptune is the planet in the solar system which is eighth from the sun.

nerve NOUN ① a long thin fibre that sends messages between your brain and other parts of your body. ② If you talk about someone's nerves, you are referring to how able they are to remain calm in a difficult situation • *It needs confidence and strong nerves.* ③ Nerve is courage • *O'Meara held his nerve to sink the putt.* ④ (*informal*) Nerve is boldness or rudeness • *He had the nerve to swear at me.* ▶ PHRASE ⑤ (*informal*) If someone **gets on your nerves**, they irritate you.

nerve-racking ADJECTIVE making you feel very worried and tense • *a nerve-racking experience.*

nervous ADJECTIVE ① worried and frightened. ② relating to or affecting your nerves. **nervously** ADVERB **nervousness** NOUN

> **nervous** ADJECTIVE
> ① = anxious, apprehensive, edgy, jittery (*informal*), jumpy, on edge, tense, toey (*Australian and New Zealand; slang*), worried
> ≠ calm

nervous breakdown NOUN an illness in which someone suffers from severe depression or anxiety and needs psychiatric treatment.

nervous system NOUN [SCIENCE] Your nervous system is the nerves in your body together with your brain and spinal cord.

nest NOUN ① a place that a bird makes to lay its eggs in; also a place that some insects and other animals make to rear their young in. ▶ VERB ② When birds nest, they build a nest and lay eggs in it.

nestle [*Said* ***ness-sl***] VERB If you nestle somewhere, you settle there comfortably, often pressing up against someone else • *A new puppy nestled in her lap.*

nestling NOUN a young bird that has not yet learned to fly and so has not left the nest.

net NOUN ① a piece of material made of threads woven together with small spaces in between. ② The net is the same as the **internet**. ▶ **ADJECTIVE** ③ A net amount is final, after everything that should be subtracted from it has been subtracted • *a net profit of £171 million*. ④ The net weight of something is its weight without its wrapping.

netball **NOUN** Netball is a game played by two teams of seven players in which each team tries to score goals by throwing a ball through a net at the top of a pole.

netting **NOUN** Netting is material made of threads or metal wires woven together with small spaces in between.

nettle **NOUN** a wild plant covered with little hairs that sting.

network **NOUN** ① a large number of lines or roads which cross each other at many points • *a small network of side roads*. ② A network of people or organisations is a large number of them that work together as a system • *the public telephone network*. ③ A television network is a group of broadcasting stations that all transmit the same programmes at the same time. ④ [ICT] a group of computers connected to each other.

neuron; also spelt **neurone** **NOUN** a cell that is part of the nervous system and conducts messages to and from the brain.

neurosis, neuroses *[Said nyoor-**roh**-siss]* **NOUN** a mental illness that causes people to have strong fears and worries.

neurotic *[Said nyoor-**rot**-ik]* **ADJECTIVE** having strong and unreasonable fears and worries • *He was almost neurotic about being followed*.

neuter *[Said **nyoo**-ter]* **VERB** ① When an animal is neutered, its reproductive organs are removed. ▶ **ADJECTIVE** ② In some languages, a neuter noun or pronoun is one which is not masculine or feminine.

neutral **ADJECTIVE** ① People who are neutral do not support either side in a disagreement or war. ② [DGT] The neutral wire in an electric plug is the one that is not earth or live. ③ [ART] A neutral colour is not definite or striking, for example pale grey. ④ [SCIENCE] In chemistry, a neutral substance is neither acid nor alkaline. ▶ **NOUN** ⑤ a person or country that does not support either side in a disagreement or war. ⑥ [DGT] Neutral is the position between the gears of a vehicle in which the gears are not connected to the engine. **neutrality** **NOUN**

> **neutral** **ADJECTIVE**
> ① = disinterested, dispassionate, impartial, nonaligned
> ≠ biased

neutralise, neutralises, neutralising, neutralised; also spelt **neutralize** **VERB** ① To neutralise something means to prevent it from working or taking effect, especially by doing or applying something that has the opposite effect. ② [SCIENCE] If you neutralise a substance, you make it neither acid nor alkaline.

neutron **NOUN** [SCIENCE] an atomic particle that has no electrical charge.

never **ADVERB** at no time in the past, present or future.

> **never** **ADVERB**
> = at no time, not ever

nevertheless **ADVERB** in spite of what has just been said • *They dress rather plainly but nevertheless look quite smart*.

new **ADJECTIVE** ① recently made, created or discovered • *a new house* • *a new plan* • *a new virus*. ② not used or owned before • *We've got a new car*. ③ different or unfamiliar • *a name which was new to me*. **newness** **NOUN**

new ADJECTIVE
① = advanced, current, fresh, ground-breaking, latest, modern, recent, ultra-modern, up-to-date, up-to-the-minute
≠ old

newborn ADJECTIVE born recently.

newcomer NOUN someone who has recently arrived in a place.

newly ADVERB recently • *the newly born baby*.

new moon NOUN The moon is a new moon when it is a thin crescent shape at the start of its four-week cycle.

news NOUN News is information about things that have happened.

news NOUN
= bulletin, disclosure, dispatch, information, intelligence, latest (*informal*), tidings (*formal*), word

newsagent NOUN a person or shop that sells newspapers and magazines.

newspaper NOUN a publication, on large sheets of paper, that is produced regularly and contains news and articles.

New Testament NOUN [RE] The New Testament is the second part of the Bible, which deals with the life of Jesus Christ and with the early Church.

New Year NOUN New Year is the time when people celebrate the start of a year.

New Zealander NOUN someone who comes from New Zealand.

next ADJECTIVE ① coming immediately after something else • *Their next child was a girl*. ② in a position nearest to something • *in the next room*. ▶ ADVERB ③ coming immediately after something else • *Steve arrived next*. ▶ PHRASE ④ If one thing is **next to** another, it is at the side of it.

next ADJECTIVE
① = ensuing, following, subsequent, succeeding
② = adjacent, adjoining, closest, nearest, neighbouring
▶ ADVERB ③ = afterwards, subsequently

next door ADJECTIVE, ADVERB in the house next to yours.

NHS In Britain, NHS is an abbreviation for 'National Health Service'.

nib NOUN the pointed end of a pen.

nibble VERB ① When you nibble something, you take small bites of it. ▶ NOUN ② a small bite of something.

nice ADJECTIVE pleasant or attractive. **nicely** ADVERB **niceness** NOUN

nice ADJECTIVE
= attractive, beautiful, charming, delightful, fantastic, fine, gorgeous, lovely

nicety, **niceties** [*Said* ***nigh**-se-tee*] NOUN a small detail • *the social niceties*.

niche [*Said* ***neesh***] NOUN ① a hollow area in a wall. ② If you say that you have found your niche, you mean that you have found a job or way of life that is exactly right for you.

nick VERB ① If you nick something, you make a small cut in its surface • *He nicked his chin*. ② (*informal*) To nick something also means to steal it. ▶ NOUN ③ a small cut in the surface of something.

nickel NOUN [SCIENCE] Nickel is a silver-coloured metallic element that is used in alloys. Its atomic number is 28 and its symbol is Ni.

nickname NOUN ① an informal name given to someone. ▶ VERB ② If you nickname someone, you give them a nickname.

A B C D E F G H I J K L M N O P Q R S T U V W X Y Z

nicotine NOUN SCIENCE Nicotine is an addictive substance found in tobacco. It is named after Jacques Nicot, who first brought tobacco to France.

niece NOUN Someone's niece is the daughter of their sister or brother.

nifty ADJECTIVE neat and pleasing or cleverly done.

Nigerian *[Said nie-**jeer**-ee-an]* ADJECTIVE ① belonging or relating to Nigeria. ▶ NOUN ② someone from Nigeria.

niggle VERB ① If something niggles you, it worries you slightly. ▶ NOUN ② a small worry that you keep thinking about.

night NOUN Night is the time between sunset and sunrise when it is dark.

nightclub NOUN a place where people go late in the evening to drink and dance.

nightfall NOUN Nightfall is the time of day when it starts to get dark.

nightie NOUN (*informal*) a nightdress.

nightly ADJECTIVE, ADVERB happening every night • *the nightly news programme*.

nightmare NOUN a very frightening dream; also used of any very unpleasant or frightening situation • *The meal itself was a nightmare*.
nightmarish ADJECTIVE

nil NOUN Nil means zero or nothing. It is used especially in sports scores.

nimble ADJECTIVE ① able to move quickly and easily. ② able to think quickly and cleverly. **nimbly** ADVERB

nine the number 9. **ninth** ADJECTIVE

nineteen the number 19. **nineteenth** ADJECTIVE

ninety, **nineties** the number 90. **ninetieth** ADJECTIVE

nip, **nips**, **nipping**, **nipped** VERB ① (*informal*) If you nip somewhere, you go there quickly. ② To nip someone or something means to pinch or squeeze them slightly. ▶ NOUN ③ a light pinch.

nirvana *[Said neer-**vah**-na]* NOUN RE Nirvana is the ultimate state of spiritual enlightenment which can be achieved in the Buddhist religion.

nitrogen NOUN SCIENCE Nitrogen is a chemical element usually found as a gas. It forms about 78 per cent of the earth's atmosphere. Nitrogen's atomic number is 7 and its symbol is N.

no INTERJECTION ① used to say that something is not true or to refuse something. ▶ ADJECTIVE ② none at all or not at all • *She gave no reason* • *You're no friend of mine*. ▶ ADVERB ③ used with a comparative to mean 'not' • *no later than July 24th*.

> **no** INTERJECTION
> ① = absolutely not, certainly not, definitely not, not at all, of course not
> ≠ yes

no. a written abbreviation for **number**.

nobility NOUN ① Nobility is the quality of being noble • *the unmistakable nobility of her character*. ② The nobility of a society are all the people who have titles and high social rank.

noble ADJECTIVE ① honest and brave, and deserving admiration. ② very impressive • *great parks with noble tall trees*. ▶ NOUN ③ a member of the nobility. **nobly** ADVERB

> **noble** ADJECTIVE
> ① = generous, honourable, magnanimous, upright, virtuous, worthy
> ≠ ignoble
> ▶ NOUN ③ = aristocrat, lord, nobleman, peer
> ≠ peasant

nobleman, **noblemen** NOUN a man who is a member of the nobility.

noblewoman, **noblewomen** NOUN a woman who is a member of the nobility.

nobody, **nobodies** PRONOUN ① not a single person. ▶ NOUN ② Someone who is a nobody is not at all important.

nocturnal ADJECTIVE ① happening at night • *a nocturnal journey through New York.* ② active at night • *a nocturnal animal.*

nod, **nods**, **nodding**, **nodded** VERB ① When you nod, you move your head up and down, usually to show agreement. ▶ NOUN ② a movement of your head up and down. **nod off** VERB If you nod off, you fall asleep.

noise NOUN a sound, especially one that is loud or unpleasant.

> **noise** NOUN
> = commotion, din, hubbub, pandemonium, racket, row, uproar
> ≠ silence

noisy, **noisier**, **noisiest** ADJECTIVE making a lot of noise or full of noise • *a noisy crowd.* **noisily** ADVERB **noisiness** NOUN

> **noisy** ADJECTIVE
> = deafening, loud, piercing, strident, tumultuous, vociferous
> ≠ quiet

nomad NOUN a person who belongs to a tribe which travels from place to place rather than living in just one place. **nomadic** ADJECTIVE

nominal ADJECTIVE ① Something that is nominal is supposed to have a particular identity or status, but in reality does not have it • *the nominal leader of his party.* ② A nominal amount of money is very small compared to the value of something • *I am prepared to do the work for a nominal fee.* **nominally** ADVERB

nominate VERB If you nominate someone for a job or position, you formally suggest that they have it. **nomination** NOUN

> **nominate** VERB
> = name, propose, recommend, select, submit, suggest

non- PREFIX not • *non-smoking.*

nonchalant [*Said* **non**-*shal-nt*] ADJECTIVE seeming calm and not worried. **nonchalance** NOUN **nonchalantly** ADVERB

nondescript ADJECTIVE Someone or something nondescript has no special or interesting qualities or details • *a nondescript coat.*

none PRONOUN not a single thing or person, or not even a small amount of something.

nonfiction NOUN [LIBRARY] Nonfiction is writing that gives facts and information rather than telling a story.

nonplussed ADJECTIVE confused and unsure about how to react.

nonsense NOUN Nonsense is foolish and meaningless words or behaviour. **nonsensical** ADJECTIVE

> **nonsense** NOUN
> = drivel, garbage (*informal*), inanity, rot, rubbish, waffle (*British*; *informal*)

nonstop ADJECTIVE, ADVERB continuing without any pauses or breaks • *nonstop excitement.*

noodle NOUN Noodles are a kind of pasta shaped into long, thin pieces.

nook NOUN (*literary*) a small sheltered place.

noon NOUN Noon is midday.

no-one; also spelt **no one** PRONOUN not a single person.

noose NOUN a loop at the end of a piece of rope, with a knot that tightens when the rope is pulled.

nor CONJUNCTION used after 'neither' or after a negative statement, to add something else that the negative statement applies to • *They had neither the time nor the money for the sport.*

norm NOUN If something is the norm, it is the usual and expected thing • *cultures where large families are the norm.*

normal ADJECTIVE usual and ordinary • *I try to lead a normal life.* **normality** NOUN

> **normal** ADJECTIVE
> = average, conventional, habitual, ordinary, regular, routine, standard, typical, usual
> ≠ unusual

normally ADVERB ① usually • *I don't normally like dancing.* ② in a way that is normal • *The foetus is developing normally.*

north NOUN ① The north is the direction to your left when you are looking towards the place where the sun rises. ② The north of a place or country is the part which is towards the north when you are in the centre. ▶ ADVERB, ADJECTIVE ③ North means towards the north • *The helicopter took off and headed north.* ▶ ADJECTIVE ④ A north wind blows from the north.

North America NOUN North America is the third largest continent, consisting of Canada, the United States and Mexico. **North American** ADJECTIVE

north-east NOUN, ADVERB, ADJECTIVE North-east is halfway between north and east.

north-eastern ADJECTIVE in or from the north-east.

northerly ADJECTIVE ① Northerly means to or towards the north. ② A northerly wind blows from the north.

northern ADJECTIVE in or from the north • *the mountains of northern Italy.*

North Pole NOUN GEOGRAPHY The North Pole is the most northerly place on the surface of the earth.

northward or **northwards** ADVERB ① Northward or northwards means towards the north • *We continued northwards.* ▶ ADJECTIVE ② The northward part of something is the north part.

north-west NOUN, ADVERB, ADJECTIVE North-west is halfway between north and west.

north-western ADJECTIVE in or from the north-west.

Norwegian *[Said nor-**wee**-jn]* ADJECTIVE ① belonging or relating to Norway. ▶ NOUN ② someone who comes from Norway. ③ Norwegian is the main language spoken in Norway.

nose NOUN ① the part of your face above your mouth which you use for smelling and breathing. ② the front part of a car or plane.

nostalgia *[Said nos-**tal**-ja]* NOUN Nostalgia is a feeling of affection for the past, and sadness that things have changed. **nostalgic** ADJECTIVE

nostril NOUN Your nostrils are the two openings in your nose which you breathe through.

nosy, **nosier**, **nosiest**; also spelt **nosey** ADJECTIVE trying to find out about things that do not concern you.

> **nosy** ADJECTIVE
> = curious, eavesdropping, inquisitive, prying

not ADVERB used to make a sentence negative, to refuse something, or to deny something.

notable ADJECTIVE important or interesting • *The production is notable for some outstanding performances.* **notably** ADVERB

notch NOUN a small V-shaped cut in a surface.

note NOUN ① a short letter. ② a written piece of information that helps you to remember something • *You should make a note of that.* ③ In music, a note is a musical sound of a particular pitch, or a written symbol that represents it. ④ a banknote. ⑤ an atmosphere, feeling or quality • *There was a note of regret in his voice* • *I'm determined to close on an optimistic note.* ▶ VERB ⑥ If you note a fact, you become aware of it or you mention it • *I noted that the rain had stopped.* ▶ PHRASE ⑦ If you **take note** of something, you pay attention to it • *The world hardly took note of this crisis.*
note down VERB If you note something down, you write it down so that you will remember it.

note NOUN
① = communication (*formal*), letter, memo, memorandum, message, reminder
② = account, jotting, record, register
⑤ = hint, tone, touch, trace
▶ VERB ⑥ = mention, notice, observe, perceive, register, remark, see

notebook NOUN a small book for writing notes in.

noted ADJECTIVE well-known and admired • *a noted opera singer.*

nothing PRONOUN not anything • *There was nothing to do.*

notice VERB ① If you notice something, you become aware of it. ▶ NOUN ② Notice is attention or awareness • *I'm glad he brought it to my notice.* ③ a written announcement. ④ Notice is also advance warning about something • *We were lucky to get you at such short notice.* ▶ PHRASE ⑤ If you **hand in your notice**, you tell your employer that you intend to leave your job after a fixed period of time.

notice VERB
① = detect, discern, note, observe, perceive, see, spot
▶ NOUN ③ = advertisement, bill, poster, sign
④ = advance warning, intimation, notification, warning

noticeable ADJECTIVE obvious and easy to see • *a noticeable improvement.*
noticeably ADVERB

noticeable ADJECTIVE
= conspicuous, evident, obvious, perceptible, unmistakable

noticeboard NOUN a board for notices.

notification NOUN a formal announcement.

notify, **notifies**, **notifying**, **notified** VERB To notify someone of something means to officially inform them of it • *You must notify us of any change of address.*

notify VERB
= advise (*formal*), inform, tell, warn

notion NOUN an idea or belief.

notorious ADJECTIVE well-known for something bad • *The river has become notorious for pollution.* **notoriously** ADVERB **notoriety** NOUN

notorious ADJECTIVE
= disreputable, infamous, scandalous

notwithstanding PREPOSITION (*formal*) in spite of • *He liked his classmate, notwithstanding his different views.*

nought the number 0.

noun NOUN [ENGLISH] [MFL] a word which refers to a person, thing or idea. Examples of nouns are 'president', 'table', 'sun' and 'beauty'.

nourish [*Said* **nur**-*rish*] VERB To nourish people or animals means to provide them with food.

nourishing ADJECTIVE Food that is nourishing makes you strong and healthy.

nourishment NOUN Nourishment is food that your body needs in order to remain healthy • *poor nourishment*.

novel NOUN ① LIBRARY a book that tells an invented story. ▸ ADJECTIVE ② new and interesting • *a very novel experience*.

novelist NOUN a person who writes novels.

novelty, **novelties** NOUN ① Novelty is the quality of being new and interesting • *The novelty had worn off*. ② something new and interesting • *Steam power was still a bit of a novelty then*. ③ a small, unusual object sold as a gift or souvenir.

November NOUN November is the eleventh month of the year. It has 30 days.

novice NOUN ① someone who is not yet experienced at something. ② someone who is preparing to become a monk or nun.

now ADVERB ① at the present time or moment. ▸ CONJUNCTION ② as a result or consequence of a particular fact • *Things have got better now there is a new board*. ▸ PHRASE ③ **Just now** means very recently • *I drove Brenda back to the camp just now*. ④ If something happens **now and then**, it happens sometimes but not regularly.

> **now** ADVERB
> ① = at once, currently, immediately, nowadays, right now, straight away, without delay

nowadays ADVERB at the present time, in contrast with in the past • *I don't go swimming much nowadays*.

nowhere ADVERB not anywhere.

noxious *[Said* ***nok****-shus]* ADJECTIVE harmful or poisonous • *a noxious gas*.

nozzle NOUN a spout fitted onto the end of a pipe or hose to control the flow of a liquid.

nuance *[Said* ***nyoo****-ahnss]* NOUN a small difference in sound, colour or meaning • *the nuances of his music*.

nuclear ADJECTIVE ① SCIENCE relating to the energy produced when the nuclei of atoms are split • *nuclear power* • *the nuclear industry*. ② relating to weapons that explode using the energy released by atoms • *nuclear war*. ③ SCIENCE relating to the structure and behaviour of the nuclei of atoms • *nuclear physics*.

nuclear reactor NOUN A nuclear reactor is a device which is used to obtain nuclear energy.

nucleus, **nuclei** *[Said* ***nyoo****-klee-uss]* NOUN ① SCIENCE The nucleus of an atom is the central part of it. It is positively charged and is made up of protons and neutrons. ② SCIENCE The nucleus of a cell is the part that contains the chromosomes and controls the growth and reproduction of the cell. ③ The nucleus of something is the basic central part of it to which other things are added • *They have retained the nucleus of the team that won the World Cup*.

nude ADJECTIVE ① naked. ▸ NOUN ② a picture or statue of a naked person. **nudity** NOUN

nudge VERB ① If you nudge someone, you push them gently, usually with your elbow. ▸ NOUN ② a gentle push.

nudist NOUN a person who believes in wearing no clothes.

nugget NOUN a small rough lump of something, especially gold.

nuisance NOUN someone or something that is annoying or inconvenient.

> **nuisance** NOUN
> = annoyance, bother, hassle (*informal*), inconvenience, irritation, pain (*informal*), pest

null PHRASE **Null and void** means not legally valid • *Other documents were declared to be null and void.*

numb ADJECTIVE ① unable to feel anything • *My legs felt numb* • *numb with grief.* ▶ VERB ② If something numbs you, it makes you unable to feel anything • *The cold numbed my fingers.*

> **numb** ADJECTIVE
> ① = dead, frozen, insensitive, paralysed
> ▶ VERB ② = dull, freeze, paralyse, stun

number NOUN ① a word or a symbol used for counting or calculating. ② Someone's number is the series of numbers that you use to telephone them. ③ A number of things is a quantity of them • *Adrian has introduced me to a large number of people.* ④ a song or piece of music. ▶ VERB ⑤ If things number a particular amount, there are that many of them • *At that time London's population numbered about 460,000.* ⑥ If you number something, you give it a number • *The picture is signed and numbered by the artist.* ⑦ To be numbered among a particular group means to belong to it • *Only the best are numbered among their champions.*

> **number** NOUN
> ① = digit, figure, numeral
> ③ = collection, crowd, horde, multitude

numerical ADJECTIVE expressed in numbers or relating to numbers • *a numerical value.*

numerous ADJECTIVE existing or happening in large numbers.

> **numerous** ADJECTIVE
> = lots of, many, several

nun NOUN a woman who has taken religious vows and lives in a convent.

nurse NOUN ① a person whose job is to look after people who are ill. ▶ VERB ② If you nurse someone, you look after them when they are ill. ③ If you nurse a feeling, you feel it strongly for a long time • *He nursed a grudge against his teacher.*

nursery, **nurseries** NOUN ① a place where young children are looked after while their parents are working. ② a room in which young children sleep and play. ③ a place where plants are grown and sold.

nursery school NOUN a school for children from three to five years old.

nursing home NOUN a privately run hospital, especially for elderly people.

nurture VERB (*formal*) If you nurture a young child or a plant, you look after it carefully.

nut NOUN ① a fruit with a hard shell and an edible centre that grows on certain trees. ② a piece of metal with a hole in the middle which a bolt screws into.

nutmeg NOUN Nutmeg is a spice used for flavouring in cooking.

nutrient NOUN [SCIENCE] Nutrients are substances that help plants or animals to grow • *the nutrients in the soil.*

nutrition NOUN [D&T] Nutrition is the food that you eat, considered from the point of view of how it helps you to grow and remain healthy • *The effects of poor nutrition are evident.* **nutritional** ADJECTIVE **nutritionist** NOUN

nutritious ADJECTIVE containing substances that help you to grow and remain healthy.

nutty, **nuttier**, **nuttiest** ADJECTIVE ① (*informal*) mad or very foolish. ② tasting of nuts.

nylon NOUN ① Nylon is a type of strong artificial material. ② Nylons are stockings or tights.

Oo

oak NOUN a large tree which produces acorns. It has a hard wood which is often used to make furniture.

OAP NOUN In Britain, an OAP is a person who receives a pension. OAP is an abbreviation for 'old age pensioner'.

oar NOUN a wooden pole with a wide, flat end, used for rowing a boat.

oasis, **oases** *[Said oh-**ay**-siss]* NOUN GEOGRAPHY a small area in a desert where water and plants are found.

oat NOUN Oats are a type of grain.

oath NOUN a formal promise, especially a promise to tell the truth in a court of law.

oath NOUN
= pledge, promise, vow

oatmeal NOUN Oatmeal is a rough flour made from oats.

OBE NOUN a British honour awarded by the King or Queen. OBE is an abbreviation for 'Officer of the Order of the British Empire' • *Jane Smith, OBE.*

obedient ADJECTIVE If you are obedient, you do what you are told to do. **obediently** ADVERB **obedience** NOUN

obedient ADJECTIVE
= law-abiding, submissive, subservient
≠ disobedient

obese *[Said oh-**bees**]* ADJECTIVE extremely fat. **obesity** NOUN

obey VERB If you obey a person or an order, you do what you are told to do.

obey VERB
= abide by, adhere to (*formal*), comply with, follow, observe
≠ disobey

obituary, **obituaries** NOUN a piece of writing about the life and achievements of someone who has just died.

object *[Said **ob**-ject]* NOUN ① anything solid that you can touch or see, and that is not alive. ② an aim or purpose. ③ The object of your feelings or actions is the person that they are directed towards. ④ MFL In grammar, the object of a verb or preposition is the word or phrase which follows it and describes the person or thing affected. ▶ VERB *[Said ob-**ject**]* ⑤ If you object to something, you dislike it or disapprove of it.

object NOUN
① = article, thing
② = aim, goal, idea, intention, objective, purpose
▶ VERB ⑤ = oppose, protest
≠ approve

objection NOUN If you have an objection to something, you dislike it or disapprove of it.

objection NOUN
= opposition, protest
≠ support

objectionable ADJECTIVE unpleasant and offensive.

objective NOUN ① an aim • *The protection of the countryside is their main objective.* ▶ ADJECTIVE ② If you are objective, you are not influenced by personal feelings or prejudices • *an objective approach*. **objectively** ADVERB **objectivity** NOUN

obligation NOUN something that you must do because it is your duty.

obligatory *[Said ob-**lig**-a-tree]* ADJECTIVE required by a rule or law • *Religious education was made obligatory*.

oblige VERB ① If you are obliged to do something, you have to do it. ② If you oblige someone, you help them. **obliging** ADJECTIVE

oblique *[Said o-**bleek**]* ADJECTIVE ① An oblique remark is not direct, and is therefore difficult to understand. ② An oblique line slopes at an angle.

obliterate VERB To obliterate something is to destroy it completely. **obliteration** NOUN

oblivion NOUN Oblivion is unconsciousness or complete lack of awareness of your surroundings. **oblivious** ADJECTIVE **obliviously** ADVERB

oblong NOUN ① a four-sided shape with two parallel short sides, two parallel long sides, and four right angles. ▸ ADJECTIVE ② shaped like an oblong.

obnoxious *[Said ob-**nok**-shuss]* ADJECTIVE extremely unpleasant.

oboe NOUN a woodwind musical instrument with a double reed. **oboist** NOUN

obscene ADJECTIVE indecent and likely to upset people • *obscene pictures*. **obscenely** ADVERB **obscenity** NOUN

obscure ADJECTIVE ① Something that is obscure is known by only a few people • *an obscure Mongolian dialect*. ② Something obscure is difficult to see or to understand • *The news was shrouded in obscure language*. ▸ VERB ③ To obscure something is to make it difficult to see or understand • *His view was obscured by trees*. **obscurity** NOUN

obscure ADJECTIVE
① = little-known, unknown
≠ famous
② = arcane (*formal*), cryptic, opaque
≠ simple
▸ VERB ③ = cloak, cloud, conceal, hide, mask, screen, shroud
≠ expose

observance NOUN The observance of a law or custom is the practice of obeying or following it.

observant ADJECTIVE Someone who is observant notices things that are not easy to see.

observant ADJECTIVE
= attentive, perceptive, vigilant, watchful

observation NOUN ① Observation is the act of watching something carefully • *Success hinges on close observation*. ② something that you have seen or noticed. ③ a remark. ④ Observation is the ability to notice things that are not easy to see.

observatory, **observatories** NOUN a room or building containing telescopes and other equipment for studying the sun, moon and stars.

observe VERB ① To observe something is to watch it carefully. ② To observe something is to notice it. ③ If you observe that something is the case, you make a comment about it. ④ To observe a law or custom is to obey or follow it. **observer** NOUN **observable** ADJECTIVE

observe VERB
① = monitor, scrutinise, study, survey, view, watch
② = discover, note, notice, see, spot, witness
③ = comment, mention, remark, say, state

obsession NOUN If someone has an obsession about something, they cannot stop thinking about that thing. **obsessional** ADJECTIVE **obsessed** ADJECTIVE **obsessive** ADJECTIVE

> **obsession** NOUN
> = complex, fixation, mania, preoccupation, thing (*informal*)

obsolete ADJECTIVE out of date and no longer used.

obstacle NOUN something which is in your way and makes it difficult to do something.

> **obstacle** NOUN
> = barrier, difficulty, hindrance, hurdle, impediment, obstruction

obstetrician NOUN An obstetrician is a doctor who specialises in the care of women during pregnancy and childbirth.

obstetrics NOUN Obstetrics is the branch of medicine concerned with pregnancy and childbirth.

obstinate ADJECTIVE Someone who is obstinate is stubborn and unwilling to change their mind. **obstinately** ADVERB **obstinacy** NOUN

> **obstinate** ADJECTIVE
> = dogged, headstrong, inflexible, intractable, stubborn, wilful
> ≠ flexible

obstruct VERB If something obstructs a road or path, it blocks it. **obstruction** NOUN **obstructive** ADJECTIVE

> **obstruct** VERB
> = bar, block, choke, clog

obtain VERB If you obtain something, you get it. **obtainable** ADJECTIVE

> **obtain** VERB
> = acquire, get, get hold of, get your hands on (*informal*), procure (*formal*), secure (*formal*)

obtuse ADJECTIVE ① Someone who is obtuse is stupid or slow to understand things. ② MATHS An obtuse angle is between 90° and 180°.

obvious ADJECTIVE easy to see or understand. **obviously** ADVERB

> **obvious** ADJECTIVE
> = apparent, blatant, clear, evident, overt, palpable, plain, self-evident

occasion NOUN ① a time when something happens. ② an important event. ③ An occasion for doing something is an opportunity for doing it. ▶ VERB ④ (*formal*) To occasion something is to cause it • *damage occasioned by fire.*

> **occasion** NOUN
> ② = affair, event
> ③ = chance, opportunity, time
> ▶ VERB ④ = bring about, give rise to, induce, produce, prompt, provoke

occasional ADJECTIVE happening sometimes but not often • *an occasional outing*. **occasionally** ADVERB

> **occasional** ADJECTIVE
> = intermittent, odd, periodic, sporadic
> ≠ frequent

occult NOUN The occult is the knowledge and study of supernatural and magical forces or powers.

occupancy NOUN The occupancy of a building is the act of living or working in it.

occupant NOUN The occupants of a building are the people who live or work in it.

occupation NOUN ① a job or profession. ② a hobby or something you do for pleasure. ③ The occupation of a country is the act of invading it and taking control of it. **occupational** ADJECTIVE

occupy, **occupies**, **occupying**, **occupied** VERB ① The people who occupy a building are the people who live or work there. ② When people occupy a place, they move into it and take control of it • *Demonstrators occupied the building.* ③ To occupy a position in a system or plan is to have that position • *His phone-in show occupies a daytime slot.* ④ If something occupies you, you spend your time doing it • *That problem occupies me night and day.* **occupier** NOUN

occur, **occurs**, **occurring**, **occurred** VERB ① If something occurs, it happens or exists • *The crash occurred yesterday evening.* ② If something occurs to you, you suddenly think of it.

> **occur** VERB
> ① = appear, arise, be present, exist, happen, take place
> ② = cross your mind, dawn on, strike

occurrence NOUN ① an event. ② The occurrence of something is the fact that it happens or exists • *the occurrence of diseases.*

ocean NOUN ① the sea. ② The five oceans are the five very large areas of sea on the Earth's surface • *the Atlantic Ocean.* **oceanic** ADJECTIVE

o'clock ADVERB You use 'o'clock' after the number of the hour to say what the time is.

octave NOUN ① MUSIC the difference in pitch between the first note and the eighth note of a musical scale. ② ENGLISH eight lines of poetry together.

October NOUN October is the tenth month of the year. It has 31 days.

octopus, **octopuses** NOUN a sea creature with eight long tentacles which it uses to catch food.

odd ADJECTIVE ① Something odd is strange or unusual. ② Odd things do not match each other • *odd socks.* ③ Odd numbers are numbers that cannot be divided exactly by two.
▸ ADVERB ④ You use 'odd' after a number to say that it is approximate • *I've written twenty-odd plays.* **oddly** ADVERB **oddness** NOUN

> **odd** ADJECTIVE
> ① = bizarre, curious, funny, peculiar, queer (*old-fashioned*), singular (*formal*), strange, weird
> ≠ ordinary

oddity, **oddities** NOUN something very strange.

odds PLURAL NOUN The odds of something happening are how likely it is to happen • *The odds are against the record being beaten.*

ode NOUN ENGLISH a poem written in praise of someone or something.

odious ADJECTIVE extremely unpleasant.

odour NOUN (*formal*) a strong smell. **odorous** ADJECTIVE

odyssey [*Said* ***od**-i-see*] NOUN An odyssey is a long and eventful journey. The name comes from Odysseus, the Greek hero who wandered from adventure to adventure for ten years.

oesophagus, **oesophaguses** [*Said ee-**sof**-fag-uss*] NOUN the tube that carries food from your throat to your stomach.

oestrogen another spelling of **estrogen**.

of PREPOSITION ① consisting of or containing • *a collection of short stories* • *a cup of tea.* ② used when naming something or describing a characteristic of something • *the city of Canberra* • *a woman of great power and influence.* ③ belonging to or connected with • *a friend of Rachel* • *the cover of the book.*

off PREPOSITION, ADVERB ① indicating movement away from or out of a place • *They had just stepped off the plane*

• *She got up and marched off.* ② indicating separation or distance from a place • *some islands off the coast of Australia* • *The whole crescent has been fenced off.* ③ not working • *It was Frank's night off.* ▶ ADVERB, ADJECTIVE ④ not switched on • *He turned the radio off* • *the off switch.* ▶ ADJECTIVE ⑤ cancelled or postponed • *The concert was off.* ⑥ Food that is off has gone sour or bad. ▶ PREPOSITION ⑦ not liking or not using something • *He went right off chocolate.*

offal NOUN Offal is liver, kidneys and internal organs of animals, which can be eaten.

offence NOUN ① a crime • *a driving offence.* ▶ PHRASE ② If something **gives offence**, it upsets people. If you **take offence**, you are upset by someone or something.

offend VERB ① If you offend someone, you upset them. ② (*formal*) To offend or to offend against a law is to commit a crime. **offender** NOUN

offend VERB
① = affront, insult, outrage
≠ please

offensive ADJECTIVE ① Something offensive is rude and upsetting • *offensive behaviour.* ② Offensive actions or weapons are used in attacking someone. ▶ NOUN ③ an attack • *a full-scale offensive against the rebels.* **offensively** ADVERB

offensive ADJECTIVE
① = abusive, insulting, objectionable

offer VERB ① If you offer something to someone, you ask them if they would like it. ▶ NOUN ② something that someone says they will give you or do for you if you want them to • *Many refused the offer anyway.* ③ a specially low price for a product in a shop • *You will need a voucher to qualify for the special offer.*

offer VERB
① = hold out, tender
▶ NOUN ② = proposition, tender

offering NOUN something that is offered or given to someone.

offhand ADJECTIVE ① If someone is offhand, they are unfriendly and slightly rude. ▶ ADVERB ② If you know something offhand, you know it without having to think very hard • *I couldn't tell you offhand how long he's been here.*

office NOUN ① a room where people work at desks. ② a government department • *the Office of Fair Trading.* ③ a place where people can go for information, tickets or other services. ④ Someone who holds office has an important job or position in government or in an organisation.

officer NOUN a person with a position of authority in the armed forces, the police or a government organisation.

official ADJECTIVE ① approved by the government or by someone in authority • *the official figures.* ② done or used by someone in authority as part of their job • *official notepaper.* ▶ NOUN ③ a person who holds a position of authority in an organisation. **officially** ADVERB

official ADJECTIVE
① = authorised, certified, formal, licensed
≠ unofficial
▶ NOUN ③ = executive, officer, representative

officialdom NOUN You can refer to officials in government or other organisations as officialdom, especially when you find them difficult to deal with.

officiate VERB To officiate at a ceremony is to be in charge and perform the official part of the ceremony.

offing PHRASE If something is **in the offing**, it is likely to happen soon • *A change is in the offing.*

off-licence NOUN a shop which sells alcoholic drinks.

offline ADJECTIVE ① If a computer is offline, it is switched off or not connected to the internet. ▶ ADVERB ② If you do something offline, you do it while not connected to the internet.

offset, **offsets**, **offsetting**, **offset** VERB If one thing is offset by another thing, its effect is reduced or cancelled out by that thing • *This tedium can be offset by watching the television.*

offshoot NOUN something that has developed from another thing • *The technology we use is an offshoot of the motor industry.*

offshore ADJECTIVE, ADVERB in or from the part of the sea near the shore • *an offshore wind* • *a wreck fifteen kilometres offshore.*

offside ADJECTIVE If a soccer, rugby or hockey player is offside, they have broken the rules by moving too far forward.

offspring NOUN A person's or animal's offspring are their children.

often ADVERB happening many times or a lot of the time.

> **often** ADVERB
> = frequently, repeatedly

ogre [*Said* ***oh-gur***] NOUN a cruel, frightening giant in a fairy story.

oil NOUN ① Oil is a thick, sticky liquid used as a fuel and for lubrication. ② Oil is also a thick, greasy liquid made from plants or animals • *cooking oil* • *bath oil.* ▶ VERB ③ If you oil something, you put oil in it or on it.

oil painting NOUN An oil painting is a painting that has been painted with oil paints.

oily ADJECTIVE Something that is oily is covered with or contains oil • *an oily rag* • *oily skin.*

ointment NOUN a smooth, thick substance that you put on sore skin to heal it.

okay; also spelt **OK** ADJECTIVE (*informal*) Okay means all right • *Tell me if this sounds okay.*

> **okay** ADJECTIVE
> = acceptable, all right

old ADJECTIVE ① having lived or existed for a long time • *an old lady* • *old clothes.* ② 'Old' is used to give the age of someone or something • *This photo is five years old.* ③ 'Old' also means former • *my old art teacher.*

> **old** ADJECTIVE
> ① = aged, elderly, senior, venerable
> ≠ young
> ③ = former, one-time, previous
> ≠ new

olden PHRASE **In the olden days** means long ago.

Old English NOUN Old English was the English language from the fifth century AD until about 1100. Old English is also known as Anglo-Saxon.

old-fashioned ADJECTIVE ① Something which is old-fashioned is no longer fashionable • *old-fashioned shoes.* ② Someone who is old-fashioned believes in the values and standards of the past.

> **old-fashioned** ADJECTIVE
> ① = antiquated, archaic, dated, obsolete, outdated, outmoded, out of date, passé
> ≠ fashionable

Old Testament NOUN [RE] The Old Testament is the first part of the Christian Bible. It is also the holy book of the Jewish religion and contains writings which relate to the history of the Jews.

olive NOUN ① a small green or black fruit containing a stone. Olives are usually pickled and eaten as a snack or crushed to produce oil. ▸ ADJECTIVE, NOUN ② dark yellowish-green.

-ology SUFFIX '-ology' is used to form words that refer to the study of something • *biology* • *geology*.

Olympic Games *[Said ol-**lim**-pik]* PLURAL NOUN (*trademark*) The Olympic Games are a set of sporting contests held in a different city every four years. It originated in Ancient Greece where a contest was regularly held in Olympia to honour the god Zeus.

ombudsman NOUN The ombudsman is a person who investigates complaints against the government or a public organisation.

omelette *[Said **om**-lit]* NOUN a dish made by beating eggs together and cooking them in a flat pan.

omen NOUN something that is thought to be a sign of what will happen in the future • *John saw this success as a good omen for his trip*.

> **omen** NOUN
> = sign, warning

ominous ADJECTIVE suggesting that something unpleasant is going to happen • *an ominous sign*. **ominously** ADVERB

> **ominous** ADJECTIVE
> = sinister, threatening

omission NOUN ① something that has not been included or done • *There are some striking omissions in the survey*. ② Omission is the act of not including or not doing something • *controversy over the omission of female novelists from the shortlist*.

omit, **omits**, **omitting**, **omitted** VERB ① If you omit something, you do not include it. ② (*formal*) If you omit to do something, you do not do it.

> **omit** VERB
> ① = exclude, leave out, miss out, skip

omnibus, **omnibuses** NOUN ① a book containing a collection of stories or articles by the same author or about the same subject. ▸ ADJECTIVE ② An omnibus edition of a radio or television show contains two or more programmes that were originally broadcast separately.

omnipotent *[Said om-**nip**-a-tent]* ADJECTIVE having very great or unlimited power • *omnipotent emperors*. **omnipotence** NOUN

on PREPOSITION ① above and supported by, touching, or attached to something • *The woman was sitting on the sofa*. ② If you are on a bus, plane or train, you are inside it. ③ If something happens on a particular day, that is when it happens • *It is his birthday on Monday*. ④ If something is done on an instrument or machine, it is done using that instrument or machine • *He preferred to play on his computer*. ⑤ A book or talk on a particular subject is about that subject. ▸ ADVERB ⑥ If you have a piece of clothing on, you are wearing it. ▸ ADJECTIVE ⑦ A machine or switch that is on is working. ⑧ If an event is on, it is happening or taking place • *The race is definitely on*.

once ADVERB ① If something happens once, it happens one time only. ② If something was once true, it was true in the past, but is no longer true. ▸ CONJUNCTION ③ If something happens once another thing has happened, it happens immediately afterwards • *Once we understood the problem, we tried to find a solution*. ▸ PHRASE ④ If you do something **at once**, you do it immediately. If several things happen **at once**, they all happen at the same time.

one ① the number 1. ▶ **ADJECTIVE** ② If you refer to the one person or thing of a particular kind, you mean the only person or thing of that kind • *My one aim is to look after the horses well.* ③ One also means 'a', used when emphasising something • *They got one almighty shock.* ▶ **PRONOUN** ④ One refers to a particular thing or person • *Alf Brown's business was a good one.* ⑤ One also means people in general • *One likes to have the opportunity to chat.*

one-off **NOUN** something that happens or is made only once.

onerous *[Said* ***ohn****-er-uss]* **ADJECTIVE** *(formal)* difficult or unpleasant • *an onerous task.*

oneself **PRONOUN** 'Oneself' is used when you are talking about people in general • *One could hardly hear oneself talk.*

one-sided **ADJECTIVE** ① If an activity or relationship is one-sided, one of the people has a lot more success or involvement than the other • *a one-sided contest.* ② A one-sided argument or report considers the facts or a situation from only one point of view.

one-way **ADJECTIVE** ① One-way streets are streets along which vehicles can drive in only one direction. ② A one-way ticket is one that you can use to travel to a place, but not to travel back again.

ongoing **ADJECTIVE** continuing to happen • *an ongoing process of learning.*

onion **NOUN** a small, round vegetable with a brown skin like paper and a very strong taste.

online **ADJECTIVE** ① Online activity is carried out using the internet • *online shopping.* ② If a computer is online, it is switched on or connected to the internet. ▶ **ADVERB** ③ If you do something online, you do it while connected to the internet.

onlooker **NOUN** someone who is watching an event.

only **ADVERB** ① You use 'only' to indicate the one thing or person involved • *Only Keith knows whether he will continue.* ② You use 'only' to emphasise that something is unimportant or small • *He's only a little boy.* ③ You can use 'only' to introduce something which happens immediately after something else • *She had thought of one plan, only to discard it for another.* ▶ **ADJECTIVE** ④ If you talk about the only thing or person, you mean that there are no others • *their only hit single.* ⑤ If you are an only child, you have no brothers or sisters. ▶ **CONJUNCTION** ⑥ 'Only' also means but or except • *He was like you, only blond.* ▶ **PHRASE** ⑦ **Only too** means extremely • *I would be only too happy to swap places.*

> **only** **ADVERB**
> ① = just, merely, purely, simply, solely
> ▶ **ADJECTIVE** ④ = one, sole

onset **NOUN** The onset of something unpleasant is the beginning of it • *the onset of war.*

onslaught *[Said* ***on****-slawt]* **NOUN** a violent attack.

onto; also spelt **on to** **PREPOSITION** If you put something onto an object, you put it on it.

onus *[Rhymes with* ***bonus****]* **NOUN** *(formal)* If the onus is on you to do something, it is your duty or responsibility to do it.

onwards or **onward** **ADVERB** ① continuing to happen from a particular time • *He could not speak a word from that moment onwards.* ② travelling forwards • *Duncliffe escorted the pair onwards to his own room.*

ooze **VERB** When a thick liquid oozes, it flows slowly • *The cold mud oozed over her new footwear.*

opal NOUN a pale or whitish semiprecious stone used for making jewellery.

opaque *[Said oh-**pake**]* ADJECTIVE If something is opaque, you cannot see through it • *opaque glass windows*.

open VERB ① When you open something, or when it opens, you move it so that it is no longer closed • *She opened the door*. ② When a shop or office opens, people are able to go in. ③ To open something also means to start it • *He tried to open a bank account*. ▶ ADJECTIVE ④ Something that is open is not closed or fastened • *an open box of chocolates*. ⑤ If you have an open mind, you are willing to consider new ideas or suggestions. ⑥ Someone who is open is honest and frank. ⑦ When a shop or office is open, people are able to go in. ⑧ An open area of sea or land is a large, empty area • *open country*. ⑨ If something is open to you, it is possible for you to do it • *There is no other course open to us but to fight it out*. ⑩ If a situation is still open, it is still being considered • *Even if the case remains open, the full facts may never be revealed*. ▶ PHRASE ⑪ **In the open** means outside. ⑫ **In the open** also means not secret. **openly** ADVERB

open VERB
① = uncover, undo, unlock
≠ shut
▶ ADJECTIVE ④ = ajar, uncovered, undone, unlocked
≠ shut
⑥ = candid, frank, honest

opening ADJECTIVE ① Opening means coming first • *the opening day of the season*. ▶ NOUN ② The opening of a book or film is the first part of it. ③ a hole or gap. ④ an opportunity • *She waited for an opening to bring up the subject*.

opening ADJECTIVE
① = first, inaugural (*formal*), initial, introductory
▶ NOUN ② = beginning, commencement (*formal*), start
≠ conclusion
③ = chink, cleft, crack, gap, hole, slot, space, vent

open-minded ADJECTIVE willing to consider new ideas and suggestions.

open-plan ADJECTIVE An open-plan office or building has very few dividing walls inside.

opera NOUN a play in which the words are sung rather than spoken. **operatic** ADJECTIVE

operate VERB ① To operate is to work • *We are shocked at the way that businesses operate*. ② When you operate a machine, you make it work. ③ When surgeons operate, they cut open a patient's body to remove or repair a damaged part.

operation NOUN ① a complex planned event • *a full-scale military operation*. ② a form of medical treatment in which a surgeon cuts open a patient's body to remove or repair a damaged part. ③ MATHS any process in which a number or quantity is operated on according to a set of rules, for example addition, subtraction, multiplication and division. ▶ PHRASE ④ If something is **in operation**, it is working or being used • *The system is in operation from April to the end of September*.

operational ADJECTIVE working or able to be used • *an operational aircraft*.

operative ADJECTIVE Something that is operative is working or having an effect.

operator NOUN ① someone who operates a machine • *a forklift operator*. ② someone who runs a business • *a tour operator*. ③ someone who connects telephone calls in places such as an office or hotel.

opinion NOUN a belief or view.

> **opinion** NOUN
> = assessment, belief, estimation, judgment, point of view, view, viewpoint

opinionated ADJECTIVE Someone who is opinionated has strong views and refuses to accept that they might be wrong.

opium NOUN Opium is a drug made from the seeds of a poppy. It is used in medicine to relieve pain.

opponent NOUN someone who is against you in an argument or a contest.

opportune ADJECTIVE (*formal*) happening at a convenient time • *The king's death was opportune for the prince.*

opportunism NOUN Opportunism is taking advantage of any opportunity to gain money or power for yourself. **opportunist** NOUN

opportunity, **opportunities** NOUN a chance to do something.

oppose VERB If you oppose something, you disagree with it and try to prevent it.

> **oppose** VERB
> = fight against, resist, speak out against
> ≠ support

opposed ADJECTIVE ① If you are opposed to something, you disagree with it • *He was totally opposed to bullying in schools.* ② Opposed also means opposite or very different • *two opposed schools of thought.* ▶ PHRASE ③ If you refer to one thing **as opposed to** another, you are emphasising that it is the first thing rather than the second which concerns you • *Real spectators, as opposed to invited guests, were hard to spot.*

opposite PREPOSITION, ADVERB ① If one thing is opposite another, it is facing it • *the shop opposite the station* • *the house opposite.* ▶ ADJECTIVE ② The opposite part of something is the part farthest away from you • *the opposite side of town.* ③ If things are opposite, they are completely different • *I take the opposite view to you.* ▶ NOUN ④ If two things are completely different, they are opposites.

> **opposite** ADJECTIVE
> ③ = conflicting, contrary, contrasting, opposed, reverse
> ▶ NOUN ④ = antithesis (*formal*), contrary, converse, reverse

opposition NOUN ① If there is opposition to something, people disagree with it and try to prevent it. ② The political parties who are not in power are referred to as the opposition. ③ In a game or sports event, the opposition is the person or team that you are competing against.

> **opposition** NOUN
> ① = disapproval, hostility, resistance
> ≠ support

oppressed ADJECTIVE People who are oppressed are treated cruelly or unfairly. **oppress** VERB **oppressor** NOUN

> **oppressed** ADJECTIVE
> = downtrodden, persecuted

oppression NOUN cruel and unfair treatment of people.

> **oppression** NOUN
> = persecution, tyranny

oppressive ADJECTIVE ① If the weather is oppressive, it is hot and humid. ② An oppressive situation makes you feel dispirited or concerned • *The silence became oppressive.* ③ An oppressive system treats people cruelly or unfairly • *Some groups in the* *country were subject to oppressive laws.* **oppressively** ADVERB

opt VERB If you opt for something, you choose it. If you opt out of something, you choose not to be involved in it.

optical ADJECTIVE ① SCIENCE concerned with vision, light or images. ② relating to the appearance of things.

optician NOUN someone who tests people's eyes, and makes and sells glasses and contact lenses.

optimism NOUN Optimism is a feeling of hopefulness about the future. **optimist** NOUN

optimistic ADJECTIVE hopeful about the future. **optimistically** ADVERB

optimistic ADJECTIVE
= buoyant, confident, hopeful, positive, sanguine
≠ pessimistic

optimum ADJECTIVE the best that is possible • *50 to 80 centimetres is the optimum size.*

option NOUN a choice between two or more things. **optional** ADJECTIVE

opulent *[Said* ***op****-yool-nt]* ADJECTIVE grand and expensive-looking • *an opulent seafront estate.* **opulence** NOUN

opus, **opuses** or **opera** NOUN ① MUSIC An opus is a musical composition. 'Opus' is often used with a number, indicating its position in a series of published works by the same composer. ② ART An opus is also a great artistic work, such as a piece of writing or a painting.

or CONJUNCTION ① used to link two different things • *I didn't know whether to laugh or cry.* ② used to introduce a warning • *Do what I say or else I will fire.*

-or SUFFIX '-or' is used to form nouns from verbs • *actor* • *conductor.*

oracle NOUN ① In ancient Greece, an oracle was a place where a priest or priestess made predictions about the future. ② a prophecy made by a priest or other person with great authority or wisdom.

oral ADJECTIVE ① spoken rather than written • *oral history.* ② Oral describes things that are used in your mouth or done with your mouth • *an oral vaccine.* ▶ NOUN ③ an examination that is spoken rather than written. **orally** ADVERB

oral ADJECTIVE
① = spoken, verbal

orange NOUN ① a round citrus fruit that is juicy and sweet and has a thick reddish-yellow skin. ▶ ADJECTIVE, NOUN ② reddish-yellow.

orang-utan; also spelt **orang-utang** NOUN An orang-utan is a large ape with reddish-brown hair. Orang-utans come from the forests of Borneo and Sumatra.

orator NOUN someone who is good at making speeches.

oratory NOUN Oratory is the art and skill of making formal public speeches.

orbit NOUN ① SCIENCE the curved path followed by an object going round a planet or the sun. ▶ VERB ② If something orbits a planet or the sun, it goes round and round it.

orchard NOUN a piece of land where fruit trees are grown.

orchestra *[Said* ***or****-kess-tra]* NOUN MUSIC a large group of musicians who play musical instruments together. **orchestral** ADJECTIVE

orchestrate VERB ① To orchestrate something is to organise it very carefully in order to produce a particular result. ② To orchestrate a piece of music is to rewrite it so that it can be played by an orchestra. **orchestration** NOUN

A B C D E F G H I J K L M N O P Q R S T U V W X Y Z

orchid *[Said or-kid]* NOUN Orchids are plants with beautiful and unusual flowers.

ordain VERB When someone is ordained, they are made a member of the clergy.

ordeal NOUN a difficult and extremely unpleasant experience • *the ordeal of being arrested and charged with attempted murder.*

> **ordeal** NOUN
> = hardship, nightmare, torture, trial, tribulation (*formal*)

order NOUN ① a command given by someone in authority. ② If things are arranged or done in a particular order, they are arranged or done in that sequence • *in alphabetical order.* ③ Order is a situation in which everything is in the correct place or done at the correct time. ④ something that you ask to be brought to you or sent to you. ⑤ An order is a division of living organisms that is smaller than a class and larger than a family. ▶ VERB ⑥ To order someone to do something is to tell them firmly to do it. ⑦ When you order something, you ask for it to be brought or sent to you. ▶ PHRASE ⑧ If you do something **in order to** achieve a particular thing, you do it because you want to achieve that thing.

> **order** NOUN
> ① = command, decree, dictate, directive, instruction
> ③ = harmony, regularity, symmetry
> ≠ disorder
> ▶ VERB ⑥ = command, decree, direct, instruct, ordain
> ≠ forbid

orderly ADJECTIVE Something that is orderly is organised or arranged well.

> **orderly** ADJECTIVE
> = neat, regular, tidy
> ≠ disorderly

ordinarily ADVERB If something ordinarily happens, it usually happens.

ordinary ADJECTIVE Ordinary means not special or different in any way.

> **ordinary** ADJECTIVE
> = conventional, normal, regular, routine, standard, usual
> ≠ special

ordination NOUN When someone's ordination takes place, they are made a member of the clergy.

ordnance NOUN Weapons and other military supplies are referred to as ordnance.

ore NOUN GEOGRAPHY Ore is rock or earth from which metal can be obtained.

oregano *[Said or-rig-**gah**-no]* NOUN Oregano is a herb used for flavouring in cooking.

organ NOUN ① SCIENCE Your organs are parts of your body that have a particular function, for example your heart or lungs. ② a large musical instrument with pipes of different lengths through which air is forced. It has various keyboards which are played like a piano.

organic ADJECTIVE ① Something that is organic is produced by or found in plants or animals • *decaying organic matter.* ② Organic food is produced without the use of artificial fertilisers or pesticides. **organically** ADVERB

organisation; also spelt **organization** NOUN ① any group or business. ② The organisation of something is the act of planning and arranging it. **organisational** ADJECTIVE

> **organisation** NOUN
> ① = association, body, company, confederation, group, institution, outfit (*informal*)
> ② = organising, planning, structuring

organise; also spelt **organize** VERB ① If you organise an event, you plan and arrange it. ② If you organise things, you arrange them in a sensible order. **organised** ADJECTIVE **organiser** NOUN

> **organise** VERB
> ① = arrange, establish, jack up (*New Zealand; informal*), plan, set up

organism NOUN SCIENCE any living animal, plant, fungus or bacterium.

organist NOUN someone who plays the organ.

orgy, **orgies** [*Said* **or**-*jee*] NOUN You can refer to a period of intense activity as an orgy of that activity • *an orgy of violence.*

Orient NOUN (*literary*) The Orient is eastern and south-eastern Asia.

oriental ADJECTIVE relating to eastern or south-eastern Asia.

orientated ADJECTIVE If someone is interested in a particular thing, you can say that they are orientated towards it • *These people are very career-orientated.*

orientation NOUN You can refer to an organisation's activities and aims as its orientation • *Poland's political and military orientation.*

oriented ADJECTIVE Oriented means the same as orientated.

orienteering NOUN Orienteering is a sport in which people run from one place to another in the countryside, using a map and compass to guide them.

origin NOUN ① You can refer to the beginning or cause of something as its origin or origins. ② You can refer to someone's family background as their origin or origins • *She was of Swedish origin.*

> **origin** NOUN
> ① = derivation, root, source
> ② = ancestry, descent, extraction, lineage, stock

original ADJECTIVE ① Original describes things that existed at the beginning, rather than being added later, or things that were the first of their kind to exist • *the original owner of the cottage.* ② Original means imaginative and clever • *a stunningly original idea.* ▶ NOUN ③ a work of art or a document that is the one that was first produced, and not a copy. **originally** ADVERB **originality** NOUN

> **original** ADJECTIVE
> ① = first, initial
> ② = fresh, new, novel
> ≠ unoriginal

originate VERB When something originates, or you originate it, it begins to happen or exist. **originator** NOUN

ornament NOUN a small, attractive object that you display in your home or that you wear in order to look attractive.

> **ornament** NOUN
> = adornment, bauble, decoration, knick-knack (*informal*), trinket

ornamental ADJECTIVE designed to be attractive rather than useful • *an ornamental lake.*

ornate ADJECTIVE Something that is ornate has a lot of decoration on it.

orphan NOUN ① a child whose parents are dead. ▶ VERB ② If a child is orphaned, its parents have died.

orphanage NOUN a place where orphans are looked after.

orthodox ADJECTIVE ① Orthodox beliefs or methods are the ones that most people have or use and that are considered standard. ② People who

are orthodox believe in the older, more traditional ideas of their religion or political party. ③ RE The Orthodox Church is the part of the Christian Church which separated from the western European Church in the 11th century and is the main church in Greece and Russia.
orthodoxy NOUN

osmosis *[Said oz-**moh**-siss]* NOUN SCIENCE Osmosis is the process by which a liquid moves through a semipermeable membrane from a weaker solution to a more concentrated one.

osprey *[Said **oss**-pree]* NOUN a large bird of prey which catches fish with its feet.

ostensibly ADVERB If something is done ostensibly for a reason, that seems to be the reason for it • *Byrnes submitted his resignation, ostensibly on medical grounds.*

ostentatious ADJECTIVE ① Something that is ostentatious is intended to impress people, for example by looking expensive • *ostentatious sculptures.* ② People who are ostentatious try to impress other people with their wealth or importance. **ostentatiously** ADVERB **ostentation** NOUN

ostentatious ADJECTIVE
① = extravagant, flamboyant, flashy, grandiose, pretentious, showy

ostrich NOUN The ostrich is the largest bird in the world. Ostriches cannot fly.

other ADJECTIVE, PRONOUN ① Other people or things are different people or things • *All the other children had gone home* • *One of the cabinets came from the palace; the other is a copy.* ▶ PHRASE ② **The other day** or **the other week** means recently • *She had bought four pairs of shoes the other day.*

otherwise ADVERB ① You use 'otherwise' to say a different situation would exist if a particular fact or occurrence was not the case • *You had to learn to swim pretty quickly, otherwise you sank.* ② 'Otherwise' means apart from the thing mentioned • *She had written to her daughter, but otherwise refused to take sides.* ③ 'Otherwise' also means in a different way • *The majority voted otherwise.*

otter NOUN a small, furry animal with a long tail. Otters swim well and eat fish.

ought *[Said **awt**]* VERB If you say that someone ought to do something, you mean that they should do it • *He ought to see a doctor.*

ounce NOUN a unit of weight equal to one sixteenth of a pound or about 28.35 grams.

our ADJECTIVE 'Our' refers to something belonging or relating to the speaker or writer and one or more other people • *We recently sold our house.*

ours PRONOUN 'Ours' refers to something belonging or relating to the speaker or writer and one or more other people • *a friend of ours from Korea.*

ourselves PRONOUN ① 'Ourselves' is used when the same speaker or writer and one or more other people do an action and are affected by it • *We haven't damaged ourselves too badly.* ② 'Ourselves' is used to emphasise 'we' • *We ourselves were delighted at the news.*

oust VERB If you oust someone, you force them out of a job or a place • *Cole was ousted from the board.*

out ADVERB ① towards the outside of a place • *Two dogs rushed out of the house.* ② not at home • *She was out when I rang last night.* ③ in the open air • *They are playing out in bright sunshine.* ④ no longer shining or burning • *The lights went out.*

▸ ADJECTIVE ⑤ on strike • *Over 800 construction workers are out in sympathy.* ⑥ unacceptable or unfashionable • *Miniskirts are out.* ⑦ incorrect • *Logan's timing was out in the first two rounds.*

out-and-out ADJECTIVE entire or complete • *an out-and-out lie.*

outback NOUN In Australia, the outback is the remote parts where very few people live.

outbreak NOUN If there is an outbreak of something unpleasant, such as war, it suddenly occurs.

> **outbreak** NOUN
> = eruption, explosion

outburst NOUN ① a sudden, strong expression of an emotion, especially anger • *John broke into an angry outburst about how unfairly the work was divided.* ② a sudden occurrence of violent activity • *an outburst of gunfire.*

outcast NOUN someone who is rejected by other people.

outcome NOUN a result • *the outcome of the election.*

outcrop NOUN a large piece of rock that sticks out of the ground.

outcry, **outcries** NOUN If there is an outcry about something, a lot of people are angry about it • *a public outcry over alleged fraud.*

outdated ADJECTIVE no longer in fashion.

outdo, **outdoes**, **outdoing**, **outdid**, **outdone** VERB If you outdo someone, you do a particular thing better than they do.

> **outdo** VERB
> = go one better than, outshine, surpass, top

outdoor ADJECTIVE happening or used outside • *outdoor activities.*

outdoors ADVERB outside • *It was too chilly to sit outdoors.*

outer ADJECTIVE The outer parts of something are the parts furthest from the centre • *the outer door of the office.*

outer space NOUN Outer space is everything beyond the earth's atmosphere.

outfit NOUN ① a set of clothes. ② (*informal*) an organisation.

outgoing ADJECTIVE ① Outgoing describes someone who is leaving a job or place • *the outgoing President.* ② Someone who is outgoing is friendly and not shy.

outgrow, **outgrows**, **outgrowing**, **outgrew**, **outgrown** VERB ① If you outgrow a piece of clothing, you grow too big for it. ② If you outgrow a way of behaving, you stop it because you have grown older and more mature.

outhouse NOUN a small building in the grounds of a house to which it belongs.

outing NOUN a trip made for pleasure.

outlandish ADJECTIVE very unusual or odd • *outlandish clothes.*

outlaw VERB ① If something is outlawed, it is made illegal. ▸ NOUN ② In the past, an outlaw was a criminal.

outlay NOUN an amount of money spent on something • *a cash outlay of $300.*

outlet NOUN ① An outlet for your feelings or ideas is a way of expressing them. ② a hole or pipe through which water or air can flow away. ③ a shop which sells goods made by a particular manufacturer.

outline VERB ① If you outline a plan or idea, you explain it in a general way. ② You say that something is outlined when you can see its shape because there is a light behind it. ▸ NOUN ③ a general explanation or description of something. ④ The outline of something is its shape.

A B C D E F G H I J K L M N O P Q R S T U V W X Y Z

outline VERB
① = sketch, summarise
▶ NOUN ③ = rundown (*informal*), summary, synopsis
④ = contours, figure, form, shape, silhouette

outlive VERB To outlive someone is to live longer than they do.

outlook NOUN ① Your outlook is your general attitude towards life. ② The outlook of a situation is the way it is likely to develop • *The outlook for the business is uncertain.*

outlook NOUN
① = attitude, perspective, view
② = future, prospects

outlying ADJECTIVE Outlying places are far from cities.

outmoded ADJECTIVE old-fashioned and no longer useful • *an outmoded form of transport.*

outnumber VERB If there are more of one group than of another, the first group outnumbers the second.

out of PREPOSITION ① If you do something out of a particular feeling, you are motivated by that feeling • *Out of curiosity she went along.* ② 'Out of' also means from • *old instruments made out of wood.* ③ If you are out of something, you no longer have any of it • *I do hope we're not out of fuel again.* ④ If you are out of the rain, sun or wind, you are sheltered from it. ⑤ You also use 'out of' to indicate proportion. For example, one out of five means one in every five.

out of date ADJECTIVE old-fashioned and no longer useful.

out of date ADJECTIVE
= antiquated, archaic, obsolete, old-fashioned, outdated, outmoded
≠ modern

outpatient NOUN Outpatients are people who receive treatment in hospital without staying overnight.

outpost NOUN a small collection of buildings a long way from a main centre • *a remote mountain outpost.*

output NOUN ① Output is the amount of something produced by a person or organisation. ② ICT The output of a computer is the information that it produces.

outrage VERB ① If something outrages you, it angers and shocks you • *I was outraged at what had happened to her.* ▶ NOUN ② Outrage is a feeling of anger and shock. ③ something very shocking or violent. **outrageous** ADJECTIVE **outrageously** ADVERB

outright ADJECTIVE [*Said* **owt**-*rite*] ① absolute • *an outright rejection.* ▶ ADVERB [*Said owt*-**rite**] ② in an open and direct way • *Have you asked him outright?* ③ completely and totally • *I own the company outright.*

outset NOUN The outset of something is the beginning of it • *the outset of his journey.*

outshine, **outshines**, **outshining**, **outshone** VERB If you outshine someone, you perform better than they do.

outside NOUN ① The outside of something is the part which surrounds or encloses the rest of it. ▶ PREPOSITION ② on or to the exterior of • *outside the house.* ③ Outside also means not included in something • *outside office hours.* ▶ ADJECTIVE ④ Outside means not inside • *an outside toilet.* ▶ ADVERB ⑤ out of doors.

outside NOUN
① = exterior, facade, face, surface
≠ inside
▶ ADJECTIVE ④ = exterior, external, outdoor, outer, outward, surface
≠ inside

outsider NOUN ① someone who does not belong to a particular group.

a b c d e f g h i j k l m n **o** p q r s t u v w x y z

② a competitor considered unlikely to win in a race.

outsize or **outsized** ADJECTIVE much larger than usual • *outsize feet.*

outskirts PLURAL NOUN The outskirts of a city or town are the parts around the edge of it.

> **outskirts** PLURAL NOUN
> = edge, perimeter, periphery

outspoken ADJECTIVE Outspoken people give their opinions openly, even if they shock other people.

outstanding ADJECTIVE ① extremely good • *The collection contains hundreds of outstanding works of art.* ② Money that is outstanding is still owed • *an outstanding mortgage of many thousands of pounds.*

> **outstanding** ADJECTIVE
> ① = brilliant, excellent, exceptional, first-class, first-rate, great, superb
> ② = due, overdue, owing, payable, unpaid

outstretched ADJECTIVE If your arms are outstretched, they are stretched out as far as possible.

outstrip, **outstrips**, **outstripping**, **outstripped** VERB If one thing outstrips another thing, it becomes bigger or more successful or moves faster than the other thing.

outward ADJECTIVE, ADVERB
① Outward means away from a place or towards the outside • *the outward journey.* ▸ ADJECTIVE ② The outward features of someone are the ones they appear to have, rather than the ones they actually have • *She never showed any outward signs of emotion.*
outwardly ADVERB

outwards ADVERB away from a place or towards the outside • *The door opened outwards.*

outweigh VERB If you say that the advantages of something outweigh its disadvantages, you mean that the advantages are more important than the disadvantages.

outwit, **outwits**, **outwitting**, **outwitted** VERB If you outwit someone, you use your intelligence to defeat them.

oval NOUN ① a round shape, similar to a circle but wider in one direction than the other. ▸ ADJECTIVE ② shaped like an oval • *an oval table.*

ovary, **ovaries** [*Said* ***oh**-var-ree*] NOUN SCIENCE A woman's ovaries are the two organs in her body that produce eggs.

ovation NOUN a long burst of applause.

oven NOUN the part of a cooker that you use for baking or roasting food.

over PREPOSITION ① Over something means directly above it or covering it • *the picture over the fireplace* • *He put his hands over his eyes.* ② A view over an area is a view across that area • *The pool and terrace look out over the sea.* ③ If something is over a road or river, it is on the opposite side of the road or river. ④ Something that is over a particular amount is more than that amount. ⑤ 'Over' indicates a topic of discussion • *A customer was arguing over the bill.* ⑥ If something happens over a period of time, it happens during that period • *I went to New Zealand over Christmas.* ▸ ADVERB, PREPOSITION ⑦ If you lean over, you bend your body in a particular direction • *He bent over and rummaged in a drawer* • *She was hunched over her keyboard.* ▸ ADVERB ⑧ 'Over' is used to indicate a position • *over by the window* • *Come over here.* ⑨ If something rolls or turns over, it is moved so that its other side is facing upwards • *He flipped over the envelope.* ▸ ADJECTIVE ⑩ Something that is over is completely finished. ▸ PHRASE ⑪ **All over** a place means everywhere in

that place • *studios all over America.*
▶ NOUN ⑫ In cricket, an over is a set of six balls bowled by a bowler from the same end of the pitch.

over PREPOSITION
④ = above, exceeding, in excess of, more than
▶ ADJECTIVE ⑩ = at an end, complete, done, finished, gone, past, up

overall ADJECTIVE ① Overall means taking into account all the parts or aspects of something • *The overall quality of pupils' work had shown a marked improvement.* ▶ ADVERB ② taking into account all the parts of something • *Overall, things are not really too bad.* ▶ NOUN ③ (*in plural*) Overalls are a piece of clothing that looks like trousers and a jacket combined. You wear overalls to protect your other clothes when you are working. ④ An overall is a piece of clothing like a coat that you wear to protect your other clothes when you are working.

overawed ADJECTIVE If you are overawed by something, you are very impressed by it and a little afraid of it.

overbearing ADJECTIVE trying to dominate other people • *Mozart had a difficult relationship with his overbearing father.*

overboard ADVERB If you fall overboard, you fall over the side of a ship into the water.

overcame the past tense of **overcome**.

overcast ADJECTIVE If it is overcast, the sky is covered by cloud.

overcoat NOUN a thick, warm coat.

overcome, **overcomes**, **overcoming**, **overcame**, **overcome** VERB ① If you overcome a problem or a feeling, you manage to deal with it or control it. ▶ ADJECTIVE ② If you are overcome by a feeling, you feel it very strongly.

overcome VERB
① = conquer, get the better of, master, surmount, triumph over, vanquish (*literary*)

overcrowded ADJECTIVE If a place is overcrowded, there are too many things or people in it.

overdo, **overdoes**, **overdoing**, **overdid**, **overdone** VERB If you overdo something, you do it too much or in an exaggerated way • *It is important never to overdo new exercises.*

overdose NOUN a larger dose of a drug than is safe.

overdraft NOUN an agreement with a bank that allows someone to spend more money than they have in their account.

overdrawn ADJECTIVE If someone is overdrawn, they have taken more money from their bank account than the account has in it.

overdue ADJECTIVE If someone or something is overdue, they are late • *The payments are overdue.*

overestimate VERB If you overestimate something, you think that it is bigger, more important or better than it really is • *We had overestimated his popularity.*

overflow, **overflows**, **overflowing**, **overflowed**, **overflown** VERB If a liquid overflows, it spills over the edges of its container. If a river overflows, it flows over its banks.

overgrown ADJECTIVE A place that is overgrown is covered with weeds because it has not been looked after • *an overgrown path.*

overhang, **overhangs**, **overhanging**, **overhung** VERB If one thing overhangs another, it sticks out sideways above it • *old trees whose branches overhang a footpath.*

overhaul VERB ① If you overhaul something, you examine it thoroughly and repair any faults. ▸ **NOUN** ② If you give something an overhaul, you examine it and repair or improve it.

overhead **ADJECTIVE** ① Overhead means above you • *overhead cables.* ▸ **ADVERB** ② Overhead means above you • *seagulls flying overhead.*

overhear, **overhears**, **overhearing**, **overheard** **VERB** If you overhear someone's conversation, you hear what they are saying to someone else.

overhung the past tense and past participle of **overhang**.

overjoyed **ADJECTIVE** extremely pleased • *Colm was overjoyed to see me.*

overland **ADJECTIVE, ADVERB** travelling across land rather than going by sea or air • *an overland trek to India* • *Wray was returning to England overland.*

overlap, **overlaps**, **overlapping**, **overlapped** **VERB** If one thing overlaps another, one part of it covers part of the other thing.

overload **VERB** If you overload someone or something, you give them too much to do or to carry.

overlook **VERB** ① If a building or window overlooks a place, it has a view over that place. ② If you overlook something, you ignore it or do not notice it.

> **overlook** **VERB**
> ② = disregard, forget, ignore, miss, neglect, turn a blind eye to

overly **ADVERB** excessively • *I'm not overly fond of puddings.*

overnight **ADVERB** ① during the night • *Further rain was forecast overnight.* ② suddenly • *Good players don't become bad ones overnight.* ▸ **ADJECTIVE** ③ during the night. ④ sudden • *an overnight success.* ⑤ for use when you go away for one or two nights • *an overnight bag.*

overpower **VERB** ① If you overpower someone, you seize them despite their struggles, because you are stronger than them. ② If a feeling overpowers you, it affects you very strongly. **overpowering** **ADJECTIVE**

overran the past tense of **overrun**.

overrate **VERB** If you overrate something, you think that it is better or more important than it really is. **overrated** **ADJECTIVE**

overreact **VERB** If you overreact, you react in an extreme way.

overriding **ADJECTIVE** more important than anything else • *an overriding duty.*

overrule **VERB** To overrule a person or their decisions is to decide that their decisions are incorrect.

> **overrule** **VERB**
> = overturn, reverse

overrun, **overruns**, **overrunning**, **overran**, **overrun** **VERB** ① If an army overruns a country, it occupies it very quickly. ② If animals or plants overrun a place, they spread quickly over it. ③ If an event overruns, it continues for longer than it was meant to.

oversaw the past tense of **oversee**.

overseas **ADVERB** ① abroad • *travelling overseas.* ▸ **ADJECTIVE** ② abroad • *an overseas tour.* ③ from abroad • *overseas students.*

oversee, **oversees**, **overseeing**, **oversaw**, **overseen** **VERB** To oversee a job is to make sure it is done properly. **overseer** **NOUN**

> **oversee** **VERB**
> = be in charge of, coordinate, direct, manage, preside, supervise

overshadow **VERB** If something is overshadowed, it is made unimportant by something else that is better or more important.

oversight **NOUN** something which

you forget to do or fail to notice.

overstate VERB If you overstate something, you exaggerate its importance.

overstep, **oversteps**, **overstepping**, **overstepped** PHRASE If you **overstep the mark**, you behave in an unacceptable way.

overt ADJECTIVE open and obvious • *overt signs of stress*. **overtly** ADVERB

overtake, **overtakes**, **overtaking**, **overtook**, **overtaken** VERB If you overtake someone, you pass them because you are moving faster than them.

overthrow, **overthrows**, **overthrowing**, **overthrew**, **overthrown** VERB If a government is overthrown, it is removed from power by force.

> **overthrow** VERB
> = bring down, depose, oust, topple

overtime NOUN ① Overtime is time that someone works in addition to their normal working hours. ▶ ADVERB ② If someone works overtime, they do work in addition to their normal working hours.

overtones PLURAL NOUN If something has overtones of an emotion or attitude, it suggests it without showing it openly • *the political overtones of the trial*.

overtook the past tense of **overtake**.

overture NOUN ① a piece of music that is the introduction to an opera or play. ② If you make overtures to someone, you approach them because you want to start a friendly or business relationship with them.

overturn VERB ① To overturn something is to turn it upside down or onto its side. ② If someone overturns a legal decision, they change it by using their higher authority.

> **overturn** VERB
> ① = capsize, knock down, knock over, tip over, topple, upset
> ② = overrule, reverse

overview NOUN a general understanding or description of a situation.

overweight ADJECTIVE too fat, and therefore unhealthy.

> **overweight** ADJECTIVE
> = fat, hefty, obese, stout

overwhelm VERB ① If you are overwhelmed by something, it affects you very strongly • *The priest appeared overwhelmed by the news*. ② If one group of people overwhelms another, they gain complete control or victory over them. **overwhelming** ADJECTIVE **overwhelmingly** ADVERB

overwork VERB If you overwork, you work too hard.

overwrought [*Said oh-ver-**rawt***] ADJECTIVE extremely upset • *He didn't get angry or overwrought*.

owe VERB ① If you owe someone money, they have lent it to you and you have not yet paid it back. ② If you owe a quality or skill to someone, they are responsible for giving it to you • *He owes his success to his mother*. ③ If you say that you owe someone gratitude or loyalty, you mean that they deserve it from you.

owl NOUN Owls are birds of prey that hunt at night. They have large eyes and short, hooked beaks.

own ADJECTIVE ① If something is your own, it belongs to you or is associated with you • *She stayed in her own house*. ▶ VERB ② If you own something, it belongs to you. ▶ PHRASE ③ **On your own** means alone.

> **own** ADJECTIVE
> ① = personal, private
> ▶ VERB ② = have, keep, possess

▸ **PHRASE** ③ = alone, by yourself, independently, unaided

owner NOUN The owner of something is the person it belongs to.

owner NOUN
= possessor, proprietor

ownership NOUN If you have ownership of something, you own it • *He shared the ownership of a sailing dinghy.*

ox, **oxen** NOUN Oxen are cattle which are used for carrying or pulling things.

oxide NOUN a compound of oxygen and another chemical element.

oxygen NOUN SCIENCE Oxygen is a chemical element in the form of a colourless gas. It makes up about 21 per cent of the earth's atmosphere. With an extremely small number of exceptions, living things need oxygen to live, and things cannot burn without it. Oxygen's atomic number is 8 and its symbol is O.

oxymoron, **oxymora** or **oxymorons** NOUN ENGLISH two words that contradict each other placed beside each other, for example 'deafening silence'.

oyster NOUN Oysters are large, flat shellfish. Some oysters can be eaten, and others produce pearls.

oz an abbreviation for 'ounce' or 'ounces'.

ozone NOUN Ozone is a form of oxygen that is poisonous and has a strong smell. There is a layer of ozone high above the earth's surface.

ozone layer NOUN The ozone layer is that part of the earth's atmosphere that protects living things from the harmful radiation of the sun.

Pp

p ① an abbreviation for 'pence'. ② a written abbreviation for 'page'. The plural is pp.

pa NOUN In New Zealand, a pa is a Māori village or settlement.

pace NOUN ① The pace of something is the speed at which it moves or happens. ② a step; also used as a measurement of distance. ▸ VERB ③ If you pace up and down, you continually walk around because you are anxious or impatient.

pacemaker NOUN a small electronic device put into someone's heart to control their heartbeat.

Pacific *[Said pas-**sif**-ik]* NOUN The Pacific is the ocean separating North and South America from Asia and Australia.

pacifist NOUN someone who is opposed to all violence and war. **pacifism** NOUN

pacify, pacifies, pacifying, pacified VERB If you pacify someone who is angry, you calm them.

> **pacify** VERB
> = appease, calm, mollify, placate, soothe

pack VERB ① If you pack, you put things neatly into a suitcase, bag or box. ② If people pack into a place, it becomes crowded with them. ▸ NOUN ③ a bag or rucksack carried on your back. ④ a packet or collection of something • *a pack of fish fingers*. ⑤ A pack of playing cards is a complete set. ⑥ A pack of dogs or wolves is a group of them. **pack in** VERB *(informal)* If you pack something in, you stop doing it. **pack up** VERB If you pack up your belongings, you put them in a bag because you are leaving.

package NOUN ① a small parcel. ② a set of proposals or offers presented as a whole • *a package of beauty treatments*. **packaged** ADJECTIVE

packaging NOUN [DGT] Packaging is the container or wrapping in which an item is sold or sent.

packed ADJECTIVE very full • *The church was packed with people*.

packet NOUN a thin cardboard box or paper container in which something is sold.

pact NOUN a formal agreement or treaty.

pad, pads, padding, padded NOUN ① a thick, soft piece of material. ② a number of pieces of paper fixed together at one end. ③ The pads of an animal such as a cat or dog are the soft, fleshy parts on the bottom of its paws. ④ a flat surface from which helicopters take off or rockets are launched. ▸ VERB ⑤ If you pad something, you put a pad inside it or over it to protect it or change its shape. ⑥ If you pad around, you walk softly. **padding** NOUN

paddle NOUN ① a short pole with a broad blade at one or both ends, used to move a small boat or a canoe. ▸ VERB ② If someone paddles a boat, they move it using a paddle. ③ If you paddle, you walk in shallow water.

paddock NOUN a small field where horses are kept.

paddy, **paddies** NOUN A paddy or paddy field is an area in which rice is grown.

padlock NOUN ① a lock made up of a metal case with a U-shaped bar attached to it, which can be put through a metal loop and then closed. It is unlocked by turning a key in the lock on the case. ▶ VERB ② If you padlock something, you lock it with a padlock.

paediatrician [*Said pee-dee-ya-**trish**-n*]; also spelt **pediatrician** NOUN a doctor who specialises in treating children.

paediatrics [*Said pee-dee-**ya**-triks*]; also spelt **pediatrics** NOUN Paediatrics is the area of medicine which deals with children's diseases. **paediatric** ADJECTIVE

pagan [*Said **pay**-gan*] ADJECTIVE ① involving beliefs and worship outside the main religions of the world • *pagan myths and cults*. ▶ NOUN ② someone who believes in a pagan religion. **paganism** NOUN

page, **pages**, **paging**, **paged** NOUN ① one side of one of the pieces of paper in a book or magazine; also the sheet of paper itself. ② In medieval times, a page was a young boy servant who was learning to be a knight. ▶ VERB ③ To page someone is to send a signal or message to a small electronic device which they are carrying.

pageant [*Said **paj**-jent*] NOUN a grand, colourful show or parade.

paid the past tense and past participle of **pay**.

pail NOUN a bucket.

pain NOUN ① Pain is an unpleasant feeling of physical hurt. ② Pain is also an unpleasant feeling of deep unhappiness. ▶ VERB ③ If something pains you, it makes you very unhappy. **painless** ADJECTIVE **painlessly** ADVERB

> **pain** NOUN
> ① = ache, discomfort, irritation, soreness, trouble, twinge
> ② = agony, anguish, distress, grief, misery

painful ADJECTIVE ① causing emotional pain. ② causing physical pain. **painfully** ADVERB

> **painful** ADJECTIVE
> ① = distressing, grievous, saddening, unpleasant
> ② = aching, excruciating, sore, tender

painkiller NOUN a drug that reduces or stops pain.

painstaking ADJECTIVE very careful and thorough • *years of painstaking research*.

paint NOUN ① [ART] Paint is a coloured liquid used to decorate buildings, or to make a picture. ▶ VERB ② [ART] If you paint something or paint a picture of it, you make a picture of it using paint. ③ [DGT] When you paint something such as a wall, you cover it with paint. **painter** NOUN **painting** NOUN

pair NOUN ① two things of the same type or that do the same thing • *a pair of earrings*. ② You use 'pair' when referring to certain objects which have two main matching parts • *a pair of scissors*. ▶ VERB ③ When people pair off, they become grouped in pairs. ④ If you pair up with someone, you agree to do something together.

Pakistani [*Said pah-kiss-**tah**-nee*] ADJECTIVE ① belonging or relating to Pakistan. ▶ NOUN ② someone who comes from Pakistan.

pal NOUN (*informal*) a friend.

palace NOUN a large, grand house, especially the official home of a king or queen.

palatable ADJECTIVE Palatable food tastes pleasant.

palate *[Said **pall**-lat]* NOUN ① the top of the inside of your mouth. ② Someone's palate is their ability to judge good food and drink • *dishes to tempt every palate*.

pale ADJECTIVE rather white and without much colour or brightness.

> **pale** ADJECTIVE
> = ashen, colourless, faded, sallow, wan, white

Palestinian ADJECTIVE ① belonging or relating to the region of Palestine, between the River Jordan and the Mediterranean. ▸ NOUN ② an Arab who comes from Palestine.

palette NOUN [ART] a flat piece of wood on which an artist mixes colours.

pall *[Rhymes with **fall**]* VERB ① If something palls, it becomes less interesting or less enjoyable • *This record palls after ten minutes*. ▸ NOUN ② a thick cloud of smoke. ③ a cloth covering a coffin.

palm NOUN ① A palm or palm tree is a tropical tree with no branches and a crown of long leaves. ② the flat surface of your hand which your fingers bend towards.

palpable ADJECTIVE obvious and easily sensed • *Happiness was palpable in the air*.
palpably ADVERB

paltry *[Said **pawl**-tree]* ADJECTIVE A paltry sum of money is a very small amount.

pamper VERB If you pamper someone, you give them too much kindness and comfort.

pamphlet NOUN [ENGLISH] a very thin book in paper covers giving information about something.

pan, pans, panning, panned NOUN ① a round metal container with a long handle, used for cooking things in on top of a cooker. ▸ VERB ② When a film camera pans, it moves in a wide sweep. ③ *(informal)* To pan something is to criticise it strongly.

panacea *[Said pan-nass-**see**-ah]* NOUN something that is supposed to cure everything.

panache *[Said pan-**nash**]* NOUN Something that is done with panache is done confidently and stylishly.

pancake NOUN a thin, flat piece of fried batter which can be served with savoury or sweet fillings.

pancreas *[Said **pang**-kree-ass]* NOUN [SCIENCE] The pancreas is an organ in the body situated behind the stomach. It produces insulin and enzymes that help with digestion.

panda NOUN A panda or giant panda is a large animal rather like a bear that lives in China. It has black fur with large patches of white.

pandemonium *[Said pan-dim-**moan**-ee-um]* NOUN Pandemonium is a state of noisy confusion • *scenes of pandemonium*.

pander VERB If you pander to someone, you do everything they want.

pane NOUN a sheet of glass in a window or door.

panel NOUN ① a small group of people who are chosen to do something • *a panel of judges*. ② a flat piece of wood that is part of a larger object • *door panels*. ③ A control panel is a surface containing switches and instruments to operate a machine.
panelled ADJECTIVE

panelling NOUN Panelling is rectangular pieces of wood covering an inside wall.

pang NOUN a sudden strong feeling of sadness or pain.

panic, **panics**, **panicking**, **panicked** NOUN ① Panic is a sudden overwhelming feeling of fear or anxiety. ▶ VERB ② If you panic, you become so afraid or anxious that you cannot act sensibly.

> **panic** NOUN
> ① = alarm, dismay, fear, fright, hysteria, terror
> ▶ VERB ② = become hysterical, go to pieces, lose your nerve

panorama NOUN an extensive view over a wide area of land • *a fine panorama over the hills.* **panoramic** ADJECTIVE

pant VERB If you pant, you breathe quickly and loudly through your mouth.

panther NOUN a large wild animal belonging to the cat family, especially the black leopard.

pantomime NOUN a musical play, usually based on a fairy story and performed at Christmas.

pantry, **pantries** NOUN a small room where food is kept.

pants PLURAL NOUN ① Pants are a piece of underwear with holes for your legs and elastic around the waist or hips. ② In American English, pants are trousers.

papaya NOUN a fruit with sweet yellow flesh that grows in the West Indies and tropical Australia.

paper NOUN ① Paper is a material made from wood pulp and used for writing on or wrapping things. ② a newspaper. ③ (*in plural*) Papers are official documents, for example a passport for identification. ④ part of a written examination. ▶ VERB ⑤ If you paper a wall, you put wallpaper on it.

paperback NOUN a book with a thin cardboard cover.

paperwork NOUN Paperwork is the part of a job that involves dealing with letters and records.

paprika NOUN Paprika is a red powder made from a kind of pepper.

par PHRASE ① Something that is **on a par** with something else is similar in quality or amount • *This match was on a par with the German Cup Final.* ② Something that is **below par** or **under par** is below its normal standard. ▶ NOUN ③ In golf, par is the number of strokes which it is thought a good player should take for a hole or all the holes on a particular golf course.

parable NOUN [RE] a short story which makes a moral or religious point.

parachute [*Said* ***par****-rash-oot*] NOUN a circular piece of fabric attached by lines to a person or package so that they can fall safely to the ground from an aircraft.

parade NOUN ① a line of people or vehicles standing or moving together as a display. ▶ VERB ② When people parade, they walk together in a group as a display.

> **parade** NOUN
> ① = cavalcade, march, pageant, procession, tattoo

Paradise NOUN According to some religions, Paradise is a wonderful place where good people go when they die.

paradox NOUN something that contains two ideas that seem to contradict each other • *The paradox of exercise is that while you use a lot of energy, it seems to generate more.* **paradoxical** ADJECTIVE

paraffin NOUN Paraffin is a strong-smelling liquid which is used as a fuel.

paragon NOUN someone whose behaviour is perfect in some way • *a paragon of elegance.*

paragraph NOUN [ENGLISH] a section of a piece of writing. Paragraphs begin on a new line.

parallel NOUN ① Something that is a parallel to something else has similar qualities or features to it. ▶ ADJECTIVE ② [MATHS] If two lines are parallel, they are the same distance apart along the whole of their length.

parallelogram NOUN [MATHS] a four-sided shape in which each side is parallel to the opposite side.

paralyse VERB If something paralyses you, it causes loss of feeling and movement in your body.

paralysis *[Said par-**ral**-liss-iss]* NOUN Paralysis is loss of the power to move.

paramedic *[Said par-ram-**med**-dik]* NOUN a person who does some types of medical work, for example for the ambulance service.

parameter *[Said par-**ram**-met-ter]* NOUN a limit which affects the way something is done • *the general parameters set by the president.*

paramilitary ADJECTIVE A paramilitary organisation has a military structure but is not the official army of a country.

paramount ADJECTIVE more important than anything else • *Safety is paramount.*

paranoia *[Said par-ran-**noy**-ah]* NOUN Paranoia is a mental illness in which someone believes that other people are trying to harm them.

paranoid *[Said **par**-ran-noyd]* ADJECTIVE Someone who is paranoid believes wrongly that other people are trying to harm them.

parapet NOUN a low wall along the edge of a bridge or roof.

paraphernalia *[Said par-raf-fan-**ale**-yah]* NOUN Someone's paraphernalia is all their belongings or equipment.

paraphrase NOUN ① A paraphrase of a piece of writing or speech is the same thing said in a different way • *a paraphrase of the popular song.* ▶ VERB ② If you paraphrase what someone has said, you express it in a different way.

parasite NOUN a small animal or plant that lives on or inside a larger animal or plant. **parasitic** ADJECTIVE

paratroops or **paratroopers** PLURAL NOUN Paratroops are soldiers trained to be dropped by parachute.

parcel, parcels, parcelling, parcelled NOUN ① something wrapped up in paper. ▶ VERB ② If you parcel something up, you make it into a parcel.

parched ADJECTIVE ① If the ground is parched, it is very dry and in need of water. ② *(informal)* If you are parched, you are very thirsty.

parchment NOUN Parchment is thick yellowish paper of very good quality.

pardon INTERJECTION ① You say **pardon** or **I beg your pardon** to express surprise or apology, or when you have not heard what someone has said. ▶ VERB ② If you pardon someone, you forgive them for doing something wrong.

pare VERB When you pare fruit or vegetables, you cut off the skin.

parent NOUN Your parents are the people who caused you to be born and who usually look after you while you grow up. **parental** ADJECTIVE

> **parent** NOUN
> = father, mother, old *(Australian and New Zealand; informal)*

parentage NOUN A person's parentage is their parents and ancestors.

parish NOUN an area with its own church and often its own elected council.

parishioner NOUN Parishioners are the people who live in a parish and attend its church.

parity NOUN (*formal*) If there is parity between things, they are equal • *By 1943 the USA had achieved a rough parity of power with the British.*

park NOUN ① a public area with grass and trees. ② a private area of grass and trees around a large country house. ▸ VERB ③ When someone parks a vehicle, they drive it into a position where it can be left. **parked** ADJECTIVE **parking** NOUN

parliament NOUN [CITIZENSHIP] the group of elected representatives who make the laws of a country. **parliamentary** ADJECTIVE

parlour NOUN (*old-fashioned*) a sitting room.

parochial [*Said par-**roe**-key-yal*] ADJECTIVE concerned only with local matters • *narrow parochial interests.*

parody, **parodies**, **parodying**, **parodied** NOUN ① an amusing imitation of the style of an author or of a familiar situation. ▸ VERB ② If you parody something, you make a parody of it.

> **parody** NOUN
> ① = imitation, satire, spoof (*informal*), takeoff (*informal*)

parole NOUN When prisoners are given parole, they are released early on condition that they behave well.

parrot NOUN a brightly coloured tropical bird with a curved beak.

parry, **parries**, **parrying**, **parried** VERB ① If you parry a question, you cleverly avoid answering it • *My searching questions are simply parried with evasions.* ② If you parry a blow, you push aside your attacker's arm to defend yourself.

parsley NOUN Parsley is a herb with curly or flat leaves used for flavouring in cooking.

parsnip NOUN a long, pointed, cream-coloured root vegetable.

part NOUN ① one of the pieces or aspects of something. ② one of the roles in a play or film, played by an actor or actress. ③ Someone's part in something is their involvement in it • *He was jailed for eleven years for his part in the plot.* ▸ PHRASE ④ If you **take part** in an activity, you do it together with other people. ▸ VERB ⑤ If things that are next to each other part, they move away from each other. ⑥ If two people part, they leave each other.

> **part** NOUN
> ① = bit, fraction, fragment, piece, portion, section
> ③ = capacity, duty, function, involvement, role
> ▸ PHRASE ④ = be instrumental in, be involved in, have a hand in, join in, participate in, play a part in

partake, **partakes**, **partaking**, **partook**, **partaken** VERB (*formal*) If you partake of food, you eat it • *She partook of the refreshments offered.*

partial ADJECTIVE ① not complete or whole • *a partial explanation* • *partial success.* ② liking something very much • *I'm very partial to marigolds.* ③ supporting one side in a dispute, rather than being fair and without bias. **partially** ADVERB

participate VERB [CITIZENSHIP] If you participate in an activity, you take part in it. **participant** NOUN **participation** NOUN

> **participate** VERB
> = be involved in, engage in, enter into, join in, take part

particle NOUN ① [SCIENCE] a basic unit of matter, such as an atom, molecule or electron. ② a very small piece of something.

particular ADJECTIVE ① relating or belonging to only one thing or person

• *That particular place is dangerous.* ② especially great or intense • *Pay particular attention to the oral part of the exam.* ③ Someone who is particular has high standards and is not easily satisfied. **particularly** ADVERB

particular ADJECTIVE
① = distinct, exact, express, peculiar, precise, specific
② = exceptional, marked, notable, singular, special, uncommon
③ = choosy (*informal*), exacting, fastidious, fussy, meticulous

parting NOUN an occasion when one person leaves another.

partisan ADJECTIVE ① favouring or supporting one person or group • *a partisan crowd.* ▸ NOUN ② a member of an unofficial armed force fighting to free their country from enemy occupation • *Norwegian partisans in World War II.*

partition NOUN ① a screen separating one part of a room or vehicle from another. ② Partition is the division of a country into independent areas. ▸ VERB ③ To partition something is to divide it into separate parts.

partly ADVERB to some extent but not completely.

partly ADVERB
= in part (*formal*), in some measure (*formal*), partially, to some degree, to some extent

partner NOUN ① Someone's partner is the person they are married to or are living with. ② Your partner is the person you are doing something with, for example in a dance or a game. ③ Business partners are joint owners of their business. ▸ VERB ④ If you partner someone, you are their partner for a game or social occasion. **partnership** NOUN

partner NOUN
① = husband, mate, spouse, wife
② = companion, date, plus-one (*informal*), team-mate

partridge NOUN a brown game bird with a round body and a short tail.

part-time ADJECTIVE involving work for only a part of the working day or week.

party, **parties** NOUN ① a social event held for people to enjoy themselves. ② CITIZENSHIP an organisation whose members share the same political beliefs and campaign for election to government. ③ a group who are doing something together. ④ (*formal*) one of the people involved in a legal agreement or dispute.

party NOUN
① = celebration, function, gathering, get-together (*informal*), hooley, hoolie, reception
② = alliance, clique, coalition, faction, grouping
③ = band, crew, gang, squad, team, unit

pass VERB ① To pass something is to move past it. ② To pass in a particular direction is to move in that direction • *We passed through the gate.* ③ If you pass something to someone, you hand it to them or transfer it to them. ④ If you pass a period of time doing something, you spend it that way • *He hoped to pass the long night in meditation.* ⑤ When a period of time passes, it happens and finishes. ⑥ If you pass a test, you are considered to be of an acceptable standard. ⑦ When a new law or proposal is passed, it is formally approved. ⑧ When a judge passes sentence on someone, the judge states what the punishment will be. ⑨ If you pass the ball in a ball game, you throw, kick or hit it to another player in your team. ▶ **NOUN** ⑩ the transfer of the ball in a ball game to another player in the same team. ⑪ an official document that allows you to go somewhere. ⑫ a narrow route between mountains. **pass away** or **pass on** **VERB** Someone who has passed away has died. **pass out** **VERB** If someone passes out, they faint. **pass up** **VERB** (*informal*) If you pass up an opportunity, you do not take advantage of it.

> **pass VERB**
> ① = exceed, go beyond, outdo, outstrip, overtake, surpass
> ⑥ = get through, graduate, qualify, succeed
> ≠ fail
> ▶ **NOUN** ⑪ = identification, passport, ticket

passable **ADJECTIVE** of an acceptable standard • *a passable imitation of his dad.*

passage **NOUN** ① a space that connects two places. ② a long, narrow corridor. ③ a section of a book or piece of music.

> **passage NOUN**
> ① = channel, course, path, road, route, way
> ② = aisle, corridor, hall, lobby
> ③ = excerpt, extract, quotation, section

passenger **NOUN** a person travelling in a vehicle, aircraft or ship.

passer-by, **passers-by** **NOUN** someone who is walking past someone or something.

passing **ADJECTIVE** lasting only for a short time • *a passing phase.*

passion **NOUN** ① Passion is a very strong feeling of attraction. ② Passion is also any strong emotion.

> **passion NOUN**
> ② = emotion, excitement, fire, intensity, warmth, zeal

passionate **ADJECTIVE** involving very strong feelings about something. **passionately** **ADVERB**

> **passionate ADJECTIVE**
> = ardent, emotional, heartfelt, impassioned, intense, strong

passive **ADJECTIVE** ① remaining calm and showing no feeling when provoked. ▶ **NOUN** ② ENGLISH In grammar, the passive or passive voice is the form of the verb in which the person or thing to which an action is being done is the grammatical subject of the sentence, and is given more emphasis as a result. For example, the passive of *The committee rejected your application* is *Your application was rejected by the committee*. **passively** **ADVERB** **passivity** **NOUN**

> **passive ADJECTIVE**
> ① = docile, receptive, resigned, submissive

Passover **NOUN** RE The Passover is an eight-day Jewish festival held in spring.

passport **NOUN** an official identification document which you need to show when you travel abroad.

password **NOUN** ① a secret word known to only a few people. It allows people on the same side to recognise a friend. ② ICT a word or series of numbers and letters that you need to know to get into a computer, mobile phone, security system, etc.

past **NOUN** ① The past is the period of time before the present. ▶ **ADJECTIVE** ② Past things are things that happened or existed before the present • *the past 30 years.* ③ ENGLISH MFL The past tense of a verb is the form used to express something that happened in the past. ▶ **PREPOSITION**, **ADVERB** ④ You use 'past' when you are telling the time • *It was ten past eleven.* ⑤ If you go past something, you move towards it and continue until you are on the other side • *They drove rapidly past their cottage.* ▶ PREPOSITION ⑥ Something that is past a place is situated on the other side of it • *It's just past the church there.*

past NOUN
① = antiquity, days gone by, former times, long ago
▶ ADJECTIVE ② = ancient, bygone, former, olden, previous
≠ future
▶ PREPOSITION ⑥ = beyond, by, over

pasta NOUN Pasta is a dried mixture of flour, eggs and water, formed into different shapes.

paste NOUN ① Paste is a soft, rather sticky mixture that can be easily spread • *tomato paste.* ▶ VERB ② If you paste something onto a surface, you stick it with glue.

pastel ADJECTIVE ① Pastel colours are pale and soft. ▶ NOUN ② [ART] Pastels are small sticks of coloured crayon, used for drawing pictures.

pastime NOUN a hobby or something you do just for pleasure.

pastime NOUN
= activity, diversion, hobby, recreation

pastor NOUN a member of the clergy in charge of a congregation.

pastoral ADJECTIVE ① characteristic of peaceful country life and landscape • *pastoral scenes.* ② relating to the duties of the clergy in caring for the needs of their parishioners, or of a school in caring for the needs of its students • *a pastoral visit* • *Most schools have some system of pastoral care.*

pastry, **pastries** NOUN ① Pastry is a mixture of flour, fat and water, rolled flat and used for making pies. ② a small cake.

past tense NOUN [ENGLISH] [MFL] In grammar, the past tense is the tense of a verb that you use mainly to refer to things that happened or existed before the time of writing or speaking.

pasture NOUN Pasture is an area of grass on which farm animals graze.

pasty, **pastier**, **pastiest**; **pasties** ADJECTIVE ① *[Rhymes with* ***hasty****]* Someone who is pasty looks pale and unhealthy. ▶ NOUN ② *[Said* ***pass****-tee]* a small pie containing meat and vegetables.

pat, **pats**, **patting**, **patted** VERB ① If you pat something, you tap it lightly with your hand held flat. ▶ NOUN ② a small lump of butter.

patch NOUN ① a piece of material used to cover a hole in something. ② an area of a surface that is different in appearance from the rest • *a bald patch.* ▶ VERB ③ If you patch something, you mend it by fixing a patch over the hole. **patch up** VERB If you patch something up, you mend it hurriedly or temporarily.

patchwork ADJECTIVE ① A patchwork quilt is made from many small pieces of material sewn together. ▶ NOUN ② Something that is a patchwork is made up of many parts.

patchy, **patchier**, **patchiest** ADJECTIVE Something that is patchy is unevenly spread or incomplete in parts • *patchy fog on the hills.*

patent NOUN ① an official right given to an inventor to be the only person or company allowed to make or sell a new product. ▶ VERB ② If you patent something, you obtain a patent for it. ▶ ADJECTIVE ③ obvious • *This was patent nonsense.* **patently** ADVERB

paternal ADJECTIVE relating to a father • *paternal pride.*

paternity NOUN Paternity is the state or fact of being a father.

path NOUN ① a strip of ground for people to walk on. ② Your path is the area ahead of you and the direction in which you are moving.

> **path** NOUN
> ① = footpath, pathway, towpath, track, trail, way
> ② = course, direction, passage, route, way

pathetic ADJECTIVE ① If something is pathetic, it makes you feel pity. ② Pathetic also means very poor or unsuccessful • *a pathetic attempt*. **pathetically** ADVERB

> **pathetic** ADJECTIVE
> ① = heartbreaking, sad
> ② = feeble, lamentable, pitiful, poor, sorry

pathological ADJECTIVE extreme and uncontrollable • *a pathological fear of snakes*. **pathologically** ADVERB

pathology NOUN Pathology is the study of diseases and the way they develop. **pathologist** NOUN

pathos [*Said* ***pay****-thoss*] NOUN Pathos is a quality in literature or art that causes great sadness or pity.

pathway NOUN a path.

patience NOUN Patience is the ability to stay calm in a difficult or irritating situation.

> **patience** NOUN
> = calmness, composure, cool (*slang*), restraint, tolerance

patient ADJECTIVE ① If you are patient, you stay calm in a difficult or irritating situation. ▶ NOUN ② a person receiving medical treatment from a doctor or in a hospital. **patiently** ADVERB

> **patient** ADJECTIVE
> ① = calm, composed, long-suffering, philosophical, serene
> ≠ impatient
> ▶ NOUN ② = case, sick person

patio, **patios** NOUN a paved area close to a house.

patriarch [*Said* ***pay****-tree-ark*] NOUN a man who is the head of a family in a society in which power passes from father to son. **patriarchy** NOUN **patriarchal** ADJECTIVE

patrician ADJECTIVE (*formal*) belonging to a family of high rank.

patriot NOUN someone who loves their country and feels very loyal towards it. **patriotic** ADJECTIVE **patriotism** NOUN

patrol, **patrols**, **patrolling**, **patrolled** VERB ① When soldiers, police or guards patrol an area, they walk or drive around to make sure there is no trouble. ▶ NOUN ② a group of people patrolling an area.

patron NOUN ① a person who supports or gives money to artists, writers or musicians. ② The patrons of a hotel, pub or shop are the people who use it. **patronage** NOUN

patronise; also spelt **patronize** VERB ① If someone patronises you, they treat you kindly, but in a way that suggests that you are less intelligent than them or inferior to them. ② If you patronise a hotel, pub or shop, you are a customer there. **patronising** ADJECTIVE

patron saint NOUN The patron saint of a group of people or place is a saint who is believed to look after them.

patter VERB ① If something patters on a surface, it makes quick, light tapping sounds. ▶ NOUN ② a series of light tapping sounds • *a patter of light rain*.

pattern NOUN ① a decorative design of repeated shapes. ② The pattern of something is the way it is usually done or happens • *a perfectly normal pattern of behaviour*. ③ a diagram or shape used as a guide for making

something, for example clothes.
patterned ADJECTIVE

pattern NOUN
① = design, motif
③ = design, diagram, plan, stencil, template

pauper NOUN (*old-fashioned*) a very poor person.

pause VERB ① If you pause, you stop what you are doing for a short time. ▶ NOUN ② a short period when you stop what you are doing.

pause VERB
① = break, delay, halt, rest, take a break, wait
▶ NOUN ② = break, halt, interruption, interval, rest, stoppage

pave VERB When an area of ground is paved, it is covered with flat blocks of stone or concrete.

pavement NOUN a path with a hard surface at the side of a road.

pavilion NOUN a building at a sports ground where players can wash and change.

paw NOUN ① The paws of an animal such as a cat or bear are its feet with claws and soft pads. ▶ VERB ② If an animal paws something, it hits it or scrapes at it with its paws.

pawn VERB ① If you pawn something, you leave it with a pawnbroker in exchange for money. ▶ NOUN ② the smallest and least valuable playing piece in chess.

pay, pays, paying, paid VERB ① When you pay money to someone, you give it to them because you are buying something or owe it to them. ② If it pays to do something, it is to your advantage to do it • *They say it pays to advertise.* ③ If you pay for something that you have done, you suffer as a result. ④ If you pay attention to something, you give it your attention. ⑤ If you pay a visit to someone, you visit them. ▶ NOUN ⑥ Someone's pay is their salary or wages.

pay VERB
① = compensate, honour, settle
② = be advantageous, be worthwhile
▶ NOUN ⑥ = earnings, fee, income, payment, salary, wages

payable ADJECTIVE An amount of money that is payable has to be paid or can be paid • *All fees are payable in advance.*

payment NOUN ① Payment is the act of paying money. ② a sum of money paid.

payment NOUN
② = advance, deposit, instalment, premium, remittance

payroll NOUN Someone who is on an organisation's payroll is employed and paid by them.

PC NOUN ① In Britain, PC is an abbreviation for 'police constable'. ② a personal computer. ▶ ADJECTIVE ③ short for **politically correct**.

PE an abbreviation for 'physical education'.

pea NOUN Peas are small, round, green seeds that grow in pods and are eaten as a vegetable.

peace NOUN ① Peace is a state of calm and quiet when there is no disturbance of any kind. ② When a country is at peace, it is not at war.
peaceable ADJECTIVE

peace NOUN
① = calm, quiet, silence, stillness, tranquillity
② = armistice, cessation of hostilities, truce
≠ war

peaceful ADJECTIVE quiet and calm.
peacefully ADVERB

peaceful ADJECTIVE
= calm, placid, quiet, serene, still, tranquil

peach NOUN ① a soft, round fruit with yellow flesh and a yellow and red skin. ▸ ADJECTIVE ② pale orange with a hint of pink.

peacock NOUN a large bird with green and blue feathers. The male has a long tail which it can spread out in a fan.

peak NOUN ① The peak of an activity or process is the point at which it is strongest or most successful. ② the pointed top of a mountain. ▸ VERB ③ When something peaks, it reaches its highest value or its greatest level of success. **peaked** ADJECTIVE

> **peak** NOUN
> ① = climax, culmination, high point, zenith
> ② = brow, crest, pinnacle, summit, top
> ▸ VERB ③ = be at its height, climax, come to a head, culminate, reach its highest point

peanut NOUN Peanuts are small oval nuts that grow under the ground.

pear NOUN a fruit which is narrow at the top and wide and rounded at the bottom.

pearl NOUN a hard, round, creamy-white object used to make jewellery. Pearls grow inside the shell of an oyster.

peasant NOUN In some countries, a peasant is a person who works on the land.

peat NOUN Peat is dark-brown decaying plant material found in cool, wet regions. Dried peat can be used as fuel.

pebble NOUN a smooth, round stone.

peck VERB ① If a bird pecks something, it bites at it quickly with its beak. ② If you peck someone on the cheek, you give them a quick kiss. ▸ NOUN ③ a quick bite by a bird. ④ a quick kiss on the cheek.

peculiar ADJECTIVE ① strange and perhaps unpleasant. ② relating or belonging only to a particular person or thing • *a gesture peculiar to her.* **peculiarly** ADVERB **peculiarity** NOUN

> **peculiar** ADJECTIVE
> ① = bizarre, curious, funny, odd, queer (*old-fashioned*), strange, weird
> ② = distinctive, distinguishing, individual, personal, special, unique

pedal, **pedals**, **pedalling**, **pedalled** NOUN ① a control lever on a machine or vehicle that you press with your foot. ▸ VERB ② When you pedal a bicycle, you push the pedals round with your feet to move along.

pedantic ADJECTIVE If a person is pedantic, they are too concerned with unimportant details and traditional rules.

peddle VERB Someone who peddles something sells it.

pedestal NOUN a base on which a statue stands.

pedestrian NOUN ① someone who is walking. ▸ ADJECTIVE ② Pedestrian means ordinary and rather dull • *a pedestrian performance.*

pedestrian crossing NOUN a specially marked place where you can cross the road safely.

pediatrician another spelling of **paediatrician**.

pediatrics another spelling of **paediatrics**.

pedigree ADJECTIVE ① A pedigree animal is descended from a single breed and its ancestors are known and recorded. ▸ NOUN ② Someone's pedigree is their background or ancestry.

peek VERB ① If you peek at something, you have a quick look at it • *I peeked round the corner.* ▸ NOUN ② a quick look at something.

peek VERB
① = glance, peep, snatch a glimpse, sneak a look
▸ NOUN ② = glance, glimpse, look, peep

peel NOUN ① The peel of a fruit is the skin when it has been removed. ▸ VERB ② When you peel fruit or vegetables, you remove the skin. ③ If a surface is peeling, it is coming off in thin layers. **peelings** PLURAL NOUN

peep VERB ① If you peep at something, you have a quick look at it. ② If something peeps out from behind something else, a small part of it becomes visible • *a handkerchief peeping out of his breast pocket*. ▸ NOUN ③ a quick look at something.

peer VERB ① If you peer at something, you look at it very hard. ▸ NOUN ② a member of the nobility. ③ Your peers are the people who are of the same age and social status as yourself.

peerage NOUN ① The peers in a country are called the peerage. ② A peerage is also the rank of being a peer.

peer group NOUN Your peer group is the people who are of the same age and social status as yourself.

peerless ADJECTIVE so magnificent that nothing can equal it • *a peerless cast of actors*.

peg, **pegs**, **pegging**, **pegged** NOUN ① a plastic or wooden clip used for hanging wet clothes on a line. ② a hook on a wall where you can hang things. ▸ VERB ③ If you peg clothes on a line, you fix them there with pegs. ④ If a price is pegged at a certain level, it is fixed at that level.

pejorative *[Said pej-**jor**-ra-tiv]* ADJECTIVE A pejorative word expresses criticism.

pelican NOUN a large water bird with a pouch beneath its beak in which it stores fish.

pellet NOUN a small ball of paper, lead or other material.

pelt VERB ① If you pelt someone with things, you throw the things with force at them. ② (*informal*) If you pelt along, you run very fast. ▸ NOUN ③ the skin and fur of an animal.

pelvis NOUN the wide, curved group of bones at hip level at the base of your spine. **pelvic** ADJECTIVE

pen, **pens**, **penning**, **penned** NOUN ① a long, thin instrument used for writing with ink. ② a small fenced area in which farm animals are kept for a short time. ▸ VERB ③ (*literary*) If someone pens a letter or article, they write it. ④ If you are penned in or penned up, you have to remain in an uncomfortably small area.

penal ADJECTIVE relating to the punishment of criminals.

penalise; also spelt **penalize** VERB If you are penalised, you are made to suffer some disadvantage as a punishment for something.

penalty, **penalties** NOUN ① a punishment or disadvantage that someone is made to suffer. ② In soccer, a penalty is a free kick at goal that is given to the attacking team if the defending team have committed a foul near their goal.

penance NOUN If you do penance, you do something unpleasant to show that you are sorry for something wrong that you have done.

pence a plural form of **penny**.

penchant *[Said **pon**-shon]* NOUN (*formal*) If you have a penchant for something, you have a particular liking for it • *a penchant for crime*.

pencil NOUN a long, thin stick of wood with graphite in the centre, used for drawing or writing.

pendant NOUN a piece of jewellery attached to a chain and worn round the neck.

pending (*formal*) ADJECTIVE ① Something that is pending is waiting to be dealt with or will happen soon. ▶ PREPOSITION ② Something that is done pending a future event is done until the event happens • *The army should stay in the west pending a future war.*

pendulum NOUN a rod with a weight at one end in a clock which swings regularly from side to side to control the clock.

penetrate VERB To penetrate an area that is difficult to get into is to succeed in getting into it.
penetration NOUN

penetrating ADJECTIVE ① loud and high-pitched • *a penetrating voice.* ② having or showing deep understanding • *penetrating questions.*

penguin NOUN A penguin is a black and white bird with webbed feet and small wings like flippers. Penguins are found mainly in the Antarctic.

penicillin NOUN Penicillin is a powerful antibiotic obtained from fungus and used to treat infections.

peninsula NOUN GEOGRAPHY an area of land almost surrounded by water.

penis NOUN SCIENCE A man's penis is the part of his body used for urination and reproduction.

pennant NOUN a triangular flag, especially one used by ships as a signal.

penniless ADJECTIVE Someone who is penniless has no money.

penny, **pennies** or **pence** NOUN a unit of currency in Britain and some other countries. In Britain a penny is worth one-hundredth of a pound.

pension [*Said* ***pen**-shn*] NOUN a regular sum of money paid to an old or retired person.

pensioner NOUN an old or retired person who gets a pension paid by the state.

pensive ADJECTIVE deep in thought.

pentathlon [*Said pen-**tath**-lon*] NOUN a sports contest in which athletes compete in five different events.

penthouse NOUN a luxurious flat at the top of a building.

pent-up ADJECTIVE Pent-up emotions have been held back for a long time without release.

pent-up ADJECTIVE
= inhibited, repressed, suppressed

penultimate ADJECTIVE The penultimate thing in a series is the one before the last.

people, **peoples**, **peopling**, **peopled** PLURAL NOUN ① People are men, women and children. ▶ NOUN ② all the men, women and children of a particular country or race. ▶ VERB ③ If an area is peopled by a particular group, that group of people live there.

people PLURAL NOUN
① = human beings, humanity, humans, mankind
▶ NOUN ② = citizens, inhabitants, population, public

pepper NOUN ① a hot-tasting powdered spice used for flavouring in cooking. ② a hollow green, orange, red or yellow fruit eaten as a vegetable, with sweet-flavoured flesh.

peppermint NOUN Peppermint is a plant with a strong taste. It is used for making sweets and in medicine.

per PREPOSITION 'Per' is used to mean 'each' when expressing rates and ratios • *The class meets two evenings per week.*

perceive VERB If you perceive something that is not obvious, you see it or realise it.

per cent PHRASE You use **per cent** to talk about amounts as a proportion of a hundred. An amount that is 10 per cent (10%) of a larger amount is equal to 10 hundredths of the larger amount • *20 per cent of voters have still not decided who to vote for.*

percentage NOUN [MATHS] a fraction expressed as a number of hundredths • *How do you show one fifth as a percentage?*

perceptible ADJECTIVE Something that is perceptible can be seen • *a barely perceptible nod.*

perception NOUN ① Perception is the recognition of things using the senses, especially the sense of sight. ② Someone who has perception realises or notices things that are not obvious. ③ Your perception of something or someone is your understanding of them.

perceptive ADJECTIVE Someone who is perceptive realises or notices things that are not obvious. **perceptively** ADVERB

> **perceptive** ADJECTIVE
> = acute, astute, aware, penetrating, sharp

perch VERB ① If you perch on something, you sit on the edge of it. ② When a bird perches on something, it stands on it. ▶ NOUN ③ a short rod for a bird to stand on. ④ an edible freshwater fish.

percussion ADJECTIVE, NOUN [MUSIC] Percussion instruments or percussion are musical instruments that you hit to produce sounds. **percussionist** NOUN

perennial ADJECTIVE continually occurring or never ending • *The damp cellar was a perennial problem.*

perfect ADJECTIVE *[Said* ***per****-fect]* ① of the highest standard and without fault • *His English was perfect.* ② complete or absolute • *They have a perfect right to say so.* ③ [ENGLISH] [MFL] In grammar, the perfect tenses of a verb are used to talk about things that happened before a particular time. The **present perfect** is formed in English with the present tense of 'have' and the past participle of the main verb, as in 'She has spoken'. The **past perfect** is formed with 'had' and the past participle of the main verb, as in 'She had spoken'. ▶ VERB *[Said per-****fect****]* ④ If you perfect something, you make it as good as it can possibly be. **perfectly** ADVERB **perfection** NOUN

> **perfect** ADJECTIVE
> ① = expert, faultless, flawless, masterly, polished, skilled
> ≠ imperfect
> ② = absolute, complete, consummate, sheer, unmitigated, utter
> ▶ VERB ④ = hone, improve, polish, refine

perfectionist NOUN someone who always tries to do everything perfectly.

perforated ADJECTIVE Something that is perforated has had small holes made in it. **perforation** NOUN

perform VERB ① To perform a task or action is to do it. ② [DRAMA] To perform is to act, dance or play music in front of an audience. **performer** NOUN

> **perform** VERB
> ① = carry out, complete, do, execute, fulfil
> ② = act, do, play, present, put on, stage

performance NOUN ① [DRAMA] an entertainment provided for an audience. ② The performance of a task or action is the doing of it. ③ Someone's or something's performance is how successful they are • *the poor performance of the local economy.*

perfume NOUN ① Perfume is a pleasant-smelling liquid for putting on the body. ② The perfume of something is its pleasant smell. **perfumed** ADJECTIVE

perfunctory ADJECTIVE done quickly without interest or care • *a perfunctory kiss.*

perhaps ADVERB You use 'perhaps' when you are not sure whether something is true or possible.

> **perhaps** ADVERB
> = conceivably, it could be, maybe, possibly

peril NOUN (*formal*) Peril is great danger. **perilous** ADJECTIVE **perilously** ADVERB

perimeter NOUN [MATHS] The perimeter of a closed figure or shape is the length of its boundary.

period NOUN ① a particular length of time. ② one of the parts the day is divided into at school. ③ A woman's period is the monthly bleeding from her womb. ▸ ADJECTIVE ④ relating to a historical period of time • *period furniture.* **periodic** ADJECTIVE **periodically** ADVERB

> **period** NOUN
> ① = interval, spell, stretch, term, time, while

periodical NOUN a magazine.

peripheral [*Said per-**rif**-fer-ral*] ADJECTIVE ① of little importance in comparison with other things • *a peripheral activity.* ② on or relating to the edge of an area.

periphery, **peripheries** NOUN The periphery of an area is its outside edge.

perish VERB ① (*formal*) If someone or something perishes, they are killed or destroyed. ② If fruit or fabric perishes, it rots. **perishable** ADJECTIVE

perjury NOUN (*Law*) If someone commits perjury, they tell a lie in court while under oath. **perjure** VERB

perk NOUN ① an extra, such as a company car, offered by an employer in addition to a salary. Perk is an abbreviation for 'perquisite'. ▸ VERB ② (*informal*) When someone perks up, they become more cheerful. **perky** ADJECTIVE

perm NOUN ① If you have a perm, your hair is curled and treated with chemicals to keep the curls for several months. ▸ VERB ② To perm someone's hair means to put a perm in it.

permanent ADJECTIVE lasting for ever, or present all the time. **permanently** ADVERB **permanence** NOUN

> **permanent** ADJECTIVE
> = abiding, constant, enduring, eternal, lasting, perpetual
> ≠ temporary

permeate VERB To permeate something is to spread through it and affect every part of it • *A sense of optimism permeates everything that the organisation does.*

permissible ADJECTIVE allowed by the rules.

permission NOUN If you have permission to do something, you are allowed to do it.

> **permission** NOUN
> = approval, assent (*formal*), authorisation, consent, go-ahead, licence
> ≠ ban

permissive ADJECTIVE A permissive society allows things which some people disapprove of. **permissiveness** NOUN

permit, **permits**, **permitting**, **permitted** VERB ① To permit something is to allow it or make it possible. ▶ NOUN ② an official document which says that you are allowed to do something.

permit VERB
① = allow, authorise, enable, give the green light to, grant, sanction
≠ ban
▶ NOUN ② = authorisation, licence, pass, passport, permission, warrant

pernicious ADJECTIVE (*formal*) very harmful • *the pernicious influence of television*.

peroxide NOUN Peroxide is a chemical used for bleaching hair or as an antiseptic.

perpendicular ADJECTIVE MATHS upright, or at right angles to a horizontal line.

perpetrate VERB (*formal*) To perpetrate a crime is to commit it. **perpetrator** NOUN

perpetual ADJECTIVE never ending • *a perpetual toothache*. **perpetually** ADVERB **perpetuity** NOUN

perpetuate VERB To perpetuate a situation or belief is to cause it to continue • *The television series will perpetuate the myths*.

perplexed ADJECTIVE If you are perplexed, you are puzzled and do not know what to do.

persecute VERB To persecute someone is to treat them cruelly and unfairly over a long period of time. **persecution** NOUN **persecutor** NOUN

persecute VERB
= hound, ill-treat, oppress, pick on, torment, torture

persevere VERB If you persevere, you keep trying to do something and do not give up. **perseverance** NOUN

Persian [*Said per-zhn*] ADJECTIVE, NOUN an old word for **Iranian**, used especially when referring to the older forms of the language.

persist VERB ① If something undesirable persists, it continues to exist. ② If you persist in doing something, you continue in spite of opposition or difficulty. **persistence** NOUN **persistent** ADJECTIVE

person, **people** or **persons** NOUN ① a man, woman or child. ② MFL In grammar, the first person is the speaker (I), the second person is the person being spoken to (you), and the third person is anyone else being referred to (he, she, they).

person NOUN
① = human, human being, individual, living soul, soul

personal ADJECTIVE ① Personal means belonging or relating to a particular person rather than to people in general • *my personal feeling*. ② Personal matters relate to your feelings, relationships and health which you may not wish to discuss with other people. **personally** ADVERB

personal ADJECTIVE
① = individual, own, particular, peculiar, private, special

personality, **personalities** NOUN ① Your personality is your character and nature. ② a famous person in entertainment or sport.

personality NOUN
① = character, identity, individuality, make-up, nature, psyche
② = big name, celebrity, famous name, household name, star

personification NOUN ① ENGLISH Personification is a form of imagery in which something inanimate is described as if it has human qualities, for example 'The trees sighed and whispered as the impatient breeze stirred their branches'. ② Someone who is the personification of some quality is a living example of that quality • *He was the personification of evil.*

personify, **personifies**, **personifying**, **personified** VERB ① Someone who personifies a particular quality seems to be a living example of it. ② If you personify a thing or concept, you write or speak of it as if it has human abilities or qualities, for example 'The sun is trying to come out'.

personnel [*Said per-son-**nell***] NOUN The personnel of an organisation are the people who work for it.

perspective NOUN ① A particular perspective is one way of thinking about something. ② ART Perspective is a method artists use to make some people and things seem further away than others.

perspiration NOUN Perspiration is the moisture that appears on your skin when you are hot or frightened.

persuade VERB If someone persuades you to do something or persuades you that something is true, they make you do it or believe it by giving you very good reasons. **persuasion** NOUN **persuasive** ADJECTIVE

persuade VERB
= bring round (*informal*), coax, induce, sway, talk into, win over

pertaining ADJECTIVE (*formal*) If information or questions are pertaining to a place or thing, they are about that place or thing • *issues pertaining to women.*

pertinent ADJECTIVE especially relevant to the subject being discussed • *He asks pertinent questions.*

perturbed ADJECTIVE Someone who is perturbed is worried.

Peruvian [*Said per-**roo**-vee-an*] ADJECTIVE ① belonging or relating to Peru. ▶ NOUN ② someone who comes from Peru.

pervade VERB Something that pervades a place is present and noticeable throughout it • *a fear that pervades the community.* **pervasive** ADJECTIVE

perverse ADJECTIVE Someone who is perverse deliberately does things that are unreasonable or harmful. **perversely** ADVERB **perversity** NOUN

pervert VERB (*formal*) To pervert something is to interfere with it so that it is no longer what it should be • *a conspiracy to pervert the course of justice.*

perverted ADJECTIVE ① Someone who is perverted has disgusting or unacceptable behaviour or ideas. ② Something that is perverted is completely wrong • *a perverted sense of value.*

peso, **pesos** [*Said **pay**-soh*] NOUN the main unit of currency in several South American countries.

pessimism NOUN Pessimism is the tendency to believe that bad things will happen. **pessimist** NOUN

pessimistic ADJECTIVE believing that bad things will happen. **pessimistically** ADVERB

pessimistic ADJECTIVE
= despondent, gloomy, glum, hopeless
≠ optimistic

pest NOUN ① an insect or small animal which damages plants or food supplies. ② (*informal*) someone who keeps bothering or annoying you.

pest NOUN
① = bane, blight, scourge
② = bane, bore, nuisance, pain (*informal*), pain in the neck (*informal*)

pester VERB If you pester someone, you keep bothering them or asking them to do something.

pester VERB
= annoy, badger, bother, bug (*informal*), drive someone up the wall (*slang*), get on someone's nerves (*informal*)

pesticide NOUN SCIENCE Pesticides are chemicals sprayed onto plants to kill insects and grubs.

pet, **pets**, **petting**, **petted** NOUN ① a tame animal kept at home. ▶ ADJECTIVE ② Someone's pet theory or pet project is something that they particularly support or feel strongly about. ▶ VERB ③ If you pet a person or animal, you stroke them affectionately.

petal NOUN The petals of a flower are the coloured outer parts.

petite [*Said pet-**teet***] ADJECTIVE A woman who is petite is small and slim.

petition NOUN ① a document demanding official action which is signed by a lot of people. ② a formal request to a court for legal action to be taken. ▶ VERB ③ If you petition someone in authority, you make a formal request to them • *I petitioned the government for permission to visit its country.*

petrified ADJECTIVE If you are petrified, you are very frightened.

petrol NOUN SCIENCE Petrol is a liquid obtained from petroleum and used as a fuel for motor vehicles.

petroleum NOUN Petroleum is thick, dark oil found under the earth or under the sea bed.

petty, **pettier**, **pettiest** ADJECTIVE ① Petty things are small and unimportant. ② Petty behaviour consists of doing small things which are selfish and unkind.

petty ADJECTIVE
① = insignificant, measly (*informal*), trifling, trivial, unimportant
② = cheap, mean, small-minded

petulant ADJECTIVE showing unreasonable and childish impatience or anger. **petulantly** ADVERB **petulance** NOUN

pew NOUN a long wooden seat with a back, which people sit on in church.

pewter NOUN Pewter is a silvery-grey metal made from a mixture of tin and lead.

pH NOUN SCIENCE The pH of a solution or of the soil is a measurement of how acid or alkaline it is. Acid solutions have a pH of less than 7 and alkaline solutions have a pH greater than 7. pH is an abbreviation for 'potential of hydrogen'.

phantom NOUN ① a ghost. ▶ ADJECTIVE ② imagined or unreal • *a phantom illness.*

pharaoh [*Said **fair**-oh*] NOUN The pharaohs were kings of ancient Egypt.

pharmaceutical [*Said far-mass-**yoo**-tik-kl*] ADJECTIVE connected with the industrial production of medicines.

pharmacist NOUN a person who is qualified to prepare and sell medicines.

pharmacy, **pharmacies** NOUN a shop where medicines are sold.

phase NOUN ① a particular stage in the development of something. ▶ VERB ② To phase something is to cause it to happen gradually in stages.

PhD NOUN a degree awarded to someone who has done advanced research in a subject. PhD is an abbreviation for 'Doctor of Philosophy'.

pheasant NOUN a large, long-tailed game bird.

phenomenal [*Said fin-**nom**-in-nal*] ADJECTIVE extraordinarily great or good. **phenomenally** ADVERB

phenomenon, **phenomena** NOUN something that happens or exists, especially something remarkable or something being considered in a scientific way • *a well-known geographical phenomenon.*

philanthropist *[Said fil-**lan**-throp-pist]* NOUN someone who freely gives help or money to people in need. **philanthropic** ADJECTIVE **philanthropy** NOUN

philistine NOUN If you call someone a philistine, you mean that they do not like art, literature or music.

philosophical or **philosophic** ADJECTIVE Someone who is philosophical does not get upset when disappointing things happen.

philosophy, **philosophies** NOUN ① Philosophy is the study or creation of ideas about existence, knowledge or beliefs. ② a set of beliefs that a person has. **philosopher** NOUN

phobia NOUN a great fear or hatred of something • *The man had a phobia about flying.* **phobic** ADJECTIVE

-phobia SUFFIX '-phobia' means 'fear of' • *claustrophobia.*

phoenix *[Said **fee**-niks]* NOUN an imaginary bird which, according to myth, burns itself to ashes every five hundred years and rises from the fire again.

phone NOUN ① a piece of electronic equipment which allows you to speak to someone in another place by keying in or dialling their number. ▸ VERB ② If you phone someone, you key in or dial their number and speak to them using a phone.

-phone SUFFIX '-phone' means 'giving off sound' • *telephone* • *gramophone.*

phoney, **phonier**, **phoniest**; **phoneys**; also spelt **phony** *(informal)* ADJECTIVE ① false and intended to deceive. ▸ NOUN ② Someone who is a phoney pretends to have qualities they do not possess.

photo, **photos** NOUN *(informal)* a photograph.

photocopier NOUN a machine which makes instant copies of documents by photographing them.

photocopy, **photocopies**, **photocopying**, **photocopied** [LIBRARY] NOUN ① a copy of a document produced by a photocopier. ▸ VERB ② If you photocopy a document, you make a copy of it using a photocopier.

photogenic ADJECTIVE Someone who is photogenic always looks nice in photographs.

photograph NOUN ① a picture made using a camera. ▸ VERB ② When you photograph someone, you take a picture of them by using a camera. **photographer** NOUN **photography** NOUN

photographic ADJECTIVE connected with photography.

photosynthesis NOUN [SCIENCE] Photosynthesis is the process by which the action of sunlight on the chlorophyll in plants produces the substances that keep the plants alive.

phrase NOUN ① a group of words considered as a unit. ▸ VERB ② If you phrase something in a particular way, you choose those words to express it • *I should have phrased that better.*

physical ADJECTIVE ① concerning the body rather than the mind. ② relating to things that can be touched or seen, especially with regard to their size or shape • *the physical characteristics of their machinery* • *the physical world.* **physically** ADVERB

physical education NOUN Physical education consists of lessons in which gymnastics or sports are taught.

physician NOUN a doctor.

physics NOUN Physics is the scientific study of matter, energy, gravity, electricity, heat and sound. **physicist** NOUN

physiology NOUN Physiology is the scientific study of the way the bodies of living things work.

physiotherapy NOUN Physiotherapy is medical treatment which involves exercise and massage. **physiotherapist** NOUN

physique *[Said fiz-**zeek**]* NOUN A person's physique is the shape and size of their body.

pi *[Rhymes with **fly**]* NOUN MATHS Pi is a number, approximately 3.142 and symbolised by the Greek letter π. Pi is the ratio of the circumference of a circle to its diameter.

piano, **pianos** MUSIC NOUN ① a large musical instrument with a row of black and white keys. When the keys are pressed, little hammers hit wires to produce the different notes. ② In music, piano is an instruction to play or sing something quietly. **pianist** NOUN

pick VERB ① To pick something is to choose it. ② If you pick a flower or fruit, or pick something from a place, you remove it with your fingers. ③ If someone picks a lock, they open it with a piece of wire instead of a key. ▸ NOUN ④ The pick of a group of people or things are the best ones in it. ⑤ a pickaxe. **pick on** VERB If you pick on someone, you criticise them unfairly or treat them unkindly. **pick out** VERB If you pick out someone or something, you recognise them when they are difficult to see, or you choose them from among other things. **pick up** VERB If you pick someone or something up, you collect them from the place where they are waiting.

> **pick** VERB
> ① = choose, decide upon, hand-pick, opt for, select, settle on
> ② = gather, harvest, pluck
> ▸ NOUN ④ = elite, flower, pride
> ▸ **pick on** = bait, tease, torment

picket VERB ① When a group of people picket a place of work, they stand outside to persuade other workers to join a strike. ▸ NOUN ② someone who is picketing a place.

pickings PLURAL NOUN Pickings are goods or money that can be obtained very easily • *rich pickings*.

pickle NOUN ① Pickle or pickles consists of vegetables or fruit preserved in vinegar or salt water. ▸ VERB ② To pickle food is to preserve it in vinegar or salt water.

picnic, **picnics**, **picnicking**, **picnicked** NOUN ① a meal eaten out of doors. ▸ VERB ② People who are picnicking are having a picnic.

pictorial ADJECTIVE relating to or using pictures • *a pictorial record of the railway*.

picture NOUN ① a drawing, painting or photograph of someone or something. ② If you have a picture of something in your mind, you have an idea or impression of it. ▸ VERB ③ If someone is pictured in a newspaper or magazine, a photograph of them is printed in it. ④ If you picture something, you think of it and imagine it clearly • *That is how I always picture him*.

> **picture** NOUN
> ① = drawing, illustration, painting, photograph, portrait, selfie (*informal*), sketch
> ▸ VERB ④ = conceive of, imagine, see, visualise

picturesque *[Said pik-chur-**esk**]* ADJECTIVE A place that is picturesque is very attractive and unspoiled.

pie NOUN a dish of meat, vegetables or fruit covered with pastry.

piece NOUN ① a portion or part of something. ② something that has been written or created, such as a work of art or a musical composition. ③ a coin • *a 50 pence piece.* ▶ VERB ④ If you piece together a number of things, you gradually put them together to make something complete.

> **piece** NOUN
> ① = bit, chunk, fragment, part, portion, slice
> ② = article, composition, creation, study, work
> ▶ VERB ④ = assemble, join, mend, patch together, repair, restore

piecemeal ADVERB, ADJECTIVE done gradually and at irregular intervals • *He built up a piecemeal knowledge of the subject, but it was not complete.*

pier NOUN a large structure which sticks out into the sea at a seaside town, and which people can walk along.

pierce VERB If a sharp object pierces something, it goes through it, making a hole.

> **pierce** VERB
> = bore, drill, lance, penetrate, puncture

piercing ADJECTIVE ① A piercing sound is high-pitched and unpleasant. ② Someone with piercing eyes seems to look at you very intensely.

piety [*Said* **pie**-*it-tee*] NOUN Piety is strong and devout religious belief or behaviour.

pig NOUN a farm animal kept for its meat. It has pinkish skin, short legs, and a snout.

> **pig** NOUN
> = hog, piggy (*informal*), porker, swine

pigeon NOUN a largish bird with grey feathers, often seen in towns.

pigeonhole NOUN one of the sections in a frame on a wall where letters can be left.

piggyback NOUN If you give someone a piggyback, you carry them on your back, supporting them under their knees.

pigment NOUN a substance that gives something a particular colour. **pigmentation** NOUN

pike NOUN ① a large freshwater fish of northern countries with strong teeth. ② a medieval weapon consisting of a pointed metal blade attached to a long pole.

pile NOUN ① a quantity of things lying one on top of another. ② the soft surface of a carpet consisting of many threads standing on end. ③ (*in plural*) Piles are painful swellings that appear in the veins inside or just outside a person's anus. ▶ VERB ④ If you pile things somewhere, you put them one on top of the other.

> **pile** NOUN
> ① = heap, hoard, mound, mountain, stack
> ② = down, fur, nap
> ▶ VERB ④ = heap, hoard, stack

pile-up NOUN (*informal*) a road accident involving several vehicles.

pilgrim NOUN [RE] a person who travels to a holy place for religious reasons. **pilgrimage** NOUN

pill NOUN ① a small, hard tablet of medicine that you swallow. ② The pill is a type of drug that women can take regularly to prevent pregnancy.

pillage VERB If a group of people pillage a place, they steal from it using violence.

pillar NOUN ① a tall, narrow, solid structure, usually supporting part of a building. ② Someone who is

A B C D E F G H I J K L M N O P Q R S T U V W X Y Z

described as a pillar of a particular group is an active and important member of it • *a pillar of the Church*.

pillory, **pillories**, **pillorying**, **pilloried** VERB If someone is pilloried, they are criticised severely by a lot of people.

pillow NOUN a rectangular cushion which you rest your head on when you are in bed.

pilot NOUN ① a person who is trained to fly an aircraft. ② a person who goes on board ships to guide them through local waters to a port. ▸ VERB ③ To pilot something is to control its movement or to guide it. ④ To pilot a scheme or product is to test it to see if it would be successful.

pin NOUN ① a thin, pointed piece of metal used to fasten together things such as pieces of fabric or paper. ▸ VERB ② If you pin something somewhere, you fasten it there with a pin or a drawing pin. ③ If someone pins you in a particular position, they hold you there so that you cannot move. ④ If you try to pin something down, you try to get or give a clear and exact description of it or statement about it.

PIN NOUN a security number used by the holder of a cash card or credit card. PIN is an abbreviation for 'personal identification number'.

pinch VERB ① If you pinch something, you squeeze it between your thumb and first finger. ② (*informal*) If someone pinches something, they steal it. ▸ NOUN ③ A pinch of something is the amount that you can hold between your thumb and first finger • *a pinch of salt*.

pinched ADJECTIVE If someone's face is pinched, it looks thin and pale.

pine NOUN ① A pine or pine tree is an evergreen tree with very thin leaves. ▸ VERB ② If you pine for something, you are sad because you cannot have it.

pineapple NOUN a large, oval fruit with sweet, yellow flesh and a thick, lumpy brown skin.

ping-pong NOUN the same as **table tennis**.

pink ADJECTIVE pale reddish-white.

pinnacle NOUN ① a tall pointed piece of stone or rock. ② The pinnacle of something is its best or highest level • *the pinnacle of his career*.

pinpoint VERB If you pinpoint something, you explain or discover exactly what or where it is.

pinstripe ADJECTIVE Pinstripe cloth has very narrow vertical stripes.

pint NOUN a unit of liquid volume equal to one eighth of a gallon or about 0.568 litres.

pioneer *[Said pie-on-**ear**]* NOUN ① Someone who is a pioneer in a particular activity is one of the first people to develop it. ▸ VERB ② Someone who pioneers a new process or invention is the first person to develop it.

pious *[Said **pie**-uss]* ADJECTIVE very religious and moral.

pip NOUN Pips are the hard seeds in a fruit.

pipe NOUN ① a long, hollow tube through which liquid or gas can flow. ② an object used for smoking tobacco. It consists of a small hollow bowl attached to a tube. ▸ VERB ③ To pipe a liquid or gas somewhere is to transfer it through a pipe.

pipeline NOUN a large underground pipe that carries oil or gas over a long distance.

piper NOUN a person who plays the bagpipes.

piping NOUN Piping consists of pipes and tubes.

pirate NOUN Pirates were sailors who attacked and robbed other ships.

Pisces *[Said* ***pie****-seez]* **NOUN** Pisces is the twelfth sign of the zodiac, represented by two fish. People born between February 19th and March 20th are born under this sign.

pistol **NOUN** a small gun held in the hand.

piston **NOUN** a cylinder or disc that slides up and down inside a tube. Pistons make parts of engines move.

pit **NOUN** ① a large hole in the ground. ② a small hollow in the surface of something. ③ a coal mine.

> **pit** **NOUN**
> ① = chasm, hole, pothole

pitch **NOUN** ① [PE] an area of ground marked out for playing a game such as football. ② [MUSIC] The pitch of a sound is how high or low it is. ③ a black substance used in road tar and also for making boats and roofs waterproof. ▶ **VERB** ④ If you pitch something somewhere, you throw it with a lot of force. ⑤ If you pitch something at a particular level of difficulty, you set it at that level • *Any film must be pitched at a level to suit its intended audience.* ⑥ When you pitch a tent, you fix it in an upright position.

pitcher **NOUN** a large jug.

pitfall **NOUN** The pitfalls of a situation are its difficulties or dangers.

pith **NOUN** the white substance between the outer skin and the flesh of an orange or lemon.

pitiful **ADJECTIVE** Someone or something that is pitiful is in such a sad or weak situation that you feel pity for them.

pittance **NOUN** a very small amount of money.

pitted **ADJECTIVE** covered in small hollows • *Nails often become pitted.*

pity, **pities, pitying, pitied** **VERB** ① If you pity someone, you feel very sorry for them. ▶ **NOUN** ② Pity is a feeling of being sorry for someone. ③ If you say that it is a pity about something, you are expressing your disappointment about it.

> **pity** **VERB**
> ① = feel for, feel sorry for, sympathise with
> ▶ **NOUN** ② = charity, compassion, kindness, mercy, sympathy, understanding
> ③ = crime (*informal*), crying shame, shame

pivot **VERB** ① If something pivots, it balances or turns on a central point • *The keel pivots on a large stainless steel pin.* ▶ **NOUN** ② the central point on which something balances or turns.

pivotal **ADJECTIVE** A pivotal role, point or figure is very important to the success of something • *This was a pivotal moment in Stevenson's career.*

pixie **NOUN** an imaginary little creature in fairy stories.

pizza *[Said* ***peet****-sah]* **NOUN** a flat piece of dough covered with cheese, tomato and other savoury food.

placard **NOUN** a large notice carried at a demonstration or displayed in a public place.

placate **VERB** If you placate someone, you stop them feeling angry by doing something to please them.

place **NOUN** ① any point, building or area. ② the position where something belongs • *She set the holder in its place on the table.* ③ a space at a table set with cutlery where one person can eat. ④ If you have a place in a group or at a college, you are a member or are accepted as a student. ⑤ a particular point or stage in a sequence of things • *second place in the race.* ▶ **PHRASE** ⑥ When something **takes place**, it happens. ▶ **VERB** ⑦ If you place something somewhere,

A B C D E F G H I J K L M N O P Q R S T U V W X Y Z

you put it there. ⑧ If you place an order, you order something.

place NOUN
① = area, location, point, position, site, spot
▸ PHRASE ⑥ = come about, go on, happen, occur
▸ VERB ⑦ = deposit, locate, plant, position, put, situate

placebo, **placebos** *[Said plas-**see**-boh]* NOUN a substance given to a patient in place of a drug and from which, though it has no active ingredients, the patient may imagine they get some benefit.

placenta, **placentas** *[Said plas-**sen**-tah]* NOUN SCIENCE The placenta is the mass of veins and tissues in the womb of a pregnant woman or animal. It gives the foetus food and oxygen.

placid ADJECTIVE calm and not easily excited or upset. **placidly** ADVERB

plagiarism *[Said **play**-jer-rizm]* NOUN Plagiarism is copying someone else's work or ideas and pretending that it is your own. **plagiarist** NOUN **plagiarise** VERB

plague, **plagues**, **plaguing**, **plagued** *[Said **playg**]* NOUN ① Plague is a very infectious disease that kills large numbers of people. ② A plague of unpleasant things is a large number of them occurring at the same time • *a plague of rats.* ▸ VERB ③ If problems plague you, they keep causing you trouble.

plaice NOUN an edible European flat fish.

plaid *[Said **plad**]* NOUN Plaid is woven material with a tartan design.

plain ADJECTIVE ① very simple in style with no pattern or decoration • *plain walls.* ② obvious and easy to recognise or understand • *plain language.* ③ A person who is plain is not at all beautiful or attractive. ▸ ADVERB ④ You can use 'plain' before a noun or adjective to emphasise it • *You were just plain stupid.* ▸ NOUN ⑤ a large, flat area of land with very few trees. **plainly** ADVERB

plain ADJECTIVE
① = austere, bare, spartan, stark ≠ fancy
② = clear, comprehensible, distinct, evident, obvious, unmistakable

plaintiff NOUN a person who has brought a court case against another person.

plan, **plans**, **planning**, **planned** NOUN ① a method of achieving something that has been worked out beforehand. ② a detailed diagram or drawing of something that is to be made. ▸ VERB ③ If you plan something, you decide in detail what it is to be and how to do it. ④ If you are planning to do something, you intend to do it • *They plan to marry in the summer.*

plan NOUN
① = method, proposal, scheme, strategy, system
② = blueprint, diagram, layout, scale drawing
▸ VERB ③ = arrange, design, devise, draft, formulate

plane NOUN ① a vehicle with wings and engines that enable it to fly. ② a flat surface. ③ You can refer to the standard at which something is done as a particular plane • *I want to take gymnastics to a higher plane.* ④ a tool with a flat bottom with a sharp blade in it. You move it over a piece of wood to remove thin pieces from the surface. ▸ VERB ⑤ If you plane a piece of wood, you smooth its surface with a plane.

planet NOUN a round object in space which moves around the sun or a star and is lit by light from it. **planetary** ADJECTIVE

plank NOUN a long rectangular piece of wood.

plankton NOUN Plankton is a layer of tiny plants and animals that live just below the surface of a sea or lake.

plant NOUN ① a living thing that grows in the earth and has stems, leaves and roots. ② a factory or power station • *a giant bottling plant*. ▸ VERB ③ When you plant a seed or plant, you put it into the ground. ④ If you plant something somewhere, you put it there firmly or secretly.

plantation NOUN ① a large area of land where crops such as tea, cotton or sugar are grown. ② a large number of trees planted together.

plaque *[Rhymes with **black**]* NOUN ① a flat piece of metal which is fixed to a wall and has an inscription in memory of a famous person or event. ② Plaque is a substance which forms around your teeth and consists of bacteria, saliva and food.

plasma *[Said **plaz**-mah]* NOUN Plasma is the clear fluid part of blood.

plaster NOUN ① Plaster is a paste made of sand, lime and water, which is used to form a smooth surface for inside walls and ceilings. ② a strip of sticky material with a small pad, used for covering cuts on your body. ▸ VERB ③ To plaster a wall is to cover it with a layer of plaster. ▸ PHRASE ④ If your arm or leg is **in plaster**, it has a plaster cast on it to protect a broken bone. **plasterer** NOUN

plastered ADJECTIVE ① If something is plastered to a surface, it is stuck there. ② If something is plastered with things, they are all over its surface.

plastic NOUN ① Plastic is a substance made by a chemical process that can be moulded when soft to make a wide range of objects. ▸ ADJECTIVE ② made of plastic.

plastic surgery NOUN Plastic surgery is surgery to replace or repair damaged skin or to improve a person's appearance by changing the shape of their features.

plate NOUN ① a flat dish used to hold food. ② a flat piece of metal or other hard material used for various purposes in machinery or building • *heavy steel plates used in shipbuilding*. ③ GEOGRAPHY a large part of the earth's surface.

plateau, **plateaus** or **plateaux** *[Rhymes with **snow**]* NOUN GEOGRAPHY a large area of high and fairly flat land.

platform NOUN ① a raised structure on which someone or something can stand. ② the raised area in a railway station where passengers get on and off trains.

platinum NOUN Platinum is a valuable silver-coloured metal. Its atomic number is 78 and its symbol is Pt.

platitude NOUN a statement made as if it were significant but which has become meaningless or boring because it has been used so many times before.

platonic ADJECTIVE A platonic relationship is simply one of friendship and does not involve romantic attraction.

platoon NOUN a small group of soldiers, commanded by a lieutenant.

platter NOUN a large serving plate.

platypus NOUN A platypus or duck-billed platypus is an Australian mammal which lives in rivers. It has brown fur, webbed feet, and a bill like a duck.

plaudits PLURAL NOUN (*formal*) Plaudits are expressions of admiration.

plausible ADJECTIVE An explanation that is plausible seems likely to be true. **plausibility** NOUN

play VERB ① When children play, they take part in games or use toys. ② When you play a sport or match, you take part in it. ③ If an actor plays a character in a play or film, he or she performs that role. ④ If you play a musical instrument, you produce music from it. ⑤ If you play recorded music, you operate a machine in order to produce that music. ▸ NOUN ⑥ a piece of drama performed in the theatre or on television. **player** NOUN

> **play** VERB
> ① = amuse yourself, entertain yourself, frolic, have fun
> ② = compete, participate, take on, take part, vie with
> ▸ NOUN ⑥ = comedy, drama, pantomime, show, tragedy

playboy NOUN a rich man who spends his time enjoying himself.

playful ADJECTIVE ① friendly and light-hearted • *a playful kiss on the tip of his nose*. ② lively • *a playful puppy*. **playfully** ADVERB

playground NOUN a special area for children to play in.

playgroup NOUN an informal kind of school for very young children where they learn by playing.

playing field NOUN an area of grass where people play sports.

playwright NOUN [ENGLISH] [DRAMA] a person who writes plays.

plaza [*Said* **plah**-*za*] NOUN an open square in a city.

plea NOUN ① an emotional request • *a plea for help*. ② In a court of law, someone's plea is their statement that they are guilty or not guilty.

plead VERB ① If you plead with someone, you ask them in an intense emotional way to do something. ② When a person pleads guilty or not guilty, they state in court that they are guilty or not guilty of a crime.

> **plead** VERB
> ① = appeal, ask, beg, beseech (*literary*), implore

pleasant ADJECTIVE ① enjoyable or attractive. ② friendly or charming. **pleasantly** ADVERB

> **pleasant** ADJECTIVE
> ① = agreeable, delightful, enjoyable, lekker (*South African; slang*), lovely, nice, pleasurable
> ≠ unpleasant
> ② = affable, amiable, charming, friendly, likable, likeable, nice
> ≠ unpleasant

please ADVERB ① You say please when you are asking someone politely to do something. ▸ VERB ② If something pleases you, it makes you feel happy and satisfied.

> **please** VERB
> ② = amuse, charm, delight, entertain

pleased ADJECTIVE happy or satisfied.

> **pleased** ADJECTIVE
> = contented, delighted, glad, happy, satisfied

pleasing ADJECTIVE attractive, satisfying or enjoyable • *a pleasing appearance*.

pleasure NOUN ① Pleasure is a feeling of happiness, satisfaction or enjoyment. ② an activity that you enjoy. **pleasurable** ADJECTIVE

> **pleasure** NOUN
> ① = amusement, enjoyment, happiness, joy, satisfaction

pleat NOUN a permanent fold in fabric made by folding one part over another.

plebiscite [*Said* **pleb**-*iss-ite*] NOUN (*formal*) a vote on a matter of national importance in which all the voters in a country can take part.

pledge NOUN ① a solemn promise. ▶ VERB ② If you pledge something, you promise that you will do it or give it.

plentiful ADJECTIVE existing in large numbers or amounts and readily available • *Fruit and vegetables were plentiful.* **plentifully** ADVERB

> **plentiful** ADJECTIVE
> = abundant, ample, bountiful, copious, infinite
> ≠ scarce

plenty NOUN If there is plenty of something, there is a lot of it.

> **plenty** NOUN
> = enough, great deal, heaps (*informal*), lots (*informal*), plethora

plethora [*Said* ***pleth****-thor-ah*] NOUN A plethora of something is an amount that is greater than you need.

pliable ADJECTIVE ① If something is pliable, you can bend it without breaking it. ② Someone who is pliable can be easily influenced or controlled.

pliers PLURAL NOUN Pliers are a small tool with metal jaws for holding small objects and bending wire.

plight NOUN Someone's plight is the very difficult or dangerous situation that they are in • *the plight of the refugees.*

plinth NOUN a block of stone on which a statue or pillar stands.

plod, **plods**, **plodding**, **plodded** VERB If you plod somewhere, you walk there slowly and heavily.

plonk VERB (*informal*) If you plonk something down, you put it down heavily and carelessly.

plot, **plots**, **plotting**, **plotted** NOUN ① a secret plan made by a group of people. ② ENGLISH The plot of a novel or play is the story. ③ a small piece of land. ▶ VERB ④ If people plot to do something, they plan it secretly • *His family is plotting to disinherit him.* ⑤ If someone plots the course of a plane or ship on a map, or plots a graph, they mark the points in the correct places.

> **plot** NOUN
> ① = conspiracy, intrigue, plan, scheme
> ② = narrative, scenario, story, story line
> ▶ VERB ④ = conspire, hatch, plan, scheme

plough [*Rhymes with* ***cow***] NOUN ① a large farming tool that is pulled across a field to turn the soil over before planting seeds. ▶ VERB ② When someone ploughs land, they use a plough to turn over the soil.

ploy NOUN a clever plan or way of behaving in order to get something that you want.

pluck VERB ① To pluck a fruit or flower is to remove it with a sharp pull. ② To pluck a chicken or other dead bird means to pull its feathers out before cooking it. ③ When you pluck a stringed instrument, you pull the strings and let them go. ▶ NOUN ④ Pluck is courage. **plucky** ADJECTIVE

plug, **plugs**, **plugging**, **plugged** NOUN ① a plastic object with metal prongs that can be pushed into a socket to connect an appliance to the electricity supply. ② a disc of rubber or metal with which you block up the hole in a sink or bath. ▶ VERB ③ If you plug a hole, you block it with something.

> **plug** NOUN
> ② = bung, cork, stopper
> ▶ VERB ③ = block, fill, seal

plum NOUN a small fruit with a smooth red or yellow skin and a large stone in the middle.

plumage *[Said* ***ploom****-mage]* NOUN A bird's plumage is its feathers.

plumber NOUN a person who connects and repairs water pipes.

plumbing NOUN The plumbing in a building is the system of water pipes, sinks and toilets.

plume NOUN a large, brightly coloured feather.

plummet, **plummets**, **plummeting**, **plummeted** VERB If something plummets, it falls very quickly • *Sales have plummeted.*

plump ADJECTIVE rather fat • *a small plump baby.*

> **plump** ADJECTIVE
> = beefy (*informal*), burly, chubby, fat, stout, tubby

plunder VERB If someone plunders a place, they steal things from it.

plunge VERB ① If something plunges, it falls suddenly. ② If you plunge an object into something, you push it in quickly. ③ If you plunge into an activity or state, you suddenly become involved in it or affected by it • *The United States had just plunged into the war.* ▸ NOUN ④ a sudden fall.

plural NOUN [ENGLISH] [MFL] the form of a word that is used to refer to two or more people or things, for example the plural of 'chair' is 'chairs', and the plural of 'mouse' is 'mice'.

pluralism NOUN Pluralism is the belief that it is possible for different social and religious groups to live together peacefully while keeping their own beliefs and traditions. **pluralist** ADJECTIVE, NOUN

plus ① You use 'plus' to show that one number is being added to another • *Two plus two equals four.* ② You can use 'plus' when you mention an additional item • *He wrote a history of Scotland plus a history of British literature.* ▸ ADJECTIVE ③ slightly more than the number mentioned • *a career of 25 years plus.*

plush ADJECTIVE (*informal*) very expensive and smart • *a plush hotel.*

Pluto NOUN Pluto is a dwarf planet in the solar system.

ply, **plies**, **plying**, **plied** VERB ① If you ply someone with things or questions, you keep giving them things or asking them questions. ② To ply a trade is to do a particular job as your work. ▸ NOUN ③ Ply is the thickness of wool or thread, measured by the number of strands it is made from.

plywood NOUN Plywood is wooden board made from several thin sheets of wood glued together under pressure.

p.m. used to specify times between 12 noon and 12 midnight, eg *He went to bed at 9 p.m.* It is an abbreviation for the Latin phrase 'post meridiem', which means 'after noon'.

pneumatic *[Said new-****mat****-ik]* ADJECTIVE [DGT] operated by or filled with compressed air • *a pneumatic drill.*

pneumonia *[Said new-****moan****-ee-ah]* NOUN Pneumonia is a serious disease which affects a person's lungs and makes breathing difficult.

poach VERB ① If someone poaches animals from someone else's land, they illegally catch the animals for food. ② When you poach food, you cook it gently in hot liquid. **poacher** NOUN

pocket NOUN ① a small pouch that forms part of a piece of clothing. ② A pocket of something is a small area of it • *There are still pockets of resistance.*

pocket money NOUN Pocket money is an amount of money given regularly to children by their parents.

pod NOUN a long, narrow seed container that grows on plants such as peas or beans.

podium NOUN a small platform, often one on which someone stands to make a speech.

poem NOUN a piece of writing in which the words are arranged in short rhythmic lines, often with a rhyme.

poet NOUN a person who writes poems.

poetic ADJECTIVE ① very beautiful and expressive • *a pure and poetic love*. ② relating to poetry. **poetically** ADVERB

poetry NOUN Poetry is poems, considered as a form of literature.

poignant [*Said* **poyn**-*yant*] ADJECTIVE Something that is poignant has a strong emotional effect on you, often making you feel sad • *a moving and poignant moment*. **poignancy** NOUN

point NOUN ① an opinion or fact expressed by someone • *You've made a good point*. ② a quality • *Tact was never her strong point*. ③ the purpose or meaning something has • *He completely missed the point in most of his argument*. ④ a position or time • *At some point during the party, a fight erupted*. ⑤ a single mark in a competition. ⑥ the thin, sharp end of something such as a needle or knife. ⑦ The points of a compass are the 32 directions indicated on it. ⑧ The decimal point in a number is the dot separating the whole number from the fraction. ⑨ On a railway track, the points are the levers and rails which enable a train to move from one track to another. ▸ VERB ⑩ If you point at something, you stick out your finger to show where it is. ⑪ If something points in a particular direction, it faces that way.

point NOUN
② = attribute, characteristic, feature, quality, side, trait
③ = aim, goal, intention, object, purpose
⑥ = nib, prong, tip

point-blank ADJECTIVE ① Something that is shot at point-blank range is shot with a gun held very close to it. ▸ ADVERB ② If you say something point-blank, you say it directly without explanation or apology.

pointed ADJECTIVE ① A pointed object has a thin, sharp end. ② Pointed comments express criticism. **pointedly** ADVERB

pointer NOUN a piece of information which helps you to understand something • *Here are a few pointers to help you make a choice*.

pointless ADJECTIVE Something that is pointless has no purpose. **pointlessly** ADVERB

point of view, **points of view** NOUN Your point of view is your opinion about something or your attitude towards it.

poise NOUN Someone who has poise is calm and dignified.

poised ADJECTIVE If you are poised to do something, you are ready to do it at any moment.

poison NOUN ① Poison is a substance that can kill people or animals if they swallow it or absorb it. ▸ VERB ② To poison someone is to try to kill them with poison.

poison NOUN
① = toxin, venom

poisonous ADJECTIVE containing something that causes death or illness.

poisonous ADJECTIVE
= noxious, toxic, venomous

poke VERB ① If you poke someone or

something, you push at them quickly with your finger or a sharp object. ② Something that pokes out of another thing appears from underneath or behind it • *roots poking out of the earth.* ▶ **NOUN** ③ a sharp jab or prod.

poke VERB
① = dig, elbow, jab, nudge, prod, stab
▶ **NOUN** ③ = dig, jab, nudge, prod

poker NOUN ① Poker is a card game in which the players make bets on the cards dealt to them. ② a long metal rod used for moving coals or logs in a fire.

polar ADJECTIVE relating to the area around the North and South Poles.

polar bear NOUN a large white bear which lives in the area around the North Pole.

pole NOUN ① a long rounded piece of wood or metal. ② The earth's poles are the two opposite ends of its axis • *the North Pole.*

Pole NOUN someone who comes from Poland.

pole vault NOUN The pole vault is an athletics event in which contestants jump over a high bar using a long flexible pole to lift themselves into the air.

police PLURAL NOUN ① CITIZENSHIP The police are the people who are officially responsible for making sure that people obey the law. ▶ **VERB** ② To police an area is to keep law and order there by means of the police or an armed force.

policeman, policemen NOUN a man who is a member of a police force.

policewoman, policewomen NOUN a woman who is a member of a police force.

policy, policies NOUN ① a set of plans, especially in politics or business • *the new economic policy.* ② An insurance policy is a document which shows an agreement made with an insurance company.

polio NOUN Polio is an infectious disease that is caused by a virus and often results in paralysis. Polio is short for 'poliomyelitis'.

polish VERB ① If you polish something, you put polish on it or rub it with a cloth to make it shine. ② If you polish a skill or technique you have, you work on it in order to improve it. ▶ **NOUN** ③ Polish is a substance that you put on an object to clean it and make it shine • *shoe polish.* ④ Something that has polish is elegant and of good quality. **polished ADJECTIVE**

polish VERB
① = buff, shine, wax
② = brush up, improve, perfect, refine
▶ **NOUN** ④ = class (*informal*), elegance, finesse, grace, refinement, style

Polish [*Said* ***pole**-ish*] **ADJECTIVE** ① belonging or relating to Poland. ▶ **NOUN** ② Polish is the main language spoken in Poland.

polite ADJECTIVE ① Someone who is polite has good manners and behaves considerately towards other people. ② Polite society is cultivated and refined. **politely ADVERB**

polite ADJECTIVE
① = civil, courteous, respectful, well-behaved, well-mannered
≠ rude
② = cultured, genteel, refined, sophisticated, urbane

politeness NOUN the quality of having good manners and behaving considerately.

politeness NOUN
= civility, courtesy, decency, etiquette

political ADJECTIVE ① GEOGRAPHY relating to the state, government or public administration. ② relating to or interested in politics. **politically** ADVERB

politically correct ADJECTIVE careful not to offend or designed not to offend minority or disadvantaged groups.

politician NOUN a person involved in the government of a country.

politics NOUN HISTORY Politics is the activity and planning concerned with achieving power and control in a country or organisation.

polka NOUN a fast dance in which couples dance together in circles around the room.

poll NOUN ① a survey in which people are asked their opinions about something. ② (*in plural*) A political election can be referred to as the polls. ▸ VERB ③ If you are polled on something, you are asked your opinion about it as part of a survey.

pollen NOUN SCIENCE Pollen is a fine yellow powder produced by flowers in order to fertilise other flowers of the same species.

pollutant NOUN a substance that causes pollution.

pollute VERB To pollute water or air is to make it dirty and dangerous to use or live in. **polluted** ADJECTIVE

pollute VERB
= contaminate, infect, poison, taint

pollution NOUN GEOGRAPHY Pollution of the environment happens when dirty, dangerous or unwanted substances get into the air, water or soil.

polo NOUN Polo is a game played between two teams of players on horseback. The players use wooden hammers with long handles to hit a ball.

polyester NOUN DGT a synthetic fibre, used especially to make clothes.

polygamy *[Said pol-**lig**-gam-ee]* NOUN Polygamy is having more than one wife at the same time. **polygamous** ADJECTIVE

polystyrene NOUN Polystyrene is a very light plastic, used especially as insulating material or to make containers.

polythene NOUN SCIENCE Polythene is a type of plastic that is used to make thin sheets or bags.

polyunsaturated ADJECTIVE Polyunsaturated oils and margarines are made mainly from vegetable fats and are considered to be healthier than most other oils. **polyunsaturate** NOUN

pomegranate NOUN a round fruit with a thick reddish skin. It contains a lot of small seeds.

pomp NOUN Pomp is the use of ceremony, fine clothes and decorations on special occasions • *Sir Patrick was buried with much pomp.*

pompous ADJECTIVE behaving in a way that is too serious and self-important. **pomposity** NOUN

pompous ADJECTIVE
= arrogant, grandiose, ostentatious, pretentious, puffed up

pond NOUN a small, usually man-made area of water.

ponder VERB If you ponder, you think about something deeply • *He was pondering the problem when Phillipson drove up.*

ponder VERB
= brood, consider, contemplate, mull over, reflect, think

ponderous ADJECTIVE dull, slow and serious • *the ponderous commentary.* **ponderously** ADVERB

pong NOUN (*informal*) an unpleasant smell.

pontiff NOUN (*formal*) The pontiff is the Pope.

pony, ponies NOUN a small horse.

ponytail NOUN a hairstyle in which long hair is tied at the back of the head and hangs down like a tail.

poodle NOUN a type of dog with curly hair.

pool NOUN ① a small area of still water. ② Pool is a game in which players try to hit coloured balls into pockets around the table using long sticks called cues. ③ A pool of people, money or things is a group or collection used or shared by several people. ④ (*in plural*) The pools are a competition in which people try to guess the results of football matches. ▸ VERB ⑤ If people pool their resources, they gather together the things they have so that they can be shared or used by all of them.

poor ADJECTIVE ① Poor people have very little money and few possessions. ② Poor places are inhabited by people with little money and show signs of neglect. ③ You use 'poor' to show sympathy • *Poor you!* ④ 'Poor' also means of a low quality or standard • *a poor performance.*

> **poor** ADJECTIVE
> ① = broke (*informal*), destitute, hard up (*informal*), impoverished, penniless, poverty-stricken
> ≠ rich
> ④ = feeble, inferior, mediocre, second-rate, shoddy, unsatisfactory

poorly ADJECTIVE ① feeling unwell or ill. ▸ ADVERB ② badly • *a poorly planned operation.*

pop, pops, popping, popped NOUN ① Pop is modern music played and enjoyed especially by young people. ② (*informal*) You can refer to fizzy, nonalcoholic drinks as pop. ③ a short, sharp sound. ▸ VERB ④ If something pops, it makes a sudden sharp sound. ⑤ (*informal*) If you pop something somewhere, you put it there quickly • *I'd just popped the pie in the oven.* ⑥ (*informal*) If you pop somewhere, you go there quickly • *His mother popped out to buy him an ice cream.*

popcorn NOUN Popcorn is a snack consisting of grains of maize heated until they puff up and burst.

Pope NOUN [RE] The Pope is the head of the Roman Catholic Church.

poppy, poppies NOUN a plant with a large, red flower on a hairy stem.

populace NOUN (*formal*) The populace of a country is its people.

popular ADJECTIVE ① liked or approved of by a lot of people. ② involving or intended for ordinary people • *the popular press.* **popularly** ADVERB **popularity** NOUN **popularise** VERB

> **popular** ADJECTIVE
> ① = fashionable, favourite, in demand, in favour, sought-after, well-liked
> ≠ unpopular
> ② = common, conventional, general, universal

populate VERB The people or animals that populate an area live there.

population NOUN The population of a place is the people who live there, or the number of people living there.

porcelain NOUN Porcelain is a delicate, hard material used to make crockery and ornaments.

porch NOUN a covered area at the entrance to a building.

pore NOUN ① The pores in your skin or on the surface of a plant are very small holes which allow moisture to pass through. ▸ VERB ② If you pore over a piece of writing or a diagram, you study it carefully.

A B C D E F G H I J K L M N O P Q R S T U V W X Y Z

pork NOUN Pork is meat from a pig which has not been salted or smoked.

porridge NOUN Porridge is a thick, sticky food made from oats cooked in water or milk.

port NOUN ① a town or area which has a harbour or docks. ② Port is a kind of strong, sweet red wine. ▸ ADJECTIVE ③ The port side of a ship is the left side when you are facing the front.

-port SUFFIX '-port' comes at the end of words that have something to do with 'carrying' in their meaning • *transport*.

portable ADJECTIVE designed to be easily carried • *a portable speaker*.

porter NOUN ① a person whose job is to be in charge of the entrance of a building, greeting and directing visitors. ② A porter in a railway station or hospital is a person whose job is to carry or move things.

portfolio, **portfolios** NOUN ① a thin, flat case for carrying papers. ② A portfolio is also a group of selected duties, investments or items of artwork • *the education portfolio* • *Choose your share portfolio wisely*.

portion NOUN a part or amount of something • *a portion of fresh fruit*.

> **portion** NOUN
> = bit, chunk, helping, part, piece, segment, serving

portrait NOUN [ART] a picture or photograph of someone.

portray VERB When an actor, artist or writer portrays someone or something, they represent or describe them. **portrayal** NOUN

Portuguese [*Said por-tyoo-**geez***] ADJECTIVE ① belonging or relating to Portugal. ▸ NOUN ② someone who comes from Portugal. ③ Portuguese is the main language spoken in Portugal and Brazil.

pose VERB ① If something poses a problem, it is the cause of the problem. ② If you pose a question, you ask it. ③ If you pose as someone else, you pretend to be that person in order to deceive people. ▸ NOUN ④ a way of standing, sitting or lying • *Mr Clark assumes a pose for the photographer*.

> **pose** VERB
> ② = ask, put, submit
> ③ = impersonate, masquerade as, pass yourself off as, pretend to be

posh ADJECTIVE (*informal*) ① smart, fashionable and expensive • *a posh restaurant*. ② upper-class • *the man with the posh voice*.

> **posh** ADJECTIVE
> ① = classy (*informal*), elegant, exclusive, fashionable, smart, stylish, up-market
> ② = aristocratic, genteel, upper-class
> ≠ common

position NOUN ① [DRAMA] The position of someone or something is the place where they are or ought to be • *Would the cast take their positions, please*. ② When someone or something is in a particular position, they are sitting or lying in that way • *I raised myself to a sitting position*. ③ a job or post in an organisation. ④ The position that you are in at a particular time is the situation that you are in • *This puts the president in a difficult position*. ▸ VERB ⑤ To position something somewhere is to put it there • *Llewelyn positioned a cushion behind Joanna's back*.

> **position** NOUN
> ① = location, place, point, whereabouts
> ▸ VERB ⑤ = arrange, lay out, locate, place, put

positive ADJECTIVE ① completely sure

about something • *I was positive he'd known about that money.* ② confident and hopeful • *I felt very positive about everything.* ③ showing approval or encouragement • *I anticipate a positive response.* ④ providing definite proof of something • *positive evidence.* ⑤ MATHS A positive number is greater than zero. **positively** ADVERB

positive ADJECTIVE
① = certain, confident, convinced, sure
③ = constructive, helpful
≠ negative
④ = clear, clear-cut, conclusive, concrete, firm

possess VERB ① If you possess a particular quality, you have it. ② If you possess something, you own it. ③ If a feeling or belief possesses you, it strongly influences you • *Absolute terror possessed her.* **possessor** NOUN

possess VERB
① = be blessed with, be born with, enjoy, have
② = acquire, control, hold, occupy, seize, take over

possession NOUN ① If something is in your possession or if you are in possession of it, you have it. ② Your possessions are the things that you own or that you have with you.

possession NOUN
① = control, custody, ownership, tenure
② = assets, belongings, effects, estate, property, things

possessive ADJECTIVE ① A person who is possessive about someone or something wants to keep them to themselves. ▸ NOUN ② In grammar, the possessive is the form of a noun or pronoun used to show possession • *my car* • *That's hers.*

possibility, **possibilities** NOUN something that might be true or might happen • *the possibility of a ban.*

possibility NOUN
= chance, hope, likelihood, odds, prospect, risk

possible ADJECTIVE ① likely to happen or able to be done • *the best possible result.* ② likely or capable of being true or correct • *I can think of no possible explanation.* **possibly** ADVERB

possible ADJECTIVE
① = attainable, feasible, practicable, viable, workable
≠ impossible
② = conceivable, imaginable, likely, potential

possum NOUN In Australian and New Zealand English, a possum is a phalanger, a marsupial with thick fur and a long tail.

post NOUN ① The post is the system by which letters and parcels are collected and delivered. ② a job or official position in an organisation. ③ a strong, upright pole fixed into the ground • *They are tied to a post.* ④ a message or article published on a website. ▸ VERB ⑤ If you post a letter, you send it to someone by putting it into a postbox. ⑥ If you are posted somewhere, you are sent by your employers to work there. ⑦ If you post a message or article, you publish it on a website. **postal** ADJECTIVE

post- PREFIX after a particular time or event • *his postwar career.*

postage NOUN Postage is the money that you pay to send letters and parcels by post.

postcard NOUN a card, often with a picture on one side, which you write on and send without an envelope.

postcode NOUN a short sequence of letters and numbers at the end of an address which helps the post office to sort the mail.

poster NOUN a large notice or picture

that is stuck on a wall as an advertisement or for decoration.

posterior NOUN (*humorous*) A person's posterior is their bottom.

posterity NOUN (*formal*) You can refer to the future and the people who will be alive then as posterity • *to record the voyage for posterity*.

posthumous [*Said* ***poss****-tyum-uss*] ADJECTIVE happening or awarded after a person's death • *a posthumous medal*. **posthumously** ADVERB

postman, **postmen** NOUN someone who collects and delivers letters and parcels sent by post.

postmortem NOUN a medical examination of a dead body to find out how the person died.

post office NOUN ① The Post Office is the national organisation responsible for postal services. ② a building where you can buy stamps and post letters.

postpone VERB If you postpone an event, you arrange for it to take place at a later time than was originally planned. **postponement** NOUN

> **postpone** VERB
> = adjourn, defer, delay, put back, put off, shelve

posture NOUN Your posture is the position or manner in which you hold your body.

pot NOUN a deep round container; also used to refer to its contents.

potato, **potatoes** NOUN a white vegetable that has a brown or red skin and grows underground.

potent ADJECTIVE effective or powerful • *a potent cocktail*. **potency** NOUN

potential ADJECTIVE ① capable of becoming the thing mentioned • *potential customers* • *potential sources of finance*. ▶ NOUN ② Your potential is your ability to achieve success in the future. **potentially** ADVERB

> **potential** ADJECTIVE
> ① = likely, possible, probable
> ▶ NOUN ② = ability, aptitude, capability, capacity, power, wherewithal

pothole NOUN ① a hole in the surface of a road caused by bad weather or traffic. ② an underground cavern.

potion NOUN a drink containing medicine, poison or supposed magical powers.

potted ADJECTIVE Potted meat or fish is cooked and put into a small sealed container to preserve it.

potter NOUN ① a person who makes pottery. ▶ VERB ② If you potter about, you pass the time doing pleasant, unimportant things.

pottery NOUN ① Pottery is pots, dishes and other items made from clay and fired in a kiln. ② Pottery is also the craft of making pottery.

potty, **potties**; **pottier**, **pottiest** NOUN ① a bowl which a small child can sit on and use instead of a toilet. ▶ ADJECTIVE ② (*informal*) crazy or foolish.

pouch NOUN ① a small, soft container with a fold-over top. ② Animals like kangaroos have a pouch, which is a pocket of skin in which they carry their young.

poultry NOUN Chickens, turkeys and other birds kept for their meat or eggs are referred to as poultry.

pounce VERB If an animal or person pounces on something, they leap and grab it.

pound NOUN ① The pound is the main unit of currency in Britain and in some other countries. ② a unit of weight equal to 16 ounces or about 0.454 kilograms. ▶ VERB ③ If you pound something, you hit it repeatedly with your fist • *Someone was pounding on the door.* ④ If you pound a substance, you crush it into a powder or paste • *Wooden mallets were used to pound the meat.* ⑤ If your heart is pounding, it is beating very strongly and quickly. ⑥ If you pound somewhere, you run there with heavy noisy steps.

pour VERB ① If you pour a liquid out of a container, you make it flow out by tipping the container. ② If something pours somewhere, it flows there quickly and in large quantities • *Sweat poured down his face.* ③ When it is raining heavily, you can say that it is pouring.

pour VERB
② = course, flow, gush, run, spout, stream

pout VERB If you pout, you stick out your lips or bottom lip.

poverty NOUN GEOGRAPHY the state of being very poor.

poverty NOUN
= destitution, hardship, insolvency, want

powder NOUN ① Powder consists of many tiny particles of a solid substance. ▸ VERB ② If you powder a surface, you cover it with powder. **powdery** ADJECTIVE

power NOUN ① Someone who has power has a lot of control over people and activities. ② Someone who has the power to do something has the ability to do it • *the power of speech.* ③ Power is also the authority to do something • *the power of arrest.* ④ The power of something is the physical strength that it has to move things. ⑤ Power is energy obtained, for example, by burning fuel or using the wind or waves. ⑥ MATHS In maths, a power is the product of a number multiplied by itself a certain number of times. For example, the third power of 10 is 1000. ⑦ SCIENCE In physics, power is the energy transferred from one thing to another in one second. It is measured in watts. ▸ VERB ⑧ Something that powers a machine provides the energy for it to work.

power NOUN
① = ascendancy (*formal*), control, dominion (*formal*), sovereignty, supremacy
③ = authority, authorisation, licence, privilege, right
④ = brawn, might, strength, vigour

powerful ADJECTIVE ① able to control people and events. ② having great physical strength. ③ having a strong effect. **powerfully** ADVERB

powerful ADJECTIVE
① = commanding, dominant, influential
② = mighty, strapping, strong, sturdy, vigorous
≠ weak
③ = compelling, convincing, effective, forceful, persuasive, telling

powerless ADJECTIVE unable to control or influence events • *I was powerless to save her.*

powerless ADJECTIVE
= helpless, impotent, incapable

power station NOUN a place where electricity is generated.

practicable ADJECTIVE If a task or plan is practicable, it can be carried out successfully • *a practicable option.*

practical ADJECTIVE ① The practical aspects of something are those that involve experience and real situations rather than ideas or theories • *the practical difficulties of teaching science.* ② sensible and likely to be effective • *practical low-heeled shoes.* ③ Someone who is practical is able to deal effectively and sensibly with problems. ▸ NOUN ④ an examination in which you make or perform something rather than simply write. **practicality** NOUN

practical ADJECTIVE
① = applied, pragmatic
② = functional, sensible
≠ impractical
③ = accomplished, experienced, proficient, seasoned, skilled, veteran

practically ADVERB ① almost but not completely or exactly • *The house was practically a wreck.* ② in a practical way • *practically minded.*

practice NOUN ① You can refer to something that people do regularly as a practice • *the practice of shaking hands.* ② Practice is regular training or exercise • *I need more practice to improve my football skills.* ③ A doctor's or lawyer's practice is his or her business.

practice NOUN
① = custom, habit, method, routine, way
② = drill, exercise, preparation, rehearsal, training

practise VERB ① If you practise something, you do it regularly in order to improve. ② People who practise a religion, custom or craft regularly take part in the activities associated with it • *a practising Buddhist.* ③ Someone who practises medicine or law works as a doctor or lawyer.

practise VERB
① = polish, rehearse, train
② = do, follow, observe

practised ADJECTIVE Someone who is practised at doing something is very skilful at it • *a practised performer.*

practitioner NOUN You can refer to someone who works in a particular profession as a practitioner • *a medical practitioner.*

pragmatic ADJECTIVE A pragmatic way of considering or doing something is a practical rather than theoretical way • *He is pragmatic about the risks involved.* **pragmatically** ADVERB **pragmatism** NOUN

prairie NOUN a large area of flat, grassy land in North America.

praise VERB ① If you praise someone or something, you express strong approval of their qualities or achievements. ▸ NOUN ② Praise is what is said or written in approval of someone's qualities or achievements.

praise VERB
① = admire, applaud, approve, congratulate, pay tribute to
≠ criticise
▸ NOUN ② = accolade, approval, commendation, congratulation, tribute
≠ criticism

pram NOUN a baby's cot on wheels.

prance VERB Someone who is prancing around is walking with exaggerated movements.

prank NOUN a childish trick.

prawn NOUN a small, pink, edible shellfish with a long tail.

pray VERB [RE] When someone prays, they speak to God to give thanks or to ask for help.

prayer NOUN ① [RE] Prayer is the activity of praying. ② [RE] the words said when someone prays.

pre- PREFIX 'Pre-' means before a particular time or event • *pre-war.*

preach VERB When someone preaches, they give a short talk on a religious or moral subject as part of a church service. **preacher** NOUN

precarious ADJECTIVE ① If your situation is precarious, you may fail in what you are doing at any time. ② Something that is precarious is likely to fall because it is not well balanced or secured. **precariously** ADVERB

precaution NOUN an action that is intended to prevent something from happening • *It's still worth taking precautions against accidents.* **precautionary** ADJECTIVE

precaution NOUN
= insurance, preventative measure, protection, provision, safeguard

precede VERB ① Something that precedes another thing happens or occurs before it. ② If you precede someone somewhere, you go in front of them. **preceding** ADJECTIVE

precedence [Said *press-id-ens*] NOUN If something takes precedence over other things, it is the most important thing and should be dealt with first.

precedent NOUN An action or decision that is regarded as a precedent is used as a guide in taking similar action or decisions later.

precinct NOUN ① A shopping precinct is a pedestrian shopping area. ② (*in plural, formal*) The precincts of a place are its buildings and land.

precious ADJECTIVE Something that is precious is valuable or very important and should be looked after or used carefully.

precious ADJECTIVE
= expensive, invaluable, priceless, prized, valuable
≠ worthless

precipice [Said ***press**-sip-piss*] NOUN a very steep rock face.

precipitate VERB (*formal*) If something precipitates an event or situation, it causes it to happen suddenly.

precipitation NOUN GEOGRAPHY Precipitation is any kind of moisture that falls from the sky; used especially when stating the amount that falls during a particular period.

precise ADJECTIVE exact and accurate in every detail • *precise measurements.* **precisely** ADVERB **precision** NOUN

precise ADJECTIVE
= accurate, actual, correct, exact, particular, specific, very
≠ vague

preclude VERB (*formal*) If something precludes an event or situation, it prevents it from happening • *The meal precluded serious conversation.*

precocious ADJECTIVE Precocious children behave in a way that seems too advanced for their age.

preconceived ADJECTIVE Preconceived ideas about something have been formed without any real experience or information. **preconception** NOUN

precondition NOUN If something is a precondition for another thing, it must happen before the second thing can take place.

precursor NOUN A precursor of something that exists now is a similar thing that existed at an earlier time • *real tennis, an ancient precursor of the modern game.*

predator [Said ***pred**-dat-tor*] NOUN SCIENCE an animal that kills and eats other animals. **predatory** ADJECTIVE

predecessor NOUN Someone's predecessor is a person who used to do their job before.

predetermined ADJECTIVE decided in advance or controlled by previous events rather than left to chance.

predicament NOUN a difficult situation.

predicament NOUN
= fix (*informal*), hot water (*informal*), jam (*informal*), scrape (*informal*), tight spot (*informal*)

predict VERB If someone predicts an event, they say that it will happen in the future.

predict VERB
= forecast, foresee, foretell, prophesy

prediction NOUN something that is forecast.

prediction NOUN
= forecast, prophecy

predominant ADJECTIVE more important or more noticeable than anything else in a particular set of people or things • *Yellow is the predominant colour in the house.* **predominantly** ADVERB

predominate VERB If one type of person or thing predominates, it is the most common, frequent or noticeable • *Fresh flowers predominate in the bouquet.* **predominance** NOUN

pre-eminent ADJECTIVE recognised as being the most important in a particular group • *the pre-eminent experts in the area.* **pre-eminence** NOUN

pre-empt VERB (*formal*) If you pre-empt something, you prevent it by doing something else which makes it pointless or impossible • *By resigning, he pre-empted the decision to sack him.*

preen VERB When a bird preens its feathers, it cleans them using its beak.

preface [*Said* ***pref**-fiss*] NOUN an introduction at the beginning of a book explaining what the book is about or why it was written.

prefect NOUN a pupil who has special duties at a school.

prefer, **prefers**, **preferring**, **preferred** VERB If you prefer one thing to another, you like it better than the other thing. **preferable** ADJECTIVE **preferably** ADVERB

prefer VERB
= be partial to, favour, go for, incline towards, like better

preference [*Said* ***pref**-fer-enss*] NOUN ① If you have a preference for something, you like it more than other things • *a preference for tea over coffee.* ② When making a choice, if you give preference to one type of person or thing, you try to choose that type.

preferential ADJECTIVE A person who gets preferential treatment is treated better than others.

prefix NOUN ENGLISH a letter or group of letters added to the beginning of a word to make a new word, for example 'semi-', 'pre-' and 'un-'.

pregnant ADJECTIVE A woman who is pregnant has a baby developing in her womb. **pregnancy** NOUN

prehistoric ADJECTIVE HISTORY existing at a time in the past before anything was written down.

prejudice NOUN ① Prejudice is an unreasonable and unfair dislike or preference formed without carefully examining the facts. ② Prejudice is also an intolerance towards certain people or groups • *racial prejudice.* **prejudiced** ADJECTIVE **prejudicial** ADJECTIVE

prejudice NOUN
① = bias, partiality, preconception
② = bigotry, chauvinism, discrimination, racism, sexism

preliminary ADJECTIVE Preliminary activities take place before something starts, in preparation for it • *the preliminary rounds of the competition.*

prelude NOUN Something that is an introduction to a more important event can be described as a prelude to that event.

premature ADJECTIVE happening too early, or earlier than expected • *premature baldness*. **prematurely** ADVERB

premeditated ADJECTIVE planned in advance • *a premeditated attack*.

premier NOUN ① The leader of a government is sometimes referred to as the premier. ② In Australia, a premier is the leader of a State government. ▶ ADJECTIVE ③ considered to be the best or most important • *Wellington's premier jewellers*.

premiere *[Said* ***prem****-mee-er]* NOUN the first public performance of a new play or film.

premise *[Said* ***prem****-iss]* NOUN ① *(in plural)* The premises of an organisation are all the buildings it occupies on one site. ② a statement which you suppose is true and use as the basis for an idea or argument.

premium NOUN ① A sum of money paid regularly to an insurance company for an insurance policy. ② an extra sum of money that has to be paid • *Paying a premium for space is worthwhile*.

premonition *[Said prem-on-****ish****-on]* NOUN a feeling that something unpleasant is going to happen.

> **premonition** NOUN
> = foreboding, funny feeling *(informal)*, omen, sign

preoccupation NOUN If you have a preoccupation with something, it is very important to you and you keep thinking about it.

preoccupied ADJECTIVE Someone who is preoccupied is deep in thought or totally involved with something.

> **preoccupied** ADJECTIVE
> = absorbed, engrossed, immersed, oblivious, wrapped up

preparatory ADJECTIVE Preparatory activities are done before doing something else in order to prepare for it.

prepare VERB If you prepare something, you make it ready for a particular purpose or event • *He was preparing the meal*. **preparation** NOUN

prepared ADJECTIVE If you are prepared to do something, you are willing to do it.

preposterous ADJECTIVE extremely unreasonable and ridiculous • *a preposterous statement*.

prerequisite *[Said pree-****rek****-wiz-zit]* NOUN *(formal)* Something that is a prerequisite for another thing must happen or exist before the other thing is possible • *Self-esteem is a prerequisite for a happy life*.

prerogative *[Said prir-****rog****-at-tiv]* NOUN *(formal)* Something that is the prerogative of a person is their special privilege or right.

prescribe VERB When a doctor prescribes treatment, he or she states what treatment a patient should have.

prescription NOUN a piece of paper on which the doctor has written the name of a medicine needed by a patient.

presence NOUN ① Someone's presence in a place is the fact of their being there • *His presence made me happy*. ② If you are in someone's presence, you are in the same place as they are. ③ Someone who has presence has an impressive appearance or manner.

present ADJECTIVE *[Said* ***prez****-ent]* ① If someone is present somewhere, they are there • *He had been present at the birth of his son*. ② A present situation is one that exists now rather than in the past or the future. ③ ENGLISH | MFL

The present tense of a verb is the form used to express something that is happening in the present. ▶ **NOUN** [*Said* ***prez****-ent*] ④ The present is the period of time that is taking place now. ⑤ something that you give to someone for them to keep. ▶ **VERB** [*Said pri-****zent***] ⑥ If you present someone with something, you give it to them • *She presented a bravery award to the girl*. ⑦ Something that presents a difficulty or a challenge causes it or provides it. ⑧ The person who presents a radio or television show introduces each part or each guest. **presenter NOUN**

present ADJECTIVE
① = at hand, here, in attendance, there, to hand
≠ absent
▶ **NOUN** ⑤ = bonsela (*South African*), donation, gift, offering
▶ **VERB** ⑥ = award, bestow, donate, give, grant, hand out

presentable ADJECTIVE neat or attractive and suitable for people to see.

presentation NOUN ① the act of presenting or a way of presenting something. ② The presentation of a piece of work is the way it looks or the impression it gives. ③ To give a presentation is to give a talk or demonstration to an audience of something you have been studying or working on.

present-day ADJECTIVE existing or happening now • *present-day farming practices*.

presently ADVERB ① If something will happen presently, it will happen soon • *I'll finish the job presently*. ② Something that is presently happening is happening now • *Some progress is presently being made*.

present tense NOUN ENGLISH MFL In grammar, the present tense is the tense of a verb that you use mainly to talk about things that happen or exist at the time of writing or speaking.

preservative NOUN a substance or chemical that stops things decaying.

preserve VERB ① If you preserve something, you take action so that it remains as it is. ② If you preserve food, you treat it to prevent it from decaying. ▶ **NOUN** ③ Preserves are foods such as jam or chutney that have been made with a lot of sugar or vinegar. **preservation NOUN**

preside VERB A person who presides over a formal event is in charge of it.

president NOUN ① In a country which has no king or queen, the president is the elected leader • *the President of the United States of America*. ② The president of an organisation is the person who has the highest position. **presidency NOUN** **presidential ADJECTIVE**

press VERB ① If you press something, you push it or hold it firmly against something else • *Lisa pressed his hand* • *Press the blue button*. ② If you press clothes, you iron them. ③ If you press for something, you try hard to persuade someone to agree to it • *She was pressing for improvements to the education system*. ④ If you press charges, you make an accusation against someone which has to be decided in a court of law. ▶ **NOUN** ⑤ Newspapers and the journalists who work for them are called the press.

press VERB
① = compress, crush, mash, push, squeeze
③ = beg, implore, petition, plead, pressurise, urge

press conference NOUN When someone gives a press conference, they have a meeting to answer questions put by reporters.

pressing ADJECTIVE Something that is pressing needs to be dealt with immediately • *pressing needs*.

pressure NOUN ① SCIENCE Pressure is the force that is produced by pushing on something. ② PSHE If you are under pressure, you have too much to do and not enough time, or someone is trying hard to persuade you to do something. ▸ VERB ③ If you pressure someone, you try hard to persuade them to do something.

pressurise; also spelt **pressurize** VERB If you pressurise someone, you try hard to persuade them to do something.

prestige [*Said press-**teezh***] NOUN If you have prestige, people admire you because of your position. **prestigious** ADJECTIVE

presumably ADVERB If you say that something is presumably the case, you mean you assume that it is • *Your audience, presumably, are younger*.

presume [*Said priz-**yoom***] VERB If you presume something, you think that it is the case although you have no proof. **presumption** NOUN

presumptuous ADJECTIVE Someone who behaves in a presumptuous way does things that they have no right to do.

pretence NOUN a way of behaving that is false and intended to deceive people.

pretend VERB If you pretend that something is the case, you try to make people believe that it is, although in fact it is not • *Latimer pretended not to notice*.

> **pretend** VERB
> = counterfeit, fake, falsify, feign, pass yourself off as

pretender NOUN A pretender to a throne or title is someone who claims it but whose claim is being questioned.

pretension NOUN Someone with pretensions claims that they are more important than they really are.

pretentious ADJECTIVE Someone or something that is pretentious is trying to seem important when in fact they are not.

> **pretentious** ADJECTIVE
> = affected, conceited, ostentatious, pompous, snobbish

pretext NOUN a false reason given to hide the real reason for doing something.

pretty, **prettier**, **prettiest** ADJECTIVE ① attractive in a delicate way. ▸ ADVERB ② (*informal*) quite or rather • *He spoke pretty good English*. **prettily** ADVERB **prettiness** NOUN

> **pretty** ADJECTIVE
> ① = attractive, beautiful, cute, lovely
> ▸ ADVERB ② = fairly, kind of (*informal*), quite, rather

prevail VERB ① If a custom or belief prevails in a particular place, it is normal or most common there • *This attitude has prevailed in Britain for many years*. ② If someone or something prevails, they succeed in their aims • *In recent years better sense has prevailed*. **prevailing** ADJECTIVE

prevalent ADJECTIVE very common or widespread • *the hooliganism so prevalent today*. **prevalence** NOUN

prevent VERB If you prevent something, you stop it from happening or being done. **preventable** ADJECTIVE **prevention** NOUN

> **prevent** VERB
> = avert, foil, hinder, impede, stop, thwart

preventive or **preventative** ADJECTIVE intended to help prevent things such as disease or crime • *preventive health care.*

preview NOUN ① an opportunity to see something, such as a film or exhibition, before it is shown to the public. ② ICT a part of a computer program which allows you to look at what you have keyed or added to a document or spreadsheet as it will appear when it is printed.

previous ADJECTIVE happening or existing before something else in time or position • *previous reports* • *the previous year.* **previously** ADVERB

> **previous** ADJECTIVE
> = earlier, former, one-time, past, preceding, prior

prey [*Rhymes with **say***] NOUN ① The creatures that an animal hunts and eats are called its prey. ▶ VERB ② An animal that preys on a particular kind of animal lives by hunting and eating it.

price NOUN ① The price of something is the amount of money you have to pay to buy it. ▶ VERB ② To price something at a particular amount is to fix its price at that amount.

> **price** NOUN
> ① = amount, charge, cost, fee, figure, value
> ▶ VERB ② = cost, estimate, put a price on, value

priceless ADJECTIVE Something that is priceless is so valuable that it is difficult to work out how much it is worth.

pricey, pricier, priciest ADJECTIVE (*informal*) expensive.

prick VERB ① If you prick something, you stick a sharp pointed object into it. ▶ NOUN ② a small, sharp pain caused when something pricks you.

pride NOUN ① Pride is a feeling of satisfaction you have when you have done something well. ② Pride is also a feeling of being better than other people. ③ A pride of lions is a group of them. ▶ VERB ④ If you pride yourself on a quality or skill, you are proud of it • *She prides herself on punctuality.*

priest NOUN ① RE a member of the clergy in some Christian Churches. ② RE In many non-Christian religions, a priest is a man who has special duties in the place where people worship. **priestly** ADJECTIVE

priestess NOUN a female priest in a non-Christian religion.

priesthood NOUN The priesthood is the position of being a priest.

prim, primmer, primmest ADJECTIVE Someone who is prim always behaves very correctly and is easily shocked by anything rude.

> **prim** ADJECTIVE
> = proper, prudish, puritanical, strait-laced

primarily ADVERB You use 'primarily' to indicate the main or most important feature of something • *I still rated people primarily on their looks.*

primary ADJECTIVE 'Primary' is used to describe something that is extremely important for someone or something • *the primary aim of his research.*

primary school NOUN a school for children aged up to 11.

primate NOUN ① an archbishop. ② a member of the group of animals which includes humans, monkeys and apes.

prime ADJECTIVE ① main or most important • *a prime cause of brain damage.* ② of the best quality • *in prime condition.* ▶ NOUN ③ Someone's prime is the stage when they are at their strongest, most active or most successful. ▶ **VERB** ④ If you prime someone, you give them information about something in advance to prepare them • *We are primed for every lesson.*

prime ADJECTIVE
① = chief, leading, main, principal
② = best, choice, first-rate, select, superior

prime minister NOUN The prime minister is the leader of the government.

primeval *[Said pry-**mee**-vl]*; also spelt **primaeval** ADJECTIVE belonging to a very early period in the history of the world.

primitive ADJECTIVE ① connected with a society that lives very simply without industries or a writing system • *the primitive peoples of the world.* ② very simple, basic or old-fashioned • *a very small primitive cottage.*

primitive ADJECTIVE
② = crude, rough, rude, rudimentary, simple

primrose NOUN a small plant that has pale yellow flowers in spring.

prince NOUN a male member of a royal family, especially the son of a king or queen. **princely** ADJECTIVE

princess NOUN a female member of a royal family, usually the daughter of a king or queen, or the wife of a prince.

principal ADJECTIVE ① main or most important • *the principal source of food.* ▶ NOUN ② the person in charge of a school or college. **principally** ADVERB

principal ADJECTIVE
① = chief, first, foremost, main, major, primary, prime

principality, **principalities** NOUN a country ruled by a prince.

principle NOUN ① a belief you have about the way you should behave • *a woman of principle.* ② a general rule or scientific law which explains how something happens or works • *the principle of evolution in nature.*

principle NOUN
① = conscience, integrity, morals, scruples, sense of duty
② = axiom, canon, doctrine, fundamental, law

print VERB ① To print a newspaper or book is to reproduce it in large quantities using a mechanical or electronic copying process. ② If you print when you are writing, you do not join the letters together. ▶ NOUN ③ The letters and numbers on the pages of a book or newspaper are referred to as the print. ④ a photograph, or a printed copy of a painting. ⑤ Footprints and fingerprints can be referred to as prints.

printer, **printers** NOUN ① a machine that can be connected to a computer to reproduce copies of documents or pictures on paper. ② a person or company that prints newspapers or books.

printing NOUN the process of producing printed material such as books and newspapers.

prior ADJECTIVE ① planned or done at an earlier time • *I have a prior engagement.* ▶ PHRASE ② Something that happens **prior to** a particular time or event happens before it.

prioritise; also spelt **prioritize** VERB To prioritise things is to decide which is the most important and deal with it first.

priority, **priorities** NOUN something that needs to be dealt with first • *The priority is building homes.*

prise VERB If you prise something open or away from a surface, you force it open or away • *She prised his fingers loose.*

prism NOUN ① an object made of clear glass with many flat sides. It separates light passing through it into the colours of the rainbow. ② MATHS A prism is any polyhedron with two identical parallel ends and sides which are parallelograms.

prison NOUN a building where criminals are kept in captivity.

> **prison** NOUN
> = dungeon, jail, nick (*British, Australian and New Zealand; slang*), penal institution

prisoner NOUN someone who is kept in prison or held in captivity against their will.

> **prisoner** NOUN
> = captive, convict, hostage

pristine [*Said priss-teen*] ADJECTIVE (*formal*) very clean or new and in perfect condition.

private ADJECTIVE ① for the use of one person rather than people in general • *a private bathroom*. ② taking place between a small number of people and kept secret from others • *a private conversation*. ③ owned or run by individuals or companies rather than by the state • *a private company*. ▶ NOUN ④ a soldier of the lowest rank.
privacy NOUN **privately** ADVERB

> **private** ADJECTIVE
> ① = exclusive, individual, personal, special
> ② = clandestine (*formal*), confidential, secret
> ≠ public

private school NOUN a school that does not receive money from the government, and which parents pay for their children to attend.

privatise; also spelt **privatize** VERB If the government privatises a state-owned industry or organisation, it allows it to be bought and owned by a private individual or group.

privilege NOUN a special right or advantage given to a person or group • *the privileges of monarchy*. **privileged** ADJECTIVE

privy ADJECTIVE (*formal*) If you are privy to something secret, you have been told about it.

prize NOUN ① a reward given to the winner of a competition or game. ▶ ADJECTIVE ② of the highest quality or standard • *his prize dahlia*. ▶ VERB ③ Something that is prized is wanted and admired for its value or quality.

> **prize** NOUN
> ① = accolade, award, honour, trophy
> ▶ ADJECTIVE ② = award-winning, first-rate, outstanding, top
> ▶ VERB ③ = cherish, esteem, treasure, value

pro, **pros** NOUN ① (*informal*) a professional. ▶ PHRASE ② The **pros and cons** of a situation are its advantages and disadvantages.

pro- PREFIX 'Pro-' means supporting or in favour of • *pro-democracy protests*.

probability, **probabilities** NOUN ① The probability of something happening is how likely it is to happen • *the probability of success*. ② If something is a probability, it is likely to happen • *The probability is that you will be feeling better*.

> **probability** NOUN
> ① = chances, likelihood, odds, prospect

probable ADJECTIVE Something that is probable is likely to be true or correct, or likely to happen • *the most probable outcome*.

> **probable** ADJECTIVE
> = apparent, feasible, likely, on the cards, plausible
> ≠ improbable

probably ADVERB Something that is probably the case is likely but not certain.

> **probably** ADVERB
> = doubtless, in all probability, likely, presumably

probation NOUN Probation is a period of time during which a person convicted of a crime is supervised by a probation officer instead of being sent to prison. **probationary** ADJECTIVE

probe VERB ① If you probe, you ask a lot of questions to discover the facts about something. ▸ NOUN ② a long thin instrument used by doctors and dentists when examining a patient.

problem NOUN ① an unsatisfactory situation that causes difficulties. ② a puzzle or question that you solve using logical thought or mathematics. **problematic** ADJECTIVE

> **problem** NOUN
> ① = difficulty, predicament, quandary, trouble
> ② = conundrum, puzzle, riddle

procedure NOUN a way of doing something, especially the correct or usual way • *It's standard procedure.* **procedural** ADJECTIVE

> **procedure** NOUN
> = method, policy, practice, process, strategy, system

proceed VERB ① If you proceed to do something, you start doing it, or continue doing it • *She proceeded to tell them.* ② (*formal*) If you proceed in a particular direction, you move in that direction • *The taxi proceeded along a lonely road.*

> **proceed** VERB
> ① = begin, carry on, continue, get under way, go on, start
> ≠ cease
> ② = advance, continue, go on, make your way, progress, travel

proceedings PLURAL NOUN ① You can refer to an organised and related series of events as the proceedings • *She was determined to see the proceedings from start to finish.* ② Legal proceedings are legal action taken against someone.

process NOUN ① a series of actions intended to achieve a particular result or change. ▸ PHRASE ② If you are **in the process** of doing something, you have started doing it but have not yet finished. ▸ VERB ③ When food is processed, it is prepared in factories before it is sold. ④ When information is processed, it is put through a system or into a computer to organise it.

> **process** NOUN
> ① = course of action, means, method, procedure, system
> ▸ VERB ③ = deal with, dispose of, handle, take care of

procession NOUN a group of people or vehicles moving in a line, often as part of a ceremony.

processor NOUN ICT In computing, a processor is the central chip in a computer which controls its operations.

proclaim VERB If someone proclaims something, they announce it or make it known • *You have proclaimed your innocence.* **proclamation** NOUN

procure VERB (*formal*) If you procure something, you obtain it.

prod, **prods, prodding, prodded** VERB If you prod something, you give it a push with your finger or with something pointed.

prodigy, **prodigies** [*Said* ***prod**-dij-ee*] NOUN someone who shows an extraordinary natural ability at an early age.

produce VERB [*Said pro-**dyoos***] ① To produce something is to make it or cause it • *a factory producing circuits for computers*. ② If you produce something from somewhere, you bring it out so it can be seen. ▶ **NOUN** [*Said* ***prod****-yoos*] ③ Produce is food that is grown to be sold • *fresh produce*.

produce VERB
① = construct, create, invent, make, manufacture
② = advance, bring forward, bring to light, put forward

producer NOUN The producer of a record, film or show is the person in charge of making it or putting it on.

product NOUN ① something that is made to be sold • *high-quality products*. ② MATHS The product of two or more numbers or quantities is the result of multiplying them together. ③ SCIENCE a substance formed in a chemical reaction.

product NOUN
① = commodity, goods, merchandise, produce

production NOUN ① DGT Production is the process of manufacturing or growing something in large quantities • *modern methods of production*. ② Production is also the amount of goods manufactured or food grown by a country or company • *Production has fallen by 13.2%*. ③ A production of a play, opera or other show is a series of performances of it.

productive ADJECTIVE ① To be productive means to produce a large number of things • *Farms were more productive in these areas*. ② If something such as a meeting is productive, good or useful things happen as a result of it.

productive ADJECTIVE
① = fertile, fruitful, prolific
≠ unproductive
② = constructive, useful, valuable, worthwhile
≠ unproductive

productivity NOUN Productivity is the rate at which things are produced or dealt with.

profane ADJECTIVE (*formal*) showing disrespect for a religion or religious things • *profane language*.

profess VERB ① (*formal*) If you profess to do or have something, you claim to do or have it. ② If you profess a feeling or opinion, you express it • *He professes a lasting affection for Trinidad*.

profession NOUN ① a type of job that requires advanced education or training. ② You can use 'profession' to refer to all the people who have a particular profession • *the medical profession*.

profession NOUN
① = business, career, occupation

professional ADJECTIVE ① Professional means relating to the work of someone who is qualified in a particular profession • *I think you need professional advice*. ② Professional also describes activities when they are done to earn money rather than as a hobby • *professional football*. ③ A professional piece of work is of a very high standard. ▶ **NOUN** ④ a person who has been trained in a profession. ⑤ someone who plays a sport to earn money rather than as a hobby.

professor NOUN the senior teacher in a department of a British university. **professorial ADJECTIVE**

proficient ADJECTIVE If you are proficient at something, you can do it well. **proficiency NOUN**

proficient ADJECTIVE
= able, accomplished, adept, capable, competent, efficient, skilful, skilled
≠ incompetent

profile NOUN ① Your profile is the outline of your face seen from the side. ② A profile of someone is a short description of their life and character.

profit NOUN ① When someone sells something, the profit is the amount they gain by selling it for more than it cost them to buy or make. ▶ VERB ② If you profit from something, you gain or benefit from it. **profitable** ADJECTIVE

profit NOUN
① = earnings, proceeds, revenue, surplus, takings
≠ loss
▶ VERB ② = capitalise on, exploit, make the most of, take advantage of

profound ADJECTIVE ① great in degree or intensity • *a profound need to please.* ② showing great and deep intellectual understanding • *a profound question.* **profoundly** ADVERB **profundity** NOUN

program, programs, programming, programmed [ICT] NOUN ① a set of instructions that a computer follows to perform a particular task. ▶ VERB ② When someone programs a computer, they write a program and put it into the computer. **programmer** NOUN

programme NOUN ① a planned series of events • *a programme of official engagements.* ② a particular piece presented as a unit on television or radio, such as a play, show or discussion. ③ a booklet giving information about a play, concert or show that you are attending.

programme NOUN
① = agenda, schedule, timetable
② = broadcast, show

progress NOUN ① Progress is the process of gradually improving or getting near to achieving something • *Gerry is now making some real progress towards fitness.* ② The progress of something is the way in which it develops or continues • *news on the progress of the war.* ▶ PHRASE ③ Something that is **in progress** is happening • *A cricket match was in progress.* ▶ VERB ④ If you progress, you become more advanced or skilful. ⑤ To progress is to continue • *As the evening progressed, sadness turned to rage.* **progression** NOUN

progress NOUN
① = advance, breakthrough, headway, improvement
▶ VERB ④ = advance, blossom, develop, improve

progressive ADJECTIVE ① having modern ideas about how things should be done. ② happening gradually • *a progressive illness.*

prohibit VERB If someone prohibits something, they forbid it or make it illegal. **prohibition** NOUN

prohibit VERB
= ban, forbid, outlaw, prevent
≠ allow

prohibitive ADJECTIVE If the cost of something is prohibitive, it is so high that people cannot afford it.

project NOUN *[Said **pro**-ject]* ① a carefully planned attempt to achieve something or to study something over a period of time. ▶ VERB *[Said pro-**ject**]* ② Something that is projected is planned or expected to happen in the future • *The population aged 65 or over is projected to increase.* ③ To project an image onto a screen is to make it appear there using equipment such as a projector. ④ Something that projects sticks out beyond a surface or edge. **projection** NOUN

projector NOUN a piece of equipment which produces a large image on a screen by shining light through a photographic slide or film strip.

proletariat NOUN (*formal*) Working-class people are sometimes referred to as the proletariat. **proletarian** ADJECTIVE

a b c d e f g h i j k l m n o p q r s t u v w x y z

proliferate VERB If things proliferate, they quickly increase in number. **proliferation** NOUN

prolific ADJECTIVE producing a lot of something • *this prolific artist.*

prologue NOUN a speech or section that introduces a play or book.

prolong VERB If you prolong something, you make it last longer. **prolonged** ADJECTIVE

prom NOUN (*informal*) a concert at which some of the audience stand.

promenade [*Said prom-min-**ahd***] NOUN a road or path next to the sea at a seaside resort.

prominent ADJECTIVE ① Prominent people are well-known and important. ② Something that is prominent is very noticeable • *a prominent nose.* **prominence** NOUN **prominently** ADVERB

> **prominent** ADJECTIVE
> ① = eminent, famous, important, notable, noted, renowned, well-known
> ② = conspicuous, eye-catching, jutting, noticeable, obvious, pronounced, striking

promise VERB ① If you promise to do something, you say that you will definitely do it. ② Something that promises to have a particular quality shows signs that it will have that quality • *This promised to be a very long night.* ▸ NOUN ③ a statement made by someone that they will definitely do something • *He made a promise to me.* ④ Someone or something that shows promise seems likely to be very successful. **promising** ADJECTIVE

> **promise** VERB
> ① = assure, give your word, guarantee, pledge, vow
> ② = hint at, indicate, show signs of
> ▸ NOUN ③ = assurance, guarantee, pledge, undertaking, vow

promontory, promontories [*Said prom-mon-tree*] NOUN an area of high land sticking out into the sea.

promote VERB ① If someone promotes something, they try to make it happen. ② If someone promotes a product such as a film or a book, they try to make it popular by advertising. ③ If someone is promoted, they are given a more important job at work. **promoter** NOUN **promotion** NOUN

> **promote** VERB
> ① = back, support
> ② = advertise, plug (*informal*), publicise
> ③ = elevate, upgrade

prompt VERB ① If something prompts someone to do something, it makes them decide to do it • *Curiosity prompted him to push at the door.* ② If you prompt someone when they stop speaking, you tell them what to say next or encourage them to continue. ▸ ADVERB ③ exactly at the time mentioned • *Wednesday morning at 10.40 prompt.* ▸ ADJECTIVE ④ A prompt action is done without any delay • *a prompt reply.* **promptly** ADVERB

> **prompt** VERB
> ① = cause, induce, inspire, motivate, spur
> ② = coax, remind
> ▸ ADVERB ③ = exactly, on the dot, precisely, sharp
> ▸ ADJECTIVE ④ = immediate, instant, instantaneous, quick, rapid, swift

prone ADJECTIVE ① If you are prone to something, you have a tendency to be affected by it or to do it • *She is prone to headaches.* ② If you are prone, you are lying flat and face downwards • *lying prone on the grass.*

> **prone** ADJECTIVE
> ① = disposed, given, inclined, liable, susceptible
> ② = face down, prostrate

pronoun NOUN [ENGLISH] [MFL] In grammar, a pronoun is a word that is used to replace a noun. 'He', 'she' and 'them' are all pronouns.

pronounce VERB [ENGLISH] [MFL] When you pronounce a word, you say it.

pronounced ADJECTIVE very noticeable • *He talks with a pronounced lowland accent.*

pronunciation [*Said pron-nun-see-**ay**-shn*] NOUN the way a word is usually said.

proof NOUN If you have proof of something, you have evidence which shows that it is true or exists.

> **proof** NOUN
> = confirmation, evidence, testimony, verification

prop, **props**, **propping**, **propped** VERB ① If you prop an object somewhere, you support it or rest it against something • *The barman propped himself against the counter.* ▶ NOUN ② a stick or other object used to support something. ③ The props in a play are all the objects and furniture used by the actors.

propaganda NOUN [HISTORY] Propaganda is exaggerated or false information that is published or broadcast in order to influence people.

propagate VERB ① If people propagate an idea, they spread it to try to influence many other people. ② If you propagate plants, you grow more of them from an original one.
propagation NOUN

propel, **propels**, **propelling**, **propelled** VERB To propel something is to cause it to move in a particular direction.

propeller NOUN a device on a boat or aircraft with rotating blades which make the boat or aircraft move.

propensity, **propensities** NOUN (*formal*) a tendency to behave in a particular way.

proper ADJECTIVE ① real and satisfactory • *He was no nearer having a proper job.* ② correct or suitable • *Put things in their proper place.* ③ accepted or conventional • *a proper wedding.*
properly ADVERB

> **proper** ADJECTIVE
> ② = appropriate, apt, correct, fitting, right, suitable
> ≠ improper
> ③ = accepted, conventional, orthodox

property, **properties** NOUN ① A person's property is the things that belong to them. ② a building and the land belonging to it. ③ a characteristic or quality • *Mint has powerful healing properties.*

> **property** NOUN
> ① = assets, belongings, effects, estate, possessions
> ③ = attribute, characteristic, feature, hallmark, quality, trait

prophecy, **prophecies** [*Said **prof**-iss-see*] NOUN a statement about what someone believes will happen in the future.

prophet NOUN [RE] a person who predicts what will happen in the future.

prophetic ADJECTIVE correctly predicting what will happen • *It was a prophetic warning.*

proportion NOUN ① A proportion of an amount or group is a part of it • *a tiny proportion of the population.* ② The proportion of one amount to another is its size in comparison with the other amount • *the highest proportion of women to men.* ③ (*in plural*) You can refer to the size of something as its proportions • *a red umbrella of vast proportions.*

> **proportion** NOUN
> ① = percentage, quota, segment, share

A B C D E F G H I J K L M N O P Q R S T U V W X Y Z

proportional or **proportionate** ADJECTIVE If one thing is proportional to another, it remains the same size in comparison with the other • *proportional increases in profit*. **proportionally** or **proportionately** ADVERB

proportional representation NOUN Proportional representation is a system of voting in elections in which the number of representatives of each party is in proportion to the number of people who voted for it.

proposal NOUN a plan that has been suggested • *business proposals*.

propose VERB ① If you propose a plan or idea, you suggest it. ② If you propose to do something, you intend to do it • *And how do you propose to do that?* ③ When someone proposes a toast to a particular person, they ask people to drink a toast to that person. ④ If someone proposes to another person, they ask that person to marry them.

proposition NOUN ① a statement expressing a theory or opinion. ② an offer or suggestion • *I made her a proposition*.

proprietor NOUN The proprietor of a business is the owner.

propriety NOUN (*formal*) Propriety is what is socially or morally acceptable • *a model of propriety*.

propulsion NOUN Propulsion is the power that moves something.

prose NOUN Prose is ordinary written language in contrast to poetry.

prosecute VERB If someone is prosecuted, they are charged with a crime and have to stand trial. **prosecutor** NOUN

prosecution NOUN The lawyers who try to prove that a person on trial is guilty are called the prosecution.

prospect NOUN ① If there is a prospect of something happening, there is a possibility that it will happen • *There was little prospect of going home*. ② Someone's prospects are their chances of being successful in the future. ▶ VERB ③ If someone prospects for gold or oil, they look for it. **prospector** NOUN

> **prospect** NOUN
> ① = expectation, hope, outlook, promise

prospective ADJECTIVE 'Prospective' is used to say that someone wants to be or is likely to be something. For example, the prospective owner of something is the person who wants to own it.

prospectus NOUN a booklet giving details about a college or a company.

prosper VERB When people or businesses prosper, they are successful and make a lot of money. **prosperous** ADJECTIVE **prosperity** NOUN

prostrate ADJECTIVE lying face downwards on the ground.

protagonist NOUN (*formal*) ① a main character in a play or story. ② Someone who is a protagonist of an idea or movement is a leading supporter of it.

protect VERB To protect someone or something is to prevent them from being harmed or damaged. **protective** ADJECTIVE **protector** NOUN

protection NOUN ① the act of preventing harm or damage. ② something that keeps a person or thing safe.

> **protection** NOUN
> ② = barrier, buffer, cover, safeguard, shelter

protein NOUN [SCIENCE] Protein is a complex compound consisting of amino acid chains, found in many foods and essential for all living things.

protest VERB *[Said pro-**test**]* ① If you protest about something, you say or demonstrate publicly that you disagree with it • *They protested against the new law.* ▶ NOUN *[Said **pro**-test]* ② a demonstration or statement showing that you disagree with something. **protester** NOUN

> **protest** VERB
> ① = complain, disagree, disapprove, object, oppose
> ▶ NOUN ② = complaint, objection, outcry

Protestant NOUN, ADJECTIVE [RE] (a member) of one of the Christian Churches which separated from the Catholic Church in the 16th century.

protestation NOUN a strong declaration that something is true or not true • *his protestations of love.*

protocol NOUN Protocol is the system of rules about the correct way to behave in formal situations.

proton NOUN [SCIENCE] a particle which forms part of the nucleus of an atom and has a positive electrical charge.

prototype NOUN [D&T] a first model of something that is made so that the design can be tested and improved.

protracted ADJECTIVE lasting longer than usual • *a protracted dispute.*

protrude VERB (*formal*) If something is protruding from a surface or edge, it is sticking out. **protrusion** NOUN

proud ADJECTIVE ① feeling pleasure and satisfaction at something you own or have achieved • *I was proud of our players today.* ② having great dignity and self-respect • *too proud to ask for money.* **proudly** ADVERB

> **proud** ADJECTIVE
> ① = gratified, honoured, pleased

prove, proves, proving, proved or **proven** VERB ① To prove that something is true is to provide evidence that it is definitely true • *A letter from Kathleen proved that he lived there.* ② If something proves to be the case, it becomes clear that it is so • *His first impressions of her proved wrong.*

> **prove** VERB
> ① = ascertain, confirm, demonstrate, establish, verify
> ≠ disprove

proverb NOUN a short sentence which gives advice or makes a comment about life. **proverbial** ADJECTIVE

provide VERB ① If you provide something for someone, you give it to them or make it available for them. ② If you provide for someone, you give them the things they need.

> **provide** VERB
> ① = contribute, equip, furnish, outfit, supply

providence NOUN Providence is God or a force which is believed to arrange the things that happen to us.

province NOUN ① one of the areas into which some large countries are divided, each province having its own administration. ② (*in plural*) You can refer to the parts of a country which are not near the capital as the provinces.

provincial ADJECTIVE ① connected with the parts of a country outside the capital • *a provincial theatre.* ② narrow-minded and lacking sophistication.

provision NOUN ① The provision of something is the act of making it available to people • *the provision of health care.* ② (*in plural*) Provisions are supplies of food.

provisional ADJECTIVE A provisional arrangement has not yet been made definite and so might be changed.

proviso, **provisos** *[Said prov-**eye**-zoh]* NOUN a condition in an agreement.

provocation NOUN an act done deliberately to annoy someone.

provocative ADJECTIVE intended to annoy people or make them react • *a provocative speech.*

provoke VERB ① If you provoke someone, you deliberately try to make them angry. ② If something provokes an unpleasant reaction, it causes it • *illness provoked by tension or worry.*

> **provoke** VERB
> ① = anger, annoy, enrage, goad, insult, irritate, tease
> ② = cause, evoke, produce, prompt, rouse, set off, spark off

prowess NOUN Prowess is outstanding ability • *his prowess at tennis.*

prowl VERB If a person or animal prowls around, they move around quietly and secretly, as if hunting.

proximity NOUN *(formal)* Proximity is nearness to someone or something.

proxy PHRASE If you do something **by proxy**, someone else does it on your behalf • *voting by proxy.*

prudent ADJECTIVE behaving in a sensible and cautious way • *It is prudent to plan ahead.* **prudence** NOUN **prudently** ADVERB

prune NOUN ① a dried plum. ▸ VERB ② When someone prunes a tree or shrub, they cut back some of the branches.

pry, **pries**, **prying**, **pried** VERB If someone is prying, they are trying to find out about something secret or private.

> **pry** VERB
> = interfere, intrude, poke your nose in *(informal)*, poke your nose into *(informal)*, snoop *(informal)*

PS PS is written before an additional message at the end of a letter. PS is an abbreviation for 'postscript'.

pseudonym *[Said **syoo**-doe-nim]* NOUN a name an author uses rather than their real name.

psyche *[Said **sigh**-kee]* NOUN your mind and your deepest feelings.

psychiatry NOUN Psychiatry is the branch of medicine concerned with mental health. **psychiatrist** NOUN **psychiatric** ADJECTIVE

psychic ADJECTIVE having unusual mental powers such as the ability to read people's minds or predict the future.

psychoanalysis NOUN Psychoanalysis is the examination and treatment of someone who has mental health problems by encouraging them to talk about their feelings and past events in order to discover the cause of the illness. **psychoanalyst** NOUN **psychoanalyse** VERB

psychology NOUN Psychology is the scientific study of the mind and of the reasons for people's behaviour. **psychological** ADJECTIVE **psychologist** NOUN

psychopath NOUN a person with a psychiatric disorder who can commit antisocial or violent acts without feeling guilt. **psychopathic** ADJECTIVE

psychosis, **psychoses** *[Said sigh-**koe**-siss]* NOUN a severe mental illness that causes people to interpret reality in a different way from the people around them. **psychotic** ADJECTIVE

PTO PTO is an abbreviation for 'please turn over'. It is written at the bottom of a page to indicate that the writing continues on the other side.

pub NOUN a building where people go to buy and drink alcoholic or soft drinks.

puberty *[Said pyoo-ber-tee]* NOUN Puberty is the stage when a person's body changes from that of a child into that of an adult.

pubic *[Said pyoo-bik]* ADJECTIVE relating to the area around and above a person's genitals.

public NOUN ① You can refer to people in general as the public. ▸ ADJECTIVE ② relating to people in general • *There was some public support for the idea.* ③ provided for everyone to use, or open to anyone • *public transport.*
publicly ADVERB

> **public** NOUN
> ① = masses, nation, people, populace, society
> ▸ ADJECTIVE ② = civic, general, popular, universal
> ③ = communal, community, open to the public, universal
> ≠ private

publican NOUN a person who owns or manages a pub.

publication NOUN ① The publication of a book is the act of printing it and making it available. ② a book or magazine • *medical publications.*

publicise; also spelt **publicize** VERB When someone publicises a fact or event, they advertise it and make it widely known.

> **publicise** VERB
> = advertise, plug (*informal*), promote

publicity NOUN Publicity is information or advertisements about an item or event.

> **publicity** NOUN
> = advertising, plug (*informal*), promotion

public school NOUN In Britain, a public school is a school that is privately run and that charges fees for the pupils to attend.

public servant NOUN In Australia and New Zealand, a public servant is someone who works in the public service.

public service NOUN In Australia and New Zealand, the public service is the government departments responsible for the administration of the country.

publish VERB LIBRARY When a company publishes a book, newspaper or magazine, they print copies of it and distribute it.
publishing NOUN

> **publish** VERB
> = bring out, post, print, put out

publisher NOUN LIBRARY The publisher of a book, newspaper or magazine is the person or company that prints copies of it and distributes it.

pudding NOUN ① a sweet cake mixture cooked with fruit or other flavouring and served hot. ② You can refer to the sweet course of a meal as the pudding.

puddle NOUN a small shallow pool of liquid.

puerile *[Said pyoo-rile]* ADJECTIVE Puerile behaviour is silly and childish.

puff VERB ① To puff on a cigarette or pipe is to smoke it. ② If you are puffing, you are breathing loudly and quickly with your mouth open. ③ If something puffs out or puffs up, it swells and becomes larger and rounder. ▸ NOUN ④ a small amount of air or smoke that is released.

pug NOUN a small, short-haired dog with a flat nose.

pull VERB ① When you pull something, you hold it and move it towards you. ② When something is pulled by a vehicle or animal, it is attached to it and moves along behind it • *Four oxen can pull a single* *plough.* ③ When you pull a curtain or blind, you move it so that it covers or uncovers the window. ④ If you pull a muscle, you injure it by stretching it too far or too quickly. ⑤ When a vehicle pulls away, pulls out or pulls in, it moves in that direction. ▶ **NOUN** ⑥ The pull of something is its attraction or influence • *the pull of the past.* **pull down VERB** When a building is pulled down, it is deliberately destroyed. **pull out VERB** If you pull out of something, you leave it or decide not to continue with it • *The German government has pulled out of the project.* **pull through VERB** When someone pulls through, they recover from a serious illness.

pull VERB
① = drag, draw, haul, tow, tug, yank
≠ push
▶ **NOUN** ⑥ = attraction, lure, magnetism

pulley NOUN DGT a device for lifting heavy weights. The weight is attached to a rope which passes over a wheel or series of wheels.

pullover NOUN a woollen piece of clothing that covers the top part of your body.

pulmonary ADJECTIVE relating to the lungs or to the veins and arteries carrying blood between the lungs and the heart.

pulp NOUN If something is turned into a pulp, it is crushed until it is soft and moist.

pulpit *[Said **pool**-pit]* **NOUN** the small raised platform in a church where a member of the clergy stands to preach.

pulse NOUN ① Your pulse is the regular beating of blood through your body, the rate of which you can feel at your wrists and elsewhere. ② The seeds of beans, peas and lentils are called pulses when they are used for food. ▶ **VERB** ③ If something is pulsing, it is moving or vibrating with rhythmic, regular movements • *She could feel the blood pulsing in her eardrums.*

pummel, pummels, pummelling, pummelled VERB If you pummel something, you beat it with your fists.

pump NOUN ① a machine that is used to force a liquid or gas to move in a particular direction. ② Pumps are light shoes with flat soles which people wear for sport or leisure. ▶ **VERB** ③ To pump a liquid or gas somewhere is to force it to flow in that direction, using a pump. ④ If you pump money into something, you put a lot of money into it.

pumpkin NOUN a very large, round, orange fruit eaten as a vegetable.

pun NOUN a clever and amusing use of words so that what you say has two different meanings, such as *my dog's a champion boxer.*

punch VERB ① If you punch someone, you hit them hard with your fist. ▶ **NOUN** ② a hard blow with the fist. ③ a tool used for making holes. ④ Punch is a drink made from a mixture of wine, spirits and fruit.

punctual ADJECTIVE arriving at the correct time. **punctually ADVERB punctuality NOUN**

punctual ADJECTIVE
= in good time, on time, prompt

punctuate VERB ① Something that is punctuated by a particular thing is interrupted by it at intervals • *a grey day punctuated by bouts of rain.* ② ENGLISH When you punctuate a piece of writing, you put punctuation into it.

punctuation NOUN ENGLISH The marks in writing such as full stops, question marks and commas are called punctuation or punctuation marks.

puncture NOUN ① If a tyre has a puncture, a small hole has been made in it and it has become flat. ▸ VERB ② To puncture something is to make a small hole in it.

pungent ADJECTIVE having a strong, often unpleasant, smell or taste. **pungency** NOUN

punish VERB To punish someone who has done something wrong is to make them suffer because of it.

> **punish** VERB
> = discipline, penalise, rap someone's knuckles, sentence, throw the book at

punishment NOUN something unpleasant done to someone because they have done something wrong.

> **punishment** NOUN
> = penalty, retribution

punitive [Said *pyoo-nit-tiv*] ADJECTIVE harsh and intended to punish people • *punitive military action.*

Punjabi [Said *pun-**jah**-bee*] ADJECTIVE ① belonging or relating to the Punjab, a state in north-western India. ▸ NOUN ② someone who comes from the Punjab. ③ Punjabi is a language spoken in the Punjab.

punk NOUN Punk or punk rock is an aggressive style of rock music.

punt NOUN a long, flat-bottomed boat. You move it along by pushing a pole against the river bottom.

puny, **punier**, **puniest** ADJECTIVE very small and weak.

> **puny** ADJECTIVE
> = feeble, frail, sickly, skinny, weak

pup NOUN a young dog. Some other young animals such as seals are also called pups.

pupil NOUN ① The pupils at a school are the children who go there. ② Your pupils are the small, round, black areas in the centre of your eyes.

> **pupil** NOUN
> ① = scholar (*South African*), schoolboy, schoolchild, schoolgirl, student

puppet NOUN a doll or toy animal that is moved by pulling strings or by putting your hand inside its body.

puppy, **puppies** NOUN a young dog.

purchase VERB ① When you purchase something, you buy it. ▸ NOUN ② something you have bought. **purchaser** NOUN

pure ADJECTIVE ① Something that is pure is not mixed with anything else • *pure wool* • *pure white.* ② Pure also means clean and free from harmful substances • *The water is pure enough to drink.* ③ People who are pure have not done anything considered to be sinful. ④ Pure also means complete and total • *a matter of pure luck.* **purity** NOUN

> **pure** ADJECTIVE
> ② = clean, germ-free, pasteurised, spotless, sterilised
> ≠ impure
> ④ = absolute, complete, outright, sheer, unmitigated, utter

purely ADVERB involving only one feature and not including anything else • *purely professional.*

purge VERB To purge something is to remove undesirable things from it • *to purge the country of criminals.*

purify, **purifies**, **purifying**, **purified** VERB To purify something is to remove all dirty or harmful substances from it. **purification** NOUN

purist NOUN someone who believes that something should be done in a particular, correct way • *a football purist.*

puritan NOUN someone who believes in strict moral principles and avoids physical pleasures. **puritanical** ADJECTIVE

purple NOUN, ADJECTIVE reddish-blue.

purport *[Said pur-**port**]* VERB (*formal*) Something that purports to be or have a particular thing claims to be or have it • *a country which purports to disapprove of smokers.*

purpose NOUN ① The purpose of something is the reason for it • *the purpose of the meeting.* ② If you have a particular purpose, this is what you want to achieve • *To make music is my purpose in life.* ▸ PHRASE ③ If you do something **on purpose**, you do it deliberately. **purposely** ADVERB **purposeful** ADJECTIVE

> **purpose** NOUN
> ① = aim, function, intention, object, point, reason
> ▸ PHRASE ③ = by design, deliberately, intentionally, knowingly, purposely

purr VERB When a cat purrs, it makes a low vibrating sound because it is contented.

purse NOUN ① a small leather or fabric container for carrying money. ▸ VERB ② If you purse your lips, you move them into a tight, rounded shape.

pursue, **pursues**, **pursuing**, **pursued** VERB ① If you pursue an activity or plan, you do it or make efforts to achieve it • *I decided to pursue a career in photography.* ② If you pursue someone, you follow them to try to catch them. **pursuer** NOUN **pursuit** NOUN

purveyor NOUN (*formal*) A purveyor of goods or services is a person who sells them or provides them.

push VERB ① When you push something, you press it using force in order to move it. ② If you push someone into doing something, you force or persuade them to do it • *His agent pushed him into auditioning for a part.* ③ (*informal*) Someone who pushes drugs sells them illegally. **push off** VERB (*informal*) If you tell someone to push off, you are telling them rudely to go away.

> **push** VERB
> ① = press, ram, shove, thrust
> ≠ pull
> ② = encourage, persuade, press, urge

pushchair NOUN a small folding chair on wheels in which a baby or toddler can be wheeled around.

pushing PREPOSITION Someone who is pushing a particular age is nearly that age • *pushing sixty.*

pushover NOUN (*informal*) ① something that is easy. ② someone who is easily persuaded or defeated.

pushy, **pushier**, **pushiest** ADJECTIVE (*informal*) behaving in a forceful and determined way.

> **pushy** ADJECTIVE
> = aggressive, ambitious, assertive, bossy (*formal*), forceful, obtrusive

pussy, **pussies** NOUN (*informal*) a cat.

put, **puts**, **putting**, **put** VERB ① When you put something somewhere, you move it into that place or position. ② If you put an idea or remark in a particular way, you express it that way • *I think you've put that very well.* ③ To put someone or something in a particular state or situation means to cause them to be in it • *It puts us both in an awkward position.* ④ You can use 'put' to express an estimate of the size or importance of something • *Her wealth is now put at £290 million.* **put down** VERB ① To put someone down is to criticise them and make them appear foolish. ② If an animal is put down, it is killed because it is very ill or dangerous. **put off** VERB ① If you put something off, you delay doing it. ② To put someone off is to discourage them. **put out** VERB ① If you put a fire out or put the light out, you make it stop burning or shining. ② If you are put out, you are annoyed or upset. **put up** VERB If you put up resistance to something, you argue or fight against it • *She put up a tremendous struggle.* **put up with** VERB If you put up with something, you tolerate it even though you disagree with it or dislike it.

put VERB
① = deposit, lay, place, position, rest
② = phrase, word
▸ **put down** ① = belittle, criticise, find fault with, humiliate ▸ **put off** ① = defer, delay, postpone, put back, put on ice, reschedule ▸ **put up with** = abide, bear, stand, stand for, stomach, tolerate

putt NOUN In golf, a putt is a gentle stroke made when the ball is near the hole.

putting NOUN Putting is a game played on a small grass course with no obstacles. You hit a ball gently with a club so that it rolls towards one of a series of holes around the course.

putty NOUN Putty is a paste used to fix panes of glass into frames.

puzzle VERB ① If something puzzles you, it confuses you and you do not understand it • *There was something about her that puzzled me.* ▸ NOUN ② A puzzle is a game or question that requires a lot of thought to complete or solve. **puzzled** ADJECTIVE **puzzlement** NOUN

puzzle VERB
① = baffle, bewilder, confuse, mystify, stump
▸ NOUN ② = brain-teaser (*informal*), poser, problem, riddle

PVC NOUN PVC is a plastic used for making clothing, pipes and many other things. PVC is an abbreviation for 'polyvinyl chloride'.

pygmy, **pygmies** [*Said* ***pig****-mee*]; also spelt **pigmy** NOUN a very small person, especially one who belongs to a racial group in which all the people are small.

pyjamas PLURAL NOUN Pyjamas are loose trousers and a jacket or top that you wear in bed.

pylon NOUN a very tall metal structure which carries overhead electricity cables.

pyramid NOUN ① a three-dimensional shape with a flat base and flat triangular sides sloping upwards to a point. ② HISTORY The Pyramids are ancient stone structures built over the tombs of Egyptian kings and queens.

python NOUN a large snake that kills animals by squeezing them with its body.

Qq

quack VERB When a duck quacks, it makes a loud, harsh sound.

quadriceps NOUN [PE] a large muscle in four parts at the front of your thigh.

quadruple *[Said kwod-**roo**-pl]* VERB When an amount or number quadruples, it becomes four times as large as it was.

quagmire *[Said **kwag**-mire]* NOUN a soft, wet area of land which you sink into if you walk on it.

quail NOUN ① a type of small game bird with a round body and short tail. ▶ VERB ② If you quail, you feel or look afraid.

quaint ADJECTIVE attractively old-fashioned or unusual • *quaint customs*. **quaintly** ADVERB

quake VERB If you quake, you shake and tremble because you are very frightened.

Quaker NOUN [RE] a member of a Christian group, the Society of Friends.

qualification NOUN ① Your qualifications are your skills and achievements, especially as officially recognised at the end of a course of training or study. ② something you add to a statement to make it less strong • *It is a good novel and yet cannot be recommended without qualification*.

> **qualification** NOUN
> ① = ability, accomplishment, achievement, capability, quality, skill
> ② = condition, exception, modification, reservation

qualify, **qualifies**, **qualifying**, **qualified** VERB ① [PE] When you qualify, you pass the examinations or tests that you need to pass to do a particular job or to take part in a sporting event. ② If you qualify a statement, you add a detail or explanation to make it less strong • *I would qualify that by putting it into context*. ③ If you qualify for something, you become entitled to have it • *You qualify for a discount*. **qualified** ADJECTIVE

> **qualify** VERB
> ① = become licensed, gain qualifications, get certified, graduate

quality, **qualities** NOUN ① The quality of something is how good it is • *The quality of food is very poor*. ② a characteristic • *These qualities are essential for success*.

> **quality** NOUN
> ① = calibre, distinction, grade, merit, value, worth
> ② = aspect, characteristic, feature, mark, property, trait

qualm *[Said **kwahm**]* NOUN If you have qualms about what you are doing, you worry that it might not be right.

quandary, **quandaries** *[Said **kwon**-dree]* NOUN If you are in a quandary, you cannot decide what to do.

quango, **quangos** NOUN a body responsible for a particular area of public administration, which is financed by the government but is outside direct government control.

Quango is short for 'quasi-autonomous non-governmental organisation'.

quantity, **quantities** NOUN ① an amount you can measure or count • *a small quantity of the mixture*. ② Quantity is the amount of something that there is • *emphasis on quantity rather than quality*.

> **quantity** NOUN
> ① = amount, number, part, sum
> ② = extent, measure, size, volume

quarantine *[Said **kwor**-an-teen]* NOUN If an animal is in quarantine, it is kept away from other animals for a time because it might have an infectious disease.

quarrel, **quarrels**, **quarrelling**, **quarrelled** NOUN ① an angry argument. ▶ VERB ② If people quarrel, they have an angry argument.

> **quarrel** NOUN
> ① = argument, disagreement, dispute, feud, fight, row, squabble
> ▶ VERB ② = argue, bicker, clash, fall out (*informal*), fight, row, squabble

quarry, **quarries**, **quarrying**, **quarried** *[Said **kwor**-ree]* NOUN ① a place where stone is removed from the ground by digging or blasting. ② A person's or animal's quarry is the animal that they are hunting. ▶ VERB ③ To quarry stone means to remove it from a quarry by digging or blasting.

quarter NOUN ① one of four equal parts. ② an American coin worth 25 cents. ③ You can refer to a particular area in a city as a quarter • *the French quarter*. ④ You can use 'quarter' to refer vaguely to a particular person or group of people • *You are very popular in certain quarters*. ⑤ (*in plural*) A soldier's or a servant's quarters are the rooms that they live in.

quarterly, **quarterlies** ADJECTIVE ① Quarterly means happening regularly every three months • *my quarterly report*. ▶ NOUN ② a magazine or journal published every three months.

quartet *[Said kwor-**tet**]* NOUN a group of four musicians who sing or play together; also a piece of music written for four instruments or singers.

quartz NOUN Quartz is a kind of hard, shiny crystal used in making very accurate watches and clocks.

quash *[Said **kwosh**]* VERB To quash a decision or judgment means to reject it officially • *The judges quashed their convictions*.

quay *[Said **kee**]* NOUN a place where boats are tied up and loaded or unloaded.

queasy, **queasier**, **queasiest** *[Said **kwee**-zee]* ADJECTIVE feeling slightly sick. **queasiness** NOUN

> **queasy** ADJECTIVE
> = ill, nauseous, queer (*old-fashioned*), sick, unwell

queen NOUN ① a female monarch or a woman married to a king. ② a female bee or ant which can lay eggs. ③ In chess, the queen is the most powerful piece and can move in any direction. ④ In a pack of cards, a queen is a card with a picture of a queen on it.

queer ADJECTIVE Queer means very strange.

quell VERB ① To quell a rebellion or riot means to put an end to it by using force. ② If you quell a feeling such as fear or grief, you stop yourself from feeling it • *trying to quell the loneliness*.

quench VERB If you quench your thirst, you have a drink so that you are no longer thirsty.

query, **queries**, **querying**, **queried** *[Said qweer-ree]* NOUN ① a question. ▶ VERB ② If you query something, you ask about it because you think it might not be right • *No-one queried my decision.*

> **query** NOUN
> ① = inquiry, question
> ≠ response
> ▶ VERB ② = challenge, dispute, object to, question

quest NOUN a long search for something.

question NOUN ① a sentence which asks for information. ② If there is some question about something, there is doubt about it. ③ a problem that needs to be discussed • *Can we get back to the question of the car?* ▶ VERB ④ If you question someone, you ask them questions. ⑤ If you question something, you express doubts about it • *He never stopped questioning his own beliefs.* ▶ PHRASE ⑥ If something is **out of the question**, it is impossible.

> **question** NOUN
> ③ = issue, motion, point, subject, topic
> ▶ VERB ④ = examine, interrogate, probe, quiz
> ≠ answer
> ⑤ = challenge, dispute, distrust, doubt, query, suspect

questionable ADJECTIVE possibly not true or not honest.

question mark NOUN the punctuation mark (?) which is used at the end of a question.

questionnaire NOUN a list of questions which asks for information.

queue, **queues**, **queuing** or **queueing**, **queued** *[Said kyoo]* NOUN ① a line of people or vehicles waiting for something. ▶ VERB ② When people queue, they stand in a line waiting for something.

quibble VERB ① If you quibble, you argue about something unimportant. ▶ NOUN ② a minor objection.

quiche *[Said keesh]* NOUN a tart with a savoury filling.

quick ADJECTIVE ① moving with great speed. ② lasting only a short time • *a quick chat.* ③ happening without any delay • *a quick response.* ④ intelligent and able to understand things easily.

> **quick** ADJECTIVE
> ① = brisk, fast, hasty, rapid, speedy, swift
> ≠ slow
> ② = brief, cursory, hasty, hurried, perfunctory
> ≠ long
> ③ = hasty, prompt, sudden

quickly ADVERB with great speed.

> **quickly** ADVERB
> = fast, hastily, hurriedly, rapidly, speedily, swiftly
> ≠ slowly

quicksand NOUN an area of deep wet sand that you sink into if you walk on it.

quid, **quid** NOUN (*informal*) In British English, a pound in money.

quiet ADJECTIVE ① Someone or something that is quiet makes very little noise or no noise at all. ② Quiet also means peaceful • *a quiet evening at home.* ③ A quiet event happens with very little fuss or publicity • *a quiet wedding.* ▶ NOUN ④ Quiet is silence. **quietly** ADVERB **quietness** NOUN

> **quiet** ADJECTIVE
> ① = hushed, inaudible, low, silent, soft
> ≠ noisy
> ② = calm, mild, peaceful, restful, serene, tranquil
> ▶ NOUN ④ = calmness, peace, serenity, silence, stillness, tranquillity
> ≠ noise

quieten VERB To quieten someone means to make them become quiet.

quill NOUN ① a pen made from a feather. ② A bird's quills are the large feathers on its wings and tail. ③ A porcupine's quills are its spines.

quilt NOUN A quilt for a bed is a cover, especially a cover that is padded.

quince NOUN a sour-tasting fruit used for making jam and marmalade.

quintessential ADJECTIVE (*formal*) A person or thing that is quintessential seems to represent the basic nature of something in a pure, concentrated form • *It was the quintessential Hollywood party.*

quintet [*Said kwin-**tet***] NOUN a group of five musicians who sing or play together; also a piece of music written for five instruments or singers.

quip, **quips**, **quipping**, **quipped** NOUN ① an amusing or clever remark. ▶ VERB ② To quip means to make an amusing or clever remark.

quirk NOUN ① an odd habit or characteristic • *an interesting quirk of human nature.* ② an unexpected event or development • *a quirk of fate.* **quirky** ADJECTIVE

quit, **quits**, **quitting**, **quit** VERB If you quit something, you leave it or stop doing it • *Leigh quit his job as a salesman.*

> **quit** VERB
> = discontinue, give up, leave, resign, retire, stop

quite ADVERB ① fairly but not very • *quite old.* ② completely • *Jane lay quite still.* ▶ PHRASE ③ You use **quite a** to emphasise that something is large or impressive • *It was quite a party.*

> **quite** ADVERB
> ① = fairly, moderately, rather, reasonably, somewhat
> ② = absolutely, completely, entirely, fully, perfectly, totally

quiver VERB ① If something quivers, it trembles. ▶ NOUN ② a trembling movement • *a quiver of panic.*

quiz, **quizzes**, **quizzing**, **quizzed** NOUN ① a game in which the competitors are asked questions to test their knowledge. ▶ VERB ② If you quiz someone, you question them closely about something.

quizzical [*Said **kwiz**-ik-kl*] ADJECTIVE amused and questioning • *a quizzical smile.*

quota NOUN a number or quantity of something which is officially allowed • *a quota of three foreign players allowed in each team.*

quotation NOUN an extract from a book or speech which is quoted.

quote VERB ① If you quote something that someone has written or said, you repeat their exact words. ② If you quote a fact, you state it because it supports what you are saying. ▶ NOUN ③ an extract from a book or speech. ④ an estimate of how much a piece of work will cost.

> **quote** VERB
> ① = cite, extract, recite, repeat

Qur'an another spelling of **Koran**.

Rr

A B C D E F G H I J K L M N O P Q **R** S T U V W X Y Z

RAAF In Australia, RAAF is an abbreviation for 'Royal Australian Air Force'.

rabbi, **rabbis** *[Said* ***rab****-by]* NOUN a Jewish religious leader.

rabbit NOUN a small mammal with long ears.

rabble NOUN a noisy, disorderly crowd.

rabid ADJECTIVE ① used to describe someone with very strong views that you do not approve of • *a rabid Nazi*. ② A rabid dog or other animal has rabies.

rabies *[Said* ***ray****-beez]* NOUN an infectious disease which causes people and animals, especially dogs, to go mad and die.

raccoon; also spelt **racoon** NOUN a small North American mammal with a long striped tail.

race NOUN ① a competition to see who is fastest, for example in running or driving. ② one of the major groups that human beings can be divided into according to their physical features. ▸ VERB ③ If you race someone, you compete with them in a race. ④ If you race something or if it races, it goes at its greatest rate • *Her heart raced uncontrollably*. ⑤ If you race somewhere, you go there as quickly as possible • *The hares raced away out of sight*. **racing** NOUN

> **race** NOUN
> ② = ethnic group, nation, people
> ▸ VERB ⑤ = dash, fly, hurry, run, speed, tear

racecourse NOUN a grass track, sometimes with jumps, along which horses race.

racehorse NOUN a horse trained to run in races.

racial ADJECTIVE relating to the different races that people belong to • *racial harmony*. **racially** ADVERB

rack NOUN ① a piece of equipment for holding things or hanging things on. ▸ VERB ② If you are racked by something, you suffer because of it • *She was racked by guilt*. ▸ PHRASE ③ (*informal*) If you **rack your brains**, you try hard to think of or remember something.

racket NOUN ① If someone is making a racket, they are making a lot of noise. ② an illegal way of making money • *a racket selling fake designer bags*. ③ Racket is another spelling of **racquet**.

> **racket** NOUN
> ① = clamour, commotion, din, hubbub, noise, row, rumpus
> ② = enterprise, fraud, scheme

racquet; also spelt **racket** NOUN a bat with strings across it used in tennis and similar games.

radar NOUN Radar is equipment used to track ships or aircraft that are out of sight by using radio signals that are reflected back from the object and shown on a screen.

radiant ADJECTIVE ① Someone who is radiant is so happy that it shows in their face. ② glowing brightly. **radiance** NOUN

radiate VERB ① If things radiate from a place, they form a pattern like lines spreading out from the centre of a circle. ② If you radiate a quality or emotion, it shows clearly in your face and behaviour • *He radiated health.*

radiation NOUN [SCIENCE] the stream of particles given out by a radioactive substance.

radiator NOUN ① a hollow metal device for heating a room, usually connected to a central heating system. ② the part of a car that is filled with water to cool the engine.

radical NOUN ① Radicals are people who think there should be great changes in society, and try to make them happen. ▸ ADJECTIVE ② very significant, important or basic • *a radical change in the law.* **radically** ADVERB **radicalism** NOUN

radio, **radios**, **radioing**, **radioed** NOUN ① Radio is a system of sending sound over a distance by transmitting electrical signals. ② Radio is also the broadcasting of programmes to the public by radio. ③ a piece of equipment for listening to radio programmes. ▸ VERB ④ To radio someone means to send them a message by radio • *The pilot radioed that a fire had started.*

radioactive ADJECTIVE giving off powerful and harmful rays. **radioactivity** NOUN

radiotherapy NOUN the treatment of diseases such as cancer using radiation. **radiotherapist** NOUN

radish NOUN a small salad vegetable with a red skin and white flesh and a hot taste.

radius, **radii** or **radiuses** NOUN [MATHS] The radius of a circle is the length of a straight line drawn from its centre to its circumference.

RAF In Britain, RAF is an abbreviation for 'Royal Air Force'.

raffle NOUN a competition in which people buy numbered tickets and win a prize if they have the ticket that is chosen.

raft NOUN a floating platform made from long pieces of wood tied together.

rafter NOUN Rafters are the sloping pieces of wood that support a roof.

rag NOUN ① a piece of old cloth used to clean or wipe things. ② If someone is dressed in rags, they are wearing old torn clothes.

rage NOUN ① Rage is great anger. ▸ VERB ② To rage about something means to speak angrily about it. ③ If something such as a storm or battle is raging, it is continuing with great force or violence • *The fire still raged out of control.*

> **rage** NOUN
> ① = anger, frenzy, fury, wrath
> ▸ VERB ② = be furious, fume, lose your temper, rave, storm
> ③ = be at its height, rampage, storm, surge

ragged ADJECTIVE Ragged clothes are old and torn.

raid VERB ① To raid a place means to enter it by force to attack it or steal something. ▸ NOUN ② the raiding of a building or a place • *an armed raid on a bank.*

> **raid** VERB
> ① = assault, attack, break into, invade, plunder
> ▸ NOUN ② = attack, break-in, foray

rail NOUN ① a fixed horizontal bar used as a support or for hanging things on. ② Rails are the steel bars which trains run along. ③ Rail is the railway considered as a means of transport • *I plan to go by rail.*

a b c d e f g h i j k l m n o p q r s t u v w x y z

railing NOUN Railings are a fence made from metal bars.

railway NOUN a route along which trains travel on steel rails.

rain NOUN ① water falling from the clouds in small drops. ▸ VERB ② When it is raining, rain is falling. **rainy** ADJECTIVE

> **rain** NOUN
> ① = deluge, downpour, drizzle, rainfall, showers
> ▸ VERB ② = drizzle, pour, teem

rainbow NOUN an arch of different colours that sometimes appears in the sky when it is raining.

raincoat NOUN a waterproof coat.

rainfall NOUN the amount of rain that falls in a place during a particular period.

rainforest NOUN GEOGRAPHY a dense forest of tall trees where there is a lot of rain.

rainwater NOUN rain that has been stored.

raise VERB ① If you raise something, you make it higher • *She went to the window and raised the blinds* • *a drive to raise standards of literacy*. ② If you raise your voice, you speak more loudly. ③ To raise money for a cause means to get people to donate money towards it. ④ To raise a child means to look after it until it is grown up. ⑤ If you raise a subject, you mention it.

> **raise** VERB
> ① = elevate, heave, hoist, lift
> ≠ lower
> ④ = bring up, nurture, rear
> ⑤ = advance, bring up, broach, introduce, moot, suggest

raisin NOUN Raisins are dried grapes.

rake NOUN a garden tool with a row of metal teeth and a long handle. **rake up** VERB If you rake up something embarrassing from the past, you remind someone about it.

rally, rallies, rallying, rallied NOUN ① a large public meeting held to show support for something. ② a competition in which vehicles are raced over public roads. ③ In tennis or squash, a rally is a continuous series of shots exchanged by the players. ▸ VERB ④ When people rally to something, they gather together to continue a struggle or to support something.

ram VERB ① If one vehicle rams another, it crashes into it. ② To ram something somewhere means to push it there firmly • *He rammed his key into the lock*. ▸ NOUN ③ an adult male sheep.

RAM NOUN ICT a storage space which can be filled with data but which loses its contents when the machine is switched off. RAM stands for 'random access memory'.

Ramadan NOUN RE the ninth month of the Muslim year, during which Muslims eat and drink nothing during daylight.

ramble NOUN ① a long walk in the countryside. ▸ VERB ② To ramble means to go for a ramble. ③ To ramble also means to talk in a confused way • *He then started rambling and repeating himself*. **rambler** NOUN

> **ramble** NOUN
> ① = excursion, hike, stroll, walk
> ▸ VERB ② = amble, stray, stroll, walk, wander
> ③ = babble, chatter

ramification NOUN The ramifications of a decision or plan are all its consequences and effects.

ramp NOUN a sloping surface connecting two different levels.

rampage VERB ① To rampage means to rush about wildly causing damage. ▸ PHRASE ② To go **on the rampage** means to rush about in a wild or violent way.

rampage VERB
① = go berserk, rage, run amok, run riot
▸ PHRASE ② = amok, berserk, wild

rampant ADJECTIVE If something such as crime or disease is rampant, it is growing or spreading uncontrollably.

ramshackle ADJECTIVE A ramshackle building is in very poor condition.

ran the past tense of **run**.

ranch NOUN a large farm where cattle or horses are reared, especially in the USA.

rancid *[Said* ***ran****-sid]* ADJECTIVE Rancid food has gone bad.

rancour *[Said* ***rang****-kur]* NOUN *(formal)* Rancour is bitter hatred. **rancorous** ADJECTIVE

rand NOUN The rand is the main unit of currency in South Africa.

random ADJECTIVE ① A random choice or arrangement is not based on any definite plan. ▸ PHRASE ② If you do something **at random**, you do it without any definite plan • *He chose his victims at random*. **randomly** ADVERB

random ADJECTIVE
① = aimless, arbitrary, haphazard, indiscriminate, spot
▸ PHRASE ② = aimlessly, arbitrarily, haphazardly, indiscriminately, randomly

rang the past tense of **ring**.

range NOUN ① The range of something is the maximum distance over which it can reach things or detect things • *This mortar has a range of 15,000 metres*. ② a number of different things of the same kind • *A wide range of colours are available*. ③ a set of values on a scale • *The average age range is between 35 and 55*. ④ A range of mountains is a line of them. ⑤ A rifle range or firing range is a place where people practise shooting at targets. ▸ VERB ⑥ When a set of things ranges between two points, they vary within these points on a scale • *prices ranging between £370 and £1200*.

range NOUN
① = bounds, extent, field, limits, province, scope
② = assortment, class, gamut, selection, series, variety
▸ VERB ⑥ = extend, go, run, stretch, vary

ranger NOUN someone whose job is to look after a forest or park.

rank NOUN ① Someone's rank is their official level in a job or profession. ② The ranks are the ordinary members of the armed forces, rather than the officers. ③ The ranks of a group are its members • *We welcomed five new members to our ranks*. ④ a row of people or things. ▸ VERB ⑤ To rank as something means to have that status or position on a scale • *His dismissal ranks as the worst humiliation he has ever known*. ▸ ADJECTIVE ⑥ complete and absolute • *rank stupidity*. ⑦ having a strong, unpleasant smell • *the rank smell of unwashed clothes*.

rank NOUN
① = class, echelon, grade, level, standing, station, status
④ = column, file, line, row
▸ ADJECTIVE ⑥ = absolute, complete, downright, sheer, unmitigated, utter

ransack VERB To ransack a place means to disturb everything and leave it in a mess, in order to search for or steal something.

ransom NOUN money that is demanded to free someone who has been kidnapped.

rant VERB To rant means to talk loudly in an excited or angry way.

rap, raps, rapping, rapped VERB ① If you rap something, you hit it with a series of quick blows. ▶ NOUN ② a quick knock or blow on something • *A rap on the door signalled his arrival.* ③ Rap is a style of poetry spoken to music with a strong rhythmic beat.

rapid ADJECTIVE happening or moving very quickly • *rapid industrial expansion* • *He took a few rapid steps.* **rapidly** ADVERB **rapidity** NOUN

rapport [*Said rap-**por***] NOUN (*formal*) If there is a rapport between two people, they find it easy to understand each other's feelings and attitudes.

rapt ADJECTIVE If you are rapt, you are so interested in something that you are not aware of other things • *sitting with rapt attention in front of the screen.*

rapture NOUN Rapture is a feeling of extreme delight. **rapturous** ADJECTIVE **rapturously** ADVERB

rare ADJECTIVE ① Something that is rare is not common or does not happen often • *a rare flower* • *Such major disruptions are rare.* ② Rare meat has been lightly cooked. **rarely** ADVERB

> **rare** ADJECTIVE
> ① = exceptional, few, scarce, sparse, sporadic, uncommon, unusual
> ≠ common

rarefied [*Said **rare**-if-eyed*] ADJECTIVE seeming to have little connection with ordinary life • *He grew up in a rarefied literary atmosphere.*

raring ADJECTIVE If you are raring to do something, you are very eager to do it.

rarity, rarities NOUN ① something that is interesting or valuable because it is unusual. ② The rarity of something is the fact that it is not common.

rash ADJECTIVE ① If you are rash, you do something hasty and foolish. ▶ NOUN ② an area of red spots that appear on your skin when you are ill or have an allergy. ③ A rash of events is a lot of them happening in a short time • *a rash of strikes.* **rashly** ADVERB

> **rash** ADJECTIVE
> ① = foolhardy, hasty, impetuous, impulsive, reckless
> ▶ NOUN ② = eruption, outbreak
> ③ = epidemic, flood, plague, spate, wave

rasp VERB ① To rasp means to make a harsh unpleasant sound. ▶ NOUN ② a coarse file with rows of raised teeth, used for smoothing wood or metal.

raspberry, raspberries NOUN a small, red soft fruit that grows on a bush.

rat NOUN a long-tailed animal which looks like a large mouse.

rate NOUN ① The rate of something is the speed or frequency with which it happens • *New diet books appear at the rate of nearly one a week.* ② The rate of interest is its level • *a further cut in interest rates.* ③ the cost or charge for something. ④ In some countries, rates are a local tax paid by people who own buildings. ▶ PHRASE ⑤ If you say **at this rate** something will happen, you mean it will happen if things continue in the same way • *At this rate we'll be lucky to get home before six.* ⑥ You say **at any rate** when you want to add to or amend what you have just said • *He is the least appealing character, to me at any rate.* ▶ VERB ⑦ The way you rate someone or something is your opinion of them • *He was rated as one of England's top young players.*

> **rate** NOUN
> ① = frequency, pace, speed, tempo, velocity
> ③ = charge, cost, fee, price, tariff
> ▶ VERB ⑦ = appraise, class, consider, count, rank, regard

rather **ADVERB** ① Rather means to a certain extent • *We got along rather well* • *The reality is rather more complex.* ▶ **PHRASE** ② If you **would rather** do a particular thing, you would prefer to do it. ③ If you do one thing **rather than** another, you choose to do the first thing instead of the second.

> **rather** **ADVERB**
> ① = fairly, pretty (*informal*), quite, relatively, slightly, somewhat

ratify, **ratifies**, **ratifying**, **ratified** **VERB** (*formal*) To ratify a written agreement means to approve it formally, usually by signing it. **ratification** **NOUN**

rating **NOUN** ① a score based on the quality or status of something. ② The ratings are statistics showing how popular each television programme is.

ratio, **ratios** **NOUN** ① a relationship which shows how many times one thing is bigger than another • *The adult to child ratio is 1 to 6.* ② MATHS a relationship between two numbers, which shows how many times one number goes into another • *The ratio of 1 to 6 is shown as 1:6.*

ration **NOUN** ① Your ration of something is the amount you are allowed to have. ② Rations are the food given each day to a soldier or member of an expedition. ▶ **VERB** ③ When something is rationed, you are only allowed a limited amount of it, because there is a shortage.

rational **ADJECTIVE** When people are rational, their judgments are based on reason rather than emotion. **rationally** **ADVERB** **rationality** **NOUN**

> **rational** **ADJECTIVE**
> = enlightened, logical, reasonable, sensible

rationale [*Said rash-on-**nahl***] **NOUN** The rationale for a course of action or for a belief is the set of reasons on which it is based.

rattle **VERB** ① When something rattles, it makes short, regular knocking sounds. ② If something rattles you, it upsets you • *He was obviously rattled by events.* ▶ **NOUN** ③ the noise something makes when it rattles. ④ a baby's toy which makes a noise when it is shaken.

raucous [*Said **raw**-kuss*] **ADJECTIVE** A raucous voice is loud and rough.

ravage (*formal*) **VERB** ① To ravage something means to seriously harm or damage it • *a country ravaged by floods.* ▶ **NOUN** ② The ravages of something are its damaging effects • *the ravages of two world wars.*

rave **VERB** ① If someone raves, they talk in an angry, uncontrolled way • *He started raving about being treated badly.* ② (*informal*) If you rave about something, you talk about it very enthusiastically. ▶ **ADJECTIVE** ③ (*informal*) If something gets a rave review, it is praised enthusiastically. ▶ **NOUN** ④ (*informal*) a large party with electronic dance music.

> **rave** **VERB**
> ① = babble, rage, rant
> ② = be wild about (*informal*), enthuse, gush

raven **NOUN** ① a large black bird with a deep, harsh call. ▶ **ADJECTIVE** ② Raven hair is black and shiny.

ravenous **ADJECTIVE** very hungry.

ravine **NOUN** a deep, narrow valley with steep sides.

raving **ADJECTIVE** ① If someone is raving, they are speaking in a strange, wild way. ▶ **NOUN** ② Someone's ravings are strange things they write or say.

ravioli [*Said rav-ee-**oh**-lee*] **NOUN** Ravioli consists of small squares of pasta filled with meat or other ingredients and served with a sauce.

ravishing ADJECTIVE Someone or something that is ravishing is very beautiful • *a ravishing landscape*.

raw ADJECTIVE ① Raw food has not been cooked. ② A raw substance is in its natural state • *raw sugar*. ③ If part of your body is raw, the skin has come off or been rubbed away. ④ Someone who is raw is too young or too new in a job or situation to know how to behave.

raw material NOUN Raw materials are the natural substances used to make something.

ray NOUN ① a beam of light or radiation. ② A ray of hope is a small amount that makes an unpleasant situation seem slightly better. ③ a large sea fish with eyes on the top of its body, and a long tail.

raze VERB To raze a building, town or forest means to completely destroy it • *The town was razed to the ground during the occupation*.

razor NOUN a tool that people use for shaving.

re- PREFIX ① 'Re-' is used to form nouns and verbs that refer to the repetition of an action or process • *reread* • *remarry*. ② 'Re-' is also used to form verbs that refer to going back to a previous condition • *refresh* • *renew*.

reach VERB ① When you reach a place, you arrive there. ② When you reach for something, you stretch out your arm to it. ③ If something reaches a place or point, it extends as far as that place or point • *She has a cloak that reaches to the ground*. ④ If something or someone reaches a stage or level, they get to it • *Unemployment has reached record levels*. ⑤ To reach an agreement or decision means to succeed in achieving it. ▶ PHRASE ⑥ If a place is **within reach**, you can get there • *a cycle route well within reach of most people*. ⑦ If something is **out of reach**, you cannot get it to it by stretching out your arm • *Store out of reach of children*.

reach VERB
① = arrive at, get as far as, get to, make
③ = extend to, go as far as
④ = arrive at, attain, climb to, fall to, rise to

react VERB When you react to something, you behave in a particular way because of it • *He reacted badly to the news*.

reaction NOUN ① Your reaction to something is what you feel, say or do because of it • *Reaction to the visit is mixed*. ② Your reactions are your ability to move quickly in response to something that happens • *Squash requires fast reactions*. ③ If there is a reaction against something, it becomes unpopular • *a reaction against the government*.

reaction NOUN
① = acknowledgment, answer, feedback, response
③ = backlash, counterbalance

reactionary, **reactionaries** ADJECTIVE ① Someone who is reactionary tries to prevent political or social change. ▶ NOUN ② Reactionaries are reactionary people.

reactor NOUN a device which is used to produce nuclear energy.

read, **reads**, **reading**, **read** VERB ① When you read, you look at something written and follow it or say it aloud. ② If you can read someone's moods or mind, you can judge what they are feeling or thinking. ③ When you read a meter or gauge, you look at it and record the figure on it. ④ If you read a subject at university, you study it.

read VERB
① = glance at, look at, pore over, scan, study
② = comprehend, decipher, interpret

reader NOUN ① The readers of a newspaper or magazine are the people who read it regularly. ② At a university, a reader is a senior lecturer just below the rank of professor.

readership NOUN The readership of a newspaper or magazine consists of the people who read it regularly.

readily ADVERB ① willingly and eagerly • *She readily agreed to see Alex.* ② easily done or quickly obtainable • *Help is readily available.*

reading NOUN ① Reading is the activity of reading books. ② The reading on a meter or gauge is the figure or measurement it shows.

readjust *[Said ree-aj-**just**]* VERB ① If you readjust, you adapt to a new situation. ② If you readjust something, you alter it to a different position.

ready ADJECTIVE ① having reached the required stage, or prepared for action or use • *In a few days' time the plums will be ready to eat.* ② willing or eager to do something • *She says she's not ready for university.* ③ easily produced or obtained • *ready cash.* **readiness** NOUN

ready ADJECTIVE
① = organised, prepared, primed, ripe, set
② = agreeable, eager, happy, keen, willing
③ = accessible, available, convenient, handy

ready-made ADJECTIVE already made and therefore able to be used immediately.

reaffirm VERB To reaffirm something means to state it again • *He reaffirmed his support for the campaign.*

real ADJECTIVE ① actually existing and not imagined or invented. ② genuine and not imitation • *Who's to know if they're real diamonds?* ③ true or actual and not mistaken • *This was the real reason for her call.*

real ADJECTIVE
① = actual, authentic, concrete, factual, genuine, legitimate, tangible, true
≠ imaginary
② = authentic, bona fide, dinkum (*Australian and New Zealand; informal*), genuine, honest, rightful, sincere, true, unaffected
≠ fake

real estate NOUN Real estate is property in the form of land and buildings rather than personal possessions.

realise; also spelt **realize** VERB ① If you realise something, you become aware of it. ② (*formal*) If your hopes or fears are realised, what you hoped for or feared actually happens • *Our worst fears were realised.* ③ To realise a sum of money means to receive it as a result of selling goods or shares. **realisation** NOUN

realise VERB
① = appreciate, comprehend, grasp, recognise, understand

realism NOUN Realism is the recognition of the true nature of a situation • *a triumph of muddled thought over realism and common sense.* **realist** NOUN

realistic ADJECTIVE ① recognising and accepting the true nature of a situation. ② representing things in a way that is true to real life • *His novels are more realistic than his short stories.* **realistically** ADVERB

realistic ADJECTIVE
① = down-to-earth, level-headed, matter-of-fact, practical, sensible, sober
② = authentic, faithful, lifelike, true

reality NOUN ① Reality is the real nature of things, rather than the way someone imagines it • *Fiction and reality were increasingly blurred.* ② If something has become reality, it actually exists or is actually happening.

reality NOUN
① = authenticity, fact, realism, truth

really ADVERB ① used to add emphasis to what is being said • *I'm not really surprised.* ② used to indicate that you are talking about the true facts about something • *What was really going on?*

really ADVERB
① = absolutely, certainly, extremely, remarkably, terribly, truly, very
② = actually, in fact, in reality, truly

realm [*Said* ***relm***] NOUN (*formal*) ① You can refer to any area of thought or activity as a realm • *the realm of politics.* ② a country with a king or queen • *defence of the realm.*

reap VERB ① To reap a crop such as corn means to cut and gather it. ② When people reap benefits or rewards, they get them as a result of hard work or careful planning.
reaper NOUN

reappear VERB When people or things reappear, you can see them again, because they have come back • *The stolen ring reappeared three years later in a pawn shop.* **reappearance** NOUN

reappraisal NOUN (*formal*) If there is a reappraisal, people think about something and decide whether they want to change it • *a reappraisal of the government's economic policies.*

rear NOUN ① The rear of something is the part at the back. ▸ VERB ② To rear children or young animals means to bring them up until they are able to look after themselves. ③ When a horse rears, it raises the front part of its body, so that its front legs are in the air.

rearrange VERB To rearrange something means to organise or arrange it in a different way.

reason NOUN ① The reason for something is the fact or situation which explains why it happens or which causes it to happen. ② If you have reason to believe or feel something, there are definite reasons why you believe it or feel it • *He had every reason to be upset.* ③ Reason is the ability to think and make judgments. ▸ VERB ④ If you reason that something is true, you decide it is true after considering all the facts. ⑤ If you reason with someone, you persuade them to accept sensible arguments.

reason NOUN
① = cause, grounds, incentive, motive, purpose
③ = intellect, judgment, rationality, reasoning, sense
▸ VERB ⑤ = bring round (*informal*), persuade, win over

reasonable ADJECTIVE ① Reasonable behaviour is fair and sensible. ② If an explanation is reasonable, there are good reasons for thinking it is correct. ③ A reasonable amount is a fairly large amount. ④ A reasonable price is fair and not too high.
reasonably ADVERB

reasonable ADJECTIVE
① = fair, moderate, rational, sane, sensible, sober, steady, wise
② = justifiable, legitimate, logical, sensible, sound, understandable
④ = cheap, competitive, fair, inexpensive, low, modest

reasoning NOUN Reasoning is the process by which you reach a conclusion after considering all the facts.

reassess VERB If you reassess something, you consider whether it still has the same value or importance. **reassessment** NOUN

reassure VERB If you reassure someone, you say or do things that make them less worried. **reassurance** NOUN

> **reassure** VERB
> = bolster, cheer up, comfort, encourage

rebate NOUN money paid back to someone who has paid too much tax or rent.

rebel, **rebels**, **rebelling**, **rebelled** NOUN *[Said* ***reb****-l]* ① HISTORY Rebels are people who are fighting their own country's army to change the political system. ② Someone who is a rebel rejects society's values and behaves differently from other people. ▶ VERB *[Said ri-****bel****]* ③ To rebel means to fight against authority or reject accepted values.

> **rebel** VERB
> ③ = defy, mutiny, resist, revolt

rebellion NOUN HISTORY A rebellion is organised and often violent opposition to authority.

> **rebellion** NOUN
> = insurrection, mutiny, revolt, revolution, uprising

rebellious ADJECTIVE unwilling to obey and likely to rebel against authority.

rebound VERB When something rebounds, it bounces or springs back after hitting a solid surface.

rebuff VERB ① If you rebuff someone, you reject what they offer • *She rebuffed their offers of help.* ▶ NOUN ② a rejection of an offer.

rebuild, **rebuilds**, **rebuilding**, **rebuilt** VERB When a town or building is rebuilt, it is built again after being damaged or destroyed.

rebuke *[Said rib-****yook****]* VERB To rebuke someone means to speak severely to them about something they have done.

recall VERB ① To recall something means to remember it. ② If you are recalled to a place, you are ordered to return there. ③ If a company recalls products, it asks people to return them because they are faulty.

recap, **recaps**, **recapping**, **recapped** VERB ① To recap means to repeat and summarise the main points of an explanation or discussion. ▶ NOUN ② a summary of the main points of an explanation or discussion.

recapture VERB ① When you recapture a pleasant feeling, you experience it again • *She may never recapture that past assurance.* ② When soldiers recapture a place, they capture it from the people who took it from them. ③ When animals or prisoners are recaptured, they are caught after they have escaped.

recede VERB ① When something recedes, it moves away into the distance. ② If a man's hair is receding, he is starting to go bald at the front.

receipt *[Said ris-****seet****]* NOUN ① a piece of paper confirming that money or goods have been received. ② In a shop or theatre, the money received is often called the receipts • *Box-office receipts were down last month.* ③ *(formal)* The receipt of something is the receiving of it • *You have to sign here and acknowledge receipt.*

receive VERB ① When you receive something, someone gives it to you, or you get it after it has been sent to you. ② To receive something also means to have it happen to you • *injuries she received in a car crash.* ③ When you receive visitors or guests, you welcome them. ④ If something is received in a particular way, that is how people react to it • *The decision has been received with great disappointment.*

> **receive** VERB
> ① = accept, be given, get, pick up, take
> ② = encounter, suffer, sustain, undergo
> ③ = entertain, greet, meet, take in, welcome

receiver NOUN the part of a telephone you hold near to your ear and mouth.

recent ADJECTIVE Something recent happened a short time ago. **recently** ADVERB

> **recent** ADJECTIVE
> = current, fresh, new, present-day, up-to-date

reception NOUN ① In a hotel or office, reception is the place near the entrance where appointments or enquiries are dealt with. ② a formal party. ③ The reception someone or something gets is the way people react to them • *Her tour met with a rapturous reception.* ④ If your radio or television gets good reception, the sound or picture is clear.

receptionist NOUN The receptionist in a hotel or office deals with people when they arrive, answers the telephone, and arranges appointments.

receptive ADJECTIVE Someone who is receptive to ideas or suggestions is willing to consider them.

recess NOUN ① a period when no work is done by a committee or parliament • *the Christmas recess.* ② a place where part of a wall has been built further back than the rest.

recession NOUN a period when a country's economy is less successful and more people become unemployed.

> **recession** NOUN
> = decline, depression, downturn, slump

recharge VERB To recharge a battery means to charge it with electricity again after it has been used.

recipe *[Said* ***res****-sip-ee]* NOUN ① DGT a list of ingredients and instructions for cooking something. ② If something is a recipe for disaster or for success, it is likely to result in disaster or success.

recipient NOUN The recipient of something is the person receiving it.

reciprocal ADJECTIVE ① A reciprocal agreement involves two people, groups or countries helping each other in a similar way • *a reciprocal agreement on trade.* ▶ NOUN ② MATHS If one number is the reciprocal of another number, the two numbers give a product of 1 when they are multiplied together • *The reciprocal of 2 is 0.5.*

reciprocate VERB If you reciprocate someone's feelings or behaviour, you feel or behave in the same way towards them.

recital NOUN a performance of music or poetry, usually by one person.

recite VERB If you recite a poem or something you have learnt, you say it aloud. **recitation** NOUN

reckless ADJECTIVE showing a complete lack of care about danger or damage • *a reckless tackle.* **recklessly** ADVERB **recklessness** NOUN

reckon VERB ① *(informal)* If you reckon that something is true, you think it is true • *I reckoned he was still fond of her.* ② *(informal)* If someone reckons to do something, they claim or expect to do it • *Officers on the case are reckoning to charge someone shortly.* ③ To reckon an amount means to calculate it. ④ If you reckon on something, you rely on it happening when making your plans • *He reckons on being world champion.* ⑤ If you had not reckoned with something, you had not expected it and therefore were unprepared when it happened • *Giles had not reckoned with the strength of Sally's feelings.*

> **reckon** VERB
> ① = assume, believe, consider, judge, suppose, think
> ③ = calculate, count, estimate, figure out, work out

reckoning NOUN a calculation • *There were a thousand or so, by my reckoning.*

reclaim VERB ① When you reclaim something, you collect it after leaving it somewhere or losing it. ② To reclaim land means to make it suitable for use, for example by draining it. **reclamation** NOUN

recline VERB To recline means to lie or lean back at an angle • *a photo of him reclining on his bed.*

recluse NOUN Someone who is a recluse lives alone and avoids other people. **reclusive** ADJECTIVE

recognise; also spelt **recognize** VERB ① If you recognise someone or something, you realise that you know who or what they are • *The receptionist recognised me at once.* ② To recognise something also means to accept and acknowledge it • *The RAF recognised him as an outstanding pilot.* **recognition** NOUN **recognisable** ADJECTIVE **recognisably** ADVERB

> **recognise** VERB
> ① = identify, know, place, spot
> ② = acknowledge, appreciate, honour, salute

recoil VERB To recoil from something means to draw back in shock or horror.

recommend VERB If you recommend something to someone, you praise it and suggest they try it. **recommendation** NOUN

reconcile VERB ① To reconcile two things that seem to oppose one another, means to make them work or exist together successfully • *The designs reconciled style with comfort.* ② When people are reconciled, they become friendly again after a quarrel. ③ If you reconcile yourself to an unpleasant situation, you accept it. **reconciliation** NOUN

reconnaissance *[Said rik-**kon**-iss-sanss]* NOUN Reconnaissance is the gathering of military information by soldiers, planes or satellites.

reconsider VERB To reconsider something means to think about it again to decide whether to change it. **reconsideration** NOUN

reconstruct VERB ① To reconstruct something that has been damaged means to build it again. ② To reconstruct a past event means to get a complete description of it from small pieces of information. **reconstruction** NOUN

> **reconstruct** VERB
> ① = rebuild, recreate, regenerate, renovate, restore
> ② = build up, deduce, piece together

record NOUN *[Said **rek**-ord]* ① If you keep a record of something, you keep a written account or store information in a computer • *medical records.* ② a round, flat piece of plastic on which music has been recorded. ③ an achievement which is the best of its type. ④ Your record is what is known about your achievements or past activities • *He had a distinguished* *war record.* ▶ **VERB** [*Said ri-**kord***] ⑤ If you record information, you write it down or put it into a computer. ⑥ To record sound means to preserve it on tape or disc, or digitally. ▶ **ADJECTIVE** [*Said **rek**-ord*] ⑦ higher, lower, better or worse than ever before • *Profits were at a record level.*

> **record** **NOUN**
> ① = account, archive, file, journal, minute, register
> ④ = background, career, curriculum vitae, track record (*informal*)
> ▶ **VERB** ⑤ = blog, document, enter, log, note, register, write down

recorder **NOUN** a small woodwind instrument.

recording **NOUN** A recording of something is a tape, disc etc of it.

recount **VERB** [*Said ri-**kownt***] ① If you recount a story, you tell it. ▶ **NOUN** [*Said **ree**-kownt*] ② a second count of votes in an election when the result is very close.

recoup [*Said rik-**koop***] **VERB** If you recoup money that you have spent or lost, you get it back.

recourse **NOUN** (*formal*) If you have recourse to something, you use it to help you • *The members settled their differences without recourse to war.*

recover **VERB** ① To recover from an illness or unhappy experience means to get well again or get over it. ② If you recover a lost object or your ability to do something, you get it back.

> **recover** **VERB**
> ① = convalesce, get better, get well, improve, recuperate, revive
> ② = get back, recapture, recoup, regain, retrieve

recovery **NOUN** ① the act of getting better again. ② the act of getting something back.

> **recovery** **NOUN**
> ① = healing, improvement, recuperation, revival
> ② = recapture, reclamation, restoration, retrieval

recreate **VERB** To recreate something means to succeed in making it happen or exist again • *a museum that faithfully recreates an old farmhouse.*

recreation [*Said rek-kree-**ay**-shn*] **NOUN** Recreation is all the things that you do for enjoyment in your spare time. **recreational** **ADJECTIVE**

recrimination **NOUN** Recriminations are accusations made by people about each other.

recruit **VERB** ① To recruit people means to get them to join a group or help with something. ▶ **NOUN** ② someone who has joined the army or some other organisation. **recruitment** **NOUN**

> **recruit** **VERB**
> ① = draft, enlist, enrol, muster
> ▶ **NOUN** ② = beginner, convert, novice, trainee

rectangle **NOUN** MATHS a four-sided shape with four right angles. **rectangular** **ADJECTIVE**

rectify, **rectifies**, **rectifying**, **rectified** **VERB** (*formal*) If you rectify something that is wrong, you put it right.

rector **NOUN** a Church of England priest in charge of a parish.

rectory, **rectories** **NOUN** a house where a rector lives.

rectum **NOUN** (*technical*) the bottom end of the tube down which waste food passes out of your body. **rectal** **ADJECTIVE**

recuperate **VERB** When you recuperate, you gradually recover after being ill or injured. **recuperation** **NOUN**

recur, **recurs**, **recurring**, **recurred** VERB If something recurs, it happens or occurs again • *His hamstring injury recurred after the first game.* **recurrence** NOUN **recurrent** ADJECTIVE

recurring ADJECTIVE ① happening or occurring many times • *a recurring dream.* ② [MATHS] A recurring digit is one that is repeated over and over again after the decimal point.

recycle VERB [GEOGRAPHY] To recycle used products means to process them so that they can be used again • *recycled glass.*

red, **redder**, **reddest** NOUN, ADJECTIVE ① Red is the colour of blood or of a ripe tomato. ▸ADJECTIVE ② Red hair is between red and brown in colour.

redeem VERB ① If a feature redeems an unpleasant thing or situation, it makes it seem less bad. ② If you redeem yourself, you do something that gives people a good opinion of you again. ③ If you redeem something, you get it back by paying for it. ④ [RE] In Christianity, Jesus Christ is said to have redeemed the human race by paying the price of his life to save them from sin and death.

redemption NOUN Redemption is the state of being redeemed.

red-handed PHRASE To **catch someone red-handed** means to catch them doing something wrong.

red-hot ADJECTIVE Red-hot metal has been heated to such a high temperature that it has turned red.

redress (*formal*) VERB ① To redress a wrong means to put it right. ▸NOUN ② If you get redress for harm done to you, you are compensated for it.

red tape NOUN Red tape is official rules and procedures that seem unnecessary and cause delay. In the 18th century, red tape was used to bind official government documents.

reduce VERB ① To reduce something means to make it smaller in size or amount. ② You can use 'reduce' to say that someone or something is changed to a weaker or inferior state • *She reduced them to tears* • *The village was reduced to rubble.*

reduce VERB
① = curtail, cut, cut down, decrease, diminish, lessen, lower, shorten
≠ increase
② = degrade, demote, downgrade, drive, force

reduction NOUN When there is a reduction in something, it is made smaller.

redundancy, **redundancies** NOUN ① Redundancy is the state of being redundant. ② The number of redundancies is the number of people made redundant.

redundant ADJECTIVE ① When people are made redundant, they lose their jobs because there is no more work for them or no money to pay them. ② When something becomes redundant, it is no longer needed.

reed NOUN ① Reeds are hollow stemmed plants that grow in shallow water or wet ground. ② a thin piece of cane or metal inside some wind instruments which vibrates when air is blown over it.

reef NOUN [GEOGRAPHY] a long line of rocks or coral close to the surface of the sea.

reek VERB ① To reek of something means to smell strongly and unpleasantly of it. ▸NOUN ② If there is a reek of something, there is a strong unpleasant smell of it.

reel NOUN ① a cylindrical object around which you wrap something; often part of a device which you turn as a control. ② a fast Scottish dance. ▸VERB ③ When someone reels, they move unsteadily as if they are going to fall. ④ If your mind is reeling, you are confused because you have too much to think about. **reel off** VERB If you reel off information, you repeat it from memory quickly and easily.

re-elect VERB When someone is re-elected, they win an election again and are able to stay in power.

refer, **refers**, **referring**, **referred** VERB ① If you refer to something, you mention it. ② If you refer to a book or record, you look at it to find something out. ③ When a problem or issue is referred to someone, they are formally asked to deal with it • *The case was referred to the European Court.*

> **refer** VERB
> ① = allude, bring up, cite, mention
> ② = consult, look up

referee NOUN ① the official who controls a football game or a boxing or wrestling match. ② someone who gives a reference to a person who is applying for a job.

reference NOUN ① A reference to something or someone is a mention of them. ② Reference is the act of referring to something or someone for information or advice • *He makes that decision without reference to her.* ③ a number or name that tells you where to find information or identifies a document. ④ If someone gives you a reference when you apply for a job, they write a letter about your abilities.

referendum, **referendums** or **referenda** NOUN a vote in which all the people in a country are officially asked whether they agree with a policy or proposal.

refine VERB To refine a raw material such as oil or sugar means to process it to remove impurities.

refined ADJECTIVE ① very polite and well-mannered. ② processed to remove impurities.

> **refined** ADJECTIVE
> ① = civilised, genteel, gentlemanly, ladylike, polite
> ≠ common
> ② = distilled, filtered, processed, pure, purified

refinement NOUN ① Refinements are minor improvements. ② Refinement is politeness and good manners.

refinery, **refineries** NOUN a factory where substances such as oil or sugar are refined.

reflect VERB ① If something reflects an attitude or situation, it shows what it is like • *His off-duty hobbies reflected his maritime interests.* ② If something reflects light or heat, the light or heat bounces off it. ③ When something is reflected in a mirror or water, you can see its image in it. ④ MATHS If something reflects, its direction is reversed. ⑤ When you reflect, you think about something. **reflective** ADJECTIVE **reflectively** ADVERB

reflection NOUN ① If something is a reflection of something else, it shows what it is like • *This is a terrible reflection of the times.* ② an image in a mirror or water. ③ SCIENCE Reflection is the process by which light and heat are bounced off a surface. ④ MATHS In maths, reflection is also the turning back of something on itself • *reflection of an axis.* ⑤ Reflection is also thought • *After days of reflection she decided to leave.*

reflex NOUN ① A reflex or reflex action is a sudden uncontrollable movement that you make as a result of pressure or a blow. ② If you have good reflexes, you respond very quickly when something unexpected happens. ▸ ADJECTIVE ③ MATHS A reflex angle is between 180° and 360°.

reform NOUN ① Reforms are major changes to laws or institutions • *a programme of economic reform.* ▶ VERB ② When laws or institutions are reformed, major changes are made to them. ③ When people reform, they stop committing crimes or doing other unacceptable things. **reformer** NOUN

reform NOUN
① = amendment, correction, improvement, rehabilitation
▶ VERB ② = amend, better, correct, rectify, rehabilitate

Reformation NOUN [HISTORY] The Reformation was a religious and political movement in Europe in the 16th century that began as an attempt to reform the Roman Catholic Church, but ended in the establishment of the Protestant Churches.

refrain VERB ① (*formal*) If you refrain from doing something, you do not do it • *Please refrain from running in the corridors.* ▶ NOUN ② [MUSIC] The refrain of a song is a short, simple part, repeated after each verse.

refresh VERB ① If something refreshes you when you are hot or tired, it makes you feel cooler or more energetic • *A glass of fruit juice will refresh you.* ▶ PHRASE ② To **refresh someone's memory** means to remind them of something they had forgotten.

refresh VERB
① = brace, enliven, rejuvenate, revive, stimulate

refreshing ADJECTIVE You say that something is refreshing when it is pleasantly different from what you are used to • *She is a refreshing contrast to her father.*

refreshment NOUN Refreshments are drinks and small amounts of food provided at an event.

refrigerator NOUN an electrically cooled container in which you store food to keep it fresh.

refuel, refuels, refuelling, refuelled VERB When an aircraft or vehicle is refuelled, it is filled with more fuel.

refuge NOUN ① a place where you go for safety. ② If you take refuge, you go somewhere for safety or behave in a way that will protect you • *They took refuge in a bomb shelter* • *Father Rowan took refuge in silence.*

refuge NOUN
① = asylum, harbour, haven, sanctuary, shelter

refugee NOUN Refugees are people who have been forced to leave their country and live elsewhere.

refund NOUN [*Said* **re***-fund*] ① money returned to you because you have paid too much for something or because you have returned goods. ▶ VERB [*Said re-***fund**] ② To refund someone's money means to return it to them after they have paid for something with it.

refurbish VERB (*formal*) To refurbish a building means to decorate it and repair damage. **refurbishment** NOUN

refusal NOUN A refusal is when someone says firmly that they will not do, allow or accept something.

refuse[1] [*Said rif-***yooz**] VERB ① If you refuse to do something, you say or decide firmly that you will not do it. ② If someone refuses something, they do not allow it or do not accept it • *The United States has refused him a visa* • *He offered me a second drink which I refused.*

refuse VERB
① = abstain (*formal*), decline, withhold
② = decline, reject, spurn, turn down
≠ accept

refuse² [*Said* ***ref**-yoos*] **NOUN** Refuse is rubbish or waste.

> **refuse NOUN**
> = garbage (*informal*), junk (*informal*), litter, rubbish, trash, waste

refute VERB (*formal*) To refute a theory or argument means to prove that it is wrong.

regain VERB To regain something means to get it back.

regal ADJECTIVE very grand and suitable for a king or queen • *regal splendour*. **regally ADVERB**

regard VERB ① To regard someone or something in a particular way means to think of them in that way or have that opinion of them • *We all regard him as a friend* • *Many disapprove of the tax, regarding it as unfair*. ② (*literary*) To regard someone in a particular way also means to look at them in that way • *She regarded him curiously for a moment*. ▸ **NOUN** ③ If you have a high regard for someone, you have a very good opinion of them. ▸ **PHRASE** ④ **Regarding, as regards, with regard to** and **in regard to** are all used to indicate what you are talking or writing about • *There was always some question regarding education* • *As regards the war, he believed in victory at any price*. ⑤ 'Regards' is used in various expressions to express friendly feelings • *Give my regards to your husband*.

> **regard VERB**
> ① = consider, judge, look on, see, think of, view
> ② = contemplate, eye, gaze, look, scrutinise, watch

regardless PREPOSITION, ADVERB done or happening in spite of something else • *He led from the front, regardless of the danger*.

regatta NOUN a race meeting for sailing or rowing boats.

regenerate VERB (*formal*) To regenerate something means to develop and improve it after it has been declining • *a scheme to regenerate the docks area of the city*. **regeneration NOUN**

regent NOUN someone who rules in place of a king or queen who is ill or too young to rule.

reggae NOUN Reggae is a type of music, originally from the West Indies, with a strong beat.

regime [*Said ray-**jeem***] **NOUN** a system of government, and the people who are ruling a country • *a communist regime*.

regiment NOUN a large group of soldiers commanded by a colonel. **regimental ADJECTIVE**

regimented ADJECTIVE very strictly controlled • *the regimented life of the orphanage*. **regimentation NOUN**

region NOUN ① [GEOGRAPHY] a large area of land. ② You can refer to any area or part as a region • *the pelvic region of the body*. ▸ **PHRASE** ③ **In the region of** means approximately • *The scheme will cost in the region of six million*. **regional ADJECTIVE regionally ADVERB**

> **region NOUN**
> ① = area, district, land, locality, quarter, sector, territory, tract, zone

register NOUN ① an official list or record of things • *the electoral register*. ② (*technical*) a style of speaking or writing used in particular circumstances or social occasions. ▸ **VERB** ③ When something is registered, it is recorded on an official list • *The car was registered in my name*. ④ If an instrument registers a measurement, it shows it. ⑤ If your face registers a feeling, it expresses it. **registration NOUN**

registrar NOUN ① a person who keeps official records of births, marriages and deaths. ② At a college or university, the registrar is a senior administrative official. ③ a senior hospital doctor.

registration number NOUN the sequence of letters and numbers on the front and back of a motor vehicle that identify it.

registry, **registries** NOUN a place where official records are kept.

regret, **regrets**, **regretting**, **regretted** VERB ① If you regret something, you are sorry that it happened. ② You can say that you regret something as a way of apologising • *We regret any inconvenience to passengers.* ▶ NOUN ③ If you have regrets, you are sad or sorry about something. **regretful** ADJECTIVE **regretfully** ADVERB

> **regret** VERB
> ① = be sorry, grieve, lament, mourn, repent
> ▶ NOUN ③ = grief, pang of conscience, penitence, remorse, repentance, sorrow

regrettable ADJECTIVE unfortunate and undesirable • *a regrettable accident.* **regrettably** ADVERB

regular ADJECTIVE ① even and equally spaced • *soft music with a regular beat.* ② [MATHS] A regular shape has equal angles and equal sides • *a regular polygon.* ③ Regular events or activities happen often and according to a pattern, for example each day or each week • *The trains to London are fairly regular.* ④ If you are a regular customer or visitor somewhere, you go there often. ⑤ usual or normal • *I was filling in for the regular receptionist.* ⑥ having a well balanced appearance • *a regular geometrical shape.* ▶ NOUN ⑦ People who go to a place often are known as its regulars. **regularly** ADVERB **regularity** NOUN

> **regular** ADJECTIVE
> ① = consistent, constant, even, periodic, rhythmic, steady, uniform
> ≠ irregular
> ⑤ = customary, everyday, habitual, normal, ordinary, routine, typical, usual

regulate VERB To regulate something means to control the way it operates • *Sweating helps to regulate the body's temperature.* **regulator** NOUN

regulation NOUN ① Regulations are official rules. ② Regulation is the control of something • *regulation of the betting industry.*

rehabilitate VERB To rehabilitate someone who has been ill or in prison means to help them lead a normal life. **rehabilitation** NOUN

rehearsal NOUN [DRAMA] a practice of a performance in preparation for the actual event.

rehearse VERB [DRAMA] To rehearse a performance means to practise it in preparation for the actual event.

reign [*Said* **rain**] VERB ① When a king or queen reigns, he or she rules a country. ② You can say that something reigns when it is a noticeable feature of a situation or period of time • *Panic reigned after his assassination.* ▶ NOUN ③ [HISTORY] The reign of a king or queen is the period during which he or she reigns.

rein NOUN ① Reins are the thin leather straps which you hold when you are riding a horse. ▶ PHRASE ② To **keep a tight rein on** someone or something means to control them firmly.

reincarnation NOUN [RE] People who believe in reincarnation believe that when you die, you are born again as another creature.

reindeer, **reindeer** NOUN Reindeer are

deer with large antlers that live in northern regions.

reinforce VERB ① To reinforce something means to strengthen it • *a reinforced steel barrier*. ② If something reinforces an idea or claim, it provides evidence to support it.

reinforcement NOUN ① Reinforcements are additional soldiers sent to join an army in battle. ② Reinforcement is the reinforcing of something.

reinstate VERB ① To reinstate someone means to give them back a position they have lost. ② To reinstate something means to bring it back • *Parliament voted against reinstating capital punishment*. **reinstatement** NOUN

reiterate *[Said ree-**it**-er-ate]* VERB *(formal)* If you reiterate something, you say it again. **reiteration** NOUN

reject VERB *[Said re-**ject**]* ① If you reject a proposal or request, you do not accept it or agree to it. ② If you reject a belief, political system or way of life, you decide that it is not for you. ▸ NOUN *[Said **re**-ject]* ③ a product that cannot be used, because there is something wrong with it. **rejection** NOUN

reject VERB
① = decline, deny, rebuff, refuse, renounce *(formal)*, say no to, spurn, turn down, unfollow, unfriend
≠ accept

rejoice VERB To rejoice means to be very pleased about something • *The whole country rejoiced after his downfall*.

rejoice VERB
= be overjoyed, celebrate, delight, glory

rejoin VERB If you rejoin someone, you go back to them soon after leaving them • *She rejoined her friends in the pool*.

rejuvenate *[Said ree-**joo**-vin-ate]* VERB To rejuvenate someone means to make them feel young again. **rejuvenation** NOUN

relapse NOUN If a sick person has a relapse, their health suddenly gets worse after improving.

relate VERB ① If something relates to something else, it is connected or concerned with it • *The statistics relate only to western Germany*. ② If you can relate to someone, you can understand their thoughts and feelings. ③ To relate a story means to tell it.

relation NOUN ① If there is a relation between two things, they are similar or connected in some way • *This theory bears no relation to reality*. ② Your relations are the members of your family. ③ Relations between people are their feelings and behaviour towards each other • *Relations between brother and sister had not improved*.

relation NOUN
① = bearing, bond, connection, correlation, link, relationship
② = kin, kinsman, kinswoman, relative

relationship NOUN ① The relationship between two people or groups is the way they feel and behave towards each other. ② PSHE a close friendship, especially one involving romantic feelings. ③ The relationship between two things is the way in which they are connected • *the relationship between slavery and the sugar trade*.

relationship NOUN
① = affinity, association, bond, connection, rapport
③ = connection, correlation, link, parallel

relative ADJECTIVE ① compared to other things or people of the same kind • *The fighting resumed after a period of relative calm* • *He is a relative novice*. ② You use 'relative' when comparing the size or quality of two things • *the relative strengths of the British and German forces*. ▶ **NOUN** ③ Your relatives are the members of your family.

relax **VERB** ① If you relax, you become calm and your muscles lose their tension. ② If you relax your hold, you hold something less tightly. ③ To relax something also means to make it less strict or controlled • *The rules governing student conduct were relaxed*. **relaxation** **NOUN**

relax **VERB**
① = laze, rest, take it easy, unwind

relay **NOUN** *[Said* ***re****-lay]* ① PE A relay race or relay is a race between teams, with each team member running one part of the race. ▶ **VERB** *[Said re-****lay****]* ② To relay a television or radio signal means to send it on. ③ If you relay information, you tell it to someone else.

release **VERB** ① To release someone or something means to set them free or remove restraints from them. ② To release something also means to issue it or make it available • *He is releasing an album of love songs*. ▶ **NOUN** ③ When the release of someone or something takes place, they are set free. ④ A press release or publicity release is an official written statement given to reporters. ⑤ A new release is a new film or record that has just become available.

release **VERB**
① = deliver, discharge, extricate, free, let go, liberate, set free
② = issue, launch, publish, put out
▶ **NOUN** ③ = discharge, emancipation, freedom, liberation, liberty

relegate **VERB** To relegate something or someone means to give them a less important position or status. **relegation** **NOUN**

relent **VERB** If someone relents, they agree to something they had previously not allowed.

relentless **ADJECTIVE** never stopping and never becoming less intense • *the relentless rise of business closures*. **relentlessly** **ADVERB**

relentless **ADJECTIVE**
= incessant, nonstop, persistent, sustained, unrelenting, unremitting

relevant **ADJECTIVE** If something is relevant, it is connected with and is appropriate to what is being discussed • *We have passed all relevant information on to the police*. **relevance** **NOUN**

relevant **ADJECTIVE**
= applicable, apposite, appropriate, apt, pertinent
≠ irrelevant

reliable **ADJECTIVE** ① Reliable people and things can be trusted to do what you want. ② If information is reliable, you can assume that it is correct. **reliably** **ADVERB** **reliability** **NOUN**

reliable **ADJECTIVE**
① = dependable, faithful, safe, sound, staunch, sure, true, trustworthy
≠ unreliable

reliant **ADJECTIVE** If you are reliant on someone or something, you depend on them • *They are not wholly reliant on charity*. **reliance** **NOUN**

relic **NOUN** ① Relics are objects or customs that have survived from an earlier time. ② an object regarded as holy because it is thought to be connected with a saint.

relief **NOUN** ① If you feel relief, you are glad and thankful because a bad situation is over or has been avoided.

② Relief is also money, food or clothing provided for people who are in need.

relieve VERB ① If something relieves an unpleasant feeling, it makes it less unpleasant • *Meditation can help relieve stress.* ② (*formal*) If you relieve someone, you do their job or duty for a period. ③ If someone is relieved of their duties, they are dismissed from their job. ④ If you relieve yourself, you urinate.

religion NOUN ① RE Religion is the belief in a god or gods and all the activities connected with such beliefs. ② RE a system of religious belief.

religious ADJECTIVE ① connected with religion • *religious worship.* ② RE Someone who is religious has a strong belief in a god or gods.

> **religious** ADJECTIVE
> ① = devotional, divine, doctrinal, holy, sacred, scriptural, spiritual, theological
> ② = devout, God-fearing, godly, pious, righteous

religiously ADVERB If you do something religiously, you do it regularly as a duty • *He stuck religiously to the rules.*

relinquish [*Said ril-**ling**-kwish*] VERB (*formal*) If you relinquish something, you give it up.

relish VERB ① If you relish something, you enjoy it • *He relished the idea of getting some cash.* ▶ NOUN ② Relish is enjoyment • *He told me with relish of the wonderful times he had.* ③ Relish is also a savoury sauce or pickle.

relive VERB If you relive a past experience, you remember it and imagine it happening again.

relocate VERB If people or businesses are relocated, they are moved to a different place. **relocation** NOUN

reluctant ADJECTIVE If you are reluctant to do something, you are unwilling to do it. **reluctance** NOUN

> **reluctant** ADJECTIVE
> = averse, disinclined, hesitant, loath, slow, unwilling
> ≠ eager

reluctantly ADVERB If you do something reluctantly, you do it although you do not want to.

rely, **relies**, **relying**, **relied** VERB ① If you rely on someone or something, you need them and depend on them • *She has to rely on payments from her parents.* ② If you can rely on someone to do something, you can trust them to do it • *They can always be relied on to turn up.*

remain VERB ① If you remain in a particular place, you stay there. ② If you remain in a particular state, you stay the same and do not change • *The two men remained silent.* ③ Something that remains still exists or is left over • *Huge amounts of weapons remain to be collected.*

> **remain** VERB
> ① = be left, linger, stay behind, wait
> ② = continue, endure, go on, last, stay, survive

remainder NOUN ① The remainder of something is the part that is left • *He gulped down the remainder of his coffee.* ② the amount left over when one number cannot be exactly divided by another • *For 10 ÷ 3, the remainder is 1.*

> **remainder** NOUN
> ① = balance, last, others, remains, remnants, rest

remand VERB ① If a judge remands someone who is accused of a crime, the trial is postponed and the person is ordered to come back at a later date. ▶ PHRASE ② If someone is **on remand**, they are in prison waiting for their trial to begin.

remark VERB ① If you remark on something, you mention it or comment on it • *She had remarked on the boy's improvement.* ▶ NOUN ② something you say, often in a casual way.

> **remark** VERB
> ① = comment, mention, observe, say, state
> ▶ NOUN ② = comment, observation, statement, utterance, word

remarkable ADJECTIVE impressive and unexpected • *It was a remarkable achievement.* **remarkably** ADVERB

remarry, **remarries**, **remarrying**, **remarried** VERB If someone remarries, they get married again.

remedial ADJECTIVE ① Remedial activities are to help someone improve their health after they have been ill. ② Remedial exercises are designed to improve someone's ability in something • *the remedial reading class.*

remedy, **remedies**, **remedying**, **remedied** NOUN ① a way of dealing with a problem • *a remedy for colic.* ▶ VERB ② If you remedy something that is wrong, you correct it • *We have to remedy the situation immediately.*

remember VERB ① If you can remember someone or something from the past, you can bring them into your mind or think about them. ② If you remember to do something, you do it when you intended to • *Ben had remembered to book reservations.*

> **remember** VERB
> ① = call to mind, recall, recognise, retain
> ≠ forget

remembrance NOUN If you do something in remembrance of a dead person, you are showing that they are remembered with respect and affection.

remind VERB ① If someone reminds you of a fact, they say something to make you think about it • *Remind me to buy a bottle of water, will you?* ② If someone reminds you of another person, they look similar and make you think of them.

> **remind** VERB
> ① = bring back to, jog someone's memory, make someone remember, put in mind, refresh someone's memory

reminder NOUN ① If one thing is a reminder of another, the first thing makes you think of the second • *a reminder of better times.* ② a note sent to tell someone they have forgotten to do something.

reminiscent ADJECTIVE Something that is reminiscent of something else reminds you of it.

remission NOUN When prisoners get remission for good behaviour, their sentences are reduced.

remit (*formal*) VERB *[Said ri-**mit**]* ① To remit money to someone means to send it to them in payment for something. ▶ NOUN *[Said **ree**-mit]* ② The remit of a person or committee is the subject or task they are responsible for • *Their remit is to research into a wide range of health problems.*

remnant NOUN a small part of something left after the rest has been used or destroyed.

remorse NOUN (*formal*) Remorse is a strong feeling of guilt. **remorseful** ADJECTIVE

remote ADJECTIVE ① Remote areas are far away from places where most people live. ② far away in time • *the remote past.* ③ If you say a person is remote, you mean they do not want to be friendly • *She is severe, solemn and remote.* ④ If there is only a remote possibility of something happening, it is unlikely to happen. **remoteness** NOUN

remote ADJECTIVE
① = distant, far-off, inaccessible, isolated, lonely, outlying
② = distant, far-off
③ = aloof, cold, detached, distant, reserved, withdrawn
④ = poor, slender, slight, slim, small

remote control NOUN Remote control is a system of controlling a machine or vehicle from a distance using radio or electronic signals.

remotely ADVERB used to emphasise a negative statement • *He isn't remotely keen.*

removal NOUN ① The removal of something is the act of taking it away. ② A removal company transports furniture from one building to another.

remove VERB ① If you remove something from a place, you take it off or away. ② If you are removed from a position of authority, you are not allowed to continue your job. ③ If you remove an undesirable feeling or attitude, you get rid of it • *Most of her fears had been removed.* **removable** ADJECTIVE

remove VERB
① = delete, detach, eject, eliminate, erase, extract, get rid of, take away, take off, take out, withdraw

Renaissance *[Said ren-**nay**-sonss]* NOUN HISTORY The Renaissance was a period from the 14th to 16th centuries in Europe when there was a great revival in the arts and learning.

renal ADJECTIVE concerning the kidneys • *renal failure.*

rename VERB If you rename something, you give it a new name.

render VERB You can use 'render' to say that something is changed into a different state • *The bomb was quickly rendered harmless.*

rendezvous *[Said ron-day-voo]* NOUN ① a meeting • *Baxter arranged a six o'clock rendezvous.* ② a place where you have arranged to meet someone • *The pub became a popular rendezvous.*

rendition NOUN (*formal*) a performance of a play, poem or piece of music.

renew VERB ① To renew an activity or relationship means to begin it again. ② To renew a licence or contract means to extend the period of time for which it is valid. **renewal** NOUN

renew VERB
① = begin again, recommence, re-establish, reopen, resume

renewable ADJECTIVE ① able to be renewed. ▶ NOUN ② GEOGRAPHY a renewable form of energy, such as wind power or solar power.

renounce VERB (*formal*) If you renounce something, you reject it or give it up. **renunciation** NOUN

renounce VERB
= disown, give up, reject, relinquish

renovate VERB If you renovate an old building or machine, you repair it and restore it to good condition. **renovation** NOUN

renovate VERB
= do up, modernise, recondition, refurbish, repair, restore, revamp

renowned *[Rhymes with **sound**]* ADJECTIVE well-known for something good • *He is not renowned for his patience.* **renown** NOUN

rent VERB ① If you rent something, you pay the owner a regular sum of money in return for being able to use it. ▶ NOUN ② Rent is the amount of money you pay regularly to rent land or accommodation.

rental ADJECTIVE ① concerned with

the renting out of goods and services • *Scotland's largest car rental company.* ▶ **NOUN** ② the amount of money you pay when you rent something.

reorganise; also spelt **reorganize** **VERB** To reorganise something means to organise it in a new way in order to make it more efficient or acceptable. **reorganisation NOUN**

rep (*informal*) **NOUN** ① A rep is a travelling salesperson. Rep is an abbreviation for **representative**. ▶ **PHRASE** ② When actors work **in rep**, they are working with a repertory company.

repair NOUN ① something you do to mend something that is damaged or broken. ▶ **VERB** ② If you repair something, you mend it.

repair NOUN
① = darn, mend, patch, restoration
▶ **VERB** ② = fix, mend, patch, patch up, renovate, restore

repay, **repays**, **repaying**, **repaid VERB** ① To repay money means to give it back to the person who lent it. ② If you repay a favour, you do something to help the person who helped you. **repayment NOUN**

repay VERB
① = pay back, refund, settle up

repeal VERB If the government repeals a law, it cancels it so that it is no longer valid.

repeat VERB ① If you repeat something, you say, write or do it again. ② If you repeat what someone has said, you tell someone else about it • *I trust you not to repeat that to anyone.* ▶ **NOUN** ③ something which is done or happens again • *the number of repeats shown on TV*. **repeated ADJECTIVE repeatedly ADVERB**

repeat VERB
① = echo, reiterate, say again

repel, **repels**, **repelling**, **repelled VERB** ① If something repels you, you find it horrible and disgusting. ② When soldiers repel an attacking force, they successfully defend themselves against it. ③ [SCIENCE] When a magnetic pole repels an opposite pole, it forces the opposite pole away.

repel VERB
① = disgust, offend, revolt, sicken
≠ attract
② = drive off, repulse, resist

repellent ADJECTIVE ① (*formal*) horrible and disgusting • *I found him repellent.* ▶ **NOUN** ② Repellents are chemicals used to keep insects or other creatures away.

repent VERB (*formal*) If you repent, you are sorry for something bad you have done. **repentance NOUN repentant ADJECTIVE**

repercussion NOUN The repercussions of an event are the effects it has at a later time.

repertoire [*Said* ***rep****-et-twar*] **NOUN** A performer's repertoire is all the pieces of music or dramatic parts he or she has learned and can perform.

repertory, **repertories NOUN** ① Repertory is the practice of performing a small number of plays in a theatre for a short time, using the same actors in each play. ② In Australian, New Zealand and South African English, repertory is the same as **repertoire**.

repetition NOUN ① If there is a repetition of something, it happens again • *We don't want a repetition of last week's fiasco.* ② [ENGLISH] Repetition is when a word, phrase or sound is repeated, for example to emphasise a point or to make sure it is understood, or for poetic effect.

repetitive ADJECTIVE A repetitive activity involves a lot of repetition and is boring • *dull and repetitive work.*

replace VERB ① When one thing replaces another, the first thing takes the place of the second. ② If you replace something that is damaged or lost, you get a new one. ③ If you replace something, you put it back where it was before • *She replaced the receiver.*

> **replace** VERB
> ① = succeed, supersede, supplant, take over from, take the place of

replacement NOUN ① The replacement for someone or something is the person or thing that takes their place. ② The replacement of a person or thing happens when they are replaced by another person or thing.

> **replacement** NOUN
> ① = proxy, stand-in, substitute, successor, surrogate

replay VERB *[Said re-**play**]* ① If a match is replayed, the teams play it again. ② If you replay a recording, you play it again • *Replay the first few seconds of the DVD please.* ▸ NOUN *[Said **re**-play]* ③ a match that is played for a second time.

replenish VERB *(formal)* If you replenish something, you make it full or complete again.

replica NOUN an accurate copy of something • *a replica of Columbus's ship.*
replicate VERB

reply, **replies**, **replying**, **replied** VERB ① If you reply to something, you say or write an answer. ▸ NOUN ② what you say or write when you answer someone.

> **reply** VERB
> ① = answer, counter, respond, retort, return
> ▸ NOUN ② = answer, response, retort

report VERB ① If you report that something has happened, you tell someone about it or give an official account of it • *He reported the theft to the police.* ② To report someone to an authority means to make an official complaint about them. ③ If you report to a person or place, you go there and say you have arrived. ▸ NOUN ④ an account of an event or situation.

> **report** VERB
> ① = cover, describe, inform of, notify, state
> ▸ NOUN ④ = account, description, statement

reporter NOUN someone who writes news articles or broadcasts news reports.

repossess VERB If a shop or company repossesses goods that have not been paid for, they take them back.

represent VERB ① If you represent someone, you act on their behalf • *lawyers representing relatives of the victims.* ② If a sign or symbol represents something, it stands for it. ③ To represent something in a particular way means to describe it in that way • *The popular press tends to represent him as a hero.*

> **represent** VERB
> ② = mean, stand for, symbolise
> ③ = depict, describe, picture, portray, show

representation NOUN ① Representation is the state of being represented by someone • *Was there any student representation?* ② You can describe a picture or statue of someone as a representation of them.

representative NOUN ① a person chosen to act on behalf of another person or a group. ▸ ADJECTIVE ② A representative selection is typical of the group it belongs to • *The photos chosen are not representative of his work.*

representative NOUN
① = agent, delegate, deputy, proxy, spokesman, spokeswoman
▶ ADJECTIVE ② = characteristic, illustrative, typical

repress VERB ① If you repress a feeling, you succeed in not showing or feeling it • *I couldn't repress my anger any longer.* ② To repress people means to restrict their freedom and control them by force. **repression** NOUN

repressive ADJECTIVE Repressive governments use force and unjust laws to restrict and control people.

reprieve [Said rip-**preev**] VERB ① If someone who has been sentenced to death is reprieved, their sentence is changed and they are not killed. ▶ NOUN ② a delay before something unpleasant happens • *The zoo won a reprieve from closure.*

reprimand VERB ① If you reprimand someone, you officially tell them that they should not have done something. ▶ NOUN ② something said or written by a person in authority when they are reprimanding someone.

reprisal NOUN Reprisals are violent actions taken by one group of people against another group that has harmed them.

reproach (formal) NOUN ① If you express reproach, you show that you feel sad and angry about what someone has done • *a long letter of reproach.* ▶ VERB ② If you reproach someone, you tell them, rather sadly, that they have done something wrong. **reproachful** ADJECTIVE **reproachfully** ADVERB

reproduce VERB ① To reproduce something means to make a copy of it. ② SCIENCE When living things reproduce, they produce more of their own kind • *Bacteria reproduce by splitting into two.*

reproduction NOUN ① a modern copy of a painting or piece of furniture. ② SCIENCE Reproduction is the process by which a living thing produces more of its kind • *the study of animal reproduction.*

reproductive ADJECTIVE relating to the reproduction of living things • *the female reproductive system.*

reptile NOUN a cold-blooded animal, such as a snake or a lizard, which has scaly skin and lays eggs. **reptilian** ADJECTIVE

republic NOUN a country which has a president rather than a king or queen. **republican** NOUN, ADJECTIVE **republicanism** NOUN

repulsive ADJECTIVE horrible and disgusting.

reputable ADJECTIVE known to be good and reliable • *a well-established and reputable firm.*

reputation NOUN The reputation of something or someone is the opinion that people have of them • *The college had a good reputation.*

reputation NOUN
= character, name, renown, repute, standing, stature

reputed ADJECTIVE If something is reputed to be true, some people say that it is true • *He is the reputed writer of a number of the plays.* **reputedly** ADVERB

request VERB ① If you request something, you ask for it politely or formally. ▶ NOUN ② If you make a request for something, you request it.

request VERB
① = ask, beg, seek
▶ NOUN ② = appeal, application, call, plea

requiem [Said **rek**-wee-em] NOUN ① A requiem or requiem mass is a mass celebrated for someone who has recently died. ② a piece of music for singers and an orchestra, originally written for a requiem mass • *Mozart's Requiem.*

require VERB ① If you require something, you need it. ② If you are required to do something, you have to do it because someone says you must • *The rules require employers to provide safety training.*

require VERB
① = demand, depend on, be in need of, need, want (*informal*)
② = compel, demand, direct, instruct, oblige, order

requirement NOUN something that you must have or must do • *A good degree is a requirement for entry.*

requirement NOUN
= demand, essential, necessity, need, specification

requisite (*formal*) ADJECTIVE ① necessary for a particular purpose • *She filled in the requisite paperwork.* ▶ NOUN ② something that is necessary for a particular purpose.

rescue, rescues, rescuing, rescued VERB ① If you rescue someone, you save them from a dangerous or unpleasant situation. ▶ NOUN ② Rescue is help which saves someone from a dangerous or unpleasant situation. **rescuer** NOUN

research NOUN ① Research is work that involves studying something and trying to find out facts about it. ▶ VERB ② If you research something, you try to discover facts about it. **researcher** NOUN

research NOUN
① = analysis, examination, exploration, investigation, study
▶ VERB ② = analyse, examine, explore, google, investigate, study

resemblance NOUN If there is a resemblance between two things, they are similar to each other • *There was a remarkable resemblance between them.*

resemblance NOUN
= analogy, correspondence, likeness, parallel, similarity

resemble VERB To resemble something means to be similar to it.

resemble VERB
= bear a resemblance to, be like, be similar to, look like, parallel, take after

resent VERB If you resent something, you feel bitter and angry about it.

resent VERB
= be angry about, be offended by, dislike, object to, take offence at

resentful ADJECTIVE bitter and angry • *He felt very resentful about losing his job.* **resentfully** ADVERB

resentful ADJECTIVE
= aggrieved, angry, bitter, embittered, huffy, indignant, offended

resentment NOUN a feeling of anger or bitterness.

resentment NOUN
= anger, animosity, bitterness, grudge, huff, indignation, rancour (*formal*)

reservation NOUN ① If you have reservations about something, you are not sure that it is right. ② If you make a reservation, you book a place in advance. ③ an area of land set aside for American Indian peoples • *a Cherokee reservation.*

reserve VERB ① If something is reserved for a particular person or purpose, it is kept specially for them. ▶ NOUN ② a supply of something for future use. ③ In sport, a reserve is someone who is available to play in case one of the team is unable to play.

A B C D E F G H I J K L M N O P Q R S T U V W X Y Z

④ A nature reserve is an area of land where animals, birds or plants are officially protected. ⑤ If someone shows reserve, they keep their feelings hidden. **reserved** ADJECTIVE

reserve VERB
① = hoard, hold, keep, put by, save, set aside, stockpile, store
▸ NOUN ② = cache, fund, hoard, stock, stockpile, store, supply

reservoir *[Said **rez**-ev-wahr]* NOUN a lake used for storing water before it is supplied to people.

reshuffle NOUN a reorganisation of people or things.

reside *[Said riz-**zide**]* VERB *(formal)* ① If someone resides somewhere, they live there or are staying there. ② If a quality resides in something, the quality is in that thing.

residence *(formal)* NOUN ① A residence is a house. ▸ PHRASE ② If you **take up residence** somewhere, you go and live there.

resident NOUN ① A resident of a house or area is someone who lives there. ▸ ADJECTIVE ② If someone is resident in a house or area, they live there.

residential ADJECTIVE ① A residential area contains mainly houses rather than offices or factories. ② providing accommodation • *residential care for elderly people.*

residue NOUN a small amount of something that remains after most of it has gone • *an increase in toxic residues found in drinking water.* **residual** ADJECTIVE

resign VERB ① If you resign from a job, you formally announce that you are leaving it. ② If you resign yourself to an unpleasant situation, you realise that you have to accept it. **resigned** ADJECTIVE

resign VERB
① = abdicate, hand in your notice, leave, quit, step down *(informal)*
② = accept, bow, reconcile yourself

resignation NOUN ① Someone's resignation is a formal statement of their intention to leave a job. ② Resignation is the reluctant acceptance of an unpleasant situation or fact.

resilient ADJECTIVE [PSHE] able to recover quickly from unpleasant or damaging events. **resilience** NOUN

resin NOUN ① Resin is a sticky substance produced by some trees. ② Resin is also a substance produced chemically and used to make plastics.

resist VERB ① If you resist something, you refuse to accept it and try to prevent it • *The pay squeeze will be fiercely resisted by the unions.* ② If you resist someone, you fight back against them.

resist VERB
① = defy, fight, oppose, refuse, struggle against
≠ accept

resistance NOUN ① Resistance to something such as change is a refusal to accept it. ② Resistance to an attack consists of fighting back • *The demonstrators offered no resistance.* ③ Your body's resistance to germs or disease is its power to not be harmed by them. ④ [SCIENCE] Resistance is also the power of a substance to resist the flow of an electrical current through it.

resistant ADJECTIVE ① opposed to something and wanting to prevent it • *People were very resistant to change.* ② If something is resistant to a particular thing, it is not harmed or affected by it • *Certain insects are resistant to this spray.*

resolute *[Said* ***rez****-ol-loot]* **ADJECTIVE** (*formal*) Someone who is resolute is determined not to change their mind. **resolutely ADVERB**

resolution NOUN ① Resolution is determination. ② If you make a resolution, you promise yourself to do something. ③ a formal decision taken at a meeting. ④ ENGLISH The resolution of a problem is the solving of it.

resolve VERB ① If you resolve to do something, you firmly decide to do it. ② If you resolve a problem, you find a solution to it. ▸ **NOUN** ③ Resolve is absolute determination.

> **resolve VERB**
> ① = decide, determine, intend, make up your mind
> ② = clear up, find a solution to, overcome, solve, sort out, work out
> ▸ **NOUN** ③ = determination, resolution, tenacity

resonance NOUN ① Resonance is sound produced by an object vibrating as a result of another sound nearby. ② Resonance is also a deep, clear and echoing quality of sound.

resonate VERB If something resonates, it vibrates and produces a deep, strong sound.

resort VERB ① If you resort to a course of action, you do it because you have no alternative. ▸ **NOUN** ② a place where people spend their holidays. ▸ **PHRASE** ③ If you do something **as a last resort**, you do it because you can find no other way of solving a problem.

resounding ADJECTIVE ① loud and echoing • *a resounding round of applause.* ② A resounding success is a great success.

resource NOUN The resources of a country, organisation or person are the materials, money or skills they have.

resourceful ADJECTIVE A resourceful person is good at finding ways of dealing with problems. **resourcefulness NOUN**

respect VERB ① If you respect someone, you have a good opinion of their character or ideas. ② If you respect someone's rights or wishes, you do not do things that they would not like, or would consider wrong • *It is about time they started respecting the law.* ▸ **NOUN** ③ If you have respect for someone, you have a good opinion of them. ▸ **PHRASE** ④ You can say **in this respect** to refer to a particular feature • *At least in this respect we are equals.*

> **respect VERB**
> ① = admire, have a good opinion of, have a high opinion of, honour, look up to, think highly of, venerate (*formal*)
> ≠ disrespect
> ▸ **NOUN** ③ = admiration, esteem, regard, reverence
> ≠ disrespect

respectable ADJECTIVE ① considered to be acceptable and morally correct • *respectable families.* ② adequate or reasonable • *a respectable rate of economic growth.* **respectability NOUN** **respectably ADVERB**

> **respectable ADJECTIVE**
> ① = decent, good, honourable, proper, reputable, upright, worthy
> ② = appreciable, considerable, decent, fair, reasonable

respectful ADJECTIVE showing respect for someone • *Our children are always respectful to their elders.* **respectfully ADVERB**

respective ADJECTIVE belonging or relating individually to the people or things just mentioned • *They went into their respective rooms to pack.*

respectively ADVERB in the same order as the items just mentioned

• *Amanda and Emily finished first and second respectively*.

respiration NOUN SCIENCE Your respiration is your breathing.

respiratory ADJECTIVE SCIENCE relating to breathing • *respiratory diseases*.

respite NOUN (*formal*) a short rest from something unpleasant.

respond VERB When you respond to something, you react to it by doing or saying something.

respondent NOUN ① a person who answers a questionnaire or a request for information. ② In a court case, the respondent is the defendant.

response NOUN Your response to an event is your reaction or reply to it • *There has been no response to his remarks yet*.

responsibility, **responsibilities** NOUN ① PSHE CITIZENSHIP If you have responsibility for something, it is your duty to deal with it or look after it • *The garden was to have been his responsibility*. ② If you accept responsibility for something that has happened, you agree that you caused it or were to blame • *We must all accept responsibility for our own mistakes*.

responsibility NOUN
① = duty, obligation, onus
② = blame, fault, guilt, liability

responsible ADJECTIVE ① If you are responsible for something, it is your job to deal with it. ② If you are responsible for something bad that has happened, you are to blame for it. ③ If you are responsible to someone, that person is your boss and tells you what you have to do. ④ A responsible person behaves properly and sensibly without needing to be supervised. ⑤ A responsible job involves making careful judgments about important matters. **responsibly** ADVERB

responsible ADJECTIVE
① = in charge, in control
② = at fault, guilty, to blame
④ = dependable, level-headed, reliable, sensible, sound, trustworthy
≠ irresponsible

responsive ADJECTIVE ① quick to show interest and pleasure. ② taking notice of events and reacting in an appropriate way • *The course is responsive to students' needs*.

rest NOUN ① The rest of something is all the remaining parts of it. ② If you have a rest, you sit or lie quietly and relax. ▸ VERB ③ If you rest, you relax and do not do anything active for a while.

rest NOUN
① = balance, others, remainder, surplus
② = break, holiday, leisure, relaxation, respite
▸ VERB ③ = have a break, idle, laze, put your feet up, relax, sit down, take it easy

restaurant [*Said* ***rest**-er-ront*] NOUN a place where you can buy and eat a meal.

restaurateur [*Said rest-er-a-**tur***] NOUN someone who owns or manages a restaurant.

restful ADJECTIVE Something that is restful helps you feel calm and relaxed.

restless ADJECTIVE finding it hard to remain still or relaxed because of boredom or impatience. **restlessly** ADVERB **restlessness** NOUN

restless ADJECTIVE
= edgy, fidgety, fretful, jumpy, on edge, unsettled

restore VERB ① To restore something means to cause it to exist again or to return to its previous state • *He was* *anxious to restore his reputation*. ②To restore an old building or work of art means to clean and repair it. **restoration** NOUN

> **restore** VERB
> ① = re-establish, reinstate, reintroduce, return
> ② = fix up, mend, rebuild, reconstruct, refurbish, renovate, repair

restrain VERB To restrain someone or something means to hold them back or prevent them from doing what they want to.

> **restrain** VERB
> = contain, control, curb, hamper, hinder, hold back, inhibit

restrained ADJECTIVE behaving in a controlled way.

restraint NOUN ① Restraints are rules or conditions that limit something • *wage restraints*. ② Restraint is calm, controlled behaviour.

restrict VERB ① If you restrict something, you prevent it becoming too large or varied. ② To restrict people or animals means to limit their movement or actions. **restrictive** ADJECTIVE

> **restrict** VERB
> ② = confine, contain, hamper, handicap, impede, inhibit, limit, restrain

restriction NOUN a rule or situation that limits what you can do • *financial restrictions*.

> **restriction** NOUN
> = constraint, control, curb, limitation, regulation, restraint, stipulation

result NOUN ① The result of an action or situation is the situation that is caused by it • *As a result of the incident he got a two-year suspension*. ② The result is also the final marks, figures or situation at the end of an exam, calculation or contest • *election results* • *The result was calculated to three decimal places*. ▶ VERB ③ If something results in a particular event, it causes that event to happen. ④ If something results from a particular event, it is caused by that event • *The fire had resulted from carelessness*. **resultant** ADJECTIVE

> **result** NOUN
> ① = consequence, effect, outcome, product, upshot
> ▶ VERB ③ = bring about, cause, lead to
> ④ = arise, derive, develop, ensue, follow, happen, stem

resume *[Said riz-**yoom**]* VERB If you resume an activity or position, you return to it after a break. **resumption** NOUN

resurgence NOUN If there is a resurgence of an attitude or activity, it reappears and grows stronger. **resurgent** ADJECTIVE

resurrect VERB If you resurrect something, you make it exist again after it has disappeared or ended. **resurrection** NOUN

resuscitate *[Said ris-**suss**-it-tate]* VERB If you resuscitate someone, you make them conscious again after an accident. **resuscitation** NOUN

retail NOUN The retail price is the price at which something is sold in the shops. **retailer** NOUN

retain VERB To retain something means to keep it. **retention** NOUN

retaliate VERB If you retaliate, you do something to harm or upset someone because they have already acted in a similar way against you. **retaliation** NOUN

retaliate VERB
= get back (*informal*), get even (*informal*), get your own back (*informal*), hit back (*informal*), pay back, take revenge

rethink, **rethinks**, **rethinking**, **rethought** VERB If you rethink something, you think about how it should be changed • *We have to rethink our strategy*.

reticent ADJECTIVE Someone who is reticent is unwilling to tell people about things. **reticence** NOUN

retina NOUN SCIENCE the light-sensitive part at the back of your eyeball, which receives an image and sends it to your brain.

retinue NOUN a group of helpers or friends travelling with an important person.

retire VERB ① When older people retire, they give up work. ② (*formal*) If you retire, you leave to go into another room, or to bed • *She retired early with a good book*. **retired** ADJECTIVE **retirement** NOUN

retort VERB ① To retort means to reply angrily. ▸ NOUN ② a short, angry reply.

retract VERB ① If you retract something you have said, you say that you did not mean it. ② When something is retracted, it moves inwards or backwards • *The undercarriage was retracted shortly after takeoff*. **retraction** NOUN **retractable** ADJECTIVE

retreat VERB ① To retreat means to move backwards away from something or someone. ② If you retreat from something difficult or unpleasant, you avoid doing it. ▸ NOUN ③ If an army moves away from the enemy, this is referred to as a retreat. ④ a quiet place that you can go to rest or do things in private.

retreat VERB
① = back away, back off, draw back, pull back, withdraw
≠ advance
▸ NOUN ③ = departure, evacuation, flight, withdrawal
≠ advance
④ = haven, refuge, sanctuary

retribution NOUN (*formal*) Retribution is punishment • *the threat of retribution*.

retrieve VERB If you retrieve something, you get it back. **retrieval** NOUN

retriever NOUN a large dog often used by hunters to bring back birds and animals which have been shot.

retrospect PHRASE When you consider something **in retrospect**, you think about it afterwards and often have a different opinion from the one you had at the time • *In retrospect, I probably shouldn't have resigned*.

retrospective ADJECTIVE ① concerning things that happened in the past. ② taking effect from a date in the past. **retrospectively** ADVERB

return VERB ① When you return to a place, you go back after you have been away. ② If you return something to someone, you give it back to them. ③ When you return a ball during a game, you hit it back to your opponent. ④ When a judge or jury returns a verdict, they announce it. ▸ NOUN ⑤ Your return is your arrival back at a place. ⑥ The return on an investment is the profit or interest you get from it. ⑦ a ticket for the journey to a place and back again. ▸ PHRASE ⑧ If you do something **in return** for a favour, you do it to repay the favour.

return VERB
① = come back, go back, reappear, turn back
② = give back, pay back, refund, repay

reunion NOUN a party or meeting for people who have not seen each other for a long time.

reunite VERB If people are reunited, they meet again after they have been separated for some time.

rev, **revs**, **revving**, **revved** (*informal*) VERB ① When you rev the engine of a vehicle, you press the accelerator to increase the engine speed. ▸ NOUN ② The speed of an engine is measured in revolutions per minute, referred to as revs • *I noticed that the engine revs had dropped*.

revamp VERB To revamp something means to improve or repair it.

reveal VERB ① To reveal something means to tell people about it • *They were not ready to reveal any of the details*. ② If you reveal something that has been hidden, you uncover it. ▸ NOUN ③ an occasion when something that has been kept secret is shown or explained • *The series is building up to the big reveal*.

reveal VERB
① = announce, disclose, divulge, get off your chest (*informal*), let on
② = bring to light, lay bare, uncover, unearth, unveil

revel, **revels**, **revelling**, **revelled** VERB If you revel in a situation, you enjoy it very much. **revelry** NOUN

revelation NOUN ① a surprising or interesting fact made known to people. ② If an experience is a revelation, it makes you realise or learn something.

revenge NOUN ① Revenge involves hurting someone who has hurt you. ▸ VERB ② If you revenge yourself on someone who has hurt you, you hurt them in return.

revenge NOUN
① = reprisal, retaliation, retribution, vengeance
▸ VERB ② = avenge, get even (*informal*), get your own back (*informal*), hit back (*informal*), pay back, retaliate

revenue NOUN Revenue is money that a government, company or organisation receives • *government tax revenues*.

revered ADJECTIVE If someone is revered, he or she is respected and admired • *He is still revered as the father of the nation*.

reverence NOUN Reverence is a feeling of great respect.

Reverend ADJECTIVE Reverend is a title used before the name of a member of the clergy • *the Reverend George Young*.

reversal NOUN If there is a reversal of a process or policy, it is changed to the opposite process or policy.

reverse VERB ① When someone reverses a process, they change it to the opposite process • *They won't reverse the decision to increase prices*. ② If you reverse the order of things, you arrange them in the opposite order. ③ When you reverse a car, you drive it backwards. ▸ NOUN ④ The reverse is the opposite of what has just been said or done. ▸ ADJECTIVE ⑤ Reverse means opposite to what is usual or to what has just been described.

reverse VERB
① = change, invalidate, overrule, overturn, retract
▸ NOUN ④ = contrary, converse, opposite

reversible ADJECTIVE Reversible clothing can be worn with either side on the outside.

revert VERB (*formal*) To revert to a former state or type of behaviour means to go back to it.

review NOUN ① an article or an item on television or radio, giving an opinion of a new book, play or film. ② When there is a review of a situation or system, it is examined to decide whether changes are needed. ▶ VERB ③ To review a book, play or film means to write an account expressing an opinion of it. ④ To review something means to examine it to decide whether changes are needed. **reviewer** NOUN

> **review** NOUN
> ① = commentary, criticism, notice
> ② = analysis, examination, report, study, survey

revise VERB ① If you revise something, you alter or correct it. ② When you revise for an examination, you go over your work to learn things thoroughly. **revision** NOUN

> **revise** VERB
> ① = amend, correct, edit, refresh, revamp, update

revive VERB ① When a feeling or practice is revived, it becomes active or popular again. ② If someone who has fainted revives, they become conscious again. **revival** NOUN

> **revive** VERB
> ① = rally, resuscitate

revolt NOUN ① HISTORY a violent attempt by a group of people to change their country's political system. ▶ VERB ② HISTORY When people revolt, they fight against the authority that governs them. ③ If something revolts you, it is so horrible that you feel disgust.

revolting ADJECTIVE horrible and disgusting • *The smell in the cell was revolting.*

revolution NOUN ① HISTORY a violent attempt by a large group of people to change the political system of their country. ② an important change in an area of human activity • *the Industrial Revolution.* ③ one complete turn in a circle.

revolutionary, revolutionaries ADJECTIVE ① involving great changes • *a revolutionary new cooling system.* ▶ NOUN ② a person who takes part in a revolution.

revolve VERB ① If something revolves round something else, it centres on that as the most important thing • *My job revolves around the telephone.* ② When something revolves, it turns in a circle around a central point • *The moon revolves round the earth.*

revolver NOUN a small gun held in the hand.

revulsion NOUN Revulsion is a strong feeling of disgust or disapproval.

reward PSHE NOUN ① something you are given because you have done something good. ▶ VERB ② If you reward someone, you give them a reward.

> **reward** NOUN
> ① = bonus, bounty, payment, prize

rewarding ADJECTIVE Something that is rewarding gives you a lot of satisfaction.

rewind, rewinds, rewinding, rewound VERB If you rewind a tape on a tape recorder or video, you make the tape go backwards.

rhetoric NOUN *[Said **ret**-or-ik]* Rhetoric is speech or writing that is intended to impress people.

rhetorical ADJECTIVE ① A rhetorical question is one which is asked in order to make a statement rather than to get an answer. ② Rhetorical language is intended to be grand and impressive.

rhino NOUN *(informal)* a rhinoceros.

A B C D E F G H I J K L M N O P Q R S T U V W X Y Z

rhinoceros NOUN a large African or Asian animal with one or two horns on its nose.

rhododendron NOUN an evergreen bush with large coloured flowers.

rhubarb NOUN Rhubarb is a plant with long red stems which can be cooked with sugar and eaten.

rhyme ENGLISH VERB ① If two words rhyme, they have a similar sound • *Sally rhymes with valley.* ▶ NOUN ② a word that rhymes with another. ③ a short poem with rhyming lines.

rhythm NOUN ① MUSIC Rhythm is a regular movement or beat. ② a regular pattern of changes, for example, in the seasons. **rhythmic** ADJECTIVE **rhythmically** ADVERB

> **rhythm** NOUN
> ① = beat, pulse, tempo, time

rib NOUN Your ribs are the curved bones that go from your backbone to your chest.

ribbon NOUN a long, narrow piece of cloth used for decoration.

rice NOUN Rice is a tall grass that produces edible grains. Rice is grown in warm countries on wet ground.

rich ADJECTIVE ① Someone who is rich has a lot of money and possessions. ② Something that is rich in something contains a large amount of it • *Liver is particularly rich in vitamin A.* ③ Rich food contains a large amount of fat, oil or sugar. ④ Rich colours, smells and sounds are strong and pleasant. **richness** NOUN

> **rich** ADJECTIVE
> ① = affluent, loaded (*slang*), opulent, prosperous, wealthy, well off
> ≠ poor
> ② = abundant, fertile, plentiful

richly ADVERB ① If someone is richly rewarded, they are rewarded well with something valuable. ② If you feel strongly that someone deserves something, you can say it is richly deserved.

rickety ADJECTIVE likely to collapse or break • *a rickety wooden jetty.*

rickshaw NOUN a hand-pulled cart used in Asia for carrying passengers.

ricochet, **ricochets**, **ricocheting** or **ricochetting**, **ricocheted** or **ricochetted** *[Said* ***rik****-osh-ay]* VERB When a bullet ricochets, it hits a surface and bounces away from it.

rid, **rids**, **ridding**, **rid** PHRASE ① When you **get rid of** something you do not want, you remove or destroy it. ▶ VERB ② (*formal*) To rid a place of something unpleasant means to succeed in removing it.

> **rid** PHRASE
> ① = dispose of, dump, eject, jettison, remove, weed out

ridden the past participle of **ride**.

riddle NOUN ① a puzzle which seems to be nonsense, but which has an entertaining solution. ② Something that is a riddle puzzles and confuses you.

ride, **rides**, **riding**, **rode**, **ridden** VERB ① When you ride a horse or a bike, you sit on it and control it as it moves along. ② When you ride in a car, you travel in it. ▶ NOUN ③ a journey on a horse or bike or in a vehicle.

rider NOUN ① a person riding on a horse or bicycle. ② an additional statement which changes or puts a condition on what has already been said.

ridge NOUN ① a long, narrow piece of high land. ② a raised line on a flat surface.

ridicule VERB ① To ridicule someone means to make fun of them in an unkind way. ▶ NOUN ② Ridicule is unkind laughter and mockery.

ridiculous ADJECTIVE very foolish. **ridiculously** ADVERB

ridiculous ADJECTIVE
= absurd, laughable, ludicrous, preposterous

rife ADJECTIVE (*formal*) very common • *Unemployment was rife.*

rifle NOUN ① a gun with a long barrel. ▸ VERB ② When someone rifles something, they make a quick search through it to steal things.

rift NOUN ① a serious quarrel between friends that damages their friendship. ② a split in something solid, especially in the ground.

rig, **rigs**, **rigging**, **rigged** VERB ① If someone rigs an election or contest, they dishonestly arrange for a particular person to succeed. ▸ NOUN ② a large structure used for extracting oil or gas from the ground or sea bed. **rig up** VERB If you rig up a device or structure, you make it quickly and fix it in place • *They had even rigged up a makeshift aerial.*

right ADJECTIVE, ADVERB ① correct and in accordance with the facts • *That clock never tells the right time* • *That's absolutely right.* ② 'Right' means on or towards the right side of something. ▸ ADJECTIVE ③ The right choice or decision is the best or most suitable one. ④ The right people or places are those that have influence or are socially admired • *He was always to be seen in the right places.* ⑤ The right side of something is the side intended to be seen and to face outwards. ▸ NOUN ⑥ 'Right' is used to refer to principles of morally correct behaviour • *At least he knew right from wrong.* ⑦ PSHE CITIZENSHIP If you have a right to do something, you are morally or legally entitled to do it. ⑧ The right is one of the two sides of something. For example, when you look at the word 'to', the 'o' is to the right of the 't'. ⑨ The Right refers to people who support the political ideas of capitalism and conservatism rather than socialism. ▸ ADVERB ⑩ 'Right' is used to emphasise a precise place • *I'm right here.* ⑪ 'Right' means immediately • *I had to decide right then.* ▸ VERB ⑫ If you right something, you correct it or put it back in an upright position. **rightly** ADVERB

right ADJECTIVE, ADVERB
① = accurate, correct, exact, factual, genuine, precise, strict, true, valid ≠ wrong
▸ ADJECTIVE ③ = acceptable, appropriate, desirable, done, fit, fitting, okay, OK, proper, seemly (*old-fashioned*), suitable
▸ NOUN ⑥ = equity, fairness, honour, integrity, justice, legality, morality, virtue

right angle NOUN MATHS an angle of 90°.

righteous ADJECTIVE Righteous people behave in a way that is morally good and religious.

rightful ADJECTIVE Someone's rightful possession is one which they have a moral or legal right to. **rightfully** ADVERB

right-handed ADJECTIVE, ADVERB Someone who is right-handed does things such as writing and painting with their right hand.

right-wing ADJECTIVE believing more strongly in capitalism or conservatism, or less strongly in socialism, than other members of the same party or group. **right-winger** NOUN

right-wing ADJECTIVE
= conservative, Tory (*British*)

rigid ADJECTIVE ① Rigid laws or systems cannot be changed and are considered severe. ② A rigid object is stiff and does not bend easily. **rigidly** ADVERB **rigidity** NOUN

> **rigid** ADJECTIVE
> ① = fixed, inflexible, set, strict, stringent
> ② = firm, hard, solid, stiff
> ≠ flexible

rigorous ADJECTIVE very careful and thorough. **rigorously** ADVERB

rigour NOUN (*formal*) The rigours of a situation are the things which make it hard or unpleasant • *the rigours of his world tour.*

rim NOUN the outside or top edge of an object such as a wheel or a cup. **rimmed** ADJECTIVE

rind NOUN Rind is the thick outer skin of fruit, cheese or bacon.

ring, **rings**, **ringing**, **ringed**, **rang**, **rung** VERB ① If you ring someone, you phone them. ② When a bell rings, it makes a clear, loud sound. ③ To ring something means to draw a circle around it. ④ If something is ringed with something else, it has that thing all the way around it • *The courthouse was ringed with police.* ▸ NOUN ⑤ the sound made by a bell. ⑥ a small circle of metal worn on your finger. ⑦ an object or group of things in the shape of a circle. ⑧ At a boxing match or circus, the ring is the place where the fight or performance takes place. ⑨ an organised group of people who are involved in an illegal activity • *an international spy ring.*

> **ring** VERB
> ② = chime, clang, peal, resonate, toll
> ▸ NOUN ⑦ = band, circle, hoop, loop, round
> ⑨ = band, cell, clique, syndicate

ringer NOUN ① a person or thing that is almost identical to another. ② In Australian English, a ringer is someone who works on a sheep farm. ③ In Australian and New Zealand English, a ringer is also the fastest shearer in a woolshed.

ringleader NOUN the leader of a group of people who get involved in mischief or crime.

rink NOUN a large indoor area for ice-skating or roller-skating.

rinse VERB ① When you rinse something, you wash it in clean water. ▸ NOUN ② a liquid you can put on your hair to give it a different colour.

riot NOUN ① When there is a riot, a crowd of people behave noisily and violently. ▸ VERB ② To riot means to behave noisily and violently. ▸ PHRASE ③ To **run riot** means to behave in a wild and uncontrolled way.

> **riot** NOUN
> ① = anarchy, disorder, disturbance, mob violence, strife
> ▸ VERB ② = go on the rampage, rampage, run riot, take to the streets

rip, **rips**, **ripping**, **ripped** VERB ① When you rip something, you tear it violently. ② If you rip something away, you remove it quickly and violently. ▸ NOUN ③ a long split in cloth or paper. **rip off** VERB (*informal*) If someone rips you off, they cheat you by charging you too much money.

RIP an abbreviation often written on gravestones, meaning 'rest in peace'.

ripe ADJECTIVE ① When fruit or grain is ripe, it is fully developed and ready to be eaten. ② If a situation is ripe for something to happen, it is ready for it. **ripeness** NOUN

ripen VERB When crops ripen, they become ripe.

ripper NOUN (*informal*) In Australian and New Zealand English, a ripper is an excellent person or thing.

ripple NOUN ① Ripples are little waves on the surface of calm water.

② If there is a ripple of laughter or applause, people laugh or applaud gently for a short time. ▶ **VERB** ③ When the surface of water ripples, little waves appear on it.

rise, **rises**, **rising**, **rose**, **risen** **VERB** ① If something rises, it moves upwards. ② (*formal*) When you rise, you stand up. ③ To rise also means to get out of bed. ④ When the sun rises, it first appears. ⑤ The place where a river rises is where it begins. ⑥ If land rises, it slopes upwards. ⑦ If a sound or wind rises, it becomes higher or stronger. ⑧ If an amount rises, it increases. ⑨ If you rise to a challenge or a remark, you respond to it rather than ignoring it • *He rose to the challenge with enthusiasm.* ⑩ When people rise up, they start fighting against people in authority. ▶ **NOUN** ⑪ an increase. ⑫ Someone's rise is the process by which they become more powerful or successful • *his rise to fame.*

rise **VERB**
① = ascend, climb, go up, move up
⑧ = go up, grow, increase, intensify, mount
≠ fall
▶ **NOUN** ⑪ = improvement, increase, upsurge
≠ fall

riser **NOUN** An early riser is someone who likes to get up early in the morning.

risk **NOUN** ① PSHE a chance that something unpleasant or dangerous might happen. ▶ **VERB** ② If you risk something unpleasant, you do something knowing that the unpleasant thing might happen as a result • *If he doesn't play, he risks losing his place in the team.* ③ If you risk someone's life, you put them in a dangerous situation in which they might be killed. **risky** **ADJECTIVE**

risk **NOUN**
① = danger, gamble, peril, pitfall
▶ **VERB** ② = chance, dare, gamble, jeopardise, put in jeopardy

rite **NOUN** a religious ceremony.

ritual **NOUN** ① a series of actions carried out according to the custom of a particular society or group • *This is the most ancient of the Buddhist rituals.* ▶ **ADJECTIVE** ② Ritual activities happen as part of a tradition or ritual • *fasting and ritual dancing.* **ritualistic** **ADJECTIVE**

rival, **rivals**, **rivalling**, **rivalled** **NOUN** ① Your rival is the person you are competing with. ▶ **VERB** ② If something rivals something else, it is of the same high standard or quality • *As a holiday destination, South Africa rivals Kenya for weather.*

rival **NOUN**
① = adversary, antagonist, challenger, opponent
▶ **VERB** ② = be a match for, equal, match

rivalry, **rivalries** **NOUN** Rivalry is active competition between people.

river **NOUN** a natural feature consisting of water flowing for a long distance between two banks.

rivet **NOUN** a short, round pin with a flat head which is used to fasten sheets of metal together.

riveting **ADJECTIVE** If you find something riveting, you find it fascinating and it holds your attention • *I find tennis riveting.*

road **NOUN** a long piece of hard ground specially surfaced so that people and vehicles can travel along it easily.

road **NOUN**
= motorway, route, street, track

road rage **NOUN** Road rage is aggressive behaviour by a driver as a reaction to the behaviour of another driver.

road train NOUN in Australia, a road train is a line of linked trailers pulled by a truck, used for transporting cattle or sheep.

roadworks PLURAL NOUN Roadworks are repairs being done on a road.

roam VERB If you roam around, you wander around without any particular purpose • *Hens were roaming around the yard.*

roar VERB ① If something roars, it makes a very loud noise. ② To roar with laughter or anger means to laugh or shout very noisily. ③ When a lion roars, it makes a loud, angry sound. ▶ NOUN ④ a very loud noise.

roast VERB ① When you roast meat or other food, you cook it using dry heat in an oven or over a fire. ▶ ADJECTIVE ② Roast meat has been roasted. ▶ NOUN ③ a piece of meat that has been roasted.

rob, **robs**, **robbing**, **robbed** VERB ① If someone robs you, they steal your possessions. ② If you rob someone of something they need or deserve, you deprive them of it • *He robbed me of my childhood.*

rob VERB
① = burgle, con (*informal*), defraud, loot, steal from, swindle

robber NOUN Robbers are people who steal money or property using force or threats • *bank robbers.*

robbery, **robberies** NOUN Robbery is the act of stealing money or property using force or threats.

robe NOUN a long, loose piece of clothing which covers the body • *He knelt in his white robes before the altar.*

robin NOUN a small bird with a red breast.

robot NOUN ① a machine which is programmed to move and perform tasks automatically. ② in South African English, a robot is a set of traffic lights.

robust ADJECTIVE very strong and healthy. **robustly** ADVERB

rock NOUN ① Rock is the hard mineral substance that forms the surface of the earth. ② a large piece of rock • *She picked up a rock and threw it into the lake.* ③ Rock or rock music is music with simple tunes and a very strong beat. ④ Rock is also a sweet shaped into long, hard sticks, sold in holiday resorts. ▶ VERB ⑤ When something rocks or when you rock it, it moves regularly backwards and forwards or from side to side • *She rocked the baby.* ⑥ If something rocks people, it shocks and upsets them • *Palermo was rocked by a crime wave.* ▶ PHRASE ⑦ If someone's marriage or relationship is **on the rocks**, it is unsuccessful and about to end.

rock and roll NOUN Rock and roll is a style of music with a strong beat that was especially popular in the 1950s.

rocket NOUN ① a space vehicle, usually shaped like a long pointed tube. ② an explosive missile • *They fired rockets into a number of government buildings.* ③ a firework that explodes when it is high in the air. ▶ VERB ④ If prices rocket, they increase very quickly.

rocking chair NOUN a chair on two curved pieces of wood that rocks backwards and forwards when you sit in it.

rocky, **rockier**, **rockiest** ADJECTIVE covered with rocks.

rod NOUN a long, thin pole or bar, usually made of wood or metal • *a fishing rod.*

rode the past tense of **ride**.

rodent NOUN a small mammal with sharp front teeth which it uses for gnawing.

rodeo, **rodeos** NOUN a public entertainment in which cowboys show different skills.

roe NOUN Roe is the eggs of a fish.

rogue NOUN ① You can refer to a man who behaves dishonestly as a rogue. ▸ ADJECTIVE ② a vicious animal that lives apart from its herd or pack.

role; also spelt **rôle** NOUN ① Someone's role is their position and function in a situation or society. ② DRAMA An actor's role is the character that he or she plays • *her first leading role*.

roll VERB ① When something rolls or when you roll it, it moves along a surface, turning over and over. ② When vehicles roll along, they move • *Tanks rolled into the village*. ③ If you roll your eyes, you make them turn up or go from side to side. ④ If you roll something flexible into a cylinder or ball, you wrap it several times around itself • *He rolled up the bag with the money in it*. ▸ NOUN ⑤ A roll of paper or cloth is a long piece of it that has been rolled into a tube • *a roll of wrapping paper*. ⑥ a small, rounded, individually baked piece of bread. ⑦ an official list of people's names • *the electoral roll*. ⑧ A roll on a drum is a long, rumbling sound made on it.
roll up VERB ① If you roll up something flexible, you wrap it several times around itself. ② If you roll up your sleeves or trousers, you fold them over from the bottom to make them shorter. ③ (*informal*) If you roll up, you arrive.

roller NOUN ① a cylinder that turns round in a machine or piece of equipment. ② Rollers are tubes which you can wind your hair around to make it curly.

roller-coaster NOUN a pleasure ride at a fair, consisting of a small railway that goes up and down very steep slopes.

rolling pin NOUN a cylinder used for rolling pastry dough to make it flat.

ROM NOUN ICT ROM is a storage device that holds data permanently and cannot be altered by the programmer. ROM stands for 'read only memory'.

Roman Catholic RE ADJECTIVE ① relating or belonging to the branch of the Christian Church that accepts the Pope in Rome as its leader. ▸ NOUN ② someone who belongs to the Roman Catholic Church.
Roman Catholicism NOUN

romance NOUN ① a relationship between two people who are in love with each other. ② Romance is the pleasure and excitement of doing something new and unusual • *the romance of foreign travel*. ③ LIBRARY a novel about a love affair.

Romanian [*Said roe-**may**-nee-an*]; also spelt **Rumanian** ADJECTIVE ① belonging or relating to Romania. ▸ NOUN ② someone who comes from Romania. ③ Romanian is the main language spoken in Romania.

romantic ADJECTIVE ① A romantic person has ideas that are not realistic, for example about love or about ways of changing society • *a romantic idealist*. ② connected with love • *a romantic relationship*. ③ Something that is romantic is beautiful in a way that strongly affects your feelings • *It is one of the most romantic ruins in Scotland*. ④ Romantic describes a style of music, literature and art popular in Europe in the late 18th and early 19th centuries, which emphasised feeling and imagination rather than order and form. **romantically** ADVERB **romanticism** NOUN

romantic ADJECTIVE
② = amorous, loving, tender

roo, **roos** NOUN (*informal*) In Australian English, a roo is a kangaroo.

roof NOUN ① The roof of a building or car is the covering on top of it. ② The roof of your mouth or of a cave is the highest part.

roofing NOUN Roofing is material used for covering roofs.

rooftop NOUN the outside part of the roof of a building.

room NOUN ① a separate section in a building, divided from other rooms by walls. ② If there is room somewhere, there is enough space for things to be fitted in or for people to do what they want to do • *There wasn't enough room for his gear.*

> **room** NOUN
> ① = chamber, office
> ② = capacity, elbow room, space

roost NOUN ① a place where birds rest or build their nests. ▸ VERB ② When birds roost, they settle somewhere for the night.

root NOUN ① The roots of a plant are the parts that grow under the ground. ② The root of a hair is the part beneath the skin. ③ You can refer to the place or culture that you grew up in as your roots. ④ The root of something is its original cause or basis • *We got to the root of the problem.* ▸ VERB ⑤ To root through things means to search through them, pushing them aside • *She rooted through his bag.* **root out** VERB If you root something or someone out, you find them and force them out • *a major drive to root out corruption.*

rooted ADJECTIVE developed from or strongly influenced by something • *songs rooted in traditional African music.*

rope NOUN ① a thick, strong length of twisted cord. ▸ VERB ② If you rope one thing to another, you tie them together with rope.

rosary, **rosaries** NOUN a string of beads that Roman Catholics use for counting prayers.

rose ① Rose is the past tense of **rise**. ▸ NOUN ② a large garden flower which has a pleasant smell and grows on a bush with thorns. ▸ NOUN, ADJECTIVE ③ reddish-pink.

rosemary NOUN Rosemary is a herb with fragrant spiky leaves, used for flavouring in cooking.

rosette NOUN a large badge of coloured ribbons gathered into a circle, which is worn as a prize in a competition or to support a political party.

roster NOUN a list of people who take it in turn to do a particular job • *He put himself first on the new roster for domestic chores.*

rostrum, **rostrums** or **rostra** NOUN a raised platform on which someone stands to speak to an audience or conduct an orchestra.

rosy, **rosier**, **rosiest** ADJECTIVE ① reddish-pink. ② If a situation seems rosy, it is likely to be good or successful. ③ If a person looks rosy, they have pink cheeks and look healthy.

rot, **rots**, **rotting**, **rotted** VERB ① When food or wood rots, it decays and can no longer be used. ② When something rots another substance, it causes it to decay • *Sugary drinks rot your teeth.* ▸ NOUN ③ Rot is the condition that affects things when they rot • *The timber frame was not protected against rot.*

> **rot** VERB
> ① = decay, decompose, fester, spoil
> ▸ NOUN ③ = decay, deterioration, mould

rota NOUN a list of people who take turns to do a particular job.

rotate VERB [MATHS] When something rotates, it turns with a circular movement • *He rotated the camera 180°.* **rotation** NOUN

rotor NOUN ① The rotor is the part of a machine that turns. ② The rotors or rotor blades of a helicopter are the four long, flat pieces of metal on top of it which rotate and lift it off the ground.

rotten ADJECTIVE ① decayed and no longer of use • *The front bay window is rotten.* ② (*informal*) of very poor quality • *I think it's a rotten idea.* ③ (*informal*) very unfair, unkind or unpleasant • *That's a rotten thing to say!*

> **rotten** ADJECTIVE
> ① = bad, decayed, decomposed, mouldy, sour
> ② = inferior, lousy (*slang*), poor, unsatisfactory

rouble [*Said* ***roo**-bl*] NOUN the main unit of currency in Russia.

rough [*Said* ***ruff***] ADJECTIVE ① uneven and not smooth. ② not using enough care or gentleness • *Don't be so rough or you'll break it.* ③ difficult or unpleasant • *Teenagers have been given a rough time.* ④ approximately correct • *At a rough guess it is five times more profitable.* ⑤ If the sea is rough, there are large waves because of bad weather. ⑥ A rough town or area has a lot of crime or violence. ▶ NOUN, ADJECTIVE ⑦ A rough or a rough sketch is a drawing or description that shows the main features but does not show the details. ▶ NOUN ⑧ On a golf course, the rough is the part of the course next to a fairway where the grass has not been cut. **roughly** ADVERB **roughness** NOUN

> **rough** ADJECTIVE
> ① = bumpy, craggy, rocky, rugged, uneven
> ≠ smooth
> ③ = difficult, hard, tough, unpleasant
> ④ = approximate, estimated, sketchy, vague

roulette [*Said roo-**let***] NOUN Roulette is a gambling game in which a ball is dropped onto a revolving wheel with numbered holes in it.

round ADJECTIVE ① Something round is shaped like a ball or a circle. ② complete or whole • *round numbers.* ▶ PREPOSITION, ADVERB ③ If something is round something else, it surrounds it. ④ The distance round something is the length of its circumference or boundary • *I'm about two inches larger round the waist.* ⑤ You can refer to an area near a place as the area round it • *There's nothing to do round here.* ▶ PREPOSITION ⑥ If something moves round you, it keeps moving in a circle with you in the centre. ⑦ When someone goes to the other side of something, they have gone round it. ▶ ADVERB, PREPOSITION ⑧ If you go round a place, you go to different parts of it to look at it • *We went round the museum.* ▶ ADVERB ⑨ If you turn or look round, you turn so you are facing in a different direction. ⑩ When someone comes round, they visit you • *He came round with a bunch of flowers.* ▶ NOUN ⑪ one of a series of events • *After round three, two Americans shared the lead.* ⑫ If you buy a round of drinks, you buy a drink for each member of the group you are with. **round up** VERB If you round up people or animals, you gather them together.

> **round** ADJECTIVE
> ① = circular, cylindrical, rounded, spherical
> ▶ NOUN ⑪ = lap, period, session, stage

roundabout NOUN ① a meeting point of several roads with a circle in the centre which vehicles have to travel around. ② a circular platform which rotates and which children can ride on in a playground. ③ the same as a merry-go-round.

rounded ADJECTIVE curved in shape, without any points or sharp edges.

rounders NOUN a game played by two teams, in which a player scores points by hitting a ball and running around four sides of a square pitch.

round-the-clock ADJECTIVE happening continuously.

rouse VERB ① If someone rouses you, they wake you up. ② If you rouse yourself to do something, you make yourself get up and do it. ③ If something rouses you, it makes you feel very emotional and excited.

rout *[Rhymes with **out**]* VERB To rout your opponents means to defeat them completely and easily.

route *[Said **root**]* NOUN a way from one place to another.

> **route** NOUN
> = channel, course, itinerary, path, road, way

routine ADJECTIVE ① Routine activities are done regularly. ▶ NOUN ② the usual way or order in which you do things. ③ a boring repetition of tasks. **routinely** ADVERB

> **routine** ADJECTIVE
> ① = everyday, normal, ordinary, regular, standard, typical, usual
> ▶ NOUN ② = order, pattern, practice, procedure, programme, schedule, system

roving ADJECTIVE ① wandering or roaming • *roving gangs of youths*. ② not restricted to any particular location or area • *a roving reporter*.

row[1] *[Rhymes with **snow**]* NOUN ① A row of people or things is several of them arranged in a line. ▶ VERB ② When you row a boat, you use oars to make it move through the water.

> **row** NOUN
> ① = bank, column, line, queue, rank

row[2] *[Rhymes with **now**]* NOUN ① a serious argument. ② If someone is making a row, they are making too much noise. ▶ VERB ③ If people are rowing, they are quarrelling noisily.

> **row** NOUN
> ① = altercation, argument, quarrel, squabble

rowdy, **rowdier**, **rowdiest** ADJECTIVE rough and noisy.

> **rowdy** ADJECTIVE
> = boisterous, noisy, unruly, wild

royal ADJECTIVE ① belonging to or involving a queen, a king or a member of their family. ② 'Royal' is used in the names of organisations appointed or supported by a member of a royal family. ▶ NOUN ③ (*informal*) Members of the royal family are sometimes referred to as the royals.

> **royal** ADJECTIVE
> ① = imperial, regal, sovereign

royalist NOUN someone who supports their country's royal family.

royalty, **royalties** NOUN ① The members of a royal family are sometimes referred to as royalty. ② Royalties are payments made to authors and musicians from the sales of their books or records.

rub, **rubs**, **rubbing**, **rubbed** VERB If you rub something, you move your hand or a cloth backwards and forwards over it. **rub out** VERB To rub out something written means to remove it by rubbing it with a rubber or a cloth.

rubber NOUN ① Rubber is a strong elastic substance used for making tyres, boots and other products. ② a small piece of rubber used to rub out pencil mistakes.

rubbish NOUN ① Rubbish is unwanted things or waste material. ② (*informal*) You can refer to nonsense or something of very poor quality as rubbish.

rubbish NOUN
① = garbage (*informal*), litter, refuse (*formal*), trash, waste
② = drivel, garbage, gibberish, nonsense

rubble NOUN Bits of old brick and stone are referred to as rubble.

ruby, **rubies** NOUN a type of red jewel.

rucksack NOUN a bag with shoulder straps for carrying things on your back.

rudder NOUN a piece of wood or metal at the back of a boat or plane which is moved to make the boat or plane turn.

rude ADJECTIVE ① not polite. ② embarrassing or offensive • *rude jokes*. ③ unexpected and unpleasant • *a rude awakening*. **rudely** ADVERB **rudeness** NOUN

rude ADJECTIVE
① = disrespectful, impertinent, impudent, insolent
≠ polite
③ = abrupt, unpleasant, violent

rudimentary ADJECTIVE (*formal*) very basic or not developed • *He had only a rudimentary knowledge of French*.

ruff NOUN ① a stiff circular collar with many pleats in it, worn especially in the 16th century. ② a thick band of fur or feathers around the neck of a bird or animal.

ruffle VERB ① If you ruffle someone's hair, you move your hand quickly backwards and forwards over their head. ② If something ruffles you, it makes you annoyed or upset. ▶ NOUN ③ Ruffles are small folds made in a piece of material for decoration.

rug NOUN ① a small, thick carpet. ② a blanket which you can use to cover your knees or for sitting on outdoors.

rugby NOUN Rugby is a game played by two teams, who try to kick and throw an oval ball to their opponents' end of the pitch. Rugby League is played with 13 players in each side; Rugby Union is played with 15 players in each side.

rugged ADJECTIVE ① rocky and wild • *the rugged west coast of Ireland*. ② having strong features • *his rugged good looks*.

ruin VERB ① If you ruin something, you destroy or spoil it completely. ② If someone is ruined, they have lost all their money. ▶ NOUN ③ Ruin is the state of being destroyed or completely spoilt. ④ A ruin or the ruins of something refers to the parts that are left after it has been severely damaged • *the ruins of a thirteenth-century monastery*.

ruin VERB
① = break, damage, destroy, devastate, impair, mar, mess up, spoil, undo, wreck
▶ NOUN ③ = decay, destruction, devastation, disrepair, downfall, fall
④ = remains, shell, wreck

rule NOUN ① Rules are statements which tell you what you are allowed to do. ▶ VERB ② To rule a country or group of people means to have power over it and be in charge of its affairs. ③ (*formal*) When someone in authority rules on a particular matter, they give an official decision about it. ▶ PHRASE ④ **As a rule** means usually or generally • *As a rule, I eat my meals in front of the TV*. **rule out** VERB ① If you rule out an idea or course of action, you reject it. ② If one thing rules out another, it prevents it from happening or being possible • *The accident ruled out a future for him in football*.

rule NOUN
① = decree, guideline, law, order, regulation
▶ VERB ② = administer, be in power, govern, lead, reign

▶ PHRASE ④ = generally, mainly, normally, on the whole, usually

ruler NOUN ① a person who rules a country. ② a long, flat piece of wood or plastic with straight edges marked in centimetres or inches, used for measuring or drawing straight lines.

ruler NOUN
① = commander, governor, head of state, leader, monarch, sovereign

rum NOUN Rum is a strong alcoholic drink made from sugar cane juice.

rumble VERB ① If something rumbles, it makes a continuous low noise • *Another train rumbled past the house.* ▶ NOUN ② a continuous low noise • *the distant rumble of traffic.*

rummage VERB If you rummage somewhere, you search for something, moving things about carelessly.

rumour NOUN ① a story that people are talking about, which may or may not be true. ▶ VERB ② If something is rumoured, people are suggesting that it has happened.

rumour NOUN
① = gossip, hearsay, whisper, word

rump NOUN ① An animal's rump is its rear end. ② Rump or rump steak is meat cut from the rear end of a cow.

run, runs, running, ran, run VERB ① When you run, you move quickly, leaving the ground during each stride. ② If you say that a road or river runs in a particular direction, you are describing its course. ③ If you run your hand or an object over something, you move it over it. ④ If someone runs in an election, they stand as a candidate • *He announced he would run for President.* ⑤ If you run a business or an activity, you are in charge of it. ⑥ If you run an experiment, a computer program, or a tape, you start it and let it continue • *He ran a series of computer checks.* ⑦ To run a car means to have it and use it. ⑧ If you run someone somewhere in a car, you drive them there • *Could you run me up to town?* ⑨ If you run water, you turn on a tap to make it flow • *We heard him running the kitchen tap.* ⑩ If your nose is running, it is producing a lot of mucus. ⑪ If the dye in something runs, the colour comes out when it is washed. ⑫ If a feeling runs through your body, it affects you quickly and strongly. ⑬ If an amount is running at a particular level, it is at that level • *Inflation is currently running at 2.6 per cent.* ⑭ If someone or something is running late, they have taken more time than was planned. ⑮ If an event or contract runs for a particular time, it lasts for that time. ▶ NOUN ⑯ If you go for a run, you run for pleasure or exercise. ⑰ a journey somewhere • *It was quite a run to the village.* ⑱ If a play or show has a run of a particular length of time, it is on for that time. ⑲ A run of success or failure is a series of successes or failures. ⑳ In cricket or baseball, a player scores one run by running between marked places on the pitch after hitting the ball. **run away** VERB If you run away from a place, you leave it suddenly and secretly.
run down VERB ① To run someone down means to criticise them strongly. ② To run down an organisation means to reduce its size and activity. **run out** VERB If you run out of something, you have no more left. **run over** VERB If someone is run over, they are hit by a moving vehicle.

run VERB
① = bolt, gallop, jog, sprint
⑤ = administer, be in charge of, control, direct, look after, manage

runaway NOUN a person who has escaped from a place or left it secretly and hurriedly.

rundown ADJECTIVE ① tired and not well. ② neglected and in poor condition. ▶ NOUN ③ (*informal*) If you give someone the rundown on a situation, you tell them the basic, important facts about it.

rung ① Rung is the past participle of **ring**. ▶ NOUN ② The rungs on a ladder are the bars that form the steps.

runner NOUN ① a person who runs, especially as a sport. ② a person who takes messages or runs errands. ③ A runner on a plant such as a strawberry is a long shoot from which a new plant develops. ④ The runners on drawers and ice-skates are the thin strips on which they move.

runner-up, **runners-up** NOUN a person or team that comes second in a race or competition.

running ADJECTIVE ① continuing without stopping over a period of time • *a running commentary*. ② Running water is flowing rather than standing still.

runny, **runnier**, **runniest** ADJECTIVE ① more liquid than usual • *Warm the honey until it becomes runny*. ② If someone's nose or eyes are runny, liquid is coming out of them.

runway NOUN a long strip of ground used by aeroplanes for taking off or landing.

rupee [*Said roo-**pee***] NOUN the main unit of currency in India, Pakistan and some other countries.

rupture NOUN ① a severe injury in which part of your body tears or bursts open. ▶ VERB ② To rupture part of the body means to cause it to tear or burst • *a ruptured spleen*.

rural ADJECTIVE GEOGRAPHY relating to or involving the countryside.

ruse NOUN (*formal*) an action which is intended to trick someone.

rush VERB ① To rush means to move fast or do something quickly. ② If you rush someone into doing something, you make them do it without allowing them enough time to think. ▶ NOUN ③ If you are in a rush, you are busy and do not have enough time to do things. ④ If there is a rush for something, there is a sudden increase in demand for it • *There was a rush for tickets*. ⑤ Rushes are plants with long, thin stems that grow near water.

> **rush** VERB
> ① = dash, fly, gush, hasten, hurry, race, run, scurry, shoot
> ② = hurry, hustle, press, pressurise, push
> ▶ NOUN ③ = bustle, dash, hurry, race, scramble, stampede

rush hour NOUN The rush hour is one of the busy parts of the day when most people are travelling to or from work.

Russian ADJECTIVE ① belonging or relating to Russia. ▶ NOUN ② someone who comes from Russia. ③ Russian is the main language spoken in Russia.

rust NOUN ① Rust is a reddish-brown substance that forms on iron or steel which has been in contact with water and which is decaying gradually. ▶ NOUN, ADJECTIVE ② reddish-brown. ▶ VERB ③ When a metal object rusts, it becomes covered in rust.

rustic ADJECTIVE simple in a way considered to be typical of the countryside • *a rustic old log cabin*.

rustle VERB When something rustles, it makes soft sounds as it moves.
rustling ADJECTIVE, NOUN

rusty, **rustier**, **rustiest** ADJECTIVE ① affected by rust • *a rusty iron gate.* ② If someone's knowledge is rusty, it is not as good as it used to be because they have not used it for a long time • *My German is a bit rusty these days.*

rut NOUN ① a deep, narrow groove in the ground made by the wheels of a vehicle. ▶ PHRASE ② If someone is **in a rut**, they have become fixed in their way of doing things.

ruthless ADJECTIVE very harsh or cruel • *a ruthless dictator.* **ruthlessness** NOUN **ruthlessly** ADVERB

rye NOUN a type of grass that produces light brown grain.

Ss

Sabbath NOUN RE The Sabbath is the day of the week when members of some religious groups, especially Jews and Christians, do not work.

sabotage *[Said **sab**-ot-ahj]* NOUN ① the deliberate damaging of things such as machinery and railway lines. ▸ VERB ② If something is sabotaged, it is deliberately damaged. **saboteur** NOUN

sabre NOUN ① a heavy curved sword. ② a light sword used in fencing.

sachet *[Said **sash**-ay]* NOUN a small closed packet, containing a small amount of something such as sugar or shampoo.

sack NOUN ① a large bag made of rough material used for carrying or storing goods. ▸ VERB ② (*informal*) If someone is sacked, they are dismissed from their job by their employer. ▸ PHRASE ③ (*informal*) If someone gets **the sack**, they are dismissed from their job by their employer.

> **sack** VERB
> ② = discharge, dismiss, fire (*informal*)
> ▸ PHRASE ③ = discharge, dismissal, termination of employment (*formal*)

sacrament NOUN RE an important Christian ceremony such as communion, baptism or marriage.

sacred *[Said **say**-krid]* ADJECTIVE holy, or connected with religion or religious ceremonies • *sacred ground*.

sacrifice *[Said **sak**-riff-ice]* VERB ① If you sacrifice something valuable or important, you give it up. ② To sacrifice an animal means to kill it as an offering to a god. ▸ NOUN ③ the killing of an animal as an offering to a god or gods. ④ the action of giving something up. **sacrificial** ADJECTIVE

> **sacrifice** VERB
> ① = forego, forfeit, give up, surrender
> ▸ NOUN ④ = renunciation, self-denial

sacrilege *[Said **sak**-ril-ij]* NOUN Sacrilege is behaviour that shows great disrespect for something holy. **sacrilegious** ADJECTIVE

sacrosanct *[Said **sak**-roe-sangkt]* ADJECTIVE regarded as too important to be criticised or changed • *Freedom of the press is sacrosanct*.

sad ADJECTIVE ① If you are sad, you feel unhappy. ② Something sad makes you feel unhappy • *a sad story*. **sadly** ADVERB

> **sad** ADJECTIVE
> ① = blue, dejected, depressed, dismal, down, downcast, gloomy, glum, grief-stricken, low, melancholy (*literary*), mournful, unhappy, wistful
> ≠ happy
> ② = depressing, dismal, gloomy, harrowing, heart-rending, melancholy, mournful, moving, pathetic, poignant, tragic, upsetting

sadden VERB If something saddens you, it makes you feel sad.

saddle NOUN ① a leather seat that you sit on when you are riding a horse. ② The saddle on a bicycle is the seat. ▸ VERB ③ If you saddle a horse, you put a saddle on it.

sadism *[Said **say**-diz-m]* NOUN Sadism is the obtaining of pleasure from making people suffer pain or humiliation. **sadist** NOUN **sadistic** ADJECTIVE **sadistically** ADVERB

sadness NOUN the feeling of being unhappy.

> **sadness** NOUN
> = dejection, depression, despondency, melancholy (*literary*), unhappiness
> ≠ happiness

safari, **safaris** NOUN an expedition for hunting or observing wild animals, especially in Africa.

safe ADJECTIVE ① PSHE Something that is safe does not cause harm or danger. ② If you are safe, you are not in any danger. ③ If it is safe to say something, you can say it with little risk of being wrong. ▸ NOUN ④ a strong metal box with special locks, in which you can keep valuable things. **safely** ADVERB

> **safe** ADJECTIVE
> ① = harmless, innocuous
> ≠ dangerous
> ② = all right, in safe hands, okay, OK, out of danger, out of harm's way, protected, safe and sound, secure

safeguard VERB ① To safeguard something means to protect it. ▸ NOUN ② something designed to protect people or things.

> **safeguard** VERB
> ① = defend, guard, look after, preserve, protect, save, shield
> ▸ NOUN ② = barrier, cover, defence, protection

safekeeping NOUN If something is given to you for safekeeping, it is given to you to look after.

safety NOUN the state of being safe from harm or danger.

> **safety** NOUN
> = immunity, protection, security
> ≠ danger

sag, **sags**, **sagging**, **sagged** VERB When something sags, it hangs down loosely or sinks downwards in the middle. **sagging** ADJECTIVE

saga *[Said **sah**-ga]* NOUN a very long story, usually with many different adventures • *a saga of rivalry, honour and love.*

sage NOUN ① (*literary*) a very wise person. ② Sage is also a herb used for flavouring in cooking.

Sagittarius *[Said saj-it-**tair**-ee-uss]* NOUN Sagittarius is the ninth sign of the zodiac, represented by a creature who is half horse, half man, holding a bow and arrow. People born between November 22nd and December 21st are born under this sign.

said the past tense and past participle of **say**.

sail NOUN ① Sails are large pieces of material attached to a ship's mast. The wind blows against the sail and moves the ship. ▸ VERB ② When a ship sails, it moves across water. ③ If you sail somewhere, you go there by ship.

sailor NOUN a member of a ship's crew.

saint NOUN a person who after death is formally recognised by a Christian Church as deserving special honour because of having lived a very holy life.

saintly ADJECTIVE behaving in a very good or holy way.

sake PHRASE ① If you do something **for someone's sake**, you do it to help or please them. ② You use **for the sake of** to say why you are doing something • *a one-off expedition for interest's sake.*

salad NOUN a mixture of raw vegetables.

salami *[Said sal-**lah**-mee]* NOUN Salami is a kind of spicy sausage.

salary, **salaries** NOUN a regular monthly payment to an employee. **salaried** ADJECTIVE

sale NOUN ① The sale of goods is the selling of them. ② an occasion when a shop sells things at reduced prices. ③ *(in plural)* The sales of a product are the numbers that are sold.

saleable ADJECTIVE easy to sell or suitable for being sold.

salesman NOUN a man who sells products for a company.

saleswoman NOUN a woman who sells products for a company.

salient *[Said **say**-lee-ent]* ADJECTIVE *(formal)* The salient points or facts are the important ones.

saliva *[Said sal-**live**-a]* NOUN Saliva is the watery liquid in your mouth that helps you chew and digest food.

salmon, **salmons** or **salmon** *[Said **sam**-on]* NOUN a large edible silver-coloured fish with pink flesh.

salmonella *[Said sal-mon-**nell**-a]* NOUN Salmonella is a kind of bacteria which can cause severe food poisoning.

salon NOUN a place where hairdressers work.

saloon NOUN ① a car with a fixed roof and a separate boot. ② in the Wild West of America, a place where alcoholic drinks were sold and drunk.

salt NOUN ① Salt is a white substance found naturally in sea water. It is used to flavour and preserve food. ② SCIENCE a chemical compound formed from an acid base.

salty, **saltier**, **saltiest** ADJECTIVE containing salt or tasting of salt.

> **salty** ADJECTIVE
> = brak *(South African)*, briny, salted

salute NOUN ① a formal sign of respect. Soldiers give a salute by raising their right hand to their forehead. ▶ VERB ② If you salute someone, you give them a salute.

salvage VERB ① If you salvage things, you save them, for example from a wrecked ship or a destroyed building. ▶ NOUN ② You refer to things saved from a wrecked ship or destroyed building as salvage.

salvation NOUN ① When someone's salvation takes place, they are saved from harm or evil. ② To be someone's salvation means to save them from harm or evil.

salvo, **salvos** or **salvoes** NOUN the firing of several guns or missiles at the same time.

same ADJECTIVE *(usually preceded by the)* ① If two things are the same, they are like one another. ② Same means just one thing and not two different ones • *They were born in the same town.*

> **same** ADJECTIVE
> ① = alike, equal, equivalent, identical, indistinguishable
> ≠ different

Samoan ADJECTIVE ① belonging or relating to Samoa. ▶ NOUN ② someone who comes from Samoa.

sample NOUN ① A sample of something is a small amount of it that you can try or test • *a free sample of a new product.* ▶ VERB ② If you sample something, you try it • *I sampled his cooking.*

samurai *[Said **sam**-oor-eye]* NOUN A samurai was a member of an ancient Japanese warrior class.

sanctimonious *[Said sank-tim-**moan**-ee-uss]* ADJECTIVE pretending to be very religious and virtuous.

sanction VERB ① To sanction something means to officially approve of it or allow it. ▶ NOUN ② Sanction is official approval of something. ③ a severe punishment or penalty intended to make people obey the law. ④ Sanctions are sometimes taken by countries against a country that has broken international law.

sanction VERB
① = allow, approve, authorise, back, endorse, permit, support
≠ veto
▶ NOUN ② = approval, authorisation, backing, blessing, permission, support
④ = ban, boycott, embargo, penalties

sanctity NOUN If you talk about the sanctity of something, you are saying that it should be respected because it is very important • *the sanctity of marriage*.

sanctuary, **sanctuaries** NOUN ① a place where you are safe from harm or danger. ② a place where wildlife is protected • *a bird sanctuary*.

sand NOUN ① Sand consists of tiny pieces of stone. Beaches are made of sand. ▶ VERB ② If you sand something, you rub sandpaper over it to make it smooth.

sandal NOUN Sandals are light open shoes with straps, worn in warm weather.

sandpaper NOUN DGT Sandpaper is strong paper with a coating of sand on it, used for rubbing surfaces to make them smooth.

sandstone NOUN Sandstone is a type of rock formed from sand, often used for building.

sandwich NOUN ① two slices of bread with a filling between them. ▶ VERB ② If one thing is sandwiched between two others, it is in a narrow space between them • *a small shop sandwiched between a bar and an office*.

sandy, **sandier**, **sandiest** ADJECTIVE ① A sandy area is covered with sand. ② Sandy hair is light orange-brown.

sane ADJECTIVE ① If someone is sane, they have a normal and healthy mind. ② A sane action is sensible and reasonable.

sane ADJECTIVE
① = lucid, normal, rational
≠ mad
② = judicious (*formal*), level-headed, rational, reasonable, sensible, sound

sang the past tense of **sing**.

sanguine [*Said sang-gwin*] ADJECTIVE (*formal*) cheerful and confident.

sanitary ADJECTIVE Sanitary means concerned with keeping things clean and hygienic • *improving sanitary conditions*.

sanitation NOUN Sanitation is the process of keeping places clean and hygienic, especially by providing a sewage system and clean water supply.

sanity NOUN Your sanity is your ability to think and act normally and reasonably.

sank the past tense of **sink**.

sap, **saps**, **sapping**, **sapped** VERB ① If something saps your strength or confidence, it gradually weakens and destroys it. ▶ NOUN ② Sap is the watery liquid in plants.

sapphire NOUN a blue precious stone.

sarcastic ADJECTIVE saying or doing the opposite of what you really mean in order to mock or insult someone • *a sarcastic remark*. **sarcasm** NOUN **sarcastically** ADVERB

sarcastic ADJECTIVE
= caustic, ironic, sardonic, satirical

sardine NOUN a small edible sea fish.

sardonic ADJECTIVE mocking or scornful • *a sardonic grin*. **sardonically** ADVERB

sari, saris *[Said* ***sah****-ree]* NOUN a piece of clothing worn especially by Indian women, consisting of a long piece of material folded around the body.

sartorial ADJECTIVE (*formal*) relating to clothes • *sartorial elegance*.

sash NOUN a long piece of cloth worn round the waist or over one shoulder.

sat the past tense and past participle of **sit**.

Satan NOUN Satan is the Devil.

satanic *[Said sa-****tan****-ik]* ADJECTIVE caused by or influenced by Satan • *satanic forces*.

satchel NOUN a leather or cloth bag with a long strap.

satellite NOUN ① a spacecraft sent into orbit round the earth to collect information or as part of a communications system. ② a natural object in space that moves round a planet or star.

satin NOUN Satin is a kind of smooth, shiny silk.

satire NOUN Satire is the use of mocking or ironical humour, especially in literature, to show how foolish or wicked some people are. **satirical** ADJECTIVE

satisfaction NOUN Satisfaction is the feeling of pleasure you get when you do something you wanted or needed to do.

satisfactory ADJECTIVE acceptable or adequate • *a satisfactory explanation*. **satisfactorily** ADVERB

> **satisfactory** ADJECTIVE
> = acceptable, adequate, all right, good enough, passable, sufficient
> ≠ unsatisfactory

satisfied ADJECTIVE happy because you have got what you want.

> **satisfied** ADJECTIVE
> = content, contented, happy, pleased
> ≠ disappointed

satisfy, satisfies, satisfying, satisfied VERB ① To satisfy someone means to give them enough of something to make them pleased or contented. ② To satisfy someone that something is the case means to convince them of it. ③ To satisfy the requirements for something means to fulfil them.

> **satisfy** VERB
> ① = gratify, indulge, please
> ② = convince, persuade, put someone's mind at rest, reassure
> ③ = fulfil, meet

satisfying ADJECTIVE Something that is satisfying gives you a feeling of pleasure and fulfilment.

saturated ADJECTIVE ① very wet. ② If a place is saturated with things, it is completely full of them • *If you thought the area was already saturated with supermarkets, think again*. **saturation** NOUN

Saturday NOUN the day between Friday and Sunday.

Saturn NOUN Saturn is the planet in the solar system which is sixth from the sun.

sauce NOUN a liquid eaten with food to give it more flavour.

saucepan NOUN a deep metal cooking pot with a handle and a lid.

saucer NOUN a small curved plate for a cup.

saucy, saucier, sauciest ADJECTIVE cheeky in an amusing way.

Saudi *[Rhymes with* ***cloudy****]* ADJECTIVE ① belonging or relating to Saudi Arabia. ▶ NOUN ② someone who comes from Saudi Arabia.

sauna *[Said* ***saw****-na]* NOUN If you have a sauna, you go into a very hot room in order to sweat, then have a cold bath or shower.

saunter **VERB** To saunter somewhere means to walk there slowly and casually.

sausage **NOUN** a mixture of minced meat and herbs formed into a tubular shape and served cooked.

savage **ADJECTIVE** ① cruel and violent • *savage fighting.* ▶ **NOUN** ② If you call someone a savage, you mean that they are violent and uncivilised. ▶ **VERB** ③ If an animal savages you, it attacks you and bites you. **savagely** **ADVERB**

> **savage** **ADJECTIVE**
> ① = barbaric, barbarous, brutal, cruel, ferocious, inhuman, vicious, violent
> ▶ **NOUN** ② = barbarian, beast, brute, lout, monster
> ▶ **VERB** ③ = attack, bite, maul

savagery **NOUN** Savagery is cruel and violent behaviour.

save **VERB** ① If you save someone, you rescue them • *He saved my life.* ② If you save someone or something, you keep them safe. ③ If you save something, you keep it so that you can use it later • *He'd saved up enough money for the deposit.* ④ To save time, money or effort means to prevent it from being wasted • *You could have saved us the trouble.* ▶ **PREPOSITION** ⑤ (*formal*) Save means except • *I was alone in the house save for a very old woman.*

> **save** **VERB**
> ① = come to someone's rescue, deliver, redeem, rescue, salvage
> ② = keep safe, preserve, protect, safeguard
> ③ = hoard, keep, put by, reserve, set aside
> ≠ waste

saving **NOUN** ① a reduction in the amount of time or money used. ② (*in plural*) Your savings are the money you have saved.

saviour **NOUN** ① If someone saves you from danger, you can refer to them as your saviour. ▶ **PROPER NOUN** ② **RE** In Christianity, the Saviour is Jesus Christ.

savour **VERB** If you savour something, you take your time with it and enjoy it fully • *I settled down and savoured a cup of strong coffee.*

savoury **ADJECTIVE** ① Savoury is salty or spicy. ② Something that is not very savoury is not very pleasant or respectable • *the less savoury places.*

saw, **saws**, **sawing**, **sawed**, **sawn** ① Saw is the past tense of **see**. ▶ **VERB** ② If you saw something, you cut it with a saw. ▶ **NOUN** ③ a tool, with a blade with sharp teeth along one edge, for cutting wood.

sawdust **NOUN** Sawdust is the fine powder produced when you saw wood.

saxophone **NOUN** a curved metal wind instrument often played in jazz bands.

say, **says**, **saying**, **said** **VERB** ① When you say something, you speak words. ② 'Say' is used to give an example • *a maximum fee of, say, a million.* ▶ **NOUN** ③ If you have a say in something, you can give your opinion and influence decisions.

> **say** **VERB**
> ① = announce, declare, mention, remark, state, utter
> ▶ **NOUN** ③ = voice, vote

saying **NOUN** a well-known sentence or phrase that tells you something about human life.

> **saying** **NOUN**
> = adage, axiom, maxim, proverb

scab **NOUN** a hard, dry covering that forms over a wound. **scabby** **ADJECTIVE**

scaffolding NOUN Scaffolding is a framework of poles and boards that is used by workmen to stand on while they are working on the outside structure of a building.

scald [*Said* ***skawld***] VERB ① If you scald yourself, you burn yourself with very hot liquid or steam. ▶ NOUN ② a burn caused by scalding.

scale NOUN ① The scale of something is its size or extent • *the sheer scale of the disaster*. ② a set of levels or numbers used for measuring things. ③ GEOGRAPHY The scale of a map, plan or model is the relationship between the size of something in the map, plan or model and its size in the real world • *a scale of 1:30,000*. ④ MUSIC an upward or downward sequence of musical notes. ⑤ The scales of a fish or reptile are the small pieces of hard skin covering its body. ⑥ (*in plural*) Scales are a piece of equipment used for weighing things. ▶ VERB ⑦ If you scale something high, you climb it.

scallop NOUN Scallops are edible shellfish with two flat fan-shaped shells.

scalp NOUN ① Your scalp is the skin under the hair on your head. ② the piece of skin and hair removed when someone is scalped. ▶ VERB ③ To scalp someone means to remove the skin and hair from their head in one piece.

scalpel NOUN a knife with a thin, sharp blade, used by surgeons.

scaly, **scalier**, **scaliest** ADJECTIVE covered with scales.

scam NOUN (*informal*) an illegal trick, usually done to get money from a person.

scamper VERB To scamper means to move quickly and lightly.

scan VERB ① If you scan something, you look at all of it carefully • *I scanned the horizon to the north-east*. ② If you scan a piece of writing, you read it very quickly to find the important or interesting parts. ③ If a machine scans something, it examines it by means of a beam of light or X-rays. ④ ENGLISH If the words of a poem scan, they fit into a regular, rhythmical pattern. ⑤ ENGLISH If you scan a line of poetry you count the number of beats or metrical feet it has. ▶ NOUN ⑥ an examination or search by a scanner • *a brain scan*.

scandal NOUN a situation or event that people think is shocking and immoral. **scandalous** ADJECTIVE

Scandinavia [*Said skan-din-****nay****-vee-a*] NOUN Scandinavia is the name given to a group of countries in Northern Europe, including Norway, Sweden, Denmark and sometimes Finland and Iceland. **Scandinavian** NOUN, ADJECTIVE

scanner NOUN ① a machine which is used to examine, identify or record things by means of a beam of light or X-rays. ② ICT a machine which converts text or images into a form that can be stored on a computer.

scant ADJECTIVE You use 'scant' to show that there is not as much of something as there should be • *Some drivers pay scant attention to the laws of the road*.

scapegoat NOUN If someone is made a scapegoat, they are blamed for something, although it may not be their fault.

scar, **scars**, **scarring**, **scarred** NOUN ① a mark left on your skin after a wound has healed. ② a permanent effect on someone's mind that results from a very unpleasant experience • *the scars of war*. ▶ VERB ③ If an injury scars you, it leaves a permanent mark on your skin.

④ If an unpleasant experience scars you, it has a permanent effect on you.

scarce ADJECTIVE If something is scarce, there is not very much of it.
scarcity NOUN

scarce ADJECTIVE
= few, rare, uncommon, unusual
≠ common

scarcely ADVERB Scarcely means hardly • *I can scarcely hear her.*

scare VERB ① If something scares you, it frightens you. ▶ NOUN ② If something gives you a scare, it scares you. ③ If there is a scare about something, a lot of people are worried about it • *a health scare.*
scared ADJECTIVE

scare VERB
① = alarm, frighten, give someone a fright, intimidate, startle, terrify, terrorise, unnerve
▶ NOUN ② = fright, shock, start
③ = alert, hysteria, panic

scarecrow NOUN an object shaped like a person, put in a field to scare birds away.

scarf, **scarfs** or **scarves** NOUN a piece of cloth worn round your neck or head to keep you warm.

scarlet NOUN, ADJECTIVE bright red.

scary, **scarier**, **scariest** ADJECTIVE (*informal*) frightening.

scary ADJECTIVE
= alarming, chilling, creepy (*informal*), eerie, frightening, hair-raising, spooky, terrifying, unnerving

scathing [*Said* ***skayth**-ing*] ADJECTIVE harsh and scornful • *They were scathing about his job.*

scatter VERB ① To scatter things means to throw or drop them all over an area. ② If people scatter, they suddenly move away in different directions.

scatter VERB
① = shower, sow, sprinkle, throw about
≠ gather

scattering NOUN A scattering of things is a small number of them spread over a large area • *the scattering of islands.*

scavenge VERB If you scavenge for things, you search for them among waste and rubbish. **scavenger** NOUN

scenario [*Said sin-**nar**-ee-oh*] NOUN ① DRAMA The scenario of a film or play is a summary of its plot. ② the way a situation could possibly develop in the future • *the worst possible scenario.*

scene NOUN ① ENGLISH DRAMA part of a play or film in which a series of events happen in one place. ② Pictures and views are sometimes called scenes • *a village scene.* ③ The scene of an event is the place where it happened. ④ an area of activity • *the music scene.*

scene NOUN
② = landscape, panorama, view
③ = location, place, setting, site, spot
④ = arena, business, environment, world

scenery NOUN ① In the countryside, you can refer to everything you see as the scenery. ② In a theatre, the scenery is the painted cloth on the stage which represents the place where the action is happening.

scenery NOUN
① = landscape, panorama, surroundings, terrain, view

scenic ADJECTIVE A scenic place or route has nice views.

scent NOUN ① a smell, especially a pleasant one. ② Scent is perfume. ▶ VERB ③ When an animal scents something, it becomes aware of it by smelling it.

sceptic *[Said* ***skep****-tik]* **NOUN** someone who has doubts about things that other people believe. **scepticism** **NOUN**

sceptical *[Said* ***skep****-tik-kl]* **ADJECTIVE** If you are sceptical about something, you have doubts about it. **sceptically** **ADVERB**

schedule *[Said* ***shed****-yool]* **NOUN** ① a plan that gives a list of events or tasks, together with the times at which each thing should be done. ▶ **VERB** ② If something is scheduled to happen, it has been planned and arranged • *Their journey was scheduled for the beginning of May.*

scheme, **schemes, scheming, schemed** **NOUN** ① a plan or arrangement • *a five-year development scheme.* ▶ **VERB** ② When people scheme, they make secret plans.

schism *[Said* ***skizm****]* **NOUN** a split or division within a group or organisation.

schizophrenia *[Said skit-soe-****free****-nee-a]* **NOUN** Schizophrenia is a serious mental illness which prevents someone relating their thoughts and feelings to what is happening around them. **schizophrenic** **ADJECTIVE**

scholar **NOUN** ① a person who studies an academic subject and knows a lot about it. ② In South African English, a scholar is a school pupil.

scholarly **ADJECTIVE** having or showing a lot of knowledge.

scholarship **NOUN** ① If you get a scholarship to a school or university, your studies are paid for by the school or university or by some other organisation. ② Scholarship is academic study and knowledge.

school **NOUN** ① a place where children are educated. ② University departments and colleges are sometimes called schools • *My oldest son is in medical school.* ③ You can refer to a large group of dolphins or fish as a school. ▶ **VERB** ④ When someone is schooled in something, they are taught it • *They were schooled in the modern techniques.*

schoolchild **NOUN** Schoolchildren are children who go to school. **schoolboy** **NOUN** **schoolgirl** **NOUN**

schooling **NOUN** Your schooling is the education you get at school.

schooner **NOUN** a sailing ship.

science **NOUN** ① Science is the study of the nature and behaviour of natural things and the knowledge obtained about them. ② a branch of science, for example physics or biology.

science fiction **NOUN** Stories about events happening in the future or in other parts of the universe are called science fiction.

scientific **ADJECTIVE** ① relating to science or to a particular science • *scientific knowledge.* ② done in a systematic way, using experiments or tests • *this scientific method.* **scientifically** **ADVERB**

scientist **NOUN** an expert in one of the sciences who does work connected with it.

scintillating *[Said* ***sin****-til-late-ing]* **ADJECTIVE** lively and witty • *scintillating conversation.*

scissors **PLURAL NOUN** Scissors are a cutting tool with two sharp blades.

scoff **VERB** ① If you scoff, you speak in a scornful, mocking way about something. ② *(informal)* If you scoff food, you eat it quickly and greedily.

scold **VERB** If you scold someone, you tell them off.

> **scold** **VERB**
> = chide, lecture, rebuke, reprimand, tell off *(informal)*, tick off *(informal)*

scone *[Said **skon** or **skoan**]* NOUN Scones are small cakes made from flour and fat and usually eaten with butter.

scoop VERB ① If you scoop something up, you pick it up using a spoon or the palm of your hand. ▶ NOUN ② an object like a large spoon which is used for picking up food such as ice cream.

scooter NOUN ① a small, light motorcycle. ② a simple cycle which a child rides by standing on it and pushing the ground with one foot.

scope NOUN ① If there is scope for doing something, the opportunity to do it exists. ② The scope of something is the whole subject area which it deals with or includes.

-scope SUFFIX '-scope' is used to form nouns meaning an instrument used for observing or detecting • *microscope* • *telescope*.

scorching ADJECTIVE extremely hot • *another scorching summer*.

score VERB ① If you score in a game, you get a goal, run or point. ② To score in a game also means to record the score obtained by the players. ③ If you score a success or victory, you achieve it. ④ To score a surface means to cut a line into it. ▶ NOUN ⑤ The score in a game is the number of goals, runs or points obtained by the two teams. ⑥ Scores of things means very many of them • *Ros entertained scores of celebrities*. ⑦ (*old-fashioned*) A score is twenty. ⑧ MUSIC The score of a piece of music is the written version of it.
scorer NOUN

scorn NOUN ① Scorn is great contempt • *a look of scorn*. ▶ VERB ② If you scorn someone, you treat them with great contempt. ③ (*formal*) If you scorn something, you refuse to accept it.

scorn NOUN
① = contempt, derision, disdain, mockery
▶ VERB ② = despise, disdain, look down on, slight

scornful ADJECTIVE showing contempt • *his scornful comment*.
scornfully ADVERB

scornful ADJECTIVE
= contemptuous, disdainful, scathing, sneering, supercilious, withering

Scorpio NOUN Scorpio is the eighth sign of the zodiac, represented by a scorpion. People born between October 23rd and November 21st are born under this sign.

scorpion NOUN an animal that looks like a small lobster, with a long tail with a poisonous sting on the end.

Scot NOUN ① a person who comes from Scotland. ▶ ADJECTIVE ② Scots means the same as **Scottish**.

scotch NOUN Scotch is whisky made in Scotland.

Scotsman, **Scotsmen** NOUN a man who comes from Scotland.

Scotswoman, **Scotswomen** NOUN a woman who comes from Scotland.

Scottish ADJECTIVE belonging or relating to Scotland.

scoundrel NOUN (*old-fashioned*) a man who cheats and deceives people.

scour VERB ① If you scour a place, you look all over it in order to find something • *The police scoured the area*. ② If you scour something such as a pan, you clean it by rubbing it with something rough.

scourge *[Rhymes with **urge**]* NOUN something that causes a lot of suffering • *hay fever, that scourge of summer*.

scout NOUN ① a boy who is a member of the Scout Association, an organisation for boys which aims to develop character and responsibility. ② someone who is sent to an area to find out the position of an enemy army. ▶ **VERB** ③ If you scout around for something, you look around for it.

scowl **VERB** ① If you scowl, you frown because you are angry • *They were scowling at me.* ▶ **NOUN** ② an angry expression.

scrabble **VERB** If you scrabble at something, you scrape at it with your hands or feet.

scramble **VERB** ① If you scramble over something, you climb over it using your hands to help you. ▶ **NOUN** ② a motorcycle race over rough ground.

scrap, **scraps, scrapping, scrapped** **NOUN** ① A scrap of something is a very small piece of it • *a scrap of cloth.* ② *(in plural)* Scraps are pieces of leftover food. ▶ **ADJECTIVE, NOUN** ③ Scrap metal or scrap is metal from old machinery or cars that can be re-used. ▶ **VERB** ④ If you scrap something, you get rid of it • *They considered scrapping passport controls.*

scrapbook **NOUN** a book in which you stick things such as pictures or newspaper articles.

scrape **VERB** ① If you scrape a surface, you rub a rough or sharp object against it. ② If something scrapes, it makes a harsh noise by rubbing against something • *his shoes scraping across the stone ground.*

> **scrape** **VERB**
> ① = graze, scour, scratch, scuff, skin
> ② = grate, grind, rasp, scratch

scratch **VERB** ① To scratch something means to make a small cut on it accidentally • *They were always getting scratched by cats.* ② If you scratch, you rub your skin with your nails because it is itching. ▶ **NOUN** ③ a small cut.

scrawl **VERB** ① If you scrawl something, you write it in a careless and untidy way. ▶ **NOUN** ② You can refer to careless and untidy writing as a scrawl.

scrawny, **scrawnier, scrawniest** **ADJECTIVE** thin and bony • *a small scrawny man.*

scream **VERB** ① If you scream, you shout or cry in a loud, high-pitched voice. ▶ **NOUN** ② a loud, high-pitched cry.

> **scream** **VERB**
> ① = cry, howl, screech, shout, shriek, squeal, yell
> ▶ **NOUN** ② = cry, howl, screech, shriek, squeal, yell

screech **VERB** ① To screech means to make an unpleasant high-pitched noise • *The car wheels screeched.* ▶ **NOUN** ② an unpleasant high-pitched noise.

screen **NOUN** ① a flat vertical surface on which a picture is shown • *a television screen.* ② a vertical panel used to separate different parts of a room or to protect something. ▶ **VERB** ③ To screen a film or television programme means to show it. ④ If you screen someone, you put something in front of them to protect them.

screenplay **NOUN** The screenplay of a film is the script.

screw **NOUN** ① a small, sharp piece of metal used for fixing things together or for fixing something to a wall. ▶ **VERB** ② If you screw things together, you fix them together using screws. ③ If you screw something onto something else, you fix it there by twisting it round and round • *He screwed the top on the ink bottle.* **screw up** **VERB** If you screw something up, you twist it or squeeze it so that it no longer has its proper shape • *Amy screwed up her face.*

screwdriver NOUN a tool for turning screws.

scribble VERB ① If you scribble something, you write it quickly and roughly. ② To scribble also means to make meaningless marks • *When Caroline was five she scribbled on a wall.* ▸ NOUN ③ You can refer to something written or drawn quickly and roughly as a scribble.

script NOUN DRAMA the written version of a play or film.

scripture NOUN RE Scripture refers to sacred writings, especially the Bible. **scriptural** ADJECTIVE

scroll NOUN a long roll of paper or parchment with writing on it.

scrub, **scrubs**, **scrubbing**, **scrubbed** VERB ① If you scrub something, you clean it with a stiff brush and water. ▸ NOUN ② If you give something a scrub, you scrub it. ③ GEOGRAPHY Scrub consists of low trees and bushes.

scruff NOUN The scruff of your neck is the back of your neck or collar.

scruffy, **scruffier**, **scruffiest** ADJECTIVE dirty and untidy • *four scruffy youths.*

scruffy ADJECTIVE
= ragged, seedy, shabby, tatty, unkempt
≠ smart

scrum NOUN When rugby players form a scrum, they form a group and push against each other with their heads down in an attempt to get the ball.

scrupulous ADJECTIVE ① always doing what is honest or morally right. ② paying very careful attention to detail • *a long and scrupulous search.* **scrupulously** ADVERB

scrutinise; also spelt **scrutinize** VERB If you scrutinise something, you examine it very carefully.

scrutinise VERB
= examine, inspect, pore over, scan, search, study

scrutiny NOUN If something is under scrutiny, it is being observed very carefully.

scuba diving NOUN Scuba diving is the sport of swimming underwater while breathing from tanks of compressed air on your back.

scuff VERB ① If you scuff your feet, you drag them along the ground when you are walking. ② If you scuff your shoes, you mark them by scraping or rubbing them.

scuffle NOUN ① a short, rough fight. ▸ VERB ② When people scuffle, they fight roughly.

sculpt VERB When something is sculpted, it is carved or shaped in stone, wood or clay.

sculptor NOUN someone who makes sculptures.

sculpture NOUN ① a work of art produced by carving or shaping stone or clay. ② Sculpture is the art of making sculptures.

scum NOUN Scum is a layer of a dirty substance on the surface of a liquid.

scurrilous [*Said* ***skur**-ril-luss*] ADJECTIVE abusive and damaging to someone's good name • *scurrilous stories.*

scurry, **scurries**, **scurrying**, **scurried** VERB To scurry means to run quickly with short steps.

scuttle VERB ① To scuttle means to run quickly. ② To scuttle a ship means to sink it deliberately by making holes in the bottom. ▸ NOUN ③ a container for coal.

scythe [*Said* ***sythe***] NOUN a tool with a long handle and a curved blade used for cutting grass or grain.

sea NOUN ① The sea is the salty water that covers much of the earth's surface. ② A sea of people or things is a very large number of them • *a sea of red flags*.

seagull NOUN Seagulls are common white, grey and black birds that live near the sea.

seal NOUN ① an official mark on a document which shows that it is genuine. ② a piece of wax fixed over the opening of a container. ③ a large mammal with flippers that lives partly on land and partly in the sea. ▶ VERB ④ If you seal an envelope, you stick down the flap. ⑤ If you seal an opening, you cover it securely so that air, gas or liquid cannot get through.

sea lion NOUN a type of large seal.

seam NOUN ① a line of stitches joining two pieces of cloth. ② A seam of coal is a long, narrow layer of it beneath the ground.

seaman, seamen NOUN a sailor.

search VERB ① If you search for something, you look for it in several places. ② If a person is searched their body and clothing are examined to see if they are hiding anything. ▶ NOUN ③ an attempt to find something.

> **search** VERB
> ① = comb, forage, fossick (*Australian and New Zealand*), google, hunt, look, scour, seek, sift
> ▶ NOUN ③ = hunt, quest

search engine NOUN a service on the internet which enables users to search for items of interest.

searching ADJECTIVE intended to discover the truth about something • *searching questions*.

searing ADJECTIVE A searing pain is very sharp.

seashore NOUN The seashore is the land along the edge of the sea.

seasick ADJECTIVE feeling sick because of the movement of a boat. **seasickness** NOUN

seaside NOUN The seaside is an area next to the sea.

season NOUN ① The seasons are the periods into which a year is divided and which have their own typical weather conditions. The seasons are spring, summer, autumn and winter. ② a period of the year when something usually happens • *the football season* • *the hunting season*. ▶ VERB ③ If you season food, you add salt, pepper or spices to it.

seasonal ADJECTIVE happening during one season or one time of the year • *seasonal work*.

seasoned ADJECTIVE very experienced • *a seasoned professional*.

seasoning NOUN Seasoning is flavouring such as salt and pepper.

season ticket NOUN a train or bus ticket that you can use as many times as you like within a certain period.

seat NOUN ① something you can sit on. ② The seat of a piece of clothing is the part that covers your bottom. ③ If someone wins a seat in parliament, they are elected. ▶ VERB ④ If you seat yourself somewhere, you sit down. ⑤ If a place seats a particular number of people, it has enough seats for that number • *The theatre seats 570 people*.

seat belt NOUN a strap that you fasten across your body for safety when travelling in a car or an aircraft.

seating NOUN The seating in a place is the number or arrangement of seats there.

seaweed NOUN Plants that grow in the sea are called seaweed.

secateurs [*Said sek-at-**turz***] PLURAL NOUN Secateurs are small shears for pruning garden plants.

secluded ADJECTIVE quiet and hidden from view • *a secluded beach*. **seclusion** NOUN

second ADJECTIVE *[Said* ***sek**-ond]* ① The second item in a series is the one counted as number two. ▶ NOUN *[Said* ***sek**-ond]* ② one of the sixty parts that a minute is divided into. ③ Seconds are goods that are sold cheaply because they are slightly faulty. ▶ VERB ④ *[Said* ***sek**-ond]* If you second a proposal, you formally agree with it so that it can be discussed or voted on. ⑤ *[Said si-**kond**]* If you are seconded somewhere, you are sent there temporarily to work. **secondly** ADVERB

secondary ADJECTIVE ① Something that is secondary is less important than something else. ② Secondary education is education for pupils between the ages of eleven and eighteen.

secondary school NOUN a school for pupils between the ages of eleven and eighteen.

second-class ADJECTIVE ① Second-class things are regarded as less important than other things of the same kind • *He has been treated as a second-class citizen.* ② Second-class services are cheaper and therefore slower or less comfortable than first-class ones.

second-hand ADJECTIVE, ADVERB ① Something that is second-hand has already been owned by someone else • *a second-hand car.* ② If you hear a story second-hand, you hear it indirectly, rather than from the people involved.

second-rate ADJECTIVE of poor quality • *a second-rate movie.*

secret ADJECTIVE ① Something that is secret is told to only a small number of people and hidden from everyone else • *a secret meeting.* ▶ NOUN ② a fact told to only a small number of people and hidden from everyone else. **secretly** ADVERB **secrecy** NOUN

secret ADJECTIVE
① = closet (*informal*), confidential, covert, furtive, hidden, undercover, underground

secret agent NOUN a spy.

secretary, secretaries NOUN ① a person employed by an organisation to keep records, write letters, and do office work. ② Ministers in charge of some government departments are also called secretaries • *the Health Secretary.* **secretarial** ADJECTIVE

secrete *[Said sik-**kreet**]* VERB ① When part of a plant or animal secretes a liquid, it produces it. ② (*formal*) If you secrete something somewhere, you hide it. **secretion** NOUN

secretive ADJECTIVE Secretive people tend to hide their feelings and intentions.

secretive ADJECTIVE
= cagey (*informal*), reserved, reticent

secret service NOUN A country's secret service is the government department in charge of espionage.

sect NOUN a religious or political group which has broken away from a larger group.

sectarian *[Said sek-**tair**-ee-an]* ADJECTIVE strongly supporting a particular sect • *sectarian violence.*

section NOUN A section of something is one of the parts it is divided into • *this section of the motorway.*

section NOUN
= division, instalment, part, piece, portion, segment

sector NOUN ① A sector of something, especially a country's economy, is one part of it • *the private sector.* ② MATHS A sector of a circle is one of the two parts formed when you draw two straight lines from the centre to the circumference.

secular ADJECTIVE having no connection

with religion • *secular education.*

secure VERB ① *(formal)* If you secure something, you manage to get it • *They secured the rights to her story.* ② If you secure a place, you make it safe from harm or attack. ③ To secure something also means to fasten it firmly • *One end was secured to the pier.* ▶ ADJECTIVE ④ If a place is secure, it is tightly locked or well protected. ⑤ If an object is secure, it is firmly fixed in place. ⑥ If you feel secure, you feel safe and confident. **securely** ADVERB

secure VERB
① = acquire, gain, get, obtain, procure *(formal)*
② = fortify, make impregnable, make safe, strengthen
③ = attach, bind, fasten, fix, lock, moor, tie up
≠ release
▶ ADJECTIVE ④ = fortified, impregnable, protected, safe, shielded
⑤ = fastened, firm, fixed, locked, solid, stable, tight
⑥ = confident, protected, reassured, relaxed, safe
≠ insecure

security NOUN ① Security means all the precautions taken to protect a place • *The airports have increased the level of security.* ② A feeling of security is a feeling of being safe.

sedate *[Said sid-**date**]* ADJECTIVE ① quiet and dignified. ▶ VERB ② To sedate someone means to give them a drug to calm them down or make them sleep. **sedately** ADVERB

sedative *[Said **sed**-at-tiv]* NOUN ① a drug that calms you down or makes you sleep. ▶ ADJECTIVE ② having a calming or soothing effect • *antihistamines which have a sedative effect.* **sedation** NOUN

sedentary *[Said **sed**-en-tree]* ADJECTIVE A sedentary occupation is one in which you spend most of your time sitting down.

sediment NOUN ① Sediment is solid material that settles at the bottom of a liquid • *A bottle of beer with sediment in it is usually a guarantee of quality.* ② GEOGRAPHY Sediment is also small particles of rock that have been worn down and deposited together by water, ice and wind.

sedimentary ADJECTIVE GEOGRAPHY Sedimentary rocks are formed from fragments of shells or rocks that have become compressed. Sandstone and limestone are sedimentary rocks.

seduce VERB If you are seduced into doing something, you are persuaded to do it because it seems very attractive.

seductive ADJECTIVE Something seductive is very attractive and tempting. **seductively** ADVERB

see, **sees**, **seeing**, **saw**, **seen** VERB ① If you see something, you are looking at it or you notice it. ② If you see someone, you visit them or meet them • *I went to see my dentist.* ③ If you see someone to a place, you accompany them there. ④ To see something also means to realise or understand it • *I see what you mean.* ⑤ If you say you will see what is happening, you mean you will find out. ⑥ If you say you will see if you can do something, you mean you will try to do it. ⑦ If you see that something is done, you make sure that it is done. ⑧ If you see to something, you deal with it. ⑨ 'See' is used to say that an event takes place during a particular period of time • *The next couple of years saw two momentous developments.* ▶ PHRASE ⑩ *(informal)* **Seeing that** or **seeing as** means because • *I took John for lunch, seeing as it was his birthday.* ▶ NOUN ⑪ A bishop's see is his diocese.

see VERB
① = behold, discern, glimpse, look, notice, observe, perceive, sight, spot
④ = appreciate, comprehend, follow, get, grasp, realise, understand
⑤ = ascertain, determine, discover, find out

seed NOUN ① SCIENCE The seeds of a plant are the small, hard parts from which new plants can grow. ② The seeds of a feeling or process are its beginning or origins • *the seeds of mistrust*.

seedling NOUN a young plant grown from a seed.

seedy, seedier, seediest ADJECTIVE untidy and shabby • *a seedy hotel*.

seek, seeks, seeking, sought VERB (*formal*) ① To seek something means to try to find it, obtain it or achieve it • *The police were still seeking information*. ② If you seek to do something, you try to do it • *De Gaulle sought to reunite the country*.

seek VERB
① = be after, hunt, look for, search for
② = aim, aspire to, attempt, endeavour, strive, try

seem VERB If something seems to be the case, it appears to be the case or you think it is the case • *He seemed such a quiet chap*.

seem VERB
= appear, give the impression, look, look like

seeming ADJECTIVE appearing to be real or genuine • *this seeming disregard for human life*. **seemingly** ADVERB

seep VERB If a liquid or gas seeps through something, it flows through very slowly.

seething ADJECTIVE If you are seething about something, you are very angry but it does not show.

segment NOUN ① A segment of something is one part of it. ② The segments of an orange or grapefruit are the sections which you can divide it into. ③ MATHS A segment of a circle is one of the two parts formed when you draw a straight line across it.

segregate VERB To segregate two groups of people means to keep them apart from each other. **segregated** ADJECTIVE **segregation** NOUN

seize VERB ① If you seize something, you grab it firmly • *He seized the phone*. ② To seize a place or to seize control of it means to take control of it quickly and suddenly. ③ If you seize an opportunity, you take advantage of it. ④ If you seize on something, you immediately show great interest in it • *MPs have seized on a new report*. **seize up** VERB ① If a part of your body seizes up, it becomes stiff and painful. ② If an engine seizes up, it becomes jammed and stops working.

seize VERB
① = grab, grasp, snatch
② = annex, appropriate, confiscate, hijack, impound

seizure [*Said* ***seez****-yer*] NOUN ① a sudden violent attack of an illness, especially a heart attack or a fit. ② If there is a seizure of power, a group of people suddenly take control using force.

seldom ADVERB not very often • *They seldom speak to each other*.

select VERB ① If you select something, you choose it. ▸ ADJECTIVE ② of good quality • *a select social club*. **selector** NOUN

select VERB
① = choose, decide on, opt for, pick, settle on, single out, take
▸ ADJECTIVE ② = choice, exclusive, first-class, first-rate, hand-picked, prime, special, superior

selection NOUN ① Selection is the choosing of people or things • *the selection of parliamentary candidates.* ② A selection of people or things is a set of them chosen from a larger group. ③ The selection of goods in a shop is the range of goods available • *a good selection of shoes.*

selective ADJECTIVE choosing things carefully • *I am selective about what I eat.* **selectively** ADVERB

self, **selves** NOUN Your self is your basic personality or nature • *Hershey is her normal dependable self.*

self- PREFIX ① done to yourself or by yourself • *self-help* • *self-control.* ② doing something automatically • *a self-loading rifle.*

self-assured ADJECTIVE behaving in a way that shows confidence in yourself.

self-centred ADJECTIVE thinking only about yourself and not about other people.

self-confessed ADJECTIVE admitting to having bad habits or unpopular opinions • *a self-confessed liar.*

self-confident ADJECTIVE confident of your own abilities or worth. **self-confidence** NOUN

self-conscious ADJECTIVE nervous and easily embarrassed, and worried about what other people think of you. **self-consciously** ADVERB

self-control NOUN PSHE Self-control is the ability to restrain yourself and not show your feelings.

self-defence NOUN Self-defence is the use of special physical techniques to protect yourself when someone attacks you.

self-employed ADJECTIVE working for yourself and organising your own finances, rather than working for an employer.

self-esteem NOUN PSHE Your self-esteem is your good opinion of yourself.

self-evident ADJECTIVE Self-evident facts are completely obvious and need no proof or explanation.

selfie NOUN (*informal*) a photograph taken by pointing a camera at yourself.

self-indulgent ADJECTIVE allowing yourself to do or have things you enjoy, especially as a treat.

self-interest NOUN If you do something out of self-interest, you do it for your own benefit rather than to help other people.

selfish ADJECTIVE caring only about yourself, and not about other people. **selfishly** ADVERB **selfishness** NOUN

> **selfish** ADJECTIVE
> = egoistic, egoistical, egotistic, egotistical, greedy, self-centred

selfless ADJECTIVE putting other people's interests before your own.

self-raising ADJECTIVE Self-raising flour contains baking powder to make cakes and bread rise when they are baked.

self-respect NOUN Self-respect is a belief in your own worth and opinions.

self-righteous ADJECTIVE convinced that you are better or more virtuous than other people. **self-righteousness** NOUN

self-service ADJECTIVE A self-service shop or restaurant is one where you serve yourself.

self-sufficient ADJECTIVE ① producing or making everything you need, and so not needing to buy things. ② able to live in a way in which you do not need other people.

sell, **sells**, **selling**, **sold** VERB ① If you sell something, you let someone have it in return for money. ② If a shop sells something, it has it available for people to buy • *a tobacconist that sells stamps.* ③ If something sells, people buy it • *This book will sell.* **seller** NOUN **sell out** VERB If a shop has sold out of something, it has sold it all.

> **sell** VERB
> ① = deal in, hawk, peddle, trade in
> ≠ buy
> ② = deal in, stock, trade in
> ≠ buy

semblance NOUN If there is a semblance of something, it seems to exist, although it might not really exist • *an effort to restore a semblance of normality.*

semi- PREFIX 'Semi-' means half or partly • *semiskilled workers.*

semifinal NOUN The semifinals are the two matches in a competition played to decide who plays in the final. **semifinalist** NOUN

seminar NOUN a meeting of a small number of university students or teachers to discuss a particular topic.

Senate NOUN The Senate is the smaller, more important of the two councils in the government of some countries, for example Australia, Canada and the USA.

senator NOUN a member of a Senate.

send, **sends, sending, sent** VERB ① If you send something to someone, you arrange for it to be delivered to them. ② To send a radio signal or message means to transmit it. ③ If you send someone somewhere, you tell them to go there or arrange for them to go. ④ If you send for someone, you send a message asking them to come and see you. ⑤ If you send off for something, you write and ask for it to be sent to you. ⑥ To send people or things in a particular direction means to make them move in that direction • *It should have sent him tumbling from the saddle.* **send up** VERB If you send someone or something up, you imitate them and make fun of them.

> **send** VERB
> ① = dispatch, forward, remit
> ② = broadcast, stream, transmit

senile ADJECTIVE If elderly people become senile, they become confused and cannot look after themselves. **senility** NOUN

senior ADJECTIVE ① The senior people in an organisation or profession have the highest and most important jobs. ▶ NOUN ② Someone who is your senior is older than you. **seniority** NOUN

> **senior** ADJECTIVE
> ① = best, better, high-ranking, superior
> ≠ junior

senior citizen NOUN an elderly person, especially one receiving a retirement pension.

sensation NOUN ① a feeling, especially a physical feeling. ② If something is a sensation, it causes great excitement and interest.

sensational ADJECTIVE ① causing great excitement and interest. ② (*informal*) extremely good • *a sensational party.* **sensationally** ADVERB

sense NOUN ① Your senses are the physical abilities of sight, hearing, smell, touch and taste. ② a feeling • *a sense of guilt.* ③ A sense of a word is one of its meanings. ④ Sense is the ability to think and behave sensibly. ▶ VERB ⑤ If you sense something, you become aware of it. ▶ PHRASE ⑥ If something **makes sense**, you can understand it or it seems sensible • *It makes sense to find out as much as you can.*

sense NOUN
② = consciousness, feeling, impression
④ = brains (*informal*), common sense, intelligence, judgment, reason, wisdom
▶ VERB ⑤ = be aware of, feel, get the impression, have a hunch, realise

senseless ADJECTIVE ① A senseless action has no meaning or purpose • *senseless destruction*. ② If someone is senseless, they are unconscious.

sensibility NOUN Your sensibility is your ability to experience deep feelings • *a man of sensibility rather than reason*.

sensible ADJECTIVE showing good sense and judgment. **sensibly** ADVERB

sensible ADJECTIVE
= down-to-earth, judicious (*formal*), practical, prudent, rational, sound, wise
≠ foolish

sensitive ADJECTIVE ① If you are sensitive to other people's feelings, you understand them. ② If you are sensitive about something, you are worried or easily upset about it • *He was sensitive about his height*. ③ A sensitive subject or issue needs to be dealt with carefully because it can make people angry or upset. ④ Something that is sensitive to a particular thing is easily affected or harmed by it. **sensitively** ADVERB

sensitive ADJECTIVE
② = easily offended, easily upset, thin-skinned, touchy

sensitivity NOUN ① the quality of being sensitive. ② the ability of a plant or animal to respond to external stimuli such as light, sound, movement or temperature.

sensor NOUN an instrument which reacts to physical conditions such as light or heat.

sensual [*Said* **senss**-*yool*] ADJECTIVE giving pleasure to your physical senses rather than to your mind • *the sensual rhythm of his voice*. **sensuality** NOUN

sensuous ADJECTIVE giving pleasure through the senses. **sensuously** ADVERB

sentence NOUN ① a group of words which make a statement, question or command. When written down a sentence begins with a capital letter and ends with a full stop. ② In a law court, a sentence is a punishment given to someone who has been found guilty. ▶ VERB ③ When a guilty person is sentenced, they are told officially what their punishment will be.

sentiment NOUN ① a feeling, attitude or opinion • *I doubt my parents share my sentiments*. ② Sentiment consists of feelings such as tenderness or sadness • *There's no room for sentiment in business*.

sentimental ADJECTIVE ① feeling or expressing tenderness or sadness to an exaggerated extent • *sentimental love stories*. ② relating to a person's emotions • *things of sentimental value*. ③ ENGLISH Sentimental literature is intended to provoke an emotional response to the story, rather than relying on the reader's own natural response. **sentimentality** NOUN

sentimental ADJECTIVE
① = maudlin, mushy (*informal*), nostalgic, sloppy (*informal*), slushy (*informal*)

sentinel NOUN (*old-fashioned*) a sentry.

sentry NOUN a soldier who keeps watch and guards a camp or building.

separate ADJECTIVE [*Said* **sep**-*ir-it*] ① If something is separate from something else, the two things are

a b c d e f g h i j k l m n o p q r s t u v w x y z

not connected. ▶ **VERB** *[Said* ***sep****-ir-ate]* ② To separate people or things means to cause them to be apart from each other. ③ If people or things separate, they move away from each other. ④ If a married couple separate, they decide to live apart. **separately** **ADVERB** **separation** **NOUN**

> **separate** **ADJECTIVE**
> ① = detached, disconnected, discrete, divorced, isolated, unconnected
> ≠ connected
> ▶ **VERB** ② = detach, disconnect, divide
> ≠ connect
> ④ = break up, divorce, part, split up

sepia *[Said* ***see****-pee-a]* **ADJECTIVE, NOUN** deep brown, like the colour of old photographs.

September **NOUN** September is the ninth month of the year. It has 30 days.

septic **ADJECTIVE** If a wound becomes septic, it becomes infected with poison.

sequel **NOUN** ① A sequel to a book or film is another book or film which continues the story. ② The sequel to an event is a result or consequence of it • *There's a sequel to my egg story.*

sequence **NOUN** ① A sequence of events is a number of them coming one after the other • *the whole sequence of events that had brought me to this place.* ② The sequence in which things are arranged is the order in which they are arranged • *Do things in the right sequence.*

> **sequence** **NOUN**
> ① = chain, course, cycle, progression, series, string, succession
> ② = arrangement, order, pattern, progression, structure

sequin **NOUN** Sequins are small, shiny, coloured discs sewn on clothes to decorate them.

Serbian **ADJECTIVE** ① belonging or relating to Serbia. ▶ **NOUN** ② someone who comes from Serbia.

serenade **VERB** ① If you serenade someone you love, you sing or play music to them outside their window. ▶ **NOUN** ② a song sung outside a person's window by someone who loves them.

serene **ADJECTIVE** peaceful and calm • *She had a serene air.* **serenely** **ADVERB** **serenity** **NOUN**

sergeant **NOUN** ① a noncommissioned officer of middle rank in the army or air force. ② a police officer just above a constable in rank.

serial **NOUN** a story which is broadcast or published in a number of parts over a period of time • *a television serial.*

series, **series** **NOUN** ① A series of things is a number of them coming one after the other • *a series of loud explosions.* ② A radio or television series is a set of programmes with the same title.

> **series** **NOUN**
> ① = chain, run, sequence, string, succession

serious **ADJECTIVE** ① A serious problem or situation is very bad and worrying. ② Serious matters are important and should be thought about carefully. ③ If you are serious about something, you are sincere about it • *You are really serious about having a baby.* ④ People who are serious are thoughtful, quiet and do not laugh much. **seriousness** **NOUN**

> **serious** **ADJECTIVE**
> ① = acute, alarming, bad, critical, dangerous, extreme, grave (*formal*), grievous, grim, intense, precarious, severe, worrying
> ② = crucial, deep, difficult,

far-reaching, grave (*formal*), important, momentous, pressing, profound, significant, urgent, weighty
≠ funny
③ = earnest, genuine, heartfelt, honest, in earnest, resolute, resolved, sincere
④ = earnest, grave, humourless, pensive, sober, solemn, staid, stern

seriously ADVERB ① You say seriously to emphasise that you mean what you say • *Seriously, though, something must be done.* ▸ PHRASE ② If you **take something seriously**, you regard it as important.

sermon NOUN a talk on a religious or moral subject given as part of a church service.

serpent NOUN (*literary*) a snake.

serrated ADJECTIVE having a row of V-shaped points along the edge, like a saw • *green serrated leaves.*

servant NOUN someone who is employed to work in another person's house.

serve VERB ① If you serve a country, an organisation or a person, you do useful work for them. ② To serve as something means to act or be used as that thing • *the room that served as their office.* ③ If something serves people in a particular place, it provides them with something they need • *a recycling plant which serves the whole of the county.* ④ If you serve food or drink to people, you give it to them. ⑤ To serve customers in a shop means to help them and provide them with what they want. ⑥ To serve a prison sentence or an apprenticeship means to spend time doing it. ⑦ When you serve in tennis or badminton, you throw the ball or shuttlecock into the air and hit it over the net to start playing. ▸ NOUN ⑧ the act of serving in tennis or badminton.

server NOUN ① ICT a computer or computer program which supplies information or resources to a number of computers on a network. ② a spoon or fork used for serving food • *salad servers.*

service NOUN ① a system organised to provide something for the public • *the bus service.* ② Some government organisations are called services • *the diplomatic service.* ③ The services are the army, the navy and the air force. ④ If you give your services to a person or organisation, you work for them or help them in some way • *services to the community.* ⑤ In a shop or restaurant, service is the process of being served. ⑥ a religious ceremony. ⑦ When it is your service in a game of tennis or badminton, it is your turn to serve. ⑧ (*in plural*) Motorway services consist of a petrol station, restaurant, shop and toilets. ▸ VERB ⑨ When a machine or vehicle is serviced, it is examined and adjusted so that it will continue working efficiently.

serviceman, servicemen NOUN a man in the army, navy or air force.

service station NOUN a garage that sells petrol, oil, spare parts and snacks.

servicewoman, servicewomen NOUN a woman in the army, navy or air force.

serving NOUN ① a helping of food. ▸ ADJECTIVE ② A serving spoon or dish is used for serving food.

session NOUN ① a meeting of an official group • *the emergency session of the Indiana Supreme Court.* ② a period during which meetings are held regularly • *the end of the parliamentary session.* ③ The period during which an activity takes place can also be called a session • *a yoga session.*

set, sets, setting, set NOUN ① Several things make a set when they belong together or form a group • *a set of weights.* ② MATHS In maths, a set is a collection of numbers or other things which are treated as a group. ③ A television set is a television. ④ The set for a play or film is the scenery or furniture on the stage or in the studio. ⑤ In tennis, a set is a group of six or more games. There are usually several sets in a match. ▸ VERB ⑥ If something is set somewhere, that is where it is • *The house was set back from the beach.* ⑦ When the sun sets, it goes below the horizon. ⑧ When you set the table, you prepare it for a meal by putting plates and cutlery on it. ⑨ When you set a clock or a control, you adjust it to a particular point or position. ⑩ If you set someone a piece of work or a target, you give it to them to do or to achieve. ⑪ When something such as jelly or cement sets, it becomes firm or hard. ▸ ADJECTIVE ⑫ Something that is set is fixed and not varying • *a set charge.* ⑬ If you are set to do something, you are ready or likely to do it. ⑭ If you are set on doing something, you are determined to do it. ⑮ If a play or story is set at a particular time or in a particular place, the events in it take place at that time or in that place.
set about VERB If you set about doing something, you start doing it.
set back VERB If something sets back a project or scheme, it delays it.
set off VERB ① When you set off, you start a journey. ② To set something off means to cause it to start. **set out** VERB ① When you set out, you start a journey. ② If you set out to do something, you start trying to do it.
set up VERB If you set something up, you make all the necessary preparations for it • *We have done all we can about setting up a system of communication.*

set NOUN
① = batch, kit, outfit, series
▸ VERB ⑥ = deposit, lay, locate, place, position, put, rest, stick
▸ ADJECTIVE ⑫ = arranged, established, firm, fixed, predetermined, scheduled
⑭ = bent on, determined, intent on
▸ **set up** = arrange, establish, install, institute, organise

setback NOUN PSHE something that stops you from making progress.

settee NOUN a long comfortable seat for two or three people to sit on.

setter NOUN a long-haired breed of dog originally used in hunting.

setting NOUN ① The setting of something is its surroundings or circumstances • *The Irish setting made the story realistic.* ② The settings on a machine are the different positions to which the controls can be adjusted.

settle VERB ① To settle an argument means to put an end to it • *The dispute was settled.* ② If something is settled, it has all been decided and arranged. ③ If you settle on something or settle for it, you choose it • *We settled for orange juice and coffee.* ④ When you settle a bill, you pay it. ⑤ If you settle in a place, you make it your permanent home. ⑥ If you settle yourself somewhere, you sit down and make yourself comfortable. ⑦ If something settles, it sinks slowly down and comes to rest • *A black dust settled on the walls.* **settle down** VERB ① When someone settles down, they start living a quiet life in one place, especially when they get married. ② To settle down means to become quiet or calm.

settle VERB
① = clear up, decide, dispose of, put an end to, reconcile, resolve, straighten out

② = agree, arrange, decide on, determine, fix
⑤ = make your home, move to, people, populate

settlement NOUN ① an official agreement between people who have been involved in a conflict • *the last chance for a peaceful settlement.* ② GEOGRAPHY a place where people have settled and built homes.

settler NOUN someone who settles in a new country • *the first settlers in Cuba.*

seven the number 7.

seventeen the number 17. **seventeenth** ADJECTIVE

seventh ADJECTIVE ① The seventh item in a series is the one counted as number seven. ▶ NOUN ② one of seven equal parts.

seventy, **seventies** the number 70. **seventieth** ADJECTIVE

sever VERB ① To sever something means to cut it off or cut right through it. ② If you sever a connection with someone or something, you end it completely • *She severed her ties with England.*

several ADJECTIVE Several people or things means a small number of them.

several ADJECTIVE
= assorted, some, sundry, various

severe ADJECTIVE ① extremely bad or unpleasant • *severe stomach pains.* ② stern and harsh • *Perhaps I was too severe with that young man.* **severely** ADVERB **severity** NOUN

severe ADJECTIVE
① = acute, critical, deep, dire, extreme, grave (*formal*), intense, serious, terrible
≠ mild
② = disapproving, grim, hard, harsh, stern, strict

sew, **sews**, **sewing**, **sewed**, **sewn** [*Said so*] VERB DGT When you sew things together, you join them using a needle and thread. **sewing** NOUN

sewage [*Said soo-ij*] NOUN Sewage is dirty water and waste which is carried away in sewers.

sewer NOUN an underground channel that carries sewage to a place where it is treated to make it harmless.

sewerage NOUN Sewerage is the system by which sewage is carried away and treated.

sex NOUN ① The sexes are the two groups, male and female, into which people and animals are divided. ② The sex of a person or animal is their characteristic of being either male or female. ③ Sex is the physical activity by which people and animals produce young.

sexism NOUN Sexism is discrimination against the members of one gender, usually women. **sexist** ADJECTIVE, NOUN

sextet NOUN ① MUSIC a group of six musicians who sing or play together; also a piece of music written for six instruments or singers. ② ENGLISH six lines of poetry together, especially linked by a pattern of rhyme.

sexual ADJECTIVE ① connected with the act of sex or with people's desire for sex • *sexual attraction.* ② relating to the difference between males and females • *sexual equality.* ③ relating to the biological process by which people and animals produce young • *sexual reproduction.* **sexually** ADVERB

sexuality [*Said seks-yoo-al-it-ee*] NOUN ① A person's sexuality is their ability to experience sexual feelings. ② You can refer to a person's sexuality when you are talking about whether they are sexually attracted to people of the same sex or a different sex.

shabby, **shabbier**, **shabbiest** **ADJECTIVE** ① old and worn in appearance • *a shabby overcoat*. ② dressed in old, worn-out clothes • *a shabby figure crouching in a doorway*. ③ behaving in a mean or unfair way • *shabby treatment*. **shabbily ADVERB**

> **shabby ADJECTIVE**
> ① = dilapidated, ragged, scruffy, seedy, tatty, threadbare, worn
> ③ = contemptible, despicable, dirty, mean, rotten (*informal*)

shack NOUN a small hut.

shackle NOUN ① In the past, shackles were two metal rings joined by a chain fastened around a prisoner's wrists or ankles. ▸ **VERB** ② To shackle someone means to put shackles on them. ③ (*literary*) If you are shackled by something, it restricts or hampers you.

shade NOUN ① Shade is an area of darkness and coolness which the sun does not reach • *The table was in the shade*. ② a lampshade. ③ The shades of a colour are its different forms. For example, olive green is a shade of green. ▸ **VERB** ④ If a place is shaded by trees or buildings, they prevent the sun from shining on it. ⑤ If you shade your eyes, you put your hand in front of them to protect them from a bright light.

shadow NOUN ① the dark shape made when an object prevents light from reaching a surface. ② Shadow is darkness caused by light not reaching a place. ▸ **VERB** ③ To shadow someone means to follow them and watch them closely.

shadow cabinet NOUN The shadow cabinet consists of the leaders of the main opposition party, each of whom is concerned with a particular policy.

shadowy ADJECTIVE ① A shadowy place is dark and full of shadows. ② A shadowy figure or shape is difficult to see because it is dark or misty.

shady, **shadier**, **shadiest ADJECTIVE** A shady place is sheltered from sunlight by trees or buildings.

shaft NOUN ① a vertical passage, for example one for a lift or one in a mine. ② A shaft of light is a beam of light. ③ DGT A shaft in a machine is a rod which revolves and transfers movement in the machine • *the drive shaft*.

shaggy, **shaggier**, **shaggiest ADJECTIVE** Shaggy hair or fur is long and untidy.

shake, **shakes**, **shaking**, **shook**, **shaken VERB** ① To shake something means to move it quickly from side to side or up and down. ② If something shakes, it moves from side to side or up and down with small, quick movements. ③ If your voice shakes, it trembles because you are nervous or angry. ④ If something shakes you, it shocks and upsets you. ⑤ When you shake your head, you move it from side to side in order to say 'no'. ▸ **NOUN** ⑥ If you give something a shake, you shake it. ▸ **PHRASE** ⑦ When you **shake hands** with someone, you grasp their hand as a way of greeting them.

> **shake VERB**
> ① = agitate, brandish, flourish, wave
> ② = jolt, quake, quiver, shiver, shudder, tremble, vibrate
> ④ = distress, disturb, rattle (*informal*), shock, unnerve, upset

shaky, **shakier**, **shakiest ADJECTIVE** rather weak and unsteady • *Confidence in the economy is still shaky*. **shakily ADVERB**

> **shaky ADJECTIVE**
> = rickety, tottering, trembling, unstable, unsteady, wobbly

shall VERB ① If I say I shall do something, I mean that I intend to do it. ② If I say something shall happen,

I am emphasising that it will definitely happen, or I am ordering it to happen • *You shall go to the ball!* ③ 'Shall' is also used in questions when you are asking what to do, or making a suggestion • *Shall we sit down?* • *Shall I go and check for you?*

shallow ADJECTIVE ① Shallow means not deep. ② Shallow also means not involving serious thought or sincere feelings • *a well-meaning but shallow man*.

sham NOUN ① Something that is a sham is not real or genuine. ▸ ADJECTIVE ② not real or genuine • *a sham display of affection*.

shambles NOUN (*informal*) If an event is a shambles, it is confused and badly organised.

shame NOUN ① Shame is the feeling of guilt or embarrassment you get when you know you have done something wrong or foolish. ② Shame is also something that makes people lose respect for you • *the scenes that brought shame to English soccer*. ③ If you say something is a shame, you mean you are sorry about it • *It's a shame you can't come round*. ▸ INTERJECTION ④ (*informal*) In South African English, you say 'Shame!' to show sympathy. ▸ VERB ⑤ If something shames you, it makes you feel ashamed. ⑥ If you shame someone into doing something, you force them to do it by making them feel ashamed not to • *Two children shamed their parents into giving up cigarettes*.

> **shame** NOUN
> ① = embarrassment, humiliation, ignominy
> ② = discredit, disgrace, dishonour, scandal
> ▸ VERB ⑤ = disgrace, embarrass, humiliate

shameful ADJECTIVE If someone's behaviour is shameful, they ought to be ashamed of it. **shamefully** ADVERB

shameless ADJECTIVE behaving in an indecent or unacceptable way, but showing no shame • *shameless dishonesty*. **shamelessly** ADVERB

> **shameless** ADJECTIVE
> = barefaced, brazen, flagrant, unabashed, unashamed

shampoo NOUN ① Shampoo is a soapy liquid used for washing your hair. ▸ VERB ② When you shampoo your hair, you wash it with shampoo.

shanty NOUN ① a small, rough hut. ② A sea shanty is a song sailors used to sing.

shape NOUN ① The shape of something is the form or pattern of its outline, for example whether it is round or square. ② MATHS something with a definite form, for example a circle or triangle. ③ The shape of something such as an organisation is its structure and size. ▸ VERB ④ If you shape an object, you form it into a particular shape • *Shape the dough into an oblong*. ⑤ To shape something means to cause it to develop in a particular way • *events that shaped the lives of some of the leading characters*.

> **shape** NOUN
> ① = contours, figure, form, lines, outline
> ▸ VERB ④ = fashion, form, make, model, mould

shapeless ADJECTIVE not having a definite shape.

shapely ADJECTIVE having an attractive figure.

shard NOUN a small fragment of pottery, glass or metal.

share VERB ① If two people share something, they both use it, do it or have it • *We shared a bottle of orange juice*. ② If you share an idea or a piece of news with someone, you tell it to them. ▸ **NOUN** ③ A share of something is a portion of it. ④ The shares of a company are the equal parts into which its ownership is divided. People can buy shares as an investment. **share out VERB** If you share something out, you give it out equally among a group of people.

share VERB
① = divide, split
▸ **NOUN** ③ = allotment, portion, quota, ration

shareholder NOUN a person who owns shares in a company.

shark NOUN ① Sharks are large, powerful fish with sharp teeth. ② (*informal*) a person who cheats people out of money.

sharp, **sharpest ADJECTIVE** ① A sharp object has a fine edge or point that is good for cutting or piercing things. ② A sharp outline or distinction is easy to see. ③ A sharp person is quick to notice or understand things. ④ A sharp change is sudden and significant • *a sharp rise in prices*. ⑤ If you say something in a sharp way, you say it firmly and rather angrily. ⑥ A sharp sound is short, sudden and quite loud. ⑦ A sharp pain is a sudden pain. ⑧ A sharp taste is slightly sour. ⑨ A musical instrument or note that is sharp is slightly too high in pitch. ▸ **ADVERB** ⑩ If something happens at a certain time sharp, it happens at that time precisely • *You'll begin at eight o'clock sharp*. ▸ **NOUN** ⑪ In music, a sharp is a note or key a semitone higher than that described by the same letter. It is represented by the symbol (♯). **sharply ADVERB sharpness NOUN**

sharp ADJECTIVE
① = jagged, keen, pointed, razor-sharp
≠ blunt
③ = alert, astute, bright, observant, perceptive, quick, quick-witted
④ = abrupt, marked, sudden

sharpen VERB ① To sharpen an object means to make its edge or point sharper. ② If your senses or abilities sharpen, you become quicker at noticing or understanding things. ③ If you voice sharpens, you begin to speak more angrily or harshly. ④ If something sharpens the disagreements between people, it makes them greater.

shatter VERB ① If something shatters, it breaks into a lot of small pieces. ② If something shatters your hopes or beliefs, it destroys them completely. ③ If you are shattered by an event or piece of news, you are shocked and upset by it.

shattered ADJECTIVE (*informal*) completely exhausted • *He must be absolutely shattered after all his efforts*.

shattering ADJECTIVE making you feel shocked and upset • *a shattering event*.

shave, **shaves**, **shaving**, **shaved VERB** ① When a person shaves, they remove hair from a part of their body with a razor. ② If you shave off part of a piece of wood, you cut thin pieces from it. ▸ **NOUN** ③ When a man has a shave, he shaves.

shaven ADJECTIVE If part of someone's body is shaven, it has been shaved.

shawl NOUN a large piece of woollen cloth worn round a person's head or shoulders or used to wrap a baby in.

she PRONOUN 'She' is used to refer to a woman or girl whose identity is clear. 'She' is also used to refer to a country, a ship or a car.

sheaf, **sheaves NOUN** ① A sheaf of papers is a bundle of them. ② A sheaf of corn is a bundle of ripe corn tied together.

shear, **shears**, **shearing**, **sheared**, **shorn** VERB To shear a sheep means to cut off its wool.

shearer NOUN someone whose job is to shear sheep.

sheath NOUN a covering for the blade of a knife.

shed, **sheds**, **shedding**, **shed** NOUN ① a small building used for storing things. ▸ VERB ② When an animal sheds hair or skin, some of its hair or skin drops off. When a tree sheds its leaves, its leaves fall off. ③ (*formal*) To shed something also means to get rid of it • *The firm is to shed 700 jobs.* ④ If a lorry sheds its load, the load falls off the lorry onto the road. ⑤ If you shed tears, you cry.

sheen NOUN a gentle brightness on the surface of something.

sheep, **sheep** NOUN A sheep is a farm animal with a thick woolly coat. Sheep are kept for meat and wool.

sheepdog NOUN a breed of dog often used for controlling sheep.

sheepish ADJECTIVE If you look sheepish, you look embarrassed because you feel shy or foolish. **sheepishly** ADVERB

sheepskin NOUN Sheepskin is the skin and wool of a sheep, used for making rugs and coats.

sheer ADJECTIVE ① Sheer means complete and total • *sheer exhaustion.* ② A sheer cliff or drop is vertical. ③ Sheer fabrics are very light and delicate.

> **sheer** ADJECTIVE
> ① = absolute, complete, pure, total, unqualified, utter
> ② = perpendicular, steep, vertical
> ③ = delicate, fine, lightweight, thin
> ≠ thick

sheet NOUN ① a large rectangular piece of cloth used to cover a bed. ② A sheet of paper is a rectangular piece of it. ③ A sheet of glass or metal is a large, flat piece of it.

sheik [*Said shake*]; also spelt **sheikh** NOUN an Arab chief or ruler.

shelf, **shelves** NOUN a flat piece of wood, metal or glass fixed to a wall and used for putting things on.

shell NOUN ① The shell of an egg or nut is its hard covering. ② The shell of a tortoise, snail or crab is the hard protective covering on its back. ③ The shell of a building or other structure is its frame • *The room was just an empty shell.* ④ a container filled with explosives that can be fired from a gun. ▸ VERB ⑤ If you shell peas or nuts, you remove their natural covering. ⑥ To shell a place means to fire large explosive shells at it.

shellfish, **shellfish** or **shellfishes** NOUN a small sea creature with a shell.

shelter NOUN ① a small building made to protect people from bad weather or danger. ② If a place provides shelter, it provides protection from bad weather or danger. ▸ VERB ③ If you shelter in a place, you stay there and are safe. ④ If you shelter someone, you provide them with a place to stay when they are in danger.

> **shelter** NOUN
> ① = hostel, refuge, sanctuary
> ② = asylum, cover, harbour, haven, protection, refuge, safety, sanctuary
> ▸ VERB ③ = hide, huddle, take cover
> ④ = harbour, hide, protect, shield

sheltered ADJECTIVE ① A sheltered place is protected from wind and rain. ② If you lead a sheltered life, you do not experience unpleasant or upsetting things. ③ Sheltered accommodation is accommodation designed for old or disabled people.

shelve VERB If you shelve a plan, you decide to postpone it for a while.

shepherd NOUN ① a person who looks after sheep. ▶ VERB ② If you shepherd someone somewhere, you accompany them there.

sheriff NOUN ① In America, a sheriff is a person elected to enforce the law in a county. ② In Australia, a sheriff is an administrative officer of the Supreme Court who carries out writs and judgments.

sherry, **sherries** NOUN Sherry is a kind of strong wine.

shield NOUN ① a large piece of a strong material like metal or plastic which soldiers or police officers carry to protect themselves. ② If something is a shield against something, it gives protection from it. ▶ VERB ③ To shield someone means to protect them from something.

shift VERB ① If you shift something, you move it. If something shifts, it moves • *to shift the rubble.* ② If an opinion or situation shifts, it changes slightly. ▶ NOUN ③ A shift in an opinion or situation is a slight change. ④ a set period during which people work • *the night shift.*

shilling NOUN a former British, Australian and New Zealand coin worth one-twentieth of a pound.

shimmer VERB ① If something shimmers, it shines with a faint, flickering light. ▶ NOUN ② a faint, flickering light.

shin, **shins**, **shinning**, **shinned** NOUN ① Your shin is the front part of your leg between your knee and your ankle. ▶ VERB ② If you shin up a tree or pole, you climb it quickly by gripping it with your hands and legs.

shine, **shines**, **shining**, **shone** VERB ① When something shines, it gives out or reflects a bright light • *The stars shone brilliantly.* ② If you shine a torch or lamp somewhere, you point it there.

shine VERB
① = beam, gleam, glow, radiate, shimmer, sparkle

shingle NOUN ① GEOGRAPHY Shingle consists of small pebbles on the seashore. ② Shingles are small wooden roof tiles. ③ Shingles is a disease that causes a painful red rash, especially around the waist.

shining ADJECTIVE ① Shining things are very bright, usually because they are reflecting light • *shining stainless steel tables.* ② A shining example of something is a very good or typical example of that thing • *a shining example of courage.*

shining ADJECTIVE
① = bright, brilliant, gleaming, luminous, radiant, shimmering, sparkling

shiny, **shinier**, **shiniest** ADJECTIVE Shiny things are bright and look as if they have been polished • *a shiny brass plate.*

ship, **ships**, **shipping**, **shipped** NOUN ① a large boat which carries passengers or cargo. ▶ VERB ② If people or things are shipped somewhere, they are transported there.

-ship SUFFIX '-ship' is used to form nouns that refer to a condition or position • *fellowship.*

shipment NOUN ① a quantity of goods that are transported somewhere • *a shipment of olive oil.* ② The shipment of goods is the transporting of them.

shipping NOUN ① Shipping is the transport of cargo on ships. ② You can also refer to ships generally as shipping • *Attention all shipping!*

shipwreck NOUN When there is a shipwreck, a ship is destroyed in an accident at sea • *He was drowned in a shipwreck.*

shipyard NOUN a place where ships are built and repaired.

shire NOUN ① In Britain, 'shire' is an old word for a county. ② In Australia, a shire is a rural district with its own local council.

shirk VERB To shirk a task means to avoid doing it.

shirt NOUN a piece of clothing worn on the upper part of the body, with a collar, sleeves, and buttons down the front.

shiver VERB ① When you shiver, you tremble slightly because you are cold or scared. ▶ NOUN ② a slight trembling caused by cold or fear.

shoal NOUN A shoal of fish is a large group of them swimming together.

shock NOUN ① If you have a shock, you have a sudden upsetting experience. ② Shock is a person's emotional and physical condition when something very unpleasant or upsetting has happened to them. ③ In medicine, shock is a serious physical condition in which the blood cannot circulate properly because of an injury. ④ a slight movement in something when it is hit by something else • *The straps help to absorb shocks.* ⑤ A shock of hair is a thick mass of it. ▶ VERB ⑥ If something shocks you, it upsets you because it is unpleasant and unexpected • *I was shocked by his appearance.* ⑦ You can say that something shocks you when it offends you because it is rude or immoral. **shocked** ADJECTIVE

> **shock** NOUN
> ① = blow, bombshell, distress, trauma
> ▶ VERB ⑥ = numb, paralyse, shake, stagger, stun, traumatise
> ⑦ = appal, disgust, offend, outrage

shocking ADJECTIVE ① (*informal*) very bad • *a shocking set of exam results.* ② disgusting or horrifying • *shocking images.*

shod the past tense and past participle of **shoe**.

shoddy, **shoddier**, **shoddiest** ADJECTIVE badly made or done • *a shoddy piece of work.*

shoe, **shoes**, **shoeing**, **shod** NOUN ① Shoes are strong coverings for your feet. They cover most of your foot, but not your ankle. ▶ VERB ② To shoe a horse means to fix horseshoes onto its hooves.

shoestring NOUN (*informal*) If you do something on a shoestring, you do it using very little money.

shone the past tense and past participle of **shine**.

shook the past tense of **shake**.

shoot, **shoots**, **shooting**, **shot** VERB ① To shoot a person or animal means to kill or injure them by firing a gun at them. ② To shoot an arrow means to fire it from a bow. ③ If something shoots in a particular direction, it moves there quickly and suddenly • *They shot back into Green Street.* ④ When a film is shot, it is filmed • *The whole film was shot in California.* ⑤ In games such as football or hockey, to shoot means to kick or hit the ball towards the goal. ▶ NOUN ⑥ an occasion when people hunt animals or birds with guns. ⑦ a plant that is beginning to grow, or a new part growing from a plant.

shooting NOUN an incident in which someone is shot.

shop, **shops**, **shopping**, **shopped** NOUN ① a place where things are sold. ② a place where a particular type of work is done • *a bicycle repair shop.* ▶ VERB ③ When you shop, you go to the shops to buy things. **shopper** NOUN

> **shop** NOUN
> ① = boutique, market, store, supermarket

shopkeeper NOUN someone who owns or manages a small shop.

shoplifting NOUN Shoplifting is stealing goods from shops.
shoplifter NOUN

shopping NOUN Your shopping is the goods you have bought from the shops.

shore NOUN ① The shore of a sea, lake or wide river is the land along the edge of it. ▶ VERB ② If you shore something up, you reinforce it or strengthen it • *a short-term solution to shore up the worst defence in the League.*

shoreline NOUN the edge of a sea, lake or wide river.

shorn ① Shorn is the past participle of **shear**. ▶ ADJECTIVE ② Grass or hair that is shorn is cut very short.

short ADJECTIVE ① not lasting very long. ② small in length, distance or height • *a short climb* • *the short road.* ③ not using many words • *a short speech.* ④ If you are short with someone, you speak to them crossly. ⑤ If you have a short temper, you get angry very quickly. ⑥ If you are short of something, you do not have enough of it. ⑦ If a name is short for another name, it is a short version of it. ▶ NOUN ⑧ (*in plural*) Shorts are trousers with short legs. ▶ ADVERB ⑨ If you stop short of a place, you do not quite reach it. ▶ PHRASE ⑩ **Short of** is used to say that a level or amount has not quite been reached • *a hundred votes short of a majority.*

> **short** ADJECTIVE
> ① = brief, fleeting, momentary, short-lived
> ≠ long
> ② = diminutive, little, small, tiny
> ≠ tall
> ③ = brief, concise, succinct, terse

shortage NOUN If there is a shortage of something, there is not enough of it.

> **shortage** NOUN
> = dearth, deficiency, lack, scarcity, shortfall, want
> ≠ abundance

shortcoming NOUN Shortcomings are faults or weaknesses.

shortcut NOUN ① a quicker way of getting somewhere than the usual route. ② a quicker way of doing something • *Stencils have been used as a shortcut to hand painting.*

shorten VERB If you shorten something or if it shortens, it becomes shorter • *This might help to shorten the conversation.*

> **shorten** VERB
> = abbreviate, cut, trim
> ≠ lengthen

shortfall NOUN If there is a shortfall in something, there is less than you need.

shorthand NOUN Shorthand is a way of writing in which signs represent words or syllables. It is used to write down quickly what someone is saying.

short-list NOUN ① a list of people selected from a larger group, from which one person is finally selected for a job or prize. ▶ VERB ② If someone is short-listed for a job or prize, they are put on a short-list.

shortly ADVERB ① Shortly means soon • *I'll be back shortly.* ② If you speak to someone shortly, you speak to them in a cross and impatient way.

short-sighted ADJECTIVE ① If you are short-sighted, you cannot see things clearly when they are far away. ② A short-sighted decision does not take account of the way things may develop in the future.

short-term ADJECTIVE happening or having an effect within a short time or for a short time.

shot ① Shot is the past tense and past participle of **shoot**. ▶ NOUN ② the act of firing a gun. ③ Someone who is a good shot can shoot accurately. ④ In football, golf and tennis, a shot is the act of kicking or hitting the ball. ⑤ a photograph or short film sequence • *I'd like to get some shots of the river.* ⑥ (*informal*) If you have a shot at something, you try to do it.

shotgun NOUN a gun that fires a lot of small pellets all at once.

shot put NOUN In athletics, the shot put is an event in which the contestants throw a heavy metal ball called a shot as far as possible. **shot putter** NOUN

should VERB ① You use 'should' to say that something ought to happen • *Ward should have done better.* ② You also use 'should' to say that you expect something to happen • *He should have heard by now.* ③ (*formal*) You can use 'should' to announce that you are about to do or say something • *I should like to express my thanks to the Professor.* ④ 'Should' is used in conditional sentences • *If you should see Kerr, tell him I have his umbrella.* ⑤ 'Should' is sometimes used in 'that' clauses • *It is inevitable that you should go.* ⑥ If you say that you should think something, you mean that it is probably true • *I should think that's unlikely.*

shoulder NOUN ① Your shoulders are the parts of your body between your neck and the tops of your arms. ▶ VERB ② If you shoulder something heavy, you put it across one of your shoulders to carry it. ③ If you shoulder the responsibility or blame for something, you accept it.

shout NOUN ① a loud call or cry. ▶ VERB ② If you shout something, you say it very loudly • *He shouted something to his brother.* **shout down** VERB If you shout someone down, you prevent them from being heard by shouting at them.

shout NOUN
① = bellow, cry, roar, scream, yell
▶ VERB ② = bawl, bellow, call, cry, roar, scream, yell

shove VERB ① If you shove someone or something, you push them roughly • *He shoved his wallet into a back pocket.* ▶ NOUN ② a rough push. **shove off** VERB (*informal*) If you tell someone to shove off, you are telling them angrily and rudely to go away.

shovel, **shovels**, **shovelling**, **shovelled** NOUN ① a tool like a spade, used for moving earth or snow. ▶ VERB ② If you shovel earth or snow, you move it with a shovel.

show, **shows**, **showing**, **showed**, **shown** VERB ① To show that something exists or is true means to prove it • *The survey showed that 29 per cent would now approve the treaty.* ② If a picture shows something, it represents it • *The painting shows supporters and crowd scenes.* ③ If you show someone something, you let them see it • *Show me your passport.* ④ If you show someone to a room or seat, you lead them there. ⑤ If you show someone how to do something, you demonstrate it to them. ⑥ If something shows, it is visible. ⑦ If something shows a quality or characteristic, you can see that it has it • *Her sketches and watercolours showed promise.* ⑧ If you show your feelings, you let people see them • *She was flustered, but too proud to show it.* ⑨ If you show affection or mercy, you behave in an affectionate or merciful way • *the first person who showed me some affection.* ⑩ To show a film or television programme means to let the public see it. ▸ **NOUN** ⑪ a form of light entertainment at the theatre or on television. ⑫ an exhibition • *the Napier Antiques Show*. ⑬ A show of a feeling or attitude is behaviour in which you show it • *a show of optimism*. ▸ **PHRASE** ⑭ If something is **on show**, it is being exhibited for the public to see. **show off** **VERB** (*informal*) If someone is showing off, they are trying to impress people. **show up** **VERB** ① (*informal*) If you show up, you arrive at a place. ② If something shows up, it can be seen clearly • *Her bones were too soft to show up on an X-ray*.

show **VERB**
① = demonstrate, prove
⑤ = demonstrate, instruct, teach
⑦ = demonstrate, display, indicate, manifest (*formal*), reveal
▸ **NOUN** ⑫ = display, exhibition, presentation
⑬ = air, display, pose, pretence, semblance

show business **NOUN** Show business is entertainment in the theatre, films and television.

showdown **NOUN** (*informal*) a major argument or conflict intended to end a dispute.

shower **NOUN** ① a device which sprays you with water so that you can wash yourself. ② If you have a shower, you wash yourself by standing under a shower. ③ a short period of rain. ④ You can refer to a lot of things falling at once as a shower • *a shower of confetti*. ▸ **VERB** ⑤ If you shower, you have a shower. ⑥ If you are showered with a lot of things, they fall on you.

showing **NOUN** A showing of a film or television programme is a presentation of it so that the public can see it.

showjumping **NOUN** Showjumping is a horse-riding competition in which the horses jump over a series of high fences.

show-off **NOUN** (*informal*) someone who tries to impress people with their knowledge or skills.

showroom **NOUN** a shop where goods such as cars or electrical appliances are displayed.

showy, **showier**, **showiest** **ADJECTIVE** large or bright and intended to impress people • *a showy house*.

shrank the past tense of **shrink**.

shrapnel **NOUN** Shrapnel consists of small pieces of metal scattered from an exploding shell.

shred, **shreds**, **shredding**, **shredded** **VERB** ① If you shred something, you cut or tear it into very small pieces. ▸ **NOUN** ② A shred of paper or material is a small, narrow piece of it. ③ If there is not a shred of something, there is absolutely none of it • *He was left without a shred of self-esteem*.

shrewd **ADJECTIVE** Someone who is shrewd is intelligent and makes good judgments. **shrewdly** **ADVERB** **shrewdness** **NOUN**

shrewd **ADJECTIVE**
= astute, canny, crafty, perceptive, sharp, smart

shriek **NOUN** ① a high-pitched scream. ▸ **VERB** ② If you shriek, you make a high-pitched scream.

shrill **ADJECTIVE** A shrill sound is unpleasantly high-pitched and piercing. **shrilly** **ADVERB**

shrill **ADJECTIVE**
= penetrating, piercing, sharp

shrimp **NOUN** a small edible shellfish with a long tail and many legs.

shrine **NOUN** [RE] a place of worship associated with a sacred person or object.

A B C D E F G H I J K L M N O P Q R S T U V W X Y Z

shrink, **shrinks**, **shrinking**, **shrank**, **shrunk** VERB ① If something shrinks, it becomes smaller. ② If you shrink from something, you move away from it because you are afraid of it. **shrinkage** NOUN

shrink VERB
① = contract, diminish, dwindle, get smaller, narrow
≠ grow

shrivel, **shrivels**, **shrivelling**, **shrivelled** VERB When something shrivels, it becomes dry and withered.

shroud NOUN ① a cloth in which a dead body is wrapped before it is buried. ▶ VERB ② If something is shrouded in darkness or fog, it is hidden by it.

shrub NOUN a low, bushy plant.

shrug, **shrugs**, **shrugging**, **shrugged** VERB ① If you shrug your shoulders, you raise them slightly as a sign of indifference of if you don't know something. ▶ NOUN ② If you give a shrug of your shoulders, you shrug them.

shrunk the past participle of **shrink**.

shrunken ADJECTIVE (*formal*) Someone or something that is shrunken has become smaller than it used to be • *a shrunken old man*.

shudder VERB ① If you shudder, you tremble with fear or horror. ② If a machine or vehicle shudders, it shakes violently. ▶ NOUN ③ a shiver of fear or horror.

shuffle VERB ① If you shuffle, you walk without lifting your feet properly off the ground. ② If you shuffle about, you move about and fidget because you feel uncomfortable or embarrassed. ③ If you shuffle a pack of cards, you mix them up before you begin a game. ▶ NOUN ④ the way someone walks when they shuffle.

shun, **shuns**, **shunning**, **shunned** VERB If you shun someone or something, you deliberately avoid them.

shunt VERB (*informal*) If you shunt people or things to a place, you move them there • *You are shunted from room to room*.

shut, **shuts**, **shutting**, **shut** VERB ① If you shut something, you close it. ② When a shop or pub shuts, it is closed and you can no longer go into it. ▶ ADJECTIVE ③ If something is shut, it is closed. **shut down** VERB When a factory or business is shut down, it is closed permanently. **shut up** VERB (*informal*) If you shut up, you stop talking.

shut VERB
① = close, fasten, slam
≠ open
▶ ADJECTIVE ③ = closed, fastened, sealed
≠ open

shutter NOUN Shutters are hinged wooden or metal covers fitted on the outside or inside of a window.

shuttle ADJECTIVE ① A shuttle service is an air, bus or train service which makes frequent journeys between two places. ▶ NOUN ② a plane used in a shuttle service.

shy, **shyer**, **shyest**; **shies**, **shying**, **shied** ADJECTIVE ① A shy person is nervous and uncomfortable in the company of other people. ▶ VERB ② When a horse shies, it moves away suddenly because something has frightened it. ③ If you shy away from doing something, you avoid doing it because you are afraid or nervous. **shyly** ADVERB **shyness** NOUN

shy ADJECTIVE
① = bashful, reserved, retiring, self-conscious, timid
≠ bold

sibling NOUN (*formal*) Your siblings are your brothers and sisters.

sick ADJECTIVE ① If you are sick, you are ill. ② If you feel sick, you feel as if you are going to vomit. If you are sick, you vomit. ③ (*informal*) If you are sick of doing something, you feel you have been doing it too long. ④ (*informal*) A sick joke or story deals with death or suffering in an unpleasantly frivolous way. ▶ PHRASE ⑤ If something **makes you sick**, it makes you angry. **sickness** NOUN

> **sick** ADJECTIVE
> ① = ailing, laid up (*informal*), poorly (*British; informal*), under the weather (*informal*), unwell
> ≠ well
> ② = ill, nauseous, queasy
> ③ = bored, fed up, tired, weary

sicken VERB If something sickens you, it makes you feel disgusted. **sickening** ADJECTIVE

sickle NOUN a tool with a short handle and a curved blade used for cutting grass or grain.

sickly, **sicklier**, **sickliest** ADJECTIVE ① A sickly person or animal is weak and unhealthy. ② Sickly also means very unpleasant to smell or taste.

side NOUN ① Side refers to a position to the left or right of something • *the two armchairs on either side of the fireplace*. ② The sides of a boundary or barrier are the two areas it separates • *this side of the border*. ③ Your sides are the parts of your body from your armpits down to your hips. ④ The sides of something are its outside surfaces, especially the surfaces which are not its front or back. ⑤ The sides of a hill or valley are the parts that slope. ⑥ The two sides in a war, argument or relationship are the two people or groups involved. ⑦ A particular side of something is one aspect of it • *the sensitive, caring side of human nature*. ▶ ADJECTIVE ⑧ situated on a side of a building or vehicle • *the side door*. ⑨ A side road is a small road leading off a larger one. ⑩ A side issue is an issue that is less important than the main one. ▶ VERB ⑪ If you side with someone in an argument, you support them.

> **side** NOUN
> ① = edge, verge
> ⑥ = camp, faction, party, team
> ▶ VERB ⑪ = agree with, stand up for, support, take the part of

sideboard NOUN ① a long, low cupboard for plates and glasses. ② (*in plural*) A man's sideboards are his sideburns.

sideburns PLURAL NOUN A man's sideburns are areas of hair growing on his cheeks in front of his ears.

side effect NOUN The side effects of a drug are the effects it has in addition to its main effects.

sidekick NOUN (*informal*) Someone's sidekick is their close friend who spends a lot of time with them.

sideline NOUN an extra job in addition to your main job.

sideshow NOUN Sideshows are stalls at a fairground.

sidestep, **sidesteps**, **sidestepping**, **sidestepped** VERB If you sidestep a difficult problem or question, you avoid dealing with it.

sidewalk NOUN In American English, a sidewalk is a pavement.

sideways ADVERB ① from or towards the side of something or someone. ▶ ADJECTIVE ② to or from one side • *a sideways step*.

siding NOUN a short railway track beside the main tracks, where engines and carriages are left when not in use.

siege [*Said seej*] NOUN HISTORY a military operation in which an army surrounds a place and prevents food or help from reaching the people inside.

sieve *[Said siv]* **NOUN** ① a kitchen tool made of mesh, used for sifting or straining things. ▸ **VERB** ② If you sieve a powder or liquid, you pass it through a sieve.

sift **VERB** ① If you sift a powdery substance, you pass it through a sieve to remove lumps. ② If you sift through something such as evidence, you examine it all thoroughly.

sigh **VERB** ① When you sigh, you let out a deep breath. ▸ **NOUN** ② the breath you let out when you sigh.

sight **NOUN** ① Sight is the ability to see • *His sight was so poor that he could not follow the cricket.* ② something you see • *It was a ghastly sight.* ③ *(in plural)* Sights are interesting places which tourists visit. ▸ **VERB** ④ If you sight someone or something, you see them briefly or suddenly • *He had been sighted in Cairo.* ▸ **PHRASE** ⑤ If something is **in sight**, you can see it. If it is **out of sight**, you cannot see it.

> **sight** **NOUN**
> ① = eyesight, visibility, vision
> ② = display, scene, spectacle
> ▸ **VERB** ④ = see, spot

sighted **ADJECTIVE** Someone who is sighted can see.

sighting **NOUN** A sighting of something rare or unexpected is an occasion when it is seen.

sightseeing **NOUN** Sightseeing is visiting the interesting places that tourists usually visit. **sightseer** **NOUN**

sign **NOUN** ① a mark or symbol that always has a particular meaning, for example in mathematics or music. ② a gesture with a particular meaning. ③ A sign can also consist of words, a picture or a symbol giving information or a warning. ④ A sign is an event or happening that some people believe God has sent as a warning or instruction to an individual or to people in general. ⑤ If there are signs of something, there is evidence that it exists or is happening • *We are now seeing the first signs of recovery.* ▸ **VERB** ⑥ If you sign a document, you write your name on it • *He hurriedly signed the death certificate.* ⑦ If you sign, you communicate by using sign language. **sign on** **VERB** ① If you sign on for a job or course, you officially agree to do it by signing a contract. ② When people sign on, they officially state that they are unemployed and claim benefit from the state. **sign up** **VERB** If you sign up for a job or course, you officially agree to do it.

> **sign** **NOUN**
> ① = character, emblem, logo, mark, symbol
> ③ = board, notice, placard
> ⑤ = clue, evidence, hint, indication, symptom, token, trace

signal, **signals**, **signalling**, **signalled** **NOUN** ① a gesture, sound or action intended to give a message to someone. ② A railway signal is a piece of equipment beside the track which tells train drivers whether to stop or not. ▸ **VERB** ③ If you signal to someone, you make a gesture or sound to give them a message.

> **signal** **NOUN**
> ① = beacon, cue, gesture, sign
> ▸ **VERB** ③ = beckon, gesticulate, gesture, motion, nod, sign, wave

signature **NOUN** If you write your signature, you write your name the way you usually write it.

significant **ADJECTIVE** large or important • *a significant amount*

• *a significant victory*. **significance** NOUN **significantly** ADVERB

significant ADJECTIVE
= considerable, important, impressive, marked, notable, pronounced, striking
≠ insignificant

signify, **signifies**, **signifying**, **signified** VERB A gesture that signifies something has a particular meaning • *She screwed up her face to signify her disgust*.

sign language NOUN Sign language is a way of communicating using your hands, used especially by deaf people.

signpost NOUN a road sign with information on it such as the name of a town and how far away it is.

Sikh *[Said seek]* NOUN RE a person who believes in Sikhism, an Indian religion which separated from Hinduism in the 16th century and which teaches that there is only one God. **Sikhism** NOUN

silence NOUN ① Silence is quietness. ② Someone's silence about something is their failure or refusal to talk about it. ▶ VERB ③ To silence someone or something means to stop them talking or making a noise.

silence NOUN
① = calm, hush, lull, peace, quiet, stillness
≠ noise
② = dumbness, muteness, reticence, speechlessness
▶ VERB ③ = deaden, gag, muffle, quiet, quieten, stifle, still, suppress

silent ADJECTIVE ① If you are silent, you are not saying anything. ② If you are silent about something, you do not tell people about it. ③ When something is silent, it makes no noise. ④ A silent film has only pictures and no sound. **silently** ADVERB

silent ADJECTIVE
① = dumb, mute, speechless, taciturn, wordless
③ = hushed, quiet, soundless, still
≠ noisy

silhouette *[Said sil-loo-**ett**]* NOUN the outline of a dark shape against a light background. **silhouetted** ADJECTIVE

silicon NOUN SCIENCE Silicon is an element found in sand, clay and stone. It is used to make glass and also to make parts of computers. Its atomic number is 14 and its symbol is Si.

silk NOUN Silk is a fine, soft cloth made from a substance produced by silkworms.

silken ADJECTIVE (*literary*) smooth and soft • *silken hair*.

silky, **silkier**, **silkiest** ADJECTIVE smooth and soft.

sill NOUN a ledge at the bottom of a window.

silly, **sillier**, **silliest** ADJECTIVE foolish or childish.

silly ADJECTIVE
= absurd, daft (*British; informal*), foolish, idiotic, inane, ridiculous, stupid

silt NOUN GEOGRAPHY Silt is fine sand or soil which is carried along by a river.

silver NOUN ① SCIENCE Silver is a valuable greyish-white metallic element used for making jewellery and ornaments. Its atomic number is 47 and its symbol is Ag. ② Silver is also coins made from silver or from silver-coloured metal • *He's won a handful of silver on the fruit machine*. ③ In a house, the silver is all the things made from silver, especially the cutlery. ▶ ADJECTIVE, NOUN ④ greyish-white.

silver medal NOUN a medal made from silver awarded to the competitor who comes second in a competition.

silvery ADJECTIVE having the appearance or colour of silver • *the silvery moon*.

similar ADJECTIVE ① If one thing is similar to another, or if two things are similar, they are like each other. ② In maths, two triangles are similar if the angles in one correspond exactly to the angles in the other. **similarly** ADVERB

> **similar** ADJECTIVE
> ① = alike, analogous, comparable, like, uniform
> ≠ different

similarity NOUN If there is a similarity between things, they are alike in some way.

> **similarity** NOUN
> = analogy, likeness, resemblance, sameness
> ≠ difference

simmer VERB When food simmers, it cooks gently at just below boiling point.

simple ADJECTIVE ① Something that is simple is uncomplicated and easy to understand or do. ② Simple also means plain and not elaborate in style • *a simple coat*. ③ A simple way of life is uncomplicated. ④ You use 'simple' to emphasise that what you are talking about is the only important thing • *simple stubbornness*. **simplicity** NOUN

> **simple** ADJECTIVE
> ① = easy, elementary, straightforward, uncomplicated, understandable
> ≠ complicated
> ② = basic, classic, clean, plain, severe
> ≠ elaborate

simplify, **simplifies**, **simplifying**, **simplified** VERB To simplify something means to make it easier to do or understand. **simplification** NOUN

> **simplify** VERB
> = make simpler, streamline

simplistic ADJECTIVE too simple or naive • *a rather simplistic approach to the subject*.

simply ADVERB ① Simply means merely • *It was simply a question of making the decision*. ② You use 'simply' to emphasise what you are saying • *It is simply not true*. ③ If you say or write something simply, you do it in a way that makes it easy to understand.

simulate VERB To simulate something means to imitate it • *The wood has been painted to simulate stone* • *He simulated shock*.

simulation NOUN ① Simulation is the process of simulating something or the result of simulating it. ② (*technical*) A simulation is an attempt to solve a problem by representing it mathematically, often on a computer.

simulator NOUN A simulator is a device designed to reproduce actual conditions, for example in order to train pilots or astronauts.

simultaneous ADJECTIVE Things that are simultaneous happen at the same time. **simultaneously** ADVERB

sin, **sins**, **sinning**, **sinned** NOUN ① [RE] Sin is wicked and immoral behaviour. ▶ VERB ② To sin means to do something wicked and immoral.

> **sin** NOUN
> ① = crime, evil, offence, wickedness, wrong
> ▶ VERB ② = do wrong

since PREPOSITION, CONJUNCTION, ADVERB ① Since means from a particular time until now • *I've been waiting patiently since half past three.* ▶ **ADVERB** ② Since also means at some time after a particular time in the past • *The band split up and he has since gone solo.* ▶ **CONJUNCTION** ③ Since also means because • *I'm forever on a diet, since I put on weight easily.*

sincere **ADJECTIVE** If you are sincere, you say things that you really mean • *a sincere expression of friendliness.*
sincerity **NOUN**

> **sincere** **ADJECTIVE**
> = genuine, heartfelt, real, wholehearted
> ≠ insincere

sincerely **ADVERB** ① If you say or feel something sincerely, you mean it or feel it genuinely. ▶ **PHRASE** ② You write **Yours sincerely** before your signature at the end of a letter in which you have named the person you are writing to in the greeting at the beginning of the letter. For example, if you began your letter 'Dear Mr Brown' you would use 'Yours sincerely'.

sinful **ADJECTIVE** [RE] wicked and immoral.

sing, **sings**, **singing**, **sang**, **sung** **VERB** ① When you sing, you make musical sounds with your voice, usually producing words that fit a tune. ② When birds or insects sing, they make pleasant sounds. **singer** **NOUN**

single **ADJECTIVE** ① Single means only one and not more • *A single shot was fired.* ② People who are single are not married. ③ A single bed or bedroom is for one person. ④ A single ticket is a one-way ticket. ▶ **NOUN** ⑤ a recording of one or two short pieces of music on a small record, CD or download. ⑥ Singles is a game of tennis, badminton or squash between just two players. **single out** **VERB** If you single someone out from a group, you give them special treatment • *He'd been singled out for some special award.*

> **single** **ADJECTIVE**
> ① = lone, one, only, sole, solitary
> ② = unattached, unmarried
> ③ = individual, separate

single-handed **ADVERB** If you do something single-handed, you do it on your own, without any help.

single-minded **ADJECTIVE** A single-minded person has only one aim and is determined to achieve it.

singly **ADVERB** If people do something singly, they do it on their own or one by one.

singular **NOUN** ① [MFL] In grammar, the singular is the form of a word that refers to just one person or thing. ▶ **ADJECTIVE** ② (*formal*) unusual and remarkable • *her singular beauty.*
singularity **NOUN** **singularly** **ADVERB**

> **singular** **ADJECTIVE**
> ② = exceptional, extraordinary, rare, remarkable, uncommon, unique, unusual

sinister **ADJECTIVE** seeming harmful or evil • *something cold and sinister about him.*

> **sinister** **ADJECTIVE**
> = evil, forbidding, menacing, ominous, threatening

sink, **sinks**, **sinking**, **sank**, **sunk** **NOUN** ① a basin with taps supplying water, usually in a kitchen or bathroom. ▶ **VERB** ② If something sinks, it moves downwards, especially through water • *An Indian cargo ship sank in icy seas.* ③ To sink a ship means to cause it to sink by attacking it. ④ If an amount or value sinks, it decreases. ⑤ If you sink into an unpleasant state, you gradually pass into it • *He sank into black despair.* ⑥ To sink something sharp into an object means to make it go deeply into it • *The tiger sank its teeth into his leg.* **sink in** VERB When a fact sinks in, you fully understand it or realise it • *The truth was at last sinking in.*

sinner NOUN someone who has committed a sin.

sinus NOUN Your sinuses are the air passages in the bones of your skull, just behind your nose.

sip, sips, sipping, sipped VERB ① If you sip a drink, you drink it by taking a small amount at a time. ▸ NOUN ② a small amount of drink that you take into your mouth.

siphon [*Said* ***sigh****-fn*]; also spelt **syphon** VERB If you siphon off a liquid, you draw it out of a container through a tube and transfer it to another place.

sir NOUN ① Sir is a polite, formal way of addressing a man. ② Sir is also the title used in front of the name of a knight or baronet.

siren NOUN a warning device, for example on a police car, which makes a loud wailing noise.

sirloin NOUN Sirloin is a prime cut of beef from the lower part of a cow's back.

sister NOUN ① Your sister is a girl or woman who has the same parents as you. ② a member of a female religious order. ③ In a hospital, a sister is a senior nurse who supervises a ward. ▸ ADJECTIVE ④ Sister means closely related to something or very similar to it • *Voyager 2 and its sister ship, Voyager 1.*

sisterhood NOUN Sisterhood is a strong feeling of companionship between women.

sister-in-law, sisters-in-law NOUN Someone's sister-in-law is the sister of their husband or wife, or their sibling's wife.

sit, sits, sitting, sat VERB ① If you are sitting, your weight is supported by your buttocks rather than your feet. ② When you sit or sit down somewhere, you lower your body until you are sitting. ③ If you sit an examination, you take it. ④ (*formal*) When a parliament, law court or other official body sits, it meets and officially carries out its work.

sitcom NOUN (*informal*) a television comedy series which shows characters in amusing situations that are similar to everyday life.

site NOUN ① a piece of ground where a particular thing happens or is situated • *a building site.* ② A site is the same as a website. ▸ VERB ③ If something is sited in a place, it is built or positioned there.

sitting NOUN ① one of the times when a meal is served. ② one of the occasions when a parliament or law court meets and carries out its work.

sitting room NOUN a room in a house where people sit and relax.

situated ADJECTIVE If something is situated somewhere, that is where it is • *a town situated 45 minutes from Geneva.*

situation NOUN ① what is happening in a particular place at a particular time • *the political situation.* ② The situation of a building or town is its surroundings • *a beautiful situation.*

> **situation** NOUN
> ① = case, circumstances, plight, scenario, state of affairs

six the number 6.

sixteen the number 16. **sixteenth** ADJECTIVE

sixth ADJECTIVE ① The sixth item in a series is the one counted as number six. ▸ NOUN ② one of six equal parts.

sixth sense NOUN You say that someone has a sixth sense when they know something instinctively, without having any evidence of it.

sixty, **sixties** the number 60. **sixtieth** ADJECTIVE

sizable; also spelt **sizeable** ADJECTIVE fairly large • *a sizable amount of money.*

size NOUN ① The size of something is how big or small it is • *the size of the audience.* ② The size of something is also the fact that it is very large • *the sheer size of Australia.* ③ one of the standard graded measurements of clothes and shoes. **size up** VERB If you size up people or situations, you look at them carefully and make a judgment about them.

> **size** NOUN
> ① = dimensions, extent, proportions
> ② = bulk, immensity

sizzle VERB If something sizzles, it makes a hissing sound like the sound of frying food.

skate, **skates**, **skating**, **skated** NOUN ① Skates are ice skates or roller skates. ② a flat edible sea fish. ▶ VERB ③ If you skate, you move about on ice wearing ice skates. ④ If you skate round a difficult subject, you avoid discussing it.

skateboard NOUN a narrow board on wheels, which you stand on and ride for fun.

skeleton NOUN Your skeleton is the framework of bones in your body.

sketch NOUN ① [ART] a quick, rough drawing. ② A sketch of a situation or incident is a brief description of it. ③ a short, humorous piece of acting, usually forming part of a comedy show. ▶ VERB ④ If you sketch something, you draw it quickly and roughly.

sketchy, **sketchier**, **sketchiest** ADJECTIVE giving only a rough description or account • *Details surrounding his death are sketchy.*

skew *[Said skyoo]* or **skewed** ADJECTIVE in a slanting position, rather than straight or upright.

skewer NOUN ① a long metal pin used to hold pieces of food together during cooking. ▶ VERB ② If you skewer something, you push a skewer through it.

ski, **skis**, **skiing**, **skied** NOUN ① Skis are long pieces of wood, metal or plastic that you fasten to special boots so you can move easily on snow. ▶ VERB ② When you ski, you move on snow wearing skis, especially as a sport.

skid, **skids**, **skidding**, **skidded** VERB If a vehicle skids, it slides in an uncontrolled way, for example because the road is wet or icy.

skilful ADJECTIVE If you are skilful at something, you can do it very well. **skilfully** ADVERB

> **skilful** ADJECTIVE
> = able, accomplished, adept, competent, expert, masterly, proficient, skilled
> ≠ incompetent

skill NOUN ① Skill is the knowledge and ability that enables you to do something well. ② a type of work or technique which requires special training and knowledge.

> **skill** NOUN
> ① = ability, competence, dexterity, expertise, facility, knack, proficiency

skilled ADJECTIVE ① A skilled person has the knowledge and ability to do something well. ② Skilled work is work which can only be done by people who have had special training.

> **skilled** ADJECTIVE
> ① = able, accomplished, competent, experienced, expert, masterly, professional, proficient, skilful, trained
> ≠ incompetent

skim, **skims**, **skimming**, **skimmed** VERB ① If you skim something from the surface of a liquid, you remove it. ② If something skims a surface, it moves along just above it • *seagulls skimming the waves*. ③ If you skim a piece of writing, you read through it quickly and without taking in the details.

skimmed milk NOUN Skimmed milk has had the cream removed.

skin, **skins**, **skinning**, **skinned** NOUN ① Your skin is the natural covering of your body. An animal skin is the skin and fur of a dead animal. ② The skin of a fruit or vegetable is its outer covering. ③ a solid layer which forms on the surface of a liquid. ▶ VERB ④ If you skin a dead animal, you remove its skin. ⑤ If you skin a part of your body, you accidentally graze it.

skinny, **skinnier**, **skinniest** ADJECTIVE extremely thin.

skinny ADJECTIVE
= bony, emaciated, lean, scrawny, thin, underfed, undernourished
≠ plump

skip, **skips**, **skipping**, **skipped** VERB ① If you skip along, you move along jumping from one foot to the other. ② (*informal*) If you skip something, you miss it out or avoid doing it • *It is all too easy to skip meals*. ▶ NOUN ③ Skips are the movements you make when you skip. ④ a large metal container for holding rubbish and rubble.

skipper NOUN (*informal*) The skipper of a ship or boat is its captain.

skirmish NOUN a short, rough fight.

skirt NOUN ① A skirt is a piece of clothing which fastens at the waist and hangs down over the legs. ▶ VERB ② Something that skirts an area is situated around the edge of it. ③ If you skirt something, you go around the edge of it • *We skirted the town*. ④ If you skirt a problem, you avoid dealing with it • *He was skirting the real question*.

skull NOUN Your skull is the bony part of your head which surrounds your brain.

skunk NOUN a small black and white mammal from North America which gives off an unpleasant smell when it is frightened.

sky, **skies** NOUN The sky is the space around the earth which you can see when you look upwards.

skylight NOUN a window in a roof or ceiling.

skyline NOUN The skyline is the line where the sky meets buildings or the ground • *the New York City skyline*.

Skype NOUN (*trademark*) ① a computer program for making phone calls and video calls on the internet. ▶ VERB ② If you Skype someone, you use a computer program to speak to them on the internet.

skyscraper NOUN a very tall building.

slab NOUN a thick, flat piece of something.

slack ADJECTIVE ① Something that is slack is loose and not firmly stretched or positioned. ② A slack period is one in which there is not much work to do. ▶ NOUN ③ The slack in a rope is the part that hangs loose. ④ (*in plural*, *old-fashioned*) Slacks are casual trousers. **slackness** NOUN

slacken VERB ① If something slackens, it becomes slower or less intense • *The rain had slackened to a drizzle*. ② To slacken also means to become looser • *Her grip slackened on Arnold's arm*.

slag, **slags**, **slagging**, **slagged** NOUN ① Slag is the waste material left when ore has been melted down to remove the metal • *a slag heap*. ▶ VERB ② (*informal*) To slag someone off means to criticise them in an unpleasant way, usually behind their back.

slain the past participle of **slay**.

slalom *[Said* ***slah****-lom]* **NOUN** a skiing competition in which the competitors have to twist and turn quickly to avoid obstacles.

slam, slams, slamming, slammed **VERB** ① If you slam a door or if it slams, it shuts noisily and with great force. ② If you slam something down, you put it down violently • *She slammed the phone down.*

slander **NOUN** ① Slander is something untrue and malicious said about someone. ▶ **VERB** ② To slander someone means to say untrue and malicious things about them. **slanderous** **ADJECTIVE**

> **slander** **NOUN**
> ① = libel, scandal, slur, smear
> ▶ **VERB** ② = libel, malign, smear

slang **NOUN** Slang consists of very informal words and expressions.

slant **VERB** ① If something slants, it slopes • *The back can be adjusted to slant into the most comfortable position.* ② If news or information is slanted, it is presented in a biased way. ▶ **NOUN** ③ a slope. ④ A slant on a subject is one way of looking at it, especially a biased one.

slap, slaps, slapping, slapped **VERB** ① If you slap someone, you hit them with the palm of your hand. ② If you slap something onto a surface, you put it there quickly and noisily. ▶ **NOUN** ③ If you give someone a slap, you slap them.

slash **VERB** ① If you slash something, you make a long, deep cut in it. ② *(informal)* To slash money means to reduce it greatly • *Car makers could be forced to slash prices.* ▶ **NOUN** ③ a diagonal line that separates letters, words or numbers, for example in the number 340/21/K.

slate **NOUN** ① Slate is a dark grey rock that splits easily into thin layers. ② Slates are small, flat pieces of slate used for covering roofs. ▶ **VERB** ③ *(informal)* If critics slate a play, film or book, they criticise it severely.

slaughter **VERB** ① To slaughter a large number of people means to kill them unjustly or cruelly. ② To slaughter farm animals means to kill them for meat. ▶ **NOUN** ③ Slaughter is the killing of many people.

slave **NOUN** ① someone who is forced to work for another person. ▶ **VERB** ② If you slave for someone, you work very hard for them. **slavery** **NOUN**

slay, slays, slaying, slew, slain **VERB** *(literary)* To slay someone means to kill them.

sleazy, sleazier, sleaziest **ADJECTIVE** A sleazy place looks dirty, run-down and not respectable.

sled or **sledge** **NOUN** a vehicle on runners used for travelling over snow.

sledgehammer **NOUN** a large, heavy hammer.

sleek **ADJECTIVE** ① Sleek hair is smooth and shiny. ② Someone who is sleek looks rich and dresses elegantly.

sleep, sleeps, sleeping, slept **NOUN** ① Sleep is the natural state of rest in which your eyes are closed and you are unconscious. ② If you have a sleep, you sleep for a while • *He'll be ready for a sleep soon.* ▶ **VERB** ③ When you sleep, you rest in a state of sleep. ▶ **PHRASE** ④ If a sick or injured animal **is put to sleep**, it is painlessly killed.

> **sleep** **NOUN**
> ① = doze, hibernation, kip *(British; slang)*, nap, slumber, snooze *(informal)*
> ▶ **VERB** ③ = doze, hibernate, kip *(British; slang)*, slumber, snooze *(informal)*, take a nap

sleeper NOUN ① You use 'sleeper' to say how deeply someone sleeps • *I'm a very heavy sleeper*. ② a bed on a train, or a train which has beds on it. ③ Railway sleepers are the large beams that support the rails of a railway track.

sleeping bag NOUN a large, warm bag for sleeping in, especially when you are camping.

sleepover NOUN a gathering or party at which friends spend the night at another friend's house.

sleepy, sleepier, sleepiest ADJECTIVE ① tired and ready to go to sleep. ② A sleepy town or village is very quiet. **sleepily** ADVERB **sleepiness** NOUN

> **sleepy** ADJECTIVE
> ① = drowsy, lethargic, sluggish
> ② = dull, quiet

sleet NOUN Sleet is a mixture of rain and snow.

sleeve NOUN The sleeves of a piece of clothing are the parts that cover your arms. **sleeveless** ADJECTIVE

sleigh [*Said* ***slay***] NOUN a sledge.

slender ADJECTIVE ① attractively thin and graceful. ② small in amount or degree • *the first slender hopes of peace*.

> **slender** ADJECTIVE
> ① = lean, slight, slim
> ② = faint, remote, slight, slim, small

slept the past tense and past participle of **sleep**.

sleuth [*Said* ***slooth***] NOUN (*old-fashioned*) a detective.

slew VERB ▸ ① Slew is the past tense of **slay**. ② If a vehicle slews, it slides or skids • *The bike slewed into the crowd*.

slice NOUN ① A slice of cake, bread or other food is a piece of it cut from a larger piece. ② a kitchen tool with a broad, flat blade • *a fish slice*. ③ In sport, a slice is a stroke in which the player makes the ball go to one side, rather than straight ahead. ▸ VERB ④ If you slice food, you cut it into thin pieces. ⑤ To slice through something means to cut or move through it quickly, like a knife • *The ship sliced through the water*.

slick ADJECTIVE ① A slick action is done quickly and smoothly • *slick passing and strong running*. ② A slick person speaks easily and persuasively but is not sincere • *a slick TV presenter*. ▸ NOUN ③ An oil slick is a layer of oil floating on the surface of the sea or a lake.

slide, slides, sliding, slid VERB ① When something slides, it moves smoothly over or against something else. ▸ NOUN ② a small piece of photographic film which can be projected onto a screen so that you can see the picture. ③ a small piece of glass on which you put something that you want to examine through a microscope. ④ In a playground, a slide is a structure with a steep, slippery slope for children to slide down.

slight ADJECTIVE ① Slight means small in amount or degree • *a slight dent*. ② A slight person has a slim body. ▸ PHRASE ③ **Not in the slightest** means not at all • *This doesn't surprise me in the slightest*. ▸ VERB ④ If you slight someone, you insult them by behaving rudely towards them. ▸ NOUN ⑤ A slight is an example of rude or insulting behaviour. **slightly** ADVERB

> **slight** ADJECTIVE
> ① = insignificant, minor, negligible, small, trivial
> ≠ large

slim, slimmer, slimmest; slims, slimming, slimmed ADJECTIVE ① A slim person is attractively thin. ② A slim object is thinner than usual • *a slim book*. ③ If there is only a slim chance that something will happen, it is unlikely to happen. ▸ **VERB** ④ If you are slimming, you are trying to lose weight. **slimmer NOUN**

slime NOUN Slime is an unpleasant, thick, slippery substance.

slimy, slimier, slimiest ADJECTIVE ① covered in slime. ② Slimy people are friendly and pleasant in an insincere way.

sling, slings, slinging, slung VERB ① (*informal*) If you sling something somewhere, you throw it there. ② If you sling a rope between two points, you attach it so that it hangs loosely between them. ▸ **NOUN** ③ a piece of cloth tied round a person's neck to support a broken or injured arm. ④ a device made of ropes or cloth used for carrying things.

slip, slips, slipping, slipped VERB ① If you slip, you accidentally slide and lose your balance. ② If something slips, it slides out of place accidentally • *One of the knives slipped from her grasp*. ③ If you slip somewhere, you go there quickly and quietly • *She slipped out of the house*. ④ If you slip something somewhere, you put it there quickly and quietly. ⑤ If something slips to a lower level or standard, it falls to that level or standard • *The shares slipped to an all-time low*. ▸ **NOUN** ⑥ a small mistake. ⑦ A slip of paper is a small piece of paper. ⑧ a piece of clothing worn under a dress or skirt. **slip up VERB** (*informal*) If you slip up, you make a mistake.

> **slip VERB**
> ③ = creep, sneak, steal
> ▸ **NOUN** ⑥ = blunder, error, mistake

slipper NOUN Slippers are loose, soft shoes that you wear indoors.

slippery ADJECTIVE ① smooth, wet or greasy, and difficult to hold or walk on. ② (*informal*) You describe a person as slippery when they cannot be trusted.

slipstream NOUN The slipstream of a car or plane is the flow of air directly behind it.

slit, slits, slitting, slit VERB ① If you slit something, you make a long, narrow cut in it. ▸ **NOUN** ② a long, narrow cut or opening.

slither VERB To slither somewhere means to move there by sliding along the ground in an uneven way • *The snake slithered into the water*.

sliver NOUN a small, thin piece of something.

slob NOUN (*informal*) a lazy, untidy person.

slog, slogs, slogging, slogged VERB (*informal*) ① If you slog at something, you work hard and steadily at it • *They are still slogging away at algebra*. ② If you slog somewhere, you move along with difficulty • *people willing to slog round the streets delivering catalogues*.

slogan NOUN a short, easily remembered phrase used in advertising or by a political party.

> **slogan NOUN**
> = jingle, motto

slop, slops, slopping, slopped VERB ① If a liquid slops, it spills over the edge of a container in a messy way. ② (*in plural*) You can refer to dirty water or liquid waste as slops.

slope NOUN ① a flat surface that is at an angle, so that one end is higher than the other. ② The slope of something is the angle at which it slopes. ▸ **VERB** ③ If a surface slopes, it is at an angle. ④ If something slopes, it leans to one side rather than being upright • *sloping handwriting*.

> **slope NOUN**
> ① = gradient, incline, ramp
> ▸ **VERB** ③ = fall, rise, slant

sloppy, **sloppier**, **sloppiest** ADJECTIVE (*informal*) ① very messy or careless • *two sloppy performances.* ② foolishly sentimental • *some sloppy love story.* **sloppily** ADVERB **sloppiness** NOUN

slot, **slots**, **slotting**, **slotted** NOUN ① a narrow opening in a machine or container, for example for putting coins in. ▶ VERB ② When you slot something into something else, you put it into a space where it fits.

sloth [*Rhymes with **growth***] NOUN ① (*formal*) Sloth is laziness. ② a South and Central American animal that moves very slowly and hangs upside down from the branches of trees.

slouch VERB If you slouch, you stand or sit with your shoulders and head drooping forwards.

Slovak ADJECTIVE ① belonging or relating to Slovakia. ▶ NOUN ② someone who comes from Slovakia. ③ Slovak is the language spoken in Slovakia.

Slovene, **Slovenes** ADJECTIVE ① belonging or relating to Slovenia. ▶ NOUN ② someone who comes from Slovenia. ③ Slovene is the language spoken in Slovenia.

slow ADJECTIVE ① moving, happening or doing something with very little speed • *His progress was slow.* ② Someone who is slow is not very clever. ③ If a clock or watch is slow, it shows a time earlier than the correct one. ▶ VERB ④ If something slows, slows down or slows up, it moves or happens more slowly. **slowness** NOUN

> **slow** ADJECTIVE
> ① = gradual, leisurely, lingering, ponderous, sluggish, unhurried
> ≠ fast
> ▶ VERB ④ = check, decelerate

slowly ADVERB not quickly or hurriedly.

> **slowly** ADVERB
> = by degrees, gradually, unhurriedly
> ≠ quickly

slow motion NOUN Slow motion is movement which is much slower than normal, especially in a film • *It all seemed to happen in slow motion.*

sludge NOUN Sludge is thick mud or sewage.

slug NOUN ① a small, slow-moving creature with a slimy body, like a snail without a shell. ② (*informal*) A slug of a strong alcoholic drink is a mouthful of it.

sluggish ADJECTIVE moving slowly and without energy • *the sluggish waters.* **sluggishly** ADVERB

slum NOUN a poor, run-down area of a city.

slumber (*literary*) NOUN ① Slumber is sleep. ▶ VERB ② When you slumber, you sleep.

slump VERB ① If an amount or a value slumps, it falls suddenly by a large amount. ② If you slump somewhere, you fall or sit down heavily • *He slumped against the side of the car.* ▶ NOUN ③ a sudden, severe drop in an amount or value • *the slump in house prices.* ④ a time when there is economic decline and high unemployment.

slung the past tense and past participle of **sling**.

slur, **slurs**, **slurring**, **slurred** NOUN ① an insulting remark. ▶ VERB ② When people slur their speech, they do not say their words clearly, often because they are drunk or ill.

slush NOUN ① Slush is wet melting snow. ② (*informal*) You can refer to sentimental love stories as slush. **slushy** ADJECTIVE

sly, **slyer** or **slier**, **slyest** or **sliest** ADJECTIVE ① A sly expression or remark shows that you know something other people do not know

• *a sly smile.* ② A sly person is cunning and good at deceiving people. **slyly** ADVERB

sly ADJECTIVE
② = crafty, cunning, devious, scheming, underhand, wily

smack VERB ① If you smack someone, you hit them with your open hand. ② If something smacks of something else, it reminds you of it • *His tale smacks of fantasy.* ▶ NOUN ③ If you give someone a smack, you smack them. ④ a loud, sharp noise • *He landed with a smack on the tank.*

small ADJECTIVE ① Small means not large in size, number or amount. ② Small means not important or significant • *small changes.* ▶ NOUN ③ The small of your back is the narrow part where your back curves slightly inwards.
smallness NOUN

small ADJECTIVE
① = little, miniature, minute, minuscule, tiny
≠ large
② = inconsequential, insignificant, little, minor, negligible, petty, slight, trifling, trivial, unimportant

smallpox NOUN Smallpox is a serious contagious disease that causes a fever and a rash.

small talk NOUN Small talk is conversation about unimportant things.

smart ADJECTIVE ① A smart person is clean and neatly dressed. ② Smart means clever • *a smart idea.* ③ A smart movement is quick and sharp. ④ A smart machine or system is one that uses computer technology. ▶ VERB ⑤ If a wound smarts, it stings. ⑥ If you are smarting from criticism or unkindness, you are feeling upset by it. **smartly** ADVERB **smartness** NOUN

smart ADJECTIVE
① = chic, elegant, neat, spruce, stylish
≠ scruffy
② = astute, bright, canny, clever, ingenious, intelligent, shrewd
≠ dumb

smarten VERB If you smarten something up, you make it look neater and tidier.

smartphone NOUN a mobile phone allowing access to the internet.

smash VERB ① If you smash something, you break it into a lot of pieces by hitting it or dropping it. ② To smash through something such as a wall means to go through it by breaking it. ③ To smash against something means to hit it with great force • *An immense wave smashed against the hull.* ▶ NOUN ④ (*informal*) If a play or film is a smash or a smash hit, it is very successful. ⑤ a car crash. ⑥ In tennis, a smash is a stroke in which the player hits the ball downwards very hard.

smashing ADJECTIVE (*informal*) If you describe something as smashing, you mean you like it very much.

smattering NOUN A smattering of knowledge or information is a very small amount of it • *a smattering of Russian.*

smear NOUN ① a dirty, greasy mark on a surface • *a smear of pink lipstick.* ② an untrue and malicious rumour. ▶ VERB ③ If something smears a surface, it makes dirty, greasy marks on it • *The blade was chipped and smeared.* ④ If you smear a surface with a thick substance, you spread a layer of the substance over the surface.

smell, **smells**, **smelling**, **smelled** or **smelt** NOUN ① The smell of something is a quality it has which you perceive through your nose

• *a smell of damp wood.* ② Your sense of smell is your ability to smell things. ▶ **VERB** ③ If something smells, it has a quality you can perceive through your nose, especially an unpleasant quality. ④ If you smell something, you become aware of it through your nose. ⑤ If you can smell something such as danger or trouble, you feel it is present or likely to happen.

smell NOUN
① = aroma, fragrance, odour, perfume, pong (*British and Australian; informal*), reek, scent, stench, stink
▶ **VERB** ④ = scent, sniff

smelly, **smellier**, **smelliest** **ADJECTIVE** having a strong, unpleasant smell.

smelly ADJECTIVE
= foul, reeking, stinking
≠ fragrant

smelt **VERB** To smelt a metal ore means to heat it until it melts, so that the metal can be extracted.

smile **VERB** ① When you smile, the corners of your mouth move outwards and slightly upwards because you are pleased or amused. ▶ **NOUN** ② the expression you have when you smile.

smile VERB
① = beam, grin, smirk
▶ **NOUN** ② = beam, grin, smirk

smirk **VERB** ① When you smirk, you smile in a sneering or sarcastic way • *The boy smirked and turned the volume up.* ▶ **NOUN** ② a sneering or sarcastic smile.

smith **NOUN** someone who makes things out of iron, gold or another metal.

smitten **ADJECTIVE** If you are smitten with someone or something, you are very impressed with or enthusiastic about them • *They were totally smitten with each other.*

smock **NOUN** a loose garment like a long blouse.

smog **NOUN** Smog is a mixture of smoke and fog which occurs in some industrial cities.

smoke **NOUN** ① Smoke is a mixture of gas and small particles sent into the air when something burns. ▶ **VERB** ② If something is smoking, smoke is coming from it. ③ When someone smokes a cigarette or pipe, they suck smoke from it into their mouth and blow it out again. ④ To smoke fish or meat means to hang it over burning wood so that the smoke preserves it and gives it a pleasant flavour • *smoked bacon.* **smoker** **NOUN** **smoking** **NOUN**, **ADJECTIVE**

smoky, **smokier**, **smokiest** **ADJECTIVE** A smoky place is full of smoke.

smooth **ADJECTIVE** ① A smooth surface has no roughness and no holes in it. ② A smooth liquid or mixture has no lumps in it. ③ A smooth movement or process happens evenly and steadily • *smooth acceleration.* ④ Smooth also means successful and without problems • *staff responsible for the smooth running of the hall.* ▶ **VERB** ⑤ If you smooth something, you move your hands over it to make it smooth and flat. **smoothly** **ADVERB** **smoothness** **NOUN**

smooth ADJECTIVE
① = glassy, glossy, polished, silky, sleek
≠ rough

smoothie **NOUN** a thick type of drink made in an electric blender from milk, fruit and crushed ice.

smother **VERB** ① If you smother a fire, you cover it with something to put it out. ② To smother a person means to cover their face with something so that they cannot breathe. ③ To smother someone also means to give them too much love and protection. ④ If you smother an emotion, you control it so that people do not notice it • *They tried to smother their glee.*

smothered ADJECTIVE completely covered with something • *a spectacular trellis smothered in climbing roses.*

smoulder VERB ① When something smoulders, it burns slowly, producing smoke but no flames. ② If a feeling is smouldering inside you, you feel it very strongly but do not show it • *smouldering with resentment.*

smudge NOUN ① a dirty or blurred mark or a smear on something. ▶ VERB ② If you smudge something, you make it dirty or messy by touching it or marking it.

smug, **smugger**, **smuggest** ADJECTIVE Someone who is smug is very pleased with how good or clever they are. **smugly** ADVERB **smugness** NOUN

> **smug** ADJECTIVE
> = complacent, conceited, self-satisfied, superior

smuggle VERB To smuggle things or people into or out of a place means to take them there illegally or secretly.

smuggler NOUN someone who smuggles goods illegally into a country.

snack NOUN a light, quick meal.

snag, **snags**, **snagging**, **snagged** NOUN ① a small problem or disadvantage • *There is one snag: it is not true.* ② (*informal*) In Australian and New Zealand English, a snag is a sausage. ▶ VERB ③ If you snag your clothing, you damage it by catching it on something sharp.

> **snag** NOUN
> ① = catch (*informal*), difficulty, disadvantage, drawback, problem

snail NOUN a small, slow-moving creature with a long, shiny body and a shell on its back.

snake NOUN ① a long, thin, scaly reptile with no legs. ▶ VERB ② Something that snakes moves in long winding curves • *The queue snaked out of the shop.*

snap, **snaps**, **snapping**, **snapped** VERB ① If something snaps or if you snap it, it breaks with a sharp cracking noise. ② If you snap something into a particular position, you move it there quickly with a sharp sound. ③ If an animal snaps at you, it shuts its jaws together quickly as if to bite you. ④ If someone snaps at you, they speak in a sharp, unfriendly way. ⑤ If you snap someone, you take a quick photograph of them. ▶ NOUN ⑥ the sound of something snapping. ⑦ (*informal*) a photograph taken quickly and casually. ▶ ADJECTIVE ⑧ A snap decision or action is taken suddenly without careful thought.

snapper NOUN a fish with edible pink flesh, found in waters around Australia, New Zealand and the US.

snapshot NOUN a photograph taken quickly and casually.

snare NOUN ① a trap for catching birds or small animals. ▶ VERB ② To snare an animal or bird means to catch it using a snare.

snarl VERB ① When an animal snarls, it bares its teeth and makes a fierce growling noise. ② If you snarl, you say something in a fierce, angry way. ▶ NOUN ③ the noise an animal makes when it snarls.

snatch VERB ① If you snatch something, you reach out for it quickly and take it. ② If you snatch an amount of time or an opportunity, you quickly make use of it. ▶ NOUN ③ If you make a snatch at something, you reach out for it quickly to try to take it. ④ A snatch of conversation or song is a very small piece of it.

sneak VERB ① If you sneak somewhere, you go there quickly trying not to be seen or heard. ② If you sneak something somewhere, you take it there secretly. ▸ NOUN ③ (*informal*) someone who tells people in authority that someone else has done something wrong.

sneak VERB
① = lurk, sidle, slip, steal
② = slip, smuggle, spirit

sneaker NOUN Sneakers are casual shoes with rubber soles.

sneaking ADJECTIVE If you have a sneaking feeling about something or someone, you have this feeling rather reluctantly • *I had a sneaking suspicion that she was enjoying herself.*

sneaky, **sneakier**, **sneakiest** ADJECTIVE (*informal*) Someone who is sneaky does things secretly rather than openly.

sneaky ADJECTIVE
= crafty, deceitful, devious, dishonest, mean, slippery, sly, untrustworthy

sneer VERB ① If you sneer at someone or something, you show by your expression and your comments that you think they are stupid or inferior. ▸ NOUN ② the expression on someone's face when they sneer.

sneeze VERB ① When you sneeze, you suddenly take in breath and blow it down your nose noisily, because something has irritated the inside of your nose. ▸ NOUN ② an act of sneezing.

snide ADJECTIVE A snide comment or remark criticises someone in a nasty but indirect way.

sniff VERB ① When you sniff, you breathe in air through your nose hard enough to make a sound. ② If you sniff something, you smell it by sniffing. ③ You can say that a person sniffs at something when they do not think very much of it • *Bessie sniffed at his household arrangements.* ▸ NOUN ④ the noise you make when you sniff. ⑤ A sniff of something is a smell of it • *a sniff at the flowers.*

snigger VERB ① If you snigger, you laugh in a quiet, disrespectful way • *They were sniggering at her accent.* ▸ NOUN ② a quiet, disrespectful laugh.

snip, **snips**, **snipping**, **snipped** VERB ① If you snip something, you cut it with scissors or shears in a single quick action. ▸ NOUN ② a small cut made by scissors or shears.

snippet NOUN A snippet of something such as information or news is a small piece of it.

snob NOUN ① someone who admires upper-class people and looks down on lower-class people. ② someone who believes that they are better than other people. **snobbery** NOUN **snobbish** ADJECTIVE

snooker NOUN Snooker is a game played on a large table covered with smooth green cloth. Players score points by hitting different coloured balls into side pockets using a long stick called a cue.

snoop VERB (*informal*) Someone who is snooping is secretly looking round a place to find out things.

snooze (*informal*) VERB ① If you snooze, you sleep lightly for a short time, especially during the day. ▸ NOUN ② a short, light sleep.

snore VERB ① When a sleeping person snores, they make a loud noise each time they breathe. ▸ NOUN ② the noise someone makes when they snore.

snorkel NOUN a tube you can breathe through when you are swimming just under the surface of the sea. **snorkelling** NOUN

snort VERB ① When people or animals snort, they force breath out through their nose in a noisy way • *Sarah snorted with laughter.* ▶ NOUN ② the noise you make when you snort.

snout NOUN An animal's snout is its nose.

snow NOUN ① Snow consists of flakes of ice crystals which fall from the sky in cold weather. ▶ VERB ② When it snows, snow falls from the sky.

snowball NOUN ① a ball of snow for throwing. ▶ VERB ② When something such as a project snowballs, it grows rapidly.

snowman, **snowmen** NOUN a large mound of snow moulded into the shape of a person.

snub, **snubs**, **snubbing**, **snubbed** VERB ① To snub someone means to behave rudely towards them, especially by making an insulting remark or ignoring them. ▶ NOUN ② an insulting remark or a piece of rude behaviour. ▶ ADJECTIVE ③ A snub nose is short and turned-up.

snuff NOUN Snuff is powdered tobacco which people take by sniffing it up their noses.

snug, **snugger**, **snuggest** ADJECTIVE A snug place is warm and comfortable. If you are snug, you are warm and comfortable. **snugly** ADVERB

snuggle VERB If you snuggle somewhere, you cuddle up more closely to something or someone.

so ADVERB ① 'So' is used to refer to what has just been mentioned • *Had he locked the car? If so, where were the keys?* ② 'So' is used to mean also • *He laughed, and so did Jarvis.* ③ 'So' can be used to mean 'therefore' • *It's a bit expensive, so I don't think I will get one.* ④ 'So' is used when you are talking about the degree or extent of something • *Why are you so cruel?* ⑤ 'So' is used before words like 'much' and 'many' to say that there is a definite limit to something • *There are only so many questions that can be asked about the record.* ▶ PHRASE ⑥ **So that** and **so as** are used to introduce the reason for doing something • *to die so that you might live.*

soak VERB ① To soak something or leave it to soak means to put it in a liquid and leave it there. ② When a liquid soaks something, it makes it very wet. ③ When something soaks up a liquid, the liquid is drawn up into it.

soak VERB
② = bathe, permeate, steep, wet

soaked ADJECTIVE extremely wet.

soaking ADJECTIVE If something is soaking, it is very wet.

soap NOUN Soap is a substance made of natural oils and fats and used for washing yourself. **soapy** ADJECTIVE

soap opera NOUN a popular television drama serial about people's daily lives.

soar VERB ① If an amount soars, it quickly increases by a great deal • *Property prices soared.* ② If something soars into the air, it quickly goes up into the air. **soaring** ADJECTIVE

sob, **sobs**, **sobbing**, **sobbed** VERB ① When someone sobs, they cry in a noisy way, breathing in short breaths. ▶ NOUN ② the noise made when you cry.

sober ADJECTIVE ① If someone is sober, they are not drunk. ② Sober also means serious and thoughtful. ③ Sober colours are plain and rather dull. **soberly** ADVERB **sober up** VERB To sober up means to become sober after being drunk.

sobering ADJECTIVE Something which is sobering makes you serious and thoughtful • *the sobering lesson of the last year*.

so-called ADJECTIVE You use 'so-called' to say that the name by which something is called is incorrect or misleading • *so-called environmentally-friendly products*.

soccer NOUN Soccer is a game played by two teams of eleven players who try to kick or head a ball into the opposing team's net.

sociable ADJECTIVE Sociable people are friendly and enjoy talking to other people. **sociability** NOUN

> **sociable** ADJECTIVE
> = friendly, gregarious, outgoing

social ADJECTIVE ① to do with society or life within a society • *people from similar social backgrounds*. ② to do with leisure activities that involve meeting other people. **socially** ADVERB

socialise; also spelt **socialize** VERB When people socialise, they meet other people socially, for example at parties.

socialism NOUN Socialism is the political belief that the state should own industries on behalf of the people and that everyone should be equal. **socialist** ADJECTIVE, NOUN

social media PLURAL NOUN [ICT] websites and applications used by large groups of people to share information and to develop social and professional contacts.

social networking site, **social networking sites** NOUN [ICT] a website where users can connect with other people to chat and share photographs and videos.

social security NOUN Social security is a system by which the government pays money regularly to people who have no other income or only a very small income.

social work NOUN Social work involves giving help and advice to people with serious financial or family problems. **social worker** NOUN

society, **societies** NOUN ① [CITIZENSHIP] Society is the people in a particular country or region • *a major problem in society*. ② an organisation for people who have the same interest or aim • *the school debating society*. ③ Society is also rich, upper-class, fashionable people.

> **society** NOUN
> ① = civilisation, culture
> ② = association, circle, club, fellowship, group, guild, institute, league, organisation, union

sociology NOUN Sociology is the study of human societies and the relationships between groups in these societies. **sociological** ADJECTIVE **sociologist** NOUN

sock NOUN Socks are pieces of clothing covering your foot and ankle.

socket NOUN ① a place on a wall or on a piece of electrical equipment into which you can put a plug or bulb. ② Any hollow part or opening into which another part fits can be called a socket • *eye sockets*.

sod NOUN (*literary*) The sod is the surface of the ground, together with the grass and roots growing in it.

soda NOUN ① Soda is the same as **soda water**. ② Soda is also sodium in the form of crystals or a powder, and is used for baking or cleaning.

soda water NOUN Soda water is fizzy water used for mixing with alcoholic drinks or fruit juice.

sodden ADJECTIVE soaking wet.

sodium NOUN [SCIENCE] Sodium is a silvery-white chemical element which combines with other chemicals. Salt is a sodium compound. Sodium's atomic number is 11 and its symbol is Na.

sofa NOUN a long comfortable seat with a back and arms for two or three people.

soft ADJECTIVE ① Something soft is not hard, stiff or firm. ② Soft also means very gentle • *a soft breeze.* ③ A soft sound or voice is quiet and not harsh. ④ A soft colour or light is not bright. **softly** ADVERB

> **soft** ADJECTIVE
> ① = flexible, pliable, squashy, supple, yielding
> ≠ hard
> ③ = gentle, low, mellow, muted, quiet, subdued

soft drink NOUN any cold, nonalcoholic drink.

soften VERB ① If something is softened or softens, it becomes less hard, stiff or firm. ② If you soften, you become more sympathetic and less critical • *Phillida softened as she spoke.*

software NOUN [ICT] Computer programs are known as software.

soggy, **soggier**, **soggiest** ADJECTIVE unpleasantly wet or full of water.

soil NOUN ① Soil is the top layer on the surface of the earth in which plants grow. ▸ VERB ② If you soil something, you make it dirty. **soiled** ADJECTIVE

> **soil** NOUN
> ① = clay, dirt, earth, ground
> ▸ VERB ② = dirty, foul, pollute, smear, spatter, stain
> ≠ clean

solace [*Said* **sol**-*iss*] NOUN (*literary*) Solace is something that makes you feel less sad • *I found solace in writing.*

solar ADJECTIVE ① [SCIENCE] relating or belonging to the sun. ② using the sun's light and heat as a source of energy • *a solar-powered calculator.*

solar system NOUN The solar system is the sun and all the planets, comets and asteroids that orbit round it.

sold the past tense and past participle of **sell**.

soldier NOUN a person in an army.

sole, **soles**, **soling**, **soled** ADJECTIVE ① The sole thing or person of a particular type is the only one of that type. ▸ NOUN ② The sole of your foot or shoe is the underneath part. ③ a flat seawater fish which you can eat. ▸ VERB ④ When a shoe is soled, a sole is fitted to it.

solely ADVERB If something involves solely one thing, it involves that thing and nothing else.

solemn ADJECTIVE Solemn means serious rather than cheerful or humorous. **solemnly** ADVERB **solemnity** NOUN

> **solemn** ADJECTIVE
> = earnest, grave (*formal*), serious, sober, staid

solicitor NOUN a lawyer who gives legal advice and prepares legal documents and cases.

solid ADJECTIVE ① A solid substance or object is hard or firm, and not in the form of a liquid or gas. ② You say that something is solid when it is not hollow • *solid steel.* ③ You say that a structure is solid when it is strong and not likely to fall down • *solid fences.* ④ You use 'solid' to say that something happens for a period of time without interruption • *I cried for two solid days.* ▸ NOUN ⑤ a solid substance or object. **solidly** ADVERB

> **solid** ADJECTIVE
> ① = firm, hard
> ③ = stable, strong, sturdy, substantial

solidarity NOUN If a group of people show solidarity, they show unity and support for each other.

soliloquy, **soliloquies** *[Said sol-lill-ok-wee]* NOUN [ENGLISH] a speech in a play made by a character who is alone on the stage.

solitary ADJECTIVE ① A solitary activity is one that you do on your own. ② A solitary person or animal spends a lot of time alone. ③ If there is a solitary person or object somewhere, there is only one.

solitary confinement NOUN A prisoner in solitary confinement is being kept alone in a prison cell.

solitude NOUN Solitude is the state of being alone.

solitude NOUN
= isolation, loneliness, privacy, seclusion

solo, **solos** NOUN ① a piece of music played or sung by one person alone. ▶ ADJECTIVE ② A solo performance or activity is done by one person alone • *my first solo flight*. ▶ ADVERB ③ Solo means alone • *to sail solo around the world*.

soloist NOUN a person who performs a solo.

solstice NOUN one of the two times in the year when the sun is at its furthest point south or north of the equator.

soluble ADJECTIVE [SCIENCE] A soluble substance is able to dissolve in liquid.

solution NOUN ① a way of dealing with a problem or difficult situation • *a quick solution to our problem*. ② The solution to a riddle or a puzzle is the answer. ③ [SCIENCE] a liquid in which a solid substance has been dissolved.

solve VERB If you solve a problem or a question, you find a solution or answer to it.

solve VERB
= clear up, crack, decipher, get to the bottom of, resolve, work out

solvent ADJECTIVE ① If a person or company is solvent, they have enough money to pay all their debts. ▶ NOUN ② [SCIENCE] a liquid that can dissolve other substances. **solvency** NOUN

Somali, **Somalis** ADJECTIVE ① belonging or relating to Somalia. ▶ NOUN ② The Somalis are a group of people who live in Somalia. ③ Somali is the language spoken by Somalis.

sombre ADJECTIVE ① Sombre colours are dark and dull. ② A sombre person is serious, sad or gloomy.

some ① You use 'some' to refer to a quantity or number when you are not stating the quantity or number exactly • *There's some money on the table*. ② You use 'some' to emphasise that a quantity or number is fairly large • *She had been there for some days*. ▶ ADVERB ③ You use 'some' in front of a number to show that it is not exact • *a fishing village some seven miles north*.

somebody PRONOUN You use 'somebody' to refer to a person without saying exactly who you mean.

some day ADVERB Some day means at a date in the future that is unknown or that has not yet been decided.

somehow ADVERB ① You use 'somehow' to say that you do not know how something was done or will be done • *You'll find a way of doing it somehow*. ② You use 'somehow' to say that you do not know the reason for something • *Somehow it didn't feel quite right*.

someone PRONOUN You use 'someone' to refer to a person without saying exactly who you mean.

somersault NOUN a forwards or backwards roll in which the head is placed on the ground and the body is brought over it.

something PRONOUN You use 'something' to refer to anything that is not a person without saying exactly what you mean.

sometime ADVERB ① at a time in the future or the past that is unknown or that has not yet been fixed • *He has to find out sometime.* ▶ ADJECTIVE ② (*formal*) 'Sometime' is used to say that a person had a particular job or role in the past • *a sometime actor, dancer and singer.*

sometimes ADVERB occasionally, rather than always or never.

> **sometimes** ADVERB
> = at times, every now and then, every so often, from time to time, now and again, now and then, occasionally, once in a while

somewhat ADVERB to some extent or degree • *The future seemed somewhat bleak.*

somewhere ADVERB ① 'Somewhere' is used to refer to a place without stating exactly where it is • *There has to be a file somewhere.* ② 'Somewhere' is used when giving an approximate amount, number or time • *somewhere between the winter of 2009 and the summer of 2011.*

son NOUN Someone's son is their male child.

sonar NOUN Sonar is equipment on a ship which calculates the depth of the sea or the position of an underwater object using sound waves.

sonata NOUN [MUSIC] a piece of classical music, usually in three or more movements, for piano or for another instrument with or without piano.

song NOUN a piece of music with words that are sung to the music.

songbird NOUN a bird that produces musical sounds like singing.

son-in-law, **sons-in-law** NOUN Someone's son-in-law is the husband of their grown-up child.

sonnet NOUN [ENGLISH] a poem with 14 lines, in which lines rhyme according to fixed patterns.

soon ADVERB If something is going to happen soon, it will happen in a very short time.

> **soon** ADVERB
> = any minute now, before long, in a minute, in the near future, presently, shortly
> ≠ later

soot NOUN Soot is black powder which rises in the smoke from a fire. **sooty** ADJECTIVE

soothe VERB ① If you soothe someone who is angry or upset, you make them calmer. ② Something that soothes pain makes the pain less severe. **soothing** ADJECTIVE

sophisticated ADJECTIVE ① Sophisticated people have refined or cultured tastes or habits. ② A sophisticated machine or device is made using advanced and complicated methods. **sophistication** NOUN

> **sophisticated** ADJECTIVE
> ① = cosmopolitan, cultivated, cultured, refined, urbane
> ② = advanced, complex, complicated, elaborate, intricate, refined
> ≠ simple

soppy, **soppier**, **soppiest** ADJECTIVE (*informal*) silly or foolishly sentimental.

soprano, **sopranos** NOUN [MUSIC] a woman, girl or boy with a singing voice in the highest range of musical notes.

sorcerer *[Said* ***sor****-ser-er]* **NOUN** a person who performs magic by using the power of evil spirits.

sorcery **NOUN** Sorcery is magic that uses the power of evil spirits.

sordid **ADJECTIVE** ① dishonest or immoral • *a rather sordid business.* ② dirty, unpleasant or miserable • *the sordid guest house.*

sore **ADJECTIVE** ① If part of your body is sore, it causes you pain and discomfort. ② (*literary*) 'Sore' is used to emphasise something • *The President is in sore need of friends.* ▶ **NOUN** ③ a painful place where your skin has become infected. **sorely** **ADVERB** **soreness** **NOUN**

> **sore** **ADJECTIVE**
> ① = inflamed, painful, raw, sensitive, smarting, tender

sorghum *[Said* ***saw****-gum]* **NOUN** a type of tropical grass that is grown for hay, grain and syrup.

sorrow **NOUN** ① Sorrow is deep sadness or regret. ② Sorrows are things that cause sorrow • *the sorrows of this world.*

> **sorrow** **NOUN**
> ① = grief, heartache, melancholy (*literary*), misery, mourning, pain, regret, sadness, unhappiness, woe (*formal*)
> ≠ joy
> ② = hardship, heartache, misfortune, trouble, woe (*formal*), worry
> ≠ joy

sorry, **sorrier**, **sorriest** **ADJECTIVE** ① If you are sorry about something, you feel sadness or regret about it. ② feeling sympathy for someone. ③ 'Sorry' is used to describe people and things that are in a bad physical or mental state • *She was in a pretty sorry state when we found her.*

> **sorry** **ADJECTIVE**
> ① = apologetic, penitent, regretful, remorseful, repentant
> ② = moved, sympathetic
> ③ = deplorable, miserable, pathetic, pitiful, poor, sad, wretched

sort **NOUN** ① The different sorts of something are the different types of it. ▶ **VERB** ② To sort things means to arrange them into different groups or sorts. **sort out** **VERB** If you sort out a problem or misunderstanding, you deal with it and find a solution to it.

> **sort** **NOUN**
> ① = brand, category, class, group, kind, make, species, style, type, variety
> ▶ **VERB** ② = arrange, categorise, classify, divide, grade, group, separate

SOS **NOUN** An SOS is a signal that you are in danger and need help.

so-so **ADJECTIVE** (*informal*) neither good nor bad • *The food is so-so.*

soufflé *[Said* ***soo****-flay]*; also spelt **souffle** **NOUN** a light, fluffy food made from beaten egg whites and other ingredients that is baked in the oven.

sought the past tense and past participle of **seek**.

soul **NOUN** ① RE A person's soul is the spiritual part of them that is supposed to continue after their body is dead. ② People also use 'soul' to refer to a person's mind, character, thoughts and feelings. ③ 'Soul' can be used to mean person • *There was not a soul there.* ④ Soul is a type of pop music.

sound **NOUN** ① SCIENCE Sound is everything that can be heard. It is caused by vibrations travelling through air or water to your ear. ② A particular sound is something that you hear. ③ The sound of someone or

something is the impression you have of them through what other people have told you • *I like the sound of your father's grandfather.* ▸ **VERB** ④ If something sounds or if you sound it, it makes a noise. ⑤ To sound something deep, such as a well or the sea, means to measure how deep it is using a weighted line or sonar.
▸ **ADJECTIVE** ⑥ in good condition • *a guarantee that a house is sound.* ⑦ reliable and sensible • *The logic behind the argument seems sound.* **soundly ADVERB**

> **sound NOUN**
> ① = din, hubbub, noise, racket, tone
> ≠ silence
> ▸ **VERB** ④ = blow, chime, clang, peal, ring, set off, toll
> ▸ **ADJECTIVE** ⑥ = all right, fine, fit, healthy, in good condition, intact, robust
> ⑦ = down-to-earth, good, reasonable, reliable, sensible, solid, valid

soundtrack NOUN The soundtrack of a film is the part you hear, especially the music.

soup NOUN Soup is liquid food made by cooking meat, fish or vegetables in water.

sour ADJECTIVE ① If something is sour, it has a sharp, acid taste. ② Sour milk has an unpleasant taste because it is no longer fresh. ③ A sour person is bad-tempered and unfriendly.
▸ **VERB** ④ If a friendship, situation or attitude sours or if something sours it, it becomes less friendly, enjoyable or hopeful.

> **sour ADJECTIVE**
> ① = acid, bitter, pungent, sharp, tart
> ≠ sweet
> ② = curdled, off, rancid
> ③ = disagreeable, embittered, jaundiced, tart

source NOUN ① The source of something is the person, place or thing that it comes from • *the source of his confidence.* ② A source is a person or book that provides information for a news story or for research.
③ GEOGRAPHY The source of a river or stream is the place where it begins.

> **source NOUN**
> ① = beginning, cause, derivation, origin, originator

sour grapes PLURAL NOUN You describe someone's behaviour as sour grapes when they say something is worthless but secretly want it and cannot have it.

south NOUN ① The south is the direction to your right when you are looking towards the place where the sun rises. ② The south of a place or country is the part which is towards the south when you are in the centre.
▸ **ADVERB, ADJECTIVE** ③ South means towards the south • *The taxi headed south* • *the south end of the site.*
▸ **ADJECTIVE** ④ A south wind blows from the south.

South America NOUN South America is the fourth largest continent. It has the Pacific Ocean on its west side, the Atlantic on the east, and the Antarctic to the south. South America is joined to Central America by the Isthmus of Panama.
South American ADJECTIVE

south-east NOUN, ADVERB, ADJECTIVE South-east is halfway between south and east.

south-eastern ADJECTIVE in or from the south-east.

southerly ADJECTIVE ① Southerly means to or towards the south.
② A southerly wind blows from the south.

southern ADJECTIVE in or from the south.

Southern Cross NOUN The Southern Cross is a small group of stars which can be seen from the southern part of the earth, and which is represented on the national flags of Australia and New Zealand.

South Pole NOUN GEOGRAPHY The South Pole is the most southerly place on the surface of the earth.

southward or **southwards** ADVERB ① Southward or southwards means towards the south • *the dusty road which led southwards.* ▶ ADJECTIVE ② The southward part of something is the south part.

south-west NOUN, ADVERB, ADJECTIVE South-west is halfway between south and west.

south-western ADJECTIVE in or from the south-west.

souvenir NOUN something you keep to remind you of a holiday, place or event.

> **souvenir** NOUN
> = keepsake, memento, relic, reminder

sovereign *[Said* ***sov****-rin]* NOUN ① a king, queen or royal ruler of a country. ② In the past, a sovereign was a British gold coin worth one pound. ▶ ADJECTIVE ③ A sovereign state or country is independent and not under the authority of any other country.

sovereignty *[Said* ***sov****-rin-tee]* NOUN Sovereignty is the political power that a country has to govern itself.

Soviet *[Said* ***soh****-vee-et]* HISTORY ADJECTIVE ① belonging or relating to the Soviet Union, a former country consisting of Russia and neighbouring states. ▶ NOUN ② The people and the government of the Soviet Union were sometimes referred to as the Soviets.

sow[1], **sowing, sowed, sown** *[Said* ***soh****]* VERB ① To sow seeds or sow an area of land with seeds means to plant them in the ground. ② To sow undesirable feelings or attitudes means to cause them • *You have sown discontent.*

sow[2], **sows** *[Rhymes with* ***now****]* NOUN an adult female pig.

soya NOUN Soya flour, margarine, oil and milk are made from soya beans.

spa NOUN a place where water containing minerals bubbles out of the ground, at which people drink or bathe in the water to improve their health.

space NOUN ① Space is the area that is empty or available in a place, building or container. ② Space is the area beyond the earth's atmosphere surrounding the stars and planets. ③ a gap between two things • *the space between the tables.* ④ Space can also refer to a period of time • *two incidents in the space of a week.* ▶ VERB ⑤ If you space a series of things, you arrange them with gaps between them.

> **space** NOUN
> ① = accommodation, capacity, room
> ③ = blank, distance, gap, interval
> ④ = interval, period, span, time, while

spacecraft NOUN a rocket or other vehicle that can travel in space.

spaceship NOUN a spacecraft that carries people through space.

spacious ADJECTIVE having or providing a lot of space • *the spacious living room.*

> **spacious** ADJECTIVE
> = ample, broad, expansive, extensive, huge, large, vast

spade NOUN ① a tool with a flat metal blade and a long handle used for digging. ② Spades is one of the four suits in a pack of playing cards. It is marked by a black symbol like a heart-shaped leaf with a stem.

spaghetti *[Said spag-**get**-ee]* **NOUN** Spaghetti consists of long, thin pieces of pasta.

spam **NOUN** unwanted emails, usually containing advertising.

span, **spans**, **spanning**, **spanned** **NOUN** ① the period of time during which something exists or functions • *looking back today over a span of 40 years.* ② The span of something is the total length of it from one end to the other. ▸ **VERB** ③ If something spans a particular length of time, it lasts throughout that time • *a career that spanned 50 years.* ④ A bridge that spans something stretches right across it.

Spaniard *[Said **span**-yard]* **NOUN** someone who comes from Spain.

spaniel **NOUN** a dog with long drooping ears and a silky coat.

Spanish **ADJECTIVE** ① belonging or relating to Spain. ▸ **NOUN** ② Spanish is the main language spoken in Spain, and is also spoken by many people in Central and South America.

spanner **NOUN** a tool with a specially shaped end that fits round a nut to turn it.

spar, **spars**, **sparring**, **sparred** **VERB** ① When boxers spar, they hit each other with light punches for practice. ② To spar with someone also means to argue with them, but not in an unpleasant or serious way. ▸ **NOUN** ③ a strong pole that a sail is attached to on a yacht or ship.

spare **ADJECTIVE** ① extra to what is needed • *What does she do in her spare time?* ▸ **NOUN** ② a thing that is extra to what is needed. ▸ **VERB** ③ If you spare something for a particular purpose, you make it available • *Few troops could be spared to go abroad.* ④ If someone is spared an unpleasant experience, they are prevented from suffering it • *The class was spared the misery of detention.*

> **spare** **ADJECTIVE**
> ① = extra, free, superfluous, surplus
> ▸ **VERB** ③ = afford, give, let someone have
> ④ = let off (*informal*), pardon, relieve of, save from

sparing **ADJECTIVE** If you are sparing with something, you use it in very small quantities. **sparingly** **ADVERB**

spark **NOUN** ① a tiny, bright piece of burning material thrown up by a fire. ② a small flash of light caused by electricity. ③ A spark of feeling is a small amount of it • *that tiny spark of excitement.* ▸ **VERB** ④ If something sparks, it throws out sparks. ⑤ If one thing sparks another thing off, it causes the second thing to start happening • *The tragedy sparked off a wave of sympathy among staff.*

sparkle **VERB** ① If something sparkles, it shines with a lot of small, bright points of light. ▸ **NOUN** ② Sparkles are small, bright points of light. **sparkling** **ADJECTIVE**

> **sparkle** **VERB**
> ① = gleam, glisten, glitter, shimmer, twinkle

sparrow **NOUN** a common small bird with brown and grey feathers.

sparse **ADJECTIVE** small in number or amount and spread out over an area • *the sparse audience.* **sparsely** **ADVERB**

spartan **ADJECTIVE** A spartan way of life is very simple with no luxuries • *spartan accommodation.*

spasm **NOUN** ① a sudden tightening of the muscles. ② a sudden, short burst of something • *a spasm of fear.*

spat the past tense and past participle of **spit**.

spate **NOUN** A spate of things is a large number of them that happen or appear in a rush • *a recent spate of first novels from older writers.*

spatial *[Said* ***spay****-shl]* **ADJECTIVE** to do with size, area or position.

spawn **NOUN** ① Spawn is a jelly-like substance containing the eggs of fish or amphibians. ▶ **VERB** ② When fish or amphibians spawn, they lay their eggs. ③ If something spawns something else, it causes it • *The depressed economy spawned the riots.*

speak, **speaks**, **speaking**, **spoke**, **spoken** **VERB** ① When you speak, you use your voice to say words. ② If you speak a foreign language, you know it and can use it.
speak out **VERB** To speak out about something means to publicly state an opinion about it.

speaker **NOUN** ① a person who is speaking, especially someone making a speech. ② A speaker on a device that reproduces sound is a loudspeaker.

spear **NOUN** ① a weapon consisting of a long pole with a sharp point. ▶ **VERB** ② To spear something means to push or throw a spear or other pointed object into it.

spearhead **VERB** If someone spearheads a campaign, they lead it.

spec **PHRASE** If you do something **on spec**, you do it hoping for a result but without any certainty • *He turned up at the same event on spec.*

special **ADJECTIVE** ① Something special is more important or better than other things of its kind. ② Special describes someone who is officially appointed, or something that is needed for a particular purpose • *Karen actually had to get special permission to go there.* ③ Special also describes something that belongs or relates to only one particular person, group or place • *the special needs of the chronically sick.*

special **ADJECTIVE**
① = exceptional, important, significant, unique
≠ ordinary
③ = characteristic, distinctive, individual, particular, peculiar, specific
≠ general

specialise; also spelt **specialize** **VERB** If you specialise in something, you make it your speciality • *a shop specialising in ceramics.* **specialisation** **NOUN**

specialised; also spelt **specialized** **ADJECTIVE** developed for a particular purpose or trained in a particular area of knowledge • *a specialised sales team.*

specialist **NOUN** ① someone who has a particular skill or who knows a lot about a particular subject • *a skin specialist.* ▶ **ADJECTIVE** ② having a skill or knowing a lot about a particular subject • *a specialist teacher.* **specialism** **NOUN**

speciality, **specialities** **NOUN** A person's speciality is something they are especially good at or know a lot about • *Roses are her speciality.*

specially **ADVERB** If something has been done specially for a particular person or purpose, it has been done only for that person or purpose.

species *[Said* ***spee****-sheez]* **NOUN** SCIENCE a division of plants or animals whose members have the same characteristics and are able to breed with each other.

specific **ADJECTIVE** ① particular • *specific areas of difficulty.* ② precise and exact • *She will ask for specific answers.*
specifically **ADVERB**

specification **NOUN** DGT a detailed description of what is needed for something, such as the necessary features in the design of something • *I like to build it to my own specifications.*

specify, **specifies**, **specifying**, **specified** VERB To specify something means to state or describe it precisely • *In his will he specified that these documents were never to be removed.*

> **specify** VERB
> = be specific about, indicate, name, spell out, state, stipulate

specimen NOUN A specimen of something is an example or small amount of it which gives an idea of what the whole is like • *a specimen of your writing.*

speck NOUN a very small stain or amount of something.

speckled ADJECTIVE Something that is speckled is covered in very small marks or spots.

spectacle NOUN ① a strange or interesting sight or scene • *an astonishing spectacle.* ② a grand and impressive event or performance.

spectacular ADJECTIVE ① Something spectacular is very impressive or dramatic. ▸ NOUN ② a grand and impressive show or performance.

spectator NOUN a person who is watching something.

> **spectator** NOUN
> = bystander, eyewitness, observer, onlooker, witness

spectre NOUN ① a frightening idea or image • *the spectre of war.* ② a ghost.

spectrum, **spectra** or **spectrums** NOUN ① [ART] The spectrum is the range of different colours produced when light passes through a prism or a drop of water. A rainbow shows the colours in a spectrum. ② A spectrum of opinions or emotions is a range of them.

speculate VERB If you speculate about something, you think about it and form opinions about it. **speculation** NOUN

speculative ADJECTIVE ① A speculative piece of information is based on guesses and opinions rather than known facts. ② Someone with a speculative expression seems to be trying to guess something • *His mother regarded him with a speculative eye.*

speech NOUN ① Speech is the ability to speak or the act of speaking. ② a formal talk given to an audience. ③ In a play, a speech is a group of lines spoken by one of the characters.

> **speech** NOUN
> ② = address, discourse, lecture, talk

speechless ADJECTIVE Someone who is speechless is unable to speak for a short time because something has shocked them.

speed, **speeds**, **speeding**, **sped** or **speeded** NOUN ① The speed of something is the rate at which it moves or happens. ② Speed is very fast movement or travel. ▸ VERB ③ If you speed somewhere, you move or travel there quickly. ④ Someone who is speeding is driving a vehicle faster than the legal speed limit.

> **speed** NOUN
> ① = haste, hurry, momentum, pace, rapidity, swiftness, velocity
> ▸ VERB ③ = career, flash, gallop, race, rush, tear

speedboat NOUN a small, fast motorboat.

speed limit NOUN The speed limit is the maximum speed at which vehicles are legally allowed to drive on a particular road.

speedway NOUN Speedway is the sport of racing lightweight motorcycles on special tracks.

speedy, **speedier**, **speediest** ADJECTIVE done very quickly. **speedily** ADVERB

spell, **spells**, **spelling**, **spelt** or **spelled** VERB ① When you spell a word, you

name or write its letters in order. ② When letters spell a word, they form that word when put together in a particular order. ③ If something spells a particular result, it suggests that this will be the result • *This haphazard method could spell disaster for you*. ▸ NOUN ④ A spell of something is a short period of it • *a spell of rough weather*. ⑤ a word or sequence of words used to perform magic.
spell out VERB If you spell something out, you explain it in detail • *I don't have to spell it out, do I?*

spellbound ADJECTIVE so fascinated by something that you cannot think about anything else • *She had sat spellbound through the film*.

spelling NOUN The spelling of a word is the correct order of letters in it.

spend, **spends**, **spending**, **spent** VERB ① When you spend money, you buy things with it. ② To spend time or energy means to use it.

spent ADJECTIVE ① Spent describes things which have been used and therefore cannot be used again • *spent matches*. ② If you are spent, you are exhausted and have no energy left.

sperm NOUN a cell produced in the reproductive organ of a male animal which can enter a female animal's egg and fertilise it.

spew VERB ① When things spew from something or when it spews them out, they come out of it in large quantities. ② (*informal*) To spew means to vomit.

sphere NOUN ① a perfectly round object, such as a ball. ② An area of activity or interest can be referred to as a sphere of activity or interest.
spherical ADJECTIVE

spice NOUN ① Spice is powder or seeds from a plant added to food to give it flavour. ② Spice is something which makes life more exciting • *Variety is the spice of life*. ▸ VERB ③ To spice food means to add spice to it. ④ If you spice something up, you make it more exciting or lively.

spicy, **spicier**, **spiciest** ADJECTIVE strongly flavoured with spices.

spider NOUN a small insect-like creature with eight legs that spins webs to catch insects for food.

spike NOUN ① a long pointed piece of metal. ② The spikes on a sports shoe are the pointed pieces of metal attached to the sole. ③ Some other long pointed objects are called spikes • *beautiful pink flower spikes*.

spiky, **spikier**, **spikiest** ADJECTIVE Something spiky has sharp points.

spill, **spills**, **spilling**, **spilled** or **spilt** VERB ① If you spill something or if it spills, it accidentally falls or runs out of a container. ② If people or things spill out of a place, they come out of it in large numbers.

spillage NOUN the spilling of something, or something that has been spilt • *the oil spillage in the Shetlands*.

spin, **spins**, **spinning**, **spun** VERB ① If something spins, it turns quickly around a central point. ② When spiders spin a web, they give out a sticky substance and make it into a web. ③ When people spin, they make thread by twisting together pieces of fibre using a machine. ④ If your head is spinning, you feel dizzy or confused. ▸ NOUN ⑤ a rapid turn around a central point • *a golf club which puts more spin on the ball*. **spin out** VERB If you spin something out, you make it last longer than it otherwise would.

> **spin** VERB
> ① = pirouette, revolve, rotate, turn, whirl

spinach [*Said* ***spin****-itch*] NOUN Spinach is a vegetable with large green leaves.

spinal ADJECTIVE to do with the spine.

spine NOUN ① Your spine is your backbone. ② Spines are long, sharp points on an animal's body or on a plant.

spin-off NOUN something useful that unexpectedly results from an activity.

spinster NOUN (*old-fashioned*) a woman who has never married.

spiral, **spirals**, **spiralling**, **spiralled** NOUN ① a continuous curve which winds round and round, with each curve above or outside the previous one. ▶ ADJECTIVE ② in the shape of a spiral • *a spiral staircase*. ▶ VERB ③ If something spirals, it moves up or down in a spiral curve • *The aircraft spiralled down*. ④ If an amount or level spirals, it rises or falls quickly at an increasing rate • *Prices have spiralled recently*.

spire NOUN The spire of a church is the tall cone-shaped structure on top.

spirit NOUN ① Your spirit is the part of you that is not physical and that is connected with your deepest thoughts and feelings. ② RE The spirit of a dead person is a nonphysical part that is believed to remain alive after death. ③ a supernatural being, such as a ghost. ④ Spirit is liveliness, energy and self-confidence • *a band full of spirit*. ⑤ Spirit can refer to an attitude • *his old fighting spirit*. ⑥ (*in plural*) Spirits can describe how happy or unhappy someone is • *in good spirits*. ⑦ Spirits are strong alcoholic drinks such as whisky and gin. ▶ VERB ⑧ If you spirit someone or something into or out of a place, you get them in or out quickly and secretly.

spirit NOUN
① = life force, soul
③ = apparition, ghost, phantom, spectre, sprite
④ = animation, energy, enthusiasm, fire, force, vigour, zest

spirited ADJECTIVE showing energy and courage.

spiritual ADJECTIVE ① to do with people's thoughts and beliefs, rather than their bodies and physical surroundings. ② RE to do with people's religious beliefs • *spiritual guidance*. ▶ NOUN ③ a religious song originally sung by enslaved Black people in America. **spiritually** ADVERB **spirituality** NOUN

spit, **spits**, **spitting**, **spat** NOUN ① Spit is saliva. ② a long stick made of metal or wood which is pushed through a piece of meat so that it can be hung over a fire and cooked. ③ GEOGRAPHY a long, flat, narrow piece of land sticking out into the sea. ▶ VERB ④ If you spit, you force saliva or some other substance out of your mouth. ⑤ (*informal*) When it is spitting, it is raining very lightly.

spite PHRASE ① If you do something **in spite of** something else, you do the first thing even though the second thing makes it unpleasant or difficult • *In spite of all the gossip, Virginia stayed behind*. ▶ VERB ② If you do something to spite someone, you do it deliberately to hurt or annoy them. ▶ NOUN ③ If you do something out of spite, you do it to hurt or annoy someone.

spite PHRASE
① = despite, even though, notwithstanding, regardless of, though
▶ NOUN ③ = ill will, malevolence, malice, spitefulness, venom

spiteful ADJECTIVE A spiteful person does or says nasty things to people deliberately to hurt them.

spiteful ADJECTIVE
= catty (*informal*), cruel, malevolent, malicious, nasty, snide, venomous, vindictive

splash VERB ① If you splash around in water, your movements disturb the water in a noisy way. ② If liquid splashes something, it scatters over it in a lot of small drops. ▸ NOUN ③ A splash is the sound made when something hits or falls into water. ④ A splash of liquid is a small quantity of it that has been spilt on something. **splash out** VERB To splash out on something means to spend a lot of money on it.

splatter VERB When something is splattered with a substance, the substance is splashed all over it • *fur coats splattered with paint*.

spleen NOUN Your spleen is an organ near your stomach which controls the quality of your blood.

splendid ADJECTIVE ① very good indeed • *a splendid career*. ② beautiful and impressive • *a splendid old mansion*. **splendidly** ADVERB

splendid ADJECTIVE
① = cracking (*British, Australian and New Zealand; informal*), excellent, fantastic (*informal*), fine, glorious, great (*informal*), marvellous, wonderful
② = gorgeous, grand, imposing, impressive, magnificent, superb

splendour NOUN ① If something has splendour, it is beautiful and impressive. ② (*in plural*) The splendours of something are its beautiful and impressive features.

splint NOUN a long piece of wood or metal fastened to a broken limb to hold it in place.

splinter NOUN ① a thin, sharp piece of wood or glass which has broken off a larger piece. ▸ VERB ② If something splinters, it breaks into thin, sharp pieces.

split, **splits**, **splitting**, **split** VERB ① If something splits or if you split it, it divides into two or more parts. ② If something such as wood or fabric splits, a long crack or tear appears in it. ③ If people split something, they share it between them. ▸ NOUN ④ A split in a piece of wood or fabric is a crack or tear. ⑤ A split between two things is a division or difference between them • *the split between rugby league and rugby union*. **split up** VERB If two people split up, they end their relationship or marriage.

split VERB
① = diverge, fork, part, separate
② = burst, come apart, crack, rip
▸ NOUN ④ = crack, fissure, rip, tear
⑤ = breach, breakup, divergence, division, rift, schism

split second NOUN an extremely short period of time.

splitting ADJECTIVE A splitting headache is a very painful headache.

splutter VERB ① If someone splutters, they speak in a confused way because they are embarrassed. ② If something splutters, it makes a series of short, sharp sounds.

spoil, **spoils**, **spoiling**, **spoiled** or **spoilt** VERB ① If you spoil something, you prevent it from being successful or satisfactory. ② To spoil children means to give them everything they want, with harmful effects on their character. ③ To spoil someone also means to give them something nice as a treat.

spoil VERB
① = damage, destroy, harm, impair, mar, mess up, ruin, wreck
② = cosset, indulge, pamper

spoke ① Spoke is the past tense of **speak**. ▸ NOUN ② The spokes of a wheel are the bars which connect the hub to the rim.

A B C D E F G H I J K L M N O P Q R S T U V W X Y Z

spoken the past participle of **speak**.

spokesperson NOUN someone who speaks on behalf of another person or a group. **spokesman** NOUN **spokeswoman** NOUN

sponge NOUN ① a sea creature with a body made up of many cells. ② part of the very light skeleton of a sponge, used for bathing and cleaning. ③ A sponge or sponge cake is a very light cake. ▸ VERB ④ If you sponge something, you clean it by wiping it with a wet sponge.

sponsor VERB ① To sponsor something, such as an event or someone's training, means to support it financially • *The visit was sponsored by the London Natural History Society*. ② If you sponsor someone who is doing something for charity, you agree to give them a sum of money for the charity if they manage to do it. ③ If you sponsor a proposal or suggestion, you officially put it forward and support it • *the MP who sponsored the Bill*. ▸ NOUN ④ a person or organisation sponsoring something or someone. **sponsorship** NOUN

spontaneous ADJECTIVE ① Spontaneous acts are not planned or arranged in advance. ② A spontaneous event happens because of processes within something rather than being caused by things outside it • *spontaneous bleeding*. **spontaneously** ADVERB **spontaneity** NOUN

spoof NOUN something such as an article or television programme that seems to be about a serious matter but is actually a joke.

spooky, **spookier**, **spookiest** ADJECTIVE eerie and frightening.

> **spooky** ADJECTIVE
> = creepy (*informal*), eerie, frightening, ghostly, haunted, scary (*informal*), supernatural, uncanny

spool NOUN a cylindrical object onto which thread, tape or film can be wound.

spoon NOUN an object shaped like a small shallow bowl with a long handle, used for eating, stirring and serving food.

spoonful, **spoonfuls** or **spoonsful** NOUN the amount held by a spoon.

sporadic ADJECTIVE happening at irregular intervals • *a few sporadic attempts at keeping a diary*. **sporadically** ADVERB

spore NOUN [SCIENCE] Spores are cells produced by bacteria and nonflowering plants such as fungi which develop into new bacteria or plants.

sport NOUN ① Sports are games and other enjoyable activities which need physical effort and skill. ② (*informal*) You say that someone is a sport when they accept defeat or teasing cheerfully • *Be a sport, Minister!* ▸ VERB ③ If you sport something noticeable or unusual, you wear it • *One girl sported a bowler hat*.

sporting ADJECTIVE ① relating to sport. ② behaving in a fair and decent way.

sports car NOUN a low, fast car, usually with room for only two people.

sportsman or **sportswoman** NOUN a person who takes part in sports and is good at them.

sportsmanship NOUN Sportsmanship is the behaviour of a good sportsman or sportswoman, for example fairness, generosity and cheerfulness when losing.

sporty, **sportier**, **sportiest** ADJECTIVE ① A sporty car is fast and flashy. ② A sporty person is good at sports.

spot, **spots**, **spotting**, **spotted** NOUN ① Spots are small, round, coloured areas on a surface. ② Spots on a person's skin are small lumps, usually caused by an infection or allergy. ③ A spot of something is a small amount of it • *spots of rain*. ④ A place can be called a spot • *the most beautiful spot in the garden*. ▶ VERB ⑤ If you spot something, you notice it. ▶ PHRASE ⑥ If you do something **on the spot**, you do it immediately.

spot NOUN
① = blemish, blot, blotch, mark, smudge, speck
④ = location, place, point, position, scene, site
▶ VERB ⑤ = catch sight of, detect, discern, observe, see, sight

spotless ADJECTIVE perfectly clean. **spotlessly** ADVERB

spotlight, **spotlights**, **spotlighting**, **spotlit** or **spotlighted** NOUN ① DRAMA a powerful light which can be directed to light up a small area. ▶ VERB ② If something spotlights a situation or problem, it draws the public's attention to it • *a national campaign to spotlight the problem*.

spot-on ADJECTIVE (*informal*) exactly correct or accurate.

spotted ADJECTIVE Something spotted has a pattern of spots on it.

spotter NOUN a person whose hobby is looking out for things of a particular kind • *a train spotter*.

spotty, **spottier**, **spottiest** ADJECTIVE Someone who is spotty has spots or pimples on their skin, especially on their face.

spouse NOUN Someone's spouse is the person they are married to.

spout VERB ① When liquid or flame spouts out of something, it shoots out in a long stream. ② When someone spouts what they have learned, they say it in a boring way. ▶ NOUN ③ a tube with a lip-like end for pouring liquid • *a teapot with a long spout*.

sprain VERB ① If you sprain a joint, you accidentally damage it by twisting it violently. ▶ NOUN ② the injury caused by spraining a joint.

sprang the past tense of **spring**.

sprawl VERB ① If you sprawl somewhere, you sit or lie there with your legs and arms spread out. ② A place that sprawls is spread out over a large area • *a Monday market which sprawls all over town*. ▶ NOUN ③ anything that spreads in an untidy and uncontrolled way • *a sprawl of skyscrapers*. **sprawling** ADJECTIVE

spray NOUN ① Spray consists of many drops of liquid splashed or forced into the air • *A spray of water shot upwards from the fountain*. ② Spray is also a liquid kept under pressure in a can or other container • *hair spray*. ③ a piece of equipment for spraying liquid • *a garden spray*. ④ A spray of flowers or leaves consists of several of them on one stem. ▶ VERB ⑤ To spray a liquid over something means to cover it with drops of the liquid.

spread, **spreads**, **spreading**, **spread** VERB ① If you spread something out, you open it out or arrange it so that it can be seen or used easily • *He spread the map out on his knees*. ② If you spread a substance on a surface, you put a thin layer on the surface. ③ If something spreads, it gradually reaches or affects more people • *The news spread quickly*. ④ If something spreads over a period of time, it happens regularly or continuously over that time • *His four international appearances were spread over eight years*. ⑤ If something such as work is spread, it is distributed evenly. ▶ NOUN ⑥ The spread of something is the extent to which it gradually reaches or affects more people • *the* *spread of technology*. ⑦ A spread of ideas, interests or other things is a wide variety of them. ⑧ soft food put on bread • *cheese spread*.

spread VERB
① = extend, fan out, open, sprawl, unfold, unfurl, unroll
② = apply, coat, cover, overlay, plaster, smear, smother
③ = circulate, grow, expand, increase, proliferate, travel
▸ NOUN ⑥ = diffusion, expansion, extent, growth, increase, progression, proliferation, upsurge

spreadsheet NOUN [ICT] a computer program that is used for entering and arranging figures, used mainly for financial planning.

spree NOUN a period of time spent doing something enjoyable • *a shopping spree*.

sprig NOUN ① a small twig with leaves on it. ② In Australian and New Zealand English, sprigs are studs on the sole of a football boot.

sprightly, **sprightlier**, **sprightliest** ADJECTIVE lively and active.

spring, **springs**, **springing**, **sprang**, **sprung** NOUN ① Spring is the season between winter and summer. ② a coil of wire which returns to its natural shape after being pressed or pulled. ③ a place where water comes up through the ground. ④ an act of springing • *With a spring he had opened the door*. ▸ VERB ⑤ To spring means to jump upwards or forwards • *Martha sprang to her feet*. ⑥ If something springs in a particular direction, it moves suddenly and quickly • *The door sprang open*. ⑦ If one thing springs from another, it is the result of it • *The failures sprang from three facts*.

springboard NOUN ① a flexible board on which a diver or gymnast jumps to gain height. ② If something is a springboard for an activity or enterprise, it makes it possible for it to begin.

springbok NOUN ① a small South African antelope which moves in leaps. ② A Springbok is a person who has represented South Africa in a sports team.

spring onion NOUN a small onion with long green shoots, often eaten raw in salads.

sprinkle VERB If you sprinkle a liquid or powder over something, you scatter it over it.

sprinkling NOUN A sprinkling of something is a small quantity of it • *a light sprinkling of snow*.

sprint NOUN ① a short, fast race. ▸ VERB ② To sprint means to run fast over a short distance.

sprinter NOUN an athlete who runs fast over short distances.

sprout VERB ① When something sprouts, it grows. ② If things sprout up, they appear rapidly • *Their houses sprouted up in that region*. ▸ NOUN ③ A sprout is the same as a **brussels sprout**.

spruce NOUN ① an evergreen tree with needle-like leaves. ▸ ADJECTIVE ② Someone who is spruce is very neat and smart. ▸ VERB ③ To spruce something up means to make it neat and smart.

sprung the past participle of **spring**.

spun the past tense and past participle of **spin**.

spur, **spurs**, **spurring**, **spurred** VERB ① If something spurs you to do something or spurs you on, it encourages you to do it. ▸ NOUN ② Something that acts as a spur encourages a person to do something. ③ Spurs are sharp metal points attached to the heels of a rider's boots and used to urge a horse on. ▶ PHRASE ④ If you do something **on the spur of the moment**, you do it suddenly, without planning it.

spurious [*Said* ***spyoor**-ee-uss*] ADJECTIVE not genuine or real.

spurn VERB If you spurn something, you refuse to accept it • *You spurned his last offer.*

spurt VERB ① When a liquid or flame spurts out of something, it comes out quickly in a thick, powerful stream. ▶ NOUN ② A spurt of liquid or flame is a thick powerful stream of it • *a small spurt of blood.* ③ A spurt of activity or effort is a sudden, brief period of it.

spy, spies, spying, spied NOUN ① a person sent to find out secret information about a country or organisation. ▶ VERB ② Someone who spies tries to find out secret information about another country or organisation. ③ If you spy on someone, you watch them secretly. ④ If you spy something, you notice it.

squabble VERB ① When people squabble, they quarrel about something trivial. ▶ NOUN ② a quarrel.

> **squabble** VERB
> ① = argue, bicker, fall out (*informal*), feud, fight, quarrel, row, wrangle
> ▶ NOUN ② = altercation, argument, barney (*British, Australian and New Zealand; informal*), disagreement, dispute, fight, quarrel, row, tiff

squad NOUN a small group chosen to do a particular activity • *the fraud squad* • *the England football squad.*

squadron NOUN a section of one of the armed forces, especially the air force.

squalid ADJECTIVE ① dirty, untidy and in bad condition. ② Squalid activities are unpleasant and often dishonest.

squall NOUN a brief, violent storm.

squalor NOUN Squalor consists of bad or dirty conditions or surroundings.

squander VERB To squander money or resources means to waste them • *They have squandered huge amounts of money.*

square NOUN ① MATHS a shape with four equal sides and four right angles. ② In a town or city, a square is a flat, open place, bordered by buildings or streets. ③ MATHS The square of a number is the number multiplied by itself. For example, the square of 3, written 3^2, is 3 x 3. ▶ ADJECTIVE ④ shaped like a square • *her delicate square face.* ⑤ 'Square' is used before units of length when talking about the area of something • *24 square metres.* ⑥ 'Square' is used after units of length when you are giving the length of each side of something square • *a towel measuring a foot square.* ▶ VERB ⑦ MATHS If you square a number, you multiply it by itself.

squarely ADVERB ① Squarely means directly rather than indirectly or at an angle • *I looked squarely in the mirror.* ② If you approach a subject squarely, you consider it fully, without trying to avoid unpleasant aspects of it.

squash VERB ① If you squash something, you press it, so that it becomes flat or loses its shape. ▶ NOUN ② If there is a squash in a place, there are a lot of people squashed in it. ③ Squash is a game in which two players hit a small rubber ball against the walls of a court using rackets. ④ Squash is a drink made from fruit juice, sugar and water.

squat, squats, squatting, squatted; squatter, squattest VERB ① If you squat down, you crouch, balancing on your feet with your legs bent. ② A person who squats in an unused building lives there as a squatter.

▸ NOUN ③ a building used by squatters. ▸ ADJECTIVE ④ short and thick.

squatter NOUN ① a person who lives in an unused building without permission and without paying rent. ② In Australian English, a squatter is someone who owns a large amount of land for sheep or cattle farming. ③ In Australia and New Zealand in the past, a squatter was someone who rented land from the King or Queen.

squawk VERB ① When a bird squawks, it makes a loud, harsh noise. ▸ NOUN ② a loud, harsh noise made by a bird.

squeak VERB ① If something squeaks, it makes a short, high-pitched sound. ▸ NOUN ② a short, high-pitched sound. **squeaky** ADJECTIVE

squeal VERB ① When things or people squeal, they make long, high-pitched sounds. ▸ NOUN ② a long, high-pitched sound.

squeamish ADJECTIVE easily upset by unpleasant sights or situations.

squeeze VERB ① When you squeeze something, you press it firmly from two sides. ② If you squeeze something into a small amount of time or space, you manage to fit it in. ▸ NOUN ③ If you give something a squeeze, you squeeze it • *She gave my hand a quick squeeze.* ④ If getting into something is a squeeze, it is just possible to fit into it • *It would take four comfortably, but six would be a squeeze.*

squid NOUN a sea creature with a long soft body and many tentacles.

squint VERB ① If you squint at something, you look at it with your eyes screwed up. ▸ NOUN ② If someone has a squint, their eyes look in different directions from each other.

squire NOUN HISTORY In a village, the squire was a gentleman who owned a large house with a lot of land.

squirm VERB If you squirm, you wriggle and twist your body about, usually because you are nervous or embarrassed.

squirrel NOUN a small furry mammal with a long bushy tail.

squirt VERB ① If a liquid squirts, it comes out of a narrow opening in a thin, fast stream. ▸ NOUN ② a thin, fast stream of liquid.

Sri Lankan [*Said shree-**lang**-kan*] ADJECTIVE ① belonging or relating to Sri Lanka. ▸ NOUN ② someone who comes from Sri Lanka.

stab, **stabs**, **stabbing**, **stabbed** VERB ① To stab someone means to wound them by pushing a knife into their body. ② To stab at something means to push at it sharply with your finger or with something long and narrow. ▸ PHRASE ③ (*informal*) If you **have a stab** at something, you try to do it. ▸ NOUN ④ You can refer to a sudden unpleasant feeling as a stab of something • *He felt a stab of guilt.*

stable ADJECTIVE ① not likely to change or come to an end suddenly • *I am in a stable relationship.* ② firmly fixed or balanced and not likely to move, wobble or fall. ▸ NOUN ③ a building in which horses are kept. **stability** NOUN **stabilise** VERB

staccato [*Said stak-**kah**-toe*] ADJECTIVE consisting of a series of short, sharp, separate sounds.

stack NOUN ① A stack of things is a pile of them, one on top of the other. ▸ VERB ② If you stack things, you arrange them one on top of the other in a pile.

stadium NOUN a sports ground with rows of seats around it.

staff NOUN ① The staff of an organisation are the people who work for it. ▸ VERB ② To staff an organisation means to find and employ people to work in it. ③ If an organisation is staffed by particular people, they are the people who work for it.

> **staff** NOUN
> ① = employees, personnel, team, workers, workforce

stag NOUN an adult male deer.

stage NOUN ① a part of a process that lasts for a period of time. ② DRAMA In a theatre, the stage is a raised platform where the actors or entertainers perform. ③ DRAMA You can refer to the profession of acting as the stage. ▸ VERB ④ If someone stages a play or event, they organise it and present it or take part in it.

> **stage** NOUN
> ① = lap, period, phase, point, step
> ▸ VERB ④ = arrange, engineer, mount, orchestrate, organise

stagger VERB ① If you stagger, you walk unsteadily, for example because you are ill. ② If something staggers you, it amazes you. ③ If events are staggered, they are arranged so that they do not all happen at the same time. **staggering** ADJECTIVE **staggered** ADJECTIVE

stagnant ADJECTIVE Stagnant water is not flowing and is unhealthy and dirty.

staid ADJECTIVE serious and dull.

stain NOUN ① a mark on something that is difficult to remove. ▸ VERB ② If a substance stains something, the thing becomes marked or coloured by it.

> **stain** NOUN
> ① = blot, mark, spot
> ▸ VERB ② = dirty, mark, soil, spot

stained glass NOUN Stained glass is coloured pieces of glass held together with strips of lead.

stainless steel NOUN Stainless steel is a metal made from steel and chromium which does not rust.

stair NOUN Stairs are a set of steps inside a building going from one floor to another.

staircase NOUN a set of stairs.

stairway NOUN a set of stairs.

stake PHRASE ① If something is **at stake**, it might be lost or damaged if something else is not successful • *The whole future of the company was at stake.* ▸ VERB ② If you say you would stake your money, life or reputation on the success or truth of something, you mean you would risk it • *He is prepared to stake his own career on this.* ▸ NOUN ③ If you have a stake in something such as a business, you own part of it and its success is important to you. ④ a pointed wooden post that can be hammered into the ground and used as a support. ⑤ (*in plural*) The stakes involved in something are the things that can be lost or gained.

stale ADJECTIVE ① Stale food or air is no longer fresh. ② If you feel stale, you have no new ideas and are bored.

> **stale** ADJECTIVE
> ① = flat, old, sour, stagnant
> ≠ fresh

stalemate NOUN ① Stalemate is a situation in which neither side in an argument or contest can win. ② In chess, stalemate is a situation in which a player cannot make any move permitted by the rules, so that the game ends and no-one wins.

stalk [*Said* ***stawk***] NOUN ① The stalk of a flower or leaf is its stem. ▸ VERB ② To stalk a person or animal means to follow them quietly in order to catch, kill or observe them. ③ If someone stalks into a room, they walk in a stiff, proud or angry way.

stall NOUN ① a large table containing goods for sale or information. ② (*in plural*) In a theatre, the stalls are the seats at the lowest level, in front of the stage. ▸ VERB ③ When a vehicle stalls, the engine suddenly stops. ④ If you stall when someone asks you to do something, you try to avoid doing it until a later time.

stallion NOUN an adult male horse that can be used for breeding.

stamina NOUN Stamina is the physical or mental energy needed to do something for a very long time.

stammer VERB ① When someone stammers, they speak with difficulty, repeating words and sounds and hesitating awkwardly. ▸ NOUN ② Someone who has a stammer tends to stammer when they speak.

stamp NOUN ① a small piece of gummed paper which you stick on a letter or parcel before posting it. ② a small block with a pattern cut into it, which you press onto an inky pad and make a mark with it on paper; also the mark made by the stamp. ③ If something bears the stamp of a particular quality or person, it shows clear signs of that quality or of the person's style or characteristics. ▸ VERB ④ If you stamp a piece of paper, you make a mark on it using a stamp. ⑤ If you stamp, you lift your foot and put it down hard on the ground. **stamp out** VERB To stamp something out means to put an end to it • *We must stamp out bullying in schools.*

stampede VERB ① When a group of animals stampede, they run in a wild, uncontrolled way. ▸ NOUN ② a group of animals stampeding.

stance NOUN Your stance on a particular matter is your attitude and way of dealing with it • *He takes no particular stance on animal rights.*

stand, **stands**, **standing**, **stood** VERB ① If you are standing, you are upright, your legs are straight, and your weight is supported by your feet. When you stand up, you get into a standing position. ② If something stands somewhere, that is where it is • *The house stands alone on the top of a small hill.* ③ If you stand something somewhere, you put it there in an upright position • *Stand the containers on bricks.* ④ If a decision or offer stands, it is still valid • *My offer still stands.* ⑤ You can use 'stand' when describing the state or condition of something • *Youth unemployment stands at 35 per cent.* ⑥ If a letter stands for a particular word, it is an abbreviation for that word. ⑦ If you say you will not stand for something, you mean you will not tolerate it. ⑧ If something can stand a situation or test, it is good enough or strong enough not to be damaged by it. ⑨ If you cannot stand something, you cannot bear it • *I can't stand that woman.* ⑩ If you stand in an election, you are one of the candidates. ▸ PHRASE ⑪ When someone **stands trial**, they are tried in a court of law. ▸ NOUN ⑫ a stall or very small shop outdoors or in a large public building. ⑬ a large structure at a sports ground, where the spectators sit. ⑭ a piece of furniture designed to hold something • *an umbrella stand.*

stand by VERB ① If you stand by to provide help or take action, you are ready to do it if necessary. ② If you stand by while something happens, you do nothing to stop it.

stand down VERB If someone stands down, they resign from their job or position. **stand in** VERB If you stand in for someone, you take their place while they are ill or away. **stand out**

VERB If something stands out, it can be easily noticed or is more important than other similar things.
stand up **VERB** ① If something stands up to rough treatment, it is not damaged or harmed. ② If you stand up to someone who is criticising or attacking you, you defend yourself.

standard **NOUN** ① a level of quality or achievement that is considered acceptable • *The work is not up to standard.* ② (*in plural*) Standards are moral principles of behaviour. ▶ **ADJECTIVE** ③ usual, normal and correct • *The practice became standard procedure for most motor companies.*

standard **NOUN**
① = calibre, criterion, guideline, level, norm, quality, requirement
② = ethics, ideals, morals, principles, rules, scruples, values
▶ **ADJECTIVE** ③ = accepted, correct, customary, normal, orthodox, regular, usual

standardise; also spelt **standardize** **VERB** To standardise things means to change them so that they all have a similar set of features • *We have decided to standardise our equipment.*

stand-by **NOUN** ① something available for use when you need it • *a useful stand-by.* ▶ **ADJECTIVE** ② A stand-by ticket is a cheap ticket that you buy just before a theatre performance or a flight if there are any seats left.

stand-in **NOUN** someone who takes a person's place while the person is ill or away • *The school had to employ a stand-in while the teacher was ill.*

standing **ADJECTIVE** ① permanently in existence or used regularly • *a standing joke.* ▶ **NOUN** ② A person's standing is their status and reputation. ③ 'Standing' is used to say how long something has existed • *a friend of 20 years' standing.*

standpoint **NOUN** If you consider something from a particular standpoint, you consider it from that point of view • *from a military standpoint.*

standstill **NOUN** If something comes to a standstill, it stops completely.

stank the past tense of **stink**.

stanza **NOUN** [ENGLISH] a verse of a poem.

staple **NOUN** ① Staples are small pieces of wire that hold sheets of paper firmly together. You insert them with a stapler. ▶ **VERB** ② If you staple sheets of paper, you fasten them together with staples. ▶ **ADJECTIVE** ③ A staple food forms a regular and basic part of someone's everyday diet.

star, **stars**, **starring**, **starred** **NOUN** ① a large ball of burning gas in space that appears as a point of light in the sky at night. ② a shape with four or more points sticking out in a regular pattern. ③ Famous actors, sports players and musicians are referred to as stars. ④ (*in plural*) The horoscope in a newspaper or magazine can be referred to as the stars • *I'm a Virgo, but don't read my stars every day.* ▶ **VERB** ⑤ If an actor or actress stars in a film or if the film stars that person, he or she has one of the most important parts in it.

star **NOUN**
③ = celebrity, idol, luminary (*literary*)

starboard **ADJECTIVE** The starboard side of a ship is the right-hand side when you are facing the front.

starch **NOUN** ① Starch is a substance used for stiffening fabric such as cotton and linen. ② [SCIENCE] Starch is a carbohydrate found in foods such as bread and potatoes. ▶ **VERB** ③ To starch fabric means to stiffen it with starch.

stare VERB ① If you stare at something, you look at it for a long time. ▸ NOUN ② a long fixed look at something.

stare VERB
① = gaze, look

starfish, **starfishes** or **starfish** NOUN a flat, star-shaped sea creature with five limbs.

stark ADJECTIVE ① harsh, unpleasant and plain • *the stark choice.* ▸ PHRASE ② If someone is **stark naked**, they have no clothes on at all.

start VERB ① If something starts, it begins to take place or comes into existence • *When does the party start?* ② If you start to do something, you begin to do it • *Susie started to cry.* ③ If you start something, you cause it to begin or to come into existence • *as good a time as any to start a business.* ④ If you start a machine or car, you operate the controls to make it work. ⑤ If you start, your body suddenly jerks because of surprise or fear. ▸ NOUN ⑥ The start of something is the point or time at which it begins. ⑦ If you do something with a start, you do it with a sudden jerky movement because of surprise or fear • *I awoke with a start.*

start VERB
① = arise, begin, come into being, come into existence, commence (*formal*), get under way, originate
≠ finish
② = begin, commence (*formal*), embark upon, proceed, set about
≠ stop
③ = begin, create, establish, found, get going, inaugurate (*formal*), initiate, instigate, institute, introduce, launch, open, pioneer, set in motion, set up, trigger
≠ stop
▸ NOUN ⑥ = beginning, birth, commencement (*formal*), dawn, foundation, inauguration (*formal*), inception (*formal*), initiation, onset, opening, outset
≠ finish

starter NOUN a small quantity of food served as the first part of a meal.

startle VERB If something sudden and unexpected startles you, it surprises you and makes you slightly frightened. **startled** ADJECTIVE **startling** ADJECTIVE

starve VERB ① If people are starving, they are suffering from a serious lack of food and are likely to die. ② To starve a person or animal means to prevent them from having any food. ③ (*informal*) If you say you are starving, you mean you are very hungry. ④ If someone or something is starved of something they need, they are suffering because they are not getting enough of it • *The hospital was starved of cash.* **starvation** NOUN

stash VERB (*informal*) If you stash something away in a secret place, you store it there to keep it safe.

state NOUN ① The state of something is its condition, what it is like, or its circumstances. ② Countries are sometimes referred to as states • *the state of Denmark.* ③ Some countries are divided into regions called states which make some of their own laws • *the State of Vermont.* ④ You can refer to the government or administration of a country as the state. ▸ PHRASE ⑤ If you are **in a state**, you are nervous or upset and unable to control your emotions. ▸ ADJECTIVE ⑥ A state ceremony involves the ruler or leader of a country. ▸ VERB ⑦ If you state something, you say it or write it, especially in a formal way.

state NOUN
① = circumstances, condition, plight, position, predicament, shape, situation

② = country, kingdom, land, nation, republic
▶ VERB ⑦ = affirm, articulate, assert, declare, express, say, specify

stately home NOUN In Britain, a stately home is a very large old house which belongs to an upper-class family.

statement NOUN ① something you say or write when you give facts or information in a formal way. ② a document provided by a bank showing all the money paid into and out of an account during a period of time.

statement NOUN
① = account, announcement, bulletin, declaration, explanation, proclamation, report, testimony

state school NOUN a school maintained and financed by the government in which education is free.

statesman, **statesmen** NOUN an important and experienced politician.

static ADJECTIVE ① never moving or changing • *The temperature remains fairly static.* ▶ NOUN ② SCIENCE Static or static electricity is an electrical charge caused by friction. It builds up in metal objects.

station NOUN ① a building and platforms where trains stop for passengers. ② A bus or coach station is a place where some buses start their journeys. ③ A radio station is the frequency on which a particular company broadcasts. ④ In Australian and New Zealand English, a station is a large sheep or cattle farm. ⑤ (*old-fashioned*) A person's station is their position or rank in society. ▶ VERB ⑥ Someone who is stationed somewhere is sent there to work or do a particular job • *Her husband was stationed in Vienna.*

stationary ADJECTIVE not moving • *a stationary car.*

stationery NOUN Stationery is paper, pens and other writing equipment.

statistic NOUN ① Statistics are facts obtained by analysing numerical information. ② Statistics is the branch of mathematics that deals with the analysis of numerical information. **statistical** ADJECTIVE **statistically** ADVERB

statistician [*Said stat-iss-**tish**-an*] NOUN a person who studies or works with statistics.

statue NOUN a sculpture of a person.

stature NOUN ① Someone's stature is their height and size. ② Someone's stature is also their importance and reputation • *the desire to gain international stature.*

status [*Said **stay**-tuss*] NOUN ① A person's status is their position and importance in society. ② Status is also the official classification given to someone or something • *I am not sure what your legal status is.*

status NOUN
① = position, prestige, rank, standing

status quo [*Said stay-tuss **kwoh***] NOUN The status quo is the situation that exists at a particular time • *They want to keep the status quo.*

statute NOUN a law. **statutory** ADJECTIVE

staunch ADJECTIVE ① A staunch supporter is a strong and loyal supporter • *a staunch supporter of the Royal family.* ▶ VERB ② If you staunch blood, you stop it from flowing out of a wound.

stave NOUN ① MUSIC A stave is the five lines that music is written on. ▶ VERB ② If you stave something off, you try to delay or prevent it.

stay VERB ① If you stay in a place, you do not move away from it • *She stayed in bed until noon.* ② If you stay at a hotel or a friend's house, you spend some time there as a guest or visitor. ③ If you stay in a particular state, you continue to be in it • *I stayed awake the first night.* ④ In Scottish and South African English, to stay in a place can also mean to live there. ▶ NOUN ⑤ a short time spent somewhere • *a very pleasant stay in Cornwall.*

> **stay** VERB
> ① = hang around (*informal*), linger, loiter, remain, tarry, wait

stead PHRASE (*formal*) Something that will stand someone **in good stead** will be useful to them in the future.

steadfast ADJECTIVE refusing to change or give up. **steadfastly** ADVERB

> **steadfast** ADJECTIVE
> = constant, faithful, firm, immovable, resolute, staunch, steady, unshakeable

steady, **steadier**, **steadiest**; **steadies**, **steadying**, **steadied** ADJECTIVE ① continuing or developing gradually without major interruptions or changes • *a steady rise in profits.* ② firm and not shaking or wobbling • *O'Brien held out a steady hand.* ③ A steady look or voice is calm and controlled. ④ Someone who is steady is sensible and reliable. ▶ VERB ⑤ When you steady something, you hold on to prevent it from shaking or wobbling. ⑥ When you steady yourself, you control and calm yourself. **steadily** ADVERB

> **steady** ADJECTIVE
> ① = consistent, constant, continuous, even, nonstop, regular, uninterrupted
> ② = firm, secure, stable
> ▶ VERB ⑤ = brace, secure, stabilise, support

steak NOUN ① Steak is good-quality beef without much fat. ② A fish steak is a large piece of fish.

steal, **steals**, **stealing**, **stole**, **stolen** VERB ① To steal something means to take it without permission and without intending to return it. ② To steal somewhere means to move there quietly and secretively.

> **steal** VERB
> ① = appropriate, nick (*British, Australian and New Zealand; slang*), pilfer, pinch (*informal*), swipe (*slang*), take
> ② = creep, slip, sneak, tiptoe

stealth [*Rhymes with* ***health***] NOUN If you do something with stealth, you do it quietly and secretively. **stealthy** ADJECTIVE **stealthily** ADVERB

steam NOUN ① Steam is the hot vapour formed when water boils. ▶ ADJECTIVE ② Steam engines are operated using steam as a means of power. ▶ VERB ③ If something steams, it gives off steam. ④ To steam food means to cook it in steam. **steamy** ADJECTIVE

steamer NOUN ① a ship powered by steam. ② a container with small holes in the bottom in which you steam food.

steel NOUN ① Steel is a very strong metal containing mainly iron with a small amount of carbon. ▶ VERB ② To steel yourself means to prepare to deal with something unpleasant.

steep ADJECTIVE ① A steep slope rises sharply and is difficult to go up. ② larger than is reasonable • *a steep price increase.* ▶ VERB ③ To steep something in a liquid means to soak it thoroughly. **steeply** ADVERB

> **steep** ADJECTIVE
> ① = sheer, vertical
> ≠ gradual

② = excessive, extortionate, high, unreasonable
▸ VERB ③ = immerse, marinate, soak

steeped ADJECTIVE If a person or place is steeped in a particular quality, they are surrounded by it or have been deeply influenced by it • *an industry steeped in tradition*.

steeple NOUN a tall pointed structure on top of a church tower.

steeplechase NOUN a long horse race in which the horses jump over obstacles such as hedges and water jumps.

steer VERB ① To steer a vehicle or boat means to control it so that it goes in the right direction. ② To steer someone towards a particular course of action means to influence and direct their behaviour or thoughts.

stem, **stems**, **stemming**, **stemmed** NOUN ① The stem of a plant is the long, thin central part above the ground that carries the leaves and flowers. ② The stem of a glass is the long, narrow part connecting the bowl to the base. ▸ VERB ③ If a problem stems from a particular situation, that situation is the original starting point or cause of the problem. ④ If you stem the flow of something, you restrict it or stop it from spreading • *to stem the flow of blood*.

stench NOUN a very strong, unpleasant smell.

stencil, **stencils**, **stencilling**, **stencilled** NOUN ① a thin sheet with a cut-out pattern through which ink or paint passes to form the pattern on the surface below. ▸ VERB ② To stencil a design on a surface means to create it using a stencil.

step, **steps**, **stepping**, **stepped** NOUN ① If you take a step, you lift your foot and put it down somewhere else. ② one of a series of actions that you take in order to achieve something. ③ a raised flat surface, usually one of a series that you can walk up or down. ▸ VERB ④ If you step in a particular direction, you move your foot in that direction. ⑤ If someone steps down or steps aside from an important position, they resign.
step in VERB If you step in, you become involved in a difficult situation in order to help to resolve it.
step up VERB If you step up the rate of something, you increase it.

stepping stone NOUN ① Stepping stones are a line of large stones that you walk on to cross a shallow river. ② a job or event that is regarded as a stage in your progress, especially in your career.

stereo ADJECTIVE A stereo recording or music system is one in which the sound is directed through two speakers.

stereotype [PSHE] NOUN ① a fixed image or set of characteristics that people consider to represent a particular type of person or thing • *the stereotype of the polite, industrious Japanese*. ▸ VERB ② If you stereotype someone, you assume they are a particular type of person and will behave in a particular way.

sterile ADJECTIVE ① Sterile means completely clean and free from germs. ② A sterile person or animal is unable to produce offspring.
sterility NOUN

sterile ADJECTIVE
① = antiseptic, germ-free, sterilised
② = barren, unproductive
≠ fertile

sterilise; also spelt **sterilize** VERB ① To sterilise something means to make it completely clean and free from germs, usually by boiling it or treating it with an antiseptic. ② If a person or animal is sterilised, they have an operation that makes it impossible for them to produce offspring.

sterling NOUN ① Sterling is the money system of the United Kingdom. ▶ ADJECTIVE ② excellent in quality • *Volunteers are doing sterling work.*

stern ADJECTIVE ① very serious and strict • *a stern father* • *a stern warning.* ▶ NOUN ② The stern of a boat is the back part.

steroid NOUN Steroids are chemicals that occur naturally in your body. Sometimes sportsmen and sportswomen illegally take them as drugs to improve their performance.

stethoscope NOUN a device used by doctors to listen to a patient's heart and breathing, consisting of earpieces connected to a hollow tube and a small disc.

stew NOUN ① a dish of small pieces of savoury food cooked together slowly in a liquid. ▶ VERB ② To stew meat, vegetables or fruit means to cook them slowly in a liquid.

steward NOUN ① a man who works on a ship or plane looking after passengers and serving meals. ② a person who helps to direct the public at a race, march or other event.

stewardess NOUN a woman who works on a ship or plane looking after passengers and serving meals.

stick, **sticks**, **sticking**, **stuck** NOUN ① a long, thin piece of wood. ② A stick of something is a long, thin piece of it • *a stick of celery.* ▶ VERB ③ If you stick a long or pointed object into something, you push it in. ④ If you stick one thing to another, you attach it with glue or sticky tape. ⑤ If one thing sticks to another, it becomes attached and is difficult to remove. ⑥ If a movable part of something sticks, it becomes fixed and will no longer move or work properly • *My gears keep sticking.* ⑦ (*informal*) If you stick something somewhere, you put it there. ⑧ If you stick by someone, you continue to help and support them. ⑨ If you stick to something, you keep to it and do not change to something else • *He should have stuck to the old ways of doing things.* ⑩ When people stick together, they stay together and support each other. **stick out** VERB ① If something sticks out, it projects from something else. ② To stick out also means to be very noticeable. **stick up** VERB ① If something sticks up, it points upwards from a surface. ② (*informal*) If you stick up for a person or principle, you support or defend them.

> **stick** NOUN
> ① = bat, cane, mace, pole, rod, truncheon, twig, wand
> ▶ VERB ③ = dig, insert, jab, poke, push, put, ram, shove, stuff, thrust
> ④ = attach, bond, fix, fuse, glue, paste
> ⑤ = adhere (*formal*), bond, cling, fuse
> ⑥ = catch, jam, lodge, snag

sticker NOUN a small piece of paper or plastic with writing or a picture on it, that you stick onto a surface.

sticky, **stickier**, **stickiest** ADJECTIVE ① A sticky object is covered with a substance that can stick to other things • *sticky hands.* ② Sticky paper or tape has glue on one side so that you can stick it to a surface. ③ (*informal*) A sticky situation is difficult or embarrassing to deal with. ④ Sticky weather is unpleasantly hot and humid.

> **sticky** ADJECTIVE
> ① = adhesive, tacky

stiff ADJECTIVE ① DGT Something that is stiff is firm and not easily bent. ② If you feel stiff, your muscles or joints ache when you move. ③ Stiff behaviour is formal and not friendly or relaxed. ④ Stiff also means difficult or severe • *stiff competition for places*. ⑤ A stiff breeze is blowing strongly. ▶ **ADVERB** ⑥ (*informal*) If you are bored stiff or scared stiff, you are very bored or very scared. **stiffly ADVERB stiffness NOUN**

stiff ADJECTIVE
① = firm, hard, rigid, solid, taut
≠ limp
③ = cold, forced, formal, stilted, unnatural, wooden
④ = arduous, difficult, exacting, formidable, hard, rigorous, tough

stiffen VERB ① If you stiffen, you suddenly stop moving and your muscles become tense • *I stiffened with tension*. ② If your joints or muscles stiffen, they become sore and difficult to bend or move. ③ If fabric or material is stiffened, it is made firmer so that it does not bend easily.

stifle [*Said sty-fl*] **VERB** ① If the atmosphere stifles you, you feel you cannot breathe properly. ② To stifle something means to stop it from happening or continuing • *Martin stifled a yawn*. **stifling ADJECTIVE**

stigma NOUN If something has a stigma attached to it, people consider it unacceptable or a disgrace • *the stigma of poverty*.

stiletto, stilettos NOUN Stilettos are women's shoes with very high, narrow heels.

still ADVERB ① If a situation still exists, it has continued to exist and it exists now. ② If something could still happen, it might happen although it has not happened yet. ③ 'Still' emphasises that something is the case in spite of other things • *Whatever you think of him, he's still your father*. ▶ **ADVERB, ADJECTIVE** ④ Still means staying in the same position without moving • *Sit still* • *The air was still*. ▶ **ADJECTIVE** ⑤ A still place is quiet and peaceful with no signs of activity. ▶ **NOUN** ⑥ a photograph taken from a film or video. **stillness NOUN**

still ADVERB, ADJECTIVE
④ = calm, inert, motionless, stationary, tranquil

stillborn ADJECTIVE A stillborn baby is dead when it is born.

stilt NOUN ① Stilts are long upright poles on which a building is built, for example on wet land. ② Stilts are also two long pieces of wood or metal on which people balance and walk.

stilted ADJECTIVE formal, unnatural and rather awkward • *a stilted conversation*.

stimulant NOUN a drug or other substance that makes your body work faster, increasing your heart rate and making it difficult to sleep.

stimulate VERB ① To stimulate something means to encourage it to begin or develop • *to stimulate discussion*. ② If something stimulates you, it gives you new ideas and enthusiasm. **stimulating ADJECTIVE stimulation NOUN**

stimulus, stimuli NOUN something that causes a process or event to begin or develop.

sting, stings, stinging, stung VERB ① If a creature or plant stings you, it pricks your skin and injects a substance which causes pain. ② If a part of your body stings, you feel a sharp tingling pain there. ③ If someone's remarks sting you, they make you feel upset and hurt. ▶ **NOUN** ④ A creature's sting is the part it stings you with.

stink, stinks, stinking, stank, stunk VERB ① Something that stinks smells very unpleasant. ▶ **NOUN** ② a very unpleasant smell.

stint NOUN a period of time spent doing a particular job • *a three-year stint in the army.*

stipulate VERB (*formal*) If you stipulate that something must be done, you state clearly that it must be done. **stipulation NOUN**

stir, stirs, stirring, stirred VERB ① When you stir a liquid, you move it around using a spoon or a stick. ② To stir means to move slightly. ③ If something stirs you, it makes you feel strong emotions • *The power of the singing stirred me.* ▶ **NOUN** ④ If an event causes a stir, it causes general excitement or shock • *two books which have caused a stir.*

stirring ADJECTIVE ① causing excitement, emotion and enthusiasm • *a stirring account of the action.* ▶ **NOUN** ② If there is a stirring of emotion, people begin to feel it.

stitch VERB ① When you stitch pieces of material together, you use a needle and thread to sew them together. ② To stitch a wound means to use a special needle and thread to hold the edges of skin together. ▶ **NOUN** ③ one of the pieces of thread that can be seen where material has been sewn. ④ one of the pieces of thread that can be seen where a wound has been stitched • *He had eleven stitches in his lip.* ⑤ If you have a stitch, you feel a sharp pain at the side of your abdomen, usually because you have been running or laughing.

stock NOUN ① Stocks are shares bought as an investment in a company; also the amount of money raised by the company through the issue of shares. ② A shop's stock is the total amount of goods it has for sale. ③ If you have a stock of things, you have a supply ready for use. ④ The stock an animal or person comes from is the type of animal or person they are descended from • *She was descended from Scots Highland stock.* ⑤ Stock is farm animals. ⑥ Stock is a liquid made from boiling meat, bones or vegetables together in water. Stock is used as a base for soups, stews and sauces. ▶ **VERB** ⑦ A shop that stocks particular goods keeps a supply of them to sell. ⑧ If you stock a shelf or cupboard, you fill it with food or other things. ▶ **ADJECTIVE** ⑨ A stock expression or way of doing something is one that is commonly used. **stock up VERB** If you stock up on something, you buy a supply of it.

stock NOUN
① = bonds, investments, shares
② = goods, merchandise (*formal*)
③ = reserve, reservoir, stockpile, store, supply
④ = ancestry, descent, extraction, lineage, origin, parentage
▶ **VERB** ⑦ = deal in, sell, supply, trade in
▶ **ADJECTIVE** ⑨ = hackneyed, overused, routine, standard, stereotyped, typical, usual

stockbroker NOUN A stockbroker is a person whose job is to buy and sell shares for people who want to invest money.

stock exchange NOUN a place where there is trading in stocks and shares • *the New York Stock Exchange.*

stocking NOUN Stockings are long pieces of thin clothing that cover the leg.

stockman, stockmen NOUN a man who looks after sheep or cattle on a farm.

stock market NOUN The stock market is the organisation and activity involved in buying and selling stocks and shares.

stockpile VERB ① If someone stockpiles something, they store large quantities of it for future use. ▶ NOUN ② a large store of something.

> **stockpile** VERB
> ① = accumulate, amass, collect, gather, hoard, save, stash (*informal*), store up
> ▶ NOUN ② = arsenal, cache, hoard, reserve, stash (*informal*), stock, store

stocky, **stockier**, **stockiest** ADJECTIVE A stocky person is rather short, but broad and solid-looking.

> **stocky** ADJECTIVE
> = chunky, solid, sturdy

stoke VERB To stoke a fire means to keep it burning by moving or adding fuel.

stole the past tense of **steal**.

stolen the past participle of **steal**.

stomach NOUN ① Your stomach is the organ inside your body where food is digested. ② You can refer to the front part of your body above your waist as your stomach. ▶ VERB ③ If you cannot stomach something, you strongly dislike it and cannot accept it.

> **stomach** NOUN
> ② = belly, paunch, puku (*New Zealand*), tummy (*informal*)

stone NOUN ① Stone is the hard solid substance found in the ground and used for building. ② a small piece of rock. ③ The stone in a fruit such as a plum or cherry is the large seed in the centre. ④ a unit of weight equal to 14 pounds or about 6.35 kilograms. ⑤ You can refer to a jewel as a stone • *a diamond ring with three stones*. ▶ VERB ⑥ To stone something or someone means to throw stones at them.

stony, **stonier**, **stoniest** ADJECTIVE ① Stony ground is rough and contains a lot of stones or rocks. ② If someone's expression is stony, it shows no friendliness or sympathy.

stood the past tense and past participle of **stand**.

stool NOUN a seat with legs but no back or arms.

stoop VERB ① If you stoop, you stand or walk with your shoulders bent forwards. ② If you would not stoop to something, you would not disgrace yourself by doing it.

stop, **stops**, **stopping**, **stopped** VERB ① If you stop doing something, you no longer do it. ② If an activity or process stops, it comes to an end or no longer happens. ③ If a machine stops, it no longer functions or it is switched off. ④ To stop something means to prevent it. ⑤ If people or things that are moving stop, they no longer move. ⑥ If you stop somewhere, you stay there for a short while. ▶ PHRASE ⑦ To **put a stop to** something means to prevent it from happening or continuing. ▶ NOUN ⑧ a place where a bus, train or other vehicle stops during a journey. ⑨ If something that is moving comes to a stop, it no longer moves.

> **stop** VERB
> ① = cease, cut out (*informal*), desist, discontinue, end, quit
> ≠ start
> ② = cease, come to an end, conclude, end, finish, halt
> ≠ start
> ④ = arrest, check, prevent

stoppage NOUN If there is a stoppage, people stop work because of a disagreement with their employer.

stopper NOUN a piece of glass or cork that fits into the neck of a jar or bottle.

stopwatch NOUN a watch that can be started and stopped by pressing buttons, which is used to time events.

storage NOUN The storage of something is the keeping of it somewhere until it is needed.

store NOUN ① a shop. ② A store of something is a supply kept for future use. ③ a place where things are kept while they are not used. ▶ VERB ④ When you store something somewhere, you keep it there until it is needed. ▶ PHRASE ⑤ Something that is **in store for** you is going to happen to you in the future.

> **store** NOUN
> ② = cache, fund, hoard, reserve, reservoir, stock, stockpile, supply
> ③ = depot, storeroom, warehouse
> ▶ VERB ④ = hoard, keep, save, stash (*informal*), stockpile

storeroom NOUN a room where things are kept until they are needed.

storey, **storeys** NOUN A storey of a building is one of its floors or levels.

storm NOUN ① When there is a storm, there is heavy rain, a strong wind, and often thunder and lightning. ② If something causes a storm, it causes an angry or excited reaction • *His words caused a storm of protest.* ▶ VERB ③ If someone storms out, they leave quickly, noisily and angrily. ④ To storm means to say something in a loud, angry voice • *'It's a fiasco!' he stormed.* ⑤ If people storm a place, they attack it. **stormy** ADJECTIVE

story, **stories** NOUN ① ENGLISH a description of imaginary people and events written or told to entertain people. ② The story of something or someone is an account of the important events that have happened to them • *his life story.*

> **story** NOUN
> ① = account, anecdote, legend, narrative, tale, yarn

stout ADJECTIVE ① rather fat. ② thick, strong and sturdy • *stout walking shoes.* ③ determined, firm and strong • *He can outrun the stoutest opposition.* **stoutly** ADVERB

stove NOUN a piece of equipment for heating a room or for cooking.

stow VERB ① If you stow something somewhere or stow it away, you store it until it is needed. ② If someone stows away in a ship or plane, they hide in it to go somewhere secretly without paying.

straddle VERB ① If you straddle something, you stand or sit with one leg on either side of it. ② If something straddles a place, it crosses it, linking different parts together • *The town straddles a river.*

straight ADJECTIVE, ADVERB ① continuing in the same direction without curving or bending • *the straight path* • *Amy stared straight ahead of her.* ② upright or level rather than sloping or bent • *Keep your arms straight.* ▶ ADVERB ③ immediately and directly • *We will go straight to the hotel.* ▶ ADJECTIVE ④ neat and tidy • *Get this room straight.* ⑤ honest, frank and direct • *They wouldn't give me a straight answer.* ⑥ A straight choice involves only two options.

> **straight** ADJECTIVE, ADVERB
> ② = erect, even, horizontal, level, perpendicular, upright, vertical
> ≠ crooked
> ▶ ADJECTIVE ⑤ = blunt, candid, forthright, frank, honest, outright, plain, point-blank

straightaway ADVERB If you do something straightaway, you do it immediately.

straighten VERB ① To straighten something means to remove any bends or curves from it. ② To straighten something also means to make it neat and tidy. ③ To straighten out a confused situation means to organise and deal with it.

straightforward ADJECTIVE ① easy and involving no problems. ② honest, open and frank.

> **straightforward** ADJECTIVE
> ① = basic, easy, elementary, lo-fi, routine, simple, uncomplicated
> ≠ complicated
> ② = candid, direct, forthright, frank, honest, open, plain, straight
> ≠ devious

strain NOUN ① Strain is worry and nervous tension. ② If a strain is put on something, it is affected by a strong force which may damage it. ③ You can refer to an aspect of someone's character, remarks or work as a strain • *There was a strain of bitterness in his voice.* ④ You can refer to distant sounds of music as strains of music. ⑤ A particular strain of plant is a variety of it • *strains of rose.* ▸ VERB ⑥ To strain something means to force it or use it more than is reasonable or normal. ⑦ If you strain a muscle, you injure it by moving awkwardly. ⑧ To strain food means to pour away the liquid from it.

> **strain** NOUN
> ① = anxiety, pressure, stress, tension
> ▸ VERB ⑥ = overwork, tax

strained ADJECTIVE ① worried and anxious. ② If a relationship is strained, people feel unfriendly and do not trust each other.

strait NOUN ① You can refer to a narrow strip of sea as a strait or the straits • *the Straits of Hormuz.* ② (*in plural*) If someone is in a bad situation, you can say they are in difficult straits.

straitjacket NOUN a special jacket used to tie the arms of a violent person tightly around their body.

strand NOUN ① A strand of thread or hair is a single long piece of it. ② You can refer to a part of a situation or idea as a strand of it • *the different strands of the problem.*

stranded ADJECTIVE If someone or something is stranded somewhere, they are stuck and cannot leave.

strange ADJECTIVE ① unusual or unexpected. ② not known, seen or experienced before • *alone in a strange country.* **strangely** ADVERB **strangeness** NOUN

> **strange** ADJECTIVE
> ① = abnormal, bizarre, curious, extraordinary, funny, odd, peculiar, queer (*old-fashioned*), uncommon, weird
> ② = alien, exotic, foreign, new, novel, unfamiliar

stranger NOUN ① someone you have never met before. ② If you are a stranger to a place or situation, you have not been there or experienced it before.

strangle VERB To strangle someone means to kill them by squeezing their throat. **strangulation** NOUN

strangled ADJECTIVE A strangled sound is unclear and muffled.

stranglehold NOUN To have a stranglehold on something means to have control over it and prevent it from developing.

strap, **straps**, **strapping**, **strapped** NOUN ① a narrow piece of leather or cloth, used to fasten or hold things together. ▸ VERB ② To strap something means to fasten it with a strap.

strapping ADJECTIVE tall, strong and healthy-looking.

strata the plural of **stratum**.

strategic [*Said strat-**tee**-jik*] ADJECTIVE planned or intended to achieve something or to gain an advantage • *a strategic plan.* **strategically** ADVERB

strategy, **strategies** NOUN ① PSHE a plan for achieving something.

② Strategy is the skill of planning the best way to achieve something, especially in war. **strategist** NOUN

stratum, **strata** NOUN [SCIENCE] The strata in the earth's surface are the different layers of rock.

straw NOUN ① Straw is the dry, yellowish stalks from cereal crops. ② a hollow tube of paper or plastic which you use to suck a drink into your mouth. ▸ PHRASE ③ If something is **the last straw**, it is the latest in a series of bad events and makes you feel you cannot stand any more.

strawberry, **strawberries** NOUN a small red fruit with tiny seeds in its skin.

stray VERB ① When people or animals stray, they wander away from where they should be. ② If your thoughts stray, you stop concentrating. ▸ ADJECTIVE ③ A stray dog or cat is one that has wandered away from home. ④ Stray things are separated from the main group of things of their kind • *a stray piece of lettuce*. ▸ NOUN ⑤ a stray dog or cat.

streak NOUN ① a long mark or stain. ② If someone has a particular streak, they have that quality in their character. ③ A lucky or unlucky streak is a series of successes or failures. ▸ VERB ④ If something is streaked with a colour, it has lines of the colour in it. ⑤ To streak somewhere means to move there very quickly. **streaky** ADJECTIVE

stream NOUN ① a small river. ② You can refer to a steady flow of something as a stream • *a constant stream of people*. ③ In a school, a stream is a group of children of the same age and ability. ▸ VERB ④ To stream somewhere means to move in a continuous flow in large quantities • *Rain streamed down the windscreen*.

streamline VERB ① To streamline a vehicle, aircraft or boat means to improve its shape so that it moves more quickly and efficiently. ② To streamline an organisation means to make it more efficient by removing parts of it.

street NOUN a road in a town or village, usually with buildings along it.

strength NOUN ① Your strength is your physical energy and the power of your muscles. ② Strength can refer to the degree of someone's confidence or courage. ③ You can refer to power or influence as strength • *The campaign against factory closures gathered strength*. ④ Someone's strengths are their good qualities and abilities. ⑤ The strength of an object is the degree to which it can stand rough treatment. ⑥ The strength of a substance is the amount of other substances that it contains • *coffee with sugar and milk in it at the correct strength*. ⑦ The strength of a feeling or opinion is the degree to which it is felt or supported. ⑧ The strength of a relationship is its degree of closeness or success. ⑨ The strength of a group is the total number of people in it. ▸ PHRASE ⑩ If people do something **in strength**, a lot of them do it together • *The press were here in strength*.

strength NOUN
① = brawn, might, muscle, stamina
≠ weakness
⑦ = force, intensity, potency, power, vehemence, vigour
≠ weakness

strengthen VERB ① To strengthen something means to give it more power, influence or support and make it more likely to succeed. ② To strengthen an object means to improve it or add to its structure so that it can withstand rough treatment.

strengthen VERB
① = consolidate, encourage, harden, stiffen, toughen
≠ weaken
② = bolster, brace, fortify, reinforce, support
≠ weaken

strenuous *[Said* ***stren****-yoo-uss]* ADJECTIVE involving a lot of effort or energy. **strenuously** ADVERB

stress NOUN ① Stress is worry and nervous tension. ② Stresses are strong physical forces applied to an object. ③ ENGLISH Stress is emphasis put on a word or part of a word when it is pronounced, making it slightly louder. ▶ VERB ④ If you stress a point, you emphasise it and draw attention to its importance. **stressful** ADJECTIVE

stress NOUN
① = anxiety, hassle *(informal)*, pressure, strain, tension, worry
▶ VERB ④ = accentuate, emphasise, repeat, underline

stretch VERB ① Something that stretches over an area extends that far. ② When you stretch, you hold out part of your body as far as you can. ③ To stretch something soft or elastic means to pull it to make it longer or bigger. ▶ NOUN ④ A stretch of land or water is an area of it. ⑤ A stretch of time is a period of time.

stretch VERB
① = continue, cover, extend, go on, hang, last, reach, spread
② = extend, reach, straighten
≠ bend
▶ NOUN ④ = area, expanse, extent, sweep, tract
⑤ = period, run, space, spell, stint, term, time

stretcher NOUN a long piece of material with a pole along each side, used to carry an injured person.

strewn ADJECTIVE If things are strewn about, they are scattered about untidily • *The costumes were strewn all over the floor.*

stricken ADJECTIVE severely affected by something unpleasant.

strict ADJECTIVE ① Someone who is strict controls other people very firmly. ② A strict rule must always be obeyed absolutely. ③ The strict meaning of something is its precise and accurate meaning. ④ You can use 'strict' to describe someone who never breaks the rules or principles of a particular belief • *a strict Muslim.*

strict ADJECTIVE
① = authoritarian, firm, rigid, rigorous, stern, stringent
③ = accurate, exact, meticulous, particular, precise, true

strictly ADVERB ① Strictly means only for a particular purpose • *I was in it strictly for the money.* ▶ PHRASE ② You say **strictly speaking** to correct a statement or add more precise information • *Somebody pointed out that, strictly speaking, electricity was a discovery, not an invention.*

stride, **strides**, **striding**, **strode**, **stridden** VERB ① To stride along means to walk quickly with long steps. ▶ NOUN ② a long step; also the length of a step.

strident *[Said* ***stry****-dent]* ADJECTIVE loud, harsh and unpleasant.

strife NOUN *(formal)* Strife is trouble, conflict and disagreement.

strike, **strikes**, **striking**, **struck** NOUN ① If there is a strike, people stop working as a protest. ② A hunger strike is a refusal to eat anything as a protest. A rent strike is a refusal to pay rent. ③ a military attack • *the threat of air strikes.* ▶ VERB ④ To strike someone or something means to hit them. ⑤ If an illness, disaster or enemy strikes, it suddenly affects or attacks someone. ⑥ If a thought strikes you, it comes into your mind. ⑦ If you are struck by something, you are impressed by it. ⑧ When a clock strikes, it makes a sound to indicate the time. ⑨ To strike a deal with someone means to come to an agreement with them. ⑩ If someone strikes oil or gold, they discover it in the ground. ⑪ If you strike a match, you rub it against something to make it burst into flame. **strike off** VERB If a professional person is struck off for bad behaviour, their name is removed from an official register and they are not allowed to practise their profession. **strike out** VERB If someone strikes out, they go off to do something different on their own. **strike up** VERB To strike up a conversation or friendship means to begin it.

striker NOUN ① Strikers are people who are refusing to work as a protest. ② in soccer, a player whose function is to attack and score goals.

striking ADJECTIVE very noticeable because of being unusual or very attractive. **strikingly** ADVERB

string, **strings**, **stringing**, **strung** NOUN ① String is thin cord made of twisted threads. ② You can refer to a row or series of similar things as a string of them • *a string of islands* • *a string of injuries*. ③ The strings of a musical instrument are tightly stretched lengths of wire or nylon which vibrate to produce the notes. ④ (*in plural*) The section of an orchestra consisting of stringed instruments is called the strings. **string along** VERB (*informal*) To string someone along means to deceive them by letting them believe you have the same desires, hopes or plans as them. **string out** VERB ① If things are strung out, they are spread out in a long line. ② To string something out means to make it last longer than necessary.

stringent ADJECTIVE Stringent laws or conditions are very severe or are strictly controlled • *stringent security checks*.

strip, **strips**, **stripping**, **stripped** NOUN ① A strip of something is a long, narrow piece of it. ② A comic strip is a series of drawings which tell a story. ③ A sports team's strip is the clothes worn by the team when playing a match. ▸ VERB ④ If you strip, you take off all your clothes. ⑤ To strip something means to remove whatever is covering its surface. ⑥ To strip someone of their property or rights means to take their property or rights away from them officially.

stripe NOUN Stripes are long, thin lines, usually of different colours. **striped** ADJECTIVE

strive, **strives**, **striving**, **strove**, **striven** VERB If you strive to do something, you make a great effort to achieve it.

> **strive** VERB
> = attempt, do your best, do your utmost, endeavour (*formal*), make an effort, seek, try

strode the past tense of **stride**.

stroke VERB ① If you stroke something, you move your hand smoothly and gently over it. ▸ NOUN ② If someone has a stroke, they suddenly lose consciousness as a result of a blockage or rupture in a blood vessel in the brain. A stroke can result in damage to speech and paralysis. ③ The strokes of a brush or pen are the movements that you make with it. ④ The strokes of a clock are the sounds that indicate the hour. ⑤ A swimming stroke is a particular style of swimming. ▸ PHRASE ⑥ If you have **a stroke of luck**, then you are lucky and something good happens to you.

stroll VERB ① To stroll along means to walk slowly in a relaxed way. ▶ NOUN ② a slow, pleasurable walk.

stroller NOUN In Australian and American English, a stroller is a pushchair.

strong ADJECTIVE ① Someone who is strong has powerful muscles. ② You also say that someone is strong when they are confident and have courage. ③ Strong objects are able to withstand rough treatment. ④ Strong also means great in degree or intensity • *a strong wind*. ⑤ A strong argument or theory is supported by a lot of evidence. ⑥ If a group or organisation is strong, it has a lot of members or influence. ⑦ You can use 'strong' to say how many people there are in a group • *The audience was about two dozen strong*. ⑧ Your strong points are the things you are good at. ⑨ A strong economy or currency is stable and successful. ⑩ A strong liquid or drug contains a lot of a particular substance. ▶ ADVERB ⑪ If someone or something is still going strong, they are still healthy or working well after a long time. **strongly** ADVERB

strong ADJECTIVE
① = athletic, brawny, burly, muscular, powerful, strapping, well-built
≠ weak
③ = durable, hard-wearing, heavy-duty, reinforced, sturdy, substantial, tough, well-built
≠ fragile
④ = acute, ardent, deep, fervent, fierce, intense, keen, passionate, profound, vehement, violent, zealous
≠ faint

stronghold NOUN ① a place that is held and defended by an army. ② A stronghold of an attitude or belief is a place in which the attitude or belief is strongly held • *a Conservative stronghold*.

strove the past tense of **strive**.

struck the past tense and past participle of **strike**.

structure NOUN ① DGT The structure of something is the way it is made, built or organised. ② something that has been built or constructed. ▶ VERB ③ DGT To structure something means to arrange it into an organised pattern or system. **structural** ADJECTIVE **structurally** ADVERB

structure NOUN
① = arrangement, construction, design, make-up, organisation
② = building, construction, edifice

struggle VERB ① If you struggle to do something, you try hard to do it in difficult circumstances. ② When people struggle, they twist and move violently during a fight. ▶ NOUN ③ Something that is a struggle is difficult to achieve and takes a lot of effort. ④ a fight.

struggle VERB
① = strain, strive, toil, work
▶ NOUN ③ = effort, labour, toil, work

strum, strums, strumming, strummed VERB To strum a guitar means to play it by moving your fingers backwards and forwards across all the strings.

strung the past tense and past participle of **string**.

strut, struts, strutting, strutted VERB ① To strut means to walk in a stiff, proud way with your chest out and your head high. ▶ NOUN ② a piece of wood or metal which strengthens or supports part of a building or structure.

Stuart HISTORY **NOUN** Stuart was the family name of the monarchs who ruled Scotland from 1371 to 1714 and England from 1603 to 1714.

stub, **stubs**, **stubbing**, **stubbed** **NOUN** ① The stub of a pencil or cigarette is the short piece that remains when the rest has been used. ② The stub of a ticket is the small part that you keep. ▸ **VERB** ③ If you stub your toe, you hurt it by accidentally kicking something. **stub out** **VERB** To stub out a cigarette means to put it out by pressing the end against something.

stubble **NOUN** ① The short stalks remaining in the ground after a crop is harvested are called stubble. ② If a man has stubble on his face, he has very short hair growing there because he has not shaved recently.

stubborn **ADJECTIVE** ① Someone who is stubborn is determined not to change their opinion or course of action. ② A stubborn stain is difficult to remove. **stubbornly** **ADVERB** **stubbornness** **NOUN**

> **stubborn** **ADJECTIVE**
> ① = dogged, inflexible, obstinate, tenacious, wilful

stuck ① Stuck is the past tense and past participle of **stick**. ▸ **ADJECTIVE** ② If something is stuck in a particular position, it is fixed or jammed and cannot be moved • *His car's stuck in a snowdrift*. ③ If you are stuck, you are unable to continue what you were doing because it is too difficult. ④ If you are stuck somewhere, you are unable to get away.

stud **NOUN** ① a small piece of metal fixed into something. ② A male horse or other animal that is kept for stud is kept for breeding purposes.

studded **ADJECTIVE** decorated with small pieces of metal or precious stones.

student **NOUN** a person studying at university or college.

studied **ADJECTIVE** A studied action or response has been carefully planned and is not natural • *She sipped her glass of white wine with studied boredom*.

studio, **studios** **NOUN** ① a room where a photographer or painter works. ② a room containing special equipment where records, films or radio or television programmes are made.

studious [*Said* ***styoo**-dee-uss*] **ADJECTIVE** spending a lot of time studying.

studiously **ADVERB** carefully and deliberately • *She was studiously ignoring me*.

study, **studies**, **studying**, **studied** **VERB** ① If you study a particular subject, you spend time learning about it. ② If you study something, you look at it carefully • *He studied the map in silence*. ▸ **NOUN** ③ Study is the activity of studying a subject • *the serious study of medieval archaeology*. ④ Studies are subjects which are studied • *media studies*. ⑤ a piece of research on a particular subject • *a detailed study of the world's most remote places*. ⑥ a room used for writing and studying.

> **study** **VERB**
> ① = learn, read up, swot (*British, Australian and New Zealand; informal*)
> ② = contemplate, examine, pore over
> ▸ **NOUN** ③ = lessons, research, school work, swotting (*British, Australian and New Zealand; informal*)

stuff **NOUN** ① You can refer to a substance or group of things as stuff. ▸ **VERB** ② (*informal*) If you stuff something somewhere, you push it there quickly and roughly. ③ If you stuff something with a substance or objects, you fill it with the substance or objects.

stuff NOUN
① = apparatus, belongings, equipment, gear, kit, material, substance, tackle, things
▶ VERB ② = cram, force, jam, push, ram, shove, squeeze, thrust
③ = cram, fill, load, pack

stuffing NOUN Stuffing is a mixture of small pieces of food put inside poultry or a vegetable before it is cooked.

stuffy, **stuffier**, **stuffiest** ADJECTIVE ① very formal and old-fashioned. ② If it is stuffy in a room, there is not enough fresh air.

stuffy ADJECTIVE
① = dull, formal, old-fashioned, staid, strait-laced
② = close, heavy, muggy, oppressive, stale, stifling

stumble VERB ① If you stumble while you are walking or running, you trip and almost fall. ② If you stumble when speaking, you make mistakes when pronouncing the words. ③ If you stumble across something or stumble on it, you find it unexpectedly.

stump NOUN ① a small part of something that is left when the rest has been removed • *the stump of a dead tree*. ② In cricket, the stumps are the three upright wooden sticks that support the bails, forming the wicket. ▶ VERB ③ (*informal*) If a question or problem stumps you, you cannot think of an answer or solution.

stun, **stuns**, **stunning**, **stunned** VERB ① If you are stunned by something, you are very shocked by it. ② To stun a person or animal means to knock them unconscious with a blow to the head.

stung the past tense and past participle of **sting**.

stunk the past participle of **stink**.

stunning ADJECTIVE very beautiful or impressive • *a stunning first novel*.

stunt NOUN ① an unusual or dangerous and exciting action that someone does to get publicity or as part of a film. ▶ VERB ② To stunt the growth or development of something means to prevent it from developing as it should.

stupendous ADJECTIVE very large or impressive • *a stupendous amount of money*. **stupendously** ADVERB

stupid ADJECTIVE showing lack of good judgment or intelligence and not at all sensible. **stupidly** ADVERB

stupid ADJECTIVE
= absurd, daft (*British; informal*), dim, foolish, idiotic, inane, obtuse (*formal*), thick
≠ clever

stupidity NOUN a lack of intelligence or good judgment.

stupidity NOUN
= absurdity, folly, foolishness, inanity, silliness

sturdy, **sturdier**, **sturdiest** ADJECTIVE strong and firm and unlikely to be damaged or injured • *a sturdy chest of drawers*.

sturdy ADJECTIVE
= durable, hardy, robust, solid, substantial, stout, strong, well-built
≠ fragile

sturgeon [*Said stur-jon*] NOUN a large edible fish, the eggs of which are also eaten and are known as caviar.

stutter NOUN ① Someone who has a stutter finds it difficult to speak smoothly and often repeats sounds through being unable to complete a word. ▶ VERB ② When someone stutters, they hesitate or repeat sounds when speaking.

style NOUN ① The style of something is the general way in which it is done or presented, often showing the attitudes of the people involved. ② A person or place that has style is smart, elegant and fashionable. ③ The style of something is its design • *new windows that fit in with the style of the house.* ▶ VERB ④ To style a piece of clothing or a person's hair means to design and create its shape.

> **style** NOUN
> ① = approach, manner, method, mode, technique, way
> ② = chic, elegance, flair, sophistication, taste

stylised; also spelt **stylized** ADJECTIVE using a particular artistic or literary form as a basis rather than being natural or spontaneous • *a stylised picture of a Japanese garden.*

stylish ADJECTIVE smart, elegant and fashionable. **stylishly** ADVERB

suave [*Said swahv*] ADJECTIVE charming, polite and confident • *a suave Italian.*

subconscious NOUN ① Your subconscious is the part of your mind that can influence you without your being aware of it. ▶ ADJECTIVE ② happening or existing in someone's subconscious and therefore not directly realised or understood by them • *a subconscious fear of rejection.* **subconsciously** ADVERB

subcontinent NOUN a large mass of land, often consisting of several countries, and forming part of a continent • *the Indian subcontinent.*

subdue, **subdues**, **subduing**, **subdued** VERB ① To subdue a person or group of people is to bring them under control by using force. ② To subdue a colour, light or emotion means to make it less bright or strong.

> **subdue** VERB
> ① = crush, defeat, overcome, overpower, quell, vanquish (*literary*)

subdued ADJECTIVE ① rather quiet and sad. ② not very noticeable or bright.

subject NOUN ① The subject of writing or a conversation is the thing or person being discussed. ② MFL In grammar, the subject is the word or words representing the person or thing doing the action expressed by the verb. For example, in the sentence 'My cat keeps catching birds', 'my cat' is the subject. ③ an area of study. ④ The subjects of a king or queen are the people who are ruled by them. ▶ VERB ⑤ To subject someone to something means to make them experience it • *He was subjected to constant interruption.* ▶ ADJECTIVE ⑥ Someone or something that is subject to something is affected by it • *He was subject to attacks at various times.*

> **subject** NOUN
> ① = issue, matter, object, point, question, theme, topic
> ▶ VERB ⑤ = expose, put through, submit

subjective ADJECTIVE influenced by personal feelings and opinion rather than based on fact or rational thought.

sublime ADJECTIVE Something that is sublime is wonderful and affects people emotionally • *sublime music.*

submarine NOUN a ship that can travel beneath the surface of the sea.

submerge VERB ① To submerge means to go beneath the surface of a liquid. ② If you submerge yourself in an activity, you become totally involved in it.

submission NOUN ① Submission is a state in which someone accepts the control of another person • *Now he must beat us into submission.* ② The submission of a proposal or application is the act of sending it for consideration.

submissive ADJECTIVE behaving in a quiet, obedient way.

submit, **submits**, **submitting**, **submitted** VERB ① If you submit to something, you accept it because you are not powerful enough to resist it. ② If you submit an application or proposal, you send it to someone for consideration.

submit VERB
① = agree, bow, capitulate, comply, give in, surrender, yield (*formal*)
≠ resist
② = hand in, present, propose, put forward, send in, table, tender
≠ withdraw

subordinate NOUN [*Said sub-**ord**-in-it*] ① A person's subordinate is someone who is in a less important position than them. ▶ ADJECTIVE [*Said sub-**ord**-in-it*] ② If one thing is subordinate to another, it is less important • *The House of Lords would always remain subordinate to the Commons.* ▶ VERB [*Said sub-**ord**-in-ate*] ③ To subordinate one thing to another means to treat it as being less important.

subscribe VERB ① If you subscribe to a particular belief or opinion, you support it or agree with it. ② If you subscribe to a magazine, you pay to receive regular copies. **subscriber** NOUN

subscription NOUN a sum of money that you pay regularly to belong to an organisation or to receive regular copies of a magazine.

subsequent ADJECTIVE happening or coming into existence at a later time than something else • *the December uprising and the subsequent political violence.* **subsequently** ADVERB

subservient ADJECTIVE Someone who is subservient does whatever other people want them to do.

subside VERB ① To subside means to become less intense or quieter • *Her excitement suddenly subsided.* ② If water or the ground subsides, it sinks to a lower level.

subsidence [*Said sub-**side**-ins*] NOUN If a place is suffering from subsidence, parts of the ground have sunk to a lower level.

subsidiary, **subsidiaries** [*Said sub-**sid**-yer-ee*] NOUN ① a company which is part of a larger company. ▶ ADJECTIVE ② treated as being of less importance and additional to another thing • *Drama is offered as a subsidiary subject.*

subsidise; also spelt **subsidize** VERB To subsidise something means to provide part of the cost of it • *He feels the government should do much more to subsidise films.* **subsidised** ADJECTIVE

subsidy, **subsidies** NOUN a sum of money paid to help support a company or provide a public service.

substance NOUN ① Anything which is a solid, a powder, a liquid or a paste can be referred to as a substance. ② If a speech or piece of writing has substance, it is meaningful or important • *a good speech, but there was no substance.*

substance NOUN
① = element, fabric, material, stuff

substantial ADJECTIVE ① very large in degree or amount • *a substantial pay rise.* ② large and strongly built • *a substantial stone building.*

substantially ADVERB Something that is substantially true is generally or mostly true.

substitute VERB ① To substitute one

thing for another means to use it instead of the other thing or to put it in the other thing's place. ② MATHS to replace one mathematical element with another. ▶ **NOUN** ③ If one thing is a substitute for another, it is used instead of it or put in its place. **substitution NOUN**

> **substitute VERB**
> ① = exchange, interchange, replace, swap, switch
> ▶ **NOUN** ③ = deputy, proxy, replacement, representative, surrogate

subterfuge *[Said **sub**-ter-fyooj]* **NOUN** Subterfuge is the use of deceitful or dishonest methods.

subtitle NOUN A film with subtitles has a printed translation of the dialogue at the bottom of the screen.

subtle *[Said **sut**-tl]* **ADJECTIVE** ① very fine, delicate or small in degree • *a subtle change*. ② using indirect methods to achieve something. **subtly ADVERB subtlety NOUN**

subtract VERB If you subtract you remove one number from another.

> **subtract VERB**
> = deduct, take away, take from
> ≠ add

suburb NOUN an area of a town or city that is away from its centre.

suburban ADJECTIVE ① relating to a suburb or suburbs. ② dull and conventional.

suburbia NOUN You can refer to the suburbs of a city as suburbia.

subversive ADJECTIVE ① intended to destroy or weaken a political system • *subversive activities*. ▶ **NOUN** ② Subversives are people who try to destroy or weaken a political system. **subversion NOUN**

subvert VERB *(formal)* To subvert something means to cause it to weaken or fail • *a cunning campaign to subvert the music industry*.

subway NOUN ① a footpath that goes underneath a road. ② an underground railway.

succeed VERB ① To succeed means to achieve the result you intend. ② To succeed someone means to be the next person to have their job. ③ If one thing succeeds another, it comes after it in time • *The explosion was succeeded by a crash*. **succeeding ADJECTIVE**

> **succeed VERB**
> ① = be successful, do well, flourish, make it *(informal)*, prosper, thrive, triumph, work
> ≠ fail
> ② = replace, take over from

success NOUN ① Success is the achievement of something you have been trying to do. ② Someone who is a success has achieved an important position or made a lot of money.

> **success NOUN**
> ① = celebrity, eminence, fame, prosperity, triumph, victory, wealth
> ≠ failure
> ② = celebrity, hit, sensation, star, triumph, winner
> ≠ failure

successful ADJECTIVE having achieved what you intended to do. **successfully ADVERB**

> **successful ADJECTIVE**
> = flourishing, lucrative, profitable, rewarding, thriving, top

succession NOUN ① A succession of things is a number of them occurring one after the other. ② When someone becomes the next person to have an important position, you can refer to this event as their succession to this position • *his succession to the throne*. ▶ **PHRASE** ③ If something happens a number of weeks, months or years **in succession**, it happens that number of times without a break • *Borg won Wimbledon five years in succession.*

successive ADJECTIVE occurring one after the other without a break • *three successive victories.*

successor NOUN Someone's successor is the person who takes their job when they leave.

succinct *[Said suk-**singkt**]* ADJECTIVE expressing something clearly and in very few words. **succinctly** ADVERB

succulent ADJECTIVE Succulent food is juicy and delicious.

succumb VERB If you succumb to something, you are unable to resist it any longer • *She never succumbed to temptation.*

such ADJECTIVE, PRONOUN ① You use 'such' to refer to the person or thing you have just mentioned, or to someone or something similar • *Naples or Palermo or some such place.* ▶ PHRASE ② You can use **such as** to introduce an example of something • *herbal teas such as camomile.* ③ You can use **such as it is** to indicate that something is not great in quality or quantity • *The action, such as it is, is set in Egypt.* ④ You can use **such and such** when you want to refer to something that is not specific • *A good trick is to ask whether they have seen such and such a film.* ▶ ADJECTIVE ⑤ 'Such' can be used for emphasising • *I have such a terrible sense of guilt.*

suck VERB ① If you suck something, you hold it in your mouth and pull at it with your cheeks and tongue, usually to get liquid out of it. ② To suck something in a particular direction means to draw it there with a powerful force. **suck up** VERB (*informal*) To suck up to someone means to do things to please them in order to obtain praise or approval.

sucker NOUN ① (*informal*) If you call someone a sucker, you mean that they are easily fooled or cheated. ② Suckers are pads on the bodies of some animals and insects which they use to cling to a surface. ③ A sucker is also a cup-shaped piece of plastic or rubber on an object that sticks to a surface when pressed flat.

suction NOUN ① Suction is the force involved when a substance is drawn or sucked from one place to another. ② Suction is the process by which two surfaces stick together when the air between them is removed • *They stay there by suction.*

Sudanese *[Said soo-dan-**neez**]* ADJECTIVE ① belonging or relating to the Sudan. ▶ NOUN ② someone who comes from the Sudan.

sudden ADJECTIVE happening quickly and unexpectedly • *a sudden cry.* **suddenly** ADVERB **suddenness** NOUN

sudden ADJECTIVE
= abrupt, hasty, quick, swift, unexpected
≠ gradual

sue, **sues**, **suing**, **sued** VERB To sue someone means to start a legal case against them, usually to claim money from them.

suede *[Said **swayd**]* NOUN Suede is a thin, soft leather with a rough surface.

suffer VERB ① If someone is suffering pain, or suffering as a result of an unpleasant situation, they are badly affected by it. ② If something suffers as a result of neglect or a difficult situation, its condition or quality becomes worse • *The bus service is suffering.* **sufferer** NOUN **suffering** NOUN

suffer VERB
① = bear, endure, experience, go through, sustain, undergo

suffice VERB (*formal*) If something suffices, it is enough or adequate for a purpose.

sufficient ADJECTIVE If a supply or quantity is sufficient for a purpose, there is enough of it available. **sufficiently** ADVERB

> **sufficient** ADJECTIVE
> = adequate, ample, enough
> ≠ insufficient

suffix NOUN [ENGLISH] a group of letters which is added to the end of a word to form a new word, for example '-ology' or '-itis'.

suffocate VERB To suffocate means to die as a result of having too little air or oxygen to breathe. **suffocation** NOUN

suffrage NOUN Suffrage is the right to vote in political elections.

suffused ADJECTIVE (*literary*) If something is suffused with light or colour, light or colour has gradually spread over it.

sugar NOUN Sugar is a sweet substance used to sweeten food or drinks. Sugar is obtained from sugar cane or sugar beet.

sugar beet, **sugar beets** NOUN a plant with white roots from which sugar is obtained.

sugar cane, **sugar canes** NOUN a tropical plant with thick stems from which sugar is obtained.

suggest VERB ① If you suggest a plan or idea to someone, you mention it as a possibility for them to consider. ② If something suggests a particular thought or impression, it makes you think in that way or gives you that impression • *Nothing you say suggests he is worried.*

> **suggest** VERB
> ① = advise, advocate, propose, recommend
> ② = hint, imply, indicate, insinuate, intimate

suggestion NOUN ① a plan or idea that is mentioned as a possibility for someone to consider. ② A suggestion of something is a very slight indication or faint sign of it • *a suggestion of dishonesty.*

> **suggestion** NOUN
> ① = plan, proposal, proposition, recommendation
> ② = hint, indication, insinuation, intimation, trace

suggestive ADJECTIVE Something that is suggestive of a particular thing gives a slight hint or sign of it. **suggestively** ADVERB

suicidal ADJECTIVE ① People who are suicidal want to kill themselves. ② Suicidal behaviour is so dangerous that it is likely to result in death • *a suicidal leap.* **suicidally** ADVERB

suicide NOUN People who die by suicide deliberately kill themselves.

suicide bomber NOUN a terrorist who carries out a bomb attack, knowing that he or she will be killed in the explosion. **suicide bombing** NOUN

suit NOUN ① a matching jacket and trousers or skirt. ② In a court of law, a suit is a legal action taken by one person against another. ③ one of four different types of card in a pack of playing cards. The four suits are hearts, clubs, diamonds and spades. ▸ VERB ④ If a situation or course of action suits you, it is appropriate or acceptable for your purpose. ⑤ If a piece of clothing or a colour suits you, you look good when you are wearing it. ⑥ If you do something to suit yourself, you do it because you want to and without considering other people.

> **suit** VERB
> ④ = be acceptable to, do, please, satisfy

suitable ADJECTIVE right or acceptable for a particular purpose or occasion. **suitability** NOUN **suitably** ADVERB

> **suitable** ADJECTIVE
> = acceptable, appropriate, apt, fit, fitting, proper, right, satisfactory
> ≠ unsuitable

suitcase NOUN a case in which you carry your clothes when you are travelling.

suite [*Said* ***sweet***] NOUN ① In a hotel, a suite is a set of rooms. ② a set of matching furniture or bathroom fittings.

suited ADJECTIVE right or appropriate for a particular purpose or person • *He is well suited to be minister for the arts.*

suitor NOUN (*old-fashioned*) A person's suitor is someone who wants to marry them.

sulk VERB Someone who is sulking is showing their annoyance by being silent and moody.

sulky, **sulkier**, **sulkiest** ADJECTIVE showing annoyance by being silent and moody.

> **sulky** ADJECTIVE
> = huffy, moody, petulant, resentful, sullen

sullen ADJECTIVE behaving in a bad-tempered and disagreeably silent way. **sullenly** ADVERB

sulphur NOUN [SCIENCE] Sulphur is a pale yellow nonmetallic element which burns with a very unpleasant smell. Its atomic number is 16 and its symbol is S.

sultan NOUN In some Muslim countries, the ruler of the country is called the sultan.

sum, **sums**, **summing**, **summed** NOUN ① an amount of money. ② In arithmetic, a sum is a calculation. ③ The sum of something is the total amount of it. **sum up** VERB If you sum something up, you briefly describe its main points.

> ▶ **sum up** = recapitulate, summarise

summarise; also spelt **summarize** VERB [EXAM TERM] To summarise something means to give a short account of its main points.

summary, **summaries** NOUN ① A summary of something is a short account of its main points. ▶ ADJECTIVE ② A summary action is done without delay or careful thought • *Summary punishments are common.* **summarily** ADVERB

> **summary** NOUN
> ① = outline, review, rundown, summing-up, synopsis

summer NOUN Summer is the season between spring and autumn.

summit NOUN ① The summit of a mountain is its top. ② a meeting between leaders of different countries to discuss particular issues.

summon VERB ① If someone summons you, they order you to go to them. ② If you summon up strength or energy, you make a great effort to be strong or energetic.

summons, **summonses** NOUN ① an official order to appear in court. ② an order to go to someone • *The result was a summons to headquarters.*

sumptuous ADJECTIVE Something that is sumptuous is magnificent and obviously very expensive.

sum total NOUN The sum total of a number of things is all of them added or considered together.

sun, **suns**, **sunning**, **sunned** NOUN ① The sun is the star providing heat and light for the planets revolving around it in our solar system. ② You refer to heat and light from the sun as sun • *We need a bit of sun.* ▶ VERB ③ If you sun yourself, you sit in the sunshine.

a b c d e f g h i j k l m n o p q r **s** t u v w x y z

sunbathe VERB If you sunbathe, you sit in the sunshine to get a suntan.

sunburn NOUN Sunburn is sore red skin on someone's body due to too much exposure to the rays of the sun. **sunburnt** ADJECTIVE

Sunday NOUN Sunday is the day between Saturday and Monday.

Sunday school NOUN Sunday school is a special class held on Sundays to teach children about Christianity.

sundry ADJECTIVE ① 'Sundry' is used to refer to several things or people of various sorts • *sundry journalists and lawyers*. ▶ PHRASE ② **All and sundry** means everyone.

sunflower NOUN a tall plant with very large yellow flowers.

sung the past participle of **sing**.

sunglasses PLURAL NOUN Sunglasses are spectacles with dark lenses that you wear to protect your eyes from the sun.

sunk the past participle of **sink**.

sunken ADJECTIVE ① having sunk to the bottom of the sea, a river, or a lake • *sunken ships*. ② A sunken object or area has been constructed below the level of the surrounding area • *a sunken garden*. ③ curving inwards • *Her cheeks were sunken*.

sunlight NOUN Sunlight is the bright light produced when the sun is shining. **sunlit** ADJECTIVE

sunny, **sunnier**, **sunniest** ADJECTIVE When it is sunny, the sun is shining.

sunrise NOUN Sunrise is the time in the morning when the sun first appears, and the colours produced in the sky at that time.

sunset NOUN Sunset is the time in the evening when the sun disappears below the horizon, and the colours produced in the sky at that time.

sunshine NOUN Sunshine is the bright light produced when the sun is shining.

suntan NOUN If you have a suntan, the sun has turned your skin brown. **suntanned** ADJECTIVE

super ADJECTIVE very nice or very good • *a super party*.

superb ADJECTIVE very good indeed. **superbly** ADVERB

> **superb** ADJECTIVE
> = breathtaking, excellent, exquisite, magnificent, marvellous, outstanding, splendid, superior, unrivalled, wonderful

superficial ADJECTIVE ① involving only the most obvious or most general aspects of something • *a superficial knowledge of music*. ② not having a deep, serious or genuine interest in anything • *a superficial and rather silly character*. ③ Superficial wounds are not very deep or severe. **superficially** ADVERB

superfluous [*Said soo-**per**-floo-uss*] ADJECTIVE (*formal*) unnecessary or no longer needed.

superhuman ADJECTIVE having much greater power or ability than is normally expected of humans • *superhuman strength*.

superintendent NOUN ① a police officer above the rank of inspector. ② a person whose job is to be responsible for a particular thing • *the superintendent of prisons*.

superior ADJECTIVE ① better or of higher quality than other similar things. ② in a position of higher authority than another person. ③ showing too much pride and self-importance • *Jerry smiled in a superior way*. ▶ NOUN ④ Your superiors are people who are in a higher position than you in society or an organisation. **superiority** NOUN

superior ADJECTIVE
① = better, choice, de luxe, exceptional, first-rate, surpassing, unrivalled
≠ inferior
③ = condescending, disdainful, haughty, lofty, patronising, snobbish, stuck-up (*informal*), supercilious
▸ NOUN ④ = boss, manager, senior, supervisor
≠ inferior

superlative [*Said soo-**per**-lat-tiv*] NOUN ① ENGLISH In grammar, the superlative is the form of an adjective which indicates that the person or thing described has more of a particular quality than anyone or anything else. For example, 'quickest', 'best' and 'easiest' are all superlatives. ▸ ADJECTIVE ② (*formal*) very good indeed • *a superlative performance*.

supermarket NOUN a shop selling food and household goods arranged so that you can help yourself and pay for everything at a till by the exit.

supernatural ADJECTIVE ① Something that is supernatural, for example ghosts or witchcraft, cannot be explained by normal scientific laws. ▸ NOUN ② You can refer to supernatural things as the supernatural.

superpower NOUN a very powerful and influential country such as the USA.

supersede [*Said soo-per-**seed***] VERB If something supersedes another thing, it replaces it because it is more modern • *New York superseded Paris as the centre for modern art*.

supersonic ADJECTIVE A supersonic aircraft can travel faster than the speed of sound.

superstar NOUN You can refer to a very famous entertainer or sports player as a superstar.

superstition NOUN Superstition is a belief in things like magic and powers that bring good or bad luck. **superstitious** ADJECTIVE

supervise VERB To supervise someone means to check and direct what they are doing to make sure that they do it correctly. **supervision** NOUN **supervisor** NOUN

supervise VERB
= be in charge of, direct, have charge of, keep an eye on, manage, oversee, run

supper NOUN Supper is a meal eaten in the evening or a snack eaten before you go to bed.

supplant VERB (*formal*) To supplant someone or something means to take their place • *By the 1930s the wristwatch had supplanted the pocket watch*.

supple ADJECTIVE able to bend and move easily.

supplement VERB ① To supplement something means to add something to it to improve it • *Many village men supplemented their wages by fishing for salmon*. ▸ NOUN ② something that is added to something else to improve it. ③ a separate part of a newspaper or magazine, often dealing with a particular subject.

supplement VERB
① = add to, augment, complement, reinforce, top up
▸ NOUN ② = addition, appendix, complement, extra

supplementary ADJECTIVE added to something else to improve it • *supplementary doses of vitamin E*.

supplier NOUN a firm which provides particular goods.

supply, **supplies**, **supplying**, **supplied** VERB ① To supply someone with something means to provide it or send it to them. ▸ NOUN ② A supply of something is an amount available for use • *the world's supply of precious metals.* ③ (*in plural*) Supplies are food and equipment for a particular purpose.

> **supply** VERB
> ① = equip, furnish, give, provide
> ▸ NOUN ② = cache, fund, hoard, reserve, stock, stockpile, store
> ③ = equipment, provisions, rations, stores

support VERB ① If you support someone, you agree with their aims and want them to succeed. ② If you support someone who is in difficulties, you are kind, encouraging and helpful to them. ③ If something supports an object, it is underneath it and holding it up. ④ To support someone or something means to prevent them from falling by holding them. ⑤ To support someone financially means to provide them with money. ▸ NOUN ⑥ an object that is holding something up. ⑦ [PSHE] Moral support is encouragement given to someone to help them do something difficult. ⑧ Financial support is money that is provided for someone or something. **supportable** ADJECTIVE

> **support** VERB
> ① = back, champion, defend, promote, second, side with, uphold
> ≠ oppose
> ② = encourage, help
> ③ = bolster, brace, hold up, prop up, reinforce
> ▸ NOUN ⑥ = brace, foundation, pillar, post, prop

supporter NOUN a person who agrees with or helps someone.

> **supporter** NOUN
> = adherent (*formal*), advocate, ally, champion, fan, follower, sponsor

supportive ADJECTIVE A supportive person is encouraging and helpful to someone who is in difficulties.

suppose VERB ① If you suppose that something is the case, you think that it is likely • *I supposed that would be too obvious.* ▸ PHRASE ② You can say **I suppose** when you are not entirely certain or enthusiastic about something • *Yes, I suppose he could come.* ▸ CONJUNCTION ③ You can use 'suppose' or 'supposing' when you are considering or suggesting a possible situation or action • *Supposing he were to break down under interrogation?*

> **suppose** VERB
> ① = assume, believe, expect, guess, imagine, presume, think

supposed ADJECTIVE ① 'Supposed' is used to express doubt about something that is generally believed • *the supposed culprit.* ② If something is supposed to be done or to happen, it is planned, expected or required to be done or to happen • *You are supposed to report it to the police* • *It was supposed to be this afternoon.* ③ Something that is supposed to be the case is generally believed or thought to be so • *Wimbledon is supposed to be the best tournament of them all.* **supposedly** ADVERB

> **supposed** ADJECTIVE
> ② = expected, meant, obliged, required
> ③ = alleged, assumed, believed, meant, presumed, reputed, rumoured

supposition NOUN something that is believed or assumed to be true • *the supposition that science requires an ordered universe.*

suppress VERB ① If an army or government suppresses an activity, it prevents people from doing it. ② If someone suppresses a piece of

information, they prevent it from becoming generally known. ③ If you suppress your feelings, you stop yourself expressing them.
suppression NOUN

suppress VERB
① = crush, quash, quell, stamp out, stop
③ = conceal, contain, curb, repress, restrain, smother, stifle

supremacy *[Said soo-**prem**-mass-ee]* NOUN If a group of people has supremacy over others, it is more powerful than the others.

supreme ADJECTIVE ① 'Supreme' is used as part of a title to indicate the highest level of an organisation or system • *the Supreme Court*. ② 'Supreme' is used to emphasise the greatness of something • *the supreme achievement of the human race*.
supremely ADVERB

supreme ADJECTIVE
② = chief, foremost, greatest, highest, leading, paramount, pre-eminent, principal, top, ultimate

surcharge NOUN an additional charge.

sure ADJECTIVE ① If you are sure about something, you have no doubts about it. ② If you are sure of yourself, you are very confident. ③ If something is sure to happen, it will definitely happen. ④ Sure means reliable or accurate • *a sure sign that something is wrong*. ▶ PHRASE ⑤ If you **make sure** about something, you check it or take action to see that it is done. ▶ INTERJECTION ⑥ Sure is an informal way of saying 'yes' • *'Can I come too?' – 'Sure'*.

sure ADJECTIVE
① = certain, clear, convinced, definite, positive, satisfied
≠ unsure
④ = definite, dependable, foolproof, infallible, reliable, trustworthy, undeniable

surely ADVERB 'Surely' is used to emphasise the belief that something is the case • *Surely these people here knew that?*

surf VERB ① When you surf, you take part in the sport of surfing. ② When you surf the internet, you go from website to website reading the information. ▶ NOUN ③ Surf is the white foam that forms on the top of waves when they break near the shore.

surface NOUN ① The surface of something is the top or outside area of it. ② The surface of a situation is what can be seen easily rather than what is hidden or not immediately obvious. ▶ VERB ③ If someone surfaces, they come up from under water to the surface.

surfboard NOUN a long narrow lightweight board used for surfing.

surf club NOUN In Australia, a surf club is an organisation of lifesavers in charge of safety on a particular beach, and which often provides leisure facilities.

surfeit *[Said **sur**-fit]* NOUN If there is a surfeit of something, there is too much of it.

surfing NOUN Surfing is a sport which involves riding towards the shore on the top of a large wave while standing on a surfboard.

surge NOUN ① a sudden great increase in the amount of something • *a surge of panic*. ▶ VERB ② If something surges, it moves suddenly and powerfully • *The soldiers surged forwards*.

surgeon NOUN a doctor who performs operations.

surgery, **surgeries** NOUN ① Surgery is

medical treatment involving cutting open part of the patient's body to treat the damaged part. ②The room or building where a doctor or dentist works is called a surgery. ③A period of time during which a doctor is available to see patients is called surgery • *evening surgery*.

surgical ADJECTIVE used in or involving a medical operation • *surgical gloves*. **surgically** ADVERB

surly, **surlier**, **surliest** ADJECTIVE rude and bad-tempered. **surliness** NOUN

surmise VERB (*formal*) To surmise something means to guess it • *I surmised it was of French manufacture*.

surname NOUN Your surname is your last name, which you share with other members of your family.

surpass VERB (*formal*) To surpass someone or something means to be better than them.

surplus NOUN If there is a surplus of something there is more of it than is needed.

surprise NOUN ①an unexpected event. ②Surprise is the feeling caused when something unexpected happens. ▶VERB ③If something surprises you, it gives you a feeling of surprise. ④If you surprise someone, you do something they were not expecting. **surprising** ADJECTIVE

> **surprise** NOUN
> ①= bombshell, revelation, shock, start
> ②= amazement, astonishment, incredulity, wonder
> ▶VERB ③= amaze, astonish, astound, jolt, stagger, stun, take aback

surreal ADJECTIVE very strange and dreamlike.

surrender VERB ①To surrender means to stop fighting and agree that the other side has won. ②If you surrender to a temptation or feeling, you let it take control of you. ③To surrender something means to give it up to someone else • *The gallery director surrendered his keys*. ▶NOUN ④Surrender is a situation in which one side in a fight agrees that the other side has won and gives in.

> **surrender** VERB
> ①= capitulate, give in, submit, succumb (*formal*), yield (*formal*)
> ③= cede, give up, relinquish, renounce, yield (*formal*)
> ▶NOUN ④= capitulation, submission

surreptitious [*Said sur-rep-**tish**-uss*] ADJECTIVE A surreptitious action is done secretly or so that no-one will notice • *a surreptitious glance*. **surreptitiously** ADVERB

surrogate ADJECTIVE ①acting as a substitute for someone or something. ▶NOUN ②a person or thing that acts as a substitute.

surround VERB ①To surround someone or something means to be situated all around them. ▶NOUN ②The surround of something is its outside edge or border.

> **surround** VERB
> ①= encircle, enclose, encompass, envelop, hem in

surrounding ADJECTIVE The surrounding area of a particular place is the area around it • *the surrounding countryside*.

surveillance [*Said sur-**vay**-lanss*] NOUN Surveillance is the close watching of a person's activities by the police or army.

survey VERB [*Said sur-**vay***] ①To survey something means to look carefully at the whole of it. ②To survey a building or piece of land means to examine it carefully in order to make a report or plan of its structure and features. ▶NOUN [*Said **sir**-vay*] ③A survey of something is a detailed examination of it, often in the form of a report.

surveyor NOUN a person whose job is to survey buildings or land.

survival NOUN Survival is being able to continue living or existing in spite of great danger or difficulties • *There was no hope of survival.*

survive VERB To survive means to continue to live or exist in spite of great danger or difficulties • *a German monk who survived the shipwreck.* **survivor** NOUN

survive VERB
= endure, last, live, outlive, pull through

susceptible ADJECTIVE If you are susceptible to something, you are likely to be influenced or affected by it • *Elderly people are more susceptible to infection.* **susceptibility** NOUN

suspect VERB *[Said sus-**pekt**]* ① If you suspect something, you think that it is likely or is probably true • *I suspected that the report would be sent.* ② If you suspect something, you have doubts about its reliability or genuineness • *Given his previous behaviour, I suspected his remorse.* ③ If you suspect someone of doing something wrong, you think that they have done it. ▸ NOUN *[Said **sus**-pekt]* ④ someone who is thought to be guilty of a crime. ▸ ADJECTIVE *[Said **sus**-pekt]* ⑤ If something is suspect, it cannot be trusted or relied upon • *a rather suspect holy man.*

suspect VERB
① = believe, feel, guess, suppose
② = distrust, doubt, mistrust
▸ ADJECTIVE ⑤ = dodgy (*British, Australian and New Zealand; informal*), doubtful, dubious, fishy (*informal*), questionable

suspend VERB ① If something is suspended, it is hanging from somewhere • *the television set suspended above the bar.* ② To suspend an activity or event means to delay it or stop it for a while. ③ If someone is suspended from their job, they are told not to do it for a period of time, usually as a punishment.

suspense NOUN Suspense is a state of excitement or anxiety caused by having to wait for something.

suspension NOUN ① The suspension of something is the delaying or stopping of it. ② A person's suspension is their removal from a job for a period of time, usually as a punishment. ③ The suspension of a vehicle consists of springs and shock absorbers which provide a smooth ride. ④ a liquid mixture in which very small bits of a solid material are contained and are not dissolved.

suspicion NOUN ① Suspicion is the feeling of not trusting someone or the feeling that something is wrong. ② a feeling that something is likely to happen or is probably true • *the suspicion that more could have been achieved.*

suspicion NOUN
① = distrust, doubt, misgiving, mistrust, scepticism
② = hunch, idea, impression

suspicious ADJECTIVE ① If you are suspicious of someone, you do not trust them. ② 'Suspicious' is used to describe things that make you think that there is something wrong with a situation • *suspicious circumstances.* **suspiciously** ADVERB

suspicious ADJECTIVE
① = apprehensive, distrustful, doubtful, sceptical, wary
② = dodgy (*British, Australian and New Zealand; informal*), doubtful, dubious, fishy (*informal*), funny, questionable, shady (*informal*), suspect

sustain VERB ① To sustain something

means to continue it for a period of time • *Their team-mates were unable to sustain the challenge.* ② If something sustains you, it gives you energy and strength. ③ (*formal*) To sustain an injury or loss means to suffer it.

sustainable ADJECTIVE ① capable of being sustained. ② If economic development or energy resources are sustainable they are capable of being maintained at a steady level without exhausting natural resources or causing ecological damage • *sustainable forestry.*

sustenance NOUN (*formal*) Sustenance is food and drink.

swab, swabs, swabbing, swabbed NOUN ① a small piece of cotton wool used for cleaning a wound. ▸ VERB ② To swab something means to clean it using a large mop and a lot of water. ③ To swab a wound means to clean it or take specimens from it using a swab.

swag NOUN (*informal*) ① goods or valuables, especially ones which have been gained dishonestly. ② in Australian and New Zealand English, a swag is the bundle of possessions belonging to a tramp. ③ In Australian and New Zealand English, swags of something is lots of it.

swagger VERB ① To swagger means to walk in a proud, exaggerated way. ▸ NOUN ② an exaggerated walk.

swallow VERB ① If you swallow something, you make it go down your throat and into your stomach. ② When you swallow, you move your throat muscles as if you were swallowing something, especially when you are nervous. ▸ NOUN ③ a bird with pointed wings and a long forked tail.

swam the past tense of **swim**.

swamp NOUN ① an area of permanently wet land. ▸ VERB ② If something is swamped, it is covered or filled with water. ③ If you are swamped by things, you have more than you are able to deal with • *She was swamped with calls.* **swampy** ADJECTIVE

swan NOUN a large, usually white, bird with a long neck that lives on rivers or lakes.

swap, swaps, swapping, swapped [*Rhymes with* ***stop***] VERB To swap one thing for another means to replace the first thing with the second, often by making an exchange with another person • *Webb swapped shirts with a Leeds player.*

swap VERB
= barter, exchange, interchange, switch, trade

swarm NOUN ① A swarm of insects is a large group of them flying together. ▸ VERB ② When bees or other insects swarm, they fly together in a large group. ③ If people swarm somewhere, a lot of people go there quickly and at the same time • *the crowds of office workers who swarm across the bridge.* ④ If a place is swarming with people, there are a lot of people there.

swashbuckling ADJECTIVE 'Swashbuckling' is used to describe people who have the exciting behaviour or appearance of pirates.

swastika [*Said* ***swoss****-tik-ka*] NOUN a symbol in the shape of a cross with each arm bent over at right angles. It was the official symbol of the Nazis in Germany, but in India it is a good luck sign.

swat, swats, swatting, swatted VERB To swat an insect means to hit it sharply in order to kill it.

swathe [*Rhymes with* ***bathe***] NOUN ① a long strip of cloth that is wrapped around something • *swathes of white* *silk*. ② A swathe of land is a long strip of it.

swathed ADJECTIVE If someone is swathed in something, they are wrapped in it • *She was swathed in towels*.

sway VERB ① To sway means to lean or swing slowly from side to side. ② If something sways you, it influences your judgment. ▸ NOUN ③ (*literary*) Sway is the power to influence people • *under the sway of more powerful neighbours*.

swear, **swears**, **swearing**, **swore**, **sworn** VERB ① To swear means to say words that are considered to be very rude or blasphemous. ② If you swear to something, you state solemnly that you will do it or that it is true. ③ If you swear by something, you firmly believe that it is a reliable cure or solution • *Some people swear by extra vitamins*. **swear in** VERB When someone is sworn in to a new position, they solemnly promise to fulfil the duties and are officially appointed.

sweat NOUN ① Sweat is the salty liquid produced by your body when you are hot or afraid. ▸ VERB ② When you sweat, sweat comes through the pores in your skin in order to lower the temperature of your body.

sweater NOUN a knitted piece of clothing covering your upper body and arms.

sweatshirt NOUN a piece of clothing made of thick cotton, covering your upper body and arms.

sweaty, **sweatier**, **sweatiest** ADJECTIVE covered or soaked with sweat.

Swede NOUN someone who comes from Sweden.

Swedish ADJECTIVE ① belonging or relating to Sweden. ▸ NOUN ② Swedish is the main language spoken in Sweden.

sweep, **sweeps**, **sweeping**, **swept** VERB ① If you sweep the floor, you use a brush to gather up dust or rubbish from it. ② To sweep things off a surface means to push them all off with a quick, smooth movement. ③ If something sweeps from one place to another, it moves there very quickly • *A gust of wind swept over the terrace*. ④ If an attitude or new fashion sweeps a place, it spreads rapidly through it • *a phenomenon that is sweeping America*. ▸ NOUN ⑤ If you do something with a sweep of your arm, you do it with a wide curving movement of your arm.

sweeping ADJECTIVE ① A sweeping curve or movement is long and wide. ② A sweeping statement is based on a general assumption rather than on careful thought. ③ affecting a lot of people to a great extent • *sweeping changes*.

sweet ADJECTIVE ① containing a lot of sugar • *a mug of sweet tea*. ② pleasant and satisfying • *sweet success*. ③ A sweet smell is soft and fragrant. ④ A sweet sound is gentle and tuneful. ⑤ attractive and pleasant • *a sweet little baby*. ▸ NOUN ⑥ Things such as toffees, chocolates and mints are sweets. ⑦ a dessert. **sweetly** ADVERB **sweetness** NOUN

> **sweet** ADJECTIVE
> ① = cloying, sugary, sweetened
> ≠ sour
> ③ = aromatic, fragrant, perfumed, sweet-smelling
> ④ = harmonious, mellow, melodious, musical, tuneful
> ▸ NOUN ⑥ = candy (*American*), confectionery, lolly (*Australian and New Zealand*), sweetie

sweet corn NOUN Sweet corn is a long stalk covered with juicy yellow seeds that can be eaten as a vegetable.

sweeten VERB To sweeten food means

to add sugar or another sweet substance to it.

sweetener NOUN a very sweet, artificial substance that can be used instead of sugar.

sweetheart NOUN ① You can call someone who you are very fond of 'sweetheart'. ② (*old-fashioned*) A young person's sweetheart is their boyfriend or girlfriend.

sweet tooth NOUN If you have a sweet tooth, you like sweet food very much.

swell, **swells**, **swelling**, **swelled**, **swollen** VERB ① If something swells, it becomes larger and rounder • *It causes the abdomen to swell*. ② If an amount swells, it increases in number. ▶ NOUN ③ The regular up and down movement of the waves at sea can be called a swell.

swelling NOUN ① an enlarged area on your body as a result of injury or illness. ② The swelling of something is an increase in its size.

sweltering ADJECTIVE If the weather is sweltering, it is very hot.

swept the past tense and past participle of **sweep**.

swerve VERB To swerve means to suddenly change direction to avoid colliding with something.

> **swerve** VERB
> = swing, turn, veer

swift ADJECTIVE ① happening or moving very quickly • *a swift glance*. ▶ NOUN ② a bird with narrow crescent-shaped wings. **swiftly** ADVERB **swiftness** NOUN

> **swift** ADJECTIVE
> ① = brisk, express, fast, hurried, prompt, quick, rapid, speedy
> ≠ slow

swig, **swigs**, **swigging**, **swigged** (*informal*) VERB ① To swig a drink means to drink it in large mouthfuls, usually from a bottle. ▶ NOUN ② If you have a swig of a drink, you take a large mouthful of it.

swill VERB ① To swill something means to pour water over it to clean it • *Swill the can out thoroughly*. ▶ NOUN ② Swill is a liquid mixture containing waste food that is fed to pigs.

swim, **swims**, **swimming**, **swam**, **swum** VERB ① To swim means to move through water using various movements with parts of the body. ② If things are swimming, it seems as if everything you see is moving and you feel dizzy. ▶ NOUN ③ If you go for a swim, you go into water to swim for pleasure. **swimmer** NOUN

swimming NOUN Swimming is the activity of moving through water using your arms and legs.

swimming pool NOUN a large hole that has been tiled and filled with water for swimming.

swimsuit NOUN a piece of clothing worn for swimming.

swindle VERB ① To swindle someone means to deceive them to obtain money or property. ▶ NOUN ② a trick in which someone is cheated out of money or property. **swindler** NOUN

swine NOUN ① (*old-fashioned*) A swine is another name for a pig. ② (*informal*) If you call someone a swine, you mean they are nasty and spiteful.

swing, **swings**, **swinging**, **swung** VERB ① If something swings, it moves repeatedly from side to side from a fixed point. ② If someone or something swings in a particular direction, they turn quickly or move in a sweeping curve in that direction. ▶ NOUN ③ a seat hanging from a frame or a branch, which you sit on and move backwards and forwards. ④ A swing in opinion is a significant change in people's opinion.

swipe VERB ① To swipe at something means to try to hit it making a curving movement with the arm. ② (*informal*) To swipe something means to steal it. ③ To swipe a credit card means to pass it through a machine that electronically reads the information stored in the card. ▸ NOUN ④ To take a swipe at something means to swipe at it.

swirl VERB To swirl means to move quickly in circles • *The black water swirled around his legs.*

swish VERB ① To swish means to move quickly through the air making a soft sound • *The curtains swished back.* ▸ NOUN ② the sound made when something swishes.

Swiss, **Swiss** ADJECTIVE ① belonging or relating to Switzerland. ▸ NOUN ② someone who comes from Switzerland.

switch NOUN ① a small control for an electrical device or machine. ② a change • *a switch in routine.* ▸ VERB ③ To switch to a different task or topic means to change to it. ④ If you switch things, you exchange one for the other. **switch off** VERB To switch off a light or machine means to stop it working by pressing a switch. **switch on** VERB To switch on a light or machine means to start it working by pressing a switch.

switchboard NOUN The switchboard in an organisation is the part where all telephone calls are received.

swivel, **swivels**, **swivelling**, **swivelled** VERB ① To swivel means to turn round on a central point. ▸ ADJECTIVE ② A swivel chair or lamp is made so that you can move the main part of it while the base remains in a fixed position.

swollen a past participle of **swell**.

swoon VERB (*literary*) To swoon means to faint as a result of strong emotion.

swoop VERB To swoop means to move downwards through the air in a fast curving movement • *A flock of pigeons swooped low over the square.*

swop another spelling of **swap**.

sword [*Said* **sord**] NOUN a weapon consisting of a very long blade with a short handle.

swordfish, **swordfishes** or **swordfish** NOUN a large sea fish with an upper jaw which sticks out like a sword.

swore the past tense of **swear**.

sworn the past participle of **swear**.

swum the past participle of **swim**.

swung the past tense and past participle of **swing**.

sycamore [*Said* **sik-am-mor**] NOUN a tree that has large leaves with five points.

syllable NOUN [ENGLISH] a part of a word that contains a single vowel sound and is pronounced as a unit. For example, 'book' has one syllable and 'reading' has two.

syllabus, **syllabuses** or **syllabi** NOUN The subjects that are studied for a particular course or examination are called the syllabus.

symbol NOUN a shape, design or idea that is used to represent something • *The fish has long been a symbol of Christianity.*

> **symbol** NOUN
> = emblem, emoticon, figure, logo, mark, representation, sign, token

symbolic ADJECTIVE Something that is symbolic has a special meaning that is considered to represent something else • *Six tons of ivory were burned in a symbolic ceremony.*

symbolise; also spelt **symbolize** VERB If a shape, design or idea symbolises something, it is regarded as being a symbol of it • *In China and Japan the carp symbolises courage.* **symbolism** NOUN

symmetrical ADJECTIVE [MATHS] If something is symmetrical, it could be split into two halves, one being the exact reflection of the other. **symmetrically** ADVERB

symmetry NOUN [MATHS] Something that has symmetry is symmetrical.

sympathetic ADJECTIVE ① A sympathetic person shows kindness and understanding to other people. ② If you are sympathetic to a proposal or an idea, you approve of it.

sympathise; also spelt **sympathize** VERB To sympathise with someone who is in difficulties means to show them understanding and care.

sympathiser; also spelt **sympathizer** NOUN People who support a particular cause can be referred to as sympathisers.

sympathy, **sympathies** NOUN ① Sympathy is kindness and understanding towards someone who is in difficulties. ② If you have sympathy with someone's ideas or actions, you agree with them. ▸ PHRASE ③ If you do something **in sympathy** with someone, you do it to show your support for them.

> **sympathy** NOUN
> ① = compassion, empathy, pity, understanding

symphony, **symphonies** NOUN a piece of music for an orchestra, usually in four movements.

symptom NOUN ① something wrong with your body that is a sign of an illness. ② Something that is considered to be a sign of a bad situation can be referred to as a symptom of it • *another symptom of the unrest sweeping across the country.* **symptomatic** ADJECTIVE

synagogue [*Said* **sin**-a-gog] NOUN [RE] a building where Jewish people meet for worship and religious instruction.

synchronise [*Said* **sing**-kron-nize]; also spelt **synchronize** VERB ① To synchronise two actions means to do them at the same time and speed. ② To synchronise watches means to set them to show exactly the same time as each other. **synchronisation** NOUN

syndicate NOUN an association of business people formed to carry out a particular project.

syndrome NOUN ① a medical condition characterised by a particular set of symptoms • *Down's syndrome.* ② You can refer to a typical set of characteristics as a syndrome • *the syndrome of skipping from one wonder diet to the next.*

synod [*Said* **sin**-od] NOUN a council of church leaders which meets regularly to discuss religious and moral issues.

synonym NOUN [ENGLISH] If two words have the same or a very similar meaning, they are synonyms.

synonymous ADJECTIVE ① Two words that are synonymous have the same or very similar meanings. ② If two things are closely associated, you can say that one is synonymous with the other • *New York is synonymous with the Statue of Liberty.*

synopsis, **synopses** NOUN a summary of a book, play or film.

syntax NOUN [ENGLISH] The syntax of a language is its grammatical rules and the way its words are arranged.

synthesis, **syntheses** NOUN A synthesis of different ideas or styles is a blended combination of them. **synthesise** VERB

synthetic ADJECTIVE made from artificial substances rather than natural ones.

Syrian [*Said* **sirr**-ee-an] ADJECTIVE ① belonging or relating to Syria.

▶ **NOUN** ② someone who comes from Syria.

syringe *[Said si-**rinj**]* **NOUN** a hollow tube with a part which is pushed down inside and a fine hollow needle at one end, used for injecting or extracting liquids.

syrup **NOUN** a thick sweet liquid made by boiling sugar with water. **syrupy** **ADJECTIVE**

system **NOUN** ① LIBRARY an organised way of doing or arranging something according to a fixed plan or set of rules. ② People sometimes refer to the government and administration of the country as the system. ③ You can also refer to a set of equipment as a system • *an old stereo system.* ④ In biology, a system of a particular kind is the set of organs that perform that function • *the immune system.*

system **NOUN**
① = arrangement, method, procedure, routine, structure, technique

systematic **ADJECTIVE** following a fixed plan and done in an efficient way • *a systematic study.*
systematically **ADVERB**

Tt

tab NOUN a small extra piece that is attached to something, for example on a curtain so it can be hung on a pole.

tabby, **tabbies** NOUN a cat whose fur has grey, brown or black stripes.

table NOUN ① a piece of furniture with a flat horizontal top supported by one or more legs. ② a set of facts or figures arranged in rows or columns. ▸ VERB ③ If you table something such as a proposal, you say formally that you want it to be discussed.

tablecloth NOUN a cloth used to cover a table and keep it clean.

tablespoon NOUN a large spoon used for serving food; also the amount that a tablespoon contains.

tablet NOUN ① any small, round pill made of powdered medicine. ② a slab of stone with words cut into it. ③ ICT a small mobile personal computer with a screen that is manipulated by swiping or tapping with the hand.

table tennis NOUN Table tennis is a game for two or four people in which you use bats to hit a small hollow ball over a low net across a table.

tabloid NOUN ENGLISH a newspaper with small pages, short news stories, and lots of photographs.

taboo, **taboos** NOUN ① a social custom that some words, subjects or actions must be avoided because they are considered embarrassing or offensive • *We have a powerful taboo against boasting.* ② a religious custom that forbids people to do something. ▸ ADJECTIVE ③ forbidden or disapproved of • *a taboo subject.*

tacit *[Said **tass**-it]* ADJECTIVE understood or implied without actually being said or written. **tacitly** ADVERB

taciturn *[Said **tass**-it-urn]* ADJECTIVE Someone who is taciturn does not talk very much and so seems unfriendly.

tack NOUN ① a short nail with a broad, flat head. ② If you change tack, you start to use a different method for dealing with something. ▸ VERB ③ If you tack something to a surface, you nail it there with tacks. ④ If you tack a piece of fabric, you sew it with long loose stitches.

tackle VERB ① If you tackle a difficult task, you start dealing with it in a determined way. ② If you tackle someone in a game such as soccer, you try to get the ball away from them. ③ If you tackle someone about something, you talk to them about it in order to get something changed or dealt with. ▸ NOUN ④ A tackle in sport is an attempt to get the ball away from your opponent. ⑤ Tackle is the equipment used for fishing.

tacky, **tackier**, **tackiest** ADJECTIVE ① slightly sticky to touch • *The cream feels tacky to the touch.* ② (*informal*) badly made and in poor taste • *tacky furniture.*

tact NOUN Tact is the ability to see when a situation is difficult or delicate and to handle it without upsetting people. **tactless** ADJECTIVE **tactlessly** ADVERB

tact NOUN
= delicacy, diplomacy, discretion, sensitivity

tactful ADJECTIVE behaving with or showing tact. **tactfully** ADVERB

tactful ADJECTIVE
= diplomatic, discreet, sensitive
≠ tactless

tactic NOUN ① Tactics are the methods you use to achieve what you want, especially to win a game. ② Tactics are also the ways in which troops and equipment are used in order to win a battle.

tactical ADJECTIVE relating to or using tactics • *England made some tactical errors in the game.* **tactically** ADVERB

tactile ADJECTIVE involving the sense of touch.

taffeta [*Said **taf**-fit-a*] NOUN Taffeta is a stiff, shiny fabric that is used mainly for making women's clothes.

tag, **tags**, **tagging**, **tagged** NOUN a small label made of cloth, paper or plastic.

tail NOUN ① The tail of an animal, bird or fish is the part extending beyond the end of its body. ② Tail can be used to mean the end part of something • *the tail of the plane.* ③ (*in plural*) If a man is wearing tails, he is wearing a formal jacket which has two long pieces hanging down at the back. ▸ VERB ④ (*informal*) If you tail someone, you follow them in order to find out where they go and what they do. ▸ ADJECTIVE, ADVERB ⑤ The 'tails' side of a coin is the side which does not have a person's head. **tail off** VERB If something tails off, it becomes gradually less.

tailback NOUN a long queue of traffic stretching back from whatever is blocking the road.

tailor NOUN ① a person who makes, alters and repairs clothes, especially for men. ▸ VERB ② If something is tailored for a particular purpose, it is specially designed for it.

tailor-made ADJECTIVE suitable for a particular person or purpose, or specifically designed for them.

taint VERB ① To taint something is to spoil it by adding something undesirable to it. ▸ NOUN ② an undesirable quality in something which spoils it.

take, **takes**, **taking**, **took**, **taken** VERB ① 'Take' is used to show what action or activity is being done • *Amy took a bath* • *She took her driving test.* ② If something takes a certain amount of time, or a particular quality or ability, it requires it • *He takes three hours to get ready.* ③ If you take something, you put your hand round it and hold it or carry it • *Here, let me take your coat.* ④ If you take someone somewhere, you drive them there by car or lead them there. ⑤ If you take something that is offered to you, you accept it • *He had to take the job.* ⑥ If you take the responsibility or blame for something, you accept responsibility or blame. ⑦ If you take something that does not belong to you, you steal it. ⑧ If you take pills or medicine, you swallow them. ⑨ If you can take something painful, you can bear it • *We can't take much more of this.* ⑩ If you take someone's advice, you do what they say you should do. ⑪ If you take a person's temperature or pulse, you measure it. ⑫ If you take a car or train, or a road or route, you use it to go from one place to another. ▸ PHRASE ⑬ If you **take care of** someone or something, you look after them. ⑭ If you **take care of** a problem or situation, you deal with it and get it sorted. **take after** VERB If you take after someone in your family, you look or behave like them. **take down** VERB If you take down what someone is saying, you write it down. **take in** VERB ① If someone is taken in, they are deceived. ② If you take something in, you understand it. **take off** VERB When an aeroplane takes off, it leaves the ground and begins to fly. **takeoff** NOUN **take over** VERB To take something over means to start controlling it. **takeover** NOUN **take to** VERB If you take to someone or something, you like them immediately.

take VERB
② = demand, require
③ = bear (*formal*), bring, carry, convey (*formal*), ferry, fetch, transport
④ = bring, conduct (*formal*), escort, guide, lead, usher
▸ PHRASE ⑬ = care for, look after, mind, nurse, protect, tend, watch
≠ neglect
⑭ = attend to, cope with, deal with, handle, manage, see to
▸ **take in** ① = con (*informal*), deceive, dupe, fool, mislead, trick ② = absorb, appreciate, assimilate, comprehend, digest, get, grasp, understand

takeaway NOUN ① a shop or restaurant that sells hot cooked food to be eaten elsewhere. ② a hot cooked meal bought from a takeaway.

takings PLURAL NOUN Takings are the money that a shop or cinema gets from selling its goods or tickets.

tale NOUN a story.

talent NOUN Talent is the natural ability to do something well. **talented** ADJECTIVE

talent NOUN
= ability, aptitude, capacity, flair, genius, gift, knack

talisman [*Said* ***tal****-iz-man*] NOUN an object which you believe has magic powers to protect you or bring luck.

talk VERB ① When you talk, you say things to someone. ② If people talk, especially about other people's private affairs, they gossip about them • *The neighbours might talk.* ③ If you talk on or about something, you make an informal speech about it. ▸ NOUN ④ Talk is discussion or gossip. ⑤ an informal speech about something. **talk down** VERB If you talk down to someone, you talk to them in a way that shows that you think you are more important or clever than them.

talk NOUN
④ = chat, chatter, conversation
⑤ = address, discourse, lecture, sermon, speech

talkative ADJECTIVE talking a lot.

talkative ADJECTIVE
= chatty, communicative, long-winded

tall ADJECTIVE ① of more than average or normal height. ② having a particular height • *a wall ten metres tall.* ▸ PHRASE ③ If you describe something as **a tall story**, you mean that it is difficult to believe because it is so unlikely.

tall ADJECTIVE
① = high, lanky, lofty, soaring, towering
≠ short

tally, **tallies**, **tallying**, **tallied** NOUN ① an informal record of amounts which you keep adding to as you go along • *He ended with a reasonable goal tally last season.* ▸ VERB ② If numbers or statements tally, they are exactly the same or they give the same results or conclusions.

tambourine NOUN a percussion instrument made of a skin stretched tightly over a circular frame, with small round pieces of metal around the edge that jingle when the tambourine is beaten or shaken.

tame ADJECTIVE ① A tame animal or bird is not afraid of people and is not violent towards them. ② Something that is tame is uninteresting and lacks excitement or risk • *The report was pretty tame.* ▸ VERB ③ If you tame people or things, you bring them under control. ④ To tame a wild animal or bird is to train it to be obedient and live with humans.

tamper VERB If you tamper with something, you interfere or meddle with it.

tan, **tans**, **tanning**, **tanned** NOUN ① If you have a tan, your skin is darker than usual because you have been in the sun. ▸ VERB ② To tan an animal's hide is to turn it into leather by treating it with chemicals. ▸ ADJECTIVE ③ Something that is tan is of a light yellowish-brown colour • *a tan dress.*

tandem NOUN a bicycle designed for two riders sitting one behind the other.

tang NOUN a strong, sharp smell or flavour • *the tang of lemon.* **tangy** ADJECTIVE

tangerine NOUN ① a type of small sweet orange with a loose rind. ▸ NOUN, ADJECTIVE ② reddish-orange.

tangible [*Said* ***tan****-jib-bl*] ADJECTIVE clear or definite enough to be easily seen or felt • *tangible proof.*

tangle NOUN ① a mass of things such as hairs or fibres knotted or coiled together and difficult to separate. ▸ VERB ② If you are tangled in wires or ropes, you are caught or trapped in them so that it is difficult to get free.

> **tangle** NOUN
> ① = jumble, knot, mass, mat, muddle, web
> ▸ VERB ② = catch, jumble, knot, twist

tango, **tangos** NOUN A tango is a Latin American dance using long gliding steps and sudden pauses; also a piece of music composed for this dance.

tank NOUN ① a large container for storing liquid or gas. ② an armoured military vehicle which moves on tracks and is equipped with guns or rockets.

tanker NOUN a ship or lorry designed to carry large quantities of gas or liquid • *a petrol tanker.*

tannin NOUN a brown or yellow substance found in plants and used in making leather.

tantalising; also spelt **tantalizing** ADJECTIVE Something that is tantalising makes you feel hopeful and excited, although you know that you probably will not be able to have what you want • *a tantalising glimpse of riches to come.*

tantamount ADJECTIVE If you say that something is tantamount to something else, you mean that it is almost the same as it • *That would be tantamount to treason.*

tantrum NOUN a noisy and sometimes violent outburst of temper, especially by a child.

Tanzanian [*Said tan-zan-****nee****-an*] ADJECTIVE ① belonging or relating to Tanzania. ▸ NOUN ② someone who comes from Tanzania.

tap, **taps**, **tapping**, **tapped** NOUN ① a device that you turn to control the flow of liquid or gas from a pipe or container. ② the action of hitting something lightly; also the sound that this action makes. ▸ VERB ③ If you tap something or tap on it, you hit it lightly. ④ If a telephone is tapped, a device is fitted to it so that someone can listen secretly to the calls.

tape NOUN ① Tape is plastic ribbon covered with a magnetic substance and used to record sounds, pictures and computer data. ② A tape is a recording of sounds, pictures or computer data. ③ Tape is a long, thin strip of fabric that is used for binding or fastening. ④ Tape is also a strip of sticky plastic which you use for sticking things together. ▶ **VERB** ⑤ If you tape sounds or television pictures, you record them. ⑥ If you tape one thing to another, you attach them using sticky tape.

tape measure **NOUN** a strip of plastic or metal that is marked off in inches or centimetres and used for measuring things.

taper **VERB** ① Something that tapers becomes thinner towards one end. ▶ **NOUN** ② a thin candle.

tape recorder **NOUN** a machine used for recording sounds onto magnetic tape, and for playing these sounds back.

tapestry, **tapestries** **NOUN** a piece of heavy cloth with designs embroidered on it.

tar **NOUN** Tar is a thick, black, sticky substance which is used in making roads.

target **NOUN** ① something which you aim at when firing weapons. ② The target of an action or remark is the person or thing at which it is directed • *You become a target for our hatred.* ③ Your target is the result that you are trying to achieve.

tariff **NOUN** ① a tax that a government collects on imported goods. ② any list of prices or charges.

tarmac **NOUN** Tarmac is a material used for making road surfaces. It consists of crushed stones mixed with tar.

tarnish **VERB** ① If metal tarnishes, it becomes stained and loses its shine. ② If something tarnishes your reputation, it spoils it and causes people to lose their respect for you.

tarpaulin **NOUN** a sheet of heavy waterproof material used as a protective covering.

tarragon **NOUN** Tarragon is a herb with narrow green leaves used in cooking.

tart **NOUN** ① a pastry case with a sweet filling. ▶ **ADJECTIVE** ② Something that is tart is sour or sharp to taste. ③ A tart remark is unpleasant and cruel.

tartan **NOUN** Tartan is a woollen fabric from Scotland with checks of various colours and sizes, depending on which clan it belongs to.

task **NOUN** any piece of work which has to be done.

> **task** **NOUN**
> = assignment, chore, duty, job, mission, undertaking

Tasmanian devil **NOUN** a black-and-white marsupial of Tasmania, which eats flesh.

taste **NOUN** ① Your sense of taste is your ability to recognise the flavour of things in your mouth. ② The taste of something is its flavour. ③ If you have a taste of food or drink, you have a small amount of it to see what it is like. ④ If you have a taste for something, you enjoy it • *a taste for publicity*. ⑤ If you have a taste of something, you experience it • *my first taste of defeat*. ⑥ A person's taste is their choice in the things they like to buy or have around them • *His taste in music is great*. ▶ **VERB** ⑦ When you can taste something in your mouth, you are aware of its flavour. ⑧ If you taste food or drink, you have a small amount of it to see what it is like. ⑨ If food or drink tastes of something, it has that flavour.

> **taste** **NOUN**
> ② = flavour, tang
> ③ = bite, mouthful, sip
> ④ = appetite, fondness, liking, penchant (*formal*)

A B C D E F G H I J K L M N O P Q R S **T** U V W X Y Z

tasteful ADJECTIVE attractive and elegant. **tastefully** ADVERB

tasteless ADJECTIVE ① vulgar and unattractive. ② A tasteless remark or joke is offensive. ③ Tasteless food has very little flavour.

> **tasteless** ADJECTIVE
> ① = flashy, garish, gaudy, tacky (*informal*), tawdry, vulgar
> ≠ tasteful
> ③ = bland, insipid
> ≠ tasty

tasty, **tastier**, **tastiest** ADJECTIVE having a pleasant flavour.

> **tasty** ADJECTIVE
> = appetising, delicious, lekker (*South African; slang*), luscious, palatable
> ≠ tasteless

tatters PHRASE Clothes that are **in tatters** are badly torn. **tattered** ADJECTIVE

tattoo, **tattoos**, **tattooing**, **tattooed** VERB ① If someone tattoos you or tattoos a design on you, they draw it on your skin by pricking little holes and filling them with coloured dye. ▸ NOUN ② a picture or design tattooed on someone's body. ③ a public military display of exercises and music.

tatty, **tattier**, **tattiest** ADJECTIVE worn out or untidy and rather dirty.

taught the past tense and past participle of **teach**.

taunt VERB ① To taunt someone is to speak to them about their weaknesses or failures in order to make them angry or upset. ▸ NOUN ② an offensive remark intended to make a person angry or upset.

Taurus NOUN Taurus is the second sign of the zodiac, represented by a bull. People born between April 20th and May 20th are born under this sign.

taut ADJECTIVE stretched very tight • *taut wires*.

tavern NOUN (*old-fashioned*) a pub.

tawdry, **tawdrier**, **tawdriest** [*Said taw-dree*] ADJECTIVE cheap, gaudy and of poor quality.

tawny NOUN, ADJECTIVE brownish-yellow.

tax NOUN ① Tax is an amount of money that the people in a country have to pay to the government so that it can provide public services such as health care and education. ▸ VERB ② If a sum of money is taxed, a certain amount of it has to be paid to the government. ③ If goods are taxed, a certain amount of their price has to be paid to the government. ④ If a person or company is taxed, they have to pay a certain amount of their income to the government. ⑤ If something taxes you, it makes heavy demands on you • *They must be told not to tax your patience*. **taxation** NOUN

> **tax** NOUN
> ① = duty, excise, levy (*formal*), tariff
> ▸ VERB ⑤ = drain, exhaust, sap, strain, stretch

taxi, **taxis**, **taxiing**, **taxied** NOUN ① a car with a driver which you hire to take you to where you want to go. ▸ VERB ② When an aeroplane taxis, it moves slowly along the runway before taking off or after landing.

tea NOUN ① Tea is the dried leaves of an evergreen shrub found in Asia. ② Tea is a drink made by brewing the leaves of the tea plant in hot water; also a cup of this. ③ Tea is also any drink made with hot water and leaves or flowers • *peppermint tea*. ④ Tea is a meal taken in the late afternoon or early evening.

teach, **teaches**, **teaching**, **taught** VERB ① If you teach someone something, you give them instructions so that

they know about it or know how to do it. ② If you teach a subject, you help students learn about a subject at school, college or university.
teaching NOUN

teach VERB
① = coach, drill, educate, instruct, school, train, tutor

teacher NOUN a person who teaches other people, especially children.

teacher NOUN
= coach, don, guru, instructor, lecturer, master, mistress, professor, tutor

teak NOUN Teak is a hard wood which comes from a large Asian tree.

team NOUN ① a group of people who work together or play together against another group in a sport or game. ▸ VERB ② If you team up with someone, you join them and work together with them.

team NOUN
① = band, crew, gang, group, side, squad, troupe
▸ VERB ② = collaborate, cooperate, join forces, link up, pair up, unite, work together

teamwork NOUN Teamwork is the ability of a group of people to work well together.

teapot NOUN a round pot with a handle, a lid and a spout, used for brewing and pouring tea.

tear¹, **tears** [*Rhymes with **fear***] NOUN Tears are the drops of salty liquid that come out of your eyes when you cry.

tear², **tears**, **tearing**, **tore**, **torn** [*Rhymes with **hair***] NOUN ① a hole that has been made in something. ▸ VERB ② If you tear something, it is damaged by being pulled so that a hole appears in it. ③ If you tear somewhere, you rush there • *He tore through busy streets in a high-speed chase.*

tear NOUN
① = hole, ladder, rip, rupture, scratch, split
▸ VERB ② = ladder, rip, rupture, scratch, shred, split
③ = charge, dart, dash, fly, race, shoot, speed, zoom

tearaway NOUN someone who is wild and uncontrollable.

tearful ADJECTIVE about to cry or crying gently. **tearfully** ADVERB

tease VERB ① If you tease someone, you deliberately make fun of them or embarrass them because it amuses you. ▸ NOUN ② someone who enjoys teasing people.

tease VERB
① = make fun of, mock, needle (*informal*), taunt

teaspoon NOUN a small spoon used for stirring drinks; also the amount that a teaspoon holds.

tea tree NOUN a tree found in Australia and New Zealand with leaves that yield an oil used as an antiseptic • *Tea tree oil has many uses.*

tech NOUN (*informal*) a technical college.

technical ADJECTIVE ① involving machines, processes and materials used in industry, transport and communications. ② skilled in practical and mechanical things rather than theories and ideas. ③ involving a specialised field of activity • *I never understood the technical jargon.*

technicality, **technicalities** NOUN ① The technicalities of a process or activity are the detailed methods used to do it. ② an exact detail of a law or a set of rules, especially one some people might not notice • *The verdict may have been based on a technicality.*

technically ADVERB If something is

technically true or correct, it is true or correct when you consider only the facts, rules or laws, but may not be important or relevant in a particular situation • *Technically, they were not supposed to drink on duty*.

technician NOUN someone whose job involves skilled practical work with scientific equipment.

technique NOUN ① a particular method of doing something • *these techniques of manufacture*. ② Technique is skill and ability in an activity which is developed through training and practice • *Jim's unique vocal technique*.

technology, **technologies** NOUN ① DGT Technology is the study of the application of science and scientific knowledge for practical purposes in industry, farming, medicine or business. ② a particular area of activity that requires scientific methods and knowledge • *computer technology*. **technological** ADJECTIVE **technologically** ADVERB

teddy, **teddies** NOUN A teddy or teddy bear is a stuffed toy that looks like a friendly bear.

tedious [*Said* ***tee****-dee-uss*] ADJECTIVE boring and lasting for a long time • *the tedious task of clearing up*.

tedium [*Said* ***tee****-dee-um*] NOUN the quality of being boring and lasting for a long time • *the tedium of unemployment*.

tee, **tees**, **teeing**, **teed** NOUN the small wooden or plastic peg on which a golf ball is placed before the golfer first hits it. **tee off** VERB To tee off is to hit the golf ball from the tee, or to start a round of golf.

teem VERB ① If a place is teeming with people or things, there are a lot of them moving about. ② If it teems, it rains very heavily • *The rain was teeming down*.

teenage ADJECTIVE ① aged between thirteen and nineteen. ② typical of people aged between thirteen and nineteen • *teenage fashion*. **teenager** NOUN

teens PLURAL NOUN Your teens are the period of your life when you are between thirteen and nineteen years old.

teeter VERB To teeter is to shake or sway slightly in an unsteady way and seem about to fall over.

teeth the plural of **tooth**.

teetotal [*Said tee-****toe****-tl*] ADJECTIVE Someone who is teetotal never drinks alcohol. **teetotaller** NOUN

telecommunications NOUN Telecommunications is the science and activity of sending signals and messages over long distances using electronic equipment.

telegram NOUN a message sent by telegraph.

telegraph NOUN The telegraph is a system of sending messages over long distances using electrical or radio signals.

telephone NOUN ① a piece of electrical equipment for talking directly to someone who is in a different place. ▸ VERB ② If you telephone someone, you speak to them using a telephone.

telescope NOUN a long instrument shaped like a tube which has lenses which make distant objects appear larger and nearer.

televise VERB If an event is televised, it is filmed and shown on television.

television NOUN a piece of electronic equipment which receives pictures and sounds by electrical signals over a distance.

tell, **tells**, **telling**, **told** VERB ① If you tell someone something, you let them know about it. ② If you tell someone to do something, you order or advise them to do it. ③ If you can tell something, you are able to judge correctly what is happening or what the situation is • *I could tell he was scared*. ④ If an unpleasant or tiring experience begins to tell, it begins to have a serious effect • *The pressure began to tell*.

tell VERB
① = inform, notify
② = command, direct (*formal*), instruct, order
③ = discern, see

teller NOUN a person who receives or gives out money in a bank.

telling ADJECTIVE Something that is telling has an important effect, often because it shows the true nature of a situation • *a telling account of the war*.

telltale ADJECTIVE A telltale sign reveals information • *the sad telltale signs of a recent accident*.

telly, **tellies** NOUN (*informal*) a television.

temerity [*Said tim-**mer**-it-ee*] NOUN If someone has the temerity to do something, they do it even though it upsets or annoys other people • *She had the temerity to call him Bob*.

temp NOUN (*informal*) an employee who works for short periods of time in different places.

temper NOUN ① Your temper is the frame of mind or mood you are in. ② a sudden outburst of anger. ▶ PHRASE ③ If you **lose your temper**, you become very angry. ▶ VERB ④ To temper something is to make it more acceptable or suitable • *curiosity tempered with some caution*.

temperament [*Said **tem**-pra-ment*] NOUN Your temperament is your nature or personality, shown in the way you react towards people and situations • *an artistic temperament*.

temperamental ADJECTIVE Someone who is temperamental has moods that change often and suddenly.

temperate ADJECTIVE GEOGRAPHY A temperate place has weather that is neither extremely hot nor extremely cold.

temperature NOUN ① SCIENCE The temperature of something is how hot or cold it is. ② Your temperature is the temperature of your body. ▶ PHRASE ③ If you **have a temperature**, the temperature of your body is higher than it should be, because you are ill.

tempest NOUN (*literary*) a violent storm.

tempestuous [*Said tem-**pest**-yoo-uss*] ADJECTIVE violent or strongly emotional • *a tempestuous relationship*.

template NOUN a shape or pattern cut out in wood, metal, plastic or card which you draw or cut around to reproduce that shape or pattern.

temple NOUN ① RE a building used for the worship of a god in various religions • *a Buddhist temple*. ② Your temples are the flat parts on each side of your forehead.

tempo, **tempos** or **tempi** NOUN ① The tempo of something is the speed at which it happens • *the slow tempo of change*. ② MUSIC The tempo of a piece of music is its speed.

temporary ADJECTIVE lasting for only a short time. **temporarily** ADVERB

temporary ADJECTIVE
= ephemeral (*formal*), fleeting, interim, momentary, passing, provisional, transient (*formal*), transitory
≠ permanent

tempt VERB ① If you tempt someone, you try to persuade them to do something by offering them something they want. ② If you are tempted to do something, you want to do it but you think it might be wrong or harmful • *He was tempted to reply with sarcasm.*

tempt VERB
① = entice, lure, seduce

temptation NOUN ① Temptation is the state you are in when you want to do or have something, even though you know it might be wrong or harmful. ② something that you want to do or have, even though you know it might be wrong or harmful.

ten the number 10. **tenth** ADJECTIVE

tenacious *[Said tin-**nay**-shuss]* ADJECTIVE determined and not giving up easily. **tenaciously** ADVERB **tenacity** NOUN

tenant NOUN someone who pays rent for the place they live in, or for land or buildings that they use. **tenancy** NOUN

tend VERB ① If something tends to happen, it happens usually or often. ② If you tend someone or something, you look after them • *the way we tend our cattle.*

tend VERB
① = be apt, be inclined, be liable, be prone, have a tendency
② = care for, look after, nurse, take care of

tendency, **tendencies** NOUN a trend or type of behaviour that happens very often • *a tendency to be critical.*

tendency NOUN
= inclination, leaning, propensity

tender ADJECTIVE ① Someone who is tender has gentle and caring feelings. ② If someone is at a tender age, they are young and do not know very much about life. ③ Tender meat is easy to cut or chew. ④ If a part of your body is tender, it is painful and sore. ▶ VERB ⑤ If someone tenders an apology or their resignation, they offer it. ▶ NOUN ⑥ a formal offer to supply goods or to do a job for a particular price.

tender ADJECTIVE
① = affectionate, caring, compassionate, gentle, kind, loving, sensitive, warm
≠ tough
④ = aching, bruised, inflamed, painful, raw, sensitive, sore
▶ VERB ⑤ = hand in, offer
▶ NOUN ⑥ = bid, estimate, package, submission

tendon NOUN SCIENCE a strong cord of tissue which joins a muscle to a bone.

tenement *[Said **ten**-em-ent]* NOUN a large house or building divided into many flats.

tenet NOUN The tenets of a theory or belief are the main ideas it is based upon.

tenner NOUN (*informal*) a ten-pound or ten-dollar note.

tennis NOUN Tennis is a game played by two or four players on a rectangular court in which a ball is hit by players over a central net.

tenor NOUN ① a man who sings in a fairly high voice. ② The tenor of something is the general meaning or mood that it expresses • *the whole tenor of his poetry had changed.* ▶ ADJECTIVE ③ A tenor recorder, saxophone or other musical instrument has a range of notes of a fairly low pitch.

tense ADJECTIVE ① If you are tense, you are nervous and cannot relax. ② A tense situation or period of time is one that makes people nervous and worried. ③ If your body is tense, your muscles are tight. ▶ VERB ④ If you tense, or if your muscles tense, your muscles become tight and stiff. ▶ NOUN ⑤ The tense of a verb is the form which shows whether you are talking about the past, present or future.

tense ADJECTIVE
① = anxious, edgy, jittery (*informal*), jumpy, nervous, uptight (*informal*)
≠ calm
② = anxious, nerve-racking, stressful
③ = rigid, strained, taut, tight
≠ relaxed

tension NOUN ① Tension is the feeling of nervousness or worry that you have when something dangerous or important is happening. ② DGT The tension in a rope or wire is how tightly it is stretched.

tent NOUN a shelter made of canvas or nylon held up by poles and pinned down with pegs and ropes.

tentacle NOUN The tentacles of an animal such as an octopus are the long, thin parts that it uses to feel and hold things.

tentative ADJECTIVE acting or speaking cautiously because of being uncertain or afraid. **tentatively** ADVERB

tenterhooks PLURAL NOUN If you are on tenterhooks, you are nervous and excited about something that is going to happen.

tenuous [*Said* ***ten**-yoo-uss*] ADJECTIVE If an idea or connection is tenuous, it is so slight and weak that it may not really exist or may easily cease to exist • *a very tenuous friendship*.

tenure [*Said* ***ten**-yoor*] NOUN ① Tenure is the legal right to live in a place or to use land or buildings for a period of time. ② Tenure is the period of time during which someone holds an important job • *His tenure ended in 2014*.

tepid ADJECTIVE Tepid liquid is only slightly warm.

term NOUN ① a fixed period of time • *her second term as manager*. ② one of the periods of time that each year is divided into at a school or college. ③ a name or word used for a particular thing. ④ (*in plural*) The terms of an agreement are the conditions that have been accepted by the people involved in it. ⑤ If you express something in particular terms, you express it using a particular type of language or in a way that clearly shows your attitude • *The young priest spoke of her in glowing terms*. ▶ PHRASE ⑥ If you **come to terms with** something difficult or unpleasant, you learn to accept it. ▶ VERB ⑦ To term something is to give it a name or to describe it • *He termed my performance memorable*.

term NOUN
① = period, session, spell, stretch, time
③ = designation, expression, name, word
④ = conditions, provisions, proviso, stipulations

terminal ADJECTIVE ① A terminal illness or disease cannot be cured and causes death gradually. ▶ NOUN ② a place where vehicles, passengers or goods begin or end a journey. ③ A computer terminal is a keyboard and a visual display unit that is used to put information into or get information out of a computer. ④ one of the parts of an electrical device through which electricity enters or leaves. **terminally** ADVERB

terminate VERB When you terminate something or when it terminates, it stops or ends. **termination** NOUN

terminology, terminologies NOUN The terminology of a subject is the set of special words and expressions used in it.

terminus [*Said* ***ter**-min-uss*] NOUN a place where a bus or train route ends.

termite NOUN Termites are small white insects that feed on wood.

terrace NOUN ① a row of houses joined together. ② a flat area of stone next to a building where people can sit.

terracotta NOUN a type of brown pottery with no glaze.

terrain NOUN The terrain of an area is the type of land there • *the region's hilly terrain.*

terrestrial ADJECTIVE involving the earth or land.

terrible ADJECTIVE ① serious and unpleasant • *a terrible illness.* ② (*informal*) very bad or of poor quality • *Paddy's terrible haircut.*

> **terrible** ADJECTIVE
> ① = appalling, awful, desperate, dreadful, frightful (*old-fashioned*), horrendous, horrible, horrid (*old-fashioned*), rotten (*informal*)
> ② = abysmal, appalling, awful, dire, dreadful, horrible, rotten (*informal*)
> ≠ excellent

terribly ADVERB very or very much • *I was terribly upset.*

terrier NOUN a small, short-bodied dog.

terrific ADJECTIVE ① (*informal*) very pleasing or impressive • *a terrific film.* ② great in amount, degree or intensity • *a terrific blow on the head.*
terrifically ADVERB

terrify, **terrifies**, **terrifying**, **terrified** VERB If something terrifies you, it makes you feel extremely frightened.

territorial ADJECTIVE involving or relating to the ownership of a particular area of land or water • *a territorial dispute.*

territory, **territories** NOUN ① The territory of a country is the land that it controls. ② An animal's territory is an area which it regards as its own and defends when other animals try to enter it.

> **territory** NOUN
> ① = area, country, district, domain, dominion, land, province, state

terror NOUN ① Terror is great fear or panic. ② something that makes you feel very frightened.

terrorise; also spelt **terrorize** VERB If someone terrorises you, they frighten you by threatening you or being violent to you.

terrorism NOUN Terrorism is the use of violence for political reasons.
terrorist NOUN, ADJECTIVE

terse ADJECTIVE A terse statement is short and rather unfriendly.

tertiary [*Said ter-shar-ee*] ADJECTIVE ① third in order or importance. ② Tertiary education is education at university or college level.

test VERB ① When you test something, you try it to find out what it is, what condition it is in, or how well it works. ② If you test someone, you ask them questions to find out how much they know.
▸ NOUN ③ a deliberate action or experiment to find out whether something works or how well it works. ④ a set of questions or tasks given to someone to find out what they know or can do.

> **test** VERB
> ① = assess, check, try, try out
> ▸ NOUN ③ = assessment, check, trial

testament NOUN ① (*Law*) a will. ② a copy of either the Old or the New Testament of the Bible.

test case NOUN a legal case that becomes an example for deciding other similar cases.

testicle NOUN [SCIENCE] A man's testicles are the two sex glands beneath the penis that produce sperm.

testify, **testifies**, **testifying**, **testified** VERB ① When someone testifies, they make a formal statement, especially in a court of law • *He later testified at the inquiry.* ② To testify to something is to show that it is likely to be true • *a consultant's certificate testifying to her good health.*

testimonial *[Said tess-tim-**moh**-nee-al]* NOUN a statement saying how good someone or something is.

testimony, **testimonies** NOUN A person's testimony is a formal statement they make, especially in a court of law.

testing ADJECTIVE Testing situations or problems are very difficult to deal with • *It is a testing time for his team.*

test match NOUN one of a series of international cricket or rugby matches.

testosterone *[Said tess-**toss**-ter-rone]* NOUN Testosterone is a hormone that produces male characteristics.

test tube NOUN a small cylindrical glass container that is used in chemical experiments.

tetanus *[Said **tet**-ah-nuss]* NOUN Tetanus is a painful infectious disease caused by germs getting into wounds.

tether VERB ① If you tether an animal, you tie it to a post. ▶ PHRASE ② If you are **at the end of your tether**, you are extremely tired and have no more patience or energy left to deal with your problems.

Teutonic *[Said tyoo-**tonn**-ik]* ADJECTIVE *(formal)* involving or related to German people.

text NOUN ① The text of a book is the main written part of it, rather than the pictures or index. ② Text is any written material. ③ a book or other piece of writing used for study or an exam at school or college. ④ Text is short for 'text message'. ▶ VERB ⑤ If you text someone, you send them a text message. **textual** ADJECTIVE

textbook NOUN a book about a particular subject for students to use.

textile NOUN DGT a woven cloth or fabric.

text message NOUN a written message sent using a mobile phone.

texture NOUN The texture of something is the way it feels when you touch it.

> **texture** NOUN
> = consistency, feel

Thai, **Thais** ADJECTIVE ① belonging or relating to Thailand. ▶ NOUN ② someone who comes from Thailand. ③ Thai is the main language spoken in Thailand.

than PREPOSITION, CONJUNCTION ① You use 'than' to link two parts of a comparison • *She was older than me.* ② You use 'than' to link two parts of a contrast • *Players would rather play than train.*

thank VERB When you thank someone, you show that you are grateful for something, usually by saying 'thank you'.

thankful ADJECTIVE happy and relieved about something. **thankfully** ADVERB

thankless ADJECTIVE A thankless job or task involves doing a lot of hard work that other people do not notice or are not grateful for • *Referees have a thankless task.*

thanks PLURAL NOUN ① When you express your thanks to someone, you tell or show them how grateful you are for something. ▶ PHRASE ② If something happened **thanks to** someone or something, it happened because of them • *I'm as prepared as I can be, thanks to you.* ▶ INTERJECTION ③ You say 'thanks' to show that you are grateful for something.

thanksgiving NOUN ① Thanksgiving is an act of thanking God, especially in prayer or in a religious ceremony. ② In the United States, Thanksgiving is a public holiday in the autumn.

thank you INTERJECTION You say 'thank you' to show that you are grateful to someone for something.

that ADJECTIVE, PRONOUN ① 'That' or 'those' is used to refer to things or people already mentioned or known about • *That man was waving.* ▶ CONJUNCTION ② 'That' is used to introduce a clause • *I said that I was coming home.* ▶ PRONOUN ③ 'That' is also used to introduce a relative clause • *I followed Alex to a door that led inside.*

thatch NOUN ① Thatch is straw and reeds used to make roofs. ▶ VERB ② To thatch a roof is to cover it with thatch.

thaw VERB ① When snow or ice thaws, it melts. ② When you thaw frozen food, or when it thaws, it returns to its normal state in a warmer atmosphere. ③ When people who are unfriendly thaw, they begin to be more friendly and relaxed. ▶ NOUN ④ a period of warmer weather in winter when snow or ice melts.

the ADJECTIVE The definite article 'the' is used when you are talking about something that is known about, that has just been mentioned, or that you are going to give details about.

theatre [Said **thee**-uh-tuh] NOUN ① DRAMA a building where plays and other entertainments are performed on a stage. ② Theatre is work such as writing, producing and acting in plays. ③ An operating theatre is a room in a hospital designed and equipped for surgical operations.

theatrical [Said thee-**at**-rik-kl] ADJECTIVE ① DRAMA involving the theatre or performed in a theatre • *his theatrical career.* ② Theatrical behaviour is exaggerated, unnatural and done for effect. **theatrically** ADVERB

thee PRONOUN (*old-fashioned*) Thee means you.

theft NOUN Theft is the crime of stealing.

> **theft** NOUN
> = robbery, stealing, thieving

their ADJECTIVE 'Their' refers to something belonging or relating to people or things, other than yourself or the person you are talking to, which have already been mentioned • *It was their fault.*

theirs PRONOUN 'Theirs' refers to something belonging or relating to people or things, other than yourself or the person you are talking to, which have already been mentioned • *Amy had been Helen's friend, not theirs.*

them PRONOUN 'Them' refers to things or people, other than yourself or the people you are talking to, which have already been mentioned • *He picked up the pillows and threw them to the floor.*

theme NOUN ① ENGLISH a main idea or topic in a piece of writing, painting, film or music • *the main theme of the book.* ② a tune, especially one played at the beginning and end of a television or radio programme.

themselves PRONOUN ① 'Themselves' is used when people, other than yourself or the person you are talking to, do an action and are affected by it • *They think they've made a fool of themselves.* ② 'Themselves' is used to emphasise 'they' • *He was as excited as they themselves were.*

then ADVERB at a particular time in the past or future • *I'd left home by then.*

theologian *[Said thee-ol-**loe**-jee-an]* NOUN someone who studies religion and the nature of God.

theology NOUN [RE] Theology is the study of religion and God.
theological ADJECTIVE

theoretical ADJECTIVE ① based on or to do with ideas of a subject rather than the practical aspects. ② not proved to exist or be true.
theoretically ADVERB

theory, **theories** NOUN ① an idea or set of ideas that is meant to explain something • *Darwin's theory of evolution*. ② Theory is the set of rules and ideas that a particular subject or skill is based upon. ▶ PHRASE ③ You use **in theory** to say that although something is supposed to happen, it may not in fact happen • *In theory, prices should rise by 2 per cent*.

> **theory** NOUN
> ① = conjecture (*formal*), hypothesis (*formal*), supposition, surmise (*formal*)

therapeutic *[Said ther-ap-**yoo**-tik]* ADJECTIVE ① If something is therapeutic, it helps you to feel happier and more relaxed • *Laughing is therapeutic*. ② In medicine, therapeutic treatment is designed to treat a disease or to improve a person's health.

therapy NOUN Therapy is the treatment of mental or physical illness, often without the use of drugs or operations. **therapist** NOUN

there ADVERB ① in, at or to that place, point or case • *He's sitting over there*. ▶ PRONOUN ② 'There' is used to say that something exists or does not exist, or to draw attention to something • *There are flowers on the table*.

thereby ADVERB (*formal*) as a result of the event or action mentioned • *They had recruited 200 new members, thereby making the day worthwhile*.

therefore ADVERB as a result.

> **therefore** ADVERB
> = as a result, consequently, for that reason, hence (*formal*), so, thus

thermal ADJECTIVE ① to do with or caused by heat • *thermal energy*. ② Thermal clothes are specially designed to keep you warm in cold weather.

thermometer NOUN [SCIENCE] an instrument for measuring the temperature of a room or a person's body.

thermostat NOUN a device used to control temperature, for example on a central heating system.

thesaurus, **thesauruses** *[Said this-**saw**-russ]* NOUN [LIBRARY] a reference book in which words with similar meanings are grouped together.

these the plural of **this**.

thesis, **theses** *[Said **thee**-siss]* NOUN a long piece of writing, based on research, that is done as part of a university degree.

they PRONOUN ① 'They' refers to people or things, other than you or the people you are talking to, that have already been mentioned • *They married two years later*. ② 'They' is sometimes used instead of 'he' or 'she' where the gender of the person is unknown or unspecified. Some people consider this to be incorrect • *Someone could have a nasty accident if they tripped over that*.

thick ADJECTIVE ① Something thick has a large distance between its two opposite surfaces. ② If something is a particular amount thick, it measures that amount between its two sides. ③ Thick means growing or grouped closely together and in large quantities • *thick dark hair*. ④ Thick liquids contain little water and do not flow easily • *thick soup*. ⑤ (*informal*) A thick person is stupid or slow to understand things.

thick ADJECTIVE
① = fat, wide
≠ thin
③ = bristling, dense, lush, luxuriant
≠ sparse
④ = clotted, concentrated, condensed
≠ watery

thicken VERB If something thickens, it becomes thicker • *The clouds thickened*.

thicken VERB
= clot, condense, congeal, set
≠ thin

thicket NOUN a small group of trees growing closely together.

thief, **thieves** NOUN a person who steals.

thief NOUN
= burglar, crook (*informal*), mugger (*informal*), pickpocket, robber, shoplifter

thieving NOUN Thieving is the act of stealing.

thigh NOUN Your thighs are the top parts of your legs, between your knees and your hips.

thin, **thinner**, **thinnest**; **thins**, **thinning**, **thinned** ADJECTIVE ① Something that is thin is much narrower than it is long. ② A thin person or animal has very little fat on their body. ③ Thin liquids contain a lot of water • *thin soup*. ▶ VERB ④ If you thin something such as paint or soup, you add water or other liquid to it.

thin ADJECTIVE
① = fine, narrow, slim
≠ thick
② = emaciated, lean, skinny, slender, slim
≠ fat
③ = dilute, diluted, runny, watery, weak
≠ thick

thing NOUN ① an object, rather than a plant, an animal or a human being. ② (*in plural*) Your things are your clothes or possessions.

thing NOUN
① = article, object
② = belongings, effects, gear (*informal*), possessions, stuff

think, **thinks**, **thinking**, **thought** VERB ① When you think about ideas or problems, you use your mind to consider them. ② If you think something, you have the opinion that it is true or the case • *I think she has a secret boyfriend*. ③ If you think of something, you remember it or it comes into your mind. ④ If you think a lot of someone or something, you admire them or think they are good.

think VERB
① = consider, contemplate, deliberate, meditate, mull over, muse (*literary*), ponder, reflect
② = believe, consider, deem (*formal*), hold, imagine, judge, reckon (*informal*)

third ADJECTIVE ① The third item in a series is the one counted as number three. ▶ NOUN ② one of three equal parts.

Third World NOUN The poorer countries of Africa, Asia and South America can be referred to as the Third World.

thirst NOUN ① If you have a thirst, you feel a need to drink something. ② A thirst for something is a very strong desire for it • *a thirst for money*. **thirsty** ADJECTIVE **thirstily** ADVERB

thirteen the number 13. **thirteenth** ADJECTIVE

thirty, **thirties** the number 30. **thirtieth** ADJECTIVE

this ADJECTIVE, PRONOUN ① 'This' is used to refer to something or someone that is nearby or has just been mentioned • *This is Robert.* ② 'This' is used to refer to the present time or place • *this week.*

thistle NOUN a wild plant with prickly-edged leaves and purple flowers.

thong NOUN a long narrow strip of leather.

thorn NOUN one of many sharp points growing on some plants and trees.

thorny, thornier, thorniest ADJECTIVE ① covered with thorns. ② A thorny subject or question is difficult to discuss or answer.

thorough [*Said* **thur**-*ruh*] ADJECTIVE ① done very carefully and completely • *a thorough examination.* ② A thorough person is very careful in what they do and makes sure nothing has been missed out. **thoroughly** ADVERB

thorough ADJECTIVE
① = complete, comprehensive, exhaustive, full, intensive, meticulous, painstaking, scrupulous

thoroughbred NOUN an animal that has parents that are of the same high quality breed.

thoroughfare NOUN a main road in a town.

those the plural of **that**.

thou PRONOUN (*old-fashioned*) Thou means you.

though [*Rhymes with* ***show***] CONJUNCTION ① despite the fact that • *Meg felt cold, even though the sun was out.* ② if • *It looks as though you were right.*

thought ① Thought is the past tense and past participle of **think**. ▶ NOUN ② an idea that you have in your mind. ③ Thought is the activity of thinking • *She was lost in thought.* ④ Thought is a particular way of thinking or a particular set of ideas • *this school of thought.*

thought NOUN
② = idea, notion, opinion, view
③ = consideration, contemplation, deliberation, meditation, reflection, thinking

thoughtful ADJECTIVE ① When someone is thoughtful, they are quiet and serious because they are thinking about something. ② A thoughtful person remembers what other people want or need, and tries to be kind to them. **thoughtfully** ADVERB

thoughtful ADJECTIVE
① = contemplative, pensive, reflective
② = attentive, caring, considerate, kind
≠ thoughtless

thoughtless ADJECTIVE A thoughtless person forgets or ignores what other people want, need or feel. **thoughtlessly** ADVERB

thoughtless ADJECTIVE
= insensitive, tactless
≠ thoughtful

thousand the number 1000. **thousandth** ADJECTIVE

thrash VERB ① To thrash someone is to beat them by hitting them with something. ② To thrash someone in a contest or fight is to defeat them completely. ③ To thrash out a problem or an idea is to discuss it in detail until a solution is reached.

thread NOUN ① a long, fine piece of cotton, silk, nylon or wool. ② The thread on something such as a screw or the top of a container is the raised spiral line of metal or plastic round it. ③ The thread of an argument or story is an idea or theme that connects the different parts of it. ▶ VERB ④ When you thread something, you pass thread, tape or cord through it. ⑤ If you thread your way through people or things, you carefully make your way through them.

threadbare ADJECTIVE Threadbare cloth or clothing is old and thin.

threat NOUN ① a statement that someone will harm you, especially if you do not do what they want. ② anything or anyone that seems likely to harm you. ③ If there is a threat of something unpleasant happening, it is very possible that it will happen.

> **threat** NOUN
> ① = menace, threatening remark
> ② = hazard, menace, risk

threaten VERB ① If you threaten to harm someone or threaten to do something that will upset them, you say that you will do it. ② If someone or something threatens a person or thing, they are likely to harm them.

> **threaten** VERB
> ① = make threats to, menace
> ② = endanger, jeopardise, put at risk, put in jeopardy

three the number 3.

three-dimensional ADJECTIVE MATHS A three-dimensional object or shape is not flat, but has height or depth as well as length and width.

threesome NOUN a group of three.

threshold *[Said **thresh**-hold]* NOUN ① the doorway or the floor in the doorway of a building or room. ② The threshold of something is the lowest amount, level or limit at which something happens or changes • *the tax threshold* • *His boredom threshold was exceptionally low.*

threw the past tense of **throw**.

thrice ADVERB (*old-fashioned*) If you do something thrice, you do it three times.

thrift NOUN Thrift is the practice of saving money and not wasting things.

thrifty, **thriftier**, **thriftiest** ADJECTIVE A thrifty person saves money and does not waste things.

> **thrifty** ADJECTIVE
> = careful, economical, frugal, prudent

thrill NOUN ① a sudden feeling of great excitement, pleasure or fear; also any event or experience that gives you such a feeling. ▶ VERB ② If something thrills you, or you thrill to it, it gives you a feeling of great pleasure and excitement. **thrilled** ADJECTIVE **thrilling** ADJECTIVE

> **thrill** NOUN
> ① = high (*informal*), kick (*informal*)
> ▶ VERB ② = excite, give a kick (*informal*)

thriller NOUN a book, film or play that tells an exciting story about dangerous or mysterious events.

thrive, **thrives**, **thriving**, **thrived** or **throve** VERB When people or things thrive, they are healthy, happy or successful. **thriving** ADJECTIVE

> **thrive** VERB
> = do well, flourish, prosper

throat NOUN ① the back of your mouth and the top part of the passages inside your neck. ② the front part of your neck.

throb, **throbs**, **throbbing**, **throbbed** VERB ① If a part of your body throbs, you feel a series of strong beats or dull pains. ② If something throbs, it vibrates and makes a loud, rhythmic noise • *The engines throbbed.*

throes PLURAL NOUN ① Throes are a series of violent pangs or movements • *death throes.* ▶ PHRASE ② If you are **in the throes of** something, you are deeply involved in it.

thrombosis, **thromboses** *[Said throm-**boe**-siss]* NOUN a blood clot which blocks the flow of blood in the body. Thromboses are dangerous and often fatal.

throne NOUN ① a ceremonial chair used by a king or queen on important official occasions. ② The throne is a way of referring to the position of being king or queen • *The Queen is celebrating 60 years on the throne.*

throng NOUN ① a large crowd of people. ▸ VERB ② If people throng somewhere or throng a place, they go there in great numbers • *Hundreds of city workers thronged the scene.*

throttle VERB To throttle someone is to kill or injure them by squeezing their throat.

through [Said **threw**] PREPOSITION ① moving all the way from one side of something to the other • *a path through the woods.* ② because of • *He had been exhausted through lack of sleep.* ③ during • *He has to work through the summer.* ④ If you go through an experience, it happens to you • *I don't want to go through that again.* ▸ ADJECTIVE ⑤ If you are through with something, you have finished doing it or using it.

throughout PREPOSITION ① during • *I stayed awake throughout the night.* ▸ ADVERB ② happening or existing through the whole of a place • *The house was painted brown throughout.*

throw, **throws**, **throwing**, **threw**, **thrown** VERB ① When you throw something you are holding, you move your hand quickly and let it go, so that it moves through the air. ② If you throw yourself somewhere, you move there suddenly and with force • *We threw ourselves on the ground.* ③ To throw someone into an unpleasant situation is to put them there • *It threw them into a panic.* ④ If something throws light or shadow on something else, it makes that thing have light or shadow on it. ⑤ If you throw yourself into an activity, you become actively and enthusiastically involved in it. ⑥ If you throw a fit or tantrum, you suddenly begin behaving in an uncontrolled way.

throw VERB
① = cast, chuck (*informal*), fling, hurl, lob, pitch, sling, toss

throwback NOUN something which has the characteristics of something that existed a long time ago • *Everything about her was a throwback to the fifties.*

thrush NOUN a small brown songbird.

thrust, **thrusts**, **thrusting**, **thrust** VERB ① If you thrust something somewhere, you push or move it there quickly with a lot of force. ② If you thrust your way somewhere, you move along, pushing between people or things. ▸ NOUN ③ a sudden forceful movement. ④ The main thrust of an activity or idea is the most important part of it • *the general thrust of his argument.*

thud, **thuds**, **thudding**, **thudded** NOUN ① a dull sound, usually made by a solid, heavy object hitting something soft. ▸ VERB ② If something thuds somewhere, it makes a dull sound, usually by hitting something else.

thug NOUN a very rough and violent person.

thug NOUN
= bandit, hooligan, tough, tsotsi (*South African*)

thumb NOUN ① the short, thick finger on the side of your hand. ▸ VERB ② If someone thumbs a lift, they stand at the side of the road and stick out their thumb until a driver stops and gives them a lift.

thump VERB ① If you thump someone or something, you hit them hard with your fist. ② If something thumps somewhere, it makes a fairly loud, dull sound, usually when it hits something else. ③ When your heart thumps, it beats strongly and quickly. ▸ **NOUN** ④ a hard hit • *a great thump on the back.* ⑤ a fairly loud, dull sound.

thunder **NOUN** ① Thunder is a loud cracking or rumbling noise caused by expanding air which is suddenly heated by lightning. ② Thunder is any loud rumbling noise • *the distant thunder of bombs.* ▸ **VERB** ③ When it thunders, a loud cracking or rumbling noise occurs in the sky after a flash of lightning. ④ If something thunders, it makes a loud continuous noise • *The helicopter thundered low over the trees.*

thunderbolt **NOUN** a flash of lightning, accompanied by thunder.

thunderous **ADJECTIVE** A thunderous noise is very loud • *thunderous applause.*

Thursday **NOUN** Thursday is the day between Wednesday and Friday.

thus **ADVERB** (*formal*) ① in this way • *I sat thus for nearly half an hour.* ② therefore • *She is more experienced than him, thus better paid.*

thwart **VERB** To thwart someone or their plans is to prevent them from doing or getting what they want.

thy **ADJECTIVE** (*old-fashioned*) Thy means your.

thyme [*Said* ***time***] **NOUN** Thyme is a bushy herb with very small leaves.

tiara [*Said tee-**ah**-ra*] **NOUN** a semicircular crown of jewels worn by a woman on formal occasions.

Tibetan **ADJECTIVE** ① belonging or relating to Tibet. ▸ **NOUN** ② someone who comes from Tibet.

tic **NOUN** a twitching of a group of muscles, especially the muscles in the face.

tick **NOUN** ① a written mark to show that something is correct or has been dealt with. ② The tick of a clock is the series of short sounds it makes when it is working. ③ a tiny, blood-sucking, insect-like creature that usually lives on the bodies of people or animals. ▸ **VERB** ④ To tick something written on a piece of paper is to put a tick next to it. ⑤ When a clock ticks, it makes a regular series of short sounds as it works. **ticking** **NOUN** **tick off** **VERB** (*informal*) If you tick someone off, you speak angrily to them because they have done something wrong.

ticket **NOUN** a piece of paper or card which shows that you have paid for a journey or have paid to enter a place of entertainment.

tickle **VERB** ① When you tickle someone, you move your fingers lightly over their body in order to make them laugh. ② If something tickles you, it amuses you or gives you pleasure • *Simon is tickled by the idea.*

tidal **ADJECTIVE** to do with or produced by tides • *a tidal estuary.*

tidal wave **NOUN** GEOGRAPHY a very large wave, often caused by an earthquake, that comes over land and destroys things.

tide **NOUN** ① The tide is the regular change in the level of the sea on the shore, caused by the gravitational pull of the sun and the moon. ② The tide of opinion or fashion is what the majority of people think or do at a particular time. ③ A tide of something is a large amount of it • *the tide of anger and bitterness.* **tide over** **VERB** If something will tide someone over, it will help them through a difficult period of time.

tidings **PLURAL NOUN** (*formal*) Tidings are news.

tidy, **tidier, tidiest; tidies, tidying, tidied** **ADJECTIVE** ① Something that is tidy is neat and arranged in an orderly way. ② Someone who is tidy always keeps their things neat and arranged in an orderly way. ③ (*informal*) A tidy amount of money is a fairly large amount of it. ▶ **VERB** ④ To tidy a place is to make it neat by putting things in their proper place.

> **tidy** ADJECTIVE
> ① = neat, orderly
> ≠ untidy
> ▶ **VERB** ④ = spruce up, straighten
> ≠ mess up

tie, ties, tying, tied VERB ① If you tie one thing to another or tie it in a particular position, you fasten it using cord of some kind. ② If you tie a knot or a bow in a piece of cord or cloth, you fasten the ends together to make a knot or bow. ③ Something or someone that is tied to something else is closely linked with it • *40,000 jobs are tied to the project*. ④ If you tie with someone in a competition or game, you have the same number of points. ▶ **NOUN** ⑤ a long, narrow piece of cloth worn around the neck under a shirt collar and tied in a knot at the front. ⑥ a connection or feeling that links you with a person, place or organisation • *I had very close ties with the family*.

> **tie** VERB
> ① = bind, fasten, knot, lash, rope, secure, tether, truss
> ≠ untie
> ④ = be level, draw
> ▶ **NOUN** ⑥ = affiliation, affinity, bond, connection, relationship

tied up ADJECTIVE If you are tied up, you are busy.

tier NOUN one of a number of rows or layers of something • *Take the stairs to the upper tier*.

tiff NOUN (*informal*) a small unimportant quarrel.

tiger NOUN a large meat-eating animal of the cat family. It comes from Asia and has an orange coloured coat with black stripes.

tight ADJECTIVE ① fitting closely • *The shoes are too tight*. ② firmly fastened and difficult to move • *a tight knot*. ③ stretched or pulled so as not to be slack • *a tight cord*. ④ A tight plan or arrangement allows only the minimum time or money needed to do something • *Our schedule tonight is very tight*. ▶ **ADVERB** ⑤ held firmly and securely • *He held me tight*. **tightly** ADVERB **tightness** NOUN

> **tight** ADJECTIVE
> ① = constricted, cramped, snug
> ≠ loose
> ② = firm, secure
> ③ = rigid, taut, tense
> ≠ slack

tighten VERB ① If you tighten your hold on something, you hold it more firmly. ② If you tighten a rope or chain, or if it tightens, it is stretched or pulled until it is straight. ③ If someone tightens a rule or system, they make it stricter or more efficient.

tightrope NOUN a tightly stretched rope on which an acrobat balances and performs tricks.

tights PLURAL NOUN Tights are a piece of clothing made of thin stretchy material that fit closely round a person's hips, legs and feet.

tile NOUN ① a small flat square piece of something, for example slate or carpet, that is used to cover surfaces. ▶ **VERB** ② To tile a surface is to fix tiles to it. **tiled** ADJECTIVE

till PREPOSITION, CONJUNCTION ① Till means the same as until. ▶ **NOUN** ② a drawer or box in a shop where money is kept, usually in a cash register. ▶ **VERB** ③ To till the ground is to plough it for raising crops.

tiller NOUN the handle fixed to the top of the rudder for steering a boat.

tilt VERB ① If you tilt an object or it tilts, it changes position so that one end or side is higher than the other. ▸ NOUN ② a position in which one end or side of something is higher than the other.

tilt VERB
① = incline, lean, slant, slope, tip
▸ NOUN ② = angle, gradient, incline, slant, slope

timber NOUN ① Timber is wood that has been cut and prepared ready for building and making furniture. ② The timbers of a ship or house are the large pieces of wood that have been used to build it.

timbre *[Said **tam**-ber]* NOUN [MUSIC] The timbre of a musical instrument, voice or sound is the particular quality or characteristic it has.

time NOUN ① Time is what is measured in hours, days and years • *We still have plenty of time.* ② 'Time' is used to mean a particular period or point • *I enjoyed my time in Durban.* ③ If you say it is time for something or it is time to do it, you mean that it ought to happen or be done now • *It is time for a change.* ④ 'Times' is used after numbers to indicate how often something happens • *I saw my father four times a year.* ⑤ 'Times' is used after numbers when you are saying how much bigger, smaller, better or worse one thing is compared to another • *The Belgians drink three times as much beer as the French.* ⑥ 'Times' is used in arithmetic to link numbers that are multiplied together • *Two times three is six.* ▸ VERB ⑦ If you time something for a particular time, you plan that it should happen then • *We could not have timed our arrival better.* ⑧ If you time an activity or action, you measure how long it lasts.

time NOUN
② = interval, period, spell, stretch, while
▸ VERB ⑦ = schedule, set

timeless ADJECTIVE Something timeless is so good or beautiful that it cannot be affected by the passing of time or by changes in fashion.

timely ADJECTIVE happening at just the right time • *a timely appearance.*

timer NOUN a device that measures time, especially one that is part of a machine.

timescale NOUN The timescale of an event is the length of time during which it happens.

timetable NOUN ① a plan of the times when particular activities or jobs should be done. ② a list of the times when particular trains, boats, buses or aeroplanes arrive and depart.

timid ADJECTIVE shy and having no courage or self-confidence. **timidity** NOUN **timidly** ADVERB

timid ADJECTIVE
= bashful, cowardly, diffident, nervous, shy
≠ bold

timing NOUN ① Someone's timing is their skill in judging the right moment at which to do something. ② The timing of an event is when it actually happens.

tin NOUN ① [SCIENCE] Tin is a soft, silvery-white metallic element used in alloys. Its atomic number is 50, and its symbol is Sn. ② A tin is a metal container which is filled with food and then sealed in order to preserve the food. ③ A tin is a small metal container which may have a lid • *a baking tin* • *the biscuit tin.*

tinge NOUN a small amount of something • *a tinge of envy.* **tinged** ADJECTIVE

tingle VERB ① When a part of your body tingles, you feel a slight prickling feeling in it. ▶ NOUN ② a slight prickling feeling. **tingling** NOUN, ADJECTIVE

tinker NOUN ① a person who travels from place to place mending metal pots and pans or doing other small repair jobs. ▶ VERB ② If you tinker with something, you make a lot of small changes to it in order to repair or improve it • *All he wanted was to tinker with engines.*

tinned ADJECTIVE Tinned food has been preserved by being sealed in a tin.

tinsel NOUN Tinsel is long threads with strips of shiny paper attached, used as a decoration at Christmas.

tint NOUN ① a small amount of a particular colour • *a distinct tint of green.* ▶ VERB ② If a person tints their hair, they change its colour by adding a weak dye to it. **tinted** ADJECTIVE

tiny, **tinier**, **tiniest** ADJECTIVE extremely small.

> **tiny** ADJECTIVE
> = diminutive, microscopic, miniature, minute, negligible, wee (*Scottish*)
> ≠ huge

tip, **tips**, **tipping**, **tipped** NOUN ① the end of something long and thin • *a fingertip.* ② a place where rubbish is dumped. ③ If you give someone such as a waiter a tip, you give them some money to thank them for their services. ④ a useful piece of advice or information. ▶ VERB ⑤ If you tip an object, you move it so that it is no longer horizontal or upright. ⑥ If you tip something somewhere, you pour it there quickly or carelessly. **tipped** ADJECTIVE

tipple NOUN A person's tipple is the alcoholic drink that they normally drink.

tipsy, **tipsier**, **tipsiest** ADJECTIVE slightly drunk.

tiptoe, **tiptoes**, **tiptoeing**, **tiptoed** VERB If you tiptoe somewhere, you walk there very quietly on your toes.

tirade [*Said tie-**rade***] NOUN a long, angry speech in which you criticise someone or something.

tire VERB ① If something tires you, it makes you use a lot of energy so that you want to rest or sleep. ② If you tire of something, you become bored with it.

> **tire** VERB
> ① = drain, exhaust, fatigue

tired ADJECTIVE having little energy. **tiredness** NOUN

> **tired** ADJECTIVE
> = drained, drowsy, exhausted, fatigued, sleepy, tuckered out (*American, Australian and New Zealand; informal*), weary, worn out

tireless ADJECTIVE Someone who is tireless has a lot of energy and never seems to need a rest.

tiresome ADJECTIVE A person or thing that is tiresome makes you feel irritated or bored.

tiring ADJECTIVE Something that is tiring makes you tired.

tissue [*Said **tiss**-yoo*] NOUN ① [SCIENCE] The tissue in plants and animals consists of cells that are similar in appearance and function • *scar tissue* • *dead tissue.* ② Tissue is thin paper that is used for wrapping breakable objects. ③ a small piece of soft paper that you use as a handkerchief.

tit NOUN a small European bird • *a blue tit.*

titanic ADJECTIVE very big or important.

title NOUN ① the name of a book, film or piece of music. ② a word that describes someone's rank or job • *My official title is Design Manager.*

③ the position of champion in a sports competition • *the European featherweight title.*

titled ADJECTIVE Someone who is titled has a high social rank and has a title such as 'Princess', 'Lord', 'Lady' or 'Sir'.

TNT NOUN TNT is a type of powerful explosive. It is an abbreviation for 'trinitrotoluene'.

to PREPOSITION ① 'To' is used to indicate the place that someone or something is moving towards or pointing at • *They are going to China.* ② 'To' is used to indicate the limit of something • *Goods to the value of 500 pounds.* ③ 'To' is used in ratios and rates when saying how many units of one type there are for each unit of another • *I only get about 30 kilometres to the gallon from it.* ▶ ADVERB ④ If you push or shut a door to, you close it but do not shut it completely.

toad NOUN an amphibian that looks like a frog but has a drier skin and lives less in the water.

toast NOUN ① Toast is slices of bread made brown and crisp by cooking at a high temperature. ② To drink a toast to someone is to drink an alcoholic drink in honour of them. ▶ VERB ③ If you toast bread, you cook it at a high temperature so that it becomes brown and crisp. ④ If you toast yourself, you sit in front of a fire so that you feel pleasantly warm. ⑤ To toast someone is to drink an alcoholic drink in honour of them.

toaster NOUN a piece of electrical equipment used for toasting bread.

tobacco NOUN Tobacco is the dried leaves of the tobacco plant which people smoke in pipes, cigarettes and cigars.

today ADVERB, NOUN ① Today means the day on which you are speaking or writing. ② Today also means the present period of history • *the challenges of growing up in today's society.*

toddler NOUN a small child who has just learned to walk.

to-do, to-dos NOUN A to-do is a situation in which people are very agitated or confused • *It's just like him to make such a to-do about nothing.*

toe NOUN ① Your toes are the five movable parts at the end of your foot. ② The toe of a shoe or sock is the part that covers the end of your foot.

toff NOUN (*informal, old-fashioned*) a rich person or one from an aristocratic family.

toffee NOUN Toffee is a sticky, chewy sweet made by boiling sugar and butter together with water.

together ADVERB ① If people do something together, they do it with each other. ② If two things happen together, they happen at the same time. ③ If things are joined or fixed together, they are joined or fixed to each other. ④ If things or people are together, they are very near to each other.

> **together** ADVERB
> ① = collectively, en masse, in unison, jointly, shoulder to shoulder, side by side
> ② = as one, at once, concurrently (*formal*), simultaneously, with one accord

togetherness NOUN Togetherness is a feeling of closeness and friendship.

toil VERB ① When people toil, they work hard doing unpleasant, difficult or tiring tasks or jobs. ▶ NOUN ② Toil is unpleasant, difficult or tiring work.

toilet NOUN ① a large bowl, connected by a pipe to the drains, which you use when you want to get rid of urine or faeces. ② a small room containing a toilet.

toiletries PLURAL NOUN Toiletries are the things you use when cleaning and taking care of your body, such as soap and talc.

token NOUN ① a piece of paper or card that is worth a particular amount of money and can be exchanged for goods • *book tokens*. ② a flat round piece of metal or plastic that can sometimes be used instead of money. ③ If you give something to someone as a token of your feelings for them, you give it to them as a way of showing those feelings. ▶ ADJECTIVE ④ If something is described as token, it shows that it is not being treated as important • *a token contribution to your fees*.

told Told is the past tense and past participle of **tell**.

tolerable ADJECTIVE ① able to be put up with. ② fairly satisfactory or reasonable • *a tolerable salary*.

> **tolerable** ADJECTIVE
> ① = acceptable, bearable
> ≠ unbearable
> ② = acceptable, adequate, okay, OK, passable, reasonable, so-so (*informal*)

tolerance NOUN ① A person's tolerance is their ability to accept or put up with something which may not be enjoyable or pleasant for them. ② Tolerance is the quality of allowing other people to have their own attitudes or beliefs, or to behave in a particular way, even if you do not agree or approve • *religious tolerance*.

tolerant ADJECTIVE accepting of different views and behaviour.

> **tolerant** ADJECTIVE
> = broad-minded, liberal, open-minded, understanding
> ≠ narrow-minded

tolerate VERB ① If you tolerate things that you do not approve of or agree with, you allow them. ② If you can tolerate something, you accept it, even though it is unsatisfactory or unpleasant. **toleration** NOUN

> **tolerate** VERB
> ① = accept, put up with
> ② = bear, endure, stand

toll NOUN ① The death toll in an accident is the number of people who have died in it. ② a sum of money that you have to pay in order to use a particular bridge or road. ▶ VERB ③ When someone tolls a bell, it is rung slowly, often as a sign that someone has died.

tom NOUN a male cat.

tomato, tomatoes NOUN a small round red fruit, used as a vegetable and often eaten raw in salads.

tomb NOUN a large grave for one or more corpses.

> **tomb** NOUN
> = grave, mausoleum, sarcophagus, sepulchre (*literary*), vault

tomboy NOUN a girl who likes playing rough or noisy games.

tome NOUN (*formal*) a very large heavy book.

tomorrow ADVERB, NOUN ① Tomorrow means the day after today. ② You can refer to the future, especially the near future, as tomorrow.

ton NOUN ① a unit of weight equal to 2240 pounds or about 1016 kilograms. ② (*in plural, informal*) If you have tons of something, you have a lot of it.

tonal ADJECTIVE involving the quality or pitch of a sound or of music.

tone NOUN ① Someone's tone is a quality in their voice which shows what they are thinking or feeling. ② MUSIC The tone of a musical instrument or a singer's voice is the kind of sound it has. ③ ENGLISH The tone of a piece of writing is its style and the ideas or opinions expressed in it • *I was shocked at the tone of your leading article.* ④ ART a lighter, darker or brighter shade of the same colour • *The whole room is painted in two tones of orange.* **tone down** VERB If you tone down something, you make it less forceful or severe.

tongs PLURAL NOUN Tongs consist of two long narrow pieces of metal joined together at one end. You press the pieces together to pick an object up.

tongue NOUN ① Your tongue is the soft part in your mouth that you can move and use for tasting, licking and speaking. ② a language. ③ Tongue is the cooked tongue of an ox. ④ The tongue of a shoe or boot is the piece of leather underneath the laces.

tonic NOUN ① Tonic or tonic water is a colourless, fizzy drink that has a slightly bitter flavour and is often mixed with alcoholic drinks. ② a medicine that makes you feel stronger, healthier and less tired. ③ anything that makes you feel stronger or more cheerful • *It was a tonic just being with her.*

tonight ADVERB, NOUN Tonight is the evening or night that will come at the end of today.

tonne *[Said* ***tun****]* NOUN a unit of weight equal to 1000 kilograms.

tonsillitis *[Said ton-sil-****lie****-tiss]* NOUN Tonsillitis is a painful swelling of your tonsils caused by an infection.

too ADVERB ① also or as well • *You were there too.* ② more than a desirable, necessary or acceptable amount • *We had spent too long in the sun.*

> **too** ADVERB
> ① = as well, besides, in addition, into the bargain, likewise, moreover
> ② = excessively, over-, overly, unduly, unreasonably

took the past tense of **take**.

tool NOUN ① any hand-held instrument or piece of equipment that you use to help you do a particular kind of work. ② an object, skill or idea that is needed or used for a particular purpose • *You can use the survey as a bargaining tool in the negotiations.*

> **tool** NOUN
> ① = implement, instrument, utensil

tooth, **teeth** NOUN ① Your teeth are the hard, enamel-covered objects in your mouth that you use for biting and chewing food. ② The teeth of a comb, saw or zip are the parts that stick out in a row on its edge.

toothpaste NOUN Toothpaste is a substance which you use to clean your teeth.

top, **tops**, **topping**, **topped** NOUN ① The top of something is its highest point, part or surface. ② The top of a bottle, jar or tube is its cap or lid. ③ a piece of clothing worn on the upper half of your body. ④ a toy with a pointed end on which it spins. ▶ ADJECTIVE ⑤ The top thing of a series of things is the highest one • *the top floor of the building.* ▶ VERB ⑥ If someone tops a poll or popularity chart, they do better than anyone else in it • *It has topped the bestseller lists in almost every country.* ⑦ If something tops a particular amount, it is greater than that amount • *The temperature topped 90°.* **top up** VERB To top something up is to add something to it in order to keep it at an acceptable or usable level.

top hat NOUN a tall hat with a narrow brim that men wear on special occasions.

topic NOUN a particular subject that you write about or discuss.

topical ADJECTIVE involving or related to events that are happening at the time you are speaking or writing.

topping NOUN food that is put on top of other food in order to decorate it or add to its flavour.

topple VERB If something topples, it becomes unsteady and falls over.

top-secret ADJECTIVE meant to be kept completely secret.

topsy-turvy ADJECTIVE in a confused state • *My life was truly topsy-turvy.*

Torah NOUN [RE] The Torah is Jewish law and teaching.

torch NOUN ① a small electric light carried in the hand and powered by batteries. ② a long stick with burning material wrapped around one end.

tore the past tense of **tear²**.

torment NOUN *[Said* ***tor****-ment]* ① Torment is extreme pain or unhappiness. ② something that causes extreme pain and unhappiness • *It's a torment to see them staring at me.* ▶ VERB *[Said tor-****ment****]* ③ If something torments you, it causes you extreme unhappiness.

torn ① Torn is the past participle of **tear²**. ▶ ADJECTIVE ② If you are torn between two or more things, you cannot decide which one to choose and this makes you unhappy • *torn between duty and pleasure.*

tornado, tornadoes or **tornados** *[Said tor-****nay****-doh]* NOUN a violent storm with strong circular winds around a funnel-shaped cloud.

torpedo, torpedoes, torpedoing, torpedoed *[Said tor-****pee****-doh]* NOUN ① a tube-shaped bomb that travels underwater and explodes when it hits a target. ▶ VERB ② If a ship is torpedoed, it is hit, and usually sunk, by a torpedo.

torrent NOUN ① When a lot of water is falling very rapidly, it can be said to be falling in torrents. ② A torrent of speech is a lot of it directed continuously at someone • *torrents of abuse.*

torrential ADJECTIVE Torrential rain pours down very rapidly and in great quantities.

torrid ADJECTIVE ① Torrid weather is very hot and dry. ② If something is described as torrid, it involves very strong emotions.

torso, torsos NOUN the main part of your body, excluding your head, arms and legs.

tortoise NOUN a slow-moving reptile with a large hard shell over its body into which it can pull its head and legs for protection.

tortuous ADJECTIVE ① A tortuous road is full of bends and twists. ② A tortuous piece of writing is long and complicated.

torture NOUN ① Torture is great pain that is deliberately caused to someone to punish them or get information from them. ▶ VERB ② If someone tortures another person, they deliberately cause that person great pain to punish them or get information. ③ To torture someone is also to cause them to suffer mentally • *Memory tortured her.* **torturer** NOUN

Tory, Tories NOUN In Britain, a Tory is a member or supporter of the Conservative Party.

toss VERB ① If you toss something somewhere, you throw it there lightly and carelessly. ② If you toss a coin, you decide something by throwing a coin into the air and guessing which side will face upwards when it lands. ③ If you toss your head, you move it suddenly backwards, especially when you are angry or annoyed or want your own way. ④ To toss is to move repeatedly from side to side • *We tossed and turned and tried to sleep.*

tot, tots, totting, totted NOUN ① a very young child. ② a small amount of strong alcohol such as whisky.

▶ **VERB** ③ To tot up numbers is to add them together.

total, **totals**, **totalling**, **totalled** **NOUN** ① the number you get when you add several numbers together. ▶ **ADJECTIVE** ② Total means complete • *a total failure*. ▶ **VERB** ③ When you total a set of numbers or objects, you add them all together. ④ If several numbers total a certain figure, that is the figure you get when all the numbers are added together • *Their debts totalled over 300,000 dollars*. **totally** **ADVERB**

total **NOUN**
① = aggregate, sum, whole
▶ **ADJECTIVE** ② = absolute, complete, out-and-out, outright, unconditional, undivided, unmitigated, unqualified, utter
▶ **VERB** ④ = add up to, amount to, come to

totalitarian [*Said toe-tal-it-**tair**-ee-an*] **ADJECTIVE** A totalitarian political system is one in which one political party controls everything and does not allow any other parties to exist. **totalitarianism** **NOUN**

tote (*informal*) **NOUN** ① The tote is a system of betting money on horses at a racetrack, in which all the money is divided among the people who have bet on the winning horses. Tote is an abbreviation for 'totalisator'. ▶ **VERB** ② To tote a gun means to carry it.

totter **VERB** When someone totters, they walk in an unsteady way.

touch **VERB** ① If you touch something, you put your fingers or hand on it. ② When two things touch, their surfaces come into contact • *Their knees were touching*. ③ If you are touched by something, you are emotionally affected by it • *I was touched by his thoughtfulness*. ▶ **NOUN** ④ Your sense of touch is your ability to tell what something is like by touching it. ⑤ a detail which is added to improve something • *finishing touches*. ⑥ a small amount of something • *a touch of mustard*. ▶ **PHRASE** ⑦ If you are **in touch** with someone, you are in contact with them.

touch **VERB**
① = feel, finger, handle
② = brush, graze, meet
③ = affect, move, stir

touchdown **NOUN** Touchdown is the landing of an aircraft.

touching **ADJECTIVE** causing feelings of sadness and sympathy.

touching **ADJECTIVE**
= affecting (*literary*), moving, poignant

touchy, **touchier**, **touchiest** **ADJECTIVE** ① If someone is touchy, they are easily upset or irritated. ② A touchy subject is one that needs to be dealt with carefully, because it might upset or offend people.

touchy **ADJECTIVE**
① = easily offended, sensitive, toey (*Australian and New Zealand; slang*)

tough [*Said **tuff***] **ADJECTIVE** ① A tough person is strong and independent and able to put up with hardship. ② A tough substance is difficult to break. ③ A tough task, problem or way of life is difficult or full of hardship. ④ Tough policies or actions are strict and firm • *tough measures against organised crime*. **toughly** **ADVERB** **toughness** **NOUN** **toughen** **VERB**

tough **ADJECTIVE**
① = hardened, hardy, resilient, robust, rugged, strong
② = durable, hard-wearing, leathery, resilient, robust, rugged, solid, strong, sturdy
≠ fragile
③ = arduous, difficult, exacting, hard
≠ easy

tour **NOUN** ① a long journey during

which you visit several places. ② a short trip round a place such as a city or famous building. ▶ **VERB** ③ If you tour a place, you go on a journey or a trip round it.

tourism **NOUN** Tourism is the business of providing services for people on holiday, for example hotels and sightseeing trips.

tourist GEOGRAPHY **NOUN** a person who visits places for pleasure or interest.

tournament **NOUN** PE a sports competition in which players who win a match play further matches, until just one person or team is left.

tousled **ADJECTIVE** Tousled hair is untidy.

tout **VERB** ① If someone touts something, they try to sell it. ② If someone touts for business or custom, they try to obtain it in a very direct way • *volunteers who spend days touting for donations.* ▶ **NOUN** ③ someone who sells tickets outside a sports ground or theatre, charging more than the original price.

tow **VERB** ① If a vehicle tows another vehicle, it pulls it along behind it. ▶ **NOUN** ② To give a vehicle a tow is to tow it. ▶ **PHRASE** ③ If you have someone **in tow**, they are with you because you are looking after them.

towards **PREPOSITION** ① in the direction of • *He turned towards the door.* ② about or involving • *My feelings towards Susan have changed.* ③ as a contribution for • *a huge donation towards the new opera house.* ④ near to • *We sat towards the back.*

towel **NOUN** a piece of thick, soft cloth that you use to dry yourself with.

towelling **NOUN** Towelling is thick, soft cloth that is used for making towels.

tower **NOUN** ① a tall, narrow building, sometimes attached to a larger building such as a castle or church. ▶ **VERB** ② Someone or something that towers over other people or things is much taller than them. **towering** **ADJECTIVE**

town **NOUN** ① a place with many streets and buildings where people live and work. ② Town is the central shopping and business part of a town rather than the suburbs • *She has gone into town.*

toxic **ADJECTIVE** poisonous • *toxic waste.*

toxin **NOUN** SCIENCE a poison, especially one produced by bacteria and very harmful to living creatures.

toy **NOUN** ① any object made to play with. ▶ **VERB** ② If you toy with an idea, you consider it without being very serious about it • *She toyed with the idea of telephoning him.* ③ If you toy with an object, you fiddle with it • *Jessica was toying with her glass.*

trace **VERB** ① If you trace something, you find it after looking for it • *Police are trying to trace the owner of the car.* ② EXAM TERM To trace the development of something is to find out or describe how it developed. ③ If you trace a drawing or a map, you copy it by covering it with a piece of transparent paper and drawing over the lines underneath. ▶ **NOUN** ④ a sign which shows you that someone or something has been in a place • *No trace of his father had been found.* ⑤ a very small amount of something. **tracing** **NOUN**

trace **VERB**
① = locate, track down
▶ **NOUN** ④ = evidence, hint, indication, record, sign, suggestion, whiff
⑤ = dash, drop, remnant, suspicion, tinge, touch, vestige

track **NOUN** ① a narrow road or path.

② a strip of ground with rails on it that a train travels along. ③ a piece of ground, shaped like a ring, which horses, cars or athletes race around. ④ (*in plural*) Tracks are marks left on the ground by a person or animal • *the deer tracks by the side of the path.* ▶ ADJECTIVE ⑤ In an athletics competition, the track events are the races on a running track. ▶ VERB ⑥ If you track animals or people, you find them by following their footprints or other signs that they have left behind. **track down** VERB If you track down someone or something, you find them by searching for them.

track record NOUN The track record of a person or a company is their past achievements or failures • *the track record of the film's star.*

tracksuit NOUN a loose, warm suit of trousers and a top, worn for outdoor sports.

tract NOUN ① A tract of land or forest is a large area of it. ② a pamphlet which expresses a strong opinion on a religious, moral or political subject. ③ a system of organs and tubes in an animal's or person's body that has a particular function • *the digestive tract.*

traction NOUN Traction is a form of medical treatment given to an injured limb which involves pulling it gently for long periods of time using a system of weights and pulleys.

tractor NOUN a vehicle with large rear wheels that is used on a farm for pulling machinery and other heavy loads.

trade NOUN ① Trade is the activity of buying, selling or exchanging goods or services between people, firms or countries. ② Someone's trade is the kind of work they do, especially when it requires special training in practical skills • *a joiner by trade.* ▶ VERB ③ When people, firms or countries trade, they buy, sell or exchange goods or services. ④ If you trade things, you exchange them • *Their mother had traded her rings for a few potatoes.*

> **trade** NOUN
> ① = business, commerce
> ② = business, line, line of work, occupation, profession
> ▶ VERB ③ = deal, do business, traffic

trademark NOUN a name or symbol that a manufacturer always uses on its products. Trademarks are usually protected by law so that no-one else can use them.

trader NOUN a person whose job is to buy and sell goods • *a timber trader.*

> **trader** NOUN
> = broker, dealer, merchant

tradesman, **tradesmen** NOUN a person, for example a shopkeeper, whose job is to sell goods.

trade union NOUN an organisation of workers that tries to improve the pay and conditions in a particular industry.

tradition NOUN a custom or belief that has existed for a long time without changing.

> **tradition** NOUN
> = convention, custom

traditional ADJECTIVE ① Traditional customs or beliefs have existed for a long time without changing • *her traditional Indian dress.* ② A traditional organisation or institution is one in which older methods are used rather than modern ones • *a traditional school.* **traditionally** ADVERB

> **traditional** ADJECTIVE
> ① = conventional, established
> ≠ unconventional

traditionalist NOUN someone who supports the established customs and beliefs of their society, and does not want to change them.

traffic, **traffics**, **trafficking**, **trafficked** NOUN ① Traffic is the movement of vehicles or people along a route at a particular time. ② Traffic in something such as drugs is an illegal trade in them. ▶ VERB ③ Someone who traffics in drugs or other goods buys and sells them illegally.

traffic light NOUN Traffic lights are the set of red, amber and green lights at a road junction which control the flow of traffic.

tragedy, **tragedies** *[Said* ***traj****-id-ee]* NOUN ① an event or situation that is disastrous or very sad. ② a serious story or play, that usually ends with the death of the main character.

tragic ADJECTIVE ① Something tragic is very sad because it involves death, suffering or disaster • *a tragic accident*. ② Tragic films, plays and books are sad and serious • *a tragic love story*. **tragically** ADVERB

> **tragic** ADJECTIVE
> ① = distressing, heartbreaking, heart-rending

trail NOUN ① a rough path across open country or through forests. ② a series of marks or other signs left by someone or something as they move along. ▶ VERB ③ If you trail something or it trails, it drags along behind you as you move, or it hangs down loosely • *a small plane trailing a banner*. ④ If someone trails along, they move slowly, without any energy or enthusiasm. ⑤ If a voice trails away or trails off, it gradually becomes more hesitant until it stops completely.

trailer NOUN a small vehicle which can be loaded with things and pulled behind a car.

train NOUN ① a number of carriages or trucks which are pulled by a railway engine. ② A train of thought is a connected series of thoughts. ③ A train of vehicles or people is a line or group following behind something or someone • *a train of oil tankers*. ▶ VERB ④ If you train someone, you teach them how to do something. ⑤ If you train, you learn how to do a particular job • *She trained as a serious actor*. ⑥ If you train for a sports match or a race, you prepare for it by doing exercises. **training** NOUN

> **train** VERB
> ④ = coach, drill, educate, instruct, school, teach, tutor

trainee NOUN someone who is being taught how to do a job.

trainers PLURAL NOUN Trainers are shoes with thick rubber soles, originally designed for running.

trait NOUN a particular characteristic or tendency. In literature, a trait is an aspect of a character in a story, for example, kind, greedy, funny or stupid • *a very English trait*.

traitor NOUN [HISTORY] someone who betrays their country or the group which they belong to.

trajectory, **trajectories** *[Said traj-****jek****-tor-ee]* NOUN The trajectory of an object moving through the air is the curving path that it follows.

tram NOUN a vehicle which runs on rails along the street and is powered by electricity from an overhead wire.

tramp NOUN ① a person who has no home, no job, and very little money. ② a long country walk • *I took a long, wet tramp through the fine woodlands*. ▶ VERB ③ If you tramp from one place to another, you walk with slow, heavy footsteps.

trample VERB ① If you trample on something, you tread heavily on it so that it is damaged. ② If you trample on someone or on their rights or feelings, you behave in a way that shows you don't care about them.

trampoline NOUN a piece of gymnastic equipment consisting of a large piece of strong cloth held taut by springs in a frame, on which a person jumps for exercise or fun.

trance NOUN a mental state in which someone seems to be asleep but is conscious enough to be aware of their surroundings and to respond to questions and commands.

tranquil *[Said* ***trang****-kwil]* ADJECTIVE calm and peaceful • *tranquil lakes* • *I have a tranquil mind.* **tranquillity** NOUN

transaction NOUN a business deal which involves buying and selling something.

transcend VERB If one thing transcends another, it goes beyond it or is superior to it • *The story transcends belief.*

transcript NOUN a written copy of something that is spoken.

transfer, **transfers**, **transferring**, **transferred** VERB ① If you transfer something from one place to another, you move it • *They transferred the money to the Swiss account.* ② If you transfer to a different place or job, or are transferred to it, you move to a different place or job within the same organisation. ▶ NOUN ③ the movement of something from one place to another. ④ a piece of paper with a design on one side which can be ironed or pressed onto cloth, paper or china. **transferable** ADJECTIVE

transfixed ADJECTIVE If a person is transfixed by something, they are so impressed or frightened by it that they cannot move • *Price stood transfixed at the sight of that tiny figure.*

transform VERB ① If something is transformed, it is changed completely • *The frown is transformed into a smile.* ② MATHS To transform a shape is to change how it looks, for example by translation, reflection, rotation or enlargement. **transformation** NOUN

transform VERB
① = alter, change, convert, reform, revolutionise

transfusion NOUN A transfusion or blood transfusion is a process in which blood from a healthy person is injected into the body of another person who is badly injured or ill.

transient *[Said* ***tran****-zee-ent]* ADJECTIVE Something transient does not stay or exist for very long • *transient emotions.* **transience** NOUN

transistor NOUN ① a small electrical device in something such as a television or radio which is used to control electric currents. ② A transistor or a transistor radio is a small portable radio.

transit NOUN ① Transit is the carrying of goods or people by vehicle from one place to another. ▶ PHRASE ② People or things that are **in transit** are travelling or being taken from one place to another • *damage that had occurred in transit.*

transition NOUN PSHE a change from one form, state or stage of life to another • *the transition from war to peace.*

transitional ADJECTIVE A transitional period or stage is one during which something changes from one form or state to another.

transitory ADJECTIVE lasting for only a short time.

translate VERB ① To translate something that someone has said or written is to say it or write it in a different language. ② MATHS To translate a shape is to move it up or down, or from side to side, but not change it in any other way. **translation** NOUN **translator** NOUN

translucent ADJECTIVE If something is translucent, light passes through it so that it seems to glow • *translucent petals*.

transmission NOUN ① The transmission of something involves passing or sending it to a different place or person • *the transmission of infectious diseases*. ② The transmission of television or radio programmes is the broadcasting of them. ③ a broadcast.

transmit, **transmits**, **transmitting**, **transmitted** VERB ① When a message or an electronic signal is transmitted, it is sent by radio waves. ② To transmit something to a different place or person is to pass it or send it to the place or person • *the teacher's role in transmitting knowledge*. **transmitter** NOUN

transparency, **transparencies** NOUN ① a small piece of photographic film which can be projected onto a screen. ② Transparency is the quality that an object or substance has if you can see through it.

transparent ADJECTIVE If an object or substance is transparent, you can see through it. **transparently** ADVERB

> **transparent** ADJECTIVE
> = clear, crystalline (*literary*), sheer, translucent
> ≠ opaque

transpire VERB ① (*formal*) When it transpires that something is the case, people discover that it is the case • *It transpired that he had flown off on holiday*. ② When something transpires, it happens • *You start to wonder what transpired between them*.

transplant NOUN ① a process of removing something from one place and putting it in another • *a man who needs a heart transplant*. ▸ VERB ② When something is transplanted, it is moved to a different place.

transport NOUN ① Vehicles that you travel in are referred to as transport • *public transport*. ② Transport is the moving of goods or people from one place to another • *The prices quoted include transport costs*. ▸ VERB ③ When goods or people are transported from one place to another, they are moved there.

> **transport** NOUN
> ② = removal, shipment, transportation
> ▸ VERB ③ = carry, convey (*formal*), ship, transfer

transportation NOUN Transportation is the transporting of people and things from one place to another.

transvestite NOUN a person who enjoys wearing clothes normally worn by people of the opposite gender.

trap, **traps**, **trapping**, **trapped** NOUN ① a piece of equipment or a hole that is carefully positioned in order to catch animals or birds. ② a trick that is intended to catch or deceive someone. ▸ VERB ③ Someone who traps animals catches them using traps. ④ If you trap someone, you trick them so that they do or say something which they did not want to. ⑤ If you are trapped somewhere, you cannot move or escape because something is blocking your way or holding you down. ⑥ If you are trapped, you are in an unpleasant situation that you cannot easily change. **trapper** NOUN

> **trap** NOUN
> ① = net, snare
> ▸ VERB ③ = catch, corner, snare
> ④ = dupe, trick

trapeze NOUN a bar of wood or metal hanging from two ropes on which acrobats and gymnasts swing and perform skilful movements.

trappings PLURAL NOUN The trappings of a particular rank, position or state are the clothes or equipment that go with it.

trash NOUN ① Trash is rubbish • *He picks up your trash on Mondays.* ② (*informal*) If you say that something such as a book, painting or film is trash, you mean that it is not very good.

> **trash** NOUN
> ① = garbage, refuse, rubbish, waste
> ② = garbage (*informal*), rubbish

trauma [*Said* ***traw***-*ma*] NOUN a very upsetting experience which causes great stress.

traumatic ADJECTIVE A traumatic experience is very upsetting.

travel, **travels, travelling, travelled** VERB ① To travel is to go from one place to another. ② When something reaches one place from another, you say that it travels there • *Gossip travels fast.* ▸ NOUN ③ Travel is the act of travelling • *air travel.* ④ (*in plural*) Someone's travels are the journeys that they make to places a long way from their home • *my travels in the Himalayas.* **traveller** NOUN **travelling** ADJECTIVE

> **travel** VERB
> ① = go, journey (*formal*), make your way, take a trip

traverse VERB (*formal*) If you traverse an area of land or water, you go across it or over it • *They have traversed the island from the west coast.*

travesty, **travesties** NOUN a very bad or ridiculous representation or imitation of something • *The case is a travesty of justice.*

trawl VERB When fishermen trawl, they drag a wide net behind a boat in order to catch fish.

trawler NOUN a fishing boat that is used for trawling.

tray NOUN a flat object with raised edges which is used for carrying food or drinks.

treacherous ADJECTIVE ① A treacherous person is likely to betray you and cannot be trusted. ② The ground or the sea can be described as treacherous when it is dangerous or unreliable • *treacherous mountain roads.* **treacherously** ADVERB

> **treacherous** ADJECTIVE
> ① = disloyal, faithless, unfaithful, untrustworthy
> ≠ loyal
> ② = dangerous, hazardous, perilous (*literary*)

treachery NOUN Treachery is behaviour in which someone betrays their country or a person who trusts them.

treacle NOUN Treacle is a thick, sweet syrup used to make cakes and toffee • *treacle tart.*

tread, **treads, treading, trod, trodden** VERB ① If you tread on something, you walk on it or step on it. ② If you tread something into the ground or into a carpet, you crush it in by stepping on it • *bubblegum that has been trodden into the pavement.* ▸ NOUN ③ A person's tread is the sound they make with their feet as they walk • *his heavy tread.* ④ The tread of a tyre or shoe is the pattern of ridges on it that stops it slipping.

treadmill NOUN ① an exercise machine with a continuous moving belt for walking or running on. ② Any task or job that you must keep doing even though it is unpleasant or tiring can be referred to as a treadmill

• *My life is one constant treadmill of making music.*

treason NOUN Treason is the crime of betraying your country, for example by helping its enemies.

treasure NOUN ① Treasure is a collection of gold, silver, jewels or other precious objects, especially one that has been hidden • *buried treasure.* ② Treasures are valuable works of art • *the finest art treasures in the world.* ▸ VERB ③ If you treasure something, you are very pleased that you have it and regard it as very precious • *He treasures his friendship with her.*
treasured ADJECTIVE

> **treasure** VERB
> ③ = cherish, hold dear, prize, value

treasurer NOUN a person who is in charge of the finance and accounts of an organisation.

Treasury NOUN The Treasury is the government department that deals with the country's finances.

treat VERB ① If you treat someone in a particular way, you behave that way towards them. ② If you treat something in a particular way, you deal with it that way or see it that way • *We are now treating this case as murder.* ③ When a doctor treats a patient or an illness, he or she gives them medical care and attention. ④ If something such as wood or cloth is treated, a special substance is put on it in order to protect it or give it special properties • *The carpet's been treated with a stain protector.* ⑤ If you treat someone, you buy or arrange something special for them which they will enjoy. ▸ NOUN ⑥ If you give someone a treat, you buy or arrange something special for them which they will enjoy • *my birthday treat.*
treatment NOUN

> **treat** VERB
> ① = act towards, behave towards, deal with
> ③ = care for, nurse

treatise [*Said* ***tree****-tiz*] NOUN a long formal piece of writing about a particular subject.

treaty, **treaties** NOUN a written agreement between countries in which they agree to do something or to help each other.

treble VERB ① If something trebles or is trebled, it becomes three times greater in number or amount • *Next year we can treble that amount.* ▸ ADJECTIVE ② Treble means three times as large or three times as strong as previously • *a treble dose.*

tree NOUN a large plant with a hard woody trunk, branches and leaves.

trek, **treks**, **trekking**, **trekked** VERB ① If you trek somewhere, you go on a long and difficult journey. ▸ NOUN ② a long and difficult journey, especially one made by walking.

trellis NOUN a frame made of horizontal and vertical strips of wood or metal and used to support plants.

tremble VERB ① If you tremble, you shake slightly, usually because you are frightened or cold. ② If something trembles, it shakes slightly. ③ If your voice trembles, it sounds unsteady, usually because you are frightened or upset.
trembling ADJECTIVE

tremendous ADJECTIVE ① large or impressive • *a tremendous size.* ② (*informal*) very good or pleasing • *tremendous fun.* **tremendously** ADVERB

tremor NOUN ① a shaking movement of your body which you cannot control. ② an unsteady quality in your voice, for example when you are upset. ③ a small earthquake.

trench NOUN a long narrow channel dug into the ground.

trenchant *[Said* ***trent****-shent]* ADJECTIVE Trenchant writings or comments are bold and firmly expressed.

trend NOUN a change towards doing or being something different.

trendy, **trendier**, **trendiest** ADJECTIVE (*informal*) Trendy things or people are fashionable.

> **trendy** ADJECTIVE
> = fashionable, in (*slang*), in fashion, in vogue, latest, stylish

trepidation NOUN (*formal*) Trepidation is fear or anxiety • *He saw the look of trepidation on my face.*

trespass VERB If you trespass on someone's land or property, you go onto it without their permission. **trespasser** NOUN

tresses PLURAL NOUN (*old-fashioned*) A woman's tresses are her long flowing hair.

trestle NOUN a wooden or metal structure that is used as one of the supports for a table.

trevally, **trevallies** NOUN an Australian and New Zealand fish that is caught for both food and sport.

triad *[Said* ***try****-ad]* NOUN ① (*formal*) a group of three similar things. ② MUSIC In music, a triad is a chord of three notes consisting of the tonic and the third and fifth above it.

trial NOUN ① the legal process in which a judge and jury decide whether a person is guilty of a particular crime after listening to all the evidence about it. ② an experiment in which something is tested • *Trials of the drug start next month.*

triangle NOUN ① MATHS a shape with three straight sides. ② a percussion instrument consisting of a thin steel bar bent in the shape of a triangle. **triangular** ADJECTIVE

triathlon *[Said tri-****ath****-lon]* NOUN a sports contest in which athletes compete in three different events.

tribe NOUN a group of people of the same race, who have the same customs, religion, language or land, especially when they are thought to be primitive. **tribal** ADJECTIVE

tribulation NOUN (*formal*) Tribulation is trouble or suffering • *the tribulations of everyday life.*

tribunal *[Said try-****byoo****-nl]* NOUN a special court or committee appointed to deal with particular problems • *an industrial tribunal.*

tributary, **tributaries** NOUN GEOGRAPHY a stream or river that flows into a larger river.

tribute NOUN ① A tribute is something said or done to show admiration and respect for someone • *Police paid tribute to her courage.* ② If one thing is a tribute to another, it is the result of the other thing and shows how good it is • *His success has been a tribute to hard work.*

> **tribute** NOUN
> ① = accolade (*formal*), compliment, honour, praise, testimony

trick NOUN ① an action done to deceive someone. ② Tricks are clever or skilful actions done in order to entertain people • *magic tricks.* ▸ VERB ③ If someone tricks you, they deceive you.

> **trick** NOUN
> ① = con (*informal*), deception, hoax, ploy, ruse
> ▸ VERB ③ = con (*informal*), deceive, dupe, fool, take in (*informal*)

trickery NOUN Trickery is deception • *He obtained the money by trickery.*

trickle VERB ① When a liquid trickles

somewhere, it flows slowly in a thin stream. ② When people or things trickle somewhere, they move there slowly in small numbers or quantities. ▸ **NOUN** ③ a thin stream of liquid. ④ A trickle of people or things is a small number or quantity of them.

tricky, **trickier**, **trickiest** **ADJECTIVE** difficult to do or deal with.

> **tricky** **ADJECTIVE**
> = complex, complicated, delicate, difficult, hard, problematic, puzzling, sensitive

tricycle **NOUN** a vehicle similar to a bicycle but with two wheels at the back and one at the front.

trifle **NOUN** ① A trifle means a little • *He seemed a trifle annoyed.* ② Trifles are things that are not very important or valuable. ③ a cold pudding made of layers of sponge cake, fruit, jelly and custard. ▸ **VERB** ④ If you trifle with someone or something, you treat them in a disrespectful way • *He was not to be trifled with.*

trifling **ADJECTIVE** small and unimportant.

trigger **NOUN** ① the small lever on a gun which is pulled in order to fire it. ▸ **VERB** ② If something triggers an event or triggers it off, it causes it to happen.

trillion **NOUN** ① A trillion is a million million. This is shown as one followed by twelve zeros. ② (*informal*) Trillions of things means an extremely large number of them.

trilogy, **trilogies** **NOUN** a series of three books or plays that have the same characters or are on the same subject.

trim, **trimmer**, **trimmest**; **trims**, **trimming**, **trimmed** **ADJECTIVE** ① neat, tidy and attractive. ▸ **VERB** ② To trim something is to clip small amounts off it. ③ If you trim off parts of something, you cut them off because they are not needed • *Trim off the excess marzipan.* ▸ **NOUN** ④ If something is given a trim, it is cut a little • *All styles need a trim every six to eight weeks.* ⑤ a decoration on something, especially along its edges • *a velvet trim.* **trimmed** **ADJECTIVE**

trimming **NOUN** Trimmings are extra parts added to something for decoration or as a luxury • *a turkey dinner with all the trimmings.*

trinity **NOUN** ① [RE] In the Christian religion, the Trinity is the joining of God the Father, God the Son, and God the Holy Spirit. ② (*literary*) A trinity is a group of three things or people.

trinket **NOUN** a cheap ornament or piece of jewellery.

trio, **trios** **NOUN** ① a group of three musicians who sing or play together; also a piece of music written for three instruments or singers. ② any group of three things or people together • *a trio of children's tales.*

trip, **trips**, **tripping**, **tripped** **NOUN** ① a journey made to a place. ▸ **VERB** ② If you trip, you catch your foot on something and fall over. ③ If you trip someone or trip them up, you make them fall over by making them catch their foot on something.

> **trip** **NOUN**
> ① = excursion, jaunt, journey, outing, voyage
> ▸ **VERB** ② = fall over, lose your footing, stumble

tripe **NOUN** Tripe is the stomach lining of a pig, cow or ox, which is cooked and eaten.

triple **ADJECTIVE** ① consisting of three things or three parts • *the Triple Alliance.* ▸ **VERB** ② If you triple something or if it triples, it becomes three times greater in number or size.

triplet NOUN Triplets are three children born at the same time to the same mother.

tripod *[Said* ***try****-pod]* NOUN a stand with three legs used to support something like a camera or telescope.

trite ADJECTIVE dull and not original • *his trite novels.*

triumph NOUN ① a great success or achievement. ② Triumph is a feeling of great satisfaction when you win or achieve something. ▸ VERB ③ If you triumph, you win a victory or succeed in overcoming something.

> **triumph** NOUN
> ① = success, victory
> ≠ failure
> ▸ VERB ③ = come out on top (*informal*), prevail, succeed, win
> ≠ fail

triumphal ADJECTIVE done or made to celebrate a victory or great success • *a triumphal return to Rome.*

triumphant ADJECTIVE Someone who is triumphant feels very happy because they have won a victory or have achieved something • *a triumphant shout.*

trivia PLURAL NOUN Trivia are unimportant things.

trivial ADJECTIVE Something trivial is unimportant.

> **trivial** ADJECTIVE
> = insignificant, minor, negligible, paltry, petty, slight, trifling, unimportant
> ≠ important

trod the past tense of **tread**.

trodden the past participle of **tread**.

troll NOUN ① an imaginary creature in Scandinavian mythology that lives in caves or mountains and is believed to turn to stone at daylight. ② (*slang*) a person who makes offensive or provocative posts on a website. ▸ VERB ③ (*slang*) If you troll, you deliberately make offensive or provocative posts on a website.

trolley NOUN ① a small table on wheels. ② a small cart on wheels used for carrying heavy objects • *a supermarket trolley.*

trombone NOUN a brass wind instrument with a U-shaped slide which you move to produce different notes.

troop NOUN ① Troops are soldiers. ② A troop of people or animals is a group of them. ▸ VERB ③ If people troop somewhere, they go there in a group.

trooper NOUN a low-ranking soldier in the cavalry.

trophy, **trophies** NOUN ① a cup or shield given as a prize to the winner of a competition. ② something you keep to remember a success or victory.

tropical ADJECTIVE belonging to or typical of the tropics • *a tropical island.*

tropics PLURAL NOUN GEOGRAPHY The tropics are the hottest parts of the world, between two lines of latitude, the Tropic of Cancer, 23½° north of the equator, and the Tropic of Capricorn, 23½° south of the equator.

trot, **trots**, **trotting**, **trotted** VERB ① When a horse trots, it moves at a speed between a walk and a canter, lifting its feet quite high off the ground. ② If you trot, you run or jog using small quick steps. ▸ NOUN ③ When a horse breaks into a trot, it starts trotting.

trotter NOUN A pig's trotters are its feet.

trouble NOUN ① Troubles are difficulties or problems. ② If there is trouble, people are quarrelling or fighting • *There was more trouble after the match.* ▸ PHRASE ③ If you are **in**

a b c d e f g h i j k l m n o p q r s **t** u v w x y z

trouble, you are in a situation where you may be punished because you have done something wrong. ▶ VERB ④ If something troubles you, it makes you feel worried or anxious. ⑤ If you trouble someone for something, you disturb them in order to ask them for it • *Can I trouble you for some milk?* **troubling** ADJECTIVE **troubled** ADJECTIVE

> **trouble** NOUN
> ① = bother, difficulty, hassle (*informal*), problem
> ▶ VERB ④ = agitate, bother, disturb, worry
> ⑤ = bother, disturb, impose upon, inconvenience, put out

troublesome ADJECTIVE causing problems or difficulties • *a troublesome cough*.

trough [*Said* ***troff***] NOUN a long, narrow container from which animals drink or feed.

trounce VERB If you trounce someone, you defeat them completely.

troupe [*Said* ***troop***] NOUN a group of actors, singers or dancers who work together and often travel around together.

trousers PLURAL NOUN Trousers are a piece of clothing covering the body from the waist down, enclosing each leg separately.

trout NOUN a type of freshwater fish.

trowel NOUN ① a small garden tool with a curved, pointed blade used for planting or weeding. ② a small tool with a flat blade used for spreading cement or plaster.

truant NOUN ① a child who stays away from school without permission. ▶ PHRASE ② If children **play truant**, they stay away from school without permission. **truancy** NOUN

truce NOUN an agreement between two people or groups to stop fighting for a short time.

truck NOUN ① a large motor vehicle used for carrying heavy loads. ② an open vehicle used for carrying goods on a railway.

truculent [*Said* ***truk****-yoo-lent*] ADJECTIVE bad-tempered and aggressive. **truculence** NOUN

trudge VERB ① If you trudge, you walk with slow, heavy steps. ▶ NOUN ② a slow tiring walk • *the long trudge home*.

true, **truer**, **truest** ADJECTIVE ① A true story or statement is based on facts and is not made up. ② 'True' is used to describe things or people that are genuine • *She was a true friend*. ③ True feelings are sincere and genuine. ▶ PHRASE ④ If something **comes true**, it actually happens. **truly** ADVERB

> **true** ADJECTIVE
> ① = accurate, correct, factual
> ≠ inaccurate
> ② = authentic, bona fide, genuine, real
> ≠ false

truffle NOUN ① a soft, round sweet made from chocolate. ② a round mushroom-like fungus which grows underground and is considered very good to eat.

trump NOUN In a game of cards, trumps is the suit with the highest value.

trumpet NOUN ① a brass wind instrument with a narrow tube ending in a bell-like shape. ▶ VERB ② When an elephant trumpets, it makes a sound like a very loud trumpet.

truncated ADJECTIVE Something that is truncated is made shorter.

trundle VERB If you trundle something or it trundles somewhere, it moves or rolls along slowly.

A B C D E F G H I J K L M N O P Q R S T U V W X Y Z

trunk NOUN ① the main stem of a tree from which the branches and roots grow. ② the main part of your body, excluding your head, neck, arms and legs. ③ the long flexible nose of an elephant. ④ a large, strong case or box with a hinged lid used for storing things. ⑤ (*in plural*) A man's trunks are his bathing pants or shorts.

truss VERB To truss someone or truss them up is to tie them up so that they cannot move.

trust VERB ① If you trust someone, you believe that they are honest and will not harm you. ② If you trust someone to do something, you believe they will do it successfully or properly. ③ If you trust someone with something, you give it to them or tell it to them • *One member of the group cannot be trusted with the secret.* ④ If you do not trust something, you feel that it is not safe or reliable • *I didn't trust my arms and legs to work.* ▸ NOUN ⑤ Trust is the responsibility you are given to deal with or look after important or secret things • *He had built up a position of trust.* ⑥ a financial arrangement in which an organisation looks after and invests money for someone.
trusting ADJECTIVE

trust VERB
② = count on, depend on, have confidence in, have faith in, place your trust in, rely upon

trustee NOUN someone who is allowed by law to control money or property they are keeping or investing for another person.

trustworthy ADJECTIVE A trustworthy person is reliable and responsible and can be trusted.

trusty, trustier, trustiest ADJECTIVE Trusty things and animals are considered to be reliable because they have always worked well in the past • *a trusty black labrador.*

trusty ADJECTIVE
= dependable, faithful, firm, reliable, solid, staunch, true, trustworthy

truth NOUN ① The truth is the facts about something, rather than things that are imagined or made up • *I know she was telling the truth.* ② an idea or principle that is generally accepted to be true • *the basic truths in life.*

truth NOUN
① = fact, reality

truthful ADJECTIVE A truthful person is honest and tells the truth.
truthfully ADVERB

try, tries, trying, tried VERB ① To try to do something is to make an effort to do it. ② If you try something, you use it or do it to test how useful or enjoyable it is • *Howard wanted me to try the cake.* ③ When a person is tried, they appear in court and a judge and jury decide if they are guilty after hearing the evidence. ▸ NOUN ④ an attempt to do something. ⑤ a test of something • *You gave it a try.* ⑥ In rugby, a try is scored when someone carries the ball over the goal line of the opposing team and touches the ground with it.

try VERB
① = attempt, endeavour (*formal*), make an attempt, make an effort, seek, strive
② = check out, sample, test, try out
▸ NOUN ④ = attempt, effort, endeavour (*formal*), go (*informal*), shot (*informal*)

trying ADJECTIVE A trying person or thing is difficult to deal with and makes you feel impatient or annoyed.

tryst [*Said* **trist**] NOUN an appointment or meeting, especially between lovers in a quiet, secret place.

tsar [*Said* **zar**]; also spelt **czar** NOUN a Russian emperor or king between 1547 and 1917.

T-shirt; also spelt **tee shirt** NOUN a simple short-sleeved cotton shirt with no collar.

tsunami, **tsunamis** NOUN GEOGRAPHY a large, often destructive sea wave, caused by an earthquake or volcanic eruption under the sea.

tub NOUN a wide circular container.

tuba NOUN a large brass musical instrument that can produce very low notes.

tubby, **tubbier**, **tubbiest** ADJECTIVE rather fat.

> **tubby** ADJECTIVE
> = chubby, fat, overweight, plump, podgy, portly, stout

tube NOUN ① a round, hollow pipe. ② a soft metal or plastic cylindrical container with a screw cap at one end • *a tube of toothpaste*. **tubing** NOUN

tuberculosis *[Said tyoo-ber-kyoo-**loe**-siss]* NOUN Tuberculosis is a serious infectious disease affecting the lungs.

tubular ADJECTIVE in the shape of a tube.

TUC In Britain, the TUC is an association of trade unions. TUC is an abbreviation for 'Trades Union Congress'.

tuck VERB ① If you tuck something somewhere, you put it there so that it is safe or comfortable • *She tucked the letter into her handbag*. ② If you tuck a piece of fabric into or under something, you push the loose ends inside or under it to make it tidy. ③ If something is tucked away, it is in a quiet place where few people go • *a little house tucked away in a valley*.

tucker *(informal)* NOUN ① In Australian and New Zealand English, tucker is food. ▶ VERB ② In American, Australian and New Zealand English, if you are tuckered out you are tired out.

Tudor HISTORY NOUN Tudor was the family name of the English monarchs who reigned from 1485 to 1603.

Tuesday NOUN Tuesday is the day between Monday and Wednesday.

tug, **tugs**, **tugging**, **tugged** VERB ① To tug something is to give it a quick, hard pull. ▶ NOUN ② a quick, hard pull • *He felt a tug at his arm*. ③ a small, powerful boat which tows large ships.

> **tug** VERB
> ① = drag, draw, haul, heave, jerk, pluck, pull, wrench, yank
> ▶ NOUN ② = heave, jerk, pull, wrench, yank

tug of war NOUN A tug of war is a sport in which two teams test their strength by pulling against each other on opposite ends of a rope.

tuition NOUN Tuition is the teaching of a subject, especially to one person or to a small group.

tulip NOUN a brightly coloured spring flower.

tumble VERB ① To tumble is to fall with a rolling or bouncing movement. ▶ NOUN ② a fall.

tumbler NOUN a drinking glass with straight sides.

tummy, **tummies** NOUN *(informal)* Your tummy is your stomach.

tumour *[Said **tyoo**-mur]* NOUN a mass of diseased or abnormal cells that has grown in a person's or animal's body.

tumultuous ADJECTIVE A tumultuous event or welcome is very noisy because people are happy or excited.

tuna, **tuna** *[Said **tyoo**-na]* NOUN Tuna are large fish that live in warm seas and are caught for food.

tundra NOUN GEOGRAPHY The tundra is a vast treeless Arctic region.

tune NOUN ① a series of musical notes arranged in a particular way. ▶ VERB

②To tune a musical instrument is to adjust it so that it produces the right notes. ③To tune an engine or machine is to adjust it so that it works well. ④If you tune to a particular radio or television station you turn or press the controls to select the station you want to listen to or watch. ▶ PHRASE ⑤If your voice or an instrument is **in tune**, it produces the right notes.

tune NOUN
①= melody, strains

tuneful ADJECTIVE having a pleasant and easily remembered tune.

tuner NOUN A piano tuner is a person whose job it is to tune pianos.

tunic NOUN a sleeveless garment covering the top part of the body and reaching to the hips, thighs or knees.

Tunisian *[Said tyoo-**niz**-ee-an]* ADJECTIVE ①belonging or relating to Tunisia. ▶ NOUN ②someone who comes from Tunisia.

tunnel, tunnels, tunnelling, tunnelled NOUN ①a long underground passage. ▶ VERB ②To tunnel is to make a tunnel.

turban NOUN a head-covering worn by a Hindu, Muslim or Sikh man, consisting of a long piece of cloth wound round his head.

turbine NOUN a machine or engine in which power is produced when a stream of air, gas, water or steam pushes the blades of a wheel and makes it turn round.

turbulent ADJECTIVE ①A turbulent period of history is one where there is much uncertainty, and possibly violent change. ②Turbulent air or water currents make sudden changes of direction. **turbulence** NOUN

turf, turves; turfs, turfing, turfed NOUN Turf is short, thick, even grass and the layer of soil beneath it.

turf out VERB *(informal)* To turf someone out is to force them to leave a place.

turgid *[Said **tur**-jid]* ADJECTIVE *(literary)* A turgid play, film or piece of writing is difficult to understand and rather boring.

Turk NOUN someone who comes from Turkey.

turkey, turkeys NOUN a large bird kept for food; also the meat of this bird.

Turkish ADJECTIVE ①belonging or relating to Turkey. ▶ NOUN ②Turkish is the main language spoken in Turkey.

turmoil NOUN Turmoil is a state of confusion, disorder or great anxiety • *Europe is in a state of turmoil.*

turn VERB ①When you turn, you move so that you are facing or going in a different direction. ②When you turn something or when it turns, it moves or rotates so that it faces in a different direction or is in a different position. ③If you turn your attention or thoughts to someone or something, you start thinking about them or discussing them. ④When something turns or is turned into something else, it becomes something different • *A hobby can be turned into a career.* ▶ NOUN ⑤an act of turning something so that it faces in a different direction or is in a different position. ⑥a change in the way something is happening or being done • *Her career took a turn for the worse.* ⑦If it is your turn to do something, you have the right, chance or duty to do it. ▶ PHRASE ⑧**In turn** is used to refer to people, things or actions that are in sequence one after the other. **turn down** VERB If you turn down someone's request or offer, you refuse or reject it. **turn up** VERB ①If someone or something turns up, they arrive or appear somewhere. ② If something turns up, it is found or discovered.

turn VERB
② = rotate, spin, swivel, twirl, twist
④ = change, convert, mutate, transform
▶ NOUN ⑦ = chance, go, opportunity

turning NOUN a road which leads away from the side of another road.

turning point NOUN the moment when decisions are taken and events start to move in a different direction.

turnip NOUN a round root vegetable with a white or yellow skin.

turnout NOUN The turnout at an event is the number of people who go to it.

turnover NOUN ① The turnover of people in a particular organisation or group is the rate at which people leave it and are replaced by others. ② The turnover of a company is the value of the goods or services sold during a particular period.

turnstile NOUN a revolving mechanical barrier at the entrance to places like football grounds or zoos.

turquoise [*Said* ***tur****-kwoyz*] NOUN, ADJECTIVE ① light bluish-green. ▶ NOUN ② Turquoise is a bluish-green stone used in jewellery.

turret NOUN a small narrow tower on top of a larger tower or other buildings.

turtle NOUN a large reptile with a thick shell covering its body and flippers for swimming. It lays its eggs on land but lives the rest of its life in the sea.

tussle NOUN an energetic fight or argument between two people, especially about something they both want.

tutor NOUN ① a teacher at a college or university. ② a private teacher. ▶ VERB ③ If someone tutors a person or subject, they teach that person or subject.

tutorial NOUN a teaching session involving a tutor and a small group of students.

tutu [*Said* ***too****-too*] NOUN a short, stiff skirt worn by female ballet dancers.

TV NOUN ① TV is television. ② a television set.

twang NOUN ① a sound like the one made by pulling and then releasing a tight wire. ② A twang is a nasal quality in a person's voice. ▶ VERB ③ If a tight wire or string twangs or you twang it, it makes a sound as it is pulled and then released.

tweak VERB ① If you tweak something, you twist it or pull it. ▶ NOUN ② a short twist or pull of something.

twee ADJECTIVE sweet and pretty but in bad taste or sentimental.

tweed NOUN Tweed is a thick woollen cloth.

tweet VERB ① When a small bird tweets, it makes a short, high-pitched sound. ② If you tweet, you send a message on the social networking site Twitter. ▶ NOUN ③ a short high-pitched sound made by a small bird. ④ a message sent on the social networking site Twitter.

tweezers PLURAL NOUN Tweezers are a small tool with two arms which can be closed together and are used for pulling out hairs or picking up small objects.

twelve the number 12. **twelfth** ADJECTIVE

twenty, **twenties** the number 20. **twentieth** ADJECTIVE

twice ADVERB Twice means two times.

twig NOUN a very small thin branch growing from a main branch of a tree or bush.

A B C D E F G H I J K L M N O P Q R S T U V W X Y Z

twilight *[Said twy-lite]* NOUN ① Twilight is the time after sunset when it is just getting dark. ② The twilight of something is the final stages of it • *the twilight of his career.*

twin NOUN ① If two people are twins, they have the same mother and were born on the same day. ② 'Twin' is used to describe two similar things that are close together or happen together • *the little twin islands.*

twine NOUN ① Twine is strong smooth string. ▸ VERB ② If you twine one thing round another, you twist or wind it round.

twinge NOUN ① a sudden, unpleasant feeling • *a twinge of jealousy.* ② a sudden sharp pain • *a twinge in my lower back.*

twinkle VERB ① If something twinkles, it sparkles or seems to sparkle with an unsteady light • *Her green eyes twinkled.* ▸ NOUN ② a sparkle or brightness that something has.

twirl VERB If something twirls, or if you twirl it, it spins or twists round and round.

twist VERB ① When you twist something you turn one end of it in one direction while holding the other end or turning it in the opposite direction. ② When something twists or is twisted, it moves or bends into a strange shape. ③ If you twist a part of your body, you injure it by turning it too sharply or in an unusual direction • *I've twisted my ankle.* ④ If you twist something that someone has said, you change the meaning slightly. ▸ NOUN ⑤ a twisting action or motion. ⑥ an unexpected development or event in a story or film, especially at the end • *Each day now seemed to bring a new twist to the story.*

> **twist** VERB
> ① = bend, curl, twine, weave, wring
> ② = distort, mangle, screw up
> ③ = sprain, wrench

twisted ADJECTIVE ① Something twisted has been bent or moved into a strange shape • *a tangle of twisted metal.* ② If someone's mind or behaviour is twisted, it is unpleasantly abnormal • *He's bitter and twisted.*

twit NOUN (*informal*) a silly person.

twitch VERB ① If you twitch, you make little jerky movements which you cannot control. ② If you twitch something, you give it a little jerk in order to move it. ▸ NOUN ③ a little jerky movement.

twitter VERB When birds twitter, they make short high-pitched sounds.

two the number 2.

two-faced ADJECTIVE A two-faced person is not honest in the way they behave towards other people.

> **two-faced** ADJECTIVE
> = deceitful, dishonest, disloyal, false, hypocritical, insincere, treacherous

twofold ADJECTIVE Something twofold has two equally important parts or reasons • *Their concern was twofold: personal and political.*

twosome *[Said too-sum]* NOUN two people or things that are usually seen together.

two-time VERB (*informal*) If you two-time your boyfriend or girlfriend, you deceive them, by having a romantic relationship with someone else without telling them.

two-up NOUN In Australia and New Zealand, two-up is a popular gambling game in which two coins are tossed and bets are placed on whether they land heads or tails.

tycoon NOUN a person who is successful in business and has become rich and powerful.

type NOUN ① A type of something is a class of it that has common features and belongs to a larger group of related things • *What type of dog should we get?* ② A particular type of person has a particular appearance or quality • *Andrea is the type who likes to play safe.* ▸ VERB ③ If you type something, you use a typewriter or computer keyboard to write it.

> **type** NOUN
> ① = brand, breed, class, group, kind, make, sort, species, style, variety

typewriter NOUN a machine with a keyboard with individual keys which are pressed to produce letters and numbers on a page.

typhoid *[Said* ***tie****-foyd]* NOUN Typhoid, or typhoid fever, is an infectious disease caused by dirty water or food. It produces fever and can kill.

typhoon NOUN [GEOGRAPHY] a very violent tropical storm.

typical ADJECTIVE showing the most usual characteristics or behaviour.
typically ADVERB

> **typical** ADJECTIVE
> = average, characteristic, normal, regular, representative, standard, stock, usual
> ≠ uncharacteristic

typify, typifies, typifying, typified VERB If something typifies a situation or thing, it is characteristic of it or a typical example of it • *This story is one that typifies our times.*

typing NOUN Typing is the work or activity of producing something on a typewriter or computer keyboard.

typist NOUN ① a person whose job is typing. ② a person who types in a particular way • *a painfully slow typist.*

tyranny, tyrannies NOUN ① A tyranny is cruel and unjust rule of people by a person or group • *the evils of Nazi tyranny.* ② You can refer to something which is not human but is harsh as tyranny • *the tyranny of fate.*
tyrannical ADJECTIVE

tyrant NOUN a person who treats the people he or she has authority over cruelly and unjustly.

tyre NOUN a thick ring of rubber fitted round each wheel of a vehicle and filled with air.

Uu

ubiquitous *[Said yoo-**bik**-wit-tuss]* ADJECTIVE Something that is ubiquitous seems to be everywhere at the same time • *the ubiquitous jeans.*

UFO NOUN a strange object seen in the sky, which some people believe to be a spaceship from another planet. UFO is an abbreviation for 'unidentified flying object'.

Ugandan *[Said yoo-**gan**-dan]* ADJECTIVE ① belonging or relating to Uganda. ▸ NOUN ② someone who comes from Uganda.

ugly, **uglier**, **ugliest** ADJECTIVE very unattractive in appearance.

> **ugly** ADJECTIVE
> = plain, unattractive, unsightly
> ≠ beautiful

UK an abbreviation for **United Kingdom**.

ulcer NOUN a sore area on the skin or inside the body, which takes a long time to heal • *stomach ulcers.* **ulcerous** ADJECTIVE

ulterior *[Said ul-**teer**-ee-or]* ADJECTIVE If you have an ulterior motive for doing something, you have a hidden reason for it.

ultimate ADJECTIVE ① final or eventual • *a gold medal is the ultimate goal.* ② most important or powerful • *the ultimate ambition of any player.* ▸ NOUN ③ You can refer to the best or most advanced example of something as the ultimate • *This hotel is the ultimate in luxury.* **ultimately** ADVERB

> **ultimate** ADJECTIVE
> ① = eventual, final, last
> ② = greatest, paramount, supreme, utmost
> ▸ NOUN ③ = epitome, extreme, height, peak

ultimatum *[Said ul-tim-**may**-tum]* NOUN a warning stating that unless someone meets your conditions, you will take action against them.

ultrasound NOUN SCIENCE Ultrasound is sound which cannot be heard by the human ear because its frequency is too high.

ultraviolet ADJECTIVE SCIENCE Ultraviolet light is not visible to the human eye. It is a form of radiation that causes your skin to darken after being exposed to the sun.

umbilical cord *[Said um-**bil**-lik-kl]* NOUN SCIENCE the tube of blood vessels which connects an unborn baby to its mother and through which the baby receives nutrients and oxygen.

umbrella NOUN a device that you use to protect yourself from the rain. It consists of a folding frame covered in cloth attached to a long stick.

umpire NOUN ① The umpire in cricket or tennis is the person who makes sure that the game is played according to the rules and who makes a decision if there is a dispute. ▸ VERB ② If you umpire a game, you are the umpire.

umpteen ADJECTIVE (*informal*) very many • *tomatoes and umpteen other* *plants.* **umpteenth** ADJECTIVE

unabashed ADJECTIVE not embarrassed or discouraged by something • *Samuel was unabashed.*

unabated ADJECTIVE, ADVERB continuing without any reduction in intensity or amount • *The noise continued unabated.*

unable ADJECTIVE If you are unable to do something, you cannot do it.

unacceptable ADJECTIVE If you find something unacceptable, you disapprove of it because you think it is of a very low standard.

unaccompanied ADJECTIVE alone.

unaccustomed ADJECTIVE If you are unaccustomed to something, you are not used to it.

unaffected ADJECTIVE ① not changed in any way by a particular thing • *unaffected by the recession.* ② behaving in a natural and genuine way • *the most down-to-earth, unaffected person I've ever met.*

unaided ADVERB, ADJECTIVE without help • *He was incapable of walking unaided.*

unambiguous ADJECTIVE An unambiguous statement has only one meaning.

unanimous *[Said yoon-**nan**-nim-mus]* ADJECTIVE When people are unanimous, they all agree about something. **unanimously** ADVERB **unanimity** NOUN

unannounced ADJECTIVE happening unexpectedly and without warning.

unarmed ADJECTIVE not carrying any weapons.

unassuming ADJECTIVE modest and quiet.

unattached ADJECTIVE An unattached person is not married and is not having a steady relationship with someone.

unattended ADJECTIVE not being watched or looked after • *an unattended handbag.*

unauthorised; also spelt **unauthorized** ADJECTIVE done without official permission • *unauthorised parking.*

unavoidable ADJECTIVE unable to be prevented or avoided.

unaware ADJECTIVE If you are unaware of something, you do not know about it.

> **unaware** ADJECTIVE
> = ignorant, oblivious, unconscious, unsuspecting
> ≠ aware

unawares ADVERB If something catches you unawares, it happens when you are not expecting it.

unbalanced ADJECTIVE ① with more weight or emphasis on one side than the other • *an unbalanced load* • *an unbalanced relationship.* ② slightly mad. ③ made up of parts that do not work well together • *an unbalanced lifestyle.* ④ An unbalanced account of something is an unfair one because it emphasises some things and ignores others.

unbearable ADJECTIVE Something unbearable is so unpleasant or upsetting that you feel you cannot stand it • *The pain was unbearable.* **unbearably** ADVERB

> **unbearable** ADJECTIVE
> = intolerable, oppressive, unacceptable
> ≠ tolerable

unbeatable ADJECTIVE Something that is unbeatable is the best thing of its kind.

unbelievable ADJECTIVE ① extremely great or surprising • *unbelievable courage.* ② so unlikely that you cannot believe it. **unbelievably** ADVERB

unbelievable ADJECTIVE
① = colossal, incredible, stupendous
② = implausible, improbable, inconceivable, incredible, preposterous, unconvincing
≠ believable

unborn ADJECTIVE not yet born.

unbroken ADJECTIVE continuous or complete • *ten days of almost unbroken sunshine.*

uncanny ADJECTIVE strange and difficult to explain • *an uncanny resemblance.*

uncertain ADJECTIVE ① not knowing what to do • *For a minute he looked uncertain.* ② doubtful or not known • *The outcome of the war was uncertain.* **uncertainty** NOUN

uncertain ADJECTIVE
① = doubtful, dubious, unclear, undecided
≠ certain
② = ambiguous, doubtful, indefinite, indeterminate
≠ certain

unchallenged ADJECTIVE accepted without any questions being asked • *an unchallenged decision.*

uncharacteristic ADJECTIVE not typical or usual • *My father reacted with uncharacteristic speed.*

uncle NOUN Your uncle is the brother of your mother or father, or the husband of one of your parents' siblings.

unclear ADJECTIVE confusing and not obvious.

unclear ADJECTIVE
= ambiguous, confused, vague
≠ clear

uncomfortable ADJECTIVE ① If you are uncomfortable, you are not physically relaxed and feel slight pain or discomfort. ② Uncomfortable also means slightly worried or embarrassed. **uncomfortably** ADVERB

uncomfortable ADJECTIVE
① = awkward, cramped, disagreeable, ill-fitting, painful
≠ comfortable
② = awkward, embarrassed, ill at ease, self-conscious, uneasy
≠ comfortable

uncommon ADJECTIVE ① not happening often or not seen often. ② unusually great • *She had read Cecilia's last letter with uncommon interest.* **uncommonly** ADVERB

uncommon ADJECTIVE
① = exceptional, extraordinary, few, infrequent, out of the ordinary, rare, scarce, sparse, unusual
≠ common
② = acute, exceptional, extraordinary, extreme, great, intense, remarkable

uncompromising ADJECTIVE determined not to change an opinion or aim in any way • *an uncompromising approach to life.* **uncompromisingly** ADVERB

unconcerned ADJECTIVE not interested in something or not worried about it.

unconditional ADJECTIVE with no conditions or limitations • *a full three-year unconditional guarantee.* **unconditionally** ADVERB

unconscious ADJECTIVE ① Someone who is unconscious is asleep or in a state similar to sleep as a result of a shock, accident or injury. ② If you are unconscious of something, you are not aware of it. **unconsciously** ADVERB **unconsciousness** NOUN

unconscious ADJECTIVE
① = asleep, senseless, stunned
≠ conscious
② = oblivious, unaware, unknowing, unsuspecting
≠ aware

uncontrollable ADJECTIVE If someone or something is uncontrollable, they or it cannot be controlled or stopped • *uncontrollable anger*. **uncontrollably** ADVERB

unconventional ADJECTIVE not behaving in the same way as most other people.

unconvinced ADJECTIVE not at all certain that something is true or right • *Some critics remain unconvinced by the plan*.

uncouth *[Said un-**kooth**]* ADJECTIVE bad-mannered and unpleasant.

uncover VERB ① If you uncover a secret, you find it out. ② To uncover something is to remove the cover or lid from it.

> **uncover** VERB
> ① = bring to light, expose, reveal, show up, unearth
> ② = expose, lay bare, open, reveal, unearth, unveil, unwrap

undaunted ADJECTIVE If you are undaunted by something disappointing, you are not discouraged by it.

undecided ADJECTIVE If you are undecided, you have not yet made a decision about something.

undemanding ADJECTIVE not difficult to do or deal with • *undemanding work*.

undeniable ADJECTIVE certainly true • *undeniable evidence*. **undeniably** ADVERB

under PREPOSITION ① below or beneath. ② You can use 'under' to say that a person or thing is affected by a particular situation or condition • *The country was under threat* • *It is wrong to keep animals under unnatural conditions*. ③ If someone studies or works under a particular person, that person is their teacher or their boss. ④ less than • *under five kilometres* • *children under the age of 14*. ▶ PHRASE ⑤ **Under way** means already started • *A murder investigation is already under way*.

> **under** PREPOSITION
> ① = below, beneath, underneath
> ≠ above

underarm ADJECTIVE ① under your arm • *underarm hair*. ▶ ADVERB ② If you throw a ball underarm, you throw it without raising your arm over your shoulder.

undercarriage NOUN the part of an aircraft, including the wheels, that supports the aircraft when it is on the ground.

underclass NOUN The underclass is the people in society who are the most poor and whose situation is unlikely to improve.

undercover ADJECTIVE involving secret work to obtain information • *a police undercover operation*.

undercurrent NOUN a weak, partly hidden feeling that may become stronger later.

undercut, **undercuts**, **undercutting**, **undercut** VERB ① To undercut someone's prices is to sell a product more cheaply than they do. ② If something undercuts your attempts to achieve something, it prevents them from being effective.

underdeveloped ADJECTIVE An underdeveloped country does not have modern industries, and usually has a low standard of living.

underdog NOUN The underdog in a competition is the person who seems likely to lose.

underestimate VERB If you underestimate something or someone, you do not realise how large, great or capable they are.

underfoot ADJECTIVE, ADVERB under your feet • *the icy ground underfoot*.

undergo, **undergoes**, **undergoing**, **underwent**, **undergone** VERB If you undergo something unpleasant, it happens to you.

undergo VERB
= be subjected to, endure, experience, go through, suffer

underground ADJECTIVE, ADVERB ① below the surface of the ground. ② secret, unofficial and usually illegal. ▶ NOUN ③ The underground is a railway system in which trains travel in tunnels below ground.

undergrowth NOUN Small bushes and plants growing under trees are called the undergrowth.

underhand ADJECTIVE secret and dishonest • *underhand behaviour*.

underlie, **underlies**, **underlying**, **underlay**, **underlain** VERB The thing that underlies a situation is the cause or basis of it. **underlying** ADJECTIVE

underline VERB ① If something underlines a feeling or a problem, it emphasises it. ② If you underline a word or sentence, you draw a line under it.

undermine VERB To undermine an idea, feeling or system is to make it less strong or secure • *You're trying to undermine my confidence again*.

undermine VERB
= impair, sap, subvert, weaken
≠ strengthen

underneath PREPOSITION ① below or beneath. ▶ ADVERB, PREPOSITION ② Underneath describes feelings and qualities that do not show in your behaviour • *Alex knew that underneath she was shattered*. ▶ ADJECTIVE ③ The underneath part of something is the part that touches or faces the ground.

underpants PLURAL NOUN Underpants are a piece of clothing worn by men and boys under their trousers.

underpass NOUN a road or footpath that goes under a road or railway.

underpin, **underpins**, **underpinning**, **underpinned** VERB If something underpins something else, it helps it to continue by supporting and strengthening it • *Australian skill is usually underpinned by an immense team spirit*.

underprivileged ADJECTIVE Underprivileged people have less money and fewer opportunities than other people.

underrate VERB If you underrate someone, you do not realise how clever or valuable they are.

understand, **understands**, **understanding**, **understood** VERB ① If you understand what someone says, you know what they mean. ② If you understand a situation, you know what is happening and why. ③ If you say that you understand that something is the case, you mean that you have heard that it is the case • *I understand that she's a lot better now*.

understand VERB
① = catch on (*informal*), comprehend, follow, get, grasp, see, take in
② = appreciate, comprehend, fathom, grasp, realise
③ = believe, gather, hear, learn

understandable ADJECTIVE If something is understandable, people can easily understand it. **understandably** ADVERB

understanding NOUN ① If you have an understanding of something, you have some knowledge about it. ② an informal agreement between people. ▶ ADJECTIVE ③ kind and sympathetic.

understanding NOUN
① = appreciation, comprehension, grasp, knowledge, perception
② = accord (*formal*), agreement, pact
▶ ADJECTIVE ③ = compassionate, considerate, sensitive, sympathetic

understatement NOUN a statement that does not say fully how true something is • *To say I was pleased was an understatement.*

understood the past tense and past participle of **understand**.

understudy, **understudies** NOUN someone who has learnt a part in a play so that they can act it if the main actor or actress is ill.

undertake, **undertakes**, **undertaking**, **undertook**, **undertaken** VERB When you undertake a task or job, you agree to do it.

undertaker NOUN someone whose job is to prepare bodies for burial and arrange funerals.

undertaking NOUN a task which you have agreed to do.

> **undertaking** NOUN
> = affair, business, endeavour, enterprise, job, operation, project, task, venture

undertone NOUN ① If you say something in an undertone, you say it very quietly. ② If something has undertones of a particular kind, it indirectly suggests ideas of this kind • *unsettling undertones of anger.*

undertook the past tense of **undertake**.

undervalue, **undervalues**, **undervaluing**, **undervalued** VERB If you undervalue something, you think it is less important than it really is.

underwater ADVERB, ADJECTIVE ① beneath the surface of the sea, a river or a lake. ▸ ADJECTIVE ② designed to work in water • *an underwater camera.*

underwear NOUN Your underwear is the clothing that you wear under your other clothes, next to your skin.

underwent the past tense of **undergo**.

undesirable ADJECTIVE unwelcome and likely to cause harm • *undesirable behaviour.*

undid the past tense of **undo**.

undisputed ADJECTIVE definite and without any doubt • *the undisputed champion.*

undivided ADJECTIVE If you give something your undivided attention, you concentrate on it totally.

undo, **undoes**, **undoing**, **undid**, **undone** VERB ① If you undo something that is tied up, you untie it. ② If you undo something that has been done, you reverse the effect of it.

undoing NOUN If something is someone's undoing, it is the cause of their failure.

undoubted ADJECTIVE You use 'undoubted' to emphasise something • *The event was an undoubted success.* **undoubtedly** ADVERB

undress VERB When you undress, you take off your clothes.

undue ADJECTIVE greater than is reasonable • *undue pressure.* **unduly** ADVERB

undulating ADJECTIVE (*formal*) moving gently up and down • *undulating hills.*

undying ADJECTIVE lasting forever • *his undying love for his wife.*

unearth VERB If you unearth something that is hidden, you discover it.

unearthly ADJECTIVE strange and unnatural.

uneasy ADJECTIVE If you are uneasy, you feel worried that something may be wrong. **unease** NOUN **uneasily** ADVERB **uneasiness** NOUN

> **uneasy** ADJECTIVE
> = agitated, anxious, nervous, perturbed, worried
> ≠ comfortable

unemployed ADJECTIVE ① without a

job • *an unemployed mechanic*. ▶ **PLURAL NOUN** ② The unemployed are all the people who are without a job.

unemployed ADJECTIVE
① = idle, jobless, redundant
≠ employed

unemployment NOUN Unemployment is the state of being without a job.

unending ADJECTIVE Something unending has continued for a long time and seems as if it will never stop • *unending joy*.

unenviable ADJECTIVE An unenviable situation is one that you would not like to be in.

unequal ADJECTIVE ① An unequal society does not offer the same opportunities and privileges to all people. ② Unequal things are different in size, strength or ability.

uneven ADJECTIVE ① An uneven surface is not level or smooth. ② not the same or consistent • *six lines of uneven length*. **unevenly** ADVERB

uneven ADJECTIVE
① = bumpy, not level, not smooth, rough
≠ level
② = fluctuating, inconsistent, irregular, patchy, variable
≠ even

uneventful ADJECTIVE An uneventful period of time is one when nothing interesting happens.

unexpected ADJECTIVE Something unexpected is surprising because it was not thought likely to happen. **unexpectedly** ADVERB

unexpected ADJECTIVE
= astonishing, chance, surprising, unforeseen

unfailing ADJECTIVE continuous and not weakening as time passes • *his unfailing cheerfulness*.

unfair ADJECTIVE not right or just. **unfairly** ADVERB

unfair ADJECTIVE
= unjust, wrong, wrongful
≠ fair

unfaithful ADJECTIVE If someone is unfaithful, they are not loyal.

unfamiliar ADJECTIVE If something is unfamiliar to you, or if you are unfamiliar with it, you have not seen or heard it before.

unfamiliar ADJECTIVE
= alien, exotic, foreign, new, novel, strange, unknown

unfashionable ADJECTIVE Something that is unfashionable is not popular or is no longer used by many people.

unfavourable ADJECTIVE not encouraging or promising, or not providing any advantage.

unfit ADJECTIVE ① If you are unfit, your body is not in good condition because you have not been taking enough exercise. ② Something that is unfit for a particular purpose is not suitable for that purpose.

unfold VERB ① When a situation unfolds, it develops and becomes known. ② If you unfold something that has been folded, you open it out so that it is flat.

unforeseen ADJECTIVE happening unexpectedly.

unforgettable ADJECTIVE Something unforgettable is so good or so bad that you are unlikely to forget it. **unforgettably** ADVERB

unforgivable ADJECTIVE Something unforgivable is so bad or cruel that it can never be forgiven or justified. **unforgivably** ADVERB

unfortunate ADJECTIVE ① Someone who is unfortunate is unlucky. ② If you describe an event as unfortunate, you mean that it is a pity that it happened • *an unfortunate accident*. **unfortunately** ADVERB

unfounded ADJECTIVE Something that is unfounded has no evidence to support it • *unfounded allegations*.

unfriendly ADJECTIVE ① A person who is unfriendly is not pleasant to you. ② A place that is unfriendly makes you feel uncomfortable or is not welcoming.

> **unfriendly** ADJECTIVE
> ① = aloof, antagonistic, cold, disagreeable, hostile, unkind
> ≠ friendly

ungainly ADJECTIVE moving in an awkward or clumsy way.

ungrateful ADJECTIVE not grateful or thankful.

> **ungrateful** ADJECTIVE
> = unappreciative, unthankful
> ≠ grateful

unhappy, **unhappier**, **unhappiest** ADJECTIVE ① sad and depressed. ② not pleased or satisfied • *I am unhappy at being left out*. ③ If you describe a situation as an unhappy one, you are sorry that it exists • *an unhappy state of affairs*. **unhappily** ADVERB **unhappiness** NOUN

> **unhappy** ADJECTIVE
> ① = depressed, despondent, down, miserable, sad
> ≠ happy

unhealthy ADJECTIVE ① likely to cause illness • *an unhealthy lifestyle*. ② An unhealthy person is often ill.

> **unhealthy** ADJECTIVE
> ① = bad for you, harmful, insanitary, noxious, unwholesome
> ≠ healthy
> ② = ailing, crook (*Australian and New Zealand; informal*), ill, not well, poorly (*British; informal*), sick, unwell
> ≠ healthy

unhinged ADJECTIVE Someone who is unhinged is mentally unbalanced.

unhurried ADJECTIVE Unhurried is used to describe actions or movements that are slow and relaxed.

unicorn NOUN an imaginary animal that looks like a white horse with a straight horn growing from its forehead.

unidentified ADJECTIVE You say that someone or something is unidentified when nobody knows who or what they are.

uniform NOUN ① a special set of clothes worn by people at work or school. ▸ ADJECTIVE ② Something that is uniform does not vary but is even and regular throughout. **uniformity** NOUN

unify, **unifies**, **unifying**, **unified** VERB If you unify a number of things, you bring them together. **unification** NOUN

unilateral ADJECTIVE A unilateral decision or action is one taken by only one of several groups involved in a particular situation. **unilaterally** ADVERB

unimaginable ADJECTIVE impossible to imagine or understand properly • *a fairyland of unimaginable beauty*.

unimportant ADJECTIVE having very little significance or importance.

> **unimportant** ADJECTIVE
> = insignificant, minor, paltry, slight, trivial
> ≠ important

uninhabited ADJECTIVE An uninhabited place is a place where nobody lives.

uninhibited ADJECTIVE If you are uninhibited, you behave freely and naturally and show your true feelings.

unintelligible ADJECTIVE (*formal*) impossible to understand.

uninterested ADJECTIVE If you are uninterested in something, you are not interested in it.

> **uninterested** ADJECTIVE
> = apathetic, bored, impassive, indifferent, nonchalant, passive, unconcerned
> ≠ interested

uninterrupted ADJECTIVE continuing without breaks or interruptions • *uninterrupted views.*

union NOUN ① an organisation of people or groups with mutual interests, especially workers aiming to improve their pay and conditions. ② When the union of two things takes place, they are joined together to become one thing.

> **union** NOUN
> ① = association, coalition, confederation, federation, league
> ② = amalgamation, blend, combination, fusion, mixture

unique *[Said yoo-**neek**]* ADJECTIVE ① being the only one of its kind. ② If something is unique to one person or thing, it concerns or belongs to that person or thing only • *trees and vegetation unique to the Canary islands.* **uniquely** ADVERB **uniqueness** NOUN

unisex ADJECTIVE designed to be used by both men and women • *unisex clothing.*

unison NOUN If a group of people do something in unison, they all do it together at the same time.

unit NOUN ① If you consider something as a unit, you consider it as a single complete thing. ② a group of people who work together at a particular job • *the Police Support Unit.* ③ a machine or piece of equipment which has a particular function • *a remote control unit.* ④ A unit of measurement is a fixed standard that is used for measuring things.

unite VERB If a number of people unite, they join together and act as a group.

> **unite** VERB
> = collaborate, combine, join, join forces, link up, merge, pull together, work together
> ≠ divide

United Kingdom NOUN The United Kingdom consists of Great Britain and Northern Ireland.

United Nations NOUN The United Nations is an international organisation which tries to encourage peace, cooperation and friendship between countries.

unity NOUN Where there is unity, people are in agreement and act together for a particular purpose.

universal ADJECTIVE concerning or relating to everyone in the world or every part of the universe • *Music and sports programmes have a universal appeal* • *universal destruction.* **universally** ADVERB

> **universal** ADJECTIVE
> = common, general, unlimited, widespread, worldwide

universe NOUN The universe is the whole of space, including all the stars and planets.

university, **universities** NOUN a place where students study for degrees.

unjust ADJECTIVE not fair or reasonable. **unjustly** ADVERB

unjustified ADJECTIVE If a belief or action is unjustified, there is no good reason for it.

unkempt ADJECTIVE untidy and not looked after properly • *unkempt hair.*

unkind ADJECTIVE unpleasant and rather cruel. **unkindly** ADVERB **unkindness** NOUN

> **unkind** ADJECTIVE
> = cruel, malicious, mean, nasty, spiteful, thoughtless
> ≠ kind

unknown ADJECTIVE ① If someone or something is unknown, people do not know about them or have not heard of them. ▶ NOUN ② You can refer to the things that people in general do not know about as the unknown.

> **unknown** ADJECTIVE
> ① = humble, obscure, unfamiliar, unsung
> ≠ famous

unlawful ADJECTIVE not legal • *the unlawful possession of a gun.*

unleaded ADJECTIVE Unleaded petrol has a reduced amount of lead in it in order to reduce the pollution from cars.

unleash VERB When a powerful or violent force is unleashed, it is released.

unless CONJUNCTION You use 'unless' to introduce the only circumstances in which something will not take place or is not true • *Unless it was raining, they played in the little garden.*

unlike PREPOSITION ① You can use 'unlike' to show how two people, things or situations are different from each other • *Unlike me, she enjoys ballet.* ▶ ADJECTIVE ② If one thing is unlike another, the two things are different.

> **unlike** ADJECTIVE
> ② = different from, dissimilar to, distinct from, divergent from (*formal*), far from
> ≠ like

unlikely ADJECTIVE ① If something is unlikely, it is probably not true or probably will not happen. ② strange and unexpected • *There are riches in unlikely places.*

> **unlikely** ADJECTIVE
> ① = implausible, incredible, unbelievable, unconvincing
> ≠ likely

unlimited ADJECTIVE If a supply of something is unlimited, you can have as much as you want or need.

unload VERB If you unload things from a container or vehicle, you remove them.

unlock VERB If you unlock a door or container, you open it by turning a key in the lock.

unlucky ADJECTIVE Someone who is unlucky has bad luck. **unluckily** ADVERB

> **unlucky** ADJECTIVE
> = cursed, hapless, luckless, unfortunate, wretched
> ≠ lucky

unmarked ADJECTIVE ① with no marks of damage or injury. ② with no signs or marks of identification • *unmarked police cars.*

unmistakable; also spelt **unmistakeable** ADJECTIVE Something unmistakable is so obvious that it cannot be mistaken for something else. **unmistakably** ADVERB

unmitigated ADJECTIVE (*formal*) You use unmitigated to describe a situation or quality that is completely bad • *an unmitigated disaster.*

unmoved ADJECTIVE not emotionally affected • *He is unmoved by criticism.*

unnatural ADJECTIVE ① strange and rather frightening because it is not usual • *There was an unnatural stillness.* ② artificial and not typical • *My voice sounded high-pitched and unnatural.* **unnaturally** ADVERB

unnecessary ADJECTIVE If something is unnecessary, there is no need for it to happen or be done. **unnecessarily** ADVERB

> **unnecessary** ADJECTIVE
> = needless, pointless, uncalled-for
> ≠ necessary

unnerve VERB If something unnerves you, it frightens or startles you. **unnerving** ADJECTIVE

unobtrusive ADJECTIVE Something that is unobtrusive does not draw attention to itself.

unoccupied ADJECTIVE not occupied. For example, if a house is unoccupied, there is nobody living in it.

unofficial ADJECTIVE without the approval or permission of a person in authority • *unofficial strikes*. **unofficially** ADVERB

unorthodox ADJECTIVE unusual and not generally accepted • *an unorthodox theory*.

unpack VERB When you unpack, you take everything out of a suitcase or bag.

unpaid ADJECTIVE ① If you do unpaid work, you do not receive any money for doing it. ② An unpaid bill has not yet been paid.

unpalatable ADJECTIVE ① Unpalatable food is unpleasant to eat. ② An unpalatable idea is so unpleasant that it is difficult to accept.

unparalleled ADJECTIVE greater than anything else of its kind • *an unparalleled success*.

unpleasant ADJECTIVE ① Something unpleasant causes you to have bad feelings, for example by making you uncomfortable or upset. ② An unpleasant person is unfriendly or rude. **unpleasantly** ADVERB **unpleasantness** NOUN

> **unpleasant** ADJECTIVE
> ① = bad, disagreeable, distasteful, nasty, repulsive, unpalatable
> ≠ pleasant
> ② = disagreeable, horrid (*old-fashioned*), objectionable, obnoxious, rude, unfriendly
> ≠ pleasant

unpopular ADJECTIVE disliked by most people • *an unpopular idea*.

> **unpopular** ADJECTIVE
> = detested, disliked, shunned, undesirable
> ≠ popular

unprecedented [*Said un-***press***-id-en-tid*] ADJECTIVE (*formal*) Something that is unprecedented has never happened before or is the best of its kind so far.

unpredictable ADJECTIVE If someone or something is unpredictable, you never know how they will behave or react.

> **unpredictable** ADJECTIVE
> = chance, doubtful, hit and miss (*informal*), unforeseeable
> ≠ predictable

unprepared ADJECTIVE If you are unprepared for something, you are not ready for it and are therefore surprised or at a disadvantage when it happens.

unproductive ADJECTIVE not producing anything useful.

unqualified ADJECTIVE ① having no qualifications or not having the right qualifications for a particular job • *supervision of unqualified doctors*. ② total • *an unqualified success*.

unquestionable ADJECTIVE so obviously true or real that nobody can doubt it • *His devotion is unquestionable*. **unquestionably** ADVERB

unravel, unravels, unravelling, unravelled VERB ① If you unravel something such as a twisted and knotted piece of string, you unwind it so that it is straight. ② If you unravel a mystery, you work out the answer to it.

unreal ADJECTIVE so strange that you find it difficult to believe.

unrealistic ADJECTIVE ① An unrealistic person does not face the truth about something or deal with it in a practical way. ② Something unrealistic is not true to life • *an unrealistic picture.*

unreasonable ADJECTIVE unfair and difficult to deal with or justify • *an unreasonable request.* **unreasonably** ADVERB

unrelated ADJECTIVE Things that are unrelated have no connection with each other.

unrelenting ADJECTIVE continuing in a determined way • *unrelenting criticism.*

unreliable ADJECTIVE If people, machines or methods are unreliable, you cannot rely on them.

unremitting ADJECTIVE never stopping.

unrest NOUN If there is unrest, people are angry and dissatisfied.

unrivalled ADJECTIVE better than anything else of its kind • *an unrivalled range of health and beauty treatments.*

unruly ADJECTIVE difficult to control or organise • *unruly children* • *unruly hair.*

unsatisfactory ADJECTIVE not good enough.

unsatisfactory ADJECTIVE
= disappointing, inadequate, mediocre, poor, unacceptable
≠ satisfactory

unscathed ADJECTIVE not injured or harmed as a result of a dangerous experience.

unscrupulous ADJECTIVE willing to behave dishonestly in order to get what you want.

unseemly ADJECTIVE Unseemly behaviour is not suitable for a particular situation and shows a lack of control and good manners • *an unseemly squabble.*

unseen ADJECTIVE You use 'unseen' to describe things that you cannot see or have not seen.

unsettle VERB If something unsettles you, it makes you restless or worried.

unshakable; also spelt **unshakeable** ADJECTIVE An unshakable belief is so strong that it cannot be destroyed.

unsightly ADJECTIVE very ugly • *an unsightly scar.*

unskilled ADJECTIVE Unskilled work does not require any special training or ability.

unsolicited ADJECTIVE given or happening without being asked for.

unsound ADJECTIVE ① If a conclusion or method is unsound, it is based on ideas that are likely to be wrong. ② An unsound building is likely to collapse.

unspeakable ADJECTIVE very unpleasant.

unspecified ADJECTIVE You say that something is unspecified when you are not told exactly what it is • *It was being stored in some unspecified place.*

unspoilt or **unspoiled** ADJECTIVE If you describe a place as unspoilt or unspoiled, you mean it has not been changed and it is still in its natural or original state.

unspoken ADJECTIVE An unspoken wish or feeling is one that is not mentioned to other people.

unstable ADJECTIVE ① likely to change suddenly and create difficulty or danger • *The political situation in Moscow is unstable.* ② not firm or fixed properly and likely to wobble or fall.

unsteady ADJECTIVE ① having difficulty in controlling the movement of your legs or hands • *unsteady on her feet.* ② not held or fixed securely and likely to fall over. **unsteadily** ADVERB

unsteady ADJECTIVE
② = precarious, rickety, shaky, tottering, unsafe, unstable, wobbly
≠ steady

unstuck ADJECTIVE separated from the thing that it was stuck to.

unsuccessful ADJECTIVE If you are unsuccessful, you do not succeed in what you are trying to do.
unsuccessfully ADVERB

unsuitable ADJECTIVE not right or appropriate for a particular purpose.
unsuitably ADVERB

unsuitable ADJECTIVE
= improper, inappropriate, unacceptable, unfit
≠ suitable

unsuited ADJECTIVE not appropriate for a particular task or situation • *He's totally unsuited to the job.*

unsung ADJECTIVE You use 'unsung' to describe someone who is not appreciated or praised for their good work • *George is the unsung hero of the club.*

unsure ADJECTIVE uncertain or doubtful.

unsuspecting ADJECTIVE having no idea of what is happening or going to happen • *His horse escaped and collided with an unsuspecting cyclist.*

untangle VERB If you untangle something that is twisted together, you undo the twists.

untenable ADJECTIVE (*formal*) A theory, argument or position that is untenable cannot be successfully defended.

unthinkable ADJECTIVE so shocking or awful that you cannot imagine it to be true.

untidy, **untidier**, **untidiest** ADJECTIVE not neat or well arranged. **untidily** ADVERB

untidy ADJECTIVE
= bedraggled, chaotic, cluttered, jumbled, messy, unkempt
≠ tidy

until PREPOSITION, CONJUNCTION ① If something happens until a particular time, it happens before that time and stops at that time • *The shop stayed open until midnight* • *She waited until her sister was asleep and crept out.* ② If something does not happen until a particular time, it does not happen before that time and only starts happening at that time • *It didn't rain until the middle of the afternoon* • *It was not until they arrived that they found out who he was.*

untimely ADJECTIVE happening too soon or sooner than expected • *his untimely death.*

unto PREPOSITION (*old-fashioned*) Unto means the same as to • *Nation shall speak peace unto nation.*

untold ADJECTIVE You use untold to emphasise how great or extreme something is • *The island possessed untold wealth.*

untouched ADJECTIVE ① not changed, moved or damaged • *a small village untouched by tourism.* ② If a meal is untouched, none of it has been eaten.

untoward ADJECTIVE unexpected and causing difficulties • *no untoward problems.*

untrue ADJECTIVE not true.

untrue ADJECTIVE
= erroneous (*formal*), false, fictitious, inaccurate, incorrect, misleading, mistaken
≠ true

unused ADJECTIVE ① [*Said un-**yoozd***] not yet used. ② [*Said un-**yoost***] If you are unused to something, you have not often done or experienced it.

unusual ADJECTIVE Something that is unusual does not occur very often.
unusually ADVERB

unusual ADJECTIVE
= curious, exceptional, extraordinary, rare, uncommon, unconventional
≠ common

A B C D E F G H I J K L M N O P Q R S T U V W X Y Z

unveil VERB When someone unveils a new statue or plaque, they draw back a curtain that is covering it.

unwanted ADJECTIVE Unwanted things are not desired or wanted, either by a particular person or by people in general • *He felt lonely and unwanted.*

unwarranted ADJECTIVE (*formal*) not justified or not deserved • *unwarranted fears.*

unwelcome ADJECTIVE not wanted • *an unwelcome visitor* • *unwelcome news.*

unwell ADJECTIVE If you are unwell, you are ill.

> **unwell** ADJECTIVE
> = ailing, crook (*Australian and New Zealand; informal*), ill, poorly (*British; informal*), queasy, sick
> ≠ well

unwieldy ADJECTIVE difficult to move or carry because of being large or an awkward shape.

unwilling ADJECTIVE If you are unwilling to do something, you do not want to do it. **unwillingly** ADVERB

> **unwilling** ADJECTIVE
> = averse, grudging, loath, reluctant
> ≠ willing

unwind, **unwinds**, **unwinding**, **unwound** VERB ① When you unwind after working hard, you relax. ② If you unwind something that is wrapped round something else, you undo it.

unwise ADJECTIVE foolish or not sensible.

> **unwise** ADJECTIVE
> = daft (*British; informal*), foolish, idiotic, irresponsible, rash, senseless, silly, stupid
> ≠ wise

unwitting ADJECTIVE Unwitting describes someone who becomes involved in something without realising what is really happening • *her unwitting victims.* **unwittingly** ADVERB

unworthy ADJECTIVE (*formal*) Someone who is unworthy of something does not deserve it.

unwound the past tense and past participle of **unwind**.

unwrap, **unwraps**, **unwrapping**, **unwrapped** VERB When you unwrap something, you take off the paper or covering around it.

unwritten ADJECTIVE An unwritten law is one which is generally understood and accepted without being officially laid down.

up ADVERB, PREPOSITION ① towards or in a higher place • *He ran up the stairs* • *high up in the mountains.* ② towards or in the north • *I'm flying up to Darwin.* ▶ PREPOSITION ③ If you go up a road or river, you go along it. ④ You use 'up to' to say how large something can be or what level it has reached • *traffic jams up to 15 kilometres long.* ⑤ (*informal*) If someone is up to something, they are secretly doing something they should not be doing. ⑥ If it is up to someone to do something, it is their responsibility. ▶ ADJECTIVE ⑦ If you are up, you are not in bed. ⑧ If a period of time is up, it has come to an end. ▶ ADVERB ⑨ If an amount of something goes up, it increases.

up-and-coming ADJECTIVE Up-and-coming people are likely to be successful.

upbringing NOUN Your upbringing is the way that your parents have taught you to behave.

update VERB If you update something, you make it more modern or add new information to it • *He updated his timetable for the new term.*

upgrade VERB If a person or their job is upgraded, they are given more responsibility or status and usually more money.

upheaval NOUN a big change which causes a lot of trouble.

upheld the past tense and past participle of **uphold**.

uphill ADVERB ① If you go uphill, you go up a slope. ▶ ADJECTIVE ② An uphill task requires a lot of effort and determination.

uphold, upholds, upholding, upheld VERB If someone upholds a law or a decision, they support and maintain it.

upholstery NOUN Upholstery is the soft covering on chairs and sofas that makes them comfortable.

upkeep NOUN The upkeep of something is the continual process and cost of keeping it in good condition.

> **upkeep** NOUN
> = keep, maintenance, overheads, preservation, running

upland ADJECTIVE ① An upland area is an area of high land. ▶ NOUN ② (*in plural*) Uplands are areas of high land.

uplifting ADJECTIVE something that is uplifting makes you feel happy.

upload [ICT] VERB ① If you upload data you transfer it from the memory of a computer to a larger computer system. ▶ NOUN ② a piece of data transferred in this way.

upon PREPOSITION ① (*formal*) Upon means on • *I stood upon the stair.* ② You use upon when mentioning an event that is immediately followed by another • *Upon entering the hall he took a quick glance round.* ③ If an event is upon you, it is about to happen • *The football season is upon us once more.*

upper ADJECTIVE ① referring to something that is above something else, or the higher part of something • *the upper arm.* ▶ NOUN ② the top part of a shoe.

upper class NOUN The upper classes are people who belong to a very wealthy or aristocratic group in a society.

uppermost ADJECTIVE, ADVERB ① on top or in the highest position • *the uppermost leaves* • *Lay your arms beside your body with the palms turned uppermost.* ▶ ADJECTIVE ② most important • *His family is now uppermost in his mind.*

upright ADJECTIVE, ADVERB ① standing or sitting up straight, rather than bending or lying down. ② behaving in a very respectable and moral way.

uprising NOUN If there is an uprising, a large group of people begin fighting against the existing government to bring about political changes.

uproar NOUN If there is uproar or an uproar, there is a lot of shouting and noise, often because people are angry.

uproot VERB ① If someone is uprooted, they have to leave the place where they have lived for a long time. ② If a tree is uprooted, it is pulled out of the ground.

upset, upsets, upsetting, upset ADJECTIVE [*Said up-***set**] ① worried or unhappy. ▶ VERB [*Said up-***set**] ② If something upsets you, it makes you feel worried or unhappy. ③ If you upset something, you turn it over or spill it accidentally. ▶ NOUN [*Said* ***up****-set*] ④ A stomach upset is a slight stomach illness caused by an infection or by something you have eaten.

> **upset** ADJECTIVE
> ① = agitated, distressed, frantic, hurt, troubled, unhappy
> ▶ VERB ② = agitate, bother, distress, disturb, grieve, ruffle
> ③ = capsize, knock over, overturn, spill

upshot NOUN The upshot of a series of events is the final result.

upside down ADJECTIVE, ADVERB the wrong way up.

upstage VERB If someone upstages you, they draw people's attention away from you by being more attractive or interesting.

upstairs ADVERB ① If you go upstairs in a building, you go up to a higher floor. ▸ ADJECTIVE, ADVERB ② on a higher floor or on the top floor. ▸ NOUN ③ The upstairs of a building is its upper floor or floors.

upstart NOUN someone who has risen too quickly to an important position and is too arrogant.

upstream ADVERB towards the source of a river • *They made their way upstream.*

upsurge NOUN An upsurge of something is a sudden large increase in it.

uptake NOUN You can say that someone is quick on the uptake if they understand things quickly.

uptight ADJECTIVE (*informal*) tense or annoyed.

up-to-date ADJECTIVE ① being the newest thing of its kind. ② having the latest information.

up-to-the-minute ADJECTIVE Up-to-the-minute information is the latest available information.

upturn NOUN an improvement in a situation.

upturned ADJECTIVE ① pointing upwards • *rain splashing down on her upturned face.* ② upside down • *an upturned bowl.*

upwards ADVERB ① If you move or look upwards, you move or look towards the sky or towards a higher level • *People stared upwards and pointed.* ② If an amount or rate moves upwards, it increases. **upward** ADJECTIVE

uranium [*Said yoo-**ray**-nee-um*] NOUN SCIENCE Uranium is a radioactive metallic element used in the production of nuclear power and weapons. Its atomic number is 92 and its symbol is U.

Uranus NOUN Uranus is the planet in the solar system which is seventh from the sun.

urban ADJECTIVE GEOGRAPHY relating to a town or city • *She found urban life very different from country life.*

urbane ADJECTIVE well-mannered, and comfortable in social situations.

Urdu [*Said **oor**-doo*] NOUN Urdu is the official language of Pakistan. It is also spoken by many people in India.

urge NOUN ① If you have an urge to do something, you have a strong wish to do it. ▸ VERB ② If you urge someone to do something, you try hard to persuade them to do it.

> **urge** NOUN
> ① = compulsion, desire, drive, impulse, longing, wish
> ▸ VERB ② = beg, beseech (*literary*), implore, plead, press

urgent ADJECTIVE needing to be dealt with as soon as possible. **urgently** ADVERB **urgency** NOUN

> **urgent** ADJECTIVE
> = compelling, immediate, imperative, pressing

urinal [*Said yoor-**rye**-nl*] NOUN a bowl or trough fixed to the wall in a public toilet for men to urinate in.

urinate [*Said **yoor**-rin-ate*] VERB When you urinate, you go to the toilet and get rid of urine from your body.

urine [*Said **yoor**-rin*] NOUN the waste liquid that you get rid of from your body when you go to the toilet.

URL NOUN ICT A URL is a technical name for an internet address. URL is an abbreviation for 'uniform resource locator'.

urn **NOUN** a decorated container, especially one that is used to hold the ashes of a person who has been cremated.

us **PRONOUN** A speaker or writer uses us to refer to himself or herself and one or more other people • *Why don't you tell us?*

US or **USA** an abbreviation for 'United States (of America)'.

usage **NOUN** ① the degree to which something is used, or the way in which it is used. ② the way in which words are actually used • *The terms soon entered common usage.*

USB **NOUN** ICT a socket on a computer or other electronic device where you can connect another piece of equipment, such as a keyboard, camera or flash drive. USB is an abbreviation for 'universal serial bus'.

use **VERB** *[Said* ***yooz****]* ① If you use something, you do something with it in order to do a job or achieve something • *May I use your phone?* ② If you use someone, you take advantage of them by making them do things for you. ▶ **NOUN** *[Said* ***yoos****]* ③ The use of something is the act of using it • *the use of force.* ④ If you have the use of something, you have the ability or permission to use it. ⑤ If you find a use for something, you find a purpose for it. **usable**; also spelt **useable** **ADJECTIVE** **user** **NOUN**

> **use** **VERB**
> ① = apply, employ, operate, utilise
> ▶ **NOUN** ③ = application, employment, operation, usage
> ⑤ = end, object, point, purpose

used *[Said* ***yoost****]* **VERB** ① Something that used to be done or used to be true was done or was true in the past. ▶ **PHRASE** ② If you are **used to** something, you are familiar with it and have often experienced it. ▶ **ADJECTIVE** *[Said* ***yoozd****]* ③ A used object has had a previous owner.

useful **ADJECTIVE** If something is useful, you can use it in order to do something or to help you in some way. **usefully** **ADVERB** **usefulness** **NOUN**

> **useful** **ADJECTIVE**
> = beneficial, effective, helpful, practical, valuable, worthwhile
> ≠ useless

useless **ADJECTIVE** ① If something is useless, you cannot use it because it is not suitable or helpful. ② If a course of action is useless, it will not achieve what is wanted.

> **useless** **ADJECTIVE**
> ① = futile, impractical, unproductive, unsuitable, worthless
> ≠ useful

username **NOUN** a name that someone uses when logging into a computer or website.

usher **VERB** ① If you usher someone somewhere, you show them where to go by going with them. ▶ **NOUN** ② a person who shows people where to sit at a wedding or a concert.

USSR HISTORY an abbreviation for 'Union of Soviet Socialist Republics', a country which was made up of a lot of smaller countries including Russia, but which is now broken up.

usual **ADJECTIVE** ① happening, done or used most often • *his usual seat.* ▶ **PHRASE** ② If you do something **as usual**, you do it in the way that you normally do it, or you do something that you do regularly. **usually** **ADVERB**

> **usual** **ADJECTIVE**
> ① = accustomed, common, customary, habitual, normal, regular, standard

usurp *[Said yoo-**zerp**]* VERB *(formal)* If someone usurps another person's job or title they take it when they have no right to do so.

ute *[Said **yoot**]* NOUN *(informal)* in Australian and New Zealand English, a ute is a utility truck.

utensil *[Said yoo-**ten**-sil]* NOUN Utensils are tools • *cooking utensils.*

uterus *[Said **yoo**-ter-russ]* NOUN SCIENCE A woman's uterus is her womb.

utilise; also spelt **utilize** VERB *(formal)* To utilise something is to use it. **utilisation** NOUN

utility, **utilities** NOUN ① The utility of something is its usefulness. ② a service, such as water or gas, that is provided for everyone.

utmost ADJECTIVE used to emphasise a particular quality • *I have the utmost respect for Richard.*

utter VERB ① When you utter sounds or words, you make or say them. ▶ ADJECTIVE ② Utter means complete or total • *scenes of utter chaos.* **utterly** ADVERB

utter ADJECTIVE
② = absolute, complete, consummate, out-and-out, outright, perfect, pure, sheer, thorough, total

utterance NOUN something that is said • *his first utterance.*

Vv

vacant ADJECTIVE ① If something is vacant, it is not occupied or being used. ② If a job or position is vacant, no-one holds it at present. ③ A vacant look suggests that someone does not understand something or is not very intelligent. **vacancy** NOUN **vacantly** ADVERB

vacate VERB (*formal*) If you vacate a room or job, you leave it and it becomes available for someone else.

vacation NOUN ① the period between academic terms at a university or college • *the summer vacation*. ② a holiday.

vaccinate [*Said* **vak**-*sin-ate*] VERB To vaccinate someone means to give them a vaccine, usually by injection, to protect them against a disease. **vaccination** NOUN

vaccine [*Said* **vak**-*seen*] NOUN a substance made from the germs that cause a disease, given to people to make them immune to that disease.

vacuum [*Said* **vak**-*yoom*] NOUN ① SCIENCE a space containing no air, gases or other matter. ▸ VERB ② If you vacuum something, you clean it using a vacuum cleaner.

vacuum cleaner NOUN an electric machine which cleans by sucking up dirt.

vagina [*Said vaj*-**jie**-*na*] NOUN SCIENCE A woman's vagina is the passage that connects her outer sex organs to her womb.

vague [*Said* **vayg**] ADJECTIVE ① If something is vague, it is not expressed or explained clearly, or you cannot see or remember it clearly • *vague statements*. ② Someone looks or sounds vague if they are not concentrating or thinking clearly. **vaguely** ADVERB **vagueness** NOUN

> **vague** ADJECTIVE
> ① = hazy, indefinite, indistinct, loose, uncertain, unclear
> ≠ definite

vain ADJECTIVE ① A vain action or attempt is one which is not successful • *He made a vain effort to cheer her up*. ② A vain person is very proud of their looks, intelligence or other qualities. ▸ PHRASE ③ If you do something **in vain**, you do not succeed in achieving what you intend. **vainly** ADVERB

> **vain** ADJECTIVE
> ① = abortive, fruitless, futile, unproductive, useless
> ≠ successful
> ② = conceited, egotistical, ostentatious, proud, stuck-up (*informal*)
> ▸ PHRASE ③ = fruitless, to no avail, unsuccessful, wasted

valentine NOUN ① Your valentine is someone you love and send a card to on Saint Valentine's Day, February 14th. ② A valentine or a valentine card is the card you send to the person you love on Saint Valentine's Day.

valet [*Said* **val**-*lit or* **val**-*lay*] NOUN a male servant who is employed to look after another man, particularly caring for his clothes.

valiant ADJECTIVE very brave.
valiantly ADVERB

valid ADJECTIVE ① Something that is valid is based on sound reasoning. ② A valid ticket or document is one which is officially accepted.
validity NOUN

validate VERB If something validates a statement or claim, it proves that it is true or correct.

valley NOUN GEOGRAPHY a long stretch of land between hills, often with a river flowing through it.

valour NOUN Valour is great bravery.

valuable ADJECTIVE ① having great importance or usefulness. ② worth a lot of money.

valuable ADJECTIVE
① = beneficial, helpful, important, prized, useful, worthwhile
≠ useless
② = costly, expensive, precious
≠ worthless

valuation NOUN a judgment about how much money something is worth or how good it is.

value, **values**, **valuing**, **valued** NOUN ① The value of something is its importance or usefulness • *information of great value*. ② The value of something you own is the amount of money that it is worth. ③ The values of a group or a person are the moral principles and beliefs that they think are important • *the values of liberty and equality*. ▶ VERB ④ If you value something, you think it is important and you appreciate it. ⑤ When experts value something, they decide how much money it is worth. **valued** ADJECTIVE **valuer** NOUN

value NOUN
① = advantage, benefit, effectiveness, importance, merit, use, usefulness, virtue, worth
② = cost, market price, price, selling price, worth
▶ VERB ④ = appreciate, cherish, have a high opinion of, prize, rate highly, respect, treasure
⑤ = appraise, assess, cost, estimate, evaluate, price

valve NOUN ① a part attached to a pipe or tube which controls the flow of gas or liquid. ② a small flap in your heart or in a vein which controls the flow and direction of blood.

vampire NOUN In horror stories, vampires are corpses that come out of their graves at night and suck the blood of living people.

van NOUN a covered vehicle larger than a car but smaller than a lorry, used for carrying goods.

vandal NOUN someone who deliberately damages or destroys things, particularly public property.
vandalise VERB **vandalism** NOUN

vanguard *[Said van-gard]* NOUN If someone is in the vanguard of something, they are in the most advanced part of it.

vanilla NOUN Vanilla is a flavouring for food such as ice cream, which comes from the pods of a tropical plant.

vanish VERB ① If something vanishes, it disappears • *The moon vanished behind a cloud*. ② If something vanishes, it ceases to exist • *a vanishing civilisation*.

vanish VERB
① = become invisible, be lost to view, disappear, fade, recede
≠ appear
② = become extinct, cease, cease to exist, die out, dissolve, evaporate, fade away, go away, melt away, pass

vanity NOUN Vanity is a feeling of excessive pride about your looks or abilities.

vanquish *[Said **vang**-kwish]* **VERB** (*literary*) To vanquish someone means to defeat them completely.

> **vanquish VERB**
> = beat, conquer, crush, defeat, overcome, rout, trounce

vapour NOUN SCIENCE Vapour is a mass of tiny drops of water or other liquids in the air which looks like mist.

variable ADJECTIVE ① Something that is variable is likely to change at any time. ▶ **NOUN** ② In any situation, a variable is something in it that can change. ③ MATHS a symbol such as x which can represent any value or any one of a set of values. **variability NOUN**

variance NOUN If one thing is at variance with another, the two seem to contradict each other.

variant NOUN ① A variant of something has a different form from the usual one, for example *gaol* is a variant of *jail*. ▶ **ADJECTIVE** ② alternative or different.

variation NOUN ① a change from the normal or usual pattern • *a variation of the same route*. ② a change in level, amount or quantity • *a large variation in demand*.

> **variation NOUN**
> ① = alteration, change, departure, deviation, difference, diversion

varicose veins PLURAL NOUN Varicose veins are swollen painful veins in the legs.

varied ADJECTIVE of different types, quantities or sizes.

variety, **varieties NOUN** ① If something has variety, it consists of things which are not all the same. ② A variety of things is a number of different kinds of them • *a wide variety of readers*. ③ A variety of something is a particular type of it • *a new variety of celery*. ④ Variety is a form of entertainment consisting of short unrelated acts, such as singing, dancing and comedy.

> **variety NOUN**
> ② = array, assortment, collection, medley, mixture, range
> ③ = category, class, kind, sort, strain, type

various ADJECTIVE Various means of several different types • *trees of various sorts*. **variously ADVERB**

> **various ADJECTIVE**
> = assorted, different, disparate, diverse, miscellaneous, sundry

varnish NOUN ① a liquid which when painted onto a surface gives it a hard, clear, shiny finish. ▶ **VERB** ② If you varnish something, you paint it with varnish.

vary, **varies**, **varying**, **varied VERB** ① If things vary, they change • *Weather patterns vary greatly*. ② If you vary something, you introduce changes in it • *Vary your routes as much as possible*. **varied ADJECTIVE**

> **vary VERB**
> ① = alter, alternate, change, fluctuate
> ② = alternate, diversify, modify

vascular ADJECTIVE relating to tubes or ducts that carry fluids within animals or plants.

vase NOUN a glass or china jar for flowers.

vasectomy, **vasectomies** *[Said vas-**sek**-tom-ee]* **NOUN** an operation to sterilise a man by cutting the tube in his body that carries the sperm.

Vaseline NOUN (*trademark*) Vaseline is a soft, clear jelly made from petroleum and used as an ointment or as grease.

vast ADJECTIVE extremely large.

vastly ADVERB **vastness** NOUN

vast ADJECTIVE
= colossal, enormous, giant, gigantic, great, huge, immense, massive
≠ tiny

vat NOUN a large container for liquids.

VAT *[Said **vee-ay-tee** or **vat**]* NOUN In Britain, VAT is a tax which is added to the costs of making or providing goods and services. VAT is an abbreviation for 'value-added tax'.

vault *[Rhymes with **salt**]* NOUN ① a strong secure room, often underneath a building, where valuables are stored, or underneath a church where people are buried. ② an arched roof, often found in churches. ▶ VERB ③ If you vault over something, you jump over it using your hands or a pole to help.

veal NOUN Veal is the meat from a calf.

veer VERB If something which is moving veers in a particular direction, it suddenly changes course • *The aircraft veered sharply to one side.*

vegan *[Said **vee-gn**]* NOUN someone who does not eat any food made from animal products, such as meat, eggs, cheese or milk.

vegetable NOUN ① Vegetables are edible roots or leaves such as carrots or cabbage. ▶ ADJECTIVE ② Vegetable is used to refer to any plants in contrast to animals or minerals • *vegetable life.*

vegetarian NOUN a person who does not eat meat, poultry or fish. **vegetarianism** NOUN

vegetation NOUN GEOGRAPHY Vegetation is the plants in a particular area.

vehement *[Said **vee-im-ent**]* ADJECTIVE Someone who is vehement has strong feelings or opinions and expresses them forcefully • *He wrote a letter of vehement protest.* **vehemence** NOUN **vehemently** ADVERB

vehicle *[Said **vee-ik-kl**]* NOUN ① a machine, often with an engine, used for transporting people or goods. ② something used to achieve a particular purpose or as a means of expression • *The play seemed an ideal vehicle for his music.* **vehicular** ADJECTIVE

veil *[Rhymes with **male**]* NOUN a piece of thin, soft cloth that women sometimes wear over their heads. **veiled** ADJECTIVE

vein *[Rhymes with **rain**]* NOUN ① Your veins are the tubes in your body through which your blood flows to your heart. ② Veins are the thin lines on leaves or on insects' wings. ③ A vein of a metal or a mineral is a layer of it in rock. ④ Something that is in a particular vein is in that style or mood • *in a more serious vein.*

veld *[Said **felt**]* NOUN The veld is flat high grassland in Southern Africa.

velocity NOUN (*technical*) Velocity is the speed at which something is moving in a particular direction.

velvet NOUN Velvet is a very soft material which has a thick layer of fine short threads on one side. **velvety** ADJECTIVE

vendetta NOUN a long-lasting bitter quarrel in which people try to harm each other.

vendor NOUN a person who sells something.

veneer NOUN ① You can refer to a superficial quality that someone has as a veneer of that quality • *a veneer of calm.* ② Veneer is a thin layer of wood or plastic used to cover a surface.

venerable ADJECTIVE ① A venerable person is someone you treat with respect because they are old and wise. ② Something that is venerable is impressive because it is old or important historically.

vengeance NOUN ① Vengeance is the act of harming someone because they have harmed you. ▶ PHRASE ② If something happens **with a vengeance**, it happens to a much greater extent than was expected • *It began to rain again with a vengeance.*

venison NOUN Venison is the meat from a deer.

venom NOUN ① The venom of a snake, scorpion or spider is its poison. ② Venom is a feeling of great bitterness or spitefulness towards someone • *He was glaring at me with venom.* **venomous** ADJECTIVE

vent NOUN ① a hole in something through which gases and smoke can escape and fresh air can enter • *air vents.* ▶ VERB ② If you vent strong feelings, you express them • *She wanted to vent her anger upon me.* ▶ PHRASE ③ If you **give vent** to strong feelings, you express them • *Pamela gave vent to a lot of bitterness.*

ventilate VERB To ventilate a room means to allow fresh air into it. **ventilated** ADJECTIVE

ventilation NOUN ① Ventilation is the process of breathing air in and out of the lungs. ② A ventilation system supplies fresh air into a building.

ventilator NOUN a machine that helps people breathe when they cannot breathe naturally, for example if they are very ill.

ventriloquist *[Said ven-**trill**-o-kwist]* NOUN an entertainer who can speak without moving their lips so that the words seem to come from a dummy. **ventriloquism** NOUN

venture NOUN ① something new which involves the risk of failure or of losing money • *a successful venture in television films.* ▶ VERB ② If you venture something such as an opinion, you say it cautiously or hesitantly because you are afraid it might be foolish or wrong • *I would not venture to agree.* ③ If you venture somewhere that might be dangerous, you go there.

venue *[Said **ven**-yoo]* NOUN The venue for an event is the place where it will happen.

Venus NOUN Venus is the planet in the solar system which is second from the sun.

veranda *[Said ver-**ran**-da]*; also spelt **verandah** NOUN a platform with a roof that is attached to an outside wall of a house at ground level.

verb NOUN [ENGLISH] [MFL] In grammar, a verb is a word that expresses actions and states, for example 'be', 'become', 'take' and 'run'.

verbal ADJECTIVE ① [ENGLISH] You use 'verbal' to describe things connected with words and their use • *verbal attacks on referees.* ② 'Verbal' describes things which are spoken rather than written • *a verbal agreement.* **verbally** ADVERB

verdict NOUN ① In a law court, a verdict is the decision which states whether a prisoner is guilty or not guilty. ② If you give a verdict on something, you give your opinion after thinking about it.

> **verdict** NOUN
> ② = conclusion, decision, finding, judgment, opinion

verge NOUN ① The verge of a road is the narrow strip of grassy ground at the side. ▶ PHRASE ② If you are **on the verge** of something, you are going to do it soon or it is likely to happen soon • *on the verge of crying.* ▶ VERB ③ Something that verges on something else is almost the same as it • *dark blue that verged on purple.*

verify, **verifies, verifying, verified** VERB If you verify something, you check that it is true • *None of his statements could be verified.* **verifiable** ADJECTIVE **verification** NOUN

veritable ADJECTIVE You use veritable to emphasise something • *a veritable jungle of shops.*

vermin PLURAL NOUN Vermin are small animals or insects, such as rats and cockroaches, which carry disease and damage crops.

vernacular *[Said ver-**nak**-yoo-lar]* NOUN The vernacular of a particular country or district is the language widely spoken there.

versatile ADJECTIVE ① If someone is versatile, they have many different skills. ② If a tool or material is versatile, it can be used for many different purposes. **versatility** NOUN

verse NOUN ① Verse is another word for poetry. ② one part of a poem or song, or a chapter of the Bible.

versed ADJECTIVE If you are versed in something, you know a lot about it.

version NOUN ① A version of something is a form of it in which some details are different from earlier or later forms • *a cheaper version of the aircraft.* ② Someone's version of an event is their personal description of what happened.

versus PREPOSITION Versus is used to indicate that two people or teams are competing against each other.

vertebra, **vertebrae** *[Said **ver**-tib-bra]* NOUN [SCIENCE] Vertebrae are the small bones which form a person's or animal's backbone.

vertebrate NOUN [SCIENCE] Vertebrates are any creatures which have a backbone.

vertical ADJECTIVE [MATHS] Something that is vertical points straight up and forms a ninety-degree angle with the surface on which it stands.
vertically ADVERB

vertigo NOUN Vertigo is a feeling of dizziness caused by looking down from a high place.

verve NOUN Verve is lively and forceful enthusiasm.

very ADVERB ① to a great degree • *very bad dreams.* ▶ ADJECTIVE ② 'Very' is used before words to emphasise them • *the very end of the book.* ▶ PHRASE ③ You use 'not very' to mean that something is the case only to a small degree • *You're not very like your sister.*

very ADVERB
① = deeply, extremely, greatly, highly, really, terribly

vessel NOUN ① a ship or large boat. ② *(literary)* any bowl or container in which a liquid can be kept. ③ a thin tube along which liquids such as blood or sap move in animals and plants.

vest NOUN a piece of underwear worn for warmth on the top half of the body.

vestige *[Said **vest**-ij]* NOUN *(formal)* A vestige is a tiny part of something that is left over when the rest has been used up • *They have a vestige of strength left.*

vet, **vets, vetting, vetted** NOUN ① a doctor for animals. ▶ VERB ② If you vet someone or something, you check them carefully to see if they are acceptable • *He refused to let them vet his speeches.*

veteran NOUN ① someone who has served in the armed forces, particularly during a war.
② someone who has been involved in a particular activity for a long time • *a veteran of 25 political campaigns.*

veterinary *[Said vet-er-in-ar-ee]* ADJECTIVE Veterinary is used to describe the work of a vet and the medical treatment of animals.

veterinary surgeon NOUN the same as a **vet**.

veto, vetoes, vetoing, vetoed *[Said vee-toh]* VERB ① If someone in authority vetoes something, they say no to it. ▶ NOUN ② Veto is the right that someone in authority has to say no to something • *Dr Baker has the power of veto.*

> **veto** VERB
> ① = ban, forbid, prohibit
> ▶ NOUN ② = ban, prohibition

vexed ADJECTIVE If you are vexed, you are annoyed, worried or puzzled.

VHF NOUN VHF is a range of high radio frequencies. VHF is an abbreviation for 'very high frequency'.

via PREPOSITION ① If you go to one place via another, you travel through that place to get to your destination • *He drove directly from Bonn via Paris.* ② Via also means done or achieved by making use of a particular thing or person • *to follow proceedings via newspapers or television.*

viable *[Said vy-a-bl]* ADJECTIVE Something that is viable is capable of doing what it is intended to do without extra help or financial support • *a viable business.* **viability** NOUN

viaduct *[Said vy-a-dukt]* NOUN a long, high bridge that carries a road or railway across a valley.

vibrant ADJECTIVE Something or someone that is vibrant is full of life, energy and enthusiasm. **vibrantly** ADVERB **vibrancy** NOUN

vibrate VERB [SCIENCE] If something vibrates, it moves a tiny amount backwards and forwards very quickly. **vibration** NOUN

vicar NOUN a priest in the Church of England.

vicarage NOUN a house where a vicar lives.

vice NOUN ① a serious moral fault in someone's character, such as greed, or a weakness, such as smoking. ② a tool with a pair of jaws that hold an object tightly while it is being worked on.

vice versa ADVERB 'Vice versa' is used to indicate that the reverse of what you have said is also true • *Brothers sometimes annoy their sisters, and vice versa.*

vicinity *[Said vis-sin-it-ee]* NOUN If something is in the vicinity of a place, it is in the surrounding or nearby area.

vicious ADJECTIVE cruel and violent. **viciously** ADVERB **viciousness** NOUN

victim NOUN someone who has been harmed or injured by someone or something.

victor NOUN The victor in a fight or contest is the person who wins.

Victorian ADJECTIVE ① [HISTORY] Victorian describes things that happened or were made during the reign of Queen Victoria (1837–1901). ② Victorian also describes people or things connected with the state of Victoria in Australia.

victory, victories NOUN a success in a battle or competition. **victorious** ADJECTIVE

> **victory** NOUN
> = laurels, success, superiority, triumph, win
> ≠ defeat

video, videos, videoing, videoed NOUN ① Video is the recording and showing of films and events using a video recorder, video tape and a television set. ② a sound and picture recording which can be played back on a television set. ③ a video recorder.

a b c d e f g h i j k l m n o p q r s t u v w x y z

▶ VERB ④ If you video something, you record it on magnetic tape for later viewing.

vie, **vies**, **vying**, **vied** VERB (*formal*) If you vie with someone, you compete to do something sooner than or better than they do.

Vietnamese [*Said vyet-nam-**meez***] ADJECTIVE ① belonging or relating to Vietnam. ▶ NOUN ② someone who comes from Vietnam. ③ Vietnamese is the main language spoken in Vietnam.

view NOUN ① Your views are your personal opinions • *his political views*. ② everything you can see from a particular place. ▶ VERB ③ If you view something in a particular way, you think of it in that way • *They viewed me with contempt*. ▶ PHRASE ④ You use **in view of** to specify the main fact or event influencing your actions or opinions • *He wore a lighter suit in view of the heat*. ⑤ If something is **on view**, it is being shown or exhibited to the public.

> **view** NOUN
> ① = attitude, belief, conviction, feeling, opinion, point of view
> ② = aspect, landscape, panorama, perspective, scene, spectacle
> ▶ VERB ③ = consider, deem (*formal*), judge, regard

viewer NOUN Viewers are the people who watch television.

viewpoint NOUN ① Your viewpoint is your attitude towards something. ② a place from which you get a good view of an area or event.

> **viewpoint** NOUN
> ① = attitude, belief, conviction, feeling, opinion, point of view

vigil [*Said **vij**-jil*] NOUN a period of time, especially at night, when you stay quietly in one place, for example because you are making a political protest or praying.

vigilant ADJECTIVE careful and alert to danger or trouble. **vigilance** NOUN **vigilantly** ADVERB

vigilante [*Said vij-il-**ant**-ee*] NOUN Vigilantes are unofficially organised groups of people who try to protect their community and catch and punish criminals.

vigorous ADJECTIVE energetic or enthusiastic. **vigorously** ADVERB **vigour** NOUN

Viking NOUN HISTORY The Vikings were seamen from Scandinavia who raided parts of north-western Europe from the 8th to the 11th centuries.

vile ADJECTIVE unpleasant or disgusting • *a vile accusation* • *a vile smell*.

villa NOUN a house, especially a pleasant holiday home in a country with a warm climate.

village NOUN a collection of houses and other buildings in the countryside. **villager** NOUN

villain NOUN ① someone who harms others or breaks the law. ② the main evil character in a story. **villainous** ADJECTIVE **villainy** NOUN

vindicate VERB (*formal*) If someone is vindicated, their views or ideas are proved to be right • *My friend's instincts have been vindicated*. **vindication** NOUN

vindictive ADJECTIVE Someone who is vindictive is deliberately hurtful towards someone, often as an act of revenge. **vindictiveness** NOUN

vine NOUN a trailing or climbing plant which winds itself around and over a support, especially one which produces grapes.

vinegar NOUN Vinegar is a sharp-tasting liquid made from sour wine, beer or cider, which is used for salad dressing. **vinegary** ADJECTIVE

vineyard [*Said **vin**-yard*] NOUN an area of land where grapes are grown.

vintage ADJECTIVE ① A vintage wine is a good quality wine which has been stored for a number of years to improve its quality. ② Vintage describes something which is the best or most typical of its kind • *a vintage guitar*. ③ A vintage car is one made between 1918 and 1930. ▶ NOUN ④ a grape harvest of one particular year and the wine produced from it.

vinyl NOUN Vinyl is a strong plastic used to make things such as furniture and floor coverings.

viola [*Said vee-**oh**-la*] NOUN a musical instrument like a violin, but larger and with a lower pitch.

violate VERB ① If you violate an agreement, law or promise, you break it. ② If you violate someone's peace or privacy, you disturb it. ③ If you violate a place, especially a holy place, you treat it with disrespect or violence. **violation** NOUN

violence NOUN ① Violence is behaviour which is intended to hurt or kill people. ② If you do or say something with violence, you use a lot of energy in doing or saying it, often because you are angry.

> **violence** NOUN
> ① = bloodshed, brutality, cruelty, force, savagery, terrorism
> ② = fervour, force, harshness, intensity, severity, vehemence

violent ADJECTIVE ① If someone is violent, they try to hurt or kill people. ② A violent event happens unexpectedly and with great force. ③ Something that is violent is said, felt or done with great force. **violently** ADVERB

> **violent** ADJECTIVE
> ① = bloodthirsty, brutal, cruel, murderous, savage, vicious
> ≠ gentle
> ② = powerful, raging, rough, strong, turbulent, wild
> ③ = acute, furious, intense, powerful, severe, strong

violet NOUN ① a plant with dark purple flowers. ▶ NOUN, ADJECTIVE ② bluish purple.

violin NOUN a musical instrument with four strings that is held under the chin and played with a bow. **violinist** NOUN

VIP NOUN VIPs are famous or important people. VIP is an abbreviation for 'very important person'.

viral [*Said **vie**-rul*] ADJECTIVE ① relating to or caused by a virus. ▶ ADVERB ② If a story or a video goes viral, it spreads quickly and widely among users of the internet.

virgin ADJECTIVE Something that is virgin is fresh and unused • *virgin land*.

Virgo NOUN Virgo is the sixth sign of the zodiac, represented by a girl. People born between August 23rd and September 22nd are born under this sign.

virile ADJECTIVE A virile man has all the qualities that a man is traditionally expected to have, such as strength. **virility** NOUN

virtual [*Said **vur**-tyool*] ADJECTIVE ① Virtual means that something has all the characteristics of a particular thing, but it is not formally recognised as being that thing • *The country is in a virtual state of war*. ② [ICT] Virtual objects and activities are generated by a computer to simulate real objects and activities. **virtually** ADVERB

virtual reality NOUN [ICT] Virtual reality is a situation or setting that has been created by a computer and that looks real to the person using it.

virtue NOUN ① Virtue is thinking and

doing what is morally right and avoiding what is wrong. ② a good quality in someone's character. ③ A virtue of something is an advantage • *The virtue of neatness is that you can always find things.* ▸ PHRASE ④ (*formal*) **By virtue of** means because of • *The article stuck in my mind by virtue of one detail.*

virtue NOUN
① = goodness, integrity, morality
③ = advantage, asset, attribute, merit, plus (*informal*), strength
▸ PHRASE ④ = as a result of, because of, by dint of, on account of, thanks to

virtuoso, **virtuosos** or **virtuosi** [*Said vur-tyoo-**oh**-soh*] NOUN someone who is exceptionally good at something, particularly playing a musical instrument.

virtuous ADJECTIVE behaving with or showing moral virtue. **virtuously** ADVERB

virus [*Said **vie**-russ*] NOUN ① SCIENCE a kind of germ that can cause disease. ② ICT a program that alters or damages the information stored in a computer system.

visa NOUN an official stamp, usually put in your passport, that allows you to visit a particular country.

visibility NOUN You use visibility to say how far or how clearly you can see in particular weather conditions.

visible ADJECTIVE ① able to be seen. ② noticeable or evident • *There was little visible excitement.* **visibly** ADVERB

visible ADJECTIVE
① = clear, conspicuous, distinguishable, in sight, observable, perceptible
≠ invisible
② = apparent, evident, manifest (*formal*), noticeable, obvious, plain

vision NOUN ① Vision is the ability to see clearly. ② a mental picture, in which you imagine how things might be different • *the vision of a possible future.* ③ Vision is also imaginative insight • *a total lack of vision and imagination.* ④ an unusual experience that some people claim to have, in which they see things that other people cannot see. **visionary** NOUN, ADJECTIVE

vision NOUN
② = conception, daydream, dream, fantasy, ideal, image
③ = foresight, imagination, insight, intuition
④ = apparition, hallucination, illusion, mirage, phantom, spectre

visit VERB ① If you visit someone, you go to see them and spend time with them. ② If you visit a place, you go to see it. ▸ NOUN ③ a trip to see a person or place. **visitor** NOUN

visit VERB
① = call on, go to see, look up
▸ NOUN ③ = call, stay, stop

visor [*Said **vie**-zor*] NOUN a transparent movable shield attached to a helmet, which can be pulled down to protect the eyes or face.

visual ADJECTIVE relating to sight • *a visual inspection.*

visualise [*Said **viz**-yool-eyes*]; also spelt **visualize** VERB If you visualise something, you form a mental picture of it.

vital ADJECTIVE ① necessary or very important • *vital evidence.* ② energetic, exciting and full of life • *an active and vital life outside school.* **vitally** ADVERB

vital ADJECTIVE
① = central, critical, crucial, essential, important, indispensable, necessary, pivotal
② = active, dynamic, energetic, lively, spirited, sprightly, vivacious
≠ dull

vitality NOUN People who have vitality are energetic and lively.

vitamin NOUN [SCIENCE] Vitamins are organic compounds which you need in order to remain healthy. They occur naturally in food.

vivacious [*Said viv-**vay**-shuss*] ADJECTIVE A vivacious person is attractively lively and high-spirited. **vivacity** NOUN

vivid ADJECTIVE very bright in colour or clear in detail • *vivid red paint* • *vivid memories*. **vividly** ADVERB **vividness** NOUN

vixen NOUN a female fox.

vocabulary, **vocabularies** NOUN ① [ENGLISH] Someone's vocabulary is the total number of words they know in a particular language. ② [ENGLISH] The vocabulary of a language is all the words in it.

vocal ADJECTIVE ① You say that someone is vocal if they express their opinions strongly and openly. ② [MUSIC] Vocal means involving the use of the human voice, especially in singing. **vocalist** NOUN **vocally** ADVERB

vocation NOUN ① a strong wish to do a particular job, especially one which involves serving other people. ② a profession or career.

vocational ADJECTIVE 'Vocational' is used to describe the skills needed for a particular job or profession • *vocational training*.

vociferous [*Said voe-**sif**-fer-uss*] ADJECTIVE (*formal*) Someone who is vociferous speaks a lot, or loudly, because they want to make a point strongly • *vociferous critics*. **vociferously** ADVERB

vodka NOUN a strong clear alcoholic drink which originally came from Russia.

vogue [*Said **vohg***] PHRASE If something is **the vogue** or **in vogue**, it is fashionable and popular • *Colour photographs became the vogue*.

voice NOUN ① Your voice is the sounds produced by your vocal cords, or the ability to make such sounds. ▸ VERB ② If you voice an opinion or an emotion, you say what you think or feel • *A range of opinions were voiced*.

void NOUN ① a situation which seems empty because it has no interest or excitement • *Cats fill a very large void in your life*. ② a large empty hole or space • *His feet dangled in the void*.

volatile ADJECTIVE liable to change often and unexpectedly • *The situation at work is volatile*.

volcanic ADJECTIVE A volcanic region has many volcanoes or was created by volcanoes.

volcano, **volcanoes** NOUN [GEOGRAPHY] a hill with an opening through which lava, gas and ash burst out from inside the earth onto the surface.

volition NOUN (*formal*) If you do something of your own volition, you do it because you have decided for yourself, without being persuaded by others • *He attended of his own volition*.

volley NOUN ① A volley of shots or gunfire is a lot of shots fired at the same time. ② In tennis, a volley is a stroke in which the player hits the ball before it bounces.

volleyball NOUN Volleyball is a game in which two teams hit a large ball back and forth over a high net with their hands. The ball is not allowed to bounce on the ground.

volt NOUN [SCIENCE] A volt is a unit of electrical force. One volt produces one amp of electricity when the resistance is one ohm.

voltage NOUN The voltage of an electric current is its force measured in volts.

volume NOUN ① MATHS The volume of something is the amount of space it contains or occupies. ② The volume of something is also the amount of it that there is • *a large volume of letters*. ③ The volume of a radio, TV or MP3 player is the strength of the sound that it produces. ④ a book, or one of a series of books.

voluminous *[Said vol-**loo**-min-uss]* ADJECTIVE very large or full in size or quantity • *voluminous skirts*.

voluntary ADJECTIVE ① Voluntary actions are ones that you do because you choose to do them and not because you have been forced to do them. ② Voluntary work is done by people who are not paid for what they do. **voluntarily** ADVERB

volunteer NOUN ① CITIZENSHIP someone who does work for which they are not paid • *a volunteer for Greenpeace*. ② someone who chooses to join the armed forces, especially during wartime. ▶ VERB ③ CITIZENSHIP If you volunteer to do something, you offer to do it rather than being forced into it. ④ If you volunteer information, you give it without being asked.

voluptuous *[Said vol-**lupt**-yoo-uss]* ADJECTIVE having a figure which is considered to be full and attractive. **voluptuously** ADVERB **voluptuousness** NOUN

vomit VERB ① If you vomit, food and drink comes back up from your stomach and out through your mouth. ▶ NOUN ② Vomit is partly digested food and drink that has come back up from someone's stomach and out through their mouth.

> **vomit** VERB
> ① = be sick, bring up, regurgitate

voodoo NOUN Voodoo is a form of magic practised in the Caribbean, especially in Haiti.

vote NOUN ① CITIZENSHIP Someone's vote is their choice in an election, or at a meeting where decisions are taken. ② When a group of people have a vote, they make a decision by allowing each person in the group to say what they would prefer. ③ In an election, the vote is the total number of people who have made their choice • *the average Liberal vote*. ④ If people have the vote, they have the legal right to vote in an election. ▶ VERB ⑤ CITIZENSHIP When people vote, they indicate their choice or opinion, usually by writing on a piece of paper or by raising their hand. ⑥ If you vote that a particular thing should happen, you are suggesting it should happen • *I vote that we all go to the Netherlands*. **voter** NOUN

> **vote** NOUN
> ② = ballot, plebiscite (*formal*), polls, referendum
> ▶ VERB ⑤ = cast a vote, go to the polls, opt, return
> ⑥ = propose, recommend, suggest

vouch VERB ① If you say that you can vouch for something, you mean that you have evidence from your own experience that it is true or correct. ② If you say that you can vouch for someone, you mean that you are sure that you can guarantee their good behaviour or support • *Her employer will vouch for her*.

voucher NOUN a piece of paper that can be used instead of money to pay for something.

vow VERB ① If you vow to do something, you make a solemn promise to do it • *He vowed to do better in future*. ▶ NOUN ② a solemn promise.

vowel NOUN ENGLISH a sound made without your tongue touching the roof of your mouth or your teeth, or one of the letters a, e, i, o, u, which represent such sounds.

voyage NOUN a long journey on a ship or in a spacecraft. **voyager** NOUN

vulgar ADJECTIVE ① socially unacceptable or offensive • *vulgar language.* ② showing a lack of taste or quality • *IShe thought it was a very vulgar house.* **vulgarity** NOUN **vulgarly** ADVERB

vulgar ADJECTIVE
① = coarse, rude, uncouth
≠ refined
② = common, flashy, gaudy, tacky (*informal*), tasteless, tawdry
≠ sophisticated

vulnerable ADJECTIVE weak and without protection. **vulnerably** ADVERB **vulnerability** NOUN

vulnerable ADJECTIVE
= exposed, sensitive, susceptible, weak

vulture NOUN a large bird which lives in hot countries and eats the flesh of dead animals.

vying the present participle of **vie**.

Ww

wacky, **wackier**, **wackiest** ADJECTIVE (*informal*) odd or crazy • *wacky clothes*.

wad NOUN ① A wad of papers or banknotes is a thick bundle of them. ② A wad of something is a lump of it • *a wad of cotton wool*.

wade VERB ① If you wade through water or mud, you walk slowly through it. ② If you wade through a book or document, you spend a lot of time and effort reading it because you find it dull or difficult.

wafer NOUN ① a thin, crisp, sweet biscuit often eaten with ice cream. ② a thin disc of special bread used in the Christian service of Holy Communion.

waffle [*Said* ***wof****-fl*] VERB ① When someone waffles, they talk or write a lot without being clear or without saying anything of importance. ▶ NOUN ② Waffle is vague and lengthy speech or writing. ③ a thick, crisp pancake with squares marked on it often eaten with syrup poured over it.

waft [*Said* ***wahft***] VERB If a sound or scent wafts or is wafted through the air, it moves gently through it.

wag, **wags**, **wagging**, **wagged** VERB ① When a dog wags its tail, it shakes it repeatedly from side to side. ② If you wag your finger, you move it repeatedly up and down.

wage NOUN ① A wage or wages is the regular payment made to someone each week for the work they do, especially for manual or unskilled work. ▶ VERB ② If a person or country wages a campaign or war, they start it and carry it on over a period of time.

wager NOUN a bet.

wagon; also spelt **waggon** NOUN ① a strong four-wheeled vehicle for carrying heavy loads, usually pulled by a horse or tractor. ② Wagons are also the containers for freight pulled by a railway engine.

waif NOUN a young, thin person who looks hungry and homeless.

wail VERB ① To wail is to cry loudly with sorrow or pain. ▶ NOUN ② a long, unhappy cry.

waist NOUN the middle part of your body where it narrows slightly above your hips.

waistcoat NOUN a sleeveless piece of clothing, often worn under a suit or jacket, which buttons up the front.

wait VERB ① If you wait, you spend time, usually doing little or nothing, before something happens. ② If something can wait, it is not urgent and can be dealt with later. ③ If you wait on people in a restaurant, it is your job to serve them food. ▶ NOUN ④ a period of time before something happens. ▶ PHRASE ⑤ If you **can't wait** to do something, you are very excited and eager to do it.

> **wait** VERB
> ① = linger, pause, remain, stand by, stay
> ▶ NOUN ④ = delay, interval, pause

waiter NOUN a person who works in a

restaurant, serving people with food and drink.

waiting list NOUN a list of people who have asked for something which cannot be given to them immediately, for example medical treatment.

waitress NOUN a woman who works in a restaurant, serving people with food and drink.

waive *[Said wave]* VERB If someone waives something such as a rule or a right, they decide not to insist on it being applied.

wake, **wakes, waking, woke, woken** VERB ① When you wake or when something wakes you, you become conscious again after being asleep. ▶ NOUN ② The wake of a boat or other object moving in water is the track of waves it leaves behind it. ③ a gathering of people who have got together to mourn someone's death. ▶ PHRASE ④ If one thing follows **in the wake of** another, it follows it as a result of it, or in imitation of it • *a project set up in the wake of last year's riots.* **wake up** VERB ① When you wake up or something wakes you up, you become conscious again after being asleep. ② If you wake up to a dangerous situation, you become aware of it.

> **wake** VERB
> ① = awake, come to, rouse, stir, waken

walk VERB ① When you walk, you move along by putting one foot in front of the other on the ground. ② If you walk away with or walk off with something such as a prize, you win it or achieve it easily. ▶ NOUN ③ a journey made by walking • *We'll have a quick walk.* ④ Your walk is the way you walk • *his rolling walk.* **walk out** VERB ① If you walk out on someone, you leave them suddenly. ② If workers walk out, they go on strike.

> **walk** VERB
> ① = amble, hike, march, ramble, step, stride, stroll, wander
> ▶ NOUN ③ = hike, march, ramble, stroll, trek
> ④ = carriage, gait, pace, stride

walkabout NOUN ① an informal walk amongst crowds in a public place by royalty or by some other well-known person. ② Walkabout is a period when an Aboriginal Australian wanders in the bush to return to a traditional way of life.

walker NOUN a person who walks, especially for pleasure or to keep fit.

walking stick NOUN a wooden stick which people can lean on while walking.

walkover NOUN *(informal)* a very easy victory in a competition or contest.

walkway NOUN a passage between two buildings for people to walk along.

wall NOUN ① one of the vertical sides of a building or a room. ② a long, narrow vertical structure made of stone or brick that surrounds or divides an area of land. ③ a lining or membrane enclosing a bodily cavity or structure • *the wall of the womb.*

wallaby, **wallabies** NOUN an Australian animal like a small kangaroo.

wallet NOUN a small, flat case made of leather or plastic, used for keeping paper money and sometimes credit cards.

wallop VERB *(informal)* If you wallop someone, you hit them very hard.

wallow VERB ① If you wallow in an unpleasant feeling or situation, you allow it to continue longer than is reasonable or necessary because you are getting a kind of enjoyment from it • *We're wallowing in misery.* ② When an animal wallows in mud or water, it lies or rolls about in it slowly for pleasure.

wallpaper NOUN Wallpaper is thick coloured or patterned paper for pasting onto the walls of rooms in order to decorate them.

walnut NOUN ① an edible nut with a wrinkled shape and a hard, round, light-brown shell. ② Walnut is wood from the walnut tree which is often used for making expensive furniture.

walrus, **walruses** NOUN an animal which lives in the sea and which looks like a large seal with a tough skin, coarse whiskers, and two tusks.

waltz NOUN ① a dance which has a rhythm of three beats to the bar. ▶ VERB ② If you waltz with someone, you dance a waltz with them. ③ (*informal*) If you waltz somewhere, you walk there in a relaxed and confident way.

wan [*Rhymes with* ***on***] ADJECTIVE pale and tired-looking.

wand NOUN a long, thin rod that magicians wave when they are performing tricks and magic.

wander VERB ① If you wander in a place, you walk around in a casual way. ② If your mind wanders or your thoughts wander, you lose concentration and start thinking about other things. **wanderer** NOUN

> **wander** VERB
> ① = cruise, drift, ramble, range, roam, stroll

wane VERB If a condition, attitude or emotion wanes, it becomes gradually weaker.

want VERB ① If you want something, you feel a desire to have it. ② If something is wanted, it is needed or needs to be done. ③ If someone is wanted, the police are searching for them • *John was wanted for fraud.* ▶ NOUN ④ (*formal*) A want of something is a lack of it.

> **want** VERB
> ① = covet, crave, desire, wish
> ② = be deficient in, demand, lack, need, require
> ▶ NOUN ④ = absence, deficiency, lack, scarcity, shortage
> ≠ abundance

wanting ADJECTIVE If you find something wanting or if it proves wanting, it is not as good in some way as you think it should be.

wanton ADJECTIVE A wanton action deliberately causes unnecessary harm or waste • *wanton destruction.*

war, **wars**, **warring**, **warred** NOUN ① a period of fighting between countries or states when weapons are used and many people may be killed. ② a competition between groups of people, or a campaign against something • *a trade war* • *the war against crime.* ▶ VERB ③ When two countries war with each other, they are fighting a war against each other. **warring** ADJECTIVE

> **war** NOUN
> ① = combat, conflict, fighting, hostilities, strife, warfare
> ≠ peace
> ▶ VERB ③ = battle, clash, fight

waratah [*Said wor-ra-****tah***] NOUN an Australian shrub with dark green leaves and large clusters of crimson flowers.

ward NOUN ① a room in a hospital which has beds for several people who need similar treatment. ② an area or district which forms a separate part of a political constituency or local council. ③ A ward or a ward of court is a child who is officially put in the care of an adult or a court of law, because their parents are dead or because they need protection. **ward off** VERB If you ward off a danger or an illness, you do something to prevent it from affecting or harming you.

-ward or **-wards** SUFFIX '-ward' and '-wards' form adverbs or adjectives that show the way something is moving or facing • *homeward* • *westwards*.

warden NOUN ① a person in charge of a building or institution such as a youth hostel or prison. ② an official who makes sure that certain laws or rules are obeyed in a particular place or activity • *a traffic warden*.

warder NOUN a person who is in charge of prisoners in a jail.

wardrobe NOUN ① a tall cupboard in which you can hang your clothes. ② Someone's wardrobe is their collection of clothes.

ware NOUN ① Ware is manufactured goods of a particular kind • *kitchenware*. ② Someone's wares are the things they sell, usually in the street or in a market.

warehouse NOUN a large building where raw materials or manufactured goods are stored.

warfare NOUN Warfare is the activity of fighting a war.

warhead NOUN the front end of a bomb or missile, where the explosives are carried.

warm, **warmest** ADJECTIVE ① Something that is warm has some heat, but not enough to be hot • *a warm day*. ② Warm clothes or blankets are made of a material which protects you from the cold. ③ Warm colours or sounds are pleasant and make you feel comfortable and relaxed. ④ A warm person is friendly and affectionate. ▶ VERB ⑤ If you warm something, you heat it up gently so that it stops being cold. **warmly** ADVERB **warm up** VERB If you warm up for an event or an activity, you practise or exercise gently to prepare for it.

warm ADJECTIVE
① = balmy, heated, lukewarm, pleasant, tepid
≠ cold
④ = affectionate, amiable, cordial, friendly, genial, loving
≠ unfriendly
▶ VERB ⑤ = heat, heat up, melt, thaw, warm up
≠ cool

warm-blooded ADJECTIVE An animal that is warm-blooded has a relatively high body temperature which remains constant and does not change with the surrounding temperature.

warmth NOUN ① Warmth is a moderate amount of heat. ② Someone who has warmth is friendly and affectionate.

warn VERB ① If you warn someone about a possible problem or danger, you tell them about it in advance so that they are aware of it • *I warned him what it would be like*. ② If you warn someone not to do something, you advise them not to do it, in order to avoid possible danger or punishment • *I have warned her not to train for 10 days*. **warn off** VERB If you warn someone off, you tell them to go away or to stop doing something.

warn VERB
① = alert, caution, forewarn, notify

warning NOUN something said or written to tell people of a possible problem or danger.

warning NOUN
= alarm, alert, caution, notice, premonition

warp VERB ① If something warps or is warped, it becomes bent, often

a b c d e f g h i j k l m n o p q r s t u v w x y z

because of the effect of heat or water. ② If something warps someone's mind or character, it makes them abnormal or corrupt.

warrant VERB ① (*formal*) If something warrants a particular action, it makes the action seem necessary • *no evidence to warrant a murder investigation.* ▶ NOUN ② an official document which gives permission to the police to do something • *a warrant for his arrest.*

warranty, **warranties** NOUN a guarantee • *a three-year warranty.*

warren NOUN a group of holes under the ground connected by tunnels, which rabbits live in.

warrior NOUN a fighting man or soldier, especially in former times.

warship NOUN a ship built with guns and used for fighting in wars.

wart NOUN a small, hard piece of skin which can grow on someone's face or hands.

wartime NOUN Wartime is a period of time during which a country is at war.

wary, **warier**, **wariest** ADJECTIVE cautious and on one's guard • *Michelle is wary of strangers.* **warily** ADVERB **wariness** NOUN

> **wary** ADJECTIVE
> = cautious, distrustful, guarded, suspicious, vigilant

was a past tense of **be**.

wash VERB ① If you wash something, you clean it with water and soap. ② If you wash, you clean yourself using soap and water. ③ If something is washed somewhere, it is carried there gently by water • *The infant Arthur was washed ashore.* ▶ NOUN ④ The wash is all the clothes and bedding that are washed together at one time • *a typical family's weekly wash.* ⑤ The wash in water is the disturbance and waves produced at the back of a moving boat. ▶ PHRASE ⑥ If you **wash your hands of** something or someone, you refuse to have anything more to do with it or them. **wash up** VERB ① If you wash up, you wash the dishes, pans and cutlery used in preparing and eating a meal. ② If something is washed up on land, it is carried by a river or sea and left there • *Some wreckage had been washed up on the beach.*

> **wash** VERB
> ① = bathe, cleanse, launder, rinse, scrub, shampoo
> ③ = carry off, erode, sweep away

washable ADJECTIVE able to be washed without being damaged.

washer NOUN ① a thin, flat ring of metal or plastic which is placed over a bolt before the nut is screwed on, so that it is fixed more tightly. ② In Australian English, a washer is a small piece of towelling for washing yourself.

washing NOUN Washing consists of clothes and bedding which need to be washed or are in the process of being washed and dried.

washing machine NOUN a machine for washing clothes in.

washing-up NOUN If you do the washing-up, you wash the dishes, pans and cutlery which have been used in the cooking and eating of a meal.

wasp NOUN an insect with yellow and black stripes across its body, which can sting like a bee.

wastage NOUN Wastage is loss and misuse of something • *wastage of resources.*

waste VERB ① If you waste time, money or energy, you use too much of it on something that is not important or necessary. ② If you waste an opportunity, you do not take advantage of it when it is available. ③ If you say that something is wasted on someone, you mean that it is too good, too clever, or too sophisticated for them • *This book is wasted on us*. ▸ NOUN ④ If an activity is a waste of time, money or energy, it is not important or necessary. ⑤ Waste is the use of more money or some other resource than is necessary. ⑥ Waste is also material that is no longer wanted, or material left over from a useful process • *nuclear waste*. ▸ ADJECTIVE ⑦ unwanted in its present form • *waste paper*. ⑧ Waste land is land which is not used or looked after by anyone. **waste away** VERB If someone is wasting away, they are becoming very thin and weak because they are ill or not eating properly.

> **waste** VERB
> ① = fritter away, squander, throw away
> ≠ save
> ▸ NOUN ⑤ = extravagance, misuse, squandering
> ▸ ADJECTIVE ⑦ = leftover, superfluous, unused

wasted ADJECTIVE not necessary or useful • *a wasted journey*.

wasteful ADJECTIVE extravagant or causing waste by using something in a careless and inefficient way.

> **wasteful** ADJECTIVE
> = extravagant, uneconomical
> ≠ thrifty

wasteland NOUN A wasteland is land which is of no use because it is infertile or has been misused.

wasting ADJECTIVE A wasting disease is one that gradually reduces the strength and health of the body.

watch NOUN ① a small clock usually worn on a strap on the wrist. ② a period of time during which a guard is kept over something. ▸ VERB ③ If you watch something, you look at it for some time and pay close attention to what is happening. ④ If you watch someone or something, you take care of them. ⑤ If you watch a situation, you pay attention to it or are aware of it • *I had watched Jimmy's progress with interest*. **watch out** VERB ① If you watch out for something, you keep alert to see if it is near you • *Watch out for more fog and ice*. ② If you tell someone to watch out, you are warning them to be very careful.

> **watch** NOUN
> ② = observation, supervision, surveillance
> ▸ VERB ③ = gaze at, look at, observe, pay attention, see, view
> ④ = guard, look after, mind, take care of
> ▸ **watch out** ① = be alert, be watchful, keep your eyes open, look out

watchdog NOUN ① a dog used to guard property. ② a person or group whose job is to make sure that companies do not act illegally or irresponsibly.

watchful ADJECTIVE careful to notice everything that is happening • *the watchful eye of her father*.

watchman, **watchmen** NOUN a person whose job is to guard property.

water NOUN ① Water is a clear, colourless, tasteless and odourless liquid that is necessary for all plant and animal life. ② You use 'water' or 'waters' to refer to a large area of water, such as a lake or sea • *the black waters of the lake*. ▸ VERB ③ If you water a plant or an animal, you give it water to drink. ④ If your eyes water, you have tears in them because they are hurting. ⑤ If your mouth waters, it produces extra saliva, usually because you think of or can smell something appetising. **water down** VERB If you water something down, you make it weaker.

watercolour NOUN ① Watercolours are paints for painting pictures, which are diluted with water or put on the paper using a wet brush. ② a picture which has been painted using watercolours.

watercress NOUN Watercress is a small plant which grows in streams and pools. Its leaves taste hot and are eaten in salads.

waterfall NOUN GEOGRAPHY A waterfall is water from a river or stream as it flows over the edge of a steep cliff in hills or mountains and falls to the ground below.

waterfront NOUN a street or piece of land next to an area of water such as a river or harbour.

waterlogged ADJECTIVE Land that is waterlogged is so wet that the soil cannot contain any more water, so that some water remains on the surface of the ground.

watermelon NOUN a large, round fruit which has a hard green skin and red juicy flesh.

waterproof ADJECTIVE ① not letting water pass through • *waterproof clothing.* ▸ NOUN ② a coat which keeps water out.

watershed NOUN an event or period which marks a turning point or the beginning of a new way of life • *a watershed in European history.*

water-skiing NOUN Water-skiing is the sport of skimming over the water on skis while being pulled by a boat.

water table NOUN GEOGRAPHY The water table is the level below the surface of the ground at which water can be found.

watertight ADJECTIVE ① Something that is watertight does not allow water to pass through. ② An agreement or an argument that is watertight has been so carefully put together that nobody should be able to find a fault in it.

waterway NOUN a canal, river or narrow channel of sea which ships or boats can sail along.

watery ADJECTIVE ① pale or weak • *a watery smile.* ② Watery food or drink contains a lot of water or is thin like water.

watt [*Said* ***wot***] NOUN SCIENCE a unit of power equal to one joule per second. It is named after James Watt (1736–1819), the inventor of the modern steam engine.

wattle [*Said* ***wot**-tl*] NOUN an Australian acacia tree with spikes of brightly coloured flowers.

wave VERB ① If you wave your hand, you move it from side to side, usually to say hello or goodbye. ② If you wave someone somewhere or wave them on, you make a movement with your hand to tell them which way to go. ③ If you wave something, you hold it up and move it from side to side • *The doctor waved a piece of paper at him.* ▸ NOUN ④ a ridge of water on the surface of the sea caused by wind or by tides. ⑤ A wave is the form in which some types of energy such as heat, light or sound travel through a substance. ⑥ A wave of sympathy, alarm or panic is a steady increase in it which spreads through you or through a group of people. ⑦ an increase in a type of activity or behaviour • *the crime wave.*

wave VERB
③ = brandish, flap, flourish, flutter, shake
▸ NOUN ④ = breaker, ripple, swell
⑦ = flood, movement, rush, surge, trend, upsurge

wavelength NOUN ① [SCIENCE] the distance between the same point on two adjacent waves of energy. ② the size of radio wave which a particular radio station uses to broadcast its programmes.

waver VERB ① If you waver or if your confidence or beliefs waver, you are no longer as firm, confident or sure in your beliefs • *Ben has never wavered from his belief.* ② If something wavers, it moves slightly • *The shadows wavered on the wall.*

wavy, **wavier**, **waviest** ADJECTIVE having waves or regular curves • *wavy hair.*

wax NOUN ① Wax is a solid, slightly shiny substance made of fat or oil and used to make candles and polish. ② Wax is also the sticky yellow substance in your ears. ▶ VERB ③ If you wax a surface, you treat it or cover it with a thin layer of wax, especially to polish it. ④ (*formal*) If you wax eloquent, you talk in an eloquent way.

way NOUN ① A way of doing something is the manner of doing it • *an excellent way of cooking meat.* ② The ways of a person or group are their customs or their normal behaviour • *Their ways are certainly different.* ③ The way you feel about something is your attitude to it or your opinion about it. ④ If you have a way with people or things, you are very skilful at dealing with them. ⑤ The way to a particular place is the route that you take to get there. ⑥ If you go or look a particular way, you go or look in that direction • *She glanced the other way.* ⑦ If you divide something a number of ways, you divide it into that number of parts. ⑧ Way is used with words such as 'little' or 'long' to say how far off in distance or time something is • *They lived a long way away.* ▶ PHRASE ⑨ If something or someone is **in the way**, they prevent you from moving freely or seeing clearly. ⑩ You say **by the way** when adding something to what you are saying • *By the way, I asked Brad to drop in.* ⑪ If you **go out of your way** to do something, you make a special effort to do it.

> **way** NOUN
> ① = approach, manner, means, method, procedure, technique
> ② = conduct, custom, manner, practice, style
> ⑤ = channel, course, lane, path, road, route

wayside PHRASE If someone or something **falls by the wayside**, they fail in what they are trying to do, or become forgotten and ignored.

wayward ADJECTIVE difficult to control and likely to change suddenly • *a wayward teenager.*

WC NOUN a toilet. WC is an abbreviation for 'water closet'.

we PRONOUN A speaker or writer uses 'we' to refer to himself or herself and one or more other people • *We are going to see Eddie.*

weak ADJECTIVE ① not having much strength • *weak from lack of sleep.* ② If something is weak, it is likely to break or fail • *Russia's weak economy.* ③ If you describe someone as weak, you mean they are easily influenced by other people. **weakly** ADVERB

> **weak** ADJECTIVE
> ① = delicate, faint, feeble, frail, puny, sickly, wasted
> ≠ strong
> ② = deficient, faulty, inadequate
> ③ = powerless, spineless
> ≠ resolute

weaken VERB ① If someone weakens something, they make it less strong or certain. ② If someone weakens, they become less certain about something.

weaken VERB
① = diminish, fail, flag, lessen, reduce, sap, undermine, wane
≠ strengthen

weakness NOUN ① Weakness is lack of moral or physical strength. ② If you have a weakness for something, you have a great liking for it • *a weakness for whisky.*

weakness NOUN
① = defect, flaw, fragility, frailty, imperfection, vulnerability
≠ strength
② = fondness, liking, passion, penchant (*formal*)
≠ dislike

wealth NOUN ① GEOGRAPHY Wealth is the large amount of money or property which someone owns. ② A wealth of something is a lot of it • *a wealth of information.*

wealth NOUN
① = affluence, fortune, means, money, prosperity, riches, substance
② = abundance, bounty, plenty, store
≠ shortage

wealthy, **wealthier**, **wealthiest** ADJECTIVE having a large amount of money, property or other valuable things.

wealthy ADJECTIVE
= affluent, comfortable, opulent, prosperous, rich, well-to-do
≠ poor

wean VERB To wean a baby or animal is to start feeding it food other than its mother's milk.

weapon NOUN ① an object used to kill or hurt people in a fight or war. ② anything which can be used to get the better of an opponent • *Surprise was his only weapon.* **weaponry** NOUN

wear, **wears**, **wearing**, **wore**, **worn** VERB ① When you wear something such as clothes, make-up or jewellery, you have them on your body or face. ② If you wear a particular expression, it shows on your face. ③ If something wears, it becomes thinner or worse in condition. ▸ NOUN ④ You can refer to clothes that are suitable for a particular time or occasion as a kind of wear • *beach wear.* ⑤ Wear is the amount or type of use that something has and which causes damage or change to it • *signs of wear.* **wear down** VERB If you wear people down, you weaken them by repeatedly doing something or asking them to do something. **wear off** VERB If a feeling such as pain wears off, it gradually disappears. **wear on** VERB If time wears on, it seems to pass very slowly or boringly. **wear out** VERB ① When something wears out or when you wear it out, it is used so much that it becomes thin, weak and no longer usable. ② (*informal*) If you wear someone out, you make them feel extremely tired.

wear VERB
① = be clothed in, be dressed in, don, have on, put on, sport (*informal*)
③ = corrode, erode, fray, rub, wash away
▸ NOUN ⑤ = corrosion, deterioration, erosion, use
▸ **wear out** ② = exhaust, tire, weary

wear and tear NOUN Wear and tear is the damage caused to something by normal use.

wearing ADJECTIVE Someone or something that is wearing makes you feel extremely tired.

weary, **wearier**, **weariest**; **wearies**, **wearying**, **wearied** ADJECTIVE ① very tired. ▸ VERB ② If you weary of something, you become tired of it. **wearily** ADVERB **weariness** NOUN

weary ADJECTIVE
① = drained, exhausted, fatigued, tired, tuckered out (*American, Australian and New Zealand; informal*), worn out

weasel NOUN a small wild mammal with a long, thin body and short legs.

weather NOUN ① The weather is the condition of the atmosphere at any particular time and the amount of rain, wind or sunshine occurring. ▸ VERB ② If something such as rock or wood weathers, it changes colour or shape as a result of being exposed to the wind, rain or sun. ③ If you weather a problem or difficulty, you come through it safely. ▸ PHRASE ④ If you are **under the weather**, you feel slightly ill.

weave, **weaves**, **weaving**, **wove**, **woven** VERB ① To weave cloth is to make it by crossing threads over and under each other, especially by using a machine called a loom. ② If you weave your way somewhere, you go there by moving from side to side through and round the obstacles. ▸ NOUN ③ The weave of cloth is the way in which the threads are arranged and the pattern that they form • *a tight weave*.

weaver NOUN a person who weaves cloth.

web NOUN ① a fine net of threads that a spider makes from a sticky substance which it produces in its body. ② something that has a complicated structure or pattern • *a web of lies*. ③ The Web is the same as the **World Wide Web**.

website NOUN a publication on the World Wide Web which contains information about a particular subject.

wed, **weds**, **wedding**, **wedded** or **wed** VERB (*old-fashioned*) If you wed someone or if you wed, you get married.

wedding NOUN a marriage ceremony.

wedge VERB ① If you wedge something, you force it to remain there by holding it there tightly, or by fixing something next to it to prevent it from moving • *I shut the shed door and wedged it with a log of wood*. ▸ NOUN ② a piece of something such as wood, metal or rubber with one pointed edge and one thick edge which is used to wedge something. ③ a piece of something that has a thick triangular shape • *a wedge of cheese*.

wedlock NOUN (*old-fashioned*) Wedlock is the state of being married.

Wednesday NOUN Wednesday is the day between Tuesday and Thursday.

wee ADJECTIVE In Scotland, a term for small.

weed NOUN ① a wild plant that prevents cultivated plants from growing properly. ▸ VERB ② If you weed a place, you remove the weeds from it. **weed out** VERB If you weed out unwanted things, you get rid of them.

week NOUN ① a period of seven days, especially one beginning on a Sunday and ending on a Saturday. ② A week is also the number of hours you spend at work during a week • *a 35-hour week*. ③ The week can refer to the part of a week that does not include Saturday and Sunday • *They are working during the week*.

weekday NOUN any day except Saturday and Sunday.

weekend NOUN Saturday and Sunday.

weekly, **weeklies** ADJECTIVE ① happening or appearing once a week. ▸ ADVERB ② once a week • *I see my mother weekly*. ▸ NOUN ③ A weekly is a newspaper or magazine that is published once a week.

weep, **weeps**, **weeping**, **wept** VERB ① If someone weeps, they cry.

② If something such as a wound weeps, it oozes blood or other liquid.

weigh VERB ① If something weighs a particular amount, that is how heavy it is. ② If you weigh something, you measure how heavy it is using scales. ③ If you weigh facts or words, you think about them carefully before coming to a decision or before speaking. ④ If a problem weighs on you or weighs upon you, it makes you very worried. **weigh down** VERB ① If a load weighs you down, it stops you moving easily. ② If you are weighed down by a difficulty, it is making you very worried. **weigh up** VERB If you weigh up a person or a situation, you make an assessment of them.

weight NOUN ① The weight of something is its heaviness. ② a metal object which has a certain known heaviness. Weights are used with sets of scales in order to weigh things. ③ any heavy object. ④ The weight of something is its large amount or importance which makes it hard to fight against or contradict • *the weight of the law*. ▶ VERB ⑤ If you weight something or weight it down, you make it heavier, often so that it cannot move. ▶ PHRASE ⑥ If you **pull your weight**, you work just as hard as other people involved in the same activity.

weighted ADJECTIVE A system that is weighted in favour of a particular person or group is organised in such a way that this person or group will have an advantage.

weightless ADJECTIVE SCIENCE Something that is weightless has no weight or very little weight, for example because it is in space and not affected by the Earth's gravity. **weightlessness** NOUN

weightlifting NOUN Weightlifting is the sport of lifting heavy weights in competition or for exercise. **weightlifter** NOUN

weighty, **weightier**, **weightiest** ADJECTIVE serious or important • *a weighty problem*.

weir [*Rhymes with **near***] NOUN a low dam which is built across a river to raise the water level, control the flow of water, or change its direction.

weird [*Said **weerd***] ADJECTIVE strange or odd. **weirdly** ADVERB

> **weird** ADJECTIVE
> = bizarre, curious, extraordinary, funny, odd, peculiar, singular (*formal*), strange
> ≠ ordinary

weirdo, **weirdos** [*Said **weer-doe***] NOUN (*informal*) If you call someone a weirdo, you mean they behave in a strange way.

welcome VERB ① If you welcome a visitor, you greet them in a friendly way when they arrive. ② 'Welcome' can be said as a greeting to a visitor who has just arrived. ③ If you welcome something, you approve of it and support it • *He welcomed the decision*. ▶ NOUN ④ a greeting to a visitor • *a warm welcome*. ▶ ADJECTIVE ⑤ If someone is welcome at a place, they will be warmly received there. ⑥ If something is welcome, it brings pleasure or is accepted gratefully • *a welcome rest*. ⑦ If you tell someone they are welcome to something or welcome to do something, you mean you are willing for them to have or to do it. **welcoming** ADJECTIVE

weld VERB To weld two pieces of metal together is to join them by heating their edges and fixing them together so that when they cool they harden into one piece. **welder** NOUN

welfare NOUN ① The welfare of a person or group is their general state of health and comfort. ② Welfare services are provided to help with people's living conditions and financial problems • *welfare workers*.

welfare state NOUN The welfare state is a system in which the government uses money from taxes to provide health care and education services, and to give benefits to people who are old, unemployed or sick.

well, **better**, **best**; **wells**, **welling**, **welled** ADVERB ① If something goes well, it happens in a satisfactory way • *The interview went well*. ② in a good, skilful or pleasing way • *He draws well*. ③ thoroughly and completely • *well established*. ④ kindly • *We treat our employees well*. ⑤ If something may well or could well happen, it is likely to happen. ⑥ You use 'well' to emphasise an adjective, adverb or phrase • *He was well aware of that*. ▶ ADJECTIVE ⑦ If you are well, you are healthy. ▶ PHRASE ⑧ **As well** means also • *He was a bus driver as well*. ⑨ **As well as** means in addition to • *a meal which includes meat or fish, as well as rice*. ⑩ If you say you **may as well** or **might as well** do something, you mean you will do it, not because you are keen to, but because there is nothing better to do. ▶ NOUN ⑪ a hole drilled in the ground from which water, oil or gas is obtained. ▶ VERB ⑫ If tears well or well up, they appear in someone's eyes.

well ADVERB
① = satisfactorily, smoothly, splendidly, successfully
② = ably, adequately, admirably, competently, effectively, efficiently, expertly, professionally, skilfully
≠ badly
③ = amply, closely, completely, fully, highly, meticulously, rigorously, thoroughly
④ = compassionately, considerately, favourably, humanely, kindly, with consideration
▶ ADJECTIVE ⑦ = blooming, fit, healthy, in good condition, in good health, robust, sound, strong
≠ sick

well-balanced ADJECTIVE sensible and without serious emotional problems • *a well-balanced happy teenager*.

wellbeing NOUN PSHE Someone's wellbeing is their health and happiness.

well-earned ADJECTIVE thoroughly deserved.

well-heeled ADJECTIVE (*informal*) wealthy.

well-informed ADJECTIVE having a great deal of knowledge about a subject or subjects.

well-meaning ADJECTIVE A well-meaning person tries to be helpful but is often unsuccessful.

well-off ADJECTIVE (*informal*) quite wealthy.

well-to-do ADJECTIVE quite wealthy.

well-worn ADJECTIVE ① A well-worn expression or saying has been used too often and has become boring. ② A well-worn object or piece of clothing has been used and worn so much that it looks old and shabby.

Welsh ADJECTIVE ① belonging or relating to Wales. ▶ NOUN ② Welsh is a language spoken in parts of Wales.

Welshman, **Welshmen** NOUN a man who comes from Wales.

Welshwoman, **Welshwomen** NOUN a woman who comes from Wales.

welter NOUN (*formal*) A welter of things is a large number of them that happen or appear together in a state of confusion • *a welter of rumours*.

went the past tense of **go**.

wept the past tense and past participle of **weep**.

were a past tense of **be**.

werewolf, **werewolves** NOUN In horror stories, a werewolf is a person who changes into a wolf.

west NOUN ① The west is the direction in which you look to see the sun set. ② The west of a place or country is the part which is towards the west when you are in the centre • *the west of America*. ③ The West refers to the countries of North America and western and southern Europe. ▸ ADVERB, ADJECTIVE ④ West means towards the west. ▸ ADJECTIVE ⑤ A west wind blows from the west.

westerly ADJECTIVE ① Westerly means to or towards the west. ② A westerly wind blows from the west.

western ADJECTIVE ① in or from the west. ② coming from or associated with the countries of North America and western and southern Europe • *western dress*. ▸ NOUN ③ a book or film about life in the west of America in the 19th century.

West Indian NOUN someone who comes from the West Indies.

westward or **westwards** ADVERB ① Westward or westwards means towards the west • *He stared westwards towards the clouds*. ▸ ADJECTIVE ② The westward part of something is the west part.

wet, **wetter**, **wettest**; **wets**, **wetting**, **wet** or **wetted** ADJECTIVE ① If something is wet, it is covered in water or another liquid. ② If the weather is wet, it is raining. ③ If something such as paint, ink or cement is wet, it is not yet dry or solid. ④ (*informal*) If you say someone is wet, you mean they are weak and lacking confidence • *Don't be so wet!* ▸ NOUN ⑤ In Australia, the wet is the rainy season. ▸ VERB ⑥ To wet something is to put water or some other liquid over it. ⑦ If people wet themselves or wet their beds, they urinate in their clothes or bed because they cannot control their bladder. **wetness** NOUN

wet ADJECTIVE
① = damp, drenched, moist, saturated, soaked, sodden, waterlogged
≠ dry
② = humid, misty, rainy, showery
≠ dry
▸ VERB ⑥ = dampen, irrigate, moisten, soak, spray, water
≠ dry

whack VERB If you whack someone or something, you hit them hard.

whale NOUN a very large sea mammal which breathes through a hole on the top of its head.

whaling NOUN Whaling is the work of hunting and killing whales for oil or food.

wharf, **wharves** [*Said* ***worf***] NOUN a platform beside a river or the sea, where ships load or unload.

what PRONOUN ① 'What' is used in questions • *What time is it?* ② 'What' is used in indirect questions and statements • *I don't know what you mean*. ③ 'What' can be used at the beginning of a clause to refer to something with a particular quality • *It is impossible to decide what is real and what is invented*. ▸ ADJECTIVE ④ 'What' can be used at the beginning of a clause to show that you are talking about the whole amount that is available to you • *Their spouses try to earn what money they can*. ⑤ You say 'what' to emphasise an opinion or reaction • *What nonsense!* ▸ PHRASE ⑥ You say **what about** at the beginning of a question when you are making a suggestion or offer • *What about a drink?*

whatever PRONOUN ① You use 'whatever' to refer to anything or everything of a particular type • *He said he would do whatever he could.* ② You use 'whatever' when you do not know the precise nature of something • *Whatever it is, I don't like it.* ▶ **CONJUNCTION** ③ You use 'whatever' to mean no matter what • *Whatever happens, you have to behave decently.* ▶ **ADVERB** ④ You use 'whatever' to emphasise a negative statement or a question • *You have no proof whatever* • *Whatever is wrong with you?*

whatsoever **ADVERB** You use 'whatsoever' to emphasise a negative statement • *I have no memory of it whatsoever.*

wheat **NOUN** Wheat is a cereal plant grown for its grain, which is used to make flour.

wheel **NOUN** ① DGT a circular object which turns on a rod attached to its centre. Wheels are fixed underneath vehicles so that they can move along. ② DGT The wheel of a car is its steering wheel. ▶ **VERB** ③ If you wheel something such as a bicycle, you push it. ④ If someone or something wheels, they move round in the shape of a circle • *Cameron wheeled around and hit him.*

wheelbarrow **NOUN** a small cart with a single wheel at the front, used for carrying things in the garden.

wheelchair **NOUN** a chair with wheels in which sick, injured or disabled people can move around.

wheeze **VERB** If someone wheezes, they breathe with difficulty, making a whistling sound, usually because they have a chest complaint such as asthma. **wheezy** **ADJECTIVE**

when **ADVERB** ① You use 'when' to ask what time something happened or will happen • *When are you leaving?* ▶ **CONJUNCTION** ② You use 'when' to refer to a time in the past • *I met him when I was sixteen.* ③ You use 'when' to introduce the reason for an opinion, comment or question • *How did you pass the exam when you hadn't studied for it?* ④ 'When' is used to mean although • *He drives when he could walk.*

whence **ADVERB, CONJUNCTION** (*old-fashioned*) 'Whence' means from where.

whenever **CONJUNCTION** 'Whenever' means at any time, or every time that something happens • *I still go on courses whenever I can.*

where **ADVERB** ① You use 'where' to ask which place something is in, is coming from, or is going to • *Where is Philip?* ▶ **CONJUNCTION, PRONOUN, ADVERB** ② You use 'where' when asking about or referring to something • *I hardly know where to begin.* ▶ **CONJUNCTION** ③ You use 'where' to refer to the place in which something is situated or happening • *I don't know where we are.* ④ 'Where' can introduce a clause that contrasts with the other part of the sentence • *Some people took music lessons, where others learned dance.*

whereabouts **NOUN** ① The whereabouts of a person or thing is the place where they are. ▶ **ADVERB** ② You use 'whereabouts' when you are asking more precisely where something is • *Whereabouts in Canada are you from?*

whereas **CONJUNCTION** 'Whereas' introduces a comment that contrasts with the other part of the sentence • *Her eyes were blue, whereas mine were brown.*

whereby **PRONOUN** (*formal*) 'Whereby' means by which • *a new system whereby you pay the bill quarterly.*

whereupon **CONJUNCTION** (*formal*) 'Whereupon' means at which point • *His enemies rejected his message, whereupon he tried again.*

wherever **CONJUNCTION** ① 'Wherever' means in every place or situation

• *Alex heard the same thing wherever he went.* ② You use 'wherever' to show that you do not know where a place or person is • *the nearest police station, wherever that is.*

wherewithal NOUN If you have the wherewithal to do something, you have enough money to do it.

whet, **whets**, **whetting**, **whetted** PHRASE To **whet someone's appetite** for something means to increase their desire for it.

whether CONJUNCTION You use 'whether' when you are talking about two or more alternatives • *I don't know whether that's true or false.*

which ADJECTIVE, PRONOUN ① You use 'which' to ask about alternatives or to refer to a choice between alternatives • *Which room are you in?* ▸ PRONOUN ② 'Which' at the beginning of a clause identifies the thing you are talking about or gives more information about it • *certain wrongs which exist in our society.*

whichever ADJECTIVE, PRONOUN You use 'whichever' when you are talking about different alternatives or possibilities • *Make your pizzas round or square, whichever you prefer.*

whiff NOUN ① a slight smell of something. ② a slight sign or trace of something • *a whiff of criticism.*

while CONJUNCTION ① If something happens while something else is happening, the two things happen at the same time. ② While also means but • *The first issue is free, while the second costs £5.* ▸ NOUN ③ a period of time • *a little while earlier.* ▸ PHRASE ④ If an action or activity is **worth your while**, it will be helpful or useful to you if you do it. **while away** VERB If you while away the time in a particular way, you pass the time that way because you have nothing else to do.

whilst CONJUNCTION Whilst means the same as while.

whim NOUN a sudden desire or fancy.

whim NOUN
= craze, fad (*informal*), fancy, impulse, urge

whimper VERB ① When children or animals whimper, they make soft, low, unhappy sounds. ② If you whimper something, you say it in an unhappy or frightened way, as if you are about to cry.

whimsical ADJECTIVE unusual and slightly playful • *an endearing, whimsical charm.*

whine VERB ① To whine is to make a long, high-pitched noise, especially one which sounds sad or unpleasant. ② If someone whines about something, they complain about it in an annoying way. ▸ NOUN ③ A whine is the noise made by something or someone whining.

whinge, **whinges**, **whingeing**, **whinged** VERB If someone whinges about something, they complain about it in an annoying way.

whip, **whips**, **whipping**, **whipped** NOUN ① a thin piece of leather or rope attached to a handle, which is used for hitting people or animals. ▸ VERB ② If you whip a person or animal, you hit them with a whip. ③ When the wind whips something, it strikes it. ④ If you whip something out or off, you take it out or off very quickly • *She had whipped off her glasses.* ⑤ If you whip cream, you beat it until it is thick and frothy or stiff. **whip up** VERB If you whip up a strong emotion, you make people feel it • *The thought whipped up his temper.*

whirl VERB ① When something whirls, or when you whirl it round, it turns round very fast. ▸ NOUN ② You can refer to a lot of intense activity as a whirl of activity.

whirlpool NOUN a small circular area in a river or the sea where the water is moving quickly round and round so that objects floating near it are pulled into its centre.

whirlwind NOUN ① a tall column of air which spins round and round very fast. ▶ ADJECTIVE ② more rapid than usual • *a whirlwind tour*.

whisk VERB ① If you whisk someone or something somewhere, you take them there quickly • *We were whisked away into a private room*. ② If you whisk eggs or cream, you stir air into them quickly. ▶ NOUN ③ a kitchen tool used for quickly stirring air into eggs or cream.

whisker NOUN The whiskers of an animal such as a cat or mouse are the long, stiff hairs near its mouth.

whisky, **whiskies** NOUN Whisky is a strong alcoholic drink made from grain such as barley.

whisper VERB ① When you whisper, you talk to someone very quietly, using your breath and not your throat. ▶ NOUN ② If you talk in a whisper, you whisper.

whistle VERB ① When you whistle a tune or whistle, you produce a clear musical sound by forcing your breath out between your lips. ② If something whistles, it makes a loud, high sound • *The kettle whistled*. ▶ NOUN ③ A whistle is the sound something or someone makes when they whistle. ④ a small metal tube that you blow into to produce a whistling sound.

white NOUN, ADJECTIVE ① White is the lightest possible colour. ② Someone who is white has a pale skin and is of European origin. ▶ ADJECTIVE ③ If someone goes white, their face becomes very pale because they are afraid, shocked or ill. ④ White coffee contains milk or cream. ▶ NOUN ⑤ The white of an egg is the transparent liquid surrounding the yolk which turns white when it is cooked. **whiteness** NOUN

whiteboard NOUN a white board on which people can write or draw using special coloured pens.

white-collar ADJECTIVE White-collar workers work in offices rather than doing manual work • *a white-collar union*.

whitewash NOUN ① Whitewash is a mixture of lime and water used for painting walls white. ② an attempt to hide unpleasant facts • *the refusal to accept official whitewash in the enquiry*.

whiting NOUN a sea fish related to the cod.

whittle VERB If you whittle a piece of wood, you shape it by shaving or cutting small pieces off it.
whittle away or **whittle down** VERB To whittle away at something or to whittle it down means to make it smaller or less effective • *The 250 entrants had been whittled down to 34*.

whizz; also spelt **whiz** (*informal*) VERB ① If you whizz somewhere, you move there quickly • *Could you whizz down to the shop and get me some milk?* ▶ NOUN ② If you are a whizz at something, you are very good at it.

who PRONOUN ① You use 'who' when you are asking about someone's identity • *Who gave you that black eye?* ② 'Who' at the beginning of a clause refers to the person or people you are talking about • *a shipyard worker who wants to be a postman*.

whoever PRONOUN ① 'Whoever' means the person who • *Whoever bought it for you has to make the claim*. ② 'Whoever' also means no matter who • *I pity him, whoever he is*. ③ 'Whoever' is used in questions to give emphasis to 'who' • *Whoever thought of such a thing?*

whole ADJECTIVE ① indicating all of something • *Have the whole cake.* ▸ NOUN ② the full amount of something • *the whole of Africa.* ▸ ADVERB ③ in one piece • *He swallowed it whole.* ▸ PHRASE ④ You use **as a whole** to emphasise that you are talking about all of something • *The country as a whole is in a very odd mood.* ⑤ You say **on the whole** to mean that something is generally true • *On the whole, we should be glad they are gone.*
wholeness NOUN

whole ADJECTIVE
① = complete, entire, full, total, uncut, undivided
▸ NOUN ② = aggregate, all, everything, lot, sum total, total

wholehearted ADJECTIVE enthusiastic and totally sincere • *wholehearted approval.*
wholeheartedly ADVERB

wholemeal ADJECTIVE Wholemeal flour is made from the complete grain of the wheat plant, including the husk.

wholesale ADJECTIVE, ADVERB ① Wholesale refers to the activity of buying goods cheaply in large quantities and selling them again, especially to shopkeepers • *We buy fruit and vegetables wholesale.* ▸ ADJECTIVE ② Wholesale also means done to an excessive extent • *the wholesale destruction of wild plant species.*
wholesaler NOUN

wholesome ADJECTIVE ① Something that is wholesome is good and likely to improve your life, behaviour or health • *good wholesome entertainment.* ② If you describe a person as wholesome, you mean that their appearance suggests health and wellbeing • *wholesome individuals who will make a positive contribution to society.*

wholly [*Said* ***hoe**-lee*] ADVERB completely.

whom PRONOUN 'Whom' is the object form of 'who' • *the girl whom Albert would marry.*

whoop VERB ① If you whoop, you shout loudly in a happy or excited way. ▸ NOUN ② a loud cry of happiness or excitement • *whoops of delight.*

whooping cough [*Said* ***hoop**-ing*] NOUN Whooping cough is an acute infectious disease which makes people cough violently and produce a loud sound when they breathe.

whose PRONOUN ① You use 'whose' to ask who something belongs to • *Whose gun is this?* ② You use 'whose' at the beginning of a clause which gives information about something relating or belonging to the thing or person you have just mentioned • *a wealthy gentleman whose mansion is for sale.*

why ADVERB, PRONOUN You use 'why' when you are asking about the reason for something, or talking about it • *Why did you do it?* • *He wondered why she suddenly looked happier.*

wick NOUN the cord in the middle of a candle, which you set alight.

wicked ADJECTIVE ① very bad • *a wicked thing to do.* ② mischievous in an amusing or attractive way • *a wicked sense of humour.* **wickedly** ADVERB
wickedness NOUN

wicked ADJECTIVE
① = atrocious, bad, depraved, evil, sinful, vicious
② = impish, mischievous, naughty

wicker ADJECTIVE A wicker basket or chair is made from twigs, canes or reeds that have been woven together.

wicket NOUN ① In cricket, the wicket is one of the two sets of stumps and bails at which the bowler aims the ball. ② The grass between the wickets on a cricket pitch is also called the wicket.

wide ADJECTIVE ① measuring a large distance from one side to the other. ② If there is a wide variety, range or selection of something, there are many different kinds of it • *a wide range of colours*. ▶ ADVERB ③ If you open or spread something wide, you open it to its fullest extent. **widely** ADVERB

wide ADJECTIVE
① = ample, baggy, broad, expansive, extensive, full, immense, large, roomy, spacious, sweeping, vast, voluminous
≠ narrow
② = ample, broad, catholic, comprehensive, encyclopedic, exhaustive, extensive, far-ranging, immense, inclusive, large, vast, wide-ranging
≠ narrow
▶ ADVERB ③ = completely, fully, right out

widen VERB ① If something widens or if you widen it, it becomes bigger from one side to the other. ② You can say that something widens when it becomes greater in size or scope • *the opportunity to widen your outlook*.

wide-ranging ADJECTIVE extending over a variety of different things or over a large area • *a wide-ranging survey*.

widespread ADJECTIVE existing or happening over a large area or to a great extent • *the widespread use of chemicals*.

widespread ADJECTIVE
= broad, common, extensive, pervasive, prevalent, rife

widow NOUN a woman whose spouse has died.

widowed ADJECTIVE If someone is widowed, their husband or wife has died.

widower NOUN a man whose spouse has died.

width NOUN The width of something is the distance from one side or edge to the other.

wield [*Said* ***weeld***] VERB ① If you wield a weapon or tool, you carry it and use it. ② If someone wields power, they have it and are able to use it.

wife, **wives** NOUN A person's wife is the woman they are married to.

Wi-Fi NOUN [ICT] a system of accessing the internet from machines such as laptop computers that aren't physically connected to a network.

wig NOUN a false head of hair worn to cover someone's own hair or to hide their baldness.

wiggle VERB ① If you wiggle something, you move it up and down or from side to side with small jerky movements. ▶ NOUN ② a small jerky movement.

wild ADJECTIVE ① Wild animals, birds and plants live and grow in natural surroundings and are not looked after by people. ② Wild land is natural and has not been cultivated • *wild areas of countryside*. ③ Wild weather or sea is stormy and rough. ④ Wild behaviour is excited and uncontrolled. ⑤ A wild idea or scheme is original and crazy. ▶ NOUN ⑥ The wild is a free and natural state of living • *There are about 200 left in the wild*. ⑦ The wilds are remote areas where few people live, far away from towns. **wildly** ADVERB

wild ADJECTIVE
① = fierce, free, natural, uncultivated, undomesticated, untamed, warrigal (*Australian; literary*)
③ = howling, raging, rough, stormy, violent
④ = boisterous, rowdy, turbulent, uncontrolled, wayward

wilderness NOUN an area of natural land which is not cultivated.

wildfire NOUN If something spreads like wildfire, it spreads very quickly.

wildlife NOUN Wildlife means wild animals and plants.

Wild West NOUN The Wild West was the western part of the United States when it was first being settled by Europeans.

wiles PLURAL NOUN Wiles are clever or crafty tricks used to persuade people to do something • *You are going to need all your wiles to get a pay rise from the new boss.*

wilful ADJECTIVE ① Wilful actions or attitudes are deliberate and often intended to hurt someone • *wilful damage.* ② Someone who is wilful is obstinate and determined to get their own way • *a wilful little boy.* **wilfully** ADVERB

will[1] VERB ① You use 'will' to form the future tense • *Robin will be quite annoyed.* ② You use 'will' to say that you intend to do something • *I will not deceive you.* ③ You use 'will' when inviting someone to do or have something • *Will you have another coffee?* ④ You use 'will' when asking or telling someone to do something • *Will you do me a favour?* • *You will do as I say.* ⑤ You use 'will' to say that you are assuming something to be the case • *As you will have gathered, I was surprised.*

will[2] VERB ① If you will something to happen, you try to make it happen by mental effort • *I willed my eyes to open.* ② If you will something to someone, you leave it to them when you die • *Penbrook Farm is willed to her.* ▸ NOUN ③ Will is the determination to do something • *the will to win.* ④ If something is the will of a person or group, they want it to happen • *the will of the people.* ⑤ a legal document in which you say what you want to happen to your money and property when you die. ▸ PHRASE ⑥ If you can do something **at will**, you can do it whenever you want.

> **will** VERB
> ② = bequeath, leave, pass on
> ▸ NOUN ③ = determination, purpose, resolution, resolve, willpower
> ④ = choice, inclination, mind, volition, wish

willing ADJECTIVE ready and eager to do something • *a willing helper.* **willingly** ADVERB **willingness** NOUN

> **willing** ADJECTIVE
> = agreeable, eager, game (*informal*), happy, prepared, ready
> ≠ unwilling

willow NOUN A willow or willow tree is a tree with long, thin branches and narrow leaves that often grows near water.

wilt VERB ① If a plant wilts, it droops because it needs more water or is dying. ② If someone wilts, they gradually lose strength or confidence • *James visibly wilted under pressure.*

wily, **wilier**, **wiliest** [*Said* ***wie**-lee*] ADJECTIVE clever and cunning.

wimp NOUN (*informal*) someone who is feeble and timid.

win, **wins**, **winning**, **won** VERB ① If you win a fight, game or argument, you defeat your opponent. ② If you win something, you succeed in obtaining it. ▸ NOUN ③ a victory in a game or contest. **win over** VERB If you win someone over, you persuade them to support you.

> **win** VERB
> ① = be victorious, come first, prevail, succeed, triumph
> ≠ lose
> ② = achieve, attain, gain, get, secure (*formal*)
> ▸ NOUN ③ = success, triumph, victory
> ≠ defeat

wince VERB When you wince, the

muscles of your face tighten suddenly because of pain, fear or distress.

winch NOUN ① a machine used to lift heavy objects. It consists of a cylinder around which a rope or chain is wound. ▶ VERB ② If you winch an object or person somewhere, you lift, lower or pull them using a winch.

wind[1] *[Rhymes with **tinned**]* NOUN ① a current of air moving across the earth's surface. ② Your wind is the ability to breathe easily • *Brown had recovered her wind.* ③ Wind is air swallowed with food or drink, or gas produced in your stomach, which causes discomfort. ④ MUSIC The wind section of an orchestra is the group of musicians who play wind instruments.

wind[2], **winds, winding, wound** *[Rhymes with **mind**]* VERB ① If a road or river winds in a particular direction, it twists and turns in that direction. ② When you wind something round something else, you wrap it round it several times. ③ When you wind a clock or machine or wind it up, you turn a key or handle several times to make it work. **wind up** VERB ① When you wind up something such as an activity or a business, you finish it or close it. ② If you wind up in a particular place, you end up there.

windfall NOUN a sum of money that you receive unexpectedly.

windmill NOUN a machine for grinding grain or pumping water. It is driven by vanes or sails turned by the wind.

window NOUN a space in a wall or roof or in the side of a vehicle, usually with glass in it so that light can pass through and people can see in or out.

windowsill NOUN a ledge along the bottom of a window, either on the inside or outside of a building.

windpipe NOUN Your windpipe is the tube which carries air into your lungs when you breathe. The technical name for windpipe is **trachea**.

windscreen NOUN the glass at the front of a vehicle through which the driver looks.

windsurfing NOUN Windsurfing is the sport of moving along the surface of the sea or a lake standing on a board with a sail on it.

windswept ADJECTIVE A windswept place is exposed to strong winds • *a windswept beach.*

windy, windier, windiest ADJECTIVE If it is windy, there is a lot of wind.

wine NOUN Wine is the red or white alcoholic drink which is normally made from grapes.

wing NOUN ① A bird's or insect's wings are the parts of its body that it uses for flying. ② An aeroplane's wings are the long, flat parts on each side that support it while it is in the air. ③ A wing of a building is a part which sticks out from the main part or which has been added later. ④ A wing of an organisation, especially a political party, is a group within it with a particular role or particular beliefs • *the left wing of the party.* ⑤ *(in plural)* The wings in a theatre are the sides of the stage which are hidden from the audience. **winged** ADJECTIVE

wink VERB ① When you wink, you close one eye briefly, often as a signal that something is a joke or a secret. ▶ NOUN ② the closing of your eye when you wink.

winner NOUN The winner of a prize, race or competition is the person or thing that wins it.

> **winner** NOUN
> = champion, conqueror, victor
> ≠ loser

winning ADJECTIVE ① The winning team or entry in a competition is the one that has won. ② attractive and charming • *a winning smile.*

winter NOUN Winter is the season between autumn and spring.

wintry ADJECTIVE Something wintry has features that are typical of winter • *the wintry dawn.*

wipe VERB ① If you wipe something, you rub its surface lightly to remove dirt or liquid. ② If you wipe dirt or liquid off something, you remove it using a cloth or your hands • *Anne wiped the tears from her eyes.* **wipe out** VERB To wipe out people or places is to destroy them completely.

wire NOUN ① Wire is metal in the form of a long, thin, flexible thread which can be used to make or fasten things or to conduct an electric current. ▸ VERB ② If you wire one thing to another, you fasten them together using wire. ③ DGT If you wire something or wire it up, you connect it so that electricity can pass through it. **wired** ADJECTIVE

wireless NOUN (*old-fashioned*) a radio.

wiring NOUN The wiring in a building is the system of wires that supply electricity to the rooms.

wiry, **wirier**, **wiriest** ADJECTIVE ① Wiry people are thin but with strong muscles. ② Wiry things are stiff and rough to the touch • *wiry hair.*

wisdom NOUN ① Wisdom is the ability to use experience and knowledge in order to make sensible decisions or judgments. ② If you talk about the wisdom of an action or a decision, you are talking about how sensible it is.

wisdom NOUN
① = discernment, insight, judgment, knowledge, reason
≠ foolishness

wise ADJECTIVE ① Someone who is wise can use their experience and knowledge to make sensible decisions and judgments. ▸ PHRASE ② If you say that someone is **none the wiser** or **no wiser**, you mean that they know no more about something than they did before • *I left the lesson none the wiser.*

wise ADJECTIVE
① = informed, judicious (*formal*), perceptive, rational, sensible, shrewd
≠ foolish

wisecrack NOUN a clever remark, intended to be amusing but often unkind.

wish NOUN ① a longing or desire for something, often something difficult to achieve or obtain. ② something desired or wanted • *That wish came true two years later.* ③ (*in plural*) Good wishes are expressions of hope that someone will be happy or successful • *best wishes on your birthday.* ▸ VERB ④ If you wish to do something, you want to do it • *We wished to return.* ⑤ If you wish something were the case, you would like it to be the case, but know it is not very likely • *I wish I were tall.*

wish NOUN
① = desire, hankering, hunger, longing, urge, want
▸ VERB ④ = desire, hunger, long, thirst, want, yearn

wishbone NOUN a V-shaped bone in the breast of most birds.

wishful thinking NOUN If someone's hope or wish is wishful thinking, it is unlikely to come true.

wistful ADJECTIVE sadly thinking about something, especially something you want but cannot have • *A wistful look came into her eyes.* **wistfully** ADVERB

A B C D E F G H I J K L M N O P Q R S T U V W X Y Z

wit NOUN ① Wit is the ability to use words or ideas in an amusing and clever way. ② Wit means sense • *They haven't got the wit to realise what they're doing*. ③ (*in plural*) Your wits are the ability to think and act quickly in a difficult situation • *the man who lived by his wits*. ▶ PHRASE ④ If someone is **at their wits' end**, they are so worried and exhausted by problems or difficulties that they do not know what to do.

witch NOUN a woman claimed to have magic powers and to be able to use them for good or evil.

witchcraft NOUN Witchcraft is the skill or art of using magic powers, especially evil ones.

with PREPOSITION ① If you are with someone, you are in their company • *He was at home with me*. ② 'With' is used to show who your opponent is in a fight or competition • *next week's game with Brazil*. ③ 'With' can mean using or having • *Apply the colour with a brush* • *a bloke with a moustache*. ④ 'With' is used to show how someone does something or how they feel • *She looked at him with hatred*. ⑤ 'With' can mean concerning • *a problem with her telephone bill*. ⑥ 'With' is used to show support • *Are you with us or against us?*

withdraw, **withdraws**, **withdrawing**, **withdrew**, **withdrawn** VERB ① If you withdraw something, you remove it or take it out • *He withdrew the money from his bank account*. ② If you withdraw to another place, you leave where you are and go there • *He withdrew to his study*. ③ If you withdraw from an activity, you back out of it • *They withdrew from the conference*.

withdraw VERB
① = draw out, extract, remove, take out
③ = back out, leave, pull out, retire, retreat

withdrawal NOUN ① The withdrawal of something is the act of taking it away • *the withdrawal of Russian troops*. ② The withdrawal of a statement is the act of saying formally that you wish to change or deny it. ③ an amount of money you take from your bank or building society account.

withdrawn ① Withdrawn is the past participle of **withdraw**. ▶ ADJECTIVE ② unusually shy or quiet.

withdrew the past tense of **withdraw**.

wither VERB ① When something withers or withers away, it becomes weaker until it no longer exists. ② If a plant withers, it wilts or shrivels up and dies.

wither VERB
① = decline, fade
② = droop, shrivel, wilt

withering ADJECTIVE A withering look or remark makes you feel ashamed, stupid or inferior.

withhold, **withholds**, **withholding**, **withheld** VERB (*formal*) If you withhold something that someone wants, you do not let them have it.

within PREPOSITION, ADVERB ① Within means in or inside. ▶ PREPOSITION ② Within can mean not going beyond certain limits • *Stay within the budget*. ③ Within can mean before a period of time has passed • *You must write back within fourteen days*.

without PREPOSITION ① Without means not having, feeling or showing • *Didier looked on without emotion*. ② Without can mean not using • *You can't get in without a key*. ③ Without can mean not in someone's company • *He went without me*. ④ Without can indicate that something does not happen when something else happens • *Stone signalled the ship, again without response*.

withstand, **withstands**, **withstanding**, **withstood** VERB When something or someone withstands a force or action, they survive it or do not give in to it • *ships designed to withstand the North Atlantic winter*.

witness NOUN ① someone who has seen an event such as an accident and can describe what happened. ② someone who appears in a court of law to say what they know about a crime or other event. ③ someone who writes their name on a document that someone else has signed, to confirm that it is really that person's signature. ▶ VERB ④ (*formal*) If you witness an event, you see it.

witness NOUN
① = bystander, eyewitness, observer, onlooker, spectator
▶ VERB ④ = be present at, observe, see, watch

witty, **wittier**, **wittiest** ADJECTIVE amusing in a clever way • *this witty novel*. **wittily** ADVERB

witty ADJECTIVE
= amusing, brilliant, clever, funny, humorous, sparkling

wives the plural of **wife**.

wizard NOUN a man in a fairy story who has magic powers.

wizardry NOUN Wizardry is something that is very cleverly done • *technological wizardry*.

wobble VERB If something wobbles, it shakes or moves from side to side because it is loose or unsteady • *a cyclist who wobbled into my path*.

wobbly, **wobblier**, **wobbliest** ADJECTIVE unsteady • *a wobbly table*.

woe (*literary*) NOUN ① Woe is great unhappiness or sorrow. ② (*in plural*) Someone's woes are their problems or misfortunes.

wok NOUN a large bowl-shaped metal pan used for Chinese-style cooking.

woke the past tense of **wake**.

woken the past participle of **wake**.

wolf, **wolves**; **wolfs**, **wolfing**, **wolfed** NOUN ① a wild animal related to the dog. Wolves hunt in packs and kill other animals for food. ▶ VERB ② (*informal*) If you wolf food or wolf it down, you eat it up quickly and greedily.

woman, **women** NOUN ① an adult female human being. ② Woman can refer to women in general • *a problem affecting both man and woman*.

woman NOUN
① = dame (*slang*), female, girl, lady, lass, sheila (*Australian and New Zealand; informal*), vrou (*South African*)
≠ man

womanhood NOUN Womanhood is the state of being a woman rather than a girl • *on the verge of womanhood*.

womb [*Said* ***woom***] NOUN A woman's womb is the part inside her body where her unborn baby grows.

wombat [*Said* ***wom-bat***] NOUN a short-legged furry Australian mammal which eats plants.

women the plural of **woman**.

won the past tense and past participle of **win**.

wonder VERB ① If you wonder about something, you think about it with curiosity or doubt. ② If you wonder at something, you are surprised and amazed at it • *He wondered at her anger*. ▶ NOUN ③ Wonder is a feeling of surprise and amazement. ④ something or someone that surprises and amazes people • *the wonders of science*.

wonder VERB
① = ask yourself, ponder, puzzle, speculate

② = be amazed, be astonished, boggle, marvel
▸ NOUN ④ = marvel, miracle, phenomenon, spectacle

wonderful ADJECTIVE ① making you feel very happy and pleased • *It was wonderful to be together.* ② very impressive • *Nature is a wonderful thing.*
wonderfully ADVERB

wonderful ADJECTIVE
① = excellent, great (*informal*), marvellous, superb, tremendous
② = amazing, astounding, incredible, magnificent, remarkable

wondrous ADJECTIVE (*literary*) amazing and impressive.

wont [*Rhymes with* ***don't***] ADJECTIVE (*old-fashioned*) If someone is wont to do something, they do it often • *a gesture he was wont to use when preaching.*

woo VERB ① If you woo people, you try to get them to help or support you • *attempts to woo the women's vote.* ② (*old-fashioned*) If you woo someone you are attracted to, you try to get them to marry you.

wood NOUN ① Wood is the substance which forms the trunks and branches of trees. ② a large area of trees growing near each other.

wooded ADJECTIVE covered in trees • *a wooded area nearby.*

wooden ADJECTIVE made of wood • *a wooden box.*

woodland NOUN Woodland is land that is mostly covered with trees.

woodwind ADJECTIVE Woodwind instruments are musical instruments such as flutes, oboes, clarinets and bassoons, that are played by being blown into.

woodwork NOUN ① Woodwork refers to the parts of a house, such as stairs, doors or window-frames, that are made of wood. ② Woodwork is the craft or skill of making things out of wood.

woody, **woodier**, **woodiest** ADJECTIVE ① Woody plants have hard tough stems. ② A woody area has a lot of trees in it.

wool NOUN ① Wool is the hair that grows on sheep and some other animals. ② Wool is also yarn spun from the wool of animals which is used to knit, weave and make such things as clothes, blankets and carpets.

woollen ADJECTIVE ① made from wool. ▸ NOUN ② Woollens are clothes made of wool.

woolly, **woollier**, **woolliest** ADJECTIVE ① made of wool or looking like wool • *a woolly hat.* ② If you describe people or their thoughts as woolly, you mean that they seem confused and unclear.

word NOUN ① a single unit of language in speech or writing which has a meaning. ② a remark • *a word of praise.* ③ a brief conversation • *Could I have a word?* ④ A word can also be a message • *The word is that Sharon is exhausted.* ⑤ Your word is a promise • *He gave me his word.* ⑥ The word can be a command • *I gave the word to start.* ⑦ (*in plural*) The words of a play or song are the spoken or sung text. ▸ VERB ⑧ When you word something, you choose your words in order to express your ideas accurately or acceptably • *the best way to word our invitations.*

word NOUN
② = comment, remark, statement, utterance
③ = chat, conversation, discussion, talk
④ = announcement, bulletin, communication, information, intelligence, message, news
⑤ = assurance, oath, pledge, promise, word of honour

A B C D E F G H I J K L M N O P Q R S T U V **W** X Y Z

wording NOUN The wording of a piece of writing or a speech is the words used in it, especially when these words have been carefully chosen to have a certain effect.

word processor NOUN [ICT] a computer program or a computer which is used to produce printed documents.

wore the past tense of **wear**.

work VERB ① People who work have a job which they are paid to do • *My husband works for a national newspaper.* ② When you work, you do the tasks that your job involves. ③ To work the land is to cultivate it. ④ If someone works a machine, they control or operate it. ⑤ If a machine works, it operates properly and effectively • *The radio doesn't work.* ⑥ If something such as an idea or a system works, it is successful • *The housing benefit system is not working.* ⑦ If something works its way into a particular position, it gradually moves there • *The cable had worked loose.* ▸ NOUN ⑧ People who have work or who are in work have a job which they are paid to do • *She's trying to find work.* ⑨ Work is the tasks that have to be done. ⑩ something done or made • *a work of art.* ⑪ [SCIENCE] In physics, work is transfer of energy. It is calculated by multiplying a force by the distance moved by the point to which the force has been applied. Work is measured in joules. ⑫ (*in plural*) A works is a place where something is made by an industrial process • *the old steel works.* ⑬ Works are large-scale building, digging or general construction activities • *building works.* **work out** VERB ① If you work out a solution to a problem, you find the solution. ② If a situation works out in a particular way, it happens in that way. **work up** VERB ① If you work up to something, you gradually progress towards it. ② If you work yourself up or work someone else up, you make yourself or the other person very upset or angry about something. **worked up** ADJECTIVE

> **work** VERB
> ② = labour, slave, slog away, toil
> ≠ laze
> ▸ NOUN ⑧ = craft, employment, job, livelihood, occupation, profession
> ⑨ = assignment, business, chore, duty, job, task, yakka (*Australian and New Zealand; informal*)
> ▸ **work out** ① = calculate, figure out, resolve, solve ② = develop, go, happen, turn out

workable ADJECTIVE Something workable can operate successfully or can be used for a particular purpose • *a workable solution* • *This plan simply isn't workable.*

workaholic NOUN a person who finds it difficult to stop working and do other things.

worker NOUN a person employed in a particular industry or business • *a defence worker.*

> **worker** NOUN
> = craftsman, employee, labourer, workman

workforce NOUN The workforce is all the people who work in a particular place.

working class NOUN The working class or working classes are the group of people in society who do not own much property and who do jobs which involve physical rather than intellectual skills.

workload NOUN the amount of work that a person or a machine has to do.

workman, **workmen** NOUN a man whose job involves using physical rather than intellectual skills.

workmanship NOUN Workmanship is the skill with which something is made or a job is completed.

workmate NOUN Someone's workmate is the fellow worker with whom they do their job.

workout NOUN a session of physical exercise or training.

workshop NOUN ① a room or building that contains tools or machinery used for making or repairing things • *an engineering workshop*. ② a period of discussion or practical work in which a group of people learn about a particular subject • *a theatre workshop*.

world NOUN ① The world is the earth, the planet we live on. ② You can use 'world' to refer to people generally • *The eyes of the world are upon me*. ③ Someone's world is the life they lead and the things they experience • *We come from different worlds*. ④ A world is a division or section of the earth, its history, or its people, such as the Arab World or the Ancient World. ⑤ A particular world is a field of activity and the people involved in it • *the world of football*. ▶ ADJECTIVE ⑥ 'World' is used to describe someone or something that is one of the best or most important of its kind • *a world leader*. ▶ PHRASE ⑦ If you **think the world** of someone, you like or admire them very much.

worldly, **worldlier**, **worldliest** ADJECTIVE ① relating to the ordinary activities of life rather than spiritual things • *opportunities for worldly pleasures*. ② experienced and knowledgeable about life.

world war NOUN a war that involves countries all over the world.

worldwide ADJECTIVE throughout the world • *a worldwide flu epidemic*.

World Wide Web NOUN The World Wide Web is a system of linked documents accessed via the internet.

worm NOUN ① a small thin animal without bones or legs, which lives in the soil or off other creatures. ② an insect such as a beetle or moth at a very early stage in its life. ③ a computer program that makes many copies of itself within a network, usually harming the system. ▶ VERB ④ If you worm an animal, you give it medicine in order to kill the worms that are living as parasites in its intestines. **worm out** VERB If you worm information out of someone, you gradually persuade them to give you it.

worn ① Worn is the past participle of **wear**. ▶ ADJECTIVE ② damaged or thin because of long use. ③ looking old or exhausted • *He appeared frail and worn*.

worn-out ADJECTIVE ① used until it is too thin or too damaged to be of further use • *a worn-out cardigan*. ② extremely tired • *You must be worn-out after the drive*.

> **worn-out** ADJECTIVE
> ① = broken-down, tattered, threadbare, worn
> ② = exhausted, fatigued, prostrate, tired, weary

worried ADJECTIVE unhappy and anxious about a problem or about something unpleasant that might happen.

> **worried** ADJECTIVE
> = anxious, bothered, concerned, nervous, troubled, uneasy
> ≠ unconcerned

worry, **worries**, **worrying**, **worried** VERB ① If you worry, you feel anxious and fearful about a problem or about something unpleasant that might happen. ② If something worries you, it causes you to feel uneasy or fearful • *a puzzle which had worried her all her life*. ③ If you worry someone with a problem, you disturb or bother them

by telling them about it • *I didn't want to worry the boys with this.* ④ If a dog worries sheep or other animals, it frightens or harms them by chasing them or biting them. ▶ **NOUN** ⑤ Worry is a feeling of unhappiness and unease caused by a problem or by thinking of something unpleasant that might happen • *the major source of worry.* ⑥ a person or thing that causes you to feel anxious or uneasy • *Inflation is the least of our worries.*
worrying **ADJECTIVE**

worry **VERB**
① = be anxious, brood, feel uneasy, fret
③ = bother, hassle (*informal*), pester, plague, trouble
▶ **NOUN** ⑤ = anxiety, apprehension, concern, fear, misgiving, unease

worse **ADJECTIVE, ADVERB** ① Worse is the comparative form of **bad** and **badly**. ② If someone who is ill gets worse, they become more ill than before. ▶ **PHRASE** ③ If someone or something is **none the worse** for something, they have not been harmed by it • *He appeared none the worse for the accident.*

worsen **VERB** If a situation worsens, it becomes more difficult or unpleasant • *The weather conditions worsened.*

worsen **VERB**
= decline, degenerate, deteriorate, go downhill (*informal*)
≠ improve

worse off **ADJECTIVE** If you are worse off, you have less money or are in a more unpleasant situation than before • *There are people much worse off than me.*

worship, worships, worshipping, worshipped **VERB** ① RE If you worship a god, you show your love and respect by praying or singing hymns. ② If you worship someone or something, you love them or admire them very much. ▶ **NOUN** ③ Worship is the feeling of respect, love or admiration you feel for something or someone. **worshipper** **NOUN**

worship **VERB**
① = glorify, honour, praise, pray to, venerate (*formal*)
≠ dishonour
② = adore, idolise, love
≠ despise
▶ **NOUN** ③ = admiration, adoration, adulation, devotion, homage, praise

worst **ADJECTIVE, ADVERB** Worst is the superlative of **bad** and **badly**.

worth **PREPOSITION** ① If something is worth a sum of money, it has that value • *a house worth $850,000.* ② If something is worth doing, it deserves to be done. ▶ **NOUN** ③ A particular amount of money's worth of something is the quantity of it that you can buy for that money • *five pounds' worth of petrol.* ④ Someone's worth is the value or usefulness they are considered to have.

worthless **ADJECTIVE** having no real value or use • *a worthless piece of junk.*

worthless **ADJECTIVE**
= meaningless, paltry, poor, trifling, trivial, useless, valueless
≠ valuable

worthwhile **ADJECTIVE** important enough to justify the time, money or effort spent on it • *a worthwhile career.*

worthy, worthier, worthiest **ADJECTIVE** If someone or something is worthy of something, they deserve it • *a worthy champion.*

would **VERB** ① You use 'would' to say what someone thought was going to happen • *We were sure it would be a success.* ② You use 'would' when you are referring to the result or effect of a possible situation • *If readers can help I would be most grateful.* ③ You use 'would' when referring to someone's willingness to do something • *I wouldn't change places with him if you paid me*. ④ You use 'would' in polite questions • *Would you like some lunch?*

would-be ADJECTIVE wanting to be or claiming to be • *a would-be pop singer*.

wound[1] [*Rhymes with **spooned***] NOUN ① an injury to part of your body, especially a cut in your skin and flesh. ▸ VERB ② If someone wounds you, they damage your body using a gun, knife or other weapon. ③ If you are wounded by what someone says or does, your feelings are hurt. **wounded** ADJECTIVE

wound[2] [*Rhymes with **sound***] the past tense and past participle of **wind**[2].

wove the past tense of **weave**.

woven the past participle of **weave**.

wow INTERJECTION Wow is an expression of admiration or surprise.

wraith, **wraiths** [*Said **rayth***] NOUN (*literary*) A wraith is a ghost or apparition.

wrangle VERB ① If you wrangle with someone, you argue noisily or angrily, often about something unimportant. ▸ NOUN ② an argument that is difficult to settle. **wrangling** NOUN

wrap, **wraps**, **wrapping**, **wrapped** VERB ① If you wrap something or wrap something up, you fold a piece of paper or cloth tightly around it to cover or enclose it. ② If you wrap paper or cloth round something, you put or fold the paper round it. ③ If you wrap your arms, fingers or legs round something, you coil them round it. **wrap up** VERB If you wrap up, you put warm clothes on.

wrapped up ADJECTIVE (*informal*) If you are wrapped up in a person or thing, you give that person or thing all your attention.

wrapper NOUN a piece of paper, plastic or foil which covers and protects something that you buy • *sweet wrappers*.

wrapping NOUN Wrapping is the material used to cover and protect something.

wrath [*Said **roth***] NOUN (*literary*) Wrath is great anger • *The manager faced the wrath of the fans*.

wreak [*Said **reek***] VERB To wreak havoc or damage is to cause it.

wreath [*Said **reeth***] NOUN an arrangement of flowers and leaves, often in the shape of a circle, which is put on a grave as a sign of remembrance for the dead person.

wreck VERB ① If someone wrecks something, they break it, destroy it, or spoil it completely. ② If a ship is wrecked, it has been so badly damaged that it can no longer sail. ▸ NOUN ③ a vehicle which has been badly damaged in an accident. ④ If you say someone is a wreck, you mean that they are in very poor physical or mental health or completely exhausted. **wrecked** ADJECTIVE

wreckage NOUN Wreckage is what remains after something has been badly damaged or destroyed.

wrench VERB ① If you wrench something, you give it a sudden and violent twist or pull • *Nick wrenched open the door*. ② If you wrench a limb or a joint, you twist and injure it. ▸ NOUN ③ a metal tool with parts which can be adjusted to fit around nuts or bolts to loosen or tighten them. ④ a painful parting from someone or something.

wrest [*Said **rest***] VERB (*formal*) If you wrest something from someone else you take it from them violently or with effort • *to try and wrest control of the island from the Mafia*.

a b c d e f g h i j k l m n o p q r s t u v w x y z

wrestle VERB ① If you wrestle someone or wrestle with them, you fight them by holding or throwing them, but not hitting them. ② When you wrestle with a problem, you try to deal with it. **wrestler** NOUN

wrestling NOUN Wrestling is a sport in which two people fight and try to win by throwing or holding their opponent on the ground.

wretched *[Said* ***ret****-shid]* ADJECTIVE ① very unhappy or unfortunate • *a wretched childhood*. ② *(informal)* You use wretched to describe something or someone you feel angry about or dislike • *a wretched bully*.

wriggle VERB ① If someone wriggles, they twist and turn their body or a part of their body using quick movements • *He wriggled his arms and legs*. ② If you wriggle somewhere, you move there by twisting and turning • *I wriggled out of the van*. **wriggly** ADJECTIVE

wring, wrings, wringing, wrung VERB ① When you wring a wet cloth or wring it out, you squeeze the water out of it by twisting it. ② If you wring your hands, you hold them together and twist and turn them, usually because you are worried or upset. ③ If someone wrings a bird's neck, they kill the bird by twisting and breaking its neck.

wrinkle NOUN ① Wrinkles are lines in someone's skin, especially on the face, which form as they grow old. ▸ VERB ② If something wrinkles, folds or lines develop on it • *Fold the paper carefully so that it doesn't wrinkle*. ③ When you wrinkle your nose, forehead or eyes, you tighten the muscles in your face so that the skin folds into lines. **wrinkled** ADJECTIVE **wrinkly** ADJECTIVE

wrist NOUN the part of your body between your hand and your arm which bends when you move your hand.

writ NOUN a legal document that orders a person to do or not to do a particular thing.

write, writes, writing, wrote, written VERB ① When you write something, you use a pen or pencil to form letters, words or numbers on a surface. ② If you write something such as a poem, a book or a piece of music, you create it. ③ When you write to someone or write them a letter, you express your feelings in a letter. ④ When someone writes something such as a cheque, they put the necessary information on it and sign it. ⑤ When you write data you transfer it to a computer's memory. **write down** VERB If you write something down, you record it on a piece of paper. **write up** VERB If you write up something, you write a full account of it, often using notes that you have made.

writer NOUN ① a person who writes books, stories or articles as a job. ② The writer of something is the person who wrote it.

writhe VERB If you writhe, you twist and turn your body, often because you are in pain.

writing NOUN ① Writing is something that has been written or printed • *Apply in writing for the information*. ② Your writing is the way you write with a pen or pencil. ③ Writing is also a piece of written work, especially the style of language used • *witty writing*. ④ An author's writings are his or her written works.

written ① Written is the past participle of **write**. ▸ ADJECTIVE ② taken down in writing • *a written agreement*.

wrong ADJECTIVE ① not working properly or unsatisfactory • *There was* *something wrong with the car*. ② not correct or truthful • *the wrong answer*. ③ bad or immoral • *It is wrong to kill people*. ▶ NOUN ④ an unjust action or situation • *the wrongs of our society*. ▶ VERB ⑤ If someone wrongs you, they treat you in an unfair or unjust way. **wrongly** ADVERB

wrong ADJECTIVE
② = false, faulty, incorrect, mistaken, unsound, untrue
≠ right
③ = bad, crooked, evil, illegal, immoral, unfair, unjust
≠ right
▶ NOUN ④ = abuse, crime, grievance, injustice, sin

wrongful ADJECTIVE A wrongful act is regarded as illegal, unfair or immoral • *wrongful imprisonment*. **wrongfully** ADVERB

wrote the past tense of **write**.

wrought iron NOUN Wrought iron is a pure type of iron that is formed into decorative shapes.

wrung the past tense and past participle of **wring**.

wry ADJECTIVE A wry expression shows that you find a situation slightly amusing because you know more about it than other people. **wryly** ADVERB **wryness** NOUN

A B C D E F G H I J K L M N O P Q R S T U V W X Y Z

X or **x** ① 'X' is used to represent the name of an unknown or secret person or place • *The witness was referred to as Mr X throughout the trial.* ② In algebra, 'x' is used as a symbol to represent a number whose value is not known. ③ People sometimes write 'X' on a map to mark a precise position. ④ 'X' is used to represent a kiss at the bottom of a letter, a vote on a ballot paper, or the signature of someone who cannot write.

xenophobia *[Said zen-nof-**foe**-bee-a]* NOUN a fear or strong dislike of people from other countries.
xenophobic ADJECTIVE

Xerox *[Said **zeer**-roks]* NOUN *(trademark)* ① a machine that makes photographic copies of sheets of paper with writing or printing on them. ② a copy made by a Xerox machine.

Xmas NOUN *(informal)* Xmas means the same as Christmas.

X-ray NOUN ① a stream of radiation of very short wavelength that can pass through some solid materials. X-rays are used by doctors to examine the bones or organs inside a person's body. ② a picture made by sending X-rays through someone's body in order to examine the inside of it.
▶ VERB ③ If you are X-rayed, a picture is made of the inside of your body by passing X-rays through it.

xylophone *[Said **zy**-lo-fone]* NOUN a musical instrument made of a row of wooden bars of different lengths. It is played by hitting the bars with special hammers.

Yy

-y SUFFIX -y forms nouns • *anarchy*.

yacht *[Said yot]* NOUN a boat with sails or an engine, used for racing or for pleasure trips.

yachting NOUN Yachting is the sport or activity of sailing a yacht.

yachtsman, **yachtsmen** NOUN a man who sails a yacht.

yachtswoman, **yachtswomen** NOUN a woman who sails a yacht.

yak NOUN a type of long-haired ox with long horns, found mainly in Tibet.

yakka or **yacker** NOUN (*informal*) In Australian and New Zealand English, yakka or yacker is work.

yank (*informal*) VERB ① If you yank something, you pull or jerk it suddenly with a lot of force. ▶ NOUN ② A Yank is an American.

Yankee NOUN (*informal*) the same as a Yank.

yard NOUN ① a unit of length equal to 36 inches or about 91.4 centimetres. ② an enclosed area that is usually next to a building and is often used for a particular purpose • *a ship repair yard*.

yardstick NOUN someone or something you use as a standard against which to judge other people or things • *He had no yardstick by which to judge university*.

yarn NOUN ① DGT Yarn is thread used for knitting or making cloth. ② (*informal*) a story that someone tells, often with invented details to make it more interesting or exciting • *fishermen's yarns*.

yawn VERB ① When you yawn, you open your mouth wide and take in more air than usual. You often yawn when you are tired or bored. ② A gap or opening that yawns is large and wide. ▶ NOUN ③ an act of yawning.

yawning ADJECTIVE A yawning gap or opening is very wide.

ye (*old-fashioned*) PRONOUN ① Ye is used to mean 'you'. ▶ ADJECTIVE ② Ye is also used to mean 'the'.

yeah INTERJECTION (*informal*) Yeah means 'yes'.

year NOUN ① a period of twelve months or 365 days (366 days in a leap year), which is the time taken for the earth to travel once around the sun. ② a period of twelve consecutive months, not always January to December, on which administration or organisation is based • *the current financial year*. ▶ PHRASE ③ If something happens **year in, year out**, it happens every year • *a tradition kept up year in, year out*.

yearling NOUN an animal between one and two years old.

yearn *[Rhymes with* ***learn****]* VERB If you yearn for something, you want it very much indeed • *He yearned to sleep*. **yearning** NOUN

yeast NOUN SCIENCE Yeast is a kind of fungus which is used to make bread rise, and to make liquids ferment in order to produce alcohol.

yell VERB ① If you yell, you shout loudly, usually because you are angry, excited or in pain. ▶ **NOUN** ② a loud shout.

yellow **NOUN, ADJECTIVE** ① Yellow is the colour of buttercups, egg yolks and lemons. ▶ **VERB** ② When something yellows or is yellowed, it becomes yellow, often because it is old. ▶ **ADJECTIVE** ③ (*informal*) If you say someone is yellow, you mean they are cowardly. **yellowish** **ADJECTIVE**

yellow fever **NOUN** Yellow fever is a serious infectious disease that is found in tropical countries. It causes fever and jaundice.

yelp **VERB** ① When people or animals yelp, they give a sudden, short cry. ▶ **NOUN** ② a sudden, short cry.

yen **NOUN** ① The yen is the main unit of currency in Japan. ② (*informal*) If you have a yen to do something, you have a strong desire to do it • *Mike had a yen to try cycling*.

yes **INTERJECTION** You use 'yes' to agree with someone, to say that something is true, or to accept something.

yes **INTERJECTION**
= aye (*Scottish; informal*), okay, sure, ya (*South African*), yeah (*informal*), yup (*informal*)
≠ no

yesterday **NOUN, ADVERB** ① Yesterday is the day before today. ② You also use 'yesterday' to refer to the past • *Leave yesterday's sadness behind you*.

yet **ADVERB** ① If something has not happened yet, it has not happened up to the present time • *It isn't quite dark yet*. ② If something should not be done yet, it should not be done now, but later • *Don't switch off yet*. ③ 'Yet' can mean there is still a possibility that something can happen • *We'll make a soldier of you yet*. ④ You can use 'yet' when you want to say how much longer a situation will continue • *The service doesn't start for an hour yet*. ⑤ 'Yet' can be used for emphasis • *She'd changed her mind yet again*. ▶ **CONJUNCTION** ⑥ You can use 'yet' to introduce a fact which is rather surprising • *He isn't a smoker yet he always carries a lighter*.

yew **NOUN** an evergreen tree with bright red berries.

Yiddish **NOUN** Yiddish is a language derived mainly from German, which many Jewish people of European origin speak.

yield **VERB** ① If you yield to someone or something, you stop resisting and give in to them • *Russia recently yielded to US pressure*. ② If you yield something that you have control of or responsibility for, you surrender it • *They refused to yield control of their weapons*. ③ If something yields, it breaks or gives way • *The handle would yield to her grasp*. ④ To yield something is to produce it • *One season's produce yields food for the following year*. ▶ **NOUN** ⑤ A yield is an amount of food, money or profit produced from a given area of land or from an investment.

yob **NOUN** (*informal*) a noisy, badly behaved boy or young man.

yoga [*Said* ***yoe**-ga*] **NOUN** Yoga is a Hindu method of mental and physical exercise or discipline.

yogurt [*Said* ***yog**-gurt or **yoe**-gurt*]; also spelt **yoghurt** **NOUN** Yogurt is a slightly sour thick liquid made from milk that has had bacteria added to it.

yoke **NOUN** ① a wooden bar attached to two collars which is laid across the necks of animals such as oxen to hold them together, and to which a plough or other tool may be attached. ② (*literary*) If people are under a yoke of some kind, they are being oppressed • *People are still suffering under the yoke of slavery*.

yolk *[Rhymes with* ***joke****]* **NOUN** the yellow part in the middle of an egg.

Yom Kippur *[Said yom kip-****poor****]* **NOUN** RE Yom Kippur is an annual Jewish religious holiday, which is a day of fasting and prayers. It is also called the Day of Atonement.

yonder **ADVERB, ADJECTIVE** *(old-fashioned)* over there • *There's an island yonder.*

yore **PHRASE** *(old-fashioned)* **Of yore** means existing a long time ago • *nostalgia for the days of yore.*

you **PRONOUN** ① 'You' refers to the person or group of people that a person is speaking or writing to. ② 'You' also refers to people in general • *You can get a two-bedroom villa quite cheaply here.*

young **ADJECTIVE** ① A young person, animal or plant has not lived very long and is not yet mature. ▸ **PLURAL NOUN** ② The young are young people in general. ③ The young of an animal are its babies.

> **young** **ADJECTIVE**
> ① = adolescent, immature, infant, junior, juvenile, little, youthful
> ≠ old
> ▸ **PLURAL NOUN** ③ = babies, brood, family, litter, little ones, offspring

youngster **NOUN** a child or young person.

your **ADJECTIVE** ① 'Your' means belonging or relating to the person or group of people that someone is speaking to • *I do like your name.* ② 'Your' is used to show that something belongs or relates to people in general • *Some of these chemicals can cause serious damage to your health.*

yours **PRONOUN** 'Yours' refers to something belonging or relating to the person or group of people that someone is speaking to • *His hair is longer than yours.*

yourself, **yourselves** **PRONOUN** ① 'Yourself' is used when the person being spoken to does the action and is affected by it • *Why can't you do it yourself?* ② 'Yourself' is used to emphasise 'you' • *Do you yourself want to go?*

youth **NOUN** ① Someone's youth is the period of their life before they are a fully mature adult. ② Youth is the quality or condition of being young and often inexperienced. ③ a boy or young man. ④ The youth are young people thought of as a group • *the youth of today.* **youthful** **ADJECTIVE**

yo-yo, **yo-yos** **NOUN** a round wooden or plastic toy attached to a piece of string. You play by making the yo-yo rise and fall on the string.

Yule **NOUN** *(old-fashioned)* Yule means Christmas.

yuppie **NOUN** A yuppie is a young, middle-class person who earns a lot of money which he or she spends on himself or herself.

a b c d e f g h i j k l m n o p q r s t u v w x y z

Zz

Zambian *[Said **zam**-bee-an]* ADJECTIVE ① belonging or relating to Zambia. ▶ NOUN ② someone who comes from Zambia.

zany, **zanier**, **zaniest** ADJECTIVE (*informal*) odd and ridiculous • *zany humour.*

zap, **zaps**, **zapping**, **zapped** VERB (*informal*) ① To zap someone is to kill them, usually by shooting. ② To zap also is to move somewhere quickly • *I zapped over to Paris.*

zeal NOUN Zeal is very great enthusiasm. **zealous** ADJECTIVE **zealously** ADVERB

zealot *[Said **zel**-lot]* NOUN a person who acts with very great enthusiasm, especially in following a political or religious cause.

zebra NOUN a type of African wild horse with black and white stripes over its body.

Zen or **Zen Buddhism** NOUN [RE] Zen is a form of Buddhism that concentrates on learning through meditation and intuition.

zenith NOUN (*literary*) The zenith of something is the time when it is at its most successful or powerful • *the zenith of his military career.*

zero, **zeros** or **zeroes**, **zeroing**, **zeroed** ① nothing or the number 0. ② Zero is freezing point, 0° Centigrade. ▶ ADJECTIVE ③ Zero means there is none at all of a particular thing • *His chances are zero.* **zero in** VERB To zero in on a target is to aim at or to move towards it • *The headlines zeroed in on the major news stories.*

zero NOUN
① = nil, nothing, nought

zest NOUN ① Zest is a feeling of pleasure and enthusiasm • *zest for life.* ② Zest is a quality which adds extra flavour or interest to something • *brilliant ideas to add zest to your wedding list.* ③ The zest of an orange or lemon is the outside of the peel which is used to flavour food or drinks.

zigzag, **zigzags**, **zigzagging**, **zigzagged** NOUN ① a line which has a series of sharp, angular turns to the right and left in it, like a continuous series of 'W's. ▶ VERB ② To zigzag is to move forward by going at an angle first right and then left • *He zigzagged his way across the racecourse.*

Zimbabwean *[Said zim-**bahb**-wee-an]* ADJECTIVE ① belonging or relating to Zimbabwe. ▶ NOUN ② someone who comes from Zimbabwe.

zinc NOUN [SCIENCE] Zinc is a bluish-white metallic element used in alloys and to coat other metals to stop them rusting. Its atomic number is 30 and its symbol is Zn.

zip, **zips**, **zipping**, **zipped** NOUN ① a long narrow fastener with two rows of teeth that are closed or opened by a small clip pulled between them. ▶ VERB ② When you zip something or zip it up, you fasten it using a zip.

zipper NOUN the same as a **zip**.

zodiac *[Said **zoe**-dee-ak]* NOUN The zodiac is an imaginary strip in the sky which contains the planets and stars which astrologers think are important influences on people. It is divided into 12 sections, each with a special name and symbol.

zombie NOUN ① (*informal*) If you refer to someone as a zombie, you mean that they seem to be unaware of what is going on around them and to act without thinking about what they are doing. ② In voodoo, a zombie is a dead person who has been brought back to life by witchcraft.

zone NOUN an area that has particular features or properties • *a war zone.*

zoo, **zoos** NOUN a place where live animals are kept so that people can look at them.

zoology *[Said zoo-**ol**-loj-jee]* NOUN Zoology is the scientific study of animals. **zoological** ADJECTIVE **zoologist** NOUN

zoom VERB ① To zoom is to move very quickly • *They zoomed to safety.* ② If a camera zooms in on something, it gives a close-up picture of it.

zucchini *[Said zoo-**keen**-nee]* PLURAL NOUN Zucchini are small vegetable marrows with dark green skin. They are also called **courgettes**.

Zulu, **Zulus** *[Said **zoo**-loo]* NOUN ① The Zulus are a group of Black people who live in southern Africa. ② Zulu is the language spoken by the Zulus.